Dear Future Business Leader,

By using this book to prepare for the GMAT® exam, you are taking a very important step toward gaining admission to a high-quality business or management program and achieving a rewarding career in management. I applaud your decision.

The Graduate Management Admission Council® developed the GMAT exam more than 50 years ago to help leading graduate schools of business and management choose the applicants who best suit their programs. Programs that use GMAT scores in selective admissions have helped establish the MBA degree as a hallmark of excellence worldwide and have raised the credibility of other graduate-level management and specialized programs. Today, the test is used by more than 5,200 graduate programs and is given to test-takers daily in more than 110 countries around the world.

This 13th edition of *The Official Guide for GMAT® Review* includes study material for the new Integrated Reasoning section, which makes its debut in June 2012. Four new question types will incorporate advances in technology and measurement to test your ability to integrate information from multiple sources and in multiple formats to make reasoned conclusions. These skills were identified by schools as important for incoming management students to have in an increasingly data-driven world, and their inclusion on the test reflects GMAC's ongoing commitment to evolving with the needs of management programs and students.

Why do GMAT scores matter so much? Other admissions factors—such as work experience, grades, admissions essays, and interviews—can say something about who you are and what you have done in your career, but only your GMAT scores can tell schools how you are likely to perform academically in the courses that are fundamental to graduate management degrees.

Management programs that require you to take the GMAT exam really care about the quality of their student body. And excellent students mean a stronger program, a more enriching learning environment, and a more valuable degree for you to take into the professional world. By enrolling in a school that uses the GMAT exam for your graduate management degree, you will maximize the value of your degree, and that value will pay off in many ways, throughout your career.

I wish you great success in preparing for this important next step in your professional education, and I wish you a very rewarding management career.

Sincerely,

David A. Wilson
President and CEO
Graduate Management Admission Council®

1.0   What Is the GMAT® Exam?

13th EDITION
REVIEW

The **only** study guide by the creators of the test

- More than 900 questions from past GMAT® exams

- NEW! Companion website includes 50 Integrated Reasoning questions

- Diagnostic section helps you assess where to focus your test-prep efforts

~The~
OFFICIAL
Guide

From the Graduate Management Admission Council®

THE OFFICIAL GUIDE FOR GMAT® REVIEW, 13TH EDITION

For details of our global editorial offices, for customer services and for information about how to apply for permission to reuse the copyright material in this book please see our website at www.wiley.com.

John Wiley & Sons, Ltd, also publishes its books in a variety of electronic formats and by print-on-demand. Not all content that is available in standard print versions of this book may appear or be packaged in all book formats. If you have purchased a version of this book that did not include media that is referenced by or accompanies a standard print version, you may request this media by visiting http://booksupport.wiley.com. For more information about Wiley products, visit us at www.wiley.com.

Library of Congress Control Number: 2011945676

A catalogue record for this book is available from the British Library.

ISBN: 978-1-119-96187-1 (pbk)
ISBN: 978-1-118-22414-4; 978-1-118-24179-0; 978-1-118-23738-0 (ebk)

Printed in Great Britain by TJ International Ltd, Padstow, Cornwall.

10 9 8 7 6 5 4 3

Book production by Wiley Publishing, Inc. Composition Services
Charles Forster, Designer
Mike Wilson, Production Designer

Updates to this book are available on the Downloads tab at this site: http://www.wiley.com/WileyCDA/WileyTitle/productCd-1118109791.html. If a Downloads tab does not appear at this link, there are no updates at this time.

Table of Contents

NEW!

1.0 What Is the GMAT® Exam?

The Graduate Management Admission Test® (GMAT®) exam is a standardized exam used in admissions decisions by more than 5,200 graduate management programs worldwide. It helps you gauge, and demonstrate to schools, your academic potential for success in graduate level management studies.

The four-part exam measures your Analytical Writing, Verbal, Quantitative, and Integrated Reasoning skills—higher-order reasoning skills that management faculty worldwide have identified as important for incoming students to have. Unlike undergraduate grades and curricula, which vary in their meaning across regions and institutions, your GMAT scores provide a standardized, statistically reliable measure of how you are likely to perform academically in the core curriculum of a graduate management program. The GMAT exam's validity, appropriateness, and value in admissions have been well-established through numerous academic studies.

The GMAT exam is delivered entirely in English and solely on computer. It is not a test of business knowledge, subject matter mastery, English vocabulary, or advanced computational skills. The GMAT exam also does not measure other factors related to success in graduate management study, such as job experience, leadership ability, motivation, and interpersonal skills. Your GMAT score is intended to be used as one admissions criterion among other, more subjective, criteria, such as admissions essays and interviews.

1.1 Why Take the GMAT® Exam?

Launched in 1954 by a group of nine business schools to provide a uniform measure of the academic skills needed to succeed in their programs, the GMAT exam is now used by more than 5,200 graduate management programs at approximately 1,900 institutions worldwide.

Using GMAT scores helps institutions select the most qualified applicants and ensure that the applicants they admit are up to the academic rigors of their programs. When you consider which programs to apply to, you can look at a school's use of the GMAT exam as one indicator of quality. Schools that use the GMAT exam typically list score ranges or average scores in their class profiles, so you may also find these profiles helpful in gauging the academic competitiveness of a program you are considering and how well your performance on the exam compares with that of the students enrolled in the program.

Myth -vs- FACT

M – If I don't score in the 90th percentile, I won't get into any school I choose.

F – Very few people get very high scores.

Fewer than 50 of the more than 200,000 people taking the GMAT exam each year get a perfect score of 800. Thus, while you may be exceptionally capable, the odds are against your achieving a perfect score. Also, the GMAT exam is just one piece of your application packet. Admissions officers use GMAT scores in conjunction with undergraduate records, application essays, interviews, letters of recommendation, and other information when deciding whom to accept into their programs.

No matter how well you perform on the GMAT exam, you should contact the schools that interest you to learn more about them and to ask how they use GMAT scores and other criteria (such as your undergraduate grades, essays, and letters of recommendation) in their admissions processes. School admissions offices, web sites, and materials published by schools are the primary sources of information when you are doing research about where you might want to go to business school.

For more information on the GMAT exam, test registration, appropriate uses of GMAT scores, sending your scores to schools, and applying to business school, please visit our web site at mba.com.

1.2 GMAT® Exam Format

The GMAT exam consists of four separately timed sections (see the table on the next page). The test starts with one Analytical Writing Assessment (AWA) essay prompt, and you will have 30 minutes to type your essay on a computer keyboard. The AWA is followed immediately by the 30-minute Integrated Reasoning section, which features 12 question prompts in four different question formats. The test ends with two 75-minute, multiple-choice sections: the Quantitative section, with 37 questions, and the Verbal section, with 41.

The Verbal and Quantitative sections of the GMAT exam are computer adaptive, which means that the test draws from a large bank of questions to tailor itself to your ability level, and you won't get many questions that are much too hard or too easy for you. The first question will be of medium difficulty. As you answer each question, the computer scores your answer and uses it—as well as your responses to any preceding questions—to select the next question.

> ## Myth -vs- **FACT**
>
> **M – Getting an easier question means I answered the last one wrong.**
>
> **F – Getting an easier question does not necessarily mean you got the previous question wrong.**
>
> To ensure that everyone receives the same content, the test selects a specific number of questions of each type. The test may call for your next question to be a relatively difficult problem-solving item involving arithmetic operations. But, if there are no more relatively difficult problem-solving items involving arithmetic, you might be given an easier item.
>
> Most people are not skilled at estimating item difficulty, so don't worry when taking the test or waste valuable time trying to determine the difficulty of the questions you are answering.

Computer-adaptive tests become more difficult the more questions you answer correctly, but if you get a question that seems easier than the last one, it does not necessarily mean you answered the last question incorrectly. The test has to cover a range of content, both in the type of question asked and the subject matter presented.

Because the computer uses your answers to select your next questions, you may not skip questions or go back and change your answer to a previous question. If you don't know the answer to a question, try to eliminate as many choices as possible, then select the answer you think is best. If you answer a question incorrectly by mistake—or correctly by lucky guess—your answers to subsequent questions will lead you back to questions that are at the appropriate skill level for you.

Though the individual questions are different, the content mixture is the same for every GMAT exam. Your score is determined by the difficulty and statistical characteristics of the questions you answer as well as the number of questions you answer correctly. By adapting to each test-taker, the GMAT exam is able to accurately and efficiently gauge skill levels over a full range of abilities, from very high to very low.

The test includes the types of questions found in this book and in the online Integrated Reasoning component, but the format and presentation of the questions are different on the computer. When you take the test:

- Only one question or question prompt at a time is presented on the computer screen.

- The answer choices for the multiple-choice questions will be preceded by circles, rather than by letters.

- Different question types appear in random order in the multiple-choice and Integrated Reasoning sections of the test.

- You must select your answer using the computer.

- You must choose an answer and confirm your choice before moving on to the next question.

- You may not go back to previous screens to change answers to previous questions.

Format of the GMAT® Exam		
	Questions	Timing
Analytical Writing Analysis of an Argument	1	30 min.

Integrated Reasoning
    Multi-Source Reasoning
    Table Analysis
    Graphics Interpretation
    Two-Part Analysis
	12	30 min.

Optional break		

Quantitative
    Problem Solving
    Data Sufficiency
	37	75 min.

Optional break		

Verbal
    Reading Comprehension
    Critical Reasoning
    Sentence Correction
	41	75 min.

	Total Time:	210 min.

1.3 What Is the Content of the Test Like?

The GMAT exam measures higher-order analytical skills encompassing several types of reasoning. The Analytical Writing Assessment asks you to analyze the reasoning behind an argument and respond in writing; the Integrated Reasoning section asks you to interpret and synthesize information from multiple sources and in different formats to make reasoned conclusions; the Quantitative section asks you to reason quantitatively using basic arithmetic, algebra, and geometry;

and the Verbal section asks you to read and comprehend written material and to reason and evaluate arguments.

Test questions may address a variety of subjects, but all of the information you need to answer the questions will be included on the exam, with no outside knowledge of the subject matter necessary. The GMAT exam is not a test of business knowledge, English vocabulary, or advanced computational skills. You will need to read and write in English and have basic math and English skills to perform well on the test, but its difficulty comes from the required analytical abilities, which are developed over time.

The questions in this book are organized by question type and from easiest to most difficult, but keep in mind that when you take the test, you may see different types of questions in any order within each section.

1.4 Integrated Reasoning Section

The Integrated Reasoning section measures your ability to understand and evaluate multiple sources and types of information—graphic, numeric, and verbal—as they relate to one another; use both quantitative and verbal reasoning to solve complex problems; and solve multiple problems in relation to one another.

Four types of questions are used in the Integrated Reasoning section:

- Multi-Source Reasoning
- Table Analysis
- Graphics Interpretation
- Two-Part Analysis

Integrated Reasoning questions may be quantitative, verbal, or a combination of both. You will have to interpret graphics and sort tables to extract meaning from data, but advanced statistical knowledge and spreadsheet manipulation skills are not necessary. You will have access to an online calculator with basic functions for the Integrated Reasoning section, but note that the calculator is *not* available on the Quantitative section.

To review the Integrated Reasoning question types and test-taking tips, see chapter 10. For practice questions of each format, with full answer explanations, please visit the Integrated Reasoning online component using your unique access code found in the back of this book.

1.5 Quantitative Section

The GMAT Quantitative section measures your ability to reason quantitatively, solve quantitative problems, and interpret graphic data.

Two types of multiple-choice questions are used in the Quantitative section:

- Problem Solving
- Data Sufficiency

Both are intermingled throughout the Quantitative section, and both require basic knowledge of arithmetic, elementary algebra, and commonly known concepts of geometry.

To review the basic mathematical concepts that you will need to answer Quantitative questions, see the math review in chapter 4. For test-taking tips specific to the question types in the Quantitative section, practice questions, and answer explanations, see chapters 5 and 6.

1.6 Verbal Section

The GMAT Verbal section measures your ability to read and comprehend written material, and to reason and evaluate arguments. The Verbal section includes reading sections from several different content areas. Although you may be generally familiar with some of the material, neither the reading passages nor the questions assume detailed knowledge of the topics discussed.

Three types of multiple-choice questions are intermingled throughout the Verbal section:

- Reading Comprehension
- Critical Reasoning
- Sentence Correction

All three require basic knowledge of the English language, but the Verbal section is not a test of advanced vocabulary.

For test-taking tips specific to each question type in the Verbal section, practice questions, and answer explanations, see chapters 7 through 9.

1.7 Analytical Writing Assessment

The Analytical Writing Assessment (AWA) consists of one 30-minute writing task: Analysis of an Argument. The AWA measures your ability to think critically, communicate your ideas, and formulate an appropriate and constructive critique. You will type your essay on a computer keyboard.

For test-taking tips, sample essay responses, answer explanations, and sample Analysis of an Argument topics, see chapter 11.

1.8 What Computer Skills Will I Need?

The GMAT exam requires only minimal computer skills. You will type your AWA essay on the computer keyboard using standard word-processing keystrokes. In the Integrated Reasoning and multiple-choice sections, you select your responses using either your computer mouse or the keyboard. The Integrated Reasoning section includes basic computer navigation and functions, such as clicking on tabs and using drop-down menus to sort tables and select answers.

To learn more about the specific skills required to take the GMAT exam, download GMATPrep® software, the free test-preparation software from mba.com/gmatprep.

1.9 What Are the Test Centers Like?

The GMAT exam is administered under standardized conditions at test centers worldwide. Each test center has a proctored testing room with individual computer workstations that allow you to sit for the exam under quiet conditions and with some privacy. You will be able to take two optional breaks—one after completing the Integrated Reasoning section and another between the Quantitative and Verbal sections. You may not take notes or scratch paper with you into the testing room, but an erasable notepad and marker will be provided for you to use during the test.

1.10 How Are Scores Calculated?

Verbal and Quantitative sections are scored on a scale of 0 to 60, with scores below 6 or above 51 extremely rare. The Total GMAT score ranges from 200 to 800 and is based on your performance in these two sections. Your score is determined by:

- The number of questions you answer
- The number of questions you answer correctly or incorrectly
- The level of difficulty and other statistical characteristics of each question

Your Verbal, Quantitative, and Total GMAT scores are determined by a complex mathematical procedure that takes into account the difficulty of the questions that were presented to you and how you answered them. When you answer the easier questions correctly, you get a chance to answer harder questions, making it possible to earn a higher score. After you have completed all the questions on the test, or when your time is expired, the computer will calculate your scores. Your scores on the Verbal and Quantitative sections are combined to produce your Total score.

The Analytical Writing Assessment consists of one writing task, Analysis of an Argument, and your essay will be scored two times independently. Essays are evaluated by college and university faculty members from a variety of disciplines, including management education, who rate the overall quality of your critical thinking and writing. (For details on how readers are qualified, visit mba.com.) In addition, your response may be scored by an automated scoring program designed to reflect the judgment of expert readers.

Your essay is scored on a scale of 0 to 6, with 6 being the highest score and 0 the lowest. A score of zero is given for responses that are off-topic, are in a foreign language, merely attempt to copy the topic, consist only of keystroke characters, or are blank. Your AWA score is typically the average of two independent ratings. If the independent scores vary by more than a point, a third reader adjudicates, but because of ongoing training and monitoring, discrepancies are rare.

Your Analytical Writing Assessment and Integrated Reasoning scores are computed and reported separately from the other sections of the test and have no effect on your Verbal, Quantitative, or Total scores. The schools that you have designated to receive your scores may receive a copy of your Analytical Writing Assessment essay with your score report. Your own copy of your score report will not include your essay.

Like your AWA score, your Integrated Reasoning score will not count toward your Total score. A score scale for Integrated Reasoning will be available by April 2012 on mba.com.

Appendix A contains the 2011 percentile ranking tables that explain the distribution of GMAT scaled scores across all GMAT tests-takers during the period beginning July 2008 and ending June 2011. These ranking tables do not include Integrated Reasoning scores.

1.11 Test Development Process

The GMAT exam is developed by experts who use standardized procedures to ensure high-quality, widely appropriate test material. All questions are subjected to independent reviews and are revised or discarded as necessary. Multiple-choice questions are tested during GMAT exam administrations. Analytical Writing Assessment tasks are tested on mba.com registrants and then assessed for their fairness and reliability. For more information on test development, see mba.com.

2.0 How to Prepare

2.0 How to Prepare

2.1 How Should I Prepare to Take the Test?

The GMAT exam was designed specifically to measure academic skills needed for management education, and the test contains several question formats unique to the GMAT exam. At a minimum, you should be familiar with the test format and the question formats before you sit for the test. Because the GMAT exam is a timed exam, you should practice answering test questions not only to better understand the question formats and the skills they require, but also to help you learn to pace yourself so you can finish each section when you sit for the exam.

Because the exam measures reasoning rather than subject matter knowledge, you most likely will not find it helpful to memorize facts. You do not need to study advanced English vocabulary or mathematical concepts, but you should be sure your grasp of basic arithmetic, algebra, and geometry is sound enough that you can use these skills in quantitative problem-solving. Likewise, you do not need to study advanced vocabulary words, but you should have a firm understanding of basic English vocabulary and grammar for reading, writing, and reasoning.

> ### Myth -vs- **FACT**
>
> M – **You may need very advanced math skills to get a high GMAT score.**
>
> F – **The math skills tested on the GMAT exam are quite basic.**
>
> The GMAT exam only requires basic quantitative analytic skills. You should review the math skills (algebra, geometry, basic arithmetic) presented in this book, but the required skill level is low. The difficulty of GMAT Quantitative questions stems from the logic and analysis used to solve the problems and not the underlying math skills.

This book and other study materials released by the Graduate Management Admission Council contain questions that have been retired from the GMAT exam. All questions that appear or have appeared on the GMAT exam are copyrighted and owned by the GMAC, which does not license them to be reprinted elsewhere. Accessing live Integrated Reasoning, Quantitative, or Verbal test questions in advance or sharing test content during or after you take the test is a serious violation, which could cause your scores to be canceled and schools to be notified. In cases of a serious violation, you may be banned from future testing, and other legal remedies may be pursued.

2.2 What About Practice Tests?

The Quantitative and Verbal sections of the GMAT exam are computer adaptive, and the Integrated Reasoning section includes questions that require you to use the computer to sort tables and navigate to different sources of information. GMATPrep® software will help you prepare for the test. The software is available for download at no charge for those who have created an account on mba.com. The software includes two full-length GMAT exams, including computer-adaptive Quantitative and Verbal sections; plus additional practice questions; information about the test; and tutorials to help you become familiar with how the GMAT exam will appear on the computer screen at the test center.

To maximize your free practice exams, you should download the software as you start to prepare for the test. Take one practice test to familiarize yourself with the exam and to get an idea of how you might score. As your test date approaches, after you have studied using this book and other study materials, take the second practice test to determine whether you need to shift your focus to other areas you need to strengthen. Note that the practice tests may include questions that are also published in this book.

2.3 How Should I Use the Diagnostic Test?

This book contains a Diagnostic Test to help you determine the types of Quantitative and Verbal questions that you need to practice most. You should take the Diagnostic Test around the same time that you take the first GMATPrep sample test. The Diagnostic Test will give you a rating—*below average*, *average*, *above average*, or *excellent*—of your skills in each type of GMAT test question. These ratings will help you identify areas to focus on as you prepare for the GMAT exam.

The Diagnostic Test does not include Integrated Reasoning or Analysis of an Argument questions.

Use the results of the Diagnostic Test to help you select the right chapter of this book to start with. Next, read the introductory material carefully, and answer the practice questions in that chapter. Remember, the questions in the chapters are organized by difficulty, from easiest to most difficult. Make sure you follow the directions for each type of question and try to work as quickly and as efficiently as possible. Then review the explanations for the correct answers, spending as much time as necessary to familiarize yourself with the range of questions or problems presented.

2.4 Where Can I Get Additional Practice?

If you would like additional practice, *The Official Guide for GMAT® Verbal Review* and *The Official Guide for GMAT® Quantitative Review* include even more practice questions that are not published in this book. For an on-the-go solution, you can purchase *The Official Guide for GMAT® Review* app, available in both Apple and Android platforms. Please note that the Official GMAT mobile app is a mobile version of *The Official Guide for GMAT® Review*. Although it has interactive features not available in the print edition, it uses the same questions published in the printed guide. The Official GMAT mobile app and other books and study materials are available at mba.com/store.

2.5 General Test-Taking Suggestions

Specific test-taking strategies for individual question types are presented later in this book. The following are general suggestions to help you perform your best on the test.

1. **Use your time wisely.**
   Although the GMAT exam stresses accuracy more than speed, it is important to use your time wisely. On average, you will have about 1¾ minutes for each Verbal question, about 2 minutes for each Quantitative question, and about 2½ minutes for each Integrated Reasoning question, some of which have multiple questions. Once you start the test, an onscreen clock will show the time you have left. You can hide this display if you want, but it is a good idea to check the clock periodically to monitor your progress. The clock will automatically alert you when 5 minutes remain for the section you are working on.

2. **Answer practice questions ahead of time.**
   After you become generally familiar with all question types, use the practice questions in this book and the online Integrated Reasoning component to prepare for the actual test. It may be useful to time yourself as you answer the practice questions to get an idea of how long you will have for each question when you sit for the actual test, as well as to determine whether you are answering quickly enough to finish the test in the allotted time.

3. **Read all test directions carefully.**

   The directions explain exactly what is required to answer each question type. If you read hastily, you may miss important instructions and lower your score. To review directions during the test, click on the Help icon. But be aware that the time you spend reviewing directions will count against your time allotment for that section of the test.

4. **Read each question carefully and thoroughly.**

   Before you answer a question, determine exactly what is being asked and then select the best choice. Never skim a question or the possible answers; skimming may cause you to miss important information or nuances.

5. **Do not spend too much time on any one question.**

   If you do not know the correct answer, or if the question is too time-consuming, try to eliminate choices you know are wrong, select the best of the remaining answer choices, and move on to the next question. Not completing sections and randomly guessing answers to questions at the end of each test section can significantly lower your score. As long as you have worked on each section, you will receive a score even if you do not finish one or more section in the allotted time. But you will not earn points for questions you never get to see.

6. **Confirm your answers ONLY when you are ready to move on.**

   On the Quantitative and Verbal sections, once you have selected your answer to a multiple-choice question, you will be asked to confirm it. Once you confirm your response, you cannot go back and change it. You may not skip questions. In the Integrated Reasoning section, there may be several questions based on information provided in the same question prompt. When there is more than one response on a single screen, you can change your response to any of the questions on the screen before moving on to the next screen. But you may not navigate back to a previous screen to change any responses.

7. **Plan your essay answer before you begin to write.**

   The best way to approach the Analysis of an Argument section is to read the directions carefully, take a few minutes to think about the question, and plan a response before you begin writing. Take care to organize your ideas and develop them fully, but leave time to reread your response and make any revisions that you think would improve it.

Myth -vs- **FACT**

M – **It is more important to respond correctly to the test questions than it is to finish the test.**

F – **There is a severe penalty for not completing the GMAT exam.**

If you are stumped by a question, give it your best guess and move on. If you guess incorrectly, the computer program will likely give you an easier question, which you are likely to answer correctly, and the computer will rapidly return to giving you questions matched to your ability. If you don't finish the test, your score will be reduced greatly. Failing to answer five verbal questions, for example, could reduce your score from the 91st percentile to the 77th percentile. Pacing is important.

Myth -vs- **FACT**

M – **The first 10 questions are critical and you should invest the most time on those.**

F – **All questions count.**

It is true that the computer-adaptive testing algorithm uses the first 10 questions to obtain an initial estimate of your ability; however, that is only an *initial* estimate. As you continue to answer questions, the algorithm self-corrects by computing an updated estimate on the basis of all the questions you have answered, and then administers items that are closely matched to this new estimate of your ability. Your final score is based on all your responses and considers the difficulty of all the questions you answered. Taking additional time on the first 10 questions will not game the system and can hurt your ability to finish the test.

3.0 Diagnostic Test

3.0 Diagnostic Test

Like the practice sections later in the book, the Diagnostic Test uses questions from real GMAT® exams. The purpose of the Diagnostic Test is to help you determine how skilled you are in answering each of the five types of questions on the GMAT exam: problem solving, data sufficiency, reading comprehension, critical reasoning, and sentence correction.

Scores on the Diagnostic Test are designed to help you answer the question, "If all the questions on the GMAT exam were like the questions in this section, how well would I do?" Your scores are classified as being *excellent, above average, average,* or *below average,* relative to the scores of other test-takers. You can use this information to focus your test-preparation activities.

Instructions

1. Take your time answering these questions. The Diagnostic Test is not timed.

2. If you are stumped by a question, you should guess and move on, just like you should do on the real GMAT exam.

3. You can take one segment at a time, if you want. It is better to finish an entire section (Quantitative or Verbal) in one sitting, but this is not a requirement.

4. You can go back and change your answers in the Diagnostic Test.

5. After you take the test, check your answers using the answer key that follows the test. The number of correct answers is your raw score.

6. Convert your raw score, using the table provided.

Note: The Diagnostic Test is designed to give you guidance on how to prepare for the GMAT exam; however, a strong score on one type of question does not guarantee that you will perform as well on the real GMAT exam. The statistical reliability of scores on the Diagnostic Test ranges from 0.75 to 0.89, and the subscale classification is about 85%–90% accurate, meaning that your scores on the Diagnostic Test are a good, but not perfect, measure of how you are likely to perform on the real test. Use the tests on the free online software to obtain a good estimate of your expected GMAT Verbal, Quantitative, and Total scores.

You should not compare the number of questions you got right in each section. Instead, you should compare how your responses are rated in each section.

3.1 Quantitative Questions

Problem Solving

Solve the problem and indicate the best of the answer choices given.
<u>Numbers:</u> All numbers used are real numbers.
<u>Figures:</u> All figures accompanying problem solving questions are intended to provide information useful in solving the problems. Figures are drawn as accurately as possible. Exceptions will be clearly noted. Lines shown as straight are straight, and lines that appear jagged are also straight. The positions of points, angles, regions, etc., exist in the order shown, and angle measures are greater than zero. All figures lie in a plane unless otherwise indicated.

1. Last month a certain music club offered a discount to preferred customers. After the first compact disc purchased, preferred customers paid $3.99 for each additional compact disc purchased. If a preferred customer purchased a total of 6 compact discs and paid $15.95 for the first compact disc, then the dollar amount that the customer paid for the 6 compact discs is equivalent to which of the following?

   (A) $5(4.00)+15.90$
   (B) $5(4.00)+15.95$
   (C) $5(4.00)+16.00$
   (D) $5(4.00-0.01)+15.90$
   (E) $5(4.00-0.05)+15.95$

2. The average (arithmetic mean) of the integers from 200 to 400, inclusive, is how much greater than the average of the integers from 50 to 100, inclusive?

   (A) 150
   (B) 175
   (C) 200
   (D) 225
   (E) 300

3. The sequence $a_1, a_2, a_3,...,a_n,...$ is such that $a_n = \dfrac{a_{n-1}+a_{n-2}}{2}$ for all $n \geq 3$. If $a_3 = 4$ and $a_5 = 20$, what is the value of a_6 ?

   (A) 12
   (B) 16
   (C) 20
   (D) 24
   (E) 28

4. Among a group of 2,500 people, 35 percent invest in municipal bonds, 18 percent invest in oil stocks, and 7 percent invest in both municipal bonds and oil stocks. If 1 person is to be randomly selected from the 2,500 people, what is the probability that the person selected will be one who invests in municipal bonds but NOT in oil stocks?

   (A) $\dfrac{9}{50}$
   (B) $\dfrac{7}{25}$
   (C) $\dfrac{7}{20}$
   (D) $\dfrac{21}{50}$
   (E) $\dfrac{27}{50}$

5. A closed cylindrical tank contains 36π cubic feet of water and is filled to half its capacity. When the tank is placed upright on its circular base on level ground, the height of the water in the tank is 4 feet. When the tank is placed on its side on level ground, what is the height, in feet, of the surface of the water above the ground?

   (A) 2
   (B) 3
   (C) 4
   (D) 6
   (E) 9

6. A marketing firm determined that, of 200 households surveyed, 80 used neither Brand A nor Brand B soap, 60 used only Brand A soap, and for every household that used both brands of soap, 3 used only Brand B soap. How many of the 200 households surveyed used both brands of soap?

    (A)   15
    (B)   20
    (C)   30
    (D)   40
    (E)   45

7. A certain club has 10 members, including Harry. One of the 10 members is to be chosen at random to be the president, one of the remaining 9 members is to be chosen at random to be the secretary, and one of the remaining 8 members is to be chosen at random to be the treasurer. What is the probability that Harry will be either the member chosen to be the secretary or the member chosen to be the treasurer?

    (A) $\frac{1}{720}$
    (B) $\frac{1}{80}$
    (C) $\frac{1}{10}$
    (D) $\frac{1}{9}$
    (E) $\frac{1}{5}$

8. If a certain toy store's revenue in November was $\frac{2}{5}$ of its revenue in December and its revenue in January was $\frac{1}{4}$ of its revenue in November, then the store's revenue in December was how many times the average (arithmetic mean) of its revenues in November and January?

    (A) $\frac{1}{4}$
    (B) $\frac{1}{2}$
    (C) $\frac{2}{3}$
    (D)   2
    (E)   4

9. A researcher computed the mean, the median, and the standard deviation for a set of performance scores. If 5 were to be added to each score, which of these three statistics would change?

    (A)   The mean only
    (B)   The median only
    (C)   The standard deviation only
    (D)   The mean and the median
    (E)   The mean and the standard deviation

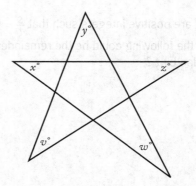

10. In the figure shown, what is the value of $v + x + y + z + w$?

    (A)   45
    (B)   90
    (C)   180
    (D)   270
    (E)   360

11. Of the three-digit integers greater than 700, how many have two digits that are equal to each other and the remaining digit different from the other two?

    (A)   90
    (B)   82
    (C)   80
    (D)   45
    (E)   36

12. Positive integer y is 50 percent of 50 percent of positive integer x, and y percent of x equals 100. What is the value of x ?

    (A)   50
    (B)   100
    (C)   200
    (D)   1,000
    (E)   2,000

13. If s and t are positive integers such that $\frac{s}{t} = 64.12$, which of the following could be the remainder when s is divided by t ?

    (A)   2
    (B)   4
    (C)   8
    (D)   20
    (E)   45

14. Of the 84 parents who attended a meeting at a school, 35 volunteered to supervise children during the school picnic and 11 volunteered both to supervise children during the picnic and to bring refreshments to the picnic. If the number of parents who volunteered to bring refreshments was 1.5 times the number of parents who neither volunteered to supervise children during the picnic nor volunteered to bring refreshments, how many of the parents volunteered to bring refreshments?

    (A)   25
    (B)   36
    (C)   38
    (D)   42
    (E)   45

15. The product of all the prime numbers less than 20 is closest to which of the following powers of 10 ?

    (A) 10^9
    (B) 10^8
    (C) 10^7
    (D) 10^6
    (E) 10^5

16. If $\sqrt{3-2x} = \sqrt{2x}+1$, then $4x^2 =$

    (A)   1
    (B)   4
    (C) $2-2x$
    (D) $4x-2$
    (E) $6x-1$

17. If $n = \sqrt{\frac{16}{81}}$, what is the value of $\sqrt{n}$?

    (A) $\frac{1}{9}$
    (B) $\frac{1}{4}$
    (C) $\frac{4}{9}$
    (D) $\frac{2}{3}$
    (E) $\frac{9}{2}$

18. If n is the product of the integers from 1 to 8, inclusive, how many different prime factors greater than 1 does n have?

    (A)   Four
    (B)   Five
    (C)   Six
    (D)   Seven
    (E)   Eight

19. If k is an integer and $2 < k < 7$, for how many different values of k is there a triangle with sides of lengths 2, 7, and k ?

    (A)   One
    (B)   Two
    (C)   Three
    (D)   Four
    (E)   Five

20. A right circular cone is inscribed in a hemisphere so that the base of the cone coincides with the base of the hemisphere. What is the ratio of the height of the cone to the radius of the hemisphere?

    (A) $\sqrt{3}:1$
    (B) $1:1$
    (C) $\frac{1}{2}:1$
    (D) $\sqrt{2}:1$
    (E) $2:1$

21. John deposited $10,000 to open a new savings account that earned 4 percent annual interest, compounded quarterly. If there were no other transactions in the account, what was the amount of money in John's account 6 months after the account was opened?

    (A) $10,100
    (B) $10,101
    (C) $10,200
    (D) $10,201
    (E) $10,400

22. A container in the shape of a right circular cylinder is $\frac{1}{2}$ full of water. If the volume of water in the container is 36 cubic inches and the height of the container is 9 inches, what is the diameter of the base of the cylinder, in inches?

    (A) $\frac{16}{9\pi}$
    (B) $\frac{4}{\sqrt{\pi}}$
    (C) $\frac{12}{\sqrt{\pi}}$
    (D) $\sqrt{\frac{2}{\pi}}$
    (E) $4\sqrt{\frac{2}{\pi}}$

23. If the positive integer x is a multiple of 4 and the positive integer y is a multiple of 6, then xy must be a multiple of which of the following?

    I. 8
    II. 12
    III. 18

    (A) II only
    (B) I and II only
    (C) I and III only
    (D) II and III only
    (E) I, II, and III

24. Aaron will jog from home at x miles per hour and then walk back home by the same route at y miles per hour. How many miles from home can Aaron jog so that he spends a total of t hours jogging and walking?

    (A) $\dfrac{xt}{y}$

    (B) $\dfrac{x+t}{xy}$

    (C) $\dfrac{xyt}{x+y}$

    (D) $\dfrac{x+y+t}{xy}$

    (E) $\dfrac{y+t}{x} - \dfrac{t}{y}$

Data Sufficiency

Each <u>data sufficiency</u> problem consists of a question and two statements, labeled (1) and (2), which contain certain data. Using these data and your knowledge of mathematics and everyday facts (such as the number of days in July or the meaning of the word *counterclockwise*), decide whether the data given are sufficient for answering the question and then indicate one of the following answer choices:

A   Statement (1) ALONE is sufficient, but statement (2) alone is not sufficient.
B   Statement (2) ALONE is sufficient, but statement (1) alone is not sufficient.
C   BOTH statements TOGETHER are sufficient, but NEITHER statement ALONE is sufficient.
D   EACH statement ALONE is sufficient.
E   Statements (1) and (2) TOGETHER are not sufficient.

<u>Note:</u> In data sufficiency problems that ask for the value of a quantity, the data given in the statements are sufficient only when it is possible to determine exactly one numerical value for the quantity.

<u>Example:</u>

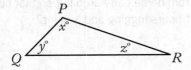

In $\triangle PQR$, what is the value of x ?

(1) $PQ = PR$
(2) $y = 40$

<u>Explanation:</u> According to statement (1) $PQ = PR$; therefore, $\triangle PQR$ is isosceles and $y = z$. Since $x + y + z = 180$, it follows that $x + 2y = 180$. Since statement (1) does not give a value for y, you cannot answer the question using statement (1) alone. According to statement (2), $y = 40$; therefore, $x + z = 140$. Since statement (2) does not give a value for z, you cannot answer the question using statement (2) alone. Using both statements together, since $x + 2y = 180$ and the value of y is given, you can find the value of x. Therefore, BOTH statements (1) and (2) TOGETHER are sufficient to answer the question, but NEITHER statement ALONE is sufficient.

<u>Numbers:</u> All numbers used are real numbers.

<u>Figures:</u>
- Figures conform to the information given in the question, but will not necessarily conform to the additional information given in statements (1) and (2).
- Lines shown as straight are straight, and lines that appear jagged are also straight.
- The positions of points, angles, regions, etc., exist in the order shown, and angle measures are greater than zero.
- All figures lie in a plane unless otherwise indicated.

25. If the units digit of integer n is greater than 2, what is the units digit of n ?

    (1) The units digit of n is the same as the units digit of n^2.
    (2) The units digit of n is the same as the units digit of n^3.

26. What is the value of the integer p ?
    (1) Each of the integers 2, 3, and 5 is a factor of p.
    (2) Each of the integers 2, 5, and 7 is a factor of p.

27. If the length of Wanda's telephone call was rounded up to the nearest whole minute by her telephone company, then Wanda was charged for how many minutes for her telephone call?

    (1) The total charge for Wanda's telephone call was $6.50.
    (2) Wanda was charged $0.50 more for the first minute of the telephone call than for each minute after the first.

28. What is the perimeter of isosceles triangle MNP ?

    (1) $MN = 16$
    (2) $NP = 20$

29. In a survey of retailers, what percent had purchased computers for business purposes?

    (1) 85 percent of the retailers surveyed who owned their own store had purchased computers for business purposes.
    (2) 40 percent of the retailers surveyed owned their own store.

30. The only gift certificates that a certain store sold yesterday were worth either $100 each or $10 each. If the store sold a total of 20 gift certificates yesterday, how many gift certificates worth $10 each did the store sell yesterday?

    (1) The gift certificates sold by the store yesterday were worth a total of between $1,650 and $1,800.
    (2) Yesterday the store sold more than 15 gift certificates worth $100 each.

31. Is the standard deviation of the set of measurements $x_1, x_2, x_3, x_4, \ldots, x_{20}$ less than 3 ?

    (1) The variance for the set of measurements is 4.
    (2) For each measurement, the difference between the mean and that measurement is 2.

32. Is the range of the integers 6, 3, y, 4, 5, and x greater than 9 ?

    (1) $y > 3x$
    (2) $y > x > 3$

33. Is $\dfrac{5^{x+2}}{25} < 1$?

    (1) $5^x < 1$
    (2) $x < 0$

34. Of the companies surveyed about the skills they required in prospective employees, 20 percent required both computer skills and writing skills. What percent of the companies surveyed required neither computer skills nor writing skills?

    (1) Of those companies surveyed that required computer skills, half required writing skills.
    (2) 45 percent of the companies surveyed required writing skills but not computer skills.

35. What is the value of $w + q$?

    (1) $3w = 3 - 3q$
    (2) $5w + 5q = 5$

36. If X and Y are points in a plane and X lies inside the circle C with center O and radius 2, does Y lie inside circle C ?

    (1) The length of line segment XY is 3.
    (2) The length of line segment OY is 1.5.

37. Is $x > y$?

    (1) $x = y + 2$
    (2) $\dfrac{x}{2} = y - 1$

38. If Paula drove the distance from her home to her college at an average speed that was greater than 70 kilometers per hour, did it take her less than 3 hours to drive this distance?

    (1) The distance that Paula drove from her home to her college was greater than 200 kilometers.

    (2) The distance that Paula drove from her home to her college was less than 205 kilometers.

39. In the xy-plane, if line k has negative slope and passes through the point $(-5, r)$, is the x-intercept of line k positive?

    (1) The slope of line k is −5.

    (2) $r > 0$

40. If $5,000 invested for one year at p percent simple annual interest yields $500, what amount must be invested at k percent simple annual interest for one year to yield the same number of dollars?

    (1) $k = 0.8p$

    (2) $k = 8$

41. If $\frac{x+y}{z} > 0$, is $x < 0$?

    (1) $x < y$

    (2) $z < 0$

42. Does the integer k have at least three different positive prime factors?

    (1) $\frac{k}{15}$ is an integer.

    (2) $\frac{k}{10}$ is an integer.

43. In City X last April, was the average (arithmetic mean) daily high temperature greater than the median daily high temperature?

    (1) In City X last April, the sum of the 30 daily high temperatures was 2,160°.

    (2) In City X last April, 60 percent of the daily high temperatures were less than the average daily high temperature.

44. If m and n are positive integers, is $\left(\sqrt{m}\right)^n$ an integer?

    (1) $\left(\sqrt{m}\right)$ is an integer.

    (2) $\left(\sqrt{n}\right)$ is an integer.

45. Of the 66 people in a certain auditorium, at most 6 people have their birthdays in any one given month. Does at least one person in the auditorium have a birthday in January?

    (1) More of the people in the auditorium have their birthday in February than in March.

    (2) Five of the people in the auditorium have their birthday in March.

46. Last year the average (arithmetic mean) salary of the 10 employees of Company X was $42,800. What is the average salary of the same 10 employees this year?

    (1) For 8 of the 10 employees, this year's salary is 15 percent greater than last year's salary.

    (2) For 2 of the 10 employees, this year's salary is the same as last year's salary.

47. In a certain classroom, there are 80 books, of which 24 are fiction and 23 are written in Spanish. How many of the fiction books are written in Spanish?

    (1) Of the fiction books, there are 6 more that are not written in Spanish than are written in Spanish.

    (2) Of the books written in Spanish, there are 5 more nonfiction books than fiction books.

48. If p is the perimeter of rectangle Q, what is the value of p?

    (1) Each diagonal of rectangle Q has length 10.

    (2) The area of rectangle Q is 48.

3.2 Verbal Questions

Reading Comprehension

Each of the <u>reading comprehension</u> questions is based on the content of a passage. After reading the passage, answer all questions pertaining to it on the basis of what is <u>stated</u> or <u>implied</u> in the passage. For each question, select the best answer of the choices given.

Line   According to economic signaling theory, consumers may perceive the frequency with which an unfamiliar brand is advertised as a cue that the brand is of high quality. The notion that
(5)   highly advertised brands are associated with high-quality products does have some empirical support. Marquardt and McGann found that heavily advertised products did indeed rank high on certain measures of product quality. **Because**
(10)   **large advertising expenditures represent a significant investment on the part of a manufacturer, only companies that expect to recoup these costs in the long run, through consumers' repeat purchases of the product,**
(15)   **can afford to spend such amounts.**
        However, two studies by Kirmani have found that although consumers initially perceive expensive advertising as a signal of high brand quality, at some level of spending the manufacturer's
(20)   advertising effort may be perceived as unreasonably high, implying low manufacturer confidence in product quality. If consumers perceive excessive advertising effort as a sign of a manufacturer's desperation, the result may be less favorable
(25)   brand perceptions. In addition, a third study by Kirmani, of print advertisements, found that the use of color affected consumer perception of brand quality. Because consumers recognize that color advertisements are more expensive than
(30)   black and white, the point at which repetition of an advertisement is perceived as excessive comes sooner for a color advertisement than for a black-and-white advertisement.

1.   Which of the following best describes the purpose of the sentence in lines 10–15 ?

(A)   To show that economic signaling theory fails to explain a finding

(B)   To introduce a distinction not accounted for by economic signaling theory

(C)   To account for an exception to a generalization suggested by Marquardt and McGann

(D)   To explain why Marquardt and McGann's research was conducted

(E)   To offer an explanation for an observation reported by Marquardt and McGann

2.   The primary purpose of the passage is to

(A)   present findings that contradict one explanation for the effects of a particular advertising practice

(B)   argue that theoretical explanations about the effects of a particular advertising practice are of limited value without empirical evidence

(C)   discuss how and why particular advertising practices may affect consumers' perceptions

(D)   contrast the research methods used in two different studies of a particular advertising practice

(E)   explain why a finding about consumer responses to a particular advertising practice was unexpected

3. Kirmani's research, as described in the passage, suggests which of the following regarding consumers' expectations about the quality of advertised products?

   (A) Those expectations are likely to be highest if a manufacturer runs both black-and-white and color advertisements for the same product.

   (B) Those expectations can be shaped by the presence of color in an advertisement as well as by the frequency with which an advertisement appears.

   (C) Those expectations are usually high for frequently advertised new brands but not for frequently advertised familiar brands.

   (D) Those expectations are likely to be higher for products whose black-and-white advertisements are often repeated than for those whose color advertisements are less often repeated.

   (E) Those expectations are less definitively shaped by the manufacturer's advertisements than by information that consumers gather from other sources.

4. Kirmani's third study, as described in the passage, suggests which of the following conclusions about a black-and-white advertisement?

   (A) It can be repeated more frequently than a comparable color advertisement could before consumers begin to suspect low manufacturer confidence in the quality of the advertised product.

   (B) It will have the greatest impact on consumers' perceptions of the quality of the advertised product if it appears during periods when a color version of the same advertisement is also being used.

   (C) It will attract more attention from readers of the print publication in which it appears if it is used only a few times.

   (D) It may be perceived by some consumers as more expensive than a comparable color advertisement.

   (E) It is likely to be perceived by consumers as a sign of higher manufacturer confidence in the quality of the advertised product than a comparable color advertisement would be.

5. The passage suggests that Kirmani would be most likely to agree with which of the following statements about consumers' perceptions of the relationship between the frequency with which a product is advertised and the product's quality?

   (A) Consumers' perceptions about the frequency with which an advertisement appears are their primary consideration when evaluating an advertisement's claims about product quality.

   (B) Because most consumers do not notice the frequency of advertisement, it has little impact on most consumers' expectations regarding product quality.

   (C) Consumers perceive frequency of advertisement as a signal about product quality only when the advertisement is for a product that is newly on the market.

   (D) The frequency of advertisement is not always perceived by consumers to indicate that manufacturers are highly confident about their products' quality.

   (E) Consumers who try a new product that has been frequently advertised are likely to perceive the advertisement's frequency as having been an accurate indicator of the product's quality.

Line   The idea of the brain as an information
        processor—a machine manipulating blips of energy
        according to fathomable rules—has come to
        dominate neuroscience. However, one enemy of
(5)   the brain-as-computer metaphor is John R. Searle,
        a philosopher who argues that since computers
        simply follow algorithms, they cannot deal with
        important aspects of human thought such as
        meaning and content. Computers are syntactic,
(10)   rather than semantic, creatures. People, on the
        other hand, understand meaning because they have
        something Searle obscurely calls the causal powers
        of the brain.
            Yet how would a brain work if not by reducing
(15)   what it learns about the world to information—some
        kind of code that can be transmitted from neuron
        to neuron? What else could meaning and content
        be? If the code can be cracked, a computer should
        be able to simulate it, at least in principle. But
(20)   even if a computer could simulate the workings
        of the mind, Searle would claim that the machine
        would not really be thinking; it would just be acting
        as if it were. His argument proceeds thus: if a
        computer were used to simulate a stomach, with
(25)   the stomach's churnings faithfully reproduced on a
        video screen, the machine would not be digesting
        real food. It would just be blindly manipulating the
        symbols that generate the visual display.
            Suppose, though, that a stomach were simulated
(30)   using plastic tubes, a motor to do the churning, a
        supply of digestive juices, and a timing mechanism.
        If food went in one end of the device, what came out
        the other end would surely be digested food. Brains,
        unlike stomachs, are information processors, and if
(35)   one information processor were made to simulate
        another information processor, it is hard to see
        how one and not the other could be said to think.
        Simulated thoughts and real thoughts are made of
        the same element: information. The representations
(40)   of the world that humans carry around in their heads
        are already simulations. To accept Searle's argument,
        one would have to deny the most fundamental notion
        in psychology and neuroscience: that brains work
        by processing information.

6. The main purpose of the passage is to

    (A)   propose an experiment
    (B)   analyze a function
    (C)   refute an argument
    (D)   explain a contradiction
    (E)   simulate a process

7. Which of the following is most consistent with Searle's
    reasoning as presented in the passage?

    (A)   Meaning and content cannot be reduced to
           algorithms.
    (B)   The process of digestion can be simulated
           mechanically, but not on a computer.
    (C)   Simulated thoughts and real thoughts are
           essentially similar because they are composed
           primarily of information.
    (D)   A computer can use "causal powers" similar to
           those of the human brain when processing
           information.
    (E)   Computer simulations of the world can achieve
           the complexity of the brain's representations of
           the world.

8. The author of the passage would be most likely to
    agree with which of the following statements about the
    simulation of organ functions?

    (A)   An artificial device that achieves the functions of
           the stomach could be considered a valid model
           of the stomach.
    (B)   Computer simulations of the brain are best used
           to crack the brain's codes of meaning and
           content.
    (C)   Computer simulations of the brain challenge
           ideas that are fundamental to psychology and
           neuroscience.
    (D)   Because the brain and the stomach both act as
           processors, they can best be simulated by
           mechanical devices.
    (E)   The computer's limitations in simulating
           digestion suggest equal limitations in computer-
           simulated thinking.

9. It can be inferred that the author of the passage believes that Searle's argument is flawed by its failure to

   (A) distinguish between syntactic and semantic operations

   (B) explain adequately how people, unlike computers, are able to understand meaning

   (C) provide concrete examples illustrating its claims about thinking

   (D) understand how computers use algorithms to process information

   (E) decipher the code that is transmitted from neuron to neuron in the brain

10. From the passage, it can be inferred that the author would agree with Searle on which of the following points?

    (A) Computers operate by following algorithms.

    (B) The human brain can never fully understand its own functions.

    (C) The comparison of the brain to a machine is overly simplistic.

    (D) The most accurate models of physical processes are computer simulations.

    (E) Human thought and computer-simulated thought involve similar processes of representation.

11. Which of the following most accurately represents Searle's criticism of the brain-as-computer metaphor, as that criticism is described in the passage?

    (A) The metaphor is not experimentally verifiable.

    (B) The metaphor does not take into account the unique powers of the brain.

    (C) The metaphor suggests that a brain's functions can be simulated as easily as those of a stomach.

    (D) The metaphor suggests that a computer can simulate the workings of the mind by using the codes of neural transmission.

    (E) The metaphor is unhelpful because both the brain and the computer process information.

Line Women's grassroots activism and their vision
of a new civic consciousness lay at the heart of
social reform in the United States throughout the
Progressive Era, the period between the depression
(5) of 1893 and America's entry into the Second
World War. Though largely disenfranchised except
for school elections, white middle-class women
reformers won a variety of victories, notably in
the improvement of working conditions, especially
(10) for women and children. Ironically, though,
child labor legislation pitted women of different
classes against one another. To the reformers,
child labor and industrial home work were equally
inhumane practices that should be outlawed, but,
(15) as a number of women historians have recently
observed, working-class mothers did not always
share this view. Given the precarious finances of
working-class families and the necessity of pooling
the wages of as many family members as possible,
(20) working-class families viewed the passage and
enforcement of stringent child labor statutes as a
personal economic disaster and made strenuous
efforts to circumvent child labor laws. Yet
reformers rarely understood this resistance in terms
(25) of the desperate economic situation of working-
class families, interpreting it instead as evidence
of poor parenting. This is not to dispute women
reformers' perception of child labor as a terribly
exploitative practice, but their understanding of
(30) child labor and their legislative solutions for ending
it failed to take account of the economic needs of
working-class families.

12. The primary purpose of the passage is to

(A) explain why women reformers of the Progressive Era failed to achieve their goals

(B) discuss the origins of child labor laws in the late nineteenth and early twentieth centuries

(C) compare the living conditions of working-class and middle-class women in the Progressive Era

(D) discuss an oversight on the part of women reformers of the Progressive Era

(E) revise a traditional view of the role played by women reformers in enacting Progressive Era reforms

13. The *view* mentioned in line 17 of the passage refers to which of the following?

(A) Some working-class mothers' resistance to the enforcement of child labor laws

(B) Reformers' belief that child labor and industrial home work should be abolished

(C) Reformers' opinions about how working-class families raised their children

(D) Certain women historians' observation that there was a lack of consensus between women of different classes on the issue of child labor and industrial home work

(E) Working-class families' fears about the adverse consequences that child labor laws would have on their ability to earn an adequate living

14. The author of the passage mentions the observations of women historians (lines 15–17) most probably in order to

(A) provide support for an assertion made in the preceding sentence (lines 10–12)

(B) raise a question that is answered in the last sentence of the passage (lines 27–32)

(C) introduce an opinion that challenges a statement made in the first sentence of the passage

(D) offer an alternative view to the one attributed in the passage to working-class mothers

(E) point out a contradiction inherent in the traditional view of child labor reform as it is presented in the passage

15. The passage suggests that which of the following was a reason for the difference of opinion between working-class mothers and women reformers on the issue of child labor?

    (A) Reformers' belief that industrial home work was preferable to child labor outside the home

    (B) Reformers' belief that child labor laws should pertain to working conditions but not to pay

    (C) Working-class mothers' resentment at reformers' attempts to interfere with their parenting

    (D) Working-class mothers' belief that child labor was an inhumane practice

    (E) Working-class families' need for every employable member of their families to earn money

16. The author of the passage asserts which of the following about women reformers who tried to abolish child labor?

    (A) They alienated working-class mothers by attempting to enlist them in agitating for progressive causes.

    (B) They underestimated the prevalence of child labor among the working classes.

    (C) They were correct in their conviction that child labor was deplorable but shortsighted about the impact of child labor legislation on working-class families.

    (D) They were aggressive in their attempts to enforce child labor legislation, but were unable to prevent working-class families from circumventing them.

    (E) They were prevented by their nearly total disenfranchisement from making significant progress in child labor reform.

17. According to the passage, one of the most striking achievements of white middle-class women reformers during the Progressive Era was

    (A) gaining the right to vote in school elections

    (B) mobilizing working-class women in the fight against child labor

    (C) uniting women of different classes in grassroots activism

    (D) improving the economic conditions of working-class families

    (E) improving women's and children's working conditions

Critical Reasoning

Each of the <u>critical reasoning</u> questions is based on a short argument, a set of statements, or a plan of action. For each question, select the best answer of the choices given.

18. Vasquez-Morrell Assurance specializes in insuring manufacturers. Whenever a policyholder makes a claim, a claims adjuster determines the amount that Vasquez-Morrell is obligated to pay. Vasquez-Morrell is cutting its staff of claims adjusters by 15 percent. To ensure that the company's ability to handle claims promptly is affected as little as possible by the staff cuts, consultants recommend that Vasquez-Morrell lay off those adjusters who now take longest, on average, to complete work on claims assigned to them.

    Which of the following, if true, most seriously calls into question the consultants' criterion for selecting the staff to be laid off?

    (A) If the time that Vasquez-Morrell takes to settle claims increases significantly, it could lose business to other insurers.

    (B) Supervisors at Vasquez-Morrell tend to assign the most complex claims to the most capable adjusters.

    (C) At Vasquez-Morrell, no insurance payments are made until a claims adjuster has reached a final determination on the claim.

    (D) There are no positions at Vasquez-Morrell to which staff currently employed as claims adjusters could be reassigned.

    (E) The premiums that Vasquez-Morrell currently charges are no higher than those charged for similar coverage by competitors.

19. Prolonged spells of hot, dry weather at the end of the grape-growing season typically reduce a vineyard's yield, because the grapes stay relatively small. In years with such weather, wine producers can make only a relatively small quantity of wine from a given area of vineyards. Nonetheless, in regions where wine producers generally grow their own grapes, analysts typically expect a long, hot, dry spell late in the growing season to result in increased revenues for local wine producers.

    Which of the following, if true, does most to justify the analysts' expectation?

    (A) The lower a vineyard's yield, the less labor is required to harvest the grapes.

    (B) Long, hot, dry spells at the beginning of the grape-growing season are rare, but they can have a devastating effect on a vineyard's yield.

    (C) Grapes grown for wine production are typically made into wine at or near the vineyard in which they were grown.

    (D) When hot, dry spells are followed by heavy rains, the rains frequently destroy grape crops.

    (E) Grapes that have matured in hot, dry weather make significantly better wine than ordinary grapes.

20. In the past, most children who went sledding in the winter snow in Verland used wooden sleds with runners and steering bars. Ten years ago, smooth plastic sleds became popular; they go faster than wooden sleds but are harder to steer and slow. The concern that plastic sleds are more dangerous is clearly borne out by the fact that the number of children injured while sledding was much higher last winter than it was 10 years ago.

    Which of the following, if true in Verland, most seriously undermines the force of the evidence cited?

(A)   A few children still use traditional wooden sleds.

(B)   Very few children wear any kind of protective gear, such as helmets, while sledding.

(C)   Plastic sleds can be used in a much wider variety of snow conditions than wooden sleds can.

(D)   Most sledding injuries occur when a sled collides with a tree, a rock, or another sled.

(E)   Because the traditional wooden sleds can carry more than one rider, an accident involving a wooden sled can result in several children being injured.

21.   Metal rings recently excavated from seventh-century settlements in the western part of Mexico were made using the same metallurgical techniques as those used by Ecuadorian artisans before and during that period. These techniques are sufficiently complex to make their independent development in both areas unlikely. Since the people of these two areas were in cultural contact, archaeologists hypothesize that the metallurgical techniques used to make the rings found in Mexico were learned by Mexican artisans from Ecuadorian counterparts.

Which of the following would it be most useful to establish in order to evaluate the archaeologists' hypothesis?

(A)   Whether metal objects were traded from Ecuador to western Mexico during the seventh century

(B)   Whether travel between western Mexico and Ecuador in the seventh century would have been primarily by land or by sea

(C)   Whether artisans from western Mexico could have learned complex metallurgical techniques from their Ecuadorian counterparts without actually leaving western Mexico

(D)   Whether metal tools were used in the seventh-century settlements in western Mexico

(E)   Whether any of the techniques used in the manufacture of the metal rings found in western Mexico are still practiced among artisans in Ecuador today

22.   Following several years of declining advertising sales, the *Greenville Times* reorganized its advertising sales force. Before reorganization, the sales force was organized geographically, with some sales representatives concentrating on city-center businesses and others concentrating on different outlying regions. The reorganization attempted to increase the sales representatives' knowledge of clients' businesses by having each sales representative deal with only one type of industry or of retailing. After the reorganization, revenue from advertising sales increased.

In assessing whether the improvement in advertising sales can properly be attributed to the reorganization, it would be most helpful to find out which of the following?

(A)   What proportion of the total revenue of the *Greenville Times* is generated by advertising sales?

(B)   Has the circulation of the *Greenville Times* increased substantially in the last two years?

(C)   Among all the types of industry and retailing that use the *Greenville Times* as an advertising vehicle, which type accounts for the largest proportion of the newspaper's advertising sales?

(D)   Do any clients of the sales representatives of the *Greenville Times* have a standing order with the *Times* for a fixed amount of advertising per month?

(E)   Among the advertisers in the *Greenville Times*, are there more types of retail business or more types of industrial business?

23. Motorists in a certain country frequently complain that traffic congestion is much worse now than it was 20 years ago. No real measure of how much traffic congestion there was 20 years ago exists, but the motorists' complaints are almost certainly unwarranted. The country's highway capacity has tripled in the last twenty years, thanks to a vigorous highway construction program, whereas the number of automobiles registered in the country has increased by only 75 percent.

    Which of the following, if true, most seriously weakens the argument?

    (A) Most automobile travel is local, and the networks of roads and streets in the country's settled areas have changed little over the last 20 years.

    (B) Gasoline prices are high, and miles traveled per car per year have not changed much over the last 20 years.

    (C) The country's urban centers have well-developed public transit systems that carry most of the people who commute into those centers.

    (D) The average age of automobiles registered in the country is lower now than it was 20 years ago.

    (E) Radio stations have long been broadcasting regular traffic reports that inform motorists about traffic congestion.

24. The percentage of households with an annual income of more than $40,000 is higher in Merton County than in any other county. However, the percentage of households with an annual income of $60,000 or more is higher in Sommer County.

    If the statements above are true, which of the following must also be true?

    (A) The percentage of households with an annual income of $80,000 is higher in Sommer County than in Merton County.

    (B) Merton County has the second highest percentage of households with an annual income of $60,000 or more.

    (C) Some households in Merton County have an annual income between $40,000 and $60,000.

    (D) The number of households with an annual income of more than $40,000 is greater in Merton County than in Sommer County.

    (E) Average annual household income is higher in Sommer County than in Merton County.

25. Tiger beetles are such fast runners that they can capture virtually any nonflying insect. However, when running toward an insect, a tiger beetle will intermittently stop and then, a moment later, resume its attack. Perhaps the beetles cannot maintain their pace and must pause for a moment's rest; but an alternative hypothesis is that while running, tiger beetles are unable to adequately process the resulting rapidly changing visual information and so quickly go blind and stop.

Which of the following, if discovered in experiments using artificially moved prey insects, would support one of the two hypotheses and undermine the other?

(A) When a prey insect is moved directly toward a beetle that has been chasing it, the beetle immediately stops and runs away without its usual intermittent stopping.

(B) In pursuing a swerving insect, a beetle alters its course while running and its pauses become more frequent as the chase progresses.

(C) In pursuing a moving insect, a beetle usually responds immediately to changes in the insect's direction, and it pauses equally frequently whether the chase is up or down an incline.

(D) If, when a beetle pauses, it has not gained on the insect it is pursuing, the beetle generally ends its pursuit.

(E) The faster a beetle pursues an insect fleeing directly away from it, the more frequently the beetle stops.

26. Guillemots are birds of Arctic regions. They feed on fish that gather beneath thin sheets of floating ice, and they nest on nearby land. Guillemots need 80 consecutive snow-free days in a year to raise their chicks, so until average temperatures in the Arctic began to rise recently, the guillemots' range was limited to the southernmost Arctic coast. Therefore, if the warming continues, the guillemots' range will probably be enlarged by being extended northward along the coast.

Which of the following, if true, most seriously weakens the argument?

(A) Even if the warming trend continues, there will still be years in which guillemot chicks are killed by an unusually early snow.

(B) If the Arctic warming continues, guillemots' current predators are likely to succeed in extending their own range farther north.

(C) Guillemots nest in coastal areas, where temperatures are generally higher than in inland areas.

(D) If the Arctic warming continues, much of the thin ice in the southern Arctic will disappear.

(E) The fish that guillemots eat are currently preyed on by a wider variety of predators in the southernmost Arctic regions than they are farther north.

27. Some batches of polio vaccine used around 1960 were contaminated with SV40, a virus that in monkeys causes various cancers. Some researchers now claim that this contamination caused some cases of a certain cancer in humans, mesothelioma. This claim is not undercut by the fact that a very careful survey made in the 1960s of people who had received the contaminated vaccine found no elevated incidence of any cancer, since _____.

(A) most cases of mesothelioma are caused by exposure to asbestos

(B) in some countries, there was no contamination of the vaccine

(C) SV40 is widely used in laboratories to produce cancers in animals

(D) mesotheliomas take several decades to develop

(E) mesothelioma was somewhat less common in 1960 than it is now

28. Gortland has long been narrowly self-sufficient in both grain and meat. However, as per capita income in Gortland has risen toward the world average, per capita consumption of meat has also risen toward the world average, and it takes several pounds of grain to produce one pound of meat. Therefore, since per capita income continues to rise, whereas domestic grain production will not increase, Gortland will soon have to import either grain or meat or both.

    Which of the following is an assumption on which the argument depends?

    (A) The total acreage devoted to grain production in Gortland will soon decrease.

    (B) Importing either grain or meat will not result in a significantly higher percentage of Gortlanders' incomes being spent on food than is currently the case.

    (C) The per capita consumption of meat in Gortland is increasing at roughly the same rate across all income levels.

    (D) The per capita income of meat producers in Gortland is rising faster than the per capita income of grain producers.

    (E) People in Gortland who increase their consumption of meat will not radically decrease their consumption of grain.

29. The Hazelton coal-processing plant is a major employer in the Hazelton area, but national environmental regulations will force it to close if it continues to use old, polluting processing methods. However, to update the plant to use newer, cleaner methods would be so expensive that the plant will close unless it receives the tax break it has requested. In order to prevent a major increase in local unemployment, the Hazelton government is considering granting the plant's request.

Which of the following would be most important for the Hazelton government to determine before deciding whether to grant the plant's request?

(A) Whether the company that owns the plant would open a new plant in another area if the present plant were closed

(B) Whether the plant would employ far fewer workers when updated than it does now

(C) Whether the level of pollutants presently being emitted by the plant is high enough to constitute a health hazard for local residents

(D) Whether the majority of the coal processed by the plant is sold outside the Hazelton area

(E) Whether the plant would be able to process more coal when updated than it does now

30. A physically active lifestyle has been shown to help increase longevity. In the Wistar region of Bellaria, the average age at death is considerably higher than in any other part of the country. Wistar is the only mountainous part of Bellaria. A mountainous terrain makes even such basic activities as walking relatively strenuous; it essentially imposes a physically active lifestyle on people. Clearly, this circumstance explains the long lives of people in Wistar.

Which of the following, if true, most seriously weakens the argument?

(A) In Bellaria all medical expenses are paid by the government, so that personal income does not affect the quality of health care a person receives.

(B) The Wistar region is one of Bellaria's least populated regions.

(C) Many people who live in the Wistar region have moved there in middle age or upon retirement.

(D) The many opportunities for hiking, skiing, and other outdoor activities that Wistar's mountains offer make it a favorite destination for vacationing Bellarians.

(E) Per capita spending on recreational activities is no higher in Wistar than it is in other regions of Bellaria.

31. Cheever College offers several online courses via remote computer connection, in addition to traditional classroom-based courses. A study of student performance at Cheever found that, overall, the average student grade for online courses matched that for classroom-based courses. In this calculation of the average grade, course withdrawals were weighted as equivalent to a course failure, and the rate of withdrawal was much lower for students enrolled in classroom-based courses than for students enrolled in online courses.

If the statements above are true, which of the following must also be true of Cheever College?

(A) Among students who did not withdraw, students enrolled in online courses got higher grades, on average, than students enrolled in classroom-based courses.

(B) The number of students enrolled per course at the start of the school term is much higher, on average, for the online courses than for the classroom-based courses.

(C) There are no students who take both an online and a classroom-based course in the same school term.

(D) Among Cheever College students with the best grades, a significant majority take online, rather than classroom-based, courses.

(E) Courses offered online tend to deal with subject matter that is less challenging than that of classroom-based courses.

32. For years the beautiful Renaissance buildings in Palitito have been damaged by exhaust from the many tour buses that come to the city. There has been little parking space, so most buses have idled at the curb during each stop on their tour, and idling produces as much exhaust as driving. The city has now provided parking that accommodates a third of the tour buses, so damage to Palitito's buildings from the buses' exhaust will diminish significantly.

Which of the following, if true, most strongly supports the argument?

(A) The exhaust from Palitito's few automobiles is not a significant threat to Palitito's buildings.

(B) Palitito's Renaissance buildings are not threatened by pollution other than engine exhaust.

(C) Tour buses typically spend less than one-quarter of the time they are in Palitito transporting passengers from one site to another.

(D) More tourists come to Palitito by tour bus than by any other single means of transportation.

(E) Some of the tour buses that are unable to find parking drive around Palitito while their passengers are visiting a site.

33. During the 1980s and 1990s, the annual number of people who visited the Sordellian Mountains increased continually, and many new ski resorts were built. Over the same period, however, the number of visitors to ski resorts who were caught in avalanches decreased, even though there was no reduction in the annual number of avalanches in the Sordellian Mountains.

Which of the following, if true in the Sordellian Mountains during the 1980s and 1990s, most helps to explain the decrease?

(A) Avalanches were most likely to happen when a large new snowfall covered an older layer of snow.

(B) Avalanches destroyed at least some buildings in the Sordellian Mountains in every year.

(C) People planning new ski slopes and other resort facilities used increasingly accurate information about which locations are likely to be in the path of avalanches.

(D) The average length of stay for people visiting the Sordellian Mountains increased slightly.

(E) Construction of new ski resorts often led to the clearing of wooded areas that had helped to prevent avalanches.

34. A year ago, Dietz Foods launched a yearlong advertising campaign for its canned tuna. Last year Dietz sold 12 million cans of tuna compared to the 10 million sold during the previous year, an increase directly attributable to new customers brought in by the campaign. Profits from the additional sales, however, were substantially less than the cost of the advertising campaign. Clearly, therefore, the campaign did nothing to further Dietz's economic interests.

Which of the following, if true, most seriously weakens the argument?

(A) Sales of canned tuna account for a relatively small percentage of Dietz Foods' profits.

(B) Most of the people who bought Dietz's canned tuna for the first time as a result of the campaign were already loyal customers of other Dietz products.

(C) A less expensive advertising campaign would have brought in significantly fewer new customers for Dietz's canned tuna than did the campaign Dietz Foods launched last year.

(D) Dietz made money on sales of canned tuna last year.

(E) In each of the past five years, there was a steep, industry-wide decline in sales of canned tuna.

Sentence Correction

Each of the <u>sentence correction</u> questions presents a sentence, part or all of which is underlined. Beneath the sentence you will find five ways of phrasing the underlined part. The first of these repeats the original; the other four are different. Follow the requirements of standard written English to choose your answer, paying attention to grammar, word choice, and sentence construction. Select the answer that produces the most effective sentence; your answer should make the sentence clear, exact, and free of grammatical error. It should also minimize awkwardness, ambiguity, and redundancy.

35. Unlike <u>the buildings in Mesopotamian cities, which were arranged haphazardly, the same basic plan was followed for all cities of the Indus Valley: with houses</u> laid out on a north-south, east-west grid, and houses and walls were built of standard-size bricks.

    (A) the buildings in Mesopotamian cities, which were arranged haphazardly, the same basic plan was followed for all cities of the Indus Valley: with houses

    (B) the buildings in Mesopotamian cities, which were haphazard in arrangement, the same basic plan was used in all cities of the Indus Valley: houses were

    (C) the arrangement of buildings in Mesopotamian cities, which were haphazard, the cities of the Indus Valley all followed the same basic plan: houses

    (D) Mesopotamian cities, in which buildings were arranged haphazardly, the cities of the Indus Valley all followed the same basic plan: houses were

    (E) Mesopotamian cities, which had buildings that were arranged haphazardly, the same basic plan was used for all cities in the Indus Valley: houses that were

36. New data from United States Forest Service ecologists show <u>that for every dollar spent on controlled small-scale burning, forest thinning, and the training of fire-management personnel, it saves seven dollars that would not be spent on having to extinguish</u> big fires.

    (A) that for every dollar spent on controlled small-scale burning, forest thinning, and the training of fire-management personnel, it saves seven dollars that would not be spent on having to extinguish

    (B) that for every dollar spent on controlled small-scale burning, forest thinning, and the training of fire-management personnel, seven dollars are saved that would have been spent on extinguishing

    (C) that for every dollar spent on controlled small-scale burning, forest thinning, and the training of fire-management personnel saves seven dollars on not having to extinguish

    (D) for every dollar spent on controlled small-scale burning, forest thinning, and the training of fire-management personnel, that it saves seven dollars on not having to extinguish

    (E) for every dollar spent on controlled small-scale burning, forest thinning, and the training of fire-management personnel, that seven dollars are saved that would not have been spent on extinguishing

37. Like the grassy fields and old pastures that the upland sandpiper needs for feeding and nesting when it returns in May after wintering in the Argentine Pampas, <u>the sandpipers vanishing in the northeastern United States is a result of residential and industrial development and of changes in</u> farming practices.

    (A) the sandpipers vanishing in the northeastern United States is a result of residential and industrial development and of changes in

    (B) the bird itself is vanishing in the northeastern United States as a result of residential and industrial development and of changes in

    (C) that the birds themselves are vanishing in the northeastern United States is due to residential and industrial development and changes to

    (D) in the northeastern United States, sandpipers' vanishing due to residential and industrial development and to changes in

    (E) in the northeastern United States, the sandpipers' vanishing, a result of residential and industrial development and changing

38. The results of two recent unrelated studies support the idea that dolphins may share certain cognitive abilities with humans and great apes; the studies indicate <u>dolphins as capable of recognizing themselves in mirrors—an ability that is often considered a sign of self-awareness—and to grasp spontaneously</u> the mood or intention of humans.

    (A) dolphins as capable of recognizing themselves in mirrors—an ability that is often considered a sign of self-awareness—and to grasp spontaneously

    (B) dolphins' ability to recognize themselves in mirrors—an ability that is often considered as a sign of self-awareness—and of spontaneously grasping

    (C) dolphins to be capable of recognizing themselves in mirrors—an ability that is often considered a sign of self-awareness—and to grasp spontaneously

    (D) that dolphins have the ability of recognizing themselves in mirrors—an ability that is often considered as a sign of self-awareness—and spontaneously grasping

    (E) that dolphins are capable of recognizing themselves in mirrors—an ability that is often considered a sign of self-awareness—and of spontaneously grasping

39. According to scholars, the earliest writing was probably not a direct rendering of speech, but <u>was more likely to begin as</u> a separate and distinct symbolic system of communication, and only later merged with spoken language.

    (A) was more likely to begin as

    (B) more than likely began as

    (C) more than likely beginning from

    (D) it was more than likely begun from

    (E) it was more likely that it began

40. In 1995 Richard Stallman, a well-known critic of the patent system, testified in Patent Office hearings that, to test the system, a colleague of his had managed to win a patent for one of Kirchhoff's <u>laws, an observation about electric current first made in 1845 and</u> now included in virtually every textbook of elementary physics.

    (A) laws, an observation about electric current first made in 1845 and

    (B) laws, which was an observation about electric current first made in 1845 and it is

    (C) laws, namely, it was an observation about electric current first made in 1845 and

    (D) laws, an observation about electric current first made in 1845, it is

    (E) laws that was an observation about electric current, first made in 1845, and is

41. Excavators at the Indus Valley site of Harappa in eastern Pakistan say the discovery of inscribed shards dating to circa 2800–2600 B.C. indicate their development of a Harappan writing system, the use of inscribed seals impressed into clay for marking ownership, and the standardization of weights for trade or taxation occurred many decades, if not centuries, earlier than was previously believed.

    (A) indicate their development of a Harappan writing system, the use of

    (B) indicate that the development of a Harappan writing system, using

    (C) indicates that their development of a Harappan writing system, using

    (D) indicates the development of a Harappan writing system, their use of

    (E) indicates that the development of a Harappan writing system, the use of

42. The Supreme Court has ruled that public universities can collect student activity fees even with students' objections to particular activities, so long as the groups they give money to will be chosen without regard to their views.

    (A) with students' objections to particular activities, so long as the groups they give money to will be

    (B) if they have objections to particular activities and the groups that are given the money are

    (C) if they object to particular activities, but the groups that the money is given to have to be

    (D) from students who object to particular activities, so long as the groups given money are

    (E) though students have an objection to particular activities, but the groups that are given the money be

43. Despite the increasing number of women graduating from law school and passing bar examinations, the proportion of judges and partners at major law firms who are women have not risen to a comparable extent.

    (A) the proportion of judges and partners at major law firms who are women have not risen to a comparable extent

    (B) the proportion of women judges and partners at major law firms have not risen comparably

    (C) the proportion of judges and partners at major law firms who are women has not risen comparably

    (D) yet the proportion of women judges and partners at major law firms has not risen to a comparable extent

    (E) yet the proportion of judges and partners at major law firms who are women has not risen comparably

44. Seldom more than 40 feet wide and 12 feet deep, but it ran 363 miles across the rugged wilderness of upstate New York, the Erie Canal connected the Hudson River at Albany to the Great Lakes at Buffalo, providing the port of New York City with a direct water link to the heartland of the North American continent.

    (A) Seldom more than 40 feet wide and 12 feet deep, but it ran 363 miles across the rugged wilderness of upstate New York, the Erie Canal connected

    (B) Seldom more than 40 feet wide or 12 feet deep but running 363 miles across the rugged wilderness of upstate New York, the Erie Canal connected

    (C) It was seldom more than 40 feet wide and 12 feet deep, and ran 363 miles across the rugged wilderness of upstate New York, but the Erie Canal, connecting

    (D) The Erie Canal was seldom more than 40 feet wide or 12 feet deep and it ran 363 miles across the rugged wilderness of upstate New York, which connected

    (E) The Erie Canal, seldom more than 40 feet wide and 12 feet deep, but running 363 miles across the rugged wilderness of upstate New York, connecting

45. In 1923, the Supreme Court declared a minimum wage for women and children in the District of Columbia as unconstitutional, and ruling that it was a form of price-fixing and, as such, an abridgment of the right of contract.

    (A) the Supreme Court declared a minimum wage for women and children in the District of Columbia as unconstitutional, and

    (B) the Supreme Court declared as unconstitutional a minimum wage for women and children in the District of Columbia, and

    (C) the Supreme Court declared unconstitutional a minimum wage for women and children in the District of Columbia,

    (D) a minimum wage for women and children in the District of Columbia was declared unconstitutional by the Supreme Court,

    (E) when the Supreme Court declared a minimum wage for women and children in the District of Columbia as unconstitutional,

46. Researchers have found that individuals who have been blind from birth, and who thus have never seen anyone gesture, nevertheless make hand motions when speaking just as frequently and in virtually the same way as sighted people do, and that they will gesture even when conversing with another blind person.

    (A) who thus have never seen anyone gesture, nevertheless make hand motions when speaking just as frequently and in virtually the same way as sighted people do, and that they will gesture

    (B) who thus never saw anyone gesturing, nevertheless make hand motions when speaking just as frequent and in virtually the same way as sighted people did, and that they will gesture

    (C) who thus have never seen anyone gesture, nevertheless made hand motions when speaking just as frequently and in virtually the same way as sighted people do, as well as gesturing

    (D) thus never having seen anyone gesture, nevertheless made hand motions when speaking just as frequent and in virtually the same way as sighted people did, as well as gesturing

    (E) thus never having seen anyone gesture, nevertheless to make hand motions when speaking just as frequently and in virtually the same way as sighted people do, and to gesture

47. Like embryonic germ cells, which are cells that develop early in the formation of the fetus and that later generate eggs or sperm, embryonic stem cells have the ability of developing themselves into different kinds of body tissue.

    (A) embryonic stem cells have the ability of developing themselves into different kinds of body tissue

    (B) embryonic stem cells have the ability to develop into different kinds of body tissue

    (C) in embryonic stem cells there is the ability to develop into different kinds of body tissue

    (D) the ability to develop themselves into different kinds of body tissue characterizes embryonic stem cells

    (E) the ability of developing into different kinds of body tissue characterizes embryonic stem cells

48. Critics contend that the new missile is a weapon whose importance is largely symbolic, more a tool for manipulating people's perceptions than to fulfill a real military need.

    (A) for manipulating people's perceptions than to fulfill

    (B) for manipulating people's perceptions than for fulfilling

    (C) to manipulate people's perceptions rather than that it fulfills

    (D) to manipulate people's perceptions rather than fulfilling

    (E) to manipulate people's perceptions than for fulfilling

49. As an actress and, more importantly, as a teacher of acting, Stella Adler was one of the most influential artists in the American theater, who trained several generations of actors including Marlon Brando and Robert De Niro.

    (A) Stella Adler was one of the most influential artists in the American theater, who trained several generations of actors including

    (B) Stella Adler, one of the most influential artists in the American theater, trained several generations of actors who include

    (C) Stella Adler was one of the most influential artists in the American theater, training several generations of actors whose ranks included

    (D) one of the most influential artists in the American theater was Stella Adler, who trained several generations of actors including

    (E) one of the most influential artists in the American theater, Stella Adler, trained several generations of actors whose ranks included

50. By developing the Secure Digital Music Initiative, the recording industry associations of North America, Japan, and Europe hope to create a standardized way of distributing songs and full-length recordings on the Internet that will protect copyright holders and foil the many audio pirates who copy and distribute digital music illegally.

    (A) of distributing songs and full-length recordings on the Internet that will protect copyright holders and foil the many audio pirates who copy and distribute

    (B) of distributing songs and full-length recordings on the Internet and to protect copyright holders and foiling the many audio pirates copying and distributing

    (C) for distributing songs and full-length recordings on the Internet while it protects copyright holders and foils the many audio pirates who copy and distribute

    (D) to distribute songs and full-length recordings on the Internet while they will protect copyright holders and foil the many audio pirates copying and distributing

    (E) to distribute songs and full-length recordings on the Internet and it will protect copyright holders and foiling the many audio pirates who copy and distribute

51. Whereas a ramjet generally cannot achieve high speeds without the initial assistance of a rocket, high speeds can be attained by scramjets, or supersonic combustion ramjets, in that they reduce airflow compression at the entrance of the engine and letting air pass through at supersonic speeds.

    (A) high speeds can be attained by scramjets, or supersonic combustion ramjets, in that they reduce

    (B) that high speeds can be attained by scramjets, or supersonic combustion ramjets, is a result of their reducing

    (C) the ability of scramjets, or supersonic combustion ramjets, to achieve high speeds is because they reduce

    (D) scramjets, or supersonic combustion ramjets, have the ability of attaining high speeds when reducing

    (E) scramjets, or supersonic combustion ramjets, can attain high speeds by reducing

52. It will not be possible to implicate melting sea ice in the coastal flooding that many global warming models have projected: just like a glass of water that will not overflow due to melting ice cubes, so melting sea ice does not increase oceanic volume.

    (A) like a glass of water that will not overflow due to melting ice cubes,

    (B) like melting ice cubes that do not cause a glass of water to overflow,

    (C) a glass of water will not overflow because of melting ice cubes,

    (D) as melting ice cubes that do not cause a glass of water to overflow,

    (E) as melting ice cubes do not cause a glass of water to overflow,

3.3 Quantitative and Verbal Answer Keys

Quantitative

1. A	17. D	33. D
2. D	18. A	34. C
3. E	19. A	35. D
4. B	20. B	36. B
5. B	21. D	37. A
6. A	22. E	38. B
7. E	23. B	39. E
8. E	24. C	40. D
9. D	25. C	41. C
10. C	26. E	42. C
11. C	27. E	43. B
12. C	28. E	44. A
13. E	29. E	45. D
14. B	30. A	46. E
15. C	31. D	47. D
16. E	32. C	48. C

Verbal

1. E	19. E	37. B
2. C	20. C	38. E
3. B	21. A	39. B
4. A	22. B	40. A
5. D	23. A	41. E
6. C	24. C	42. D
7. A	25. B	43. C
8. A	26. D	44. B
9. B	27. D	45. C
10. A	28. E	46. A
11. B	29. B	47. B
12. D	30. C	48. B
13. B	31. A	49. C
14. A	32. C	50. A
15. E	33. C	51. E
16. C	34. E	52. E
17. E	35. D	
18. B	36. B	

3.4 Interpretive Guide

The following table provides a guide for interpreting your score, on the basis of the number of questions you got right.

Interpretive Guide				
	Excellent	Above Average	Average	Below Average
Problem Solving	19-24	16-18	10-15	0-9
Data Sufficiency	19-24	16-18	10-15	0-9
Reading Comprehension	16-17	14-15	9-13	0-8
Critical Reasoning	14-17	9-13	6-8	0-5
Sentence Correction	16-18	11-15	8-10	0-7

Remember, you should not compare the number of questions you got right in each section. Instead, you should compare how your response rated in each section.

3.5 Quantitative Answer Explanations

Problem Solving

The following discussion is intended to familiarize you with the most efficient and effective approaches to the kinds of problems common to problem solving questions. The particular questions in this chapter are generally representative of the kinds of quantitative questions you will encounter on the GMAT exam. Remember that it is the problem solving strategy that is important, not the specific details of a particular question.

1. Last month a certain music club offered a discount to preferred customers. After the first compact disc purchased, preferred customers paid $3.99 for each additional compact disc purchased. If a preferred customer purchased a total of 6 compact discs and paid $15.95 for the first compact disc, then the dollar amount that the customer paid for the 6 compact discs is equivalent to which of the following?

   (A) $5(4.00)+15.90$
   (B) $5(4.00)+15.95$
   (C) $5(4.00)+16.00$
   (D) $5(4.00-0.01)+15.90$
   (E) $5(4.00-0.05)+15.95$

   Arithmetic Operations on rational numbers

   The cost of the 6 compact discs, with $15.95 for the first one and $3.99 for the other 5 discs, can be expressed as $5(3.99)+15.95$. It is clear from looking at the answer choices that some regrouping of the values is needed because none of the answer choices uses $3.99 in the calculation.

   If $4.00 is used instead of $3.99, each one of the 5 additional compact discs is calculated at $0.01 too much, and the total cost is $5(0.01) = \$0.05$ too high. There is an overage of $0.05 that must be subtracted from the $15.95, or thus $15.95 - \$0.05 = \$15.90$. Therefore, the cost can be expressed as 5(4.00) + 15.90.

   The correct answer is A.

2. The average (arithmetic mean) of the integers from 200 to 400, inclusive, is how much greater than the average of the integers from 50 to 100, inclusive?

   (A) 150
   (B) 175
   (C) 200
   (D) 225
   (E) 300

   Arithmetic Statistics

   In the list of integers from 200 to 400 inclusive, the middle value is 300. For every integer above 300, there exists an integer below 300 that is the same distance away from 300; thus the average of the integers from 200 to 400, inclusive, will be kept at 300. In the same manner, the average of the integers from 50 to 100, inclusive, is 75.

   The difference is $300 - 75 = 225$.

   The correct answer is D.

3. The sequence a_1, a_2, a_3,...,a_n,... is such that $a_n = \dfrac{a_{n-1} + a_{n-2}}{2}$ for all $n \ge 3$. If $a_3 = 4$ and $a_5 = 20$, what is the value of a_6?

   (A) 12
   (B) 16
   (C) 20
   (D) 24
   (E) 28

Algebra Applied problems

According to this formula, it is necessary to know the two prior terms in the sequence to determine the value of a term; that is, it is necessary to know both a_{n-1} and a_{n-2} to find a_n. Therefore, to find a_6, the values of a_5 and a_4 must be determined. To find a_4, let $a_n = a_5$, which makes $a_{n-1} = a_4$ and $a_{n-2} = a_3$. Then, by substituting the given values into the formula

$$a_n = \frac{a_{n-1} + a_{n-2}}{2}$$

$$a_5 = \frac{a_4 + a_3}{2}$$

$$20 = \frac{a_4 + 4}{2} \qquad \text{substitute known values}$$

$$40 = a_4 + 4 \qquad \text{multiply both sides}$$

$$36 = a_4 \qquad \text{subtract 4 from both sides}$$

Then, letting $a_n = a_6$, substitute the known values:

$$a_6 = \frac{a_5 + a_4}{2}$$

$$a_6 = \frac{20 + 36}{2} \qquad \text{substitute known values}$$

$$a_6 = \frac{56}{2} \qquad \text{simplify}$$

$$a_6 = 28$$

The correct answer is E.

4. Among a group of 2,500 people, 35 percent invest in municipal bonds, 18 percent invest in oil stocks, and 7 percent invest in both municipal bonds and oil stocks. If 1 person is to be randomly selected from the 2,500 people, what is the probability that the person selected will be one who invests in municipal bonds but NOT in oil stocks?

(A) $\frac{9}{50}$

(B) $\frac{7}{25}$

(C) $\frac{7}{20}$

(D) $\frac{21}{50}$

(E) $\frac{27}{50}$

Arithmetic Probability

Since there are 2,500 people, $2,500(0.35) = 875$ people invest in municipal bonds, and $2,500(0.07) = 175$ of those people invest in both municipal bonds and oil stocks. Therefore, there are $875 - 175 = 700$ people who invest in municipal bonds but not in oil stocks. Probability of an event =

$$\frac{\text{Number of desired outcomes}}{\text{Total number of outcomes that can occur}}.$$

Probability of investing in municipal bonds but not in oil stocks $= \frac{700}{2,500} = \frac{7}{25}$.

The correct answer is B.

5. A closed cylindrical tank contains 36π cubic feet of water and is filled to half its capacity. When the tank is placed upright on its circular base on level ground, the height of the water in the tank is 4 feet. When the tank is placed on its side on level ground, what is the height, in feet, of the surface of the water above the ground?

(A) 2

(B) 3

(C) 4

(D) 6

(E) 9

Geometry Volume

Since the cylinder is half full, it will be filled to half its height, whether it is upright or on its side. When the cylinder is on its side, half its height is equal to its radius.

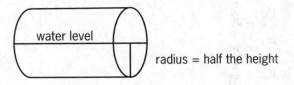

radius = half the height

Using the information about the volume of water in the upright cylinder, solve for this radius to determine the height of the water when the cylinder is on its side.

$V = \pi r^2 h$ volume $= (\pi)(\text{radius}^2)(\text{height})$

$36\pi = \pi r^2 h$ known volume of water is 36π

$36 = r^2(4)$ substitute 4 for h; divide both sides by π

$9 = r^2$ solve for r

$3 = r$ radius = height of the water in the cylinder on its side

The correct answer is B.

6. A marketing firm determined that, of 200 households surveyed, 80 used neither Brand A nor Brand B soap, 60 used only Brand A soap, and for every household that used both brands of soap, 3 used only Brand B soap. How many of the 200 households surveyed used both brands of soap?

(A) 15
(B) 20
(C) 30
(D) 40
(E) 45

Arithmetic Operations on rational numbers

Since it is given that 80 households use neither Brand A nor Brand B, then $200 - 80 = 120$ must use Brand A, Brand B, or both. It is also given that 60 households use only Brand A and that three times as many households use Brand B exclusively as use both brands. If x is the number of households that use both Brand A and Brand B, then $3x$ use Brand B alone. A Venn diagram can be helpful for visualizing the logic of the given information for this item:

Brand A   Brand B

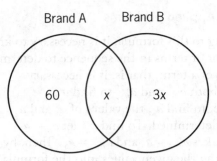

All the sections in the circles can be added up and set equal to 120, and then the equation can be solved for x:

$60 + x + 3x = 120$

$60 + 4x = 120$ combine like terms

$4x = 60$ subtract 60 from both sides

$x = 15$ divide both sides by 4

The correct answer is A.

7. A certain club has 10 members, including Harry. One of the 10 members is to be chosen at random to be the president, one of the remaining 9 members is to be chosen at random to be the secretary, and one of the remaining 8 members is to be chosen at random to be the treasurer. What is the probability that Harry will be either the member chosen to be the secretary or the member chosen to be the treasurer?

(A) $\frac{1}{720}$

(B) $\frac{1}{80}$

(C) $\frac{1}{10}$

(D) $\frac{1}{9}$

(E) $\frac{1}{5}$

Arithmetic Probability

Two probabilities must be calculated here: (1) the probability of Harry's being chosen for secretary and (2) the probability of Harry's being chosen for treasurer. For any probability, the probability of an event's occurring =

$$\frac{\text{number of desired outcomes}}{\text{total number of outcomes that can occur}}.$$

(1)   If Harry is to be secretary, he first CANNOT have been chosen for president, and then he must be chosen for secretary. The probability that he will be chosen for president is $\frac{1}{10}$, so the probability of his NOT being chosen for president is $1 - \frac{1}{10} = \frac{9}{10}$. Then, the probability of his being chosen for secretary is $\frac{1}{9}$.

Once he is chosen, the probability that he will be selected for treasurer is 0, so the probability that he will NOT be selected for treasurer is $1 - 0 = 1$. Thus, the probability that Harry will be chosen for secretary is $\left(\frac{9}{10}\right)\left(\frac{1}{9}\right)(1) = \frac{1}{10}$.

(2)   If Harry is to be treasurer, he needs to be NOT chosen for president, then NOT chosen for secretary, and then finally chosen for treasurer.

The probability that he will NOT be chosen for president is again $1 - \frac{1}{10} = \frac{9}{10}$. The probability of his NOT being chosen for secretary is $1 - \frac{1}{9} = \frac{8}{9}$. The probability of his being chosen for treasurer is $\frac{1}{8}$, so the probability that Harry will be chosen for treasurer is $\left(\frac{9}{10}\right)\left(\frac{8}{9}\right)\left(\frac{1}{8}\right) = \frac{1}{10}$.

(3)   So, finally, the probability of Harry's being chosen as either secretary or treasurer is thus $\frac{1}{10} + \frac{1}{10} = \frac{2}{10} = \frac{1}{5}$.

The correct answer is E.

8.   If a certain toy store's revenue in November was $\frac{2}{5}$ of its revenue in December and its revenue in January was $\frac{1}{4}$ of its revenue in November, then the store's revenue in December was how many times the average (arithmetic mean) of its revenues in November and January?

(A) $\frac{1}{4}$

(B) $\frac{1}{2}$

(C) $\frac{2}{3}$

(D)   2

(E)   4

Arithmetic Statistics

Let n be the store's revenue in November, d be the store's revenue in December, and j be the store's revenue in January. The information from the problem can be expressed as $n = \frac{2}{5}d$ and $j = \frac{1}{4}n$. Substituting $\frac{2}{5}d$ for n in the second equation gives $j = \frac{1}{4}\left(\frac{2}{5}d\right) = \frac{1}{10}d$. Then, the average of the revenues in November and January can be found by using these values in the formula

$$\text{average} = \frac{\text{sum of values}}{\text{number of values}}, \text{ as follows:}$$

$$\text{average} = \frac{\frac{2}{5}d + \frac{1}{10}d}{2} = \frac{\frac{4}{10}d + \frac{1}{10}d}{2} = \frac{\frac{5}{10}d}{2} = \frac{1}{2}d\left(\frac{1}{2}\right) = \frac{1}{4}d$$

Solve for the store's revenue in December by multiplying both sides of this equation by 4:

$$\text{average} = \frac{1}{4}d$$

$$4(\text{average}) = d$$

Thus, the store's revenue in December was 4 times its average revenue in November and January.

The correct answer is E.

9.   A researcher computed the mean, the median, and the standard deviation for a set of performance scores. If 5 were to be added to each score, which of these three statistics would change?

(A)   The mean only
(B)   The median only
(C)   The standard deviation only
(D)   The mean and the median
(E)   The mean and the standard deviation

Arithmetic Statistics

If 5 were added to each score, the mean would go up by 5, as would the median. However, the spread of the values would remain the same, simply centered around a new value. So, the standard deviation would **NOT** change.

The correct answer is D.

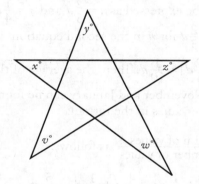

10.   In the figure shown, what is the value of $v + x + y + z + w$?

(A)   45
(B)   90
(C)   180
(D)   270
(E)   360

Geometry Angles and their measure

In the following figure, the center section of the star is a pentagon.

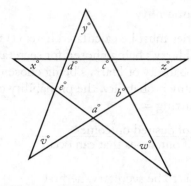

The sum of the interior angles of any polygon is $180(n-2)$, where n is the number of sides. Thus, $a + b + c + d + e = 180(5-2) = 180(3) = 540$.

Each of the interior angles of the pentagon defines a triangle with two of the angles at the points of the star. This gives the following five equations:

$a + x + z = 180$
$b + v + y = 180$
$c + x + w = 180$
$d + v + z = 180$
$e + y + w = 180$

Summing these 5 equations gives:
$a + b + c + d + e + 2v + 2x + 2y + 2z + 2w = 900$.

Substituting 540 for $a + b + c + d + e$ gives:
$540 + 2v + 2x + 2y + 2z + 2w = 900$.

From this:

$2v + 2x + 2y + 2z + 2w = 360$ subtract 540 from both sides

$2(v + x + y + z + w) = 360$ factor out 2 on the left side

$v + x + y + z + w = 180$ divide both sides by 2

The correct answer is C.

11.   Of the three-digit integers greater than 700, how many have two digits that are equal to each other and the remaining digit different from the other two?

(A)   90
(B)   82
(C)   80
(D)   45
(E)   36

Arithmetic Properties of numbers

In three-digit integers, there are three pairs of digits that can be the same while the other digit is different: tens and ones, hundreds and tens, and hundreds and ones. In each of these pairs, there are 9 options for having the third digit be different from the other two. The single exception to this is in the 700–799 set, where the number 700 cannot be included because the problem calls for integers "greater than 700." So, in the 700–799 set, there are only 8 options for when the tens and ones are the same. This is shown in the table below.

Number of digits available for the third digit when two given digits are the same			
Same	701–799	800–899	900–999
tens and ones	8	9	9
hundreds and tens	9	9	9
hundreds and ones	9	9	9

Thus, of the three-digit integers greater than 700, there are $9(9) - 1 = 80$ numbers that have two digits that are equal to each other when the remaining digit is different from these two.

The correct answer is C.

12. Positive integer y is 50 percent of 50 percent of positive integer x, and y percent of x equals 100. What is the value of x ?

    (A)   50
    (B)   100
    (C)   200
    (D)   1,000
    (E)   2,000

Arithmetic; Algebra Percents; Simultaneous equations

Because y is a positive integer, y percent is notated as $\frac{y}{100}$. According to the problem, $y = 0.50(0.50x)$ and $\left(\frac{y}{100}\right)x = 100$.

The first equation simplifies to $y = 0.25x$, and multiplying the second equation by 100 gives $xy = 10,000$.

Substituting the simplified first equation into this second equation gives:

$x(0.25x) = 10,000$

$0.25x^2 = 10,000$ simplify left side

$x^2 = 40,000$ divide both sides by 0.25

$x = 200$ solve for the value of x

The correct answer is C.

13. If s and t are positive integers such that $\frac{s}{t} = 64.12$, which of the following could be the remainder when s is divided by t ?

    (A)   2
    (B)   4
    (C)   8
    (D)   20
    (E)   45

Arithmetic Operations on rational numbers

By using a long division model, it can be seen that the remainder after dividing s by t is $s - 64t$:

$$\begin{array}{r} 64 \\ t{\overline{\smash{\big)}\,s}} \\ \underline{-64t} \\ s - 64t \end{array}$$

Then, the given equation can be written as $64.12t = s$. By splitting portions of t into its integer multiple and its decimal multiple, this becomes $64t + 0.12t = s$, or $0.12t = s - 64t$, which is the remainder. So, $0.12t = $ remainder. Test the answer choices to find the situation in which t is an integer.

A	$0.12t = 2$ or $t = 16.67$	NOT an integer
B	$0.12t = 4$ or $t = 33.33$	NOT an integer
C	$0.12t = 8$ or $t = 66.67$	NOT an integer
D	$0.12t = 20$ or $t = 166.67$	NOT an integer
E	$0.12t = 45$ or $t = 375$	INTEGER

The correct answer is E.

14. Of the 84 parents who attended a meeting at a school, 35 volunteered to supervise children during the school picnic and 11 volunteered both to supervise children during the picnic and to bring refreshments to the picnic. If the number of parents who volunteered to bring refreshments was 1.5 times the number of parents who neither volunteered to supervise children during the picnic nor volunteered to bring refreshments, how many of the parents volunteered to bring refreshments?

(A) 25
(B) 36
(C) 38
(D) 42
(E) 45

Arithmetic Operations on rational numbers

Out of the 35 parents who agreed to supervise children during the school picnic, 11 parents are also bringing refreshments, so $35 - 11 = 24$ parents are only supervising children. Let x be the number of parents who volunteered to bring refreshments, and let y be the number of parents who declined to supervise or to bring refreshments. The fact that the number of parents who volunteered to bring refreshments is 1.5 times the number who did not volunteer at all can then be expressed as $x = 1.5\,y$. A Venn diagram, such as the one below, can be helpful in answering problems of this kind.

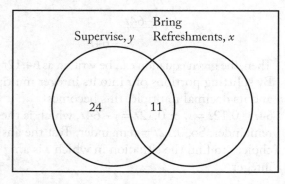

Then, the sum of the sections can be set equal to the total number of parents at the picnic, and the equation can be solved for y:

$y + 24 + x = 84$	sum of sections = total parents at picnic
$y + x = 60$	subtract 24 from each side
$y = 60 - x$	subtract x from each side

Then, substituting the value $60 - x$ for y in the equation $x = 1.5y$ gives the following:

$x = 1.5(60 - x)$	
$x = 90 - 1.5x$	distribute the 1.5
$2.5x = 90$	add 1.5x to both sides
$x = 36$	divide both sides by 2.5

The correct answer is B.

15. The product of all the prime numbers less than 20 is closest to which of the following powers of 10 ?

(A) 10^9
(B) 10^8
(C) 10^7
(D) 10^6
(E) 10^5

Arithmetic Properties of numbers

The prime numbers less than 20 are 2, 3, 5, 7, 11, 13, 17, and 19. Their product is 9,699,690 (arrived at as follows: $2 \times 3 \times 5 \times 7 \times 11 \times 13 \times 17 \times 19 = 9,699,690$). This is closest to $10,000,000 = 10^7$ ($10 \times 10 \times 10 \times 10 \times 10 \times 10 \times 10 = 10,000,000$).

The correct answer is C.

16. If $\sqrt{3 - 2x} = \sqrt{2x} + 1$ then, $4x^2 =$

(A) 1
(B) 4
(C) $2 - 2x$
(D) $4x - 2$
(E) $6x - 1$

Algebra Second-degree equations

Work with the equation to create $4x^2$ on one side.

$$\sqrt{3-2x} = \sqrt{2x} + 1$$
$$\left(\sqrt{3-2x}\right)^2 = \left(\sqrt{2x}+1\right)^2 \qquad \text{square both sides}$$
$$3 - 2x = 2x + 2\sqrt{2x} + 1$$
$$2 - 4x = 2\sqrt{2x} \qquad \text{move all non-square-root terms to one side (i.e., subtract } 2x \text{ and } 1)$$
$$1 - 2x = \sqrt{2x} \qquad \text{divide both sides by 2}$$
$$\left(1-2x\right)^2 = \left(\sqrt{2x}\right)^2 \qquad \text{square both sides}$$
$$1 - 4x + 4x^2 = 2x$$
$$4x^2 = 6x - 1 \qquad \text{isolate the } 4x^2 \text{ (add } 4x \text{ and subtract 1 from both sides)}$$

The correct answer is E.

17. If $n = \sqrt{\dfrac{16}{81}}$, what is the value of $\sqrt{n}$?

   (A) $\dfrac{1}{9}$

   (B) $\dfrac{1}{4}$

   (C) $\dfrac{4}{9}$

   (D) $\dfrac{2}{3}$

   (E) $\dfrac{9}{2}$

Arithmetic Operations on radical expressions

Work the problem.

Since $n = \sqrt{\dfrac{16}{81}} = \dfrac{4}{9}$, then $\sqrt{n} = \sqrt{\dfrac{4}{9}} = \dfrac{2}{3}$.

The correct answer is D.

18. If n is the product of the integers from 1 to 8, inclusive, how many different prime factors greater than 1 does n have?

   (A) Four
   (B) Five
   (C) Six
   (D) Seven
   (E) Eight

Arithmetic Properties of numbers

If n is the product of the integers from 1 to 8, then its prime factors will be the prime numbers from 1 to 8. There are four prime numbers between 1 and 8: 2, 3, 5, and 7.

The correct answer is A.

19. If k is an integer and $2 < k < 7$, for how many different values of k is there a triangle with sides of lengths 2, 7, and k ?

   (A) One
   (B) Two
   (C) Three
   (D) Four
   (E) Five

Geometry Triangles

In a triangle, the sum of the smaller two sides must be larger than the largest side.

For k values 3, 4, 5, and 6, the only triangle possible is 2, 7, and $k = 6$ because only $2 + 6 > 7$. For k values 3, 4, and 5, the sum of the smaller two sides is not larger than the third side; thus, 6 is the only possible value of k that satisfies the conditions.

The correct answer is A.

20. A right circular cone is inscribed in a hemisphere so that the base of the cone coincides with the base of the hemisphere. What is the ratio of the height of the cone to the radius of the hemisphere?

    (A) $\sqrt{3}:1$

    (B) $1:1$

    (C) $\frac{1}{2}:1$

    (D) $\sqrt{2}:1$

    (E) $2:1$

    Geometry Volume

    As the diagram below shows, the height of the cone will be the radius of the hemisphere, so the ratio is 1:1.

    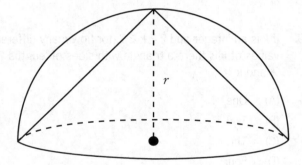

    The correct answer is B.

21. John deposited $10,000 to open a new savings account that earned 4 percent annual interest, compounded quarterly. If there were no other transactions in the account, what was the amount of money in John's account 6 months after the account was opened?

    (A) $10,100

    (B) $10,101

    (C) $10,200

    (D) $10,201

    (E) $10,400

    Arithmetic Operations on rational numbers

    Since John's account is compounded quarterly, he receives $\frac{1}{4}$ of his annual interest, or 1%, every 3 months. This is added to the amount already in the account to accrue interest for the

next quarter. After 6 months, this process will have occurred twice, so the amount in John's account will then be

$$(\$10,000)(1.01)(1.01) = \$10,000(1.01)^2 = \$10,201$$

The correct answer is D.

22. A container in the shape of a right circular cylinder is $\frac{1}{2}$ full of water. If the volume of water in the container is 36 cubic inches and the height of the container is 9 inches, what is the diameter of the base of the cylinder, in inches?

    (A) $\frac{16}{9\pi}$

    (B) $\frac{4}{\sqrt{\pi}}$

    (C) $\frac{12}{\sqrt{\pi}}$

    (D) $\sqrt{\frac{2}{\pi}}$

    (E) $4\sqrt{\frac{2}{\pi}}$

    Geometry Volume

    For a right cylinder, volume = π (radius)²(height). Since the volume of water is 36 cubic inches and since this represents $\frac{1}{2}$ the container, the water is occupying $\frac{1}{2}$ the container's height, or $9\left(\frac{1}{2}\right) = 4.5$ inches. Let r be the radius of the cylinder.

    $36 = \pi r^2 (4.5)$

    $8 = \pi r^2$ divide both sides by 4.5

    $\frac{8}{\pi} = r^2$ divide both sides by π

    $\sqrt{\frac{8}{\pi}} = r$ take the square root of both sides

    $\frac{2\sqrt{2}}{\sqrt{\pi}} = r$ simplify the $\sqrt{8}$ to get the radius

Then, since the diameter is twice the length of the radius, the diameter equals

$$2\left(\frac{2\sqrt{2}}{\sqrt{\pi}}\right) = 4\frac{\sqrt{2}}{\sqrt{\pi}} = 4\sqrt{\frac{2}{\pi}} \, .$$

The correct answer is E.

23. If the positive integer x is a multiple of 4 and the positive integer y is a multiple of 6, then xy must be a multiple of which of the following?

   I. 8
  II. 12
  III. 18

(A)   II only
(B)   I and II only
(C)   I and III only
(D)   II and III only
(E)   I, II, and III

Arithmetic Properties of numbers

The product xy must be a multiple of $4(6) = 24$ and any of its factors. Test each alternative.

   I. $\frac{24}{8} = 3$ 8 is a factor of 24
                     MUST be a multiple of 8

  II. $\frac{24}{12} = 2$ 12 is a factor of 24
                     MUST be a multiple of 12

  III. $\frac{24}{18} = 1\frac{1}{3}$ 18 is NOT a factor of 24
                     NEED NOT be a multiple of 18

The correct answer is B.

24. Aaron will jog from home at x miles per hour and then walk back home by the same route at y miles per hour. How many miles from home can Aaron jog so that he spends a total of t hours jogging and walking?

(A) $\dfrac{xt}{y}$

(B) $\dfrac{x+t}{xy}$

(C) $\dfrac{xyt}{x+y}$

(D) $\dfrac{x+y+t}{xy}$

(E) $\dfrac{y+t}{x} - \dfrac{t}{y}$

Algebra Simplifying algebraic expressions

Let j be the number of hours Aaron spends jogging; then let $t - j$ be the total number of hours he spends walking. It can be stated that Aaron jogs a distance of xj miles and walks a distance of $y(t - j)$ miles. Because Aaron travels the same route, the miles jogged must equal the miles walked, and they can be set equal.

$xj = y(t - j)$ set number of miles equal to
                          each other

$xj = yt - jy$ distribute the y

$xj + jy = yt$ add jy to both sides to get all
                       terms with j to one side

$j(x + y) = yt$ factor out the j

$j = \dfrac{yt}{x + y}$ divide both sides by $x + y$

So, the number of hours Aaron spends jogging is $j = \dfrac{yt}{x + y}$.

The number of miles he can jog is xj or, by substitution of this value of j, $x\left(\dfrac{yt}{x + y}\right) = \dfrac{xyt}{x + y}$.

The correct answer is C.

Data Sufficiency

The following section on data sufficiency is intended to familiarize you with the most efficient and effective approaches to the kinds of problems common to data sufficiency. The particular questions in this chapter are generally representative of the kinds of data sufficiency questions you will encounter on the GMAT exam. Remember that it is the problem solving strategy that is important, not the specific details of a particular question.

25. If the units digit of integer n is greater than 2, what is the units digit of n ?

    (1) The units digit of n is the same as the units digit of n^2.

    (2) The units digit of n is the same as the units digit of n^3.

Arithmetic Arithmetic operations

If the units digit of n is greater than 2, then it can only be the digits 3, 4, 5, 6, 7, 8, or 9.

(1) To solve this problem, it is necessary to find a digit that is the same as the units digit of its square. For example, both 43 squared (1,849) and 303 squared (91,809) have a units digit of 9, which is different from the units digit of 43 and 303. However, 25 squared (625) and 385 squared (148,225) both have a units digit of 5, and 16 and 226 both have a units digit of 6 and their squares (256 and 51,076, respectively) do, too. However, there is no further information to choose between 5 or 6; NOT sufficient.

(2) Once again, 5 and 6 are the only numbers which, when cubed, will both have a 5 or 6 respectively in their units digits. However, the information given does not distinguish between them; NOT sufficient.

Since (1) and (2) together yield the same information but with no direction as to which to choose, there is not enough information to determine the answer.

The correct answer is E; both statements together are still not sufficient.

26. What is the value of the integer p ?

    (1) Each of the integers 2, 3, and 5 is a factor of p.

    (2) Each of the integers 2, 5, and 7 is a factor of p.

Arithmetic Properties of numbers

(1) These are factors of p, but it is not clear that they are the only factors of p; NOT sufficient.

(2) These are factors of p, but it is not clear that they are the only factors of p; NOT sufficient.

Taken together, (1) and (2) overlap, but again there is no clear indication that these are the only factors of p.

The correct answer is E; both statements together are still not sufficient.

27. If the length of Wanda's telephone call was rounded up to the nearest whole minute by her telephone company, then Wanda was charged for how many minutes for her telephone call?

    (1) The total charge for Wanda's telephone call was $6.50.

    (2) Wanda was charged $0.50 more for the first minute of the telephone call than for each minute after the first.

Arithmetic Arithmetic operations

(1) This does not give any information as to the call's cost per minute; NOT sufficient.

(2) From this, it can be determined only that the call was longer than one minute and that the charge for the first minute was $0.50 more than the charge for each succeeding minute; NOT sufficient.

Taking (1) and (2) together, the number of minutes cannot be determined as long as the cost of each minute after the first is unknown. For example, if the cost of each minute after the first minute were $0.40, then the cost of the first minute would be $0.90. Then the total cost of the other minutes would be $6.50 − $0.90 = $5.60, and $5.60 ÷ $0.40 would yield 14. In this case, the time of the call would be $1 + 14 = 15$ minutes. If, however, the cost of each minute after the first minute were $0.15, then the cost of the first minute would be $0.65. Then $6.50 − $0.65 would be $5.85, and this in turn, when divided by $0.15, would yield 39 minutes, for a total call length of 40 minutes. More information on the cost of each minute after the first minute is still needed.

The correct answer is E;
both statements together are still not sufficient.

28. What is the perimeter of isosceles triangle *MNP* ?

   (1) $MN = 16$
   (2) $NP = 20$

Geometry Triangles

The perimeter of a triangle is the sum of all three sides. In the case of an isosceles triangle, two of the sides are equal. To determine the perimeter of this triangle, it is necessary to know both the length of an equal side and the length of the base of the triangle.

   (1) Only gives the length of one side; NOT sufficient.

   (2) Only gives the length of one side; NOT sufficient.

Since it is unclear whether *MN* or *NP* is one of the equal sides, it is not possible to determine the length of the third side or the perimeter of the triangle. The perimeter could be either $((2)(16)) + 20 = 52$ or $((2)(20)) + 16 = 56$.

The correct answer is E;
both statements together are still not sufficient.

29. In a survey of retailers, what percent had purchased computers for business purposes?

   (1) 85 percent of the retailers surveyed who owned their own store had purchased computers for business purposes.

   (2) 40 percent of the retailers surveyed owned their own store.

Arithmetic Percents

   (1) With only this, it cannot be known what percent of the retailers not owning their own store had purchased computers, and so it cannot be known how many retailers purchased computers overall; NOT sufficient.

   (2) While this permits the percent of owners and nonowners in the survey to be deduced, the overall percent of retailers who had purchased computers cannot be determined; NOT sufficient.

Using the information from both (1) and (2), the percent of surveyed owner-retailers who had purchased computers can be deduced, and the percent of nonowner-retailers can also be deduced. However, the information that would permit a determination of either the percent of nonowner-retailers who had purchased computers or the overall percent of all retailers (both owners and nonowners) who had purchased computers is still not provided.

The correct answer is E;
both statements together are still not sufficient.

30. The only gift certificates that a certain store sold yesterday were worth either $100 each or $10 each. If the store sold a total of 20 gift certificates yesterday, how many gift certificates worth $10 each did the store sell yesterday?

   (1) The gift certificates sold by the store yesterday were worth a total of between $1,650 and $1,800.

   (2) Yesterday the store sold more than 15 gift certificates worth $100 each.

Algebra Applied problems; Simultaneous equations; Inequalities

Let *x* represent the number of $100 certificates sold, and let *y* represent the number of $10 certificates sold. Then the given information can be expressed as $x + y = 20$ or thus $y = 20 − x$. The value of the $100 certificates sold is $100x$, and the value of the $10 certificates sold is $10y$.

(1)   From this, it is known that $100x + 10y > 1{,}650$. Since $y = 20 - x$, this value can be substituted for y, and the inequality can be solved for x:

$$100x + 10y > 1{,}650$$

$100x + 10(20 - x) > 1{,}650$	substitute for y
$100x + 200 - 10x > 1{,}650$	distribute
$90x + 200 > 1{,}650$	simplify
$90x > 1{,}450$	subtract 200 from both sides

$$x > 16.1$$

Thus, more than 16 of the $100 certificates were sold. If 17 $100 certificates were sold, then it must be that 3 $10 certificates were also sold for a total of $1,730, which satisfies the condition of being between $1,650 and $1,800. If, however, 18 $100 certificates were sold, then it must be that 2 $10 certificates were sold, and this totals $1,820, which is more than $1,800 and fails to satisfy the condition. Therefore, 3 of the $10 certificates were sold; SUFFICIENT.

(2)   From this it can be known only that the number of $10 certificates sold was 4 or fewer; NOT sufficient.

The correct answer is A; statement 1 alone is sufficient.

31.   Is the standard deviation of the set of measurements x_1, x_2, x_3, x_4, ..., x_{20} less than 3 ?

(1)   The variance for the set of measurements is 4.

(2)   For each measurement, the difference between the mean and that measurement is 2.

Arithmetic Statistics

In determining the standard deviation, the difference between each measurement and the mean is squared, and then the squared differences are added and divided by the number of measurements. The quotient is the variance and the positive square root of the variance is the standard deviation.

(1)   If the variance is 4, then the standard deviation $= \sqrt{4} = 2$, which is less than 3; SUFFICIENT.

(2)   For each measurement, the difference between the mean and that measurement is 2. Therefore, the square of each difference is 4, and the sum of all the squares is $4 \times 20 = 80$. The standard deviation is $\sqrt{\dfrac{80}{20}} = \sqrt{4} = 2$, which is less than 3; SUFFICIENT.

The correct answer is D; each statement alone is sufficient.

32.   Is the range of the integers 6, 3, y, 4, 5, and x greater than 9 ?

(1) $y > 3x$

(2) $y > x > 3$

Arithmetic Statistics

The range of a set of integers is equal to the difference between the largest integer and the smallest integer. The range of the set of integers 3, 4, 5, and 6 is 3, which is derived from $6 - 3$.

(1)   Although it is known that $y > 3x$, the value of x is unknown. If, for example, $x = 1$, then the value of y would be greater than 3. However, if $x = 2$, then the value of y would be greater than 6, and, since 6 would no longer be the largest integer, the range would be affected. Because the actual values of x and y are unknown, the value of the range is also unknown; NOT sufficient.

(2)   If $x > 3$ and $y > x$, then x could be 4 and y could be 5. Then the range of the 6 integers would still be $6 - 3$ or 3. However, if x were 4 and y were 15, then the range of the 6 integers would be $15 - 3$, or 12. There is no means to establish the values of x and y, beyond the fact that they both are greater than 3; NOT sufficient.

Taking (1) and (2) together, it is known that $x > 3$ and that $y > 3x$. Since the smallest integer that x could be is thus 4, then $y > 3(4)$ or $y > 12$. Therefore, the integer y must be 13 or larger. When y is equal to 13, the range of the 6 integers is $13 - 3 = 10$, which is larger than 9. As y increases in value, the value of the range will also increase.

The correct answer is C; both statements together are sufficient.

33. Is $\dfrac{5^{x+2}}{25} < 1$?

    (1) $5^x < 1$

    (2) $x < 0$

Algebra Inequalities

Note that $x^{r+s} = \left(x^r\right)\left(x^s\right)$.

(1) If $5^x < 1$, then $\dfrac{5^{x+2}}{25} < 1$ since

$$\frac{5^{x+2}}{25} = \frac{5^x \cdot 5^2}{25} = 5^x; \text{ SUFFICIENT.}$$

(2) If $x < 0$, then

$x + 2 < 2$	add 2 to both sides
$5^{x+2} < 5^2$	because $a < b$ implies $5^a < 5^b$
$\dfrac{5^{x+2}}{25} < 1$	divide both sides by $5^2 = 25$;

SUFFICIENT.

**The correct answer is D;
each statement alone is sufficient.**

34. Of the companies surveyed about the skills they required in prospective employees, 20 percent required both computer skills and writing skills. What percent of the companies surveyed required neither computer skills nor writing skills?

    (1) Of those companies surveyed that required computer skills, half required writing skills.

    (2) 45 percent of the companies surveyed required writing skills but not computer skills.

Arithmetic Percents

The surveyed companies could be placed into one of the following four categories:

1. Requiring computer skills and requiring writing skills

2. Requiring computer skills but not requiring writing skills

3. Not requiring computer skills but requiring writing skills

4. Not requiring either computer skills or writing skills

It is given that 20 percent of the surveyed companies fell into category 1. It is necessary to determine what percent of the surveyed companies fell into category 4.

(1) This helps identify the percentage in category 2. Since $\frac{1}{2}$ the companies that required computer skills also required writing skills (i.e., those in category 1), then the other $\frac{1}{2}$ of the companies that required computer skills did not require writing skills (thus category 2 = category 1). However, this information only establishes that 20 percent required computer skills, but not writing skills; NOT sufficient.

(2) While this establishes category 3, that is, that 45 percent required writing skills but not computer skills, no further information is available; NOT sufficient.

Taking (1) and (2) together, the first three categories add up to 85 percent $(20 + 20 + 45)$. Therefore, category 4 would be equal to $100 - 85 = 15$ percent of the surveyed companies required neither computer skills nor writing skills.

**The correct answer is C;
both statements together are sufficient.**

35. What is the value of $w + q$?

    (1) $3w = 3 - 3q$

    (2) $5w + 5q = 5$

Algebra First- and second-degree equations

(1) If $3q$ is added to both sides of this equation, it can be rewritten as $3w + 3q = 3$. When each term is then divided by 3, it yields $w + q = 1$; SUFFICIENT.

(2) When each term in this equation is divided by 5, it becomes $w + q = 1$; SUFFICIENT.

**The correct answer is D;
each statement alone is sufficient.**

36. If X and Y are points in a plane and X lies inside the circle C with center O and radius 2, does Y lie inside circle C?

    (1) The length of line segment XY is 3.

    (2) The length of line segment OY is 1.5.

    Geometry Circles

    (1) The maximum distance between two points that lie on a circle is equal to the diameter, or 2 times the radius. Since the radius of circle C is 2, the diameter in this case is 4. It cannot be assumed, however, that X and Y are points on the diameter; X can lie anywhere within the circle. When the distance between X and Y is 3, it is still possible either that Y is within the circle or that Y is outside the circle; NOT sufficient.

    (2) If the length of the line segment OY is 1.5 and the circle has a radius of 2, then the distance from the center O to point Y is less than the radius, and point Y must therefore lie within the circle; SUFFICIENT.

    **The correct answer is B;
    statement 2 alone is sufficient.**

37. Is $x > y$?

    (1) $x = y + 2$

    (2) $\frac{x}{2} = y - 1$

    Algebra First- and second-degree equations

    (1) Since 2 has to be added to y in order to make it equal to x, it can be reasoned that $x > y$; SUFFICIENT.

    (2) Multiplying both sides of this equation by 2 results in $x = 2(y - 1)$ or $x = 2y - 2$. If y were 0, then x would be -2, and y would be greater than x. If y were a negative number like -2, then $x = 2(-2) - 2 = -6$, and again y would be greater than x. However, if y were a positive number such as 4, then $x = 2(4) - 2 = 6$, and $x > y$. Since there is no other information concerning the value of y, it cannot be determined if $x > y$; NOT sufficient.

    **The correct answer is A;
    statement 1 alone is sufficient.**

38. If Paula drove the distance from her home to her college at an average speed that was greater than 70 kilometers per hour, did it take her less than 3 hours to drive this distance?

    (1) The distance that Paula drove from her home to her college was greater than 200 kilometers.

    (2) The distance that Paula drove from her home to her college was less than 205 kilometers.

    Arithmetic Distance problem

    A distance problem uses the formula distance = rate × time. To find the time, the formula would be rearranged as time = $\frac{\text{distance}}{\text{rate}}$. To solve this problem, it is necessary to know the rate (given here as 70 kilometers per hour) and the distance.

    (1) If D is the distance Paula drove then $D > 200$ and $\frac{D}{70} > \frac{200}{70} = 2\frac{6}{7}$ so $t > 2\frac{6}{7}$ and t may or may not be less than 3; NOT sufficient.

    (2) If D is the distance Paula drove then $D < 205$ and $\frac{D}{70} < \frac{205}{70} = 2\frac{13}{14}$ so $t < 2\frac{13}{14} < 3$; SUFFICIENT.

    **The correct answer is B;
    statement 2 alone is sufficient.**

39. In the xy-plane, if line k has negative slope and passes through the point $(-5, r)$, is the x-intercept of line k positive?

    (1) The slope of line k is -5.

    (2) $r > 0$

Geometry Coordinate geometry

The x-intercept is the x-coordinate of the point in which the line k crosses the x-axis and would have the coordinates $(x,0)$.

(1)   Knowing the slope of the line does not help in determining the x-intercept, since from point $(-5,r)$ the line k extends in both directions. Without knowing the value of r, the x-intercept could be -5 if r were 0, or it could be other numbers, both positive and negative, depending on the value of r; NOT sufficient.

(2)   Knowing that $r > 0$ suggests that the x-intercept is not -5; the point $(-5,r)$, where r is a positive number, does lie in quadrant II. It could, however, be any point with an x-coordinate of -5 in that quadrant and line k could have any negative slope, and so the line k would vary with the value of r. Therefore, the x-intercept of line k cannot be determined; NOT sufficient.

Using (1) and (2) together does not help in the determination of the x-intercept, since the point $(-5,r)$ could have any positive y-coordinate and thus line k could cross the x-axis at many different places.

The correct answer is E;
both statements together are still not sufficient.

40.   If \$5,000 invested for one year at p percent simple annual interest yields \$500, what amount must be invested at k percent simple annual interest for one year to yield the same number of dollars?

(1) $k = 0.8p$
(2) $k = 8$

Arithmetic Interest problem

With simple annual interest, the formula to use is interest = principal × rate × time. It is given that $\$500 = \$5,000 \times \dfrac{p}{100} \times 1$ (year), so $p = 10$ percent interest.

(1)   If p is 10 percent, then $k = 0.8\,p$ is 0.08. Using the same formula, the time is again 1 year; the interest is the same amount; and the rate is 0.08, or 8 percent. Thus, \$500 = principal $\times 0.08 \times 1$, or principal = \$6,250; SUFFICIENT.

(2)   If $k = 8$, then the rate is 8 percent, and the same formula and procedure as above are employed again; SUFFICIENT.

The correct answer is D;
each statement alone is sufficient.

41.   If $\dfrac{x+y}{z} > 0$, is $x < 0$?

(1) $x < y$
(2) $z < 0$

Algebra Inequalities

If $\dfrac{x+y}{z} > 0$, then either one of two cases holds true. Either $(x + y) > 0$ **and** $z > 0$, or $(x + y) < 0$ **and** $z < 0$. In other words, in order for the term to be greater than zero, it must be true that either 1) both the numerator and denominator are greater than 0 or 2) both the numerator and denominator are less than 0.

(1)   Regardless of whether $(x + y)$ is positive or negative, the positive or negative value of z must be in agreement with the sign of $(x + y)$ in order for $\dfrac{x+y}{z} > 0$. However, there is no information about z here; NOT sufficient.

(2)   If $z < 0$, then $(x + y)$ must be less than 0. However, this statement gives no information about $(x + y)$; NOT sufficient.

This can be solved using (1) and (2) together. From (2), it is known that $z < 0$, and, going back to the original analysis, for the term to be greater than zero, $(x + y)$ must also be less than 0. If $x + y < 0$ then $x < -y$. But $x < y$ from (1) so

$$x + x < -y + y$$
$$2x < 0$$
$$x < 0.$$

The correct answer is C;
both statements together are sufficient.

42. Does the integer k have at least three different positive prime factors?

    (1) $\dfrac{k}{15}$ is an integer.

    (2) $\dfrac{k}{10}$ is an integer.

    Arithmetic Properties of numbers

    (1) The prime factors of 15 are 3 and 5. So in this case, k has at least 2 different positive prime factors, but it is unknown if there are more positive prime factors; NOT sufficient.

    (2) The prime factors of 10 are 2 and 5, showing that k has at least these 2 different positive prime factors, but k might or might not have more; NOT sufficient.

    Taking (1) and (2) together, since k is divisible by both 10 and 15, it must be divisible by their different positive prime factors of 2, 3, and 5. Thus k has at least 3 different positive prime factors.

    **The correct answer is C;
    both statements together are sufficient.**

43. In City X last April, was the average (arithmetic mean) daily high temperature greater than the median daily high temperature?

    (1) In City X last April, the sum of the 30 daily high temperatures was 2,160°.

    (2) In City X last April, 60 percent of the daily high temperatures were less than the average daily high temperature.

    Arithmetic Statistics

    The formula for calculating the arithmetic mean, or the average, is as follows:

    $$\text{Average} = \frac{\text{sum of } v \text{ values}}{v}$$

    (1) These data will produce an average of $\dfrac{2160}{30} = 72°$ for last April in City X. However, there is no information regarding the median for comparison; NOT sufficient.

    (2) The median is the middle temperature of the data. As such, 50 percent of the daily high temperatures will be at or above the median, and 50 percent will be at or below the median. If 60 percent of the daily high temperatures were less than the average daily high temperature, then the average of the daily highs must be greater than the median; SUFFICIENT.

    **The correct answer is B;
    statement 2 alone is sufficient.**

44. If m and n are positive integers, is $\left(\sqrt{m}\right)^n$ an integer?

    (1) $\left(\sqrt{m}\right)$ is an integer.

    (2) $\left(\sqrt{n}\right)$ is an integer.

    Arithmetic Properties of numbers

    (1) If $\left(\sqrt{m}\right)$ is an integer and n is a positive integer, then $\left(\sqrt{m}\right)^n$ is an integer because an integer raised to a positive integer is an integer; SUFFICIENT.

    (2) The information that $\left(\sqrt{n}\right)$ is an integer is not helpful in answering the question. For example, if $m = 2$ and $n = 9$, $\sqrt{9} = 3$, which is an integer, but $\left(\sqrt{2}\right)^9 = \left(16\sqrt{2}\right)$, which is not an integer. But if $m = 4$ and $n = 9$, then $\sqrt{9} = 3$, which is an integer, and $\left(\sqrt{4}\right)^9 = 2^9 = 512$ is an integer; NOT sufficient.

    **The correct answer is A;
    statement 1 alone is sufficient.**

45. Of the 66 people in a certain auditorium, at most 6 people have birthdays in any one given month. Does at least one person in the auditorium have a birthday in January?

    (1) More of the people in the auditorium have birthdays in February than in March.

    (2) Five of the people in the auditorium have birthdays in March.

Algebra Sets and functions

Because it is given that 6 is the greatest number of individuals who can have birthdays in any particular month, these 66 people could be evenly distributed across 11 of the 12 months of the year. That is to say, it could be possible for the distribution to be $11 \times 6 = 66$, and thus any given month, such as January, would not have a person with a birthday. Assume that January has no people with birthdays, and see if this assumption is disproved.

(1) The information that more people have February birthdays than March birthdays indicates that the distribution is not even. Therefore, March is underrepresented and must thus have fewer than 6 birthdays. Since no month can have more than 6 people with birthdays, and every month but January already has as many people with birthdays as it can have, January has to have at least 1 person with a birthday; SUFFICIENT.

(2) Again, March is underrepresented with only 5 birthdays, and none of the other months can have more than 6 birthdays. Therefore, the extra birthday (from March) must occur in January; SUFFICIENT.

**The correct answer is D;
each statement alone is sufficient.**

46. Last year the average (arithmetic mean) salary of the 10 employees of Company X was $42,800. What is the average salary of the same 10 employees this year?

    (1) For 8 of the 10 employees, this year's salary is 15 percent greater than last year's salary.

    (2) For 2 of the 10 employees, this year's salary is the same as last year's salary.

Arithmetic Statistics

(1) Since all 10 employees did not receive the same 15 percent increase, it cannot be assumed that the mean this year is 15 percent higher than last year. It remains unknown whether these 8 salaries were the top 8 salaries, the bottom 8 salaries, or somewhere in-between. Without this type of information from last year, the mean for this year cannot be determined; NOT sufficient.

(2) If 2 salaries remained the same as last year, then 8 salaries changed. Without further information about the changes, the mean for this year cannot be determined; NOT sufficient.

Even taking (1) and (2) together, it remains impossible to tell the mean salary for this year without additional data.

**The correct answer is E;
both statements together are still not sufficient.**

47. In a certain classroom, there are 80 books, of which 24 are fiction and 23 are written in Spanish. How many of the fiction books are written in Spanish?

    (1) Of the fiction books, there are 6 more that are not written in Spanish than are written in Spanish.

    (2) Of the books written in Spanish, there are 5 more nonfiction books than fiction books.

Algebra Sets and functions

Let x represent the fiction books that are written in Spanish. A table could be set up like the one below, filling in the information that is known or able to be known:

	Spanish	Non-Spanish	Total
Fiction	x		24
Nonfiction			56
Total	23	57	80

(1) If x represents the fiction books written in Spanish, then $x + 6$ can now be used to represent the fiction books that are not written in Spanish. From the table above, it can be seen then that $x + x + 6 = 24$, or $2x = 18$. Therefore, x, or the number of fiction books written in Spanish, is 9; SUFFICIENT.

(2) If x represents the fiction books written in Spanish, then $x + 5$ can now be used to represent the nonfiction books written in Spanish. From the table, it can be said that $x + x + 5 = 23$, or $2x = 18$. Therefore, x, or the number of fiction books written in Spanish, is 9; SUFFICIENT.

The correct answer is D; each statement alone is sufficient.

48. If p is the perimeter of rectangle Q, what is the value of p?

(1) Each diagonal of rectangle Q has length 10.

(2) The area of rectangle Q is 48.

Geometry Rectangles; Perimeter; Area

The perimeter of a rectangle is equal to 2 times the rectangle's length plus 2 times the rectangle's width, or $p = 2l + 2w$. The diagonals of a rectangle are equal. In a rectangle, because a diagonal forms a right triangle, the length of a diagonal is equal to the square root of the length squared plus the width squared, or $d = \sqrt{l^2 + w^2}$.

(1) If a diagonal $= 10$, then $10 = \sqrt{l^2 + w^2}$, or, by squaring both sides, $100 = l^2 + w^2$. Without knowing the value or the relationship between the other two sides of the right triangle, it is impossible to solve for l or w, and thus for the perimeter of the rectangle; NOT sufficient.

(2) If the area of the rectangle is 48, then it can be stated that $lw = 48$. However, without further information, the perimeter cannot be determined. For example, l could be 6 and w could be 8, and the perimeter would then be $12 + 16 = 28$. However, it could also be that l is 4 and w is 12, and in that case the perimeter would be $8 + 24 = 32$; NOT sufficient.

Using (1) and (2) together, it is possible to solve this problem. Since from (2) $lw = 48$, then $w = \dfrac{48}{l}$. Substituting this into $100 = l^2 + w^2$ from (1) the equation can be solved as follows:

$100 = l^2 + \left(\dfrac{48}{l}\right)^2$ substitution

$100l^2 = l^4 + 2,304$ multiply both sides by l^2

$l^4 - 100l^2 + 2,304 = 0$ move all terms to one side

$(l^2 - 64)(l^2 - 36) = 0$ factor like a quadratic

$l^2 = 64,\ l^2 = 36$ solve for l^2

Since l is a length, it must be positive, so l is either 8 or 6. When $l = 8$, $w = \dfrac{48}{8} = 6$, and when $l = 6$, $w = \dfrac{48}{6} = 8$, both of which give the same perimeter.

The correct answer is C; both statements together are sufficient.

3.6 Verbal Answer Explanations

Reading Comprehension

The following discussion is intended to familiarize you with the most efficient and effective approaches to the kinds of problems common to reading comprehension. The particular questions in this chapter are generally representative of the kinds of reading comprehension questions you will encounter on the GMAT exam. Remember that it is the problem solving strategy that is important, not the specific details of a particular question.

Questions 1–5 refer to the passage on page 27.

1. Which of the following best describes the purpose of the sentence in lines 10–15?

    (A) To show that economic signaling theory fails to explain a finding

    (B) To introduce a distinction not accounted for by economic signaling theory

    (C) To account for an exception to a generalization suggested by Marquardt and McGann

    (D) To explain why Marquardt and McGann's research was conducted

    (E) To offer an explanation for an observation reported by Marquardt and McGann

Logical structure

Marquardt and McGann found a correlation between highly advertised products and high-quality products. The connection can be explained by understanding that companies may invest heavily in such advertising, anticipating that recurring purchases of high-quality products will eventually recover these advertising costs. The consumers will continue to buy these products over time because of loyalty to their high quality. The statement in bold provides this explanation for the correlation noted by Marquardt and McGann.

A The sentence does not explain a failure of the economic signaling theory.

B Economic signaling theory is about perceptions of quality, but this explanation is about actual quality and its correlation with advertising.

C No exception is mentioned in Marquardt and McGann's work.

D The sentence does not examine why or how the research was undertaken.

E **Correct.** This statement provides an explanation of why highly advertised products *did indeed rank high on certain measures of product quality.*

The correct answer is E.

2. The primary purpose of the passage is to

    (A) present findings that contradict one explanation for the effects of a particular advertising practice

    (B) argue that theoretical explanations about the effects of a particular advertising practice are of limited value without empirical evidence

    (C) discuss how and why particular advertising practices may affect consumers' perceptions

    (D) contrast the research methods used in two different studies of a particular advertising practice

    (E) explain why a finding about consumer responses to a particular advertising practice was unexpected

Main idea

The primary purpose can be determined only by evaluating the whole passage. The first paragraph discusses consumers' perceptions of quality based on frequency of advertising. The second paragraph discusses three studies that show how consumers base their evaluations of products on the kinds of advertising they see. Therefore, the purpose of the whole passage is to show how consumers' perceptions of products are shaped by certain advertising practices.

A   The passage shows that expensive advertising works to a certain point, but not after it; this method examines a continuum, not a contradiction.

B   Most of the passage is devoted to empirical evidence.

C   **Correct.** The passage shows how the frequency and the kind of advertising influence consumers' perceptions about the quality of the products advertised.

D   The passage reports the findings of four studies but does not mention research methods.

E   The passage does not indicate that any of the findings were unexpected.

The correct answer is C.

3.   Kirmani's research, as described in the passage, suggests which of the following regarding consumers' expectations about the quality of advertised products?

(A)   Those expectations are likely to be highest if a manufacturer runs both black-and-white and color advertisements for the same product.

(B)   Those expectations can be shaped by the presence of color in an advertisement as well as by the frequency with which an advertisement appears.

(C)   Those expectations are usually high for frequently advertised new brands but not for frequently advertised familiar brands.

(D)   Those expectations are likely to be higher for products whose black-and-white advertisements are often repeated than for those whose color advertisements are less often repeated.

(E)   Those expectations are less definitively shaped by the manufacturer's advertisements than by information that consumers gather from other sources.

Inference

The question's use of the word *suggests* means that the answer depends on making an inference. This research is discussed in the second paragraph. Kirmani found that too much advertising tended to make the consumers believe that manufacturers were desperate. The use of color was also found to affect consumers' perceptions of brand quality. Realizing that color advertising is more expensive than black-and-white, consumers react more quickly to what they perceive to be its overuse than they do to a repetition of black-and-white advertisements.

A   This situation is not discussed in the research, at least as it is reported in this passage.

B   Correct. It can be inferred that consumers' perceptions of product quality are influenced by the use of color in an advertisement and by the frequency of the advertisement's appearance.

C   The research does not make a distinction between new and familiar brands.

D   The research indicates only that consumers can tolerate black-and-white advertisements for a longer time than color advertisements before dismissing them as excessive.

E   There is no discussion of what consumers learn from other sources.

The correct answer is B.

4.   Kirmani's third study, as described in the passage, suggests which of the following conclusions about a black-and-white advertisement?

(A)   It can be repeated more frequently than a comparable color advertisement could before consumers begin to suspect low manufacturer confidence in the quality of the advertised product.

(B)   It will have the greatest impact on consumers' perceptions of the quality of the advertised product if it appears during periods when a color version of the same advertisement is also being used.

(C)   It will attract more attention from readers of the print publication in which it appears if it is used only a few times.

(D)   It may be perceived by some consumers as more expensive than a comparable color advertisement.

(E)   It is likely to be perceived by consumers as a sign of higher manufacturer confidence in the quality of the advertised product than a comparable color advertisement would be.

Inference

Kirmani's third study is discussed in the final two sentences. Consumers suspect expensive advertising results from a manufacturer's lack of confidence in the quality of the product. Consumers reach the point at which they find advertising *excessive* more quickly with color advertising than with black-and-white advertising because they understand that the addition of color increases advertising expenses. It is reasonable to infer that the reverse is also true and thus that consumers will tolerate lengthier repetitions of black-and-white advertising without becoming suspicious of product quality.

A   Correct. Consumers find color advertising excessive more quickly and thus can be expected to find black-and-white advertising excessive less quickly.

B   The study does not discuss concurrent appearances of color and black-and-white advertisements for the same product.

C   The sole conclusion about frequency is that consumers can tolerate a greater frequency of black-and-white advertisements than color advertisements.

D   It is stated that consumers understand that color advertisements are more expensive.

E   The research certainly does not report this finding.

The correct answer is A.

5. The passage suggests that Kirmani would be most likely to agree with which of the following statements about consumers' perceptions of the relationship between the frequency with which a product is advertised and the product's quality?

(A) Consumers' perceptions about the frequency with which an advertisement appears are their primary consideration when evaluating an advertisement's claims about product quality.

(B) Because most consumers do not notice the frequency of advertisement, it has little impact on most consumers' expectations regarding product quality.

(C) Consumers perceive frequency of advertisement as a signal about product quality only when the advertisement is for a product that is newly on the market.

(D) The frequency of advertisement is not always perceived by consumers to indicate that manufacturers are highly confident about their products' quality.

(E) Consumers who try a new product that has been frequently advertised are likely to perceive the advertisement's frequency as having been an accurate indicator of the product's quality.

Inference

The first sentence of the second paragraph provides the answer to this question: *at some level of spending the manufacturer's advertising effort may be perceived as unreasonably high, implying low manufacturer confidence in product quality.* Thus, it is logical to assume that if a product is advertised too frequently, consumers may believe that the manufacturer is spending excessive amounts on advertising because that manufacturer is not confident of the product's quality.

A Kirmani's research, as reported here, does not support this claim.

B Kirmani's research examines how consumers respond to the frequency of advertising; the research does not indicate that consumers do not notice frequency.

C The research does not distinguish between new and familiar products.

D **Correct.** Excessive advertising may lead consumers to believe that the manufacturer lacks confidence in the quality of the product.

E Kirmani's research does not specifically address new products.

The correct answer is D.

Questions 6–11 refer to the passage on page 29.

6. The main purpose of the passage is to

(A) propose an experiment
(B) analyze a function
(C) refute an argument
(D) explain a contradiction
(E) simulate a process

Main idea

Determining the main purpose comes from considering the passage as a whole. The first paragraph begins by noting that *the idea of the brain as an information processor* is generally accepted by neuroscientists. The author then presents Searle as an *enemy* of this position and explains Searle's belief that human thought is more than information processing. The second paragraph questions Searle's position, and the third asserts that the brain is an information processor, refuting Searle's argument.

A   The author uses the idea of a mechanical simulation of a stomach as a metaphor for a computer's simulation of thought; this is not a proposal for an experiment.

B   The author analyzes Searle's position, but no function is analyzed.

C   **Correct.** The author explains Searle's argument in order to refute it.

D   The author points out a weakness in Searle's thinking, but not a contradiction.

E   The simulation of a process is included as a metaphor, but it is not essential to the passage.

The correct answer is C.

7.   Which of the following is most consistent with Searle's reasoning as presented in the passage?

(A)   Meaning and content cannot be reduced to algorithms.

(B)   The process of digestion can be simulated mechanically, but not on a computer.

(C)   Simulated thoughts and real thoughts are essentially similar because they are composed primarily of information.

(D)   A computer can use "causal powers" similar to those of the human brain when processing information.

(E)   Computer simulations of the world can achieve the complexity of the brain's representations of the world.

Evaluation

Searle's position is stated in the first paragraph: because computers merely follow algorithms, *they cannot deal with important aspects of human thought such as meaning and content*. Thus, Searle believes that meaning and content cannot be reduced to algorithms.

A   **Correct.** Searle believes that meaning and content cannot be reduced to algorithms.

B   The author argues for the mechanical simulation, but offers no evidence that Searle would agree.

C   This statement reflects the author's position, but it is the opposite of Searle's.

D   Searle asserts that only people, not computers, have *the causal powers of the brain*.

E   The passage does not discuss computer simulations of the world.

The correct answer is A.

8.   The author of the passage would be most likely to agree with which of the following statements about the simulation of organ functions?

(A)   An artificial device that achieves the functions of the stomach could be considered a valid model of the stomach.

(B)   Computer simulations of the brain are best used to crack the brain's codes of meaning and content.

(C)   Computer simulations of the brain challenge ideas that are fundamental to psychology and neuroscience.

(D)   Because the brain and the stomach both act as processors, they can best be simulated by mechanical devices.

(E)   The computer's limitations in simulating digestion suggest equal limitations in computer-simulated thinking.

Application

To answer this question, think about how the author would respond to each statement. Anticipating the author's response depends on understanding the author's point of view. In this passage, the author is arguing against Searle's view of the brain and in favor of the brain as information processor. The author believes that the computer can be a model of the brain and uses the example of the mechanical stomach to support his position on simulations.

A **Correct.** The first two sentences of the third paragraph imply that a mechanical device is a valid model.

B The author believes a computer can simulate the brain but does not comment on how these simulations should be used. There is no way to predict the author's reaction to this statement.

C The author would reject this statement since neuroscience and psychology do in fact see the brain as an information processor.

D The author agrees that both the brain and the stomach act as processors; believes that the computer, a nonmechanical device, can simulate the brain; and offers a way that a mechanical device could simulate the stomach. The author does not suggest that mechanical devices are the best way to simulate both their processes.

E This statement reflects Searle's viewpoint, which the author rejects.

The correct answer is A.

9. It can be inferred that the author of the passage believes that Searle's argument is flawed by its failure to

(A) distinguish between syntactic and semantic operations

(B) explain adequately how people, unlike computers, are able to understand meaning

(C) provide concrete examples illustrating its claims about thinking

(D) understand how computers use algorithms to process information

(E) decipher the code that is transmitted from neuron to neuron in the brain

Inference

The author's attitude toward Searle's argument is apparent in the first paragraph, which ends with the author's summary of what Searle is saying. Computers understand structures, Searle argues, but only people understand meaning. How do people understand meaning? The author notes that Searle is not able to answer this question and is able only to assert that people have *causal powers of the brain*.

A The author makes it clear in the first paragraph that Searle does distinguish between the two. In Searle's view computers are syntactic, interpreting structure or arrangement, rather than semantic, understanding meaning.

B **Correct.** The first paragraph ends with the contrast between people and computers: *People, on the other hand, understand meaning because they have something Searle obscurely calls the causal powers of the brain.* By calling Searle's explanation obscure, the author implies that Searle has not adequately clarified how people understand meaning.

C Nothing in the passage criticizes Searle for not providing concrete examples. Indeed, in the second paragraph, the author anticipates how Searle would react to one concrete example, the computer simulation of the stomach.

D In the first paragraph, the author says that Searle argues that *computers simply follow algorithms*; whether or not Searle understands how they use algorithms is irrelevant.

E Since, as the author suggests in the first paragraph, Searle does not believe information could be a code transmitted from neuron to neuron, he cannot be expected to decipher that code.

The correct answer is B.

10. From the passage, it can be inferred that the author would agree with Searle on which of the following points?

    (A) Computers operate by following algorithms.
    (B) The human brain can never fully understand its own functions.
    (C) The comparison of the brain to a machine is overly simplistic.
    (D) The most accurate models of physical processes are computer simulations.
    (E) Human thought and computer-simulated thought involve similar processes of representation.

Inference

An inference requires going beyond the material explicitly stated in the passage to the author's ideas that underlie that material. The author and Searle take opposite points of view on the brain as information processor. Their area of agreement is narrow. However, they do both agree that computers work by following algorithms.

A Correct. The first paragraph explains that Searle dismisses computers because they *simply follow algorithms*; while the author disagrees with Searle on virtually every other point, no disagreement is voiced here.

B The first paragraph shows this to be Searle's position, but not the author's.

C The first paragraph shows this to be Searle's position, but not the author's.

D The second paragraph explains Searle's rejection of this position.

E The final paragraph establishes this as the author's position, but not Searle's.

The correct answer is A.

11. Which of the following most accurately represents Searle's criticism of the brain-as-computer metaphor, as that criticism is described in the passage?

    (A) The metaphor is not experimentally verifiable.
    (B) The metaphor does not take into account the unique powers of the brain.
    (C) The metaphor suggests that a brain's functions can be simulated as easily as those of a stomach.
    (D) The metaphor suggests that a computer can simulate the workings of the mind by using the codes of neural transmission.
    (E) The metaphor is unhelpful because both the brain and the computer process information.

Inference

Searle's criticism of the brain-as-computer metaphor is discussed in the first paragraph. Computers are merely machines; only people are endowed with *causal powers of the brain* that allow them to understand meaning and content.

A Searle does not believe in the value of the metaphor, so its verification is beside the point.

B Correct. Searle believes that people have something computers do not, *causal powers of the brain* for understanding *important aspects of human thought*.

C Comparing the brain to a computer, the metaphor does not make this suggestion.

D In the second paragraph, the author says, *but even if a computer could simulate the workings of the mind*, making it clear that presently it cannot; this statement does not reflect why Searle rejects the metaphor.

E This is not the basis of Searle's objection since he does not accept the premise that the brain is an information processor.

The correct answer is B.

Questions 12–17 refer to the passage on page 31.

12. The primary purpose of the passage is to

    (A) explain why women reformers of the Progressive Era failed to achieve their goals

    (B) discuss the origins of child labor laws in the late nineteenth and early twentieth centuries

    (C) compare the living conditions of working-class and middle-class women in the Progressive Era

    (D) discuss an oversight on the part of women reformers of the Progressive Era

    (E) revise a traditional view of the role played by women reformers in enacting Progressive Era reforms

Main idea

Understanding the author's purpose comes only from reflecting on the passage as a whole. The beginning of the passage notes the success of middle-class women reformers in improving working conditions for women and children. The middle discusses the position of working-class mothers, who were more concerned with the economic survival of their families than with labor reform and consequently tried to circumvent the laws. The close of the passage observes that, although middle-class reformers were right to point out exploitation of children, they failed to understand the economic plight of working-class families, who needed the income earned by every possible member. The purpose of this passage is to show the failure of middle-class reformers to understand the economic position of working-class families.

A. Lines 6–10 emphasize the victories of the reformers.

B. The passage discusses the effects, rather than the origins, of child labor laws.

C. Living conditions of middle-class and working-class women are not compared.

D. Correct. As is made clear, especially in the final sentence of the passage, women reformers failed to understand the economic needs of working-class families.

E. A traditional view is not compared with a newer, revised view of the reformers.

The correct answer is D.

13. The *view* mentioned in line 17 of the passage refers to which of the following?

    (A) Some working-class mothers' resistance to the enforcement of child labor laws

    (B) Reformers' belief that child labor and industrial home work should be abolished

    (C) Reformers' opinions about how working-class families raised their children

    (D) Certain women historians' observation that there was a lack of consensus between women of different classes on the issue of child labor and industrial home work

    (E) Working-class families' fears about the adverse consequences that child labor laws would have on their ability to earn an adequate living

Inference

To find what this appearance of *view* refers to, it is necessary to look back to the beginning of the sentence. *This view,* not shared by working-class mothers, refers to the reformers' conviction that *child labor and industrial home work were equally inhumane practices that should be outlawed.*

A   *This view* must refer back to a point already stated; resistance to child labor laws is not discussed until the following sentence.

B   **Correct.** *This view* refers to the position of reformers stated earlier in the same sentence: that *child labor and industrial home work...should be outlawed.*

C   *This view* must refer back to a point already stated; the reformers' belief that resistance to child labor laws was due to poor parenting is discussed later in the passage.

D   A number of women historians have said that working-class mothers did not always share the *view* of middle-class women reformers about child labor.

E   *This view* must refer back to a point already stated; the fears of working-class families are examined in the following sentence.

The correct answer is B.

14. The author of the passage mentions the observations of women historians (lines 15–17) most probably in order to

(A)   provide support for an assertion made in the preceding sentence (lines 10–12)

(B)   raise a question that is answered in the last sentence of the passage (lines 27–32)

(C)   introduce an opinion that challenges a statement made in the first sentence of the passage

(D)   offer an alternative view to the one attributed in the passage to working-class mothers

(E)   point out a contradiction inherent in the traditional view of child labor reform as it is presented in the passage

Evaluation

In lines 10–12, the author asserts that child labor laws *pitted women of different classes against one another.* The view of the middle-class women reformers is stated, and then, to show that working-class mothers did not hold the same opinion, the author turns to the recent work of women historians to support this statement.

A   **Correct.** The author uses the recent work of women historians to support the statement that women of different social classes were pitted against one another.

B   The women historians *have recently observed*; the verb *observed* introduces a statement rather than a question.

C   The reference to women historians has to do with working-class mothers; it does not challenge women's activism and role in social reform.

D   The passage supports what the women historians say about working-class mothers.

E   The author does not define or present the *traditional* view of child labor reform, nor is any inherent contradiction pointed out.

The correct answer is A.

15. The passage suggests that which of the following was a reason for the difference of opinion between working-class mothers and women reformers on the issue of child labor?

(A)   Reformers' belief that industrial home work was preferable to child labor outside the home

(B)   Reformers' belief that child labor laws should pertain to working conditions but not to pay

(C)   Working-class mothers' resentment at reformers' attempts to interfere with their parenting

(D)   Working-class mothers' belief that child labor was an inhumane practice

(E)   Working-class families' need for every employable member of their families to earn money

Inference

The question's use of the word *suggests* means that the answer depends on making an inference. Lines 12–23 examine the different views of middle-class reformers and working-class mothers on child labor laws. While the reformers saw child labor as an *inhumane* practice that should be *outlawed*, working class mothers understood *the necessity of pooling the wages of as many family members as possible* and viewed child labor legislation as *a personal economic disaster*.

A   Lines 12–14 show that reformers regarded both kinds of work as *equally inhumane practices that should be outlawed*.

B   Pay is not specifically discussed in the passage.

C   Lines 24–27 indicate that the reformers believed working-class resistance to child labor laws was a sign of poor parenting, but nothing is said about the working-class response to this view.

D   Lines 12–17 say that the reformers held this position, but *working class mothers did not always share this view*.

E   **Correct.** Lines 17–23 explain that working-class families needed *the wages of as many family members as possible*.

The correct answer is E.

16. The author of the passage asserts which of the following about women reformers who tried to abolish child labor?

(A)   They alienated working-class mothers by attempting to enlist them in agitating for progressive causes.

(B)   They underestimated the prevalence of child labor among the working classes.

(C)   They were correct in their conviction that child labor was deplorable but shortsighted about the impact of child labor legislation on working-class families.

(D)   They were aggressive in their attempts to enforce child labor legislation, but were unable to prevent working-class families from circumventing them.

(E)   They were prevented by their nearly total disenfranchisement from making significant progress in child labor reform.

Supporting ideas

This question is based on information explicitly stated in the final sentence of the passage. Women reformers viewed *child labor as a terribly exploitative practice* but they *failed to take account of the economic needs of working-class families*.

A   The passage does not say that reformers tried to enlist working-class mothers in progressive causes.

B   No evidence is offered to support such a statement.

C   **Correct.** The final sentence makes clear that the reformers recognized child labor as *exploitative* but did not understand *the economic needs of working-class families*.

D   The reformers' activities involved promoting legislation; there is no evidence in the passage that the reformers themselves attempted to enforce these laws.

E   Lines 6–10 show that the reformers improved working conditions for women and children, despite their disenfranchisement.

The correct answer is C.

17. According to the passage, one of the most striking achievements of white middle-class women reformers during the Progressive Era was

    (A) gaining the right to vote in school elections
    (B) mobilizing working-class women in the fight against child labor
    (C) uniting women of different classes in grassroots activism
    (D) improving the economic conditions of working-class families
    (E) improving women's and children's working conditions

Supporting ideas

The question's use of the phrase *according to the passage* indicates that the answer can be found through careful reading of the passage. This question is based on information explicitly stated in lines 7–10, which state that *white middle-class women reformers won a variety of victories, notably in the improvement of working conditions, especially for women and children.*

A   Lines 6–7 show that women already had the right to vote in school elections.

B   Lines 20–24 show that working-class families tried to *circumvent child labor laws.*

C   Lines 11–12 say that one product of grassroots activism, child labor legislation, *pitted women of different classes against one another.*

D   Lines 31–32 say that the reformers *failed to take account of the economic needs of working-class families.*

E   **Correct.** The passage states that reformers improved the working conditions of women and children.

The correct answer is E.

Critical Reasoning

The following discussion is intended to familiarize you with the most efficient and effective approaches to critical reasoning questions. The particular questions in this chapter are generally representative of the kinds of critical reasoning questions you will encounter on the GMAT exam. Remember that it is the problem solving strategy that is important, not the specific details of a particular question.

18. Vasquez-Morrell Assurance specializes in insuring manufacturers. Whenever a policyholder makes a claim, a claims adjuster determines the amount that Vasquez-Morrell is obligated to pay. Vasquez-Morrell is cutting its staff of claims adjusters by 15 percent. To ensure that the company's ability to handle claims promptly is affected as little as possible by the staff cuts, consultants recommend that Vasquez-Morrell lay off those adjusters who now take longest, on average, to complete work on claims assigned to them.

    Which of the following, if true, most seriously calls into question the consultants' criterion for selecting the staff to be laid off?

    (A) If the time that Vasquez-Morrell takes to settle claims increases significantly, it could lose business to other insurers.

    (B) Supervisors at Vasquez-Morrell tend to assign the most complex claims to the most capable adjusters.

    (C) At Vasquez-Morrell, no insurance payments are made until a claims adjuster has reached a final determination on the claim.

    (D) There are no positions at Vasquez-Morrell to which staff currently employed as claims adjusters could be reassigned.

    (E) The premiums that Vasquez-Morrell currently charges are no higher than those charged for similar coverage by competitors.

Evaluation of a Plan

Situation   An insurance company must reduce its staff of claims adjusters. To ensure continuing promptness in handling claims, consultants advise the company to lay off those adjusters who take the longest to complete claims.

Reasoning   *What problem could there be with the criterion?* The consultants' criterion is the time an adjuster takes to settle a claim. However, some claims are naturally more complicated and require more time. If it is true that the company now assigns these time-consuming cases to its most capable adjusters, then these adjusters would be likely to be the ones who take longest to complete their cases. Laying off the adjusters who take the longest would thus mean laying off the company's most capable staff, which could very well decrease its ability to handle claims promptly.

A   The consultants' advice makes sense if increased time to handle claims causes the company to lose business.

B   **Correct.** This statement properly identifies the problem with the consultants' criterion.

C   This statement merely describes the process of handling a claim; it does not provide any information about the criterion for layoffs.

D   The consultants make no recommendations for reassigning staff, so indicating that there are no positions available does not call their advice into question.

E   The consultants do not recommend a change in premiums; noting that they are similar to competitors' premiums does not undermine the plan that the consultants recommend.

The correct answer is B.

19. Prolonged spells of hot, dry weather at the end of the grape-growing season typically reduce a vineyard's yield, because the grapes stay relatively small. In years with such weather, wine producers can make only a relatively small quantity of wine from a given area of vineyards. Nonetheless, in regions where wine producers generally grow their own grapes, analysts typically expect a long, hot, dry spell late in the growing season to result in increased revenues for local wine producers.

Which of the following, if true, does most to justify the analysts' expectation?

(A) The lower a vineyard's yield, the less labor is required to harvest the grapes.

(B) Long, hot, dry spells at the beginning of the grape-growing season are rare, but they can have a devastating effect on a vineyard's yield.

(C) Grapes grown for wine production are typically made into wine at or near the vineyard in which they were grown.

(D) When hot, dry spells are followed by heavy rains, the rains frequently destroy grape crops.

(E) Grapes that have matured in hot, dry weather make significantly better wine than ordinary grapes.

Argument Construction

Situation   Hot, dry weather at the end of the grape-growing season reduces yield, so winemakers can only produce a small quantity of wine. However, analysts expect that this weather will increase winemakers' revenues.

Reasoning   *What additional piece of information explains the analysts' expectations?* The same conditions that lead to low quantity also lead to something that increases revenues. What could this be? If these weather conditions lead to higher-quality wine that will sell for higher prices, the analysts' expectations for increased revenues are justified.

A   Lower labor costs mean less expenditure for the winemakers; this does not explain how revenues would increase.

B   This statement about low yields does not explain an increase in revenues.

C   The proximity of production to the vineyard is irrelevant to the question of how hot, dry weather can be responsible for decreased yield and increased revenues.

D   This statement gives another example of weather's effect on grape crops, but it does not explain how revenues are increased.

E   **Correct.** This statement properly provides the explanation that the weather conditions will lead to better wines. With better wines typically commanding higher prices, the winemakers will gain the increased revenues that the analysts anticipate.

The correct answer is E.

20. In the past, most children who went sledding in the winter snow in Verland used wooden sleds with runners and steering bars. Ten years ago, smooth plastic sleds became popular; they go faster than wooden sleds but are harder to steer and slow. The concern that plastic sleds are more dangerous is clearly borne out by the fact that the number of children injured while sledding was much higher last winter than it was 10 years ago.

Which of the following, if true in Verland, most seriously undermines the force of the evidence cited?

(A) A few children still use traditional wooden sleds.

(B) Very few children wear any kind of protective gear, such as helmets, while sledding.

(C) Plastic sleds can be used in a much wider variety of snow conditions than wooden sleds can.

(D) Most sledding injuries occur when a sled collides with a tree, a rock, or another sled.

(E) Because the traditional wooden sleds can carry more than one rider, an accident involving a wooden sled can result in several children being injured.

Argument Evaluation

Situation   Ten years ago, wooden sleds began to be replaced by plastic sleds that go faster but are harder to control. Plastic sleds are more dangerous than wooden sleds because more children suffered injuries last year than they did 10 years ago.

Reasoning   *What weakens this argument?* This argument depends on a comparison of two kinds of sleds. Any evidence that would either strengthen or weaken the argument must indicate a comparison. Evidence that applies only to one kind of sled or to both kinds of sleds equally cannot weaken this argument. Consider the implications of the evidence presented in the answer choices. If plastic sleds can be used in a wider variety of conditions than wooden sleds can, then plastic sleds can be used more frequently. It is possible that more frequent use, rather than the sleds themselves, has led to more accidents.

A   The limited use of some wooden sleds does not weaken the argument.

B   The absence of protective gear would affect accidents with both kinds of sleds.

C   **Correct.** This statement weakens the argument by providing an alternate explanation for the increased accidents.

D   This statement is true of accidents with both kinds of sleds.

E   This explains why wooden sleds may be dangerous but does not weaken the argument that plastic sleds are even more dangerous.

The correct answer is C.

21. Metal rings recently excavated from seventh-century settlements in the western part of Mexico were made using the same metallurgical techniques as those used by Ecuadorian artisans before and during that period. These techniques are sufficiently complex to make their independent development in both areas unlikely. Since the people of these two areas were in cultural contact, archaeologists hypothesize that the metallurgical techniques used to make the rings found in Mexico were learned by Mexican artisans from Ecuadorian counterparts.

    Which of the following would it be most useful to establish in order to evaluate the archaeologists' hypothesis?

    (A) Whether metal objects were traded from Ecuador to western Mexico during the seventh century

    (B) Whether travel between western Mexico and Ecuador in the seventh century would have been primarily by land or by sea

    (C) Whether artisans from western Mexico could have learned complex metallurgical techniques from their Ecuadorian counterparts without actually leaving western Mexico

    (D) Whether metal tools were used in the seventh-century settlements in western Mexico

    (E) Whether any of the techniques used in the manufacture of the metal rings found in western Mexico are still practiced among artisans in Ecuador today

Argument Evaluation

Situation Metal rings excavated from seventh-century settlements in western Mexico were made with the same complex techniques used in Ecuador before and during a period when the two cultures were known to be in contact. Mexican artisans are thought to have learned the techniques from Ecuadorian artisans.

Reasoning *What point could best be applied in evaluating this hypothesis?* Consider what specific information would help to assess the archaeologists' theory. It is given that the two areas had some cultural contact. If it were determined that metal objects were traded from one culture to the other, it could be possible that the metalworking techniques were passed along as well. Such evidence would be relevant to the hypothesis that Mexican artisans saw the work of their Ecuadorian counterparts and, from this exchange, learned the techniques to make the metal rings.

A **Correct.** This statement properly identifies information that would be useful in the evaluation of the archaeologists' hypothesis.

B The means of travel is irrelevant to the hypothesis about the source of the techniques.

C The hypothesis is not about where Mexican artisans learned the techniques, but whether they learned them from the Ecuadorians.

D The existence of metal tools provides no helpful information in establishing whether the Ecuadorians were the source of the metallurgical techniques.

E The comparison to the present day is irrelevant to the hypothesis.

The correct answer is A.

22. Following several years of declining advertising sales, the *Greenville Times* reorganized its advertising sales force. Before reorganization, the sales force was organized geographically, with some sales representatives concentrating on city-center businesses and others concentrating on different outlying regions. The reorganization attempted to increase the sales representatives' knowledge of clients' businesses by having each sales representative deal with only one type of industry or of retailing. After the reorganization, revenue from advertising sales increased.

In assessing whether the improvement in advertising sales can properly be attributed to the reorganization, it would be most helpful to find out which of the following?

(A) What proportion of the total revenue of the *Greenville Times* is generated by advertising sales?

(B) Has the circulation of the *Greenville Times* increased substantially in the last two years?

(C) Among all the types of industry and retailing that use the *Greenville Times* as an advertising vehicle, which type accounts for the largest proportion of the newspaper's advertising sales?

(D) Do any clients of the sales representatives of the *Greenville Times* have a standing order with the *Times* for a fixed amount of advertising per month?

(E) Among the advertisers in the *Greenville Times*, are there more types of retail business or more types of industrial business?

Evaluation of a Plan

Situation   In the face of declining advertising sales, a newspaper reorganizes its sales force so that sales representatives have a better understanding of businesses. Revenue from advertising sales increased after the reorganization.

Reasoning   *What additional evidence would help determine the source of the increased revenue?* In order to attribute the increased revenue to the reorganization of the sales force, other possible causes must be eliminated. Newspaper advertising rates are linked to circulation; when circulation increases, higher rates can be charged and revenues will increase. An alternate explanation might be a significant rise in circulation, so it would be particularly helpful to know if circulation had increased.

A   The question concerns only increased revenue from advertising sales; the proportion of advertising revenue to total revenue is outside the scope of the question.

B   Correct. This statement provides another possible explanation for increased revenue of advertising sales, and so the answer to this question would help to clarify the reason for the increased revenue.

C   Knowing how the advertising sales break down by type of business might be useful for other purposes, but it does not help to show the cause of the increase.

D   A fixed amount of advertising would not explain increased revenue, so the answer to this question would be irrelevant.

E   Distinguishing between the types of businesses will not contribute to determining whether the reorganization was responsible for the increased revenue.

The correct answer is B.

23. Motorists in a certain country frequently complain that traffic congestion is much worse now than it was 20 years ago. No real measure of how much traffic congestion there was 20 years ago exists, but the motorists' complaints are almost certainly unwarranted. The country's highway capacity has tripled in the last twenty years, thanks to a vigorous highway construction program, whereas the number of automobiles registered in the country has increased by only 75 percent.

Which of the following, if true, most seriously weakens the argument?

(A) Most automobile travel is local, and the networks of roads and streets in the country's settled areas have changed little over the last twenty years.

(B) Gasoline prices are high, and miles traveled per car per year have not changed much over the last 20 years.

(C) The country's urban centers have well-developed public transit systems that carry most of the people who commute into those centers.

(D) The average age of automobiles registered in the country is lower now than it was 20 years ago.

(E) Radio stations have long been broadcasting regular traffic reports that inform motorists about traffic congestion.

Argument Evaluation

Situation   Motorists complain that traffic congestion in their country is much worse than it was twenty years ago. But these complaints have no basis since the highway capacity in this country has tripled in the same period, whereas the number of cars registered has risen by only 75 percent.

Reasoning   *Which point most undermines the argument that the complaints are unwarranted?* Consider that the response to the generalized complaints about congestion discusses only the topic of highway capacity. What if the congestion that motorists are complaining about is not on highways but on local roads? Discovering that travel tends to be local in this country and that the local roads have not been improved in the last twenty years would seriously weaken the argument.

A   **Correct.** This statement properly identifies a weakness in the argument: the response to the broad complaint addresses a different subject, highway capacity, not the issue of traffic congestion encountered by most motorists.

B   If high gas prices actually prevented motorists from driving, and if motorists' driving habits were the same as they were twenty years ago, then these points should strengthen the argument that there is no basis for their complaints.

C   The number of commuters who use public transit does not affect the argument that the motorists' complaints have no basis.

D   The age of registered cars is irrelevant to the argument.

E   The radio broadcasts attest to the existence of traffic, but not to its increase, so they do not affect the argument.

The correct answer is A.

24. The percentage of households with an annual income of more than $40,000 is higher in Merton County than in any other county. However, the percentage of households with an annual income of $60,000 or more is higher in Sommer County.

If the statements above are true, which of the following must also be true?

(A) The percentage of households with an annual income of $80,000 is higher in Sommer County than in Merton County.

(B) Merton County has the second highest percentage of households with an annual income of $60,000 or more.

(C) Some households in Merton County have an annual income between $40,000 and $60,000.

(D) The number of households with an annual income of more than $40,000 is greater in Merton County than in Sommer County.

(E) Average annual household income is higher in Sommer County than in Merton County.

Argument Construction

Situation   The percentage of households with annual incomes of more than $40,000 is higher in Merton County than in any other county; the percentage of households with annual incomes of $60,000 or more is higher in Sommer County.

Reasoning   *On the basis of this information, what point must be true?* The given information makes clear that Merton County has some households that exceed $40,000 in annual income. Sommer County has a higher percentage of households with annual incomes at or above $60,000. A higher percentage of the Merton County households must in turn have annual incomes of $60,000 or less. Thus, the annual income of some households in Merton County is between $40,000 and $60,000.

A   Since it is possible that there are no households with an annual income of $80,000 in Sommer County, this statement does not follow from the situation.

B   It is not possible to make this determination on the basis of the available evidence; Merton County may have no households at all with an income of more than $60,000.

C   **Correct.** This statement properly identifies a conclusion that can be drawn from the given information: in order for the percentage of $40,000-plus incomes to be higher in Merton county than any other county while Sommer has the highest percentage of $60,000-plus incomes, there must be some households in Merton County that bring in between $40,000 and $60,000 annually.

D   On the basis of information about the *percentages* of households, it is not possible to arrive at this conclusion about the *number* of households.

E   From the given information, it is not possible to determine where the average income is greater. It is entirely possible that the number of $60,000-plus incomes in Sommer County is quite small and that the number of $40,000-plus incomes in Merton County is substantial.

The correct answer is C.

25. Tiger beetles are such fast runners that they can capture virtually any nonflying insect. However, when running toward an insect, a tiger beetle will intermittently stop and then, a moment later, resume its attack. Perhaps the beetles cannot maintain their pace and must pause for a moment's rest; but an alternative hypothesis is that while running, tiger beetles are unable to adequately process the resulting rapidly changing visual information and so quickly go blind and stop.

Which of the following, if discovered in experiments using artificially moved prey insects, would support one of the two hypotheses and undermine the other?

(A) When a prey insect is moved directly toward a beetle that has been chasing it, the beetle immediately stops and runs away without its usual intermittent stopping.

(B) In pursuing a swerving insect, a beetle alters its course while running and its pauses become more frequent as the chase progresses.

(C) In pursuing a moving insect, a beetle usually responds immediately to changes in the insect's direction, and it pauses equally frequently whether the chase is up or down an incline.

(D) If, when a beetle pauses, it has not gained on the insect it is pursuing, the beetle generally ends its pursuit.

(E) The faster a beetle pursues an insect fleeing directly away from it, the more frequently the beetle stops.

Argument Evaluation

Situation Two hypotheses are offered to explain the sudden stop that tiger beetles make while pursuing their prey: (1) they cannot maintain the rapid pace and must rest, and (2) they run too quickly to process visual information and so temporarily go blind.

Reasoning *What point would strengthen one of the two hypotheses and weaken the other?* Consider the information provided in each answer choice, remembering that information that supports one hypothesis must necessarily detract from the other. Any information that is not about pursuit or that affects the two hypotheses equally may be dismissed from consideration. If the frequency of stopping increases when the beetle follows a swerving insect and must constantly change its course, then the second hypothesis is strengthened; the beetle's pauses increase as the variety of visual information that it needs to deal with increases.

A The hypotheses concern ongoing pursuit; since this information is not about the beetle's continuing pursuit of prey, it neither strengthens nor weakens either hypothesis.

B **Correct.** This statement provides information that strengthens the second hypothesis: the swerving pursuit and the resulting continual course adjustments appear to be forcing the beetle to stop with increasing frequency to sort out the erratic visual information.

C In this experiment, since neither vision nor tiredness appears to be problematic, the beetle could be stopping for either reason; this information neither strengthens nor weakens either hypothesis.

D This information is irrelevant since both the hypotheses are about mid-pursuit behaviors.

E The correlation of frequency of stops with speed affects both hypotheses equally; the pauses could be equally due to an inability to maintain the pace or due to a need to process the visual information.

The correct answer is B.

26. Guillemots are birds of Arctic regions. They feed on fish that gather beneath thin sheets of floating ice, and they nest on nearby land. Guillemots need 80 consecutive snow-free days in a year to raise their chicks, so until average temperatures in the Arctic began to rise recently, the guillemots' range was limited to the southernmost Arctic coast. Therefore, if the warming continues, the guillemots' range will probably be enlarged by being extended northward along the coast.

Which of the following, if true, most seriously weakens the argument?

(A) Even if the warming trend continues, there will still be years in which guillemot chicks are killed by an unusually early snow.

(B) If the Arctic warming continues, guillemots' current predators are likely to succeed in extending their own range farther north.

(C) Guillemots nest in coastal areas, where temperatures are generally higher than in inland areas.

(D) If the Arctic warming continues, much of the thin ice in the southern Arctic will disappear.

(E) The fish that guillemots eat are currently preyed on by a wider variety of predators in the southernmost Arctic regions than they are farther north.

Argument Evaluation

Situation   In the southern Arctic, guillemots find their prey beneath thin sheets of ice, nest nearby, and require 80 snow-free days to raise their young. A warming trend means that their range may be enlarged by extending northward along the coast.

Reasoning   *Which point weakens the argument about the enlargement of the guillemots' range?* How could the birds move northward and simultaneously not enlarge their range? Consider the assumption implied by the idea of *enlargement*. If the guillemots lost their southern habitat, then their northward move would be a displacement rather than an enlargement. If their source of food was no longer available to them in the southern Arctic, then they would abandon that area as part of their range.

A   An exceptional year is not an argument against an enlarged range because *an unusually early snow* could happen in the southern Arctic as well.

B   If their current predators also migrate northward, then the guillemots' situation has not changed, so this is not an argument against their enlarged range.

C   The argument suggests that they will move not inland, but *northward along the coast*.

D   Correct. This statement properly identifies a factor that weakens the argument: the guillemots' move northward would not enlarge their range if they lost their food source, fish found under thin ice, in the southern Arctic.

E   The possibility that they may find prey more easily in the north does not mean that they would abandon the southern Arctic, and so this point does not weaken the argument.

The correct answer is D.

27. Some batches of polio vaccine used around 1960 were contaminated with SV40, a virus that in monkeys causes various cancers. Some researchers now claim that this contamination caused some cases of a certain cancer in humans, mesothelioma. This claim is not undercut by the fact that a very careful survey made in the 1960s of people who had received the contaminated vaccine found no elevated incidence of any cancer, since _____.

(A)   most cases of mesothelioma are caused by exposure to asbestos

(B)   in some countries, there was no contamination of the vaccine

(C)   SV40 is widely used in laboratories to produce cancers in animals

(D)   mesotheliomas take several decades to develop

(E)   mesothelioma was somewhat less common in 1960 than it is now

Argument Construction

Situation   Researchers claim that contaminated polio vaccine administered in 1960 caused some cases of mesothelioma, a type of cancer. Their claim is not undermined by the results of a 1960s survey showing that those who received the contaminated vaccine had no elevated incidence of cancer.

Reasoning   *Why did the survey results not challenge the researchers' claim?* The survey did not reveal a higher incidence of mesothelioma. This question then requires completing a sentence that establishes cause. What could be the reason that the people surveyed in the 1960s showed no signs of the disease? If the disease takes decades to develop, then those people surveyed would not yet have shown any signs of it; less than a decade had passed between their exposure to the vaccine and the survey.

A   The contaminated vaccine is said to have caused *some* cases, not *most*; the question remains why the survey results pose no obstacle to the researchers' claim.

B   The claim is only about contaminated vaccine, not uncontaminated vaccine.

C   That the virus can cause cancers in laboratory animals had already been provided as a given; this additional information is irrelevant to the survey of people who received contaminated vaccine.

D   Correct. This statement properly identifies the reason that the survey does not call into question the researchers' claim: the people surveyed in the 1960s showed no signs of disease because the cancer takes decades to develop.

E   The frequency of mesothelioma in the general population is not related to the claim that contaminated vaccine caused the disease in a specific population.

The correct answer is D.

28. Gortland has long been narrowly self-sufficient in both grain and meat. However, as per capita income in Gortland has risen toward the world average, per capita consumption of meat has also risen toward the world average, and it takes several pounds of grain to produce one pound of meat. Therefore, since per capita income continues to rise, whereas domestic grain production will not increase, Gortland will soon have to import either grain or meat or both.

Which of the following is an assumption on which the argument depends?

(A) The total acreage devoted to grain production in Gortland will soon decrease.

(B) Importing either grain or meat will not result in a significantly higher percentage of Gortlanders' incomes being spent on food than is currently the case.

(C) The per capita consumption of meat in Gortland is increasing at roughly the same rate across all income levels.

(D) The per capita income of meat producers in Gortland is rising faster than the per capita income of grain producers.

(E) People in Gortland who increase their consumption of meat will not radically decrease their consumption of grain.

Argument Construction

Situation   A country previously self-sufficient in grain and meat will soon have to import one or the other or both. Consumption of meat has risen as per capita income has risen, and it takes several pounds of grain to produce one pound of meat.

Reasoning   *What conditions must be true for the conclusion to be true?* Meat consumption is rising. What about grain consumption? A sharp reduction in the amount of grain consumed could compensate for increased meat consumption, making the conclusion false. If people did radically decrease their grain consumption, it might not be necessary to import grain or meat or both. Since the argument concludes that the imports are necessary, it assumes grain consumption will not plunge.

A   The argument makes no assumptions about the acreage devoted to grain; it assumes only that the demand for grain will rise.

B   The argument does not discuss the percentage of their income that Gortlanders spend on food, so an assumption about this topic is not needed.

C   The argument involves only meat consumption in general, not its distribution by income level.

D   Since the argument does not refer to the incomes of meat producers and grain producers, it cannot depend on an assumption about them.

E   **Correct.** This statement properly identifies the assumption that there will be no great decrease in grain consumption.

The correct answer is E.

29. The Hazelton coal-processing plant is a major employer in the Hazelton area, but national environmental regulations will force it to close if it continues to use old, polluting processing methods. However, to update the plant to use newer, cleaner methods would be so expensive that the plant will close unless it receives the tax break it has requested. In order to prevent a major increase in local unemployment, the Hazelton government is considering granting the plant's request.

   Which of the following would be most important for the Hazelton government to determine before deciding whether to grant the plant's request?

   (A)   Whether the company that owns the plant would open a new plant in another area if the present plant were closed

   (B)   Whether the plant would employ far fewer workers when updated than it does now

   (C)   Whether the level of pollutants presently being emitted by the plant is high enough to constitute a health hazard for local residents

   (D)   Whether the majority of the coal processed by the plant is sold outside the Hazelton area

   (E)   Whether the plant would be able to process more coal when updated than it does now

Evaluation of a Plan

Situation   Because of the expenses of mandatory updating, a plant that is a major employer in the local area will close unless it receives the tax break it has requested from the local government.

Reasoning   *What point is most critical to the evaluation of the request?* Consider the information provided in the answer choices. The plant is important to the local government primarily because it is a major employer of local residents. What if updating the plant significantly reduced the number of employees needed? It is crucial for the local government to determine whether the plant will continue to employ the same number of people once it has updated.

A   The local government is concerned only with the local area, so a new site outside that area is irrelevant.

B   Correct. This statement properly identifies a factor that is critical to the plant's argument and the local government's decision.

C   Updating is mandatory under national environmental regulations, whether the local residents are affected by the plant's pollutants or not.

D   At issue is the plant's role as a major employer; where its product is sold is irrelevant.

E   The amount of coal processed by the updated plant is irrelevant to the critical issue of the number of people employed to process that coal.

The correct answer is B.

30. A physically active lifestyle has been shown to help increase longevity. In the Wistar region of Bellaria, the average age at death is considerably higher than in any other part of the country. Wistar is the only mountainous part of Bellaria. A mountainous terrain makes even such basic activities as walking relatively strenuous; it essentially imposes a physically active lifestyle on people. Clearly, this circumstance explains the long lives of people in Wistar.

Which of the following, if true, most seriously weakens the argument?

(A) In Bellaria all medical expenses are paid by the government, so that personal income does not affect the quality of health care a person receives.

(B) The Wistar region is one of Bellaria's least populated regions.

(C) Many people who live in the Wistar region have moved there in middle age or upon retirement.

(D) The many opportunities for hiking, skiing, and other outdoor activities that Wistar's mountains offer make it a favorite destination for vacationing Bellarians.

(E) Per capita spending on recreational activities is no higher in Wistar than it is in other regions of Bellaria.

Argument Evaluation

Situation   People in one region of a country live longer than people in other areas. The higher average age at time of death is attributed to the healthy lifestyle of the people in this region, where the mountainous terrain demands a physically active life.

Reasoning   *What point weakens the argument?* Consider what assumption underlies the argument that the physically active lifestyle required of living in Wistar is responsible for its residents' relative longevity. The mountainous environment necessitates lifelong levels of rigorous physical activity that build a more robust population. What if a significant portion of the population has not been conditioned since childhood to the demands of the terrain? It is assumed here that the healthy lifestyle imposed by the terrain has shaped residents from birth and accounts for their longer life span. If many residents only moved there later in life, the argument is weakened.

A   The argument is not about the quality of health care throughout the country, but the length of the residents' lives in a particular region.

B   The rate of population density does not affect the argument.

C   **Correct.** This statement properly identifies a point that weakens the argument.

D   The area's popularity as a vacation destination does not affect the longevity of the local residents.

E   The argument establishes that merely living in the region is strenuous; the spending on recreational activities is irrelevant.

The correct answer is C.

31. Cheever College offers several online courses via remote computer connection, in addition to traditional classroom-based courses. A study of student performance at Cheever found that, overall, the average student grade for online courses matched that for classroom-based courses. In this calculation of the average grade, course withdrawals were weighted as equivalent to a course failure, and the rate of withdrawal was much lower for students enrolled in classroom-based courses than for students enrolled in online courses.

If the statements above are true, which of the following must also be true of Cheever College?

(A) Among students who did not withdraw, students enrolled in online courses got higher grades, on average, than students enrolled in classroom-based courses.

(B) The number of students enrolled per course at the start of the school term is much higher, on average, for the online courses than for the classroom-based courses.

(C) There are no students who take both an online and a classroom-based course in the same school term.

(D) Among Cheever College students with the best grades, a significant majority take online, rather than classroom-based, courses.

(E) Courses offered online tend to deal with subject matter that is less challenging than that of classroom-based courses.

Argument Construction

Situation   A comparison of online and classroom courses showed similar average grades. In determining average grades, a course withdrawal was weighted as a course failure. The rate of withdrawal was higher from online than from classroom courses.

Reasoning   *What conclusion about the courses can be derived from this comparison?* Consider the ramifications of the methodology used to calculate the grade averages for the two types of courses. Because of course withdrawals, the online courses experienced a higher rate of failure, but the average grade for these courses still matched the average grade for classroom courses. From this it is logical to conclude that, for the two averages to match, the students who remained in the online courses must have had higher initial average grades than those in classroom courses.

A   **Correct.** This statement properly identifies the logical conclusion that the higher percentage of withdrawals from online classes requires higher grades, on average, to compensate for the higher rate of failure.

B   A number of students cannot be derived from a discussion of average grades and rates of withdrawal.

C   This conclusion cannot be determined on the basis of the information provided.

D   The information is about average grades; the argument does not provide any basis for a conclusion about best grades.

E   It is impossible to determine the difficulty of subject matter from this information.

The correct answer is A.

32. For years the beautiful Renaissance buildings in Palitito have been damaged by exhaust from the many tour buses that come to the city. There has been little parking space, so most buses have idled at the curb during each stop on their tour, and idling produces as much exhaust as driving. The city has now provided parking that accommodates a third of the tour buses, so damage to Palitito's buildings from the buses' exhaust will diminish significantly.

Which of the following, if true, most strongly supports the argument?

(A) The exhaust from Palitito's few automobiles is not a significant threat to Palitito's buildings.

(B) Palitito's Renaissance buildings are not threatened by pollution other than engine exhaust.

(C) Tour buses typically spend less than one-quarter of the time they are in Palitito transporting passengers from one site to another.

(D) More tourists come to Palitito by tour bus than by any other single means of transportation.

(E) Some of the tour buses that are unable to find parking drive around Palitito while their passengers are visiting a site.

Argument Evaluation

Situation   Tour buses have damaged Renaissance buildings with their exhaust fumes because lack of parking has kept the buses idling at curbs. Providing new parking for a third of the buses should significantly reduce the damage caused by the exhaust.

Reasoning   *What point strengthens the argument?* The argument for reduced damage relies on the reduction of the vehicles' exhaust fumes. Any additional evidence regarding the extent to which the vehicular emissions are likely to be reduced also supports the argument for the benefits of the new parking spaces. Learning that tour buses spend not just a few minutes but most of their time idling at the curb strengthens the argument. The new parking spaces will allow a third of the tour buses to spend 75 percent of their time with their engines off, causing no damage at all.

A   If automobile exhaust is not a threat, the argument is not affected.

B   This statement does not address the question of whether the new parking will reduce the damage caused by engine exhaust from the buses.

C   **Correct.** This statement properly cites a factor that supports the argument: since most of the buses' time has been spent producing damaging exhaust, the new parking should reduce the damage significantly.

D   This statement about tourists' chosen means of transportation is irrelevant to the issue of what the buses do while in the city.

E   It is given that the new parking will only provide space for a third of the buses, and thus some buses will continue to idle and some to drive around, continuing to contribute equally to the building damage. This statement does not strengthen the argument.

The correct answer is C.

33. During the 1980s and 1990s, the annual number of people who visited the Sordellian Mountains increased continually, and many new ski resorts were built. Over the same period, however, the number of visitors to ski resorts who were caught in avalanches decreased, even though there was no reduction in the annual number of avalanches in the Sordellian Mountains.

    Which of the following, if true in the Sordellian Mountains during the 1980s and 1990s, most helps to explain the decrease?

    (A) Avalanches were most likely to happen when a large new snowfall covered an older layer of snow.
    (B) Avalanches destroyed at least some buildings in the Sordellian Mountains in every year.
    (C) People planning new ski slopes and other resort facilities used increasingly accurate information about which locations are likely to be in the path of avalanches.
    (D) The average length of stay for people visiting the Sordellian Mountains increased slightly.
    (E) Construction of new ski resorts often led to the clearing of wooded areas that had helped prevent avalanches.

Argument Construction

Situation   Over a certain period, new ski resorts accommodated an increasing number of visitors at the same time that fewer visitors were caught in avalanches. Yet there were no fewer avalanches than usual during this period.

Reasoning   *What explains the apparent contradiction of increased visitors but fewer visitors caught in avalanches?* More resort visitors would imply more avalanche-related accidents, but the average has shifted so that fewer visitors are being caught in the avalanches. It must be that fewer visitors are exposed to this danger; consider the answer choices to identify a logical reason for this improvement in their exposure. If the likely paths of avalanches had become better understood, that information would have been applied to identify safer locations for new ski slopes and ski resorts. The facilities would thus have been built well out of the way of avalanches, resulting in fewer visitors trapped in avalanches.

A   This likelihood would remain true from year to year; it does not explain the decrease.

B   This point does not explain why fewer visitors were caught in these avalanches.

C   **Correct.** This statement properly identifies a factor that explains the decreased number of accidents.

D   The greater length of stay would seem to expose visitors to greater danger.

E   This information points to an expected increase, rather than decrease, in visitors who might be caught by avalanches.

The correct answer is C.

34. A year ago, Dietz Foods launched a yearlong advertising campaign for its canned tuna. Last year Dietz sold 12 million cans of tuna compared to the 10 million sold during the previous year, an increase directly attributable to new customers brought in by the campaign. Profits from the additional sales, however, were substantially less than the cost of the advertising campaign. Clearly, therefore, the campaign did nothing to further Dietz's economic interests.

Which of the following, if true, most seriously weakens the argument?

(A) Sales of canned tuna account for a relatively small percentage of Dietz Foods' profits.

(B) Most of the people who bought Dietz's canned tuna for the first time as a result of the campaign were already loyal customers of other Dietz products.

(C) A less expensive advertising campaign would have brought in significantly fewer new customers for Dietz's canned tuna than did the campaign Dietz Foods launched last year.

(D) Dietz made money on sales of canned tuna last year.

(E) In each of the past five years, there was a steep, industry-wide decline in sales of canned tuna.

Argument Evaluation

Situation   An advertising campaign was responsible for increased sales of canned tuna. Since the profits from the increased sales were less than the costs of the campaign, the campaign did not contribute to the company's economic interests.

Reasoning   *Which point weakens the argument?* Consider the basis of the argument: if profits are lower than costs, the campaign made no contribution to the company's financial well-being. In what case might this be untrue? What if the advertising campaign reversed an industry-wide trend of declining sales? If Dietz experienced increasing sales, while other companies experienced decreased sales, then the campaign did contribute to the economic interests of the company, and the argument is considerably weakened.

A   The issue is not the percentage of profits that canned tuna contributes, but the success of the advertising campaign.

B   If the customers bought the tuna because of the campaign, it is irrelevant to the argument that they also bought other Dietz products.

C   This information neither strengthens nor weakens the argument.

D   The argument is not about profits only, but about whether the advertising campaign contributed to the economic interests of the company.

E   **Correct.** This statement properly identifies a factor that weakens the argument: the campaign secured the benefits of increased sales at a time when the entire industry was experiencing a decline in sales.

The correct answer is E.

Sentence Correction

The following discussion is intended to familiarize you with the most efficient and effective approaches to sentence correction questions. The particular questions in this chapter are generally representative of the kinds of sentence correction questions you will encounter on the GMAT exam. Remember that it is the problem solving strategy that is important, not the specific details of a particular question.

35. Unlike the buildings in Mesopotamian cities, which were arranged haphazardly, the same basic plan was followed for all cities of the Indus Valley: with houses laid out on a north-south, east-west grid, and houses and walls were built of standard-size bricks.

    (A) the buildings in Mesopotamian cities, which were arranged haphazardly, the same basic plan was followed for all cities of the Indus Valley: with houses

    (B) the buildings in Mesopotamian cities, which were haphazard in arrangement, the same basic plan was used in all cities of the Indus Valley: houses were

    (C) the arrangement of buildings in Mesopotamian cities, which were haphazard, the cities of the Indus Valley all followed the same basic plan: houses

    (D) Mesopotamian cities, in which buildings were arranged haphazardly, the cities of the Indus Valley all followed the same basic plan: houses were

    (E) Mesopotamian cities, which had buildings that were arranged haphazardly, the same basic plan was used for all cities in the Indus Valley: houses that were

Comparison-contrast; Modifying clause

The contrast introduced by *unlike* must be logical and clear. Contrasting *the buildings in Mesopotamian cities* with *the same basic plan* does not make sense; *Mesopotamian cities* should be contrasted with *the cities of the Indus Valley*. Also, it needs to be clear that it was the *buildings* in the cities that *were arranged haphazardly* rather than the *cities*. The second half of the sentence needs *houses were laid out* to be parallel in structure to *and houses and walls were built*.

A   Illogically contrasts *the buildings in Mesopotamian cities* with *the same basic plan*; not clear whether *which were arranged haphazardly* modifies *cities* or *buildings*; *with houses* lacks parallelism and is confusing.

B   Illogically contrasts *the buildings in Mesopotamian cities* with *the same basic plan*; does not clarify what *which were haphazard in arrangement* modifies.

C   Illogically contrasts *the arrangement of buildings* with *the cities of the Indus Valley*; not clear whether *which were haphazard* modifies *buildings* or *cities*; *houses* not followed by a verb.

D   **Correct.** In this sentence, *Mesopotamian cities* are properly contrasted with *the cities of the Indus Valley*; *in which buildings were arranged haphazardly* expresses the idea clearly; and *houses* is followed by *were* as required.

E   Illogically contrasts *Mesopotamian cities* with *the same basic plan*; *houses that were* lacks parallelism and is confusing.

The correct answer is D.

36. New data from United States Forest Service ecologists show that for every dollar spent on controlled small-scale burning, forest thinning, and the training of fire-management personnel, it saves seven dollars that would not be spent on having to extinguish big fires.

    (A) that for every dollar spent on controlled small-scale burning, forest thinning, and the training of fire-management personnel, it saves seven dollars that would not be spent on having to extinguish

(B)   that for every dollar spent on controlled small-scale burning, forest thinning, and the training of fire-management personnel, seven dollars are saved that would have been spent on extinguishing

(C)   that for every dollar spent on controlled small-scale burning, forest thinning, and the training of fire-management personnel saves seven dollars on not having to extinguish

(D)   for every dollar spent on controlled small-scale burning, forest thinning, and the training of fire-management personnel, that it saves seven dollars on not having to extinguish

(E)   for every dollar spent on controlled small-scale burning, forest thinning, and the training of fire-management personnel, that seven dollars are saved that would not have been spent on extinguishing

Logical predication; Rhetorical construction

The pronoun *it* (*it saves seven dollars*) has no referent. Making *seven dollars* the subject of the clause eliminates this problem, and it also fulfills a reader's expectation that after the phrase beginning *for every dollar* another specific amount will be given to balance it. This change in structure also allows the awkward and wordy clause *that would not be spent on having to extinguish* to be rewritten so that *spent* balances *saved*: *seven dollars are saved that would have been spent on extinguishing*, and the unnecessary *having to* is omitted.

A   *It* has no referent; *not be spent* is awkward; *on having to extinguish* is wordy.

B   **Correct.** This sentence properly uses *seven dollars* as the subject of the clause to balance *every dollar* in the introductory phrase; the phrasing is concise and parallel.

C   *Saves* does not have a subject; construction is not a complete sentence; *not having to extinguish* is wordy and awkward.

D   *That* introduces a subordinate rather than main clause, making a sentence fragment; *it* has no referent; *not having to extinguish* is wordy and awkward.

E   Introductory *that* makes a sentence fragment; *that would not have been spent on extinguishing* is awkward and illogical.

The correct answer is B.

37.   Like the grassy fields and old pastures that the upland sandpiper needs for feeding and nesting when it returns in May after wintering in the Argentine Pampas, <u>the sandpipers vanishing in the northeastern United States is a result of residential and industrial development and of changes in</u> farming practices.

(A)   the sandpipers vanishing in the northeastern United States is a result of residential and industrial development and of changes in

(B)   the bird itself is vanishing in the northeastern United States as a result of residential and industrial development and of changes in

(C)   that the birds themselves are vanishing in the northeastern United States is due to residential and industrial development and changes to

(D)   in the northeastern United States, sandpipers' vanishing due to residential and industrial development and to changes in

(E)   in the northeastern United States, the sandpipers' vanishing, a result of residential and industrial development and changing

Comparison; Sentence structure

The comparison introduced by *like* must be logical and clear; the point of this comparison is that both the habitat and the bird are disappearing for similar reasons. The comparison must use comparable grammatical components; *the bird itself* is a noun phrase and matches the noun phrases *grassy fields* and *old pastures*.

A   Illogically compares *the sandpipers vanishing* to *grassy fields and old pastures*; omits apostrophe in *sandpipers' vanishing*; wordy.

B   **Correct.** This sentence properly compares *the bird itself* to *grassy fields and old pastures*; *is vanishing* as the verb strengthens the sentence by making the comparison clearer.

C   Does not finish the comparison begun with *like* but instead substitutes a clause (*that the birds themselves are vanishing*).

D   Illogically compares *the sandpipers' vanishing* to *grassy fields and old pastures*; creates a sentence fragment.

E   Illogically compares *the sandpipers' vanishing* to *grassy fields and old pastures*; creates a sentence fragment.

The correct answer is B.

38. The results of two recent unrelated studies support the idea that dolphins may share certain cognitive abilities with humans and great apes; the studies indicate <u>dolphins as capable of recognizing themselves in mirrors—an ability that is often considered a sign of self-awareness—and to grasp spontaneously</u> the mood or intention of humans.

   (A)   dolphins as capable of recognizing themselves in mirrors—an ability that is often considered a sign of self-awareness—and to grasp spontaneously

   (B)   dolphins' ability to recognize themselves in mirrors—an ability that is often considered as a sign of self-awareness—and of spontaneously grasping

   (C)   dolphins to be capable of recognizing themselves in mirrors—an ability that is often considered a sign of self-awareness—and to grasp spontaneously

   (D)   that dolphins have the ability of recognizing themselves in mirrors—an ability that is often considered as a sign of self-awareness—and spontaneously grasping

   (E)   that dolphins are capable of recognizing themselves in mirrors—an ability that is often considered a sign of self-awareness—and of spontaneously grasping

Grammatical construction; Parallelism

In the context of this sentence, *the studies indicate* must introduce a clause; the clause must begin with *that* and have a subject, *dolphins*, and a verb, *are* (the complete verb phrase would be *are capable of*). The two capabilities should be parallel: *capable of recognizing…and of spontaneously grasping*.

   A   Context requires a clause, but this construction is not a clause; *capable of recognizing* is not parallel to *to grasp spontaneously*.

   B   Construction is not a clause, and a clause is required; *dolphins' ability to recognize* is not parallel to *of spontaneously grasping*.

   C   A clause is required following *the studies indicate*; *to be capable of recognizing* is not parallel to *to grasp spontaneously*.

   D   *Have the ability of* is wordy and unidiomatic; *of recognizing* and *spontaneously grasping* are not parallel.

   E   **Correct.** *That* introduces the subordinate clause necessary to complete this sentence properly; *of recognizing* and *of spontaneously grasping* are parallel.

The correct answer is E.

39. According to scholars, the earliest writing was probably not a direct rendering of speech, but <u>was more likely to begin as</u> a separate and distinct symbolic system of communication, and only later merged with spoken language.

   (A)   was more likely to begin as

   (B)   more than likely began as

   (C)   more than likely beginning from

   (D)   it was more than likely begun from

   (E)   it was more likely that it began

Idiom; Verb form

This sentence is a comparison in which *probably not x* is balanced by *but more than likely y*. When *more* is used in the comparative form of an adjective (*more difficult*) or adverb (*more likely*), it is followed by *than*. The words used to show the comparison between *x* and *y*, *but more than likely*, must also introduce the correct verb form, allowing *y* to fit grammatically into the rest of the sentence. The subject of the sentence has three verbs, all of which should be parallel: *the earliest writing was…began…merged. Was…to begin* is not parallel and results in a construction that is not grammatically correct.

A   In this context, *more likely* is not a complete idiomatic expression; *was…to begin* is not parallel to *was* and *merged*.

B   **Correct.** In this sentence, *more than likely* is the correct comparative construction; the simple past tense *began*, parallel to *was* and *merged*, fits grammatically into the sentence.

C   Subject should be followed by three verbs; *beginning from* is not a verb.

D   Use of the pronoun *it* makes this construction a main clause, in which case the comma after *communication* must be omitted and *began* must be used to be parallel to *merged*; *was…begun* is not the correct tense.

E   In this awkward, unclear, and wordy construction, the first *it* must be followed by *is*, not *was*, because the theory is current; the second *it* acts as the subject of the subordinate clause, and this usage requires the omission of the comma after *communication*.

The correct answer is B.

40.   In 1995 Richard Stallman, a well-known critic of the patent system, testified in Patent Office hearings that, to test the system, a colleague of his had managed to win a patent for one of Kirchhoff's <u>laws, an observation about electric current first made in 1845 and</u> now included in virtually every textbook of elementary physics.

(A)   laws, an observation about electric current first made in 1845 and

(B)   laws, which was an observation about electric current first made in 1845 and it is

(C)   laws, namely, it was an observation about electric current first made in 1845 and

(D)   laws, an observation about electric current first made in 1845, it is

(E)   laws that was an observation about electric current, first made in 1845, and is

Logical predication; Parallelism

The function of the entire long phrase (*observation…physics*) that follows *one of Kirchhoff's laws* is to describe that law. It is a noun phrase in apposition, which means that it has the same syntactic relation to all the other parts of the sentence that the noun phrase *one of Kirchhoff's laws* does. Within the long modifying phrase, parallelism is maintained by balancing *an observation…first made* with *and now included*.

A   **Correct.** In this sentence, the noun phrase in apposition properly identifies and explains the law, using parallel structure and concise expression.

B   *Which* is ambiguous because it could refer to *one* or to *laws*; *it is* violates the parallelism of *first made* and *now included*.

C   *It* is ambiguous; the introduction of *it was* does not allow this construction to fit grammatically into the sentence.

D   The referent of *it* is unclear; *it is* creates a run-on sentence and violates the parallelism of *first made* and *now included*.

E   *That* appears to refer to *laws* rather than *one*, but the verb is singular; setting off the phrase *first made in 1845* in commas distorts meaning; *is* violates parallelism.

The correct answer is A.

41. Excavators at the Indus Valley site of Harappa in eastern Pakistan say the discovery of inscribed shards dating to circa 2800–2600 B.C. <u>indicate their development of a Harappan writing system, the use of</u> inscribed seals impressed into clay for marking ownership, and the standardization of weights for trade or taxation occurred many decades, if not centuries, earlier than was previously believed.

    (A) indicate their development of a Harappan writing system, the use of

    (B) indicate that the development of a Harappan writing system, using

    (C) indicates that their development of a Harappan writing system, using

    (D) indicates the development of a Harappan writing system, their use of

    (E) indicates that the development of a Harappan writing system, the use of

Agreement; Idiom; Parallelism

In long sentences such as this one, the relationship between parts of the sentence may be difficult to see. Here, the main clause of the sentence is *excavators…say* and the logical sequence that follows is *the discovery…indicates that*. The subject of this first subordinate clause is the singular noun *discovery*, which should be followed by the singular verb *indicates* rather than by the plural *indicate*, as is done in the original sentence. *Their*, used with either *development* or *use*, has no clear or logical referent in any of the alternatives. The subject of the following subordinate (*that*) clause, which has *occurred* as its verb, is a series of three phrases, which must be parallel, especially in a sentence of this length and complexity: *the development of…, the use of…, and the standardization of…*.

A *Indicate* does not agree with *discovery*; the pronoun *their* has no logical referent, and *their development* is not parallel to *the use* and *the standardization*.

B *Indicate* does not agree with *discovery*; *using* is not parallel to *the development* and *the standardization*.

C *Their* has no logical referent; the series of three elements should be parallel, but here all are different.

D The pronoun *their* has no logical referent, and *their use* is not parallel to *the development* and *the standardization*; the preferred sentence structure would have *indicates* followed by *that* when introducing a clause.

E **Correct.** In this sentence, *indicates* agrees with *discovery* and is followed by *that* to introduce a clause; the three parallel phrases begin with an article (*the*), a noun, and the preposition *of*.

The correct answer is E.

42. The Supreme Court has ruled that public universities can collect student activity fees even <u>with students' objections to particular activities, so long as the groups they give money to will be</u> chosen without regard to their views.

    (A) with students' objections to particular activities, so long as the groups they give money to will be

    (B) if they have objections to particular activities and the groups that are given the money are

    (C) if they object to particular activities, but the groups that the money is given to have to be

    (D) from students who object to particular activities, so long as the groups given money are

    (E) though students have an objection to particular activities, but the groups that are given the money be

Logical predication; Rhetorical construction

The underlined portion of the sentence fails to establish a clear relationship among *universities*, *students*, and *groups*. To which of these three does *they* refer? It would appear that the *universities* must give the money, but *they* does not have a referent. Furthermore, *they* is followed by *their views*, and in this case *their* must refer to *groups*. Wordy and awkward phrasing as well as an unnecessary shift in verb tense (*will be chosen*) compound the difficulty of understanding this sentence in its original form.

A *With students' objections…*is awkward and dense; *they* does not have a referent; the future *will be* is incorrect since the Supreme Court *has* already *ruled*.

B   Referent for *they* is *student activity fees*, which cannot possibly *have objections...*; the use of *and* is illogical.

C   *They* refers to student *activity fees* rather than *students*; *but* does not have the requisite sense of *with the provision that*; *have to be* is wordy.

D   Correct. In this sentence, *from students who object* is clear and idiomatic; *so long as* is used appropriately; *groups given money* eliminates the problem of a pronoun without a referent; *are* is the proper tense.

E   *Have an objection* is an unnecessarily wordy way to say *object*; the verb *be* does not complete the latter part of the sentence.

The correct answer is D.

43. Despite the increasing number of women graduating from law school and passing bar examinations, <u>the proportion of judges and partners at major law firms who are women have not risen to a comparable extent</u>.

(A) the proportion of judges and partners at major law firms who are women have not risen to a comparable extent

(B) the proportion of women judges and partners at major law firms have not risen comparably

(C) the proportion of judges and partners at major law firms who are women has not risen comparably

(D) yet the proportion of women judges and partners at major law firms has not risen to a comparable extent

(E) yet the proportion of judges and partners at major law firms who are women has not risen comparably

Agreement; Rhetorical construction

When a number of plural nouns appear in phrases between a singular subject and the verb, it can be easy to overlook the true subject of the verb. Here, *judges*, *partners*, *firms*, and *women* all occur between the singular subject, *proportion*, and the verb, which should also be singular, *has risen*. Concise expression is particularly important in a long construction; *to a comparable extent* may be more concisely expressed as *comparably*.

A   Plural verb, *have risen*, does not agree with the singular subject, *proportion*.

B   *Have risen* does not agree with *proportion*; here, *women* applies only to *judges*, not to *partners at major law firms*.

C   Correct. In this sentence, *has risen* agrees with *proportion*, and *comparably* is more concise than *to a comparable extent*. The modifying clause *who are women* follows (1) *judges* and (2) *partners at major law firms* as closely as is possible given the content of the sentence; this positioning has the virtue of being clear in its meaning.

D   The contrast has already been introduced by *despite*, so the addition of *yet* is illogical and ungrammatical; *to a comparable extent* is wordy.

E   *Despite* introduces the contrast; adding *yet* is illogical and results in an ungrammatical construction.

The correct answer is C.

44. <u>Seldom more than 40 feet wide and 12 feet deep, but it ran 363 miles across the rugged wilderness of upstate New York, the Erie Canal connected</u> the Hudson River at Albany to the Great Lakes at Buffalo, providing the port of New York City with a direct water link to the heartland of the North American continent.

(A) Seldom more than 40 feet wide and 12 feet deep, but it ran 363 miles across the rugged wilderness of upstate New York, the Erie Canal connected

(B) Seldom more than 40 feet wide and 12 feet deep but running 363 miles across the rugged wilderness of upstate New York, the Erie Canal connected

(C) It was seldom more than 40 feet wide and 12 feet deep, and ran 363 miles across the rugged wilderness of upstate New York, but the Erie Canal, connecting

(D) The Erie Canal was seldom more than 40 feet wide or 12 feet deep and it ran 363 miles across the rugged wilderness of upstate New York, which connected

(E) The Erie Canal, seldom more than 40 feet wide and 12 feet deep, but running 363 miles across the rugged wilderness of upstate New York, connecting

Logical predication; Grammatical construction

The phrase *seldom…deep* is the first half of a modifier that describes *the Erie Canal*. However, because a comma incorrectly follows *deep*, this phrase appears to be the entire modifier, which must agree with the noun or pronoun that immediately follows it. This phrase cannot modify the conjunction *but*, and *it* has no referent; *but it ran* is not a logical or grammatical construction following the modifying phrase. Substituting *running* for *it ran* creates an adjective phrase parallel to the first adjective phrase (*seldom…deep*). To contrast the small size reported in the first phrase with the great distance reported in the second, the two phrases may be joined with *but*; together they create a single modifier correctly modifying *the Erie Canal. The Erie Canal* is then the subject of the sentence and requires the verb *connected* to provide a logical statement.

A *But it ran* cannot logically or grammatically follow the modifying phrase.

B **Correct.** This sentence properly has the single modifier consisting of two contrasting parts.

C Neither *and* nor *but* acts as a logical connector; the use of *connecting* results in a sentence fragment.

D The paired concepts of width and depth should be joined by *and*, not *or*; this construction calls for two main clauses to be separated by a comma after *deep*; *which* is ambiguous.

E The two halves of the modifier should not be separated by a comma after *deep*; the subject is awkwardly and confusingly placed at a great distance from the predicate; the use of *connecting* rather than *connected* creates a sentence fragment.

The correct answer is B.

45. In 1923, the Supreme Court declared a minimum wage for women and children in the District of Columbia as unconstitutional, and ruling that it was a form of price-fixing and, as such, an abridgment of the right of contract.

(A) the Supreme Court declared a minimum wage for women and children in the District of Columbia as unconstitutional, and

(B) the Supreme Court declared as unconstitutional a minimum wage for women and children in the District of Columbia, and

(C) the Supreme Court declared unconstitutional a minimum wage for women and children in the District of Columbia,

(D) a minimum wage for women and children in the District of Columbia was declared unconstitutional by the Supreme Court,

(E) when the Supreme Court declared a minimum wage for women and children in the District of Columbia as unconstitutional,

Idiom; Grammatical construction

This sentence depends on the correct use of an idiom: *the court declares x unconstitutional.* The inverted form should be used here because of the long phrases involved: *the court declares unconstitutional x. The Supreme Court* is the subject of the sentence; *declared* is the verb. *Ruling… contract* acts a modifier describing the action of the main clause; because the modifier is subordinate to the main clause, the conjunction *and* must be omitted. *And* is used to join two independent clauses, not a clause and its modifier.

A *Declared…as unconstitutional* is not the correct idiom; the use of *and* creates an ungrammatical construction.

B *Declared as unconstitutional* is not the correct idiom; the use of *and* creates an ungrammatical construction.

C   **Correct.** In this sentence, the correct idiom is used, and the modifier is grammatically and logically attached to the main clause.

D   Passive voice construction is weak and wordy; its use causes the modifier to be misplaced and ambiguous.

E   *Declared…as unconstitutional* is not the correct idiom; *when* transforms the main clause into a subordinate clause, resulting in a sentence fragment.

The correct answer is C.

46. Researchers have found that individuals who have been blind from birth, and <u>who thus have never seen anyone gesture, nevertheless make hand motions when speaking just as frequently and in virtually the same way as sighted people do, and that they will gesture</u> even when conversing with another blind person.

(A)   who thus have never seen anyone gesture, nevertheless make hand motions when speaking just as frequently and in virtually the same way as sighted people do, and that they will gesture

(B)   who thus never saw anyone gesturing, nevertheless make hand motions when speaking just as frequent and in virtually the same way as sighted people did, and that they will gesture

(C)   who thus have never seen anyone gesture, nevertheless made hand motions when speaking just as frequently and in virtually the same way as sighted people do, as well as gesturing

(D)   thus never having seen anyone gesture, nevertheless made hand motions when speaking just as frequent and in virtually the same way as sighted people did, as well as gesturing

(E)   thus never having seen anyone gesture, nevertheless to make hand motions when speaking just as frequently and in virtually the same way as sighted people do, and to gesture

Parallelism; Verb form; Diction

The researchers have found (1) *that individuals… make hand motions…as sighted people do* and (2) *that they will gesture…with another blind person.* In the original sentence, the two findings are reported in two parallel subordinate clauses introduced by *that.* The verb tenses are logical and parallel: *who have been blind* and *who have never seen* indicate a condition that began in the past and continues in the present; *make* and *do* refer to present actions. The verb *make* (*hand motions*) is correctly modified by the adverb *frequently* to show how the action of the verb is carried out. The emphatic future *will gesture* is properly used here with *even* to emphasize the extreme or the unexpected.

A   **Correct.** Although the original sentence is complicated, the parallelism of its structure and phrasing allows its meaning to be clear and its expression effective.

B   Verbs *saw* and *did* indicate action completed in the past; the simple past tense is not appropriate in either case; the adjective *frequent* cannot modify the verb; awkward and muddy.

C   *Made* indicates past action, but the present tense is logically required; *as well as gesturing* violates the parallelism of the two subordinate (*that*) clauses; choppy and unclear.

D   *Having seen* is not parallel to *have been*; *made* and *did* do not show ongoing action; *frequent* incorrectly modifies the verb; *as well as gesturing* destroys the parallelism of the two subordinate (*that*) clauses; awkward and unclear.

E   Replacing the verb *make* with the infinitive *to make* results in an ungrammatical construction that fails to complete the sentence.

The correct answer is A.

47. Like embryonic germ cells, which are cells that develop early in the formation of the fetus and that later generate eggs or sperm, <u>embryonic stem cells have the ability of developing themselves into different kinds of body tissue.</u>

(A) embryonic stem cells have the ability of developing themselves into different kinds of body tissue

(B) embryonic stem cells have the ability to develop into different kinds of body tissue

(C) in embryonic stem cells there is the ability to develop into different kinds of body tissue

(D) the ability to develop themselves into different kinds of body tissue characterizes embryonic stem cells

(E) the ability of developing into different kinds of body tissue characterizes embryonic stem cells

Idiom; Grammatical construction

Two constructions create problems in the original sentence. The first is the unidiomatic construction *have the ability of developing*; *ability* must be followed by an infinitive, *to develop*, not a phrase. The second problematic construction is *to develop themselves into*. In this biological context, the verb *develop* means to progress from an earlier to a later stage; it is used intransitively, which means that it cannot take an object. The pronoun *themselves* acts as an object, creating a construction that is not grammatical or logical. Omitting the pronoun removes the problem.

A *Ability* is incorrectly followed by *of developing*; a pronoun cannot follow *develop*, when it is used, as it is here, in its intransitive sense.

B **Correct.** *Ability* is properly followed by the infinitive in this sentence, and the pronoun *themselves* is omitted.

C This awkward and wordy construction violates the parallelism of *like embryonic germ cells…embryonic stem cells…*.

D The two parts of the comparison must be parallel; *like embryonic germ cells* must be followed by *embryonic stem cells*, not *the ability to develop*.

E *Ability* is followed by the unidiomatic *of developing* rather than *to develop*; the main clause must begin with *embryonic stem cells* to balance and complete *like embryonic germ cells*.

The correct answer is B.

48. Critics contend that the new missile is a weapon whose importance is largely symbolic, more a tool <u>for manipulating people's perceptions than to fulfill</u> a real military need.

(A) for manipulating people's perceptions than to fulfill

(B) for manipulating people's perceptions than for fulfilling

(C) to manipulate people's perceptions rather than that it fulfills

(D) to manipulate people's perceptions rather than fulfilling

(E) to manipulate people's perceptions than for fulfilling

Parallelism

This sentence uses the comparative construction *more x than y* where *x* and *y* must be parallel. Here, *x* is *a tool for manipulating people's perceptions*, and *y* is *to fulfill a real military need*. *A tool* does not need to be repeated in the second half of the comparison because it is understood, but the wording of the two phrases does need to match. There are two acceptable solutions: (1) *for manipulating* can be followed by *for fulfilling* or (2) *to manipulate* can be followed by *to fulfill*.

A *For manipulating* is not parallel to *to fulfill*.

B **Correct.** *For manipulating* and *for fulfilling* are parallel in this sentence.

C *To manipulate* is not parallel to *that it fulfills*.

D *To manipulate* is not parallel to *fulfilling*.

E *To manipulate* is not parallel to *for fulfilling*.

The correct answer is B.

49. As an actress and, more importantly, as a teacher of acting, Stella Adler was one of the most influential artists in the American theater, who trained several generations of actors including Marlon Brando and Robert De Niro.

    (A) Stella Adler was one of the most influential artists in the American theater, who trained several generations of actors including

    (B) Stella Adler, one of the most influential artists in the American theater, trained several generations of actors who include

    (C) Stella Adler was one of the most influential artists in the American theater, training several generations of actors whose ranks included

    (D) one of the most influential artists in the American theater was Stella Adler, who trained several generations of actors including

    (E) one of the most influential artists in the American theater, Stella Adler, trained several generations of actors whose ranks included

Logical predication

The original sentence contains a number of modifiers, but not all of them are correctly expressed. The clause *who trained…* describes *Stella Adler*, yet a relative clause such as this one must be placed immediately after the noun or pronoun it modifies, and this clause follows *theater* rather than *Adler*. Replacing *who trained* with *training* corrects the error because the phrase *training…* modifies the whole preceding clause rather than the single preceding noun. *Several generations of actors including* shows the same error in reverse; *including* modifies the whole phrase, but the two actors named are not *generations of actors*. The more limiting clause *whose ranks included* (referring to *actors*) is appropriate here.

A   Relative (*who*) clause follows *theater* rather than *Adler*; *including* refers to *generations of actors*, when the reference should be to *actors* only.

B   This construction, in which the subject is both preceded and followed by modifiers, is awkward; the verbs should be consistently in the past tense, but *include* is present tense.

C   **Correct.** In this sentence, substituting *training* for *who trained* and *whose ranks included* for *including* eliminates the modification errors.

D   Introductory modifier must be immediately followed by *Stella Adler*, not *one…*; *including* refers to *generations of actors* rather than to *actors* only.

E   Introductory modifier must be immediately followed by *Stella Adler*, not *one*.

The correct answer is C.

50. By developing the Secure Digital Music Initiative, the recording industry associations of North America, Japan, and Europe hope to create a standardized way of distributing songs and full-length recordings on the Internet that will protect copyright holders and foil the many audio pirates who copy and distribute digital music illegally.

    (A) of distributing songs and full-length recordings on the Internet that will protect copyright holders and foil the many audio pirates who copy and distribute

    (B) of distributing songs and full-length recordings on the Internet and to protect copyright holders and foiling the many audio pirates copying and distributing

    (C) for distributing songs and full-length recordings on the Internet while it protects copyright holders and foils the many audio pirates who copy and distribute

    (D) to distribute songs and full-length recordings on the Internet while they will protect copyright holders and foil the many audio pirates copying and distributing

    (E) to distribute songs and full-length recordings on the Internet and it will protect copyright holders and foiling the many audio pirates who copy and distribute

Parallelism

The original sentence depends on the parallelism of its verbs to make its point clearly and effectively. *A standardized way…will protect* and (*will* understood) *foil*; *pirates…copy and distribute.* In the first pair of parallel verbs, *will* does not need to be repeated because it is understood.

A **Correct.** The verbs *will protect* and (*will*) *foil* are parallel in this sentence, as are the verbs *copy* and *distribute*.

B *And to protect* distorts meaning, suggesting that protection comes in addition to *the standardized way*; *foiling* is not parallel to *to protect*.

C *Way for* should instead be *way of*; the pronoun reference in *while it protects* is ambiguous; construction suggests that protection comes from something other than the *standardized way*.

D Pronoun *they* has no referent; use of *while* suggests that protection comes from something other than the *standardized way* of distribution.

E *And it will protect* distorts meaning, suggesting that protection comes in addition to *the standardized way*; *will protect* and *foiling* are not parallel.

The correct answer is A.

51. Whereas a ramjet generally cannot achieve high speeds without the initial assistance of a rocket, <u>high speeds can be attained by scramjets, or supersonic combustion ramjets, in that they reduce</u> airflow compression at the entrance of the engine and letting air pass through at supersonic speeds.

(A) high speeds can be attained by scramjets, or supersonic combustion ramjets, in that they reduce

(B) that high speeds can be attained by scramjets, or supersonic combustion ramjets, is a result of their reducing

(C) the ability of scramjets, or supersonic combustion ramjets, to achieve high speeds is because they reduce

(D) scramjets, or supersonic combustion ramjets, have the ability of attaining high speeds when reducing

(E) scramjets, or supersonic combustion ramjets, can attain high speeds by reducing

Rhetorical construction

The underlined portion of the original sentence is wordy and ineffective. Transforming it from passive (*high speeds can be attained by scramjets*) to active voice (*scramjets can attain high speeds*) eliminates much of the problem. As the subject of the main clause, *scramjets* correctly parallels *a ramjet*, the subject of the subordinate clause; the contrast is thus clearly and effectively drawn. *In that they reduce* is wordy and awkward; it can be replaced by the more concise phrase *by reducing*.

A Passive voice contributes to a wordy, awkward, and ineffective construction; *in that they reduce* is also wordy and awkward.

B Passive voice and subordinate (*that*) clause constructions are wordy, awkward, and ineffective.

C *The ability…is because* is not a grammatical construction; *scramjets*, not *the ability*, should be parallel to *a ramjet*.

D *Have the ability of attaining* is wordy; *when* does not indicate the cause-and-effect relationship.

E **Correct.** *Scramjets* parallels *a ramjet* for an effective contrast in this sentence; the active voice is clear and concise; *by reducing* shows how scramjets attain high speeds.

The correct answer is E.

52. It will not be possible to implicate melting sea ice in the coastal flooding that many global warming models have projected: just <u>like a glass of water that will not overflow due to melting ice cubes,</u> so melting sea ice does not increase oceanic volume.

(A) like a glass of water that will not overflow due to melting ice cubes,

(B) like melting ice cubes that do not cause a glass of water to overflow,

(C) a glass of water will not overflow because of melting ice cubes,

(D) as melting ice cubes that do not cause a glass of water to overflow,

(E) as melting ice cubes do not cause a glass of water to overflow,

Diction; Parallelism

The preposition *like* introduces nouns and noun phrases; the conjunction *as* introduces verbs or clauses, so *as* is required here. The comparative construction used here is *just as x so y*; *x* and *y* must be parallel. The *y* clause is written in effective subject-verb-object order: *melting sea ice does not increase oceanic volume*. The original wordy, awkward *x* clause is not parallel. To make it parallel, *melting ice cubes* should be the subject of the clause, *do not cause...to overflow* the verb phrase, and a *glass of water* the object.

A   *Like* is used in place of *as*; the two elements of comparison are not parallel.

B   *Like* is used in place of *as*; *that* violates parallelism.

C   *As* or *just as* is needed to introduce the clause; the two clauses are not parallel.

D   *That* violates the parallelism of the two clauses and creates an ungrammatical construction.

E   **Correct.** This sentence has *just as* properly introducing the first clause, and the two clauses are parallel.

The correct answer is E.

4.0 Math Review

4.0 Math Review

Although this chapter provides a review of some of the mathematical concepts of arithmetic, algebra, and geometry, it is not intended to be a textbook. You should use this chapter to familiarize yourself with the kinds of topics that are tested in the GMAT® exam. You may wish to consult an arithmetic, algebra, or geometry book for a more detailed discussion of some of the topics.

Section 4.1, "Arithmetic," includes the following topics:

1. Properties of Integers
2. Fractions
3. Decimals
4. Real Numbers
5. Ratio and Proportion
6. Percents
7. Powers and Roots of Numbers
8. Descriptive Statistics
9. Sets
10. Counting Methods
11. Discrete Probability

Section 4.2, "Algebra," does not extend beyond what is usually covered in a first-year high school algebra course. The topics included are as follows:

1. Simplifying Algebraic Expressions
2. Equations
3. Solving Linear Equations with One Unknown
4. Solving Two Linear Equations with Two Unknowns
5. Solving Equations by Factoring
6. Solving Quadratic Equations
7. Exponents
8. Inequalities
9. Absolute Value
10. Functions

Section 4.3, "Geometry," is limited primarily to measurement and intuitive geometry or spatial visualization. Extensive knowledge of theorems and the ability to construct proofs, skills that are usually developed in a formal geometry course, are not tested. The topics included in this section are the following:

1. Lines
2. Intersecting Lines and Angles
3. Perpendicular Lines
4. Parallel Lines
5. Polygons (Convex)
6. Triangles
7. Quadrilaterals
8. Circles
9. Rectangular Solids and Cylinders
10. Coordinate Geometry

Section 4.4, "Word Problems," presents examples of and solutions to the following types of word problems:

1. Rate Problems
2. Work Problems
3. Mixture Problems
4. Interest Problems
5. Discount
6. Profit
7. Sets
8. Geometry Problems
9. Measurement Problems
10. Data Interpretation

4.1 Arithmetic

1. Properties of Integers

An *integer* is any number in the set {. . . –3, –2, –1, 0, 1, 2, 3, . . .}. If x and y are integers and $x \neq 0$, then x is a *divisor* (*factor*) of y provided that $y = xn$ for some integer n. In this case, y is also said to be *divisible* by x or to be a *multiple* of x. For example, 7 is a divisor or factor of 28 since $28 = (7)(4)$, but 8 is not a divisor of 28 since there is no integer n such that $28 = 8n$.

If x and y are positive integers, there exist unique integers q and r, called the *quotient* and *remainder*, respectively, such that $y = xq + r$ and $0 \leq r < x$. For example, when 28 is divided by 8, the quotient is 3 and the remainder is 4 since $28 = (8)(3) + 4$. Note that y is divisible by x if and only if the remainder r is 0; for example, 32 has a remainder of 0 when divided by 8 because 32 is divisible by 8. Also, note that when a smaller integer is divided by a larger integer, the quotient is 0 and the remainder is the smaller integer. For example, 5 divided by 7 has the quotient 0 and the remainder 5 since $5 = (7)(0) + 5$.

Any integer that is divisible by 2 is an *even integer*; the set of even integers is {. . . –4, –2, 0, 2, 4, 6, 8, . . .}. Integers that are not divisible by 2 are *odd integers*; {. . . –3, –1, 1, 3, 5, . . .} is the set of odd integers.

If at least one factor of a product of integers is even, then the product is even; otherwise the product is odd. If two integers are both even or both odd, then their sum and their difference are even. Otherwise, their sum and their difference are odd.

A *prime* number is a positive integer that has exactly two different positive divisors, 1 and itself. For example, 2, 3, 5, 7, 11, and 13 are prime numbers, but 15 is not, since 15 has four different positive divisors, 1, 3, 5, and 15. The number 1 is not a prime number since it has only one positive divisor. Every integer greater than 1 either is prime or can be uniquely expressed as a product of prime factors. For example, $14 = (2)(7)$, $81 = (3)(3)(3)(3)$, and $484 = (2)(2)(11)(11)$.

The numbers –2, –1, 0, 1, 2, 3, 4, 5 are *consecutive integers*. Consecutive integers can be represented by n, $n + 1$, $n + 2$, $n + 3$, . . . , where n is an integer. The numbers 0, 2, 4, 6, 8 are *consecutive even integers*, and 1, 3, 5, 7, 9 are *consecutive odd integers*. Consecutive even integers can be represented by $2n$, $2n + 2$, $2n + 4$, . . . , and consecutive odd integers can be represented by $2n + 1$, $2n + 3$, $2n + 5$, . . . , where n is an integer.

Properties of the integer 1. If n is any number, then $1 \cdot n = n$, and for any number $n \neq 0$, $n \cdot \frac{1}{n} = 1$.

The number 1 can be expressed in many ways; for example, $\frac{n}{n} = 1$ for any number $n \neq 0$.

Multiplying or dividing an expression by 1, in any form, does not change the value of that expression.

Properties of the integer 0. The integer 0 is neither positive nor negative. If n is any number, then $n + 0 = n$ and $n \cdot 0 = 0$. Division by 0 is not defined.

2. Fractions

In a fraction $\frac{n}{d}$, n is the *numerator* and d is the *denominator*. The denominator of a fraction can never be 0, because division by 0 is not defined.

Two fractions are said to be *equivalent* if they represent the same number. For example, $\frac{8}{36}$ and $\frac{14}{63}$ are equivalent since they both represent the number $\frac{2}{9}$. In each case, the fraction is reduced to lowest terms by dividing both numerator and denominator by their *greatest common divisor* (gcd). The gcd of 8 and 36 is 4 and the gcd of 14 and 63 is 7.

Addition and subtraction of fractions.

Two fractions with the same denominator can be added or subtracted by performing the required operation with the numerators, leaving the denominators the same. For example, $\frac{3}{5} + \frac{4}{5} = \frac{3+4}{5} = \frac{7}{5}$ and $\frac{5}{7} - \frac{2}{7} = \frac{5-2}{7} = \frac{3}{7}$. If two fractions do not have the same denominator, express them as equivalent fractions with the same denominator. For example, to add $\frac{3}{5}$ and $\frac{4}{7}$, multiply the numerator and denominator of the first fraction by 7 and the numerator and denominator of the second fraction by 5, obtaining $\frac{21}{35}$ and $\frac{20}{35}$, respectively; $\frac{21}{35} + \frac{20}{35} = \frac{41}{35}$.

For the new denominator, choosing the *least common multiple* (lcm) of the denominators usually lessens the work. For $\frac{2}{3} + \frac{1}{6}$, the lcm of 3 and 6 is 6 (not $3 \times 6 = 18$), so

$$\frac{2}{3} + \frac{1}{6} = \frac{2}{3} \times \frac{2}{2} + \frac{1}{6} = \frac{4}{6} + \frac{1}{6} = \frac{5}{6}.$$

Multiplication and division of fractions.

To multiply two fractions, simply multiply the two numerators and multiply the two denominators.

For example, $\frac{2}{3} \times \frac{4}{7} = \frac{2 \times 4}{3 \times 7} = \frac{8}{21}$.

To divide by a fraction, invert the divisor (that is, find its *reciprocal*) and multiply. For example,

$$\frac{2}{3} \div \frac{4}{7} = \frac{2}{3} \times \frac{7}{4} = \frac{14}{12} = \frac{7}{6}.$$

In the problem above, the reciprocal of $\frac{4}{7}$ is $\frac{7}{4}$. In general, the reciprocal of a fraction $\frac{n}{d}$ is $\frac{d}{n}$, where n and d are not zero.

Mixed numbers.

A number that consists of a whole number and a fraction, for example, $7\frac{2}{3}$, is a mixed number:

$7\frac{2}{3}$ means $7 + \frac{2}{3}$.

To change a mixed number into a fraction, multiply the whole number by the denominator of the fraction and add this number to the numerator of the fraction; then put the result over the

denominator of the fraction. For example, $7\frac{2}{3} = \frac{(3 \times 7) + 2}{3} = \frac{23}{3}$.

3. Decimals

In the decimal system, the position of the period or *decimal point* determines the place value of the digits. For example, the digits in the number 7,654.321 have the following place values:

Thousands		Hundreds	Tens	Ones or units		Tenths	Hundredths	Thousandths
7	,	6	5	4	.	3	2	1

Some examples of decimals follow.

$$0.321 = \frac{3}{10} + \frac{2}{100} + \frac{1}{1,000} = \frac{321}{1,000}$$

$$0.0321 = \frac{0}{10} + \frac{3}{100} + \frac{2}{1,000} + \frac{1}{10,000} = \frac{321}{10,000}$$

$$1.56 = 1 + \frac{5}{10} + \frac{6}{100} = \frac{156}{100}$$

Sometimes decimals are expressed as the product of a number with only one digit to the left of the decimal point and a power of 10. This is called *scientific notation*. For example, 231 can be written as 2.31×10^2 and 0.0231 can be written as 2.31×10^{-2}. When a number is expressed in scientific notation, the exponent of the 10 indicates the number of places that the decimal point is to be moved in the number that is to be multiplied by a power of 10 in order to obtain the product. The decimal point is moved to the right if the exponent is positive and to the left if the exponent is negative. For example, 2.013×10^4 is equal to 20,130 and 1.91×10^{-4} is equal to 0.000191.

Addition and subtraction of decimals.

To add or subtract two decimals, the decimal points of both numbers should be lined up. If one of the numbers has fewer digits to the right of the decimal point than the other, zeros may be inserted to the right of the last digit. For example, to add 17.6512 and 653.27, set up the numbers in a column and add:

$$
\begin{array}{r}
17.6512 \\
+\ 653.2700 \\
\hline
670.9212
\end{array}
$$

Likewise for 653.27 minus 17.6512:

$$
\begin{array}{r}
653.2700 \\
-\ 17.6512 \\
\hline
635.6188
\end{array}
$$

Multiplication of decimals.

To multiply decimals, multiply the numbers as if they were whole numbers and then insert the decimal point in the product so that the number of digits to the right of the decimal point is equal to the sum of the numbers of digits to the right of the decimal points in the numbers being multiplied. For example:

$$
\begin{array}{r}
2.09 \quad \left(2\text{ digits to the right}\right) \\
\times\ 1.3 \quad \left(1\text{ digit to the right}\right) \\
\hline
627 \\
2090 \\
\hline
2.717 \quad \left(2+1=3\text{ digits to the right}\right)
\end{array}
$$

Division of decimals.

To divide a number (the dividend) by a decimal (the divisor), move the decimal point of the divisor to the right until the divisor is a whole number. Then move the decimal point of the dividend the same number of places to the right, and divide as you would by a whole number. The decimal point in the quotient will be directly above the decimal point in the new dividend. For example, to divide 698.12 by 12.4:

$$
12.4\overline{)698.12}
$$

will be replaced by:

$$
124\overline{)6981.2}
$$

and the division would proceed as follows:

$$
\begin{array}{r}
56.3 \\
124\overline{)6981.2} \\
\underline{620} \\
781 \\
\underline{744} \\
372 \\
\underline{372} \\
0
\end{array}
$$

4. Real Numbers

All *real* numbers correspond to points on the number line and all points on the number line correspond to real numbers. All real numbers except zero are either positive or negative.

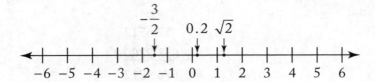

On a number line, numbers corresponding to points to the left of zero are negative and numbers corresponding to points to the right of zero are positive. For any two numbers on the number line, the number to the left is less than the number to the right; for example,

$$-4 < -3 < -\frac{3}{2} < -1, \text{ and } 1 < \sqrt{2} < 2.$$

To say that the number n is between 1 and 4 on the number line means that $n > 1$ and $n < 4$, that is, $1 < n < 4$. If n is "between 1 and 4, inclusive," then $1 \le n \le 4$.

The distance between a number and zero on the number line is called the *absolute value* of the number. Thus 3 and -3 have the same absolute value, 3, since they are both three units from zero. The absolute value of 3 is denoted $|3|$. Examples of absolute values of numbers are

$$|-5| = |5| = 5, \left|-\frac{7}{2}\right| = \frac{7}{2}, \text{ and } |0| = 0.$$

Note that the absolute value of any nonzero number is positive.

Here are some properties of real numbers that are used frequently. If x, y, and z are real numbers, then

(1) $x + y = y + x$ and $xy = yx$.
    For example, $8 + 3 = 3 + 8 = 11$, and $(17)(5) = (5)(17) = 85$.

(2) $(x + y) + z = x + (y + z)$ and $(xy)z = x(yz)$.
    For example, $(7 + 5) + 2 = 7 + (5 + 2) = 7 + (7) = 14$, and $(5\sqrt{3})(\sqrt{3}) = (5)(\sqrt{3}\sqrt{3}) = (5)(3) = 15$.

(3) $xy + xz = x(y + z)$.
    For example, $718(36) + 718(64) = 718(36 + 64) = 718(100) = 71,800$.

(4) If x and y are both positive, then $x + y$ and xy are positive.

(5) If x and y are both negative, then $x + y$ is negative and xy is positive.

(6) If x is positive and y is negative, then xy is negative.

(7) If $xy = 0$, then $x = 0$ or $y = 0$. For example, $3y = 0$ implies $y = 0$.

(8) $|x + y| \le |x| + |y|$. For example, if $x = 10$ and $y = 2$, then $|x + y| = |12| = 12 = |x| + |y|$; and if $x = 10$ and $y = -2$, then $|x + y| = |8| = 8 < 12 = |x| + |y|$.

5. Ratio and Proportion

The *ratio* of the number a to the number b $(b \neq 0)$ is $\frac{a}{b}$.

A ratio may be expressed or represented in several ways. For example, the ratio of 2 to 3 can be written as 2 to 3, 2:3, or $\frac{2}{3}$. The order of the terms of a ratio is important. For example, the ratio of the number of months with exactly 30 days to the number with exactly 31 days is $\frac{4}{7}$, not $\frac{7}{4}$.

A *proportion* is a statement that two ratios are equal; for example, $\frac{2}{3} = \frac{8}{12}$ is a proportion. One way to solve a proportion involving an unknown is to cross multiply, obtaining a new equality. For example, to solve for n in the proportion $\frac{2}{3} = \frac{n}{12}$, cross multiply, obtaining $24 = 3n$; then divide both sides by 3, to get $n = 8$.

6. Percents

Percent means *per hundred* or *number out of 100*. A percent can be represented as a fraction with a denominator of 100, or as a decimal. For example:

$$37\% = \frac{37}{100} = 0.37.$$

To find a certain percent of a number, multiply the number by the percent expressed as a decimal or fraction. For example:

$$20\% \text{ of } 90 = 0.2 \times 90 = 18$$

or

$$20\% \text{ of } 90 = \frac{20}{100} \times 90 = \frac{1}{5} \times 90 = 18.$$

Percents greater than 100%.

Percents greater than 100% are represented by numbers greater than 1. For example:

$$300\% = \frac{300}{100} = 3$$
$$250\% \text{ of } 80 = 2.5 \times 80 = 200.$$

Percents less than 1%.

The percent 0.5% means $\frac{1}{2}$ of 1 percent. For example, 0.5% of 12 is equal to $0.005 \times 12 = 0.06$.

Percent change.

Often a problem will ask for the percent increase or decrease from one quantity to another quantity. For example, "If the price of an item increases from \$24 to \$30, what is the percent increase in price?" To find the percent increase, first find the amount of the increase; then divide this increase by the original amount, and express this quotient as a percent. In the example above, the percent increase would be found in the following way: the amount of the increase is $(30 - 24) = 6$. Therefore, the percent increase is $\frac{6}{24} = 0.25 = 25\%$.

Likewise, to find the percent decrease (for example, the price of an item is reduced from \$30 to \$24), first find the amount of the decrease; then divide this decrease by the original amount, and express this quotient as a percent. In the example above, the amount of decrease is $(30 - 24) = 6$. Therefore, the percent decrease is $\frac{6}{30} = 0.20 = 20\%$.

Note that the percent increase from 24 to 30 is not the same as the percent decrease from 30 to 24.

In the following example, the increase is greater than 100 percent: If the cost of a certain house in 1983 was 300 percent of its cost in 1970, by what percent did the cost increase?

If n is the cost in 1970, then the percent increase is equal to $\frac{3n - n}{n} = \frac{2n}{n} = 2$, or 200%.

7. Powers and Roots of Numbers

When a number k is to be used n times as a factor in a product, it can be expressed as k^n, which means the nth power of k. For example, $2^2 = 2 \times 2 = 4$ and $2^3 = 2 \times 2 \times 2 = 8$ are powers of 2.

Squaring a number that is greater than 1, or raising it to a higher power, results in a larger number; squaring a number between 0 and 1 results in a smaller number. For example:

$$3^2 = 9 \qquad (9 > 3)$$
$$\left(\frac{1}{3}\right)^2 = \frac{1}{9} \qquad \left(\frac{1}{9} < \frac{1}{3}\right)$$
$$(0.1)^2 = 0.01 \qquad (0.01 < 0.1)$$

A *square root* of a number n is a number that, when squared, is equal to n. The square root of a negative number is not a real number. Every positive number n has two square roots, one positive and the other negative, but $\sqrt{n}$ denotes the positive number whose square is n. For example, $\sqrt{9}$ denotes 3. The two square roots of 9 are $\sqrt{9} = 3$ and $-\sqrt{9} = -3$.

Every real number r has exactly one real *cube root*, which is the number s such that $s^3 = r$. The real cube root of r is denoted by $\sqrt[3]{r}$. Since $2^3 = 8$, $\sqrt[3]{8} = 2$. Similarly, $\sqrt[3]{-8} = -2$, because $(-2)^3 = -8$.

8. Descriptive Statistics

A list of numbers, or numerical data, can be described by various statistical measures. One of the most common of these measures is the *average*, or *(arithmetic) mean*, which locates a type of "center" for the data. The average of n numbers is defined as the sum of the n numbers divided by n. For example, the average of 6, 4, 7, 10, and 4 is $\frac{6 + 4 + 7 + 10 + 4}{5} = \frac{31}{5} = 6.2$.

The *median* is another type of center for a list of numbers. To calculate the median of n numbers, first order the numbers from least to greatest; if n is odd, the median is defined as the middle number, whereas if n is even, the median is defined as the average of the two middle numbers. In the example above, the numbers, in order, are 4, 4, 6, 7, 10, and the median is 6, the middle number.

For the numbers 4, 6, 6, 8, 9, 12, the median is $\dfrac{6+8}{2} = 7$. Note that the mean of these numbers is 7.5.

The median of a set of data can be less than, equal to, or greater than the mean. Note that for a large set of data (for example, the salaries of 800 company employees), it is often true that about half of the data is less than the median and about half of the data is greater than the median; but this is not always the case, as the following data show.

3, 5, 7, 7, 7, 7, 7, 7, 8, 9, 9, 9, 9, 10, 10

Here the median is 7, but only $\dfrac{2}{15}$ of the data is less than the median.

The *mode* of a list of numbers is the number that occurs most frequently in the list. For example, the mode of 1, 3, 6, 4, 3, 5 is 3. A list of numbers may have more than one mode. For example, the list 1, 2, 3, 3, 3, 5, 7, 10, 10, 10, 20 has two modes, 3 and 10.

The degree to which numerical data are spread out or dispersed can be measured in many ways. The simplest measure of dispersion is the *range*, which is defined as the greatest value in the numerical data minus the least value. For example, the range of 11, 10, 5, 13, 21 is $21 - 5 = 16$. Note how the range depends on only two values in the data.

One of the most common measures of dispersion is the *standard deviation*. Generally speaking, the more the data are spread away from the mean, the greater the standard deviation. The standard deviation of n numbers can be calculated as follows: (1) find the arithmetic mean, (2) find the differences between the mean and each of the n numbers, (3) square each of the differences, (4) find the average of the squared differences, and (5) take the nonnegative square root of this average. Shown below is this calculation for the data 0, 7, 8, 10, 10, which have arithmetic mean 7.

x	$x - 7$	$(x-7)^2$
0	−7	49
7	0	0
8	1	1
10	3	9
10	3	9
	Total	68

Standard deviation $\sqrt{\dfrac{68}{5}} \approx 3.7$

Notice that the standard deviation depends on every data value, although it depends most on values that are farthest from the mean. This is why a distribution with data grouped closely around the mean will have a smaller standard deviation than will data spread far from the mean. To illustrate this, compare the data 6, 6, 6.5, 7.5, 9, which also have mean 7. Note that the numbers in the second set of data seem to be grouped more closely around the mean of 7 than the numbers in the first set. This is reflected in the standard deviation, which is less for the second set (approximately 1.1) than for the first set (approximately 3.7).

There are many ways to display numerical data that show how the data are distributed. One simple way is with a *frequency distribution*, which is useful for data that have values occurring with varying frequencies. For example, the 20 numbers

−4	0	0	−3	−2	−1	−1	0	−1	−4
−1	−5	0	−2	0	−5	−2	0	0	−1

are displayed on the next page in a frequency distribution by listing each different value x and the frequency f with which x occurs.

Data Value x	Frequency f
−5	2
−4	2
−3	1
−2	3
−1	5
0	7
Total	20

From the frequency distribution, one can readily compute descriptive statistics:

Mean: $= \dfrac{(-5)(2)+(-4)(2)+(-3)(1)+(-2)(3)+(-1)(5)+(0)(7)}{20} = -1.6$

Median: −1 (the average of the 10th and 11th numbers)

Mode: 0 (the number that occurs most frequently)

Range: $0 - (-5) = 5$

Standard deviation: $\sqrt{\dfrac{(-5+1.6)^2(2)+(-4+1.6)^2(2)+\dots+(0+1.6)^2(7)}{20}} \approx 1.7$

9. Sets

In mathematics a *set* is a collection of numbers or other objects. The objects are called the *elements* of the set. If S is a set having a finite number of elements, then the number of elements is denoted by $|S|$. Such a set is often defined by listing its elements; for example, $S = \{-5, 0, 1\}$ is a set with $|S| = 3$.

The order in which the elements are listed in a set does not matter; thus $\{-5, 0, 1\} = \{0, 1, -5\}$.

If all the elements of a set S are also elements of a set T, then S is a *subset* of T; for example, $S = \{-5, 0, 1\}$ is a subset of $T = \{-5, 0, 1, 4, 10\}$.

For any two sets A and B, the *union* of A and B is the set of all elements that are in A *or* in B *or* in both. The *intersection* of A and B is the set of all elements that are both in A *and* in B. The union is denoted by $A \cup B$ and the intersection is denoted by $A \cap B$. As an example, if $A = \{3, 4\}$ and $B = \{4, 5, 6\}$, then $A \cup B = \{3, 4, 5, 6\}$ and $A \cap B = \{4\}$. Two sets that have no elements in common are said to be *disjoint* or *mutually exclusive*.

The relationship between sets is often illustrated with a *Venn diagram* in which sets are represented by regions in a plane. For two sets S and T that are not disjoint and neither is a subset of the other, the intersection $S \cap T$ is represented by the shaded region of the diagram below.

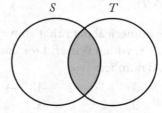

This diagram illustrates a fact about any two finite sets S and T: the number of elements in their union equals the sum of their individual numbers of elements minus the number of elements in their intersection (because the latter are counted twice in the sum); more concisely,

$$|S \cup T| = |S| + |T| - |S \cap T|.$$

This counting method is called the general addition rule for two sets. As a special case, if S and T are disjoint, then

$$|S \cup T| = |S| + |T|$$

since $|S \cap T| = 0$.

10. Counting Methods

There are some useful methods for counting objects and sets of objects without actually listing the elements to be counted. The following principle of multiplication is fundamental to these methods.

If an object is to be chosen from a set of m objects and a second object is to be chosen from a different set of n objects, then there are mn ways of choosing both objects simultaneously.

As an example, suppose the objects are items on a menu. If a meal consists of one entree and one dessert and there are 5 entrees and 3 desserts on the menu, then there are $5 \times 3 = 15$ different meals that can be ordered from the menu. As another example, each time a coin is flipped, there are two possible outcomes, heads and tails. If an experiment consists of 8 consecutive coin flips, then the experiment has 2^8 possible outcomes, where each of these outcomes is a list of heads and tails in some order.

A symbol that is often used with the multiplication principle is the *factorial*. If n is an integer greater than 1, then n factorial, denoted by the symbol $n!$, is defined as the product of all the integers from 1 to n. Therefore,

$$2! = (1)(2) = 2,$$
$$3! = (1)(2)(3) = 6,$$
$$4! = (1)(2)(3)(4) = 24, \text{ etc.}$$

Also, by definition, $0! = 1! = 1$.

The factorial is useful for counting the number of ways that a set of objects can be ordered. If a set of n objects is to be ordered from 1st to nth, then there are n choices for the 1st object, $n-1$ choices for the 2nd object, $n-2$ choices for the 3rd object, and so on, until there is only 1 choice for the nth object. Thus, by the multiplication principle, the number of ways of ordering the n objects is

$$n(n-1)(n-2)\cdots(3)(2)(1) = n!.$$

For example, the number of ways of ordering the letters A, B, and C is $3!$, or 6:

ABC, ACB, BAC, BCA, CAB, and CBA.

These orderings are called the *permutations* of the letters A, B, and C.

A permutation can be thought of as a selection process in which objects are selected one by one in a certain order. If the order of selection is not relevant and only k objects are to be selected from a larger set of n objects, a different counting method is employed.

Specifically, consider a set of n objects from which a complete selection of k objects is to be made without regard to order, where $0 \le k \le n$. Then the number of possible complete selections of k objects is called the number of *combinations* of n objects taken k at a time and is denoted by $\binom{n}{k}$.

The value of $\binom{n}{k}$ is given by $\binom{n}{k} = \dfrac{n!}{k!(n-k)!}$.

Note that $\binom{n}{k}$ is the number of k-element subsets of a set with n elements. For example, if $S = \{A, B, C, D, E\}$, then the number of 2-element subsets of S, or the number of combinations of 5 letters taken 2 at a time, is $\binom{5}{2} = \dfrac{5!}{2!3!} = \dfrac{120}{(2)(6)} = 10$.

The subsets are {A, B}, {A, C}, {A, D}, {A, E}, {B, C}, {B, D}, {B, E}, {C, D}, {C, E}, and {D, E}.

Note that $\binom{5}{2} = 10 = \binom{5}{3}$ because every 2-element subset chosen from a set of 5 elements corresponds to a unique 3-element subset consisting of the elements *not* chosen.

In general, $\binom{n}{k} = \binom{n}{n-k}$.

11. Discrete Probability

Many of the ideas discussed in the preceding three topics are important to the study of discrete probability. Discrete probability is concerned with *experiments* that have a finite number of *outcomes*. Given such an experiment, an *event* is a particular set of outcomes. For example, rolling a number cube with faces numbered 1 to 6 (similar to a 6-sided die) is an experiment with 6 possible outcomes: 1, 2, 3, 4, 5, or 6. One event in this experiment is that the outcome is 4, denoted {4}; another event is that the outcome is an odd number: {1, 3, 5}.

The probability that an event E occurs, denoted by $P(E)$, is a number between 0 and 1, inclusive. If E has no outcomes, then E is *impossible* and $P(E) = 0$; if E is the set of all possible outcomes of the experiment, then E is *certain* to occur and $P(E) = 1$. Otherwise, E is possible but uncertain, and $0 < P(E) < 1$. If F is a subset of E, then $P(F) \le P(E)$. In the example above, if the probability of each of the 6 outcomes is the same, then the probability of each outcome is $\dfrac{1}{6}$, and the outcomes are said to be *equally likely*. For experiments in which all the individual outcomes are equally likely, the probability of an event E is

$$P(E) = \frac{\text{The number of outcomes in } E}{\text{The total number of possible outcomes}}.$$

In the example, the probability that the outcome is an odd number is

$$P(\{1, 3, 5\}) = \frac{|\{1, 3, 5\}|}{6} = \frac{3}{6} = \frac{1}{2}.$$

Given an experiment with events E and F, the following events are defined:
"*not E*" is the set of outcomes that are not outcomes in E;
"*E or F*" is the set of outcomes in E or F or both, that is, $E \cup F$;
"*E and F*" is the set of outcomes in both E and F, that is, $E \cap F$.

The probability that E does not occur is $P(\text{not } E) = 1 - P(E)$. The probability that "$E$ or F" occurs is $P(E \text{ or } F) = P(E) + P(F) - P(E \text{ and } F)$, using the general addition rule at the end of section 4.1.9 ("Sets"). For the number cube, if E is the event that the outcome is an odd number, $\{1, 3, 5\}$, and F is the event that the outcome is a prime number, $\{2, 3, 5\}$, then $P(E \text{ and } F) = P(\{3, 5\}) = \dfrac{2}{6} = \dfrac{1}{3}$ and so $P(E \text{ or } F) = P(E) + P(F) - P(E \text{ and } F) = \dfrac{3}{6} + \dfrac{3}{6} - \dfrac{2}{6} = \dfrac{4}{6} = \dfrac{2}{3}$.

Note that the event "E or F" is $E \cup F = \{1, 2, 3, 5\}$, and hence $P(E \text{ or } F) = \dfrac{|\{1, 2, 3, 5\}|}{6} = \dfrac{4}{6} = \dfrac{2}{3}$.

If the event "E and F" is impossible (that is, $E \cap F$ has no outcomes), then E and F are said to be *mutually exclusive* events, and $P(E \text{ and } F) = 0$. Then the general addition rule is reduced to $P(E \text{ or } F) = P(E) + P(F)$.

This is the special addition rule for the probability of two mutually exclusive events.

Two events A and B are said to be *independent* if the occurrence of either event does not alter the probability that the other event occurs. For one roll of the number cube, let $A = \{2, 4, 6\}$ and let $B = \{5, 6\}$. Then the probability that A occurs is $P(A) = \dfrac{|A|}{6} = \dfrac{3}{6} = \dfrac{1}{2}$, while, *presuming B occurs*, the probability that A occurs is

$$\frac{|A \cap B|}{|B|} = \frac{|\{6\}|}{|\{5, 6\}|} = \frac{1}{2}.$$

Similarly, the probability that B occurs is $P(B) = \dfrac{|B|}{6} = \dfrac{2}{6} = \dfrac{1}{3}$, while, *presuming A occurs*, the probability that B occurs is

$$\frac{|B \cap A|}{|A|} = \frac{|\{6\}|}{|\{2, 4, 6\}|} = \frac{1}{3}.$$

Thus, the occurrence of either event does not affect the probability that the other event occurs. Therefore, A and B are independent.

The following multiplication rule holds for any independent events E and F: $P(E \text{ and } F) = P(E)P(F)$.

For the independent events A and B above, $P(A \text{ and } B) = P(A)P(B) = \left(\dfrac{1}{2}\right)\left(\dfrac{1}{3}\right) = \left(\dfrac{1}{6}\right)$.

Note that the event "A and B" is $A \cap B = \{6\}$, and hence $P(A \text{ and } B) = P(\{6\}) = \dfrac{1}{6}$. It follows from the general addition rule and the multiplication rule above that if E and F are independent, then

$$P(E \text{ or } F) = P(E) + P(F) - P(E)P(F).$$

For a final example of some of these rules, consider an experiment with events A, B, and C for which $P(A) = 0.23$, $P(B) = 0.40$, and $P(C) = 0.85$. Also, suppose that events A and B are mutually exclusive and events B and C are independent. Then

$$P(A \text{ or } B) = P(A) + P(B) \quad (\text{since } A \text{ or } B \text{ are mutually exclusive})$$
$$= 0.23 + 0.40$$
$$= 0.63$$
$$P(B \text{ or } C) = P(B) + P(C) - P(B)P(C) \quad (\text{by independence})$$
$$= 0.40 + 0.85 - (0.40)(0.85)$$
$$= 0.91$$

Note that $P(A \text{ or } C)$ and $P(A \text{ and } C)$ cannot be determined using the information given. But it can be determined that A and C are *not* mutually exclusive since $P(A) + P(C) = 1.08$, which is greater than 1, and therefore cannot equal $P(A \text{ or } C)$; from this it follows that $P(A \text{ and } C) \geq 0.08$. One can also deduce that $P(A \text{ and } C) \leq P(A) = 0.23$, since $A \cap C$ is a subset of A, and that $P(A \text{ or } C) \geq P(C) = 0.85$ since C is a subset of $A \cup C$. Thus, one can conclude that $0.85 \leq P(A \text{ or } C) \leq 1$ and $0.08 \leq P(A \text{ and } C) \leq 0.23$.

4.2 Algebra

Algebra is based on the operations of arithmetic and on the concept of an *unknown quantity*, or *variable*. Letters such as x or n are used to represent unknown quantities. For example, suppose Pam has 5 more pencils than Fred. If F represents the number of pencils that Fred has, then the number of pencils that Pam has is $F + 5$. As another example, if Jim's present salary S is increased by 7%, then his new salary is $1.07S$. A combination of letters and arithmetic operations, such as

$F + 5$, $\dfrac{3x^2}{2x - 5}$, and $19x^2 - 6x + 3$, is called an *algebraic expression*.

The expression $19x^2 - 6x + 3$ consists of the *terms* $19x^2$, $-6x$, and 3, where 19 is the *coefficient* of x^2, -6 is the coefficient of x^1, and 3 is a *constant term* (or coefficient of $x^0 = 1$). Such an expression is called a *second degree* (or *quadratic*) *polynomial in x* since the highest power of x is 2. The expression $F + 5$ is a *first degree* (or *linear*) *polynomial in F* since the highest power of F is 1. The expression $\dfrac{3x^2}{2x - 5}$ is not a polynomial because it is not a sum of terms that are each powers of x multiplied by coefficients.

1. Simplifying Algebraic Expressions

Often when working with algebraic expressions, it is necessary to simplify them by factoring or combining *like* terms. For example, the expression $6x + 5x$ is equivalent to $(6 + 5)x$, or $11x$. In the expression $9x - 3y$, 3 is a factor common to both terms: $9x - 3y = 3(3x - y)$. In the expression $5x^2 + 6y$, there are no like terms and no common factors.

If there are common factors in the numerator and denominator of an expression, they can be divided out, provided that they are not equal to zero.

For example, if $x \neq 3$, then $\dfrac{x - 3}{x - 3}$ is equal to 1; therefore,

$$\frac{3xy - 9y}{x - 3} = \frac{3y(x - 3)}{x - 3}$$

$$= (3y)(1)$$

$$= 3y$$

To multiply two algebraic expressions, each term of one expression is multiplied by each term of the other expression. For example:

$$(3x - 4)(9y + x) = 3x(9y + x) - 4(9y + x)$$

$$= (3x)(9y) + (3x)(x) + (-4)(9y) + (-4)(x)$$

$$= 27xy + 3x^2 - 36y - 4x$$

An algebraic expression can be evaluated by substituting values of the unknowns in the expression. For example, if $x = 3$ and $y = -2$, then $3xy - x^2 + y$ can be evaluated as

$$3(3)(-2) - (3)^2 + (-2) = -18 - 9 - 2 = -29$$

2. Equations

A major focus of algebra is to solve equations involving algebraic expressions. Some examples of such equations are

$$5x - 2 = 9 - x \quad \text{(a linear equation with one unknown)}$$

$$3x + 1 = y - 2 \quad \text{(a linear equation with two unknowns)}$$

$$5x^2 + 3x - 2 = 7x \quad \text{(a quadratic equation with one unknown)}$$

$$\frac{x(x - 3)(x^2 + 5)}{x - 4} = 0 \quad \text{(an equation that is factored on one side with 0 on the other)}$$

The *solutions* of an equation with one or more unknowns are those values that make the equation true, or "satisfy the equation," when they are substituted for the unknowns of the equation. An equation may have no solution or one or more solutions. If two or more equations are to be solved together, the solutions must satisfy all the equations simultaneously.

Two equations having the same solution(s) are *equivalent equations*. For example, the equations

$$2 + x = 3$$

$$4 + 2x = 6$$

each have the unique solution $x = 1$. Note that the second equation is the first equation multiplied by 2. Similarly, the equations

$$3x - y = 6$$

$$6x - 2y = 12$$

have the same solutions, although in this case each equation has infinitely many solutions. If any value is assigned to x, then $3x - 6$ is a corresponding value for y that will satisfy both equations; for example, $x = 2$ and $y = 0$ is a solution to both equations, as is $x = 5$ and $y = 9$.

3. Solving Linear Equations with One Unknown

To solve a linear equation with one unknown (that is, to find the value of the unknown that satisfies the equation), the unknown should be isolated on one side of the equation. This can be done by performing the same mathematical operations on both sides of the equation. Remember that if the same number is added to or subtracted from both sides of the equation, this does not change the equality; likewise, multiplying or dividing both sides by the same nonzero number does not change the equality. For example, to solve the equation $\frac{5x - 6}{3} = 4$ for x, the variable x can be isolated using the following steps:

$$5x - 6 = 12 \quad \left(\text{multiplying by } 3\right)$$
$$5x = 18 \quad \left(\text{adding } 6\right)$$
$$x = \frac{18}{5} \quad \left(\text{dividing by } 5\right)$$

The solution, $\frac{18}{5}$, can be checked by substituting it for x in the original equation to determine whether it satisfies that equation:

$$\frac{5\left(\frac{18}{5}\right) - 6}{3} = \frac{18 - 6}{3} = \frac{12}{3} = 4$$

Therefore, $x = \frac{18}{5}$ is the solution.

4. Solving Two Linear Equations with Two Unknowns

For two linear equations with two unknowns, if the equations are equivalent, then there are infinitely many solutions to the equations, as illustrated at the end of section 4.2.2 ("Equations"). If the equations are not equivalent, then they have either a unique solution or no solution. The latter case is illustrated by the two equations:

$$3x + 4y = 17$$
$$6x + 8y = 35$$

Note that $3x + 4y = 17$ implies $6x + 8y = 34$, which contradicts the second equation. Thus, no values of x and y can simultaneously satisfy both equations.

There are several methods of solving two linear equations with two unknowns. With any method, if a contradiction is reached, then the equations have no solution; if a trivial equation such as $0 = 0$ is reached, then the equations are equivalent and have infinitely many solutions. Otherwise, a unique solution can be found.

One way to solve for the two unknowns is to express one of the unknowns in terms of the other using one of the equations, and then substitute the expression into the remaining equation to obtain an equation with one unknown. This equation can be solved and the value of the unknown substituted into either of the original equations to find the value of the other unknown. For example, the following two equations can be solved for x and y.

$$\begin{aligned}(1)\ \ 3x + 2y &= 11 \\ (2)\ \ \ x - y &= 2\end{aligned}$$

In equation (2), $x = 2 + y$. Substitute $2 + y$ in equation (1) for x:

$$\begin{aligned}3(2 + y) + 2y &= 11 \\ 6 + 3y + 2y &= 11 \\ 6 + 5y &= 11 \\ 5y &= 5 \\ y &= 1\end{aligned}$$

If $y = 1$, then $x - 1 = 2$ and $x = 2 + 1 = 3$.

There is another way to solve for x and y by eliminating one of the unknowns. This can be done by making the coefficients of one of the unknowns the same (disregarding the sign) in both equations and either adding the equations or subtracting one equation from the other. For example, to solve the equations

$$\begin{aligned}(1)\ \ 6x + 5y &= 29 \\ (2)\ \ 4x - 3y &= -6\end{aligned}$$

by this method, multiply equation (1) by 3 and equation (2) by 5 to get

$$\begin{aligned}18x + 15y &= 87 \\ 20x - 15y &= -30\end{aligned}$$

Adding the two equations eliminates y, yielding $38x = 57$, or $x = \dfrac{3}{2}$. Finally, substituting $\dfrac{3}{2}$ for x in one of the equations gives $y = 4$. These answers can be checked by substituting both values into both of the original equations.

5. Solving Equations by Factoring

Some equations can be solved by factoring. To do this, first add or subtract expressions to bring all the expressions to one side of the equation, with 0 on the other side. Then try to factor the nonzero side into a product of expressions. If this is possible, then using property (7) in section 4.1.4 ("Real Numbers") each of the factors can be set equal to 0, yielding several simpler equations that possibly can be solved. The solutions of the simpler equations will be solutions of the factored equation. As an example, consider the equation $x^3 - 2x^2 + x = -5(x - 1)^2$:

$$\begin{aligned}x^3 - 2x^2 + x + 5(x - 1)^2 &= 0 \\ x(x^2 - 2x + 1) + 5(x - 1)^2 &= 0 \\ x(x - 1)^2 + 5(x - 1)^2 &= 0 \\ (x + 5)(x - 1)^2 &= 0 \\ x + 5 = 0 \text{ or } (x - 1)^2 &= 0 \\ x = -5 \text{ or } x &= 1.\end{aligned}$$

For another example, consider $\dfrac{x(x-3)(x^2+5)}{x-4} = 0$. A fraction equals 0 if and only if its numerator equals 0. Thus, $x(x-3)(x^2+5) = 0$:

$$x = 0 \text{ or } x - 3 = 0 \text{ or } x^2 + 5 = 0$$
$$x = 0 \text{ or } x = 3 \text{ or } x^2 + 5 = 0.$$

But $x^2 + 5 = 0$ has no real solution because $x^2 + 5 > 0$ for every real number. Thus, the solutions are 0 and 3.

The solutions of an equation are also called the *roots* of the equation. These roots can be checked by substituting them into the original equation to determine whether they satisfy the equation.

6. Solving Quadratic Equations

The standard form for a *quadratic equation* is

$$ax^2 + bx + c = 0,$$

where a, b, and c are real numbers and $a \neq 0$; for example:

$$x^2 + 6x + 5 = 0$$
$$3x^2 - 2x = 0, \text{ and}$$
$$x^2 + 4 = 0$$

Some quadratic equations can easily be solved by factoring. For example:

$$(1) \qquad x^2 + 6x + 5 = 0$$
$$(x+5)(x+1) = 0$$
$$x + 5 = 0 \text{ or } x + 1 = 0$$
$$x = -5 \text{ or } x = -1$$

$$(2) \qquad 3x^2 - 3 = 8x$$
$$3x^2 - 8x - 3 = 0$$
$$(3x+1)(x-3) = 0$$
$$3x + 1 = 0 \text{ or } x - 3 = 0$$
$$x = -\frac{1}{3} \text{ or } x = 3$$

A quadratic equation has at most two real roots and may have just one or even no real root. For example, the equation $x^2 - 6x + 9 = 0$ can be expressed as $(x-3)^2 = 0$, or $(x-3)(x-3) = 0$; thus the only root is 3. The equation $x^2 + 4 = 0$ has no real root; since the square of any real number is greater than or equal to zero, $x^2 + 4$ must be greater than zero.

An expression of the form $a^2 - b^2$ can be factored as $(a-b)(a+b)$.

For example, the quadratic equation $9x^2 - 25 = 0$ can be solved as follows.

$$(3x-5)(3x+5) = 0$$
$$3x - 5 = 0 \text{ or } 3x + 5 = 0$$
$$x = \frac{5}{3} \text{ or } x = -\frac{5}{3}$$

If a quadratic expression is not easily factored, then its roots can always be found using the *quadratic formula*: If $ax^2 + bx + c = 0$ $(a \neq 0)$, then the roots are

$$x = \frac{-b + \sqrt{b^2 - 4ac}}{2a} \text{ and } x = \frac{-b - \sqrt{b^2 - 4ac}}{2a}$$

These are two distinct real numbers unless $b^2 - 4ac \leq 0$. If $b^2 - 4ac = 0$, then these two expressions for x are equal to $-\dfrac{b}{2a}$, and the equation has only one root. If $b^2 - 4ac < 0$, then $\sqrt{b^2 - 4ac}$ is not a real number and the equation has no real roots.

7. Exponents

A positive integer exponent of a number or a variable indicates a product, and the positive integer is the number of times that the number or variable is a factor in the product. For example, x^5 means $(x)(x)(x)(x)(x)$; that is, x is a factor in the product 5 times.

Some rules about exponents follow.

Let x and y be any positive numbers, and let r and s be any positive integers.

(1) $\left(x^r\right)\left(x^s\right) = x^{(r+s)}$; for example, $\left(2^2\right)\left(2^3\right) = 2^{(2+3)} = 2^5 = 32$.

(2) $\dfrac{x^r}{x^s} = x^{(r-s)}$; for example, $\dfrac{4^5}{4^2} = 4^{5-2} = 4^3 = 64$.

(3) $\left(x^r\right)\left(y^r\right) = (xy)^r$; for example, $\left(3^3\right)\left(4^3\right) = 12^3 = 1{,}728$.

(4) $\left(\dfrac{x}{y}\right)^r = \dfrac{x^r}{y^r}$; for example, $\left(\dfrac{2}{3}\right)^3 = \dfrac{2^3}{3^3} = \dfrac{8}{27}$.

(5) $\left(x^r\right)^s = x^{rs} = \left(x^s\right)^r$; for example, $\left(x^3\right)^4 = x^{12} = \left(x^4\right)^3$.

(6) $x^{-r} = \dfrac{1}{x^r}$; for example, $3^{-2} = \dfrac{1}{3^2} = \dfrac{1}{9}$.

(7) $x^0 = 1$; for example, $6^0 = 1$.

(8) $x^{\frac{r}{s}} = \left(x^{\frac{1}{s}}\right)^r = \left(x^r\right)^{\frac{1}{s}} = \sqrt[s]{x^r}$; for example, $8^{\frac{2}{3}} = \left(8^{\frac{1}{3}}\right)^2 = \left(8^2\right)^{\frac{1}{3}} = \sqrt[3]{8^2} = \sqrt[3]{64} = 4$

and $9^{\frac{1}{2}} = \sqrt{9} = 3$.

It can be shown that rules 1–6 also apply when r and s are not integers and are not positive, that is, when r and s are any real numbers.

8. Inequalities

An *inequality* is a statement that uses one of the following symbols:

$\neq$ not equal to

$>$ greater than

$\geq$ greater than or equal to

$<$ less than

$\leq$ less than or equal to

Some examples of inequalities are $5x - 3 < 9$, $6x \geq y$, and $\frac{1}{2} < \frac{3}{4}$. Solving a linear inequality with one unknown is similar to solving an equation; the unknown is isolated on one side of the inequality. As in solving an equation, the same number can be added to or subtracted from both sides of the inequality, or both sides of an inequality can be multiplied or divided by a positive number without changing the truth of the inequality. However, multiplying or dividing an inequality by a negative number reverses the order of the inequality. For example, $6 > 2$, but $(-1)(6) < (-1)(2)$.

To solve the inequality $3x - 2 > 5$ for x, isolate x by using the following steps:

$$3x - 2 > 5$$
$$3x > 7 \quad (\text{adding 2 to both sides})$$
$$x > \frac{7}{3} \quad (\text{dividing both sides by 3})$$

To solve the inequality $\frac{5x - 1}{-2} < 3$ for x, isolate x by using the following steps:

$$\frac{5x - 1}{-2} < 3$$
$$5x - 1 > -6 \quad (\text{multiplying both sides by } -2)$$
$$5x > -5 \quad (\text{adding 1 to both sides})$$
$$x > -1 \quad (\text{dividing both sides by 5})$$

9. Absolute Value

The absolute value of x, denoted $|x|$, is defined to be x if $x \geq 0$ and $-x$ if $x < 0$. Note that $\sqrt{x^2}$ denotes the nonnegative square root of x^2, and so $\sqrt{x^2} = |x|$.

10. Functions

An algebraic expression in one variable can be used to define a *function* of that variable. A function is denoted by a letter such as f or g along with the variable in the expression. For example, the expression $x^3 - 5x^2 + 2$ defines a function f that can be denoted by

$$f(x) = x^3 - 5x^2 + 2.$$

The expression $\frac{2z + 7}{\sqrt{z + 1}}$ defines a function g that can be denoted by

$$g(z) = \frac{2z + 7}{\sqrt{z + 1}}.$$

The symbols "$f(x)$" or "$g(z)$" do not represent products; each is merely the symbol for an expression, and is read "f of x" or "g of z."

Function notation provides a short way of writing the result of substituting a value for a variable. If $x = 1$ is substituted in the first expression, the result can be written $f(1) = -2$, and $f(1)$ is called the "value of f at $x = 1$." Similarly, if $z = 0$ is substituted in the second expression, then the value of g at $z = 0$ is $g(0) = 7$.

Once a function $f(x)$ is defined, it is useful to think of the variable x as an input and $f(x)$ as the corresponding output. In any function there can be no more than one output for any given input. However, more than one input can give the same output; for example, if $h(x) = |x + 3|$, then $h(-4) = 1 = h(-2)$.

The set of all allowable inputs for a function is called the *domain* of the function. For f and g defined above, the domain of f is the set of all real numbers and the domain of g is the set of all numbers greater than −1. The domain of any function can be arbitrarily specified, as in the function defined by "$h(x) = 9x - 5$ for $0 \le x \le 10$." Without such a restriction, the domain is assumed to be all values of x that result in a real number when substituted into the function.

The domain of a function can consist of only the positive integers and possibly 0. For example,

$$a(n) = n^2 + \frac{n}{5} \text{ for } n = 0,\ 1,\ 2,\ 3,\ \dots .$$

Such a function is called a *sequence* and $a(n)$ is denoted by a_n. The value of the sequence a_n at $n = 3$ is $a_3 = 3^2 + \frac{3}{5} = 9.60$. As another example, consider the sequence defined by $b_n = (-1)^n (n!)$ for $n = 1,\ 2,\ 3,\ \dots .$ A sequence like this is often indicated by listing its values in the order $b_1,\ b_2,\ b_3,\ \dots,\ b_n,\ \dots$ as follows:

$-1, 2, -6, \dots, (-1)^n(n!), \dots$, and $(-1)^n(n!)$ is called the nth term of the sequence.

4.3 Geometry

1. Lines

In geometry, the word "line" refers to a straight line that extends without end in both directions.

$$\overline{\underset{P}{\bullet} \qquad \underset{Q}{\bullet}}\ \ell$$

The line above can be referred to as line PQ or line ℓ. The part of the line from P to Q is called a *line segment*. P and Q are the *endpoints* of the segment. The notation $\overline{PQ}$ is used to denote line segment PQ and PQ is used to denote the length of the segment.

2. Intersecting Lines and Angles

If two lines intersect, the opposite angles are called *vertical angles* and have the same measure. In the figure

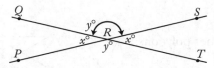

$\angle PRQ$ and $\angle SRT$ are vertical angles and $\angle QRS$ and $\angle PRT$ are vertical angles. Also, $x + y = 180°$ since PRS is a straight line.

3. Perpendicular Lines

An angle that has a measure of 90° is a *right angle*. If two lines intersect at right angles, the lines are *perpendicular*. For example:

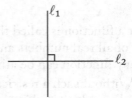

ℓ_1 and ℓ_2 above are perpendicular, denoted by $\ell_1 \perp \ell_2$. A right angle symbol in an angle of intersection indicates that the lines are perpendicular.

4. Parallel Lines

If two lines that are in the same plane do not intersect, the two lines are *parallel*. In the figure

lines ℓ_1 and ℓ_2 are parallel, denoted by $\ell_1 \parallel \ell_2$. If two parallel lines are intersected by a third line, as shown below, then the angle measures are related as indicated, where $x + y = 180°$.

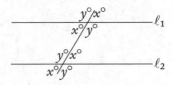

5. Polygons (Convex)

A *polygon* is a closed plane figure formed by three or more line segments, called the *sides* of the polygon. Each side intersects exactly two other sides at their endpoints. The points of intersection of the sides are *vertices*. The term "polygon" will be used to mean a convex polygon, that is, a polygon in which each interior angle has a measure of less than 180°.

The following figures are polygons:

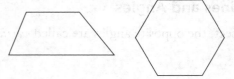

The following figures are not polygons:

A polygon with three sides is a *triangle*; with four sides, a *quadrilateral*; with five sides, a *pentagon*; and with six sides, a *hexagon*.

The sum of the interior angle measures of a triangle is 180°. In general, the sum of the interior angle measures of a polygon with n sides is equal to $(n-2)180°$. For example, this sum for a pentagon is $(5-2)180° = (3)180° = 540°$.

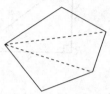

Note that a pentagon can be partitioned into three triangles and therefore the sum of the angle measures can be found by adding the sum of the angle measures of three triangles.

The *perimeter* of a polygon is the sum of the lengths of its sides.

The commonly used phrase "area of a triangle" (or any other plane figure) is used to mean the area of the region enclosed by that figure.

6. Triangles

There are several special types of triangles with important properties. But one property that all triangles share is that the sum of the lengths of any two of the sides is greater than the length of the third side, as illustrated below.

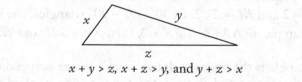

$x + y > z$, $x + z > y$, and $y + z > x$

An *equilateral* triangle has all sides of equal length. All angles of an equilateral triangle have equal measure. An *isosceles* triangle has at least two sides of the same length. If two sides of a triangle have the same length, then the two angles opposite those sides have the same measure. Conversely, if two angles of a triangle have the same measure, then the sides opposite those angles have the same length. In isosceles triangle *PQR* below, $x = y$ since $PQ = QR$.

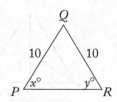

A triangle that has a right angle is a *right* triangle. In a right triangle, the side opposite the right angle is the *hypotenuse*, and the other two sides are the *legs*. An important theorem concerning right triangles is the *Pythagorean theorem*, which states: In a right triangle, the square of the length of the hypotenuse is equal to the sum of the squares of the lengths of the legs.

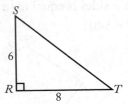

In the figure above, $\triangle RST$ is a right triangle, so $\left(RS\right)^2 + \left(RT\right)^2 = \left(ST\right)^2$. Here, $RS = 6$ and $RT = 8$, so $ST = 10$, since $6^2 + 8^2 = 36 + 64 = 100 = \left(ST\right)^2$ and $ST = \sqrt{100}$. Any triangle in which the lengths of the sides are in the ratio 3:4:5 is a right triangle. In general, if a, b, and c are the lengths of the sides of a triangle and $a^2 + b^2 = c^2$, then the triangle is a right triangle.

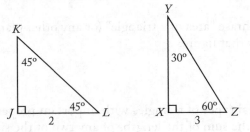

In $45°\text{–}45°\text{–}90°$ triangles, the lengths of the sides are in the ratio $1\text{:}1\text{:}\sqrt{2}$. For example, in $\triangle JKL$, if $JL = 2$, then $JK = 2$ and $KL = 2\sqrt{2}$. In $30°\text{–}60°\text{–}90°$ triangles, the lengths of the sides are in the ratio $1\text{:}\sqrt{3}\text{:}2$. For example, in $\triangle XYZ$, if $XZ = 3$, then $XY = 3\sqrt{3}$ and $YZ = 6$.

The *altitude* of a triangle is the segment drawn from a vertex perpendicular to the side opposite that vertex. Relative to that vertex and altitude, the opposite side is called the *base*.

The area of a triangle is equal to:

$$\frac{\left(\text{the length of the altitude}\right) \times \left(\text{the length of the base}\right)}{2}$$

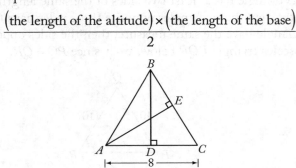

In $\triangle ABC$, $\overline{BD}$ is the altitude to base $\overline{AC}$ and $\overline{AE}$ is the altitude to base $\overline{BC}$. The area of $\triangle ABC$ is equal to

$$\frac{BD \times AC}{2} = \frac{5 \times 8}{2} = 20.$$

The area is also equal to $\dfrac{AE \times BC}{2}$. If $\triangle ABC$ above is isosceles and $AB = BC$, then altitude $\overline{BD}$ bisects the base; that is, $AD = DC = 4$. Similarly, any altitude of an equilateral triangle bisects the side to which it is drawn.

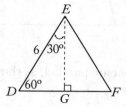

In equilateral triangle DEF, if $DE = 6$, then $DG = 3$ and $EG = 3\sqrt{3}$. The area of $\triangle DEF$ is equal to $\dfrac{3\sqrt{3} \times 6}{2} = 9\sqrt{3}$.

7. Quadrilaterals

A polygon with four sides is a *quadrilateral*. A quadrilateral in which both pairs of opposite sides are parallel is a *parallelogram*. The opposite sides of a parallelogram also have equal length.

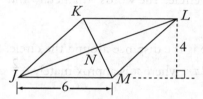

In parallelogram $JKLM$, $\overline{JK} \parallel \overline{LM}$ and $JK = LM$; $\overline{KL} \parallel \overline{JM}$ and $KL = JM$.

The diagonals of a parallelogram bisect each other (that is, $KN = NM$ and $JN = NL$).

The area of a parallelogram is equal to

$$\left(\text{the length of the altitude}\right) \times \left(\text{the length of the base}\right).$$

The area of $JKLM$ is equal to $4 \times 6 = 24$.

A parallelogram with right angles is a *rectangle*, and a rectangle with all sides of equal length is a *square*.

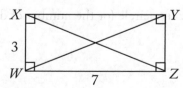

The perimeter of $WXYZ = 2(3) + 2(7) = 20$ and the area of $WXYZ$ is equal to $3 \times 7 = 21$.

The diagonals of a rectangle are equal; therefore $WY = XZ = \sqrt{9 + 49} = \sqrt{58}$.

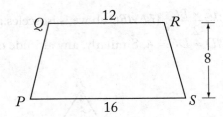

A quadrilateral with two sides that are parallel, as shown above, is a *trapezoid*. The area of trapezoid *PQRS* may be calculated as follows:

$$\frac{1}{2}(\text{the sum of the lengths of the bases})(\text{the height}) = \frac{1}{2}(QR + PS)(8) = \frac{1}{2}(28 \times 8) = 112.$$

8. Circles

A *circle* is a set of points in a plane that are all located the same distance from a fixed point (the *center* of the circle).

A *chord* of a circle is a line segment that has its endpoints on the circle. A chord that passes through the center of the circle is a *diameter* of the circle. A *radius* of a circle is a segment from the center of the circle to a point on the circle. The words "diameter" and "radius" are also used to refer to the lengths of these segments.

The *circumference* of a circle is the distance around the circle. If r is the radius of the circle, then the circumference is equal to $2\pi r$, where π is approximately $\frac{22}{7}$ or 3.14. The *area* of a circle of radius r is equal to πr^2.

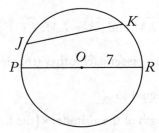

In the circle above, O is the center of the circle and $\overline{JK}$ and $\overline{PR}$ are chords. $\overline{PR}$ is a diameter and $\overline{OR}$ is a radius. If $OR = 7$, then the circumference of the circle is $2\pi(7) = 14\pi$ and the area of the circle is $\pi(7)^2 = 49\pi$.

The number of degrees of arc in a circle (or the number of degrees in a complete revolution) is 360.

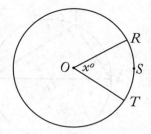

In the circle with center O above, the length of arc RST is $\frac{x}{360}$ of the circumference of the circle; for example, if $x = 60$, then arc RST has length $\frac{1}{6}$ of the circumference of the circle.

A line that has exactly one point in common with a circle is said to be *tangent* to the circle, and that common point is called the *point of tangency*. A radius or diameter with an endpoint at the point of tangency is perpendicular to the tangent line, and, conversely, a line that is perpendicular to a radius or diameter at one of its endpoints is tangent to the circle at that endpoint.

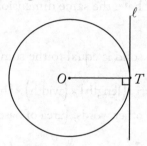

The line ℓ above is tangent to the circle and radius $\overline{OT}$ is perpendicular to ℓ.

If each vertex of a polygon lies on a circle, then the polygon is *inscribed* in the circle and the circle is *circumscribed* about the polygon. If each side of a polygon is tangent to a circle, then the polygon is *circumscribed* about the circle and the circle is *inscribed* in the polygon.

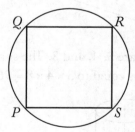 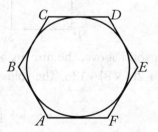

In the figure above, quadrilateral $PQRS$ is inscribed in a circle and hexagon $ABCDEF$ is circumscribed about a circle.

If a triangle is inscribed in a circle so that one of its sides is a diameter of the circle, then the triangle is a right triangle.

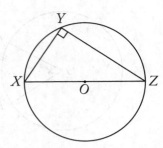

In the circle above, $\overline{XZ}$ is a diameter and the measure of $\angle XYZ$ is $90°$.

9. Rectangular Solids and Cylinders

A *rectangular solid* is a three-dimensional figure formed by 6 rectangular surfaces, as shown below. Each rectangular surface is a *face*. Each solid or dotted line segment is an *edge*, and each point at which the edges meet is a *vertex*. A rectangular solid has 6 faces, 12 edges, and 8 vertices. Opposite faces are parallel rectangles that have the same dimensions. A rectangular solid in which all edges are of equal length is a *cube*.

The *surface area* of a rectangular solid is equal to the sum of the areas of all the faces. The *volume* is equal to

$$(\text{length}) \times (\text{width}) \times (\text{height});$$

in other words, $(\text{area of base}) \times (\text{height}).$

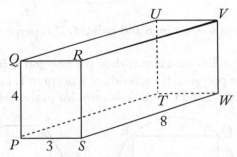

In the rectangular solid above, the dimensions are 3, 4, and 8. The surface area is equal to $2(3 \times 4) + 2(3 \times 8) + 2(4 \times 8) = 136$. The volume is equal to $3 \times 4 \times 8 = 96$.

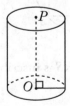

The figure above is a right circular *cylinder*. The two bases are circles of the same size with centers O and P, respectively, and altitude (height) $\overline{OP}$ is perpendicular to the bases. The surface area of a right circular cylinder with a base of radius r and height h is equal to $2(\pi r^2) + 2\pi rh$ (the sum of the areas of the two bases plus the area of the curved surface).

The volume of a cylinder is equal to $\pi r^2 h$, that is,

$$(\text{area of base}) \times (\text{height}).$$

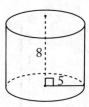

In the cylinder above, the surface area is equal to

$$2(25\pi) + 2\pi(5)(8) = 130\pi,$$

and the volume is equal to

$$25\pi(8) = 200\pi.$$

10. Coordinate Geometry

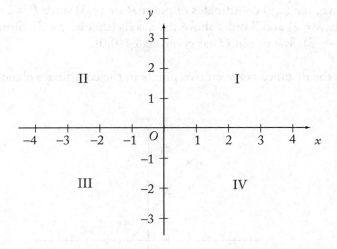

The figure above shows the (rectangular) *coordinate plane*. The horizontal line is called the *x-axis* and the perpendicular vertical line is called the *y-axis*. The point at which these two axes intersect, designated *O*, is called the *origin*. The axes divide the plane into four quadrants, I, II, III, and IV, as shown.

Each point in the plane has an *x-coordinate* and a *y-coordinate*. A point is identified by an ordered pair (x,y) of numbers in which the *x*-coordinate is the first number and the *y*-coordinate is the second number.

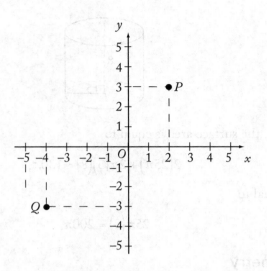

In the graph above, the (x,y) coordinates of point P are $(2,3)$ since P is 2 units to the right of the y-axis (that is, $x = 2$) and 3 units above the x-axis (that is, $y = 3$). Similarly, the (x,y) coordinates of point Q are $(-4,-3)$. The origin O has coordinates $(0,0)$.

One way to find the distance between two points in the coordinate plane is to use the Pythagorean theorem.

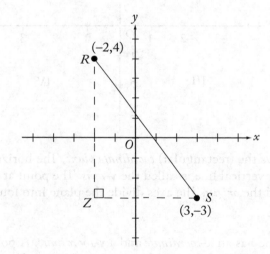

To find the distance between points R and S using the Pythagorean theorem, draw the triangle as shown. Note that Z has (x,y) coordinates $(-2,-3)$, $RZ = 7$, and $ZS = 5$. Therefore, the distance between R and S is equal to

$$\sqrt{7^2 + 5^2} = \sqrt{74}.$$

For a line in the coordinate plane, the coordinates of each point on the line satisfy a linear equation of the form $y = mx + b$ (or the form $x = a$ if the line is vertical). For example, each point on the line on the next page satisfies the equation $y = -\dfrac{1}{2}x + 1$. One can verify this for the points $(-2,2)$, $(2,0)$, and $(0,1)$ by substituting the respective coordinates for x and y in the equation.

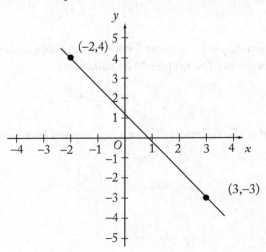

In the equation $y = mx + b$ of a line, the coefficient m is the *slope* of the line and the constant term b is the *y-intercept* of the line. For any two points on the line, the slope is defined to be the ratio of the difference in the y-coordinates to the difference in the x-coordinates. Using $(-2, 2)$ and $(2, 0)$ above, the slope is

$$\frac{\text{The difference in the } y\text{-coordinates}}{\text{The difference in the } x\text{-coordinates}} = \frac{0 - 2}{2 - (-2)} = \frac{-2}{4} = -\frac{1}{2}.$$

The y-intercept is the y-coordinate of the point at which the line intersects the y-axis. For the line above, the y-intercept is 1, and this is the resulting value of y when x is set equal to 0 in the equation $y = -\frac{1}{2}x + 1$. The *x-intercept* is the x-coordinate of the point at which the line intersects the x-axis. The x-intercept can be found by setting $y = 0$ and solving for x. For the line $y = -\frac{1}{2}x + 1$, this gives

$$-\frac{1}{2}x + 1 = 0$$

$$-\frac{1}{2}x = -1$$

$$x = 2$$

Thus, the x-intercept is 2.

Given any two points (x_1, y_1) and (x_2, y_2) with $x_1 \neq x_2$, the equation of the line passing through these points can be found by applying the definition of slope. Since the slope is $m = \frac{y_2 - y_1}{x_2 - x_1}$, then using a point known to be on the line, say (x_1, y_1), any point (x, y) on the line must satisfy $\frac{y - y_1}{x - x_1} = m$, or $y - y_1 = m(x - x_1)$. (Using (x_2, y_2) as the known point would yield an equivalent equation.) For example, consider the points $(-2, 4)$ and $(3, -3)$ on the line below.

The slope of this line is $\dfrac{-3-4}{3-(-2)} = \dfrac{-7}{5}$, so an equation of this line can be found using the point $(3,-3)$ as follows:

$$y - \left(-3\right) = -\frac{7}{5}\left(x - 3\right)$$

$$y + 3 = -\frac{7}{5}x + \frac{21}{5}$$

$$y = -\frac{7}{5}x + \frac{6}{5}$$

The y-intercept is $\dfrac{6}{5}$. The *x-intercept* can be found as follows:

$$0 = -\frac{7}{5}x + \frac{6}{5}$$

$$\frac{7}{5}x = \frac{6}{5}$$

$$x = \frac{6}{7}$$

Both of these intercepts can be seen on the graph.

If the slope of a line is negative, the line slants downward from left to right; if the slope is positive, the line slants upward. If the slope is 0, the line is horizontal; the equation of such a line is of the form $y = b$ since $m = 0$. For a vertical line, slope is not defined, and the equation is of the form $x = a$, where a is the x-intercept.

There is a connection between graphs of lines in the coordinate plane and solutions of two linear equations with two unknowns. If two linear equations with unknowns x and y have a unique solution, then the graphs of the equations are two lines that intersect in one point, which is the solution. If the equations are equivalent, then they represent the same line with infinitely many points or solutions. If the equations have no solution, then they represent parallel lines, which do not intersect.

There is also a connection between functions (see section 4.2.10) and the coordinate plane. If a function is graphed in the coordinate plane, the function can be understood in different and useful ways. Consider the function defined by

$$f\left(x\right) = -\frac{7}{5}x + \frac{6}{5}.$$

If the value of the function, $f(x)$, is equated with the variable y, then the graph of the function in the xy-coordinate plane is simply the graph of the equation

$$y = -\frac{7}{5}x + \frac{6}{5}$$

shown above. Similarly, any function $f(x)$ can be graphed by equating y with the value of the function:

$$y = f\left(x\right).$$

So for any x in the domain of the function f, the point with coordinates $(x, f(x))$ is on the graph of f, and the graph consists entirely of these points.

As another example, consider a quadratic polynomial function defined by $f(x) = x^2 - 1$. One can plot several points $(x, f(x))$ on the graph to understand the connection between a function and its graph:

x	$f(x)$
-2	3
-1	0
0	-1
1	0
2	3

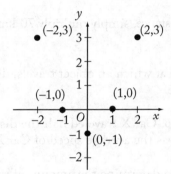

If all the points were graphed for $-2 \le x \le 2$, then the graph would appear as follows.

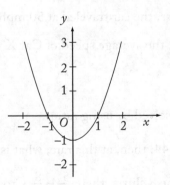

The graph of a quadratic function is called a *parabola* and always has the shape of the curve above, although it may be upside down or have a greater or lesser width. Note that the roots of the equation $f(x) = x^2 - 1 = 0$ are $x = 1$ and $x = -1$; these coincide with the x-intercepts since x-intercepts are found by setting $y = 0$ and solving for x. Also, the y-intercept is $f(0) = -1$ because this is the value of y corresponding to $x = 0$. For any function f, the x-intercepts are the solutions of the equation $f(x) = 0$ and the y-intercept is the value $f(0)$.

4.4 Word Problems

Many of the principles discussed in this chapter are used to solve word problems. The following discussion of word problems illustrates some of the techniques and concepts used in solving such problems.

1. Rate Problems

The distance that an object travels is equal to the product of the average speed at which it travels and the amount of time it takes to travel that distance, that is,

$$\text{Rate} \times \text{Time} = \text{Distance.}$$

Example 1: If a car travels at an average speed of 70 kilometers per hour for 4 hours, how many kilometers does it travel?

Solution: Since rate × time = distance, simply multiply 70 km/hour × 4 hours. Thus, the car travels 280 kilometers in 4 hours.

To determine the average rate at which an object travels, divide the total distance traveled by the total amount of traveling time.

Example 2: On a 400-mile trip, Car X traveled half the distance at 40 miles per hour (mph) and the other half at 50 mph. What was the average speed of Car X ?

Solution: First it is necessary to determine the amount of traveling time. During the first 200 miles, the car traveled at 40 mph; therefore, it took $\frac{200}{40} = 5$ hours to travel the first 200 miles. During the second 200 miles, the car traveled at 50 mph; therefore, it took $\frac{200}{50} = 4$ hours to travel the second 200 miles. Thus, the average speed of Car X was $\frac{400}{9} = 44\frac{4}{9}$ mph. Note that the average speed is *not* $\frac{40 + 50}{2} = 45$.

Some rate problems can be solved by using ratios.

Example 3: If 5 shirts cost $44, then, at this rate, what is the cost of 8 shirts?

Solution: If c is the cost of the 8 shirts, then $\frac{5}{44} = \frac{8}{c}$. Cross multiplication results in the equation

$$5c = 8 \times 44 = 352$$
$$c = \frac{352}{5} = 70.40$$

The 8 shirts cost $70.40.

2. Work Problems

In a work problem, the rates at which certain persons or machines work alone are usually given, and it is necessary to compute the rate at which they work together (or vice versa).

The basic formula for solving work problems is $\frac{1}{r} + \frac{1}{s} = \frac{1}{h}$, where r and s are, for example, the number of hours it takes Rae and Sam, respectively, to complete a job when working alone, and h is the number of hours it takes Rae and Sam to do the job when working together. The reasoning is that in 1 hour Rae does $\frac{1}{r}$ of the job, Sam does $\frac{1}{s}$ of the job, and Rae and Sam together do $\frac{1}{h}$ of the job.

Example 1: If Machine X can produce 1,000 bolts in 4 hours and Machine Y can produce 1,000 bolts in 5 hours, in how many hours can Machines X and Y, working together at these constant rates, produce 1,000 bolts?

Solution:

$$\frac{1}{4} + \frac{1}{5} = \frac{1}{h}$$
$$\frac{5}{20} + \frac{4}{20} = \frac{1}{h}$$
$$\frac{9}{20} = \frac{1}{h}$$
$$9h = 20$$
$$h = \frac{20}{9} = 2\frac{2}{9}$$

Working together, Machines X and Y can produce 1,000 bolts in $2\frac{2}{9}$ hours.

Example 2: If Art and Rita can do a job in 4 hours when working together at their respective constant rates and Art can do the job alone in 6 hours, in how many hours can Rita do the job alone?

Solution:

$$\frac{1}{6} + \frac{1}{R} = \frac{1}{4}$$
$$\frac{R+6}{6R} = \frac{1}{4}$$
$$4R + 24 = 6R$$
$$24 = 2R$$
$$12 = R$$

Working alone, Rita can do the job in 12 hours.

3. Mixture Problems

In mixture problems, substances with different characteristics are combined, and it is necessary to determine the characteristics of the resulting mixture.

Example 1: If 6 pounds of nuts that cost $1.20 per pound are mixed with 2 pounds of nuts that cost $1.60 per pound, what is the cost per pound of the mixture?

Solution: The total cost of the 8 pounds of nuts is

$$6(\$1.20) + 2(\$1.60) = \$10.40.$$

The cost per pound is
$$\frac{\$10.40}{8} = \$1.30.$$

Example 2: How many liters of a solution that is 15 percent salt must be added to 5 liters of a solution that is 8 percent salt so that the resulting solution is 10 percent salt?

Solution: Let n represent the number of liters of the 15% solution. The amount of salt in the 15% solution [$0.15n$] plus the amount of salt in the 8% solution [$(0.08)(5)$] must be equal to the amount of salt in the 10% mixture $\left[0.10(n+5)\right]$. Therefore,

$$0.15n + 0.08(5) = 0.10(n+5)$$
$$15n + 40 = 10n + 50$$
$$5n = 10$$
$$n = 2 \text{ liters}$$

Two liters of the 15% salt solution must be added to the 8% solution to obtain the 10% solution.

4. Interest Problems

Interest can be computed in two basic ways. With simple annual interest, the interest is computed on the principal only and is equal to $(\text{principal}) \times (\text{interest rate}) \times (\text{time})$. If interest is compounded, then interest is computed on the principal as well as on any interest already earned.

Example 1: If $8,000 is invested at 6 percent simple annual interest, how much interest is earned after 3 months?

Solution: Since the annual interest rate is 6%, the interest for 1 year is

$$(0.06)(\$8,000) = \$480.$$

The interest earned in 3 months is
$$\frac{3}{12}(\$480) = \$120.$$

Example 2: If $10,000 is invested at 10 percent annual interest, compounded semiannually, what is the balance after 1 year?

Solution: The balance after the first 6 months would be

$$10,000 + (10,000)(0.05) = \$10,500.$$

The balance after one year would be $10,500 + (10,500)(0.05) = \$11,025.$

Note that the interest rate for each 6-month period is 5%, which is half of the 10% annual rate. The balance after one year can also be expressed as

$$10{,}000\left(1 + \frac{0.10}{2}\right)^{2} \text{ dollars.}$$

5. Discount

If a price is discounted by n percent, then the price becomes $(100 - n)$ percent of the original price.

Example 1: A certain customer paid \$24 for a dress. If that price represented a 25 percent discount on the original price of the dress, what was the original price of the dress?

Solution: If p is the original price of the dress, then $0.75p$ is the discounted price and $0.75\,p = \$24$, or $p = \$32$. The original price of the dress was \$32.

Example 2: The price of an item is discounted by 20 percent and then this reduced price is discounted by an additional 30 percent. These two discounts are equal to an overall discount of what percent?

Solution: If p is the original price of the item, then $0.8p$ is the price after the first discount. The price after the second discount is $(0.7)(0.8\,p) = 0.56\,p$. This represents an overall discount of 44 percent $(100\% - 56\%)$.

6. Profit

Gross profit is equal to revenues minus expenses, or selling price minus cost.

Example: A certain appliance costs a merchant \$30. At what price should the merchant sell the appliance in order to make a gross profit of 50 percent of the cost of the appliance?

Solution: If s is the selling price of the appliance, then $s - 30 = (0.5)(30)$, or $s = \$45$. The merchant should sell the appliance for \$45.

7. Sets

If S is the set of numbers 1, 2, 3, and 4, you can write $S = \{1,\ 2,\ 3,\ 4\}$. Sets can also be represented by Venn diagrams. That is, the relationship among the members of sets can be represented by circles.

Example 1: Each of 25 people is enrolled in history, mathematics, or both. If 20 are enrolled in history and 18 are enrolled in mathematics, how many are enrolled in both history and mathematics?

Solution: The 25 people can be divided into three sets: those who study history only, those who study mathematics only, and those who study history and mathematics. Thus a Venn diagram may be drawn as follows, where n is the number of people enrolled in both courses, $20 - n$ is the number enrolled in history only, and $18 - n$ is the number enrolled in mathematics only.

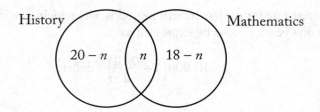

Since there is a total of 25 people, $(20 - n) + n + (18 - n) = 25$, or $n = 13$. Thirteen people are enrolled in both history and mathematics. Note that $20 + 18 - 13 = 25$, which is the general addition rule for two sets (see section 4.1.9).

Example 2: In a certain production lot, 40 percent of the toys are red and the remaining toys are green. Half of the toys are small and half are large. If 10 percent of the toys are red and small, and 40 toys are green and large, how many of the toys are red and large.

Solution: For this kind of problem, it is helpful to organize the information in a table:

	Red	Green	Total
Small	10%		50%
Large			50%
Total	40%	60%	100%

The numbers in the table are the percentages given. The following percentages can be computed on the basis of what is given:

	Red	Green	Total
Small	10%	40%	50%
Large	30%	20%	50%
Total	40%	60%	100%

Since 20% of the number of toys (n) are green and large, $0.20n = 40$ (40 toys are green and large), or $n = 200$. Therefore, 30% of the 200 toys, or $(0.3)(200) = 60$, are red and large.

8. Geometry Problems

The following is an example of a word problem involving geometry.
Example:

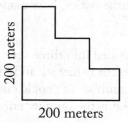

The figure above shows an aerial view of a piece of land. If all angles shown are right angles, what is the perimeter of the piece of land?

Solution: For reference, label the figure as

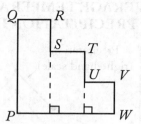

If all the angles are right angles, then $QR + ST + UV = PW$, and $RS + TU + VW = PQ$. Hence, the perimeter of the land is $2PW + 2PQ = 2 \times 200 + 2 \times 200 = 800$ meters.

9. Measurement Problems

Some questions on the GMAT involve metric units of measure, whereas others involve English units of measure. However, except for units of time, if a question requires conversion from one unit of measure to another, the relationship between those units will be given.

Example: A train travels at a constant rate of 25 meters per second. How many kilometers does it travel in 5 minutes? $\left(1 \text{ kilometer} = 1,000 \text{ meters}\right)$

Solution: In 1 minute the train travels $(25)(60) = 1,500$ meters, so in 5 minutes it travels 7,500 meters. Since 1 kilometer = 1,000 meters, it follows that 7,500 meters equals $\dfrac{7,500}{1,000}$, or 7.5 kilometers.

10. Data Interpretation

Occasionally a question or set of questions will be based on data provided in a table or graph. Some examples of tables and graphs are given below.

Example 1:

Population by Age Group	
(in thousands)	
Age	Population
17 years and under	63,376
18–44 years	86,738
45–64 years	43,845
65 years and over	24,054

How many people are 44 years old or younger?

Solution: The figures in the table are given in thousands. The answer in thousands can be obtained by adding 63,376 thousand and 86,738 thousand. The result is 150,114 thousand, which is 150,114,000.

Example 2:

AVERAGE TEMPERATURE AND PRECIPITATION IN CITY X

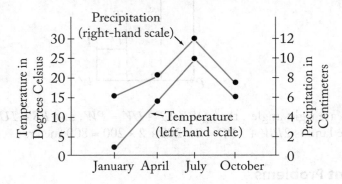

What are the average temperature and precipitation in City X during April?

Solution: Note that the scale on the left applies to the temperature line graph and the one on the right applies to the precipitation line graph. According to the graph, during April the average temperature is approximately 14° Celsius and the average precipitation is approximately 8 centimeters.

Example 3:

DISTRIBUTION OF AL'S WEEKLY NET SALARY

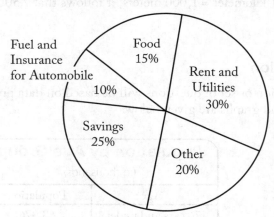

Al's weekly net salary is $350. To how many of the categories listed was at least $80 of Al's weekly net salary allocated?

Solution: In the circle graph, the relative sizes of the sectors are proportional to their corresponding values and the sum of the percents given is 100%. Note that $\frac{80}{350}$ is approximately 23%, so at least $80 was allocated to each of 2 categories—Rent and Utilities, and Savings—since their allocations are each greater than 23%.

5.0 Problem Solving

5.0 Problem Solving

The Quantitative section of the GMAT® exam uses problem solving and data sufficiency questions to gauge your skill level. This chapter focuses on problem solving questions. Remember that quantitative questions require knowledge of the following:

- Arithmetic
- Elementary algebra
- Commonly known concepts of geometry

Problem solving questions are designed to test your basic mathematical skills and understanding of elementary mathematical concepts, as well as your ability to reason quantitatively, solve quantitative problems, and interpret graphic data. The mathematics knowledge required to answer the questions is no more advanced than what is generally taught in secondary school (or high school) mathematics classes.

In these questions, you are asked to solve each problem and select the best of the five answer choices given. Begin by reading the question thoroughly to determine exactly what information is given and to make sure you understand what is being asked. Scan the answer choices to understand your options. If the problem seems simple, take a few moments to see whether you can determine the answer. Then check your answer against the choices provided.

If you do not see your answer among the choices, or if the problem is complicated, take a closer look at the answer choices and think again about what the problem is asking. See whether you can eliminate some of the answer choices and narrow down your options. If you are still unable to narrow the answer down to a single choice, reread the question. Keep in mind that the answer will be based solely on the information provided in the question—don't allow your own experience and assumptions to interfere with your ability to find the correct answer to the question.

If you find yourself stuck on a question or unable to select the single correct answer, keep in mind that you have about two minutes to answer each quantitative question. You may run out of time if you take too long to answer any one question, so you may simply need to pick the answer that seems to make the most sense. Although guessing is generally not the best way to achieve a high GMAT score, making an educated guess is a good strategy for answering questions you are unsure of. Even if your answer to a particular question is incorrect, your answers to other questions will allow the test to accurately gauge your ability level.

The following pages include test-taking strategies, directions that will apply to questions of this type, sample questions, an answer key, and explanations for all the problems. These explanations present problem solving strategies that could be helpful in answering the questions.

5.1 Test-Taking Strategies

1.   Pace yourself.

Consult the on-screen timer periodically. Work as carefully as possible, but do not spend valuable time checking answers or pondering problems that you find difficult.

2.   Use the erasable notepad provided.

Working a problem out may help you avoid errors in solving the problem. If diagrams or figures are not presented, it may help if you draw your own.

3.   Read each question carefully to determine what is being asked.

For word problems, take one step at a time, reading each sentence carefully and translating the information into equations or other useful mathematical representations.

4.   Scan the answer choices before attempting to answer a question.

Scanning the answers can prevent you from putting answers in a form that is not given (e.g., finding the answer in decimal form, such as 0.25, when the choices are given in fractional form, such as $\frac{1}{4}$). Also, if the question requires approximations, a shortcut could serve well (e.g., you may be able to approximate 48 percent of a number by using half).

5.   Don't waste time trying to solve a problem that is too difficult for you.

Make your best guess and move on to the next question.

5.2 The Directions

These directions are very similar to those you will see for problem solving questions when you take the GMAT exam. If you read them carefully and understand them clearly before sitting for the GMAT exam, you will not need to spend too much time reviewing them once the test begins.

Solve the problem and indicate the best of the answer choices given.

Numbers: All numbers used are real numbers.

Figures: A figure accompanying a problem solving question is intended to provide information useful in solving the problem. Figures are drawn as accurately as possible. Exceptions will be clearly noted. Lines shown as straight are straight, and lines that appear jagged are also straight. The positions of points, angles, regions, etc., exist in the order shown, and angle measures are greater than zero. All figures lie in a plane unless otherwise indicated.

5.3 Practice Questions

Solve the problem and indicate the best of the answer choices given.

Numbers: All numbers used are real numbers.

Figures: A figure accompanying a problem solving question is intended to provide information useful in solving the problem. Figures are drawn as accurately as possible. Exceptions will be clearly noted. Lines shown as straight are straight, and lines that appear jagged are also straight. The positions of points, angles, regions, etc., exist in the order shown, and angle measures are greater than zero. All figures lie in a plane unless otherwise indicated.

1. A project scheduled to be carried out over a single fiscal year has a budget of $12,600, divided into 12 equal monthly allocations. At the end of the fourth month of that fiscal year, the total amount actually spent on the project was $4,580. By how much was the project over its budget?

   (A) $ 380
   (B) $ 540
   (C) $1,050
   (D) $1,380
   (E) $1,430

2. For which of the following values of n is $\dfrac{100+n}{n}$ NOT an integer?

   (A)   1
   (B)   2
   (C)   3
   (D)   4
   (E)   5

3. Rectangular Floors X and Y have equal area. If Floor X is 12 feet by 18 feet and Floor Y is 9 feet wide, what is the length of Floor Y, in feet?

   (A) $13\frac{1}{2}$
   (B)   18
   (C) $18\frac{3}{4}$
   (D)   21
   (E)   24

4. A case contains c cartons. Each carton contains b boxes, and each box contains 100 paper clips. How many paper clips are contained in 2 cases?

   (A) $100bc$
   (B) $\dfrac{100b}{c}$
   (C) $200bc$
   (D) $\dfrac{200b}{c}$
   (E) $\dfrac{200}{bc}$

5. The sum of prime numbers that are greater than 60 but less than 70 is

   (A)   67
   (B)   128
   (C)   191
   (D)   197
   (E)   260

6. A rainstorm increased the amount of water stored in State J reservoirs from 124 billion gallons to 138 billion gallons. If the storm increased the amount of water in the reservoirs to 82 percent of total capacity, approximately how many billion gallons of water were the reservoirs short of total capacity prior to the storm?

   (A)   9
   (B)   14
   (C)   25
   (D)   30
   (E)   44

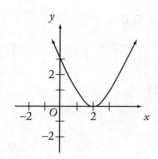

7. On the graph above, when $x = \frac{1}{2}$, $y = 2$; and when $x = 1$, $y = 1$. The graph is symmetric with respect to the vertical line at $x = 2$. According to the graph, when $x = 3$, $y =$

    (A)   −1
    (B) $-\frac{1}{2}$
    (C)   0
    (D) $\frac{1}{2}$
    (E)   1

8. When $\frac{1}{10}$ percent of 5,000 is subtracted from $\frac{1}{10}$ of 5,000, the difference is

    (A)   0
    (B)   50
    (C)   450
    (D)   495
    (E)   500

9. Which of the following is the value of $\sqrt{\sqrt[3]{0.000064}}$?

    (A)   0.004
    (B)   0.008
    (C)   0.02
    (D)   0.04
    (E)   0.2

10. Raffle tickets numbered consecutively from 101 through 350 are placed in a box. What is the probability that a ticket selected at random will have a number with a hundreds digit of 2 ?

    (A) $\frac{2}{5}$
    (B) $\frac{2}{7}$
    (C) $\frac{33}{83}$
    (D) $\frac{99}{250}$
    (E) $\frac{100}{249}$

11. When Leo imported a certain item, he paid a 7 percent import tax on the portion of the total value of the item in excess of $1,000. If the amount of the import tax that Leo paid was $87.50, what was the total value of the item?

    (A) $1,600
    (B) $1,850
    (C) $2,250
    (D) $2,400
    (E) $2,750

12. The numbers of cars sold at a certain dealership on six of the last seven business days were 4, 7, 2, 8, 3, and 6, respectively. If the number of cars sold on the seventh business day was either 2, 4, or 5, for which of the three values does the average (arithmetic mean) number of cars sold per business day for the seven business days equal the median number of cars sold per day for the seven days?

    I.   2
    II.   4
    III. 5

    (A)   II only
    (B)   III only
    (C)   I and II only
    (D)   II and III only
    (E)   I, II, and III

13. A rectangular garden is to be twice as long as it is wide. If 360 yards of fencing, including the gate, will completely enclose the garden, what will be the length of the garden, in yards?

   (A) 120
   (B) 140
   (C) 160
   (D) 180
   (E) 200

14. If $\left| y - \frac{1}{2} \right| < \frac{11}{2}$, which of the following could be a value of y ?

   (A) -11
   (B) $-\frac{11}{2}$
   (C) $\frac{11}{2}$
   (D) 11
   (E) 22

15. At a supermarket, John spent $\frac{1}{2}$ of his money on fresh fruits and vegetables, $\frac{1}{3}$ on meat products, and $\frac{1}{10}$ on bakery products. If he spent the remaining $6 on candy, how much did John spend at the supermarket?

   (A) $60
   (B) $80
   (C) $90
   (D) $120
   (E) $180

16. On Monday, a person mailed 8 packages weighing an average (arithmetic mean) of $12\frac{3}{8}$ pounds, and on Tuesday, 4 packages weighing an average of $15\frac{1}{4}$ pounds. What was the average weight, in pounds, of all the packages the person mailed on both days?

   (A) $13\frac{1}{3}$
   (B) $13\frac{13}{16}$
   (C) $15\frac{1}{2}$
   (D) $15\frac{15}{16}$
   (E) $16\frac{1}{2}$

17. $0.1 + (0.1)^2 + (0.1)^3 =$

   (A) 0.1
   (B) 0.111
   (C) 0.1211
   (D) 0.2341
   (E) 0.3

18. A carpenter constructed a rectangular sandbox with a capacity of 10 cubic feet. If the carpenter were to make a similar sandbox twice as long, twice as wide, and twice as high as the first sandbox, what would be the capacity, in cubic feet, of the second sandbox?

   (A) 20
   (B) 40
   (C) 60
   (D) 80
   (E) 100

19. A bakery opened yesterday with its daily supply of 40 dozen rolls. Half of the rolls were sold by noon, and 80 percent of the remaining rolls were sold between noon and closing time. How many dozen rolls had not been sold when the bakery closed yesterday?

   (A) 1
   (B) 2
   (C) 3
   (D) 4
   (E) 5

20. What is the 25th digit to the right of the decimal point in the decimal form of $\frac{6}{11}$?

   (A) 3
   (B) 4
   (C) 5
   (D) 6
   (E) 7

21. 150 is what percent of 30 ?

   (A) 5%
   (B) 20%
   (C) 50%
   (D) 200%
   (E) 500%

22. The ratio 2 to $\frac{1}{3}$ is equal to the ratio

    (A) 6 to 1
    (B) 5 to 1
    (C) 3 to 2
    (D) 2 to 3
    (E) 1 to 6

23. Running at the same constant rate, 6 identical machines can produce a total of 270 bottles per minute. At this rate, how many bottles could 10 such machines produce in 4 minutes?

    (A)   648
    (B)   1,800
    (C)   2,700
    (D)   10,800
    (E)   64,800

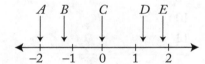

24. Of the five coordinates associated with points *A*, *B*, *C*, *D*, and *E* on the number line above, which has the greatest absolute value?

    (A) *A*
    (B) *B*
    (C) *C*
    (D) *D*
    (E) *E*

25. Of the 50 researchers in a workgroup, 40 percent will be assigned to Team A and the remaining 60 percent to Team B. However, 70 percent of the researchers prefer Team A and 30 percent prefer Team B. What is the lowest possible number of researchers who will NOT be assigned to the team they prefer?

    (A) 15
    (B) 17
    (C) 20
    (D) 25
    (E) 30

26. If *n* is a prime number greater than 3, what is the remainder when n^2 is divided by 12 ?

    (A) 0
    (B) 1
    (C) 2
    (D) 3
    (E) 5

27. $\dfrac{1}{1+\frac{1}{3}} - \dfrac{1}{1+\frac{1}{2}} =$

    (A) $-\dfrac{1}{3}$
    (B) $-\dfrac{1}{6}$
    (C) $-\dfrac{1}{12}$
    (D) $\dfrac{1}{12}$
    (E) $\dfrac{1}{3}$

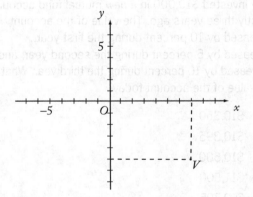

28. In the figure above, the coordinates of point *V* are

    (A) (–7,5)
    (B) (–5,7)
    (C) (5,7)
    (D) (7,5)
    (E) (7,–5)

29. A rope 40 feet long is cut into two pieces. If one piece is 18 feet longer than the other, what is the length, in feet, of the shorter piece?

(A)   9
(B)   11
(C)   18
(D)   22
(E)   29

30. A student's average (arithmetic mean) test score on 4 tests is 78. What must be the student's score on a 5th test for the student's average score on the 5 tests to be 80 ?

(A)   80
(B)   82
(C)   84
(D)   86
(E)   88

31. Lucy invested $10,000 in a new mutual fund account exactly three years ago. The value of the account increased by 10 percent during the first year, increased by 5 percent during the second year, and decreased by 10 percent during the third year. What is the value of the account today?

(A) $10,350
(B) $10,395
(C) $10,500
(D) $11,500
(E) $12,705

32. If the quotient $\frac{a}{b}$ is positive, which of the following must be true?

(A) $a > 0$
(B) $b > 0$
(C) $ab > 0$
(D) $a - b > 0$
(E) $a + b > 0$

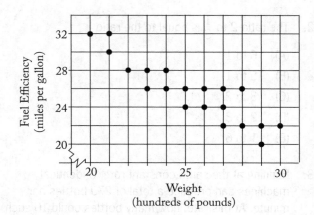

33. The dots on the graph above indicate the weights and fuel efficiency ratings for 20 cars. How many of the cars weigh more than 2,500 pounds and also get more than 22 miles per gallon?

(A)   3
(B)   5
(C)   8
(D)   10
(E)   11

34. How many minutes does it take John to type y words if he types at the rate of x words per minute?

(A) $\dfrac{x}{y}$

(B) $\dfrac{y}{x}$

(C) xy

(D) $\dfrac{60x}{y}$

(E) $\dfrac{y}{60x}$

35. $\sqrt{(16)(20)+(8)(32)} =$

(A) $4\sqrt{20}$
(B)   24
(C)   25
(D) $4\sqrt{20} + 8\sqrt{2}$
(E)   32

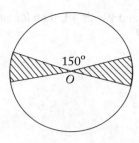

150°

O

36. If *O* is the center of the circle above, what fraction of the circular region is shaded?

    (A) $\frac{1}{12}$

    (B) $\frac{1}{9}$

    (C) $\frac{1}{6}$

    (D) $\frac{1}{4}$

    (E) $\frac{1}{3}$

37. Which of the following equations is NOT equivalent to $10y^2 = (x + 2)(x - 2)$?

    (A) $30y^2 = 3x^2 - 12$

    (B) $20y^2 = (2x - 4)(x + 2)$

    (C) $10y^2 + 4 = x^2$

    (D) $5y^2 = x^2 - 2$

    (E) $y^2 = \dfrac{x^2 - 4}{10}$

38. If Juan takes 11 seconds to run *y* yards, how many seconds will it take him to run *x* yards at the same rate?

    (A) $\dfrac{11x}{y}$

    (B) $\dfrac{11y}{x}$

    (C) $\dfrac{x}{11y}$

    (D) $\dfrac{11}{xy}$

    (E) $\dfrac{xy}{11}$

39. John has 10 pairs of matched socks. If he loses 7 individual socks, what is the greatest number of pairs of matched socks he can have left?

    (A) 7

    (B) 6

    (C) 5

    (D) 4

    (E) 3

40. What is the lowest positive integer that is divisible by each of the integers 1 through 7, inclusive?

    (A) 420

    (B) 840

    (C) 1,260

    (D) 2,520

    (E) 5,040

41. $\dfrac{1}{0.75 - 1} =$

    (A) −4

    (B) −0.25

    (C) 0.25

    (D) 0.75

    (E) 4

42. If $\dfrac{1.5}{0.2 + x} = 5$, then $x =$

    (A) −3.7

    (B) 0.1

    (C) 0.3

    (D) 0.5

    (E) 2.8

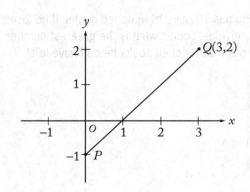

43. In the figure above, the point on segment PQ that is twice as far from P as from Q is

(A) (3,1)
(B) (2,1)
(C) (2,–1)
(D) (1.5,0.5)
(E) (1,0)

44. If n is an integer, which of the following must be even?

(A) $n+1$
(B) $n+2$
(C) $2n$
(D) $2n+1$
(E) n^2

45. If 4 is one solution of the equation $x^2 + 3x + k = 10$, where k is a constant, what is the other solution?

(A) –7
(B) –4
(C) –3
(D) 1
(E) 6

46. The sum $\frac{7}{8} + \frac{1}{9}$ is between

(A) $\frac{1}{2}$ and $\frac{3}{4}$

(B) $\frac{3}{4}$ and 1

(C) 1 and $1\frac{1}{4}$

(D) $1\frac{1}{4}$ and $1\frac{1}{2}$

(E) $1\frac{1}{2}$ and 2

47. If $x = 1 - 3t$ and $y = 2t - 1$, then for what value of t does $x = y$?

(A) $\frac{5}{2}$

(B) $\frac{3}{2}$

(C) $\frac{2}{3}$

(D) $\frac{2}{5}$

(E) 0

48. $1 - \left(\frac{1}{2} - \frac{2}{3}\right) =$

(A) $\frac{6}{5}$

(B) $\frac{7}{6}$

(C) $\frac{6}{7}$

(D) $\frac{5}{6}$

(E) 0

49. Car X averages 25.0 miles per gallon of gasoline and Car Y averages 11.9 miles per gallon. If each car is driven 12,000 miles, approximately how many more gallons of gasoline will Car Y use than Car X?

(A) 320
(B) 480
(C) 520
(D) 730
(E) 920

50. How many integers n are there such that $1 < 5n + 5 < 25$?

(A) Five
(B) Four
(C) Three
(D) Two
(E) One

51. If y is an integer, then the least possible value of $|23 - 5y|$ is

    (A) 1
    (B) 2
    (C) 3
    (D) 4
    (E) 5

52. $\sqrt{80} + \sqrt{125} =$

    (A) $9\sqrt{5}$
    (B) $20\sqrt{5}$
    (C) $41\sqrt{5}$
    (D) $\sqrt{205}$
    (E) 100

53. The average (arithmetic mean) of 10, 30, and 50 is 5 more than the average of 20, 40, and

    (A) 15
    (B) 25
    (C) 35
    (D) 45
    (E) 55

$$y = kx + 3$$

54. In the equation above, k is a constant. If $y = 17$ when $x = 2$, what is the value of y when $x = 4$?

    (A) 34
    (B) 31
    (C) 14
    (D) 11
    (E) 7

Number of Solid-Colored Marbles in Three Jars			
Jar	Number of red marbles	Number of green marbles	Total number of red and green marbles
P	x	y	80
Q	y	z	120
R	x	z	160

55. In the table above, what is the number of green marbles in Jar R?

    (A) 70
    (B) 80
    (C) 90
    (D) 100
    (E) 110

56. Four staff members at a certain company worked on a project. The amounts of time that the four staff members worked on the project were in the ratio 2 to 3 to 5 to 6. If one of the four staff members worked on the project for 30 hours, which of the following CANNOT be the total number of hours that the four staff members worked on the project?

    (A) 80
    (B) 96
    (C) 160
    (D) 192
    (E) 240

57. Company P had 15 percent more employees in December than it had in January. If Company P had 460 employees in December, how many employees did it have in January?

    (A) 391
    (B) 400
    (C) 410
    (D) 423
    (E) 445

58. A glass was filled with 10 ounces of water, and 0.01 ounce of the water evaporated each day during a 20-day period. What percent of the original amount of water evaporated during this period?

   (A)   0.002%
   (B)   0.02%
   (C)   0.2%
   (D)   2%
   (E)   20%

59. A glucose solution contains 15 grams of glucose per 100 cubic centimeters of solution. If 45 cubic centimeters of the solution were poured into an empty container, how many grams of glucose would be in the container?

   (A)   3.00
   (B)   5.00
   (C)   5.50
   (D)   6.50
   (E)   6.75

60. On a certain day, orangeade was made by mixing a certain amount of orange juice with an equal amount of water. On the next day, orangeade was made by mixing the same amount of orange juice with twice the amount of water. On both days, all the orangeade that was made was sold. If the revenue from selling the orangeade was the same for both days and if the orangeade was sold at $0.60 per glass on the first day, what was the price per glass on the second day?

   (A) $0.15
   (B) $0.20
   (C) $0.30
   (D) $0.40
   (E) $0.45

61. In the xy-plane, what is the slope of the line with equation $3x + 7y = 9$?

   (A) $-\dfrac{7}{3}$
   (B) $-\dfrac{3}{7}$
   (C) $\dfrac{3}{7}$
   (D)   3
   (E)   7

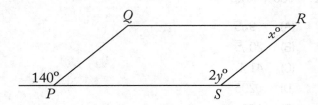

62. In the figure above, if PQRS is a parallelogram, then $y - x =$

   (A)   30
   (B)   35
   (C)   40
   (D)   70
   (E)   100

63. If 1 kilometer is approximately 0.6 mile, which of the following best approximates the number of kilometers in 2 miles?

   (A) $\dfrac{10}{3}$
   (B)   3
   (C) $\dfrac{6}{5}$
   (D) $\dfrac{1}{3}$
   (E) $\dfrac{3}{10}$

64. A certain fruit stand sold apples for $0.70 each and bananas for $0.50 each. If a customer purchased both apples and bananas from the stand for a total of $6.30, what total number of apples and bananas did the customer purchase?

    (A)   10
    (B)   11
    (C)   12
    (D)   13
    (E)   14

65. The average distance between the Sun and a certain planet is approximately 2.3×10^{14} inches. Which of the following is closest to the average distance between the Sun and the planet, in kilometers? (1 kilometer is approximately 3.9×10^{4} inches.)

    (A) 7.1×10^{8}
    (B) 5.9×10^{9}
    (C) 1.6×10^{10}
    (D) 1.6×10^{11}
    (E) 5.9×10^{11}

66. At a certain school, the ratio of the number of second graders to the number of fourth graders is 8 to 5, and the ratio of the number of first graders to the number of second graders is 3 to 4. If the ratio of the number of third graders to the number of fourth graders is 3 to 2, what is the ratio of the number of first graders to the number of third graders?

    (A)   16 to 15
    (B)   9 to 5
    (C)   5 to 16
    (D)   5 to 4
    (E)   4 to 5

67. If m is the average (arithmetic mean) of the first 10 positive multiples of 5 and if M is the median of the first 10 positive multiples of 5, what is the value of $M - m$?

    (A)   −5
    (B)   0
    (C)   5
    (D)   25
    (E)   27.5

$$A = \{2, 3, 4, 5\}$$
$$B = \{4, 5, 6, 7, 8\}$$

68. Two integers will be randomly selected from the sets above, one integer from set A and one integer from set B. What is the probability that the sum of the two integers will equal 9 ?

    (A)   0.15
    (B)   0.20
    (C)   0.25
    (D)   0.30
    (E)   0.33

69. In the coordinate plane, a circle has center (2,−3) and passes through the point (5,0). What is the area of the circle?

    (A) 3π
    (B) $3\sqrt{2}\pi$
    (C) $3\sqrt{3}\pi$
    (D) 9π
    (E) 18π

70. At a certain instant in time, the number of cars, N, traveling on a portion of a certain highway can be estimated by the formula

    $$N = \frac{20Ld}{600 + s^{2}}$$

    where L is the number of lanes in the same direction, d is the length of the portion of the highway, in feet, and s is the average speed of the cars, in miles per hour. Based on the formula, what is the estimated number of cars traveling on a $\frac{1}{2}$-mile portion of the highway if the highway has 2 lanes in the same direction and the average speed of the cars is 40 miles per hour? (5,280 feet = 1 mile)

    (A)   155
    (B)   96
    (C)   80
    (D)   48
    (E)   24

71. Yesterday's closing prices of 2,420 different stocks listed on a certain stock exchange were all different from today's closing prices. The number of stocks that closed at a higher price today than yesterday was 20 percent greater than the number that closed at a lower price. How many of the stocks closed at a higher price today than yesterday?

    (A)   484
    (B)   726
    (C)   1,100
    (D)   1,320
    (E)   1,694

72. If $y\left(\dfrac{3x-5}{2}\right) = y$ and $y \neq 0$, then $x =$

    (A) $\dfrac{2}{3}$

    (B) $\dfrac{5}{3}$

    (C) $\dfrac{7}{3}$

    (D)   1

    (E)   4

73. If $x + 5 > 2$ and $x - 3 < 7$, the value of x must be between which of the following pairs of numbers?

    (A)   −3 and 10
    (B)   −3 and 4
    (C)   2 and 7
    (D)   3 and 4
    (E)   3 and 10

74. A gym class can be divided into 8 teams with an equal number of players on each team or into 12 teams with an equal number of players on each team. What is the lowest possible number of students in the class?

    (A)   20
    (B)   24
    (C)   36
    (D)   48
    (E)   96

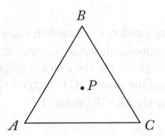

75. In the figure above, triangle ABC is equilateral, and point P is equidistant from vertices A, B, and C. If triangle ABC is rotated clockwise about point P, what is the minimum number of degrees the triangle must be rotated so that point B will be in the position where point A is now?

    (A)   60
    (B)   120
    (C)   180
    (D)   240
    (E)   270

76. At least $\dfrac{2}{3}$ of the 40 members of a committee must vote in favor of a resolution for it to pass. What is the greatest number of members who could vote against the resolution and still have it pass?

    (A)   19
    (B)   17
    (C)   16
    (D)   14
    (E)   13

77. If $n = 20! + 17$, then n is divisible by which of the following?

    I.   15
    II. 17
    III. 19

    (A) None
    (B) I only
    (C) II only
    (D) I and II
    (E) II and III

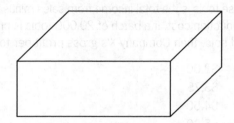

78. In the rectangular solid above, the three sides shown have areas 12, 15, and 20, respectively. What is the volume of the solid?

    (A)   60
    (B)   120
    (C)   450
    (D) 1,800
    (E) 3,600

79. After driving to a riverfront parking lot, Bob plans to run south along the river, turn around, and return to the parking lot, running north along the same path. After running 3.25 miles south, he decides to run for only 50 minutes more. If Bob runs at a constant rate of 8 minutes per mile, how many miles farther south can he run and still be able to return to the parking lot in 50 minutes?

    (A) 1.5
    (B) 2.25
    (C) 3.0
    (D) 3.25
    (E) 4.75

80. M is the sum of the reciprocals of the consecutive integers from 201 to 300, inclusive. Which of the following is true?

    (A) $\frac{1}{3} < M < \frac{1}{2}$
    (B) $\frac{1}{5} < M < \frac{1}{3}$
    (C) $\frac{1}{7} < M < \frac{1}{5}$
    (D) $\frac{1}{9} < M < \frac{1}{7}$
    (E) $\frac{1}{12} < M < \frac{1}{9}$

81. Working simultaneously at their respective constant rates, Machines A and B produce 800 nails in x hours. Working alone at its constant rate, Machine A produces 800 nails in y hours. In terms of x and y, how many hours does it take Machine B, working alone at its constant rate, to produce 800 nails?

    (A) $\dfrac{x}{x+y}$
    (B) $\dfrac{y}{x+y}$
    (C) $\dfrac{xy}{x+y}$
    (D) $\dfrac{xy}{x-y}$
    (E) $\dfrac{xy}{y-x}$

82. In the Johnsons' monthly budget, the dollar amounts allocated to household expenses, food, and miscellaneous items are in the ratio 5:2:1, respectively. If the total amount allocated to these three categories is $1,800, what is the amount allocated to food?

    (A) $900
    (B) $720
    (C) $675
    (D) $450
    (E) $225

83. There are 4 more women than men on Centerville's board of education. If there are 10 members on the board, how many are women?

    (A) 3
    (B) 4
    (C) 6
    (D) 7
    (E) 8

84. Leona bought a 1-year, $10,000 certificate of deposit that paid interest at an annual rate of 8 percent compounded semiannually. What was the total amount of interest paid on this certificate at maturity?

    (A) $10,464
    (B) $ 864
    (C) $ 816
    (D) $ 800
    (E) $ 480

85. $\dfrac{(0.0036)(2.8)}{(0.04)(0.1)(0.003)} =$

    (A) 840.0
    (B) 84.0
    (C) 8.4
    (D) 0.84
    (E) 0.084

86. Machine A produces bolts at a uniform rate of 120 every 40 seconds, and Machine B produces bolts at a uniform rate of 100 every 20 seconds. If the two machines run simultaneously, how many seconds will it take for them to produce a total of 200 bolts?

    (A) 22
    (B) 25
    (C) 28
    (D) 32
    (E) 56

87. If n is an integer greater than 6, which of the following must be divisible by 3 ?

    (A) $n(n+1)(n-4)$
    (B) $n(n+2)(n-1)$
    (C) $n(n+3)(n-5)$
    (D) $n(n+4)(n-2)$
    (E) $n(n+5)(n-6)$

88. The total cost for Company X to produce a batch of tools is $10,000 plus $3 per tool. Each tool sells for $8. The gross profit earned from producing and selling these tools is the total income from sales minus the total production cost. If a batch of 20,000 tools is produced and sold, then Company X's gross profit per tool is

    (A) $3.00
    (B) $3.75
    (C) $4.50
    (D) $5.00
    (E) $5.50

89. A dealer originally bought 100 identical batteries at a total cost of q dollars. If each battery was sold at 50 percent above the original cost per battery, then, in terms of q, for how many dollars was each battery sold?

    (A) $\dfrac{3q}{200}$

    (B) $\dfrac{3q}{2}$

    (C) $150q$

    (D) $\dfrac{q}{100}+50$

    (E) $\dfrac{150}{q}$

90. In an increasing sequence of 10 consecutive integers, the sum of the first 5 integers is 560. What is the sum of the last 5 integers in the sequence?

    (A) 585
    (B) 580
    (C) 575
    (D) 570
    (E) 565

91. If Q is an odd number and the median of Q consecutive integers is 120, what is the largest of these integers?

    (A) $\dfrac{Q-1}{2}+120$

    (B) $\dfrac{Q}{2}+119$

    (C) $\dfrac{Q}{2}+120$

    (D) $\dfrac{Q+119}{2}$

    (E) $\dfrac{Q+120}{2}$

92. A ladder of a fire truck is elevated to an angle of 60° and extended to a length of 70 feet. If the base of the ladder is 7 feet above the ground, how many feet above the ground does the ladder reach?

    (A) 35
    (B) 42
    (C) $35\sqrt{3}$
    (D) $7+35\sqrt{3}$
    (E) $7+42\sqrt{3}$

93. If Jake loses 8 pounds, he will weigh twice as much as his sister. Together they now weigh 278 pounds. What is Jake's present weight, in pounds?

    (A) 131
    (B) 135
    (C) 139
    (D) 147
    (E) 188

94. A store reported total sales of $385 million for February of this year. If the total sales for the same month last year was $320 million, approximately what was the percent increase in sales?

    (A) 2%
    (B) 17%
    (C) 20%
    (D) 65%
    (E) 83%

95. When positive integer x is divided by positive integer y, the remainder is 9. If $\dfrac{x}{y}=96.12$, what is the value of y?

    (A) 96
    (B) 75
    (C) 48
    (D) 25
    (E) 12

96. In a certain city, 60 percent of the registered voters are Democrats and the rest are Republicans. In a mayoral race, if 75 percent of the registered voters who are Democrats and 20 percent of the registered voters who are Republicans are expected to vote for Candidate A, what percent of the registered voters are expected to vote for Candidate A ?

    (A) 50%
    (B) 53%
    (C) 54%
    (D) 55%
    (E) 57%

97. $\dfrac{1}{2}+\left[\left(\dfrac{2}{3}\times\dfrac{3}{8}\right)\div 4\right]-\dfrac{9}{16}=$

    (A) $\dfrac{29}{16}$

    (B) $\dfrac{19}{16}$

    (C) $\dfrac{15}{16}$

    (D) $\dfrac{9}{13}$

    (E) 0

98. Water consists of hydrogen and oxygen, and the approximate ratio, by mass, of hydrogen to oxygen is 2:16. Approximately how many grams of oxygen are there in 144 grams of water?

    (A) 16
    (B) 72
    (C) 112
    (D) 128
    (E) 142

99. If $x(2x+1) = 0$ and $\left(x + \frac{1}{2}\right)(2x - 3) = 0$, then $x =$

   (A) -3
   (B) $-\frac{1}{2}$
   (C) 0
   (D) $\frac{1}{2}$
   (E) $\frac{3}{2}$

100. On a scale that measures the intensity of a certain phenomenon, a reading of $n + 1$ corresponds to an intensity that is 10 times the intensity corresponding to a reading of n. On that scale, the intensity corresponding to a reading of 8 is how many times as great as the intensity corresponding to a reading of 3 ?

   (A)   5
   (B)   50
   (C) 10^5
   (D) 5^{10}
   (E) $8^{10} - 3^{10}$

101. For the positive numbers, $n, n+1, n+2, n+4$, and $n+8$, the mean is how much greater than the median?

   (A)   0
   (B)   1
   (C) $n+1$
   (D) $n+2$
   (E) $n+3$

102. If $T = \frac{5}{9}(K - 32)$, and if $T = 290$, then $K =$

   (A) $\frac{1,738}{9}$
   (B)   322
   (C)   490
   (D)   554
   (E) $\frac{2,898}{5}$

103. The water from one outlet, flowing at a constant rate, can fill a swimming pool in 9 hours. The water from a second outlet, flowing at a constant rate, can fill the same pool in 5 hours. If both outlets are used at the same time, approximately what is the number of hours required to fill the pool?

   (A)   0.22
   (B)   0.31
   (C)   2.50
   (D)   3.21
   (E)   4.56

104. If a square mirror has a 20-inch diagonal, what is the approximate perimeter of the mirror, in inches?

   (A)   40
   (B)   60
   (C)   80
   (D)   100
   (E)   120

105. The present ratio of students to teachers at a certain school is 30 to 1. If the student enrollment were to increase by 50 students and the number of teachers were to increase by 5, the ratio of students to teachers would then be 25 to 1. What is the present number of teachers?

   (A)   5
   (B)   8
   (C)   10
   (D)   12
   (E)   15

106. What is the smallest integer n for which $25^n > 5^{12}$?

   (A)   6
   (B)   7
   (C)   8
   (D)   9
   (E)   10

107. Sixty percent of the members of a study group are women, and 45 percent of those women are lawyers. If one member of the study group is to be selected at random, what is the probability that the member selected is a woman lawyer?

    (A) 0.10
    (B) 0.15
    (C) 0.27
    (D) 0.33
    (E) 0.45

108. Each year for 4 years, a farmer increased the number of trees in a certain orchard by $\frac{1}{4}$ of the number of trees in the orchard the preceding year. If all of the trees thrived and there were 6,250 trees in the orchard at the end of the 4-year period, how many trees were in the orchard at the beginning of the 4-year period?

    (A) 1,250
    (B) 1,563
    (C) 2,250
    (D) 2,560
    (E) 2,752

NUMBER OF SHIPMENTS OF MANUFACTURED HOMES
IN THE UNITED STATES, 1990–2000

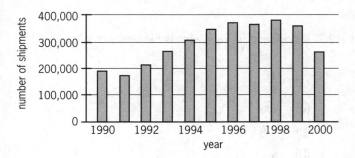

109. According to the chart shown, which of the following is closest to the median annual number of shipments of manufactured homes in the United States for the years from 1990 to 2000, inclusive?

    (A) 250,000
    (B) 280,000
    (C) 310,000
    (D) 325,000
    (E) 340,000

110. For the positive integers a, b, and k, $a^k \parallel b$ means that a^k is a divisor of b, but a^{k+1} is not a divisor of b. If k is a positive integer and $2^k \parallel 72$, then k is equal to

    (A) 2
    (B) 3
    (C) 4
    (D) 8
    (E) 18

111. If $t = \dfrac{1}{2^9 \times 5^3}$ is expressed as a terminating decimal, how many zeros will t have between the decimal point and the first nonzero digit to the right of the decimal point?

    (A) Three
    (B) Four
    (C) Five
    (D) Six
    (E) Nine

112. A certain characteristic in a large population has a distribution that is symmetric about the mean m. If 68 percent of the distribution lies within one standard deviation d of the mean, what percent of the distribution is less than $m + d$?

    (A) 16%
    (B) 32%
    (C) 48%
    (D) 84%
    (E) 92%

113. In a certain district, the ratio of the number of registered Republicans to the number of registered Democrats was $\frac{3}{5}$. After 600 additional Republicans and 500 additional Democrats registered, the ratio was $\frac{4}{5}$. After these registrations, there were how many more voters in the district registered as Democrats than as Republicans?

    (A) 100
    (B) 300
    (C) 400
    (D) 1,000
    (E) 2,500

114. In Country C, the unemployment rate among construction workers dropped from 16 percent on September 1, 1992, to 9 percent on September 1, 1996. If the number of construction workers was 20 percent greater on September 1, 1996, than on September 1, 1992, what was the approximate percent change in the number of unemployed construction workers over this period?

    (A) 50% decrease
    (B) 30% decrease
    (C) 15% decrease
    (D) 30% increase
    (E) 55% increase

115. A pharmaceutical company received $3 million in royalties on the first $20 million in sales of the generic equivalent of one of its products and then $9 million in royalties on the next $108 million in sales. By approximately what percent did the ratio of royalties to sales decrease from the first $20 million in sales to the next $108 million in sales?

    (A) 8%
    (B) 15%
    (C) 45%
    (D) 52%
    (E) 56%

116. If p is the product of the integers from 1 to 30, inclusive, what is the greatest integer k for which 3^k is a factor of p?

    (A) 10
    (B) 12
    (C) 14
    (D) 16
    (E) 18

117. If $n = 3^8 - 2^8$, which of the following is NOT a factor of n?

    (A) 97
    (B) 65
    (C) 35
    (D) 13
    (E) 5

118. Club X has more than 10 but fewer than 40 members. Sometimes the members sit at tables with 3 members at one table and 4 members at each of the other tables, and sometimes they sit at tables with 3 members at one table and 5 members at each of the other tables. If they sit at tables with 6 members at each table except one and fewer than 6 members at that one table, how many members will be at the table that has fewer than 6 members?

    (A) 1
    (B) 2
    (C) 3
    (D) 4
    (E) 5

119. In order to complete a reading assignment on time, Terry planned to read 90 pages per day. However, she read only 75 pages per day at first, leaving 690 pages to be read during the last 6 days before the assignment was to be completed. How many days in all did Terry have to complete the assignment on time?

    (A) 15
    (B) 16
    (C) 25
    (D) 40
    (E) 46

120. If $s > 0$ and $\sqrt{\dfrac{r}{s}} = s$, what is r in terms of s?

    (A) $\dfrac{1}{s}$
    (B) $\sqrt{s}$
    (C) $s\sqrt{s}$
    (D) s^3
    (E) $s^2 - s$

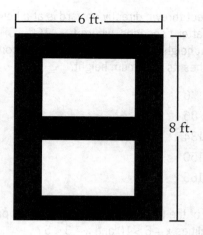

121. The front of a 6-foot-by-8-foot rectangular door has brass rectangular trim, as indicated by the shading in the figure above. If the trim is uniformly 1 foot wide, what fraction of the door's front surface is covered by the trim?

    (A) $\dfrac{13}{48}$

    (B) $\dfrac{5}{12}$

    (C) $\dfrac{1}{2}$

    (D) $\dfrac{7}{12}$

    (E) $\dfrac{5}{8}$

122. If $a = -0.3$, which of the following is true?

    (A) $a < a^2 < a^3$
    (B) $a < a^3 < a^2$
    (C) $a^2 < a < a^3$
    (D) $a^2 < a^3 < a$
    (E) $a^3 < a < a^2$

123. Mary's income is 60 percent more than Tim's income, and Tim's income is 40 percent less than Juan's income. What percent of Juan's income is Mary's income?

    (A) 124%
    (B) 120%
    (C) 96%
    (D) 80%
    (E) 64%

	City A	City B	City C	City D	City E
City A		•	•	•	•
City B			•	•	•
City C				•	•
City D					•
City E					

124. Each • in the mileage table above represents an entry indicating the distance between a pair of the five cities. If the table were extended to represent the distances between all pairs of 30 cities and each distance were to be represented by only one entry, how many entries would the table then have?

    (A) 60
    (B) 435
    (C) 450
    (D) 465
    (E) 900

125. The ratio of the length to the width of a rectangular advertising display is approximately 3.3 to 2. If the width of the display is 8 meters, what is the approximate length of the display, in meters?

    (A) 7
    (B) 11
    (C) 13
    (D) 16
    (E) 26

p, r, s, t, u

126. An arithmetic sequence is a sequence in which each term after the first is equal to the sum of the preceding term and a constant. If the list of letters shown above is an arithmetic sequence, which of the following must also be an arithmetic sequence?

I. $2p, 2r, 2s, 2t, 2u$

II. $p - 3, r - 3, s - 3, t - 3, u - 3$

III. p^2, r^2, s^2, t^2, u^2

(A) I only
(B) II only
(C) III only
(D) I and II
(E) II and III

127. If $3 < x < 100$, for how many values of x is $\frac{x}{3}$ the square of a prime number?

(A) Two
(B) Three
(C) Four
(D) Five
(E) Nine

128. A researcher plans to identify each participant in a certain medical experiment with a code consisting of either a single letter or a pair of distinct letters written in alphabetical order. What is the least number of letters that can be used if there are 12 participants, and each participant is to receive a different code?

(A) 4
(B) 5
(C) 6
(D) 7
(E) 8

129. An object thrown directly upward is at a height of h feet after t seconds, where $h = -16(t - 3)^2 + 150$. At what height, in feet, is the object 2 seconds after it reaches its maximum height?

(A)   6
(B)   86
(C)   134
(D)   150
(E)   166

130. Which of the following is equivalent to the pair of inequalities $x + 6 > 10$ and $x - 3 \leq 5$?

(A) $2 \leq x < 16$
(B) $2 \leq x < 4$
(C) $2 < x \leq 8$
(D) $4 < x \leq 8$
(E) $4 \leq x < 16$

131. David has d books, which is 3 times as many as Jeff and $\frac{1}{2}$ as many as Paula. How many books do the three of them have altogether, in terms of d?

(A) $\frac{5}{6}d$

(B) $\frac{7}{3}d$

(C) $\frac{10}{3}d$

(D) $\frac{7}{2}d$

(E) $\frac{9}{2}d$

List I: 3, 6, 8, 19

List II: x, 3, 6, 8, 19

132. If the median of the numbers in list I above is equal to the median of the numbers in list II above, what is the value of x?

(A)   6
(B)   7
(C)   8
(D)   9
(E)   10

133. There are 8 teams in a certain league and each team plays each of the other teams exactly once. If each game is played by 2 teams, what is the total number of games played?

    (A) 15
    (B) 16
    (C) 28
    (D) 56
    (E) 64

134. An operation θ is defined by the equation $a \theta b = \dfrac{a-b}{a+b}$, for all numbers a and b such that $a \neq -b$. If $a \neq -c$ and $a \theta c = 0$, then $c =$

    (A) $-a$
    (B) $-\dfrac{1}{a}$
    (C) 0
    (D) $\dfrac{1}{a}$
    (E) a

135. The price of lunch for 15 people was $207.00, including a 15 percent gratuity for service. What was the average price per person, EXCLUDING the gratuity?

    (A) $11.73
    (B) $12.00
    (C) $13.80
    (D) $14.00
    (E) $15.87

136. In Town X, 64 percent of the population are employed, and 48 percent of the population are employed males. What percent of the employed people in Town X are females?

    (A) 16%
    (B) 25%
    (C) 32%
    (D) 40%
    (E) 52%

137. At his regular hourly rate, Don had estimated the labor cost of a repair job as $336 and he was paid that amount. However, the job took 4 hours longer than he had estimated and, consequently, he earned $2 per hour less than his regular hourly rate. What was the time Don had estimated for the job, in hours?

    (A) 28
    (B) 24
    (C) 16
    (D) 14
    (E) 12

138. If $\dfrac{p}{q} < 1$, and p and q are positive integers, which of the following must be greater than 1 ?

    (A) $\sqrt{\dfrac{p}{q}}$
    (B) $\dfrac{p}{q^2}$
    (C) $\dfrac{p}{2q}$
    (D) $\dfrac{q}{p^2}$
    (E) $\dfrac{q}{p}$

139. It would take one machine 4 hours to complete a large production order and another machine 3 hours to complete the same order. How many hours would it take both machines, working simultaneously at their respective constant rates, to complete the order?

    (A) $\dfrac{7}{12}$
    (B) $1\dfrac{1}{2}$
    (C) $1\dfrac{5}{7}$
    (D) $3\dfrac{1}{2}$
    (E) 7

140. To mail a package, the rate is x cents for the first pound and y cents for each additional pound, where x > y. Two packages weighing 3 pounds and 5 pounds, respectively, can be mailed separately or combined as one package. Which method is cheaper, and how much money is saved?

    (A) Combined, with a savings of x − y cents
    (B) Combined, with a savings of y − x cents
    (C) Combined, with a savings of x cents
    (D) Separately, with a savings of x − y cents
    (E) Separately, with a savings of y cents

141. If money is invested at r percent interest, compounded annually, the amount of the investment will double in approximately $\frac{70}{r}$ years. If Pat's parents invested $5,000 in a long-term bond that pays 8 percent interest, compounded annually, what will be the approximate total amount of the investment 18 years later, when Pat is ready for college?

    (A) $20,000
    (B) $15,000
    (C) $12,000
    (D) $10,000
    (E) $ 9,000

142. On a recent trip, Cindy drove her car 290 miles, rounded to the nearest 10 miles, and used 12 gallons of gasoline, rounded to the nearest gallon. The actual number of miles per gallon that Cindy's car got on this trip must have been between

    (A) $\frac{290}{12.5}$ and $\frac{290}{11.5}$
    (B) $\frac{295}{12}$ and $\frac{285}{11.5}$
    (C) $\frac{285}{12}$ and $\frac{295}{12}$
    (D) $\frac{285}{12.5}$ and $\frac{295}{11.5}$
    (E) $\frac{295}{12.5}$ and $\frac{285}{11.5}$

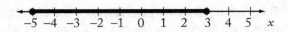

143. Which of the following inequalities is an algebraic expression for the shaded part of the number line above?

    (A) $|x| \leq 3$
    (B) $|x| \leq 5$
    (C) $|x-2| \leq 3$
    (D) $|x-1| \leq 4$
    (E) $|x+1| \leq 4$

144. A factory has 500 workers, 15 percent of whom are women. If 50 additional workers are to be hired and all of the present workers remain, how many of the additional workers must be women in order to raise the percent of women employees to 20 percent?

    (A)   3
    (B) 10
    (C) 25
    (D) 30
    (E) 35

145. In a small snack shop, the average (arithmetic mean) revenue was $400 per day over a 10-day period. During this period, if the average daily revenue was $360 for the first 6 days, what was the average daily revenue for the last 4 days?

    (A) $420
    (B) $440
    (C) $450
    (D) $460
    (E) $480

146. A certain country had a total annual expenditure of 1.2×10^{12} last year. If the population of the country was 240 million last year, what was the per capita expenditure?

    (A) $ 500
    (B) $1,000
    (C) $2,000
    (D) $3,000
    (E) $5,000

147. A certain rectangular window is twice as long as it is wide. If its perimeter is 10 feet, then its dimensions in feet are

(A) $\frac{3}{2}$ by $\frac{7}{2}$

(B) $\frac{5}{3}$ by $\frac{10}{3}$

(C) 2 by 4

(D) 3 by 6

(E) $\frac{10}{3}$ by $\frac{20}{3}$

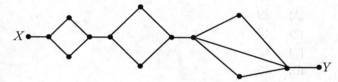

148. The diagram above shows the various paths along which a mouse can travel from point X, where it is released, to point Y, where it is rewarded with a food pellet. How many different paths from X to Y can the mouse take if it goes directly from X to Y without retracing any point along a path?

(A) 6

(B) 7

(C) 12

(D) 14

(E) 17

149. If the operation $\odot$ is defined by $x \odot y = \sqrt{xy}$ for all positive numbers x and y, then $(5 \odot 45) \odot 60 =$

(A) 30

(B) 60

(C) 90

(D) $30\sqrt{15}$

(E) $60\sqrt{15}$

150. A bar over a sequence of digits in a decimal indicates that the sequence repeats indefinitely.

What is the value of $(10^4 - 10^2)(0.00\overline{12})$?

(A) 0

(B) $0.\overline{12}$

(C) 1.2

(D) 10

(E) 12

151. At a loading dock, each worker on the night crew loaded $\frac{3}{4}$ as many boxes as each worker on the day crew. If the night crew has $\frac{4}{5}$ as many workers as the day crew, what fraction of all the boxes loaded by the two crews did the day crew load?

(A) $\frac{1}{2}$

(B) $\frac{2}{5}$

(C) $\frac{3}{5}$

(D) $\frac{4}{5}$

(E) $\frac{5}{8}$

152. A restaurant meal cost $35.50 and there was no tax. If the tip was more than 10 percent but less than 15 percent of the cost of the meal, then the total amount paid must have been between

(A) $40 and $42

(B) $39 and $41

(C) $38 and $40

(D) $37 and $39

(E) $36 and $37

153. In a weight-lifting competition, the total weight of Joe's two lifts was 750 pounds. If twice the weight of his first lift was 300 pounds more than the weight of his second lift, what was the weight, in pounds, of his first lift?

(A) 225

(B) 275

(C) 325

(D) 350

(E) 400

154. A club collected exactly $599 from its members. If each member contributed at least $12, what is the greatest number of members the club could have?

(A) 43

(B) 44

(C) 49

(D) 50

(E) 51

155. If y is the smallest positive integer such that 3,150 multiplied by y is the square of an integer, then y must be

    (A) 2
    (B) 5
    (C) 6
    (D) 7
    (E) 14

156. If [x] is the greatest integer less than or equal to x, what is the value of $[-1.6]+[3.4]+[2.7]$?

    (A) 3
    (B) 4
    (C) 5
    (D) 6
    (E) 7

157. If $\frac{4-x}{2+x} = x$, what is the value of x^2+3x-4?

    (A) −4
    (B) −1
    (C) 0
    (D) 1
    (E) 2

158. In the first week of the year, Nancy saved $1. In each of the next 51 weeks, she saved $1 more than she had saved in the previous week. What was the total amount that Nancy saved during the 52 weeks?

    (A) $1,326
    (B) $1,352
    (C) $1,378
    (D) $2,652
    (E) $2,756

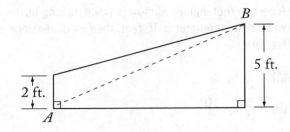

159. The trapezoid shown in the figure above represents a cross section of the rudder of a ship. If the distance from A to B is 13 feet, what is the area of the cross section of the rudder in square feet?

    (A) 39
    (B) 40
    (C) 42
    (D) 45
    (E) 46.5

160. In a certain sequence, the term x_n is given by the formula $x_n = 2x_{n-1} - \frac{1}{2}(x_{n-2})$ for all $n \geq 2$. If $x_0 = 3$ and $x_1 = 2$, what is the value of x_3?

    (A) 2.5
    (B) 3.125
    (C) 4
    (D) 5
    (E) 6.75

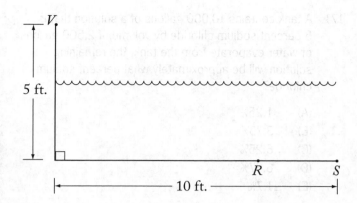

161. In the figure above, V represents an observation point at one end of a pool. From V, an object that is actually located on the bottom of the pool at point R appears to be at point S. If $VR = 10$ feet, what is the distance RS, in feet, between the actual position and the perceived position of the object?

    (A) $10 - 5\sqrt{3}$
    (B) $10 - 5\sqrt{2}$
    (C) 2
    (D) $2\frac{1}{2}$
    (E) 4

162. During a trip, Francine traveled x percent of the total distance at an average speed of 40 miles per hour and the rest of the distance at an average speed of 60 miles per hour. In terms of x, what was Francine's average speed for the entire trip?

    (A) $\dfrac{180 - x}{2}$
    (B) $\dfrac{x + 60}{4}$
    (C) $\dfrac{300 - x}{5}$
    (D) $\dfrac{600}{115 - x}$
    (E) $\dfrac{12{,}000}{x + 200}$

163. If $n = (33)^{43} + (43)^{33}$, what is the units digit of n ?

    (A) 0
    (B) 2
    (C) 4
    (D) 6
    (E) 8

164. If $x = -1$, then $\dfrac{x^4 - x^3 + x^2}{x - 1} =$

    (A) $-\dfrac{3}{2}$
    (B) $-\dfrac{1}{2}$
    (C) 0
    (D) $\dfrac{1}{2}$
    (E) $\dfrac{3}{2}$

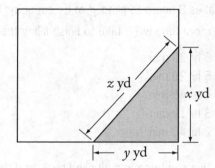

165. The shaded portion of the rectangular lot shown above represents a flower bed. If the area of the bed is 24 square yards and $x = y + 2$, then z equals

    (A) $\sqrt{13}$
    (B) $2\sqrt{13}$
    (C) 6
    (D) 8
    (E) 10

166. A border of uniform width is placed around a rectangular photograph that measures 8 inches by 10 inches. If the area of the border is 144 square inches, what is the width of the border, in inches?

    (A) 3
    (B) 4
    (C) 6
    (D) 8
    (E) 9

167. Jack is now 14 years older than Bill. If in 10 years Jack will be twice as old as Bill, how old will Jack be in 5 years?

    (A)   9
    (B)   19
    (C)   21
    (D)   23
    (E)   33

168. An empty pool being filled with water at a constant rate takes 8 hours to fill to $\frac{3}{5}$ of its capacity. How much more time will it take to finish filling the pool?

    (A)   5 hr 30 min
    (B)   5 hr 20 min
    (C)   4 hr 48 min
    (D)   3 hr 12 min
    (E)   2 hr 40 min

169. A positive number x is multiplied by 2, and this product is then divided by 3. If the positive square root of the result of these two operations equals x, what is the value of x ?

    (A) $\frac{9}{4}$
    (B) $\frac{3}{2}$
    (C) $\frac{4}{3}$
    (D) $\frac{2}{3}$
    (E) $\frac{1}{2}$

170. If $d = \frac{1}{2^3 \times 5^7}$ is expressed as a terminating decimal, how many nonzero digits will d have?

    (A)   One
    (B)   Two
    (C)   Three
    (D)   Seven
    (E)   Ten

171. A tank contains 10,000 gallons of a solution that is 5 percent sodium chloride by volume. If 2,500 gallons of water evaporate from the tank, the remaining solution will be approximately what percent sodium chloride?

    (A)   1.25%
    (B)   3.75%
    (C)   6.25%
    (D)   6.67%
    (E)   11.7%

172. For any positive integer n, the sum of the first n positive integers equals $\frac{n(n+1)}{2}$. What is the sum of all the even integers between 99 and 301 ?

    (A)   10,100
    (B)   20,200
    (C)   22,650
    (D)   40,200
    (E)   45,150

173. A committee is composed of w women and m men. If 3 women and 2 men are added to the committee, and if one person is selected at random from the enlarged committee, then the probability that a woman is selected can be represented by

    (A) $\frac{w}{m}$
    (B) $\frac{w}{w+m}$
    (C) $\frac{w+3}{m+2}$
    (D) $\frac{w+3}{w+m+3}$
    (E) $\frac{w+3}{w+m+5}$

174. How many prime numbers between 1 and 100 are factors of 7,150 ?

    (A)   One
    (B)   Two
    (C)   Three
    (D)   Four
    (E)   Five

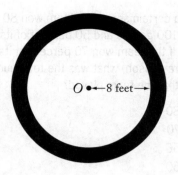

O •←— 8 feet —→

175. The figure above shows a circular flower bed, with its center at O, surrounded by a circular path that is 3 feet wide. What is the area of the path, in square feet?

(A) 25π
(B) 38π
(C) 55π
(D) 57π
(E) 64π

176. The positive integer n is divisible by 25. If $\sqrt{n}$ is greater than 25, which of the following could be the value of $\frac{n}{25}$?

(A) 22
(B) 23
(C) 24
(D) 25
(E) 26

177. Last year the price per share of Stock X increased by k percent and the earnings per share of Stock X increased by m percent, where k is greater than m. By what percent did the ratio of price per share to earnings per share increase, in terms of k and m ?

(A) $\frac{k}{m}\%$

(B) $(k-m)\%$

(C) $\frac{100(k-m)}{100+k}\%$

(D) $\frac{100(k-m)}{100+m}\%$

(E) $\frac{100(k-m)}{100+k+m}\%$

178. Of the 300 subjects who participated in an experiment using virtual-reality therapy to reduce their fear of heights, 40 percent experienced sweaty palms, 30 percent experienced vomiting, and 75 percent experienced dizziness. If all of the subjects experienced at least one of these effects and 35 percent of the subjects experienced exactly two of these effects, how many of the subjects experienced only one of these effects?

(A) 105
(B) 125
(C) 130
(D) 180
(E) 195

179. A fruit-salad mixture consists of apples, peaches, and grapes in the ratio 6:5:2, respectively, by weight. If 39 pounds of the mixture is prepared, the mixture includes how many more pounds of apples than grapes?

(A) 15
(B) 12
(C) 9
(D) 6
(E) 4

180. If $m^{-1} = -\frac{1}{3}$, then m^{-2} is equal to

(A) -9
(B) -3
(C) $-\frac{1}{9}$
(D) $\frac{1}{9}$
(E) 9

181. If $m > 0$ and x is m percent of y, then, in terms of m, y is what percent of x ?

(A) $100m$
(B) $\frac{1}{100m}$
(C) $\frac{1}{m}$
(D) $\frac{10}{m}$
(E) $\frac{10,000}{m}$

182. A photography dealer ordered 60 Model X cameras to be sold for $250 each, which represents a 20 percent markup over the dealer's initial cost for each camera. Of the cameras ordered, 6 were never sold and were returned to the manufacturer for a refund of 50 percent of the dealer's initial cost. What was the dealer's approximate profit or loss as a percent of the dealer's initial cost for the 60 cameras?

   (A)   7% loss
   (B)   13% loss
   (C)   7% profit
   (D)   13% profit
   (E)   15% profit

183. Seven pieces of rope have an average (arithmetic mean) length of 68 centimeters and a median length of 84 centimeters. If the length of the longest piece of rope is 14 centimeters more than 4 times the length of the shortest piece of rope, what is the maximum possible length, in centimeters, of the longest piece of rope?

   (A)   82
   (B)   118
   (C)   120
   (D)   134
   (E)   152

184. Lois has x dollars more than Jim has, and together they have a total of y dollars. Which of the following represents the number of dollars that Jim has?

   (A) $\dfrac{y - x}{2}$
   (B) $y - \dfrac{x}{2}$
   (C) $\dfrac{y}{2} - x$
   (D) $2y - x$
   (E) $y - 2x$

185. During a certain season, a team won 80 percent of its first 100 games and 50 percent of its remaining games. If the team won 70 percent of its games for the entire season, what was the total number of games that the team played?

   (A)   180
   (B)   170
   (C)   156
   (D)   150
   (E)   105

186. Of 30 applicants for a job, 14 had at least 4 years' experience, 18 had degrees, and 3 had less than 4 years' experience and did not have a degree. How many of the applicants had at least 4 years' experience and a degree?

   (A)   14
   (B)   13
   (C)   9
   (D)   7
   (E)   5

187. If $1 + \dfrac{1}{x} = 2 - \dfrac{2}{x}$, then x =

   (A)   −1
   (B) $\dfrac{1}{3}$
   (C) $\dfrac{2}{3}$
   (D)   2
   (E)   3

188. Last year, for every 100 million vehicles that traveled on a certain highway, 96 vehicles were involved in accidents. If 3 billion vehicles traveled on the highway last year, how many of those vehicles were involved in accidents? (1 billion = 1,000,000,000)

   (A)   288
   (B)   320
   (C)   2,880
   (D)   3,200
   (E)   28,800

189. Thirty percent of the members of a swim club have passed the lifesaving test. Among the members who have *not* passed the test, 12 have taken the preparatory course and 30 have not taken the course. How many members are there in the swim club?

    (A)   60
    (B)   80
    (C)   100
    (D)   120
    (E)   140

190. What is the difference between the sixth and the fifth terms of the sequence 2, 4, 7, ... whose *n*th term is $n + 2^{n-1}$?

    (A)   2
    (B)   3
    (C)   6
    (D)   16
    (E)   17

191. If $(x-1)^2 = 400$, which of the following could be the value of $x - 5$?

    (A)   15
    (B)   14
    (C)   −24
    (D)   −25
    (E)   −26

192. Which of the following describes all values of *x* for which $1 - x^2 \geq 0$?

    (A) $x \geq 1$
    (B) $x \leq -1$
    (C) $0 \leq x \leq 1$
    (D) $x \leq -1$ or $x \geq 1$
    (E) $-1 \leq x \leq 1$

193. The probability is $\frac{1}{2}$ that a certain coin will turn up heads on any given toss. If the coin is to be tossed three times, what is the probability that on at least one of the tosses the coin will turn up tails?

    (A) $\frac{1}{8}$
    (B) $\frac{1}{2}$
    (C) $\frac{3}{4}$
    (D) $\frac{7}{8}$
    (E) $\frac{15}{16}$

194. Of the final grades received by the students in a certain math course, $\frac{1}{5}$ are A's, $\frac{1}{4}$ are B's, $\frac{1}{2}$ are C's, and the remaining 10 grades are D's. What is the number of students in the course?

    (A)   80
    (B)   110
    (C)   160
    (D)   200
    (E)   400

195. As *x* increases from 165 to 166, which of the following must increase?

    I. $2x - 5$

    II. $1 - \frac{1}{x}$

    III. $\frac{1}{x^2 - x}$

    (A)   I only
    (B)   III only
    (C)   I and II
    (D)   I and III
    (E)   II and III

196. From the consecutive integers −10 to 10, inclusive, 20 integers are randomly chosen with repetitions allowed. What is the least possible value of the product of the 20 integers?

(A) $(-10)^{20}$
(B) $(-10)^{10}$
(C) 0
(D) $-(10)^{19}$
(E) $-(10)^{20}$

197. A rectangular box is 10 inches wide, 10 inches long, and 5 inches high. What is the greatest possible (straight-line) distance, in inches, between any two points on the box?

(A) 15
(B) 20
(C) 25
(D) $10\sqrt{2}$
(E) $10\sqrt{3}$

198. Last Sunday a certain store sold copies of Newspaper A for $1.00 each and copies of Newspaper B for $1.25 each, and the store sold no other newspapers that day. If r percent of the store's revenue from newspaper sales was from Newspaper A and if p percent of the newspapers that the store sold were copies of Newspaper A, which of the following expresses r in terms of p ?

(A) $\dfrac{100p}{125-p}$

(B) $\dfrac{150p}{250-p}$

(C) $\dfrac{300p}{375-p}$

(D) $\dfrac{400p}{500-p}$

(E) $\dfrac{500p}{625-p}$

199. $\dfrac{0.99999999}{1.0001} - \dfrac{0.99999991}{1.0003} =$

(A) 10^{-8}
(B) $3(10^{-8})$
(C) $3(10^{-4})$
(D) $2(10^{-4})$
(E) 10^{-4}

200. The ratio, by volume, of soap to alcohol to water in a certain solution is 2:50:100. The solution will be altered so that the ratio of soap to alcohol is doubled while the ratio of soap to water is halved. If the altered solution will contain 100 cubic centimeters of alcohol, how many cubic centimeters of water will it contain?

(A) 50
(B) 200
(C) 400
(D) 625
(E) 800

201. If 75 percent of a class answered the first question on a certain test correctly, 55 percent answered the second question on the test correctly, and 20 percent answered neither of the questions correctly, what percent answered both correctly?

(A) 10%
(B) 20%
(C) 30%
(D) 50%
(E) 65%

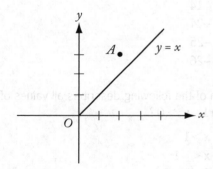

202. In the rectangular coordinate system above, the line y = x is the perpendicular bisector of segment AB (not shown), and the x-axis is the perpendicular bisector of segment BC (not shown). If the coordinates of point A are (2,3), what are the coordinates of point C ?

(A) (−3,−2)
(B) (−3,2)
(C) (2,−3)
(D) (3,−2)
(E) (2,3)

203. A store currently charges the same price for each towel that it sells. If the current price of each towel were to be increased by $1, 10 fewer of the towels could be bought for $120, excluding sales tax. What is the current price of each towel?

    (A) $ 1
    (B) $ 2
    (C) $ 3
    (D) $ 4
    (E) $12

204. If $n = 4p$, where p is a prime number greater than 2, how many different positive <u>even</u> divisors does n have, including n?

    (A) Two
    (B) Three
    (C) Four
    (D) Six
    (E) Eight

205. John and Mary were each paid x dollars in advance to do a certain job together. John worked on the job for 10 hours and Mary worked 2 hours less than John. If Mary gave John y dollars of her payment so that they would have received the same hourly wage, what was the dollar amount, in terms of y, that John was paid in advance?

    (A) $4y$
    (B) $5y$
    (C) $6y$
    (D) $8y$
    (E) $9y$

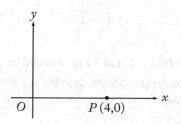

206. In the rectangular coordinate system above, if point R (not shown) lies on the positive y-axis and the area of triangle ORP is 12, what is the y-coordinate of point R?

    (A) 3
    (B) 6
    (C) 9
    (D) 12
    (E) 24

207. Car A is 20 miles behind Car B, which is traveling in the same direction along the same route as Car A. Car A is traveling at a constant speed of 58 miles per hour and Car B is traveling at a constant speed of 50 miles per hour. How many hours will it take for Car A to overtake and drive 8 miles ahead of Car B?

    (A) 1.5
    (B) 2.0
    (C) 2.5
    (D) 3.0
    (E) 3.5

208. For the past n days, the average (arithmetic mean) daily production at a company was 50 units. If today's production of 90 units raises the average to 55 units per day, what is the value of n?

    (A) 30
    (B) 18
    (C) 10
    (D) 9
    (E) 7

$$\left(\frac{x+1}{x-1}\right)^2$$

209. If $x \neq 0$ and $x \neq 1$, and if x is replaced by $\frac{1}{x}$ everywhere in the expression above, then the resulting expression is equivalent to

(A) $\left(\frac{x+1}{x-1}\right)^2$

(B) $\left(\frac{x-1}{x+1}\right)^2$

(C) $\frac{x^2+1}{1-x^2}$

(D) $\frac{x^2-1}{x^2+1}$

(E) $-\left(\frac{x-1}{x+1}\right)^2$

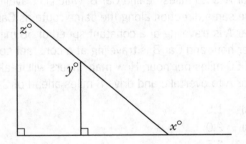

210. In the figure above, if $z = 50$, then $x + y =$

(A) 230
(B) 250
(C) 260
(D) 270
(E) 290

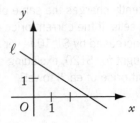

211. In the coordinate system above, which of the following is the equation of line ℓ?

(A) $2x - 3y = 6$
(B) $2x + 3y = 6$
(C) $3x + 2y = 6$
(D) $2x - 3y = -6$
(E) $3x - 2y = -6$

212. If a two-digit positive integer has its digits reversed, the resulting integer differs from the original by 27. By how much do the two digits differ?

(A) 3
(B) 4
(C) 5
(D) 6
(E) 7

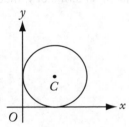

213. The circle with center C shown above is tangent to both axes. If the distance from O to C is equal to k, what is the radius of the circle, in terms of k?

(A) k

(B) $\frac{k}{\sqrt{2}}$

(C) $\frac{k}{\sqrt{3}}$

(D) $\frac{k}{2}$

(E) $\frac{k}{3}$

214. In an electric circuit, two resistors with resistances x and y are connected in parallel. In this case, if r is the combined resistance of these two resistors, then the reciprocal of r is equal to the sum of the reciprocals of x and y. What is r in terms of x and y ?

(A) xy

(B) $x + y$

(C) $\dfrac{1}{x+y}$

(D) $\dfrac{xy}{x+y}$

(E) $\dfrac{x+y}{xy}$

215. Xavier, Yvonne, and Zelda each try independently to solve a problem. If their individual probabilities for success are $\frac{1}{4}$, $\frac{1}{2}$, and $\frac{5}{8}$, respectively, what is the probability that Xavier and Yvonne, but not Zelda, will solve the problem?

(A) $\dfrac{11}{8}$

(B) $\dfrac{7}{8}$

(C) $\dfrac{9}{64}$

(D) $\dfrac{5}{64}$

(E) $\dfrac{3}{64}$

216. If $\dfrac{1}{x} - \dfrac{1}{x+1} = \dfrac{1}{x+4}$, then x could be

(A)   0
(B)   −1
(C)   −2
(D)   −3
(E)   −4

217. $\left(\dfrac{1}{2}\right)^{-3}\left(\dfrac{1}{4}\right)^{-2}\left(\dfrac{1}{16}\right)^{-1} =$

(A) $\left(\dfrac{1}{2}\right)^{-48}$

(B) $\left(\dfrac{1}{2}\right)^{-11}$

(C) $\left(\dfrac{1}{2}\right)^{-6}$

(D) $\left(\dfrac{1}{8}\right)^{-11}$

(E) $\left(\dfrac{1}{8}\right)^{-6}$

218. List T consists of 30 positive decimals, none of which is an integer, and the sum of the 30 decimals is S. The _estimated_ sum of the 30 decimals, E, is defined as follows. Each decimal in T whose tenths digit is even is rounded up to the nearest integer, and each decimal in T whose tenths digit is odd is rounded down to the nearest integer; E is the sum of the resulting integers. If $\frac{1}{3}$ of the decimals in T have a tenths digit that is even, which of the following is a possible value of $E - S$?

I.   −16
II.   6
III.   10

(A)   I only
(B)   I and II only
(C)   I and III only
(D)   II and III only
(E)   I, II, and III

219. In a certain game, a large container is filled with red, yellow, green, and blue beads worth, respectively, 7, 5, 3, and 2 points each. A number of beads are then removed from the container. If the product of the point values of the removed beads is 147,000, how many red beads were removed?

(A)   5
(B)   4
(C)   3
(D)   2
(E)   0

220. If $\dfrac{2}{1+\dfrac{2}{y}}=1$, then $y=$

   (A) -2

   (B) $-\dfrac{1}{2}$

   (C) $\dfrac{1}{2}$

   (D)   2

   (E)   3

221. If a, b, and c are consecutive positive integers and $a < b < c$, which of the following must be true?

   I. $c - a = 2$

   II. abc is an even integer.

   III. $\dfrac{a+b+c}{3}$ is an integer.

   (A)   I only
   (B)   II only
   (C)   I and II only
   (D)   II and III only
   (E)   I, II, and III

222. Of the 200 students at College T majoring in one or more of the sciences, 130 are majoring in chemistry and 150 are majoring in biology. If at least 30 of the students are not majoring in either chemistry or biology, then the number of students majoring in *both* chemistry and biology could be any number from

   (A)   20 to 50
   (B)   40 to 70
   (C)   50 to 130
   (D)   110 to 130
   (E)   110 to 150

223. If $5-\dfrac{6}{x}=x$, then x has how many possible values?

   (A)   None
   (B)   One
   (C)   Two
   (D)   A finite number greater than two
   (E)   An infinite number

224. Seed mixture X is 40 percent ryegrass and 60 percent bluegrass by weight; seed mixture Y is 25 percent ryegrass and 75 percent fescue. If a mixture of X and Y contains 30 percent ryegrass, what percent of the weight of the mixture is X ?

   (A)   10%

   (B) $33\dfrac{1}{3}\%$

   (C)   40%

   (D)   50%

   (E) $66\dfrac{2}{3}\%$

225. If n is a positive integer, then $n(n+1)(n+2)$ is

   (A)   even only when n is even
   (B)   even only when n is odd
   (C)   odd whenever n is odd
   (D)   divisible by 3 only when n is odd
   (E)   divisible by 4 whenever n is even

226. A straight pipe 1 yard in length was marked off in fourths and also in thirds. If the pipe was then cut into separate pieces at each of these markings, which of the following gives all the different lengths of the pieces, in fractions of a yard?

   (A) $\dfrac{1}{6}$ and $\dfrac{1}{4}$ only

   (B) $\dfrac{1}{4}$ and $\dfrac{1}{3}$ only

   (C) $\dfrac{1}{6}$, $\dfrac{1}{4}$, and $\dfrac{1}{3}$

   (D) $\dfrac{1}{12}$, $\dfrac{1}{6}$, and $\dfrac{1}{4}$

   (E) $\dfrac{1}{12}$, $\dfrac{1}{6}$, and $\dfrac{1}{3}$

227. If $\dfrac{0.0015 \times 10^{m}}{0.03 \times 10^{k}} = 5 \times 10^{7}$, then $m - k =$

 (A)   9
 (B)   8
 (C)   7
 (D)   6
 (E)   5

228. Right triangle PQR is to be constructed in the xy-plane so that the right angle is at P and $\overline{PR}$ is parallel to the x-axis. The x- and y-coordinates of P, Q, and R are to be integers that satisfy the inequalities $-4 \leq x \leq 5$ and $6 \leq y \leq 16$. How many different triangles with these properties could be constructed?

 (A)   110
 (B)   1,100
 (C)   9,900
 (D)   10,000
 (E)   12,100

229. How many of the integers that satisfy the inequality $\dfrac{(x+2)(x+3)}{x-2} \geq 0$ are less than 5 ?

 (A)   1
 (B)   2
 (C)   3
 (D)   4
 (E)   5

230. The value of $\dfrac{2^{-14} + 2^{-15} + 2^{-16} + 2^{-17}}{5}$ is how many times the value of 2^{-17} ?

 (A) $\dfrac{3}{2}$
 (B) $\dfrac{5}{2}$
 (C)   3
 (D)   4
 (E)   5

5.4 Answer Key

1.	A	31.	B	61.	B	91.	A
2.	C	32.	C	62.	A	92.	D
3.	E	33.	B	63.	A	93.	E
4.	C	34.	B	64.	B	94.	C
5.	B	35.	B	65.	B	95.	B
6.	E	36.	C	66.	E	96.	B
7.	E	37.	D	67.	B	97.	E
8.	D	38.	A	68.	B	98.	D
9.	E	39.	B	69.	E	99.	B
10.	A	40.	A	70.	D	100.	C
11.	C	41.	A	71.	D	101.	B
12.	B	42.	B	72.	C	102.	D
13.	A	43.	B	73.	A	103.	D
14.	C	44.	C	74.	B	104.	B
15.	C	45.	A	75.	D	105.	E
16.	A	46.	B	76.	E	106.	B
17.	B	47.	D	77.	C	107.	C
18.	D	48.	B	78.	A	108.	D
19.	D	49.	C	79.	A	109.	C
20.	C	50.	B	80.	A	110.	B
21.	E	51.	B	81.	E	111.	B
22.	A	52.	A	82.	D	112.	D
23.	B	53.	A	83.	D	113.	B
24.	A	54.	B	84.	C	114.	B
25.	A	55.	D	85.	A	115.	C
26.	B	56.	D	86.	B	116.	C
27.	D	57.	B	87.	A	117.	C
28.	E	58.	D	88.	C	118.	E
29.	B	59.	E	89.	A	119.	B
30.	E	60.	D	90.	A	120.	D

121.	D	151.	E	181.	E	211.	B
122.	B	152.	B	182.	A	212.	A
123.	C	153.	D	183.	D	213.	B
124.	B	154.	C	184.	A	214.	D
125.	C	155.	E	185.	D	215.	E
126.	D	156.	A	186.	E	216.	C
127.	B	157.	C	187.	B	217.	D
128.	B	158.	C	188.	C	218.	B
129.	B	159.	C	189.	A	219.	D
130.	D	160.	C	190.	E	220.	D
131.	C	161.	A	191.	C	221.	E
132.	B	162.	E	192.	E	222.	D
133.	C	163.	A	193.	D	223.	C
134.	E	164.	A	194.	D	224.	B
135.	B	165.	E	195.	C	225.	E
136.	B	166.	A	196.	E	226.	D
137.	B	167.	D	197.	A	227.	A
138.	E	168.	B	198.	D	228.	C
139.	C	169.	D	199.	D	229.	D
140.	A	170.	B	200.	E	230.	C
141.	A	171.	D	201.	D		
142.	D	172.	B	202.	D		
143.	E	173.	E	203.	C		
144.	E	174.	D	204.	C		
145.	D	175.	D	205.	E		
146.	E	176.	E	206.	B		
147.	B	177.	D	207.	E		
148.	C	178.	D	208.	E		
149.	A	179.	B	209.	A		
150.	E	180.	D	210.	D		

5.5 Answer Explanations

The following discussion is intended to familiarize you with the most efficient and effective approaches to the kinds of problems common to problem solving questions. The particular questions in this chapter are generally representative of the kinds of problem solving questions you will encounter on the GMAT exam. Remember that it is the problem solving strategy that is important, not the specific details of a particular question.

1. A project scheduled to be carried out over a single fiscal year has a budget of $12,600, divided into 12 equal monthly allocations. At the end of the fourth month of that fiscal year, the total amount actually spent on the project was $4,580. By how much was the project over its budget?

   (A) $ 380
   (B) $ 540
   (C) $1,050
   (D) $1,380
   (E) $1,430

   Arithmetic Operations with rational numbers

   The budget for four months is

   $\frac{\$12,600}{12} \times 4 = \$4,200$. Thus, the project was

   $\$4,580 - \$4,200 = \$380$ over budget for the first four months.

   The correct answer is A.

2. For which of the following values of n is $\frac{100+n}{n}$ NOT an integer?

   (A) 1
   (B) 2
   (C) 3
   (D) 4
   (E) 5

Arithmetic Properties of numbers

Substitute the value for n given in each answer choice into the expression, and then simplify to determine whether or not that value results in an integer.

A $\frac{100+1}{1} = \frac{101}{1} = 101$ Integer

B $\frac{100+2}{2} = \frac{102}{2} = 51$ Integer

C $\frac{100+3}{3} = \frac{103}{3} = 34.333...$ NOT an integer

D $\frac{100+4}{4} = \frac{104}{4} = 26$ Integer

E $\frac{100+5}{5} = \frac{105}{5} = 21$ Integer

Another method is to rewrite the given expression, $\frac{100+n}{n}$, as $\frac{100}{n} + \frac{n}{n} = \frac{100}{n} + 1$. This shows that the given expression is an integer exactly when $\frac{100}{n}$ is an integer. Since 100 is not divisible by 3, but 100 is divisible by 1, 2, 4, and 5, it follows that $n = 3$.

The correct answer is C.

3. Rectangular Floors X and Y have equal area. If Floor X is 12 feet by 18 feet and Floor Y is 9 feet wide, what is the length of Floor Y, in feet?

   (A) $13\frac{1}{2}$

   (B) 18

   (C) $18\frac{3}{4}$

   (D) 21

   (E) 24

   Geometry Area

   Since Floor X is a rectangle, its area is $(\text{width})(\text{length}) = (12)(18)$. It is given that this is also the area of Floor Y, so if L is the length of Floor Y, it follows that $9L = (12)(18)$, or $L = \dfrac{(12)(18)}{9} = \dfrac{(12)(\cancel{9})(2)}{\cancel{9}} = (12)(2) = 24.$

   The correct answer is E.

4. A case contains c cartons. Each carton contains b boxes, and each box contains 100 paper clips. How many paper clips are contained in 2 cases?

   (A) $100bc$

   (B) $\dfrac{100b}{c}$

   (C) $200bc$

   (D) $\dfrac{200b}{c}$

   (E) $\dfrac{200}{bc}$

   Algebra Simplifying algebraic expressions

   Each case has bc boxes, each of which has 100 paper clips. The total number of paper clips in 2 cases is thus $2(bc)(100) = 200bc$.

   The correct answer is C.

5. The sum of prime numbers that are greater than 60 but less than 70 is

   (A) 67

   (B) 128

   (C) 191

   (D) 197

   (E) 260

   Arithmetic Properties of numbers

   A prime number is a positive integer divisible by exactly two different positive divisors, 1 and itself. Note that 62, 64, 66, and 68 are also divisible by 2; 63, 66, and 69 are also divisible by 3; and 65 is also divisible by 5. The only prime numbers between 60 and 70 are 61 and 67, and $61 + 67 = 128$.

   The correct answer is B.

6. A rainstorm increased the amount of water stored in State J reservoirs from 124 billion gallons to 138 billion gallons. If the storm increased the amount of water in the reservoirs to 82 percent of total capacity, approximately how many billion gallons of water were the reservoirs short of total capacity prior to the storm?

   (A) 9

   (B) 14

   (C) 25

   (D) 30

   (E) 44

   Algebra Applied problems

   Let t be the total capacity of the reservoirs in billions of gallons. The information that the post-storm water amount of 138 billion gallons represented 82 percent of total capacity can be expressed as $0.82t = 138$. Solve for t and then estimate the value of t: $t = \dfrac{138}{0.82} \approx \dfrac{140}{0.8} = \dfrac{1,400}{8} = 175$ billion gallons. Thus, the amount the reservoirs were short of total capacity prior to the storm, in billions of gallons, was approximately $175 - 124 = 51$, so E is the best choice. A more accurate calculation gives $168.3 - 124 = 44.3$.

   The correct answer is E.

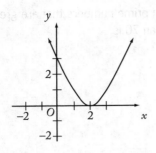

7. On the graph above, when $x = \frac{1}{2}$, $y = 2$; and when $x = 1$, $y = 1$. The graph is symmetric with respect to the vertical line at $x = 2$. According to the graph, when $x = 3$, $y =$

(A) -1
(B) $-\frac{1}{2}$
(C) 0
(D) $\frac{1}{2}$
(E) 1

Arithmetic; Algebra Interpretation of graphs; Second-degree equations

Since the graph is symmetric with respect to $x = 2$, the y value when $x = 3$ will be the same as the y value when $x = 1$, which is 1.

The correct answer is E.

8. When $\frac{1}{10}$ percent of 5,000 is subtracted from $\frac{1}{10}$ of 5,000, the difference is

(A) 0
(B) 50
(C) 450
(D) 495
(E) 500

Arithmetic Percents

Since $\frac{1}{10}$ percent is $\frac{1}{1,000}$, the difference asked for is $\left(\frac{1}{10}\right)(5,000) - \left(\frac{1}{1,000}\right)(5,000) = 500 - 5 = 495$.

The correct answer is D.

9. Which of the following is the value of $\sqrt{\sqrt[3]{0.000064}}$?

(A) 0.004
(B) 0.008
(C) 0.02
(D) 0.04
(E) 0.2

Arithmetic Operations on radical expressions

The square root and cube root evaluations are more easily carried out when 0.000064 is rewritten as 64×10^{-6}. Using this rewritten form, the value asked for is

$$\sqrt{\sqrt[3]{0.000064}} = \sqrt{\sqrt[3]{64 \times 10^{-6}}}$$
$$= \sqrt{\sqrt[3]{64} \times \sqrt[3]{10^{-6}}}$$
$$= \sqrt{4 \times 10^{-2}}$$
$$= \sqrt{4} \times \sqrt{10^{-2}}$$
$$= 2 \times 10^{-1}$$
$$= 0.2$$

The correct answer is E.

10. Raffle tickets numbered consecutively from 101 through 350 are placed in a box. What is the probability that a ticket selected at random will have a number with a hundreds digit of 2 ?

(A) $\frac{2}{5}$
(B) $\frac{2}{7}$
(C) $\frac{33}{83}$
(D) $\frac{99}{250}$
(E) $\frac{100}{249}$

Arithmetic Probability

There are 250 integers from 101 to 350 inclusive, 100 of which (that is, 200 through 299) have a hundreds digit of 2. Therefore, the probability that a ticket selected from the box at random will have a hundreds digit of 2 can be expressed as $\frac{100}{250} = \frac{2}{5}$.

The correct answer is A.

11. When Leo imported a certain item, he paid a 7 percent import tax on the portion of the total value of the item in excess of $1,000. If the amount of the import tax that Leo paid was $87.50, what was the total value of the item?

    (A) $1,600
    (B) $1,850
    (C) $2,250
    (D) $2,400
    (E) $2,750

Algebra First-degree equations

Letting x represent the total value of the item, convert the words to symbols and solve the equation.

7% of value in excess of $1,000 = 87.50

$$0.07(x - 1,000) = 87.50$$
$$x - 1,000 = 1,250$$
$$x = 2,250$$

The correct answer is C.

12. The numbers of cars sold at a certain dealership on six of the last seven business days were 4, 7, 2, 8, 3, and 6, respectively. If the number of cars sold on the seventh business day was either 2, 4, or 5, for which of the three values does the average (arithmetic mean) number of cars sold per business day for the seven business days equal the median number of cars sold per day for the seven days?

    I.   2
    II. 4
    III. 5

    (A) II only
    (B) III only
    (C) I and II only
    (D) II and III only
    (E) I, II, and III

Arithmetic Statistics

Listed in numerical order, the given numbers are 2, 3, 4, 6, 7, and 8. If the seventh number were 2 or 4, then the numbers in numerical order would be 2, 2, 3, 4, 6, 7, and 8 or 2, 3, 4, 4, 6, 7, and 8. In either case the median would be 4 and the average would be $\frac{2+2+3+4+6+7+8}{7} = \frac{32}{7}$ or $\frac{2+3+4+4+6+7+8}{7} = \frac{34}{7}$, neither of which equals 4. So, for neither of the values in I or II does the average equal the median. If the seventh number were 5, then the numbers in numerical order would be 2, 3, 4, 5, 6, 7, and 8. The median would be 5 and the average would be $\frac{2+3+4+5+6+7+8}{7} = \frac{35}{7} = 5$. Thus, for the value in III, the average equals the median.

The correct answer is B.

13. A rectangular garden is to be twice as long as it is wide. If 360 yards of fencing, including the gate, will completely enclose the garden, what will be the length of the garden, in yards?

    (A) 120
    (B) 140
    (C) 160
    (D) 180
    (E) 200

Geometry Quadrilaterals; Perimeter

Let the width of the rectangle be x. Then the length is $2x$. Since the perimeter of a rectangle is twice the sum of the length and width, it follows that

$360 = 2(x + 2x)$
$360 = 6x$
$120 = 2x$

So, the length is 120.

The correct answer is A.

14. If $\left|y - \frac{1}{2}\right| < \frac{11}{2}$, which of the following could be a value of y?

(A) -11

(B) $-\frac{11}{2}$

(C) $\frac{11}{2}$

(D) 11

(E) 22

Algebra Inequalities; Absolute value

Since $\left|y - \frac{1}{2}\right| < \frac{11}{2}$ is equivalent to $-\frac{11}{2} < y - \frac{1}{2} < \frac{11}{2}$, or $-\frac{10}{2} < y < \frac{12}{2}$, select the value that lies between $-\frac{10}{2} = -5$ and $\frac{12}{2} = 6$. That value is $\frac{11}{2}$.

The correct answer is C.

15. At a supermarket, John spent $\frac{1}{2}$ of his money on fresh fruits and vegetables, $\frac{1}{3}$ on meat products, and $\frac{1}{10}$ on bakery products. If he spent the remaining $6 on candy, how much did John spend at the supermarket?

(A) $60

(B) $80

(C) $90

(D) $120

(E) $180

Arithmetic Fractions

The amount spent was

$\frac{1}{2} + \frac{1}{3} + \frac{1}{10} = \frac{15}{30} + \frac{10}{30} + \frac{3}{30} = \frac{28}{30} = \frac{14}{15}$ of the total,

so the $6 left was $\frac{1}{15}$ of the total. It follows that the total is $(15)(\$6) = \$90$.

The correct answer is C.

16. On Monday, a person mailed 8 packages weighing an average (arithmetic mean) of $12\frac{3}{8}$ pounds, and on Tuesday, 4 packages weighing an average of $15\frac{1}{4}$ pounds. What was the average weight, in pounds, of all the packages the person mailed on both days?

(A) $13\frac{1}{3}$

(B) $13\frac{13}{16}$

(C) $15\frac{1}{2}$

(D) $15\frac{15}{16}$

(E) $16\frac{1}{2}$

Arithmetic Statistics

Since average $= \dfrac{\text{sum of values}}{\text{number of values}}$,

the information about the two shipments of packages can be expressed as

$\text{average} = \dfrac{8\left(12\frac{3}{8}\right) + 4\left(15\frac{1}{4}\right)}{12} = \dfrac{8\left(\frac{99}{8}\right) + 4\left(\frac{61}{4}\right)}{12}$

$= \dfrac{99 + 61}{12} = \dfrac{160}{12} = 13\frac{1}{3}$.

The correct answer is A.

17. $0.1 + (0.1)^2 + (0.1)^3 =$

(A) 0.1

(B) 0.111

(C) 0.1211

(D) 0.2341

(E) 0.3

Arithmetic Operations on rational numbers

Calculate the squared and the cubed term, and then add the three terms.

$0.1 + (0.1)^2 + (0.1)^3 = 0.1 + 0.01 + 0.001 = 0.111$

The correct answer is B.

18. A carpenter constructed a rectangular sandbox with a capacity of 10 cubic feet. If the carpenter were to make a similar sandbox twice as long, twice as wide, and twice as high as the first sandbox, what would be the capacity, in cubic feet, of the second sandbox?

    (A)   20
    (B)   40
    (C)   60
    (D)   80
    (E)   100

Geometry Volume

When all the dimensions of a three-dimensional object are changed by a factor of 2, the capacity, or volume, changes by a factor of $(2)(2)(2) = 2^3 = 8$. Thus the capacity of the second sandbox is $10(8) = 80$ cubic feet.

The correct answer is D.

19. A bakery opened yesterday with its daily supply of 40 dozen rolls. Half of the rolls were sold by noon, and 80 percent of the remaining rolls were sold between noon and closing time. How many dozen rolls had not been sold when the bakery closed yesterday?

    (A)   1
    (B)   2
    (C)   3
    (D)   4
    (E)   5

Arithmetic Operations on rational numbers; Percents

Since half of the 40 dozen rolls were sold by noon, then $\frac{1}{2}(40) = 20$ dozen rolls were left to be sold after noon. Because 80 percent of those 20 were sold, $100 - 80 = 20$ percent of them or $20(0.20) = 4$ dozen rolls had not been sold when the bakery closed.

The correct answer is D.

20. What is the 25th digit to the right of the decimal point in the decimal form of $\frac{6}{11}$?

    (A)   3
    (B)   4
    (C)   5
    (D)   6
    (E)   7

Arithmetic Properties of numbers

The fraction in its decimal form is $\frac{6}{11} = 0.545454\ldots$. Every odd-numbered digit to the right of the decimal point is 5, so the 25th digit must be 5.

The correct answer is C.

21. 150 is what percent of 30 ?

    (A)   5%
    (B)   20%
    (C)   50%
    (D)   200%
    (E)   500%

Arithmetic Percents

Let x be the desired percent in the problem. The given information can be expressed by the following equation, which can then be solved for x.

$$150 = 30x$$
$$\frac{(15)(10)}{(3)(10)} = x$$
$$5 = x$$

Then, 5 expressed as a percent is 500%.

The correct answer is E.

22. The ratio 2 to $\frac{1}{3}$ is equal to the ratio

    (A)   6 to 1
    (B)   5 to 1
    (C)   3 to 2
    (D)   2 to 3
    (E)   1 to 6

Arithmetic Operations on rational numbers

The ratio 2 to $\frac{1}{3}$ is the same as $\dfrac{2}{\frac{1}{3}} = 2\left(\dfrac{3}{1}\right) = 6$,

which is the same as a ratio of 6 to 1.

The correct answer is A.

23. Running at the same constant rate, 6 identical machines can produce a total of 270 bottles per minute. At this rate, how many bottles could 10 such machines produce in 4 minutes?

    (A)   648
    (B)   1,800
    (C)   2,700
    (D)   10,800
    (E)   64,800

Arithmetic Operations on rational numbers

Since there are 6 machines, each machine does $\frac{1}{6}$ of the work. Each machine can produce $270\left(\dfrac{1}{6}\right) = 45$ bottles per minute, so 10 machines can produce $45(10) = 450$ bottles per minute. Therefore, the 10 machines can produce $450(4) = 1,800$ bottles in 4 minutes.

The correct answer is B.

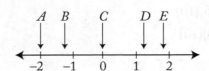

24. Of the five coordinates associated with points A, B, C, D, and E on the number line above, which has the greatest absolute value?

    (A) A
    (B) B
    (C) C
    (D) D
    (E) E

Arithmetic Properties of numbers

The absolute value of a number x is the distance between x and 0 on the number line. Point A is farthest from 0 and thus its coordinate has the greatest absolute value.

The correct answer is A.

25. Of the 50 researchers in a workgroup, 40 percent will be assigned to Team A and the remaining 60 percent to Team B. However, 70 percent of the researchers prefer Team A and 30 percent prefer Team B. What is the lowest possible number of researchers who will NOT be assigned to the team they prefer?

    (A)   15
    (B)   17
    (C)   20
    (D)   25
    (E)   30

Arithmetic Percents

The number of researchers assigned to Team A will be $(0.40)(50) = 20$, and so 30 will be assigned to Team B. The number of researchers who prefer Team A is $(0.70)(50) = 35$, and the rest, 15, prefer Team B.

If all 15 who prefer Team B are assigned to Team B, which is to have 30 researchers, then 15 who prefer Team A will need to be assigned to Team B. Alternatively, since there are only 20 spots on Team A, $35 - 20 = 15$ who prefer Team A but will have to go to Team B instead.

The correct answer is A.

26. If n is a prime number greater than 3, what is the remainder when n^2 is divided by 12 ?

    (A)   0
    (B)   1
    (C)   2
    (D)   3
    (E)   5

Arithmetic Properties of numbers

The simplest way to solve this problem is to choose a prime number greater than 3 and divide its square by 12 to see what the remainder is. For example, if $n = 5$, then $n^2 = 25$, and the remainder is 1 when 25 is divided by 12. A second prime number can be used to check the result. For example, if $n = 7$, then $n^2 = 49$, and the remainder is 1 when 49 is divided by 12. Because only one of the answer choices can be correct, the remainder must be 1.

For the more mathematically inclined, consider the remainder when each prime number n greater than 3 is divided by 6. The remainder cannot be 0 because that would imply that n is divisible by 6, which is impossible since n is a prime number. The remainder cannot be 2 or 4 because that would imply that n is even, which is impossible since n is a prime number greater than 3. The remainder cannot be 3 because that would imply that n is divisible by 3, which is impossible since n is a prime number greater than 3. Therefore, the only possible remainders when a prime number n greater than 3 is divided by 6 are 1 and 5. Thus, n has the form $6q + 1$ or $6q + 5$, where q is an integer, and, therefore, n^2 has the form $36q^2 + 12q + 1 = 12(3q^2 + q) + 1$ or $36q^2 + 60q + 25 = 12(3q^2 + 5q + 2) + 1$. In either case, n^2 has a remainder of 1 when divided by 12.

The correct answer is B.

27. $\dfrac{1}{1+\dfrac{1}{3}} - \dfrac{1}{1+\dfrac{1}{2}} =$

   (A) $-\dfrac{1}{3}$

   (B) $-\dfrac{1}{6}$

   (C) $-\dfrac{1}{12}$

   (D) $\dfrac{1}{12}$

   (E) $\dfrac{1}{3}$

Arithmetic Operations with rational numbers

Perform the arithmetic calculations as follows:

$$\frac{1}{1+\frac{1}{3}} - \frac{1}{1+\frac{1}{2}} = \frac{1}{\frac{4}{3}} - \frac{1}{\frac{3}{2}}$$

$$= \frac{3}{4} - \frac{2}{3}$$

$$= \frac{9}{12} - \frac{8}{12}$$

$$= \frac{9-8}{12}$$

$$= \frac{1}{12}$$

The correct answer is D.

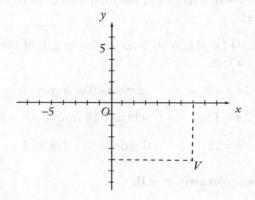

28. In the figure above, the coordinates of point V are

   (A) $(-7,5)$
   (B) $(-5,7)$
   (C) $(5,7)$
   (D) $(7,5)$
   (E) $(7,-5)$

Geometry Coordinate geometry

The x-coordinate of V is 7, and the y-coordinate of V is -5. Thus, the coordinates, (x,y), of V are $(7,-5)$.

The correct answer is E.

29. A rope 40 feet long is cut into two pieces. If one piece is 18 feet longer than the other, what is the length, in feet, of the shorter piece?

(A)   9
(B)   11
(C)   18
(D)   22
(E)   29

Algebra First-degree equations

Build an equation to express the given information and solve for the answer.

Let x = length of the shorter piece of rope in feet.

Then $x + 18$ = length of the longer piece of rope in feet.

Thus $x + (x + 18) = 40$ is the entire length of the rope in feet.

$2x + 18 = 40$	combine like terms
$2x = 22$	subtract 18 from both sides
$x = 11$	divide both sides by 2

The correct answer is B.

30. A student's average (arithmetic mean) test score on 4 tests is 78. What must be the student's score on a 5th test for the student's average score on the 5 tests to be 80 ?

(A)   80
(B)   82
(C)   84
(D)   86
(E)   88

Arithmetic Statistics

The average of the student's first 4 test scores is 78, so the sum of the first 4 test scores is $4(78) = 312$. If x represents the fifth test score, then the sum of all 5 test scores is $312 + x$ and the average of all 5 test scores is $\frac{312 + x}{5}$. But the average of all 5 test scores is 80 so

$$\frac{312 + x}{5} = 80$$

$$312 + x = 400$$

$$x = 88$$

The correct answer is E.

31. Lucy invested $10,000 in a new mutual fund account exactly three years ago. The value of the account increased by 10 percent during the first year, increased by 5 percent during the second year, and decreased by 10 percent during the third year. What is the value of the account today?

(A) $10,350
(B) $10,395
(C) $10,500
(D) $11,500
(E) $12,705

Arithmetic Percents

The first year's increase of 10 percent can be expressed as 1.10; the second year's increase of 5 percent can be expressed as 1.05; and the third year's decrease of 10 percent can be expressed as 0.90. Multiply the original value of the account by each of these yearly changes.

$$10,000(1.10)(1.05)(0.90) = 10,395$$

The correct answer is B.

32. If the quotient $\frac{a}{b}$ is positive, which of the following must be true?

(A) $a > 0$
(B) $b > 0$
(C) $ab > 0$
(D) $a - b > 0$
(E) $a + b > 0$

Arithmetic Properties of numbers

If the quotient $\frac{a}{b}$ is positive, then either a and b are both positive, or a and b are both negative.

A $a = -1$ and $b = -1$ show it NEED NOT BE TRUE that $a > 0$.

B $a = -1$ and $b = -1$ show it NEED NOT BE TRUE that $b > 0$.

C   The condition that ab is positive is exactly the same condition that $\frac{a}{b}$ is positive. Thus, it MUST BE TRUE that $ab > 0$.

D $a = 1$ and $b = 2$ show it NEED NOT BE TRUE that $a - b > 0$.

E $a = -1$ and $b = -1$ show it NEED NOT BE TRUE that $a + b > 0$.

The correct answer is C.

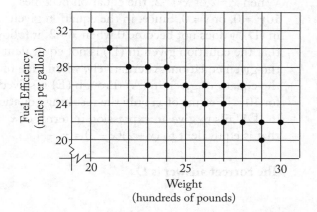

33.   The dots on the graph above indicate the weights and fuel efficiency ratings for 20 cars. How many of the cars weigh more than 2,500 pounds and also get more than 22 miles per gallon?

(A)   3
(B)   5
(C)   8
(D)   10
(E)   11

Arithmetic Interpretation of graphs and tables

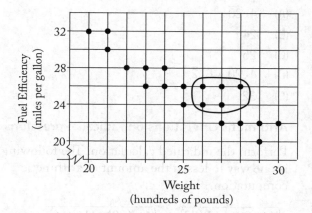

The only dots on the graph that meet the conditions of the problem are those to the right of 25 (that is, the car has a weight in excess of 2,500 pounds) and above 22 (that is, the car has a fuel efficiency over 22 miles per gallon) as shown.

The correct answer is B.

34.   How many minutes does it take John to type y words if he types at the rate of x words per minute?

(A) $\dfrac{x}{y}$

(B) $\dfrac{y}{x}$

(C) xy

(D) $\dfrac{60x}{y}$

(E) $\dfrac{y}{60x}$

Algebra First-degree equations

Let m represent the number of minutes it takes John to type y words. In this rate problem, the number of words typed = (typing rate)(time).

Thus, $y = xm$, or $m = \dfrac{y}{x}$.

The correct answer is B.

35. $\sqrt{(16)(20)+(8)(32)} =$

    (A) $4\sqrt{20}$
    (B) 24
    (C) 25
    (D) $4\sqrt{20}+8\sqrt{2}$
    (E) 32

Arithmetic Operations on radical expressions

Perform the indicated calculation. The following is one way to lessen the amount of arithmetic computation.

$$\sqrt{(16)(20)+(8)(32)} = \sqrt{(16)(20)+(16)(16)}$$
$$= \sqrt{(16)(20+16)}$$
$$= \sqrt{16}\sqrt{20+16}$$
$$= 4\sqrt{36}$$
$$= (4)(6)$$
$$= 24$$

The correct answer is B.

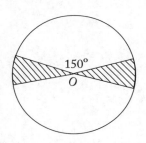

36. If *O* is the center of the circle above, what fraction of the circular region is shaded?

    (A) $\dfrac{1}{12}$

    (B) $\dfrac{1}{9}$

    (C) $\dfrac{1}{6}$

    (D) $\dfrac{1}{4}$

    (E) $\dfrac{1}{3}$

Geometry Circles and area

Vertical angles are congruent, so $150° + 150° = 300°$ of the circle is not shaded. Since there are $360°$ in a circle, this makes $360° - 300° = 60°$ of the circle shaded. The fraction of the circular region that is shaded is thus $= \dfrac{60}{360} = \dfrac{1}{6}$.

The correct answer is C.

37. Which of the following equations is NOT equivalent to $10y^2 = (x + 2)(x - 2)$?

    (A) $30y^2 = 3x^2 - 12$
    (B) $20y^2 = (2x - 4)(x + 2)$
    (C) $10y^2 + 4 = x^2$
    (D) $5y^2 = x^2 - 2$
    (E) $y^2 = \dfrac{x^2 - 4}{10}$

Algebra Simplifying algebraic expressions

When $x = 2$ or $x = -2$, the equation becomes $10y^2 = 0$, or $y = 0$. Since, in the equation given in (D), y does not become 0 when $x = 2$, it follows that the equation given in (D) is not equivalent to the given equation. Alternatively, when each of the equations given in (A) through (E) is solved for $10y^2$ in terms of x, only the resulting equation in (D) fails to give an expression in terms of x that is equivalent to $(x + 2)(x - 2) = x^2 - 4$.

The correct answer is D.

38. If Juan takes 11 seconds to run *y* yards, how many seconds will it take him to run *x* yards at the same rate?

    (A) $\dfrac{11x}{y}$

    (B) $\dfrac{11y}{x}$

    (C) $\dfrac{x}{11y}$

    (D) $\dfrac{11}{xy}$

    (E) $\dfrac{xy}{11}$

Algebra Applied problems

Juan's running rate can be expressed as $\frac{y}{11}$ yards per second. Use this value in the formula distance = (rate)(time), letting t equal the time in seconds that it will take Juan to run the distance of x yards:

$x = \frac{y}{11}t$ distance = (rate)(time)

$\frac{11x}{y} = t$ solve for t by multiplying both sides by $\frac{11}{y}$

The correct answer is A.

39. John has 10 pairs of matched socks. If he loses 7 individual socks, what is the greatest number of pairs of matched socks he can have left?

   (A) 7
   (B) 6
   (C) 5
   (D) 4
   (E) 3

Arithmetic Operations on rational numbers

Determine first the lowest number of pairs of matched socks that can be made from the 7 individual socks. The lowest number of pairs that 7 individual socks can come from is 3 full pairs plus one sock from a fourth pair. The greatest number of pairs of matched socks John can have left is therefore $10 - 4 = 6$ fully matched pairs.

The correct answer is B.

40. What is the lowest positive integer that is divisible by each of the integers 1 through 7, inclusive?

   (A) 420
   (B) 840
   (C) 1,260
   (D) 2,520
   (E) 5,040

Arithmetic Operations on rational numbers

A number that is divisible by the integers from 1 through 7 inclusive must have 2, 3, 4, 5, 6, and 7

as factors. The lowest positive integer will have no duplication of factors. The lowest common multiple of 2, 3, 4, and 6 is 12, and 5 and 7 are prime, so the lowest positive integer that is divisible by each of the integers 1 through 7 inclusive is $12(5)(7) = 420$.

The correct answer is A.

41. $\frac{1}{0.75 - 1} =$

   (A) -4
   (B) -0.25
   (C) 0.25
   (D) 0.75
   (E) 4

Arithmetic Operations with rational numbers

Perform the arithmetic calculations as follows:

$$\frac{1}{0.75 - 1} = \frac{1}{\frac{3}{4} - 1}$$

$$= \frac{1}{-\frac{1}{4}}$$

$$= -4$$

The correct answer is A.

42. If $\frac{1.5}{0.2 + x} = 5$, then $x =$

   (A) -3.7
   (B) 0.1
   (C) 0.3
   (D) 0.5
   (E) 2.8

Algebra First-degree equations

Work the problem to solve for x.

$$\frac{1.5}{0.2 + x} = 5$$

$1.5 = 1 + 5x$ multiply both sides by $0.2 + x$

$0.5 = 5x$ subtract 1 from both sides

$0.1 = x$ divide both sides by 5

The correct answer is B.

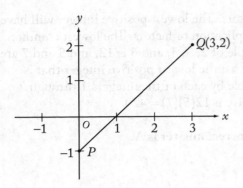

43. In the figure above, the point on segment PQ that is twice as far from P as from Q is

    (A) (3,1)
    (B) (2,1)
    (C) (2,–1)
    (D) (1.5,0.5)
    (E) (1,0)

Geometry Coordinate geometry

On a segment, a point that is twice as far from one end as the other is $\frac{1}{3}$ the distance from one end. The points (0,–1), (1,0), (2,1), and (3,2) are on segment PQ, and they divide the segment into three intervals of equal length as shown in the figure below.

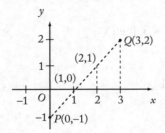

Note that the point (2,1) is twice as far from $P(0,–1)$ as from $Q(3,2)$ and also that it is $\frac{1}{3}$ the distance from Q.

The correct answer is B.

44. If n is an integer, which of the following must be even?

    (A) $n+1$
    (B) $n+2$
    (C) $2n$
    (D) $2n+1$
    (E) n^2

Arithmetic Properties of integers

A quick look at the answer choices reveals the expression $2n$ in answer choice C. $2n$ is a multiple of 2 and hence must be even.

Since only one answer choice can be correct, the other answer choices need not be checked. However, for completeness:

A $n+1$ is odd if n is even and even if n is odd. Therefore, it is not true that $n+1$ must be even.

B $n+2$ is even if n is even and odd if n is odd. Therefore, it is not true that $n+2$ must be even.

D $2n+1$ is odd whether n is even or odd. Therefore, it is not true that $2n+1$ must be even.

E n^2 is even if n is even and odd if n is odd. Therefore, it is not true that n^2 must be even.

The correct answer is C.

45. If 4 is one solution of the equation $x^2 + 3x + k = 10$, where k is a constant, what is the other solution?

    (A)   –7
    (B)   –4
    (C)   –3
    (D)   1
    (E)   6

Algebra Second-degree equations

If 4 is one solution of the equation, then substitute 4 for x and solve for k.

$$x^2 + 3x + k = 10$$
$$(4)^2 + 3(4) + k = 10$$
$$16 + 12 + k = 10$$
$$28 + k = 10$$
$$k = -18$$

Then, substitute -18 for k and solve for x.

$$x^2 + 3x - 18 = 10$$

$$x^2 + 3x - 28 = 0$$

$$(x+7)(x-4) = 0$$

$$x = -7, \; x = 4$$

The correct answer is A.

46. The sum $\frac{7}{8} + \frac{1}{9}$ is between

    (A) $\frac{1}{2}$ and $\frac{3}{4}$

    (B) $\frac{3}{4}$ and 1

    (C) 1 and $1\frac{1}{4}$

    (D) $1\frac{1}{4}$ and $1\frac{1}{2}$

    (E) $1\frac{1}{2}$ and 2

Arithmetic Operations with rational numbers

Since $\frac{1}{9} < \frac{1}{8}$, $\frac{7}{8} + \frac{1}{9} < \frac{7}{8} + \frac{1}{8} = 1$, and answer choices C, D, and E can be eliminated. Since $\frac{7}{8} > \frac{6}{8} = \frac{3}{4}$, $\frac{7}{8} + \frac{1}{9} > \frac{3}{4}$, and answer choice A can be eliminated. Thus, $\frac{3}{4} < \frac{7}{8} + \frac{1}{9} < 1$.

The correct answer is B.

47. If $x = 1 - 3t$ and $y = 2t - 1$, then for what value of t does $x = y$?

    (A) $\frac{5}{2}$

    (B) $\frac{3}{2}$

    (C) $\frac{2}{3}$

    (D) $\frac{2}{5}$

    (E) 0

Algebra Simultaneous equations

Since it is given that $x = y$, set the expressions for x and y equal to each other and solve for t.

$$1 - 3t = 2t - 1$$

$$2 = 5t \qquad \text{add } 3t \text{ and } 1 \text{ to both sides, then}$$

$$\frac{2}{5} = t \qquad \text{divide both sides by 5}$$

The correct answer is D.

48. $1 - \left(\frac{1}{2} - \frac{2}{3} \right) =$

    (A) $\frac{6}{5}$

    (B) $\frac{7}{6}$

    (C) $\frac{6}{7}$

    (D) $\frac{5}{6}$

    (E) 0

Arithmetic Operations with rational numbers

Perform the arithmetic calculations as follows:

$$1 - \left(\frac{1}{2} - \frac{2}{3} \right) = 1 - \left(\frac{3}{6} - \frac{4}{6} \right)$$

$$= 1 - \left(-\frac{1}{6} \right)$$

$$= 1 + \frac{1}{6}$$

$$= \frac{7}{6}$$

The correct answer is B.

49. Car X averages 25.0 miles per gallon of gasoline and Car Y averages 11.9 miles per gallon. If each car is driven 12,000 miles, approximately how many more gallons of gasoline will Car Y use than Car X?

    (A) 320

    (B) 480

    (C) 520

    (D) 730

    (E) 920

Arithmetic Applied problems

Car X uses 1 gallon of gasoline for every 25 miles it is driven, so Car X uses $\frac{1}{25}$ of a gallon for every 1 mile it is driven. Therefore Car X will use $(12{,}000)\left(\frac{1}{25}\right) = 480$ gallons of gasoline when it is driven 12,000 miles. Car Y uses 1 gallon of gasoline for every 11.9 or $\frac{119}{10}$ miles it is driven, so Car Y uses $\frac{10}{119}$ of a gallon for every 1 mile it is driven. Therefore Car Y will use $(12{,}000)\left(\frac{10}{119}\right) \approx (12{,}000)\left(\frac{10}{120}\right) = 1{,}000$ gallons of gasoline when it is driven 12,000 miles. Thus, Car Y will use approximately $1{,}000 - 480 = 520$ more gallons of gasoline than Car X.

The correct answer is C.

50. How many integers n are there such that $1 < 5n + 5 < 25$?

   (A) Five
   (B) Four
   (C) Three
   (D) Two
   (E) One

Algebra Inequalities

Isolate the variable in the inequalities to determine the range within which n lies.

$1 < 5n + 5 < 25$

$-4 < 5n < 20$ subtract 5 from all three values

$-\frac{4}{5} < n < 4$ divide all three values by 5

There are four integers between $-\frac{4}{5}$ and 4, namely 0, 1, 2, and 3.

The correct answer is B.

51. If y is an integer, then the least possible value of $|23 - 5y|$ is

   (A) 1
   (B) 2
   (C) 3
   (D) 4
   (E) 5

Arithmetic Absolute value; Operations with integers

Since y is an integer, $23 - 5y$ is also an integer. The task is to find the integer y for which $|23 - 5y|$ is the least. If $y \geq 0$, $-5y \leq 0$, and $23 - 5y \leq 23$. On the other hand, if $y \leq 0$, $-5y \geq 0$, and $23 - 5y \geq 23$. Therefore, the least possible value of $|23 - 5y|$ occurs at a nonnegative value of y. From the chart below, it is clear that the least possible integer value of $|23 - 5y|$ is 2, which occurs when $y = 5$.

y	$\lvert 23 - 5y \rvert$
0	23
1	18
2	13
3	8
4	3
5	2
6	7
7	12

Alternatively, since $|23 - 5y| \geq 0$, the minimum possible real value of $|23 - 5y|$ is 0. The integer value of y for which $|23 - 5y|$ is least is the integer closest to the solution of the equation $23 - 5y = 0$.

The solution is $y = \frac{23}{5} = 4.6$ and the integer closest to 4.6 is 5.

The correct answer is B.

52. $\sqrt{80} + \sqrt{125} =$

   (A) $9\sqrt{5}$
   (B) $20\sqrt{5}$
   (C) $41\sqrt{5}$
   (D) $\sqrt{205}$
   (E) 100

Arithmetic Operations with radical expressions

Rewrite each radical in the form $a\sqrt{b}$, where a and b are positive integers and b is as small as possible, and then add.

$$\sqrt{80} + \sqrt{125} = \sqrt{16(5)} + \sqrt{25(5)}$$
$$= \left(\sqrt{16}\right)\left(\sqrt{5}\right) + \left(\sqrt{25}\right)\left(\sqrt{5}\right)$$
$$= 4\sqrt{5} + 5\sqrt{5}$$
$$= 9\sqrt{5}$$

The correct answer is A.

53. The average (arithmetic mean) of 10, 30, and 50 is 5 more than the average of 20, 40, and

   (A)   15
   (B)   25
   (C)   35
   (D)   45
   (E)   55

Arithmetic Statistics

Using the formula $\dfrac{\text{sum of } n \text{ values}}{n} = \text{average}$,

the given information about the first set of numbers can be expressed in the equation $\dfrac{10 + 30 + 50}{3} = 30$. From the given information then, the average of the second set of numbers is $30 - 5 = 25$. Letting x represent the missing number, set up the equation for calculating the average for the second set of numbers, and solve for x.

$$\frac{20 + 40 + x}{3} = 25$$
$$\frac{60 + x}{3} = 25 \quad \text{simplify}$$
$$60 + x = 75 \quad \text{multiply both sides by 3}$$
$$x = 15 \quad \text{subtract 60 from both sides}$$

The correct answer is A.

$$y = kx + 3$$

54. In the equation above, k is a constant. If $y = 17$ when $x = 2$, what is the value of y when $x = 4$?

   (A)   34
   (B)   31
   (C)   14
   (D)   11
   (E)   7

Algebra First-degree equations

If $y = kx + 3$ and $y = 17$ when $x = 2$, then

$$17 = 2k + 3$$
$$14 = 2k$$
$$7 = k$$

Therefore, $y = 7x + 3$. When $x = 4$,
$y = 7(4) + 3 = 31$.

The correct answer is B.

Number of Solid-Colored Marbles in Three Jars			
Jar	Number of red marbles	Number of green marbles	Total number of red and green marbles
P	x	y	80
Q	y	z	120
R	x	z	160

55. In the table above, what is the number of green marbles in Jar R?

   (A)   70
   (B)   80
   (C)   90
   (D)   100
   (E)   110

Arithmetic; Algebra Interpretation of tables; Applied problems

First, set up an equation to find the total number of marbles in the three jars as follows:

$$x + y + y + z + x + z = 80 + 120 + 160$$

$$2x + 2y + 2z = 360 \quad \text{combine the like terms}$$

$$x + y + z = 180 \quad \text{divide both sides by 2}$$

Then, since it can be seen from the table that the number of green marbles in Jar R is z, solve for z to answer the problem. To do this most efficiently, use the information from the table for Jar P, which is that $x + y = 80$.

$$x + y + z = 180$$

$$80 + z = 180 \qquad \text{substitute 80 for } x + y$$

$$z = 100$$

The correct answer is D.

56. Four staff members at a certain company worked on a project. The amounts of time that the four staff members worked on the project were in the ratio 2 to 3 to 5 to 6. If one of the four staff members worked on the project for 30 hours, which of the following CANNOT be the total number of hours that the four staff members worked on the project?

   (A)   80
   (B)   96
   (C)   160
   (D)   192
   (E)   240

Arithmetic Ratio and proportion

For a certain value of x, the numbers of hours worked on the project by the four staff members are $2x$, $3x$, $5x$, and $6x$, for a total of $16x$. It is given that one of these four numbers is equal to 30. If $2x = 30$, then $x = 15$ and $16x = 16(15) = 240$, which is (E). If $3x = 30$, then $x = 10$ and $16x = 16(10) = 160$, which is (C). If $5x = 30$, then $x = 6$ and $16x = 16(6) = 96$, which is (B). If $6x = 30$, then $x = 5$ and $16x = 16(5) = 80$, which is (A).

The correct answer is D.

57. Company P had 15 percent more employees in December than it had in January. If Company P had 460 employees in December, how many employees did it have in January?

   (A)   391
   (B)   400
   (C)   410
   (D)   423
   (E)   445

Arithmetic Percents

It is given that 460 is 115% of the number of employees in January. Therefore, the number of employees in January was

$$\frac{460}{1.15} = \frac{460}{1.15}\left(\frac{100}{100}\right) = \left(\frac{460}{115}\right)(100) = (4)(100) = 400.$$

The correct answer is B.

58. A glass was filled with 10 ounces of water, and 0.01 ounce of the water evaporated each day during a 20-day period. What percent of the original amount of water evaporated during this period?

   (A)   0.002%
   (B)   0.02%
   (C)   0.2%
   (D)   2%
   (E)   20%

Arithmetic Percents

Since 0.01 ounce of water evaporated each day for 20 days, a total of $20(0.01) = 0.2$ ounce evaporated. Then, to find the percent of the original amount of water that evaporated, divide the amount that evaporated by the original amount and multiply by 100 to convert the decimal to a percent. Thus, $\frac{0.2}{10} \times 100 = 0.02 \times 100$ or 2%.

The correct answer is D.

59. A glucose solution contains 15 grams of glucose per 100 cubic centimeters of solution. If 45 cubic centimeters of the solution were poured into an empty container, how many grams of glucose would be in the container?

(A)   3.00
(B)   5.00
(C)   5.50
(D)   6.50
(E)   6.75

Algebra Applied problems

Let x be the number of grams of glucose in the 45 cubic centimeters of solution. The proportion comparing the glucose in the 45 cubic centimeters to the given information about the 15 grams of glucose in the entire 100 cubic centimeters of solution can be expressed as $\frac{x}{45} = \frac{15}{100}$, and thus $100x = 675$ or $x = 6.75$.

The correct answer is E.

60.   On a certain day, orangeade was made by mixing a certain amount of orange juice with an equal amount of water. On the next day, orangeade was made by mixing the same amount of orange juice with twice the amount of water. On both days, all the orangeade that was made was sold. If the revenue from selling the orangeade was the same for both days and if the orangeade was sold at $0.60 per glass on the first day, what was the price per glass on the second day?

(A) $0.15
(B) $0.20
(C) $0.30
(D) $0.40
(E) $0.45

Arithmetic Applied problems

The ratio of the amount of orangeade made and sold on the first day to amount of orangeade made and sold on the second day is 2:3, because the orangeade on the first day was 1 part orange juice and 1 part water, while on the second day it was 1 part orange juice and 2 parts water. Thus, the ratio of the number of glasses of orangeade made and sold on the first day to the number of glasses of orangeade made and sold on the second day is 2:3. Since the revenues for each day were equal and 2 glasses were sold on the first day for every 3 glasses that were sold on the second day,

$2(\$0.60) = 3p$, where p represents the price per glass at which the orangeade was sold on the second day. Therefore, $p = \left(\frac{2}{3}\right)(\$0.60) = \$0.40$.

The correct answer is D.

61.   In the xy-plane, what is the slope of the line with equation $3x + 7y = 9$?

(A) $-\frac{7}{3}$
(B) $-\frac{3}{7}$
(C) $\frac{3}{7}$
(D) 3
(E) 7

Algebra Coordinate geometry

Since the given equation of the line is equivalent to $7y = -3x + 9$, or $y = -\frac{3}{7}x + \frac{9}{7}$, the slope of the line is $-\frac{3}{7}$. Alternatively, choose 2 points lying on the line and then use the slope formula for these 2 points. For example, substitute $x = 0$ in $7y = -3x + 9$ and solve for y to get $\left(0, \frac{9}{7}\right)$, substitute $y = 0$ in $7y = -3x + 9$ and solve for x to get $(3,0)$, then use the slope formula to get $\frac{\frac{9}{7} - 0}{0 - 3} = \frac{\frac{9}{7}}{-3} = -\frac{3}{7}$.

The correct answer is B.

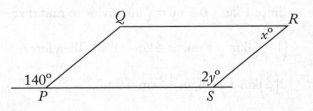

62.   In the figure above, if PQRS is a parallelogram, then $y - x =$

(A)   30
(B)   35
(C)   40
(D)   70
(E)   100

Geometry Polygons

Since *PQRS* is a parallelogram, the following must be true:

$140 = 2y$ corresponding angles are congruent

$2y + x = 180$ consecutive angles are supplementary (sum = 180°)

Solving the first equation for y gives $y = 70$. Substituting this into the second equation gives

$$2(70) + x = 180$$
$$140 + x = 180$$
$$x = 40$$

Thus, $y - x = 70 - 40 = 30$.

The correct answer is A.

63. If 1 kilometer is approximately 0.6 mile, which of the following best approximates the number of kilometers in 2 miles?

(A) $\dfrac{10}{3}$

(B) 3

(C) $\dfrac{6}{5}$

(D) $\dfrac{1}{3}$

(E) $\dfrac{3}{10}$

Arithmetic Applied problems

Since $1 \text{ km} \approx 0.6 \text{ mi} = \dfrac{3}{5}\text{mi}$, divide to find that

$\left(1 \div \dfrac{3}{5}\right)\text{km} \approx 1 \text{ mi}$, or $\dfrac{5}{3}\text{km} \approx 1 \text{ mi}$. Therefore,

$2\left(\dfrac{5}{3}\right)\text{km} \approx 2 \text{ mi}$, or $\dfrac{10}{3}\text{km} \approx 2 \text{ mi}$.

The correct answer is A.

64. A certain fruit stand sold apples for $0.70 each and bananas for $0.50 each. If a customer purchased both apples and bananas from the stand for a total of $6.30, what total number of apples and bananas did the customer purchase?

(A) 10
(B) 11
(C) 12
(D) 13
(E) 14

Algebra First-degree equations; Operations with integers

If each apple sold for $0.70, each banana sold for $0.50, and the total purchase price was $6.30, then $0.70x + 0.50y = 6.30$, where x and y are positive integers representing the number of apples and bananas, respectively, the customer purchased.

$$0.70x + 0.50y = 6.30$$
$$0.50y = 6.30 - 0.70x$$
$$0.50y = 0.70(9 - x)$$
$$y = \dfrac{7}{5}(9 - x)$$

Since y must be an integer, $9 - x$ must be divisible by 5. Furthermore, both x and y must be positive integers. For $x = 1, 2, 3, 4, 5, 6, 7, 8$, the corresponding values of $9 - x$ are 8, 7, 6, 5, 4, 3, 2, and 1. Only one of these, 5, is divisible by 5. Therefore, $x = 4$ and $y = \dfrac{7}{5}(9 - 4) = 7$ and the total number of apples and bananas the customer purchased is $4 + 7 = 11$.

The correct answer is B.

65. The average distance between the Sun and a certain planet is approximately 2.3×10^{14} inches. Which of the following is closest to the average distance between the Sun and the planet, in kilometers? (1 kilometer is approximately 3.9×10^4 inches.)

    (A) 7.1×10^8
    (B) 5.9×10^9
    (C) 1.6×10^{10}
    (D) 1.6×10^{11}
    (E) 5.9×10^{11}

Arithmetic Measurement conversion

Convert to kilometers and then estimate.

$$(2.3 \times 10^{14} \text{ in})\left(\frac{1 \text{ km}}{3.9 \times 10^4 \text{ in}}\right) = \frac{2.3 \times 10^{14}}{3.9 \times 10^4} \text{ km}$$

$$= \frac{2.3}{3.9} \times 10^{14-4} \text{ km}$$

$$\approx \frac{2}{4} \times 10^{10}$$

$$= 0.5 \times 10^{10}$$

$$= 5 \times 10^9$$

The correct answer is B.

66. At a certain school, the ratio of the number of second graders to the number of fourth graders is 8 to 5, and the ratio of the number of first graders to the number of second graders is 3 to 4. If the ratio of the number of third graders to the number of fourth graders is 3 to 2, what is the ratio of the number of first graders to the number of third graders?

    (A) 16 to 15
    (B) 9 to 5
    (C) 5 to 16
    (D) 5 to 4
    (E) 4 to 5

Arithmetic Ratio and proportion

If F, S, T, and R represent the number of first, second, third, and fourth graders, respectively, then the given ratios are: (i) $\frac{S}{R} = \frac{8}{5}$, (ii) $\frac{F}{S} = \frac{3}{4}$, and (iii) $\frac{T}{R} = \frac{3}{2}$. The desired ratio is $\frac{F}{T}$. From

(i), $S = \frac{8}{5}R$, and from (ii), $F = \frac{3}{4}S$. Combining these results, $F = \frac{3}{4}S = \frac{3}{4}\left(\frac{8}{5}R\right) = \frac{6}{5}R$. From (iii),

$T = \frac{3}{2}R$. Then $\frac{F}{T} = \frac{\frac{6}{5}R}{\frac{3}{2}R} = \frac{6}{5} \cdot \frac{2}{3} = \frac{4}{5}$. So, the

ratio of the number of first graders to the number of third graders is 4 to 5.

The correct answer is E.

67. If m is the average (arithmetic mean) of the first 10 positive multiples of 5 and if M is the median of the first 10 positive multiples of 5, what is the value of $M - m$?

    (A) -5
    (B) 0
    (C) 5
    (D) 25
    (E) 27.5

Arithmetic Statistics

The first 10 positive multiples of 5 are 5, 10, 15, 20, 25, 30, 35, 40, 45, and 50. From this, the average (arithmetic mean) of the 10 multiples, that is, $\frac{\text{sum of values}}{\text{number of values}}$, can be calculated:

$$m = \frac{5+10+15+20+25+30+35+40+45+50}{10}$$

$$= \frac{275}{10} = 27.5.$$

Since there is an even number of multiples, the median, M, is the average of the middle two numbers, 25 and 30:

$$M = \frac{25+30}{2} = 27.5.$$

Therefore, the median minus the average is:

$$M - m = 27.5 - 27.5 = 0.$$

This problem can also be solved as follows. Since the values can be grouped in pairs (i.e., 5 and 50, 10 and 45, 15 and 40, etc.), each of which is symmetric with respect to the median, it follows that the average and median are equal.

The correct answer is B.

$$A = \{2, 3, 4, 5\}$$
$$B = \{4, 5, 6, 7, 8\}$$

68. Two integers will be randomly selected from the sets above, one integer from set A and one integer from set B. What is the probability that the sum of the two integers will equal 9 ?

(A) 0.15
(B) 0.20
(C) 0.25
(D) 0.30
(E) 0.33

Arithmetic; Algebra Probability; Concepts of sets

The total number of different pairs of numbers, one from set A and one from set B is $(4)(5) = 20$. Of these 20 pairs of numbers, there are 4 possible pairs that sum to 9: 2 and 7, 3 and 6, 4 and 5, and 5 and 4. Thus, the probability that the sum of the two integers will be 9 is equal to $\frac{4}{20} = 0.20$.

The correct answer is B.

69. In the coordinate plane, a circle has center (2,–3) and passes through the point (5,0). What is the area of the circle?

(A) 3π
(B) $3\sqrt{2}\pi$
(C) $3\sqrt{3}\pi$
(D) 9π
(E) 18π

Geometry Coordinate geometry; Circles; Area

The area of a circle is given by πr^2, where r is the radius of the circle. The value of r^2 is the square of the distance from the center to a point of the circle. Using the distance formula, $r^2 = (2 - 5)^2 + (-3 - 0)^2 = 9 + 9 = 18$. Therefore, the area of the circle is 18π.

The correct answer is E.

70. At a certain instant in time, the number of cars, N, traveling on a portion of a certain highway can be estimated by the formula

$$N = \frac{20Ld}{600 + s^2}$$

where L is the number of lanes in the same direction, d is the length of the portion of the highway, in feet, and s is the average speed of the cars, in miles per hour. Based on the formula, what is the estimated number of cars traveling on a $\frac{1}{2}$-mile portion of the highway if the highway has 2 lanes in the same direction and the average speed of the cars is 40 miles per hour? (5,280 feet = 1 mile)

(A) 155
(B) 96
(C) 80
(D) 48
(E) 24

Algebra Simplifying algebraic expressions

Substitute $L = 2$, $d = \frac{1}{2}(5,280)$, and $s = 40$ into the given formula and calculate the value for N.

$$N = \frac{20(2)\left(\frac{1}{2}\right)(5,280)}{600 + 40^2}$$
$$= \frac{20(5,280)}{600 + 1,600}$$
$$= \frac{20(5,280)}{2,200}$$
$$= \frac{2(528)}{22}$$
$$= \frac{528}{11}$$
$$= 48$$

The correct answer is D.

71. Yesterday's closing prices of 2,420 different stocks listed on a certain stock exchange were all different from today's closing prices. The number of stocks that closed at a higher price today than yesterday was 20 percent greater than the number that closed at a lower price. How many of the stocks closed at a higher price today than yesterday?

    (A)   484
    (B)   726
    (C)   1,100
    (D)   1,320
    (E)   1,694

    Arithmetic Percents

    Let n be the number of stocks that closed at a lower price today than yesterday. Then $1.2n$ is the number of stocks that closed at a higher price today than yesterday, and $1.2n$ is the value asked for. Because the total number of stocks is 2,420, it follows that $n + 1.2n = 2,420$, or $2.2n = 2,420$. Therefore, $n = \dfrac{2,420}{2.2} = 1,100$, and hence $1.2n = (1.2)(1,100) = 1,320$.

    The correct answer is D.

72. If $y\left(\dfrac{3x-5}{2}\right) = y$ and $y \neq 0$, then $x =$

    (A) $\dfrac{2}{3}$

    (B) $\dfrac{5}{3}$

    (C) $\dfrac{7}{3}$

    (D)   1

    (E)   4

    Algebra First-degree equations

    Since $y \neq 0$, it is possible to simplify this equation and solve for x as follows:

    $$y\left(\dfrac{3x-5}{2}\right) = y$$

    $$\dfrac{3x-5}{2} = 1 \qquad \text{divide both sides by } y$$

$$3x - 5 = 2 \qquad \text{multiply both sides by 2}$$

$$3x = 7 \qquad \text{solve for } x$$

$$x = \dfrac{7}{3}$$

The correct answer is C.

73. If $x + 5 > 2$ and $x - 3 < 7$, the value of x must be between which of the following pairs of numbers?

    (A)   −3 and 10
    (B)   −3 and 4
    (C)   2 and 7
    (D)   3 and 4
    (E)   3 and 10

    Algebra Inequalities

    Isolate x in each given inequality. Since $x + 5 > 2$, then $x > -3$. Since $x - 3 < 7$, then $x < 10$. Thus, $-3 < x < 10$, which means the value of x must be between −3 and 10.

    The correct answer is A.

74. A gym class can be divided into 8 teams with an equal number of players on each team or into 12 teams with an equal number of players on each team. What is the lowest possible number of students in the class?

    (A)   20
    (B)   24
    (C)   36
    (D)   48
    (E)   96

    Arithmetic Properties of numbers

    The lowest value that can be divided evenly by 8 and 12 is their least common multiple (LCM). Since $8 = 2^3$ and $12 = 2^2(3)$, the LCM is $2^3(3) = 24$.

    The correct answer is B.

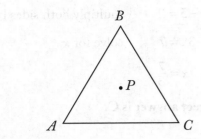

75. In the figure above, triangle *ABC* is equilateral, and point *P* is equidistant from vertices *A*, *B*, and *C*. If triangle *ABC* is rotated clockwise about point *P*, what is the minimum number of degrees the triangle must be rotated so that point *B* will be in the position where point *A* is now?

(A)   60
(B)   120
(C)   180
(D)   240
(E)   270

Geometry Angles

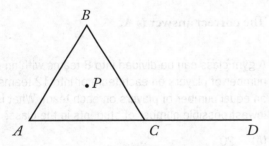

Since △*ABC* is equilateral, the measure of ∠*ACB* is 60°. Therefore, the measure of ∠*BCD* is 180° − 60° = 120°. Rotating the figure clockwise about point *P* through an angle of 120° will produce the figure shown below.

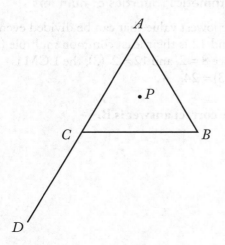

Then rotating this figure clockwise about point *P* through an angle of 120° will produce the figure shown below.

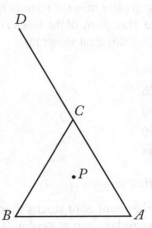

In this figure, point *B* is in the position where point *A* was in the original figure. The triangle was rotated clockwise about point *P* through 120° + 120° = 240°.

The correct answer is D.

76. At least $\frac{2}{3}$ of the 40 members of a committee must vote in favor of a resolution for it to pass. What is the greatest number of members who could vote against the resolution and still have it pass?

(A)   19
(B)   17
(C)   16
(D)   14
(E)   13

Arithmetic Operations on rational numbers

If at least $\frac{2}{3}$ of the members must vote in favor of a resolution, then no more than $\frac{1}{3}$ of the members can be voting against it. On this 40-member committee, $\frac{1}{3}(40) = 13\frac{1}{3}$, which means that no more than 13 members can vote against the resolution and still have it pass.

The correct answer is E.

77. If n = 20! + 17, then n is divisible by which of the following?

    I.   15
    II. 17
    III. 19

    (A) None
    (B) I only
    (C) II only
    (D) I and II
    (E) II and III

Arithmetic Properties of numbers

Because 20! is the product of all integers from 1 through 20, it follows that 20! is divisible by each integer from 1 through 20. In particular, 20! is divisible by each of the integers 15, 17, and 19. Since 20! and 17 are both divisible by 17, their sum is divisible by 17, and hence the correct answer will include II. If n were divisible by 15, then n – 20! would be divisible by 15. But, n – 20! = 17 and 17 is not divisible by 15. Therefore, the correct answer does not include I. If n were divisible by 19, then n – 20! would be divisible by 19. But, n – 20! = 17 and 17 is not divisible by 19. Therefore, the correct answer does not include III.

The correct answer is C.

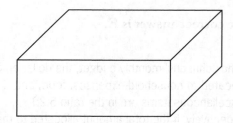

78. In the rectangular solid above, the three sides shown have areas 12, 15, and 20, respectively. What is the volume of the solid?

    (A) 60
    (B) 120
    (C) 450
    (D) 1,800
    (E) 3,600

Geometry Volume

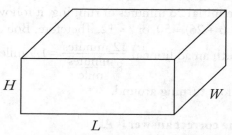

In the figure above, the areas of the three sides are given by HW, HL, and LW. Assuming $HW = 12 = (3)(4)$, $HL = 15 = (3)(5)$, and $LW = 20 = (5)(4)$, it is clear that possible choices for the edge lengths are $H = 3$, $W = 4$, and $L = 5$. Therefore, the volume of the rectangular solid is $(3)(4)(5) = 60$.

Alternatively, the product of the given areas, in some order, is $(HW)(HL)(LW) = (12)(15)(20)$. Then,

$$(HWL)^2 = (2^2 \cdot 3)(3 \cdot 5)(2^2 \cdot 5)$$
$$(HWL)^2 = (2^2 \cdot 3 \cdot 5)^2$$
$$HWL = 2^2 \cdot 3 \cdot 5$$
$$\text{volume} = 60$$

The correct answer is A.

79. After driving to a riverfront parking lot, Bob plans to run south along the river, turn around, and return to the parking lot, running north along the same path. After running 3.25 miles south, he decides to run for only 50 minutes more. If Bob runs at a constant rate of 8 minutes per mile, how many miles farther south can he run and still be able to return to the parking lot in 50 minutes?

    (A) 1.5
    (B) 2.25
    (C) 3.0
    (D) 3.25
    (E) 4.75

Algebra Applied problems

After running 3.25 miles south, Bob has been running for $(3.25 \text{ miles})\left(8 \dfrac{\text{minutes}}{\text{mile}}\right) = 26$ minutes. Thus, if t is the number of additional minutes that Bob can run south before turning around, then the number of minutes that Bob will run north, after turning around, will be $t + 26$. Since Bob will be running a total of 50 minutes after the initial 26 minutes of running, it follows that $t + (t + 26) = 50$, or $t = 12$. Therefore, Bob can run south an additional $\dfrac{12 \text{ minutes}}{8 \dfrac{\text{minutes}}{\text{mile}}} = 1.5 \text{ miles}$ before turning around.

The correct answer is A.

80. M is the sum of the reciprocals of the consecutive integers from 201 to 300, inclusive. Which of the following is true?

   (A) $\dfrac{1}{3} < M < \dfrac{1}{2}$

   (B) $\dfrac{1}{5} < M < \dfrac{1}{3}$

   (C) $\dfrac{1}{7} < M < \dfrac{1}{5}$

   (D) $\dfrac{1}{9} < M < \dfrac{1}{7}$

   (E) $\dfrac{1}{12} < M < \dfrac{1}{9}$

Arithmetic Estimation

Because $\dfrac{1}{300}$ is less than each of the 99 numbers $\dfrac{1}{201}, \dfrac{1}{202}, ..., \dfrac{1}{299}$, it follows that $\dfrac{1}{300} + \dfrac{1}{300} + \cdots + \dfrac{1}{300}$ (the sum of 99 identical values) is less than $\dfrac{1}{201} + \dfrac{1}{202} + \cdots + \dfrac{1}{299}$. Therefore, adding $\dfrac{1}{300}$ to both sides of this last inequality, it follows that $\dfrac{1}{300} + \dfrac{1}{300} + \cdots + \dfrac{1}{300}$ (the sum of 100 identical values) is less than $\dfrac{1}{201} + \dfrac{1}{202} + \cdots + \dfrac{1}{299} + \dfrac{1}{300} = M$. Hence, $(100)\left(\dfrac{1}{300}\right) < M$ or $\dfrac{1}{3} < M$. Also, because $\dfrac{1}{200}$ is greater than each of the 100 numbers $\dfrac{1}{201}$, $\dfrac{1}{202}, ..., \dfrac{1}{300}$, it follows that $\dfrac{1}{200} + \dfrac{1}{200} + \cdots + \dfrac{1}{200}$ (the sum of 100 identical values) is greater than $\dfrac{1}{201} + \dfrac{1}{202} + \cdots + \dfrac{1}{300}$. Hence, $(100)\left(\dfrac{1}{200}\right) > M$ or $\dfrac{1}{2} > M$. From $\dfrac{1}{3} < M$ and $\dfrac{1}{2} > M$, it follows that $\dfrac{1}{3} < M < \dfrac{1}{2}$.

The correct answer is A.

81. Working simultaneously at their respective constant rates, Machines A and B produce 800 nails in x hours. Working alone at its constant rate, Machine A produces 800 nails in y hours. In terms of x and y, how many hours does it take Machine B, working alone at its constant rate, to produce 800 nails?

   (A) $\dfrac{x}{x+y}$

   (B) $\dfrac{y}{x+y}$

   (C) $\dfrac{xy}{x+y}$

   (D) $\dfrac{xy}{x-y}$

   (E) $\dfrac{xy}{y-x}$

Algebra Applied problems

Let R_A and R_B be the constant rates, in nails per hour, at which Machines A and B work, respectively. Then it follows from the given information that $R_A + R_B = \dfrac{800}{x}$ and $R_A = \dfrac{800}{y}$. Hence, $\dfrac{800}{y} + R_B = \dfrac{800}{x}$, or

$$R_B = \dfrac{800}{x} - \dfrac{800}{y} = 800\left(\dfrac{1}{x} - \dfrac{1}{y}\right) = 800\left(\dfrac{y-x}{xy}\right).$$

Therefore, the time, in hours, it would take Machine B to produce 800 nails is given by

$$\dfrac{800}{800\left(\dfrac{y-x}{xy}\right)} = \dfrac{xy}{y-x}.$$

The correct answer is E.

82. In the Johnsons' monthly budget, the dollar amounts allocated to household expenses, food, and miscellaneous items are in the ratio 5:2:1, respectively. If the total amount allocated to these three categories is $1,800, what is the amount allocated to food?

   (A) $900
   (B) $720
   (C) $675
   (D) $450
   (E) $225

Algebra Applied problems

Since the ratio is 5:2:1, let $5x$ be the money allocated to household expenses, $2x$ be the money allocated to food, and $1x$ be the money allocated to miscellaneous items. The given information can then be expressed in the following equation and solved for x.

$5x + 2x + 1x = \$1,800$

$\qquad 8x = \$1,800 \qquad$ combine like terms

$\qquad x = \$225 \qquad$ divide both sides by 8

The money allocated to food is $2x = 2(\$225) = \$450$.

The correct answer is D.

83. There are 4 more women than men on Centerville's board of education. If there are 10 members on the board, how many are women?

(A) 3
(B) 4
(C) 6
(D) 7
(E) 8

Algebra Simultaneous equations; Applied problems

Let m be the number of men on the board and w be the number of women on the board. According to the problem,

$w = m + 4 \qquad$ because there are 4 more women than men and

$w + m = 10 \qquad$ because the board has a total of 10 members.

Substituting $m + 4$ for w in the second equation gives:

$m + m + 4 = 10$

$\quad 2m + 4 = 10 \qquad$ combine like terms

$\quad 2m = 6 \qquad$ subtract 4 from both sides

$\quad m = 3 \qquad$ divide both sides by 2

Using the first equation, $w = m + 4 = 3 + 4 = 7$ women on the board.

This problem can also be solved without algebra by listing the (m,w) possibilities for $w = m + 4$. These possibilities are $(0,4)$, $(1,5)$, $(2,6)$, $(3,7)$, etc., and hence the pair in which $m + w = 10$ is $(3,7)$.

The correct answer is D.

84. Leona bought a 1-year, $10,000 certificate of deposit that paid interest at an annual rate of 8 percent compounded semiannually. What was the total amount of interest paid on this certificate at maturity?

(A) $10,464
(B) $ 864
(C) $ 816
(D) $ 800
(E) $ 480

Arithmetic Operations with rational numbers

Using the formula $A = P\left(1 + \dfrac{r}{n}\right)^{nt}$, where A is the amount of money after t (1 year), P is the principal amount invested ($10,000), r is the annual interest rate (0.08), and n is the number of times compounding occurs annually (2), the given information can be expressed as follows and solved for A:

$A = (10,000)\left(1 + \dfrac{0.08}{2}\right)^{(2)(1)}$

$A = (10,000)(1.04)^2$

$A = (10,000)(1.0816)$

$A = 10,816$

Thus, since A is the final value of the certificate, the amount of interest paid at maturity is $\$10,816 - \$10,000 = \$816$.

The correct answer is C.

85. $\dfrac{(0.0036)(2.8)}{(0.04)(0.1)(0.003)} =$

   (A) 840.0
   (B) 84.0
   (C) 8.4
   (D) 0.84
   (E) 0.084

Arithmetic Operations with rational numbers

To make the calculations less tedious, convert the decimals to whole numbers times powers of 10 as follows:

$$\dfrac{(0.0036)(2.8)}{(0.04)(0.1)(0.003)} =$$

$$= \dfrac{(36 \times 10^{-4})(28 \times 10^{-1})}{(4 \times 10^{-2})(1 \times 10^{-1})(3 \times 10^{-3})}$$

$$= \dfrac{(36)(28)}{(4)(1)(3)} \times 10^{(-4-1)-(-2-1-3)}$$

$$= \dfrac{(36)(28)}{(4)(1)(3)} \times 10^{-5-(-6)}$$

$$= \dfrac{(36)(28)}{(4)(1)(3)} \times 10^{-5+6}$$

$$= \left(\dfrac{36}{3}\right)\left(\dfrac{28}{4}\right) \times 10^{-5+6}$$

$$= (12)(7) \times 10^{1}$$

$$= 84 \times 10$$

$$= 840$$

The correct answer is A.

86. Machine A produces bolts at a uniform rate of 120 every 40 seconds, and Machine B produces bolts at a uniform rate of 100 every 20 seconds. If the two machines run simultaneously, how many seconds will it take for them to produce a total of 200 bolts?

   (A) 22
   (B) 25
   (C) 28
   (D) 32
   (E) 56

Algebra Applied problems

Determine the production rates for each machine separately, and then calculate their production rate together.

Rate of Machine A $= \dfrac{120}{40} = 3$ bolts per second

Rate of Machine B $= \dfrac{100}{20} = 5$ bolts per second

Combined rate $= 3 + 5 = 8$ bolts per second

Build an equation with $s =$ the number of seconds it takes to produce 200 bolts.

$8s = 200$ (rate)(time) = amount produced

$s = 25$ solve for s

The correct answer is B.

87. If n is an integer greater than 6, which of the following must be divisible by 3 ?

   (A) $n(n+1)(n-4)$
   (B) $n(n+2)(n-1)$
   (C) $n(n+3)(n-5)$
   (D) $n(n+4)(n-2)$
   (E) $n(n+5)(n-6)$

Arithmetic Properties of numbers

The easiest and quickest way to do this problem is to choose an integer greater than 6, such as 7, and eliminate answer choices in which the value of the expression is not divisible by 3:

A $7(7+1)(7-4) = (7)(8)(3)$, which is divisible by 3, so A cannot be eliminated.

B $7(7+2)(7-1) = (7)(9)(6)$, which is divisible by 3, so B cannot be eliminated.

C $7(7+3)(7-5) = (7)(10)(2)$, which is not divisible by 3, so C can be eliminated.

D $7(7+4)(7-2)=(7)(11)(5)$, which is not divisible by 3, so D can be eliminated.

E $7(7+5)(7-6)=(7)(12)(1)$, which is divisible by 3, so E cannot be eliminated.

Choose another integer greater than 6, such as 8, and test the remaining answer choices:

A $8(8+1)(8-4)=(8)(9)(4)$, which is divisible by 3, so A cannot be eliminated.

B $8(8+2)(8-1)=(8)(10)(7)$, which is not divisible by 3, so B can be eliminated.

E $8(8+5)(8-6)=(8)(13)(2)$, which is not divisible by 3, so E can be eliminated.

Thus, A is the only answer choice that has not been eliminated.

For the more mathematically inclined, if n is divisible by 3, then the expression in each answer choice is divisible by 3. Assume, then, that n is not divisible by 3. If the remainder when n is divided by 3 is 1, then $n=3q+1$ for some integer q. All of the expressions $n-4$, $n-1$, $n+2$, and $n+5$ are divisible by 3 [i.e., $n-4=3q-3=3(q-1)$, $n-1=3q$, $n+2=3q+3=3(q+1)$, $n+5=3q+6=3(q+2)$], and none of the expressions $n-6$, $n-5$, $n-2$, $n+1$, $n+3$, and $n+4$ is divisible by 3. Therefore, if the remainder when n is divided by 3 is 1, only the expressions in answer choices A, B, and E are divisible by 3. On the other hand, if the remainder when n is divided by 3 is 2, then $n=3q+2$ for some integer q. All of the expressions $n-5$, $n-2$, $n+1$, and $n+4$ are divisible by 3 [i.e., $n-5=3q-3=3(q-1)$, $n-2=3q$, $n+1=3q+3=3(q+1)$, $n+4=3q+6=3(q+2)$], and none of the expressions $n-6$, $n-4$, $n-1$, $n+2$, $n+3$, and $n+5$ is divisible by 3. Therefore, if the remainder when n is divided by 3 is 2, only the expressions in answer choices A, C, and D are divisible by 3. Only the expression in answer choice A is divisible by 3 regardless of whether n is divisible by 3, has a remainder of 1 when divided by 3, or has a remainder of 2 when divided by 3.

The correct answer is A.

88.   The total cost for Company X to produce a batch of tools is $10,000 plus $3 per tool. Each tool sells for $8. The gross profit earned from producing and selling these tools is the total income from sales minus the total production cost. If a batch of 20,000 tools is produced and sold, then Company X's gross profit per tool is

(A) $3.00
(B) $3.75
(C) $4.50
(D) $5.00
(E) $5.50

Arithmetic Applied problems

The total cost to produce 20,000 tools is $10,000+\$3(20,000)=\$70,000$. The revenue resulting from the sale of 20,000 tools is $\$8(20,000)=\$160,000$. The gross profit is $\$160,000-\$70,000=\$90,000$, and the gross profit per tool is $\dfrac{\$90,000}{20,000}=\$4.50$.

The correct answer is C.

89.   A dealer originally bought 100 identical batteries at a total cost of q dollars. If each battery was sold at 50 percent above the original cost per battery, then, in terms of q, for how many dollars was each battery sold?

(A) $\dfrac{3q}{200}$

(B) $\dfrac{3q}{2}$

(C) $150q$

(D) $\dfrac{q}{100}+50$

(E) $\dfrac{150}{q}$

Algebra Factoring and Simplifying algebraic expressions

Since 100 batteries cost q dollars, division by 100 shows that 1 battery costs $\dfrac{q}{100}$ dollars. Then, since the selling price is 50 percent above the original cost per battery, the selling price of each battery can be expressed as $\dfrac{q}{100}(1.50)=\dfrac{q}{100}\left(\dfrac{3}{2}\right)=\dfrac{3q}{200}$.

The correct answer is A.

90. In an increasing sequence of 10 consecutive integers, the sum of the first 5 integers is 560. What is the sum of the last 5 integers in the sequence?

    (A) 585
    (B) 580
    (C) 575
    (D) 570
    (E) 565

Algebra First-degree equations

Let the first 5 consecutive integers be represented by x, $x+1$, $x+2$, $x+3$, and $x+4$. Then, since the sum of the integers is 560, $x+(x+1)+(x+2)+(x+3)+(x+4)=560$. Thus,

$$5x+10=560$$

$$5x=550 \qquad \text{solve for } x$$

$$x=110$$

The first integer in the sequence is 110, so the next integers are 111, 112, 113, and 114. From this, the last 5 integers in the sequence, and thus their sum, can be determined. The sum of the 6th, 7th, 8th, 9th, and 10th integers is $115+116+117+118+119=585$.

This problem can also be solved without algebra: The sum of the last 5 integers exceeds the sum of the first 5 integers by $1+3+5+7+9=25$ because the 6th integer exceeds the 5th integer by 1, the 7th integer exceeds the 4th integer by 3, etc.

The correct answer is A.

91. If Q is an odd number and the median of Q consecutive integers is 120, what is the largest of these integers?

    (A) $\dfrac{Q-1}{2}+120$

    (B) $\dfrac{Q}{2}+119$

    (C) $\dfrac{Q}{2}+120$

    (D) $\dfrac{Q+119}{2}$

    (E) $\dfrac{Q+120}{2}$

Arithmetic Statistics

For an odd number of data values, the median is the middle number. Thus, 120 is the middle number, and so half of the $Q-1$ remaining values are at most 120 and the other half of the $Q-1$ remaining values are at least 120. In particular, $\dfrac{Q-1}{2}$ data values lie to the right of 120 when the data values are listed in increasing order from left to right, and so the largest data value is $120+\dfrac{Q-1}{2}$. Alternatively, it is immediate that (B), (C), or (E) cannot be correct since these expressions do not have an integer value when Q is odd. For the list consisting of the single number 120 (i.e., if $Q = 1$), (D) fails because $\dfrac{Q+119}{2}=\dfrac{1+119}{2}=60\neq 120$ and (A) does not fail because $\dfrac{Q-1}{2}+120=\dfrac{1-1}{2}+120=120$.

The correct answer is A.

92. A ladder of a fire truck is elevated to an angle of 60° and extended to a length of 70 feet. If the base of the ladder is 7 feet above the ground, how many feet above the ground does the ladder reach?

    (A) 35
    (B) 42
    (C) $35\sqrt{3}$
    (D) $7+35\sqrt{3}$
    (E) $7+42\sqrt{3}$

Geometry Triangles

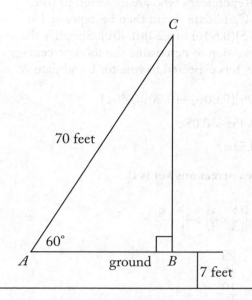

70 feet

60°

A   ground   *B*

7 feet

C

Given the figure above, determine *BC*. Then add 7 to determine how far above the ground the ladder reaches.

Triangle $\triangle ABC$ is a 30°-60°-90° triangle with hypotenuse $\overline{AC}$ of length 70 feet. Since the lengths of the sides of a 30°-60°-90° triangle are in the ratio 1:2:$\sqrt{3}$, $\frac{AB}{AC} = \frac{1}{2}$ and so $AB = \frac{1}{2}AC = 35$, and $\frac{AB}{BC} = \frac{1}{\sqrt{3}}$ and so $BC = AB\sqrt{3} = 35\sqrt{3}$. Therefore, the ladder reaches $7 + 35\sqrt{3}$ feet above the ground.

The correct answer is D.

93. If Jake loses 8 pounds, he will weigh twice as much as his sister. Together they now weigh 278 pounds. What is Jake's present weight, in pounds?

(A)   131
(B)   135
(C)   139
(D)   147
(E)   188

Algebra Systems of equations

Let J represent Jake's weight and S represent his sister's weight. Then $J - 8 = 2S$ and $J + S = 278$. Solve the second equation for S and get $S = 278 - J$. Substituting the expression for S into the first equation gives

$$J - 8 = 2(278 - J)$$
$$J - 8 = 556 - 2J$$
$$J + 2J = 556 + 8$$
$$3J = 564$$
$$J = 188$$

The correct answer is E.

94. A store reported total sales of $385 million for February of this year. If the total sales for the same month last year was $320 million, approximately what was the percent increase in sales?

(A)   2%
(B)   17%
(C)   20%
(D)   65%
(E)   83%

Arithmetic Percents

The percent increase in sales from last year to this year is 100 times the quotient of the difference in sales for the two years divided by the sales last year. Thus, the percent increase is

$$\frac{385 - 320}{320} \times 100 = \frac{65}{320} \times 100$$
$$= \frac{13}{64} \times 100$$
$$\approx \frac{13}{65} \times 100$$
$$= \frac{1}{5} \times 100$$
$$= 20\%$$

The correct answer is C.

95. When positive integer x is divided by positive integer y, the remainder is 9. If $\frac{x}{y} = 96.12$, what is the value of y?

    (A) 96
    (B) 75
    (C) 48
    (D) 25
    (E) 12

Arithmetic Properties of numbers

The remainder is 9 when x is divided by y, so $x = yq + 9$ for some positive integer q. Dividing both sides by y gives $\frac{x}{y} = q + \frac{9}{y}$. But, $\frac{x}{y} = 96.12 = 96 + 0.12$. Equating the two expressions for $\frac{x}{y}$ gives $q + \frac{9}{y} = 96 + 0.12$.

Thus, $q = 96$ and $\frac{9}{y} = 0.12$

$$9 = 0.12\,y$$

$$y = \frac{9}{0.12}$$

$$y = 75$$

The correct answer is B.

96. In a certain city, 60 percent of the registered voters are Democrats and the rest are Republicans. In a mayoral race, if 75 percent of the registered voters who are Democrats and 20 percent of the registered voters who are Republicans are expected to vote for Candidate A, what percent of the registered voters are expected to vote for Candidate A?

    (A) 50%
    (B) 53%
    (C) 54%
    (D) 55%
    (E) 57%

Arithmetic; Algebra Percents; Applied problems

Letting v be the number of registered voters in the city, then the information that 60% of the registered voters are Democrats can be expressed as $0.60v$. From this, it can be stated that $1.00v - 0.60v = 0.40v$ are Republicans. The percentage of Democrats and the percentage of Republicans who are expected to vote for Candidate A can then be expressed as $(0.75)(0.60v) + (0.20)(0.40v)$. Simplify the expression to determine the total percentage of voters expected to vote for Candidate A.

$$(0.75)(0.60v) + (0.20)(0.40v)$$

$$= 0.45v + 0.08v$$

$$= 0.53v$$

The correct answer is B.

97. $\frac{1}{2} + \left[\left(\frac{2}{3} \times \frac{3}{8}\right) \div 4\right] - \frac{9}{16} =$

    (A) $\frac{29}{16}$
    (B) $\frac{19}{16}$
    (C) $\frac{15}{16}$
    (D) $\frac{9}{13}$
    (E) 0

Arithmetic Operations on rational numbers

Perform the operations in the correct order, using least common denominators when adding or subtracting fractions:

$$\frac{1}{2} + \left[\left(\frac{2}{3} \times \frac{3}{8}\right) \div 4\right] - \frac{9}{16} = \frac{1}{2} + \left[\left(\frac{\cancel{2}^{1}}{\cancel{3}_{1}} \times \frac{\cancel{3}^{1}}{\cancel{8}_{4}}\right) \div 4\right] - \frac{9}{16}$$

$$= \frac{1}{2} + \left[\left(\frac{1}{4}\right) \div 4\right] - \frac{9}{16}$$

$$= \frac{1}{2} + \frac{1}{16} - \frac{9}{16}$$

$$= \frac{8}{16} + \frac{1}{16} - \frac{9}{16}$$

$$= \frac{8 + 1 - 9}{16}$$

$$= \frac{0}{16}$$

$$= 0$$

The correct answer is E.

98. Water consists of hydrogen and oxygen, and the approximate ratio, by mass, of hydrogen to oxygen is 2:16. Approximately how many grams of oxygen are there in 144 grams of water?

    (A) 16
    (B) 72
    (C) 112
    (D) 128
    (E) 142

    Algebra Applied problems

    The mass ratio of oxygen to water is

    $\dfrac{\text{oxygen}}{\text{oxygen} + \text{hydrogen}} = \dfrac{16}{16+2} = \dfrac{8}{9}$. Therefore, if

    x is the number of grams of oxygen in 144 grams of water, it follows that $\dfrac{x}{144} = \dfrac{8}{9}$. Now solve for x:

    $$x = \frac{8}{9} \cdot \frac{144}{1} = \frac{(8)(\cancel{3})(4)(\cancel{3})(4)}{\cancel{9}} = (8)(4)(4) = 128.$$

    The correct answer is D.

99. If $x(2x+1)=0$ and $\left(x+\dfrac{1}{2}\right)(2x-3)=0$, then $x =$

    (A) -3
    (B) $-\dfrac{1}{2}$
    (C) 0
    (D) $\dfrac{1}{2}$
    (E) $\dfrac{3}{2}$

    Algebra Second-degree equations; Simultaneous equations

    Setting each factor equal to 0, it can be seen that the solution set to the first equation is $\left\{0, -\dfrac{1}{2}\right\}$ and the solution set to the second equation is $\left\{-\dfrac{1}{2}, \dfrac{3}{2}\right\}$. Therefore, $-\dfrac{1}{2}$ is the solution to both equations.

    The correct answer is B.

100. On a scale that measures the intensity of a certain phenomenon, a reading of $n+1$ corresponds to an intensity that is 10 times the intensity corresponding to a reading of n. On that scale, the intensity corresponding to a reading of 8 is how many times as great as the intensity corresponding to a reading of 3 ?

    (A) 5
    (B) 50
    (C) 10^5
    (D) 5^{10}
    (E) $8^{10} - 3^{10}$

    Arithmetic Operations on rational numbers

    Since 8 can be obtained from 3 by "adding 1" five times, the intensity reading is greater by a factor of $(10)(10)(10)(10)(10) = 10^5$.

    The correct answer is C.

101. For the positive numbers, $n, n+1, n+2, n+4$, and $n+8$, the mean is how much greater than the median?

    (A) 0
    (B) 1
    (C) $n+1$
    (D) $n+2$
    (E) $n+3$

    Algebra Statistics

    Since the five positive numbers $n, n+1, n+2, n+4$, and $n+8$ are in ascending order, the median is the third number, which is $n+2$. The mean of the five numbers is

    $$\frac{n+(n+1)+(n+2)+(n+4)+(n+8)}{5}$$
    $$= \frac{5n+15}{5}$$
    $$= n+3$$

    Since $(n+3)-(n+2) = 1$, the mean is 1 greater than the median.

    The correct answer is B.

102. If $T = \frac{5}{9}(K - 32)$, and if $T = 290$, then $K =$

    (A) $\frac{1,738}{9}$

    (B) 322

    (C) 490

    (D) 554

    (E) $\frac{2,898}{5}$

Algebra First-degree equations

Substitute 290 for T in the equation, and solve for K.

$$T = \frac{5}{9}(K - 32)$$

$$290 = \frac{5}{9}(K - 32)$$

$$\frac{290}{1} \cdot \frac{9}{5} = K - 32$$

$$\frac{(29)(5)(2)}{1} \cdot \frac{9}{5} = K - 32$$

$$\frac{(29)(\cancel{5})(2)}{1} \cdot \frac{9}{\cancel{5}} = K - 32$$

$$522 = K - 32$$

$$554 = K$$

The correct answer is D.

103. The water from one outlet, flowing at a constant rate, can fill a swimming pool in 9 hours. The water from a second outlet, flowing at a constant rate, can fill the same pool in 5 hours. If both outlets are used at the same time, approximately what is the number of hours required to fill the pool?

    (A) 0.22

    (B) 0.31

    (C) 2.50

    (D) 3.21

    (E) 4.56

Arithmetic Operations on rational numbers

The first outlet can fill the pool at a rate of $\frac{1}{9}$ of the pool per hour, and the second can fill the pool at a rate of $\frac{1}{5}$ of the pool per hour. Together, they can fill the pool at a rate of $\frac{1}{9} + \frac{1}{5} = \frac{5}{45} + \frac{9}{45} = \frac{14}{45}$ of the pool per hour. Thus, when both outlets are used at the same time, they fill the pool in $\frac{45}{14} = 3.21$ hours.

The correct answer is D.

104. If a square mirror has a 20-inch diagonal, what is the approximate perimeter of the mirror, in inches?

    (A) 40

    (B) 60

    (C) 80

    (D) 100

    (E) 120

Geometry Perimeter; Pythagorean theorem

Let x be the length of one of the sides of the square mirror.

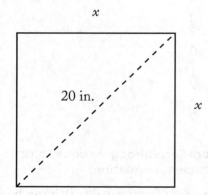

The triangles created by the diagonal are isosceles right triangles for which the Pythagorean theorem yields the following equation that can be solved for x.

$$x^2 + x^2 = 20^2$$

$$2x^2 = 400$$

$$x^2 = 200$$

$$x = \sqrt{200}$$

Therefore, the perimeter is $4x = 4\sqrt{200}$. To avoid estimating a value for $4\sqrt{200}$, note that $\left(4\sqrt{200}\right)^2 = (16)(200) = 3{,}200$, $(40)^2 = 1{,}600$, $(60)^2 = 3{,}600$, and $(80)^2 = 6{,}400$. The perimeter is closest to 60 because 3,200 is closer to 3,600 than it is to 1,600 or 6,400.

The correct answer is B.

105. The present ratio of students to teachers at a certain school is 30 to 1. If the student enrollment were to increase by 50 students and the number of teachers were to increase by 5, the ratio of students to teachers would then be 25 to 1. What is the present number of teachers?

    (A)   5
    (B)   8
    (C)   10
    (D)   12
    (E)   15

Algebra Applied problems

Let s be the present number of students, and let t be the present number of teachers. According to the problem, the following two equations apply:

$$\frac{30}{1} = \frac{s}{t} \qquad \text{Current student to teacher ratio}$$

$$\frac{s+50}{t+5} = \frac{25}{1} \qquad \text{Future student to teacher ratio}$$

Solving the first equation for s gives $s = 30t$. Substitute this value of s into the second equation, and solve for t.

$$\frac{30t + 50}{t + 5} = \frac{25}{1}$$

$30t + 50 = 25t + 125 \qquad$ multiply both sides by $t + 5$

$\qquad 5t = 75 \qquad\qquad$ simplify by subtraction

$\qquad\quad t = 15$

The correct answer is E.

106. What is the smallest integer n for which $25^n > 5^{12}$?

    (A)   6
    (B)   7
    (C)   8
    (D)   9
    (E)   10

Arithmetic Operations with rational numbers

Because $5^2 = 25$, a common base is 5. Rewrite the left side with 5 as a base: $25^n = \left(5^2\right)^n = 5^{2n}$. It follows that the desired integer is the least integer n for which $5^{2n} > 5^{12}$. This will be the least integer n for which $2n > 12$, or the least integer n for which $n > 6$, which is 7.

The correct answer is B.

107. Sixty percent of the members of a study group are women, and 45 percent of those women are lawyers. If one member of the study group is to be selected at random, what is the probability that the member selected is a woman lawyer?

    (A)   0.10
    (B)   0.15
    (C)   0.27
    (D)   0.33
    (E)   0.45

Arithmetic Probability

For simplicity, suppose there are 100 members in the study group. Since 60 percent of the members are women, there are 60 women in the group. Also, 45 percent of the women are lawyers so there are $0.45(60) = 27$ women lawyers in the study group. Therefore the probability of selecting a woman lawyer is $\frac{27}{100} = 0.27$.

The correct answer is C.

108. Each year for 4 years, a farmer increased the number of trees in a certain orchard by $\frac{1}{4}$ of the number of trees in the orchard the preceding year. If all of the trees thrived and there were 6,250 trees in the orchard at the end of the 4-year period, how many trees were in the orchard at the beginning of the 4-year period?

(A) 1,250
(B) 1,563
(C) 2,250
(D) 2,560
(E) 2,752

Arithmetic Operations on rational numbers

Increasing the number of trees each year by $\frac{1}{4}$ of the number of trees in the orchard the preceding year is equivalent to making the number of trees increase 25% per year, compounded yearly. If there were n trees at the beginning of the 4-year period, then there will be $1.25n$ trees at the end of the first year, $1.25(1.25n) = (1.25)^2n$ trees at the end of the second year, $1.25[(1.25)^2n] = (1.25)^3n$ trees at the end of the third year, and $1.25[(1.25)^3n] = (1.25)^4n$ trees at the end of the fourth year. Hence, $6,250 = (1.25)^4n$ and $n = \dfrac{6,250}{(1.25)^4}$. The arithmetic can be greatly simplified by rewriting $(1.25)^4$ as $\left(\dfrac{5}{4}\right)^4 = \dfrac{5^4}{4^4}$ and 6,250 as $(625)(10) = (5^4)(10)$. Then

$$\dfrac{6,250}{(1.25)^4} = (5^4)(10)\left(\dfrac{4^4}{5^4}\right) = (10)(4^4) = 2,560.$$

The correct answer is D.

NUMBER OF SHIPMENTS OF MANUFACTURED HOMES
IN THE UNITED STATES, 1990–2000

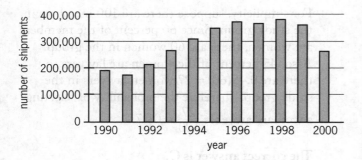

109. According to the chart shown, which of the following is closest to the median annual number of shipments of manufactured homes in the United States for the years from 1990 to 2000, inclusive?

(A) 250,000
(B) 280,000
(C) 310,000
(D) 325,000
(E) 340,000

Arithmetic Interpretation of graphs and tables; Statistics

From the chart, the approximate numbers of shipments are as follows:

Year	Number of shipments
1990	190,000
1991	180,000
1992	210,000
1993	270,000
1994	310,000
1995	350,000
1996	380,000
1997	370,000
1998	390,000
1999	360,000
2000	270,000

Since there are 11 entries in the table and 11 is an odd number, the median of the numbers of shipments is the 6th entry when the numbers of shipments are arranged in order from least to greatest. In order, from least to greatest, the first 6 entries are:

Number of shipments
180,000
190,000
210,000
270,000
270,000
310,000

The 6th entry is 310,000.

The correct answer is C.

110. For the positive integers a, b, and k, $a^k \parallel b$ means that a^k is a divisor of b, but a^{k+1} is not a divisor of b. If k is a positive integer and $2^k \parallel 72$, then k is equal to

   (A)   2
   (B)   3
   (C)   4
   (D)   8
   (E)   18

Arithmetic Property of numbers

Since $72 = (2^3)(3^2)$, it follows that 2^3 is a divisor of 72 and 2^4 is not a divisor of 72. Therefore, $2^3 \parallel 72$, and hence $k = 3$.

The correct answer is B.

111. If $t = \dfrac{1}{2^9 \times 5^3}$ is expressed as a terminating decimal, how many zeros will t have between the decimal point and the first nonzero digit to the right of the decimal point?

   (A)   Three
   (B)   Four
   (C)   Five
   (D)   Six
   (E)   Nine

Arithmetic Exponents; Operations with rational numbers

Use properties of positive integer exponents to get

$$\frac{1}{2^9 \times 5^3} = \frac{1}{2^{6+3} \times 5^3}$$

$$= \frac{1}{\left(2^6 \times 2^3\right) \times 5^3}$$

$$= \frac{1}{2^6 \times \left(2^3 \times 5^3\right)}$$

$$= \frac{1}{2^6 \times 10^3}$$

$$= \frac{1}{2^6} \times \frac{1}{10^3}$$

$$= \frac{1}{2^6} \times 10^{-3}$$

$$= \frac{1}{64} \times 10^{-3}$$

So, $t = \dfrac{1}{64} \times 10^{-3}$.

Since $\dfrac{1}{100} \times 10^{-3} < \dfrac{1}{64} \times 10^{-3} < \dfrac{1}{10} \times 10^{-3}$, then

$$0.00001 < \frac{1}{64} \times 10^{-3} < 0.0001,$$

so $0.00001 < t < 0.0001$ and t has four zeros between the decimal point and the first nonzero digit to the right of the decimal point.

The correct answer is B.

112. A certain characteristic in a large population has a distribution that is symmetric about the mean m. If 68 percent of the distribution lies within one standard deviation d of the mean, what percent of the distribution is less than $m + d$?

   (A)   16%
   (B)   32%
   (C)   48%
   (D)   84%
   (E)   92%

Arithmetic Statistics

Since 68% lies between $m - d$ and $m + d$, a total of $(100 - 68)\% = 32\%$ lies to the left of $m - d$ and to the right of $m + d$. Because the distribution is symmetric about m, half of the 32% lies to the right of $m + d$. Therefore, 16% lies to the right of $m + d$, and hence $(100 - 16)\% = 84\%$ lies to the left of $m + d$.

The correct answer is D.

113. In a certain district, the ratio of the number of registered Republicans to the number of registered Democrats was $\dfrac{3}{5}$. After 600 additional Republicans and 500 additional Democrats registered, the ratio was $\dfrac{4}{5}$. After these registrations, there were how many more voters in the district registered as Democrats than as Republicans?

   (A)   100
   (B)   300
   (C)   400
   (D)   1,000
   (E)   2,500

Algebra Applied problems

Let R and D be the numbers of registered Republicans and registered Democrats, respectively, before the additional registrations. Then, it is given that $\frac{R}{D} = \frac{3}{5}$ or $5R = 3D$. Also,

$$\frac{R+600}{D+500} = \frac{4}{5}$$

$$5(R+600) = 4(D+500)$$

$$5R + 3{,}000 = 4D + 2{,}000$$

$$3D + 3{,}000 = 4D + 2{,}000 \qquad \text{since } 5R = 3D \text{ from above}$$

$$1{,}000 = D$$

Since $D = 1{,}000$ and $5R = 3D$, it follows that $R = 600$. Finally, after the additional registrations, the number of Democrats was $1{,}000 + 500 = 1{,}500$ and the number of Republicans was $600 + 600 = 1{,}200$. The difference is $1{,}500 - 1{,}200 = 300$.

The correct answer is B.

114. In Country C, the unemployment rate among construction workers dropped from 16 percent on September 1, 1992, to 9 percent on September 1, 1996. If the number of construction workers was 20 percent greater on September 1, 1996, than on September 1, 1992, what was the approximate percent change in the number of unemployed construction workers over this period?

   (A)   50% decrease
   (B)   30% decrease
   (C)   15% decrease
   (D)   30% increase
   (E)   55% increase

Arithmetic Percents

Let U_1 and U_2 be the numbers of unemployed construction workers on September 1, 1992, and September 1, 1996, respectively, and let N be the number of construction workers on September 1, 1992. Then, from the given information, $1.2N$ is the number of construction workers on September 1, 1996, $U_1 = 0.16N$, and $U_2 = 0.09(1.2N)$. Therefore, the percent change from

September 1, 1992, to September 1, 1996, of unemployed construction workers is given by

$$\left(\frac{U_2 - U_1}{U_1} \times 100 \right)\%$$

$$= \left(\frac{0.09(1.2N) - 0.16N}{0.16N} \times 100 \right)\%$$

$$= \left(\frac{0.108 - 0.16}{0.16} \times 100 \right)\%$$

$$= \left(\frac{108 - 160}{160} \times 100 \right)\%$$

$$= \left(-\frac{13}{40} \times 100 \right)\%$$

$$\approx \left(-\frac{13}{39} \times 100 \right)\%$$

$$\approx \left(-\frac{1}{3} \times 100 \right)\%$$

$$\approx -30\%$$

The correct answer is B.

115. A pharmaceutical company received $3 million in royalties on the first $20 million in sales of the generic equivalent of one of its products and then $9 million in royalties on the next $108 million in sales. By approximately what percent did the ratio of royalties to sales decrease from the first $20 million in sales to the next $108 million in sales?

   (A)   8%
   (B)   15%
   (C)   45%
   (D)   52%
   (E)   56%

Arithmetic Percents

The ratio of royalties to sales for the first $20 million in sales is $\frac{3}{20}$, and the ratio of royalties to sales for the next $108 million in sales is $\frac{9}{108} = \frac{1}{12}$. The percent decrease in the royalties to sales ratios is 100 times the quotient of the difference in the ratios divided by the ratio of royalties to sales for the first $20 million in sales or

$$\frac{\frac{1}{12}-\frac{3}{20}}{\frac{3}{20}}\times100=\left(\frac{1}{12}-\frac{3}{20}\right)\times\frac{20}{3}\times100$$

$$=\left(\frac{1}{12}\times\frac{20}{3}-1\right)\times100$$

$$=\left(\frac{5}{9}-1\right)\times100$$

$$=-\frac{4}{9}\times100$$

$$\approx-0.44\times100$$

$$\approx45\%\text{ decrease}$$

The correct answer is C.

116. If p is the product of the integers from 1 to 30, inclusive, what is the greatest integer k for which 3^k is a factor of p?

(A) 10
(B) 12
(C) 14
(D) 16
(E) 18

Arithmetic Properties of numbers

The table below shows the numbers from 1 to 30, inclusive, that have at least one factor of 3 and how many factors of 3 each has.

Multiples of 3 between 1 and 30	Number of factors of 3
3	1
$6=2\times3$	1
$9=3\times3$	2
$12=2\times2\times3$	1
$15=3\times5$	1
$18=2\times3\times3$	2
$21=3\times7$	1
$24=2\times2\times2\times3$	1
$27=3\times3\times3$	3
$30=2\times3\times5$	1

The sum of the numbers in the right column is 14. Therefore, 3^{14} is the greatest power of 3 that is a factor of the product of the first 30 positive integers.

The correct answer is C.

117. If $n=3^8-2^8$, which of the following is NOT a factor of n?

(A) 97
(B) 65
(C) 35
(D) 13
(E) 5

Arithmetic Properties of numbers

Since 3^8-2^8 is the difference of the perfect squares $(3^4)^2$ and $(2^4)^2$, then $3^8-2^8=(3^4+2^4)(3^4-2^4)$. But 3^4-2^4 is also the difference of the perfect squares $(3^2)^2$ and $(2^2)^2$ so $3^4-2^4=(3^2+2^2)(3^2-2^2)$ and therefore $3^8-2^8=(3^4+2^4)(3^2+2^2)(3^2-2^2)$. It follows that 3^8-2^8 can be factored as $(81+16)(9+4)(9-4)=(97)(13)(5)$. Therefore, 7 is not a factor of 3^8-2^8, and hence $35=5\times7$ is not a factor of 3^8-2^8. It is easy to see that each of 97, 13, and 5 is a factor of 3^8-2^8, and so is 65, since $65=5\times13$, although this additional analysis is not needed to arrive at the correct answer.

The correct answer is C.

118. Club X has more than 10 but fewer than 40 members. Sometimes the members sit at tables with 3 members at one table and 4 members at each of the other tables, and sometimes they sit at tables with 3 members at one table and 5 members at each of the other tables. If they sit at tables with 6 members at each table except one and fewer than 6 members at that one table, how many members will be at the table that has fewer than 6 members?

(A) 1
(B) 2
(C) 3
(D) 4
(E) 5

Arithmetic Properties of numbers

Let n be the number of members that Club X has. Since the members can be equally divided into groups of 4 each with 3 left over, and the members can be equally divided into groups of 5 each with 3 left over, it follows that $n - 3$ is divisible by both 4 and 5. Therefore, $n - 3$ must be a multiple of $(4)(5) = 20$. Also, because the only multiple of 20 that is greater than 10 and less than 40 is 20, it follows that $n - 3 = 20$, or $n = 23$. Finally, when these 23 members are divided into the greatest number of groups of 6 each, there will be 5 members left over, since $23 = (3)(6) + 5$.

The correct answer is E.

119. In order to complete a reading assignment on time, Terry planned to read 90 pages per day. However, she read only 75 pages per day at first, leaving 690 pages to be read during the last 6 days before the assignment was to be completed. How many days in all did Terry have to complete the assignment on time?

    (A) 15
    (B) 16
    (C) 25
    (D) 40
    (E) 46

Algebra Applied problems

Let n be the number of days that Terry read at the slower rate of 75 pages per day. Then $75n$ is the number of pages Terry read at this slower rate, and $75n + 690$ is the total number of pages Terry needs to read. Also, $n + 6$ is the total number of days that Terry will spend on the reading assignment. The requirement that Terry average 90 pages per day is equivalent to $\dfrac{75n + 690}{n + 6} = 90$. Then

$$\frac{75n + 690}{n + 6} = 90$$
$$75n + 690 = 90n + 540$$
$$150 = 15n$$
$$10 = n$$

Therefore, the total number of days that Terry has to complete the assignment on time is $n + 6 = 10 + 6 = 16$.

The correct answer is B.

120. If $s > 0$ and $\sqrt{\dfrac{r}{s}} = s$, what is r in terms of s?

    (A) $\dfrac{1}{s}$

    (B) $\sqrt{s}$

    (C) $s\sqrt{s}$

    (D) s^3

    (E) $s^2 - s$

Algebra Equations

Solve the equation for r as follows:

$$\sqrt{\frac{r}{s}} = s$$

$\dfrac{r}{s} = s^2$ square both sides of the equation

$r = s^3$ multiply both sides by s

The correct answer is D.

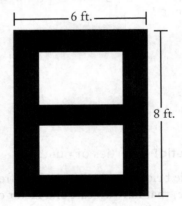

121. The front of a 6-foot-by-8-foot rectangular door has brass rectangular trim, as indicated by the shading in the figure above. If the trim is uniformly 1 foot wide, what fraction of the door's front surface is covered by the trim?

    (A) $\dfrac{13}{48}$

    (B) $\dfrac{5}{12}$

    (C) $\dfrac{1}{2}$

    (D) $\dfrac{7}{12}$

    (E) $\dfrac{5}{8}$

Geometry Area

To determine the area of the trim, find the area of the unshaded portions of the door and subtract this from the door's total area. The width of each unshaded rectangle is the width of the door minus two trim strips, or $6 - 2 = 4$ feet. The amount of height available for both unshaded rectangles is the height of the door minus three trim strips, or $8 - 3 = 5$ feet. Thus, the area of the unshaded portions is $4 \times 5 = 20$ square feet. The area of the entire door is $6 \times 8 = 48$ square feet, so the area of the trim is $48 - 20 = 28$ square feet. Therefore, the fraction of the door's front surface that is covered by the trim is $\frac{28}{48} = \frac{7}{12}$.

The correct answer is D.

122. If $a = -0.3$, which of the following is true?

(A) $a < a^2 < a^3$

(B) $a < a^3 < a^2$

(C) $a^2 < a < a^3$

(D) $a^2 < a^3 < a$

(E) $a^3 < a < a^2$

Arithmetic Operations on rational numbers

First, determine the relative values of a, a^2, and a^3, remembering that $(\text{negative})(\text{negative}) = \text{positive}$. If $a = -0.3$ then $a^2 = (-0.3)^2 = (-0.3)(-0.3) = 0.09$, and $a^3 = (-0.3)^3 = (-0.3)(-0.3)(-0.3) = -0.027$. Since $-0.3 < -0.027 < 0.09$, then $a < a^3 < a^2$.

The correct answer is B.

123. Mary's income is 60 percent more than Tim's income, and Tim's income is 40 percent less than Juan's income. What percent of Juan's income is Mary's income?

(A) 124%

(B) 120%

(C) 96%

(D) 80%

(E) 64%

Algebra; Arithmetic Applied problems; Percents

Let M be Mary's income, T be Tim's income, and J be Juan's income. Mary's income is 60 percent more than Tim's, so $M = T + 0.60T = 1.60T$. Since Tim's income is 40 percent less than Juan's income, Tim's income equals $100 - 40 = 60$ percent of Juan's income, or $T = 0.6J$. Substituting $0.6J$ for T in the first equation gives $M = 1.6(0.6J)$ or $M = 0.96J$. Thus Mary's income is 96% of Juan's income.

The correct answer is C.

	City A	City B	City C	City D	City E
City A			•	•	•
City B			•	•	•
City C				•	•
City D					•
City E					

124. Each • in the mileage table above represents an entry indicating the distance between a pair of the five cities. If the table were extended to represent the distances between all pairs of 30 cities and each distance were to be represented by only one entry, how many entries would the table then have?

(A) 60

(B) 435

(C) 450

(D) 465

(E) 900

Arithmetic Interpretation of tables

In a table with 30 cities, there are $30(30) = 900$ boxes for entries. However, since a city does not need to have any entry for a distance to and from itself, 30 entries are not needed on the diagonal through the table. Thus, the necessary number of entries is reduced to $900 - 30 = 870$ entries. Then, it is given that each pair of cities only needs one table entry, not two as the table allows; therefore, the table only needs to have $\frac{870}{2} = 435$ entries.

The correct answer is B.

125. The ratio of the length to the width of a rectangular advertising display is approximately 3.3 to 2. If the width of the display is 8 meters, what is the approximate length of the display, in meters?

    (A)   7
    (B)   11
    (C)   13
    (D)   16
    (E)   26

Algebra Applied problems

Letting l be the length of the advertising display, the proportion for the ratio of the length to the width can be expressed in the following equation, which can be solved for l:

$$\frac{3.3}{2} = \frac{l}{8}$$

$13.2 = l$ \qquad multiply both sides by 8

The correct answer is C.

$$p, r, s, t, u$$

126. An arithmetic sequence is a sequence in which each term after the first is equal to the sum of the preceding term and a constant. If the list of letters shown above is an arithmetic sequence, which of the following must also be an arithmetic sequence?

    I.   2p, 2r, 2s, 2t, 2u
    II. $p-3, r-3, s-3, t-3, u-3$
    III. p^2, r^2, s^2, t^2, u^2

    (A)   I only
    (B)   II only
    (C)   III only
    (D)   I and II
    (E)   II and III

Algebra Concepts of sets; Functions

It follows from the definition of arithmetic sequence given in the first sentence that there is a constant c such that $r-p = s-r = t-s = u-t = c$.

To test a sequence to determine whether it is arithmetic, calculate the difference of each pair of consecutive terms in that sequence to see if a constant difference is found.

I. $2r - 2p = 2(r-p) = 2c$
    $2s - 2r = 2(s-r) = 2c$
    $2t - 2s = 2(t-s) = 2c$
    $2u - 2t = 2(u-t) = 2c$ \qquad MUST be arithmetic

II. $(r-3)-(p-3) = r-p = c$ \qquad MUST be arithmetic

Since all values are just three less than the original, the same common difference applies.

III. $r^2 - p^2 = (r-p)(r+p) = c(r+p)$
     $s^2 - r^2 = (s-r)(s+r) = c(s+r)$ NEED NOT be arithmetic

Since p, r, s, t, and u are an arithmetic sequence, $r + p \neq s + r$, because $p \neq s$ unless $c = 0$.

The correct answer is D.

127. If $3 < x < 100$, for how many values of x is $\frac{x}{3}$ the square of a prime number?

    (A)   Two
    (B)   Three
    (C)   Four
    (D)   Five
    (E)   Nine

Arithmetic Properties of numbers

If $\frac{x}{3}$ is the square of a prime number, then possible values of $\frac{x}{3}$ are 2^2, 3^2, 5^2, 7^2, ... Therefore, possible values of x are $3 \times 2^2 = 12$, $3 \times 3^2 = 27$, $3 \times 5^2 = 75$, $3 \times 7^2 = 147$, ... Since only three of these values, namely 12, 27, and 75, are between 3 and 100, there are three values of x such that $\frac{x}{3}$ is the square of a prime number.

The correct answer is B.

128. A researcher plans to identify each participant in a certain medical experiment with a code consisting of either a single letter or a pair of distinct letters written in alphabetical order. What is the least number of letters that can be used if there are 12 participants, and each participant is to receive a different code?

(A) 4
(B) 5
(C) 6
(D) 7
(E) 8

Arithmetic Elementary combinatorics

None of the essential aspects of the problem is affected if the letters are restricted to be the first n letters of the alphabet, for various positive integers n. With the 3 letters a, b, and c, there are 6 codes: a, b, c, ab, ac, and bc. With the 4 letters a, b, c, and d, there are 10 codes: a, b, c, d, ab, ac, ad, bc, bd, and cd. Clearly, more than 12 codes are possible with 5 or more letters, so the least number of letters that can be used is 5.

The correct answer is B.

129. An object thrown directly upward is at a height of h feet after t seconds, where $h = -16(t-3)^2 + 150$. At what height, in feet, is the object 2 seconds after it reaches its maximum height?

(A) 6
(B) 86
(C) 134
(D) 150
(E) 166

Algebra Applied problems

Since $(t-3)^2$ is positive when $t \neq 3$ and zero when $t = 3$, it follows that the *minimum* value of $(t-3)^2$ occurs when $t = 3$. Therefore, the *maximum* value of $-16(t-3)^2$, and also the maximum value of $-16(t-3)^2 + 150$, occurs when $t = 3$. Hence, the height 2 seconds after the maximum height is the value of h when $t = 5$, or $-16(5-3)^2 + 150 = 86$.

The correct answer is B.

130. Which of the following is equivalent to the pair of inequalities $x + 6 > 10$ and $x - 3 \leq 5$?

(A) $2 \leq x < 16$
(B) $2 \leq x < 4$
(C) $2 < x \leq 8$
(D) $4 < x \leq 8$
(E) $4 \leq x < 16$

Algebra Inequalities

Solve the inequalities separately and combine the results.

$$x + 6 > 10$$
$$x > 4$$

$$x - 3 \leq 5$$
$$x \leq 8$$

Since $x > 4$, then $4 < x$. Combining $4 < x$ and $x \leq 8$ gives $4 < x \leq 8$.

The correct answer is D.

131. David has d books, which is 3 times as many as Jeff and $\frac{1}{2}$ as many as Paula. How many books do the three of them have altogether, in terms of d?

(A) $\frac{5}{6}d$

(B) $\frac{7}{3}d$

(C) $\frac{10}{3}d$

(D) $\frac{7}{2}d$

(E) $\frac{9}{2}d$

Algebra Applied problems; Simultaneous equations

Let J be the number of books that Jeff has, and let P be the number of books Paula has. Then, the given information about David's books can be expressed as $d = 3J$ and $d = \frac{1}{2}P$. Solving these two equations for J and P gives $\frac{d}{3} = J$ and $2d = P$. Thus, $d + J + P = d + \frac{d}{3} + 2d = 3\frac{1}{3}d = \frac{10}{3}d$.

The correct answer is C.

List I: 3, 6, 8, 19

List II: x, 3, 6, 8, 19

132. If the median of the numbers in list I above is equal to the median of the numbers in list II above, what is the value of x ?

   (A) 6
   (B) 7
   (C) 8
   (D) 9
   (E) 10

Arithmetic Statistics

Since list I has an even number of numbers, the median of list I is the average of the middle two numbers, so $\frac{6+8}{2} = 7$ is the median of list I.

Since list II has an odd number of numbers, the median of list II will be the middle number when the five numbers are put in ascending order. Since the median of list II must be 7 (the median of list I) and since 7 is not in list II, then x = 7.

The correct answer is B.

133. There are 8 teams in a certain league and each team plays each of the other teams exactly once. If each game is played by 2 teams, what is the total number of games played?

   (A) 15
   (B) 16
   (C) 28
   (D) 56
   (E) 64

Arithmetic Operations on rational numbers

Since no team needs to play itself, each team needs to play 7 other teams. In addition, each game needs to be counted only once, rather than once for each team that plays that game. Since two teams play each game, $\frac{8 \times 7}{2} = 28$ games are needed.

The correct answer is C.

134. An operation θ is defined by the equation $a \theta b = \frac{a-b}{a+b}$, for all numbers a and b such that $a \neq -b$. If $a \neq -c$ and $a \theta c = 0$, then c =

   (A) $-a$
   (B) $-\frac{1}{a}$
   (C) 0
   (D) $\frac{1}{a}$
   (E) a

Algebra Simplifying algebraic expressions

Substitute c for b and 0 for $a \theta c$ in the given equation, and solve for c.

$0 = \frac{a-c}{a+c}$

$0 = a-c$ \qquad multiply both sides by $a+c$

$c = a$ \qquad add c to both sides

The correct answer is E.

135. The price of lunch for 15 people was $207.00, including a 15 percent gratuity for service. What was the average price per person, EXCLUDING the gratuity?

   (A) $11.73
   (B) $12.00
   (C) $13.80
   (D) $14.00
   (E) $15.87

Arithmetic; Algebra Statistics; Applied problems

Let c be the total price of lunch for everyone excluding the gratuity. Since $207.00 is given as the total price including the 15% gratuity, the total price for the group lunch excluding the gratuity can be expressed as $207 = 1.15c$, or $\frac{\$207}{1.15} = \$180 = c$. The average price per person, or $\frac{\text{sum of } v \text{ values}}{v} = \text{average}$, was thus $\frac{\$180}{15} = \$12.00$ for each of the 15 individuals.

The correct answer is B.

136. In Town X, 64 percent of the population are employed, and 48 percent of the population are employed males. What percent of the employed people in Town X are females?

    (A) 16%
    (B) 25%
    (C) 32%
    (D) 40%
    (E) 52%

Arithmetic Percents

For simplicity, suppose that the population of Town X is 100. If 64% of the population are employed, then 64 people are employed. If 48% of the population are employed males, then 48 of the town's people are employed males. Then, there are $64 - 48 = 16$ employed females in Town X. The percent of the employed people who are females is then $\frac{16}{64} \times 100 = 25\%$.

The correct answer is B.

137. At his regular hourly rate, Don had estimated the labor cost of a repair job as $336 and he was paid that amount. However, the job took 4 hours longer than he had estimated and, consequently, he earned $2 per hour less than his regular hourly rate. What was the time Don had estimated for the job, in hours?

    (A) 28
    (B) 24
    (C) 16
    (D) 14
    (E) 12

Algebra Second-degree equations

Let r be Don's regular hourly rate and t be the number of hours he estimated the repair job to take. Then $rt = 336$ is Don's estimated labor cost. Since Don was paid $336 for doing $t + 4$ hours of work at an hourly rate of $r - 2$, it also follows that $(r - 2)(t + 4) = 336$. Then

$$(r - 2)(t + 4) = 336$$
$$rt - 2t + 4r - 8 = 336$$

$-2t + 4r - 8 = 0$	since $rt = 336$ from above
$-2t^2 + 4rt - 8t = 0$	multiply both sides by t
$-2t^2 + 4(336) - 8t = 0$	since $rt = 336$
$t^2 + 4t - 672 = 0$	divide both sides by -2
$(t - 24)(t + 28) = 0$	factor

Alternatively, from the third line above,

$-2t + 4r - 8 = 0$	
$-2t + 4\left(\frac{336}{t}\right) - 8 = 0$	since $rt = 336$ from above
	gives $r = \frac{336}{t}$
$-2t^2 + 4(336) - 8t = 0$	multiply both sides by t
$t^2 + 4t - 672 = 0$	divide both sides by -2
$(t - 24)(t + 28) = 0$	factor

So, $t - 24 = 0$, which means $t = 24$, or $t + 28 = 0$, which means $t = -28$. Since an estimated time cannot be negative, $t = 24$.

The correct answer is B.

138. If $\frac{p}{q} < 1$, and p and q are positive integers, which of the following must be greater than 1 ?

    (A) $\sqrt{\dfrac{p}{q}}$

    (B) $\dfrac{p}{q^2}$

    (C) $\dfrac{p}{2q}$

    (D) $\dfrac{q}{p^2}$

    (E) $\dfrac{q}{p}$

Arithmetic Properties of numbers

Since p and q are positive integers, $0 < \dfrac{p}{q} < 1$.

A Since $\dfrac{p}{q} < 1$, then $q > p$. Taking the square root of both sides of the inequality gives $\sqrt{q} > \sqrt{p}$. Then, $\sqrt{\dfrac{p}{q}} = \dfrac{\sqrt{p}}{\sqrt{q}}$, so here the denominator will still be larger than the numerator. CANNOT be greater than 1

B Squaring the denominator increases the denominator, which decreases the value of the fraction. CANNOT be greater than 1

C Multiplying the denominator by 2 increases the denominator, which decreases the value of the fraction. CANNOT be greater than 1

D Since $\dfrac{p}{q} < 1$, then $q > p$. When $p^2 < q$, this expression will be greater than 1, but p^2 need not be less than q. For example, if $p = 2$ and $q = 100$, $\dfrac{p}{q} = \dfrac{2}{100}$ and $\dfrac{q}{p^2} = \dfrac{100}{2^2} = \dfrac{100}{4} = 25 > 1$.

However, if $p = 3$ and $q = 4$, then $\dfrac{p}{q} = \dfrac{3}{4}$ and $\dfrac{q}{p^2} = \dfrac{4}{3^2} = \dfrac{4}{9} < 1$. NEED NOT be greater than 1

E Again, since $\dfrac{p}{q} < 1$, then $q > p$. Thus, the reciprocal, $\dfrac{q}{p}$, always has a value greater than 1 because the numerator will always be a larger positive integer than the denominator. MUST be greater than 1

The correct answer is E.

139. It would take one machine 4 hours to complete a large production order and another machine 3 hours to complete the same order. How many hours would it take both machines, working simultaneously at their respective constant rates, to complete the order?

(A) $\dfrac{7}{12}$

(B) $1\dfrac{1}{2}$

(C) $1\dfrac{5}{7}$

(D) $3\dfrac{1}{2}$

(E) 7

Arithmetic Operations on rational numbers

The first machine can complete $\dfrac{1}{4}$ of the production order in one hour, and the second machine can complete $\dfrac{1}{3}$ of the same order in one hour. Thus, working together they can complete $\dfrac{1}{4} + \dfrac{1}{3} = \dfrac{3}{12} + \dfrac{4}{12} = \dfrac{7}{12}$ of the order in one hour. Therefore, it will take $\dfrac{12}{7} = 1\dfrac{5}{7}$ hours for the two machines working simultaneously to complete the production order.

The correct answer is C.

140. To mail a package, the rate is x cents for the first pound and y cents for each additional pound, where $x > y$. Two packages weighing 3 pounds and 5 pounds, respectively, can be mailed separately or combined as one package. Which method is cheaper, and how much money is saved?

(A) Combined, with a savings of $x - y$ cents

(B) Combined, with a savings of $y - x$ cents

(C) Combined, with a savings of x cents

(D) Separately, with a savings of $x - y$ cents

(E) Separately, with a savings of y cents

Algebra Applied problems

Shipping the two packages separately would cost $1x + 2y$ for the 3-pound package and $1x + 4y$ for the 5-pound package. Shipping them together (as a single 8-pound package) would cost $1x + 7y$. By calculating the sum of the costs for shipping the two packages separately minus the cost for shipping the one combined package, it is possible to determine the difference in cost, as shown.

$\big((1x + 2y) + (1x + 4y)\big) - (1x + 7y)$ (cost for 3 lb.
\qquad\qquad\qquad\qquad\qquad\qquad + cost for 5 lb.)
\qquad\qquad\qquad\qquad\qquad\qquad − cost for 8 lb.

$= (2x + 6y) - (1x + 7y)$ \qquad combine like terms

$= 2x + 6y - 1x - 7y$ \qquad distribute the negative

$= x - y$ \qquad combine like terms

Since $x > y$, this value is positive, which means it costs more to ship two packages separately. Thus it is cheaper to mail one combined package at a cost savings of $x - y$ cents.

The correct answer is A.

141. If money is invested at r percent interest, compounded annually, the amount of the investment will double in approximately $\dfrac{70}{r}$ years. If Pat's parents invested $5,000 in a long-term bond that pays 8 percent interest, compounded annually, what will be the approximate total amount of the investment 18 years later, when Pat is ready for college?

(A) $20,000
(B) $15,000
(C) $12,000
(D) $10,000
(E) $ 9,000

Algebra Applied problems

Since the investment will double in $\dfrac{70}{r} = \dfrac{70}{8} = 8.75 \approx 9$ years, the value of the investment over 18 years can be approximated by doubling its initial value twice. Therefore, the approximate value will be ($5,000)(2)(2) = $20,000.

The correct answer is A.

142. On a recent trip, Cindy drove her car 290 miles, rounded to the nearest 10 miles, and used 12 gallons of gasoline, rounded to the nearest gallon. The actual number of miles per gallon that Cindy's car got on this trip must have been between

(A) $\dfrac{290}{12.5}$ and $\dfrac{290}{11.5}$

(B) $\dfrac{295}{12}$ and $\dfrac{285}{11.5}$

(C) $\dfrac{285}{12}$ and $\dfrac{295}{12}$

(D) $\dfrac{285}{12.5}$ and $\dfrac{295}{11.5}$

(E) $\dfrac{295}{12.5}$ and $\dfrac{285}{11.5}$

Arithmetic Estimation

The lowest number of miles per gallon can be calculated using the lowest possible miles and the highest amount of gasoline. Also, the highest number of miles per gallon can be calculated using the highest possible miles and the lowest amount of gasoline.

Since the miles are rounded to the nearest 10 miles, the number of miles is between 285 and 295. Since the gallons are rounded to the nearest gallon, the number of gallons is between 11.5 and 12.5. Therefore, the lowest number of miles per gallon is $\dfrac{\text{lowest miles}}{\text{highest gallons}} = \dfrac{285}{12.5}$ and the highest number of miles per gallon is $\dfrac{\text{highest miles}}{\text{lowest gallons}} = \dfrac{295}{11.5}$.

The correct answer is D.

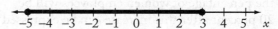

143. Which of the following inequalities is an algebraic expression for the shaded part of the number line above?

(A) $|x| \le 3$

(B) $|x| \le 5$

(C) $|x - 2| \le 3$

(D) $|x - 1| \le 4$

(E) $|x + 1| \le 4$

Algebra Inequalities

The number line above shows $-5 \le x \le 3$. To turn this into absolute value notation, as all the choices are written, the numbers need to be opposite signs of the same value.

Since the distance between -5 and 3 is 8 $(3-(-5)=8)$, that distance needs to be split in half with -4 to one side and 4 to the other. Each of these two values is 1 more than the values in the inequality above, so adding 1 to all terms in the inequality gives $-4 \le x+1 \le 4$, which is the same as $|x+1| \le 4$.

The correct answer is E.

144. A factory has 500 workers, 15 percent of whom are women. If 50 additional workers are to be hired and all of the present workers remain, how many of the additional workers must be women in order to raise the percent of women employees to 20 percent?

   (A)   3
   (B)   10
   (C)   25
   (D)   30
   (E)   35

Arithmetic; Algebra Percents;
Applied problems

Let w be the number of additional workers who must be women to satisfy the problem. It can be stated that, initially, $500(0.15)=75$ of the workers were women. Since 50 more workers are to be hired, the total workforce will increase to $500+50=550$ employees. The information that the percentage of women employees will be 20 percent after this increase can be expressed in the following equation and solved for w.

$\dfrac{75+w}{550}=0.20$

$75+w=110$ multiply both sides by 550

$w=35$ subtract 75 from both sides

The correct answer is E.

145. In a small snack shop, the average (arithmetic mean) revenue was $400 per day over a 10-day period. During this period, if the average daily revenue was $360 for the first 6 days, what was the average daily revenue for the last 4 days?

   (A) $420
   (B) $440
   (C) $450
   (D) $460
   (E) $480

Arithmetic; Algebra Statistics;
Applied problems

Let x be the average daily revenue for the last 4 days. Using the formula $\text{average} = \dfrac{\text{sum of values}}{\text{number of values}}$, the information regarding the average revenues for the 10-day and 6-day periods can be expressed as follows and solved for x:

$\$400 = \dfrac{6(\$360)+4x}{10}$

$\$4,000 = \$2,160+4x$ multiply both sides by 10

$\$1,840 = 4x$ subtract $2,160 from both sides

$\$460 = x$ divide both sides by 4

The correct answer is D.

146. A certain country had a total annual expenditure of 1.2×10^{12} last year. If the population of the country was 240 million last year, what was the per capita expenditure?

   (A) $ 500
   (B) $1,000
   (C) $2,000
   (D) $3,000
   (E) $5,000

Arithmetic Operations on rational numbers

The per capita expenditure can be calculated as follows:

$$\frac{\$1.2 \times 10^{12}}{240 \text{ million}} = \frac{\$12 \times 10^{11}}{24 \times 10^{7}}$$

$$= \$\frac{12}{24} \times \frac{10^{11}}{10^{7}}$$

$$= \$\frac{1}{2} \times 10^{11-7}$$

$$= \$0.5 \times 10^{4}$$

$$= \$5,000$$

The correct answer is E.

147. A certain rectangular window is twice as long as it is wide. If its perimeter is 10 feet, then its dimensions in feet are

(A) $\frac{3}{2}$ by $\frac{7}{2}$

(B) $\frac{5}{3}$ by $\frac{10}{3}$

(C) 2 by 4

(D) 3 by 6

(E) $\frac{10}{3}$ by $\frac{20}{3}$

Geometry Perimeter

Let l and w be the length and width in feet, respectively, of the window. Then the information in the problem can be expressed in the following two equations: $l = 2w$ since the length is twice the width and $2l + 2w = 10$ since the perimeter is 10. Substitute l for $2w$ in the second equation to get $2l + l = 10$. Therefore, $3l = 10$, or $l = \frac{10}{3}$. Then $\frac{10}{3} = 2w$ so $w = \frac{5}{3}$.

The correct answer is B.

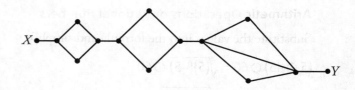

148. The diagram above shows the various paths along which a mouse can travel from point X, where it is released, to point Y, where it is rewarded with a food pellet. How many different paths from X to Y can the mouse take if it goes directly from X to Y without retracing any point along a path?

(A) 6

(B) 7

(C) 12

(D) 14

(E) 17

Arithmetic Elementary combinatorics

The total number of different paths can be found by multiplying the number of possible routes that can be taken from each intersection point of the paths to their next point of intersection. Refer to the figure below.

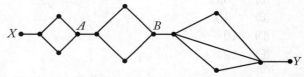

The total number of ways to get from X to A is 2, since there are only 2 paths to choose from. There are also only 2 ways to get from A to B. To get from B to Y, there are 3 possible choices. Thus, the total number of different paths is $(2)(2)(3) = 12$.

The correct answer is C.

149. If the operation $\odot$ is defined by $x \odot y = \sqrt{xy}$ for all positive numbers x and y, then $(5 \odot 45) \odot 60 =$

(A) 30

(B) 60

(C) 90

(D) $30\sqrt{15}$

(E) $60\sqrt{15}$

Arithmetic Operations on rational numbers

Substitute the values into the formula and simplify:

$$(5 \odot 45) \odot 60 = \sqrt{(5)(45)} \odot 60$$

$$= \sqrt{(5)(5)(9)} \odot 60$$

$$= (5)(3) \odot 60$$

$$= 15 \odot 60$$

$$= \sqrt{(15)(60)}$$

$$= \sqrt{(15)(15)(4)}$$

$$= (15)(2)$$

$$= 30$$

The correct answer is A.

150. A bar over a sequence of digits in a decimal indicates that the sequence repeats indefinitely.

What is the value of $\left(10^4 - 10^2\right)\left(0.00\overline{12}\right)$?

(A) 0
(B) $0.\overline{12}$
(C) 1.2
(D) 10
(E) 12

Arithmetic Operations on rational numbers

Distribute and simplify.

$$\left(10^4 - 10^2\right)\left(0.00\overline{12}\right)$$

$$= 10^4\left(0.00\overline{12}\right) - 10^2\left(0.00\overline{12}\right) \quad \text{distribute the} \; \left(0.00\overline{12}\right)$$

$$= 10,000\left(0.00\overline{12}\right) - 100\left(0.00\overline{12}\right) \quad 10^4 = 10,000 \text{ and} \; 10^2 = 100$$

$$= 12.\overline{12} - 0.\overline{12} \quad \text{multiply by multiples of 10 to move the decimals}$$

$$= 12$$

The correct answer is E.

151. At a loading dock, each worker on the night crew loaded $\frac{3}{4}$ as many boxes as each worker on the day crew. If the night crew has $\frac{4}{5}$ as many workers as the day crew, what fraction of all the boxes loaded by the two crews did the day crew load?

(A) $\frac{1}{2}$
(B) $\frac{2}{5}$
(C) $\frac{3}{5}$
(D) $\frac{4}{5}$
(E) $\frac{5}{8}$

Arithmetic Operations on rational numbers

From this, the workers on the night crew will

load $\frac{3}{4}\left(\frac{4}{5}\right) = \frac{3}{5}$ as many boxes as the day crew.

The total loaded by both the day and night crews

is thus $1 + \frac{3}{5} = \frac{5}{5} + \frac{3}{5} = \frac{8}{5}$ of the day crew's work.

Therefore, the fraction of all the boxes loaded by the two crews that was done by the day crew was

$$\frac{1}{\frac{8}{5}} = 1\left(\frac{5}{8}\right) = \frac{5}{8}.$$

The correct answer is E.

152. A restaurant meal cost $35.50 and there was no tax. If the tip was more than 10 percent but less than 15 percent of the cost of the meal, then the total amount paid must have been between

(A) $40 and $42
(B) $39 and $41
(C) $38 and $40
(D) $37 and $39
(E) $36 and $37

Arithmetic Estimation and percent

First calculate the actual total amount for the meal with a 10 percent tip and a 15 percent tip. To calculate each, multiply the cost of the meal by (1 + the percent as a decimal).

10 percent tip: 15 percent tip:

$35.50(1.10) $35.50(1.15)

$39.05 $40.825

The only answer choice that includes all values between $39.05 and $40.83 is B.

The correct answer is B.

153. In a weight-lifting competition, the total weight of Joe's two lifts was 750 pounds. If twice the weight of his first lift was 300 pounds more than the weight of his second lift, what was the weight, in pounds, of his first lift?

(A) 225
(B) 275
(C) 325
(D) 350
(E) 400

Algebra Applied problems

Let F and S be the weights, in pounds, of Joe's first and second lifts, respectively. Use these variables to set up two equations and then solve them.

$F + S = 750$	weight of two lifts was 750 pounds
$2F = S + 300$	twice the weight of first lift was 300 pounds more than the weight of second
$F = 750 - S$	Solve the first equation for F
$2(750 - S) = S + 300$	substitute $750 - S$ for F in the second equation
$1,500 - 2S = S + 300$	
$1,200 = 3S$	solve for S
$400 = S$	

Substituting this value of S back into the first equation gives $F + 400 = 750$, or $F = 350$.

The correct answer is D.

154. A club collected exactly $599 from its members. If each member contributed at least $12, what is the greatest number of members the club could have?

(A) 43
(B) 44
(C) 49
(D) 50
(E) 51

Algebra Applied problems

To determine the greatest possible number of members, first recognize that each member had to contribute the lowest amount given. Write an inequality for the individual contributions and the total amount collected, with n representing the number of members in the club. Then solve for n.

$12n \leq 599$	(least contribution)(number of members) $\leq$ total collected
$n \leq 49\frac{11}{12}$	solve for n

Since n represents individual people, it must be a whole number; the greatest possible value of n is thus 49.

This problem can also be solved as follows: The inequality $12n \leq 599$, where n is restricted to the set of positive integers, is equivalent to $12n < 600$.

Therefore, $n < \dfrac{600}{12} = \dfrac{(12)(5)(10)}{12} = (5)(10) = 50$, and the greatest such value that is an integer is 49.

The correct answer is C.

155. If y is the smallest positive integer such that 3,150 multiplied by y is the square of an integer, then y must be

(A) 2
(B) 5
(C) 6
(D) 7
(E) 14

Arithmetic Properties of numbers

To find the smallest positive integer y such that $3{,}150y$ is the square of an integer, first find the prime factorization of $3{,}150$ by a method similar to the following:

$$3{,}150 = 10 \times 315$$
$$= (2 \times 5) \times (3 \times 105)$$
$$= 2 \times 5 \times 3 \times (5 \times 21)$$
$$= 2 \times 5 \times 3 \times 5 \times (3 \times 7)$$
$$= 2 \times 3^2 \times 5^2 \times 7$$

To be a perfect square, $3{,}150y$ must have an even number of each of its prime factors. At a minimum, y must have one factor of 2 and one factor of 7 so that $3{,}150y$ has two factors of each of the primes 2, 3, 5, and 7. The smallest positive integer value of y is then $(2)(7) = 14$.

The correct answer is E.

156. If [x] is the greatest integer less than or equal to x, what is the value of $[-1.6]+[3.4]+[2.7]$?

(A) 3
(B) 4
(C) 5
(D) 6
(E) 7

Arithmetic Computation with integers

The greatest integer that is less than or equal to -1.6 is -2. It cannot be -1 because -1 is greater than -1.6. The greatest integer that is less than or equal to 3.4 is 3. It cannot be 4 because 4 is greater than 3.4. The greatest integer that is less than or equal to 2.7 is 2. It cannot be 3 because 3 is greater than 2.7. Therefore, $[-1.6]+[3.4]+[2.7] = -2+3+2 = 3$.

The correct answer is A.

157. If $\dfrac{4-x}{2+x} = x$, what is the value of $x^2 + 3x - 4$?

(A) -4
(B) -1
(C) 0
(D) 1
(E) 2

Algebra Second-degree equations

Work the problem.

$$\frac{4-x}{2+x} = x$$
$$4 - x = x(2+x) \qquad \text{multiply both sides by } (2+x)$$
$$4 - x = 2x + x^2 \qquad \text{distribute the } x$$
$$0 = x^2 + 3x - 4 \qquad \text{move all terms to right side}$$

The correct answer is C.

158. In the first week of the year, Nancy saved \$1. In each of the next 51 weeks, she saved \$1 more than she had saved in the previous week. What was the total amount that Nancy saved during the 52 weeks?

(A) \$1,326
(B) \$1,352
(C) \$1,378
(D) \$2,652
(E) \$2,756

Arithmetic Operations on rational numbers

In dollars, the total amount saved is the sum of 1, $(1 + 1)$, $(1 + 1 + 1)$, and so on, up to and including the amount saved in the 52nd week, which was \$52. Therefore, the total amount saved in dollars was $1 + 2 + 3 + \ldots + 50 + 51 + 52$. This sum can be easily evaluated by grouping the terms as $(1 + 52) + (2 + 51) + (3 + 50) + \ldots + (26 + 27)$, which results in the number 53 added to itself 26 times. Therefore, the sum is $(26)(53) = 1{,}378$.

Alternatively, the formula for the sum of the first n positive integers is $\dfrac{n(n+1)}{2}$. Therefore, the sum of the first 52 positive integers is $\dfrac{52(53)}{2} = 26(53) = 1{,}378$.

The correct answer is C.

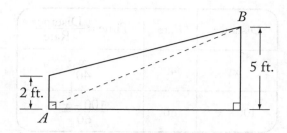

159. The trapezoid shown in the figure above represents a cross section of the rudder of a ship. If the distance from A to B is 13 feet, what is the area of the cross section of the rudder in square feet?

    (A) 39
    (B) 40
    (C) 42
    (D) 45
    (E) 46.5

Geometry Triangles and the Pythagorean theorem

The formula for calculating the area of a trapezoid is

$$\text{Area} = \frac{1}{2}(\text{base 1} + \text{base 2})(\text{height}).$$

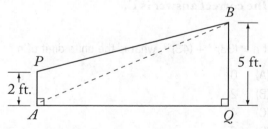

The bases of the trapezoid are given as 2 feet and 5 feet, so only the height (AQ) needs to be found. Since the dashed line $AB = 13$ feet, and triangle BQA is a right triangle, use the Pythagorean theorem to calculate AQ. Thus,

$$AQ = \sqrt{13^2 - 5^2} = \sqrt{144}, \text{ or } AQ = 12 \text{ feet.}$$

Substituting the values into the formula for calculating the area of a trapezoid:

$$\text{Area} = \frac{1}{2}(2+5)(12)$$

Area = 42 square feet.

The correct answer is C.

160. In a certain sequence, the term x_n is given by the formula $x_n = 2x_{n-1} - \frac{1}{2}(x_{n-2})$ for all $n \geq 2$. If $x_0 = 3$ and $x_1 = 2$, what is the value of x_3 ?

    (A) 2.5
    (B) 3.125
    (C) 4
    (D) 5
    (E) 6.75

Algebra Simplifying algebraic expressions

Given the formula $x_n = 2x_{n-1} - \frac{1}{2}x_{n-2}$ with $x_0 = 3$ and $x_1 = 2$, then

$$x_2 = 2x_1 - \frac{1}{2}x_0$$

$$= 2(2) - \frac{1}{2}(3)$$

$$= \frac{5}{2}$$

$$x_3 = 2x_2 - \frac{1}{2}x_1$$

$$= 2\left(\frac{5}{2}\right) - \frac{1}{2}(2)$$

$$= 5 - 1$$

$$= 4$$

The correct answer is C.

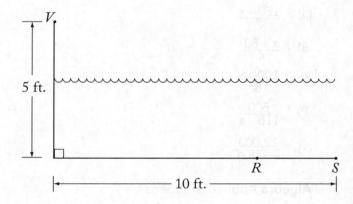

161. In the figure above, V represents an observation point at one end of a pool. From V, an object that is actually located on the bottom of the pool at point R appears to be at point S. If $VR = 10$ feet, what is the distance RS, in feet, between the actual position and the perceived position of the object?

(A) $10 - 5\sqrt{3}$

(B) $10 - 5\sqrt{2}$

(C) 2

(D) $2\frac{1}{2}$

(E) 4

Geometry Pythagorean theorem

Let P be the point 5 feet directly below V. $\triangle VPR$ is thus a right triangle.

$VP^2 + PR^2 = VR^2$ Pythagorean theorem applied to $\triangle VPR$.

$5^2 + PR^2 = 10^2$ substitute known quantities

$25 + PR^2 = 100$ solve for PR

$PR^2 = 75$

$PR = 5\sqrt{3}$

Note that $\sqrt{75} = \sqrt{25 \cdot 3} = \sqrt{25}\sqrt{3} = 5\sqrt{3}$; thus, $RS = PS - PR = 10 - 5\sqrt{3}$.

The correct answer is A.

162. During a trip, Francine traveled x percent of the total distance at an average speed of 40 miles per hour and the rest of the distance at an average speed of 60 miles per hour. In terms of x, what was Francine's average speed for the entire trip?

(A) $\dfrac{180 - x}{2}$

(B) $\dfrac{x + 60}{4}$

(C) $\dfrac{300 - x}{5}$

(D) $\dfrac{600}{115 - x}$

(E) $\dfrac{12,000}{x + 200}$

Algebra Applied problems

Assume for simplicity that the total distance of Francine's trip is 100 miles. Then the table below gives all of the pertinent information.

Distance	Rate	Time = $\dfrac{\text{Distance}}{\text{Rate}}$
x	40	$\dfrac{x}{40}$
$100 - x$	60	$\dfrac{100 - x}{60}$

The total time for Francine's trip is

$$\frac{x}{40} + \frac{100 - x}{60} = \frac{3x}{120} + \frac{2(100 - x)}{120}$$

$$= \frac{3x + 2(100 - x)}{120}$$

$$= \frac{3x + 200 - 2x}{120}$$

$$= \frac{x + 200}{120}$$

Francine's average speed over the entire trip is

$$\frac{\text{total distance}}{\text{total time}} = \frac{100}{\dfrac{x + 200}{120}} = \frac{12,000}{x + 200}.$$

The correct answer is E.

163. If $n = (33)^{43} + (43)^{33}$, what is the units digit of n?

(A) 0

(B) 2

(C) 4

(D) 6

(E) 8

Arithmetic Properties of numbers

If the units digit of an integer n is 3, then the units digits of n^1, n^2, n^3, n^4, n^5, n^6, n^7, and n^8 are, respectively, 3, 9, 7, 1, 3, 9, 7 and 1. Thus, the units digit of the powers of n form the sequence in which the digits 3, 9, 7, and 1 repeat indefinitely in that order. Since $43 = (10)(4) + 3$, the 43rd number in this sequence is 7, and therefore, the units digit $(33)^{43}$ is 7. Since $33 = (8)(4) + 1$, the 33rd number in this sequence is 3, and therefore, the units digit of $(43)^{33}$ is 3. Thus, the units digit of $(33)^{43} + (43)^{33}$ is the units digit of $7 + 3$, which is 0.

The correct answer is A.

164. If $x = -1$, then $\dfrac{x^4 - x^3 + x^2}{x - 1} =$

   (A) $-\dfrac{3}{2}$

   (B) $-\dfrac{1}{2}$

   (C) 0

   (D) $\dfrac{1}{2}$

   (E) $\dfrac{3}{2}$

Arithmetic Operations on rational numbers

Substituting the value of –1 for x in the expression results in

$$\dfrac{(-1)^4 - (-1)^3 + (-1)^2}{(-1) - 1} = \dfrac{1 - (-1) + 1}{-2} = -\dfrac{3}{2}$$

The correct answer is A.

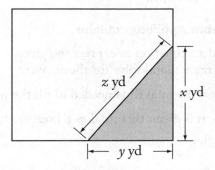

165. The shaded portion of the rectangular lot shown above represents a flower bed. If the area of the bed is 24 square yards and $x = y + 2$, then z equals

   (A) $\sqrt{13}$

   (B) $2\sqrt{13}$

   (C) 6

   (D) 8

   (E) 10

Geometry Area and the Pythagorean theorem

Using the known area of the triangular flower bed and the known length of side x of the triangle, determine the length of side z of the triangle by applying the formula for calculating the area of a triangle:

Area of a triangle $= \dfrac{1}{2}$(base)(height)

$A = \dfrac{1}{2}xy$

$24 = \dfrac{1}{2}(y + 2)(y)$ substitute 24 for area and $y + 2$ for x

$48 = y^2 + 2y$ solve for y

$0 = y^2 + 2y - 48$

$0 = (y + 8)(y - 6)$

$y + 8 = 0 \quad y - 6 = 0$

$y = -8 \quad y = 6$ eliminate $y = -8$ since it has to be a positive length

$x = 6 + 2 = 8$

Since the legs y and x of the right triangle are 6 and 8 yards long, respectively, the hypotenuse, z, must be 10 yards because 6-8-10 is a Pythagorean triple. Alternatively, the Pythagorean theorem can also be used to solve for z, where $x^2 + y^2 = z^2$. Thus, $8^2 + 6^2 = 64 + 36 = 100 = z^2$ and $\sqrt{100} = 10$.

The correct answer is E.

166. A border of uniform width is placed around a rectangular photograph that measures 8 inches by 10 inches. If the area of the border is 144 square inches, what is the width of the border, in inches?

   (A) 3

   (B) 4

   (C) 6

   (D) 8

   (E) 9

Algebra Second-degree equations

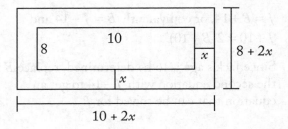

Let x be the width, in inches, of the border. The photograph with the border has dimensions $(10 + 2x)$ inches and $(8 + 2x)$ inches with an area of $(10 + 2x)(8 + 2x) = (80 + 36x + 4x^2)$ square inches. The photograph without the border has dimensions 10 inches and 8 inches with an area of $(10)(8) = 80$ square inches. The area of the border is then the difference between the areas of the photograph with and without the border or $(80 + 36x + 4x^2) - 80 = 36x + 4x^2$ square inches. It is given that the area of the border is 144 square inches so,

$$36x + 4x^2 = 144$$
$$4x^2 + 36x - 144 = 0$$
$$x^2 + 9x - 36 = 0$$
$$(x - 3)(x + 12) = 0$$

So, $x - 3 = 0$, which means $x = 3$ or $x + 12 = 0$, which means $x = -12$.

Thus, after discarding $x = -12$ since the width of the border must be positive, $x = 3$.

The correct answer is A.

167. Jack is now 14 years older than Bill. If in 10 years Jack will be twice as old as Bill, how old will Jack be in 5 years?

(A)   9
(B)   19
(C)   21
(D)   23
(E)   33

Algebra Applied problems

Let J and B be Jack's and Bill's current ages. Then the information from the problem can be expressed in the following two equations:

$J = B + 14$, or equivalently $B = J - 14$ and $J + 10 = 2(B + 10)$.

Since Jack's age is to be determined, replace B in the second equation with $J - 14$ to get an equation that can be solved for J:

$$J + 10 = 2(J - 14 + 10)$$
$$J + 10 = 2J - 8$$
$$18 = J$$

Therefore, Jack's current age is 18, and hence Jack's age in 5 years will be $18 + 5 = 23$.

The correct answer is D.

168. An empty pool being filled with water at a constant rate takes 8 hours to fill to $\frac{3}{5}$ of its capacity. How much more time will it take to finish filling the pool?

(A)   5 hr 30 min
(B)   5 hr 20 min
(C)   4 hr 48 min
(D)   3 hr 12 min
(E)   2 hr 40 min

Algebra Applied problems

Build an equation to express the given information and solve for the answer.

Let t = the total time needed to fill the pool.

Since it is given that it takes 8 hours to fill $\frac{3}{5}$ of the pool:

$$\frac{3}{5}t = 8$$
$$t = \frac{40}{3} \qquad \text{solve for } t$$
$$t = 13\frac{1}{3}$$

Thus, to calculate the time it will take to finish filling the pool:

$13\frac{1}{3} - 8 = 5\frac{1}{3}$ hours, or 5 hours 20 minutes.

The correct answer is B.

169. A positive number x is multiplied by 2, and this product is then divided by 3. If the positive square root of the result of these two operations equals x, what is the value of x ?

(A) $\dfrac{9}{4}$

(B) $\dfrac{3}{2}$

(C) $\dfrac{4}{3}$

(D) $\dfrac{2}{3}$

(E) $\dfrac{1}{2}$

Algebra Second-degree equations

Set up an equation according to the given information, and then solve for x.

First, multiply x by 2, divide that by 3, and set the square root of that equal to x:

$$\sqrt{\dfrac{2x}{3}} = x$$

To solve this equation:

$\dfrac{2x}{3} = x^2$ square both sides

$2x = 3x^2$

$0 = 3x^2 - 2x$ solve for possible values of x

$0 = x(3x - 2)$

$x = 0, \ 3x - 2 = 0$

Since $x > 0$, use $3x - 2 = 0$ to solve for x:

$3x - 2 = 0$

$3x = 2$

$x = \dfrac{2}{3}$

The correct answer is D.

170. If $d = \dfrac{1}{2^3 \times 5^7}$ is expressed as a terminating decimal, how many nonzero digits will d have?

(A) One
(B) Two
(C) Three
(D) Seven
(E) Ten

Arithmetic Operations on rational numbers

It will be helpful to use the fact that a factor that is an integer power of 10 has no effect on the number of nonzero digits a terminating decimal has.

$$\dfrac{1}{2^3 \times 5^7} = \dfrac{1}{2^3 \times 5^3} \times \dfrac{1}{5^4}$$

$$= \left(\dfrac{1}{2 \times 5}\right)^3 \times \left(\dfrac{1}{5}\right)^4$$

$$= \left(\dfrac{1}{10}\right)^3 \times \left(\dfrac{1}{5}\right)^4$$

$$= 10^{-3} \times (0.2)^4$$

$$= 10^{-3} \times (0.0016)$$

$$= 0.0000016$$

The correct answer is B.

171. A tank contains 10,000 gallons of a solution that is 5 percent sodium chloride by volume. If 2,500 gallons of water evaporate from the tank, the remaining solution will be approximately what percent sodium chloride?

(A) 1.25%
(B) 3.75%
(C) 6.25%
(D) 6.67%
(E) 11.7%

Arithmetic Operations on rational numbers; Percents

Before the evaporation occurs, the tank contains $10,000(0.05) = 500$ gallons of sodium chloride. After the evaporation occurs, the tank contains $10,000 - 2,500 = 7,500$ gallons of solution, of which 500 gallons are known to be sodium chloride. Calculate the percentage based on these postevaporation amounts:

$$\dfrac{500}{7,500} = 0.0667 = 6.67\%$$

The correct answer is D.

172. For any positive integer n, the sum of the first n positive integers equals $\dfrac{n(n+1)}{2}$. What is the sum of all the even integers between 99 and 301 ?

    (A)   10,100
    (B)   20,200
    (C)   22,650
    (D)   40,200
    (E)   45,150

Algebra Simplifying expressions; **Arithmetic** Computation with integers

The given formula translates into $1 + 2 + \ldots + n = \sum_{k=1}^{n} k = \dfrac{n(n+1)}{2}$. The sum of the even integers between 99 and 301 is the sum of the even integers from 100 through 300, or the sum of the 50th even integer through the 150th even integer. To get this sum, find the sum of the first 150 even integers and subtract the sum of the first 49 even integers. In symbols,

$$\sum_{k=1}^{150} 2k - \sum_{k=1}^{49} 2k = 2\sum_{k=1}^{150} k - 2\sum_{k=1}^{49} k$$

$$= 2\left(\frac{150(150+1)}{2}\right) - 2\left(\frac{49(49+1)}{2}\right)$$

$$= 150(151) - 49(50)$$

$$= 50\left[3(151) - 49\right]$$

$$= 50(453 - 49)$$

$$= 50(404)$$

$$= 20,200$$

The correct answer is B.

173. A committee is composed of w women and m men. If 3 women and 2 men are added to the committee, and if one person is selected at random from the enlarged committee, then the probability that a woman is selected can be represented by

(A) $\dfrac{w}{m}$

(B) $\dfrac{w}{w+m}$

(C) $\dfrac{w+3}{m+2}$

(D) $\dfrac{w+3}{w+m+3}$

(E) $\dfrac{w+3}{w+m+5}$

Arithmetic Probability

Set up an equation according to the given information regarding the values of w and m. The total number of women on the enlarged committee can be expressed as $w+3$. The total number of members on the enlarged committee can be expressed as $w+m+3+2$ or thus $w+m+5$. Then, the probability that the one person selected at random from the enlarged committee is a woman is equal to

$$\frac{\text{the number of women}}{\text{the total number of members}} = \frac{w+3}{w+m+5}.$$

The correct answer is E.

174. How many prime numbers between 1 and 100 are factors of 7,150 ?

    (A)   One
    (B)   Two
    (C)   Three
    (D)   Four
    (E)   Five

Arithmetic Properties of numbers

To find the number of prime numbers between 1 and 100 that are factors of 7,150, find the prime factorization of 7,150 using a method similar to the following:

$$7,150 = 10 \times 715$$

$$= (2 \times 5) \times (5 \times 143)$$

$$= 2 \times 5 \times 5 \times (11 \times 13)$$

Thus, 7,150 has four prime factors: 2, 5, 11, and 13.

The correct answer is D.

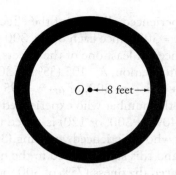

175. The figure above shows a circular flower bed, with its center at O, surrounded by a circular path that is 3 feet wide. What is the area of the path, in square feet?

(A) 25π
(B) 38π
(C) 55π
(D) 57π
(E) 64π

Geometry Area (Circles)

The flower bed and the path form two concentric circles. Since the path is 3 feet wide, the radius of the outer circle is 8 feet $+$ 3 feet $=$ 11 feet. The area of a circle can be determined using the formula: area $= \pi (\text{radius})^2$.

The area of the path can thus be found by subtracting the area of the inner circle, A_1, from the area of the outer circle, A_2.

$$A_2 - A_1 = \pi(11)^2 - \pi(8)^2 = 121\pi - 64\pi = 57\pi$$

The correct answer is D.

176. The positive integer n is divisible by 25. If $\sqrt{n}$ is greater than 25, which of the following could be the value of $\dfrac{n}{25}$?

(A) 22
(B) 23
(C) 24
(D) 25
(E) 26

Arithmetic Operations on radical expressions

If $\sqrt{n} > 25$, then $n > 25^2$. Therefore, $\dfrac{n}{25} > \dfrac{25^2}{25} =$ 25 and the only answer choice that is greater than 25 is 26.

The correct answer is E.

177. Last year the price per share of Stock X increased by k percent and the earnings per share of Stock X increased by m percent, where k is greater than m. By what percent did the ratio of price per share to earnings per share increase, in terms of k and m ?

(A) $\dfrac{k}{m}\%$

(B) $(k - m)\%$

(C) $\dfrac{100(k-m)}{100+k}\%$

(D) $\dfrac{100(k-m)}{100+m}\%$

(E) $\dfrac{100(k-m)}{100+k+m}\%$

Algebra Percents

If P and E are the price and earnings per share before the increase, then $\left(1+\dfrac{k}{100}\right)P$ and $\left(1+\dfrac{m}{100}\right)E$ are the price and earnings per share after the increase. Therefore, the percent increase in the ratio of price per share to earnings per share can be expressed as follows:

$$\left(\frac{(\text{ratio after increases}) - (\text{ratio before increases})}{(\text{ratio before increases})}\times 100\right)\%$$

$$= \left[\left(\frac{(\text{ratio after increases})}{(\text{ratio before increases})}-1\right)\times 100\right]\%$$

$$= \left[\left(\frac{\dfrac{\left(1+\dfrac{k}{100}\right)P}{\left(1+\dfrac{m}{100}\right)E}}{\dfrac{P}{E}}-1\right)\times 100\right]\%$$

$$= \left[\left(\frac{\dfrac{\left(1+\dfrac{k}{100}\right)}{\left(1+\dfrac{m}{100}\right)}\cdot\dfrac{P}{E}}{\dfrac{P}{E}}-1\right)\times 100\right]\%$$

$$= \left[\left(\cfrac{\left(1 + \cfrac{k}{100}\right)}{\cfrac{\left(1 + \cfrac{m}{100}\right)}{1}} - 1 \right) \times 100 \right] \%$$

$$= \left[\left(\cfrac{1 + \cfrac{k}{100}}{1 + \cfrac{m}{100}} - 1 \right) \times 100 \right] \%$$

$$= \left[\left(\cfrac{1 + \cfrac{k}{100}}{1 + \cfrac{m}{100}} \cdot \cfrac{100}{100} - 1 \right) \times 100 \right] \%$$

$$= \left[\left(\cfrac{100 + k}{100 + m} - 1 \right) \times 100 \right] \%$$

$$= \left(\cfrac{(100 + k) - (100 + m)}{100 + m} \times 100 \right) \%$$

$$= \left(\cfrac{k - m}{100 + m} \times 100 \right) \%$$

$$= \cfrac{100(k - m)}{100 + m} \%$$

The correct answer is D.

178. Of the 300 subjects who participated in an experiment using virtual-reality therapy to reduce their fear of heights, 40 percent experienced sweaty palms, 30 percent experienced vomiting, and 75 percent experienced dizziness. If all of the subjects experienced at least one of these effects and 35 percent of the subjects experienced exactly two of these effects, how many of the subjects experienced only one of these effects?

(A) 105
(B) 125
(C) 130
(D) 180
(E) 195

Arithmetic Applied problems

Let a be the number who experienced only one of the effects, b be the number who experienced exactly two of the effects, and c be the number

who experienced all three of the effects. Then $a + b + c = 300$, since each of the 300 participants experienced at least one of the effects. From the given information, $b = 105$ (35% of 300), which gives $a + 105 + c = 300$, or $a + c = 195$ (Eq. 1). Also, if the number who experienced sweaty palms (40% of 300, or 120) is added to the number who experienced vomiting (30% of 300, or 90), and this sum is added to the number who experienced dizziness (75% of 300, or 225), then each participant who experienced only one of the effects is counted exactly once, each participant who experienced exactly two of the effects is counted exactly twice, and each participant who experienced all three of the effects is counted exactly 3 times. Therefore, $a + 2b + 3c = 120 + 90 + 225 = 435$. Using $b = 105$, it follows that $a + 2(105) + 3c = 435$, or $a + 3c = 225$ (Eq. 2). Then solving the system defined by Eq. 1 and Eq. 2,

$$\begin{cases} a + c = 195 \\ a + 3c = 225 \end{cases} \quad \text{multiply 1st equation by } -3$$

$$\begin{cases} -3a - 3c = -585 \\ a + 3c = 225 \end{cases} \quad \text{add equations}$$

$-2a = -360$, or $a = 180$

The correct answer is D.

179. A fruit-salad mixture consists of apples, peaches, and grapes in the ratio 6:5:2, respectively, by weight. If 39 pounds of the mixture is prepared, the mixture includes how many more pounds of apples than grapes?

(A) 15
(B) 12
(C) 9
(D) 6
(E) 4

Algebra Applied problems

Using the given ratios, the information about the fruits in the mixture can be expressed as $6x + 5x + 2x = 39$, or $13x = 39$ and thus $x = 3$. There are $6x$ or $6(3) = 18$ pounds of apples and $2x$ or $2(3) = 6$ pounds of grapes. Therefore, there are $18 - 6 = 12$ more pounds of apples than pounds of grapes in 39 pounds of the mixture.

The correct answer is B.

180. If $m^{-1} = -\frac{1}{3}$, then m^{-2} is equal to

    (A)   −9
    (B)   −3
    (C) $-\frac{1}{9}$
    (D) $\frac{1}{9}$
    (E)   9

Arithmetic Negative exponents

Using rules of exponents, $m^{-2} = m^{-1 \cdot 2} = \left(m^{-1}\right)^2$,

and since $m^{-1} = -\frac{1}{3}$, $m^{-2} = \left(-\frac{1}{3}\right)^2 = \frac{1}{9}$.

The correct answer is D.

181. If $m > 0$ and x is m percent of y, then, in terms of m, y is what percent of x ?

    (A) $100m$
    (B) $\frac{1}{100m}$
    (C) $\frac{1}{m}$
    (D) $\frac{10}{m}$
    (E) $\frac{10,000}{m}$

Arithmetic Percents

The information that x is m percent of y can be expressed as $x = \frac{m}{100} y$ and solved for y as follows:

$$x = \frac{m}{100} y$$
$$\frac{100}{m} x = y$$

Then, to convert the fraction $\frac{100}{m}$ to an equivalent percent, multiply by 100, thus obtaining the value $\frac{10,000}{m}$.

The correct answer is E.

182. A photography dealer ordered 60 Model X cameras to be sold for $250 each, which represents a 20 percent markup over the dealer's initial cost for each camera.

Of the cameras ordered, 6 were never sold and were returned to the manufacturer for a refund of 50 percent of the dealer's initial cost. What was the dealer's approximate profit or loss as a percent of the dealer's initial cost for the 60 cameras?

    (A)   7% loss
    (B)   13% loss
    (C)   7% profit
    (D)   13% profit
    (E)   15% profit

Arithmetic Percents

Given that $250 is 20% greater than a camera's initial cost, it follows that the initial cost for each camera was $\left(\$\frac{250}{1.2}\right)$. Therefore, the initial cost for the 60 cameras was $60\left(\$\frac{250}{1.2}\right)$. The total revenue is the sum of the amount obtained from selling $60 - 6 = 54$ cameras for $250 each and the $\left(\frac{1}{2}\right)\left(\$\frac{250}{1.2}\right)$ refund for each of 6 cameras, or $(54)(\$250) + (6)\left(\frac{1}{2}\right)\left(\$\frac{250}{1.2}\right)$. The total profit, as a percent of the total initial cost, is

$$\left(\frac{(\text{total revenue}) - (\text{total initial cost})}{(\text{total initial cost})} \times 100\right)\% =$$

$$\left(\left(\frac{(\text{total revenue})}{(\text{total initial cost})} - 1\right) \times 100\right)\%. \text{ Using the}$$

numerical expressions obtained above,

$$\frac{(\text{total revenue})}{(\text{total initial cost})} - 1$$

$$= \frac{(54)(250) + 6\left(\frac{1}{2}\right)\left(\frac{250}{1.2}\right)}{(60)\left(\frac{250}{1.2}\right)} - 1 \qquad \text{by substitution}$$

$$= \frac{54 + 3\left(\frac{1}{1.2}\right)}{(60)\left(\frac{1}{1.2}\right)} - 1 \qquad \text{by cancelling 250s}$$

$$= \frac{54(1.2) + 3}{60} - 1 \qquad \begin{array}{l}\text{by multiplying}\\ \text{top and bottom by 1.2}\\ \text{and then cancelling 1.2}\end{array}$$

$$= \frac{67.8}{60} - 1$$

$$= 1.13 - 1$$

$$= 0.13$$

Finally, $(0.13 \times 100)\% = 13\%$, which represents a profit since it is positive.

The correct answer is D.

183. Seven pieces of rope have an average (arithmetic mean) length of 68 centimeters and a median length of 84 centimeters. If the length of the longest piece of rope is 14 centimeters more than 4 times the length of the shortest piece of rope, what is the maximum possible length, in centimeters, of the longest piece of rope?

    (A)   82
    (B)   118
    (C)   120
    (D)   134
    (E)   152

Algebra Statistics

Let a, b, c, d, e, f, and g be the lengths, in centimeters, of the pieces of rope, listed from least to greatest. From the given information it follows that $d = 84$ and $g = 4a + 14$. Therefore, listed from least to greatest, the lengths are a, b, c, 84, e, f, and $4a + 14$. The maximum value of $4a + 14$ will occur when the maximum value of a is used, and this will be the case only if the shortest 3 pieces all have the same length. Therefore, listed from least to greatest, the lengths are a, a, a, 84, e, f, and $4a + 14$. The maximum value for $4a + 14$ will occur when e and f are as small as possible. Since e and f are to the right of the median, they must be at least 84 and so 84 is the least possible value for each of e and f. Therefore, listed from least to greatest, the lengths are a, a, a, 84, 84, 84, and $4a + 14$. Since the average length is 68, it follows that $\frac{a + a + a + 84 + 84 + 84 + (4a + 14)}{7} = 68$, or $a = 30$. Hence, the maximum length of the longest piece is $(4a + 14) = [4(30) + 14] = 134$ centimeters.

The correct answer is D.

184. Lois has x dollars more than Jim has, and together they have a total of y dollars. Which of the following represents the number of dollars that Jim has?

    (A) $\dfrac{y - x}{2}$
    (B) $y - \dfrac{x}{2}$
    (C) $\dfrac{y}{2} - x$
    (D) $2y - x$
    (E) $y - 2x$

Algebra Simplifying algebraic expressions

Let J be the number of dollars that Jim has. Then, the amount that Lois has can be expressed as $J + x$ dollars. If Lois and Jim together have a total of y dollars, then:

$y = J + (J + x)$ total dollars =
                   Jim's dollars + Lois's dollars

Solve this for J to determine the number of dollars that Jim has:

$$y = 2J + x$$
$$y - x = 2J$$
$$\frac{y - x}{2} = J$$

The correct answer is A.

185. During a certain season, a team won 80 percent of its first 100 games and 50 percent of its remaining games. If the team won 70 percent of its games for the entire season, what was the total number of games that the team played?

    (A)   180
    (B)   170
    (C)   156
    (D)   150
    (E)   105

Arithmetic; Algebra Percents; Applied problems

Let G equal the number of games played by the team this season. The given information can be expressed as $(0.80)(100) + 0.50(G - 100) = 0.70G$, that is, 80 percent of the first 100 games plus 50 percent of the remaining games equals 70 percent of the total number of games played.

This equation can be solved for G to determine the answer to the problem:

$$(0.80)(100) + 0.50(G - 100) = 0.70G$$

$80 + 0.50G - 50 = 0.70G$ simplify and distribute

$30 = 0.20G$ simplify and subtract $0.05G$ from both sides

$150 = G$ multiply by 5

The correct answer is D.

186. Of 30 applicants for a job, 14 had at least 4 years' experience, 18 had degrees, and 3 had less than 4 years' experience and did not have a degree. How many of the applicants had at least 4 years' experience and a degree?

(A)   14
(B)   13
(C)   9
(D)   7
(E)   5

Arithmetic Operations on rational numbers

The problem classified the job applicants into two categories: whether they had more or less than 4 years' experience, and whether they had a degree. The given information can be summarized in the following table:

	At least 4 years' experience	Less than 4 years' experience	Total
Degree			18
No degree		3	
Total	14		30

Thus, according to the given information, $30 - 14 = 16$ applicants had less than 4 years' experience. Then, of those applicants with less than 4 years' experience, it is given that 3 applicants did not have a degree, so $16 - 3 = 13$ applicants had less than 4 years' experience and had a degree. Therefore, out of the given 18 applicants that had degrees, 13 applicants had less than 4 years' experience, so $18 - 13 = 5$ applicants had at least 4 years' experience with a degree. These results are shown in the following table.

	At least 4 years' experience	Less than 4 years' experience	Total
Degree	5	13	18
No degree		3	
Total	14	16	30

The correct answer is E.

187. If $1 + \dfrac{1}{x} = 2 - \dfrac{2}{x}$, then $x =$

(A) -1
(B) $\dfrac{1}{3}$
(C) $\dfrac{2}{3}$
(D)   2
(E)   3

Algebra First-degree equations

Work the problem to solve the equation for x.

$1 + \dfrac{1}{x} = 2 - \dfrac{2}{x}$

$x + 1 = 2x - 2$ multiply through by x

$3 = x$ solve for x by adding 2 to and subtracting x from both sides

The correct answer is E.

188. Last year, for every 100 million vehicles that traveled on a certain highway, 96 vehicles were involved in accidents. If 3 billion vehicles traveled on the highway last year, how many of those vehicles were involved in accidents? $(1 \text{ billion} = 1,000,000,000)$

(A)   288
(B)   320
(C)   2,880
(D)   3,200
(E)   28,800

Arithmetic Operations on rational numbers

According to the given information, 96 out of every 100 million vehicles were in an accident last year. Thus, of the 3 billion vehicles on the highway last year, the number of vehicles involved in accidents was:

$$\frac{96}{100,000,000} \times 3,000,000,000 =$$

$$\frac{96}{100} \times 3,000 = 96 \times 30 = 2,880 \text{ vehicles}$$

The correct answer is C.

189. Thirty percent of the members of a swim club have passed the lifesaving test. Among the members who have *not* passed the test, 12 have taken the preparatory course and 30 have not taken the course. How many members are there in the swim club?

    (A)   60
    (B)   80
    (C)   100
    (D)   120
    (E)   140

Algebra Applied problems

If 30 percent of the club members have passed the test, then 70 percent have not. Among the members who have not passed the test, 12 have taken the course and 30 have not, for a total of $12 + 30 = 42$ members who have not passed the test. Letting x represent the total number of members in the swim club, this information can be expressed as $0.70x = 42$, and so $x = 60$.

The correct answer is A.

190. What is the difference between the sixth and the fifth terms of the sequence 2, 4, 7, … whose *n*th term is $n + 2^{n-1}$?

    (A)   2
    (B)   3
    (C)   6
    (D)   16
    (E)   17

Algebra Simplifying algebraic expressions

According to the given formula, the sixth term of the sequence is $6 + 2^{6-1} = 6 + 2^5$ and the fifth term is $5 + 2^{5-1} = 5 + 2^4$. Then,

$$\left(6 + 2^5\right) - \left(5 + 2^4\right) = \left(6 - 5\right) + \left(2^5 - 2^4\right)$$

$$= 1 + 2^4\left(2 - 1\right)$$

$$= 1 + 2^4$$

$$= 1 + 16$$

$$= 17$$

The correct answer is E.

191. If $(x - 1)^2 = 400$, which of the following could be the value of $x - 5$?

    (A)   15
    (B)   14
    (C)   −24
    (D)   −25
    (E)   −26

Algebra Second-degree equations

Work the problem by taking the square root of both sides and solving for x.

$$(x - 1)^2 = 400$$

$$x - 1 = \pm 20$$

$$x - 1 = -20, \text{ or } x - 1 = 20$$

$$x = -19, \text{ or } x = 21$$

Thus, $x - 5 = -24$ or 16.

The correct answer is C.

192. Which of the following describes all values of x for which $1 - x^2 \geq 0$?

    (A) $x \geq 1$
    (B) $x \leq -1$
    (C) $0 \leq x \leq 1$
    (D) $x \leq -1$ or $x \geq 1$
    (E) $-1 \leq x \leq 1$

Algebra Inequalities

The expression $1 - x^2$ can be factored as $(1 - x)(1 + x)$. The product is positive or zero when both factors are positive or zero (this happens if $1 \geq x$ and $x \geq -1$, or equivalently if $-1 \leq x \leq 1$) or both factors are negative or zero (this happens if $1 \leq x$ and $x \leq 1$, which cannot happen), and therefore the solution is $-1 \leq x \leq 1$.

The correct answer is E.

193. The probability is $\frac{1}{2}$ that a certain coin will turn up heads on any given toss. If the coin is to be tossed three times, what is the probability that on at least one of the tosses the coin will turn up tails?

    (A) $\frac{1}{8}$

    (B) $\frac{1}{2}$

    (C) $\frac{3}{4}$

    (D) $\frac{7}{8}$

    (E) $\frac{15}{16}$

Arithmetic Probability

Another way of stating that a coin toss will turn up tails at least once is to say that it will not turn up heads every time. The probability that on at least one of the tosses the coin will not turn up heads is 1 minus the probability that the coin will turn up heads on all three tosses. Each toss is an independent event, and so the probability of getting heads all three times is $\left(\frac{1}{2}\right)^3 = \frac{1}{8}$.

Thus, the probability of not getting heads all three times (that is, getting tails at least once) is

$1 - \frac{1}{8} = \frac{7}{8}$.

The correct answer is D.

194. Of the final grades received by the students in a certain math course, $\frac{1}{5}$ are A's, $\frac{1}{4}$ are B's, $\frac{1}{2}$ are C's, and the remaining 10 grades are D's. What is the number of students in the course?

    (A) 80
    (B) 110
    (C) 160
    (D) 200
    (E) 400

Algebra Applied problems

Let x be the number of students in the course.

Then $\left(\frac{1}{5} + \frac{1}{4} + \frac{1}{2}\right)x$ or $\left(\frac{4}{20} + \frac{5}{20} + \frac{10}{20}\right)x$ or $\left(\frac{19}{20}\right)x$ of the students received grades of A, B, or C.

This means the 10 remaining grades represent $\frac{1}{20}$ of the students in the course.

Thus, $\frac{1}{20}x = 10$, and $x = 200$.

The correct answer is D.

195. As x increases from 165 to 166, which of the following must increase?

    I. $2x - 5$

    II. $1 - \frac{1}{x}$

    III. $\frac{1}{x^2 - x}$

    (A) I only
    (B) III only
    (C) I and II
    (D) I and III
    (E) II and III

Algebra Simplifying algebraic expressions

Investigate each of the functions to determine if they increase from $x = 165$ to $x = 166$.

I.   Graphically, this represents a line with positive slope. Therefore, the function increases between any two values of x. A direct computation can also be used: $\left[2(166) - 5\right] - \left[2(165) - 5\right] = 2(166 - 165) = 2$, which is positive, and thus the function increases from $x = 165$ to $x = 166$.

II. Between any two positive values of x, $\frac{1}{x}$ decreases, and hence both $-\frac{1}{x}$ and $1 - \frac{1}{x}$ increase. A direct computation can also be used:

$\left[1 - \frac{1}{166}\right] - \left[1 - \frac{1}{165}\right] =$

$\frac{1}{165} - \frac{1}{166} = \frac{166 - 165}{(165)(166)} = \frac{1}{(165)(166)}$,

which is positive, and thus the function increases from $x = 165$ to $x = 166$.

III. For $x = 165$, the denominator is $165^2 - 165 = (165)(165 - 1) = (165)(164)$, and for $x = 166$, the denominator is $166^2 - 166 = (166)(166 - 1) = (166)(165)$. Therefore, $166^2 - 166 > 165^2 - 165$, and hence

$$\frac{1}{166^2 - 166} < \frac{1}{165^2 - 165},$$

which shows that $\frac{1}{x^2 - x}$ decreases from $x = 165$ to $x = 166$.

The correct answer is C.

196. From the consecutive integers –10 to 10, inclusive, 20 integers are randomly chosen with repetitions allowed. What is the least possible value of the product of the 20 integers?

 (A) $(-10)^{20}$
 (B) $(-10)^{10}$
 (C) 0
 (D) $-(10)^{19}$
 (E) $-(10)^{20}$

Arithmetic Properties of numbers

If –10 is chosen an odd number of times and 10 is chosen the remaining number of times (for example, choose –10 once and choose 10 nineteen times, or choose –10 three times and choose 10 seventeen times), then the product of the 20 chosen numbers will be $-(10)^{20}$. Note that $-(10)^{20}$ is less than $-(10)^{19}$, the only other negative value among the answer choices.

The correct answer is E.

197. A rectangular box is 10 inches wide, 10 inches long, and 5 inches high. What is the greatest possible (straight-line) distance, in inches, between any two points on the box?

 (A) 15
 (B) 20
 (C) 25
 (D) $10\sqrt{2}$
 (E) $10\sqrt{3}$

Geometry Pythagorean theorem

The greatest possible distance between any two points in a rectangular solid is the space diagonal $\left(\overline{AD}\right)$ of the rectangular solid as shown below.

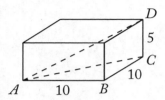

To compute the length of $\overline{AD}$, the Pythagorean theorem must be used twice as follows:

For $\triangle ABC$:

$$AC^2 = AB^2 + BC^2$$
$$AC^2 = 10^2 + 10^2$$
$$AC^2 = 200$$
$$AC = \sqrt{200}$$

For $\triangle ACD$:

$$AD^2 = AC^2 + CD^2$$
$$AD^2 = \left(\sqrt{200}\right)^2 + 5^2$$
$$AD^2 = 200 + 25$$
$$AD^2 = 225$$
$$AD = 15$$

The correct answer is A.

198. Last Sunday a certain store sold copies of Newspaper A for $1.00 each and copies of Newspaper B for $1.25 each, and the store sold no other newspapers that day. If r percent of the store's revenue from newspaper sales was from Newspaper A and if p percent of the newspapers that the store sold were copies of Newspaper A, which of the following expresses r in terms of p ?

 (A) $\dfrac{100p}{125 - p}$

 (B) $\dfrac{150p}{250 - p}$

 (C) $\dfrac{300p}{375 - p}$

 (D) $\dfrac{400p}{500 - p}$

 (E) $\dfrac{500p}{625 - p}$

Algebra Simultaneous equations

Let N be the total number of newspapers that the store sold. Then, the number of copies of

Newspaper A the store sold was p% of $N = \left(\dfrac{p}{100}\right)N$

and the revenue from those copies of Newspaper A,

in dollars, was $(1.00)\left(\dfrac{p}{100}\right)N = \left(\dfrac{p}{100}\right)N$. The

number of copies of Newspaper B the store sold was

$(100 - p)$% of $N = \left(\dfrac{100-p}{100}\right)N$ and the revenue

from those copies of Newspaper A, in dollars, was

$(1.25)\left(\dfrac{100-p}{100}\right)N = \left(\dfrac{5}{4}\right)\left(\dfrac{100-p}{100}\right)N$. The store's

total revenue from newspaper sales, in dollars,

was $\left(\dfrac{p}{100}\right)N + \left(\dfrac{5}{4}\right)\left(\dfrac{100-p}{100}\right)N$, and the fraction

of that revenue from the sale of Newspaper A was

$$\frac{\dfrac{p}{100}N}{\dfrac{p}{100}N + \left(\dfrac{5}{4}\right)\left(\dfrac{100-p}{100}\right)N} = \frac{\dfrac{p}{100}}{\dfrac{4p}{400} + \left(\dfrac{500-5p}{400}\right)}$$

$$= \frac{\dfrac{p}{100}}{\dfrac{4p+500-5p}{400}}$$

$$= \frac{\dfrac{p}{100}}{\dfrac{500-p}{400}}$$

$$= \left(\dfrac{p}{100}\right)\left(\dfrac{400}{500-p}\right)$$

$$= \frac{4p}{500-p}$$

Since r percent of the store's newspaper sales

revenue was from Newspaper A, $\dfrac{r}{100} = \dfrac{4p}{500-p}$,

and so $r = \dfrac{400p}{500-p}$.

The correct answer is D.

199. $\dfrac{0.99999999}{1.0001} - \dfrac{0.99999991}{1.0003} =$

(A) 10^{-8}

(B) $3(10^{-8})$

(C) $3(10^{-4})$

(D) $2(10^{-4})$

(E) 10^{-4}

Arithmetic Operations on rational numbers

Calculations with lengthy decimals can be avoided by writing 0.99999999 as $1 - 10^{-8}$, 0.99999991 as $1 - 9(10^{-8})$, 1.0001 as $1 + 10^{-4}$, and 1.0003 as $1 + 3(10^{-4})$. Doing this gives

$$\frac{1-10^{-8}}{1+10^{-4}} - \frac{1-9(10^{-8})}{1+3(10^{-4})}$$

$$= \frac{\left[1+10^{-4}\right]\left[1-10^{-4}\right]}{1+10^{-4}} - \frac{1-9(10^{-8})}{1+3(10^{-4})}$$

$$= \frac{1-10^{-4}}{1} - \frac{1-9(10^{-8})}{1+3(10^{-4})}$$

$$= \frac{\left[1-10^{-4}\right]\left[1+3(10^{-4})\right] - \left[1-9(10^{-8})\right]}{1+3(10^{-4})}$$

$$= \frac{1+3(10^{-4})-10^{-4}-3(10^{-8})-1+9(10^{-8})}{1+3(10^{-4})}$$

$$= \frac{2(10^{-4})+6(10^{-8})}{1+3(10^{-4})}$$

$$= \frac{\left[2(10^{-4})\right]\left[1+3(10^{-4})\right]}{1+3(10^{-4})}$$

$$= 2(10^{-4})$$

The correct answer is D.

200. The ratio, by volume, of soap to alcohol to water in a certain solution is 2:50:100. The solution will be altered so that the ratio of soap to alcohol is doubled while the ratio of soap to water is halved. If the altered solution will contain 100 cubic centimeters of alcohol, how many cubic centimeters of water will it contain?

(A) 50

(B) 200

(C) 400

(D) 625

(E) 800

Arithmetic Operations on rational numbers

From $\dfrac{\text{soap}_{\text{original}}}{\text{alcohol}_{\text{original}}} = \dfrac{2}{50}$ we get

$$\frac{\text{soap}_{\text{altered}}}{\text{alcohol}_{\text{altered}}} = 2\left(\frac{\text{soap}_{\text{original}}}{\text{alcohol}_{\text{original}}}\right) = 2\left(\frac{2}{50}\right) = \frac{2}{25},$$

and from $\dfrac{\text{soap}_{\text{original}}}{\text{water}_{\text{original}}} = \dfrac{2}{100}$ we get

$$\frac{\text{soap}_{\text{altered}}}{\text{water}_{\text{altered}}} = \frac{1}{2}\left(\frac{\text{soap}_{\text{original}}}{\text{water}_{\text{original}}}\right) = \frac{1}{2}\left(\frac{2}{100}\right) = \frac{1}{100}.$$

Therefore, the amount of soap in the altered solution can be found by solving $\dfrac{\text{soap}_{\text{altered}}}{100} = \dfrac{2}{25}$, which gives $\text{soap}_{\text{altered}} = \dfrac{2}{25} \cdot \dfrac{100}{1} = 8$, and now the amount of water in the altered solution can be found by solving $\dfrac{8}{\text{water}_{\text{altered}}} = \dfrac{1}{100}$, which gives $\text{water}_{\text{altered}} = 800$.

The correct answer is E.

201. If 75 percent of a class answered the first question on a certain test correctly, 55 percent answered the second question on the test correctly, and 20 percent answered neither of the questions correctly, what percent answered both correctly?

   (A)   10%
   (B)   20%
   (C)   30%
   (D)   50%
   (E)   65%

Arithmetic Percents

For questions of this type, it is convenient to draw a Venn diagram to represent the conditions in the problem. For example, the given information can be depicted:

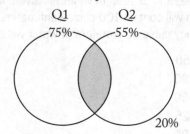

In the diagram it can be seen that the 80% of the class answering a question correctly is represented by the two circles. Let x represent the percent of the class that answered both questions correctly, that is, the shaded region above. Since the sum of the circles minus their overlap equals 80% of the class, the information given in the problem can then be expressed as $75\% + 55\% - x = 80\%$. This equation can be solved for x as follows:

$$75\% + 55\% - x = 80\%$$
$$130\% - x = 80\%$$
$$-x = -50\%$$
$$x = 50\%$$

The correct answer is D.

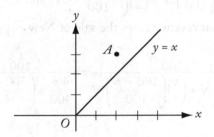

202. In the rectangular coordinate system above, the line $y = x$ is the perpendicular bisector of segment AB (not shown), and the x-axis is the perpendicular bisector of segment BC (not shown). If the coordinates of point A are (2,3), what are the coordinates of point C ?

   (A)   (–3,–2)
   (B)   (–3,2)
   (C)   (2,–3)
   (D)   (3,–2)
   (E)   (2,3)

Geometry Simple coordinate geometry

Since the line $y = x$ is the perpendicular bisector of $\overline{AB}$, B is the reflection of A through this line. In any reflection through the line $y = x$, the x-coordinate and the y-coordinate of a point become interchanged. Thus, if the coordinates of A are (2,3), the coordinates of B are (3,2).

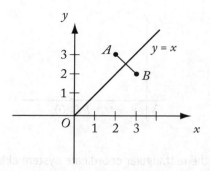

Since the x-axis is the perpendicular bisector of $\overline{BC}$, C is the reflection of B through the x-axis. In any reflection through the x-axis, the x-coordinate remains the same, and the sign of the y-coordinate changes.

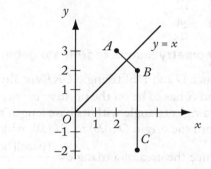

Since the coordinates of B are $(3,2)$, the coordinates of C are therefore $(3,-2)$.

The correct answer is D.

203. A store currently charges the same price for each towel that it sells. If the current price of each towel were to be increased by $1, 10 fewer of the towels could be bought for $120, excluding sales tax. What is the current price of each towel?

   (A) $ 1
   (B) $ 2
   (C) $ 3
   (D) $ 4
   (E) $12

Algebra Applied problems

Let p be the current price per towel, and let n be the number of towels that can be bought for $120. Then the information in the problem can be expressed in the following equations:

(i) $pn = 120$

(ii) $(p+1)(n-10) = 120$ or equivalently

(iii) $pn + n - 10p - 10 = 120$.

Then replace pn in (iii) with 120 to get:

$$120 + n - 10p - 10 = 120$$
$$n - 10p - 10 = 0$$
$$n - 10(p+1) = 0$$
$$n = 10(p+1)$$
$$np = 10p(p+1)$$
$$120 = 10p(p+1)$$
$$12 = p(p+1)$$
$$0 = p^2 + p - 12$$
$$0 = (p+4)(p-3)$$
$$p = 3$$

The correct answer is C.

204. If $n = 4p$, where p is a prime number greater than 2, how many different positive <u>even</u> divisors does n have, including n?

   (A)   Two
   (B)   Three
   (C)   Four
   (D)   Six
   (E)   Eight

Arithmetic Properties of numbers

Since p is a prime greater than 2, p must be odd. Therefore, the possible even divisors of $n = 4p$ are $2, 4, 2p$, and $4p$. Alternatively, choose such a prime, for example $p = 3$, and determine the number of positive even divisors that $n = 4p = 12$ has.

The correct answer is C.

205. John and Mary were each paid x dollars in advance to do a certain job together. John worked on the job for 10 hours and Mary worked 2 hours less than John. If Mary gave John y dollars of her payment so that they would have received the same hourly wage, what was the dollar amount, in terms of y, that John was paid in advance?

(A) $4y$
(B) $5y$
(C) $6y$
(D) $8y$
(E) $9y$

Algebra Applied problems

Let w be the amount of Mary and John's same hourly wage. To set their hourly pay equal, John, who worked 10 hours, needs to be paid $10w$, and Mary, who worked 8 hours, needs to be paid $8w$. Since Mary gave John y dollars, Mary now has $x - y$ dollars and John now has $x + y$ dollars. Their pay can thus be expressed as follows:

$x - y = 8w$ Mary's pay

$x + y = 10w$ John's pay

Subtract the first equation from the second and solve for w.

$2y = 2w$

$y = w$

Substitute y for w in the second equation, and solve for x, the amount each was paid in advance.

$x + y = 10y$

$x = 9y$

The correct answer is E.

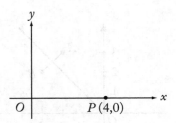

206. In the rectangular coordinate system above, if point R (not shown) lies on the positive y-axis and the area of triangle ORP is 12, what is the y-coordinate of point R ?

(A) 3
(B) 6
(C) 9
(D) 12
(E) 24

Geometry Simple coordinate geometry; Area

Since O and P of triangle ORP are already drawn and R has to be on the positive y-axis, the triangle is a right triangle with its base length the distance from the origin O (0,0) to P (4,0), which is 4.

Since the area of a triangle $= \dfrac{(\text{base})(\text{height})}{2}$,

the information about the area and base can be expressed as follows and solved for the height of triangle OPR:

$12 = \dfrac{(4)(\text{height})}{2}$

$12 = 2(\text{height})$ simplify the right side

$6 = \text{height}$ solve for the height

On the y-axis, the x-coordinate is 0 and the y-coordinate is the distance above the axis that the point is located. In this case, the y-coordinate is the height of the triangle.

The correct answer is B.

207. Car A is 20 miles behind Car B, which is traveling in the same direction along the same route as Car A. Car A is traveling at a constant speed of 58 miles per hour and Car B is traveling at a constant speed of 50 miles per hour. How many hours will it take for Car A to overtake and drive 8 miles ahead of Car B ?

(A) 1.5
(B) 2.0
(C) 2.5
(D) 3.0
(E) 3.5

Arithmetic Operations on rational numbers

Understand that Car A first has to travel 20 miles to catch up to Car B and then has to travel an additional 8 miles ahead of Car B, for a total of 28 extra miles to travel relative to Car B. It can be stated that Car A is traveling $58 - 50 = 8$ miles per hour faster than Car B. Solving the

distance = (rate)(time) formula for time yields $\frac{\text{distance}}{\text{rate}} = \text{time}$.

By substitution into this formula, it will take

Car A $\dfrac{28 \text{ miles}}{8 \text{ miles per hour}} = 3.5$ hours to overtake and drive 8 miles ahead of Car B.

The correct answer is E.

208. For the past *n* days, the average (arithmetic mean) daily production at a company was 50 units. If today's production of 90 units raises the average to 55 units per day, what is the value of *n* ?

(A) 30
(B) 18
(C) 10
(D) 9
(E) 7

Arithmetic; Algebra Statistics; Applied problems; Simultaneous equations

Let x be the total production of the past n days.

Using the formula $\text{average} = \dfrac{\text{sum of values}}{\text{number of values}}$, the information in the problem can be expressed in the following two equations:

$50 = \dfrac{x}{n}$ — daily average of 50 units over the past n days

$55 = \dfrac{x+90}{n+1}$ — increased daily average when including today's 90 units

Solving the first equation for x gives $x = 50n$. Then substituting $50n$ for x in the second equation gives the following that can be solved for n:

$$55 = \frac{50n + 90}{n+1}$$

$55(n+1) = 50n + 90$	multiply both sides by $(n+1)$
$55n + 55 = 50n + 90$	distribute the 55
$5n = 35$	subtract $50n$ and 55 from both sides
$n = 7$	divide both sides by 5

The correct answer is E.

209. If $x \neq 0$ and $x \neq 1$, and if x is replaced by $\dfrac{1}{x}$ everywhere in the expression $\left(\dfrac{x+1}{x-1}\right)^2$ above, then the resulting expression is equivalent to

(A) $\left(\dfrac{x+1}{x-1}\right)^2$

(B) $\left(\dfrac{x-1}{x+1}\right)^2$

(C) $\dfrac{x^2+1}{1-x^2}$

(D) $\dfrac{x^2-1}{x^2+1}$

(E) $-\left(\dfrac{x-1}{x+1}\right)^2$

Algebra Simplifying algebraic expressions

Substitute $\frac{1}{x}$ for x in the expression and simplify.

$$\left(\frac{\frac{1}{x}+1}{\frac{1}{x}-1}\right)^2$$

Multiply the numerator and denominator inside the parentheses by x to eliminate the compound fractions.

$$\left(\frac{x\left(\frac{1}{x}+1\right)}{x\left(\frac{1}{x}-1\right)}\right)^2$$

Distribute the x's.

$$\left(\frac{1+x}{1-x}\right)^2$$

Since this is not one of the answer choices, it is necessary to simplify further. With the knowledge that $1+x=x+1$ and $1-x=-(x-1)$, it can be stated that

$$\left(\frac{1+x}{1-x}\right)^2=\left(\frac{x+1}{-(x-1)}\right)^2=\left(-\frac{x+1}{(x-1)}\right)^2=\left(\frac{x+1}{x-1}\right)^2$$

because the negative, when squared, is positive.

The correct answer is A.

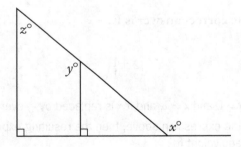

210. In the figure above, if $z=50$, then $x+y=$

    (A)   230

    (B)   250

    (C)   260

    (D)   270

    (E)   290

Geometry Angles; Measures of angles

Refer to the figure below.

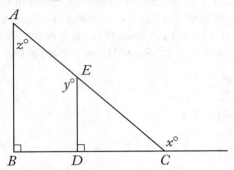

Triangle ABC is a right triangle, and segment AB is parallel to segment ED since they are both perpendicular to the same segment $\left(\overline{BC}\right)$. Therefore, $m\angle DEC = m\angle BAC = z° = 50°$. So, since $\angle DEC$ and $\angle AED$ form a straight line at E, $y+50=180$, or $y=130$.

The measure of an exterior angle of a triangle is the sum of the measures of the nonadjacent interior angles. Thus,

$$m\angle x = m\angle z + 90°, \text{ or}$$

$$m\angle x = 50° + 90° = 140°$$

Thus, $x+y=140+130=270$.

The correct answer is D.

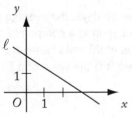

211. In the coordinate system above, which of the following is the equation of line ℓ?

    (A) $2x-3y=6$

    (B) $2x+3y=6$

    (C) $3x+2y=6$

    (D) $2x-3y=-6$

    (E) $3x-2y=-6$

Geometry Simple coordinate geometry

The line is shown going through the points $(0,2)$ and $(3,0)$. The slope of the line can be found with the formula slope $= \dfrac{\text{change in } y}{\text{change in } x} = \dfrac{y_2 - y_1}{x_2 - x_1}$ for two points (x_1, y_1) and (x_2, y_2). Thus, the slope of this line equals $\dfrac{0-2}{3-0} = -\dfrac{2}{3}$. Using the formula for a line of $y = mx + b$, where m is the slope and b is the y-intercept (in this case, 2), an equation for this line is $y = -\dfrac{2}{3}x + 2$. Since this equation must be compared to the available answer choices, the following further steps should be taken:

$y = -\dfrac{2}{3}x + 2$

$3y = -2x + 6$ multiply both sides by 3

$2x + 3y = 6$ add $2x$ to both sides

This problem can also be solved as follows. From the graph, when $x = 0$, y is positive; when $y = 0$, x is positive. This eliminates all but B and C. Of these, B is the only line containing $(0,2)$. Still another way is to use $(0,2)$ to eliminate A, C, and E, and then use $(3,0)$ to eliminate D.

The correct answer is B.

212. If a two-digit positive integer has its digits reversed, the resulting integer differs from the original by 27. By how much do the two digits differ?

(A)   3
(B)   4
(C)   5
(D)   6
(E)   7

Algebra Applied problems

Let the one two-digit integer be represented by $10t + s$, where s and t are digits, and let the other integer with the reversed digits be represented by $10s + t$. The information that the difference between the integers is 27 can be expressed in the following equation, which can be solved for the answer.

$(10s + t) - (10t + s) = 27$

$10s + t - 10t - s = 27$ distribute the negative

$9s - 9t = 27$ combine like terms

$s - t = 3$ divide both sides by 9

Thus, it is seen that the two digits s and t differ by 3.

The correct answer is A.

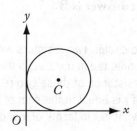

213. The circle with center C shown above is tangent to both axes. If the distance from O to C is equal to k, what is the radius of the circle, in terms of k?

(A) k

(B) $\dfrac{k}{\sqrt{2}}$

(C) $\dfrac{k}{\sqrt{3}}$

(D) $\dfrac{k}{2}$

(E) $\dfrac{k}{3}$

Geometry Circles; Simple coordinate geometry

In a circle, all distances from the circle to the center are the same and called the radius, r.

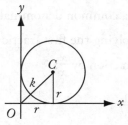

Since the horizontal distance from C to the y-axis is also a radius, the base of the triangle drawn will be r as well. This creates a right triangle, and so the Pythagorean theorem (or $a^2 + b^2 = c^2$) applies.

$r^2 + r^2 = k^2$ substitute values into Pythagorean theorem;

$2r^2 = k^2$ combine like terms

$r^2 = \dfrac{k^2}{2}$ divide both sides by 2

$r = \sqrt{\dfrac{k^2}{2}}$ take the square root of both sides

$r = \dfrac{k}{\sqrt{2}}$ simplify the square root

The correct answer is B.

214. In an electric circuit, two resistors with resistances x and y are connected in parallel. In this case, if r is the combined resistance of these two resistors, then the reciprocal of r is equal to the sum of the reciprocals of x and y. What is r in terms of x and y?

(A) xy

(B) $x+y$

(C) $\dfrac{1}{x+y}$

(D) $\dfrac{xy}{x+y}$

(E) $\dfrac{x+y}{xy}$

Algebra Applied problems

Note that two numbers are reciprocals of each other if and only if their product is 1. Thus the reciprocals of r, x, and y are $\dfrac{1}{r}$, $\dfrac{1}{x}$, and $\dfrac{1}{y}$, respectively. So, according to the problem, $\dfrac{1}{r} = \dfrac{1}{x} + \dfrac{1}{y}$. To solve this equation for r, begin by creating a common denominator on the right side by multiplying the first fraction by $\dfrac{y}{y}$ and the second fraction by $\dfrac{x}{x}$:

$\dfrac{1}{r} = \dfrac{1}{x} + \dfrac{1}{y}$

$\dfrac{1}{r} = \dfrac{y}{xy} + \dfrac{x}{xy}$

$\dfrac{1}{r} = \dfrac{x+y}{xy}$ combine the fractions on the right side

$r = \dfrac{xy}{x+y}$ invert the fractions on both sides

The correct answer is D.

215. Xavier, Yvonne, and Zelda each try independently to solve a problem. If their individual probabilities for success are $\dfrac{1}{4}$, $\dfrac{1}{2}$, and $\dfrac{5}{8}$, respectively, what is the probability that Xavier and Yvonne, but not Zelda, will solve the problem?

(A) $\dfrac{11}{8}$

(B) $\dfrac{7}{8}$

(C) $\dfrac{9}{64}$

(D) $\dfrac{5}{64}$

(E) $\dfrac{3}{64}$

Arithmetic Probability

Since the individuals' probabilities are independent, they can be multiplied to figure out the combined probability. The probability of Xavier's success is given as $\dfrac{1}{4}$, and the probability of Yvonne's success is given as $\dfrac{1}{2}$. Since the probability of Zelda's success is given as $\dfrac{5}{8}$, then the probability of her NOT solving the problem is $1 - \dfrac{5}{8} = \dfrac{3}{8}$.

Thus, the combined probability is

$\left(\dfrac{1}{4}\right)\left(\dfrac{1}{2}\right)\left(\dfrac{3}{8}\right) = \dfrac{3}{64}$.

The correct answer is E.

216. If $\dfrac{1}{x} - \dfrac{1}{x+1} = \dfrac{1}{x+4}$, then x could be

(A) 0
(B) −1
(C) −2
(D) −3
(E) −4

Algebra Second-degree equations

Solve the equation for x. Begin by multiplying all the terms by $x(x+1)(x+4)$ to eliminate the denominators.

$$\frac{1}{x} - \frac{1}{x+1} = \frac{1}{x+4}$$

$$(x+1)(x+4) - x(x+4) = x(x+1)$$

$(x+4)(x+1-x) = x(x+1)$ factor the $(x+4)$ out front on the left side

$(x+4)(1) = x(x+1)$ simplify

$x+4 = x^2 + x$ distribute the x on the right side

$4 = x^2$ subtract x from both sides

$\pm 2 = x$ take the square root of both sides

Both -2 and 2 are square roots of 4 since $(-2)^2 = 4$ and $(2)^2 = 4$. Thus, x could be -2.

This problem can also be solved as follows.

Rewrite the left side as $\dfrac{(x+1)-x}{x(x+1)} = \dfrac{1}{x(x+1)}$, then set equal to the right side to get

$\dfrac{1}{x(x+1)} = \dfrac{1}{x+4}$. Next, cross multiply:

$(1)(x+4) = x(x+1)(1)$. Therefore, $x+4 = x^2 + x$,

or $x^2 = 4$, so $x = \pm 2$.

The correct answer is C.

217. $\left(\dfrac{1}{2}\right)^{-3} \left(\dfrac{1}{4}\right)^{-2} \left(\dfrac{1}{16}\right)^{-1} =$

(A) $\left(\dfrac{1}{2}\right)^{-48}$

(B) $\left(\dfrac{1}{2}\right)^{-11}$

(C) $\left(\dfrac{1}{2}\right)^{-6}$

(D) $\left(\dfrac{1}{8}\right)^{-11}$

(E) $\left(\dfrac{1}{8}\right)^{-6}$

Arithmetic Operations on rational numbers

It is clear from the answer choices that all three factors need to be written with a common denominator, and they thus become

$$\left(\frac{1}{2}\right)^{-3} = \left(\frac{1}{2}\right)^{-3}$$

$$\left(\frac{1}{4}\right)^{-2} = \left(\left(\frac{1}{2}\right)^2\right)^{-2} = \left(\frac{1}{2}\right)^{-4}$$

$$\left(\frac{1}{16}\right)^{-1} = \left(\left(\frac{1}{2}\right)^4\right)^{-1} = \left(\frac{1}{2}\right)^{-4}$$

So, $\left(\dfrac{1}{2}\right)^{-3} \left(\dfrac{1}{4}\right)^{-2} \left(\dfrac{1}{16}\right)^{-1} =$

$\left(\dfrac{1}{2}\right)^{-3} \left(\dfrac{1}{2}\right)^{-4} \left(\dfrac{1}{2}\right)^{-4} = \left(\dfrac{1}{2}\right)^{-3-4-4} = \left(\dfrac{1}{2}\right)^{-11}.$

The correct answer is B.

218. List T consists of 30 positive decimals, none of which is an integer, and the sum of the 30 decimals is S. The estimated sum of the 30 decimals, E, is defined as follows. Each decimal in T whose tenths digit is even is rounded up to the nearest integer, and each decimal in T whose tenths digit is odd is rounded down to the nearest integer; E is the sum of the resulting integers. If $\dfrac{1}{3}$ of the decimals in T have a tenths digit that is even, which of the following is a possible value of $E - S$?

I. -16
II. 6
III. 10

(A)   I only
(B)   I and II only
(C)   I and III only
(D)   II and III only
(E)   I, II, and III

Arithmetic Operations on rational numbers

Since $\dfrac{1}{3}$ of the 30 decimals in T have an even tenths digit, it follows that $\dfrac{1}{3}(30) = 10$ decimals in T have an even tenths digit. Let T_E represent the list of these 10 decimals, let S_E represent the sum of all 10 decimals in T_E, and let E_E represent the estimated sum of all 10 decimals in T_E after rounding. The remaining 20 decimals in T have an odd tenths digit. Let T_O represent the list of these 20 remaining decimals, let S_O represent the sum of all 20 decimals in T_O, and let E_O represent the estimated sum of all 20 decimals in T_O after rounding. Note that $E = E_E + E_O$ and $S = S_E + S_O$, and hence $E - S = (E_E + E_O) - (S_E + S_O) = (E_E - S_E) + (E_O - S_O)$.

The least values of $E_E - S_E$ occur at the extreme where each decimal in T_E has tenths digit 8. Here, the difference between the rounded integer and the original decimal is greater than 0.1. (For example, the difference between the integer 15 and 14.899 that has been rounded to 15 is 0.101.) Hence, $E_E - S_E > 10(0.1) = 1$. The greatest values of $E_E - S_E$ occur at the other extreme, where each decimal in T_E has tenths digit 0. Here, the difference between the rounded integer and the original decimal is less than 1. (For example, the difference between the integer 15 and 14.001 that has been rounded to 15 is 0.999.) Hence, $E_E - S_E < 10(1) = 10$. Thus, $1 < E_E - S_E < 10$.

Similarly, the least values of $E_O - S_O$ occur at the extreme where each decimal in T_O has tenths digit 9. Here, the difference between the rounded integer and the original decimal is greater than −1. (For example, the difference between the integer 14 and 14.999 that has been rounded to 14 is −0.999.) Hence $E_O - S_O > 20(-1) = -20$. The greatest values of $E_O - S_O$ occur at the other extreme where each decimal in T_O has tenths digit 1. Here, the difference between the rounded integer and the original decimal is less than or equal to −0.1. (For example, the difference between the integer 14 and 14.1 that has been rounded to 14 is −0.1.) Hence, $E_O - S_O \leq 20(-0.1) = -2$. Thus, $-20 < E_O - S_O \leq -2$.

Adding the inequalities $1 < E_E - S_E < 10$ and $-20 < E_O - S_O \leq -2$ gives $-19 < (E_E - S_E) + (E_O - S_O) < 8$. Therefore, $-19 < (E_E + E_O) - (S_E + S_O) < 8$ and $-19 < E - S < 8$. Thus, of the values −16, 6, and 10 for $E - S$, only −16 and 6 are possible.

Note that if T contains 10 repetitions of the decimal 1.8 and 20 repetitions of the decimal 1.9, $S = 10(1.8) + 20(1.9) = 18 + 38 = 56$, $E = 10(2) + 20(1) = 40$, and $E - S = 40 - 56 = -16$. Also, if T contains 10 repetitions of the decimal 1.2 and 20 repetitions of the decimal 1.1, $S = 10(1.2) + 20(1.1) = 12 + 22 = 34$, $E = 10(2) + 20(1) = 40$, and $E - S = 40 - 34 = 6$.

The correct answer is B.

219. In a certain game, a large container is filled with red, yellow, green, and blue beads worth, respectively, 7, 5, 3, and 2 points each. A number of beads are then removed from the container. If the product of the point values of the removed beads is 147,000, how many red beads were removed?

(A)   5
(B)   4
(C)   3
(D)   2
(E)   0

Arithmetic Properties of numbers

From this, the red beads represent factors of 7 in the total point value of 147,000. Since $147,000 = 147(1,000)$, and $1,000 = 10^3$, then 147 is all that needs to be factored to determine the factors of 7. Factoring 147 yields $147 = (3)(49) = (3)(7^2)$. This means there are 2 factors of 7, or 2 red beads.

The correct answer is D.

220. If $\dfrac{2}{1+\dfrac{2}{y}} = 1$, then $y =$

(A) -2
(B) $-\dfrac{1}{2}$
(C) $\dfrac{1}{2}$
(D) 2
(E) 3

Algebra First-degree equations

Solve for y.

$$\frac{2}{1+\frac{2}{y}}=1$$

$1+\dfrac{2}{y}=2$ multiply both sides by $1+\dfrac{2}{y}$

$\dfrac{2}{y}=1$ subtract 1 from each side

$y=2$ solve for y

The correct answer is D.

221. If a, b, and c are consecutive positive integers and $a<b<c$, which of the following must be true?

    I. $c-a=2$

   II. abc is an even integer.

  III. $\dfrac{a+b+c}{3}$ is an integer.

(A)   I only
(B)   II only
(C)   I and II only
(D)   II and III only
(E)   I, II, and III

Arithmetic Properties of numbers

Since a, b, and c are consecutive positive integers and $a<b<c$, then $b=a+1$ and $c=a+2$.

I. $c-a=(a+2)-a=2$ MUST be true

II.   (odd)(even)(odd) = even   MUST be true

     (even)(odd)(even) = even   MUST be true

III. $\dfrac{a+b+c}{3}=\dfrac{a+(a+1)+(a+2)}{3}$

     $=\dfrac{3a+3}{3}=a+1=b$

     b is an integer   MUST be true

The correct answer is E.

222. Of the 200 students at College T majoring in one or more of the sciences, 130 are majoring in chemistry and 150 are majoring in biology. If at least 30 of the students are not majoring in either chemistry or biology, then the number of students majoring in *both* chemistry and biology could be any number from

(A)   20 to 50
(B)   40 to 70
(C)   50 to 130
(D)   110 to 130
(E)   110 to 150

Arithmetic Operations on rational numbers

A Venn diagram will help with this problem. There are two extremes that need to be considered: (1) having the least number of students majoring in both chemistry and biology and (2) having the greatest number of students majoring in both chemistry and biology.

(1) If at least 30 science majors are not majoring in either chemistry or biology, then at most $200-30=170$ students can be majoring in either or both. Since there are $130+150=280$ biology and chemistry majors (some of whom are individual students majoring in both areas), then there are at least $280-170=110$ majoring in both. The diagram following shows this relationship.

170 TOTAL STUDENTS
FOR CHEMISTRY AND BIOLOGY MAJORS

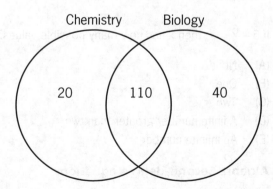

(2) The maximum number of students who can be majoring in both chemistry and biology is 130, since 130 is the number given as majoring in chemistry, the smaller of the two subject areas. Logically, there cannot be more double majors than there are majors in the smaller field. The diagram below shows this relationship in terms of the given numbers of majors in each subject area.

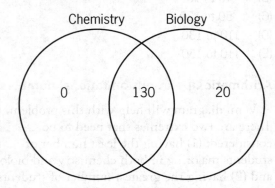

Additionally, from this diagram it can be seen that the total number of students who are majoring in chemistry, or in biology, or in both is $130 + 20 = 150$. Thus, there are $200 - 150 = 50$ students who are neither chemistry nor biology majors. This number is not in conflict with the condition that 30 is the minimum number of nonchemistry and nonbiology majors.

Thus, the number of students majoring in both chemistry and biology could be any number from a minimum of 110 to a maximum of 130.

The correct answer is D.

223. If $5 - \dfrac{6}{x} = x$, then x has how many possible values?

(A) None
(B) One
(C) Two
(D) A finite number greater than two
(E) An infinite number

Algebra Second-degree equations

Solve the equation to determine how many values are possible for x.

$$5 - \frac{6}{x} = x$$

$$5x - 6 = x^2$$

$$0 = x^2 - 5x + 6$$

$$0 = (x - 3)(x - 2)$$

$$x = 3 \text{ or } 2$$

The correct answer is C.

224. Seed mixture X is 40 percent ryegrass and 60 percent bluegrass by weight; seed mixture Y is 25 percent ryegrass and 75 percent fescue. If a mixture of X and Y contains 30 percent ryegrass, what percent of the weight of the mixture is X?

(A) 10%
(B) $33\frac{1}{3}$%
(C) 40%
(D) 50%
(E) $66\frac{2}{3}$%

Algebra Applied problems

Let X be the amount of seed mixture X in the final mixture, and let Y be the amount of seed mixture Y in the final mixture. The final mixture of X and Y needs to contain 30 percent ryegrass seed, so any other kinds of grass seed are irrelevant to the solution to this problem. The information about the ryegrass percentages for X, Y, and the final mixture can be expressed in the following equation and solved for X.

$$0.40X + 0.25Y = 0.30(X + Y)$$

$0.40X + 0.25Y = 0.30X + 0.30Y$	distribute the 0.30 on the right side
$0.10X = 0.05Y$	subtract $0.30X$ and $0.25Y$ from both sides
$X = 0.5Y$	divide both sides by 0.10

Using this, the percent of the weight of the combined mixture $(X + Y)$ that is X is

$$\frac{X}{X+Y} = \frac{0.5Y}{0.5Y + Y} = \frac{0.5Y}{1.5Y} = \frac{0.5}{1.5} = 0.33\overline{3} = 33\frac{1}{3}\%$$

The correct answer is B.

225. If n is a positive integer, then $n(n+1)(n+2)$ is

    (A) even only when n is even
    (B) even only when n is odd
    (C) odd whenever n is odd
    (D) divisible by 3 only when n is odd
    (E) divisible by 4 whenever n is even

Arithmetic Properties of numbers

The numbers n, $n+1$, and $n+2$ are consecutive integers. Therefore, either their product is (odd)(even)(odd) = even, or their product is (even)(odd)(even) = even. In either case, the product of $n(n+1)(n+2)$ is even. Thus, each of answer choices A, B, and C is false.

A statement is false if a counterexample can be shown. Test the statement using an even multiple of 3 as the value of n in the equation. When $n=6$, $n(n+1)(n+2) = 6(7)(8) = 336$. Since in this counterexample n is even but 336 is still divisible by 3, answer choice D is shown to be false.

When n is even (meaning divisible by 2), $n+2$ is also even (and also divisible by 2). So $n(n+1)(n+2)$ is always divisible by 4.

The correct answer is E.

226. A straight pipe 1 yard in length was marked off in fourths and also in thirds. If the pipe was then cut into separate pieces at each of these markings, which of the following gives all the different lengths of the pieces, in fractions of a yard?

    (A) $\frac{1}{6}$ and $\frac{1}{4}$ only

    (B) $\frac{1}{4}$ and $\frac{1}{3}$ only

    (C) $\frac{1}{6}$, $\frac{1}{4}$, and $\frac{1}{3}$

    (D) $\frac{1}{12}$, $\frac{1}{6}$, and $\frac{1}{4}$

    (E) $\frac{1}{12}$, $\frac{1}{6}$, and $\frac{1}{3}$

Arithmetic Operations on rational numbers

The number line above illustrates the markings on the pipe. Since the pipe is cut at the five markings, six pieces of pipe are produced. The length of each piece, as a fraction of a yard, is given in the following table.

Pipe piece	Length
A	$\frac{1}{4} - 0 = \frac{1}{4}$
B	$\frac{1}{3} - \frac{1}{4} = \frac{1}{12}$
C	$\frac{1}{2} - \frac{1}{3} = \frac{1}{6}$
D	$\frac{2}{3} - \frac{1}{2} = \frac{1}{6}$
E	$\frac{3}{4} - \frac{2}{3} = \frac{1}{12}$
F	$1 - \frac{3}{4} = \frac{1}{4}$

The correct answer is D.

227. If $\dfrac{0.0015 \times 10^m}{0.03 \times 10^k} = 5 \times 10^7$, then $m - k =$

    (A) 9
    (B) 8
    (C) 7
    (D) 6
    (E) 5

Arithmetic Operations on rational numbers

The left side is easier to work with when the expressions are rewritten so that integers are involved:

$$\frac{0.0015 \times 10^m}{0.03 \times 10^k} = 5 \times 10^7$$

$$\frac{15 \times 10^{m-4}}{3 \times 10^{k-2}} = 5 \times 10^7$$

$$\frac{15}{3} \times \frac{10^{m-4}}{10^{k-2}} = 5 \times 10^7$$

$$5 \times \frac{10^{m-4}}{10^{k-2}} = 5 \times 10^7$$

$$\frac{10^{m-4}}{10^{k-2}} = 10^7$$

$$10^{m-4-(k-2)} = 10^7$$

$$m - 4 - (k-2) = 7$$

$$m - k - 2 = 7$$

$$m - k = 9$$

The correct answer is A.

228. Right triangle *PQR* is to be constructed in the *xy*-plane so that the right angle is at *P* and $\overline{PR}$ is parallel to the *x*-axis. The *x*- and *y*-coordinates of *P*, *Q*, and *R* are to be integers that satisfy the inequalities $-4 \le x \le 5$ and $6 \le y \le 16$. How many different triangles with these properties could be constructed?

(A)   110
(B)   1,100
(C)   9,900
(D)   10,000
(E)   12,100

Geometry; Arithmetic Simple coordinate geometry; Elementary combinatorics

In the *xy*-plane, right triangle *PQR* is located in the rectangular region determined by $-4 \le x \le 5$ and $6 \le y \le 16$ (see following illustration).

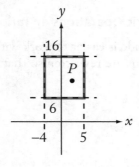

Since the coordinates of points *P*, *Q*, and *R* are integers, there are 10 possible *x* values and 11 possible *y* values, so point *P* can be any one of $10(11) = 110$ points in the rectangular area.

Since $\overline{PR}$ has to be horizontal, *R* has the same *y* value as *P* and can have 9 other *x* values. $\overline{PQ}$ has to be vertical, so *Q* has the same *x* value as *P* and can have 10 other *y* values. This gives $110(9)(10) = 9,900$ possible triangles.

The correct answer is C.

229. How many of the integers that satisfy the inequality $\frac{(x+2)(x+3)}{x-2} \ge 0$ are less than 5 ?

(A)   1
(B)   2
(C)   3
(D)   4
(E)   5

Algebra Inequalities

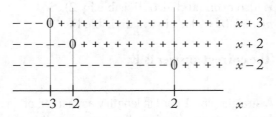

Pictorially, the number line above shows the algebraic signs of the expressions $(x + 3)$, $(x + 2)$, and $(x - 2)$. For example, $x + 3$ is 0 when $x = -3$, $x + 3$ is negative when $x < -3$, and $x + 3$ is positive when $x > -3$. The expression $\frac{(x+2)(x+3)}{x-2}$ will be positive in the intervals of the number line where the number of minus signs is even. Therefore $\frac{(x+2)(x+3)}{x-2}$ is positive for values of *x* such that $-3 < x < -2$ and for values of *x* such that $x > 2$. The only integer values of *x* in these intervals that are also less than 5 are 3 and 4. Also, $\frac{(x+2)(x+3)}{x-2}$ will be zero if and only if

$(x + 2)(x + 3) = 0$, which has two integer solutions less than 5, namely, $x = -2$ and $x = -3$. Therefore, there are four integers less than 5 that satisfy $\dfrac{(x+2)(x+3)}{x-2} \geq 0$ and those integers are $-3, -2, 3,$ and 4.

Alternatively, $\dfrac{(x+2)(x+3)}{x-2}$ will be zero if and only if $(x + 2)(x + 3) = 0$, which has two integer solutions less than 5, namely, $x = -2$ and $x = -3$.

Also, $\dfrac{(x+2)(x+3)}{x-2}$ will be positive if $(x + 2)(x + 3)$ and $x - 2$ are both positive or both negative, and for no other values of x. On the one hand, $(x + 2)(x + 3)$ will be positive when $x + 2$ and $x + 3$ are both positive, which will be the case when $x > -2$ and $x > -3$ and thus when $x > -2$. On the other hand, $(x + 2)(x + 3)$ will be positive when $x + 2$ and $x + 3$ are both negative, which will be the case when $x < -2$ and $x < -3$ and thus when $x < -3$. So, $(x + 2)(x + 3)$ will be positive when $x < -3$ or $x > -2$. (This result can also be deduced from the fact that the graph of $y = (x + 2)(x + 3)$ is a parabola with x-intercepts $(-2, 0)$ and $(-3, 0)$ that opens upward.) Since $x - 2$ will be positive when $x > 2$, it follows that $(x + 2)(x + 3)$ and $x - 2$ are both positive when $x > 2$, which includes exactly two integer values less than 5, namely, $x = 3$ and $x = 4$. There are no integer values of x such that $(x + 2)(x + 3)$ and $x - 2$ are both negative, since $(x + 2)(x + 3)$ is negative if and only if x lies between -3 and -2 and there are no integers between -3 and -2. Therefore, there are exactly 4 integer values of x less than 5 such that $\dfrac{(x+2)(x+3)}{x-2} \geq 0$. Two of the values, $x = -2$ and $x = -3$, arise from solutions to $\dfrac{(x+2)(x+3)}{x-2} = 0$, and two of the values, $x = 3$ and $x = 4$, arise from solutions to $\dfrac{(x+2)(x+3)}{x-2} > 0$.

The correct answer is D.

230. The value of $\dfrac{2^{-14}+2^{-15}+2^{-16}+2^{-17}}{5}$ is how many times the value of 2^{-17} ?

(A) $\dfrac{3}{2}$

(B) $\dfrac{5}{2}$

(C) 3

(D) 4

(E) 5

Arithmetic Negative exponents

If the value of $\dfrac{2^{-14}+2^{-15}+2^{-16}+2^{-17}}{5}$ is x times the value of 2^{-17}, then

$$x\left(2^{-17}\right) = \dfrac{2^{-14}+2^{-15}+2^{-16}+2^{-17}}{5}$$

$$x = \dfrac{\dfrac{2^{-14}+2^{-15}+2^{-16}+2^{-17}}{5}}{2^{-17}}$$

$$= \dfrac{2^{-14}+2^{-15}+2^{-16}+2^{-17}}{5} \times 2^{17}$$

$$= \dfrac{\left(2^{-14}+2^{-15}+2^{-16}+2^{-17}\right) \times 2^{17}}{5}$$

$$= \dfrac{2^{-14+17}+2^{-15+17}+2^{-16+17}+2^{-17+17}}{5}$$

$$= \dfrac{2^{3}+2^{2}+2^{1}+2^{0}}{5}$$

$$= \dfrac{8+4+2+1}{5}$$

$$= 3$$

The correct answer is C.

6.0 Data Sufficiency

6.0 Data Sufficiency

Data sufficiency questions appear in the Quantitative section of the GMAT® exam. Multiple-choice data sufficiency questions are intermingled with problem solving questions throughout the section. You will have 75 minutes to complete the Quantitative section of the GMAT exam, or about 2 minutes to answer each question. These questions require knowledge of the following topics:

- Arithmetic
- Elementary algebra
- Commonly known concepts of geometry

Data sufficiency questions are designed to measure your ability to analyze a quantitative problem, recognize which given information is relevant, and determine at what point there is sufficient information to solve a problem. In these questions, you are to classify each problem according to the five fixed answer choices, rather than find a solution to the problem.

Each data sufficiency question consists of a question, often accompanied by some initial information, and two statements, labeled (1) and (2), which contain additional information. You must decide whether the information in each statement is sufficient to answer the question or—if neither statement provides enough information—whether the information in the two statements together is sufficient. It is also possible that the statements in combination do not give enough information to answer the question.

Begin by reading the initial information and the question carefully. Next, consider the first statement. Does the information provided by the first statement enable you to answer the question? Go on to the second statement. Try to ignore the information given in the first statement when you consider whether the second statement provides information that, by itself, allows you to answer the question. Now you should be able to say, for each statement, whether it is sufficient to determine the answer.

Next, consider the two statements in tandem. Do they, together, enable you to answer the question?

Look again at your answer choices. Select the one that most accurately reflects whether the statements provide the information required to answer the question.

6.1 Test-Taking Strategies

1. Do not waste valuable time solving a problem.

You only need to determine whether sufficient information is given to solve it.

2. Consider each statement separately.

First, decide whether each statement alone gives sufficient information to solve the problem. Be sure to disregard the information given in statement (1) when you evaluate the information given in statement (2). If either, or both, of the statements give(s) sufficient information to solve the problem, select the answer corresponding to the description of which statement(s) give(s) sufficient information to solve the problem.

3. Judge the statements in tandem if neither statement is sufficient by itself.

It is possible that the two statements together do not provide sufficient information. Once you decide, select the answer corresponding to the description of whether the statements together give sufficient information to solve the problem.

4. Answer the question asked.

For example, if the question asks, "What is the value of y ?" for an answer statement to be sufficient, you must be able to find one and only one value for y. Being able to determine minimum or maximum values for an answer (e.g., $y = x + 2$) is not sufficient, because such answers constitute a range of values rather than the specific value of y.

5. Be very careful not to make unwarranted assumptions based on the images represented.

Figures are not necessarily drawn to scale; they are generalized figures showing little more than intersecting line segments and the relationships of points, angles, and regions. So, for example, if a figure described as a rectangle looks like a square, do *not* conclude that it is, in fact, a square just by looking at the figure.

If statement 1 is sufficient, then the answer must be **A or D.**

If statement 2 is not sufficient, then the answer must be **A.**

If statement 2 is sufficient, then the answer must be **D.**

If statement 1 is not sufficient, then the answer must be **B, C, or E.**

If statement 2 is sufficient, then the answer must be **B.**

If statement 2 is not sufficient, then the answer must be **C or E.**

If both statements together are sufficient, then the answer must be **C.**

If both statements together are still not sufficient, then the answer must be **E.**

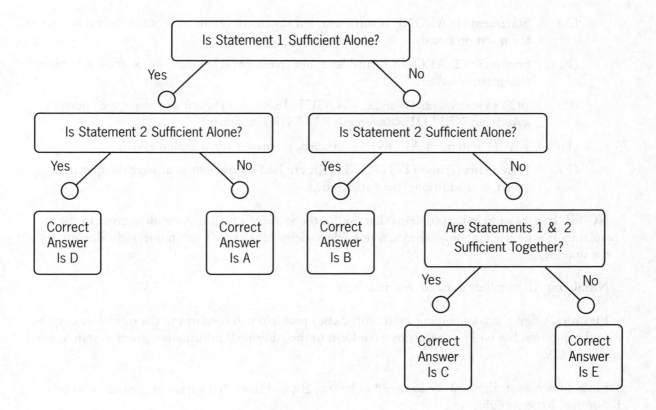

6.2 The Directions

These directions are similar to those you will see for data sufficiency questions when you take the GMAT exam. If you read the directions carefully and understand them clearly before going to sit for the test, you will not need to spend much time reviewing them when you take the GMAT exam.

Each data sufficiency problem consists of a question and two statements, labeled (1) and (2), that give data. You have to decide whether the data given in the statements are *sufficient* for answering the question. Using the data given in the statements *plus* your knowledge of mathematics and everyday facts (such as the number of days in July or the meaning of *counterclockwise*), you must indicate whether the data given in the statements are sufficient for answering the questions and then indicate one of the following answer choices:

(A)   Statement (1) ALONE is sufficient, but statement (2) alone is not sufficient to answer the question asked;

(B)   Statement (2) ALONE is sufficient, but statement (1) alone is not sufficient to answer the question asked;

(C)   BOTH statements (1) and (2) TOGETHER are sufficient to answer the question asked, but NEITHER statement ALONE is sufficient;

(D)   EACH statement ALONE is sufficient to answer the question asked;

(E)   Statements (1) and (2) TOGETHER are NOT sufficient to answer the question asked, and additional data are needed.

NOTE: In data sufficiency problems that ask for the value of a quantity, the data given in the statements are sufficient only when it is possible to determine exactly one numerical value for the quantity.

Numbers: All numbers used are real numbers.

Figures: A figure accompanying a data sufficiency problem will conform to the information given in the question but will not necessarily conform to the additional information given in statements (1) and (2).

Lines shown as straight can be assumed to be straight and lines that appear jagged can also be assumed to be straight.

You may assume that the positions of points, angles, regions, and so forth exist in the order shown and that angle measures are greater than zero degrees.

All figures lie in a plane unless otherwise indicated.

6.3 Practice Questions

Each <u>data sufficiency</u> problem consists of a question and two statements, labeled (1) and (2), which contain certain data. Using these data and your knowledge of mathematics and everyday facts (such as the number of days in July or the meaning of the word *counterclockwise*), decide whether the data given are sufficient for answering the question and then indicate one of the following answer choices:

A Statement (1) ALONE is sufficient, but statement (2) alone is not sufficient.
B Statement (2) ALONE is sufficient, but statement (1) alone is not sufficient.
C BOTH statements TOGETHER are sufficient, but NEITHER statement ALONE is sufficient.
D EACH statement ALONE is sufficient.
E Statements (1) and (2) TOGETHER are not sufficient.

<u>Note:</u> In data sufficiency problems that ask for the value of a quantity, the data given in the statements are sufficient only when it is possible to determine exactly one numerical value for quantity.

<u>Example:</u>

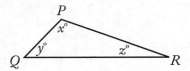

In $\triangle PQR$, what is the value of x ?

(1) $PQ = PR$
(2) $y = 40$

<u>Explanation:</u> According to statement (1) $PQ = PR$; therefore, $\triangle PQR$ is isosceles and $y = z$. Since $x + y + z = 180$, it follows that $x + 2y = 180$. Since statement (1) does not give a value for y, you cannot answer the question using statement (1) alone. According to statement (2), $y = 40$; therefore, $x + z = 140$. Since statement (2) does not give a value for z, you cannot answer the question using statement (2) alone. Using both statements together, since $x + 2y = 180$ and the value of y is given, you can find the value of x. Therefore, BOTH statements (1) and (2) TOGETHER are sufficient to answer the questions, but NEITHER statement ALONE is sufficient.

<u>Numbers:</u> All numbers used are real numbers.

<u>Figures:</u>
- Figures conform to the information given in the question, but will not necessarily conform to the additional information given in statements (1) and (2).
- Lines shown as straight are straight, and lines that appear jagged are also straight.
- The positions of points, angles, regions, etc., exist in the order shown, and angle measures are greater than zero.
- All figures lie in a plane unless otherwise indicated.

1. What is the value of $|x|$?

    (1) $x = -|x|$
    (2) $x^2 = 4$

2. What percent of a group of people are women with red hair?

    (1) Of the women in the group, 5 percent have red hair.
    (2) Of the men in the group, 10 percent have red hair.

3. In a certain class, one student is to be selected at random to read. What is the probability that a boy will read?

    (1) Two-thirds of the students in the class are boys.
    (2) Ten of the students in the class are girls.

4. If the two floors in a certain building are 9 feet apart, how many steps are there in a set of stairs that extends from the first floor to the second floor of the building?

    (1) Each step is $\frac{3}{4}$ foot high.
    (2) Each step is 1 foot wide.

5. In College X the number of students enrolled in both a chemistry course and a biology course is how much less than the number of students enrolled in neither?

    (1) In College X there are 60 students enrolled in a chemistry course.
    (2) In College X there are 85 students enrolled in a biology course.

6. A certain expressway has Exits J, K, L, and M, in that order. What is the road distance from Exit K to Exit L ?

    (1) The road distance from Exit J to Exit L is 21 kilometers.
    (2) The road distance from Exit K to Exit M is 26 kilometers.

7. If n is an integer, is $n + 1$ odd?

    (1) $n + 2$ is an even integer.
    (2) $n - 1$ is an odd integer.

8. For which type of investment, J or K, is the annual rate of return greater?

    (1) Type J returns $115 per $1,000 invested for any one-year period and type K returns $300 per $2,500 invested for any one-year period.
    (2) The annual rate of return for an investment of type K is 12 percent.

9. A citrus fruit grower receives $15 for each crate of oranges shipped and $18 for each crate of grapefruit shipped. How many crates of oranges did the grower ship last week?

    (1) Last week the number of crates of oranges that the grower shipped was 20 more than twice the number of crates of grapefruit shipped.
    (2) Last week the grower received a total of $38,700 from the crates of oranges and grapefruit shipped.

10. If Pat saved $600 of his earnings last month, how much did Pat earn last month?

    (1) Pat spent $\frac{1}{2}$ of his earnings last month for living expenses and saved $\frac{1}{3}$ of the remainder.
    (2) Of his earnings last month, Pat paid twice as much in taxes as he saved.

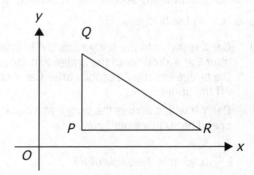

11. In the xy-plane above, is angle QPR a right angle?

    (1) Points P and Q have the same x-coordinate.
    (2) Points P and R have the same y-coordinate.

12. Water is pumped into a partially filled tank at a constant rate through an inlet pipe. At the same time, water is pumped out of the tank at a constant rate through an outlet pipe. At what rate, in gallons per minute, is the amount of water in the tank increasing?

    (1) The amount of water initially in the tank is 200 gallons.
    (2) Water is pumped into the tank at a rate of 10 gallons per minute and out of the tank at a rate of 10 gallons every $2\frac{1}{2}$ minutes.

13. Is x a negative number?

    (1) $9x > 10x$
    (2) $x + 3$ is positive.

14. If i and j are integers, is $i + j$ an even integer?

    (1) $i < 10$
    (2) $i = j$

15. What is the cube root of w?

    (1) The 5th root of w is 64.
    (2) The 15th root of w is 4.

16. If Car X followed Car Y across a certain bridge that is $\frac{1}{2}$ mile long, how many seconds did it take Car X to travel across the bridge?

    (1) Car X drove onto the bridge exactly 3 seconds after Car Y drove onto the bridge and drove off the bridge exactly 2 seconds after Car Y drove off the bridge.
    (2) Car Y traveled across the bridge at a constant speed of 30 miles per hour.

17. If $n + k = m$, what is the value of k?

    (1) $n = 10$
    (2) $m + 10 = n$

18. The number of seats in the first row of an auditorium is 18 and the number of seats in each row thereafter is 2 more than in the previous row. What is the total number of seats in the rows of the auditorium?

    (1) The number of rows of seats in the auditorium is 27.
    (2) The number of seats in the last row is 70.

19. In $\triangle PQR$, if $PQ = x$, $QR = x + 2$, and $PR = y$, which of the three angles of $\triangle PQR$ has the greatest degree measure?

    (1) $y = x + 3$
    (2) $x = 2$

$$n, 15, 12, 9, 20$$

20. What is the value of n in the list above?

    (1) $n > 12$
    (2) The median of the numbers in the list is 13.

21. What percent of the drama club members enrolled at a certain school are female students?

    (1) Of the female students enrolled at the school, 40 percent are members of the drama club.
    (2) Of the male students enrolled at the school, 25 percent are members of the drama club.

22. On a recent trip, Mary drove 50 miles. What was the average speed at which she drove the 50 miles?

    (1) She drove 30 miles at an average speed of 60 miles per hour and then drove the remaining 20 miles at an average speed of 50 miles per hour.
    (2) She drove a total of 54 minutes.

23. In Mr. Smith's class, what is the ratio of the number of boys to the number of girls?

    (1) There are 3 times as many girls as boys in Mr. Smith's class.
    (2) The number of boys is $\frac{1}{4}$ of the total number of boys and girls in Mr. Smith's class.

24. If the sequence S has 300 terms, what is the 293rd term of S?

    (1) The 298th term of S is −616, and each term of S after the first is 2 less than the preceding term.
    (2) The first term of S is −22.

25. On a certain date, Hannah invested $5,000 at x percent simple annual interest and a different amount at y percent simple annual interest. What amount did Hannah invest at y percent simple annual interest?

    (1) The total amount of interest earned by Hannah's two investments in one year was $900.
    (2) Hannah invested the $5,000 at 6 percent simple annual interest.

26. The profit from the sale of a certain appliance increases, though not proportionally, with the number of units sold. Did the profit exceed $4 million on sales of 380,000 units?

    (1) The profit exceeded $2 million on sales of 200,000 units.
    (2) The profit exceeded $5 million on sales of 350,000 units.

27. If n is an integer, is n even?

    (1) $n^2 - 1$ is an odd integer.
    (2) $3n + 4$ is an even integer.

28. Carmen currently works 30 hours per week at her part-time job. If her gross hourly wage were to increase by $1.50, how many fewer hours could she work per week and still earn the same gross weekly pay as before the increase?

    (1) Her gross weekly pay is currently $225.00.
    (2) An increase of $1.50 would represent an increase of 20 percent of her current gross hourly wage.

29. If 90 students auditioned for the school musical, how many were accepted?

    (1) $\frac{2}{3}$ of the boys and $\frac{1}{3}$ of the girls who auditioned were accepted.
    (2) 26 of the boys who auditioned were accepted.

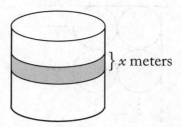

30. A circular tub has a band painted around its circumference, as shown above. What is the surface area of this painted band?

    (1) $x = 0.5$
    (2) The height of the tub is 1 meter.

$$d = 0.43t7$$

31. If t denotes the thousandths digit in the decimal representation of d above, what digit is t ?

    (1) If d were rounded to the nearest hundredth, the result would be 0.44.
    (2) If d were rounded to the nearest thousandth, the result would be 0.436.

32. If A and B are positive integers, is the product AB even?

    (1) The sum A + B is odd.
    (2) A is even.

33. The weights of all dishes of type X are exactly the same, and the weights of all dishes of type Y are exactly the same. Is the weight of 1 dish of type X less than the weight of 1 dish of type Y ?

    (1) The total weight of 3 dishes of type X and 2 dishes of type Y is less than the total weight of 2 dishes of type X and 4 dishes of type Y.
    (2) The total weight of 4 dishes of type X and 3 dishes of type Y is less than the total weight of 3 dishes of type X and 4 dishes of type Y.

34. A certain high school with a total enrollment of 900 students held a science fair for three days last week. How many of the students enrolled in the high school attended the science fair on all three days?

    (1) Of the students enrolled in the school, 30 percent attended the science fair on two or more days.
    (2) Of the students enrolled in the school, 10 percent of those that attended the science fair on at least one day attended on all three days.

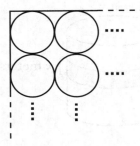

35. The inside of a rectangular carton is 48 centimeters long, 32 centimeters wide, and 15 centimeters high. The carton is filled to capacity with k identical cylindrical cans of fruit that stand upright in rows and columns, as indicated in the figure above. If the cans are 15 centimeters high, what is the value of k ?

   (1) Each of the cans has a radius of 4 centimeters.
   (2) Six of the cans fit exactly along the length of the carton.

$$\begin{cases} x - 4 = z \\ y - x = 8 \\ 8 - z = t \end{cases}$$

36. For the system of equations given, what is the value of z ?

   (1) $x = 7$
   (2) $t = 5$

37. The average (arithmetic mean) price of the 3 items that Kate purchased from a clothing store was $50. If there was no sales tax on any item that had a price of less than $80 and 6 percent sales tax on all other items, what was the total sales tax on the 3 items that Kate purchased?

   (1) The price of the most expensive item that Kate purchased from the store was $100.
   (2) The price of the least expensive item that Kate purchased from the store was $10.

38. A scientist recorded the number of eggs in each of 10 birds' nests. What was the standard deviation of the numbers of eggs in the 10 nests?

   (1) The average (arithmetic mean) number of eggs for the 10 nests was 4.
   (2) Each of the 10 nests contained the same number of eggs.

39. Terry holds 12 cards, each of which is red, white, green, or blue. If a person is to select a card randomly from the cards Terry is holding, is the probability less than $\frac{1}{2}$ that the card selected will be either red or white?

   (1) The probability that the person will select a blue card is $\frac{1}{3}$.
   (2) The probability that the person will select a red card is $\frac{1}{6}$.

40. The selling price of an article is equal to the cost of the article plus the markup. The markup on a certain television set is what percent of the selling price?

   (1) The markup on the television set is 25 percent of the cost.
   (2) The selling price of the television set is $250.

41. Is $4^{x+y} = 8^{10}$?

   (1) $x - y = 9$
   (2) $\dfrac{y}{x} = \dfrac{1}{4}$

42. Can a certain rectangular sheet of glass be positioned on a rectangular tabletop so that it covers the entire tabletop and its edges are parallel to the edges of the tabletop?

   (1) The tabletop is 36 inches wide by 60 inches long.
   (2) The area of one side of the sheet of glass is 2,400 square inches.

43. If p_1 and p_2 are the populations and r_1 and r_2 are the numbers of representatives of District 1 and District 2, respectively, the ratio of the population to the number of representatives is greater for which of the two districts?

   (1) $p_1 > p_2$
   (2) $r_2 > r_1$

44. In a random sample of 80 adults, how many are college graduates?

   (1) In the sample, the number of adults who are not college graduates is 3 times the number who are college graduates.
   (2) In the sample, the number of adults who are not college graduates is 40 more than the number who are college graduates.

	R	S	T	U
R	0	y	x	62
S	y	0	56	75
T	x	56	0	69
U	62	75	69	0

45. The table above shows the distance, in kilometers, by the most direct route, between any two of the four cities, R, S, T, and U. For example, the distance between City R and City U is 62 kilometers. What is the value of x ?

    (1) By the most direct route, the distance between S and T is twice the distance between S and R.

    (2) By the most direct route, the distance between T and U is 1.5 times the distance between R and T.

46. What is the tenths digit in the decimal representation of a certain number?

    (1) The number is less than $\frac{1}{3}$.

    (2) The number is greater than $\frac{1}{4}$.

47. Robots X, Y, and Z each assemble components at their respective constant rates. If r_x is the ratio of Robot X's constant rate to Robot Z's constant rate and r_y is the ratio of Robot Y's constant rate to Robot Z's constant rate, is Robot Z's constant rate the greatest of the three?

    (1) $r_x < r_y$

    (2) $r_y < 1$

48. If $a < x < b$ and $c < y < d$, is $x < y$?

    (1) $a < c$

    (2) $b < c$

49. How many people are directors of both Company K and Company R ?

    (1) There were 17 directors present at a joint meeting of the directors of Company K and Company R, and no directors were absent.

    (2) Company K has 12 directors and Company R has 8 directors.

50. If x and y are positive, is $\frac{x}{y}$ greater than 1 ?

    (1) $xy > 1$

    (2) $x - y > 0$

51. A clothing store acquired an item at a cost of x dollars and sold the item for y dollars. The store's gross profit from the item was what percent of its cost for the item?

    (1) $y - x = 20$

    (2) $\frac{y}{x} = \frac{5}{4}$

52. If x and y are positive, is $x < 10 < y$?

    (1) $x < y$ and $xy = 100$

    (2) $x^2 < 100 < y^2$

53. If x is an integer, is $9^x + 9^{-x} = b$?

    (1) $3^x + 3^{-x} = \sqrt{b + 2}$

    (2) $x > 0$

54. A taxi company charges f cents for the first mile of the taxi ride and m cents for each additional mile. How much does the company charge for a 10-mile taxi ride?

    (1) The company charges $0.90 for a 2-mile ride.

    (2) The company charges $1.20 for a 4-mile ride.

55. Guy's net income equals his gross income minus his deductions. By what percent did Guy's net income change on January 1, 1989, when both his gross income and his deductions increased?

    (1) Guy's gross income increased by 4 percent on January 1, 1989.

    (2) Guy's deductions increased by 15 percent on January 1, 1989.

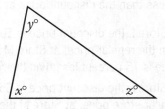

56. What is the value of z in the triangle above?

    (1) $x + y = 139$

    (2) $y + z = 108$

57. Each gift certificate sold yesterday by a certain bookstore cost either $10 or $50. If yesterday the bookstore sold more than 5 gift certificates that cost $50 each, what was the total number of gift certificates sold yesterday by the bookstore?

    (1) Yesterday the bookstore sold fewer than 10 gift certificates that cost $10 each.
    (2) The total cost of gift certificates sold yesterday by the bookstore was $460.

58. What is the tens digit of positive integer x?

    (1) x divided by 100 has a remainder of 30.
    (2) x divided by 110 has a remainder of 30.

59. Max has $125 consisting of bills each worth either $5 or $20. How many bills worth $5 does Max have?

    (1) Max has fewer than 5 bills worth $5 each.
    (2) Max has more than 5 bills worth $20 each.

60. What is the value of n in the equation $-25 + 19 + n = s$?

    (1) $s = 2$
    (2) $\dfrac{n}{s} = 4$

61. At a certain picnic, each of the guests was served either a single scoop or a double scoop of ice cream. How many of the guests were served a double scoop of ice cream?

    (1) At the picnic, 60 percent of the guests were served a double scoop of ice cream.
    (2) A total of 120 scoops of ice cream were served to all the guests at the picnic.

62. Stores L and M each sell a certain product at a different regular price. If both stores discount their regular price of the product, is the discount price at Store M less than the discount price at Store L?

    (1) At Store L the discount price is 10 percent less than the regular price; at Store M the discount price is 15 percent less than the regular price.
    (2) At Store L the discount price is $5 less than the regular store price; at Store M the discount price is $6 less than the regular price.

63. If d denotes a decimal, is $d \geq 0.5$?

    (1) When d is rounded to the nearest tenth, the result is 0.5.
    (2) When d is rounded to the nearest integer, the result is 1.

64. How many integers are there between, but not including, integers r and s?

    (1) $s - r = 10$
    (2) There are 9 integers between, but not including, $r + 1$ and $s + 1$.

65. What is the total number of coins that Bert and Claire have?

    (1) Bert has 50 percent more coins than Claire.
    (2) The total number of coins that Bert and Claire have is between 21 and 28.

66. In a survey of 200 college graduates, 30 percent said they had received student loans during their college careers, and 40 percent said they had received scholarships. What percent of those surveyed said that they had received neither student loans nor scholarships during their college careers?

    (1) 25 percent of those surveyed said that they had received scholarships but no loans.
    (2) 50 percent of those surveyed who said that they had received loans also said that they had received scholarships.

67. What is the value of integer n?

    (1) $n(n+1) = 6$
    (2) $2^{2n} = 16$

68. Three machines, K, M, and P, working simultaneously and independently at their respective constant rates, can complete a certain task in 24 minutes. How long does it take Machine K, working alone at its constant rate, to complete the task?

    (1) Machines M and P, working simultaneously and independently at their respective constant rates, can complete the task in 36 minutes.
    (2) Machines K and P, working simultaneously and independently at their respective constant rates, can complete the task in 48 minutes.

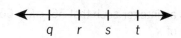

69. Of the four numbers represented on the number line above, is *r* closest to zero?

    (1) $q = -s$
    (2) $-t < q$

70. At a certain company, a test was given to a group of men and women seeking promotions. If the average (arithmetic mean) score for the group was 80, was the average score for the women greater than 85 ?

    (1)   The average score for the men was less than 75.

    (2)   The group consisted of more men than women.

71. Mary persuaded *n* friends to donate $500 each to her election campaign, and then each of these *n* friends persuaded *n* more people to donate $500 each to Mary's campaign. If no one donated more than once and if there were no other donations, what was the value of *n* ?

    (1)   The first *n* people donated $\frac{1}{16}$ of the total amount donated.

    (2)   The total amount donated was $120,000.

72. If *m* is an integer, is *m* odd?

    (1) $\frac{m}{2}$ is <u>not</u> an even integer.

    (2) $m - 3$ is an even integer.

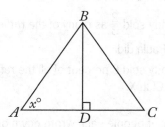

73. What is the area of triangular region *ABC* above?

    (1)   The product of *BD* and *AC* is 20.
    (2) $x = 45$

74. In the *xy*-coordinate plane, is point *R* equidistant from points (–3,–3) and (1,–3) ?

    (1)   The *x*-coordinate of point *R* is –1.
    (2)   Point *R* lies on the line *y* = –3.

75. Is the positive two-digit integer *N* less than 40 ?

    (1)   The units digit of *N* is 6 more than the tens digit.
    (2)   *N* is 4 less than 4 times the units digit.

76. Each week a certain salesman is paid a fixed amount equal to $300, plus a commission equal to 5 percent of the amount of his sales that week over $1,000. What is the total amount the salesman was paid last week?

    (1)   The total amount the salesman was paid last week is equal to 10 percent of the amount of his sales last week.

    (2)   The salesman's sales last week totaled $5,000.

77. A total of $60,000 was invested for one year. Part of this amount earned simple annual interest at the rate of *x* percent per year, and the rest earned simple annual interest at the rate of *y* percent per year. If the total interest earned by the $60,000 for that year was $4,080, what is the value of *x* ?

    (1) $x = \frac{3y}{4}$

    (2)   The ratio of the amount that earned interest at the rate of *x* percent per year to the amount that earned interest at the rate of *y* percent per year was 3 to 2.

78. At a bakery, all donuts are priced equally and all bagels are priced equally. What is the total price of 5 donuts and 3 bagels at the bakery?

    (1)   At the bakery, the total price of 10 donuts and 6 bagels is $12.90.

    (2)   At the bakery, the price of a donut is $0.15 less than the price of a bagel.

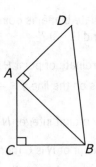

79. In the figure above, is the area of triangular region ABC equal to the area of triangular region DBA ?

    (1) $(AC)^2 = 2(AD)^2$
    (2)   ∆ABC is isosceles.

80. If r and s are positive integers, can the fraction $\frac{r}{s}$ be expressed as a decimal with only a finite number of nonzero digits?

    (1)   s is a factor of 100.
    (2)   r is a factor of 100.

81. If the ratio of the number of teachers to the number of students is the same in School District M and School District P, what is the ratio of the number of students in School District M to the number of students in School District P ?

    (1)   There are 10,000 more students in School District M than there are in School District P.
    (2)   The ratio of the number of teachers to the number of students in School District M is 1 to 20.

82. If $r > 0$ and $s > 0$, is $\frac{r}{s} < \frac{s}{r}$?

    (1) $\frac{r}{3s} = \frac{1}{4}$
    (2) $s = r + 4$

83. If k is an integer such that $56 < k < 66$, what is the value of k ?

    (1)   If k were divided by 2, the remainder would be 1.
    (2)   If k + 1 were divided by 3, the remainder would be 0.

$$k, n, 12, 6, 17$$

84. What is the value of n in the list above?

    (1) $k < n$
    (2)   The median of the numbers in the list is 10.

85. If x and y are integers, what is the value of x + y ?

    (1) $3 < \frac{x+y}{2} < 4$
    (2) $2 < x < y < 5$

86. What is the value of $b + c$?

    (1) $ab + cd + ac + bd = 6$
    (2) $a + d = 4$

87. What is the average (arithmetic mean) of j and k ?

    (1)   The average (arithmetic mean) of $j + 2$ and $k + 4$ is 11.
    (2)   The average (arithmetic mean) of j, k, and 14 is 10.

88. Paula and Sandy were among those people who sold raffle tickets to raise money for Club X. If Paula and Sandy sold a total of 100 of the tickets, how many of the tickets did Paula sell?

    (1)   Sandy sold $\frac{2}{3}$ as many of the raffle tickets as Paula did.
    (2)   Sandy sold 8 percent of all the raffle tickets sold for Club X.

89. A number of people each wrote down one of the first 30 positive integers. Were any of the integers written down by more than one of the people?

    (1)   The number of people who wrote down an integer was greater than 40.
    (2)   The number of people who wrote down an integer was less than 70.

90. Is the number of seconds required to travel d_1 feet at r_1 feet per second greater than the number of seconds required to travel d_2 feet at r_2 feet per second?

    (1) d_1 is 30 greater than d_2.
    (2) r_1 is 30 greater than r_2.

91. Last year, if Arturo spent a total of $12,000 on his mortgage payments, real estate taxes, and home insurance, how much did he spend on his real estate taxes?

    (1) Last year, the total amount that Arturo spent on his real estate taxes and home insurance was $33\frac{1}{3}$ percent of the amount that he spent on his mortgage payments.
    (2) Last year, the amount that Arturo spent on his real estate taxes was 20 percent of the total amount he spent on his mortgage payments and home insurance.

92. If a, b, c, and d are positive numbers, is $\frac{a}{b} < \frac{c}{d}$?

    (1) $0 < \frac{c-a}{d-b}$
    (2) $\left(\frac{ad}{bc}\right)^2 < \frac{ad}{bc}$

93. Is the number of members of Club X greater than the number of members of Club Y ?

    (1) Of the members of Club X, 20 percent are also members of Club Y.
    (2) Of the members of Club Y, 30 percent are also members of Club X.

94. In a certain office, 50 percent of the employees are college graduates and 60 percent of the employees are over 40 years old. If 30 percent of those over 40 have master's degrees, how many of the employees over 40 have master's degrees?

    (1) Exactly 100 of the employees are college graduates.
    (2) Of the employees 40 years old or less, 25 percent have master's degrees.

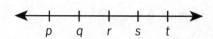

95. On the number line above, p, q, r, s, and t are five consecutive even integers in increasing order. What is the average (arithmetic mean) of these five integers?

    (1) $q + s = 24$
    (2) The average (arithmetic mean) of q and r is 11.

96. If $\lceil x \rceil$ denotes the least integer greater than or equal to x, is $\lceil x \rceil = 0$?

    (1) $-1 < x < 1$
    (2) $x < 0$

97. If x and y are integers, is $x > y$?

    (1) $x + y > 0$
    (2) $y^x < 0$

98. Is $rst = 1$?

    (1) $rs = 1$
    (2) $st = 1$

99. If r and s are the roots of the equation $x^2 + bx + c = 0$, where b and c are constants, is $rs < 0$?

    (1) $b < 0$
    (2) $c < 0$

TOTAL EXPENSES FOR THE FIVE DIVISIONS OF COMPANY H

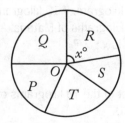

100. The figure above represents a circle graph of Company H's total expenses broken down by the expenses for each of its five divisions. If O is the center of the circle and if Company H's total expenses are $5,400,000, what are the expenses for Division R ?

    (1) $x = 94$
    (2) The total expenses for Divisions S and T are twice as much as the expenses for Division R.

101. If x is negative, is $x < -3$?

    (1) $x^2 > 9$
    (2) $x^3 < -9$

102. What is the number of cans that can be packed in a certain carton?

    (1) The interior volume of this carton is 2,304 cubic inches.
    (2) The exterior of each can is 6 inches high and has a diameter of 4 inches.

r	s	t
u	v	w
x	y	z

103. Each of the letters in the table above represents one of the numbers 1, 2, or 3, and each of these numbers occurs exactly once in each row and exactly once in each column. What is the value of r?

    (1) $v + z = 6$
    (2) $s + t + u + x = 6$

104. If [x] denotes the greatest integer less than or equal to x, is $[x] = 0$?

    (1) $5x + 1 = 3 + 2x$
    (2) $0 < x < 1$

105. Material A costs $3 per kilogram, and Material B costs $5 per kilogram. If 10 kilograms of Material K consists of x kilograms of Material A and y kilograms of Material B, is $x > y$?

    (1) $y > 4$
    (2) The cost of the 10 kilograms of Material K is less than $40.

106. While on a straight road, Car X and Car Y are traveling at different constant rates. If Car X is now 1 mile ahead of Car Y, how many minutes from now will Car X be 2 miles ahead of Car Y?

    (1) Car X is traveling at 50 miles per hour and Car Y is traveling at 40 miles per hour.
    (2) Three minutes ago Car X was $\frac{1}{2}$ mile ahead of Car Y.

107. If a certain animated cartoon consists of a total of 17,280 frames on film, how many minutes will it take to run the cartoon?

    (1) The cartoon runs without interruption at the rate of 24 frames per second.
    (2) It takes 6 times as long to run the cartoon as it takes to rewind the film, and it takes a total of 14 minutes to do both.

108. At what speed was a train traveling on a trip when it had completed half of the total distance of the trip?

    (1) The trip was 460 miles long and took 4 hours to complete.
    (2) The train traveled at an average rate of 115 miles per hour on the trip.

4, 6, 8, 10, 12, 14, 16, 18, 20, 22

109. List M (not shown) consists of 8 different integers, each of which is in the list shown. What is the standard deviation of the numbers in list M?

    (1) The average (arithmetic mean) of the numbers in list M is equal to the average of the numbers in the list shown.
    (2) List M does not contain 22.

110. Tom, Jane, and Sue each purchased a new house. The average (arithmetic mean) price of the three houses was $120,000. What was the median price of the three houses?

    (1) The price of Tom's house was $110,000.
    (2) The price of Jane's house was $120,000.

111. If x and y are integers, is xy even?

    (1) $x = y + 1$
    (2) $\frac{x}{y}$ is an even integer.

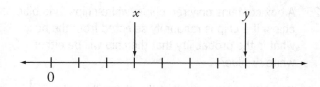

112. If the successive tick marks shown on the number line above are equally spaced and if x and y are the numbers designating the end points of intervals as shown, what is the value of y?

    (1) $x = \frac{1}{2}$

    (2) $y - x = \frac{2}{3}$

113. In triangle ABC, point X is the midpoint of side AC and point Y is the midpoint of side BC. If point R is the midpoint of line segment XC and if point S is the midpoint of line segment YC, what is the area of triangular region RCS?

    (1) The area of triangular region ABX is 32.
    (2) The length of one of the altitudes of triangle ABC is 8.

114. A department manager distributed a number of pens, pencils, and pads among the staff in the department, with each staff member receiving x pens, y pencils, and z pads. How many staff members were in the department?

    (1) The numbers of pens, pencils, and pads that each staff member received were in the ratio 2:3:4, respectively.
    (2) The manager distributed a total of 18 pens, 27 pencils, and 36 pads.

115. Machines X and Y produced identical bottles at different constant rates. Machine X, operating alone for 4 hours, filled part of a production lot; then Machine Y, operating alone for 3 hours, filled the rest of this lot. How many hours would it have taken Machine X operating alone to fill the entire production lot?

    (1) Machine X produced 30 bottles per minute.
    (2) Machine X produced twice as many bottles in 4 hours as Machine Y produced in 3 hours.

116. On a company-sponsored cruise, $\frac{2}{3}$ of the passengers were company employees and the remaining passengers were their guests. If $\frac{3}{4}$ of the company-employee passengers were managers, what was the number of company-employee passengers who were NOT managers?

    (1) There were 690 passengers on the cruise.
    (2) There were 230 passengers who were guests of the company employees.

117. The length of the edging that surrounds circular garden K is $\frac{1}{2}$ the length of the edging that surrounds circular garden G. What is the area of garden K? (Assume that the edging has negligible width.)

    (1) The area of G is 25π square meters.
    (2) The edging around G is 10π meters long.

118. For any integers x and y, $\min(x, y)$ and $\max(x, y)$ denote the minimum and the maximum of x and y, respectively. For example, $\min(5, 2) = 2$ and $\max(5, 2) = 5$. For the integer w, what is the value of $\min(10, w)$?

    (1) $w = \max(20, z)$ for some integer z.
    (2) $w = \max(10, w)$

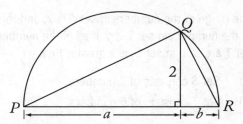

119. If arc PQR above is a semicircle, what is the length of diameter $\overline{PR}$?

    (1) $a = 4$
    (2) $b = 1$

120. A certain bookcase has 2 shelves of books. On the upper shelf, the book with the greatest number of pages has 400 pages. On the lower shelf, the book with the least number of pages has 475 pages. What is the median number of pages for all of the books on the 2 shelves?

    (1) There are 25 books on the upper shelf.
    (2) There are 24 books on the lower shelf.

121. During a 6-day local trade show, the least number of people registered in a single day was 80. Was the average (arithmetic mean) number of people registered per day for the 6 days greater than 90 ?

    (1) For the 4 days with the greatest number of people registered, the average (arithmetic mean) number registered per day was 100.

    (2) For the 3 days with the smallest number of people registered, the average (arithmetic mean) number registered per day was 85.

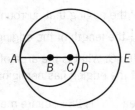

122. In the figure above, points A, B, C, D, and E lie on a line. A is on both circles, B is the center of the smaller circle, C is the center of the larger circle, D is on the smaller circle, and E is on the larger circle. What is the area of the region inside the larger circle and outside the smaller circle?

    (1) $AB = 3$ and $BC = 2$
    (2) $CD = 1$ and $DE = 4$

123. The range of the numbers in set S is x, and the range of the numbers in set T is y. If all of the numbers in set T are also in set S, is x greater than y ?

    (1) Set S consists of 7 numbers.
    (2) Set T consists of 6 numbers.

124. An employee is paid 1.5 times the regular hourly rate for each hour worked in excess of 40 hours per week, excluding Sunday, and 2 times the regular hourly rate for each hour worked on Sunday. How much was the employee paid last week?

    (1) The employee's regular hourly rate is $10.
    (2) Last week the employee worked a total of 54 hours but did not work more than 8 hours on any day.

125. A box contains only red chips, white chips, and blue chips. If a chip is randomly selected from the box, what is the probability that the chip will be either white or blue?

    (1) The probability that the chip will be blue is $\frac{1}{5}$.

    (2) The probability that the chip will be red is $\frac{1}{3}$.

126. What was the revenue that a theater received from the sale of 400 tickets, some of which were sold at the full price and the remainder of which were sold at a reduced price?

    (1) The number of tickets sold at the full price was $\frac{1}{4}$ of the total number of tickets sold.

    (2) The full price of a ticket was $25.

127. The annual rent collected by a corporation from a certain building was x percent more in 1998 than in 1997 and y percent less in 1999 than in 1998. Was the annual rent collected by the corporation from the building more in 1999 than in 1997 ?

    (1) $x > y$
    (2) $\frac{xy}{100} < x - y$

128. The hypotenuse of a right triangle is 10 cm. What is the perimeter, in centimeters, of the triangle?

    (1) The area of the triangle is 25 square centimeters.
    (2) The 2 legs of the triangle are of equal length.

129. In the xy-plane, region R consists of all the points (x,y) such that $2x + 3y \leq 6$. Is the point (r,s) in region R ?

    (1) $3r + 2s = 6$
    (2) $r \leq 3$ and $s \leq 2$

130. What is the volume of a certain rectangular solid?

    (1) Two adjacent faces of the solid have areas 15 and 24, respectively.
    (2) Each of two opposite faces of the solid has area 40.

Shipment	S1	S2	S3	S4	S5	S6
Fraction of the Total Value of the Six Shipments	$\frac{1}{4}$	$\frac{1}{5}$	$\frac{1}{6}$	$\frac{3}{20}$	$\frac{2}{15}$	$\frac{1}{10}$

131. Six shipments of machine parts were shipped from a factory on two trucks, with each shipment entirely on one of the trucks. Each shipment was labeled either S1, S2, S3, S4, S5, or S6. The table shows the value of each shipment as a fraction of the total value of the six shipments. If the shipments on the first truck had a value greater than $\frac{1}{2}$ of the total value of the six shipments, was S3 shipped on the first truck?

    (1) S2 and S4 were shipped on the first truck.
    (2) S1 and S6 were shipped on the second truck.

132. Joanna bought only $0.15 stamps and $0.29 stamps. How many $0.15 stamps did she buy?

    (1) She bought $4.40 worth of stamps.
    (2) She bought an equal number of $0.15 stamps and $0.29 stamps.

133. If x, y, and z are three-digit positive integers and if $x = y + z$, is the hundreds digit of x equal to the sum of the hundreds digits of y and z?

    (1) The tens digit of x is equal to the sum of the tens digits of y and z.
    (2) The units digit of x is equal to the sum of the units digits of y and z.

	Favorable	Unfavorable	Not Sure
Candidate M	40	20	40
Candidate N	30	35	35

134. The table above shows the results of a survey of 100 voters who each responded "Favorable" or "Unfavorable" or "Not Sure" when asked about their impressions of Candidate M and of Candidate N. What was the number of voters who responded "Favorable" for both candidates?

    (1) The number of voters who did not respond "Favorable" for either candidate was 40.
    (2) The number of voters who responded "Unfavorable" for both candidates was 10.

135. A school administrator will assign each student in a group of n students to one of m classrooms. If $3 < m < 13 < n$, is it possible to assign each of the n students to one of the m classrooms so that each classroom has the same number of students assigned to it?

    (1) It is possible to assign each of $3n$ students to one of m classrooms so that each classroom has the same number of students assigned to it.
    (2) It is possible to assign each of $13n$ students to one of m classrooms so that each classroom has the same number of students assigned to it.

136. If $°$ represents one of the operations $+$, $-$, and $\times$, is $k \circ (\ell + m) = (k \circ \ell) + (k \circ m)$ for all numbers k, ℓ, and m?

    (1) $k \circ 1$ is not equal to $1 \circ k$ for some numbers k.
    (2) $°$ represents subtraction.

137. How many of the 60 cars sold last month by a certain dealer had neither power windows nor a stereo?

    (1) Of the 60 cars sold, 20 had a stereo but not power windows.
    (2) Of the 60 cars sold, 30 had both power windows and a stereo.

138. In Jefferson School, 300 students study French or Spanish or both. If 100 of these students do not study French, how many of these students study both French and Spanish?

    (1) Of the 300 students, 60 do not study Spanish.
    (2) A total of 240 of the students study Spanish.

139. What is the median number of employees assigned per project for the projects at Company Z?

    (1) 25 percent of the projects at Company Z have 4 or more employees assigned to each project.
    (2) 35 percent of the projects at Company Z have 2 or fewer employees assigned to each project.

140. If Juan had a doctor's appointment on a certain day, was the appointment on a Wednesday?

    (1) Exactly 60 hours before the appointment, it was Monday.
    (2) The appointment was between 1:00 p.m. and 9:00 p.m.

141. Last year, a certain company began manufacturing product X and sold every unit of product X that it produced. Last year the company's total expenses for manufacturing product X were equal to $100,000 plus 5 percent of the company's total revenue from all units of product X sold. If the company made a profit on product X last year, did the company sell more than 21,000 units of product X last year?

    (1) The company's total revenue from the sale of product X last year was greater than $110,000.

    (2) For each unit of product X sold last year, the company's revenue was $5.

142. When a player in a certain game tossed a coin a number of times, 4 more heads than tails resulted. Heads or tails resulted each time the player tossed the coin. How many times did heads result?

    (1) The player tossed the coin 24 times.

    (2) The player received 3 points each time heads resulted and 1 point each time tails resulted, for a total of 52 points.

143. Beginning in January of last year, Carl made deposits of $120 into his account on the 15th of each month for several consecutive months and then made withdrawals of $50 from the account on the 15th of each of the remaining months of last year. There were no other transactions in the account last year. If the closing balance of Carl's account for May of last year was $2,600, what was the range of the monthly closing balances of Carl's account last year?

    (1) Last year the closing balance of Carl's account for April was less than $2,625.

    (2) Last year the closing balance of Carl's account for June was less than $2,675.

144. Are all of the numbers in a certain list of 15 numbers equal?

    (1) The sum of all the numbers in the list is 60.

    (2) The sum of any 3 numbers in the list is 12.

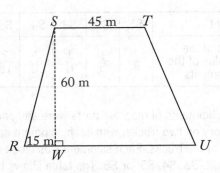

145. Quadrilateral *RSTU* shown above is a site plan for a parking lot in which side *RU* is parallel to side *ST* and *RU* is longer than *ST*. What is the area of the parking lot?

    (1) *RU* = 80 meters

    (2) *TU* = $20\sqrt{10}$ meters

146. If the average (arithmetic mean) of six numbers is 75, how many of the numbers are equal to 75 ?

    (1) None of the six numbers is less than 75.

    (2) None of the six numbers is greater than 75.

147. What was the total amount of revenue that a theater received from the sale of 400 tickets, some of which were sold at x percent of full price and the rest of which were sold at full price?

    (1) x = 50

    (2) Full-price tickets sold for $20 each.

148. Any decimal that has only a finite number of nonzero digits is a terminating decimal. For example, 24, 0.82, and 5.096 are three terminating decimals. If r and s are positive integers and the ratio $\frac{r}{s}$ is expressed as a decimal, is $\frac{r}{s}$ a terminating decimal?

    (1) $90 < r < 100$

    (2) $s = 4$

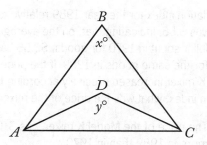

149. In the figure above, what is the value of $x + y$?

    (1) $x = 70$
    (2) $\triangle ABC$ and $\triangle ADC$ are both isosceles triangles.

150. What amount did Jean earn from the commission on her sales in the first half of 1988 ?

    (1) In 1988 Jean's commission was 5 percent of the total amount of her sales.
    (2) The amount of Jean's sales in the second half of 1988 averaged $10,000 per month more than in the first half.

151. The price per share of Stock X increased by 10 percent over the same time period that the price per share of Stock Y decreased by 10 percent. The reduced price per share of Stock Y was what percent of the original price per share of Stock X ?

    (1) The increased price per share of Stock X was equal to the original price per share of Stock Y.
    (2) The increase in the price per share of Stock X was $\frac{10}{11}$ the decrease in the price per share of Stock Y.

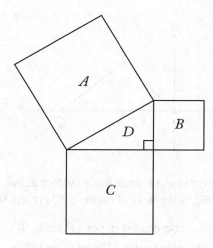

152. In the figure above, if the area of triangular region D is 4, what is the length of a side of square region A ?

    (1) The area of square region B is 9.
    (2) The area of square region C is $\frac{64}{9}$.

153. If Sara's age is exactly twice Bill's age, what is Sara's age?

    (1) Four years ago, Sara's age was exactly 3 times Bill's age.
    (2) Eight years from now, Sara's age will be exactly 1.5 times Bill's age.

154. A report consisting of 2,600 words is divided into 23 paragraphs. A 2-paragraph preface is then added to the report. Is the average (arithmetic mean) number of words per paragraph for all 25 paragraphs less than 120 ?

    (1) Each paragraph of the preface has more than 100 words.
    (2) Each paragraph of the preface has fewer than 150 words.

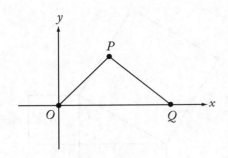

155. In the rectangular coordinate system above, if $OP < PQ$, is the area of region OPQ greater than 48 ?

   (1)   The coordinates of point P are (6,8).
   (2)   The coordinates of point Q are (13,0).

$$S = \frac{\frac{2}{n}}{\frac{1}{x} + \frac{2}{3x}}$$

156. In the expression above, if $xn \neq 0$, what is the value of S?

   (1) $x = 2n$
   (2) $n = \frac{1}{2}$

157. If n is a positive integer and $k = 5.1 \times 10^n$, what is the value of k ?

   (1) $6,000 < k < 500,000$
   (2) $k^2 = 2.601 \times 10^9$

158. If Carmen had 12 more tapes, she would have twice as many tapes as Rafael. Does Carmen have fewer tapes than Rafael?

   (1)   Rafael has more than 5 tapes.
   (2)   Carmen has fewer than 12 tapes.

159. If x is an integer, is $x|x| < 2^x$?

   (1) $x < 0$
   (2) $x = -10$

160. If n is a positive integer, is the value of $b - a$ at least twice the value of $3^n - 2^n$?

   (1) $a = 2^{n+1}$ and $b = 3^{n+1}$
   (2) $n = 3$

161. The inflation index for the year 1989 relative to the year 1970 was 3.56, indicating that, on the average, for each dollar spent in 1970 for goods, $3.56 had to be spent for the same goods in 1989. If the price of a Model K mixer increased precisely according to the inflation index, what was the price of the mixer in 1970 ?

   (1)   The price of the Model K mixer was $102.40 more in 1989 than in 1970.
   (2)   The price of the Model K mixer was $142.40 in 1989.

162. Is 5^k less than 1,000 ?

   (1) $5^{k+1} > 3,000$
   (2) $5^{k-1} = 5^k - 500$

163. Every member of a certain club volunteers to contribute equally to the purchase of a $60 gift certificate. How many members does the club have?

   (1)   Each member's contribution is to be $4.
   (2)   If 5 club members fail to contribute, the share of each contributing member will increase by $2.

164. If $x < 0$, is $y > 0$?

   (1) $\frac{x}{y} < 0$
   (2) $y - x > 0$

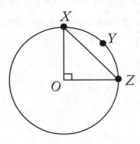

165. What is the circumference of the circle above with center O ?

   (1)   The perimeter of $\triangle OXZ$ is $20 + 10\sqrt{2}$.
   (2)   The length of arc XYZ is 5π.

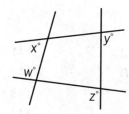

166. What is the value of $x + y$ in the figure above?

    (1) $w = 95$
    (2) $z = 125$

167. If n and k are positive integers, is $\sqrt{n+k} > 2\sqrt{n}$?

    (1) $k > 3n$
    (2) $n + k > 3n$

168. In a certain business, production index p is directly proportional to efficiency index e, which is in turn directly proportional to investment index i. What is p if $i = 70$?

    (1) $e = 0.5$ whenever $i = 60$.
    (2) $p = 2.0$ whenever $i = 50$.

169. If n is a positive integer, is $\left(\frac{1}{10}\right)^n < 0.01$?

    (1) $n > 2$
    (2) $\left(\frac{1}{10}\right)^{n-1} < 0.1$

170. If n is a positive integer, what is the tens digit of n ?

    (1) The hundreds digit of $10n$ is 6.
    (2) The tens digit of $n + 1$ is 7.

171. What is the value of $\dfrac{2t + t - x}{t - x}$?

    (1) $\dfrac{2t}{t - x} = 3$
    (2) $t - x = 5$

172. Is n an integer?

    (1) n^2 is an integer.
    (2) $\sqrt{n}$ is an integer.

173. If x, y, and z are positive integers, is $x - y$ odd?

    (1) $x = z^2$
    (2) $y = (z - 1)^2$

174. Marcia's bucket can hold a maximum of how many liters of water?

    (1) The bucket currently contains 9 liters of water.
    (2) If 3 liters of water are added to the bucket when it is half full of water, the amount of water in the bucket will increase by $\frac{1}{3}$.

6.4 Answer Key

1.	B	36.	D	71.	D	106.	D
2.	E	37.	A	72.	B	107.	D
3.	A	38.	B	73.	A	108.	E
4.	A	39.	E	74.	A	109.	C
5.	E	40.	A	75.	D	110.	B
6.	E	41.	C	76.	D	111.	D
7.	D	42.	E	77.	C	112.	D
8.	A	43.	C	78.	A	113.	A
9.	C	44.	D	79.	C	114.	E
10.	A	45.	B	80.	A	115.	B
11.	C	46.	E	81.	E	116.	D
12.	B	47.	C	82.	D	117.	D
13.	A	48.	B	83.	E	118.	D
14.	B	49.	C	84.	C	119.	D
15.	D	50.	B	85.	D	120.	C
16.	C	51.	B	86.	C	121.	A
17.	B	52.	D	87.	D	122.	D
18.	D	53.	A	88.	A	123.	E
19.	A	54.	C	89.	A	124.	E
20.	B	55.	E	90.	E	125.	B
21.	E	56.	A	91.	B	126.	E
22.	D	57.	E	92.	B	127.	B
23.	D	58.	A	93.	C	128.	D
24.	A	59.	D	94.	A	129.	E
25.	E	60.	D	95.	D	130.	C
26.	B	61.	C	96.	C	131.	B
27.	D	62.	C	97.	C	132.	A
28.	D	63.	B	98.	E	133.	A
29.	C	64.	D	99.	B	134.	A
30.	E	65.	C	100.	A	135.	B
31.	B	66.	D	101.	A	136.	D
32.	D	67.	B	102.	E	137.	E
33.	B	68.	A	103.	D	138.	D
34.	E	69.	A	104.	D	139.	C
35.	D	70.	C	105.	B	140.	C

141.	B
142.	D
143.	C
144.	B
145.	D
146.	D
147.	E
148.	B
149.	E
150.	E
151.	D
152.	D
153.	D
154.	B
155.	A
156.	A
157.	D
158.	B
159.	D
160.	A
161.	D
162.	B
163.	D
164.	A
165.	D
166.	C
167.	A
168.	B
169.	D
170.	A
171.	A
172.	B
173.	C
174.	B

6.5 Answer Explanations

The following discussion of data sufficiency is intended to familiarize you with the most efficient and effective approaches to the kinds of problems common to data sufficiency. The particular questions in this chapter are generally representative of the kinds of data sufficiency questions you will encounter on the GMAT exam. Remember that it is the problem solving strategy that is important, not the specific details of a particular question.

1. What is the value of $|x|$?

   (1) $x = -|x|$
   (2) $x^2 = 4$

   Arithmetic Absolute value

   (1) The absolute value of x, $|x|$, is always positive or 0, so this only determines that x is negative or 0; NOT sufficient.

   (2) Exactly two values of x $(x = \pm 2)$ are possible, each of which gives the value 2 for $|x|$; SUFFICIENT.

   **The correct answer is B;
   statement 2 alone is sufficient.**

2. What percent of a group of people are women with red hair?

   (1) Of the women in the group, 5 percent have red hair.
   (2) Of the men in the group, 10 percent have red hair.

   Arithmetic Percents

   In order to solve this problem, it is necessary to know the total number of people in the group and the number of women with red hair.

   (1) This indicates that 5 percent of the women have red hair, but neither the total number of women nor the total number of people in the group is known. Therefore, further information is needed; NOT sufficient.

   (2) This indicates the percent of men who have red hair, a fact that is irrelevant. It does not give information as to the total number in the group or the number of women with red hair; NOT sufficient.

With (1) and (2) taken together, the percent of men with red hair is known and the percent of the women with red hair is known, but not the percent of the group who are women with red hair. For example: if there are 100 women, including 5 red-haired women, and 100 men, including 10 red-haired men, then $\frac{5}{200} = 2.5$ percent of the group are women with red hair. On the other hand, if there are 300 women, including 15 red-haired women and 100 men, including 10 red-haired men, then $\frac{15}{400} = 3.75$ percent of the group are women with red hair.

**The correct answer is E;
both statements together are still not sufficient.**

3. In a certain class, one student is to be selected at random to read. What is the probability that a boy will read?

   (1) Two-thirds of the students in the class are boys.
   (2) Ten of the students in the class are girls.

   Arithmetic Probability

   (1) Since $\frac{2}{3}$ of the students in the class are boys, the probability that one student selected at random will be a boy is $\frac{2}{3}$; SUFFICIENT.

   (2) The desired probability is different for a class with 10 girls and 20 boys than it is for a class with 10 girls and 10 boys; NOT sufficient.

   **The correct answer is A;
   statement 1 alone is sufficient.**

4. If the two floors in a certain building are 9 feet apart, how many steps are there in a set of stairs that extends from the first floor to the second floor of the building?

   (1) Each step is $\frac{3}{4}$ foot high.

   (2) Each step is 1 foot wide.

   Arithmetic Arithmetic operations

   (1) If each step in the set of stairs is $\frac{3}{4}$ foot high and the set of stairs rises 9 feet from the first floor to the second, the number of steps must be $9 \div \frac{3}{4}$, or $\frac{9}{1} \times \frac{4}{3} = \frac{36}{3} = 12$; SUFFICIENT.

   (2) This provides no information regarding the height of the steps, and so the question cannot be answered; NOT sufficient.

   The correct answer is A; statement 1 alone is sufficient.

5. In College X the number of students enrolled in both a chemistry course and a biology course is how much less than the number of students enrolled in neither?

   (1) In College X there are 60 students enrolled in a chemistry course.

   (2) In College X there are 85 students enrolled in a biology course.

Arithmetic Sets (Venn diagrams)

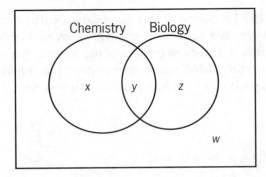

Consider the Venn diagram above, in which x represents the number of students in chemistry only, y represents the number of students in both chemistry and biology, z represents the number of students in biology only, and w represents the number of students in neither chemistry nor biology. Find the value for $w - y$.

(1) Since there are 60 students enrolled in chemistry, $x + y = 60$, but there is no way to determine the value of y. Also, no information is given for determining w. For example, if $x = y = 30$ and $w = 30$, then $w - y = 0$. However, if $x = y = 30$ and $w = 40$, then $w - y = 10$; NOT sufficient.

(2) Since there are 85 students enrolled in biology, $y + z = 85$, but there is no way to determine the value of y. Also, no information is given for determining w. For example, if $x = y = 30$, $z = 55$, and $w = 30$, then $w - y = 0$. However, if $x = y = 30$, $z = 55$, and $w = 40$, then $w - y = 10$; NOT sufficient.

Taking (1) and (2) together and subtracting the equation in (1) from the equation in (2) gives $z - x = 25$. Then, adding the equations gives $x + 2y + z = 145$, but neither gives information for finding the value of w. For example, if $x = y = 30$, $z = 55$, and $w = 30$, then $w - y = 0$. However, if $x = y = 30$, $z = 55$, and $w = 40$, then $w - y = 10$.

The correct answer is E; both statements together are still not sufficient.

6. A certain expressway has Exits J, K, L, and M, in that order. What is the road distance from Exit K to Exit L ?

   (1) The road distance from Exit J to Exit L is 21 kilometers.
   (2) The road distance from Exit K to Exit M is 26 kilometers.

   Geometry Lines

   Let JK, KL, and LM be the distances between adjacent exits.

   (1) It can only be determined that $KL = 21 - JK$; NOT sufficient.
   (2) It can only be determined that $KL = 26 - LM$; NOT sufficient.

   Statements (1) and (2) taken together do not provide any of the distances JK, LM, or JM, which would give the needed information to find KL. For example, $KL = 1$ if $JK = 20$ and $LM = 25$, while $KL = 2$ if $JK = 19$ and $LM = 24$.

   The correct answer is E; both statements together are still not sufficient.

7. If n is an integer, is $n + 1$ odd?

   (1) $n + 2$ is an even integer.
   (2) $n - 1$ is an odd integer.

   Arithmetic Properties of numbers

   (1) Since $n + 2$ is even, n is an even integer, and therefore $n + 1$ would be an odd integer; SUFFICIENT.
   (2) Since $n - 1$ is an odd integer, n is an even integer. Therefore $n + 1$ would be an odd integer; SUFFICIENT.

   The correct answer is D; each statement alone is sufficient.

8. For which type of investment, J or K, is the annual rate of return greater?

   (1) Type J returns $115 per $1,000 invested for any one-year period and type K returns $300 per $2,500 invested for any one-year period.
   (2) The annual rate of return for an investment of type K is 12 percent.

   Arithmetic Percents

   Compare the annual rates of return for Investments J and K.

   (1) For Investment J, the annual rate of return is $115 per $1,000 for any one-year period, which can be converted to a percent. For Investment K, the annual rate of return is $300 per $2,500 for any one-year period, which can also be converted to a percent. These two percents can be compared to determine which is larger; SUFFICIENT.
   (2) Investment K has an annual rate of return of 12 percent, but no information is given about the annual rate of return for Investment J; NOT sufficient.

   The correct answer is A; statement 1 alone is sufficient.

9. A citrus fruit grower receives $15 for each crate of oranges shipped and $18 for each crate of grapefruit shipped. How many crates of oranges did the grower ship last week?

   (1) Last week the number of crates of oranges that the grower shipped was 20 more than twice the number of crates of grapefruit shipped.
   (2) Last week the grower received a total of $38,700 from the crates of oranges and grapefruit shipped.

   Algebra Simultaneous equations

   If x represents the number of crates of oranges and y represents the number of crates of grapefruit, find a unique value for x.

   (1) Translating from words into symbols gives $x = 2y + 20$, but there is no information about y and no way to find a unique value for x from this equation. For example, if $y = 10$, then $x = 40$, but if $y = 100$, then $x = 220$; NOT sufficient.
   (2) Translating from words to symbols gives $15x + 18y = 38,700$, but there is no way to find a unique value for x from this equation. For example, if $y = 2,150$, then $x = 0$ and if $y = 0$, then $x = 2,580$; NOT sufficient.

Taking (1) and (2) together gives a system of two equations in two unknowns. Substituting the equation from (1) into the equation from (2) gives a single equation in the variable y. This equation can be solved for a unique value of y from which a unique value of x can be determined.

**The correct answer is C;
both statements together are sufficient.**

10. If Pat saved $600 of his earnings last month, how much did Pat earn last month?

    (1) Pat spent $\frac{1}{2}$ of his earnings last month for living expenses and saved $\frac{1}{3}$ of the remainder.

    (2) Of his earnings last month, Pat paid twice as much in taxes as he saved.

Arithmetic Operations with rational numbers

Let E be Pat's earnings last month. Find a unique value for E.

(1) Pat spent $\frac{1}{2}E$ for living expenses and so

$E - \frac{1}{2}E = \frac{1}{2}E$ remained. Pat saved $\frac{1}{3}$ of what

remained, so Pat saved $\frac{1}{3}\left(\frac{1}{2}E\right) = \frac{1}{6}E$.

But Pat saved $600, so $600 = \frac{1}{6}E$

and this gives a unique value for E; SUFFICIENT.

(2) Pat saved $600 last month and paid 2($600) in taxes, but there is no way to determine Pat's earnings last month; NOT sufficient.

**The correct answer is A;
statement 1 alone is sufficient.**

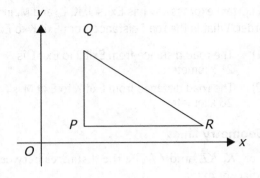

11. In the xy-plane above, is angle QPR a right angle?

    (1) Points P and Q have the same x-coordinate.

    (2) Points P and R have the same y-coordinate.

Geometry Simple coordinate geometry

(1) Because points P and Q have the same x-coordinate, it follows that side $\overline{PQ}$ is vertical (i.e., parallel to the y-axis). Therefore, angle QPR will be a right angle if and only if side $\overline{PR}$ is horizontal (i.e., parallel to the x-axis). However, depending on the location of point R in relation to point P, side $\overline{PR}$ may or may not be horizontal; NOT sufficient.

(2) Because points P and R have the same y-coordinate, it follows that side $\overline{PR}$ is horizontal. Therefore, angle QPR will be a right angle if and only if side $\overline{PQ}$ is vertical. However, depending on the location of point Q in relation to point P, side $\overline{PQ}$ may or may not be vertical; NOT sufficient.

Given (1) and (2), it follows that $\overline{PQ}$ is vertical and $\overline{PR}$ is horizontal. Therefore, angle QPR is a right angle.

**The correct answer is C;
both statements together are sufficient.**

12. Water is pumped into a partially filled tank at a constant rate through an inlet pipe. At the same time, water is pumped out of the tank at a constant rate through an outlet pipe. At what rate, in gallons per minute, is the amount of water in the tank increasing?

    (1) The amount of water initially in the tank is 200 gallons.
    (2) Water is pumped into the tank at a rate of 10 gallons per minute and out of the tank at a rate of 10 gallons every $2\frac{1}{2}$ minutes.

    Arithmetic Work Problem

    If both the rate of the water being pumped into the tank and the rate of the water being pumped out of the tank are known, then the rate at which the total amount of water in the tank is changing can be determined, but not if only one of these quantities is known.

    (1) This only gives the amount of water in the tank initially; NOT sufficient.
    (2) This information provides both the needed rates. Since the water is being pumped out of the tank at the rate of 10 gallons every $2\frac{1}{2}$ minutes, that is, 4 gallons every minute, and since 10 gallons are pumped into the tank every minute, the rate at which the water is increasing in the tank is $10 - 4 = 6$ gallons per minute; SUFFICIENT.

    The correct answer is B; statement 2 alone is sufficient.

13. Is x a negative number?

    (1) $9x > 10x$
    (2) $x + 3$ is positive.

    Arithmetic Properties of numbers

    (1) Subtracting $9x$ from both sides of $9x > 10x$ gives $0 > x$, which expresses the condition that x is negative; SUFFICIENT.
    (2) Subtracting 3 from both sides of $x + 3 > 0$ gives $x > -3$, and $x > -3$ is true for some negative numbers (such as -2 and -1) and for some numbers that aren't negative (such as 0 and 1); NOT sufficient.

    The correct answer is A; statement 1 alone is sufficient.

14. If i and j are integers, is $i + j$ an even integer?

    (1) $i < 10$
    (2) $i = j$

    Arithmetic Properties of numbers

    (1) Although $i < 10$, i could be an even integer or an odd integer less than 10. There is no information about j, so j could be an even integer or an odd integer. If i and j are both even integers, then $i + j$ is an even integer, and if i and j are both odd integers, then $i + j$ is an even integer. If, however, either i or j is an even integer and the other is an odd integer, then $i + j$ is an odd integer; NOT sufficient.
    (2) If $i = j$, then $i + j$ can also be represented as $i + i$ when i is substituted for j in the expression. This can be simplified as $2i$, and since 2 times any integer produces an even integer, then $i + j$ must be an even integer; SUFFICIENT.

    The correct answer is B; statement 2 alone is sufficient.

15. What is the cube root of w?

    (1) The 5th root of w is 64.
    (2) The 15th root of w is 4.

    Arithmetic Operations with radical expressions

    Determine the cube root of w, or determine the value of $w^{\frac{1}{3}}$.

    (1) Given the 5th root of w is 64, then $w^{\frac{1}{5}} = 64$ and $\left(w^{\frac{1}{5}}\right)^{\frac{5}{3}} = 64^{\frac{5}{3}}$. Since $\left(w^{\frac{1}{5}}\right)^{\frac{5}{3}} = w^{\left(\frac{1}{5}\right)\left(\frac{5}{3}\right)} = w^{\frac{1}{3}}$, then $w^{\frac{1}{3}} = \left(64^{\frac{5}{3}}\right) = \left(64^{\frac{1}{3}}\right)^{5} = 4^{5}$; SUFFICIENT.

    (2) Given the 15th root of w is 4, then $w^{\frac{1}{15}} = 4$ and $\left(w^{\frac{1}{15}}\right)^{5} = 4^{5}$. Since $\left(w^{\frac{1}{15}}\right)^{5} = w^{\frac{5}{15}} = w^{\frac{1}{3}}$, then $w^{\frac{1}{3}} = 4^{5}$; SUFFICIENT.

    The correct answer is D; each statement alone is sufficient.

16. If Car X followed Car Y across a certain bridge that is $\frac{1}{2}$ mile long, how many seconds did it take Car X to travel across the bridge?

    (1) Car X drove onto the bridge exactly 3 seconds after Car Y drove onto the bridge and drove off the bridge exactly 2 seconds after Car Y drove off the bridge.

    (2) Car Y traveled across the bridge at a constant speed of 30 miles per hour.

Arithmetic Rate problem

Find the number of seconds that it took Car X to cross the $\frac{1}{2}$-mile bridge.

    (1) If Car X drove onto the bridge 3 seconds after Car Y and drove off the bridge 2 seconds after Car Y, then Car X took 1 second less to cross the bridge than Car Y. Since there is no information on how long Car Y took to cross the bridge, there is no way to determine how long Car X took to cross the bridge; NOT sufficient.

    (2) If the speed of Car Y was 30 miles per hour, it took Car Y $\frac{1}{60}$ hour = 1 minute = 60 seconds to cross the bridge. However, there is no information on how long Car X took to cross the bridge; NOT sufficient.

Taking (1) and (2) together, Car X took 1 second less than Car Y to cross the bridge and Car Y took 60 seconds to cross the bridge, so Car X took $60 - 1 = 59$ seconds to cross the bridge.

**The correct answer is C;
both statements together are sufficient.**

17. If $n + k = m$, what is the value of k?

    (1) $n = 10$
    (2) $m + 10 = n$

Algebra First- and second-degree equations

It is given that $n + k = m$, so $k = m - n$. Thus, the question can be rephrased as: What is the value of $m - n$?

    (1) If $n = 10$, then $m - n = m - 10$, and the value of $m - 10$ can vary. For example, $m - 10 = 0$

if $m = 10$ and $m - 10 = 1$ if $m = 11$; NOT sufficient.

    (2) Subtracting both n and 10 from each side of $m + 10 = n$ gives $m - n = -10$, and hence the value of $m - n$ can be determined; SUFFICIENT.

**The correct answer is B;
statement 2 alone is sufficient.**

18. The number of seats in the first row of an auditorium is 18 and the number of seats in each row thereafter is 2 more than in the previous row. What is the total number of seats in the rows of the auditorium?

    (1) The number of rows of seats in the auditorium is 27.

    (2) The number of seats in the last row is 70.

Arithmetic Sequences and series

Determine the number of seats in the auditorium.

It is given that the first row has 18 seats, and since each row after the first row has 2 more seats than the previous row, the second row has 20 seats, the third row has 22 seats, and so on. The total number of seats in the auditorium can be determined if and only if the number of rows in the auditorium can be determined.

    (1) The number of rows is given to be 27, so the total number of seats can be determined; SUFFICIENT.

    (2) The last row has 70 seats. Let n be the number of rows in the auditorium. Since the first row has 18 seats, the second row has $18 + 2 = 20$ seats, and the third row has $20 + 2 = 18 + 2(2) = 22$ seats, it follows that the nth row has $18 + (n - 1)(2)$ seats. Then

$$18 + (n - 1)(2) = 70$$
$$18 + 2n - 2 = 70$$
$$2n = 54$$
$$n = 27$$

Thus the number of rows can be determined; SUFFICIENT.

**The correct answer is D;
each statement alone is sufficient.**

19. In $\triangle PQR$, if $PQ = x$, $QR = x + 2$, and $PR = y$, which of the three angles of $\triangle PQR$ has the greatest degree measure?

    (1) $y = x + 3$
    (2) $x = 2$

    Geometry Triangles

    In any triangle, the largest angle is opposite the longest side.

    (1) Since $x + 2 > x$, the longest side is either $x + 2$ or y; therefore, it is sufficient to determine whether $y > x + 2$. If $y = x + 3$ and since $x + 3 > x + 2$, it follows by substitution that $y > x + 2$; SUFFICIENT.

    (2) Substituting 2 for x yields that $PQ = 2$ and $QR = 4$, but no information is given as to the relationship of these sides with the value of y given for side PR; NOT sufficient.

    The correct answer is A; statement 1 alone is sufficient.

    $$n, 15, 12, 9, 20$$

20. What is the value of n in the list above?

    (1) $n > 12$
    (2) The median of the numbers in the list is 13.

    Arithmetic Statistics

    Determine the value of n in the list n, 15, 12, 9, 20.

    (1) Given that $n > 12$, then n can have any of the infinitely many values greater than 12; NOT sufficient.

    (2) Given that there are 5 numbers in the list and 5 is odd, the median of the list must be one of the numbers in the list—the middle number. Therefore, since none of the other numbers in the list is 13, $n = 13$; SUFFICIENT.

    The correct answer is B; statement 2 alone is sufficient.

21. What percent of the drama club members enrolled at a certain school are female students?

    (1) Of the female students enrolled at the school, 40 percent are members of the drama club.
    (2) Of the male students enrolled at the school, 25 percent are members of the drama club.

    Arithmetic Percents

    Determine what percent of drama club members are female.

    (1) Knowing that 40 percent of the females enrolled at the school are in the drama club provides no information about the male/female breakdown of the drama club; NOT sufficient.

    (2) Knowing that 25 percent of the males enrolled at the school are in the drama club provides no information about the male/female breakdown of the drama club; NOT sufficient.

    Taking (1) and (2) together does not give enough information to determine what percent of drama club members are female. For example, if the school has 100 female students and 100 male students, then the drama club would have $0.40(100) + 0.25(100) = 40 + 25 = 65$ members, $\frac{40}{65} \approx 62$ percent of whom are female. On the other hand, if the school had 40 female students and 160 male students, the drama club would have $0.40(40) + 0.25(160) = 16 + 40 = 56$ members, $\frac{16}{56} \approx 29$ percent of whom are female.

    The correct answer is E; both statements together are still not sufficient.

22. On a recent trip, Mary drove 50 miles. What was the average speed at which she drove the 50 miles?

    (1) She drove 30 miles at an average speed of 60 miles per hour and then drove the remaining 20 miles at an average speed of 50 miles per hour.
    (2) She drove a total of 54 minutes.

Arithmetic Rate problem

Mary drove 50 miles. Determine the average speed at which she drove the 50 miles.

If the time it took Mary to drive the 50 miles can be determined, then her average speed can be determined: distance = speed × time, or $\frac{distance}{speed}$ = time.

(1) It is given that she drove the first 30 miles at an average speed of 60 miles per hour, so she drove the first 30 miles in $\frac{30}{60} = \frac{1}{2}$ hour. It is also given that she drove the remaining 20 miles at an average speed of 50 miles per hour, so she drove the remaining 20 miles in $\frac{20}{50} = \frac{2}{5}$ hours. Thus, she drove the 50 miles in a total of $\frac{1}{2} + \frac{2}{5} = \frac{9}{10}$ hours, and thus her average speed for the 50 miles can be determined; SUFFICIENT.

(2) It is given that she drove a total of 54 minutes, and thus her average speed for the 50 miles can be determined; SUFFICIENT.

The correct answer is D;
each statement alone is sufficient.

23. In Mr. Smith's class, what is the ratio of the number of boys to the number of girls?

(1) There are 3 times as many girls as boys in Mr. Smith's class.

(2) The number of boys is $\frac{1}{4}$ of the total number of boys and girls in Mr. Smith's class.

Algebra Ratio and proportion

Letting B be the number of boys and G be the number of girls, determine the value of $\frac{B}{G}$.

(1) It is given that $G = 3B$, so $\frac{1}{3} = \frac{B}{G}$; SUFFICIENT.

(2) It is given that $B = \frac{1}{4}(B + G)$. Therefore, $4B = B + G$, or $3B = G$, or $\frac{B}{G} = \frac{1}{3}$; SUFFICIENT.

The correct answer is D;
each statement alone is sufficient.

24. If the sequence S has 300 terms, what is the 293rd term of S?

(1) The 298th term of S is −616, and each term of S after the first is 2 less than the preceding term.

(2) The first term of S is −22.

Arithmetic Sequences and series

Determine the 293rd term of the sequence S, or S_{293}.

(1) It is given that the 298th term of S is −616, and each term of S after the first term is 2 less than the preceding term. Therefore, $S_{298} = -616 = S_{297} - 2$, and so $S_{297} = -616 + 2 = -614$. Similarly, S_{296}, S_{295}, S_{294}, and S_{293} can be determined, each from the term preceding it; SUFFICIENT.

(2) It is given that $S_1 = -22$, but there is no information on how subsequent terms are related to S_1 and therefore no way to determine S_{293}; NOT sufficient.

The correct answer is A;
statement 1 alone is sufficient.

25. On a certain date, Hannah invested $5,000 at x percent simple annual interest and a different amount at y percent simple annual interest. What amount did Hannah invest at y percent simple annual interest?

(1) The total amount of interest earned by Hannah's two investments in one year was $900.

(2) Hannah invested the $5,000 at 6 percent simple annual interest.

Algebra Applied problems

Let $A be the amount that Hannah invested at y percent. Determine the value of A.

(1) Given that the sum of $\frac{x}{100}($5,000)$ and $\frac{y}{100}($A)$ is $900, or $50x + \frac{Ay}{100} = 900$, it is clear that more than one value of A is possible; NOT sufficient.

(2)   Given that $x = 6$, it is clear that more than one value of A is possible; NOT sufficient.

(1) and (2) together are not sufficient because more than one value of A is possible such that $50(6) + \dfrac{Ay}{100} = 900$, or $Ay = 60{,}000$. For example, $A = 10{,}000$ and $y = 6$ is possible, and $A = 20{,}000$ and $y = 3$ is also possible.

**The correct answer is E;
both statements together are still not sufficient.**

26.   The profit from the sale of a certain appliance increases, though not proportionally, with the number of units sold. Did the profit exceed $4 million on sales of 380,000 units?

(1)   The profit exceeded $2 million on sales of 200,000 units.

(2)   The profit exceeded $5 million on sales of 350,000 units.

Arithmetic Arithmetic operations; Proportions

(1)   If the profits did increase proportionally, it might be reasonable to expect a profit of $4 million on sales of 400,000 units. However, it is given that the profits do not increase proportionally. Without knowing how the profits increase, it is impossible to tell the profits on sales of 380,000 units; NOT sufficient.

(2)   It is given that the profits do increase with the number of units sold. Therefore, since the profit on sales of just 350,000 units well exceeded $4 million, then sales of $350{,}000 + 30{,}000 = 380{,}000$ units would also have a profit exceeding $4 million; SUFFICIENT.

**The correct answer is B;
statement 2 alone is sufficient.**

27.   If n is an integer, is n even?

(1) $n^2 - 1$ is an odd integer.

(2) $3n + 4$ is an even integer.

Arithmetic Properties of numbers

Determine if the integer n is even.

(1)   Since $n^2 - 1$ is odd, n^2 is even and so n is even; SUFFICIENT.

(2)   Since $3n + 4$ is even, $3n$ is even and so n is even; SUFFICIENT.

**The correct answer is D;
each statement alone is sufficient.**

28.   Carmen currently works 30 hours per week at her part-time job. If her gross hourly wage were to increase by $1.50, how many fewer hours could she work per week and still earn the same gross weekly pay as before the increase?

(1)   Her gross weekly pay is currently $225.00.

(2)   An increase of $1.50 would represent an increase of 20 percent of her current gross hourly wage.

Arithmetic Operations with rational numbers

Let w be Carmen's gross hourly wage and let n be the number of hours fewer Carmen will need to work. Find a unique value for n such that $30w = (30 - n)(w + 1.50)$.

(1)   Since Carmen's gross weekly pay is currently $225.00, then $30w = 225$ and $w = 7.50$. Substituting 7.50 for w gives $30(7.50) = (30 - n)(7.50 + 1.50)$, which can be solved for a unique value of n; SUFFICIENT.

(2)   Since 1.50 is 20 percent of Carmen's current gross hourly pay, $1.50 = 0.20w$ and $w = 7.50$. This is the same information that was gained from statement (1) and will lead to the same result; SUFFICIENT.

**The correct answer is D;
each statement alone is sufficient.**

29.   If 90 students auditioned for the school musical, how many were accepted?

(1) $\dfrac{2}{3}$ of the boys and $\dfrac{1}{3}$ of the girls who auditioned were accepted.

(2)   26 of the boys who auditioned were accepted.

Arithmetic Ratio and proportion

Determine how many of the 90 students who auditioned for the school musical were accepted.

(1)   It is given that $\frac{2}{3}$ of the boys and $\frac{1}{3}$ of the girls who auditioned were accepted, but there is no information on how many of the 90 students were boys and how many were girls. If there were 60 boys and 30 girls, for example, then $\frac{2}{3}(60)+\frac{1}{3}(30)=40+10=50$ students were accepted. On the other hand, if there were 45 boys and 45 girls, then $\frac{2}{3}(45)+\frac{1}{3}(45)=30+15=45$ students were accepted; NOT sufficient.

(2)   It is given that 26 of the boys who auditioned were accepted, but there is no information on how many girls were accepted. For example, if 50 girls were accepted, then 26 + 50 = 76 students were accepted. On the other hand, if 20 girls were accepted, then 26 + 20 = 46 students were accepted; NOT sufficient.

Taking (1) and (2) together and letting B be the number of boys who auditioned and G be the number of girls who auditioned, it follows from (2) that $26=\frac{2}{3}B$, so $B=\frac{3}{2}(26)=39$ and $G=90-39=51$. Then, from (1), the number of students accepted is $\frac{2}{3}(39)+\frac{1}{3}(51)=26+17=43$.

**The correct answer is C;
both statements together are sufficient.**

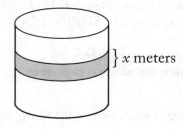

} x meters

30.   A circular tub has a band painted around its circumference, as shown above. What is the surface area of this painted band?

(1) $x = 0.5$
(2)   The height of the tub is 1 meter.

Geometry Surface area

The surface area of the band is the product of the circumference of the band and the width of the band. If both factors are known, then the area can be determined, but not if only one of these factors is known.

(1)   Only one factor, the width of the band, is known; NOT sufficient.

(2)   The circumference or the means to find the circumference is not known; NOT sufficient.

With (1) and (2) taken together, there still is no information about the circumference of the tub.

**The correct answer is E;
both statements together are still not sufficient.**

$$d = 0.43t7$$

31.   If t denotes the thousandths digit in the decimal representation of d above, what digit is t?

(1)   If d were rounded to the nearest hundredth, the result would be 0.44.
(2)   If d were rounded to the nearest thousandth, the result would be 0.436.

Arithmetic Place value; Rounding

Determine t, the thousandths digit of $d = 0.43t7$.

(1)   Since d rounded to the nearest hundredth is 0.44, t can be 5, 6, 7, 8, or 9 because each of 0.4357, 0.4367, 0.4377, 0.4387, and 0.4397 rounded to the nearest hundredth is 0.44; NOT sufficient.

(2)   Since d rounded to the nearest thousandth is 0.436 and the digit in ten-thousandths place of d is 7, the digit in thousandths place gets increased by 1 in the rounding process. Thus, $t+1=6$ and $t=5$; SUFFICIENT.

**The correct answer is B;
statement 2 alone is sufficient.**

32.   If A and B are positive integers, is the product AB even?

(1)   The sum $A + B$ is odd.
(2) A is even.

Arithmetic Properties of integers

Determine if the product of the positive integers A and B is even. This will be the case if at least one of A and B is even.

(1) Given that $A + B$ is odd, A and B cannot both be odd since the sum of two odd integers is even. Thus, at least one of A and B is even; SUFFICIENT.

(2) Given that A is even, at least one of A and B is even. The product of two even numbers is even, and the product of an even number and an odd number is even; SUFFICIENT.

**The correct answer is D;
each statement alone is sufficient.**

33. The weights of all dishes of type X are exactly the same, and the weights of all dishes of type Y are exactly the same. Is the weight of 1 dish of type X less than the weight of 1 dish of type Y ?

(1) The total weight of 3 dishes of type X and 2 dishes of type Y is less than the total weight of 2 dishes of type X and 4 dishes of type Y.

(2) The total weight of 4 dishes of type X and 3 dishes of type Y is less than the total weight of 3 dishes of type X and 4 dishes of type Y.

Algebra Inequalities

Let x be the weight of a type X dish and y be the weight of a type Y dish. Determine whether $x < y$.

(1) Given that $3x + 2y < 2x + 4y$, or $x < 2y$, it is possible that $x < y$ is true (for example, if $x = 2$ and $y = 3$) and it is possible that $x < y$ is false (for example, if $x = 3$ and $y = 2$); NOT sufficient.

(2) Given that $4x + 3y < 3x + 4y$, it follows that $x < y$; SUFFICIENT.

**The correct answer is B;
statement 2 alone is sufficient.**

34. A certain high school with a total enrollment of 900 students held a science fair for three days last week. How many of the students enrolled in the high school attended the science fair on all three days?

(1) Of the students enrolled in the school, 30 percent attended the science fair on two or more days.

(2) Of the students enrolled in the school, 10 percent of those that attended the science fair on at least one day attended on all three days.

Algebra Simultaneous equations

Let a, b, and c be the numbers of students who attended on exactly one day, exactly two days, and exactly three days, respectively, and let n be the number of students who did not attend on any of the three days. Given that $a + b + c + n = 900$, determine the value of c.

(1) Given that $(30\%)(900) = b + c$, or $b + c = 270$, more than one positive integer value for c is possible; NOT sufficient.

(2) Given that $(10\%)(a + b + c) = c$, or $a + b + c = 10c$, or $a + b = 9c$, more than one positive integer value for c is possible; NOT sufficient.

(1) and (2) together are not sufficient because more than one positive integer value for c is possible. Although there are 4 variables and only 3 linear equations involving these 4 variables, which implies there exist infinitely many *real number* solutions, the variables in the present problem are further restricted to be *positive integers*. However, specific values of c can be obtained using the equations:

  I. $a + b + c + n = 900$ (from the information in the question)

  II. $b + c = 270$ (from statement (1))

  III. $a + b = 9c$ (from statement (2))

  IV. $10c + n = 900$ (from combining I and III)

For example, if $n = 600$, then $c = 30$ from IV, $b = 240$ from II, and $a = 30$ from III. On the other hand, if $n = 500$, then $c = 40$ from IV, $b = 230$ from II, and $a = 130$ from III.

**The correct answer is E;
both statements together are still not sufficient.**

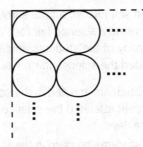

35. The inside of a rectangular carton is 48 centimeters long, 32 centimeters wide, and 15 centimeters high. The carton is filled to capacity with *k* identical cylindrical cans of fruit that stand upright in rows and columns, as indicated in the figure above. If the cans are 15 centimeters high, what is the value of *k* ?

    (1) Each of the cans has a radius of 4 centimeters.
    (2) Six of the cans fit exactly along the length of the carton.

Geometry Circles

(1) If the radius of each can is 4 centimeters, the diameter of each can is 8 centimeters. Along the 48-centimeter length of the carton, 6 cans $(48 \div 8)$ can be placed; along the 32-centimeter width of the carton, 4 cans $(32 \div 8)$ can be placed. Hence, $k = 6 \times 4 = 24$; SUFFICIENT.

(2) If 6 cans fit along the 48-centimeter length of the carton, this implies that the diameter of each can is 8 centimeters $(48 \div 6)$. Along the 32-centimeter width, 4 cans can be placed, and again $k = 6 \times 4 = 24$; SUFFICIENT.

The correct answer is D; each statement alone is sufficient.

$$\begin{cases} x - 4 = z \\ y - x = 8 \\ 8 - z = t \end{cases}$$

36. For the system of equations given, what is the value of *z* ?

    (1) $x = 7$
    (2) $t = 5$

Algebra First- and second-degree equations

(1) Since $x = 7$, then 7 can be substituted for x in the equation $x - 4 = z$, yielding $z = 3$; SUFFICIENT.

(2) If $t = 5$, then the equation $8 - z = t$ can be used to solve this question:

$8 - z = 5$	substitute for t
$3 - z = 0$	subtract 5 from both sides
$3 = z$	add z to both sides; SUFFICIENT.

The correct answer is D; each statement alone is sufficient.

37. The average (arithmetic mean) price of the 3 items that Kate purchased from a clothing store was $50. If there was no sales tax on any item that had a price of less than $80 and 6 percent sales tax on all other items, what was the total sales tax on the 3 items that Kate purchased?

    (1) The price of the most expensive item that Kate purchased from the store was $100.
    (2) The price of the least expensive item that Kate purchased from the store was $10.

Arithmetic Applied problems; Percents

Kate purchased 3 items, the average price of which was $50, and paid 6% sales tax on each item priced over $80. Determine the total sales tax that Kate paid.

Given that the average of the 3 prices is $50, it follows that the sum of the 3 prices is $(3)(\$50) = \$150$.

(1) One of the prices is $100. Therefore, the sum of the 2 remaining prices is $150 − $100 = $50. Hence, each of the remaining items has a price that is less than $80 and thus is not taxed. It follows that the total sales tax on the 3 items is the sales tax on the $100 item, which equals $(6\%)(\$100) = \$6$; SUFFICIENT.

(2) One of the prices is $10. Therefore, the sum of the 2 remaining prices is $150 − $10 = $140. If the 2 remaining prices are $70 and $70, then none of the items has

a price greater than $80, and hence the total sales tax on the 3 items is $0. If the 2 remaining prices are $40 and $100, then the total sales tax on the 3 items is (6%)($100) = $6; NOT sufficient.

This solution assumes tax is not included in the quoted prices. If tax were included in the quoted prices, then some minor adjustments in the numerical examples would be needed. However, the sufficiency of (1) and insufficiency of (2) would not be affected.

The correct answer is A; statement 1 alone is sufficient.

38. A scientist recorded the number of eggs in each of 10 birds' nests. What was the standard deviation of the numbers of eggs in the 10 nests?

    (1) The average (arithmetic mean) number of eggs for the 10 nests was 4.
    (2) Each of the 10 nests contained the same number of eggs.

Arithmetic Statistics

Note that if all the values in a data set are equal to the same number, say x, then the average of the data set is x, the difference between each data value and the average is $x - x = 0$, the sum of the squares of these differences is 0, and so the standard deviation is 0. On the other hand, if the values in a data set are not all equal to the same number, then the standard deviation will be positive.

    (1) If each of the 10 nests had 4 eggs, then the average would be 4 and the standard deviation would be 0. If 8 nests had 4 eggs, 1 nest had 3 eggs, and 1 nest had 5 eggs, then the average would be 4 and the standard deviation would be positive; NOT sufficient.

    (2) Since all of the data values are equal to the same number, the standard deviation is 0; SUFFICIENT.

The correct answer is B; statement 2 alone is sufficient.

39. Terry holds 12 cards, each of which is red, white, green, or blue. If a person is to select a card randomly from the cards Terry is holding, is the probability less than $\frac{1}{2}$ that the card selected will be either red or white?

    (1) The probability that the person will select a blue card is $\frac{1}{3}$.
    (2) The probability that the person will select a red card is $\frac{1}{6}$.

Arithmetic Probability

Determine if the probability is less than $\frac{1}{2}$ that a card selected at random from 12 cards, each of which is red, white, green, or blue, will be either red or white. That is, determine whether the number of cards that are red or white is less than $\frac{1}{2}(12) = 6$.

    (1) It is given that the probability is $\frac{1}{3}$ that the selected card will be blue. This means that $\frac{1}{3}(12) = 4$ of the cards are blue. However, there is no information about how many of the 8 remaining cards are red, how many are white, or how many are green. If, for example, there are 2 red cards, 2 white cards, and 4 green cards, then the number of cards that are red or white is 2 + 2 = 4, which is less than 6. On the other hand, if there are 3 red cards, 4 white cards, and 1 green card, then the number of cards that are red or white is 3 + 4 = 7, which is not less than 6; NOT sufficient.

    (2) It is given that the probability is $\frac{1}{6}$ that the selected card will be red. This means that $\frac{1}{6}(12) = 2$ of the cards are red. However, there is no information about how many of the 10 remaining cards are white, how many are blue, or how many are green. If, for example, there are 3 white cards, 5 blue cards, and 2 green cards, then the number of cards that are red or white is 2 + 3 = 5, which is less than 6. On the other hand, if there are 7 white cards, 1 blue card, and 2 green cards, then the number of cards that are red or white is 2 + 7 = 9, which is not less than 6; NOT sufficient.

Taking (1) and (2) together, there are 4 blue cards and 2 red cards. However, there is no information about how many of the 6 remaining cards are white or how many are green. If, for example, there are 3 white cards and 3 green cards, then the number of cards that are red or white is $2 + 3 = 5$, which is less than 6. On the other hand, if there are 5 white cards and 1 green card, then the number of cards that are red or white is $2 + 5 = 7$, which is not less than 6; NOT sufficient.

**The correct answer is E;
both statements together are still not sufficient.**

40. The selling price of an article is equal to the cost of the article plus the markup. The markup on a certain television set is what percent of the selling price?

    (1) The markup on the television set is 25 percent of the cost.
    (2) The selling price of the television set is $250.

    Algebra Percents

    Let S be the selling price of the television; C, the cost; and M, the markup, all in dollars. Then, $S = C + M$. Find the value of $\frac{M}{S}$ as a percent.

    (1) Since the markup on the television is 25 percent of the cost, $M = 0.25C$. Then, $S = C + 0.25C = 1.25C$ and $\frac{M}{S} = \frac{0.25C}{1.25C} = 0.20$, which, as a percent is 20 percent; SUFFICIENT.

    (2) The selling price of the television is $250, so $250 = S = C + M$. However, there is no information as to the values of either C or M. Therefore, it is impossible to determine the value of $\frac{M}{S}$. For example, if $C = 200$ and $M = 50$, then $\frac{M}{S} = 0.20$ or 20 percent, but if $C = 150$ and $M = 100$, then $\frac{M}{S} = 0.40$ or 40 percent; NOT sufficient.

    **The correct answer is A;
    statement 1 alone is sufficient.**

41. Is $4^{x+y} = 8^{10}$?

    (1) $x - y = 9$
    (2) $\frac{y}{x} = \frac{1}{4}$

    Algebra Properties of numbers

    The question is equivalent to determining whether $(2^2)^{x+y} = (2^3)^{10}$, which in turn is equivalent to determining whether $2^{2(x+y)} = 2^{30}$, which in turn is equivalent to determining whether $2(x + y) = 30$, or $x + y = 15$.

    (1) Given that $x - y = 9$, it is possible that $x + y = 15$ (for example, $x = 12$ and $y = 3$) and it is possible that $x + y \neq 15$ (for example, $x = 10$ and $y = 1$); NOT sufficient.

    (2) Given that $\frac{y}{x} = \frac{1}{4}$, or $x = 4y$, it is possible that $x + y = 15$ (for example, $x = 12$ and $y = 3$) and it is possible that $x + y \neq 15$ (for example, $x = 4$ and $y = 1$); NOT sufficient.

    Given (1) and (2) together, $x - y = 9$ and $x = 4y$, it follows that $4y - y = 9$, or $y = 3$, and $x = 4y = 4(3) = 12$. Therefore, $x + y = 12 + 3 = 15$.

    **The correct answer is C;
    both statements together are sufficient.**

42. Can a certain rectangular sheet of glass be positioned on a rectangular tabletop so that it covers the entire tabletop and its edges are parallel to the edges of the tabletop?

    (1) The tabletop is 36 inches wide by 60 inches long.
    (2) The area of one side of the sheet of glass is 2,400 square inches.

    Geometry Area

    Determine whether the length and width of the sheet of glass are greater than or equal to the length and width of the tabletop.

    (1) The length and width of the tabletop are given, but nothing can be determined about the dimensions of the sheet of glass; NOT sufficient.

(2) The area of the sheet of glass is given, but nothing can be determined about the dimensions of the tabletop; NOT sufficient.

(1) and (2) together are not sufficient because the information given does not specify the length and width of the sheet of glass. For example, the length and width of the sheet of glass could be 40 inches and 60 inches and, since $40 \geq 36$ and $60 \geq 60$, the answer to the question would be "Yes." On the other hand, the length and width of the sheet of glass could be 100 inches and 24 inches, and in this case the answer to the question would be "No" because 24 is not greater than or equal to 36 or 60.

**The correct answer is E;
both statements together are still not sufficient.**

43. If p_1 and p_2 are the populations and r_1 and r_2 are the numbers of representatives of District 1 and District 2, respectively, the ratio of the population to the number of representatives is greater for which of the two districts?

(1) $p_1 > p_2$

(2) $r_2 > r_1$

Algebra Ratios

Determine which ratio, $\dfrac{p_1}{r_1}$ or $\dfrac{p_2}{r_2}$, is greater.

(1) Even if $p_1 > p_2$, which ratio, $\dfrac{p_1}{r_1}$ or $\dfrac{p_2}{r_2}$, is greater depends on the values of r_1 and r_2. For example, if $p_1 = 1{,}000$, $p_2 = 500$, then $p_1 > p_2$. If $r_1 = 5$ and $r_2 = 2$, $\dfrac{p_1}{r_1} = \dfrac{1{,}000}{5} = 200$ and $\dfrac{p_2}{r_2} = \dfrac{500}{2} = 250$, so $\dfrac{p_2}{r_2} > \dfrac{p_1}{r_1}$. If however, $r_1 = 2$ and $r_2 = 5$, $\dfrac{p_1}{r_1} = \dfrac{1{,}000}{2} = 500$ and $\dfrac{p_2}{r_2} = \dfrac{500}{5} = 100$, so $\dfrac{p_1}{r_1} > \dfrac{p_2}{r_2}$; NOT sufficient.

(2) Even if $r_2 > r_1$, which ratio, $\dfrac{p_1}{r_1}$ or $\dfrac{p_2}{r_2}$, is greater depends on the values of p_1 and p_2. For example, if $r_1 = 2$, $r_2 = 5$, then $r_2 > r_1$. If $p_1 = 1{,}000$ and $p_2 = 500$, $\dfrac{p_1}{r_1} = \dfrac{1{,}000}{2} = 500$ and $\dfrac{p_2}{r_2} = \dfrac{500}{5} = 100$, so $\dfrac{p_1}{r_1} > \dfrac{p_2}{r_2}$. If,

however, $p_1 = 100$ and $p_2 = 1{,}000$, $\dfrac{p_1}{r_1} = \dfrac{100}{2} = 50$ and $\dfrac{p_2}{r_2} = \dfrac{1{,}000}{5} = 200$, so $\dfrac{p_2}{r_2} > \dfrac{p_1}{r_1}$; NOT sufficient.

Taking (1) and (2) together, $\dfrac{1}{r_2} < \dfrac{1}{r_1}$ because $r_2 > r_1$, and because populations can be assumed to be positive, $\dfrac{p_2}{r_2} < \dfrac{p_2}{r_1}$. Then, it follows that $\dfrac{p_2}{r_1} < \dfrac{p_1}{r_1}$ because $p_2 < p_1$. Combining $\dfrac{p_2}{r_2} < \dfrac{p_2}{r_1}$ and $\dfrac{p_2}{r_1} < \dfrac{p_1}{r_1}$ gives $\dfrac{p_2}{r_2} < \dfrac{p_1}{r_1}$.

**The correct answer is C;
both statements together are sufficient.**

44. In a random sample of 80 adults, how many are college graduates?

(1) In the sample, the number of adults who are <u>not</u> college graduates is 3 times the number who are college graduates.

(2) In the sample, the number of adults who are <u>not</u> college graduates is 40 more than the number who are college graduates.

Algebra First-degree equations

Let C be the number of college graduates and let N be the number who are not college graduates. Then, $C + N = 80$. Find the value of C.

(1) Since the number who are not college graduates is 3 times the number who are, $N = 3C$. Then $C + 3C = 80$, $4C = 80$, and $C = 20$; SUFFICIENT.

(2) Since the number who are not college graduates is 40 more than the number who are college graduates, $N = C + 40$. Then $C + (C + 40) = 80$, $2C + 40 = 80$, $2C = 40$, and $C = 20$; SUFFICIENT.

**The correct answer is D;
each statement alone is sufficient.**

	R	S	T	U
R	0	y	x	62
S	y	0	56	75
T	x	56	0	69
U	62	75	69	0

45. The table above shows the distance, in kilometers, by the most direct route, between any two of the four cities, R, S, T, and U. For example, the distance between City R and City U is 62 kilometers. What is the value of x ?

    (1) By the most direct route, the distance between S and T is twice the distance between S and R.

    (2) By the most direct route, the distance between T and U is 1.5 times the distance between R and T.

Arithmetic; Algebra Tables; First-degree equations

The value of x is the distance between City R and City T; the value of y is the distance between City R and City S.

(1) From this, it can be determined only that $56 = 2y$. No information is given about x; NOT sufficient.

(2) This statement yields the equation $1.5x = 69$, which be solved for x; SUFFICIENT.

The correct answer is B; statement 2 alone is sufficient.

46. What is the tenths digit in the decimal representation of a certain number?

    (1) The number is less than $\frac{1}{3}$.
    (2) The number is greater than $\frac{1}{4}$.

Arithmetic Properties of numbers

(1) Since the number is less than $\frac{1}{3}$, the tenths digit can be 0, 1, 2, or 3; NOT sufficient.

(2) Since the number is greater than $\frac{1}{4}$, the tenths digit can be 2, 3, 4, …, 9; NOT sufficient.

From (1) and (2) taken together, the number, n, is greater than $\frac{1}{4}$ but less than $\frac{1}{3}$. The tenths digit can be 2 or 3.

The correct answer is E; both statements together are still not sufficient.

47. Robots X, Y, and Z each assemble components at their respective constant rates. If r_x is the ratio of Robot X's constant rate to Robot Z's constant rate and r_y is the ratio of Robot Y's constant rate to Robot Z's constant rate, is Robot Z's constant rate the greatest of the three?

    (1) $r_x < r_y$
    (2) $r_y < 1$

Algebra Ratios

Let X, Y, and Z represent the constant rates of Robots X, Y, and Z, respectively. Then $r_x = \frac{X}{Z}$ and $r_y = \frac{Y}{Z}$. Determine if Z is the greatest of X, Y, and Z.

(1) Since $r_x < r_y$, then $\frac{X}{Z} < \frac{Y}{Z}$ and $X < Y$. However, no information is given about the value of Z in relation to the values of X and Y; NOT sufficient.

(2) Since $r_y < 1$, then $\frac{Y}{Z} < 1$ and $Y < Z$. However, no information is given about the value of X in relation to the values of Y and Z; NOT sufficient.

Taking (1) and (2) together, $X < Y$ from (1) and $Y < Z$ from (2), so $X < Z$. Thus, Z is greater than both X and Y and is the greatest of the three.

The correct answer is C; both statements together are sufficient.

48. If $a < x < b$ and $c < y < d$, is $x < y$?

    (1) $a < c$
    (2) $b < c$

Algebra Inequalities

Given $a < x < b$ and $c < y < d$, determine if $x < y$.

(1) Even though $a < c$, there is no information on the relative size of x and c. For example, if $a = 3$, $x = 10$, $b = 12$, $c = 4$, $y = 6$, and $d = 7$, $a < c$ because $3 < 4$ and $x > y$, since $10 > 6$. If, on the other hand, $a = 3$, $x = 4$, $b = 12$, $c = 4$, $y = 6$, and $d = 7$, $a < c$ because $3 < 4$ and $x < y$, since $4 < 6$. NOT sufficient.

(2) If $b < c$, then $a < x < b < c < y < d$ and so $x < y$; SUFFICIENT.

**The correct answer is B;
statement 2 alone is sufficient.**

49. How many people are directors of both Company K and Company R?

(1) There were 17 directors present at a joint meeting of the directors of Company K and Company R, and no directors were absent.

(2) Company K has 12 directors and Company R has 8 directors.

Algebra Sets

(1) This clarifies that Company K and Company R together have 17 individuals serving as directors. However, there is no information as to the distribution of the Company K directors, the Company R directors, and the joint directors; NOT sufficient.

(2) This gives the number of directors in each company but no information as to the number of joint directors; NOT sufficient.

Taking (1) and (2) together, it is known from (2) that there are 20 directorships in all. If at a joint meeting, there are only 17 people present, then $20 - 17 = 3$ people must be joint directors.

**The correct answer is C;
both statements together are sufficient.**

50. If x and y are positive, is $\frac{x}{y}$ greater than 1?

(1) $xy > 1$

(2) $x - y > 0$

Algebra Inequalities

Since, being positive, $y > 0$, it follows that $\frac{x}{y} > 1$ if and only if $x > y$.

(1) There are innumerable pairs of different numbers x and y whose product xy is greater than 1. The larger number in each pair can be either x or y; NOT sufficient.

(2) $x - y > 0$ is equivalent to $x > y$; SUFFICIENT.

**The correct answer is B;
statement 2 alone is sufficient.**

51. A clothing store acquired an item at a cost of x dollars and sold the item for y dollars. The store's gross profit from the item was what percent of its cost for the item?

(1) $y - x = 20$

(2) $\frac{y}{x} = \frac{5}{4}$

Algebra Applied problems

If the cost of an item of clothing is x and the selling price of the item is y, determine the value of $\frac{y - x}{x}$ as a percent.

(1) Although $y - x = 20$, there is no information to determine the value of x and therefore no way to determine the value of $\frac{y - x}{x}$; NOT sufficient.

(2) Since $\frac{y}{x} = \frac{5}{4}$, $y = \frac{5}{4}x$ and so $\frac{y - x}{x} =$ $\frac{\frac{5}{4}x - x}{x} = \frac{\frac{1}{4}x}{x} = \frac{1}{4}$, which is 25 percent; SUFFICIENT.

**The correct answer is B;
statement 2 alone is sufficient.**

52. If x and y are positive, is $x < 10 < y$?

(1) $x < y$ and $xy = 100$

(2) $x^2 < 100 < y^2$

Algebra Inequalities

(1) Given that $x < y$, multiply both sides by x, which is positive, to get $x^2 < xy$. Then, since

$xy = 100$, it follows that $x^2 < 100$. Similarly, multiply both sides of $x < y$ by y, which is positive, to get $xy < y^2$. Again, since $xy = 100$, it follows that $100 < y^2$. Combining $x^2 < 100$ and $100 < y^2$ gives $x^2 < 100 < y^2$, from which it follows that $\sqrt{x^2} < \sqrt{100} < \sqrt{y^2}$ and, therefore, $x < 10 < y$, since x and y are both positive; SUFFICIENT.

(2)   Given that $x^2 < 100 < y^2$, it follows that $x < 10 < y$ as shown in (1) above; SUFFICIENT.

The correct answer is D; each statement alone is sufficient.

53.   If x is an integer, is $9^x + 9^{-x} = b$?

(1) $3^x + 3^{-x} = \sqrt{b+2}$

(2) $x > 0$

Algebra Exponents

When solving this problem it is helpful to note that $(x^r)(x^{-s}) = x^{r-s}$ and that $(x^r)^2 = x^{2r}$. Note also that $x^0 = 1$.

(1)   From this, $3^x + 3^{-x} = \sqrt{b+2}$. Squaring both sides gives:

$$(3^x + 3^{-x})^2 = b+2$$
$$3^{2x} + 2(3^x \times 3^{-x}) + 3^{-2x} = b+2$$
$$9^x + 2(3^0) + 9^{-x} = b+2 \quad \text{property of exponents}$$
$$9^x + 2 + 9^{-x} = b+2 \quad \text{property of exponents}$$
$$9^x + 9^{-x} = b \quad \text{subtract 2 from both sides; SUFFICIENT.}$$

(2)   This gives no information about the relationship between x and b; NOT sufficient.

The correct answer is A; statement 1 alone is sufficient.

54.   A taxi company charges f cents for the first mile of the taxi ride and m cents for each additional mile. How much does the company charge for a 10-mile taxi ride?

(1)   The company charges $0.90 for a 2-mile ride.

(2)   The company charges $1.20 for a 4-mile ride.

Arithmetic Applied problems

If a taxi company charges f cents for the first mile and m cents for each additional mile, determine the charge for a 10-mile taxi ride, which can be expressed as $f + 9m$.

(1)   Since the charge for a 2-mile ride is $0.90, $f + m = 0.90$, and so $f + 9m = 0.90 + 8m$, but the value of m is unknown; NOT sufficient.

(2)   Since the charge for a 4-mile ride is $1.20, $f + 3m = 1.20$, and so $f + 9m = 1.20 + 6m$, but the value of m is unknown; NOT sufficient.

Taking (1) and (2) together and subtracting the equation in (1) from the equation in (2) gives $2m = 0.30$ from which $m = 0.15$. Then from (1), $f + 0.15 = 0.90$ and $f = 0.75$. Therefore, the charge for a 10-mile taxi ride is $0.75 + 9($0.15) = 2.10.

Alternatively, the graphs of $f + m = 0.90$ and $f + 3m = 1.20$ in the (f, m) coordinate plane are lines that intersect at exactly one point, and therefore values of f and m can be determined, from which $f + 9m$ can then be determined.

The correct answer is C; both statements together are sufficient.

55.   Guy's net income equals his gross income minus his deductions. By what percent did Guy's net income change on January 1, 1989, when both his gross income and his deductions increased?

(1)   Guy's gross income increased by 4 percent on January 1, 1989.

(2)   Guy's deductions increased by 15 percent on January 1, 1989.

Arithmetic Percents

Let g_b represent Guy's gross income and d_b Guy's deductions before January 1, 1989. Let g_a represent Guy's gross income and d_a Guy's deductions after January 1, 1989. Determine by what percent Guy's net income (gross income minus deductions) changed on January 1, 1989, when both his gross income and his deductions increased, or find $\dfrac{(g_a - d_a) - (g_b - d_b)}{g_b - d_b}$ as a percent.

(1)　Guy's gross income increased by 4 percent on January 1, 1989, so $g_a = 1.04 g_b$. Then,

$$\frac{(g_a - d_a) - (g_b - d_b)}{g_b - d_b} = \frac{(1.04 g_b - d_a) - (g_b - d_b)}{g_b - d_b}.$$

However, no information is given about the values of g_b, d_a, or d_b, and so

$$\frac{(g_a - d_a) - (g_b - d_b)}{g_b - d_b}$$ cannot be determined; NOT sufficient.

(2)　Guy's deductions increased by 15 percent on January 1, 1989, so $d_a = 1.15 d_b$.

Then, $$\frac{(g_a - d_a) - (g_b - d_b)}{g_b - d_b} =$$

$$\frac{(g_a - 1.15 d_b) - (g_b - d_b)}{g_b - d_b}.$$ However, no

information is given about the values of g_a, g_b, or d_b, and so $$\frac{(g_a - d_a) - (g_b - d_b)}{g_b - d_b}$$ cannot be determined; NOT sufficient.

Taking (1) and (2) together gives

$$\frac{(1.04 g_b - 1.15 d_b) - (g_b - d_b)}{g_b - d_b} = \frac{0.04 g_b - 0.15 d_b}{g_b - d_b},$$

which cannot be determined since the values of g_b and d_b are unknown.

**The correct answer is E;
both statements together are still not sufficient.**

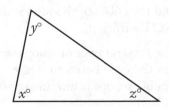

56.　What is the value of z in the triangle above?

(1)　$x + y = 139$
(2)　$y + z = 108$

Geometry Triangles

In any triangle the sum of the interior angles is $180°$; here, $x + y + z = 180$.

(1)　Since the sum of $x + y$ is known, the value of z can be determined by substituting 139 for $x + y$ in $x + y + z = 180$; SUFFICIENT.

(2)　Since the sum of $y + z$ is known, the value of x can be determined by substitution, but there is no way to determine the value of z in the sum $y + z$; NOT sufficient.

**The correct answer is A;
statement 1 alone is sufficient.**

57.　Each gift certificate sold yesterday by a certain bookstore cost either $10 or $50. If yesterday the bookstore sold more than 5 gift certificates that cost $50 each, what was the total number of gift certificates sold yesterday by the bookstore?

(1)　Yesterday the bookstore sold fewer than 10 gift certificates that cost $10 each.

(2)　The total cost of gift certificates sold yesterday by the bookstore was $460.

Arithmetic Computation with integers

Let x be the number of $10 gift certificates sold yesterday and let y be the number of $50 gift certificates sold yesterday. It is given that $y > 5$. Determine the value of $x + y$.

(1)　It is given that $x < 10$, so x could be 0, 1, 2, 3, ..., 9. Since $y > 5$, y could be 6, 7, 8, ..., and then $x + y$ could be, for example, $0 + 6 = 6$ or $2 + 8 = 10$; NOT sufficient.

(2)　It is given that $10x + 50y = 460$. Several values of x and y with $y > 5$ will satisfy this equation and give different values for $x + y$, as shown below; NOT sufficient.

x	y	$10x + 50y$	$x + y$
16	6	460	22
11	7	460	18
6	8	460	14
1	9	460	10

Taking (1) and (2) together, it can be seen from the table that all the requirements are satisfied by $x = 6$ and $y = 8$ and also by $x = 1$ and $y = 9$, but the value of $x + y$ is not uniquely determined; NOT sufficient.

**The correct answer is E;
both statements together are still not sufficient.**

58. What is the tens digit of positive integer x?

    (1) x divided by 100 has a remainder of 30.
    (2) x divided by 110 has a remainder of 30.

    Arithmetic Properties of numbers

    (1) Having a remainder of 30 when x is divided by 100 can only happen if x has a tens digit of 3 and a ones digit of 0, as in 130, 230, 630, and so forth; SUFFICIENT.

    (2) When 140 is divided by 110, the quotient is 1 R30. However, 250 divided by 110 yields a quotient of 2 R30, and 360 divided by 110 gives a quotient of 3 R30. Since there is no consistency in the tens digit, more information is needed; NOT sufficient.

    **The correct answer is A;
    statement 1 alone is sufficient.**

59. Max has $125 consisting of bills each worth either $5 or $20. How many bills worth $5 does Max have?

    (1) Max has fewer than 5 bills worth $5 each.
    (2) Max has more than 5 bills worth $20 each.

    Arithmetic Operations with integers

    Let the integer x be the number of bills worth $5 each and let the integer y be the number of bills worth $20 each. Then $5x + 20y = 125$. Determine the value of x.

    (1) Given that $x < 5$, then $x = 0, 1, 2, 3,$ or 4. If x is even, then $5x + 20y$ is even and therefore cannot equal 125. If $x = 3$, then $15 + 20y = 125$, from which it follows that $20y = 110$. But, $\frac{110}{20}$ is not an integer and $x \neq 3$. Thus, $x = 1$; SUFFICIENT.

    (2) Given that $y > 5$, then $y \geq 6$. If $y \geq 7$, then $20y \geq 140$ and so $5x + 20y \neq 125$. Therefore, $y = 6$ and $5x + 20(6) = 125$, so $x = 1$; SUFFICIENT.

    **The correct answer is D;
    each statement alone is sufficient.**

60. What is the value of n in the equation $-25 + 19 + n = s$?

    (1) $s = 2$
    (2) $\frac{n}{s} = 4$

    Algebra First- and second-degree equations

    (1) If $s = 2$, then the equation becomes $-25 + 19 + n = 2$ or $-6 + n = 2$ or $n = 8$; SUFFICIENT.

    (2) If $\frac{n}{s} = 4$, then $n = 4s$. By substituting this value of n in the given equation and simplifying, the equation becomes: $-25 + 19 + 4s = s$ or $-6 + 3s = 0$ or $s = 2$. Once s is found to be 2, the original equation can be solved as above; SUFFICIENT.

    **The correct answer is D;
    each statement alone is sufficient.**

61. At a certain picnic, each of the guests was served either a single scoop or a double scoop of ice cream. How many of the guests were served a double scoop of ice cream?

    (1) At the picnic, 60 percent of the guests were served a double scoop of ice cream.
    (2) A total of 120 scoops of ice cream were served to all the guests at the picnic.

    Arithmetic Percents

    (1) The total number of guests is unknown, and thus 60% of the total is also unknown; NOT sufficient.

    (2) The total number of scoops served is known, but the ratio between single scoops and double scoops is unknown; NOT sufficient.

    Using both statements, the ratio of the number of single scoops served to the number of double scoops served can be determined (1) and used with the total number of scoops served (2) to determine the total number of guests who were served a double scoop.

    **The correct answer is C;
    both statements together are sufficient.**

62. Stores L and M each sell a certain product at a different regular price. If both stores discount their regular price of the product, is the discount price at Store M less than the discount price at Store L ?

    (1) At Store L the discount price is 10 percent less than the regular price; at Store M the discount price is 15 percent less than the regular price.

    (2) At Store L the discount price is $5 less than the regular store price; at Store M the discount price is $6 less than the regular price.

Arithmetic Percents

Let L_r and L_d be the regular and discounted prices, respectively, at Store L, and let M_r and M_d be the regular and discounted prices, respectively, at Store M. Determine if $M_d < L_d$.

(1) Knowing that $L_d = (1 - 0.10)L_r = 0.90L_r$ and that $M_d = (1 - 0.15)M_r = 0.85M_r$ gives no information for comparing M_d and L_d; NOT sufficient.

(2) Knowing that $L_d = L_r - 5$ and that $M_d = M_r - 6$ gives no information for comparing M_d and L_d; NOT sufficient.

Taking (1) and (2) together gives $0.90L_r = L_r - 5$ and $0.85M_r = M_r - 6$, from which it follows that $0.10L_r = 5$ or $L_r = 50$ and $0.15M_r = 6$ or $M_r = 40$. Then $L_d = 50 - 5 = 45$ and $M_d = 40 - 6 = 34$. Therefore, $M_d < L_d$.

**The correct answer is C;
both statements together are sufficient.**

63. If d denotes a decimal, is $d \geq 0.5$?

    (1) When d is rounded to the nearest tenth, the result is 0.5.

    (2) When d is rounded to the nearest integer, the result is 1.

Arithmetic Rounding; Estimating

(1) In this case, for example, the value of d could range from the decimal 0.45 to 0.54. Some of these, such as 0.51 or 0.52, are greater than or equal to 0.5, and others, such as 0.47 or 0.48, are less than 0.5; NOT sufficient.

(2) When the result of rounding d to the nearest integer is 1, d could range in value from the decimal 0.50 to 1.49, which are greater than or equal to 0.5; SUFFICIENT.

**The correct answer is B;
statement 2 alone is sufficient.**

64. How many integers are there between, but not including, integers r and s ?

    (1) $s - r = 10$
    (2) There are 9 integers between, but not including, $r + 1$ and $s + 1$.

Arithmetic Properties of numbers

(1) Although the difference between s and r is 10, there are not 10 integers between them. For example, if s is 24 and r is 14, their difference is 10, but there are only 9 integers between them: 15, 16, 17, 18, 19, 20, 21, 22, and 23. This holds true for any two integers whose difference is 10; SUFFICIENT.

(2) Since r and s are the same distance apart as $r + 1$ and $s + 1$, there would still be 9 integers between r and s in this case, although the integers themselves would change; SUFFICIENT.

**The correct answer is D;
each statement alone is sufficient.**

65. What is the total number of coins that Bert and Claire have?

    (1) Bert has 50 percent more coins than Claire.
    (2) The total number of coins that Bert and Claire have is between 21 and 28.

Arithmetic Computation with integers

Determine the total number of coins Bert and Claire have. If B represents the number of coins that Bert has and C represents the number of coins that Claire has, determine $B + C$.

(1) Bert has 50% more coins than Claire, so $B = 1.5C$, and $B + C = 1.5C + C = 2.5C$, but the value of C can vary; NOT sufficient.

(2)   The total number of coins Bert and Claire have is between 21 and 28, so $21 < B + C < 28$ and, therefore, $B + C$ could be 22, 23, 24, 25, 26, or 27; NOT sufficient.

Taking (1) and (2) together, $21 < 2.5C < 28$ and then $\frac{21}{2.5} < C < \frac{28}{2.5}$ or $8.4 < C < 11.2$. If $C = 9$, then $B = (1.5)(9) = 13.5$; if $C = 10$, then $B = (1.5)(10) = 15$; and if $C = 11$, then $B = (1.5)(11) = 16.5$. Since B represents a number of coins, B is an integer. Therefore, $B = 15$, $C = 10$, and $B + C = 25$.

The correct answer is C; both statements together are sufficient.

66.   In a survey of 200 college graduates, 30 percent said they had received student loans during their college careers, and 40 percent said they had received scholarships. What percent of those surveyed said that they had received neither student loans nor scholarships during their college careers?

(1)   25 percent of those surveyed said that they had received scholarships but no loans.

(2)   50 percent of those surveyed who said that they had received loans also said that they had received scholarships.

Arithmetic Sets

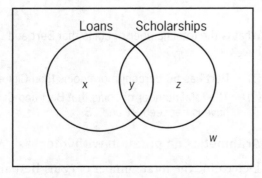

Using the variables shown on the Venn diagram above, determine the value of w. According to the information given, 30 percent had received student loans, so $x + y = 0.3(200) = 60$ and $x = 60 - y$. Also, 40 percent had received scholarships, so $y + z = 0.4(200) = 80$ and $z = 80 - y$. Then, since $x + y + z + w = 200$, $w = 200 - x - y - z = 200 - (60 - y) - y - (80 - y) =$

$60 + y$. Thus, if the value of y can be determined, then the value of w can be determined.

(1)   Since 25 percent received scholarships but no loans, $z = 80 - y = 0.25(200) = 50$ and $y = 30$; SUFFICIENT.

(2)   Since 50 percent of those who had received loans had also received scholarships, $0.5(x + y) = y$ and so $0.5(60) = 30 = y$; SUFFICIENT.

The correct answer is D; each statement alone is sufficient.

67.   What is the value of integer n?

(1) $n(n + 1) = 6$
(2) $2^{2n} = 16$

Arithmetic; Algebra Arithmetic operations; First- and second-degree equations

(1)   If $(n + 1)$ is multiplied by n, the result is $n^2 + n = 6$. If 6 is subtracted from both sides, the equation becomes $n^2 + n - 6 = 0$. This in turn can be factored as $(n + 3)(n - 2) = 0$. Therefore, n could be either -3 or 2, but there is no further information for deciding between these two values; NOT sufficient.

(2)   From $2^{2n} = 16$, 2^{2n} must equal 2^4 (since $2 \times 2 \times 2 \times 2 = 16$). Therefore, $2n = 4$ and $n = 2$; SUFFICIENT.

The correct answer is B; statement 2 alone is sufficient.

68.   Three machines, K, M, and P, working simultaneously and independently at their respective constant rates, can complete a certain task in 24 minutes. How long does it take Machine K, working alone at its constant rate, to complete the task?

(1)   Machines M and P, working simultaneously and independently at their respective constant rates, can complete the task in 36 minutes.

(2)   Machines K and P, working simultaneously and independently at their respective constant rates, can complete the task in 48 minutes.

Algebra Applied problems

Let k, m, and p be the numbers of minutes machines K, M, and P take, respectively, to complete the task. Then, Machine K can do $\frac{1}{k}$ of the task in 1 minute, Machine M can do $\frac{1}{m}$ of the task in 1 minute, and Machine P can do $\frac{1}{p}$ of the task in 1 minute. If all three machines working together can do the task in 24 minutes, then they can do $\frac{1}{24}$ of the task in 1 minute. So, $\frac{1}{k}+\frac{1}{m}+\frac{1}{p}=\frac{1}{24}$ and $\frac{1}{k}=\frac{1}{24}-\left(\frac{1}{m}+\frac{1}{p}\right)$. Determine k.

(1) Since M and P together can do the task in 36 minutes, they can do $\frac{1}{36}$ in 1 minute, and so $\frac{1}{m}+\frac{1}{p}=\frac{1}{36}$. Then $\frac{1}{k}=\frac{1}{24}-\frac{1}{36}$, which can be solved for a unique value of k; SUFFICIENT.

(2) Since K and P together can do the task in 48 minutes, they can do $\frac{1}{48}$ in 1 minute, and so $\frac{1}{k}+\frac{1}{p}=\frac{1}{48}$. From this information, there is no way to uniquely determine $\frac{1}{k}$ and therefore no way to uniquely determine k. For example, if $p=96$, then $\frac{1}{k}+\frac{1}{p}=\frac{1}{k}+\frac{1}{96}=\frac{1}{48}$ and $k=96$. On the other hand, if $p=60$, then $\frac{1}{k}+\frac{1}{p}=\frac{1}{k}+\frac{1}{60}=\frac{1}{48}$ and $k=240$. So, 96 and 240 are both possible values for k; NOT sufficient.

The correct answer is A; statement 1 alone is sufficient.

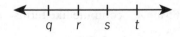

69. Of the four numbers represented on the number line above, is r closest to zero?

(1) $q=-s$
(2) $-t<q$

Algebra Order

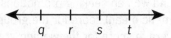

Referring to the figure above, in which it may be assumed that q, r, s, and t are different numbers, determine if r is closest to 0.

(1) Since $q=-s$, one of q and s is positive and the other is negative. Since s is to the right of q, then s is positive and q is negative. Also, 0 is halfway between q and s, so q and s are the same distance from 0. If $r=0$, then, of q, r, s, and t, r is closest to 0 because it IS 0. If $r\neq 0$, then either (i) $q<0<r<s<t$ or (ii) $q<r<0<s<t$.

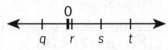

(i) If $q<0<r<s<t$, as shown above, r is closer to 0 than s is because r is between 0 and s, and r is clearly closer to 0 than t is because t is farther away from 0 than s is. Also, since q and s are the same distance from 0 and r is closer to 0 than s is, then r is closer to 0 than q is. Therefore, r is closest to 0.

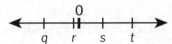

(ii) If $q<r<0<s<t$, as shown above, r is closer to 0 than q is because r is between 0 and q. Also, r is closer to 0 than s is because r is closer to 0 than q is and q and s are the same distance from 0. Moreover, r is closer to 0 than t is because t is farther away from 0 than s is. Therefore, r is closest to 0.

In each case, r is closest to 0; SUFFICIENT.

(2) If $-t<q$, then $-t$ is to the left of q. If $t=5$, $s=4$, $r=3$, and $q=-2$, then $-5<-2$, so (2) is satisfied. In this case, q is closest to 0. On the other hand, if $t=5$, $s=4$, $r=-1$, and $q=-2$, then $-5<-2$, so (2) is satisfied, but r is closest to 0; NOT sufficient.

The correct answer is A; statement 1 alone is sufficient.

70. At a certain company, a test was given to a group of men and women seeking promotions. If the average (arithmetic mean) score for the group was 80, was the average score for the women greater than 85 ?

    (1) The average score for the men was less than 75.

    (2) The group consisted of more men than women.

    Arithmetic Statistics

    The average score for a group of men and women was 80. Letting x be the average score for the women, determine whether the value of x is greater than 85.

    (1) The average score for the men was less than 75.

        Let the average score for the men be 74. (Note that $74 < 75$.)

        If there were 10 men and 10 women, then

        $$\frac{10(74) + 10x}{10 + 10} = 80$$

        $$740 + 10x = 1,600$$

        $$10x = 860$$

        $$x = 86$$

        and hence the value of x would be greater than 85.

        On the other hand, if there were 10 men and 20 women, then

        $$\frac{10(74) + 20x}{10 + 20} = 80$$

        $$740 + 20x = 2,400$$

        $$20x = 1,660$$

        $$x = 83$$

        and hence the value of x would not be greater than 85; NOT sufficient.

    (2) There were more men than women in the group.

        Let there be 20 men and 10 women. (Note that $20 > 10$.)

If the average score for the men was 74, then

$$\frac{20(74) + 10x}{20 + 10} = 80$$

$$1,480 + 10x = 2,400$$

$$10x = 920$$

$$x = 92$$

and hence the value of x would be greater than 85.

On the other hand, if the average score for the men was 94, then

$$\frac{20(94) + 10x}{20 + 10} = 80$$

$$1,880 + 10x = 2,400$$

$$10x = 520$$

$$x = 52$$

and hence the value of x would not be greater than 85; NOT sufficient.

Taking (1) and (2) together, let M be the sum of the m men's scores and let W be the sum of the w women's scores. Note that $\frac{M}{m}$ is the average score for the men and $\frac{W}{w}$ is the average score for the women. From $\frac{M+W}{m+w} = 80$ it follows that $M + W = 80(m + w) = 80m + 80w$. From (1) it follows that $\frac{M}{m} < 75$, or $75m > M$. Finally, from (2) it follows that $m > w$, or $5m > 5w$. Combining these results,

$M + W = 80m + 80w$

$75m + W > 80m + 80w$ since $75m > M$

$W > 5m + 80w$ subtract $75m$ from both sides

$W > 5w + 80w$ since $5m > 5w$

$W > 85w$ combine like terms

$\frac{W}{w} > 85$ divide by w

Hence, the average score for the women is greater than 85.

The correct answer is C;
both statements together are sufficient.

71. Mary persuaded n friends to donate $500 each to her election campaign, and then each of these n friends persuaded n more people to donate $500 each to Mary's campaign. If no one donated more than once and if there were no other donations, what was the value of n?

    (1) The first n people donated $\frac{1}{16}$ of the total amount donated.

    (2) The total amount donated was $120,000.

    Algebra Simultaneous equations

    If n is the number of friends who each contributed $500 to Mary's campaign and each persuaded n more people to contribute $500 each to the campaign, then the amount contributed to the campaign was $500\left(n^2 + n\right)$. Assuming $n > 0$, determine the value of n.

    (1) If the first n people contributed $\frac{1}{16}$ of the total amount, then

    $$500n = \frac{1}{16}(500)\left(n^2 + n\right)$$
    $$500n = \frac{1}{16}(500)(n)(n+1)$$
    $$16 = n + 1$$
    $$15 = n; \text{ SUFFICIENT.}$$

    (2) If the total amount contributed was $120,000, then

    $$500\left(n^2 + n\right) = 120,000$$
    $$n^2 + n = 240$$
    $$n^2 + n - 240 = 0$$
    $$(n+16)(n-15) = 0$$
    $$n = 15; \text{ SUFFICIENT.}$$

    Note that $n^2 + n = 240$ can be solved by inspection since $n^2 + n = n(n+1)$ and the only consecutive positive integers whose product is 240 are 15 and 16, so $n = 15$.

    Although it is not necessary to actually solve the quadratic equations in (1) and (2), it is necessary to analyze the nature of the solutions to make sure that there aren't two possible values for n.

    The correct answer is D;
    each statement alone is sufficient.

72. If m is an integer, is m odd?

    (1) $\frac{m}{2}$ is not an even integer.

    (2) $m - 3$ is an even integer.

    Algebra Properties of numbers

    (1) Since m could be either the odd integer 3 or the even integer 10 and still satisfy this condition, there is no information to show definitively whether m is odd or even; NOT sufficient.

    (2) If $m - 3$ is an even integer, then $m - 3 = 2k$ for some integer k and $m = 2k + 3 = 2(k+1) + 1$, which is odd; SUFFICIENT.

    The correct answer is B;
    statement 2 alone is sufficient.

    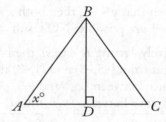

73. What is the area of triangular region ABC above?

    (1) The product of BD and AC is 20.

    (2) $x = 45$

    Geometry Triangles; Area

    The area of $\triangle ABC = \dfrac{BD \times AC}{2}$.

    (1) The product of BD and AC is given as 20, so the area of $\triangle ABC$ is $\frac{20}{2}$ or 10; SUFFICIENT.

    (2) With the measurement of x being 45, it is concluded that $\triangle ABD$ is a 45-45-90 right triangle, where the length of side BD is equal to the length of side AD. However, with no lengths of any side known, there is not enough information to calculate the area; NOT sufficient.

    The correct answer is A;
    statement 1 alone is sufficient.

74. In the xy-coordinate plane, is point R equidistant from points (–3,–3) and (1,–3) ?

    (1) The x-coordinate of point R is –1.
    (2) Point R lies on the line y = –3.

Algebra Coordinate geometry

Determine if point R is equidistant from (–3,–3) and (1,–3). Letting R = (x,y), then R will be equidistant from (–3,–3) and (1,–3) if and only if R lies on the perpendicular bisector of the line segment with endpoints (–3,–3) and (1,–3), or equivalently, if and only if R lies on the vertical line that consists of all points with x-coordinate equal to $\frac{-3+1}{2} = -1$. Therefore, determine if x = –1.

(1) Given that x = –1, then R will be equidistant from (–3,–3) and (1,–3); SUFFICIENT.

(2) Given that y = –3, then both x = –1 and x ≠ –1 are possible; NOT sufficient.

Alternatively, letting R = (x,y), then R will be equidistant from (–3,–3) and (1,–3) if and only if the distance between (x,y) and (–3,–3) is the same as the distance between (x,y) and (1,–3), or if and only if $\sqrt{(x+3)^2 + (y+3)^2} = \sqrt{(x-1)^2 + (y+3)^2}$, or if and only if $(x + 3)^2 + (y + 3)^2 = (x - 1)^2 + (y + 3)^2$, or if and only if $(x + 3)^2 = (x - 1)^2$.

(1) Given that x = –1, then $(-1 + 3)^2 = 4$ and $(-1 - 1)^2 = 4$; SUFFICIENT.

(2) Given that y = –3, then it is impossible to determine if $(x + 3)^2 = (x - 1)^2$; NOT sufficient.

The correct answer is A; statement 1 alone is sufficient.

75. Is the positive two-digit integer N less than 40 ?

    (1) The units digit of N is 6 more than the tens digit.
    (2) N is 4 less than 4 times the units digit.

Arithmetic Place value

Determine if the two-digit integer N is less than 40. Letting the tens digit be t and the units digit be u, then N = 10t + u. Determine if 10t + u < 40.

(1) Given that u = t + 6, then N = 10t + (t + 6) = 11t + 6. Since u is a digit, u = t + 6 ≤ 9, so t ≤ 3. Therefore, N = 11t + 6 ≤ 11(3) + 6 = 39; SUFFICIENT.

(2) Given that N = 4u – 4, then since u is a digit and u ≤ 9, it follows that N = 4u – 4 ≤ 4(9) – 4 = 32; SUFFICIENT.

The correct answer is D; each statement alone is sufficient.

76. Each week a certain salesman is paid a fixed amount equal to $300, plus a commission equal to 5 percent of the amount of his sales that week over $1,000. What is the total amount the salesman was paid last week?

    (1) The total amount the salesman was paid last week is equal to 10 percent of the amount of his sales last week.
    (2) The salesman's sales last week totaled $5,000.

Algebra Applied problems

Let P be the salesman's pay for last week and let S be the amount of his sales last week. Then P = 300 + 0.05(S – 1,000). Determine the value of P.

(1) Given P = 0.10S, then 0.10S = 300 + 0.05(S – 1,000). This equation can be solved for a unique value of S, from which the value of P can be determined; SUFFICIENT.

(2) Given S = 5,000, then P = 300 + 0.05(5,000 – 1,000); SUFFICIENT.

The correct answer is D; each statement alone is sufficient.

77. A total of $60,000 was invested for one year. Part of this amount earned simple annual interest at the rate of x percent per year, and the rest earned simple annual interest at the rate of y percent per year. If the total interest earned by the $60,000 for that year was $4,080, what is the value of x ?

    (1) $x = \frac{3y}{4}$
    (2) The ratio of the amount that earned interest at the rate of x percent per year to the amount that earned interest at the rate of y percent per year was 3 to 2.

Algebra Applied problems

Let X be the amount invested at x percent and let Y be the amount invested at y percent, where $X + Y = 60,000$. If $\frac{x}{100}X + \frac{y}{100}Y = 4,080$, determine the value of x.

(1) Given that $x = \frac{3}{4}y$, then $y = \frac{4}{3}x$. Since $X + Y = 60,000$, then $Y = 60,000 - X$. By substitution, $\frac{x}{100}X + \frac{y}{100}Y = 4,080$ becomes $\frac{x}{100}X + \frac{\frac{4}{3}x}{100}(60,000 - X) = 4,080$. However, because the value of X is unknown, it is impossible to determine a unique value for x; NOT sufficient.

(2) Given that $\frac{X}{Y} = \frac{3}{2}$, then $Y = \frac{2}{3}X$ and $Y = \frac{2}{3}(60,000 - Y)$, from which the values of Y and, in turn, X can be determined. However, since the value of y in the equation $\frac{x}{100}X = \frac{y}{100}Y = 4,080$ is still unknown, it is impossible to determine a unique value for x; NOT sufficient.

Taking (1) and (2) together, $\frac{x}{100}X = \frac{y}{100}Y = 4,080$ from the stem becomes $\frac{x}{100}X = \frac{\frac{4}{3}x}{100}Y = 4,080$, using the information from (1). Then, using the values of X and Y obtained from the information in (2) leaves an equation with x as the only unknown. This equation can be solved for a unique value of x.

The correct answer is C; both statements together are sufficient.

78. At a bakery, all donuts are priced equally and all bagels are priced equally. What is the total price of 5 donuts and 3 bagels at the bakery?

(1) At the bakery, the total price of 10 donuts and 6 bagels is $12.90.

(2) At the bakery, the price of a donut is $0.15 less than the price of a bagel.

Algebra Simultaneous equations

Let x be the price, in dollars, of each donut and let y be the price, in dollars, of each bagel. Find the value of $5x + 3y$.

(1) Given that $10x + 6y = 12.90$, then $5x + 3y = \frac{1}{2}(10x + 6y)$, it follows that $5x + 3y = \frac{1}{2}(12.90)$; SUFFICIENT.

(2) Given that $x = y - 0.15$, then $5x + 3y = 5(y - 0.15) + 3y = 8y - 0.75$, which varies as y varies; NOT sufficient.

The correct answer is A; statement 1 alone is sufficient.

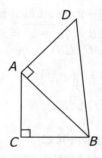

79. In the figure above, is the area of triangular region ABC equal to the area of triangular region DBA ?

(1) $(AC)^2 = 2(AD)^2$

(2) $\triangle ABC$ is isosceles.

Geometry Triangles; Area

Determine whether $\frac{1}{2}(AC)(CB) = \frac{1}{2}(AD)(AB)$ or, equivalently, whether $(AC)(CB) = (AD)(AB)$.

(1) Given that $(AC)^2 = 2(AD)^2$, then $\sqrt{2}$ and 1 could be the values of AC and AD, respectively. If, for example, $CB = \sqrt{2}$, then $AB = \sqrt{(\sqrt{2})^2 + (\sqrt{2})^2} = 2$ by the Pythagorean theorem applied to $\triangle ABC$. Hence, $(AC)(CB) = (\sqrt{2})(\sqrt{2})$ and $(AD)(AB) = (1)(2)$, from which it follows that $(AC)(CB) = (AD)(AB)$. On the other hand, if $CB = 1$, then $AB = \sqrt{(\sqrt{2})^2 + 1^2} = \sqrt{3}$ by the Pythagorean theorem applied to $\triangle ABC$. Hence, $(AC)(CB) = (\sqrt{2})(1)$ and $(AD)(AB) = (1)(\sqrt{3})$, from which it follows that $(AC)(CB) \neq (AD)(AB)$; NOT sufficient.

(2) Given that $\triangle ABC$ is isosceles then, by varying the value of AD, the area of $\triangle ABC$ may or may not be equal to the area of $\triangle DBA$. For example, if $AC = CB = 1$, then $(AC)(CB) = (1)(1) = 1$ and $AB = \sqrt{2}$ by the Pythagorean theorem applied to $\triangle ABC$. If $AD = \dfrac{1}{\sqrt{2}}$, then $(AD)(AB) = \left(\dfrac{1}{\sqrt{2}}\right)(\sqrt{2}) = 1$ and $(AC)(CB) = (AD)(AB)$. On the other hand, if $AD = 1$, $(AD)(AB) = (1)(\sqrt{2}) = \sqrt{2}$ and $(AC)(CB) \neq (AD)(AB)$; NOT sufficient.

Given (1) and (2) together, let $AC = CB = x$ be the length of the legs of the isosceles triangle ABC. Then, from $(AC)^2 = 2(AD)^2$, it follows that $x^2 = 2(AD)^2$, and hence $AD = \dfrac{x}{\sqrt{2}}$. Also, by the Pythagorean theorem applied to $\triangle ABC$, it follows that $AB = \sqrt{x^2 + x^2} = x\sqrt{2}$. Therefore, it follows that $(AC)(CB) = (x)(x) = x^2$ and $(AD)(AB) = \left(\dfrac{x}{\sqrt{2}}\right)(x\sqrt{2}) = x^2$, and so $(AC)(CB) = (AD)(AB)$.

**The correct answer is C;
both statements together are sufficient.**

80. If r and s are positive integers, can the fraction $\dfrac{r}{s}$ be expressed as a decimal with only a finite number of nonzero digits?

(1) s is a factor of 100.
(2) r is a factor of 100.

Arithmetic Properties of numbers

Determine if $\dfrac{r}{s}$, where r and s are positive integers, can be expressed as a decimal with a finite number of nonzero decimal digits.

(1) It is given that s is a factor of 100 and so $s = 1, 2, 4, 5, 10, 20, 25, 50,$ or 100. This means that $\dfrac{r}{s}$ must be one of the quotients $\dfrac{r}{1}, \dfrac{r}{2}, \dfrac{r}{4}, \dfrac{r}{5}, \dfrac{r}{10}, \dfrac{r}{20}, \dfrac{r}{25}, \dfrac{r}{50},$ or $\dfrac{r}{100}$. Thus, $\dfrac{r}{s}$ must be one of the products $r(1)$, $r(0.5)$, $r(0.25)$, $r(0.20)$, $r(0.1)$, $r(0.05)$ $r(0.04)$, $r(0.02)$, or $r(0.01)$. In each case, $\dfrac{r}{s}$ is the product of an integer and a decimal with a finite number of nonzero digits, and hence, $\dfrac{r}{s}$ can be expressed as a decimal with a finite number of nonzero digits. In fact, it suffices to note

this is true for $\dfrac{r}{100}$, since each of the other possibilities is a positive integer times $\dfrac{r}{100}$ (for example, $\dfrac{r}{20}$ is 5 times $\dfrac{r}{100}$); SUFFICIENT.

(2) It is given that r is a factor of 100. If $r = 4$ and $s = 5$, then $\dfrac{r}{s} = 0.8$, which is a decimal with a finite number of nonzero digits. On the other hand, if $r = 4$ and $s = 7$, then $\dfrac{r}{s} = 0.\overline{571428}$, which is not a decimal with a finite number of nonzero digits; NOT sufficient.

**The correct answer is A;
statement 1 alone is sufficient.**

81. If the ratio of the number of teachers to the number of students is the same in School District M and School District P, what is the ratio of the number of students in School District M to the number of students in School District P ?

(1) There are 10,000 more students in School District M than there are in School District P.

(2) The ratio of the number of teachers to the number of students in School District M is 1 to 20.

Algebra Ratios

Given that $\dfrac{T_M}{S_M} = \dfrac{T_P}{S_P}$, where T_M and S_M are the numbers of teachers and students, respectively, in District M, and T_P and S_P are the numbers of teachers and students, respectively, in District P, find the value of $\dfrac{S_M}{S_P}$.

(1) Given that $S_M = S_P + 10{,}000$, then $\dfrac{S_M}{S_P} = \dfrac{S_P + 10{,}000}{S_P}$, but the value of S_P is unknown; NOT sufficient.

(2) Given that $\dfrac{T_M}{S_M} = \dfrac{1}{20}$ and $\dfrac{T_M}{S_M} = \dfrac{T_P}{S_P}$, then $\dfrac{T_P}{S_P} = \dfrac{1}{20}$. Therefore, $S_P = 20T_P$ and $S_M = 20T_M$. It follows that $\dfrac{S_M}{S_P} = \dfrac{20T_M}{20T_P}$, but the values of T_M and T_P are unknown; NOT sufficient.

Taking (1) and (2) together, if $S_P = 1,000$,

$S_M = 1,000 + 10,000 = 11,000$, $T_P = \dfrac{1,000}{20} = 50$,

and $T_M = \dfrac{11,000}{20} = 550$, then $\dfrac{S_M}{S_P} = \dfrac{11}{1}$. However,

if $S_P = 5,000$, $S_M = 5,000 + 10,000 = 15,000$,

$T_P = \dfrac{5,000}{20} = 250$, and $T_M = \dfrac{15,000}{20} = 750$,

then $\dfrac{S_M}{S_P} = \dfrac{3}{1}$. Therefore, the value of $\dfrac{S_M}{S_P}$

cannot be determined.

The correct answer is E;
both statements together are still not sufficient.

82. If $r > 0$ and $s > 0$, is $\dfrac{r}{s} < \dfrac{s}{r}$?

   (1) $\dfrac{r}{3s} = \dfrac{1}{4}$

   (2) $s = r + 4$

Algebra Ratios

Given nonnegative numbers r and s, determine if $\dfrac{r}{s} < \dfrac{s}{r}$.

   (1) If $\dfrac{r}{3s} = \dfrac{1}{4}$, then $\dfrac{r}{s} = \dfrac{3}{4}$, $\dfrac{s}{r} = \dfrac{4}{3}$, and so

   $\dfrac{r}{s} < \dfrac{s}{r}$, since $\dfrac{3}{4} < \dfrac{4}{3}$; SUFFICIENT.

   (2) If $s = r + 4$, then $\dfrac{r}{s} = \dfrac{r}{r+4}$ and $\dfrac{s}{r} = \dfrac{r+4}{r}$.

   Since $r + 4 > r$, $\dfrac{r}{r+4} < 1$ and $\dfrac{r+4}{r} > 1$,

   so $\dfrac{r}{s} < \dfrac{s}{r}$; SUFFICIENT.

The correct answer is D;
each statement alone is sufficient.

83. If k is an integer such that $56 < k < 66$, what is the value of k ?

   (1) If k were divided by 2, the remainder would be 1.
   (2) If $k + 1$ were divided by 3, the remainder would be 0.

Arithmetic Properties of integers

Determine the value of the integer k, where $56 < k < 66$.

   (1) It is given that the remainder is 1 when k is divided by 2, which implies that k is odd.

Therefore, the value of k can be 57, 59, 61, 63, or 65; NOT sufficient.

   (2) It is given that the remainder is 0 when $k + 1$ is divided by 3, which implies that $k + 1$ is divisible by 3. Since $56 < k < 66$ (equivalently, $57 < k + 1 < 67$), the value of $k + 1$ can be 60, 63, or 66 so the value of k can be 59, 62 or 65; NOT sufficient.

Taking (1) and (2) together, 59 and 65 appear in both lists of possible values for k; NOT sufficient.

The correct answer is E;
both statements together are still not sufficient.

$k, n, 12, 6, 17$

84. What is the value of n in the list above?

   (1) $k < n$
   (2) The median of the numbers in the list is 10.

Arithmetic Statistics

Given the list $k, n, 12, 6, 17$, determine the value of n.

   (1) Although $k < n$, no information is given about the value of k or n; NOT sufficient.

   (2) Since the median of the numbers in the list is 10 and there are 5 numbers in the list, 10 is one of those 5 numbers. Therefore, $n = 10$ or $k = 10$. If $n = 10$, then the value of n has been determined. However, if $k = 10$, then n can be any number that is 10 or less, so the value of n cannot be determined; NOT sufficient.

Taking (1) and (2) together, if $k < n$ and the median of the list is 10, then 12 and 17 are to the right of the median and the list in ascending order is either 6, k, n, 12, 17 or k, 6, n, 12, 17. In either case, n is the middle number, and since the median is 10, $n = 10$.

The correct answer is C;
both statements together are sufficient.

85. If x and y are integers, what is the value of $x + y$?

   (1) $3 < \dfrac{x+y}{2} < 4$
   (2) $2 < x < y < 5$

Arithmetic Computation with integers

Determine the value of $x + y$ for integers x and y.

(1) Given that $3 < \dfrac{x + y}{2} < 4$, then $6 < x + y < 8$. Since $x + y$ is an integer and 7 is the only integer greater than 6 and less than 8, it follows that the value of $x + y$ is 7; SUFFICIENT.

(2) Given that $2 < x < y < 5$, then $2 < x < 5$, and hence $x = 3$ or $x = 4$. Likewise, $2 < y < 5$, and hence $y = 3$ or $y = 4$. With the additional restriction that $x < y$, it follows that $x = 3$ and $y = 4$, and thus $x + y = 7$; SUFFICIENT.

**The correct answer is D;
each statement alone is sufficient.**

86. What is the value of $b + c$?

(1) $ab + cd + ac + bd = 6$

(2) $a + d = 4$

Algebra First- and second-degree equations

(1) The equation $ab + cd + ac + bd = 6$ can be simplified to isolate $b + c$ by regrouping and then factoring as follows:

$$(ab + bd) + (ac + cd) = 6$$

$$b(a + d) + c(a + d) = 6$$

$$(a + d)(b + c) = 6$$

The value of $b + c$, however, cannot be determined unless the value of $a + d$ is known; NOT sufficient.

(2) This provides no information about b and c; NOT sufficient.

Since (2) provides the missing information about the needed value of $a + d$ in (1), the value of $b + c$ can be found when both (1) and (2) are used to complete the equation.

**The correct answer is C;
both statements together are sufficient.**

87. What is the average (arithmetic mean) of j and k ?

(1) The average (arithmetic mean) of $j + 2$ and $k + 4$ is 11.

(2) The average (arithmetic mean) of j, k, and 14 is 10.

Arithmetic Statistics

The average of j and k is $\dfrac{j + k}{2}$, and this value can be determined if the value of $j + k$ can be determined.

(1) It is given that $\dfrac{(j + 2) + (k + 4)}{2} = 11$.

Therefore, $\dfrac{j + k + 6}{2} = 11$, $j + k + 6 = 22$; $j + k = 16$; SUFFICIENT.

(2) It is given that $\dfrac{j + k + 14}{3} = 10$. Therefore, $j + k + 14 = 30$, $j + k = 16$; SUFFICIENT.

**The correct answer is D;
each statement alone is sufficient.**

88. Paula and Sandy were among those people who sold raffle tickets to raise money for Club X. If Paula and Sandy sold a total of 100 of the tickets, how many of the tickets did Paula sell?

(1) Sandy sold $\dfrac{2}{3}$ as many of the raffle tickets as Paula did.

(2) Sandy sold 8 percent of all the raffle tickets sold for Club X.

Algebra Simultaneous equations

If Paula sold p tickets and Sandy sold s tickets, then $p + s = 100$.

(1) Since Sandy sold $\dfrac{2}{3}$ as many tickets as Paula, $s = \dfrac{2}{3} p$. The value of p can be determined by solving the two equations simultaneously; SUFFICIENT.

(2) Since the total number of the raffle tickets sold is unknown, the number of tickets that Sandy or Paula sold cannot be determined; NOT sufficient.

**The correct answer is A;
statement 1 alone is sufficient.**

89. A number of people each wrote down one of the first 30 positive integers. Were any of the integers written down by more than one of the people?

    (1) The number of people who wrote down an integer was greater than 40.

    (2) The number of people who wrote down an integer was less than 70.

    Algebra Sets and functions

    If the number of integers to be chosen from is smaller than the number of people making the choice, then at least one of the integers has to be chosen and written down by more than one person. If the number of integers to be chosen from is the same as or greater than the number of people making the choice, it is possible that no integer will be chosen and written down more than once.

    (1) Because the number of people was greater than 30, at least one integer had to be written down by more than one person; SUFFICIENT.

    (2) It is not helpful just to know that the number of people was less than 70. If, for instance, the number of people was 35, then at least one of the 30 integers had to be written down by more than one person. If the number of people was 25 instead, it is possible that no two people wrote down the same integer; NOT sufficient.

    The correct answer is A; statement 1 alone is sufficient.

90. Is the number of seconds required to travel d_1 feet at r_1 feet per second greater than the number of seconds required to travel d_2 feet at r_2 feet per second?

    (1) d_1 is 30 greater than d_2.
    (2) r_1 is 30 greater than r_2.

    Algebra Applied problems

    Determine if $\dfrac{d_1}{r_1}$ is greater than $\dfrac{d_2}{r_2}$.

    (1) Although it is given that $d_1 = d_2 + 30$, without information about r_1 and r_2 it is impossible to determine if $\dfrac{d_1}{r_1}$ is greater than $\dfrac{d_2}{r_2}$. For example, if $d_1 = 60$, $d_2 = 30$, $r_1 = 90$, and $r_2 = 60$, then $d_1 = d_2 + 30$, but $\dfrac{d_1}{r_1} = \dfrac{2}{3}$ and $\dfrac{d_2}{r_2} = \dfrac{1}{2}$, so $\dfrac{d_1}{r_1}$ is greater than $\dfrac{d_2}{r_2}$. On the other hand, if $d_1 = 90$, $d_2 = 60$, $r_1 = 60$, and $r_2 = 30$, then $d_1 = d_2 + 30$, but $\dfrac{d_1}{r_1} = \dfrac{3}{2}$ and $\dfrac{d_2}{r_2} = 2$, so $\dfrac{d_1}{r_1}$ is not greater than $\dfrac{d_2}{r_2}$; NOT sufficient.

    (2) Although it is given that $r_1 = r_2 + 30$, without information about d_1 and d_2 it is impossible to determine if $\dfrac{d_1}{r_1}$ is greater than $\dfrac{d_2}{r_2}$. For example, if $d_1 = 60$, $d_2 = 30$, $r_1 = 90$, and $r_2 = 60$, then $r_1 = r_2 + 30$, but $\dfrac{d_1}{r_1} = \dfrac{2}{3}$ and $\dfrac{d_2}{r_2} = \dfrac{1}{2}$, so $\dfrac{d_1}{r_1}$ is greater than $\dfrac{d_2}{r_2}$. On the other hand, if $d_1 = 90$, $d_2 = 60$, $r_1 = 60$, and $r_2 = 30$, then $r_1 = r_2 + 30$, but $\dfrac{d_1}{r_1} = \dfrac{3}{2}$ and $\dfrac{d_2}{r_2} = 2$, so $\dfrac{d_1}{r_1}$ is not greater than $\dfrac{d_2}{r_2}$; NOT sufficient.

    Taking (1) and (2) together is of no more help than either (1) or (2) taken separately because the same examples used to show that (1) is not sufficient also show that (2) is not sufficient.

    The correct answer is E; both statements together are still not sufficient.

91. Last year, if Arturo spent a total of $12,000 on his mortgage payments, real estate taxes, and home insurance, how much did he spend on his real estate taxes?

    (1) Last year, the total amount that Arturo spent on his real estate taxes and home insurance was $33\dfrac{1}{3}$ percent of the amount that he spent on his mortgage payments.

    (2) Last year, the amount that Arturo spent on his real estate taxes was 20 percent of the total amount he spent on his mortgage payments and home insurance.

Arithmetic Applied problems

Let M, R, and H be the amounts that Arturo spent last year on mortgage payments, real estate taxes, and home insurance, respectively. Given that $M + R + H = 12{,}000$, determine the value of R.

(1) Given that $R + H = \frac{1}{3}M$ and $M + R + H = 12{,}000$, then $M + \frac{1}{3}M = 12{,}000$, or $M = 9{,}000$. However, the value of R cannot be determined, since it is possible that $R = 2{,}000$ (use $M = 9{,}000$ and $H = 1{,}000$) and it is possible that $R = 1{,}000$ (use $M = 9{,}000$ and $H = 2{,}000$); NOT sufficient.

(2) Given that $R = \frac{1}{5}(M + H)$, or $5R = M + H$ and $M + R + H = 12{,}000$, which can be rewritten as $(M + H) + R = 12{,}000$, then $5R + R = 12{,}000$, or $R = 2{,}000$; SUFFICIENT.

**The correct answer is B;
statement 2 alone is sufficient.**

92. If a, b, c, and d are positive numbers, is $\frac{a}{b} < \frac{c}{d}$?

(1) $0 < \frac{c-a}{d-b}$

(2) $\left(\frac{ad}{bc}\right)^2 < \frac{ad}{bc}$

Algebra Inequalities

Determine whether $\frac{a}{b} < \frac{c}{d}$, where a, b, c, and d are positive numbers.

(1) Given that $0 < \frac{c-a}{d-b}$, then $a = 2$, $b = 3$, $c = 6$, and $d = 8$ are possible values for a, b, c, and d because $\frac{c-a}{d-b} = \frac{6-2}{8-3} = \frac{4}{5}$ and $\frac{4}{5} > 0$. For these values, $\frac{a}{b} < \frac{c}{d}$ is true because $\frac{2}{3} < \frac{6}{8}$. On the other hand, $a = 4$, $b = 6$, $c = 2$, and $d = 3$ are also possible values of a, b, c, and d because $\frac{c-a}{d-b} = \frac{2-4}{3-6} = \frac{2}{3}$ and $\frac{2}{3} > 0$. For these values, $\frac{a}{b} < \frac{c}{d}$ is false because $\frac{4}{6} = \frac{2}{3}$; NOT sufficient.

(2) Given that $\left(\frac{ad}{bc}\right)^2 < \frac{ad}{bc}$, then

$\frac{ad}{bc} < 1$ dividing both sides by the positive number $\frac{ad}{bc}$

$\frac{ad}{b} < c$ multiplying both sides by the positive number c

$\frac{a}{b} < \frac{c}{d}$ dividing both sides by the positive number d; SUFFICIENT.

**The correct answer is B;
statement 2 alone is sufficient.**

93. Is the number of members of Club X greater than the number of members of Club Y ?

(1) Of the members of Club X, 20 percent are also members of Club Y.

(2) Of the members of Club Y, 30 percent are also members of Club X.

Arithmetic Sets

Let a be the number of members in Club X that do not belong to Club Y, let b be the number of members in Club Y that do not belong to Club X, and let c be the number of members that belong to both Club X and to Club Y. Determine whether $a + c > b + c$, or equivalently, whether $a > b$.

(1) If $a = 80$, $b = 79$, and $c = 20$, then 20 percent of the members of Club X are also members of Club Y (because $c = 20$ is 20 percent of $a + c = 100$) and $a > b$ is true. However, if $a = 80$, $b = 80$, and $c = 20$, then 20 percent of the members of Club X are also members of Club Y (because $c = 20$ is 20 percent of $a + c = 100$) and $a > b$ is false. Therefore, it cannot be determined whether $a > b$; NOT sufficient.

(2) If $a = 71$, $b = 70$, and $c = 30$, then 30 percent of the members of Club Y are also members of Club X (because $c = 30$ is 30 percent of $b + c = 100$) and $a > b$ is true. However, if $a = 70$, $b = 70$, and $c = 30$, then 30 percent of the members of Club Y are also members of Club X (because $c = 30$ is 30 percent of

$b + c = 100$) and $a > b$ is false. Therefore, it cannot be determined whether $a > b$; NOT sufficient.

Now assume both (1) and (2). From (1) it follows that $\frac{c}{a+c} = 0.20 = \frac{1}{5}$, or $5c = a + c$, and so $a = 4c$.

From (2) it follows that $\frac{c}{b+c} = 0.30 = \frac{3}{10}$, or $10c = 3b + 3c$, and so $7c = 3b$ and $b = \frac{7}{3}c$. Since $4c > \frac{7}{3}c$ (from the statements it can be deduced that $c > 0$), it follows that $a > b$. Therefore, (1) and (2) together are sufficient.

The correct answer is C;
both statements together are sufficient.

94. In a certain office, 50 percent of the employees are college graduates and 60 percent of the employees are over 40 years old. If 30 percent of those over 40 have master's degrees, how many of the employees over 40 have master's degrees?

(1) Exactly 100 of the employees are college graduates.

(2) Of the employees 40 years old or less, 25 percent have master's degrees.

Arithmetic Percents

(1) It is given that 50 percent of the employees are college graduates. Here, it is now known that exactly 100 of the employees are college graduates. Thus, the total number of employees in the company is 200. It is also given that 60 percent of the employees are over 40 years old, which would be $(0.60)(200)$, or 120 employees. Since it is given that 30 percent of those over 40 have master's degrees, then $(0.30)(120)$, or 36 employees are over 40 and have master's degrees; SUFFICIENT.

(2) There is no information regarding *how many* employees fall into any of the categories, and it thus cannot be determined how many employees there are in any category; NOT sufficient.

The correct answer is A;
statement 1 alone is sufficient.

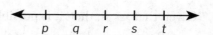

95. On the number line above, p, q, r, s, and t are five consecutive even integers in increasing order. What is the average (arithmetic mean) of these five integers?

(1) $q + s = 24$

(2) The average (arithmetic mean) of q and r is 11.

Arithmetic Properties of numbers

Since p, q, r, s, and t are consecutive even integers listed in numerical order, the 5 integers can also be given as p, $p + 2$, $p + 4$, $p + 6$, and $p + 8$. Determine the average of these 5 integers, which is the value of $\frac{p + (p+2) + (p+4) + (p+6) + (p+8)}{5} = \frac{5p + 20}{5} = p + 4$.

(1) Given that $q + s = 24$, then $(p + 2) + (p + 6) = 24$. Therefore, $2p + 8 = 24$, or $p = 8$, and hence $p + 4 = 12$; SUFFICIENT.

(2) Given that $\frac{q+r}{2} = 11$, then $q + r = (2)(11) = 22$, or $(p + 2) + (p + 4) = 22$. Therefore, $2p + 6 = 22$, or $p = 8$, and hence $p + 4 = 12$; SUFFICIENT.

The correct answer is D;
each statement alone is sufficient.

96. If $\lceil x \rceil$ denotes the least integer greater than or equal to x, is $\lceil x \rceil = 0$?

(1) $-1 < x < 1$

(2) $x < 0$

Algebra Functions

Determine if $\lceil x \rceil$, the least integer greater than or equal to x, is equal to 0, which is the same as determining if x satisfies $-1 < x \leq 0$.

(1) Given that $-1 < x < 1$, then it is possible that $\lceil x \rceil = 0$ (for example, if $x = 0$, then $\lceil x \rceil = 0$) and it is possible that $\lceil x \rceil \neq 0$ (for example, if $x = \frac{1}{2}$, then $\lceil x \rceil = 1 \neq 0$); NOT sufficient.

(2) Given that $x < 0$, then it is possible that $\lceil x \rceil = 0$ (for example, if $x = -\frac{1}{2}$, then $\lceil x \rceil = 0$) and it is possible that $\lceil x \rceil \neq 0$ (for example, if $x = -5$, then $\lceil x \rceil = -5 \neq 0$); NOT sufficient.

Taking (1) and (2) together gives $-1 < x < 0$, which implies that $\lceil x \rceil = 0$.

The correct answer is C; both statements together are sufficient.

97. If x and y are integers, is $x > y$?

   (1) $x + y > 0$
   (2) $y^x < 0$

Arithmetic Properties of integers

Determine if the integer x is greater than the integer y.

(1) It is given that $x + y > 0$, and so $-x < y$. If, for example, $x = -3$ and $y = 4$, then $x + y = -3 + 4 = 1 > 0$ and $x < y$. On the other hand, if $x = 4$ and $y = -3$, then $x + y = 4 - 3 = 1 > 0$ and $x > y$; NOT sufficient.

(2) It is given that $y^x < 0$, so $y < 0$. If, for example, $x = 3$ and $y = -2$, then $(-2)^3 = -8 < 0$ and $x > y$. On the other hand, if $x = -3$ and $y = -2$, then $(-2)^{-3} = -\frac{1}{8} < 0$ and $x < y$; NOT sufficient.

Taking (1) and (2) together, from (2) y is negative and from (1) $-x$ is less than y. Therefore, $-x$ is negative, and hence x is positive. Since x is positive and y is negative, it follows that $x > y$.

The correct answer is C; both statements together are sufficient.

98. Is $rst = 1$?

   (1) $rs = 1$
   (2) $st = 1$

Arithmetic Properties of numbers

(1) This establishes that $rs = 1$, but since the value of t is unavailable, it is unknown if $rst = 1$; NOT sufficient.

(2) Similarly, this establishes the value of st but the value of r is unknown; NOT sufficient.

Both (1) and (2) taken together are still not sufficient to determine whether or not $rst = 1$. For example, if $r = s = t = 1$, then $rs = 1$, $st = 1$, and $rst = 1$. However, if $r = t = 5$, and $s = \frac{1}{5}$, then $rs = 1$, $st = 1$, but $rst = 5$.

The correct answer is E; both statements together are still not sufficient.

99. If r and s are the roots of the equation $x^2 + bx + c = 0$, where b and c are constants, is $rs < 0$?

   (1) $b < 0$
   (2) $c < 0$

Algebra Second-degree equations

Determine whether the product of the roots to $x^2 + bx + c = 0$, where b and c are constants, is negative.

If r and s are the roots of the given equation, then $(x - r)(x - s) = x^2 + bx + c$. This implies that $x^2 - (r + s)x + rs = x^2 + bx + c$, and so $rs = c$. Therefore, rs is negative if and only if c is negative.

(1) Given that $b < 0$, then c could be negative or positive. For example, if $b = -1$ and $c = -6$, then the given equation would be $x^2 - x - 6 = (x - 3)(x + 2) = 0$, and the product of its roots would be $(3)(-2)$, which is negative. On the other hand, if $b = -6$ and $c = 5$, then the given equation would be $x^2 - 6x + 5 = (x - 5)(x - 1) = 0$, and the product of its roots would be $(5)(1)$, which is positive; NOT sufficient.

(2) Given that $c < 0$, it follows from the explanation above that $rs < 0$; SUFFICIENT.

The correct answer is B; statement 2 alone is sufficient.

TOTAL EXPENSES FOR THE
FIVE DIVISIONS OF COMPANY H

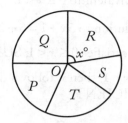

100. The figure above represents a circle graph of Company H's total expenses broken down by the expenses for each of its five divisions. If O is the center of the circle and if Company H's total expenses are $5,400,000, what are the expenses for Division R ?

    (1) $x = 94$
    (2) The total expenses for Divisions S and T are twice as much as the expenses for Division R.

Geometry Circles

In this circle graph, the expenses of Division R are equal to the value of $\frac{x}{360}$ multiplied by $5,400,000, or $15,000x$. Therefore, it is necessary to know the value of x in order to determine the expenses for Division R.

    (1) The value of x is given as 94, so the expenses of Division R can be determined; SUFFICIENT.
    (2) This gives a comparison among the expenses of some of the divisions of Company H, but no information is given about the value of x; NOT sufficient.

**The correct answer is A;
statement 1 alone is sufficient.**

101. If x is negative, is $x < -3$?

    (1) $x^2 > 9$
    (2) $x^3 < -9$

Arithmetic Properties of numbers

    (1) Given that $x^2 > 9$, it follows that $x < -3$ or $x > 3$, a result that can be obtained in a variety of ways. For example, consider the equivalent equation $\left(|x|\right)^2 > 9$ that reduces to $|x| > 3$, or consider when the two factors of $x^2 - 9$ are both positive and when the two factors of $x^2 - 9$ are both negative, or consider where the graph of the parabola $y = x^2 - 9$ is above the x-axis, etc. Since it is also given that x is negative, it follows that $x < -3$; SUFFICIENT.
    (2) Given that $x^3 < -9$, if $x = -4$, then $x^3 = -64$, and so $x^3 < -9$ and it is true that $x < -3$. However, if $x = -3$, then $x^3 = -27$, and so $x^3 < -9$, but it is not true that $x < -3$; NOT sufficient.

**The correct answer is A;
statement 1 alone is sufficient.**

102. What is the number of cans that can be packed in a certain carton?

    (1) The interior volume of this carton is 2,304 cubic inches.
    (2) The exterior of each can is 6 inches high and has a diameter of 4 inches.

Geometry Rectangular solids and cylinders

    (1) No information about the size of the cans is given; NOT sufficient.
    (2) No information about the size of the carton is given; NOT sufficient.

Taking (1) and (2) together, there is still not enough information to answer the question. If the carton is a rectangular solid that is 1 inch by 1 inch by 2,304 inches and the cans are cylindrical with the given dimensions, then 0 cans can be packed into the carton. However, if the carton is a rectangular solid that is 16 inches by 12 inches by 12 inches and the cans are cylindrical with the given dimensions, then 1 or more cans can be packed into the carton.

**The correct answer is E;
both statements together are still not sufficient.**

r	s	t
u	v	w
x	y	z

103. Each of the letters in the table above represents one of the numbers 1, 2, or 3, and each of these numbers occurs exactly once in each row and exactly once in each column. What is the value of r ?

(1) $v + z = 6$

(2) $s + t + u + x = 6$

Arithmetic Properties of numbers

In the following discussion, "row/column convention" means that each of the numbers 1, 2, and 3 appears exactly once in any given row and exactly once in any given column.

(1) Given that $v + z = 6$, then both v and z are equal to 3, since no other sum of the possible values is equal to 6. Applying the row/column convention to row 2, and then to row 3, it follows that neither u nor x can be 3. Since neither u nor x can be 3, the row/column convention applied to column 1 forces r to be 3; SUFFICIENT.

(2) If $u = 3$, then $s + t + x = 3$. Hence, $s = t = x = 1$, since the values these variables can have does not permit another possibility. However, this assignment of values would violate the row/column convention for row 1, and thus u cannot be 3. If $x = 3$, then $s + t + u = 3$. Hence, $s = t = u = 1$, since the values these variables can have does not permit another possibility. However, this assignment of values would violate the row/column convention for row 1, and thus x cannot be 3. Since neither u nor x can be 3, the row/column convention applied to column 1 forces r to be 3; SUFFICIENT.

The correct answer is D;
each statement alone is sufficient.

104. If [x] denotes the greatest integer less than or equal to x, is $[x] = 0$?

(1) $5x + 1 = 3 + 2x$

(2) $0 < x < 1$

Algebra Inequalities

It will be useful to observe that the condition $[x] = 0$ is equivalent to $0 \le x < 1$.

(1) The solution to $5x + 1 = 3 + 2x$ is $x = \dfrac{2}{3}$, which satisfies $0 \le x < 1$; SUFFICIENT.

(2) If $0 < x < 1$, then it follows that $0 \le x < 1$; SUFFICIENT.

The correct answer is D;
each statement alone is sufficient.

105. Material A costs $3 per kilogram, and Material B costs $5 per kilogram. If 10 kilograms of Material K consists of x kilograms of Material A and y kilograms of Material B, is $x > y$?

(1) $y > 4$

(2) The cost of the 10 kilograms of Material K is less than $40.

Algebra Inequalities

Since $x + y = 10$, the relation $x > y$ is equivalent to $x > 10 - x$, or $x > 5$.

(1) The given information is consistent with $x = 5.5$ and $y = 4.5$, and the given information is also consistent with $x = y = 5$. Therefore, it is possible for $x > y$ to be true and it is possible for $x > y$ to be false; NOT sufficient.

(2) Given that $3x + 5y < 40$, or $3x + 5(10 - x) < 40$, then $3x - 5x < 40 - 50$. It follows that $-2x < -10$, or $x > 5$; SUFFICIENT.

The correct answer is B;
statement 2 alone is sufficient.

106. While on a straight road, Car X and Car Y are traveling at different constant rates. If Car X is now 1 mile ahead of Car Y, how many minutes from now will Car X be 2 miles ahead of Car Y ?

(1) Car X is traveling at 50 miles per hour and Car Y is traveling at 40 miles per hour.

(2) Three minutes ago Car X was $\dfrac{1}{2}$ mile ahead of Car Y.

Arithmetic Rate problem

Simply stated, the question is how long will it take Car X to get one mile further ahead of Car Y than it is now.

(1) At their constant rates, Car X would increase its distance from Car Y by 10 miles every hour or, equivalently, 1 mile every 6 minutes; SUFFICIENT.

(2) This states that Car X increases its distance from Car Y by 0.5 mile every 3 minutes, or equivalently 1 mile every 6 minutes; SUFFICIENT.

The correct answer is D; each statement alone is sufficient.

107. If a certain animated cartoon consists of a total of 17,280 frames on film, how many minutes will it take to run the cartoon?

(1) The cartoon runs without interruption at the rate of 24 frames per second.

(2) It takes 6 times as long to run the cartoon as it takes to rewind the film, and it takes a total of 14 minutes to do both.

Arithmetic Arithmetic operations

(1) Given the frames-per-second speed, it can be determined that it takes $\frac{17,280}{24 \times 60}$ minutes to run the cartoon; SUFFICIENT.

(2) It is given both that it takes 14 minutes to run the cartoon and rewind the film and that, with the ratio 6:1 expressed as a fraction, the cartoon runs $\frac{6}{7}$ of the total time. Thus, it can be determined that running the cartoon takes $\frac{6}{7}$ of the 14 minutes; SUFFICIENT.

The correct answer is D; each statement alone is sufficient.

108. At what speed was a train traveling on a trip when it had completed half of the total distance of the trip?

(1) The trip was 460 miles long and took 4 hours to complete.

(2) The train traveled at an average rate of 115 miles per hour on the trip.

Arithmetic Applied problems

Determine the speed of the train when it had completed half the total distance of the trip.

(1) Given that the train traveled 460 miles in 4 hours, the train could have traveled at the constant rate of 115 miles per hour for 4 hours, and thus it could have been traveling 115 miles per hour when it had completed half the total distance of the trip. However, the train could have traveled 150 miles per hour for the first 2 hours (a distance of 300 miles) and 80 miles per hour for the last 2 hours (a distance of 160 miles), and thus it could have been traveling 150 miles per hour when it had completed half the total distance of the trip; NOT sufficient.

(2) Given that the train traveled at an average rate of 115 miles per hour, each of the possibilities given in the explanation for (1) could occur, since 460 miles in 4 hours gives an average speed of $\frac{460}{4} = 115$ miles per hour; NOT sufficient.

Assuming (1) and (2), each of the possibilities given in the explanation for (1) could occur. Therefore, (1) and (2) together are not sufficient.

The correct answer is E; both statements together are still not sufficient.

4, 6, 8, 10, 12, 14, 16, 18, 20, 22

109. List *M* (not shown) consists of 8 different integers, each of which is in the list shown. What is the standard deviation of the numbers in list *M* ?

(1) The average (arithmetic mean) of the numbers in list *M* is equal to the average of the numbers in the list shown.

(2) List *M* does not contain 22.

Arithmetic Statistics

If each of the 8 different numbers in list M is in the set {4, 6, 8, 10, 12, 14, 16, 18, 20, 22}, then list M can be obtained by removing 2 numbers from the given list. If s_M denotes the standard deviation of the numbers in list M, determine the value of s_M.

The average of the numbers in the given list is $\frac{4+6+8+\cdots+22}{10} = 13$, which can also be determined by observing that the numbers in the list are symmetric about 13. If s denotes the standard deviation of the given list, then

$$s^2 = \frac{(4-13)^2 + (6-13)^2 + (8-13)^2 + \cdots + (20-13)^2 + (22-13)^2}{10}$$

and

$$10s^2 = (4-13)^2 + (6-13)^2 + (8-13)^2 + \cdots + (20-13)^2 + (22-13)^2.$$

(1) It is given that the average of the numbers in list M is the same as the average of the numbers in the given list, so the average of the numbers in list M is 13 and, therefore, the sum of the numbers in list M is $8(13) = 104$. Since the sum of the numbers in the given list is $10(13) = 130$, the sum of the 2 numbers removed from the given list to create list M must be $130 - 104 = 26$. Thus, the 2 numbers could be the 2 middle values, 12 and 14, or the 2 numbers at the extremes, 4 and 22. If the numbers removed are 12 and 14, then using the reasoning shown above, $8s_M^2 = 10s^2 - (12 - 13)^2 - (14 - 13)^2 = 10s^2 - 2$. On the other hand, if 4 and 22 are the numbers removed, then $8s_M^2 = 10s^2 - (4 - 13)^2 - (22 - 13)^2 = 10s^2 - 162$. Since $10s^2 - 2 \neq 10s^2 - 162$, $8s_M^2$ can vary, and hence s_M can vary; NOT sufficient.

(2) It is given that list M does not contain 22. Since no information is given about the other number that is to be removed from the given list to create list M, it is not possible to determine the average of the numbers in list M. For example, if the other number removed is 20, then the average is

$\frac{4+6+8+\cdots+18}{8} = 11$ and

$8s_M^2 = (4-11)^2 + (6-11)^2 + (8-11)^2 + \cdots + (18-11)^2 = 176.$

But if the other number removed is 12, then the average is $\frac{4+6+8+10+14+16+18+20}{8} = 12$ and

$8s_M^2 = (4-12)^2 + \cdots + (10-12)^2 + (14-12)^2 + \cdots + (20-12)^2 = 240.$

Because $8s_M^2$ varies, so does s_M; NOT sufficient.

Taking (1) and (2) together, the sum of the 2 numbers removed from the given list to create list M must be 26 and one of those numbers is 22. Therefore, the other number is 4, and so list M consists of the numbers, 6, 8, 10, 12, 14, 16, 18, 20. Since the numbers in list M are known, s_M can be determined.

The correct answer is C; both statements together are sufficient.

110. Tom, Jane, and Sue each purchased a new house. The average (arithmetic mean) price of the three houses was $120,000. What was the median price of the three houses?

(1) The price of Tom's house was $110,000.

(2) The price of Jane's house was $120,000.

Arithmetic Statistics

Let T, J, and S be the purchase prices for Tom's, Jane's, and Sue's new houses. Given that the average purchase price is 120,000, or $T + J + S = (3)(120,000)$, determine the median purchase price.

(1) Given $T = 110,000$, the median could be 120,000 (if $J = 120,000$ and $S = 130,000$) or 125,000 (if $J = 125,000$ and $S = 125,000$); NOT sufficient.

(2) Given $J = 120,000$, the following two cases include every possibility consistent with $T + J + S = (3)(120,000)$, or $T + S = (2)(120,000)$.

(i) $T = S = 120{,}000$

(ii) One of T or S is less than 120,000 and the other is greater than 120,000.

In each case, the median is clearly 120,000; SUFFICIENT.

The correct answer is B;
statement 2 alone is sufficient.

111. If x and y are integers, is xy even?

    (1) $x = y + 1$

    (2) $\dfrac{x}{y}$ is an even integer.

Arithmetic Properties of numbers

Determine if xy is even.

    (1)   Since x and y are consecutive integers, one of these two numbers is even, and hence their product is even. For example, if x is even, then $x = 2m$ for some integer m, and thus $xy = (2m)\,y = (my)(2)$, which is an integer multiple of 2, so xy is even; SUFFICIENT.

    (2)   If $\dfrac{x}{y}$ is even, then $\dfrac{x}{y} = 2n$ for some integer n, and thus $x = 2ny$. From this it follows that $xy = (2ny)(y) = (ny^2)(2)$, which is an integer multiple of 2, so xy is even; SUFFICIENT.

The correct answer is D;
each statement alone is sufficient.

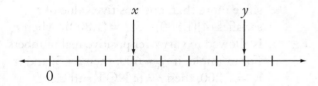

112. If the successive tick marks shown on the number line above are equally spaced and if x and y are the numbers designating the end points of intervals as shown, what is the value of y?

    (1) $x = \dfrac{1}{2}$

    (2) $y - x = \dfrac{2}{3}$

Arithmetic Properties of numbers

    (1)   If 3 tick marks represent a value of $\dfrac{1}{2}$, then 6 tick marks would represent a value of 1. From this it can be established that each subdivision of the line represents $\dfrac{1}{6}$, so the value of y is $\dfrac{7}{6}$; SUFFICIENT.

    (2)   From this, the four equal subdivisions between y and x represent a total distance of $\dfrac{2}{3}$. This implies that each subdivision of the number line has the length $\dfrac{1}{4}\left(\dfrac{2}{3}\right) = \dfrac{1}{6}$, enabling the value of y to be found; SUFFICIENT.

The correct answer is D;
each statement alone is sufficient.

113. In triangle ABC, point X is the midpoint of side AC and point Y is the midpoint of side BC. If point R is the midpoint of line segment XC and if point S is the midpoint of line segment YC, what is the area of triangular region RCS?

    (1)   The area of triangular region ABX is 32.

    (2)   The length of one of the altitudes of triangle ABC is 8.

Geometry Triangles; Area

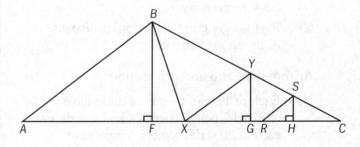

As shown in the figure above, X and Y are the midpoints of $\overline{AC}$ and $\overline{BC}$, respectively, of $\triangle ABC$, and R and S are the midpoints of $\overline{XC}$ and $\overline{YC}$, respectively. Thus, letting $AC = b$, it follows that $AX = XC = \dfrac{1}{2}b$ and $RC = \dfrac{1}{4}b$. Also, if

$\overline{BF}$, $\overline{YG}$, and $\overline{SH}$ are perpendicular to $\overline{AC}$ as shown, then ΔBFC, ΔYGC, and ΔSHC are similar triangles, since their corresponding interior angles have the same measure. Thus, letting $BF = h$, it follows that $YG = \frac{1}{2}h$ and $SH = \frac{1}{4}h$. The area of ΔRCS, which is $\frac{1}{2}\left(\frac{1}{4}b\right)\left(\frac{1}{4}h\right) = \frac{1}{32}bh$, can be determined exactly when the value of bh can be determined.

(1) Given that the area of ΔABX, which is $\frac{1}{2}(AX)(BF)$, or $\frac{1}{2}\left(\frac{1}{2}b\right)(h)$, is 32, then $bh = (4)(32)$; SUFFICIENT.

(2) Without knowing the length of the side to which the altitude is drawn, the area of ΔABC, and hence the value of bh, cannot be determined; NOT sufficient.

**The correct answer is A;
statement 1 alone is sufficient.**

114. A department manager distributed a number of pens, pencils, and pads among the staff in the department, with each staff member receiving x pens, y pencils, and z pads. How many staff members were in the department?

(1) The numbers of pens, pencils, and pads that each staff member received were in the ratio 2:3:4, respectively.

(2) The manager distributed a total of 18 pens, 27 pencils, and 36 pads.

Arithmetic Ratio and proportion

(1) Each of 10 staff members could have received 2 pens, 3 pencils, and 4 pads, or each of 20 staff members could have received 2 pens, 3 pencils, and 4 pads; NOT sufficient.

(2) There could have been 1 staff member who received 18 pens, 27 pencils, and 36 pads, or 3 staff members each of whom received 6 pens, 9 pencils, and 12 pads; NOT sufficient.

Assuming both (1) and (2), use the fact that 18:27:36 is equivalent to both 6:9:12 and 2:3:4 to obtain different possibilities for the number of

staff. Each of 3 staff members could have received 6 pens, 9 pencils, and 12 pads, or each of 9 staff members could have received 2 pens, 3 pencils, and 4 pads. Therefore, (1) and (2) together are not sufficient.

**The correct answer is E;
both statements together are still not sufficient.**

115. Machines X and Y produced identical bottles at different constant rates. Machine X, operating alone for 4 hours, filled part of a production lot; then Machine Y, operating alone for 3 hours, filled the rest of this lot. How many hours would it have taken Machine X operating alone to fill the entire production lot?

(1) Machine X produced 30 bottles per minute.

(2) Machine X produced twice as many bottles in 4 hours as Machine Y produced in 3 hours.

Algebra Rate problem

Let r_X and r_Y be the rates, in numbers of bottles produced per hour, of Machine X and Machine Y. In 4 hours Machine X produces $4r_X$ bottles working alone and in 3 hours Machine Y produces $3r_Y$ bottles working alone. Thus, $4r_X + 3r_Y$ bottles are produced when Machine X operates alone for 4 hours followed by Machine Y operating alone for 3 hours. If t is the number of hours for Machine X to produce the same number of bottles, then $4r_X + 3r_Y = \left(r_X\right)t$.

(1) Given that Machine X produces 30 bottles per minute, then $r_X = (30)(60) = 1,800$. This does not determine a unique value for t, since more than one positive value of t satisfies $(4)(1,800) + 3r_Y = (1,800)t$ when r_Y is allowed to vary over positive real numbers. For example, if $r_Y = 600$, then $t = 5$, and if $r_Y = 1,200$, then $t = 6$; NOT sufficient.

(2) Given that $4r_X = 2\left(3r_Y\right)$, so $r_X = \frac{3}{2}r_Y$. Therefore, from $4r_X + 3r_Y = \left(r_X\right)t$, it follows that $6r_Y + 3r_Y = \frac{3}{2}r_Y t$, or $6 + 3 = \frac{3}{2}t$, or $t = 6$; SUFFICIENT.

**The correct answer is B;
statement 2 alone is sufficient.**

116. On a company-sponsored cruise, $\frac{2}{3}$ of the passengers were company employees and the remaining passengers were their guests. If $\frac{3}{4}$ of the company-employee passengers were managers, what was the number of company-employee passengers who were NOT managers?

    (1) There were 690 passengers on the cruise.
    (2) There were 230 passengers who were guests of the company employees.

Arithmetic Arithmetic operations

(1) From this, since $\frac{2}{3}$ of the passengers were company employees, then $\frac{2}{3} \times 690 = 460$ passengers were company employees. Then, since $\frac{3}{4}$ of the company employees were managers, so $1 - \frac{3}{4} = \frac{1}{4}$ of the company-employee passengers were not managers. Therefore $\frac{1}{4} \times 460 = 115$ company employees were not managers; SUFFICIENT.

(2) If 230 of the passengers were guests, then this represents $1 - \frac{2}{3} = \frac{1}{3}$ of the cruise passengers. Therefore, there were $230 \times 3 = 690$ passengers altogether, $690 - 230 = 460$ of whom were company employees. Since $1 - \frac{3}{4} = \frac{1}{4}$ of the company employees were not managers, $\frac{1}{4} \times 460 = 115$ of the passengers who were company employees were not managers; SUFFICIENT.

**The correct answer is D;
each statement alone is sufficient.**

117. The length of the edging that surrounds circular garden K is $\frac{1}{2}$ the length of the edging that surrounds circular garden G. What is the area of garden K? (Assume that the edging has negligible width.)

    (1) The area of G is 25π square meters.
    (2) The edging around G is 10π meters long.

Geometry Circles; Area

Note that the length of the edging around a circular garden is equal to the circumference of the circle. The formula for the circumference of a circle, where C is the circumference and d is the diameter, is $C = \pi d$. The formula for the area of a circle, where A is the area and r is the radius, is $A = \pi r^2$. In any circle, r is equal to $\frac{1}{2}d$. If the length of the edging around K is equal to $\frac{1}{2}$ the length of the edging around G, then the circumference of K is equal to $\frac{1}{2}$ the circumference of G.

(1) Since the area of G is 25π square meters, $25\pi = \pi r^2$ or $25 = r^2$ and $5 = r$. So, if the radius of G is 5, the diameter is 10, and the circumference of G is equal to 10π. Since the circumference of K is $\frac{1}{2}$ that of G, then the circumference of K is 5π, making the diameter of K equal to 5. If the diameter of K is 5, the radius of K is 2.5, and the area of K is $\pi(2.5)^2$ or 6.25π; SUFFICIENT.

(2) If the edging around G is 10π meters long, then the circumference of G is 10π. The area of K can then by found by proceeding as in (1); SUFFICIENT.

**The correct answer is D;
each statement alone is sufficient.**

118. For any integers x and y, min(x, y) and max(x, y) denote the minimum and the maximum of x and y, respectively. For example, min$(5, 2) = 2$ and max$(5, 2) = 5$. For the integer w, what is the value of min$(10, w)$?

    (1) $w = $ max$(20, z)$ for some integer z.
    (2) $w = $ max$(10, w)$

Arithmetic Properties of numbers

If $w \geq 10$, then min$(10, w) = 10$, and if $w < 10$, then min$(10, w) = w$. Therefore, the value of min$(10, w)$ can be determined if the value of w can be determined.

(1) Given that $w = $ max$(20, z)$, then $w \geq 20$. Hence, $w \geq 10$, and so min$(10, w) = 10$; SUFFICIENT.

(2)   Given that $w = \max(10, w)$, then $w \geq 10$, and so $\min(10, w) = 10$; SUFFICIENT.

**The correct answer is D;
each statement alone is sufficient.**

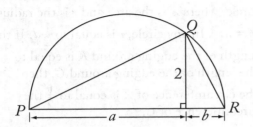

119. If arc *PQR* above is a semicircle, what is the length of diameter $\overline{PR}$?

(1) $a = 4$

(2) $b = 1$

Geometry Circles

Since angle *PQR* is inscribed in a semicircle, it is a right angle, and ΔPQR is a right triangle. ΔPQR is divided into two right triangles by the vertical line from *Q* to side $\overline{PR}$. Let $x = PQ$ and $y = QR$. The larger right triangle has hypotenuse x, so $x^2 = 4 + a^2$; the smaller right triangle has hypotenuse y, so $y^2 = 4 + b^2$. From ΔPQR, $(a + b)^2 = x^2 + y^2$, so by substitution, $(a + b)^2 = (4 + a^2) + (4 + b^2)$, and by simplification, $a^2 + 2ab + b^2 = 8 + a^2 + b^2$ or $2ab = 8$ or $ab = 4$.

(1)   If $a = 4$ is substituted in $ab = 4$, then b must be 1 and diameter *PR* is 5; SUFFICIENT.

(2)   If $b = 1$ is substituted in $ab = 4$, then a must be 4 and diameter *PR* is 5; SUFFICIENT.

**The correct answer is D;
each statement alone is sufficient.**

120. A certain bookcase has 2 shelves of books. On the upper shelf, the book with the greatest number of pages has 400 pages. On the lower shelf, the book with the least number of pages has 475 pages. What is the median number of pages for all of the books on the 2 shelves?

(1)   There are 25 books on the upper shelf.

(2)   There are 24 books on the lower shelf.

Arithmetic Statistics

(1)   The information given says nothing about the number of books on the lower shelf. If there are fewer than 25 books on the lower shelf, then the median number of pages will be the number of pages in one of the books on the upper shelf or the average number of pages in two books on the upper shelf. Hence, the median will be at most 400. If there are more than 25 books on the lower shelf, then the median number of pages will be the number of pages in one of the books on the lower shelf or the average number of pages in two books on the lower shelf. Hence, the median will be at least 475; NOT sufficient.

(2)   An analysis very similar to that used in (1) shows the information given is not sufficient to determine the median; NOT sufficient.

Given both (1) and (2), it follows that there is a total of 49 books. Therefore, the median will be the 25th book when the books are ordered by number of pages. Since the 25th book in this ordering is the book on the upper shelf with the greatest number of pages, the median is 400. Therefore, (1) and (2) together are sufficient.

**The correct answer is C;
both statements together are sufficient.**

121. During a 6-day local trade show, the least number of people registered in a single day was 80. Was the average (arithmetic mean) number of people registered per day for the 6 days greater than 90 ?

(1)   For the 4 days with the greatest number of people registered, the average (arithmetic mean) number registered per day was 100.

(2)   For the 3 days with the smallest number of people registered, the average (arithmetic mean) number registered per day was 85.

Arithmetic Statistics

Let a, b, c, d, and e be the numbers of people registered for the other 5 days, listed in increasing order. Determining if $\dfrac{80 + a + b + c + d + e}{6} > 90$ is equivalent to determining if $(80 + a + b + c + d + e) > (6)(90) = 540$, or if $a + b + c + d + e > 460$.

(1)   Given that $\dfrac{b+c+d+e}{4}=100$, then $b+c+d+e=400$. Therefore, since $a \geq 80$ (because 80 is the least of the 6 daily registration numbers), it follows that $a+b+c+d+e \geq 80+400=480$, and hence $a+b+c+d+e>460$; SUFFICIENT.

(2)   Given that $\dfrac{80+a+b}{3}=85$, then $80+a+b=$ $(3)(85)$, or $a+b=175$. Note that this is possible with each of a and b being an integer that is at least 80, such as $a=87$ and $b=88$. From $a+b=175$, the condition $a+b+c+d+e>460$ is equivalent to $175+c+d+e>460$, or $c+d+e>285$. However, using 3 integers that are each at least 88 (recall that the values of c, d, and e must be at least the value of b), it is possible for $c+d+e>285$ to hold (for example, $c=d=e=100$) and it is possible for $c+d+e>285$ not to hold (for example, $c=d=e=90$); NOT sufficient.

The correct answer is A;
statement 1 alone is sufficient.

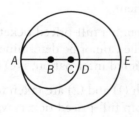

122. In the figure above, points A, B, C, D, and E lie on a line. A is on both circles, B is the center of the smaller circle, C is the center of the larger circle, D is on the smaller circle, and E is on the larger circle. What is the area of the region inside the larger circle and outside the smaller circle?

(1) $AB = 3$ and $BC = 2$
(2) $CD = 1$ and $DE = 4$

Geometry Circles

If R is the radius of the larger circle and r is the radius of the smaller circle, then the desired area is $\pi R^2 - \pi r^2$. Thus, if both the values of R and r can be determined, then the desired area can be determined.

(1)   Given that $AB = r = 3$ and $BC = 2$, then $AB + BC = R = 3 + 2 = 5$; SUFFICIENT.

(2)   Given that $CD = 1$ and $DE = 4$, then $CD + DE = R = 1 + 4 = 5$. Since $\overline{AE}$ is a diameter of the larger circle, then $AD + DE = 2R$. Also, since $\overline{AD}$ is a diameter of the smaller circle, then $AD = 2r$. Thus, $2r + DE = 2R$, or $2r + 4 = 10$, and so $r = 3$; SUFFICIENT.

The correct answer is D;
each statement alone is sufficient.

123. The range of the numbers in set S is x, and the range of the numbers in set T is y. If all of the numbers in set T are also in set S, is x greater than y?

(1)   Set S consists of 7 numbers.
(2)   Set T consists of 6 numbers.

Arithmetic Statistics

Set S has a range of x, set T has a range of y, and T is a subset of S. Determine if x is greater than y.

(1)   It is given that S contains exactly 7 numbers, but nothing additional is known about T. Thus, if $S = \{1, 2, 3, 4, 5, 6, 7\}$ and $T = \{1, 2, 3, 4, 5, 6\}$, then $x = 7 - 1 = 6$, $y = 6 - 1 = 5$, and x is greater than y. On the other hand, if $S = \{1, 2, 3, 4, 5, 6, 7\}$ and $T = \{1, 3, 4, 5, 6, 7\}$, then $x = 7 - 1 = 6$, $y = 7 - 1 = 6$, and x is not greater than y; NOT sufficient.

(2)   It is given that T contains exactly 6 numbers, but nothing additional is known about T. Since the same examples given in (1) can also be used in (2), it cannot be determined if x is greater than y; NOT sufficient.

Taking (1) and (2) together, the examples used in (1) can be used to show that it cannot be determined if x is greater than y.

The correct answer is E;
both statements together are still not sufficient.

124. An employee is paid 1.5 times the regular hourly rate for each hour worked in excess of 40 hours per week, excluding Sunday, and 2 times the regular hourly rate for each hour worked on Sunday. How much was the employee paid last week?

    (1)   The employee's regular hourly rate is $10.

    (2)   Last week the employee worked a total of 54 hours but did not work more than 8 hours on any day.

Arithmetic Arithmetic operations

The employee's pay consists of at most 40 hours at the regular hourly rate, plus any overtime pay at either 1.5 or 2 times the regular hourly rate.

    (1)   From this, the employee's regular pay for a 40-hour week is $400. However, there is no information about overtime, and so the employee's total pay cannot be calculated; NOT sufficient.

    (2)   From this, the employee worked a total of $54 - 40 = 14$ hours. However, there is no indication of how many hours were worked on Sunday (at 2 times the regular hourly rate) or another day (at 1.5 times the regular hourly rate); NOT sufficient.

With (1) and (2) taken together, there is still no way to calculate the amount of overtime pay.

The correct answer is E; both statements together are still not sufficient.

125. A box contains only red chips, white chips, and blue chips. If a chip is randomly selected from the box, what is the probability that the chip will be either white or blue?

    (1)   The probability that the chip will be blue is $\frac{1}{5}$.

    (2)   The probability that the chip will be red is $\frac{1}{3}$.

Arithmetic Probability

    (1)   Since the probability of drawing a blue chip is known, the probability of drawing a chip that is not blue (in other words, a red or white chip) can also be found. However, the probability of drawing a white or blue chip cannot be determined from this information; NOT sufficient.

    (2)   The probability that the chip will be either white or blue is the same as the probability that it will NOT be red. Thus, the probability is $1 - \frac{1}{3} = \frac{2}{3}$; SUFFICIENT.

The correct answer is B; statement 2 alone is sufficient.

126. What was the revenue that a theater received from the sale of 400 tickets, some of which were sold at the full price and the remainder of which were sold at a reduced price?

    (1)   The number of tickets sold at the full price was $\frac{1}{4}$ of the total number of tickets sold.

    (2)   The full price of a ticket was $25.

Arithmetic Arithmetic operations

    (1)   Since $\frac{1}{4}$ of the tickets were sold at full price, $\frac{3}{4} \times 400 = 300$ tickets were sold at a reduced price. However, the revenue cannot be determined from this information; NOT sufficient.

    (2)   Although a full-priced ticket cost $25, the revenue cannot be determined without additional information; NOT sufficient.

When both (1) and (2) are taken together, the revenue from full-priced tickets was $100 \times \$25 = \$2,500$, but the cost of a reduced-priced ticket is still unknown, and the theater's revenues cannot be calculated.

The correct answer is E; both statements together are still not sufficient.

127. The annual rent collected by a corporation from a certain building was x percent more in 1998 than in 1997 and y percent less in 1999 than in 1998. Was the annual rent collected by the corporation from the building more in 1999 than in 1997 ?

    (1) $x > y$

    (2) $\frac{xy}{100} < x - y$

Algebra Percents

Let A be the annual rent collected in 1997. Then the annual rent collected in 1998 is $\left(1+\frac{x}{100}\right)A$ and the annual rent collected in 1999 is $\left(1+\frac{x}{100}\right)\left(1-\frac{y}{100}\right)A$. Determine if

$$A\left(1+\frac{x}{100}\right)\left(1-\frac{y}{100}\right) > A,\text{ or equivalently, if}$$

$$\left(1+\frac{x}{100}\right)\left(1-\frac{y}{100}\right) > 1.$$

(1) Given that $x > y$, $\left(1+\frac{x}{100}\right)\left(1-\frac{y}{100}\right) > 1$ is possible by choosing $x = 100$ and $y = 10$, since $\left(1+\frac{100}{100}\right)\left(1-\frac{10}{100}\right) = (2)(0.9) = 1.8$,

and $\left(1+\frac{x}{100}\right)\left(1-\frac{y}{100}\right) \leq 1$ is possible by choosing $x = 100$ and $y = 90$, since $\left(1+\frac{100}{100}\right)\left(1-\frac{90}{100}\right) = (2)(0.1) = 0.2$; NOT sufficient.

(2) As shown below, the given inequality $\frac{xy}{100} < x - y$ is equivalent to the desired inequality, $\left(1+\frac{x}{100}\right)\left(1-\frac{y}{100}\right) > 1$, which can be justified by the following steps, where each step's inequality is equivalent to the previous step's inequality.

$\frac{xy}{10,000} < \frac{x}{100} - \frac{y}{100}$	divide both sides by 100
$0 < \frac{x}{100} - \frac{y}{100} - \frac{xy}{10,000}$	subtract $\frac{xy}{10,000}$ from both sides
$1 < 1 + \frac{x}{100} - \frac{y}{100} - \frac{xy}{10,000}$	add 1 to both sides
$1 < \left(1+\frac{x}{100}\right)\left(1-\frac{y}{100}\right)$	factor the right side; SUFFICIENT

The correct answer is B; statement 2 alone is sufficient.

128. The hypotenuse of a right triangle is 10 cm. What is the perimeter, in centimeters, of the triangle?

(1) The area of the triangle is 25 square centimeters.

(2) The 2 legs of the triangle are of equal length.

Geometry Triangles

If x and y are the lengths of the legs of the triangle, then it is given that $x^2 + y^2 = 100$. To determine the value of $x + y + 100$, the perimeter of the triangle, is equivalent to determining the value of $x + y$.

(1) Given that the area is 25, then $\frac{1}{2}xy = 25$, or $xy = 50$. Since $(x+y)^2 = x^2 + y^2 + 2xy$, it follows that $(x+y)^2 = 100 + 2(50)$, or $x + y = \sqrt{200}$; SUFFICIENT.

(2) Given that $x = y$, since $x^2 + y^2 = 100$, it follows that $2x^2 = 100$, or $x = \sqrt{50}$. Hence, $x + y = x + x = 2x = 2\sqrt{50}$; SUFFICIENT.

The correct answer is D; each statement alone is sufficient.

129. In the xy-plane, region R consists of all the points (x,y) such that $2x + 3y \leq 6$. Is the point (r,s) in region R?

(1) $3r + 2s = 6$

(2) $r \leq 3$ and $s \leq 2$

Algebra Coordinate geometry

(1) Both $(r,s) = (2,0)$ and $(r,s) = (0,3)$ satisfy the equation $3r + 2s = 6$, since $3(2) + 2(0) = 6$ and $3(0) + 2(3) = 6$. However, $2(2) + 3(0) = 4$, so (2,0) is in region R, while $2(0) + 3(3) = 9$, so (0,3) is not in region R; NOT sufficient.

(2) Both $(r,s) = (0,0)$ and $(r,s) = (3,2)$ satisfy the inequalities $r \leq 3$ and $s \leq 2$. However, $2(0) + 3(0) = 0$, so (0,0) is in region R, while $2(3) + 3(2) = 12$, so (3,2) is not in region R; NOT sufficient.

Taking (1) and (2) together, it can be seen that both $(r,s) = (2,0)$ and $(r,s) = (1,1.5)$ satisfy $3r + 2s = 6$, $r \leq 3$ and $s \leq 2$. However,

$2(2) + 3(0) = 4$, so $(2,0)$ is in region R, while $2(1) + 3(1.5) = 6.5$, so $(1,1.5)$ is not in region R. Therefore, (1) and (2) together are not sufficient.

The correct answer is E;
both statements together are still not sufficient.

---

130. What is the volume of a certain rectangular solid?

    (1) Two adjacent faces of the solid have areas 15 and 24, respectively.

    (2) Each of two opposite faces of the solid has area 40.

Geometry Rectangular solids and cylinders

(1) If the edge lengths of the rectangular solid are 3, 5, and 8, then two adjacent faces will have areas $(3)(5) = 15$ and $(3)(8) = 24$ and the volume of the rectangular solid will be $(3)(5)(8) = 120$. If the edge lengths of the rectangular solid are 1, 15, 24, then two adjacent faces will have areas $(1)(15) = 15$ and $(1)(24) = 24$ and the volume of the rectangular solid will be $(1)(15)(24) = 360$; NOT sufficient.

(2) If the edge lengths of the rectangular solid are 5, 8, and x, where x is a positive real number, then the rectangular solid will have a pair of opposite faces of area 40, namely the two faces that are 5 by 8. However, the volume is $(5)(8)(x)$, which will vary as x varies; NOT sufficient.

Taking (1) and (2) together, if the edge lengths are denoted by x, y, and z, then $xy = 15$, $xz = 24$, and $yz = 40$, and so $(xy)(xz)(yz) = (15)(24)(40)$, or $(xyz)^2 = (15)(24)(40)$. Thus, the volume of the rectangular solid is $xyz = \sqrt{(15)(24)(40)}$. Therefore, (1) and (2) together are sufficient.

The correct answer is C;
both statements together are sufficient.

Shipment	S1	S2	S3	S4	S5	S6
Fraction of the Total Value of the Six Shipments	$\frac{1}{4}$	$\frac{1}{5}$	$\frac{1}{6}$	$\frac{3}{20}$	$\frac{2}{15}$	$\frac{1}{10}$

131. Six shipments of machine parts were shipped from a factory on two trucks, with each shipment entirely on one of the trucks. Each shipment was labeled either S1, S2, S3, S4, S5, or S6. The table shows the value of each shipment as a fraction of the total value of the six shipments. If the shipments on the first truck had a value greater than $\frac{1}{2}$ of the total value of the six shipments, was S3 shipped on the first truck?

    (1) S2 and S4 were shipped on the first truck.

    (2) S1 and S6 were shipped on the second truck.

Arithmetic Operations on rational numbers

Given that the shipments on the first truck had a value greater than $\frac{1}{2}$ of the total value of the 6 shipments, determine if S3 was shipped on the first truck.

To avoid dealing with fractions, it will be convenient to create scaled values of the shipments by multiplying each fractional value by 60, which is the least common denominator of the fractions. Thus, the scaled values associated with S1, S2, S3, S4, S5, and S6 are 15, 12, 10, 9, 8, and 6, respectively. The given information is that the scaled value of the shipments on the first truck is greater than $\left(\frac{1}{2}\right)(60) = 30$.

(1) Given that the first truck includes shipments with scaled values 12 and 9, it may or may not be the case that S3 (the shipment with scaled value 10) is on the first truck. For example, the first truck could contain only S2, S3, and S4, for a total scaled value 12 + 10 + 9 = 31 > 30. Or, the first truck could contain only S1, S2, and S4, for a total scaled value 15 + 12 + 9 = 36 > 30; NOT sufficient.

(2) Given that the second truck includes shipments with scaled values 15 and 6, the second truck cannot contain S3. Otherwise, the second truck would contain shipments

with scaled values 15, 6, and 10, for a total scaled value 15 + 6 + 10 = 31, leaving at most a total scaled value 29 (which is not greater than 30) for the first truck; SUFFICIENT.

The correct answer is B; statement 2 alone is sufficient.

132. Joanna bought only $0.15 stamps and $0.29 stamps. How many $0.15 stamps did she buy?

    (1)   She bought $4.40 worth of stamps.
    (2)   She bought an equal number of $0.15 stamps and $0.29 stamps.

Algebra Simultaneous equations

Determine the value of x if x is the number of $0.15 stamps and y is the number of $0.29 stamps.

(1)   Given that $15x + 29y = 440$, then $29y = 440 - 15x$. Because x is an integer, $440 - 15x = 5(88 - 3x)$ is a multiple of 5. Therefore, $29y$ must be a multiple of 5, from which it follows that y must be a multiple of 5. Hence, the value of y must be among the numbers 0, 5, 10, 15, etc. To more efficiently test these values of y, note that $15x = 440 - 29y$, and hence $440 - 29y$ must be a multiple of 15, or equivalently, $440 - 29y$ must be a multiple of both 3 and 5. By computation, the values of $440 - 29y$ for y equal to 0, 5, 10, and 15 are 440, 295, 150, and 5. Of these, only 150, which corresponds to $y = 10$, is divisible by 3. From $15x = 440 - 29y$ it follows that $x = 10$ when $y = 10$. Therefore, $x = 10$ and $y = 10$; SUFFICIENT.

(2)   Although $x = y$, it is impossible to determine the value of x because there is no information on the total worth of the stamps Joanna bought. For example, if the total worth, in dollars, was $0.15 + 0.29$, then $x = 1$, but if the total worth was $2(0.15) + 2(0.29)$, then $x = 2$; NOT sufficient.

The correct answer is A; statement 1 alone is sufficient.

133. If x, y, and z are three-digit positive integers and if $x = y + z$, is the hundreds digit of x equal to the sum of the hundreds digits of y and z ?

    (1)   The tens digit of x is equal to the sum of the tens digits of y and z.
    (2)   The units digit of x is equal to the sum of the units digits of y and z.

Arithmetic Place value

Letting $x = 100a + 10b + c$, $y = 100p + 10q + r$, and $z = 100t + 10u + v$, where a, b, c, p, q, r, t, u, and v are digits, determine if $a = p + t$.

(1)   It is given that $b = q + u$ (which implies that $c + v \leq 9$ because if $c + v > 9$, then in the addition process a ten would need to be carried over to the tens column and b would be $q + u + 1$). Since b is a digit, $0 \leq b \leq 9$. Hence, $0 \leq q + u \leq 9$, and so $0 \leq 10(q + u) \leq 90$. Therefore, in the addition process, there are no hundreds to carry over from the tens column to the hundreds column, so $a = p + t$; SUFFICIENT.

(2)   It is given that $c = r + v$. If $x = 687$, $y = 231$, and $z = 456$, then, $y + z = 231 + 456 = 687 = x$, $r + v = 1 + 6 = 7 = c$, and $p + t = 2 + 4 = 6 = a$. On the other hand, if $x = 637$, $y = 392$, and $z = 245$, then $y + z = 392 + 245 = 637 = x$, $r + v = 2 + 5 = 7 = c$, and $p + t = 3 + 2 = 5 \neq 6 = a$; NOT sufficient.

The correct answer is A; statement 1 alone is sufficient.

	Favorable	Unfavorable	Not Sure
Candidate M	40	20	40
Candidate N	30	35	35

134. The table above shows the results of a survey of 100 voters who each responded "Favorable" or "Unfavorable" or "Not Sure" when asked about their impressions of Candidate M and of Candidate N. What was the number of voters who responded "Favorable" for both candidates?

    (1)   The number of voters who did not respond "Favorable" for either candidate was 40.
    (2)   The number of voters who responded "Unfavorable" for both candidates was 10.

Arithmetic Sets

If x is the number of voters who responded "Favorable" for both candidates, then it follows from the table that the number of voters who responded "Favorable" to at least one candidate is $40 + 30 - x = 70 - x$. This is because $40 + 30$ represents the number of voters who responded "Favorable" for Candidate M added to the number of voters who responded "Favorable" for Candidate N, a calculation that counts twice each of the x voters who responded "Favorable" for both candidates.

(1)   Given that there were 40 voters who did not respond "Favorable" for either candidate and there were 100 voters surveyed, the number of voters who responded "Favorable" to at least one candidate is $100 - 40 = 60$. Therefore, from the comments above, it follows that $70 - x = 60$, and hence $x = 10$; SUFFICIENT.

(2)   The information given affects only the numbers of voters in the categories "Unfavorable" for Candidate M only, "Unfavorable" for Candidate N only, and "Unfavorable" for both candidates. Thus, the numbers of voters in the categories "Favorable" for Candidate M only, "Favorable" for Candidate N only, and "Favorable" for both candidates are not affected. Since these latter categories are only constrained to have certain integer values that have a total sum of $70 - x$, more than one possibility exists for the value of x. For example, the numbers of voters in the categories "Favorable" for Candidate M only, "Favorable" for Candidate N only, and "Favorable" for both candidates could be 25, 15, and 15, respectively, which gives $70 - x = 25 + 15 + 15$, or $x = 15$. However, the numbers of voters in the categories "Favorable" for Candidate M only, "Favorable" for Candidate N only, and "Favorable" for both candidates could be 30, 20, and 10, respectively, which gives $70 - x = 30 + 20 + 10$, or $x = 10$; NOT sufficient.

The correct answer is A; statement 1 alone is sufficient.

135. A school administrator will assign each student in a group of n students to one of m classrooms. If $3 < m < 13 < n$, is it possible to assign each of the n students to one of the m classrooms so that each classroom has the same number of students assigned to it?

(1)   It is possible to assign each of $3n$ students to one of m classrooms so that each classroom has the same number of students assigned to it.

(2)   It is possible to assign each of $13n$ students to one of m classrooms so that each classroom has the same number of students assigned to it.

Arithmetic Properties of numbers

Determine if n is divisible by m.

(1)   Given that $3n$ is divisible by m, then n is divisible by m if $m = 9$ and $n = 27$ (note that $3 < m < 13 < n$, $3n = 81$, and $m = 9$, so $3n$ is divisible by m) and n is not divisible by m if $m = 9$ and $n = 30$ (note that $3 < m < 13 < n$, $3n = 90$, and $m = 9$, so $3n$ is divisible by m); NOT sufficient.

(2)   Given that $13n$ is divisible by m, then $13n = qm$, or $\dfrac{n}{m} = \dfrac{q}{13}$, for some integer q. Since 13 is a prime number that divides qm (because $13n = qm$) and 13 does not divide m (because $m < 13$), it follows that 13 divides q. Therefore, $\dfrac{q}{13}$ is an integer, and since $\dfrac{n}{m} = \dfrac{q}{13}$, then $\dfrac{n}{m}$ is an integer. Thus, n is divisible by m; SUFFICIENT.

The correct answer is B; statement 2 alone is sufficient.

136. If $°$ represents one of the operations $+$, $-$, and $\times$, is $k \, ° \, (\ell + m) = (k \, ° \, \ell) + (k \, ° \, m)$ for all numbers k, ℓ, and m?

(1) $k \, ° \, 1$ is not equal to $1 \, ° \, k$ for some numbers k.

(2) $°$ represents subtraction.

Arithmetic Properties of numbers

(1)   For operations $+$ and $\times$, $k \, ° \, 1$ is equal to $1 \, ° \, k$ since $k + 1 = 1 + k$ and $k \times 1 = 1 \times k$. Therefore, the operation represented must be subtraction. From this, it is possible to determine whether

$k-(\ell+m)=(k-\ell)+(k-m)$ holds for all numbers k, ℓ, and m; SUFFICIENT.

(2) The information is given directly that the operation represented is subtraction. Once again, it can be determined whether $k-(\ell+m)=(k-\ell)+(k-m)$ holds for all numbers k, ℓ, and m; SUFFICIENT.

The correct answer is D; each statement alone is sufficient.

137. How many of the 60 cars sold last month by a certain dealer had neither power windows nor a stereo?

(1) Of the 60 cars sold, 20 had a stereo but not power windows.

(2) Of the 60 cars sold, 30 had both power windows and a stereo.

Algebra Sets

(1) With this information, there are three other categories of cars that are unknown: those equipped with both a stereo and power windows, with power windows but with no stereo, and with neither power windows nor a stereo; NOT sufficient.

(2) Again there are three other categories that are unknown: those with a stereo but no power windows, with power windows with no stereo, and with neither power windows nor a stereo; NOT sufficient.

From (1) and (2) together, it can be deduced that there were $60 - 50 = 10$ cars sold that did not have a stereo. However, it is unknown and cannot be concluded from this information how many of these cars did not have a stereo but did have power windows or did not have either a stereo or power windows.

The correct answer is E; both statements together are still not sufficient.

138. In Jefferson School, 300 students study French or Spanish or both. If 100 of these students do not study French, how many of these students study both French and Spanish?

(1) Of the 300 students, 60 do not study Spanish.

(2) A total of 240 of the students study Spanish.

Algebra Sets (Venn diagrams)

One way to solve a problem of this kind is to represent the data regarding the 300 students by a Venn diagram. Let x be the number of students who study both French and Spanish, and let y be the number who do not study Spanish (i.e., those who study only French). It is given that there are 100 students who do not study French (i.e., those who study only Spanish). This information can be represented by the Venn diagram below, where $300 = x + y + 100$:

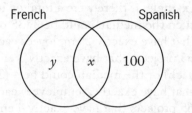

(1) This provides the value of y in the equation $300 = x + y + 100$, and the value of x (the number who study both languages) can thus be determined; SUFFICIENT.

(2) Referring to the Venn diagram above, this provides the information that 240 is the sum of $x + 100$, the number of students who study Spanish. That is, 240 is equal to the number who study both French and Spanish (x) plus the number who study only Spanish (100). Since $240 = x + 100$, the value of x and thus the number who study both languages can be determined; SUFFICIENT.

The correct answer is D; each statement alone is sufficient.

139. What is the median number of employees assigned per project for the projects at Company Z ?

(1) 25 percent of the projects at Company Z have 4 or more employees assigned to each project.

(2) 35 percent of the projects at Company Z have 2 or fewer employees assigned to each project.

Arithmetic Statistics

(1) Although 25 percent of the projects have 4 or more employees, there is essentially no information about the middle values of the numbers of employees per project. For example, if there were a total of 100 projects,

then the median could be 2 (75 projects that have exactly 2 employees each and 25 projects that have exactly 4 employees each) or the median could be 3 (75 projects that have exactly 3 employees each and 25 projects that have exactly 4 employees each); NOT sufficient.

(2) Although 35 percent of the projects have 2 or fewer employees, there is essentially no information about the middle values of the numbers of employees per project. For example, if there were a total of 100 projects, then the median could be 3 (35 projects that have exactly 2 employees each and 65 projects that have exactly 3 employees each) or the median could be 4 (35 projects that have exactly 2 employees each and 65 projects that have exactly 4 employees each); NOT sufficient.

Given both (1) and (2), $100 - (25 + 35)$ percent = 40 percent of the projects have exactly 3 employees. Therefore, when the numbers of employees per project are listed from least to greatest, 35 percent of the numbers are 2 or less and $(35 + 40)$ percent = 75 percent are 3 or less, and hence the median is 3.

**The correct answer is C;
both statements together are sufficient.**

140. If Juan had a doctor's appointment on a certain day, was the appointment on a Wednesday?

(1) Exactly 60 hours before the appointment, it was Monday.

(2) The appointment was between 1:00 p.m. and 9:00 p.m.

Arithmetic Arithmetic operations

(1) From this, it is not known at what point on Monday it was 60 hours before the appointment, and the day of the appointment cannot be known. If, for example, the specific point on Monday was 9:00 a.m., 60 hours later it would be 9:00 p.m. Wednesday, and the appointment would thus be on a Wednesday. If the specific point on Monday was instead 9:00 p.m., 60 hours later it would be 9:00 a.m. Thursday, and

the appointment would instead fall on a Thursday rather than Wednesday; NOT sufficient.

(2) No information is given about the day of the appointment; NOT sufficient.

Using (1) and (2) together, it can be determined that the point 60 hours before any time from 1:00 p.m. to 9:00 p.m. on any particular day, as given in (2), is a time between 1:00 a.m. and 9:00 a.m. two days earlier. If 60 hours before an appointment in this 1:00 p.m.–9:00 p.m. time frame it was Monday as given in (1), then the appointment had to be on a Wednesday.

**The correct answer is C;
both statements together are sufficient.**

141. Last year, a certain company began manufacturing product X and sold every unit of product X that it produced. Last year the company's total expenses for manufacturing product X were equal to $100,000 plus 5 percent of the company's total revenue from all units of product X sold. If the company made a profit on product X last year, did the company sell more than 21,000 units of product X last year?

(1) The company's total revenue from the sale of product X last year was greater than $110,000.

(2) For each unit of product X sold last year, the company's revenue was $5.

Algebra Applied problems

For a company that made a profit last year from selling product X and had total expenses for product X of $100,000 + 0.05R, where R is the total revenue for selling product X, determine whether the company sold more than 21,000 units of product X last year.

Note that since the company made a profit, revenue − cost, which is given by R − ($100,000 + 0.05R) = 0.95R − $100,000, must be positive.

(1) It is given that R > $110,000. It is possible to vary the unit price and the number of units sold so that R > $110,000 and *more than* 21,000 units were sold, and also so that R > $110,000 and *less than* 21,000 units were sold. For example, if 25,000 units were

sold for $10 per unit, then $R = 25{,}000(\$10)$ $= \$250{,}000 > \$110{,}000$ and $25{,}000 > 21{,}000$. On the other hand, if 20,000 units were sold for $10 per unit, then $R = 20{,}000(\$10) = \$200{,}000 > \$110{,}000$ and $20{,}000 < 21{,}000$; NOT sufficient.

(2) It is given that the company's revenue for each unit of product X was $5. If the company manufactured and sold x units of product X, then its revenue was $\$5x$. Because the company made a profit, $0.95(\$5x) - \$100{,}000 > 0$, and so

$$0.95(\$5x) - \$100{,}000 > 0$$
$$\$4.75 - \$100{,}000 > 0$$
$$\$4.75x > \$100{,}000$$
$$x > 21{,}052; \text{ SUFFICIENT}$$

To avoid long division in the last step, note that $4.75(21{,}000) = 99{,}750$, and thus from $4.75x > 100{,}000$ it follows that $x > 21{,}000$.

The correct answer is B;
statement 2 alone is sufficient.

142. When a player in a certain game tossed a coin a number of times, 4 more heads than tails resulted. Heads or tails resulted each time the player tossed the coin. How many times did heads result?

(1) The player tossed the coin 24 times.
(2) The player received 3 points each time heads resulted and 1 point each time tails resulted, for a total of 52 points.

Arithmetic; Algebra Probability; Applied problems; Simultaneous equations

Let h represent the number of heads that resulted and t represent the number of tails obtained by the player. Then the information given can be expressed as $h = t + 4$.

(1) The additional information can be expressed as $h + t = 24$. When this equation is paired with the given information, $h = t + 4$, there are two linear equations in two unknowns. One way to conclude that we can determine the number of heads is to solve the equations simultaneously, thereby obtaining the number of heads and the number of tails:

Solving $h = t + 4$ for t, which gives $t = h - 4$, and substituting the result in $h + t = 24$ gives $h + (h - 4) = 24$, which clearly can be solved for h. Another way to conclude that we can determine the number of heads is to note that the pair of equations represents two non-parallel lines in the coordinate plane; SUFFICIENT.

(2) The additional information provided can be expressed as $3h + t = 52$. The same comments in (1) apply here as well. For example, solving $h = t + 4$ for t, which gives $t = h - 4$, and substituting the result in $3h + t = 52$ gives $3h + (h - 4) = 52$, which clearly can be solved for h; SUFFICIENT.

The correct answer is D;
each statement alone is sufficient.

143. Beginning in January of last year, Carl made deposits of $120 into his account on the 15th of each month for several consecutive months and then made withdrawals of $50 from the account on the 15th of each of the remaining months of last year. There were no other transactions in the account last year. If the closing balance of Carl's account for May of last year was $2,600, what was the range of the monthly closing balances of Carl's account last year?

(1) Last year the closing balance of Carl's account for April was less than $2,625.
(2) Last year the closing balance of Carl's account for June was less than $2,675.

Arithmetic Statistics

(1) If Carl began making $50 withdrawals on or before May 15, his account balance on April 16 would be at least $50 greater than it was on the last day of May. Thus, his account balance on April 16 would be at least $\$2{,}600 + \$50 = \$2{,}650$, which is contrary to the information given in (1). Therefore, Carl did not begin making $50 withdrawals until June 15 or later. These observations can be used to give at least two possible ranges. Carl could have had an account balance of $2,000 on January 1, made $120 deposits in each of the first 11 months of the year, and then made a $50 withdrawal on December 15, which gives a range of monthly closing

balances of (120)(10). Also, Carl could have had an account balance of $2,000 on January 1, made $120 deposits in each of the first 10 months of the year, and then made $50 withdrawals on November 15 and on December 15, which gives a range of monthly closing balances of (120)(9); NOT sufficient.

(2) On June 1, Carl's account balance was the same as its closing balance was for May, namely $2,600. Depending on whether Carl made a $120 deposit or a $50 withdrawal on June 15, Carl's account balance on June 16 was either $2,720 or $2,550. It follows from the information given in (2) that Carl's balance on June 16 was $2,550. Therefore, Carl began making $50 withdrawals on or before June 15. These observations can be used to give at least two possible ranges. Carl could have had an account balance of $2,680 on January 1, made one $120 deposit on January 15, and then made a $50 withdrawal in each of the remaining 11 months of the year (this gives a closing balance of $2,600 for May), which gives a range of monthly closing balances of (50)(11). Also, Carl could have had an account balance of $2,510 on January 1, made $120 deposits on January 15 and on February 15, and then made a $50 withdrawal in each of the remaining 10 months of the year (this gives a closing balance of $2,600 for May), which gives a range of monthly closing balances of (50)(10); NOT sufficient.

Given both (1) and (2), it follows from the remarks above that Carl began making $50 withdrawals on June 15. Therefore, the changes to Carl's account balance for each month of last year are known. Since the closing balance for May is given, it follows that the closing balances for each month of last year are known, and hence the range of these 12 known values can be determined. Therefore, (1) and (2) together are sufficient.

The correct answer is C;
both statements together are sufficient.

144. Are all of the numbers in a certain list of 15 numbers equal?

(1) The sum of all the numbers in the list is 60.
(2) The sum of any 3 numbers in the list is 12.

Arithmetic Properties of numbers

(1) If there are 15 occurrences of the number 4 in the list, then the sum of the numbers in the list is 60 and all the numbers in the list are equal. If there are 13 occurrences of the number 4 in the list, 1 occurrence of the number 3 in the list, and 1 occurrence of the number 5 in the list, then the sum of the numbers in the list is 60 and not all the numbers in the list are equal; NOT sufficient.

(2) Given that the sum of any 3 numbers in the list is 12, arrange the numbers in the list in numerical order, from least to greatest: $a_1 \leq a_2 \leq a_3 \leq ... \leq a_{15}$.

If $a_1 < 4$, then $a_1 + a_2 + a_3 < 4 + a_2 + a_3$. Therefore, from (2), $12 < 4 + a_2 + a_3$, or $8 < a_2 + a_3$, and so at least one of the values a_2 and a_3 must be greater than 4. Because $a_2 \leq a_3$, it follows that $a_3 > 4$. Since the numbers are arranged from least to greatest, it follows that $a_4 > 4$ and $a_5 > 4$. But then $a_3 + a_4 + a_5 > 4 + 4 + 4 = 12$, contrary to (2), and so $a_1 < 4$ is not true. Therefore, $a_1 \geq 4$. Since a_1 is the least of the 15 numbers, $a_n \geq 4$ for $n = 1, 2, 3, ..., 15$.

If $a_{15} > 4$, then $a_{13} + a_{14} + a_{15} > a_{13} + a_{14} + 4$. Therefore, from (2), $12 > a_{13} + a_{14} + 4$, or $8 > a_{13} + a_{14}$, and so at least one of the values a_{13} and a_{14} must be less than 4. Because $a_{13} \leq a_{14}$, it follows that $a_{13} < 4$. Since the numbers are arranged from least to greatest, it follows that $a_{11} < 4$ and $a_{12} < 4$. But then $a_{11} + a_{12} + a_{13} < 4 + 4 + 4 = 12$, contrary to (2). Therefore, $a_{15} \leq 4$. Since a_{15} is the greatest of the 15 numbers, $a_n \leq 4$ for $n = 1, 2, 3, ..., 15$.

It has been shown that, for $n = 1, 2, 3, ..., 15$, each of $a_n \geq 4$ and $a_n \leq 4$ is true. Therefore, $a_n = 4$ for $n = 1, 2, 3, ..., 15$; SUFFICIENT.

The correct answer is B;
statement 2 alone is sufficient.

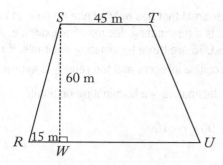

145. Quadrilateral *RSTU* shown above is a site plan for a parking lot in which side *RU* is parallel to side *ST* and *RU* is longer than *ST*. What is the area of the parking lot?

    (1) $RU = 80$ meters
    (2) $TU = 20\sqrt{10}$ meters

Geometry Area

The area of a quadrilateral region that has parallel sides of lengths a and b and altitude h is $\frac{1}{2}(a+b)h$. Therefore, it is sufficient to know the lengths of the two parallel sides and the altitude in order to find the area. The altitude is shown to be 60 m and the length of one of the parallel sides is 45 m.

(1) The length of the base of the quadrilateral, that is, the length of the second parallel side, is given. Thus, the area of the quadrilateral region, in square meters, is $\dfrac{(45+80)}{2}(60)$; SUFFICIENT.

    Alternatively, if the formula is unfamiliar, drawing the altitude from *T*, as shown in the figure below, can be helpful.

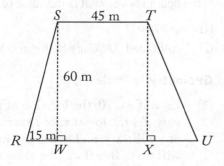

Since $ST = WX$ or 45 m, it can be seen that, in meters, $RU = 15 + 45 + XU$. Since $RU = 80$, then $80 = 15 + 45 + XU$, or

$XU = 20$. The area of *RSTU* is the sum of the areas $\left(\frac{1}{2}bh\right)$ of the two triangles $(\Delta SRW = 450\text{m}^2$ and $\Delta TUX = 600\text{m}^2)$ and the area $(l \times w)$ of the rectangle *STWX* $(2{,}700 \text{ m}^2)$. Thus, the same conclusion can be drawn.

(2) Continue to refer to the supplemental figure showing the altitude drawn from *T*. Although the length of the base of the quadrilateral is not fully known, parts of the base (*RW* as well as $WX = ST$) are known. The only missing information is the length of $\overline{XU}$. This can be found using the Pythagorean theorem with ΔTUX. Since $\overline{ST}$ and $\overline{RU}$ are parallel, $TX = SW = 60$m. It is given that $TU = 20\sqrt{10}$ m. Using the Pythagorean theorem, where $a^2 + b^2 = c^2$, yields $60^2 + XU^2 = TU^2 = \left(20\sqrt{10}\right)^2$ and by simplification, $3{,}600 + XU^2 = 4{,}000$, and thus $XU^2 = 400$ and $XU = 20$. Then, the length of $\overline{RU}$, in meters, is $15 + 45 + 20 = 80$. Since this is the information given in (1), it can similarly be used to find the area of *RSTU*; SUFFICIENT.

**The correct answer is D;
each statement alone is sufficient.**

146. If the average (arithmetic mean) of six numbers is 75, how many of the numbers are equal to 75 ?

    (1) None of the six numbers is less than 75.
    (2) None of the six numbers is greater than 75.

Arithmetic Statistics

If the average of six numbers is 75, then $\frac{1}{6}$ of the sum of the numbers is 75. Therefore, the sum of the numbers is $(6)(75)$.

(1) If one of the numbers is greater than 75, then we can write that number as $75 + x$ for some positive number x. Consequently, the sum of the 6 numbers must be at least $(5)(75) + (75 + x) = (6)(75) + x$, which is greater than $(6)(75)$, contrary to the fact that the sum is equal to $(6)(75)$. Hence, none of the numbers can be greater than 75. Since none of the numbers can be less than 75

(given information) and none of the numbers can be greater than 75, it follows that each of the numbers is equal to 75; SUFFICIENT.

(2) If one of the numbers is less than 75, then we can write that number as $75 - x$ for some positive number x. Consequently, the sum of the 6 numbers must be at most $(5)(75) + (75 - x) = (6)(75) - x$, which is less than $(6)(75)$, contrary to the fact that the sum is equal to $(6)(75)$. Hence, none of the numbers can be less than 75. Since none of the numbers can be less than 75 and none of the numbers can be greater than 75 (given information), it follows that each of the numbers is equal to 75; SUFFICIENT.

**The correct answer is D;
each statement alone is sufficient.**

147. What was the total amount of revenue that a theater received from the sale of 400 tickets, some of which were sold at x percent of full price and the rest of which were sold at full price?

(1) $x = 50$
(2) Full-price tickets sold for $20 each.

Arithmetic Percents

(1) While this reveals that *some* of the 400 tickets were sold at 50 percent of full price and *some* were sold at full price, there is no information as to the amounts in either category, nor is there any information as to the cost of a full-price ticket; NOT sufficient.

(2) Although this specifies the price of the full-price tickets, it is still unknown how many tickets were sold at full price or at a discount. Moreover, the percent of the discount is not disclosed; NOT sufficient.

While (1) and (2) together show that full-price tickets were $20 and discount tickets were 50 percent of that or $10, the number or percentage of tickets sold at either price, and thus the theater's revenue, cannot be determined.

**The correct answer is E;
both statements together are still not sufficient.**

148. Any decimal that has only a finite number of nonzero digits is a terminating decimal. For example, 24, 0.82, and 5.096 are three terminating decimals. If r and s are positive integers and the ratio $\frac{r}{s}$ is expressed as a decimal, is $\frac{r}{s}$ a terminating decimal?

(1) $90 < r < 100$
(2) $s = 4$

Arithmetic Properties of numbers

(1) This provides no information about the value of s. For example, $\frac{92}{5} = 18.4$, which terminates, but $\frac{92}{3} = 30.666\ldots$, which does not terminate; NOT sufficient.

(2) Division by the number 4 must terminate: the remainder when dividing by 4 must be 0, 1, 2, or 3, so the quotient must end with .0, .25, .5, or .75, respectively; SUFFICIENT.

**The correct answer is B;
statement 2 alone is sufficient.**

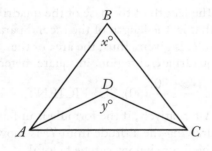

149. In the figure above, what is the value of $x + y$?

(1) $x = 70$
(2) $\triangle ABC$ and $\triangle ADC$ are both isosceles triangles.

Geometry Triangles

(1) Even if $x = 70$, the location of point D can vary. As the location of D varies, the value of y will vary, and hence the value of $x + y$ will vary. Therefore, the value of $x + y$ cannot be determined; NOT sufficient.

(2) If $\triangle ABC$ and $\triangle ADC$ are isosceles triangles, then $\angle BAC$ and $\angle BCA$ have the same

measure, and $\angle DAC$ and $\angle DCA$ have the same measure. However, since no values are given for any of the angles, there is no way to evaluate $x + y$; NOT sufficient.

Taking (1) and (2) together, $x = 70$ and $\angle BAC$ and $\angle BCA$ have the same measure. Since the sum of the measures of the angles of a triangle is $180°$, both $\angle BAC$ and $\angle BCA$ have measure $55°$ $(70 + 55 + 55 = 180)$, but there is still no information about the value of y. Therefore, the value of $x + y$ cannot be determined.

**The correct answer is E;
both statements together are still not sufficient.**

150. What amount did Jean earn from the commission on her sales in the first half of 1988 ?

(1) In 1988 Jean's commission was 5 percent of the total amount of her sales.

(2) The amount of Jean's sales in the second half of 1988 averaged $10,000 per month more than in the first half.

Arithmetic Applied problems

Let A be the amount of Jean's sales in the first half of 1988. Determine the value of A.

(1) If the amount of Jean's sales in the first half of 1988 was $10,000, then her commission in the first half of 1988 would have been $(5\%)(\$10,000) = \$500$. On the other hand, if the amount of Jean's sales in the first half of 1988 was $100,000, then her commission in the first half of 1988 would have been $(5\%)(\$100,000) = \$5,000$; NOT sufficient.

(2) No information is given that relates the amount of Jean's sales to the amount of Jean's commission; NOT sufficient.

Given (1) and (2), from (1) the amount of Jean's commission in the first half of 1988 is $(5\%)A$. From (2) the amount of Jean's sales in the second half of 1988 is $A + \$60,000$. Both statements together do not give information to determine the value of A. Therefore, (1) and (2) together are not sufficient.

**The correct answer is E;
both statements together are still not sufficient.**

151. The price per share of Stock X increased by 10 percent over the same time period that the price per share of Stock Y decreased by 10 percent. The reduced price per share of Stock Y was what percent of the original price per share of Stock X ?

(1) The increased price per share of Stock X was equal to the original price per share of Stock Y.

(2) The increase in the price per share of Stock X was $\frac{10}{11}$ the decrease in the price per share of Stock Y.

Arithmetic; Algebra Percents; Applied problems; Equations

Let x represent the original price per share of Stock X. The amount that Stock X increased per share can then be represented by $0.1x$ and the increased price per share of Stock X by $1.1x$. Let y represent the original price per share of Stock Y. The amount that Stock Y decreased per share can then be represented by $0.1y$ and the decreased price per share of Stock Y by $0.9y$. The reduced price per share of Stock Y as a percent of the original price per share of Stock X is

$$\left(\frac{0.9y}{x} \times 100\right)\% = (0.9 \times 100)\% \times \left(\frac{y}{x}\right).$$

Therefore, the question can be answered exactly when the value of $\frac{y}{x}$ can be determined.

(1) The increased price per share of Stock X is $1.1x$, and this is given as equal to y. Thus, $1.1x = y$, from which the value of $\frac{y}{x}$ can be determined; SUFFICIENT.

(2) The statement can be written as $0.1x = \frac{10}{11} \times 0.1y$, from which the value of $\frac{y}{x}$ can be determined; SUFFICIENT.

**The correct answer is D;
each statement alone is sufficient.**

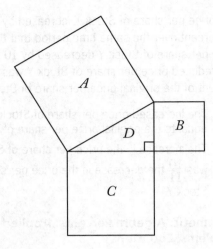

152. In the figure above, if the area of triangular region D is 4, what is the length of a side of square region A?

(1) The area of square region B is 9.

(2) The area of square region C is $\frac{64}{9}$.

Geometry Area

The area of the triangular region D can be represented by $\frac{1}{2}bh$, where b is the base of the triangle (and is equal to the length of a side of the square region C) and h is the height of the triangle (and is equal to the length of a side of the square region B). The area of any square is equal to the length of a side squared. The Pythagorean theorem is used to find the length of a side of a right triangle, when the length of the other 2 sides of the triangle are known and is represented by $a^2 + b^2 = c^2$, where a and b are the lengths of the 2 perpendicular sides of the triangle and c is the length of the hypotenuse.

Although completed calculations are provided in what follows, keep in mind that completed calculations are not needed to solve this problem.

(1) If the area of B is 9, then the length of each side is 3. Therefore, $h = 3$. Then, b can be determined, since the area of the triangle is, by substitution, $4 = \frac{1}{2}(3b)$ or $8 = 3b$ or $\frac{8}{3} = b$. Once b is known, the Pythagorean theorem can be used: $\left(\frac{8}{3}\right)^2 + 3^2 = c^2$ or $\frac{64}{9} + 9 = c^2$ or $\frac{145}{9} = c^2$. The length of a side of A is thus $\sqrt{\frac{145}{9}}$; SUFFICIENT.

(2) If the area of C is $\frac{64}{9}$, then the length of each side is $\frac{8}{3}$. Therefore, $b = \frac{8}{3}$. The area of the triangle is $A = \frac{1}{2}bh$ so $4 = \frac{1}{2}\left(\frac{8}{3}h\right)$, $8 = \frac{8}{3}h$, and $3 = h$. Once h is known, the Pythagorean theorem can be used as above; SUFFICIENT.

The correct answer is D;
each statement alone is sufficient.

153. If Sara's age is exactly twice Bill's age, what is Sara's age?

(1) Four years ago, Sara's age was exactly 3 times Bill's age.

(2) Eight years from now, Sara's age will be exactly 1.5 times Bill's age.

Algebra Applied problems

If s and b represent Sara's and Bill's ages in years, then $s = 2b$.

(1) The additional information can be expressed as $s - 4 = 3(b - 4)$, or $s = 3b - 8$. When this equation is paired with the given information, $s = 2b$, there are two linear equations in two unknowns. One way to conclude that we can determine the value of s is to solve the equations simultaneously. Setting the two expressions for s equal to each other gives $3b - 8 = 2b$, or $b = 8$. Hence, $s = 2b = (2)(8) = 16$. Another way to conclude that we can determine the value of s is to note that the pair of equations represents two non-parallel lines in the coordinate plane; SUFFICIENT.

(2) The additional information provided can be expressed as $s + 8 = 1.5(b + 8)$. The same comments in (1) apply here as well. For example, multiplying both sides of $s + 8 = 1.5(b + 8)$ by 2 gives $2s + 16 = 3b + 24$ or, using $s = 2b$, $2(2b) + 16 = 3b + 24$. Therefore, $4b - 3b = 24 - 16$, or $b = 8$. Hence, $s = 2b = (2)(8) = 16$; SUFFICIENT.

The correct answer is D;
each statement alone is sufficient.

154. A report consisting of 2,600 words is divided into 23 paragraphs. A 2-paragraph preface is then added to the report. Is the average (arithmetic mean) number of words per paragraph for all 25 paragraphs less than 120 ?

    (1) Each paragraph of the preface has more than 100 words.
    (2) Each paragraph of the preface has fewer than 150 words.

Arithmetic Statistics

Determining if the average number of words for 25 paragraphs is less than 120 is equivalent to determining if the total number of words for the 25 paragraphs is less than $(25)(120) = (25)(4)(30)$ $= (100)(30) = 3,000$. Since there are 2,600 words in the original 23 paragraphs, this is equivalent to determining if the total number of words in the 2 added paragraphs is less than $3,000 - 2,600 = 400$.

(1) The information provided implies only that the total number of words in the 2 added paragraphs is more than $(2)(100) = 200$. Therefore, the number of words could be 201, in which case the total number of added words is less than 400, or the number of words could be 400, in which case the number of added words is not less than 400; NOT sufficient.

(2) The information provided implies that the total number of words in the 2 added paragraphs is less than $(2)(150) = 300$, which in turn is less than 400; SUFFICIENT.

The correct answer is B; statement 2 alone is sufficient.

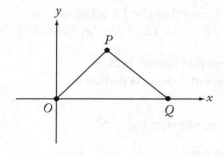

155. In the rectangular coordinate system above, if $OP < PQ$, is the area of region OPQ greater than 48 ?

    (1) The coordinates of point P are (6,8).
    (2) The coordinates of point Q are (13,0).

Geometry Coordinate Geometry; Triangles

The area of a triangle with base b and altitude h can be determined through the formula $\frac{1}{2}bh$. The altitude of a triangle is the line segment drawn from a vertex perpendicular to the side opposite that vertex. In a right triangle (formed here since it is given that the altitude is perpendicular to the side), the Pythagorean theorem states that the square of the length of the hypotenuse is equal to the sum of the squares of the lengths of the legs of the triangle.

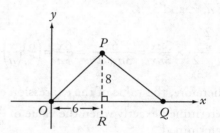

(1) The given information fixes the side lengths of $\triangle ORP$ as 6, 8, 10 (twice a 3-4-5 triangle), and the farther Q is from R (i.e., the greater the value of PQ), the greater the area of $\triangle PRQ$, and hence the greater the area of $\triangle OPQ$. If $PQ = 10$, then the area of $\triangle OPQ$ would be 48. Since it is known that $PQ > 10$ (because $10 = OP < PQ$), it follows that the area of $\triangle OPQ$ is greater than 48; SUFFICIENT.

(2) The given information implies that $OQ = 13$. However, no information is given about the height of P above the x-axis. Since the area of $\triangle ORP$ is $\frac{1}{2}$ the product of OQ and the height of P above the x-axis, it cannot be determined whether the area of $\triangle ORP$ is greater than 48. For example, if this height were 2, then the area would be $\frac{1}{2}(2)(13) = 13$, and if this height were 8, then the area would be $\frac{1}{2}(8)(13) = 52$; NOT sufficient.

The correct answer is A; statement 1 alone is sufficient.

$$S = \dfrac{\dfrac{2}{n}}{\dfrac{1}{x} + \dfrac{2}{3x}}$$

156. In the expression above, if $xn \neq 0$, what is the value of S?

(1) $x = 2n$

(2) $n = \dfrac{1}{2}$

Algebra First- and second-degree equations

It may be helpful to rewrite the given expression for S by multiplying its numerator and denominator by a common denominator of the secondary fractions (i.e., a common multiple of n, x, and $3x$):

$$\dfrac{\dfrac{2}{n}}{\dfrac{1}{x} + \dfrac{2}{3x}} \times \dfrac{3nx}{3nx} = \dfrac{6x}{3n + 2n} = \dfrac{6x}{5n} = \left(\dfrac{6}{5}\right)\left(\dfrac{x}{n}\right).$$

Therefore, the value of the expression can be determined exactly when the value of $\dfrac{x}{n}$ can be determined.

(1) From $x = 2n$ it follows that $\dfrac{x}{n} = 2$; SUFFICIENT.

(2) From $n = \dfrac{1}{2}$ it follows that $\dfrac{x}{n} = \dfrac{x}{\frac{1}{2}} = 2x$,

which can vary; NOT sufficient.

The correct answer is A; statement 1 alone is sufficient.

157. If n is a positive integer and $k = 5.1 \times 10^n$, what is the value of k?

(1) $6,000 < k < 500,000$

(2) $k^2 = 2.601 \times 10^9$

Arithmetic Properties of numbers

Given that $k = 5.1 \times 10^n$, where n is a positive integer, then the value of k must follow the pattern shown in the following table:

n	k
1	51
2	510
3	5,100
4	51,000
5	510,000
6	5,100,000
.	.
.	.
.	.

(1) Given that $6,000 < k < 500,000$, then k must have the value 51,000, and so $n = 4$; SUFFICIENT.

(2) Given that $k^2 = 2.601 \times 10^9$, then

$k = \sqrt{2.601 \times 10^9} = \sqrt{2,601 \times 10^6} = \sqrt{2,601} \times \sqrt{10^6}$
$= 51 \times 10^3 = 51,000$, and so $n = 4$; SUFFICIENT.

The correct answer is D; each statement alone is sufficient.

158. If Carmen had 12 more tapes, she would have twice as many tapes as Rafael. Does Carmen have fewer tapes than Rafael?

(1) Rafael has more than 5 tapes.

(2) Carmen has fewer than 12 tapes.

Algebra Inequalities

If C and R are the numbers of tapes that Carmen and Rafael have, respectively, then $C + 12 = 2R$, or $C = 2R - 12$. To determine if $C < R$, it is equivalent to determining if $2R - 12 < R$, or equivalently, if $R < 12$.

(1) Given that $R > 5$, it is possible that $R < 12$ (for example, if $R = 8$ and $C = 4$) and it is possible that $R \geq 12$ (for example, if $R = 12$ and $C = 12$); NOT sufficient.

(2) Given that $C < 12$, it follows that $2R - 12 < 12$, or $R < 12$; SUFFICIENT.

The correct answer is B; statement 2 alone is sufficient.

159. If x is an integer, is $x|x| < 2^x$?

(1) $x < 0$

(2) $x = -10$

Arithmetic Properties of numbers

Note that x^{-r} is equivalent to $\frac{1}{x^r}$; for example, $2^{-2} = \frac{1}{2^2} = \frac{1}{4}$.

(1) Since $|x| > 0$ when $x \neq 0$, it follows from $x < 0$ that $x|x|$ is the product of a negative number and a positive number, and hence $x|x|$ is negative. On the other hand, 2^x is positive for any number x. Since each negative number is less than each positive number, it follows that $x|x| < 2^x$; SUFFICIENT.

(2) The fact that $x = -10$ is a specific case of the argument in (1); SUFFICIENT.

**The correct answer is D;
each statement alone is sufficient.**

160. If n is a positive integer, is the value of $b - a$ at least twice the value of $3^n - 2^n$?

(1) $a = 2^{n+1}$ and $b = 3^{n+1}$

(2) $n = 3$

Algebra Exponents

If r, s, and x are real numbers with $x > 0$, then $x^{r+s} = (x^r)(x^s)$. Therefore, $2^{n+1} = (2^n)(2^1) = (2^n)(2)$ and $3^{n+1} = (3^n)(3^1) = (3^n)(3)$.

(1) From this, applying the properties of exponents:

$$b - a = 3^{n+1} - 2^{n+1} = 3(3^n) - 2(2^n)$$

Twice the value of the given expression $3^n - 2^n$ is equal to $2(3^n - 2^n)$ or $2(3^n) - 2(2^n)$. It is known that $b - a = 3(3^n) - 2(2^n)$, which is greater than $2(3^n) - 2(2^n)$. Thus, $b - a$ is at least twice the value of $3^n - 2^n$; SUFFICIENT.

(2) This statement gives no information about $b - a$; NOT sufficient.

**The correct answer is A;
statement 1 alone is sufficient.**

161. The inflation index for the year 1989 relative to the year 1970 was 3.56, indicating that, on the average, for each dollar spent in 1970 for goods, $3.56 had to be spent for the same goods in 1989. If the price of a Model K mixer increased precisely according to the inflation index, what was the price of the mixer in 1970 ?

(1) The price of the Model K mixer was $102.40 more in 1989 than in 1970.

(2) The price of the Model K mixer was $142.40 in 1989.

Arithmetic Proportions

The ratio of 1970 goods to 1989 goods is 1:3.56 or $\frac{1}{3.56}$. This ratio can be used to set up a proportion between 1970 goods and 1989 goods. Let x represent the 1970 price of the mixer. Although the 1970 price of the mixer is calculated in what follows, keep in mind that the object of this data sufficiency question is to determine whether the price can be calculated from the information given, not necessarily to actually calculate the price.

(1) From this, the 1989 price of the mixer can be expressed as $x + \$102.40$. Therefore a proportion can be set up and solved for x:

$$\frac{1}{3.56} = \frac{x}{x + \$102.40}$$

$x + \$102.40 = 3.56x$	cross multiply
$\$102.40 = 2.56x$	subtract x from both sides
$\$40 = x$	divide both sides by 2.56

The price of the mixer in 1970 was $40; SUFFICIENT.

(2) The following proportion can be set up using the information that the 1989 price of the mixer was $142.40:

$$\frac{1}{3.56} = \frac{x}{\$142.40}$$

$3.56x = \$142.40$	cross multiply
$x = \$40$	divide both sides by 3.56

The price of the mixer in 1970 was $40; SUFFICIENT.

**The correct answer is D;
each statement alone is sufficient.**

162. Is 5^k less than 1,000 ?

    (1) $5^{k+1} > 3,000$
    (2) $5^{k-1} = 5^k - 500$

Arithmetic Arithmetic operations

If x is any positive number and r and s are any positive integers, then $x^{-r} = \dfrac{1}{x^r}$ and $x^{r+s} = (x^r)(x^s)$. Therefore, $5^{k+1} = 5^k(5^1)$. When both sides of this equation are divided by 5^1 (which equals 5), the resulting equation is $\dfrac{5^{k+1}}{5} = 5^k$.

(1) If both sides of this given inequality are divided by 5, it yields $\dfrac{5^{k+1}}{5} > \dfrac{3,000}{5}$ or $5^k > 600$. Although it is known that $5^k > 600$, it is unknown if 5^k is less than 1,000; NOT sufficient.

(2) It is given that $5^{k-1} = 5^k - 500$, thus:

$5^k - 5^{k-1} = 500$ subtract 5^k from both sides; divide all terms by -1

$5^k - 5^k(5^{-1}) = 500$ property of exponents

$5^k - 5^k\left(\dfrac{1}{5}\right) = 500$ substitute for 5^{-1}

$5^k\left(1 - \dfrac{1}{5}\right) = 500$ factor out 5^k

$5^k\left(\dfrac{4}{5}\right) = 500$ simplify

$5^k = 500\left(\dfrac{5}{4}\right)$ multiply both sides by $\left(\dfrac{5}{4}\right)$

$5^k = 625$, which is less than 1,000; SUFFICIENT.

**The correct answer is B;
statement 2 alone is sufficient.**

163. Every member of a certain club volunteers to contribute equally to the purchase of a $60 gift certificate. How many members does the club have?

    (1) Each member's contribution is to be $4.
    (2) If 5 club members fail to contribute, the share of each contributing member will increase by $2.

Arithmetic; Algebra Arithmetic operations; Simultaneous equations

(1) If each member's contribution is to be $4 and the total amount to be collected is $60, then $60 \div 4 = 15$ members in the club; SUFFICIENT.

(2) Let c represent each person's contribution, and let x represent the number of members in the club. From the given information, it is known that $\dfrac{60}{x} = c$. From this, it is also known that $\dfrac{60}{x-5} = c + 2$.

These two equations can be solved simultaneously for x:

$\dfrac{60}{x-5} = \dfrac{60}{x} + 2$ substitute for c

$\dfrac{60}{x-5} = \dfrac{60 + 2x}{x}$ add fraction and whole number

$60x = (x-5)(60 + 2x)$ cross multiply

$60x = 2x^2 - 10x + 60x - 300$ multiply

$0 = 2x^2 - 10x - 300$ subtract $60x$ from both sides

$0 = 2(x - 15)(x + 10)$ factor

Therefore, x could be 15 or -10. Since there cannot be -10 members, x must be 15; so there are 15 members in the club; SUFFICIENT.

**The correct answer is D;
each statement alone is sufficient.**

164. If $x < 0$, is $y > 0$?

    (1) $\dfrac{x}{y} < 0$
    (2) $y - x > 0$

Algebra Inequalities

(1) In order for $x < 0$ and $\frac{x}{y} < 0$ to be true, y must be greater than 0. If $y = 0$, then $\frac{x}{y}$ would be undefined. If $y < 0$, then $\frac{x}{y}$ would be a positive number; SUFFICIENT.

(2) Here, if $x < 0$, then y could be 0. For example, if y was 0 and x was –3, then $y - x > 0$ would be $0 - (-3) > 0$ or $3 > 0$. The statement would also be true if y were less than 0 but greater than x. For example, if $y = -2$ and $x = -7$, then $-2 - (-7) > 0$ or $5 > 0$. Finally, this statement would also be true if $y > 0$. Without any further information, it is impossible to tell whether $y > 0$; NOT sufficient.

The correct answer is A; statement 1 alone is sufficient.

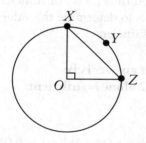

165. What is the circumference of the circle above with center O?

(1) The perimeter of $\triangle OXZ$ is $20 + 10\sqrt{2}$.
(2) The length of arc XYZ is 5π.

Geometry Circles

The circumference of the circle can be found if the radius r is known. $\triangle OXZ$ is a right triangle with $OX = OZ = r$ (since O is the center). The perimeter of $\triangle OXZ$ is the sum of OX (or r) + OZ (or r) + XZ, or the perimeter = $2r + XZ$. From the Pythagorean theorem,

$$XZ^2 = OX^2 + OZ^2$$
$$XZ^2 = r^2 + r^2$$
$$XZ = \sqrt{r^2 + r^2}$$
$$XZ = \sqrt{2r^2}$$
$$XZ = r\sqrt{2}$$

The perimeter of $\triangle OXZ$ is then $2r + r\sqrt{2}$.

(1) The perimeter of $\triangle OXZ$ is $20 + 10\sqrt{2}$. Thus, $2r + r\sqrt{2} = 20 + 10\sqrt{2} = 2(10) + 10\sqrt{2}$, and $r = 10$. Since r is known, the circumference can be found; SUFFICIENT.

(2) The length of arc XYZ is the measurement of angle XOZ divided by 360 and multiplied by the circumference. Since angle XOZ equals 90, the length of arc XYZ is thus $\frac{90}{360} = \frac{1}{4}$ of the circumference. Since $\frac{1}{4}$ of the circumference is given as equal to 5π, the circumference can be determined; SUFFICIENT.

The correct answer is D; each statement alone is sufficient.

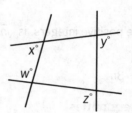

166. What is the value of $x + y$ in the figure above?

(1) $w = 95$
(2) $z = 125$

Geometry Angles

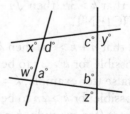

In the figure above, a, b, c, and d are the degree measures of the interior angles of the quadrilateral formed by the four lines and $a + b + c + d = 360$. Then

$$w + x + y + z$$
$$= (180 - a) + (180 - d) + (180 - c) + (180 - b)$$
$$= 720 - (a + b + c + d)$$
$$= 720 - 360$$
$$= 360.$$

Determine the value of $x + y$.

(1) Given that $w = 95$, then $95 + x + y + z = 360$ and $x + y + z = 265$. If $z = 65$, for example, then $x + y = 200$. On the other hand, if $z = 100$, then $x + y = 165$; NOT sufficient.

(2) Given that $z = 125$, then $w + x + y + 125 = 360$ and $w + x + y = 235$. If $w = 35$, for example, then $x + y = 200$. On the other hand, if $w = 100$, then $x + y = 135$; NOT sufficient.

Taking (1) and (2) together, $95 + x + y + 125 = 360$, and so $x + y = 140$. Therefore, (1) and (2) together are sufficient.

The correct answer is C; both statements together are sufficient.

167. If n and k are positive integers, is $\sqrt{n+k} > 2\sqrt{n}$?

(1) $k > 3n$
(2) $n + k > 3n$

Algebra Inequalities

Determine if $\sqrt{n+k} > 2\sqrt{n}$. Since each side is positive, squaring each side preserves the inequality, so $\sqrt{n+k} > 2\sqrt{n}$ is equivalent to $\left(\sqrt{n+k}\right)\left(\sqrt{n+k}\right) > \left(2\sqrt{n}\right)\left(2\sqrt{n}\right)$, which in turn is equivalent to $n + k > 4n$, or to $k > 3n$.

(1) Given that $k > 3n$, then $\sqrt{n+k} > 2\sqrt{n}$; SUFFICIENT.

(2) Given that $n + k > 3n$, then $k > 2n$. However, it is possible for $k > 2n$ to be true and $k > 3n$ to be false (for example, $k = 3$ and $n = 1$) and it is possible for $k > 2n$ to be true and $k > 3n$ to be true (for example, $k = 4$ and $n = 1$); NOT sufficient.

The correct answer is A; statement 1 alone is sufficient.

168. In a certain business, production index p is directly proportional to efficiency index e, which is in turn directly proportional to investment index i. What is p if $i = 70$?

(1) $e = 0.5$ whenever $i = 60$.
(2) $p = 2.0$ whenever $i = 50$.

Arithmetic Proportions

(1) This gives only values for e and i, and, while p is directly proportional to e, the nature of this proportion is unknown. Therefore, p cannot be determined; NOT sufficient.

(2) Since p is directly proportional to e, which is directly proportional to i, then p is directly proportional to i. Therefore, the following proportion can be set up: $\dfrac{p}{i} = \dfrac{2.0}{50}$. If $i = 70$, then $\dfrac{p}{70} = \dfrac{2.0}{50}$. Through cross multiplying, this equation yields $50p = 140$, or $p = 2.8$; SUFFICIENT.

The preceding approach is one method that can be used. Another approach is as follows: It is given that $p = Ke = K(Li) = (KL)i$, where K and L are the proportionality constants, and the value of $70KL$ is to be determined. Statement (1) allows us to determine the value of L, but gives nothing about K, and thus (1) is not sufficient. Statement (2) allows us to determine the value of KL, and thus (2) is sufficient.

The correct answer is B; statement 2 alone is sufficient.

169. If n is a positive integer, is $\left(\dfrac{1}{10}\right)^n < 0.01$?

(1) $n > 2$
(2) $\left(\dfrac{1}{10}\right)^{n-1} < 0.1$

Arithmetic; Algebra Properties of numbers; Inequalities

(1)
$$n > 2$$
$$-n < -2$$
$$10^{-n} < 10^{-2}$$
$$\left(10^{-1}\right)^n < 10^{-2}$$
$$\left(\dfrac{1}{10}\right)^n < 10^{-2}$$
$$\left(\dfrac{1}{10}\right)^n < 0.01$$

SUFFICIENT.

(2) $\left(\dfrac{1}{10}\right)^{n-1} < 0.1$

$\left(\dfrac{1}{10}\right)^{n-1} < 10^{-1}$

$\left(10^{-1}\right)^{n-1} < 10^{-1}$

$(10)^{(-1)(n-1)} < 10^{-1}$

$(10)^{-n+1} < 10^{-1}$

$-n+1 < -1$

$-n < -2$

$n > 2$

But, this is the inequality given in (1), which was sufficient; SUFFICIENT.

The correct answer is D; each statement alone is sufficient.

170. If n is a positive integer, what is the tens digit of n?

(1) The hundreds digit of $10n$ is 6.
(2) The tens digit of $n+1$ is 7.

Arithmetic Properties of numbers

(1) Given that the hundreds digit of $10n$ is 6, the tens digit of n is 6, since the hundreds digit of $10n$ is always equal to the tens digit of n; SUFFICIENT.

(2) Given that the tens digit of $n+1$ is 7, it is possible that the tens digit of n is 7 (for example, $n = 70$) and it is possible that the tens digit of n is 6 (for example, $n = 69$); NOT sufficient.

The correct answer is A; statement 1 alone is sufficient.

171. What is the value of $\dfrac{2t+t-x}{t-x}$?

(1) $\dfrac{2t}{t-x} = 3$
(2) $t - x = 5$

Algebra Simplifying algebraic expressions

Determine the value of $\dfrac{2t+t-x}{t-x}$.

(1) Since $\dfrac{2t}{t-x} = 3$ and

$\dfrac{2t+t-x}{t-x} = \dfrac{2t}{t-x} + \dfrac{t-x}{t-x} = \dfrac{2t}{t-x} + 1,$

it follows that $\dfrac{2t+t-x}{t-x} = 3+1$; SUFFICIENT.

(2) Given that $t - x = 5$, it follows that $\dfrac{2t+t-x}{t-x} = \dfrac{2t+5}{5} = \dfrac{2}{5}t + 1$, which can vary when the value of t varies. For example, $\dfrac{2}{5}t + 1 = 3$ if $t = 5$ (choose $x = 0$ to have $t - x = 5$) and $\dfrac{2}{5}t + 1 = 5$ if $t = 10$ (choose $x = 5$ to have $t - x = 5$); NOT sufficient.

The correct answer is A; statement 1 alone is sufficient.

172. Is n an integer?

(1) n^2 is an integer.
(2) $\sqrt{n}$ is an integer.

Arithmetic Properties of numbers

(1) Since 1^2 is an integer and $\left(\sqrt{2}\right)^2$ is an integer, the square of an integer can be an integer and the square of a non-integer can be an integer; NOT sufficient.

(2) If $\sqrt{n} = k$, where k is an integer, then $\left(\sqrt{n}\right)^2 = k^2$, or $n = k^2$. Therefore, n is the square of an integer, which in turn is an integer; SUFFICIENT.

The correct answer is B; statement 2 alone is sufficient.

173. If x, y, and z are positive integers, is $x - y$ odd?

(1) $x = z^2$
(2) $y = (z-1)^2$

Arithmetic Arithmetic operations; Properties of numbers

(1) This reveals the relationship between two of the variables but does not mention the relationship either has with y. Therefore the question cannot be answered; NOT sufficient.

(2)   If $(z-1)^2$ is expanded, the result is $z^2 - 2z + 1$. Since $y = z^2 - 2z + 1$, a substitution for y can be made in the expression $x - y$. It becomes $x - (z^2 - 2z + 1)$. However, without further information, it cannot be determined if $x - y$ is odd; NOT sufficient.

When (1) and (2) are taken together, z^2, from (1), can be substituted for x in the expression $x - (z^2 - 2z + 1)$ from (2). It then yields $z^2 - z^2 + 2z - 1$, or simply $2z - 1$, which is always an odd number regardless of the value of z. So $x - y$ is odd.

**The correct answer is C;
both statements together are sufficient.**

174. Marcia's bucket can hold a maximum of how many liters of water?

   (1)   The bucket currently contains 9 liters of water.

   (2)   If 3 liters of water are added to the bucket when it is half full of water, the amount of water in the bucket will increase by $\frac{1}{3}$.

Geometry Volume

   (1)   This statement only implies that the bucket will hold *at least* 9 liters, but the *maximum capacity* is still unknown; NOT sufficient.

   (2)   Letting c represent the maximum capacity of Marcia's bucket, the volume of water in the bucket when at half capacity can be expressed as $\frac{1}{2}c$, and if 3 liters are then added, the present volume of water in the bucket can be expressed as $\frac{1}{2}c + 3$. It is given that, when the 3 liters are added, the volume of water will increase by $\frac{1}{3}$, which is equivalent to multiplying the present volume by $\frac{4}{3}$. This becomes the expression $\frac{4}{3}\left(\frac{1}{2}c\right)$.

Therefore, it is known that $\frac{1}{2}c + 3 = \frac{4}{3}\left(\frac{1}{2}c\right)$.

This equation can be solved for c, through simplifying to $\frac{1}{2}c + 3 = \frac{2}{3}c$ then subtracting $\frac{1}{2}c$ from each side for $3 = \frac{2}{3}c - \frac{1}{2}c$, and then simplifying to $3 = \frac{1}{6}c$ or $18 = c$.

Thus the equation can be solved to determine the maximum capacity of the bucket; SUFFICIENT.

**The correct answer is B;
statement 2 alone is sufficient.**

7.0 Reading Comprehension

7.0 Reading Comprehension

Reading comprehension questions appear in the Verbal section of the GMAT® exam. The Verbal section uses multiple-choice questions to measure your ability to read and comprehend written material, to reason and evaluate arguments, and to correct written material to conform to standard written English. Because the Verbal section includes content from a variety of topics, you may be generally familiar with some of the material; however, neither the passages nor the questions assume knowledge of the topics discussed. Reading comprehension questions are intermingled with critical reasoning and sentence correction questions throughout the Verbal section of the test.

You will have 75 minutes to complete the Verbal section, or an average of about 1¾ minutes to answer each question. Keep in mind, however, that you will need time to read the written passages—and that time is not factored into the 1¾ minute average. You should therefore plan to proceed more quickly through the reading comprehension questions in order to give yourself enough time to read the passages thoroughly.

Reading comprehension questions begin with written passages up to 350 words long. The passages discuss topics from the social sciences, humanities, the physical or biological sciences, and such business-related fields as marketing, economics, and human resource management. The passages are accompanied by questions that will ask you to interpret the passage, apply the information you gather from the reading, and make inferences (or informed assumptions) based on the reading. For these questions, you will see a split computer screen. The written passage will remain visible on the left side as each question associated with that passage appears in turn on the right side. You will see only one question at a time, however. The number of questions associated with each passage may vary.

As you move through the reading comprehension sample questions, try to determine a process that works best for you. You might begin by reading a passage carefully and thoroughly, though some test-takers prefer to skim the passages the first time through, or even to read the first question before reading the passage. You may want to reread any sentences that present complicated ideas or introduce terms that are new to you. Read each question and series of answers carefully. Make sure you understand exactly what the question is asking and what the answer choices are.

If you need to, you may go back to the passage and read any parts that are relevant to answering the question. Specific portions of the passages may be highlighted in the related questions.

The following pages describe what reading comprehension questions are designed to measure, present the directions that will precede questions of this type, and describe the various question types. This chapter also provides test-taking strategies, sample questions, and detailed explanations of all the questions. The explanations further illustrate the ways in which reading comprehension questions evaluate basic reading skills.

7.1 What Is Measured

Reading comprehension questions measure your ability to understand, analyze, and apply information and concepts presented in written form. All questions are to be answered on the basis of what is stated or implied in the reading material, and no specific prior knowledge of the material is required.

The GMAT reading comprehension questions evaluate your ability to do the following:

- **Understand words and statements.**
  Although the questions do not test your vocabulary (they will not ask you to define terms), they do test your ability to interpret special meanings of terms as they are used in the reading passages. The questions will also test your understanding of the English language. These questions may ask about the overall meaning of a passage.

- **Understand logical relationships between points and concepts.**
  This type of question may ask you to determine the strong and weak points of an argument or evaluate the relative importance of arguments and ideas in a passage.

- **Draw inferences from facts and statements.**
  The inference questions will ask you to consider factual statements or information presented in a reading passage and, on the basis of that information, reach conclusions.

- **Understand and follow the development of quantitative concepts as they are presented in written material.**
  This may involve the interpretation of numerical data or the use of simple arithmetic to reach conclusions about material in a passage.

There are six kinds of reading comprehension questions, each of which tests a different skill. The reading comprehension questions ask about the following areas:

Main idea

Each passage is a unified whole—that is, the individual sentences and paragraphs support and develop one main idea or central point. Sometimes you will be told the central point in the passage itself, and sometimes it will be necessary for you to determine the central point from the overall organization or development of the passage. You may be asked in this kind of question to

- recognize a correct restatement, or paraphrasing, of the main idea of a passage

- identify the author's primary purpose or objective in writing the passage

- assign a title that summarizes, briefly and pointedly, the main idea developed in the passage

Supporting ideas

These questions measure your ability to comprehend the supporting ideas in a passage and differentiate them from the main idea. The questions also measure your ability to differentiate ideas that are *explicitly stated* in a passage from ideas that are *implied* by the author but that are not explicitly stated. You may be asked about

- facts cited in a passage

- the specific content of arguments presented by the author in support of his or her views

- descriptive details used to support or elaborate on the main idea

Whereas questions about the main idea ask you to determine the meaning of a passage *as a whole*, questions about supporting ideas ask you to determine the meanings of individual sentences and paragraphs that *contribute* to the meaning of the passage as a whole. In other words, these questions ask for the main point of *one small part* of the passage.

Inferences

These questions ask about ideas that are not explicitly stated in a passage but are *implied* by the author. Unlike questions about supporting details, which ask about information that is directly stated in a passage, inference questions ask about ideas or meanings that must be inferred from information that is directly stated. Authors can make their points in indirect ways, suggesting ideas without actually stating them. Inference questions measure your ability to understand an author's intended meaning in parts of a passage where the meaning is only suggested. These questions do not ask about meanings or implications that are remote from the passage; rather, they ask about meanings that are developed indirectly or implications that are specifically suggested by the author.

To answer these questions, you may have to

- logically take statements made by the author one step beyond their literal meanings

- recognize an alternative interpretation of a statement made by the author

- identify the intended meaning of a word used figuratively in a passage

If a passage explicitly states an effect, for example, you may be asked to infer its cause. If the author compares two phenomena, you may be asked to infer the basis for the comparison. You may be asked to infer the characteristics of an old policy from an explicit description of a new one. When you read a passage, therefore, you should concentrate not only on the explicit meaning of the author's words, but also on the more subtle meaning implied by those words.

Applying information to a context outside the passage itself

These questions measure your ability to discern the relationships between situations or ideas presented by the author and other situations or ideas that might parallel those in the passage. In this kind of question, you may be asked to

- identify a hypothetical situation that is comparable to a situation presented in the passage

- select an example that is similar to an example provided in the passage

- apply ideas given in the passage to a situation not mentioned by the author

- recognize ideas that the author would probably agree or disagree with on the basis of statements made in the passage

Unlike inference questions, application questions use ideas or situations *not* taken from the passage. Ideas and situations given in a question are *like* those given in the passage, and they parallel ideas and situations in the passage; therefore, to answer the question, you must do more than recall what you read. You must recognize the essential attributes of ideas and situations presented in the passage when they appear in different words and in an entirely new context.

Logical structure

These questions require you to analyze and evaluate the organization and logic of a passage. They may ask you

- how a passage is constructed—for instance, does it define, compare or contrast, present a new idea, or refute an idea?
- how the author persuades readers to accept his or her assertions
- the reason behind the author's use of any particular supporting detail
- to identify assumptions that the author is making
- to assess the strengths and weaknesses of the author's arguments
- to recognize appropriate counterarguments

These questions measure your ability not only to comprehend a passage but also to evaluate it critically. However, it is important for you to realize that logical structure questions do not rely on any kind of formal logic, nor do they require you to be familiar with specific terms of logic or argumentation. You can answer these questions using only the information in the passage and careful reasoning.

About the style and tone

Style and tone questions ask about the expression of a passage and about the ideas in a passage that may be expressed through its diction—the author's choice of words. You may be asked to deduce the author's attitude to an idea, a fact, or a situation from the words that he or she uses to describe it. You may also be asked to select a word that accurately describes the tone of a passage—for instance, "critical," "questioning," "objective," or "enthusiastic."

To answer this type of question, you will have to consider the language of the passage as a whole. It takes more than one pointed, critical word to make the tone of an entire passage "critical." Sometimes, style and tone questions ask what audience the passage was probably intended for or what type of publication it probably appeared in. Style and tone questions may apply to one small part of the passage or to the passage as a whole. To answer them, you must ask yourself what meanings are contained in the words of a passage beyond the literal meanings. Did the author use certain words because of their emotional content, or because a particular audience would expect to hear them? Remember, these questions measure your ability to discern meaning expressed by the author through his or her choice of words.

7.2 Test-Taking Strategies

1. **Do not expect to be completely familiar with any of the material presented in reading comprehension passages.**
   You may find some passages easier to understand than others, but all passages are designed to present a challenge. If you have some familiarity with the material presented in a passage, do not let this knowledge influence your choice of answers to the questions. Answer all questions on the basis of what is *stated or implied* in the passage itself.

2. **Analyze each passage carefully, because the questions require you to have a specific and detailed understanding of the material.**

   You may find it easier to do the analysis first, before moving to the questions. Or, you may find that you prefer to skim the passage the first time and read more carefully once you understand what a question asks. You may even want to read the question before reading the passage. You should choose the method most suitable for you.

3. **Focus on key words and phrases, and make every effort to avoid losing the sense of what is discussed in the passage.**

   Keep the following in mind:

   - Note how each fact relates to an idea or an argument.
   - Note where the passage moves from one idea to the next.
   - Separate main ideas from supporting ideas.
   - Determine what conclusions are reached and why.

4. **Read the questions carefully, making certain that you understand what is asked.**

   An answer choice that accurately restates information in the passage may be incorrect if it does not answer the question. If you need to, refer back to the passage for clarification.

5. **Read all the choices carefully.**

   Never assume that you have selected the best answer without first reading all the choices.

6. **Select the choice that answers the question best in terms of the information given in the passage.**

   Do not rely on outside knowledge of the material to help you answer the questions.

7. **Remember that comprehension—not speed—is the critical success factor when it comes to reading comprehension questions.**

7.3 The Directions

These are the directions that you will see for reading comprehension questions when you take the GMAT exam. If you read them carefully and understand them clearly before going to sit for the test, you will not need to spend too much time reviewing them once you are at the test center and the test is under way.

The questions in this group are based on the content of a passage. After reading the passage, choose the best answer to each question. Answer all questions following the passage on the basis of what is *stated or implied in the passage*.

7.4 Practice Questions

Each of the <u>reading comprehension</u> questions is based on the content of a passage. After reading the passage answer all questions pertaining to it on the basis of what is <u>stated</u> or <u>implied</u> in the passage. For each question, select the best answer of the choices given.

Line   Biologists have advanced two theories to explain
why schooling of fish occurs in so many fish species.
Because schooling is particularly widespread among
species of small fish, both theories assume that
(5)   schooling offers the advantage of some protection
from predators.
       Proponents of theory A dispute the assumption that
a school of thousands of fish is highly visible.
Experiments have shown that any fish can be seen,
(10)   even in very clear water, only within a sphere of 200
meters in diameter. When fish are in a compact group,
the spheres of visibility overlap. Thus the chance of a
predator finding the school is only slightly greater
than the chance of the predator finding a single fish
(15)   swimming alone. Schooling is advantageous to the
individual fish because a predator's chance of finding
any particular fish swimming in the school is much
smaller than its chance of finding at least one of the
same group of fish if the fish were dispersed
(20)   throughout an area.
       However, critics of theory A point out that some
fish form schools even in areas where predators are
abundant and thus little possibility of escaping
detection exists. They argue that the school continues
(25)   to be of value to its members even after detection.
They advocate theory B, the "confusion effect," which
can be explained in two different ways.
       Sometimes, proponents argue, predators simply
cannot decide which fish to attack. This indecision
(30)   supposedly results from a predator's preference for
striking prey that is distinct from the rest of the
school in appearance. In many schools the fish are
almost identical in appearance, making it difficult for a
predator to select one. The second explanation for
(35)   the "confusion effect" has to do with the sensory
confusion caused by a large number of prey moving
around the predator. Even if the predator

makes the decision to attack a particular fish,
the movement of other prey in the school can
(40)   be distracting. The predator's difficulty can be
compared to that of a tennis player trying to
hit a tennis ball when two are approaching
simultaneously.

Questions 1–4 refer to the passage above.

1. According to the passage, theory B states that which of the following is a factor that enables a schooling fish to escape predators?

   (A) The tendency of fish to form compact groups

   (B) The movement of other fish within the school

   (C) The inability of predators to detect schools

   (D) The ability of fish to hide behind one another in a school

   (E) The great speed with which a school can disperse

2. According to the passage, both theory A and theory B have been developed to explain how

   (A) fish hide from predators by forming schools

   (B) forming schools functions to protect fish from predators

   (C) schooling among fish differs from other protective behaviors

   (D) small fish are able to make rapid decisions

   (E) small fish are able to survive in an environment densely populated by large predators

3. According to one explanation of the "confusion effect," a fish that swims in a school will have greater advantages for survival if it

   (A) tends to be visible for no more than 200 meters

   (B) stays near either the front or the rear of a school

   (C) is part of a small school rather than a large school

   (D) is very similar in appearance to the other fish in the school

   (E) is medium-sized

4. The author is primarily concerned with

   (A) discussing different theories

   (B) analyzing different techniques

   (C) defending two hypotheses

   (D) refuting established beliefs

   (E) revealing new evidence

Line   Ecoefficiency (measures to minimize environmental impact through the reduction or elimination of waste from production processes) has become a goal for companies worldwide, with many realizing significant
(5)   cost savings from such innovations. Peter Senge and Goran Carstedt see this development as laudable but suggest that simply adopting ecoefficiency innovations could actually worsen environmental stresses in the future. Such innovations reduce
(10)   production waste but do not alter the number of products manufactured nor the waste generated from their use and discard; indeed, most companies invest in ecoefficiency improvements in order to increase profits and growth. Moreover, there is no
(15)   guarantee that increased economic growth from ecoefficiency will come in similarly ecoefficient ways, since in today's global markets, greater profits may be turned into investment capital that could easily be reinvested in old-style eco-inefficient industries. Even
(20)   a vastly more ecoefficient industrial system could, were it to grow much larger, generate more total waste and destroy more habitat and species than would a smaller, less ecoefficient economy. Senge and Carstedt argue that to preserve the global
(25)   environment and sustain economic growth, businesses must develop a new systemic approach that reduces total material use and total accumulated waste. Focusing exclusively on ecoefficiency, which offers a compelling business case according to
(30)   established thinking, may distract companies from pursuing radically different products and business models.

Questions 5–7 refer to the passage above.

5.   The primary purpose of the passage is to

(A)   explain why a particular business strategy has been less successful than was once anticipated

(B)   propose an alternative to a particular business strategy that has inadvertently caused ecological damage

(C)   present a concern about the possible consequences of pursuing a particular business strategy

(D)   make a case for applying a particular business strategy on a larger scale than is currently practiced

(E)   suggest several possible outcomes of companies' failure to understand the economic impact of a particular business strategy

6.   The passage mentions which of the following as a possible consequence of companies' realization of greater profits through ecoefficiency?

(A)   The companies may be able to sell a greater number of products by lowering prices.

(B)   The companies may be better able to attract investment capital in the global market.

(C)   The profits may be reinvested to increase economic growth through ecoefficiency.

(D)   The profits may be used as investment capital for industries that are not ecoefficient.

(E)   The profits may encourage companies to make further innovations in reducing production waste.

7. The passage implies that which of the following is a possible consequence of a company's adoption of innovations that increase its ecoefficiency?

(A) Company profits resulting from such innovations may be reinvested in that company with no guarantee that the company will continue to make further improvements in ecoefficiency.

(B) Company growth fostered by cost savings from such innovations may allow that company to manufacture a greater number of products that will be used and discarded, thus worsening environmental stress.

(C) A company that fails to realize significant cost savings from such innovations may have little incentive to continue to minimize the environmental impact of its production processes.

(D) A company that comes to depend on such innovations to increase its profits and growth may be vulnerable in the global market to competition from old-style eco-inefficient industries.

(E) A company that meets its ecoefficiency goals is unlikely to invest its increased profits in the development of new and innovative ecoefficiency measures.

Line   Archaeology as a profession faces two major
problems. First, it is the poorest of the poor.
Only paltry sums are available for excavating and
even less is available for publishing the results
(5)   and preserving the sites once excavated. Yet
archaeologists deal with priceless objects every day.
Second, there is the problem of illegal excavation,
resulting in museum-quality pieces being sold to the
highest bidder.
(10)   I would like to make an outrageous
suggestion that would at one stroke provide
funds for archaeology and reduce the amount
of illegal digging. I would propose that scientific
archaeological expeditions and governmental
(15)   authorities sell excavated artifacts on the open
market. Such sales would provide substantial
funds for the excavation and preservation of
archaeological sites and the publication of results.
At the same time, they would break the illegal
(20)   excavator's grip on the market, thereby decreasing
the inducement to engage in illegal activities.
    You might object that professionals excavate to
acquire knowledge, not money. Moreover, ancient
artifacts are part of our global cultural heritage,
(25)   which should be available for all to appreciate, not
sold to the highest bidder. I agree. Sell nothing that
has unique artistic merit or scientific value. But,
you might reply, everything that comes out of the
ground has scientific value. Here we part company.
(30)   Theoretically, you may be correct in claiming
that every artifact has potential scientific value.
Practically, you are wrong.
    I refer to the thousands of pottery vessels and
ancient lamps that are essentially duplicates of
(35)   one another. In one small excavation in Cyprus,
archaeologists recently uncovered 2,000 virtually
indistinguishable small jugs in a single courtyard.
Even precious royal seal impressions known as
l'melekh handles have been found in abundance
(40)   —more than 4,000 examples so far.
    The basements of museums are simply not
large enough to store the artifacts that are likely
to be discovered in the future. There is not enough
money even to catalog the finds; as a result, they

(45)   cannot be found again and become as inaccessible
as if they had never been discovered. Indeed, with
the help of a computer, sold artifacts could be more
accessible than are the pieces stored in bulging
museum basements. Prior to sale, each could be
(50)   photographed and the list of the purchasers could
be maintained on the computer. A purchaser could
even be required to agree to return the piece if it
should become needed for scientific purposes.
    It would be unrealistic to suggest that illegal
(55)   digging would stop if artifacts were sold on the
open market. But the demand for the clandestine
product would be substantially reduced. Who would
want an unmarked pot when another was available
whose provenance was known, and that was dated
(60)   stratigraphically by the professional archaeologist
who excavated it?

Questions 8–10 refer to the passage above.

8. The primary purpose of the passage is to propose

    (A) an alternative to museum display of artifacts

    (B) a way to curb illegal digging while benefiting the archaeological profession

    (C) a way to distinguish artifacts with scientific value from those that have no such value

    (D) the governmental regulation of archaeological sites

    (E) a new system for cataloging duplicate artifacts

9. The author implies that all of the following statements about duplicate artifacts are true EXCEPT

    (A) a market for such artifacts already exists

    (B) such artifacts seldom have scientific value

    (C) there is likely to be a continuing supply of such artifacts

    (D) museums are well supplied with examples of such artifacts

    (E) such artifacts frequently exceed in quality those already cataloged in museum collections

10. Which of the following is mentioned in the passage as a disadvantage of storing artifacts in museum basements?

    (A) Museum officials rarely allow scholars access to such artifacts.

    (B) Space that could be better used for display is taken up for storage.

    (C) Artifacts discovered in one excavation often become separated from each other.

    (D) Such artifacts are often damaged by variations in temperature and humidity.

    (E) Such artifacts often remain uncataloged and thus cannot be located once they are put in storage.

Line   Io and Europa, the inner two of Jupiter's four
       largest moons, are about the size of Earth's moon
       and are composed mostly or entirely of rock and
       metal. Ganymede and Callisto are larger and roughly
(5)   half ice. Thus, these four moons are somewhat
       analogous to the planets of the solar system, in which
       the rock- and metal-rich inner planets are distinct from
       the much larger gas- and ice-rich outer planets.
       Jupiter's moons are, however, more "systematic":
(10)   many of their properties vary continuously with
       distance from Jupiter. For example, Io is ice-free,
       Europa has a surface shell of ice, and while
       Ganymede and Callisto are both ice-rich, outermost
       Callisto has more.
(15)   This compositional gradient has geological
       parallels. Io is extremely geologically active, Europa
       seems to be active on a more modest scale, and
       Ganymede has undergone bouts of activity in its
       geological past. Only Callisto reveals no geological
(20)   activity. In similar fashion, Callisto's surface is very
       heavily cratered from the impact of comets and
       asteroids; Ganymede, like Earth's moon, is heavily
       cratered in parts; Europa is very lightly cratered; and
       no craters have been detected on Io, even though
(25)   Jupiter's gravity attracts comets and asteroids
       passing near it, substantially increasing the
       bombardment rate of the inner moons compared to
       that of the outer ones. But because of Io's high
       degree of geological activity, its surface undergoes
(30)   more-or-less continuous volcanic resurfacing.

Questions 11–13 refer to the passage above.

11. According to the passage, the difference in the
     amount of cratering on Callisto's and Io's respective
     surfaces can probably be explained by the difference
     between these two moons with respect to which of
     the following factors?

     (A)   Size
     (B)   Ice content
     (C)   The rate of bombardment by comets and
           asteroids
     (D)   The influence of Jupiter's other moons
     (E)   The level of geological activity

12. Which of the following best describes the purpose of
     the second paragraph of the passage?

     (A)   To provide further evidence of the systematic
           variation in the characteristics of Jupiter's four
           largest moons
     (B)   To present a comprehensive theory to explain
           the systematic variation in the characteristics of
           Jupiter's four largest moons
     (C)   To explain the significance of the systematic
           variation in the characteristics of Jupiter's four
           largest moons
     (D)   To introduce facts that contradict conventional
           assumptions about Jupiter's four largest moons
     (E)   To contrast the characteristics of Jupiter's four
           largest moons with the characteristics of the
           planets of the solar system

13. The author's reference to Jupiter's gravity in line 25 serves primarily to

    (A) indicate why the absence of craters on Io's surface is surprising

    (B) explain the presence of craters on the surface of Jupiter's four largest moons

    (C) provide an explanation for the lack of geological activity on Callisto

    (D) contrast Jupiter's characteristics with the characteristics of its four largest moons

    (E) illustrate the similarity between Jupiter's four largest moons and the planets of the solar system

Line   When Jamaican-born social activist Marcus
Garvey came to the United States in 1916, he
arrived at precisely the right historical moment.
What made the moment right was the return of
(5)   African American soldiers from the First World War
in 1918, which created an ideal constituency for
someone with Garvey's message of unity, pride,
and improved conditions for African American
communities.
(10)   Hoping to participate in the traditional American
ethos of individual success, many African American
people entered the armed forces with enthusiasm,
only to find themselves segregated from white
troops and subjected to numerous indignities. They
(15)   returned to a United States that was as segregated
as it had been before the war. Considering similar
experiences, anthropologist Anthony F. C. Wallace
has argued that when a perceptible gap arises
between a culture's expectations and the reality of
(20)   that culture, the resulting tension can inspire a
revitalization movement: an organized, conscious
effort to construct a culture that fulfills long-
standing expectations.
        Some scholars have argued that Garvey created
(25)   the consciousness from which he built, in the
1920s, the largest revitalization movement in
African American history. But such an argument
only tends to obscure the consciousness of
identity, strength, and sense of history that already
(30)   existed in the African American community. Garvey
did not create this consciousness; rather, he gave
this consciousness its political expression.

Questions 14–17 refer to the passage above.

14. According to the passage, which of the following
    contributed to Marcus Garvey's success?

    (A)   He introduced cultural and historical
           consciousness to the African American
           community.

    (B)   He believed enthusiastically in the traditional
           American success ethos.

    (C)   His audience had already formed a
           consciousness that made it receptive to his
           message.

    (D)   His message appealed to critics of African
           American support for United States military
           involvement in the First World War.

    (E)   He supported the movement to protest
           segregation that had emerged prior to his
           arrival in the United States.

15. The passage suggests that many African American
    people responded to their experiences in the armed
    forces in which of the following ways?

    (A)   They maintained as civilians their enthusiastic
           allegiance to the armed forces.

    (B)   They questioned United States involvement in
           the First World War.

    (C)   They joined political organizations to protest the
           segregation of African American troops and the
           indignities they suffered in the military.

    (D)   They became aware of the gap between their
           expectations and the realities of American
           culture.

    (E)   They repudiated Garvey's message of pride and
           unity.

16. It can be inferred from the passage that the "scholars" mentioned in line 24 believe which of the following to be true?

    (A) Revitalization resulted from the political activism of returning African American soldiers following the First World War.

    (B) Marcus Garvey had to change a number of prevailing attitudes in order for his mass movement to find a foothold in the United States.

    (C) The prevailing sensibility of the African American community provided the foundation of Marcus Garvey's political appeal.

    (D) Marcus Garvey hoped to revitalize consciousness of cultural and historical identity in the African American community.

    (E) The goal of the mass movement that Marcus Garvey helped bring into being was to build on the pride and unity among African Americans.

17. According to the passage, many African American people joined the armed forces during the First World War for which of the following reasons?

    (A) They wished to escape worsening economic conditions in African American communities.

    (B) They expected to fulfill ideals of personal attainment.

    (C) They sought to express their loyalty to the United States.

    (D) They hoped that joining the military would help advance the cause of desegregation.

    (E) They saw military service as an opportunity to fulfill Marcus Garvey's political vision.

Line   In terrestrial environments, gravity places special demands on the cardiovascular systems of animals. Gravitational pressure can cause blood to pool in the lower regions of the body, making it
(5)   difficult to circulate blood to critical organs such as the brain. Terrestrial snakes, in particular, exhibit adaptations that aid in circulating blood against the force of gravity.

The problem confronting terrestrial snakes is best
(10)   illustrated by what happens to sea snakes when removed from their supportive medium. Because the vertical pressure gradients within the blood vessels are counteracted by similar pressure gradients in the surrounding water, the distribution of blood
(15)   throughout the body of sea snakes remains about the same regardless of their orientation in space, provided they remain in the ocean. When removed from the water and tilted at various angles with the head up, however, blood pressure at their midpoint
(20)   drops significantly, and at brain level falls to zero. That many terrestrial snakes in similar spatial orientations do not experience this kind of circulatory failure suggests that certain adaptations enable them to regulate blood pressure more effectively in those
(25)   orientations.

One such adaptation is the closer proximity of the terrestrial snake's heart to its head, which helps to ensure circulation to the brain, regardless of the snake's orientation in space. The heart of sea snakes
(30)   can be located near the middle of the body, a position that minimizes the work entailed in circulating blood to both extremities. In arboreal snakes, however, which dwell in trees and often assume a vertical posture, the average distance

(35)   from the heart to the head can be as little as 15 percent of overall body length. Such a location requires that blood circulated to the tail of the snake travel a greater distance back to the heart, a problem solved by another adaptation. When
(40)   climbing, arboreal snakes often pause momentarily to wiggle their bodies, causing waves of muscle contraction that advance from the lower torso to the head. By compressing the veins and forcing blood forward, these contractions
(45)   apparently improve the flow of venous blood returning to the heart.

Questions 18–25 refer to the passage above.

18. The passage provides information in support of which of the following assertions?

(A) The disadvantages of an adaptation to a particular feature of an environment often outweigh the advantages of such an adaptation.

(B) An organism's reaction to being placed in an environment to which it is not well adapted can sometimes illustrate the problems that have been solved by the adaptations of organisms indigenous to that environment.

(C) The effectiveness of an organism's adaptation to a particular feature of its environment can only be evaluated by examining the effectiveness with which organisms of other species have adapted to a similar feature of a different environment.

(D) Organisms of the same species that inhabit strikingly different environments will often adapt in remarkably similar ways to the few features of those environments that are common.

(E) Different species of organisms living in the same environment will seldom adapt to features of that environment in the same way.

19. According to the passage, one reason that the distribution of blood in the sea snake changes little while the creature remains in the ocean is that

(A) the heart of the sea snake tends to be located near the center of its body

(B) pressure gradients in the water surrounding the sea snake counter the effects of vertical pressure gradients within its blood vessels

(C) the sea snake assumes a vertical posture less frequently than do the terrestrial and the arboreal snake

(D) the sea snake often relies on waves of muscle contractions to help move blood from the torso to the head

(E) the force of pressure gradients in the water surrounding the sea snake exceeds that of vertical pressure gradients within its circulatory system

20. It can be inferred from the passage that which of the following is true of species of terrestrial snakes that often need to assume a vertical posture?

(A) They are more likely to be susceptible to circulatory failure in vertical postures than are sea snakes.

(B) Their hearts are less likely to be located at the midpoint of their bodies than is the case with sea snakes.

(C) They cannot counteract the pooling of blood in lower regions of their bodies as effectively as sea snakes can.

(D) The blood pressure at their midpoint decreases significantly when they are tilted with their heads up.

(E) They are unable to rely on muscle contractions to move venous blood from the lower torso to the head.

21. The author describes the behavior of the circulatory system of sea snakes when they are removed from the ocean (see lines 17–20) primarily in order to

    (A) illustrate what would occur in the circulatory system of terrestrial snakes without adaptations that enable them to regulate their blood pressure in vertical orientations

    (B) explain why arboreal snakes in vertical orientations must rely on muscle contractions to restore blood pressure to the brain

    (C) illustrate the effects of circulatory failure on the behavior of arboreal snakes

    (D) illustrate the superiority of the circulatory system of the terrestrial snake to that of the sea snake

    (E) explain how changes in spatial orientation can adversely affect the circulatory system of snakes with hearts located in relatively close proximity to their heads

22. It can be inferred from the passage that which of the following is a true statement about sea snakes?

    (A) They frequently rely on waves of muscle contractions from the lower torso to the head to supplement the work of the heart.

    (B) They cannot effectively regulate their blood pressure when placed in seawater and tilted at an angle with the head pointed downward.

    (C) They are more likely to have a heart located in close proximity to their heads than are arboreal snakes.

    (D) They become acutely vulnerable to the effects of gravitational pressure on their circulatory system when they are placed in a terrestrial environment.

    (E) Their cardiovascular system is not as complicated as that of arboreal snakes.

23. The author suggests that which of the following is a disadvantage that results from the location of a snake's heart in close proximity to its head?

    (A) A decrease in the efficiency with which the snake regulates the flow of blood to the brain

    (B) A decrease in the number of orientations in space that a snake can assume without loss of blood flow to the brain

    (C) A decrease in blood pressure at the snake's midpoint when it is tilted at various angles with its head up

    (D) An increase in the tendency of blood to pool at the snake's head when the snake is tilted at various angles with its head down

    (E) An increase in the amount of effort required to distribute blood to and from the snake's tail

24. The primary purpose of the third paragraph is to

    (A) introduce a topic that is not discussed earlier in the passage

    (B) describe a more efficient method of achieving an effect discussed in the previous paragraph

    (C) draw a conclusion based on information elaborated in the previous paragraph

    (D) discuss two specific examples of phenomena mentioned at the end of the previous paragraph

    (E) introduce evidence that undermines a view reported earlier in the passage

25. In the passage, the author is primarily concerned with doing which of the following?

    (A) Explaining adaptations that enable the terrestrial snake to cope with the effects of gravitational pressure on its circulatory system

    (B) Comparing the circulatory system of the sea snake with that of the terrestrial snake

    (C) Explaining why the circulatory system of the terrestrial snake is different from that of the sea snake

    (D) Pointing out features of the terrestrial snake's cardiovascular system that make it superior to that of the sea snake

    (E) Explaining how the sea snake is able to neutralize the effects of gravitational pressure on its circulatory system

Line   In 1988 services moved ahead of
manufacturing as the main product of the United
States economy. But what is meant by "services"?
Some economists define a service as something
(5)   that is produced and consumed simultaneously, for
example, a haircut. The broader, classical definition
is that a service is an intangible something that
cannot be touched or stored. Yet electric utilities
can store energy, and computer programmers
(10)   save information electronically. Thus, the classical
definition is hard to sustain.

The United States government's definition is
more practical: services are the residual category
that includes everything that is not agriculture or
(15)   industry. Under this definition, services includes
activities as diverse as engineering and driving a
bus. However, besides lacking a strong conceptual
framework, this definition fails to recognize the
distinction between service industries and service
(20)   occupations. It categorizes workers based on their
company's final product rather than on the actual
work the employees perform. Thus, the many
service workers employed by manufacturers—
bookkeepers or janitors, for example—would
(25)   fall under the industrial rather than the services
category. Such ambiguities reveal the arbitrariness
of this definition and suggest that, although
practical for government purposes, it does not
accurately reflect the composition of the current
(30)   United States economy.

Questions 26–30 refer to the passage above.

26. The author of the passage is primarily concerned with

    (A)   discussing research data underlying several definitions

    (B)   arguing for the adoption of a particular definition

    (C)   exploring definitions of a concept

    (D)   comparing the advantages of several definitions

    (E)   clarifying some ambiguous definitions

27. In comparing the United States government's definition of services with the classical definition, the author suggests that the classical definition is

    (A)   more pragmatic

    (B)   more difficult to apply

    (C)   less ambiguous

    (D)   more widely used

    (E)   more arbitrary

28. The passage suggests which of the following about service workers in the United States?

    (A)   The number of service workers may be underestimated by the definition of services used by the government.

    (B)   There were fewer service workers than agricultural workers before 1988.

    (C)   The number of service workers was almost equal to the number of workers employed in manufacturing until 1988.

    (D)   Most service workers are employed in service occupations rather than in service industries.

    (E)   Most service workers are employed in occupations where they provide services that do not fall under the classical definition of services.

29. The author of the passage mentions which of the following as one disadvantage of the United States government's definition of services?

    (A) It is less useful than the other definitions mentioned in the passage.

    (B) It is narrower in scope than the other definitions mentioned in the passage.

    (C) It is based on the final product produced rather than on the type of work performed.

    (D) It does not recognize the diversity of occupations within the service industries.

    (E) It misclassifies many workers who are employed in service industries.

30. The author refers to "service workers employed by manufacturers" (line 23) primarily in order to point out

    (A) a type of worker not covered by the United States government's system of classifying occupations

    (B) a flaw in the United States government's definition of services

    (C) a factor that has influenced the growth of the service economy in the United States

    (D) a type of worker who is classified on the basis of work performed rather than on the basis of the company's final product

    (E) the diversity of the workers who are referred to as service workers

Line   Current feminist theory, in validating women's own stories of their experience, has encouraged scholars of women's history to view the use of women's oral narratives as the methodology, next to the use of

(5)   women's written autobiography, that brings historians closest to the "reality" of women's lives. Such narratives, unlike most standard histories, represent experience from the perspective of women, affirm the importance of women's contributions, and furnish

(10)   present-day women with historical continuity that is essential to their identity, individually and collectively.
     Scholars of women's history should, however, be as cautious about accepting oral narratives at face value as they already are about written memories.

(15)   Oral narratives are no more likely than are written narratives to provide a disinterested commentary on events or people. Moreover, the stories people tell to explain themselves are shaped by narrative devices and storytelling conventions, as well as by other

(20)   cultural and historical factors, in ways that the storytellers may be unaware of. The political rhetoric of a particular era, for example, may influence women's interpretations of the significance of their experience. Thus a woman who views the Second

(25)   World War as pivotal in increasing the social acceptance of women's paid work outside the home may reach that conclusion partly and unwittingly because of wartime rhetoric encouraging a positive view of women's participation in such work.

Questions 31–36 refer to the passage above.

31.   The passage is primarily concerned with

(A)   contrasting the benefits of one methodology with the benefits of another

(B)   describing the historical origins and inherent drawbacks of a particular methodology

(C)   discussing the appeal of a particular methodology and some concerns about its use

(D)   showing that some historians' adoption of a particular methodology has led to criticism of recent historical scholarship

(E)   analyzing the influence of current feminist views on women's interpretations of their experience

32.   According to the passage, which of the following shapes the oral narratives of women storytellers?

(A)   The conventions for standard histories in the culture in which a woman storyteller lives

(B)   The conventions of storytelling in the culture in which a woman storyteller lives

(C)   A woman storyteller's experience with distinctive traditions of storytelling developed by the women in her family of origin

(D)   The cultural expectations and experiences of those who listen to oral narratives

(E)   A woman storyteller's familiarity with the stories that members of other groups in her culture tell to explain themselves

33. The author of the passage would be most likely to make which of the following recommendations to scholars of women's history?

   (A) They should take into account their own life experiences when interpreting the oral accounts of women's historical experiences.

   (B) They should assume that the observations made in women's oral narratives are believed by the intended audience of the story.

   (C) They should treat skeptically observations reported in oral narratives unless the observations can be confirmed in standard histories.

   (D) They should consider the cultural and historical context in which an oral narrative was created before arriving at an interpretation of such a narrative.

   (E) They should rely on information gathered from oral narratives only when equivalent information is not available in standard histories.

34. Which of the following best describes the function of the last sentence of the passage?

   (A) It describes an event that historians view as crucial in recent women's history.

   (B) It provides an example of how political rhetoric may influence the interpretations of experience reported in women's oral narratives.

   (C) It provides an example of an oral narrative that inaccurately describes women's experience during a particular historical period.

   (D) It illustrates the point that some women are more aware than others of the social forces that shape their oral narratives.

   (E) It identifies the historical conditions that led to the social acceptance of women's paid work outside the home.

35. According to the passage, scholars of women's history should refrain from doing which of the following?

   (A) Relying on traditional historical sources when women's oral narratives are unavailable

   (B) Focusing on the influence of political rhetoric on women's perceptions to the exclusion of other equally important factors

   (C) Attempting to discover the cultural and historical factors that influence the stories women tell

   (D) Assuming that the conventions of women's written autobiographies are similar to the conventions of women's oral narratives

   (E) Accepting women's oral narratives less critically than they accept women's written histories

36. According to the passage, each of the following is a difference between women's oral narratives and most standard histories EXCEPT:

   (A) Women's oral histories validate the significance of women's achievements.

   (B) Women's oral histories depict experience from the point of view of women.

   (C) Women's oral histories acknowledge the influence of well-known women.

   (D) Women's oral histories present today's women with a sense of their historical relationship to women of the past.

   (E) Women's oral histories are crucial to the collective identity of today's women.

Line   Manufacturers have to do more than build large
manufacturing plants to realize economies of scale.
It is true that as the capacity of a manufacturing
operation rises, costs per unit of output fall as plant
(5)   size approaches "minimum efficient scale," where the
cost per unit of output reaches a minimum,
determined roughly by the state of existing technology
and size of the potential market. However, minimum
efficient scale cannot be fully realized unless a steady
(10)   "throughput" (the flow of materials through a plant) is
attained. The throughput needed to maintain the
optimal scale of production requires careful
coordination not only of the flow of goods through the
production process, but also of the flow of input from
(15)   suppliers and the flow of output to wholesalers and
final consumers. If throughput falls below a critical
point, unit costs rise sharply and profits disappear. A
manufacturer's fixed costs and "sunk costs" (original
capital investment in the physical plant) do not
(20)   decrease when production declines due to inadequate
supplies of raw materials, problems on the factory
floor, or inefficient sales networks. Consequently,
potential economies of scale are based on the
physical and engineering characteristics of the
(25)   production facilities—that is, on tangible capital—but
realized economies of scale are operational and
organizational, and depend on knowledge, skills,
experience, and teamwork—that is, on organized
human capabilities, or intangible capital.
(30)   The importance of investing in intangible capital
becomes obvious when one looks at what happens in
new capital-intensive manufacturing industries. Such
industries are quickly dominated, not by the first firms
to acquire technologically sophisticated plants of
(35)   theoretically optimal size, but rather by the first to
exploit the full potential of such plants. Once some
firms achieve this, a market becomes extremely hard
to enter. Challengers must construct comparable
plants and do so after the first movers have already
(40)   worked out problems with suppliers or with new
production processes. Challengers must create
distribution networks and marketing systems in
markets where first movers have all the contacts and
know-how. And challengers must recruit management
(45)   teams to compete with those that have already
mastered these functional and strategic activities.

Questions 37–41 refer to the passage above.

37.   The passage suggests that in order for a
manufacturer in a capital-intensive industry to have a
decisive advantage over competitors making similar
products, the manufacturer must

(A)   be the first in the industry to build production
facilities of theoretically optimal size

(B)   make every effort to keep fixed and sunk costs
as low as possible

(C)   be one of the first to operate its manufacturing
plants at minimum efficient scale

(D)   produce goods of higher quality than those
produced by direct competitors

(E)   stockpile raw materials at production sites in
order to ensure a steady flow of such materials

38.   The passage suggests that which of the following is
true of a manufacturer's fixed and sunk costs?

(A)   The extent to which they are determined by
market conditions for the goods being
manufactured is frequently underestimated.

(B)   If they are kept as low as possible, the
manufacturer is very likely to realize significant
profits.

(C)   They are the primary factor that determines
whether a manufacturer will realize economies
of scale.

(D)   They should be on a par with the fixed and sunk
costs of the manufacturer's competitors.

(E)   They are not affected by fluctuations in a
manufacturing plant's throughput.

39.   In the context of the passage as a whole, the second
paragraph serves primarily to

(A)   provide an example to support the argument
presented in the first paragraph

(B)   evaluate various strategies discussed in the first
paragraph

(C)   introduce evidence that undermines the
argument presented in the first paragraph

(D)   anticipate possible objections to the argument
presented in the first paragraph

(E)   demonstrate the potential dangers of a
commonly used strategy

40. The passage LEAST supports the inference that a manufacturer's throughput could be adversely affected by

    (A) a mistake in judgment regarding the selection of a wholesaler

    (B) a breakdown in the factory's machinery

    (C) a labor dispute on the factory floor

    (D) an increase in the cost per unit of output

    (E) a drop in the efficiency of the sales network

41. The primary purpose of the passage is to

    (A) point out the importance of intangible capital for realizing economies of scale in manufacturing

    (B) show that manufacturers frequently gain a competitive advantage from investment in large manufacturing facilities

    (C) argue that large manufacturing facilities often fail because of inadequate investment in both tangible and intangible capital

    (D) suggest that most new industries are likely to be dominated by firms that build large manufacturing plants early

    (E) explain why large manufacturing plants usually do not help manufacturers achieve economies of scale

Line   In the seventeenth-century Florentine textile
industry, women were employed primarily in low-
paying, low-skill jobs. To explain this segregation
of labor by gender, economists have relied on
(5)   the useful theory of human capital. According
to this theory, investment in human capital—the
acquisition of difficult job-related skills—generally
benefits individuals by making them eligible to
engage in well-paid occupations. Women's role as
(10)   child bearers, however, results in interruptions in
their participation in the job market (as compared
with men's) and thus reduces their opportunities
to acquire training for highly skilled work. In
addition, the human capital theory explains why
(15)   there was a high concentration of women workers
in certain low-skill jobs, such as weaving, but not
in others, such as combing or carding, by positing
that because of their primary responsibility in child
rearing women took occupations that could be
(20)   carried out in the home.
        There were, however, differences in pay scales
that cannot be explained by the human capital
theory. For example, male construction workers
were paid significantly higher wages than female
(25)   taffeta weavers. The wage difference between
these two low-skill occupations stems from the
segregation of labor by gender: because a limited
number of occupations were open to women, there
was a large supply of workers in their fields, and
(30)   this "overcrowding" resulted in women receiving
lower wages and men receiving higher wages.

Questions 42–44 refer to the passage above.

42.   The passage suggests that combing and carding differ
      from weaving in that combing and carding were

      (A)   low-skill jobs performed primarily by women
            employees

      (B)   low-skill jobs that were not performed in the
            home

      (C)   low-skill jobs performed by both male and
            female employees

      (D)   high-skill jobs performed outside the home

      (E)   high-skill jobs performed by both male and
            female employees

43.   Which of the following, if true, would most weaken the
      explanation provided by the human capital theory for
      women's concentration in certain occupations in
      seventeenth-century Florence?

      (A)   Women were unlikely to work outside the home
            even in occupations whose hours were flexible
            enough to allow women to accommodate
            domestic tasks as well as paid labor.

      (B)   Parents were less likely to teach occupational
            skills to their daughters than they were to their
            sons.

      (C)   Women's participation in the Florentine paid
            labor force grew steadily throughout the
            sixteenth and seventeenth centuries.

      (D)   The vast majority of female weavers in the
            Florentine wool industry had children.

      (E)   Few women worked as weavers in the Florentine
            silk industry, which was devoted to making
            cloths that required a high degree of skill to
            produce.

44. The author of the passage would be most likely to describe the explanation provided by the human capital theory for the high concentration of women in certain occupations in the seventeenth-century Florentine textile industry as

    (A) well founded though incomplete
    (B) difficult to articulate
    (C) plausible but poorly substantiated
    (D) seriously flawed
    (E) contrary to recent research

(This passage was adapted from an article written in 1992.)

Line Some observers have attributed the dramatic
growth in temporary employment that occurred in
the United States during the 1980s to increased
participation in the workforce by certain groups,
(5) such as first-time or reentering workers, who
supposedly prefer such arrangements. However,
statistical analyses reveal that demographic
changes in the workforce did not correlate with
variations in the total number of temporary
(10) workers. Instead, these analyses suggest that
factors affecting employers account for the rise
in temporary employment. One factor is product
demand: temporary employment is favored by
employers who are adapting to fluctuating demand
(15) for products while at the same time seeking
to reduce overall labor costs. Another factor
is labor's reduced bargaining strength, which
allows employers more control over the terms of
employment. Given the analyses, which reveal that
(20) growth in temporary employment now far exceeds
the level explainable by recent workforce entry
rates of groups said to prefer temporary jobs, firms
should be discouraged from creating excessive
numbers of temporary positions. Government
(25) policymakers should consider mandating benefit
coverage for temporary employees, promoting pay
equity between temporary and permanent workers,
assisting labor unions in organizing temporary
workers, and encouraging firms to assign temporary
(30) jobs primarily to employees who explicitly indicate
that preference.

Questions 45–51 refer to the passage above.

45. The primary purpose of the passage is to

   (A) present the results of statistical analyses and propose further studies

   (B) explain a recent development and predict its eventual consequences

   (C) identify the reasons for a trend and recommend measures to address it

   (D) outline several theories about a phenomenon and advocate one of them

   (E) describe the potential consequences of implementing a new policy and argue in favor of that policy

46. According to the passage, which of the following is true of the "factors affecting employers" that are mentioned in lines 10–19?

   (A) Most experts cite them as having initiated the growth in temporary employment that occurred during the 1980s.

   (B) They may account for the increase in the total number of temporary workers during the 1980s.

   (C) They were less important than demographic change in accounting for the increase of temporary employment during the 1980s.

   (D) They included a sharp increase in the cost of labor during the 1980s.

   (E) They are more difficult to account for than are other factors involved in the growth of temporary employment during the 1980s.

47. The passage suggests which of the following about the use of temporary employment by firms during the 1980s?

(A) It enabled firms to deal with fluctuating product demand far more efficiently than they did before the 1980s.

(B) It increased as a result of increased participation in the workforce by certain demographic groups.

(C) It was discouraged by government-mandated policies.

(D) It was a response to preferences indicated by certain employees for more flexible working arrangements.

(E) It increased partly as a result of workers' reduced ability to control the terms of their employment.

48. The passage suggests which of the following about the workers who took temporary jobs during the 1980s?

(A) Their jobs frequently led to permanent positions within firms.

(B) They constituted a less demographically diverse group than has been suggested.

(C) They were occasionally involved in actions organized by labor unions.

(D) Their pay declined during the decade in comparison with the pay of permanent employees.

(E) They did not necessarily prefer temporary employment to permanent employment.

49. The first sentence in the passage suggests that the "observers" mentioned in line 1 would be most likely to predict which of the following?

(A) That the number of new temporary positions would decline as fewer workers who preferred temporary employment entered the workforce

(B) That the total number of temporary positions would increase as fewer workers were able to find permanent positions

(C) That employers would have less control over the terms of workers' employment as workers increased their bargaining strength

(D) That more workers would be hired for temporary positions as product demand increased

(E) That the number of workers taking temporary positions would increase as more workers in any given demographic group entered the workforce

50. In the context of the passage, the word "excessive" (line 23) most closely corresponds to which of the following phrases?

(A) Far more than can be justified by worker preferences

(B) Far more than can be explained by fluctuations in product demand

(C) Far more than can be beneficial to the success of the firms themselves

(D) Far more than can be accounted for by an expanding national economy

(E) Far more than can be attributed to increases in the total number of people in the workforce

51. The passage mentions each of the following as an appropriate kind of governmental action EXCEPT

(A) getting firms to offer temporary employment primarily to a certain group of people

(B) encouraging equitable pay for temporary and permanent employees

(C) facilitating the organization of temporary workers by labor unions

(D) establishing guidelines on the proportion of temporary workers that firms should employ

(E) ensuring that temporary workers obtain benefits from their employers

Line   Among the myths taken as fact by the
environmental managers of most corporations is
the belief that environmental regulations affect all
competitors in a given industry uniformly. In reality,
(5)   regulatory costs—and therefore compliance—fall
unevenly, economically disadvantaging some
companies and benefiting others. For example,
a plant situated near a number of larger
noncompliant competitors is less likely to attract
(10) the attention of local regulators than is an isolated
plant, and less attention means lower costs.
Additionally, large plants can spread compliance
costs such as waste treatment across a larger
revenue base; on the other hand, some smaller
(15) plants may not even be subject to certain
provisions such as permit or reporting
requirements by virtue of their size. Finally, older
production technologies often continue to generate
toxic wastes that were not regulated when the
(20) technology was first adopted. New regulations
have imposed extensive compliance costs on
companies still using older industrial coal-fired
burners that generate high sulfur dioxide and
nitrogen oxide outputs, for example, whereas new
(25) facilities generally avoid processes that would
create such waste products. By realizing that they
have discretion and that not all industries are
affected equally by environmental regulation,
environmental managers can help their companies
(30) to achieve a competitive edge by anticipating
regulatory pressure and exploring all possibilities
for addressing how changing regulations will affect
their companies specifically.

Questions 52–55 refer to the passage above.

52. It can be inferred from the passage that a large plant might have to spend more than a similar but smaller plant on environmental compliance because the larger plant is

(A) more likely to attract attention from local regulators

(B) less likely to be exempt from permit and reporting requirements

(C) less likely to have regulatory costs passed on to it by companies that supply its raw materials

(D) more likely to employ older production technologies

(E) more likely to generate wastes that are more environmentally damaging than those generated by smaller plants

53. According to the passage, which of the following statements about sulfur dioxide and nitrogen oxide outputs is true?

(A) Older production technologies cannot be adapted so as to reduce production of these outputs as waste products.

(B) Under the most recent environmental regulations, industrial plants are no longer permitted to produce these outputs.

(C) Although these outputs are environmentally hazardous, some plants still generate them as waste products despite the high compliance costs they impose.

(D) Many older plants have developed innovative technological processes that reduce the amounts of these outputs generated as waste products.

(E) Since the production processes that generate these outputs are less costly than alternative processes, these less expensive processes are sometimes adopted despite their acknowledged environmental hazards.

54. Which of the following best describes the relationship of the statement about large plants (lines 12–17) to the passage as a whole?

    (A) It presents a hypothesis that is disproved later in the passage.

    (B) It highlights an opposition between two ideas mentioned in the passage.

    (C) It provides examples to support a claim made earlier in the passage.

    (D) It exemplifies a misconception mentioned earlier in the passage.

    (E) It draws an analogy between two situations described in the passage.

55. The primary purpose of the passage is to

    (A) address a widespread environmental management problem and suggest possible solutions

    (B) illustrate varying levels of compliance with environmental regulation among different corporations

    (C) describe the various alternatives to traditional methods of environmental management

    (D) advocate increased corporate compliance with environmental regulation

    (E) correct a common misconception about the impact of environmental regulations

Line   In *Winters v. United States* (1908), the Supreme
Court held that the right to use waters flowing through
or adjacent to the Fort Belknap Indian Reservation
was reserved to American Indians by the treaty
(5)   establishing the reservation. Although this treaty did
not mention water rights, the Court ruled that the
federal government, when it created the reservation,
intended to deal fairly with American Indians by
reserving for them the waters without which their
(10)   lands would have been useless. Later decisions, citing
Winters, established that courts can find federal rights
to reserve water for particular purposes if (1) the land
in question lies within an enclave under exclusive
federal jurisdiction, (2) the land has been formally
(15)   withdrawn from federal public lands—i.e., withdrawn
from the stock of federal lands available for private
use under federal land use laws—and set aside or
reserved, and (3) the circumstances reveal the
government intended to reserve water as well as land
(20)   when establishing the reservation.
    Some American Indian tribes have also established
water rights through the courts based on their
traditional diversion and use of certain waters prior to
the United States' acquisition of sovereignty. For
(25)   example, the Rio Grande pueblos already existed when
the United States acquired sovereignty over New
Mexico in 1848. Although they at that time became
part of the United States, the pueblo lands never
formally constituted a part of federal public lands; in
(30)   any event, no treaty, statute, or executive order has
ever designated or withdrawn the pueblos from public
lands as American Indian reservations. This fact,
however, has not barred application of the *Winters*
doctrine. What constitutes an American Indian
(35)   reservation is a question of practice, not of legal
definition, and the pueblos have always been treated
as reservations by the United States. This pragmatic
approach is buttressed by *Arizona v. California* (1963),
wherein the Supreme Court indicated that the manner
(40)   in which any type of federal reservation is created
does not affect the application to it of the *Winters*
doctrine. Therefore, the reserved water rights of
Pueblo Indians have priority over other citizens' water
rights as of 1848, the year in which pueblos must be
(45)   considered to have become reservations.

Questions 56–62 refer to the passage above.

56.   According to the passage, which of the following was
true of the treaty establishing the Fort Belknap Indian
Reservation?

(A)   It was challenged in the Supreme Court a
number of times.

(B)   It was rescinded by the federal government, an
action that gave rise to the *Winters* case.

(C)   It cited American Indians' traditional use of the
land's resources.

(D)   It failed to mention water rights to be enjoyed by
the reservation's inhabitants.

(E)   It was modified by the Supreme Court in
Arizona v. California.

57.   The passage suggests that, if the criteria discussed in
lines 10–20 were the only criteria for establishing a
reservation's water rights, which of the following would
be true?

(A)   The water rights of the inhabitants of the Fort
Belknap Indian Reservation would not take
precedence over those of other citizens.

(B)   Reservations established before 1848 would be
judged to have no water rights.

(C)   There would be no legal basis for the water
rights of the Rio Grande pueblos.

(D)   Reservations other than American Indian
reservations could not be created with reserved
water rights.

(E)   Treaties establishing reservations would have to
mention water rights explicitly in order to
reserve water for a particular purpose.

58. Which of the following most accurately summarizes the relationship between *Arizona v. California* in lines 38–42, and the criteria citing the *Winters* doctrine in lines 10–20?

    (A) *Arizona v. California* abolishes these criteria and establishes a competing set of criteria for applying the *Winters* doctrine.

    (B) *Arizona v. California* establishes that the *Winters* doctrine applies to a broader range of situations than those defined by these criteria.

    (C) *Arizona v. California* represents the sole example of an exception to the criteria as they were set forth in the *Winters* doctrine.

    (D) *Arizona v. California* does not refer to the *Winters* doctrine to justify water rights, whereas these criteria do rely on the *Winters* doctrine.

    (E) *Arizona v. California* applies the criteria derived from the *Winters* doctrine only to federal lands other than American Indian reservations.

59. The "pragmatic approach" mentioned in lines 37–38 of the passage is best defined as one that

    (A) grants recognition to reservations that were never formally established but that have traditionally been treated as such

    (B) determines the water rights of all citizens in a particular region by examining the actual history of water usage in that region

    (C) gives federal courts the right to reserve water along with land even when it is clear that the government originally intended to reserve only the land

    (D) bases the decision to recognize the legal rights of a group on the practical effect such a recognition is likely to have on other citizens

    (E) dictates that courts ignore precedents set by such cases as *Winters v. United States* in deciding what water rights belong to reserved land

60. The author cites the fact that the Rio Grande pueblos were never formally withdrawn from public lands primarily in order to do which of the following?

    (A) Suggest why it might have been argued that the *Winters* doctrine ought not to apply to pueblo lands

    (B) Imply that the United States never really acquired sovereignty over pueblo lands

    (C) Argue that the pueblo lands ought still to be considered part of federal public lands

    (D) Support the argument that the water rights of citizens other than American Indians are limited by the *Winters* doctrine

    (E) Suggest that federal courts cannot claim jurisdiction over cases disputing the traditional diversion and use of water by Pueblo Indians

61. The primary purpose of the passage is to

    (A) trace the development of laws establishing American Indian reservations

    (B) explain the legal basis for the water rights of American Indian tribes

    (C) question the legal criteria often used to determine the water rights of American Indian tribes

    (D) discuss evidence establishing the earliest date at which the federal government recognized the water rights of American Indians

    (E) point out a legal distinction between different types of American Indian reservations

62. The passage suggests that the legal rights of citizens other than American Indians to the use of water flowing into the Rio Grande pueblos are

    (A) guaranteed by the precedent set in *Arizona v. California*

    (B) abolished by the *Winters* doctrine

    (C) deferred to the Pueblo Indians whenever treaties explicitly require this

    (D) guaranteed by federal land-use laws

    (E) limited by the prior claims of the Pueblo Indians

Line   Milankovitch proposed in the early twentieth century that the ice ages were caused by variations in the Earth's orbit around the Sun. For some time this theory was considered untestable,
(5)   largely because there was no sufficiently precise chronology of the ice ages with which the orbital variations could be matched.

To establish such a chronology it is necessary to determine the relative amounts of land ice that
(10)   existed at various times in the Earth's past. A recent discovery makes such a determination possible: relative land-ice volume for a given period can be deduced from the ratio of two oxygen isotopes, 16 and 18, found in ocean sediments. Almost
(15)   all the oxygen in water is oxygen 16, but a few molecules out of every thousand incorporate the heavier isotope 18. When an ice age begins, the continental ice sheets grow, steadily reducing the amount of water evaporated from the ocean that
(20)   will eventually return to it. Because heavier isotopes tend to be left behind when water evaporates from the ocean surfaces, the remaining ocean water becomes progressively enriched in oxygen 18. The degree of enrichment can be determined
(25)   by analyzing ocean sediments of the period, because these sediments are composed of calcium carbonate shells of marine organisms, shells that were constructed with oxygen atoms drawn from the surrounding ocean. The higher the ratio of
(30)   oxygen 18 to oxygen 16 in a sedimentary specimen, the more land ice there was when the sediment was laid down.

As an indicator of shifts in the Earth's climate, the isotope record has two advantages. First, it is
(35)   a global record: there is remarkably little variation in isotope ratios in sedimentary specimens taken from different continental locations. Second, it is a more continuous record than that taken from rocks on land. Because of these advantages,
(40)   sedimentary evidence can be dated with sufficient accuracy by radiometric methods to establish a precise chronology of the ice ages. The dated isotope record shows that the fluctuations in global ice volume over the past several hundred
(45)   thousand years have a pattern: an ice age occurs roughly once every 100,000 years. These data have established a strong connection between variations in the Earth's orbit and the periodicity of the ice ages.
(50)   However, it is important to note that other factors, such as volcanic particulates or variations in the amount of sunlight received by the Earth, could potentially have affected the climate. The advantage of the Milankovitch theory is that it
(55)   is testable; changes in the Earth's orbit can be calculated and dated by applying Newton's laws of gravity to progressively earlier configurations of the bodies in the solar system. Yet the lack of information about other possible factors affecting
(60)   global climate does not make them unimportant.

Questions 63–68 refer to the passage above.

63.   In the passage, the author is primarily interested in

(A)   suggesting an alternative to an outdated research method

(B)   introducing a new research method that calls an accepted theory into question

(C)   emphasizing the instability of data gathered from the application of a new scientific method

(D)   presenting a theory and describing a new method to test that theory

(E)   initiating a debate about a widely accepted theory

64.   The author of the passage would be most likely to agree with which of the following statements about the Milankovitch theory?

(A)   It is the only possible explanation for the ice ages.

(B)   It is too limited to provide a plausible explanation for the ice ages, despite recent research findings.

(C)   It cannot be tested and confirmed until further research on volcanic activity is done.

(D)   It is one plausible explanation, though not the only one, for the ice ages.

(E)   It is not a plausible explanation for the ice ages, although it has opened up promising possibilities for future research.

65. It can be inferred from the passage that the isotope record taken from ocean sediments would be less useful to researchers if which of the following were true?

    (A) It indicated that lighter isotopes of oxygen predominated at certain times.

    (B) It had far more gaps in its sequence than the record taken from rocks on land.

    (C) It indicated that climate shifts did not occur every 100,000 years.

    (D) It indicated that the ratios of oxygen 16 and oxygen 18 in ocean water were not consistent with those found in fresh water.

    (E) It stretched back for only a million years.

66. According to the passage, which of the following is true of the ratios of oxygen isotopes in ocean sediments?

    (A) They indicate that sediments found during an ice age contain more calcium carbonate than sediments formed at other times.

    (B) They are less reliable than the evidence from rocks on land in determining the volume of land ice.

    (C) They can be used to deduce the relative volume of land ice that was present when the sediment was laid down.

    (D) They are more unpredictable during an ice age than in other climatic conditions.

    (E) They can be used to determine atmospheric conditions at various times in the past.

67. It can be inferred from the passage that precipitation formed from evaporated ocean water has

    (A) the same isotopic ratio as ocean water

    (B) less oxygen 18 than does ocean water

    (C) less oxygen 18 than has the ice contained in continental ice sheets

    (D) a different isotopic composition than has precipitation formed from water on land

    (E) more oxygen 16 than has precipitation formed from fresh water

68. It can be inferred from the passage that calcium carbonate shells

    (A) are not as susceptible to deterioration as rocks

    (B) are less common in sediments formed during an ice age

    (C) are found only in areas that were once covered by land ice

    (D) contain radioactive material that can be used to determine a sediment's isotopic composition

    (E) reflect the isotopic composition of the water at the time the shells were formed

Line　　Two works published in 1984 demonstrate
contrasting approaches to writing the history of
United States women. Buel and Buel's biography of
Mary Fish (1736–1818) makes little effort to place
(5)　her story in the context of recent historiography on
women. Lebsock, meanwhile, attempts not only to
write the history of women in one southern
community, but also to redirect two decades of
historiographical debate as to whether women
(10)　gained or lost status in the nineteenth century as
compared with the eighteenth century. Although
both books offer the reader the opportunity to
assess this controversy regarding women's status,
only Lebsock's deals with it directly. She examines
(15)　several different aspects of women's status, helping
to refine and resolve the issues. She concludes that
while women gained autonomy in some areas,
especially in the private sphere, they lost it in many
aspects of the economic sphere. More importantly,
(20)　she shows that the debate itself depends on frame
of reference: in many respects, women lost power
in relation to men, for example, as certain jobs
(delivering babies, supervising schools) were taken
over by men. Yet women also gained power in
(25)　comparison with their previous status, owning a
higher proportion of real estate, for example. In
contrast, Buel and Buel's biography provides ample
raw material for questioning the myth, fostered by
some historians, of a colonial golden age in the
(30)　eighteenth century but does not give the reader
much guidance in analyzing the controversy over
women's status.

Questions 69–74 refer to the passage above.

69.　The primary purpose of the passage is to

(A)　examine two sides of a historiographical debate

(B)　call into question an author's approach to a
historiographical debate

(C)　examine one author's approach to a
historiographical debate

(D)　discuss two authors' works in relationship to a
historiographical debate

(E)　explain the prevalent perspective on a
historiographical debate

70.　The author of the passage mentions the supervision of
schools primarily in order to

(A)　remind readers of the role education played in
the cultural changes of the nineteenth century in
the United States

(B)　suggest an area in which nineteenth-century
American women were relatively free to exercise
power

(C)　provide an example of an occupation for which
accurate data about women's participation are
difficult to obtain

(D)　speculate about which occupations were
considered suitable for United States women of
the nineteenth century

(E)　illustrate how the answers to questions about
women's status depend on particular contexts

71. With which of the following characterizations of Lebsock's contribution to the controversy concerning women's status in the nineteenth-century United States would the author of the passage be most likely to agree?

    (A) Lebsock has studied women from a formerly neglected region and time period.

    (B) Lebsock has demonstrated the importance of frame of reference in answering questions about women's status.

    (C) Lebsock has addressed the controversy by using women's current status as a frame of reference.

    (D) Lebsock has analyzed statistics about occupations and property that were previously ignored.

    (E) Lebsock has applied recent historiographical methods to the biography of a nineteenth-century woman.

72. According to the passage, Lebsock's work differs from Buel and Buel's work in that Lebsock's work

    (A) uses a large number of primary sources

    (B) ignores issues of women's legal status

    (C) refuses to take a position on women's status in the eighteenth century

    (D) addresses larger historiographical issues

    (E) fails to provide sufficient material to support its claims

73. The passage suggests that Lebsock believes that compared to nineteenth-century American women, eighteenth-century American women were

    (A) in many respects less powerful in relation to men

    (B) more likely to own real estate

    (C) generally more economically independent

    (D) more independent in conducting their private lives

    (E) less likely to work as school superintendents

74. The passage suggests that Buel and Buel's biography of Mary Fish provides evidence for which of the following views of women's history?

    (A) Women have lost power in relation to men since the colonial era.

    (B) Women of the colonial era were not as likely to be concerned with their status as were women in the nineteenth century.

    (C) The colonial era was not as favorable for women as some historians have believed.

    (D) Women had more economic autonomy in the colonial era than in the nineteenth century.

    (E) Women's occupations were generally more respected in the colonial era than in the nineteenth century.

Line   It was once believed that the brain was
        independent of metabolic processes occurring
        elsewhere in the body. In recent studies, however,
        we have discovered that the production and release
(5)   in brain neurons of the neurotransmitter serotonin
        (neurotransmitters are compounds that neurons use
        to transmit signals to other cells) depend directly on
        the food that the body processes.
          Our first studies sought to determine whether
(10)   the increase in serotonin observed in rats given
        a large injection of the amino acid tryptophan
        might also occur after rats ate meals that change
        tryptophan levels in the blood. We found that,
        immediately after the rats began to eat, parallel
(15)   elevations occurred in blood tryptophan, brain
        tryptophan, and brain serotonin levels. These
        findings suggested that the production and release
        of serotonin in brain neurons were normally coupled
        with blood-tryptophan increases. In later studies we
(20)   found that injecting insulin into a rat's bloodstream
        also caused parallel elevations in blood and brain
        tryptophan levels and in serotonin levels. We then
        decided to see whether the secretion of the animal's
        own insulin similarly affected serotonin production.
(25)   We gave the rats a carbohydrate-containing meal
        that we knew would elicit insulin secretion. As we
        had hypothesized, the blood tryptophan level and
        the concentrations of tryptophan and of serotonin
        in the brain increased after the meal.
(30)   Surprisingly, however, when we added a large
        amount of protein to the meal, brain tryptophan
        and serotonin levels fell. Since protein contains
        tryptophan, why should it depress brain tryptophan
        levels? The answer lies in the mechanism that
(35)   provides blood tryptophan to the brain cells. This
        same mechanism also provides the brain cells with
        other amino acids found in protein, such as tyrosine
        and leucine. The consumption of protein increases
        blood concentration of the other amino acids much
(40)   more, proportionately, than it does that of tryptophan.
        The more protein is in a meal, the lower is the ratio
        of the resulting blood-tryptophan concentration to
        the concentration of competing amino acids, and
        the more slowly is tryptophan provided to the brain.
(45)   Thus the more protein in a meal, the less serotonin
        subsequently produced and released.

Questions 75–83 refer to the passage above.

75.   Which of the following titles best summarizes the
       contents of the passage?

       (A)   Neurotransmitters: Their Crucial Function in
              Cellular Communication

       (B)   Diet and Survival: An Old Relationship
              Reexamined

       (C)   The Blood Supply and the Brain: A Reciprocal
              Dependence

       (D)   Amino Acids and Neurotransmitters: The
              Connection between Serotonin Levels and
              Tyrosine

       (E)   The Effects of Food Intake on the Production
              and Release of Serotonin: Some Recent Findings

76.   According to the passage, the speed with which
       tryptophan is provided to the brain cells of a rat varies
       with the

       (A)   amount of protein present in a meal

       (B)   concentration of serotonin in the brain before
              a meal

       (C)   concentration of leucine in the blood rather than
              with the concentration of tyrosine in the blood
              after a meal

       (D)   concentration of tryptophan in the brain before
              a meal

       (E)   number of serotonin-containing neurons

77.   According to the passage, when the authors began
       their first studies, they were aware that

       (A)   they would eventually need to design
              experiments that involved feeding rats high
              concentrations of protein

       (B)   tryptophan levels in the blood were difficult to
              monitor with accuracy

       (C)   serotonin levels increased after rats were fed
              meals rich in tryptophan

       (D)   there were many neurotransmitters whose
              production was dependent on metabolic
              processes elsewhere in the body

       (E)   serotonin levels increased after rats were
              injected with a large amount of tryptophan

78. According to the passage, one reason that the authors gave rats carbohydrates was to

    (A) depress the rats' tryptophan levels

    (B) prevent the rats from contracting diseases

    (C) cause the rats to produce insulin

    (D) demonstrate that insulin is the most important substance secreted by the body

    (E) compare the effect of carbohydrates with the effect of proteins

79. According to the passage, the more protein a rat consumes, the lower will be the

    (A) ratio of the rat's blood-tryptophan concentration to the amount of serotonin produced and released in the rat's brain

    (B) ratio of the rat's blood-tryptophan concentration to the concentration in its blood of the other amino acids contained in the protein

    (C) ratio of the rat's blood-tyrosine concentration to its blood-leucine concentration

    (D) number of neurotransmitters of any kind that the rat will produce and release

    (E) number of amino acids the rat's blood will contain

80. The authors' discussion of the "mechanism that provides blood tryptophan to the brain cells" (lines 34–35) is meant to

    (A) stimulate further research studies

    (B) summarize an area of scientific investigation

    (C) help explain why a particular research finding was obtained

    (D) provide supporting evidence for a controversial scientific theory

    (E) refute the conclusions of a previously mentioned research study

81. According to the passage, an injection of insulin was most similar in its effect on rats to an injection of

    (A) tyrosine

    (B) leucine

    (C) blood

    (D) tryptophan

    (E) protein

82. It can be inferred from the passage that which of the following would be LEAST likely to be a potential source of aid to a patient who was not adequately producing and releasing serotonin?

    (A) Meals consisting almost exclusively of protein

    (B) Meals consisting almost exclusively of carbohydrates

    (C) Meals that would elicit insulin secretion

    (D) Meals that had very low concentrations of tyrosine

    (E) Meals that had very low concentrations of leucine

83. It can be inferred from the passage that the authors initially held which of the following hypotheses about what would happen when they fed large amounts of protein to rats?

    (A) The rats' brain serotonin levels would not decrease.

    (B) The rats' brain tryptophan levels would decrease.

    (C) The rats' tyrosine levels would increase less quickly than would their leucine levels.

    (D) The rats would produce more insulin.

    (E) The rats would produce neurotransmitters other than serotonin.

Line   Acting on the recommendation of a British
        government committee investigating the high
        incidence in white lead factories of illness among
        employees, most of whom were women, the Home
(5)   Secretary proposed in 1895 that Parliament enact
        legislation that would prohibit women from holding
        most jobs in white lead factories. Although the
        Women's Industrial Defence Committee (WIDC),
        formed in 1892 in response to earlier legislative
(10)   attempts to restrict women's labor, did not discount
        the white lead trade's potential health dangers, it
        opposed the proposal, viewing it as yet another
        instance of limiting women's work opportunities.
        Also opposing the proposal was the Society for
(15)   Promoting the Employment of Women (SPEW),
        which attempted to challenge it by investigating the
        causes of illness in white lead factories. SPEW
        contended, and WIDC concurred, that controllable
        conditions in such factories were responsible for the
(20)   development of lead poisoning. SPEW provided
        convincing evidence that lead poisoning could be
        avoided if workers were careful and clean and if
        already extant workplace safety regulations were
        stringently enforced. However, the Women's Trade
(25)   Union League (WTUL), which had ceased in the late
        1880s to oppose restrictions on women's labor,
        supported the eventually enacted proposal, in part
        because safety regulations were generally not being
        enforced in white lead factories, where there were
(30)   no unions (and little prospect of any) to pressure
        employers to comply with safety regulations.

Questions 84–86 refer to the passage above.

84. The passage suggests that WIDC differed from WTUL
    in which of the following ways?

    (A) WIDC believed that the existing safety
        regulations were adequate to protect women's
        health, whereas WTUL believed that such
        regulations needed to be strengthened.

    (B) WIDC believed that unions could not succeed in
        pressuring employers to comply with such
        regulations, whereas WTUL believed that unions
        could succeed in doing so.

    (C) WIDC believed that lead poisoning in white lead
        factories could be avoided by controlling
        conditions there, whereas WTUL believed that
        lead poisoning in such factories could not be
        avoided no matter how stringently safety
        regulations were enforced.

    (D) At the time that the legislation concerning white
        lead factories was proposed, WIDC was
        primarily concerned with addressing health
        conditions in white lead factories, whereas
        WTUL was concerned with improving working
        conditions in all types of factories.

    (E) At the time that WIDC was opposing legislative
        attempts to restrict women's labor, WTUL had
        already ceased to do so.

85. Which of the following, if true, would most clearly support the contention attributed to SPEW in lines 17–20?

    (A) Those white lead factories that most strongly enforced regulations concerning worker safety and hygiene had the lowest incidences of lead poisoning among employees.

    (B) The incidence of lead poisoning was much higher among women who worked in white lead factories than among women who worked in other types of factories.

    (C) There were many household sources of lead that could have contributed to the incidence of lead poisoning among women who also worked outside the home in the late nineteenth century.

    (D) White lead factories were more stringent than were certain other types of factories in their enforcement of workplace safety regulations.

    (E) Even brief exposure to the conditions typically found in white lead factories could cause lead poisoning among factory workers.

86. The passage is primarily concerned with

    (A) presenting various groups' views of the motives of those proposing certain legislation

    (B) contrasting the reasoning of various groups concerning their positions on certain proposed legislation

    (C) tracing the process whereby certain proposed legislation was eventually enacted

    (D) assessing the success of tactics adopted by various groups with respect to certain proposed legislation

    (E) evaluating the arguments of various groups concerning certain proposed legislation

Line   In 1955 Maurice Duverger published *The Political Role of Women*, the first behavioralist, multinational comparison of women's electoral participation ever to use election data and survey
(5)   data together. His study analyzed women's patterns of voting, political candidacy, and political activism in four European countries during the first half of the twentieth century. Duverger's research findings were that women voted somewhat less frequently
(10)   than men (the difference narrowing the longer women had the vote) and were slightly more conservative.
       Duverger's work set an early standard for the sensitive analysis of women's electoral activities.
(15)   Moreover, to Duverger's credit, he placed his findings in the context of many of the historical processes that had shaped these activities. However, since these contexts have changed over time, Duverger's approach has proved more
(20)   durable than his actual findings. In addition, Duverger's discussion of his findings was hampered by his failure to consider certain specific factors important to women's electoral participation at the time he collected his data: the influence
(25)   of political regimes, the effects of economic factors, and the ramifications of political and social relations between women and men. Given this failure, Duverger's study foreshadowed the enduring limitations of the behavioralist approach
(30)   to the multinational study of women's political participation.

Questions 87–92 refer to the passage above.

87.   The primary purpose of the passage is to

   (A)   evaluate a research study
   (B)   summarize the history of a research area
   (C)   report new research findings
   (D)   reinterpret old research findings
   (E)   reconcile conflicting research findings

88.   According to the passage, Duverger's study was unique in 1955 in that it

   (A)   included both election data and survey data
   (B)   gathered data from sources never before used in political studies
   (C)   included an analysis of historical processes
   (D)   examined the influence on voting behavior of the relationships between women and men
   (E)   analyzed not only voting and political candidacy but also other political activities

89.   Which of the following characteristics of a country is most clearly an example of a factor that Duverger, as described in the passage, failed to consider in his study?

   (A)   A large population
   (B)   A predominantly Protestant population
   (C)   A predominantly urban population
   (D)   A one-party government
   (E)   Location in the heart of Europe

90. The author implies that Duverger's actual findings are

    (A) limited because they focus on only four countries

    (B) inaccurate in their description of the four countries in the early 1950s

    (C) out-of-date in that they are inapplicable in the four countries today

    (D) flawed because they are based on unsound data

    (E) biased by Duverger's political beliefs

91. The passage implies that, in comparing four European countries, Duverger found that the voting rates of women and men were most different in the country in which women

    (A) were most politically active

    (B) ran for office most often

    (C) held the most conservative political views

    (D) had the most egalitarian relations with men

    (E) had possessed the right to vote for the shortest time

92. The author implies that some behavioralist research involving the multinational study of women's political participation that followed Duverger's study did which of the following?

    (A) Ignored Duverger's approach

    (B) Suffered from faults similar to those in Duverger's study

    (C) Focused on political activism

    (D) Focused on the influences of political regimes

    (E) Focused on the political and social relations between women and men

Line   The majority of successful senior managers do
not closely follow the classical rational model of first
clarifying goals, assessing the problem, formulating
options, estimating likelihoods of success, making a
(5)   decision, and only then taking action to implement
the decision. Rather, in their day-by-day tactical
maneuvers, these senior executives rely on what is
vaguely termed "intuition" to manage a network of
interrelated problems that require them to deal with
(10)   ambiguity, inconsistency, novelty, and surprise; and
to integrate action into the process of thinking.

Generations of writers on management have
recognized that some practicing managers rely
heavily on intuition. In general, however, such
(15)   writers display a poor grasp of what intuition is.
Some see it as the opposite of rationality; others
view it as an excuse for capriciousness.

Isenberg's recent research on the cognitive
processes of senior managers reveals that
(20)   managers' intuition is neither of these. Rather,
senior managers use intuition in at least five distinct
ways. First, they intuitively sense when a problem
exists. Second, managers rely on intuition to
perform well-learned behavior patterns rapidly. This
(25)   intuition is not arbitrary or irrational, but is based
on years of painstaking practice and hands-on
experience that build skills. A third function of
intuition is to synthesize isolated bits of data and
practice into an integrated picture, often in
(30)   an "Aha!" experience. Fourth, some managers use
intuition as a check on the results of more rational
analysis. Most senior executives are familiar with
the formal decision analysis models and tools,
and those who use such systematic methods
(35)   for reaching decisions are occasionally leery of
solutions suggested by these methods which run
counter to their sense of the correct course of
action. Finally, managers can use intuition to bypass
in-depth analysis and move rapidly to engender a
(40)   plausible solution. Used in this way, intuition is an
almost instantaneous cognitive process in which a
manager recognizes familiar patterns.

One of the implications of the intuitive style
of executive management is that "thinking" is
(45)   inseparable from acting. Since managers often "know"
what is right before they can analyze and explain it,
they frequently act first and explain later. Analysis is
inextricably tied to action in thinking/acting cycles,
in which managers develop thoughts about their

(50)   companies and organizations not by analyzing a
problematic situation and then acting, but by acting
and analyzing in close concert. Given the great
uncertainty of many of the management issues that
they face, senior managers often instigate a course
(55)   of action simply to learn more about an issue.
They then use the results of the action to develop
a more complete understanding of the issue. One
implication of thinking/acting cycles is that action
is often part of defining the problem, not just of
(60)   implementing the solution.

Questions 93–98 refer to the passage above.

93.   According to the passage, senior managers use
intuition in all of the following ways EXCEPT to

(A)   speed up the creation of a solution to a problem

(B)   identify a problem

(C)   bring together disparate facts

(D)   stipulate clear goals

(E)   evaluate possible solutions to a problem

94.   The passage suggests which of the following about
the "writers on management" mentioned in line 12?

(A)   They have criticized managers for not following
the classical rational model of decision analysis.

(B)   They have not based their analyses on a
sufficiently large sample of actual managers.

(C)   They have relied in drawing their conclusions on
what managers say rather than on what
managers do.

(D)   They have misunderstood how managers use
intuition in making business decisions.

(E)   They have not acknowledged the role of intuition
in managerial practice.

95. Which of the following best exemplifies "an 'Aha!' experience" (line 30) as it is presented in the passage?

    (A) A manager risks taking an action whose outcome is unpredictable to discover whether the action changes the problem at hand.

    (B) A manager performs well-learned and familiar behavior patterns in creative and uncharacteristic ways to solve a problem.

    (C) A manager suddenly connects seemingly unrelated facts and experiences to create a pattern relevant to the problem at hand.

    (D) A manager rapidly identifies the methodology used to compile data yielded by systematic analysis.

    (E) A manager swiftly decides which of several sets of tactics to implement in order to deal with the contingencies suggested by a problem.

96. According to the passage, the classical model of decision analysis includes all of the following EXCEPT

    (A) evaluation of a problem

    (B) creation of possible solutions to a problem

    (C) establishment of clear goals to be reached by the decision

    (D) action undertaken in order to discover more information about a problem

    (E) comparison of the probable effects of different solutions to a problem

97. It can be inferred from the passage that which of the following would most probably be one major difference in behavior between Manager X, who uses intuition to reach decisions, and Manager Y, who uses only formal decision analysis?

    (A) Manager X analyzes first and then acts; Manager Y does not.

    (B) Manager X checks possible solutions to a problem by systematic analysis; Manager Y does not.

    (C) Manager X takes action in order to arrive at the solution to a problem; Manager Y does not.

    (D) Manager Y draws on years of hands-on experience in creating a solution to a problem; Manager X does not.

    (E) Manager Y depends on day-to-day tactical maneuvering; Manager X does not.

98. The passage provides support for which of the following statements?

    (A) Managers who rely on intuition are more successful than those who rely on formal decision analysis.

    (B) Managers cannot justify their intuitive decisions.

    (C) Managers' intuition works contrary to their rational and analytical skills.

    (D) Logical analysis of a problem increases the number of possible solutions.

    (E) Intuition enables managers to employ their practical experience more efficiently.

Line   Frazier and Mosteller assert that medical
        research could be improved by a move toward
        larger, simpler clinical trials of medical treatments.
        Currently, researchers collect far more background
(5)   information on patients than is strictly required for
        their trials—substantially more than hospitals
        collect—thereby escalating costs of data
        collection, storage, and analysis. Although limiting
        information collection could increase the risk that
(10)   researchers will overlook facts relevant to a study,
        Frazier and Mosteller contend that such risk, never
        entirely eliminable from research, would still be
        small in most studies. Only in research on entirely
        new treatments are new and unexpected variables
(15)   likely to arise.
            Frazier and Mosteller propose not only that
        researchers limit data collection on individual
        patients but also that researchers enroll more
        patients in clinical trials, thereby obtaining a more
(20)   representative sample of the total population with
        the disease under study. Often researchers restrict
        study participation to patients who have no
        ailments besides those being studied. A treatment
        judged successful under these ideal conditions can
(25)   then be evaluated under normal conditions.
        Broadening the range of trial participants, Frazier
        and Mosteller suggest, would enable researchers to
        evaluate a treatment's efficacy for diverse patients
        under various conditions and to evaluate its
(30)   effectiveness for different patient subgroups. For
        example, the value of a treatment for a progressive
        disease may vary according to a patient's stage of
        disease. Patients' ages may also affect a
        treatment's efficacy.

Questions 99–103 refer to the passage above.

99.   The passage is primarily concerned with

      (A)   identifying two practices in medical research
            that may affect the accuracy of clinical trials

      (B)   describing aspects of medical research that
            tend to drive up costs

      (C)   evaluating an analysis of certain shortcomings
            of current medical research practices

      (D)   describing proposed changes to the ways in
            which clinical trials are conducted

      (E)   explaining how medical researchers have
            traditionally conducted clinical trials and how
            such trials are likely to change

100. Which of the following can be inferred from the
      passage about a study of the category of patients
      referred to in lines 21–23?

      (A)   Its findings might have limited applicability.

      (B)   It would be prohibitively expensive in its attempt
            to create ideal conditions.

      (C)   It would be the best way to sample the total
            population of potential patients.

      (D)   It would allow researchers to limit information
            collection without increasing the risk that
            important variables could be overlooked.

      (E)   Its findings would be more accurate if it
            concerned treatments for a progressive disease
            than if it concerned treatments for a
            nonprogressive disease.

101. It can be inferred from the passage that a study limited to patients like those mentioned in lines 21–23 would have which of the following advantages over the kind of study proposed by Frazier and Mosteller?

    (A) It would yield more data and its findings would be more accurate.

    (B) It would cost less in the long term, though it would be more expensive in its initial stages.

    (C) It would limit the number of variables researchers would need to consider when evaluating the treatment under study.

    (D) It would help researchers to identify subgroups of patients with secondary conditions that might also be treatable.

    (E) It would enable researchers to assess the value of an experimental treatment for the average patient.

102. The author mentions patients' ages (line 33) primarily in order to

    (A) identify the most critical variable differentiating subgroups of patients

    (B) cast doubt on the advisability of implementing Frazier and Mosteller's proposals about medical research

    (C) indicate why progressive diseases may require different treatments at different stages

    (D) illustrate a point about the value of enrolling a wide range of patients in clinical trials

    (E) substantiate an argument about the problems inherent in enrolling large numbers of patients in clinical trials

103. According to the passage, which of the following describes a result of the way in which researchers generally conduct clinical trials?

    (A) They expend resources on the storage of information likely to be irrelevant to the study they are conducting.

    (B) They sometimes compromise the accuracy of their findings by collecting and analyzing more information than is strictly required for their trials.

    (C) They avoid the risk of overlooking variables that might affect their findings, even though doing so raises their research costs.

    (D) Because they attempt to analyze too much information, they overlook facts that could emerge as relevant to their studies.

    (E) In order to approximate the conditions typical of medical treatment, they base their methods of information collection on those used by hospitals.

Line   According to a recent theory, Archean-age gold-quartz vein systems were formed more than two billion years ago from magmatic fluids that originated from molten granite-like bodies deep
(5)   beneath the surface of the Earth. This theory is contrary to the widely held view that the systems were deposited from metamorphic fluids, that is, from fluids that formed during the dehydration of wet sedimentary rocks.
(10)   The recently developed theory has considerable practical importance. Most of the gold deposits discovered during the original gold rushes were exposed at the Earth's surface and were found because they had shed trails of alluvial gold
(15)   that were easily traced by simple prospecting methods. Although these same methods still lead to an occasional discovery, most deposits not yet discovered have gone undetected because they are buried and have no surface expression.
(20)   The challenge in exploration is therefore to unravel the subsurface geology of an area and pinpoint the position of buried minerals. Methods widely used today include analysis of aerial images that yield a broad geological overview; geophysical
(25)   techniques that provide data on the magnetic, electrical, and mineralogical properties of the rocks being investigated; and sensitive chemical tests that are able to detect the subtle chemical halos that often envelop mineralization. However,
(30)   none of these high-technology methods are of any value if the sites to which they are applied have never mineralized, and to maximize the chances of discovery the explorer must therefore pay particular attention to selecting the ground formations most
(35)   likely to be mineralized. Such ground selection relies to varying degrees on conceptual models, which take into account theoretical studies of relevant factors.
         These models are constructed primarily from
(40)   empirical observations of known mineral deposits and from theories of ore-forming processes. The explorer uses the models to identify those geological features that are critical to the formation of the mineralization being modeled, and then tries
(45)   to select areas for exploration that exhibit as many of the critical features as possible.

Questions 104–110 refer to the passage above.

104. The author is primarily concerned with

(A)   advocating a return to an older methodology

(B)   explaining the importance of a recent theory

(C)   enumerating differences between two widely used methods

(D)   describing events leading to a discovery

(E)   challenging the assumptions on which a theory is based

105. According to the passage, the widely held view of Archean-age gold-quartz vein systems is that such systems

(A)   were formed from metamorphic fluids

(B)   originated in molten granite-like bodies

(C)   were formed from alluvial deposits

(D)   generally have surface expression

(E)   are not discoverable through chemical tests

106. The passage implies that which of the following steps would be the first performed by explorers who wish to maximize their chances of discovering gold?

(A)   Surveying several sites known to have been formed more than two billion years ago

(B)   Limiting exploration to sites known to have been formed from metamorphic fluid

(C)   Using an appropriate conceptual model to select a site for further exploration

(D)   Using geophysical methods to analyze rocks over a broad area

(E)   Limiting exploration to sites where alluvial gold has previously been found

107. Which of the following statements about discoveries of gold deposits is supported by information in the passage?

(A) The number of gold discoveries made annually has increased between the time of the original gold rushes and the present.

(B) New discoveries of gold deposits are likely to be the result of exploration techniques designed to locate buried mineralization.

(C) It is unlikely that newly discovered gold deposits will ever yield as much as did those deposits discovered during the original gold rushes.

(D) Modern explorers are divided on the question of the utility of simple prospecting methods as a source of new discoveries of gold deposits.

(E) Models based on the theory that gold originated from magmatic fluids have already led to new discoveries of gold deposits.

108. It can be inferred from the passage that which of the following is easiest to detect?

(A) A gold-quartz vein system originating in magmatic fluids

(B) A gold-quartz vein system originating in metamorphic fluids

(C) A gold deposit that is mixed with granite

(D) A gold deposit that has shed alluvial gold

(E) A gold deposit that exhibits chemical halos

109. The theory mentioned in lines 1–5 relates to the conceptual models discussed in the passage in which of the following ways?

(A) It may furnish a valid account of ore-forming processes, and, hence, can support conceptual models that have great practical significance.

(B) It suggests that certain geological formations, long believed to be mineralized, are in fact mineralized, thus confirming current conceptual models.

(C) It suggests that there may not be enough similarity across Archean-age gold-quartz vein systems to warrant the formulation of conceptual models.

(D) It corrects existing theories about the chemical halos of gold deposits, and thus provides a basis for correcting current conceptual models.

(E) It suggests that simple prospecting methods still have a higher success rate in the discovery of gold deposits than do more modern methods.

110. According to the passage, methods of exploring for gold that are widely used today are based on which of the following facts?

(A) Most of the Earth's remaining gold deposits are still molten.

(B) Most of the Earth's remaining gold deposits are exposed at the surface.

(C) Most of the Earth's remaining gold deposits are buried and have no surface expression.

(D) Only one type of gold deposit warrants exploration, since the other types of gold deposits are found in regions difficult to reach.

(E) Only one type of gold deposit warrants exploration, since the other types of gold deposits are unlikely to yield concentrated quantities of gold.

Line   While the most abundant and dominant species
        within a particular ecosystem is often crucial in
        perpetuating the ecosystem, a "keystone" species,
        here defined as one whose effects are much larger
(5)   than would be predicted from its abundance, can
        also play a vital role. But because complex species
        interactions may be involved, identifying a keystone
        species by removing the species and observing
        changes in the ecosystem is problematic. It might
(10)   seem that certain traits would clearly define a
        species as a keystone species; for example,
        Pisaster ochraceus is often a keystone predator
        because it consumes and suppresses mussel
        populations, which in the absence of this starfish
(15)   can be a dominant species. But such predation on a
        dominant or potentially dominant species occurs in
        systems that do as well as in systems that do not
        have species that play keystone roles. Moreover,
        whereas *P. ochraceus* occupies an unambiguous
(20)   keystone role on wave-exposed rocky headlands, in
        more wave-sheltered habitats the impact of
        P. ochraceus predation is weak or nonexistent, and
        at certain sites sand burial is responsible for
        eliminating mussels. Keystone status appears to
(25)   depend on context, whether of particular
        geography or of such factors as community
        diversity (for example, a reduction in species
        diversity may thrust more of the remaining species
        into keystone roles) and length of species
(30)   interaction (since newly arrived species in particular
        may dramatically affect ecosystems).

Questions 111–114 refer to the passage above.

111. The passage mentions which of the following as a
     factor that affects the role of *P. ochraceus* as a
     keystone species within different habitats?

     (A) The degree to which the habitat is sheltered
          from waves

     (B) The degree to which other animals within a
          habitat prey on mussels

     (C) The fact that mussel populations are often not
          dominant within some habitats occupied by
          P. ochraceus

     (D) The size of the *P. ochraceus* population within
          the habitat

     (E) The fact that there is great species diversity
          within some habitats occupied by *P. ochraceus*

112. Which of the following hypothetical experiments most
     clearly exemplifies the method of identifying species'
     roles that the author considers problematic?

     (A) A population of seals in an Arctic habitat is
          counted in order to determine whether it is the
          dominant species in that ecosystem.

     (B) A species of fish that is a keystone species in
          one marine ecosystem is introduced into
          another marine ecosystem to see whether the
          species will come to occupy a keystone role.

     (C) In order to determine whether a species of
          monkey is a keystone species within a particular
          ecosystem, the monkeys are removed from that
          ecosystem and the ecosystem is then studied.

     (D) Different mountain ecosystems are compared
          to determine how geography affects a particular
          species' ability to dominate its ecosystem.

     (E) In a grassland experiencing a changing climate,
          patterns of species extinction are traced in
          order to evaluate the effect of climate changes
          on keystone species in that grassland.

113. Which of the following, if true, would most clearly support the argument about keystone status advanced in the last sentence of the passage (lines 24–31)?

    (A) A species of bat is primarily responsible for keeping insect populations within an ecosystem low, and the size of the insect population in turn affects bird species within that ecosystem.

    (B) A species of iguana occupies a keystone role on certain tropical islands, but does not play that role on adjacent tropical islands that are inhabited by a greater number of animal species.

    (C) Close observation of a savannah ecosystem reveals that more species occupy keystone roles within that ecosystem than biologists had previously believed.

    (D) As a keystone species of bee becomes more abundant, it has a larger effect on the ecosystem it inhabits.

    (E) A species of moth that occupies a keystone role in a prairie habitat develops coloration patterns that camouflage it from potential predators.

114. The passage suggests which of the following about the identification of a species as a keystone species?

    (A) Such an identification depends primarily on the species' relationship to the dominant species.

    (B) Such an identification can best be made by removing the species from a particular ecosystem and observing changes that occur in the ecosystem.

    (C) Such an identification is likely to be less reliable as an ecosystem becomes less diverse.

    (D) Such an identification seems to depend on various factors within the ecosystem.

    (E) Such an identification can best be made by observing predation behavior.

Line   After evidence was obtained in the 1920s that
        the universe is expanding, it became reasonable
        to ask: Will the universe continue to expand
        indefinitely, or is there enough mass in it for the
(5)   mutual attraction of its constituents to bring this
        expansion to a halt? It can be calculated that
        the critical density of matter needed to brake the
        expansion and "close" the universe is equivalent
        to three hydrogen atoms per cubic meter. But the
(10)   density of the observable universe—luminous matter
        in the form of galaxies—comes to only a fraction
        of this. If the expansion of the universe is to stop,
        there must be enough invisible matter in the
        universe to exceed the luminous matter in density
(15)   by a factor of roughly 70.

        Our contribution to the search for this "missing
        matter" has been to study the rotational velocity
        of galaxies at various distances from their center
        of rotation. It has been known for some time that
(20)   outside the bright nucleus of a typical spiral galaxy
        luminosity falls off rapidly with distance from the
        center. If luminosity were a true indicator of mass,
        most of the mass would be concentrated toward
        the center. Outside the nucleus the rotational
(25)   velocity would decrease geometrically with distance
        from the center, in conformity with Kepler's law.
        Instead we have found that the rotational velocity
        in spiral galaxies either remains constant with
        increasing distance from the center or increases
(30)   slightly. This unexpected result indicates that the
        falloff in luminous mass with distance from the
        center is balanced by an increase in nonluminous
        mass.

        Our findings suggest that as much as 90
(35)   percent of the mass of the universe is not radiating
        at any wavelength with enough intensity to be
        detected on the Earth. Such dark matter could be
        in the form of extremely dim stars of low mass,
        of large planets like Jupiter, or of black holes,
(40)   either small or massive. While it has not yet been
        determined whether this mass is sufficient to
        close the universe, some physicists consider it
        significant that estimates are converging on the
        critical value.

Questions 115–119 refer to the passage above.

115.   The passage is primarily concerned with

        (A)   defending a controversial approach
        (B)   criticizing an accepted view
        (C)   summarizing research findings
        (D)   contrasting competing theories
        (E)   describing an innovative technique

116.   The authors' study indicates that, in comparison with
        the outermost regions of a typical spiral galaxy, the
        region just outside the nucleus can be characterized
        as having

        (A)   higher rotational velocity and higher luminosity
        (B)   lower rotational velocity and higher luminosity
        (C)   lower rotational velocity and lower luminosity
        (D)   similar rotational velocity and higher luminosity
        (E)   similar rotational velocity and similar luminosity

117.   The authors' suggestion that "as much as 90 percent
        of the mass of the universe is not radiating at any
        wavelength with enough intensity to be detected on
        the Earth" (lines 34–37) would be most weakened if
        which of the following were discovered to be true?

        (A)   Spiral galaxies are less common than types of
               galaxies that contain little nonluminous matter.
        (B)   Luminous and nonluminous matter are
               composed of the same basic elements.
        (C)   The bright nucleus of a typical spiral galaxy also
               contains some nonluminous matter.
        (D)   The density of the observable universe is
               greater than most previous estimates have
               suggested.
        (E)   Some galaxies do not rotate or rotate too slowly
               for their rotational velocity to be measured.

118. It can be inferred from information presented in the passage that if the density of the universe were equivalent to significantly less than three hydrogen atoms per cubic meter, which of the following would be true as a consequence?

    (A) Luminosity would be a true indicator of mass.

    (B) Different regions in spiral galaxies would rotate at the same velocity.

    (C) The universe would continue to expand indefinitely.

    (D) The density of the invisible matter in the universe would have to be more than 70 times the density of the luminous matter.

    (E) More of the invisible matter in spiral galaxies would have to be located in their nuclei than in their outer regions.

119. The authors propose all of the following as possibly contributing to the "missing matter" in spiral galaxies EXCEPT

    (A) massive black holes

    (B) small black holes

    (C) small, dim stars

    (D) massive stars

    (E) large planets

Line   Jon Clark's study of the effect of the
         modernization of a telephone exchange on exchange
         maintenance work and workers is a solid
         contribution to a debate that encompasses two
(5)   lively issues in the history and sociology of
         technology: technological determinism and social
         constructivism.
            Clark makes the point that the characteristics of a
         technology have a decisive influence on job skills
(10)   and work organization. Put more strongly,
         technology can be a primary determinant of social
         and managerial organization. Clark believes this
         possibility has been obscured by the recent
         sociological fashion, exemplified by Braverman's
(15)   analysis, that emphasizes the way machinery
         reflects social choices. For Braverman, the shape of
         a technological system is subordinate to the
         manager's desire to wrest control of the labor
         process from the workers. Technological change is
(20)   construed as the outcome of negotiations among
         interested parties who seek to incorporate their own
         interests into the design and configuration of the
         machinery. This position represents the new
         mainstream called social constructivism.
(25)   The constructivists gain acceptance by
         misrepresenting technological determinism:
         technological determinists are supposed to believe,
         for example, that machinery imposes appropriate
         forms of order on society. The alternative to
(30)   constructivism, in other words, is to view technology
         as existing outside society, capable of directly
         influencing skills and work organization.
            Clark refutes the extremes of the constructivists
         by both theoretical and empirical arguments.
(35)   Theoretically he defines "technology" in terms of
         relationships between social and technical variables.
         Attempts to reduce the meaning of technology to
         cold, hard metal are bound to fail, for machinery is
         just scrap unless it is organized functionally and
(40)   supported by appropriate systems of operation and
         maintenance. At the empirical level Clark shows how
         a change at the telephone exchange from
         maintenance-intensive electromechanical switches
         to semielectronic switching systems altered work
(45)   tasks, skills, training opportunities, administration,
         and organization of workers. Some changes Clark
         attributes to the particular way management and
         labor unions negotiated the introduction of the
         technology, whereas others are seen as arising from

(50)   the capabilities and nature of the technology itself.
         Thus Clark helps answer the question: "When is
         social choice decisive and when are the concrete
         characteristics of technology more important?"

Questions 120–127 refer to the passage above.

120. The primary purpose of the passage is to

      (A)   advocate a more positive attitude toward
            technological change

      (B)   discuss the implications for employees of the
            modernization of a telephone exchange

      (C)   consider a successful challenge to the
            constructivist view of technological change

      (D)   challenge the position of advocates of
            technological determinism

      (E)   suggest that the social causes of technological
            change should be studied in real situations

121. Which of the following statements about the
      modernization of the telephone exchange is supported
      by information in the passage?

      (A)   The new technology reduced the role of
            managers in labor negotiations.

      (B)   The modernization was implemented without the
            consent of the employees directly affected by it.

      (C)   The modernization had an impact that went
            significantly beyond maintenance routines.

      (D)   Some of the maintenance workers felt victimized
            by the new technology.

      (E)   The modernization gave credence to the view of
            advocates of social constructivism.

122. Which of the following most accurately describes
      Clark's opinion of Braverman's position?

      (A)   He respects its wide-ranging popularity.

      (B)   He disapproves of its misplaced emphasis on
            the influence of managers.

      (C)   He admires the consideration it gives to the
            attitudes of the workers affected.

      (D)   He is concerned about its potential to impede
            the implementation of new technologies.

      (E)   He is sympathetic to its concern about the
            impact of modern technology on workers.

123. The information in the passage suggests that which of the following statements from hypothetical sociological studies of change in industry most clearly exemplifies the social constructivists' version of technological determinism?

   (A) It is the available technology that determines workers' skills, rather than workers' skills influencing the application of technology.

   (B) All progress in industrial technology grows out of a continuing negotiation between technological possibility and human need.

   (C) Some organizational change is caused by people; some is caused by computer chips.

   (D) Most major technological advances in industry have been generated through research and development.

   (E) Some industrial technology eliminates jobs, but educated workers can create whole new skills areas by the adaptation of the technology.

124. The information in the passage suggests that Clark believes that which of the following would be true if social constructivism had not gained widespread acceptance?

   (A) Businesses would be more likely to modernize without considering the social consequences of their actions.

   (B) There would be greater understanding of the role played by technology in producing social change.

   (C) Businesses would be less likely to understand the attitudes of employees affected by modernization.

   (D) Modernization would have occurred at a slower rate.

   (E) Technology would have played a greater part in determining the role of business in society.

125. According to the passage, constructivists employed which of the following to promote their argument?

   (A) Empirical studies of business situations involving technological change

   (B) Citation of managers supportive of their position

   (C) Construction of hypothetical situations that support their view

   (D) Contrasts of their view with a misstatement of an opposing view

   (E) Descriptions of the breadth of impact of technological change

126. The author of the passage uses the expression "are supposed to" in line 27 primarily in order to

   (A) suggest that a contention made by constructivists regarding determinists is inaccurate

   (B) define the generally accepted position of determinists regarding the implementation of technology

   (C) engage in speculation about the motivation of determinists

   (D) lend support to a comment critical of the position of determinists

   (E) contrast the historical position of determinists with their position regarding the exchange modernization

127. Which of the following statements about Clark's study of the telephone exchange can be inferred from information in the passage?

   (A) Clark's reason for undertaking the study was to undermine Braverman's analysis of the function of technology.

   (B) Clark's study suggests that the implementation of technology should be discussed in the context of conflict between labor and management.

   (C) Clark examined the impact of changes in the technology of switching at the exchange in terms of overall operations and organization.

   (D) Clark concluded that the implementation of new switching technology was equally beneficial to management and labor.

   (E) Clark's analysis of the change in switching systems applies only narrowly to the situation at the particular exchange that he studied.

Line   All the cells in a particular plant start out with the same complement of genes. How then can these cells differentiate and form structures as different as roots, stems, leaves, and fruits? The

(5)   answer is that only a small subset of the genes in a particular kind of cell are expressed, or turned on, at a given time. This is accomplished by a complex system of chemical messengers that in plants include hormones and other regulatory molecules.

(10)   Five major hormones have been identified: auxin, abscisic acid, cytokinin, ethylene, and gibberellin. Studies of plants have now identified a new class of regulatory molecules called oligosaccharins.

    Unlike the oligosaccharins, the five well-known

(15)   plant hormones are pleiotropic rather than specific; that is, each has more than one effect on the growth and development of plants. The five have so many simultaneous effects that they are not very useful in artificially controlling the growth of

(20)   crops. Auxin, for instance, stimulates the rate of cell elongation, causes shoots to grow up and roots to grow down, and inhibits the growth of lateral shoots. Auxin also causes the plant to develop a vascular system, to form lateral roots, and to

(25)   produce ethylene.

    The pleiotropy of the five well-studied plant hormones is somewhat analogous to that of certain hormones in animals. For example, hormones from the hypothalamus in the brain stimulate the anterior

(30)   lobe of the pituitary gland to synthesize and release many different hormones, one of which stimulates the release of hormones from the adrenal cortex. These hormones have specific effects on target organs all over the body. One hormone stimulates

(35)   the thyroid gland, for example, another the ovarian follicle cells, and so forth. In other words, there is a hierarchy of hormones.

    Such a hierarchy may also exist in plants. Oligo-saccharins are fragments of the cell wall released

(40)   by enzymes: different enzymes release different oligosaccharins. There are indications that pleiotropic plant hormones may actually function by activating the enzymes that release these other, more specific chemical messengers from the cell wall.

Questions 128–133 refer to the passage above.

128. According to the passage, the five well-known plant hormones are not useful in controlling the growth of crops because

(A) it is not known exactly what functions the hormones perform

(B) each hormone has various effects on plants

(C) none of the hormones can function without the others

(D) each hormone has different effects on different kinds of plants

(E) each hormone works on only a small subset of a cell's genes at any particular time

129. The passage suggests that the place of hypothalamic hormones in the hormonal hierarchies of animals is similar to the place of which of the following in plants?

(A) Plant cell walls

(B) The complement of genes in each plant cell

(C) A subset of a plant cell's gene complement

(D) The five major hormones

(E) The oligosaccharins

130. The passage suggests that which of the following is a function likely to be performed by an oligosaccharin?

(A) To stimulate a particular plant cell to become part of a plant's root system

(B) To stimulate the walls of a particular cell to produce other oligosaccharins

(C) To activate enzymes that release specific chemical messengers from plant cell walls

(D) To duplicate the gene complement in a particular plant cell

(E) To produce multiple effects on a particular subsystem of plant cells

131. The author mentions specific effects that auxin has on plant development in order to illustrate the

    (A) point that some of the effects of plant hormones can be harmful

    (B) way in which hormones are produced by plants

    (C) hierarchical nature of the functioning of plant hormones

    (D) differences among the best-known plant hormones

    (E) concept of pleiotropy as it is exhibited by plant hormones

132. According to the passage, which of the following best describes a function performed by oligosaccharins?

    (A) Regulating the daily functioning of a plant's cells

    (B) Interacting with one another to produce different chemicals

    (C) Releasing specific chemical messengers from a plant's cell walls

    (D) Producing the hormones that cause plant cells to differentiate to perform different functions

    (E) Influencing the development of a plant's cells by controlling the expression of the cells' genes

133. The passage suggests that, unlike the pleiotropic hormones, oligosaccharins could be used effectively to

    (A) trace the passage of chemicals through the walls of cells

    (B) pinpoint functions of other plant hormones

    (C) artificially control specific aspects of the development of crops

    (D) alter the complement of genes in the cells of plants

    (E) alter the effects of the five major hormones on plant development

Line   In the two decades between 1910 and 1930, more than ten percent of the black population of the United States left the South, where the preponderance of the black population had been
(5)   located, and migrated to northern states, with the largest number moving, it is claimed, between 1916 and 1918. It has been frequently assumed, but not proved, that the majority of the migrants in what has come to be called the Great Migration
(10)   came from rural areas and were motivated by two concurrent factors: the collapse of the cotton industry following the boll weevil infestation, which began in 1898, and increased demand in the North for labor following the cessation of European
(15)   immigration caused by the outbreak of the First World War in 1914. This assumption has led to the conclusion that the migrants' subsequent lack of economic mobility in the North is tied to rural background, a background that implies unfamiliarity
(20)   with urban living and a lack of industrial skills.
        But the question of who actually left the South has never been rigorously investigated. Although numerous investigations document an exodus from rural southern areas to southern cities prior to the
(25)   Great Migration, no one has considered whether the same migrants then moved on to northern cities. In 1910 more than 600,000 black workers, or ten percent of the black workforce, reported themselves to be engaged in "manufacturing and mechanical
(30)   pursuits," the federal census category roughly encompassing the entire industrial sector. The Great Migration could easily have been made up entirely of this group and their families. It is perhaps surprising to argue that an employed population
(35)   could be enticed to move, but an explanation lies in the labor conditions then prevalent in the South.
        About thirty-five percent of the urban black population in the South was engaged in skilled trades. Some were from the old artisan class of
(40)   slavery—blacksmiths, masons, carpenters—which had had a monopoly of certain trades, but they were gradually being pushed out by competition, mechanization, and obsolescence. The remaining sixty-five percent, more recently urbanized, worked in
(45)   newly developed industries—tobacco, lumber, coal and iron manufacture, and railroads. Wages in the South, however, were low, and black workers were aware, through labor recruiters and the black press, that they could earn more even as unskilled

(50)   workers in the North than they could as artisans in the South. After the boll weevil infestation, urban black workers faced competition from the continuing influx of both black and white rural workers, who were driven to undercut the wages
(55)   formerly paid for industrial jobs. Thus, a move north would be seen as advantageous to a group that was already urbanized and steadily employed, and the easy conclusion tying their subsequent economic problems in the North to their rural background
(60)   comes into question.

Questions 134–139 refer to the passage above.

134. The author indicates explicitly that which of the following records has been a source of information in her investigation?

(A)   United States Immigration Service reports from 1914 to 1930

(B)   Payrolls of southern manufacturing firms between 1910 and 1930

(C)   The volume of cotton exports between 1898 and 1910

(D)   The federal census of 1910

(E)   Advertisements of labor recruiters appearing in southern newspapers after 1910

135. In the passage, the author anticipates which of the following as a possible objection to her argument?

(A)   It is uncertain how many people actually migrated during the Great Migration.

(B)   The eventual economic status of the Great Migration migrants has not been adequately traced.

(C)   It is not likely that people with steady jobs would have reason to move to another area of the country.

(D)   It is not true that the term "manufacturing and mechanical pursuits" actually encompasses the entire industrial sector.

(E)   Of the African American workers living in southern cities, only those in a small number of trades were threatened by obsolescence.

136. According to the passage, which of the following is true of wages in southern cities in 1910?

    (A) They were being pushed lower as a result of increased competition.

    (B) They had begun to rise so that southern industry could attract rural workers.

    (C) They had increased for skilled workers but decreased for unskilled workers.

    (D) They had increased in large southern cities but decreased in small southern cities.

    (E) They had increased in newly developed industries but decreased in the older trades.

137. The author cites each of the following as possible influences in an African American worker's decision to migrate north in the Great Migration EXCEPT

    (A) wage levels in northern cities

    (B) labor recruiters

    (C) competition from rural workers

    (D) voting rights in northern states

    (E) the African American press

138. It can be inferred from the passage that the "easy conclusion" mentioned in line 58 is based on which of the following assumptions?

    (A) People who migrate from rural areas to large cities usually do so for economic reasons.

    (B) Most people who leave rural areas to take jobs in cities return to rural areas as soon as it is financially possible for them to do so.

    (C) People with rural backgrounds are less likely to succeed economically in cities than are those with urban backgrounds.

    (D) Most people who were once skilled workers are not willing to work as unskilled workers.

    (E) People who migrate from their birthplaces to other regions of a country seldom undertake a second migration.

139. The primary purpose of the passage is to

    (A) support an alternative to an accepted methodology

    (B) present evidence that resolves a contradiction

    (C) introduce a recently discovered source of information

    (D) challenge a widely accepted explanation

    (E) argue that a discarded theory deserves new attention

7.5 Answer Key

1.	B	29.	C	57.	C	85.	A	113.	B
2.	B	30.	B	58.	B	86.	B	114.	D
3.	D	31.	C	59.	A	87.	A	115.	C
4.	A	32.	B	60.	A	88.	A	116.	D
5.	C	33.	D	61.	B	89.	D	117.	A
6.	D	34.	B	62.	E	90.	C	118.	C
7.	B	35.	E	63.	D	91.	E	119.	D
8.	B	36.	C	64.	D	92.	B	120.	C
9.	E	37.	C	65.	B	93.	D	121.	C
10.	E	38.	E	66.	C	94.	D	122.	B
11.	E	39.	A	67.	B	95.	C	123.	A
12.	A	40.	D	68.	E	96.	D	124.	B
13.	A	41.	A	69.	D	97.	C	125.	D
14.	C	42.	B	70.	E	98.	E	126.	A
15.	D	43.	A	71.	B	99.	A	127.	C
16.	B	44.	A	72.	D	100.	A	128.	B
17.	B	45.	C	73.	C	101.	C	129.	D
18.	B	46.	E	74.	C	102.	D	130.	A
19.	B	47.	E	75.	E	103.	A	131.	E
20.	B	48.	E	76.	A	104.	B	132.	E
21.	A	49.	A	77.	E	105.	A	133.	C
22.	D	50.	A	78.	C	106.	C	134.	D
23.	E	51.	D	79.	B	107.	B	135.	C
24.	D	52.	B	80.	C	108.	D	136.	A
25.	A	53.	C	81.	D	109.	A	137.	D
26.	C	54.	C	82.	A	110.	C	138.	C
27.	B	55.	E	83.	A	111.	A	139.	D
28.	A	56.	D	84.	E	112.	C		

7.6 Answer Explanations

The following discussion of reading comprehension is intended to familiarize you with the most efficient and effective approaches to the kinds of problems common to reading comprehension. The particular questions in this chapter are generally representative of the kinds of reading comprehension questions you will encounter on the GMAT exam. Remember that it is the problem solving strategy that is important, not the specific details of a particular question.

Questions 1–4 refer to the passage on page 364.

1. According to the passage, theory B states that which of the following is a factor that enables a schooling fish to escape predators?

   (A) The tendency of fish to form compact groups
   (B) The movement of other fish within the school
   (C) The inability of predators to detect schools
   (D) The ability of fish to hide behind one another in a school
   (E) The great speed with which a school can disperse

Supporting idea

This question depends on understanding what the passage states about theory B, the "confusion effect." One element of theory B is that predators may experience sensory confusion created by large numbers of moving fish in a school.

A   The compactness of groups of schooling fish is an element of theory A, not theory B.
B   **Correct.** It is the movement of schooling fish around a predator that creates sensory confusion in the predator; this movement may distract the predator and help protect individual fish in the school.
C   According to the passage's description of theory A, predators are actually slightly more likely to detect schools than they are to detect individual fish.
D   Theory B does not involve fish hiding behind one another but rather moving around the predator.
E   The passage does not discuss the speed of dispersal of schools of fish.

The correct answer is B.

2. According to the passage, both theory A and theory B have been developed to explain how

   (A) fish hide from predators by forming schools
   (B) forming schools functions to protect fish from predators
   (C) schooling among fish differs from other protective behaviors
   (D) small fish are able to make rapid decisions
   (E) small fish are able to survive in an environment densely populated by large predators

Supporting idea

The passage states in its first paragraph that two theories were developed to explain why schooling occurs in so many fish species and that they both assume that schooling helps protect fish from predators.

A   While theory A involves an explanation of how schooling makes an individual fish less likely to be found by predators, theory B explains how schooling protects fish even when they are detected by predators.
B   **Correct.** Both theory A and theory B begin with the assumption that schooling provides protection from predators, and each theory offers a different explanation for how that protection occurs.
C   The passage does not discuss protective behaviors other than schooling.
D   The decision-making ability of predators, not schooling fish, is discussed in the passage; schooling is presented as an instinctive behavior.
E   The passage suggests that only theory B helps explain schooling behavior in environments where many predators, large or otherwise, are found, and that theory A explains schooling in areas where predators are not as abundant.

The correct answer is B.

3. According to one explanation of the "confusion effect," a fish that swims in a school will have greater advantages for survival if it

(A) tends to be visible for no more than 200 meters

(B) stays near either the front or the rear of a school

(C) is part of a small school rather than a large school

(D) is very similar in appearance to the other fish in the school

(E) is medium-sized

Inference

The "confusion effect" is discussed in the third and fourth paragraphs. The first explanation of the "confusion effect" proposes that because predators prefer to select distinctive prey, they find it difficult to select one fish from among many that look the same.

A The 200-meter visibility of fish is part of the explanation for theory A, not theory B (the "confusion effect").

B The location of an individual fish within a school is not discussed in the passage as being important to the "confusion effect."

C The size of a school of fish is not discussed as an element of the "confusion effect."

D Correct. Because predators, according to the "confusion effect," prefer to select prey that is distinct from the rest of the school, a fish that is similar in appearance to the other fish in its school would most likely enjoy a survival advantage.

E The size of a fish relative to the other fish in its school would most likely contribute to its ability to survive: that is, if it resembled other fish in size, it would be safer, based on what the passage says about the "confusion effect." Furthermore, the passage gives no reason to think that merely being medium-sized would confer any advantage (unless the other fish were medium-sized as well).

The correct answer is D.

4. The author is primarily concerned with

(A) discussing different theories

(B) analyzing different techniques

(C) defending two hypotheses

(D) refuting established beliefs

(E) revealing new evidence

Main idea

Determining the author's primary concern depends on understanding the focus of the passage as a whole. The author presents two theories that purport to account for why fish, particularly small fish, tend to school and explains the arguments of proponents of each theory.

A Correct. The author discusses two theories—identified as theory A and theory B—that account for the tendency of fish to school.

B The author is not concerned with different techniques in the passage.

C The two theories of why fish school could be referred to as hypotheses, but the author is not primarily concerned with defending them; rather, the passage explains how each attempts to account for the phenomenon in question.

D The author presents, rather than refutes, beliefs about why fish tend to school.

E The author reveals no evidence, new or otherwise, in the passage. The passage is a general discussion of scientific opinions based on existing evidence.

The correct answer is A.

Questions 5–7 refer to the passage on page 366.

5. The primary purpose of the passage is to

(A) explain why a particular business strategy has been less successful than was once anticipated

(B) propose an alternative to a particular business strategy that has inadvertently caused ecological damage

(C) present a concern about the possible consequences of pursuing a particular business strategy

(D) make a case for applying a particular business strategy on a larger scale than is currently practiced

(E) suggest several possible outcomes of companies' failure to understand the economic impact of a particular business strategy

Main idea

This question requires understanding the passage as a whole. The passage starts out defining a goal—ecoefficiency—that has become popular among companies throughout the world and that would be expected to bring overall ecological benefits. It then immediately introduces Senge and Carstedt, who have concerns about this idea. The rest of the passage is devoted to explaining their concerns, though the passage does not present a particular alternative strategy.

A   The passage never discusses whether ecoefficiency is or is not successful but only the possible consequences of it.

B   Lines 26–28 state that Senge and Carstedt believe that a *new systemic approach* must be found, but a particular alternative strategy is never offered.

C   **Correct.** After defining ecoefficiency, the rest of the passage is devoted to describing the concerns Senge and Carstedt have about it as a goal for companies.

D   The passage reports on particular concerns about the strategy and does not advocate expanding its adoption.

E   The passage is concerned with environmental impact, not economic impact.

The correct answer is C.

6. The passage mentions which of the following as a possible consequence of companies' realization of greater profits through ecoefficiency?

(A) The companies may be able to sell a greater number of products by lowering prices.

(B) The companies may be better able to attract investment capital in the global market.

(C) The profits may be reinvested to increase economic growth through ecoefficiency.

(D) The profits may be used as investment capital for industries that are not ecoefficient.

(E) The profits may encourage companies to make further innovations in reducing production waste.

Supporting ideas

This question asks for identification of an example given in the passage of what could result from the greater profits that may come with ecoefficiency. Such profits are specifically mentioned only in lines 14 and 17. The increased growth and profits referred to in line 14 are associated with increased waste generated indirectly by ecoefficient companies. The growth and profits referred to in line 17 are associated with investment of this capital in industries that may not be ecoefficient.

A   The prices of companies' products are not mentioned in the passage.

B   Greater investment in ecoefficient companies by outside sources is not mentioned in the passage.

C   The passage mentions increased profits from ecoefficiency but not the use of these profits to then increase growth through further ecoefficiency.

D   **Correct.** Lines 14–19 state explicitly that company profits from ecoefficiency may be invested in eco-inefficient industries.

E   The passage does not discuss whether companies will use increased profits from ecoefficiency to become more ecoefficient.

The correct answer is D.

7. The passage implies that which of the following is a possible consequence of a company's adoption of innovations that increase its ecoefficiency?

    (A) Company profits resulting from such innovations may be reinvested in that company with no guarantee that the company will continue to make further improvements in ecoefficiency.

    (B) Company growth fostered by cost savings from such innovations may allow that company to manufacture a greater number of products that will be used and discarded, thus worsening environmental stress.

    (C) A company that fails to realize significant cost savings from such innovations may have little incentive to continue to minimize the environmental impact of its production processes.

    (D) A company that comes to depend on such innovations to increase its profits and growth may be vulnerable in the global market to competition from old-style eco-inefficient industries.

    (E) A company that meets its ecoefficiency goals is unlikely to invest its increased profits in the development of new and innovative ecoefficiency measures.

Inference

The answer to this question will be an inference about what may result from a company's increased ecoefficiency. The passage suggests several outcomes from such an increase: a general worsening of the environment; a tendency for companies to manufacture more of particular products, which will then be thrown away by consumers; the possibility that increased profits will result in greater investment in industries that are not ecoefficient; and even the possibility that ecoefficiency might allow so much growth that more total waste will be produced and more overall wildlife habitat destroyed.

A   The passage suggests generally that ecoefficiency will increase companies' profits, but there is no suggestion that these companies will therefore then abandon ecoefficiency as a goal.

B   **Correct.** Lines 6–12 strongly suggest that it is possible that the increased growth that may come from ecoefficiency may result in more products being manufactured, which may result in more waste as those products are discarded by consumers.

C   The passage does not suggest that ecoefficiency may fail to increase a company's profits.

D   The passage suggests that ecoefficiency has allowed many companies to increase profits, but it does not suggest that eco-inefficient companies are more profitable or competitive in the global marketplace.

E   As with answer choice (A), there is no suggestion that companies are likely to abandon ecoefficient strategies once they have realized increased profits from such strategies.

The correct answer is B.

Questions 8–10 refer to the passage on page 368.

8. The primary purpose of the passage is to propose

    (A) an alternative to museum display of artifacts

    (B) a way to curb illegal digging while benefiting the archaeological profession

    (C) a way to distinguish artifacts with scientific value from those that have no such value

    (D) the governmental regulation of archaeological sites

    (E) a new system for cataloging duplicate artifacts

Main idea

After identifying in the first paragraph two problems that the field of archaeology faces, the author begins the second paragraph by explicitly stating the purpose of the essay: *I would propose that scientific archaeological expeditions and governmental authorities sell excavated artifacts on the open market.* According to the author, this proposal would both benefit the field of archaeology (line 12) and reduce illegal digging for antiquities (lines 12–13).

A   While explaining in paragraph 5 that museums often store countless artifacts unseen in their basements, the author proposes no alternative for museum display of these artifacts.

B   Correct. The author argues that selling some antiquities would help archaeology and reduce illegal digging.

C   No proposal for the grading of the artifacts is made in the passage.

D   The author does not discuss governmental regulation of the sites.

E   While the author supports one part of the proposal for selling antiquities by noting that sold artifacts could be cataloged on a computer, this is a detail rather than the main purpose of the passage.

The correct answer is B.

9.   The author implies that all of the following statements about duplicate artifacts are true EXCEPT

(A)   a market for such artifacts already exists

(B)   such artifacts seldom have scientific value

(C)   there is likely to be a continuing supply of such artifacts

(D)   museums are well supplied with examples of such artifacts

(E)   such artifacts frequently exceed in quality those already cataloged in museum collections

Inference

Duplicate artifacts are discussed throughout the passage. Because this question asks the reader to find the one statement that is NOT stated or implied in the passage, the best approach is to eliminate the four statements that are supported by the passage.

A   In the closing sentence of the passage, the author implies that the market already exists.

B   In lines 27–32, the author suggests selling artifacts that do not have *unique artistic merit or scientific value* and then states that while theoretically every artifact may have potential scientific value, in practice this is not the case. Paragraph 4 illustrates this by mentioning the many thousands of artifacts that are *essentially duplicates of one another.* Lines 51–53 imply that there are rare instances when duplicates do *become needed for scientific purposes*, so duplicates *seldom have scientific value.*

C   This statement is implied in lines 41–43, where the author notes that museum basements are *simply not large enough to store the artifacts that are likely to be discovered in the future.*

D   It can be inferred that if the duplicates cited in paragraph 4 are typical of the kinds of artifacts *stored in bulging museum basements* (lines 48–49), then museums are well supplied with such artifacts.

E   Correct. The passage does not support the assertion that the quality of duplicate objects is higher than that of museum pieces.

The correct answer is E.

10.   Which of the following is mentioned in the passage as a disadvantage of storing artifacts in museum basements?

(A)   Museum officials rarely allow scholars access to such artifacts.

(B)   Space that could be better used for display is taken up for storage.

(C)   Artifacts discovered in one excavation often become separated from each other.

(D)   Such artifacts are often damaged by variations in temperature and humidity.

(E)   Such artifacts often remain uncataloged and thus cannot be located once they are put in storage.

Supporting ideas

This question asks for specific information stated in the passage, so begin by finding the discussion of museum storage in the fifth paragraph. There, the author exposes the problems museums face: too little room and too little money. Not enough funding exists to catalog artifacts, so the artifacts *become as inaccessible as if they had never been discovered* (lines 45–46).

A   Restrictions on scholars' access to the museums' artifacts are not mentioned in the passage.

B   The author does not argue that museums should use space differently.

C   No mention is made of the separation of objects from the same excavation.

D   The author does not discuss the conditions of storage.

E   **Correct.** The author contends that many artifacts are left uncataloged and so, once shelved in the basements, they cannot be found.

The correct answer is E.

Questions 11–13 refer to the passage on page 370.

11.   According to the passage, the difference in the amount of cratering on Callisto's and Io's respective surfaces can probably be explained by the difference between these two moons with respect to which of the following factors?

(A)   Size

(B)   Ice content

(C)   The rate of bombardment by comets and asteroids

(D)   The influence of Jupiter's other moons

(E)   The level of geological activity

Supporting idea

Cratering is discussed in the second paragraph. The passage states that Callisto is heavily cratered, while Io has no detectable craters. Io is the moon closest to Jupiter, and Callisto is the farthest away. Their relative positions are accompanied by a corresponding difference in geological activity: Io is very geologically active, while Callisto is not active at all. Io's geological activity means that it is being regularly resurfaced, so it is unlikely to retain any evidence of cratering—unlike Callisto, which experiences no resurfacing, leaving its craters intact.

A   While the passage makes clear that Callisto is larger than Io, it does not address whether their relative size explains the difference in their respective amounts of cratering.

B   According to the passage, Callisto and Io differ in terms of their ice content, but nothing in the passage indicates that that content affects the cratering on their surfaces.

C   The passage states that Io experiences a higher rate of bombardment than Callisto does, but while that bombardment most likely causes cratering on Io, its surface does not retain those craters. Thus, the rate of bombardment does not, in itself, explain the difference in cratering on the surface of the two moons.

D   The only other moons of Jupiter discussed in the passage are Ganymede and Europa, and the passage does not consider their effect on the cratering of Callisto and Io.

E   **Correct.** Because Io experiences a high degree of geological activity, its surface is continuously resurfaced, which means that the surface shows no craters. Callisto, on the other hand, is not geologically active and thus is not resurfaced regularly, which explains why its surface is heavily cratered.

The correct answer is E.

12. Which of the following best describes the purpose of the second paragraph of the passage?

    (A) To provide further evidence of the systematic variation in the characteristics of Jupiter's four largest moons

    (B) To present a comprehensive theory to explain the systematic variation in the characteristics of Jupiter's four largest moons

    (C) To explain the significance of the systematic variation in the characteristics of Jupiter's four largest moons

    (D) To introduce facts that contradict conventional assumptions about Jupiter's four largest moons

    (E) To contrast the characteristics of Jupiter's four largest moons with the characteristics of the planets of the solar system

Evaluation

This question depends on understanding how the second paragraph functions in the context of the passage as a whole. The first paragraph discusses the way in which the composition of Jupiter's four largest moons varies with distance from Jupiter, and the second paragraph extends the idea of distance-based variation to geological activity and surface appearance.

A **Correct.** The second paragraph presents evidence related to the amount of geological activity and surface cratering in order to extend the first paragraph's suggestion that the characteristics of Jupiter's four largest moons vary systematically based on their distance from Jupiter.

B The passage does not offer a theory to account for the systematic variation in the characteristics of Jupiter's largest moons; it merely describes several instances of that variation.

C The second paragraph provides more examples of the systematic variation in the characteristics of Jupiter's largest moons rather than explaining that variation's significance.

D The passage describes Jupiter's moons but does not identify any conventional assumptions about those moons that are contradicted by facts introduced in the passage.

E The first paragraph suggests that Jupiter's moons exhibit differences in characteristics that are more "systematic" than are those of the planets in the solar system, but the characteristics are not themselves contrasted; in fact, the first paragraph suggests that they are similar. The second paragraph does not discuss the planets of the solar system at all.

The correct answer is A.

13. The author's reference to Jupiter's gravity in line 25 serves primarily to

    (A) indicate why the absence of craters on Io's surface is surprising

    (B) explain the presence of craters on the surface of Jupiter's four largest moons

    (C) provide an explanation for the lack of geological activity on Callisto

    (D) contrast Jupiter's characteristics with the characteristics of its four largest moons

    (E) illustrate the similarity between Jupiter's four largest moons and the planets of the solar system

Evaluation

The reference to Jupiter's gravity is part of the author's discussion of cratering on Jupiter's moons; Jupiter's gravity is strong enough to attract comets and asteroids that then bombard its inner moons. A high bombardment rate would seem to indicate that a great deal of cratering would occur on those inner moons, and yet the passage reports that, unexpectedly, on the innermost moon, Io, no craters have been detected.

A   **Correct.** Jupiter's gravity attracts comets and asteroids, which increases the bombardment rate of its inner moons, including Io. This bombardment makes it surprising that Io's surface shows no cratering.

B   The passage discusses the likely effect of Jupiter's gravity on its inner moons but not its outer moons; two of the large moons the passage discusses are outer moons.

C   According to the passage, Callisto, an outer moon, lacks geological activity because of its distance from Jupiter; Jupiter's gravity is not offered as a contributing factor to this inactivity.

D   The passage does not contrast Jupiter with its moons; rather, it compares the moons to one another.

E   The first paragraph of the passage suggests that Jupiter's moons vary in a way similar to that of the planets of the solar system, but the author does not refer to Jupiter's gravity to illustrate the similarity in this variation.

The correct answer is A.

Questions 14–17 refer to the passage on page 372.

14.   According to the passage, which of the following contributed to Marcus Garvey's success?

(A)   He introduced cultural and historical consciousness to the African American community.

(B)   He believed enthusiastically in the traditional American success ethos.

(C)   His audience had already formed a consciousness that made it receptive to his message.

(D)   His message appealed to critics of African American support for United States military involvement in the First World War.

(E)   He supported the movement to protest segregation that had emerged prior to his arrival in the United States.

Supporting idea

To answer this question, find what the passage states explicitly about how Marcus Garvey achieved his success. The passage begins by stating that Garvey arrived at the right time: that returning African American soldiers were primed to receive what he had to say about the African American community. These soldiers already held strong beliefs about their rights to opportunities for success; the passage concludes that the divide between the soldiers' expectations and their experiences led to Garvey's success.

A   The passage states that African American people were in possession of a strong cultural and historical consciousness prior to Garvey's arrival in the United States.

B   The passage attributes belief in the traditional American success ethos to African American people who joined the armed forces; it does not mention Garvey's beliefs on this subject.

C   **Correct.** African American soldiers who had experienced segregation during the First World War were ready to hear what Garvey had to say.

D   Critics of African American support for United States involvement in the First World War are not mentioned in the passage.

E   While Garvey most likely would have supported a movement to protest segregation, such a movement is not discussed in the passage.

The correct answer is C.

15. The passage suggests that many African American people responded to their experiences in the armed forces in which of the following ways?

(A) They maintained as civilians their enthusiastic allegiance to the armed forces.

(B) They questioned United States involvement in the First World War.

(C) They joined political organizations to protest the segregation of African American troops and the indignities they suffered in the military.

(D) They became aware of the gap between their expectations and the realities of American culture.

(E) They repudiated Garvey's message of pride and unity.

Inference

According to the passage, African Americans enthusiastically joined the armed services but were confronted with continued segregation, both in the military and when they returned home. The passage does not explicitly state their response to these experiences, but a response can be inferred. The second paragraph, refers to anthropologist Anthony F. C. Wallace, who argued that a revitalization movement may be brought about by the perception of a gap between expectations and reality, and such a revitalization did occur in African American communities following the First World War; thus, many African American people may have become aware of a gap such as Wallace described.

A The passage states that African American troops experienced segregation and other indignities while in the military; these experiences could reasonably be inferred to have dampened their enthusiasm for the armed forces. Regardless, the passage does not suggest an enthusiastic allegiance.

B The passage describes African American people's enthusiasm about joining the military. Although they experienced segregation and other indignities while in the military, the passage does not suggest that their opinion about involvement in the war changed.

C While African American troops may have joined political organizations, the passage does not provide any actual evidence of this having occurred.

D Correct. The fact that, as the passage states, a revitalization movement occurred in the African American community following the First World War suggests that the returning soldiers did become aware of the gap between their expectations of an improved situation with regard to segregation and the reality of continued segregation in the United States.

E The passage does not suggest that African American troops repudiated Garvey's message. On the contrary, it states that Garvey built *the largest revitalization movement in African American history*. This suggests that the members of the African American community, including the returning soldiers, were extremely receptive to Garvey's message.

The correct answer is D.

16. It can be inferred from the passage that the "scholars" mentioned in line 24 believe which of the following to be true?

(A) Revitalization resulted from the political activism of returning African American soldiers following the First World War.

(B) Marcus Garvey had to change a number of prevailing attitudes in order for his mass movement to find a foothold in the United States.

(C) The prevailing sensibility of the African American community provided the foundation of Marcus Garvey's political appeal.

(D) Marcus Garvey hoped to revitalize consciousness of cultural and historical identity in the African American community.

(E) The goal of the mass movement that Marcus Garvey helped bring into being was to build on the pride and unity among African Americans.

Inference

To determine what it is logical to infer regarding the scholars discussed in the third paragraph, look at the context in which they are mentioned. According to the passage, these scholars argue that Garvey was responsible for creating a particular consciousness within the African American community, a consciousness that the passage identifies as *identity, strength, and* [a] *sense of history*. Unlike the passage author, these scholars believe strongly in Garvey's responsibility for this consciousness, so they would most likely reject any suggestion that it existed prior to his arrival and activism.

A   According to the passage, the scholars believe that Garvey was responsible for the creation of the consciousness that led to revitalization, which suggests that revitalization resulted from Garvey's activism, not soldiers' activism.

B   **Correct.** According to the passage, the scholars believe that Garvey created the consciousness that led to his revitalization movement. This suggests that he had to change prevailing attitudes in order to foster this new consciousness.

C   According to the passage, the scholars believe that Garvey created a new consciousness in the African American community; thus, the prevailing sensibility could not have provided a foundation for his appeal.

D   According to the passage, the scholars believe that Garvey built his revitalization movement on a new consciousness of cultural and historical identity, not a previously existing one.

E   According to the passage, the scholars' position is that Garvey's movement was built on a new sense of pride and unity that he provided, and that that sense did not precede Garvey's work.

The correct answer is B.

17. According to the passage, many African American people joined the armed forces during the First World War for which of the following reasons?

(A)   They wished to escape worsening economic conditions in African American communities.

(B)   They expected to fulfill ideals of personal attainment.

(C)   They sought to express their loyalty to the United States.

(D)   They hoped that joining the military would help advance the cause of desegregation.

(E)   They saw military service as an opportunity to fulfill Marcus Garvey's political vision.

Supporting idea

This question depends on identifying what the passage states directly about African American people's reasons for joining the armed forces. The reason offered by the passage is that the African American people who entered the armed forces did so because they were *hoping to participate in the traditional American ethos of individual success*.

A   Although this is a plausible reason for entering the armed forces, the passage does not discuss economic conditions.

B   **Correct.** The passage states that African American people who joined the armed forces during the First World War wanted to achieve individual success.

C   The passage does not discuss African American people's loyalty to the United States.

D   The passage states that African American troops experienced segregation, but it does not suggest that they had hoped their joining the military would promote desegregation.

E   The passage suggests that African American troops did not become aware of Marcus Garvey's political vision until after they returned from the First World War.

The correct answer is B.

Questions 18–25 refer to the passage on page 374.

18. The passage provides information in support of which of the following assertions?

    (A) The disadvantages of an adaptation to a particular feature of an environment often outweigh the advantages of such an adaptation.

    (B) An organism's reaction to being placed in an environment to which it is not well adapted can sometimes illustrate the problems that have been solved by the adaptations of organisms indigenous to that environment.

    (C) The effectiveness of an organism's adaptation to a particular feature of its environment can only be evaluated by examining the effectiveness with which organisms of other species have adapted to a similar feature of a different environment.

    (D) Organisms of the same species that inhabit strikingly different environments will often adapt in remarkably similar ways to the few features of those environments that are common.

    (E) Different species of organisms living in the same environment will seldom adapt to features of that environment in the same way.

Application

This question requires recognizing a principle underlying the passage's overall discussion. The passage makes a general claim about terrestrial animals' need to overcome the effect of gravity on their blood circulation systems, and it then uses the specific example of terrestrial snakes to illustrate this claim. To help identify the adaptations used by terrestrial snakes, the passage describes what happens to sea snakes, which are aquatic and less affected by gravity's influence, when they are subjected to a terrestrial environment. The specific problems faced by these snakes strongly suggest that terrestrial snakes have developed ways to overcome these problems. The passage then identifies specific physiological differences between sea snakes and terrestrial snakes that demonstrate how terrestrial snakes overcome gravity's influence.

A   The passage discusses how species have successfully adapted to their specific environments and does not mention that these adaptations create disadvantages in that environment.

B   Correct. The passage discusses the problems faced by sea snakes when they are subjected to a terrestrial environment and then examines terrestrial snakes to illustrate how certain adaptations solved these problems.

C   The passage is not concerned with evaluating the effectiveness of species' adaptations to their environments; it takes for granted that these adaptations are effective.

D   The passage is concerned with how species adapt differently to different environments and not with how adaptations to different environments are similar.

E   The passage discusses how different environments affect how species have adapted, not how different species adapt to a similar environment.

The correct answer is B.

19. According to the passage, one reason that the distribution of blood in the sea snake changes little while the creature remains in the ocean is that

    (A) the heart of the sea snake tends to be located near the center of its body

    (B) pressure gradients in the water surrounding the sea snake counter the effects of vertical pressure gradients within its blood vessels

    (C) the sea snake assumes a vertical posture less frequently than do the terrestrial and the arboreal snake

    (D) the sea snake often relies on waves of muscle contractions to help move blood from the torso to the head

    (E) the force of pressure gradients in the water surrounding the sea snake exceeds that of vertical pressure gradients within its circulatory system

Supporting ideas

This question asks for an identification of factual information in the passage. Given that the contrast between sea snakes and terrestrial snakes is being used to identify adaptations used by terrestrial animals to overcome the effect of gravity on their circulation systems, the passage needs initially to illustrate why it is that sea snakes are not confronted with the same problems that gravity causes for terrestrial snakes. This information therefore needs to come fairly early in the passage.

A   The passage identifies the location of a sea snake's heart as a factor that minimizes the effort required to pump blood to both extremities but not as a cause of the even distribution of blood in sea snakes.

B   **Correct.** The passage states explicitly in lines 11–17 that while sea snakes are in the ocean, the vertical pressure gradients in their blood vessels are counteracted by the pressure gradients in the water.

C   The passage does not discuss the frequency with which any snakes assume certain postures.

D   The passage discusses muscle contractions only in relation to arboreal snakes.

E   The passage states that the vertical pressures within sea snakes' blood vessels are *counteracted* (line 13) by the water's pressure, which suggests that the pressures are equalized, not that one force exceeds the other.

The correct answer is B.

20. It can be inferred from the passage that which of the following is true of species of terrestrial snakes that often need to assume a vertical posture?

(A)   They are more likely to be susceptible to circulatory failure in vertical postures than are sea snakes.

(B)   Their hearts are less likely to be located at the midpoint of their bodies than is the case with sea snakes.

(C)   They cannot counteract the pooling of blood in lower regions of their bodies as effectively as sea snakes can.

(D)   The blood pressure at their midpoint decreases significantly when they are tilted with their heads up.

(E)   They are unable to rely on muscle contractions to move venous blood from the lower torso to the head.

Inference

This question requires using information given about how arboreal snakes, which are frequently in vertical postures, have adapted to gravity's influence to make an assumption that other terrestrial snakes that are frequently in these postures are likely to have similar adaptations. The passage implies that sea snakes have hearts at the midpoint of their bodies because the water's pressure gradients help distribute blood evenly. It then illustrates that arboreal snakes have hearts closer to their heads to help keep blood flowing to their brain when they are in vertical postures.

A   The passage does not suggest that any of the snakes mentioned are ill-adapted to their particular environments.

B   **Correct.** The passage states that arboreal snakes have hearts close to their heads and not at the midpoints of their bodies, so it is reasonable to conclude that any terrestrial snake that frequently assumes vertical postures would be unlikely to have hearts at their bodies' midpoint.

C   As with answer choice (A), the passage does not suggest that any species of snake is ill-adapted to its environment.

D   The passage states that sea snakes lose pressure at their midpoints when they are tilted on land with heads up but that terrestrial snakes do not have this problem.

E   Because arboreal snakes use muscle contractions to circulate blood when they are vertical, it is likely that most terrestrial snakes that frequently assume vertical postures also have this capability.

The correct answer is B.

21.   The author describes the behavior of the circulatory system of sea snakes when they are removed from the ocean (see lines 17–20) primarily in order to

(A)   illustrate what would occur in the circulatory system of terrestrial snakes without adaptations that enable them to regulate their blood pressure in vertical orientations

(B)   explain why arboreal snakes in vertical orientations must rely on muscle contractions to restore blood pressure to the brain

(C)   illustrate the effects of circulatory failure on the behavior of arboreal snakes

(D)   illustrate the superiority of the circulatory system of the terrestrial snake to that of the sea snake

(E)   explain how changes in spatial orientation can adversely affect the circulatory system of snakes with hearts located in relatively close proximity to their heads

Evaluation

Answering this question requires understanding why sea snakes have been brought into the passage's overall discussion about how terrestrial animals have overcome the influence of gravity on their blood circulation. The passage uses the effects that gravity has on sea snakes when they are taken out of water to identify problems that terrestrial snakes must have adapted to in order to survive.

A   **Correct.** The passage uses the problems sea snakes have when taken out of water to illustrate that without certain adaptations, terrestrial snakes would likely have similar problems.

B   The passage discusses sea snakes to illustrate problems faced by terrestrial snakes, not to explain how terrestrial snakes have adapted to gravity's influence.

C   The passage does not discuss the effects of circulatory failure on arboreal snakes.

D   The passage does not compare or contrast the effectiveness of the various adaptations used by different snakes.

E   The passage does not imply that snakes with hearts close to their heads are adversely affected by spatial positions.

The correct answer is A.

22.   It can be inferred from the passage that which of the following is a true statement about sea snakes?

(A)   They frequently rely on waves of muscle contractions from the lower torso to the head to supplement the work of the heart.

(B)   They cannot effectively regulate their blood pressure when placed in seawater and tilted at an angle with the head pointed downward.

(C)   They are more likely to have a heart located in close proximity to their heads than are arboreal snakes.

(D)   They become acutely vulnerable to the effects of gravitational pressure on their circulatory system when they are placed in a terrestrial environment.

(E)   Their cardiovascular system is not as complicated as that of arboreal snakes.

Inference

Answering this question requires understanding why sea snakes are discussed in the passage and what happens to them when they are taken out of water and subjected to the force of gravity. The second paragraph implies strongly that sea snakes will not survive certain terrestrial situations for which they are not adapted.

A   The passage associates muscle contractions to circulate blood with arboreal snakes only.

B   According to the passage, sea snakes' inability to regulate blood pressure occurs only when they are taken out of water.

C   The passage states clearly that arboreal snakes have hearts closer to their heads than do sea snakes.

D   **Correct.** The passage states that in certain postures, sea snakes placed in a terrestrial environment will lose all blood pressure at their brains, which is an acute vulnerability.

E   The passage does not provide the information needed to compare the complexity of the various snakes discussed.

The correct answer is D.

23. The author suggests that which of the following is a disadvantage that results from the location of a snake's heart in close proximity to its head?

(A) A decrease in the efficiency with which the snake regulates the flow of blood to the brain

(B) A decrease in the number of orientations in space that a snake can assume without loss of blood flow to the brain

(C) A decrease in blood pressure at the snake's midpoint when it is tilted at various angles with its head up

(D) An increase in the tendency of blood to pool at the snake's head when the snake is tilted at various angles with its head down

(E) An increase in the amount of effort required to distribute blood to and from the snake's tail

Inference

This question asks for an inference about the location of a snake's heart being closer to the brain than to the midpoint of its body. In the third paragraph, the passage states that in terrestrial snakes, which must fight the influence of gravity, the closer proximity of the heart to the head ensures blood circulation to the brain. The passage notes, however, that this makes it more difficult for such snakes to maintain blood circulation to the tail.

A The passage states that snakes have brains closer to their heads to more efficiently circulate blood to the brain.

B The passage suggests that having the heart close to the head increases the spatial orientations a snake can assume without losing blood flow to the brain, rather than decreases the number of orientations.

C The passage indicates that this is true only of sea snakes with hearts near their body's midpoint.

D The passage mentions blood pooling in the lower portions of a terrestrial organism's body but does not imply that blood can pool at a snake's head.

E **Correct.** Because, as the passage states, it is more difficult for a snake with its heart close to its head to circulate blood to the tail, and therefore its body is likely to put more effort into circulating blood to the tail.

The correct answer is E.

24. The primary purpose of the third paragraph is to

(A) introduce a topic that is not discussed earlier in the passage

(B) describe a more efficient method of achieving an effect discussed in the previous paragraph

(C) draw a conclusion based on information elaborated in the previous paragraph

(D) discuss two specific examples of phenomena mentioned at the end of the previous paragraph

(E) introduce evidence that undermines a view reported earlier in the passage

Evaluation

Answering this question requires recognizing how the passage develops its main point. The first paragraph sets up a general claim about gravity's influence on terrestrial organisms. The second paragraph then describes the ill effects that gravity has on sea snakes to identify problems that terrestrial snakes have had to adapt to. The third paragraph then uses examples to illustrate how terrestrial snakes have adapted to gravity's influence.

A The topic of the third paragraph is the adaptations developed by terrestrial snakes to survive gravity's influence, which is part of the discussion in both the first and second paragraphs.

B There is no comparison in the passage of the efficiency of the different methods used by snakes to adapt to gravity's influence.

C The third paragraph is concerned with illustrating certain adaptations used by snakes and offers no conclusions about the problems terrestrial snakes have had to adapt to, which is the topic of the second paragraph.

D **Correct.** The end of the second paragraph refers to *certain adaptations* (line 23) that the third paragraph then goes on to identify and discuss.

E The third paragraph supports the main idea of the passage and is not used to counter any claim made earlier.

The correct answer is D.

25. In the passage, the author is primarily concerned with doing which of the following?

    (A) Explaining adaptations that enable the terrestrial snake to cope with the effects of gravitational pressure on its circulatory system

    (B) Comparing the circulatory system of the sea snake with that of the terrestrial snake

    (C) Explaining why the circulatory system of the terrestrial snake is different from that of the sea snake

    (D) Pointing out features of the terrestrial snake's cardiovascular system that make it superior to that of the sea snake

    (E) Explaining how the sea snake is able to neutralize the effects of gravitational pressure on its circulatory system

Main idea

Answering this question involves assessing what the passage as a whole is attempting to do. While the passage begins by making a general claim about gravity's influence on the cardiovascular systems of terrestrial animals, it immediately points to terrestrial snakes as a good example supporting this claim. The rest of the passage is then devoted to illustrating, using the observations involving sea snakes, how gravity's influence has shaped the cardiovascular systems of terrestrial snakes.

A **Correct.** The entire passage is devoted to an explanation of how terrestrial snakes have adapted to gravity's influence.

B While the passage does compare the systems of the two snakes, it does so for the larger purpose of demonstrating gravity's influence on terrestrial snakes.

C The passage is more concerned with *how* the systems of the two snakes are different, rather than *why*, in order to identify how terrestrial snakes have adapted to gravity's influence.

D There is no judgment in the passage as to the superiority of one snake's system over the other.

E While the passage does explain how sea snakes do this, it does so only for the larger purpose of identifying how terrestrial snakes have adapted to gravity's influence.

The correct answer is A.

Questions 26–30 refer to the passage on page 378.

26. The author of the passage is primarily concerned with

    (A) discussing research data underlying several definitions

    (B) arguing for the adoption of a particular definition

    (C) exploring definitions of a concept

    (D) comparing the advantages of several definitions

    (E) clarifying some ambiguous definitions

Main idea

The author's primary concern is found by considering the passage as a whole. In the first paragraph, the author raises the central question regarding the meaning of *services* and then examines two definitions. The second paragraph analyzes the United States government's definition of *services* in more detail. The author is primarily interested in exploring different definitions of *services*.

A No research data are presented.

B The author points out the weakness of several definitions rather than giving reasons to adopt a particular one.

C **Correct.** The author considers several definitions of *services*.

D The author largely analyzes the disadvantages of the definitions.

E The author points out problems in the definitions rather than providing clarifications of the definitions themselves.

The correct answer is C.

27. In comparing the United States government's definition of services with the classical definition, the author suggests that the classical definition is

    (A) more pragmatic

    (B) more difficult to apply

    (C) less ambiguous

    (D) more widely used

    (E) more arbitrary

Inference

This question asks the reader to find information that is suggested but not directly stated in the passage. The author discusses the classical definition at the end of the first paragraph, pointing out two examples in which it does not apply and concluding that this definition is *hard to sustain*. By comparison, the government's definition is *more practical* because it is easy to apply; everything that is not agriculture or industry is defined as a service. An examination of the analysis of both definitions reveals that, according to the author, the classical definition is harder to apply.

A   The author describes the United States government's definition as *more practical* or pragmatic.

B   **Correct.** Citing two cases in which the classical definition does not apply, the author implies that this definition is harder to apply than the government's.

C   Although the United States government's definition is said to lead to *ambiguities*, the examples given to suggest difficulties with the classical definition indicate that it may be at least as ambiguous.

D   The author does not say that the classical definition is more widely used.

E   The author calls the government's definition arbitrary.

The correct answer is B.

28. The passage suggests which of the following about service workers in the United States?

(A) The number of service workers may be underestimated by the definition of services used by the government.

(B) There were fewer service workers than agricultural workers before 1988.

(C) The number of service workers was almost equal to the number of workers employed in manufacturing until 1988.

(D) Most service workers are employed in service occupations rather than in service industries.

(E) Most service workers are employed in occupations where they provide services that do not fall under the classical definition of services.

Inference

The question's use of the word *suggests* means that the answer depends on making an inference. According to the author, one of the failures of the government's definition of services is that *the many service workers employed by manufacturers—bookkeepers or janitors, for example—would fall under the industrial rather than the services category* (lines 22–26). This example shows that the number of service workers is likely to be underestimated.

A   **Correct.** Because some service workers are included in the industrial category, it is possible that the total number of service workers may be underestimated.

B   The passage does not provide the information to support this statement.

C   The author says that services moved ahead of manufacturing as the *main product* in 1988 but does not discuss the number of workers in either area.

D   The passage does not provide the information to support this statement.

E   The passage does not provide the information to support this statement.

The correct answer is A.

29. The author of the passage mentions which of the following as one disadvantage of the United States government's definition of services?

(A) It is less useful than the other definitions mentioned in the passage.

(B) It is narrower in scope than the other definitions mentioned in the passage.

(C) It is based on the final product produced rather than on the type of work performed.

(D) It does not recognize the diversity of occupations within the service industries.

(E) It misclassifies many workers who are employed in service industries.

Supporting ideas

This question is based on specific information explicitly stated in the passage. According to the author, the government's definition fails because *it categorizes workers based on their company's final product rather than on the actual work the employees perform* (lines 20–22).

A   The author calls this definition *practical for government purposes,* so for the government it is more useful than other definitions.

B   The definition *includes everything that is not agriculture or industry,* while the classical definition does not include occupations that are clearly services; the government's definition is thus not narrower.

C   Correct. Workers are categorized by the final product of their company rather than by the type of work they perform at that company.

D   Diversity of occupations within the service industries is not discussed.

E   The definition misclassifies service workers employed in manufacturing, not service industries.

The correct answer is C.

30.   The author refers to "service workers employed by manufacturers" (line 23) primarily in order to point out

(A)   a type of worker not covered by the United States government's system of classifying occupations

(B)   a flaw in the United States government's definition of services

(C)   a factor that has influenced the growth of the service economy in the United States

(D)   a type of worker who is classified on the basis of work performed rather than on the basis of the company's final product

(E)   the diversity of the workers who are referred to as service workers

Logical structure

The author discusses *the many service workers employed by manufacturers* to illustrate the failure of the government's definition to distinguish between service industries and service occupations. The resulting ambiguities, in the author's view, reveal the *arbitrariness* of the definition and its inaccuracy in reflecting the composition of the economy.

A   The worker is covered but misclassified.

B   Correct. The author uses this example to point out a serious shortcoming in the government's definition.

C   The author mentions the growth of services at the beginning of the passage but does not explore the reasons for it.

D   The situation of service workers employed by manufacturers is just the reverse; they are categorized by the company's final product, not by the work they do.

E   The author had earlier cited and illustrated the diversity of service activities that are included in the government's residual category of services; the focus here is instead the arbitrariness and inaccuracy, in the author's view, of the government's definition.

The correct answer is B.

Questions 31–36 refer to the passage on page 380.

31.   The passage is primarily concerned with

(A)   contrasting the benefits of one methodology with the benefits of another

(B)   describing the historical origins and inherent drawbacks of a particular methodology

(C)   discussing the appeal of a particular methodology and some concerns about its use

(D)   showing that some historians' adoption of a particular methodology has led to criticism of recent historical scholarship

(E)   analyzing the influence of current feminist views on women's interpretations of their experience

Main idea

This question asks for an abstract view of what the passage as a whole is primarily doing. The passage introduces a particular methodology that scholars of women's history have been encouraged to employ, explaining why the use of the methodology is supported. The passage then goes on to raise some concerns about the use of the methodology and cites one example in which caution is needed.

A   The passage is primarily concerned with only one methodology.

B   The passage mentions why the methodology had been encouraged but does not give the history of its origins; while it cautions historians to employ the methodology carefully, it is not concerned with drawbacks of its proper use.

C   **Correct.** The passage discusses why the use of a methodology is being encouraged and then offers some concerns about its use.

D   The passage does not discuss any criticism of recent scholarship in women's history.

E   There is no mention in the passage that feminist theory is influencing how women in general think about their experiences.

The correct answer is C.

32. According to the passage, which of the following shapes the oral narratives of women storytellers?

(A)   The conventions for standard histories in the culture in which a woman storyteller lives

(B)   The conventions of storytelling in the culture in which a woman storyteller lives

(C)   A woman storyteller's experience with distinctive traditions of storytelling developed by the women in her family of origin

(D)   The cultural expectations and experiences of those who listen to oral narratives

(E)   A woman storyteller's familiarity with the stories that members of other groups in her culture tell to explain themselves

Supporting ideas

This question asks for an identification of specific information provided by the passage. In the second paragraph, the passage describes certain concerns about using oral narratives. One of these concerns is that *the stories people tell to explain themselves are shaped by ... storytelling conventions* (lines 17–19) and other influences tied to the teller's cultural and historical context.

A   The passage uses *standard histories* (line 7) to refer to the usual work of scholars and not to something that influences oral narratives.

B   **Correct.** The passage raises as a concern that oral narratives may be influenced by storytelling conventions present in the culture of the speaker.

C   The passage does not mention the family of origin of women storytellers.

D   The passage does not mention the expectations of the listeners of oral narratives.

E   The passage does not discuss women storytellers' familiarity with the oral narratives belonging to other groups of women.

The correct answer is B.

33. The author of the passage would be most likely to make which of the following recommendations to scholars of women's history?

(A)   They should take into account their own life experiences when interpreting the oral accounts of women's historical experiences.

(B)   They should assume that the observations made in women's oral narratives are believed by the intended audience of the story.

(C)   They should treat skeptically observations reported in oral narratives unless the observations can be confirmed in standard histories.

(D)   They should consider the cultural and historical context in which an oral narrative was created before arriving at an interpretation of such a narrative.

(E)   They should rely on information gathered from oral narratives only when equivalent information is not available in standard histories.

Application

Answering this question involves recognizing what the author believes about oral narratives and then applying this belief to a hypothetical situation in which the author makes recommendations to scholars of women's history. While acknowledging the appeal of oral narratives to these scholars, in the second paragraph the author urges caution when using these narratives as sources of *disinterested commentary* (line 16). The passage then states that people's oral narratives are shaped by *cultural and historical factors* (line 20), which presumably relate to the cultural and historical context within which the narratives are spoken.

A   The passage does not mention the personal life experiences of scholars.

B   The passage does not mention the intended audiences of oral narratives.

C   The passage mentions *standard histories* (line 7) only as a reference to scholarly works that often have shortcomings.

D   Correct. The passage cautions that oral narratives may be biased due to cultural and historical factors, and it is therefore reasonable to suppose that the author would recommend that scholars consider this when using such information.

E   The passage does not refer to oral narratives as being valuable only for filling a gap in the available historical record.

The correct answer is D.

34.   Which of the following best describes the function of the last sentence of the passage?

(A)   It describes an event that historians view as crucial in recent women's history.

(B)   It provides an example of how political rhetoric may influence the interpretations of experience reported in women's oral narratives.

(C)   It provides an example of an oral narrative that inaccurately describes women's experience during a particular historical period.

(D)   It illustrates the point that some women are more aware than others of the social forces that shape their oral narratives.

(E)   It identifies the historical conditions that led to the social acceptance of women's paid work outside the home.

Evaluation

This question requires recognizing how a particular part of the passage is related to the overall reasoning in the passage. The first paragraph introduces a methodology and describes the methodology's appeal. The second paragraph then raises concerns about the use of the methodology, drawing attention to the cultural and historical bias that may be present in oral narratives. In line 21, the passage refers specifically to the influence *political rhetoric* may have on a woman's understanding of her experience. In the final sentence, the passage provides a specific hypothetical example of a woman at the time of the Second World War to illustrate this concern.

A   The last sentence employs a hypothetical example and does not describe a particular event as being important to historians.

B   Correct. After contending that political rhetoric may influence oral narratives, the passage uses the example of the Second World War in the final sentence to support this claim.

C   The last sentence does not provide a particular example of an oral narrative.

D   The passage does not claim that some women are more aware than others of the social forces that may bear on them.

E   The passage does not claim that social conditions during the Second World War led to acceptance of women in the workplace.

The correct answer is B.

35. According to the passage, scholars of women's history should refrain from doing which of the following?

    (A) Relying on traditional historical sources when women's oral narratives are unavailable

    (B) Focusing on the influence of political rhetoric on women's perceptions to the exclusion of other equally important factors

    (C) Attempting to discover the cultural and historical factors that influence the stories women tell

    (D) Assuming that the conventions of women's written autobiographies are similar to the conventions of women's oral narratives

    (E) Accepting women's oral narratives less critically than they accept women's written histories

Inference

Answering this question requires recognizing which option is directly inferable from information in the passage. After describing in the first paragraph why oral narratives are appealing to historians, the passage begins the second paragraph by imploring scholars of women's history to *be as cautious about accepting oral narratives ... as ... written memories* (lines 12–14). The passage then goes on to describe potential bias in oral narratives, suggesting that scholars should be as critical of them as they are of written sources.

A   The passage does not claim that traditional historical sources should be avoided by scholars.

B   The passage mentions the influence of political rhetoric merely as one example of potential bias.

C   The passage suggests that scholars *should* attempt to be aware of cultural and historical factors.

D   The passage does not discuss the conventions of women's written autobiographies.

E   **Correct.** The passage implies that written histories and oral narratives should receive the same level of critical scrutiny by scholars.

The correct answer is E.

36. According to the passage, each of the following is a difference between women's oral narratives and most standard histories EXCEPT:

    (A) Women's oral histories validate the significance of women's achievements.

    (B) Women's oral histories depict experience from the point of view of women.

    (C) Women's oral histories acknowledge the influence of well-known women.

    (D) Women's oral histories present today's women with a sense of their historical relationship to women of the past.

    (E) Women's oral histories are crucial to the collective identity of today's women.

Supporting ideas

This question asks for information that is stated in the passage, and it requires a process of elimination. In line 7, oral narratives are presented as being *unlike most standard histories*, and the passage then goes on in lines 7–11 to list characteristics of oral histories that most standard histories do not have. The answer to this question will therefore contain a characteristic of women's oral histories that is not described in lines 7–11.

A   The passage states that, unlike most standard histories, women's oral histories *affirm the importance of women's contributions* (lines 8–9).

B   The passage states that, unlike most standard histories, women's oral histories *represent experience from the perspective of women* (lines 7–8).

C   **Correct.** The passage does not mention the influence of well-known women on women's oral histories.

D   The passage states that, unlike most standard histories, women's oral histories *furnish present–day women with historical continuity* (lines 9–10).

E   The passage states that, unlike most standard histories, women's oral histories furnish a historical sense that is *essential to their identity, individually and collectively* (line 11).

The correct answer is C.

Questions 37–41 refer to the passage on page 382.

37. The passage suggests that in order for a manufacturer in a capital-intensive industry to have a decisive advantage over competitors making similar products, the manufacturer must

   (A) be the first in the industry to build production facilities of theoretically optimal size
   (B) make every effort to keep fixed and sunk costs as low as possible
   (C) be one of the first to operate its manufacturing plants at minimum efficient scale
   (D) produce goods of higher quality than those produced by direct competitors
   (E) stockpile raw materials at production sites in order to ensure a steady flow of such materials

Inference

This question asks for an inference about what a manufacturer in a capital-intensive industry must do to have an advantage over competitors making similar products. The passage addresses this question by stating that advantage accrues to those firms that are the first to exploit the full potential of optimally sized, technologically sophisticated plants. In this context, exploiting the full potential of such plants means operating them at *minimum efficient scale*. Based on the definition in the first paragraph, this means that the plant must have an output of such a size that the cost per unit of output is at a minimum.

A   The passage says that for new capital-intensive firms to dominate the market, it is not enough for them to have optimally sized plants; the plants must also be operated in a way that fully exploits their potential.
B   While keeping fixed and sunk costs low would obviously help keep overall costs low, the passage does not suggest that this is decisive in enabling a firm to have an advantage over competitors.

C   **Correct.** Being among the first manufacturers to operate plants at minimum efficient scale means that those plants are being exploited to their full potential. This strategy would most likely give such manufacturers a decisive advantage over new firms hoping to compete effectively.
D   The passage does not discuss the quality of goods made by manufacturers.
E   The passage does not suggest that stockpiling raw materials is the most efficient way to ensure a steady flow of raw materials into the manufacturing process, though the passage states that such a steady flow is a factor in achieving minimum efficient scale.

The correct answer is C.

38. The passage suggests that which of the following is true of a manufacturer's fixed and sunk costs?

   (A) The extent to which they are determined by market conditions for the goods being manufactured is frequently underestimated.
   (B) If they are kept as low as possible, the manufacturer is very likely to realize significant profits.
   (C) They are the primary factor that determines whether a manufacturer will realize economies of scale.
   (D) They should be on a par with the fixed and sunk costs of the manufacturer's competitors.
   (E) They are not affected by fluctuations in a manufacturing plant's throughput.

Inference

This question asks about what the passage implies about fixed and sunk costs. The passage states that when production declines due to certain factors, such costs remain at the same level (which may be high), and the cost per unit produced (*unit costs*) rises sharply.

A   The passage discusses the impact of market conditions on determining what the optimal size of a manufacturing plant is (which affects fixed and sunk costs). But it makes no claim about the frequency with which such an impact is "underestimated."

B   The passage emphasizes that failing to keep throughput at an efficiently high level reduces profitability because that failure results in increased cost per unit (to which, of course, the plant's fixed and sunk costs contribute). But the passage does not claim that keeping aggregate fixed and sunk costs very low is necessary in order to have the most competitive production operation.

C   The passage emphasizes that the crucial factor in achieving economies of scale is efficient operation of the production facilities, not the size of the firm's fixed and sunk costs (even though such costs are clearly in part determined by the size and design of the production facilities).

D   While a manufacturer's fixed and sunk costs may be on a par with those of the manufacturer's competitors, the passage provides no grounds for inferring that there is any need for them to be (for example, physical plants that employ different technologies may have different price tags).

E   **Correct.** According to the passage, "throughput" refers to the flow of materials through a plant. This flow can vary as a result of various factors, but fixed and sunk costs—financial resources already committed—remain the same regardless of such variation.

The correct answer is E.

39. In the context of the passage as a whole, the second paragraph serves primarily to

(A) provide an example to support the argument presented in the first paragraph

(B) evaluate various strategies discussed in the first paragraph

(C) introduce evidence that undermines the argument presented in the first paragraph

(D) anticipate possible objections to the argument presented in the first paragraph

(E) demonstrate the potential dangers of a commonly used strategy

Evaluation

This question asks about the rhetorical function of the second paragraph. While the first paragraph argues that a crucial factor in achieving economies of scale is intangible capital, or organized human capabilities, the second paragraph uses the example of new capital-intensive manufacturing industries to help show that this is indeed the case.

A   **Correct.** The second paragraph provides an example that illustrates the claims made in the first paragraph. It discusses the way in which intangible capital—e.g., distribution networks, marketing systems, smooth production processes, and qualified management teams—enables manufacturers in new capital-intensive manufacturing industries to realize economies of scale and achieve market dominance.

B   The second paragraph does, in a sense, "evaluate" investment in intangible capital: it suggests that such investment is necessary. However, investment in intangible capital is the only strategy it discusses.

C   The second paragraph supports rather than undermines the first paragraph's argument.

D   Nothing in the second paragraph suggests that there are, or could be, any objections to the first paragraph's argument.

E   The second paragraph discusses the potential positive outcomes of investing in intangible capital. It suggests that there might be negative consequences to not making such investments, but it does not indicate that avoiding such investments is a commonly used strategy.

The correct answer is A.

40. The passage LEAST supports the inference that a manufacturer's throughput could be adversely affected by

    (A) a mistake in judgment regarding the selection of a wholesaler
    (B) a breakdown in the factory's machinery
    (C) a labor dispute on the factory floor
    (D) an increase in the cost per unit of output
    (E) a drop in the efficiency of the sales network

Application

This question may be best approached by using an elimination strategy—first finding the four choices that can reasonably be inferred from the passage, and then checking to make sure that the remaining choice cannot reasonably be inferred. This requires understanding the information the passage gives about throughput, then making inferences about what can cause throughput to drop. The passage defines throughput generally as *the flow of materials through a plant* and goes on to explain that it involves coordination of the production process itself, as well as obtaining materials from suppliers and marketing and distributing the manufactured products. Anything that damages this flow of materials and products would be said to have an adverse effect on throughput.

A   Making a poor judgment about a wholesaler would most likely have an adverse effect on throughput, in that it could affect *the flow of output to wholesalers and final consumers.*

B   A breakdown in machinery would likely fall into the category of *problems on the factory floor* mentioned in the passage and would likely prove damaging to throughput because of its effect on the production process itself.

C   A labor dispute would also likely fall into the category of *problems on the factory floor* mentioned in the passage and would probably cause a decline in production and thus adversely affect throughput.

D   Correct. The passage emphasizes that changes in throughput can cause increases or decreases in costs per unit. But the passage is not committed to any claims about how changes in costs per unit might affect throughput.

E   The passage suggests that inefficient sales networks could cause a decline in production. Thus a decrease in sales efficiency would most likely adversely affect a manufacturer's ability to provide goods to consumers, and thus would create problems with throughput.

The correct answer is D.

41. The primary purpose of the passage is to

    (A) point out the importance of intangible capital for realizing economies of scale in manufacturing
    (B) show that manufacturers frequently gain a competitive advantage from investment in large manufacturing facilities
    (C) argue that large manufacturing facilities often fail because of inadequate investment in both tangible and intangible capital
    (D) suggest that most new industries are likely to be dominated by firms that build large manufacturing plants early
    (E) explain why large manufacturing plants usually do not help manufacturers achieve economies of scale

Main idea

This question depends on understanding the passage as a whole. In general, it makes an argument for investing in intangible capital as a way for manufacturers to realize economies of scale, and it supports its argument with an example.

A **Correct.** The passage focuses on intangible capital as a crucial factor in realizing economies of scale.

B According to the passage, manufacturers gain competitive advantage by building plants of optimal size that they then fully exploit; nothing in the passage suggests that large plants are frequently optimal.

C The passage assumes that manufacturers invest appropriately in tangible capital and argues that it is important for them to invest in intangible capital as well.

D The passage states that new capital-intensive manufacturing industries are dominated not by firms that are the first to build large plants, but by firms that exploit the full potential of their plants.

E The passage indicates that economies of scale can be achieved in plants of optimal size. The passage does not suggest that large plants cannot be optimal.

The correct answer is A.

Questions 42–44 refer to the passage on page 384.

42. The passage suggests that combing and carding differ from weaving in that combing and carding were

(A) low-skill jobs performed primarily by women employees

(B) low-skill jobs that were not performed in the home

(C) low-skill jobs performed by both male and female employees

(D) high-skill jobs performed outside the home

(E) high-skill jobs performed by both male and female employees

Inference

Since the question uses the word *suggests*, the answer is probably not directly stated in the passage and therefore has to be inferred. How was weaving different from carding and combing? Lines 16–17 discuss weaving, combing, and carding; all three activities are characterized as low-skill jobs. As the human capital theory notes, there was a concentration of women in certain low-skill occupations because they *could be carried out in the home* (lines 19–20); weaving was one such occupation. Since the passage implies that relatively few women worked in carding and combing, these jobs presumably could *not* be carried out in the home. Thus the passage suggests that carding and combing were low-skill jobs, mostly done by men working outside the home.

A Lines 15–17 imply that women predominated in weaving but that carding and combing were done mainly by men.

B **Correct.** Carding and combing, unlike weaving, could not be done at home.

C The passage suggests that weaving, carding, and combing were all low-skill jobs done by both men and women, although the concentrations of the genders in these jobs were different; this statement does not explain how the passage suggests that *combing and carding differ from weaving*.

D Lines 16–17 characterize all three jobs as low-skill.

E Lines 16–17 characterize all three jobs as low-skill.

The correct answer is B.

43. Which of the following, if true, would most weaken the explanation provided by the human capital theory for women's concentration in certain occupations in seventeenth-century Florence?

    (A) Women were unlikely to work outside the home even in occupations whose hours were flexible enough to allow women to accommodate domestic tasks as well as paid labor.

    (B) Parents were less likely to teach occupational skills to their daughters than they were to their sons.

    (C) Women's participation in the Florentine paid labor force grew steadily throughout the sixteenth and seventeenth centuries.

    (D) The vast majority of female weavers in the Florentine wool industry had children.

    (E) Few women worked as weavers in the Florentine silk industry, which was devoted to making cloths that required a high degree of skill to produce.

Logical structure

To answer this question, examine the logic of the explanation. How does the human capital theory explain women's concentration in certain occupations? The theory says that women's roles in childbearing made it difficult for them to acquire the skills needed in high-skill jobs. Moreover, their role in child rearing made them choose occupations that could be carried out at home. Evidence against either of these points will weaken the explanation.

A   Correct. If women of that time were generally unlikely to take any jobs outside the home, even those that allowed them to handle their domestic tasks, then these tasks are not the reason women predominated in jobs that they could do within the home, as the human capital theory posits.

B   Different levels of teaching by parents may help perpetuate job segregation, but this is quite consistent with the socially defined role that women then had as childbearers and child rearers and the explanation provided by the human capital theory.

C   The growth of women's participation in the paid labor force does not affect the explanation of occupational concentrations provided by the human capital theory.

D   The explanation suggests the women chose weaving because they had children to raise at home. The fact that the majority of weavers had children actually supports, rather than weakens, the explanation.

E   Silk weaving was a high-skill job, exactly the kind of job that women would not have in the human capital explanation. This point supports, rather than weakens, the explanation.

The correct answer is A.

44. The author of the passage would be most likely to describe the explanation provided by the human capital theory for the high concentration of women in certain occupations in the seventeenth-century Florentine textile industry as

    (A) well founded though incomplete

    (B) difficult to articulate

    (C) plausible but poorly substantiated

    (D) seriously flawed

    (E) contrary to recent research

Logical structure

This question requires an evaluation of the author's point of view. What does the author think of the human capital explanation of women's occupational concentration in the Florentine textile industry? In line 5, the author characterizes the theory as *useful*, a positive word reflecting a positive evaluation. However, the entire second paragraph is devoted to examining *differences in pay scales that cannot be explained by the human capital theory*. The author's positive view of the theory is qualified by the theory's inability to explain an important point.

A **Correct.** This statement reflects the author's generally positive evaluation, as well as concerns about insufficiencies.

B   The author articulates the theory without difficulty and does not criticize it as difficult to articulate.

C   To substantiate the theory means to provide evidence that verifies the theory. The author regards the theory's explanations of high concentration of women in certain occupations as sound, and so is unlikely to regard the theory as *poorly substantiated*.

D   If the author regarded the theory as *seriously flawed*, the passage would not describe it as *useful* (see line 5).

E   The author does not mention recent research.

The correct answer is A.

Questions 45–51 refer to the passage on page 386.

45. The primary purpose of the passage is to

(A)   present the results of statistical analyses and propose further studies

(B)   explain a recent development and predict its eventual consequences

(C)   identify the reasons for a trend and recommend measures to address it

(D)   outline several theories about a phenomenon and advocate one of them

(E)   describe the potential consequences of implementing a new policy and argue in favor of that policy

Main idea

Understanding the author's purpose comes from a careful consideration of the whole passage. The author begins by noting one explanation for the rise in temporary employment, but dismisses it, finding another explanation more likely. The author closes the passage by making specific recommendations to counter the problems caused by temporary employment.

A   The author uses statistical analyses as the basis of an explanation, but the analyses act only as support for the larger purpose of explaining a trend; no further studies are proposed.

B   The author explores possible reasons for a recent development but recommends ways to curb or change that development; the author does not predict the consequences if the situation is left unchanged or the recommendations unmet.

C **Correct.** The author examines possible reasons for the rise in temporary employment and makes specific recommendations to change the current situation.

D   The use of the phrase *several theories* is enough to make this inaccurate. Two types of explanation are suggested: employee preference or employer self-interest.

E   The author makes recommendations but provides no arguments in support of those recommendations—merely suggesting that they are aimed at discouraging employers from creating too many temporary positions.

The correct answer is C.

46. According to the passage, which of the following is true of the "factors affecting employers" that are mentioned in lines 10–19?

(A)   Most experts cite them as having initiated the growth in temporary employment that occurred during the 1980s.

(B)   They may account for the increase in the total number of temporary workers during the 1980s.

(C)   They were less important than demographic change in accounting for the increase of temporary employment during the 1980s.

(D)   They included a sharp increase in the cost of labor during the 1980s.

(E)   They are more difficult to account for than are other factors involved in the growth of temporary employment during the 1980s.

Supporting idea

This question is based on information explicitly stated in lines 10–12. The statistical analyses *suggest that factors affecting employers account for the rise in temporary employment.*

A   *Some observers* attribute the rise to the composition of the workforce; the passage does not identify what most experts believe.

B   Correct. The factors affecting employers may explain the rise in temporary employment.

C   The passage suggests that these factors were more important than demographic changes in explaining the rise.

D   Although there is some suggestion in lines 15–16 that employers at some point experienced difficulty from the cost of labor, the passage does not suggest that a sharp increase in that cost occurred in the 1980s—and even suggests that labor costs may have decreased because of labor's reduced bargaining strength.

E   The issue of how to *account for* those factors (i.e., explain why they occurred) is not raised in the passage—so the issue of whether those factors are more difficult to account for than other factors is not raised.

The correct answer is B.

47.   The passage suggests which of the following about the use of temporary employment by firms during the 1980s?

(A)   It enabled firms to deal with fluctuating product demand far more efficiently than they did before the 1980s.

(B)   It increased as a result of increased participation in the workforce by certain demographic groups.

(C)   It was discouraged by government-mandated policies.

(D)   It was a response to preferences indicated by certain employees for more flexible working arrangements.

(E)   It increased partly as a result of workers' reduced ability to control the terms of their employment.

Inference

Since the word *suggests* is used in the question, the answer is probably not directly stated in the passage and therefore has to be inferred. The author believes that the rise in temporary employment during the 1980s can be explained by two factors affecting employers: *product demand* and *labor's reduced bargaining strength.* Temporary employment allows employers to adapt their workforce to the fluctuating demand for their product. At this time, *labor's reduced bargaining strength* left employers, not workers, in greater control of the terms of employment.

A   This goes too far beyond the information provided in the passage. The passage neither says nor implies anything about efficiency levels before the 1980s.

B   The author says that *demographic changes in the workforce did not correlate with variations in the total number of temporary workers,* ruling out this explanation.

C   In 1992, the author recommended government-mandated policies because they did not exist.

D   The author says that *growth in temporary employment now far exceeds the level explainable by … groups said to prefer temporary jobs.*

E   Correct. *Labor's reduced bargaining power* resulted in employers' increased control over the terms of employment.

The correct answer is E.

48.   The passage suggests which of the following about the workers who took temporary jobs during the 1980s?

(A)   Their jobs frequently led to permanent positions within firms.

(B)   They constituted a less demographically diverse group than has been suggested.

(C)   They were occasionally involved in actions organized by labor unions.

(D)   Their pay declined during the decade in comparison with the pay of permanent employees.

(E)   They did not necessarily prefer temporary employment to permanent employment.

Inference

The question's use of the word *suggests* indicates that the answer is probably not directly stated in the passage. The author says that the rise in temporary employment *now far exceeds the level explainable by recent workforce entry rates of groups said to prefer temporary jobs*. Thus, the number of workers employed on a temporary basis is far greater than the number of workers who actually do prefer temporary employment.

A   No evidence is presented that temporary jobs led to permanent positions.

B   The passage grants that there was *increased participation in the workforce by certain groups, such as first-time or reentering workers*. This suggests more rather than less demographic diversity.

C   The role of temporary workers in labor unions is not discussed.

D   The passage does suggest that the pay of temporary workers is less than that of permanent workers, but not that the pay of temporary workers *declined*.

E   **Correct.** The passage indicates that the number of workers in temporary jobs was higher than the number of workers who stated a preference for temporary work.

The correct answer is E.

49. The first sentence in the passage suggests that the "observers" mentioned in line 1 would be most likely to predict which of the following?

(A)   That the number of new temporary positions would decline as fewer workers who preferred temporary employment entered the workforce

(B)   That the total number of temporary positions would increase as fewer workers were able to find permanent positions

(C)   That employers would have less control over the terms of workers' employment as workers increased their bargaining strength

(D)   That more workers would be hired for temporary positions as product demand increased

(E)   That the number of workers taking temporary positions would increase as more workers in any given demographic group entered the workforce

Application

These observers specifically attribute the growth of temporary employment to *increased participation in the workforce by certain groups ... who supposedly prefer such arrangements*. On the basis of the passage's first sentence, any prediction these observers might make must be about the relation between the number of workers in temporary employment and the preference of these workers for temporary employment. No other issue is discussed. A rise in temporary employment could be explained only by a rise in the number of new workers who prefer temporary jobs, and a decline in temporary employment only by a decline in the number of new workers who prefer temporary work.

A   **Correct.** By this rationale, the only reason for a decline in temporary employment would be a corresponding decline in the number of new workers who preferred temporary jobs.

B   According to the observers, temporary employment would increase only if a greater number of employers who preferred temporary jobs entered the workforce.

C   These observers are not said to consider control over the terms of employment.

D   These observers are not said to consider the relationship between product demand and temporary employment.

E   The number of workers taking temporary positions would rise only if they were composed of *certain groups, such as first-time or reentering workers*, who, the observers believe, prefer temporary work.

The correct answer is A.

50. In the context of the passage, the word "excessive" (line 23) most closely corresponds to which of the following phrases?

    (A) Far more than can be justified by worker preferences
    (B) Far more than can be explained by fluctuations in product demand
    (C) Far more than can be beneficial to the success of the firms themselves
    (D) Far more than can be accounted for by an expanding national economy
    (E) Far more than can be attributed to increases in the total number of people in the workforce

Logical structure

In its context in this passage, the word *excessive* indicates a value-judgment by the author. The author recommends that firms be *discouraged from creating excessive numbers of temporary positions* on the basis of the statistical analyses, which show that the rise in temporary employment *now far exceeds the level explainable by recent workforce entry rates of groups said to prefer temporary jobs*. In the context of lines 24–31, it is clear that the author believes that the large expansion in temporary employment exclusively serves employer interests at the expense of employee interests (including their preferences), and is, for that reason, excessive.

A **Correct.** An expansion of temporary employment that serves employer interests more than it serves employee interests (such as preferences) is considered by the author to be *excessive*.
B It is not because the expansion in temporary employment allows employers to respond to fluctuations in product demand that the author regards the expansion as *excessive*.
C The relation of temporary employment to the success of firms is not discussed.
D The relation of temporary employment to an expanding economy is not discussed.
E The author does not consider the issue of overall increases in the workforce as a whole, only the issue of increases in temporary employment.

The correct answer is A.

51. The passage mentions each of the following as an appropriate kind of governmental action EXCEPT

    (A) getting firms to offer temporary employment primarily to a certain group of people
    (B) encouraging equitable pay for temporary and permanent employees
    (C) facilitating the organization of temporary workers by labor unions
    (D) establishing guidelines on the proportion of temporary workers that firms should employ
    (E) ensuring that temporary workers obtain benefits from their employers

Supporting ideas

The author closes the passage with a list of specific recommendations. Check that list against the possible answers. By the process of elimination, choose the one recommendation the author does not make. The author recommends that government policymakers consider: 1) *mandating benefit coverage for temporary employees*, 2) *promoting pay equity between temporary and permanent workers*, 3) *assisting labor unions in organizing temporary workers*, and 4) *encouraging firms to assign temporary jobs primarily to employees who explicitly indicate that preference.*

A The author does recommend that firms assign temporary jobs to workers who prefer temporary work.
B The author does recommend that pay equity between temporary and permanent workers be encouraged.
C The author does recommend that labor unions be assisted in organizing temporary workers.
D **Correct.** The author does not recommend that such guidelines be established.
E The author does recommend that benefit coverage for temporary workers be mandated.

The correct answer is D.

Questions 52–55 refer to the passage on page 388.

52. It can be inferred from the passage that a large plant might have to spend more than a similar but smaller plant on environmental compliance because the larger plant is

(A) more likely to attract attention from local regulators

(B) less likely to be exempt from permit and reporting requirements

(C) less likely to have regulatory costs passed on to it by companies that supply its raw materials

(D) more likely to employ older production technologies

(E) more likely to generate wastes that are more environmentally damaging than those generated by smaller plants

Inference

This item depends on understanding the implications of the passage's discussion of differences between large and small plants. It asks what might be true of a larger plant that would compel it to spend more than a smaller plant on environmental compliance. The passage addresses this issue by stating that smaller plants are often not subject to the same permit or reporting requirements that larger plants are.

A The likelihood of attracting regulatory attention is discussed only in the context of comparing plants that are *isolated* with small plants that are near large noncompliant ones. The passage does not suggest that size is generally the crucial determining factor in attracting regulatory attention.

B **Correct.** According to the passage, certain permit or reporting requirements may not apply to smaller plants; this suggests that larger plants are less likely than smaller plants to be exempt from these requirements, and thus that the larger plants would have to spend more to comply.

C The passage does not discuss the passing on of regulatory costs from suppliers to plants.

D The passage does not suggest that larger plants are any more likely than smaller plants to employ older production technologies.

E The passage does not distinguish between the types of wastes emitted by larger plants and those emitted by smaller plants.

The correct answer is B.

53. According to the passage, which of the following statements about sulfur dioxide and nitrogen oxide outputs is true?

(A) Older production technologies cannot be adapted so as to reduce production of these outputs as waste products.

(B) Under the most recent environmental regulations, industrial plants are no longer permitted to produce these outputs.

(C) Although these outputs are environmentally hazardous, some plants still generate them as waste products despite the high compliance costs they impose.

(D) Many older plants have developed innovative technological processes that reduce the amounts of these outputs generated as waste products.

(E) Since the production processes that generate these outputs are less costly than alternative processes, these less expensive processes are sometimes adopted despite their acknowledged environmental hazards.

Supporting idea

This item depends on identifying what the passage states explicitly about outputs of sulfur dioxide and nitrogen oxide. The passage says that plants that produce these outputs are those that use older industrial coal-fired burners, and that such plants are subject to extensive compliance costs imposed by new regulations.

A   The passage does not address the question of whether older production technologies might be adapted to reduce outputs of sulfur dioxide and nitrogen oxide.

B   The passage states that new regulations have imposed high compliance costs on companies that produce sulfur dioxide and nitrogen oxide outputs, not that these outputs are prohibited.

C   **Correct.** The passage states that some companies are still using the older kinds of burners that generate sulfur dioxide and nitrogen oxide outputs, and that new regulations have imposed high compliance costs on these companies.

D   The passage does not address the question of whether older plants have developed new processes to reduce the amounts of sulfur dioxide and nitrogen oxide they produce.

E   Sulfur dioxide and nitrogen oxide outputs, the passage suggests, are produced only by older industrial coal-fired burners; newer facilities (using alternative processes) do not employ this technology, the expense of which is not mentioned in the passage.

The correct answer is C.

54. Which of the following best describes the relationship of the statement about large plants (lines 12–17) to the passage as a whole?

(A) It presents a hypothesis that is disproved later in the passage.

(B) It highlights an opposition between two ideas mentioned in the passage.

(C) It provides examples to support a claim made earlier in the passage.

(D) It exemplifies a misconception mentioned earlier in the passage.

(E) It draws an analogy between two situations described in the passage.

Evaluation

This question asks about the role played in the passage by the following statement: *Additionally, large plants can spread compliance costs such as waste treatment across a larger revenue base; on the other hand, some smaller plants may not even be subject to certain provisions such as permit or reporting requirements by virtue of their size.* This statement describes situations in which compliance costs for plants of different sizes may differ, which serve as evidence in support of the passage's main claim: that environmental regulations do *not* affect all competitors in a given industry uniformly.

A   The statement in question is not a hypothesis; rather, it reports factors that are known to affect the varying impact of environmental regulations.

B   This is too vague to be a good description of the kind of relationship the question asks about. The highlighted statement does present a contrast—it suggests that larger plants' compliance costs are lower under some circumstances, while smaller plants' compliance costs are lower under other circumstances. But this purports to state two facts rather than mere *ideas*; they are contrasting facts but not in any meaningful sense *opposed*, since they can easily coexist.

C   **Correct.** The statement provides examples to support the initial claim made in the passage that regulatory costs fall unevenly on competitors in an industry: large plants can spread compliance costs around, and smaller plants may not even have to pay certain costs.

D   This statement helps to dispel, not exemplify, a misconception mentioned earlier in the passage—i.e., the myth that environmental regulations affect all companies in an industry the same way.

E   The statement does not suggest that the situation of larger and smaller plants is similar (or analogous) to any other situation mentioned in the passage.

The correct answer is C.

55. The primary purpose of the passage is to

    (A) address a widespread environmental management problem and suggest possible solutions

    (B) illustrate varying levels of compliance with environmental regulation among different corporations

    (C) describe the various alternatives to traditional methods of environmental management

    (D) advocate increased corporate compliance with environmental regulation

    (E) correct a common misconception about the impact of environmental regulations

Main idea

This question depends on understanding the passage as a whole. Its first sentence indicates its main purpose: to dispel a myth about environmental regulations that is often taken as fact.

A   The passage is not about the management of any environmental problem, which would be a problem about how to prevent or undo damage to the environment. The passage primarily aims to dispel a belief that the passage says is widely held by environmental managers.

B   The passage refers to variations in firms' levels of compliance with environmental regulations, but its primary purpose is not to illustrate those varying levels, nor does it do so.

C   The passage suggests that most environmental managers are mistaken about a key concept; its primary purpose is not to describe traditional methods of environmental management or alternatives to those traditional methods, nor does it do so.

D   The passage takes no position on whether companies should increase their compliance with environmental regulation.

E   **Correct.** The passage primarily aims to dispel the belief that environmental regulations affect all companies in an industry uniformly.

The correct answer is E.

Questions 56–62 refer to the passage on page 390.

56. According to the passage, which of the following was true of the treaty establishing the Fort Belknap Indian Reservation?

    (A) It was challenged in the Supreme Court a number of times.

    (B) It was rescinded by the federal government, an action that gave rise to the *Winters* case.

    (C) It cited American Indians' traditional use of the land's resources.

    (D) It failed to mention water rights to be enjoyed by the reservation's inhabitants.

    (E) It was modified by the Supreme Court in *Arizona v. California.*

Supporting ideas

This question requires recognizing information that is explicitly stated in the passage. In the first sentence, the passage states that the Fort Belknap Indian Reservation was established by treaty. The following sentence begins by stating that this treaty *did not mention water rights* (lines 5–6); in other words, the right to use the water flowing through the reservation was not established by treaty.

A   Although the Supreme Court ruled on water rights for the reservation established by the treaty, there is no evidence in the passage that the treaty itself was ever challenged in the Supreme Court.

B   Although the *Winters* case resulted in water rights for the reservation established by the treaty, there is no evidence in the passage that the treaty was ever rescinded.

C   The passage does not mention American Indians' traditional resource use as being tied to the treaty establishing the Fort Belknap Indian Reservation.

D   **Correct.** The passage states explicitly that the treaty establishing the Fort Belknap Indian Reservation did not mention the right to use water flowing through the reservation.

E   The passage does not mention the Fort Belknap Indian Reservation or the treaty that established it in relation to *Arizona v. California.*

The correct answer is D.

57. The passage suggests that, if the criteria discussed in lines 10–20 were the only criteria for establishing a reservation's water rights, which of the following would be true?

   (A) The water rights of the inhabitants of the Fort Belknap Indian Reservation would not take precedence over those of other citizens.

   (B) Reservations established before 1848 would be judged to have no water rights.

   (C) There would be no legal basis for the water rights of the Rio Grande pueblos.

   (D) Reservations other than American Indian reservations could not be created with reserved water rights.

   (E) Treaties establishing reservations would have to mention water rights explicitly in order to reserve water for a particular purpose.

Inference

Answering this question requires making an inference based on information given in the passage. The question focuses on lines 10–20, where the passage provides a summary of the criteria used by the U.S. courts to establish water rights. The passage then explains that the Rio Grande pueblos used other means to establish water rights, noting that what *constitutes an American Indian reservation is a question of practice, not of legal definition* (lines 34–36). This strongly implies that establishing water rights for the Rio Grande pueblos required reference to legal language not contained in the criteria described in lines 10–20.

   A Since the passage says that decisions setting the criteria in lines 10–20 cited the *Winters* case—which gave water rights to the Fort Belknap Indian Reservation—one can infer that the Fort Belknap reservation met all of those criteria.

   B The criteria in lines 10–20 do not touch on specific dates of the transfer of sovereignty over particular lands.

   C **Correct.** The passage demonstrates that for the Rio Grande pueblos, it was necessary to establish water rights based on criteria not contained in lines 10–20.

   D The criteria described in lines 10–20 are not specific only to lands reserved for American Indians.

   E The passage illustrates that *Winters* established water rights in the absence of any explicit mention of water rights in the treaty.

The correct answer is C.

58. Which of the following most accurately summarizes the relationship between *Arizona v. California* in lines 38–42, and the criteria citing the *Winters* doctrine in lines 10–20?

   (A) *Arizona v. California* abolishes these criteria and establishes a competing set of criteria for applying the *Winters* doctrine.

   (B) *Arizona v. California* establishes that the *Winters* doctrine applies to a broader range of situations than those defined by these criteria.

   (C) *Arizona v. California* represents the sole example of an exception to the criteria as they were set forth in the *Winters* doctrine.

   (D) *Arizona v. California* does not refer to the *Winters* doctrine to justify water rights, whereas these criteria do rely on the *Winters* doctrine.

   (E) *Arizona v. California* applies the criteria derived from the *Winters* doctrine only to federal lands other than American Indian reservations.

Inference

This question requires inferring how one part of the passage bears on another part of the passage. The two parts referred to are the criteria described in lines 10–20 and *Arizona v. California*, which is referred to in lines 38–45. *Arizona v. California* shows that the establishment of water rights need not be tied to any previous legal definition of reservation lands but may be tied to the U.S. government's practice merely of treating the land as reserved for American Indians. The criteria described in lines 10–20 apply to situations in which the land in question has been legally identified as reservation land. So *Arizona v. California* broadened the scope of *Winters* in establishing water rights.

A   The passage illustrates that *Arizona v. California* does not supersede or deny any of the criteria in lines 10–20.

B   **Correct.** The passage suggests that *practice* and not *legal definition* (lines 34–36) allows *Winters* to be applied to situations not covered by the criteria in lines 10–20.

C   In stating that *some American Indian tribes have also established water rights* by means other than the criteria in lines 10–20, the first sentence of the second paragraph makes clear that *Arizona v. California* is not the sole exception to the criteria.

D   The passage states that *Arizona v. California* does refer to *Winters*.

E   The passage illustrates that *Arizona v. California* was directly relevant to the Pueblo Indians' water rights.

The correct answer is B.

59.   The "pragmatic approach" mentioned in lines 37–38 of the passage is best defined as one that

(A)   grants recognition to reservations that were never formally established but that have traditionally been treated as such

(B)   determines the water rights of all citizens in a particular region by examining the actual history of water usage in that region

(C)   gives federal courts the right to reserve water along with land even when it is clear that the government originally intended to reserve only the land

(D)   bases the decision to recognize the legal rights of a group on the practical effect such a recognition is likely to have on other citizens

(E)   dictates that courts ignore precedents set by such cases as *Winters v. United States* in deciding what water rights belong to reserved land

Supporting ideas

This question requires recognizing what a particular phrase in the passage is referring to. The pragmatic approach the question refers to is introduced by the passage as *this* pragmatic approach. It is therefore necessary to identify which approach the passage has already referred to in this context, which in this case is contained in the sentence just prior to the reference. This sentence states that establishing what is an American Indian reservation is a matter of the U.S. government's practice and not of any formal, legal definition.

A   **Correct.** The approach referred to as *pragmatic* involves establishing American Indian reservations based not on formal law but on the government's established practice of treating the lands as such.

B   The approach referred to as *pragmatic* is not specific to establishing water rights.

C   The approach referred to as *pragmatic* is not specific to establishing water rights.

D   The approach referred to as *pragmatic* does not refer to balancing the rights of some people with rights of others.

E   The approach referred to as *pragmatic* is shown to be consistent with and supportive of the rights established by *Winters*.

The correct answer is A.

60.   The author cites the fact that the Rio Grande pueblos were never formally withdrawn from public lands primarily in order to do which of the following?

(A)   Suggest why it might have been argued that the *Winters* doctrine ought not to apply to pueblo lands

(B)   Imply that the United States never really acquired sovereignty over pueblo lands

(C)   Argue that the pueblo lands ought still to be considered part of federal public lands

(D)   Support the argument that the water rights of citizens other than American Indians are limited by the *Winters* doctrine

(E)   Suggest that federal courts cannot claim jurisdiction over cases disputing the traditional diversion and use of water by Pueblo Indians

Evaluation

Answering this question involves recognizing how a particular part of the passage functions within the passage as a whole. The passage illustrates in the first paragraph that *Winters* was cited in the establishment of water rights based on a set of criteria that included the formal withdrawal of lands by the government. In the second paragraph, the case of the Rio Grande pueblos is introduced as an example of lands that had never been formally withdrawn by the government, raising the question of whether *Winters* would still be applicable in such situations. The passage then asserts that the situation of the pueblos *has not barred* (line 33) the application of *Winters*.

A Correct. While the passage affirms the application of *Winters* to the situation with the pueblos, it recognizes that it may initially appear that *Winters* does not apply.

B The passage states explicitly that the United States did gain official sovereignty over pueblo lands in 1848, when they *became part of the United States* (lines 27–28).

C The passage states explicitly that *the pueblo lands never formally constituted a part of federal public lands* (lines 28–29) and takes no stand on the issue of whether particular lands ought to be considered public lands.

D While one can infer that the rights of other citizens to use water could be limited by reserving water rights for residents of American Indian lands according to the *Winters* doctrine, the passage takes no stand on this issue.

E The passage does not mention the rights of federal courts to claim jurisdiction over particular water rights cases.

The correct answer is A.

61. The primary purpose of the passage is to

(A) trace the development of laws establishing American Indian reservations

(B) explain the legal basis for the water rights of American Indian tribes

(C) question the legal criteria often used to determine the water rights of American Indian tribes

(D) discuss evidence establishing the earliest date at which the federal government recognized the water rights of American Indians

(E) point out a legal distinction between different types of American Indian reservations

Main idea

This question requires recognizing the main topic of the passage, which is about the establishment of water rights on American Indian lands. Its intent is to explain or describe, and it does not take sides on any issue.

A The passage is primarily about establishing water rights, not establishing reservations.

B Correct. The passage is an explanation of water rights on American Indian lands.

C The passage describes legal criteria used to establish water rights on American Indian lands but does not take issue with them.

D The passage does not discuss the earliest date for water rights on American Indian lands.

E The passage is primarily about establishing water rights, not about types of reservations.

The correct answer is B.

62. The passage suggests that the legal rights of citizens other than American Indians to the use of water flowing into the Rio Grande pueblos are

(A) guaranteed by the precedent set in *Arizona v. California*

(B) abolished by the *Winters* doctrine

(C) deferred to the Pueblo Indians whenever treaties explicitly require this

(D) guaranteed by federal land-use laws

(E) limited by the prior claims of the Pueblo Indians

Inference

Answering this question requires recognizing what the passage implies. The passage illustrates at the beginning of the second paragraph that water rights were granted to Pueblo Indians based on their use of the water in the Rio Grande pueblos prior to U.S. sovereignty. The passage also later states that since the *Winters* doctrine applies, the water rights of Pueblo Indians *have priority over other citizens' water rights as of 1848* (lines 42–44), which implies that the water rights of citizens other than Pueblo Indians are limited.

A   The passage illustrates that *Arizona v. California* reinforced the water rights of citizens residing on American Indian reservations; it does not imply a precedent ensuring water rights for other citizens.
B   The passage states that the water rights of citizens other than Pueblo Indians are lower in priority, not abolished altogether.
C   The passage does not mention that different water rights have been defined by different treaties.
D   The passage does not mention that the water rights of citizens other than Pueblo Indians are guaranteed on pueblo lands.
E   **Correct.** The passage states that the water rights of Pueblo Indians have priority over other citizens' water rights, which thereby limits the rights of those citizens.

The correct answer is E.

Questions 63–68 refer to the passage on page 392.

63.   In the passage, the author is primarily interested in

(A)   suggesting an alternative to an outdated research method
(B)   introducing a new research method that calls an accepted theory into question
(C)   emphasizing the instability of data gathered from the application of a new scientific method
(D)   presenting a theory and describing a new method to test that theory
(E)   initiating a debate about a widely accepted theory

Main idea

This question concerns the main point of the passage. A careful examination of the overall structure of the passage will reveal the main point. In the first paragraph, the author briefly presents Milankovitch's theory and explains why it could not be tested early on. In the second and third paragraphs, the author describes how a new method allows testing of the theory and shows how evidence from the testing supports the theory. While the final paragraph acknowledges that other factors should be considered, the author's primary interest in this passage is in presenting Milankovitch's theory and the recently discovered method for testing it.

A   A new research method is described, but no previous method is discussed.
B   As described in the passage, the new method tests and confirms the theory; there is no mention that the theory is accepted or that the method casts doubt on it.
C   Nothing in the passage suggests that "instability of data" is an issue.
D   **Correct.** The author presents Milankovitch's theory and describes the oxygen isotope method of testing it.
E   The theory is nowhere said to be "widely accepted" and the author does not debate the theory.

The correct answer is D.

64.   The author of the passage would be most likely to agree with which of the following statements about the Milankovitch theory?

(A)   It is the only possible explanation for the ice ages.
(B)   It is too limited to provide a plausible explanation for the ice ages, despite recent research findings.
(C)   It cannot be tested and confirmed until further research on volcanic activity is done.
(D)   It is one plausible explanation, though not the only one, for the ice ages.
(E)   It is not a plausible explanation for the ice ages, although it has opened up promising possibilities for future research.

Application

The author's reaction to the statements about the Milankovitch theory must be based on how the author treats the theory in the passage. The first, second, and third paragraphs describe the theory and the use of a new research method to test the theory. The passage states that data from these tests *have established a strong connection between variations in the Earth's orbit and the periodicity of the ice ages*, suggesting that the author of the passage believes the theory is plausible. In the final paragraph, the author points to other factors that might be involved, suggesting that the theory might not provide a complete explanation.

A   In the last paragraph, the author suggests that because there are still other untested factors that may have effects on climate, other explanations are possible.

B   Though in the last paragraph the author points to other factors that may be involved, these are not presented by the author as indicating limitations that diminish the plausibility of the theory—they are acknowledged merely as possibilities that are not now understood—and nothing else in the passage suggests that the theory is "too limited."

C   The author shows how the theory has been tested; volcanic activity is not part of this theory.

D   Correct. The author's presentation of the theory and the tests of the theory show that the author finds the theory plausible; the mention of other factors shows the author does not think that all other explanations have been ruled out, even if they are as yet untested.

E   The theory was a plausible explanation from its beginning, but it was not testable until recently; scientists would be unlikely to try to devise means to test a theory that did not strike them as antecedently plausible.

The correct answer is D.

65.   It can be inferred from the passage that the isotope record taken from ocean sediments would be less useful to researchers if which of the following were true?

(A)   It indicated that lighter isotopes of oxygen predominated at certain times.

(B)   It had far more gaps in its sequence than the record taken from rocks on land.

(C)   It indicated that climate shifts did not occur every 100,000 years.

(D)   It indicated that the ratios of oxygen 16 and oxygen 18 in ocean water were not consistent with those found in fresh water.

(E)   It stretched back for only a million years.

Inference

To make an inference about the isotope record from ocean sediments, examine what the passage says about that record. The third paragraph discusses that record and lists its two advantages. First, it is a global record with *remarkably little variation* in samples from varied locations. Second, it is *more continuous* than the record from rocks. If either of these advantages were not true, then it is logical to infer that the record would be less useful.

A   According to lines 14–16, the lighter isotope does predominate; this is part of the record and does not affect its usefulness.

B   Correct. In lines 37–42, the author states that an advantage of the ocean record is that it is *a more continuous record than that taken from rocks on land*. If this were not true, the ocean record would be less useful.

C   If the record were to show that the shifts did not occur every 100,000 years, Milankovitch's theory would be weakened. This impact on the theory does not make the isotope record less useful to researchers. The record is useful precisely because it can offer evidence to confirm or refute such theories.

D   This inconsistency would not affect the usefulness of the ocean-water record. Researchers would simply need to accommodate the fresh-water inconsistency.

E   The record would still be useful. Lines 42–46 attest to the establishment of a pattern based on data from *the past several hundred thousand years*.

The correct answer is B.

66. According to the passage, which of the following is true of the ratios of oxygen isotopes in ocean sediments?

   (A) They indicate that sediments found during an ice age contain more calcium carbonate than sediments formed at other times.

   (B) They are less reliable than the evidence from rocks on land in determining the volume of land ice.

   (C) They can be used to deduce the relative volume of land ice that was present when the sediment was laid down.

   (D) They are more unpredictable during an ice age than in other climatic conditions.

   (E) They can be used to determine atmospheric conditions at various times in the past.

Supporting ideas

The phrase *according to the passage* suggests that the answer to the question is most likely stated in the passage. Lines 12–14 state that the relative volume of land ice can be deduced from the ratio of oxygen 18 to oxygen 16 in ocean sediments.

   A   There is no evidence in the passage about this point.

   B   The ocean record is described in lines 38–39 as *more continuous*, so it is unlikely to be less reliable. In any case, reliability is not discussed.

   C   **Correct.** Lines 12–14 explain that *the land-ice volume for a given period can be deduced from the ratio of two oxygen isotopes.*

   D   There is no evidence in the passage to support this statement.

   E   The passage does not discuss the use of this record in determining past atmospheric conditions.

The correct answer is C.

67. It can be inferred from the passage that precipitation formed from evaporated ocean water has

   (A) the same isotopic ratio as ocean water

   (B) less oxygen 18 than does ocean water

   (C) less oxygen 18 than has the ice contained in continental ice sheets

   (D) a different isotopic composition than has precipitation formed from water on land

   (E) more oxygen 16 than has precipitation formed from fresh water

Inference

Any inference about precipitation from evaporated ocean water needs to be based on what the passage says. Lines 20–22 show that *heavier isotopes tend to be left behind when water evaporates from the ocean surfaces.* Therefore, the evaporated water would contain less oxygen 18 and the remaining ocean water would contain more. It is logical to infer that precipitation formed from this evaporated water would also contain less oxygen 18.

   A   Lines 20–24 explain that the water remaining in the ocean after evaporation has more oxygen 18.

   B   **Correct.** Since *the heavier isotopes tend to be left behind*, there will be less oxygen 18 in the evaporated water and in the precipitation that forms from it.

   C   The passage suggests that the ocean water evaporates and through subsequent precipitation helps form the ice sheets, so the amount of oxygen 18 in the ice sheets should be similar to the amount in the precipitation formed from the evaporated water.

   D   The passage does not discuss precipitation formed from water on land.

   E   The passage does not discuss precipitation formed from fresh water.

The correct answer is B.

68. It can be inferred from the passage that calcium carbonate shells

    (A)   are not as susceptible to deterioration as rocks

    (B)   are less common in sediments formed during an ice age

    (C)   are found only in areas that were once covered by land ice

    (D)   contain radioactive material that can be used to determine a sediment's isotopic composition

    (E)   reflect the isotopic composition of the water at the time the shells were formed

Inference

Any inference about calcium carbonate shells needs to be based on what the passage says about these shells. Lines 24–32 explain the role of these shells in forming sediments and establishing a chronology for ice ages. The shells *were constructed with oxygen atoms drawn from the surrounding ocean*. Lines 29–32 make it clear that if the sediments reveal a higher ratio of oxygen 18, it is because more oxygen 18 had been left behind when the ocean water evaporated and contributed to the growth of continental ice sheets. It can thus be inferred that the shells that make up those sediments must reflect the proportion of oxygen 18 found in the ocean water at the time they were formed.

A   The only mention of rocks in the passage is a comparison of "gappiness" of the rock and sedimentary specimen records in lines 38–39; this information does not allow any firm inference to be made with respect to relative susceptibility to deterioration, though a more continuous record might be the result of less susceptibility to deterioration.

B   The passage does not make any reference to the relative abundance of these shells during ice ages; no such inference can be drawn.

C   The only information in the passage that might support this statement is found in lines 29–32, but that information, about the correlation between oxygen ratios in sediment specimens and land ice, describes a relation that implies nothing about distributions of such specimens.

D   Though the passage does indirectly indicate that the shells contained radioactive material, nothing in the passage suggests that radioactive material is used to determine isotopic composition.

E   **Correct.** The passage explains that oxygen atoms in the surrounding water are one of the building blocks of calcium carbonate shells. The isotopic composition of the surrounding water changes during the ice age cycles, so it is logical that the isotopic composition of the shells will change depending on when they were formed.

The correct answer is E.

Questions 69–74 refer to the passage on page 394.

69. The primary purpose of the passage is to

    (A)   examine two sides of a historiographical debate

    (B)   call into question an author's approach to a historiographical debate

    (C)   examine one author's approach to a historiographical debate

    (D)   discuss two authors' works in relationship to a historiographical debate

    (E)   explain the prevalent perspective on a historiographical debate

Main idea

This question requires understanding what the passage as a whole is attempting to do. The passage opens by introducing two books published in 1984 that both concern the history of women in the United States. The passage then makes it clear that one book deals *directly* (line 14) with the issue of women's status, while the other does not. The passage then goes on to discuss the perspective that each book takes and what each book has to offer for an assessment of women's status in the eighteenth and nineteenth centuries.

A   The two books discussed in the passage do not take different sides on a particular debate but rather are described as being more or less useful to the debate itself.

B   The passage focuses on how two different books contain information useful to a particular historiographical debate but does not call into question the approach of either book.

C   The passage focuses on two authors' works, not one.

D   Correct. The passage discusses what two different books have to offer in relation to a particular historiographical debate.

E   The passage does not describe any perspective on a particular historiographical debate as being more prevalent than any other.

The correct answer is D.

70.   The author of the passage mentions the supervision of schools primarily in order to

(A)   remind readers of the role education played in the cultural changes of the nineteenth century in the United States

(B)   suggest an area in which nineteenth-century American women were relatively free to exercise power

(C)   provide an example of an occupation for which accurate data about women's participation are difficult to obtain

(D)   speculate about which occupations were considered suitable for United States women of the nineteenth century

(E)   illustrate how the answers to questions about women's status depend on particular contexts

Evaluation

Answering this question depends on understanding what role a particular piece of information plays in the passage as a whole. The author implicitly supports Lebsock's contention (beginning at line 19) that different frames of reference can produce different perspectives on the debate about women's status in the eighteenth and nineteenth centuries. The author then summarizes different contexts cited by Lebsock to support the contention about frames of reference. As part of this summary, the author refers to *supervising schools* (line 23) as an example of a job that apparently showed women losing power.

A   The passage does not discuss the role of education in the nineteenth century.

B   The passage does mention some ways in which, according to Lebsock, *women ... gained power* (line 24) in the nineteenth century, but *supervising schools* is not among them.

C   The passage does not discuss the difficulty of obtaining data about particular occupations.

D   The passage makes no judgments about the suitability for women of any jobs in the nineteenth century.

E   Correct. The passage mentions supervising schools as part of an illustration of Lebsock's claim that the debate about women's status depends on the context being examined.

The correct answer is E.

71. With which of the following characterizations of Lebsock's contribution to the controversy concerning women's status in the nineteenth-century United States would the author of the passage be most likely to agree?

    (A) Lebsock has studied women from a formerly neglected region and time period.

    (B) Lebsock has demonstrated the importance of frame of reference in answering questions about women's status.

    (C) Lebsock has addressed the controversy by using women's current status as a frame of reference.

    (D) Lebsock has analyzed statistics about occupations and property that were previously ignored.

    (E) Lebsock has applied recent historiographical methods to the biography of a nineteenth-century woman.

Supporting ideas

Answering this question requires recognizing information explicitly given in the passage. The passage introduces the work of Lebsock in line 6 and then goes on to describe several characteristics of Lebsock's book. In lines 19–21, the author introduces Lebsock's claim that the historiographical debate about women's status is dependent on frame of reference and calls that claim important; the passage then gives an example showing how frame of reference affects views of women's status. In so doing, the author displays an implicit agreement with Lebsock's discussion on this point.

A The author of the passage portrays neither the place nor time period that Lebsock focuses on as having been neglected by historians.

B Correct. The author describes as important Lebsock's idea that frame of reference informs the debate about women's status.

C According to the passage, Lebsock's book deals with women's status in the eighteenth and nineteenth centuries, not the present status of women.

D The passage does not mention or imply that Lebsock analyzed statistics in writing her book.

E Although the passage does describe Lebsock's book as pertaining to an ongoing historiographical debate, it identifies the book's topic as *women in one southern community* (lines 7–8), not the life of a single woman.

The correct answer is B.

72. According to the passage, Lebsock's work differs from Buel and Buel's work in that Lebsock's work

    (A) uses a large number of primary sources

    (B) ignores issues of women's legal status

    (C) refuses to take a position on women's status in the eighteenth century

    (D) addresses larger historiographical issues

    (E) fails to provide sufficient material to support its claims

Supporting ideas

This question asks for recognition of information contained in the passage. In the first sentence, the passage states that Buel and Buel's work and Lebsock's work have *contrasting approaches*. The passage then proceeds, using descriptions of each work's approach, to illustrate how the works differ. The passage notes that Buel and Buel's work *makes little effort* to place its biographical subject *in the context of recent historiography on women* (lines 4–6), whereas Lebsock's work attempts *to redirect two decades of historiographical debate* about women's status.

A Primary sources are not mentioned in the passage in relation to either work discussed.

B The legal status of women is not mentioned in the passage.

C Lebsock's work is described in the passage as attempting to redirect the debate about women's status in the eighteenth and nineteenth centuries.

D Correct. The passage suggests that by not placing its subject's story in the context of historiography, Buel and Buel's work does not therefore address larger historiographical issues, as Lebsock's does.

E The passage tends to support Lebsock's views and does not refer to any lack of support for the claims made in Lebsock's work.

The correct answer is D.

73. The passage suggests that Lebsock believes that compared to nineteenth-century American women, eighteenth-century American women were

    (A) in many respects less powerful in relation to men

    (B) more likely to own real estate

    (C) generally more economically independent

    (D) more independent in conducting their private lives

    (E) less likely to work as school superintendents

Inference

This question requires making an inference based on information given in the passage. As part of the passage's description of Lebsock's contribution to the historiographical debate about women's status in the eighteenth and nineteenth centuries, Lebsock's conclusions about women's autonomy are described. As part of this description, the passage cites Lebsock's conclusion that nineteenth-century women lost economic autonomy when compared to eighteenth-century women (lines 16–19).

A   The passage states that in many ways women in the nineteenth century *lost power in relation to men* (lines 21–22), which would imply that in those respects eighteenth-century women had more power in relation to men, not less. The only increase mentioned in nineteenth-century women's power is associated with owning more real estate.

B   The passage states that more nineteenth-century women owned real estate.

C   **Correct.** As the passage states, Lebsock concluded that nineteenth-century women lost economic autonomy compared to eighteenth-century women.

D   The passage states that nineteenth-century women gained more independence in their private lives.

E   The passage cites school superintendents as an example of an occupation more likely to be held by eighteenth-century women.

The correct answer is C.

74. The passage suggests that Buel and Buel's biography of Mary Fish provides evidence for which of the following views of women's history?

    (A) Women have lost power in relation to men since the colonial era.

    (B) Women of the colonial era were not as likely to be concerned with their status as were women in the nineteenth century.

    (C) The colonial era was not as favorable for women as some historians have believed.

    (D) Women had more economic autonomy in the colonial era than in the nineteenth century.

    (E) Women's occupations were generally more respected in the colonial era than in the nineteenth century.

Inference

This question requires understanding what the passage implies. The approach that Buel and Buel's work takes is specifically described in lines 3–6 and again in lines 27–32. In lines 27–30, the passage states that Buel and Buel's work *provides ample raw material for questioning the myth ... of a colonial golden age in the eighteenth century*, referring to a myth about women's status. In describing this golden age as a myth fostered by some historians, the passage suggests that this era was not as favorable to women as these historians suggest.

A   The passage describes Lebsock's work as providing such evidence, not Buel and Buel's work.

B   The passage does not pertain to the level of concern women had for their status.

C   **Correct.** The final paragraph of the passage describes Buel and Buel's work as providing material that calls into question claims that the eighteenth century was especially favorable to women.

D   The passage refers to the economic autonomy of women in relation to Lebsock's work, not Buel and Buel's work.

E   The passage does not refer to whether any particular occupations held by women were more respected at one time or another.

The correct answer is C.

Questions 75–83 refer to the passage on page 396.

75. Which of the following titles best summarizes the contents of the passage?

    (A) Neurotransmitters: Their Crucial Function in Cellular Communication
    (B) Diet and Survival: An Old Relationship Reexamined
    (C) The Blood Supply and the Brain: A Reciprocal Dependence
    (D) Amino Acids and Neurotransmitters: The Connection between Serotonin Levels and Tyrosine
    (E) The Effects of Food Intake on the Production and Release of Serotonin: Some Recent Findings

Main idea

Finding a title that best summarizes a passage requires examining the passage as a whole. This task is made easier by the fact that the second sentence of the first paragraph provides a topic sentence stating the main idea: *In recent studies, however, we have discovered that the production and release in brain neurons of the neurotransmitter serotonin … depend directly on the food that the body processes.* In the second paragraph, the authors cite the results of several studies relating neurotransmitter levels to eating meals and to injections of insulin. In the final paragraph, the authors discuss a study of the effect of a protein-rich meal on serotonin level. Thus, the correct title must show the relationship between food eaten and serotonin produced.

A   The function of neurotransmitters is only briefly mentioned.
B   The passage does not discuss the relation between diet and survival.
C   There is no discussion of blood supply and the brain.
D   While tyrosine is briefly mentioned, this was not a main focus of the studies.
E   **Correct.** This title offers a summary of the article's contents.

The correct answer is E.

76. According to the passage, the speed with which tryptophan is provided to the brain cells of a rat varies with the

    (A) amount of protein present in a meal
    (B) concentration of serotonin in the brain before a meal
    (C) concentration of leucine in the blood rather than with the concentration of tyrosine in the blood after a meal
    (D) concentration of tryptophan in the brain before a meal
    (E) number of serotonin-containing neurons

Supporting ideas

The phrase *according to the passage* suggests that the answer is likely stated in the passage. Look at the third paragraph, which discusses variations in the speed with which tryptophan is provided to the brain. Lines 41–44 state *the more protein is in a meal … the more slowly is tryptophan provided to the brain.*

A   **Correct.** The greater the amount of protein, the more slowly tryptophan is provided.
B   The relationship is not discussed in the passage, although the concentration of serotonin *after* a meal is measured.
C   While leucine and tyrosine are mentioned, their concentrations in the blood are not compared.
D   This relationship is not discussed in the passage, although the concentration of tryptophan *after* a meal is measured.
E   The researchers do not consider the number of neurons.

The correct answer is A.

77. According to the passage, when the authors began their first studies, they were aware that

   (A) they would eventually need to design experiments that involved feeding rats high concentrations of protein

   (B) tryptophan levels in the blood were difficult to monitor with accuracy

   (C) serotonin levels increased after rats were fed meals rich in tryptophan

   (D) there were many neurotransmitters whose production was dependent on metabolic processes elsewhere in the body

   (E) serotonin levels increased after rats were injected with a large amount of tryptophan

Supporting ideas

The phrase *according to the passage* suggests that the answer is likely stated in the passage. Look at the first sentence of the second paragraph where the focus of the authors' *first studies* is explained. The investigators wanted to see if an increase in serotonin levels would be observed after rats ate meals that changed tryptophan levels in the blood. Earlier research had already established that injecting tryptophan increased serotonin levels.

A   The authors' decision to add protein came later in their studies, after they had seen the effects of eating in general.

B   The passage does not identify any problems with monitoring tryptophan levels in the blood.

C   This was the hypothesis of the first experiment, so the authors could not have known it beforehand.

D   This point is irrelevant to the authors' work; only one neurotransmitter, serotonin, is discussed.

E   **Correct.** Lines 9–12 show that this increase had already been observed.

The correct answer is E.

78. According to the passage, one reason that the authors gave rats carbohydrates was to

   (A) depress the rats' tryptophan levels

   (B) prevent the rats from contracting diseases

   (C) cause the rats to produce insulin

   (D) demonstrate that insulin is the most important substance secreted by the body

   (E) compare the effect of carbohydrates with the effect of proteins

Supporting ideas

The phrase *according to the passage* suggests that the answer is likely stated in the passage. Look at lines 22–26, which say *We then decided to see whether the secretion of the animal's own insulin similarly affected serotonin production. We gave the rats a carbohydrate-containing meal that we knew would elicit insulin secretion.* These sentences together show that the authors gave carbohydrates to the rats to cause the rats to secrete insulin.

A   Lines 26–29 show that the carbohydrate increased the blood tryptophan level.

B   Preventing disease was not part of the study.

C   **Correct.** The authors had already tried injecting insulin; they then gave the rats carbohydrates to stimulate insulin production.

D   The authors make no such claim about insulin.

E   The study involving protein came later, so this could not have been the reason for giving the rats carbohydrates.

The correct answer is C.

79. According to the passage, the more protein a rat consumes, the lower will be the

    (A) ratio of the rat's blood-tryptophan concentration to the amount of serotonin produced and released in the rat's brain

    (B) ratio of the rat's blood-tryptophan concentration to the concentration in its blood of the other amino acids contained in the protein

    (C) ratio of the rat's blood-tyrosine concentration to its blood-leucine concentration

    (D) number of neurotransmitters of any kind that the rat will produce and release

    (E) number of amino acids the rat's blood will contain

Supporting ideas

The phrase *according to the passage* suggests that the answer is likely stated in the passage. In lines 41–43, the authors state: *The more protein is in a meal, the lower is the ratio of the resulting blood-tryptophan concentration to the concentration of competing amino acids* ....

A   While lower levels of blood-tryptophan lead to lower serotonin levels, the relationship is not discussed in terms of a ratio.

B   Correct. Lines 41–43 show this to be the correct answer choice.

C   This relationship is not demonstrated in the passage.

D   This point is not made in the passage.

E   Lines 38–40 explain that *consumption of protein increases blood concentration of the other amino acids much more* .... Since proteins are made up of amino acids, eating protein would logically increase the number of amino acids.

The correct answer is B.

80. The authors' discussion of the "mechanism that provides blood tryptophan to the brain cells" (lines 34–35) is meant to

    (A) stimulate further research studies

    (B) summarize an area of scientific investigation

    (C) help explain why a particular research finding was obtained

    (D) provide supporting evidence for a controversial scientific theory

    (E) refute the conclusions of a previously mentioned research study

Logical structure

To find the purpose of this discussion, look at the context in which this reference occurs. At the beginning of the third paragraph, the authors note that, *surprisingly*, adding protein led to lower brain tryptophan and serotonin levels. The question is why were the levels lowered? *The answer lies* in the mechanism cited in lines 34–35. Therefore, the discussion of the mechanism is meant to explain a surprising research finding.

A   No further studies are mentioned.

B   There are summaries of several studies, but there is no summary of an entire area of scientific investigation.

C   Correct. The mechanism helps explain the surprising finding about lower brain tryptophan and serotonin levels.

D   No theory is advanced, nor is any evidence about it provided.

E   There is no attempt to refute any other study.

The correct answer is C.

81. According to the passage, an injection of insulin was most similar in its effect on rats to an injection of

    (A) tyrosine
    (B) leucine
    (C) blood
    (D) tryptophan
    (E) protein

Supporting ideas

Since the question refers to information given in the passage, the answer can be found by careful reading. In order to find an injection with a similar effect, look first at the effect of injecting insulin. In lines 20–22, the authors state that *injecting insulin … caused parallel elevations in blood and brain tryptophan levels and in serotonin levels.* The only other reference to injection occurs earlier in lines 10–13 where rats injected with tryptophan had increased serotonin levels; injecting tryptophan would obviously cause tryptophan levels to increase. Thus, the effects of injecting insulin were similar to the effects of injecting tryptophan.

A   No evidence suggests that tyrosine injection would have similar effects.
B   The studies did not involve injecting leucine.
C   The studies did not involve injecting blood.
D   **Correct.** According to the passage, injecting tryptophan raises serotonin and tryptophan levels just as injecting insulin does.
E   The studies involved eating protein, not injecting it; eating protein did not raise serotonin levels.

The correct answer is D.

82. It can be inferred from the passage that which of the following would be LEAST likely to be a potential source of aid to a patient who was not adequately producing and releasing serotonin?

    (A) Meals consisting almost exclusively of protein
    (B) Meals consisting almost exclusively of carbohydrates
    (C) Meals that would elicit insulin secretion
    (D) Meals that had very low concentrations of tyrosine
    (E) Meals that had very low concentrations of leucine

Inference

Since this question asks for an inference, the answer is not directly stated in the passage; it must instead be derived from the information given. What kind of meals would NOT help a patient with low serotonin levels? Meals that increased serotonin would help the patient; meals that lowered serotonin would not. According to the last sentence in the passage, *the more protein in a meal, the less serotonin subsequently produced and released.* Therefore, high-protein meals would be LEAST likely to help the patient.

A   **Correct.** Meals with very high levels of protein would tend to lower serotonin and thus to be less beneficial for the patient with inadequate serotonin levels.
B   When rats ate a carbohydrate-containing meal, serotonin increased (lines 25–29). Therefore, these meals would tend to raise serotonin levels and so help the patient.
C   In the study, meals that elicited insulin secretion raised serotonin levels.
D   Since tyrosine is an amino acid found in protein, meals low in tyrosine would be low in protein and so would tend to raise serotonin levels and help the patient.
E   Since leucine is an amino acid found in protein, meals low in leucine would be low in protein and so would tend to raise serotonin levels and help the patient.

The correct answer is A.

83. It can be inferred from the passage that the authors initially held which of the following hypotheses about what would happen when they fed large amounts of protein to rats?

   (A) The rats' brain serotonin levels would not decrease.
   (B) The rats' brain tryptophan levels would decrease.
   (C) The rats' tyrosine levels would increase less quickly than would their leucine levels.
   (D) The rats would produce more insulin.
   (E) The rats would produce neurotransmitters other than serotonin.

Inference

When the authors discuss the results of adding protein to meals, they begin with the word *surprisingly* (line 30). The use of this word indicates that the results differed from the authors' initial hypotheses. The results showed lowered serotonin. It is reasonable to conclude that the researchers initially hypothesized that serotonin levels would not decrease.

A **Correct.** The use of the word *surprisingly* in line 30 suggests that researchers thought serotonin levels would not decrease.
B The researchers had expected that tryptophan levels would not decrease, *since protein contains tryptophan* (lines 32–34).
C Since there is no discussion of the comparative levels of tyrosine and leucine, there was probably no hypothesis about these levels.
D In the passage insulin is explicitly discussed in relation to carbohydrates, and plays no role at all in the discussion of protein; this very strongly suggests that insulin production played no role in the authors' decision to feed the rats large amounts of protein.
E Serotonin is the only neurotransmitter discussed in the research, so it is unlikely that the researchers had an initial hypothesis involving other neurotransmitters.

The correct answer is A.

Questions 84–86 refer to the passage on page 398.

84. The passage suggests that WIDC differed from WTUL in which of the following ways?

   (A) WIDC believed that the existing safety regulations were adequate to protect women's health, whereas WTUL believed that such regulations needed to be strengthened.
   (B) WIDC believed that unions could not succeed in pressuring employers to comply with such regulations, whereas WTUL believed that unions could succeed in doing so.
   (C) WIDC believed that lead poisoning in white lead factories could be avoided by controlling conditions there, whereas WTUL believed that lead poisoning in such factories could not be avoided no matter how stringently safety regulations were enforced.
   (D) At the time that the legislation concerning white lead factories was proposed, WIDC was primarily concerned with addressing health conditions in white lead factories, whereas WTUL was concerned with improving working conditions in all types of factories.
   (E) At the time that WIDC was opposing legislative attempts to restrict women's labor, WTUL had already ceased to do so.

Inference

To answer this question you need to understand the differences between WIDC and WTUL as they are described in the passage. The only information about WTUL in the passage is that it had stopped opposing restrictions on women's labor in the late 1880s, and that, because existing safety regulations were not being enforced, it supported the proposal to prohibit women from working in white lead factories. WIDC, on the other hand, was formed in 1892 specifically to oppose restrictions on women's labor, and it opposed the proposal.

A   According to the passage, WIDC did believe that existing safety regulations, if enforced, could prevent lead poisoning. WTUL may or may not have believed that the safety regulations needed to be strengthened; all the passage states is that WTUL did not believe that the safety regulations were likely to be enforced.

B   The passage states that WTUL believed that because there were no unions to pressure employers, the employers would not comply with safety regulations. The passage does not present any information on which to base a conclusion about WIDC's beliefs regarding union pressure on employers.

C   Based on information in the passage, both WIDC and SPEW believed that enforcing safety regulations could protect women against lead poisoning. WIDC supported SPEW's position on the matter. WTUL believed that safety regulations were unlikely to be enforced because of the lack of unions.

D   The passage states that WIDC viewed the proposal to restrict women's employment in white lead factories as an instance of legislation designed to limit women's work opportunities—precisely the legislation that WIDC was formed to oppose. Thus, WIDC was not primarily concerned with the factories' health conditions.

E   **Correct.** WIDC began opposing legislative attempts to restrict women's labor in 1892 and continued to do so through at least 1895, when the Home Secretary proposed prohibiting women from working in white lead factories. WTUL stopped opposing restrictions on women's labor in the late 1880s, before WIDC was even founded. Thus, the passage suggests that WTUL had stopped opposing restrictions on women's labor well before WIDC worked to oppose such legislation.

The correct answer is E.

85. Which of the following, if true, would most clearly support the contention attributed to SPEW in lines 17–20?

(A)   Those white lead factories that most strongly enforced regulations concerning worker safety and hygiene had the lowest incidences of lead poisoning among employees.

(B)   The incidence of lead poisoning was much higher among women who worked in white lead factories than among women who worked in other types of factories.

(C)   There were many household sources of lead that could have contributed to the incidence of lead poisoning among women who also worked outside the home in the late nineteenth century.

(D)   White lead factories were more stringent than were certain other types of factories in their enforcement of workplace safety regulations.

(E)   Even brief exposure to the conditions typically found in white lead factories could cause lead poisoning among factory workers.

Evaluation

This question requires the reader to find a statement that would provide additional support for the contention made in the following statement: *SPEW contended, and WIDC concurred, that controllable conditions in such factories were responsible for the development of lead poisoning.* Information suggesting that when conditions were controlled, lead poisoning was less likely to develop would provide support for SPEW's contention.

A   **Correct.** If incidences of lead poisoning were low in those factories that enforced hygiene and safety regulations, that would suggest that lead poisoning was not an inevitable result of working in a white lead factory—but rather that lead poisoning was the result of poor hygiene and safety practices.

B   It would not be particularly surprising for the incidence of lead poisoning to be higher among women working in white lead factories than among women working in other kinds of factories—but such a finding would say nothing about whether controllable conditions had any effect on the development of lead poisoning.

C   The existence of household sources of lead that might contribute to lead poisoning would weaken, not support, SPEW's contention that controllable factory conditions were responsible for the development of lead poisoning.

D   If white lead factories enforced workplace safety regulations more stringently than did some other types of factories, it might be the case that SPEW's contention was incorrect: that even controlled conditions could not prevent a high incidence of lead poisoning.

E   If the conditions typically found in white lead factories were particularly bad with regard to safety and hygiene, it could conceivably be the case that SPEW's contention was true—that is, that the conditions that caused lead poisoning were controllable. But it might also be the case that an uncontrollable aspect of those conditions caused lead poisoning. Thus, this neither supports nor undermines SPEW's contention clearly.

The correct answer is A.

86.   The passage is primarily concerned with

(A)   presenting various groups' views of the motives of those proposing certain legislation

(B)   contrasting the reasoning of various groups concerning their positions on certain proposed legislation

(C)   tracing the process whereby certain proposed legislation was eventually enacted

(D)   assessing the success of tactics adopted by various groups with respect to certain proposed legislation

(E)   evaluating the arguments of various groups concerning certain proposed legislation

Main idea

Answering this question depends on identifying the overall point of the passage. The passage is mainly concerned with explaining the reasons behind the positions taken by WIDC and SPEW, which opposed the proposal to enact legislation prohibiting women from holding most white lead factory jobs, and the reasoning of WTUL, which supported the proposal.

A   The passage explains how WIDC viewed the proposal, but it does not indicate what any of the groups believed about the motivations of the Home Secretary, who made the proposal.

B   Correct. The passage contrasts the reasoning of the WIDC and SPEW, both of which believed that enforcing safety regulations would make the proposed legislation unnecessary, with the reasoning of WTUL, which thought that safety regulations were unlikely to be enforced and thus supported the proposal.

C   The passage simply states that the proposal was eventually enacted; it does not trace the process by which this occurred.

D   The passage implies that WIDC and SPEW were unsuccessful in their opposition to the proposed legislation, but it identifies only one tactic used in opposition to it: SPEW's attempt to challenge it by investigating the causes of lead poisoning.

E   The passage does not evaluate the groups' arguments concerning the proposed legislation; rather, it presents those arguments without comment on their quality or value.

The correct answer is B.

Questions 87–92 refer to the passage on page 400.

87.   The primary purpose of the passage is to

(A)   evaluate a research study

(B)   summarize the history of a research area

(C)   report new research findings

(D)   reinterpret old research findings

(E)   reconcile conflicting research findings

Main idea

Determining the primary purpose comes from examining what the author does in the entire passage. In the first paragraph, the author explains Duverger's work on women's electoral participation. In the second paragraph the author points out both the successes and failures of that work. The purpose of this passage, then, is to evaluate Duverger's study.

A   **Correct.** The author evaluates Duverger's study of women's electoral activities.
B   This passage examines only one research study, not an entire research area.
C   Duverger's work was published in 1955; its findings are not new.
D   The author explains and evaluates Duverger's findings but does not reinterpret them.
E   The author's discussion of Duverger's work does not reveal or attempt to reconcile conflicting findings.

The correct answer is A.

88.   According to the passage, Duverger's study was unique in 1955 in that it

(A)   included both election data and survey data

(B)   gathered data from sources never before used in political studies

(C)   included an analysis of historical processes

(D)   examined the influence on voting behavior of the relationships between women and men

(E)   analyzed not only voting and political candidacy but also other political activities

Supporting ideas

This question is based on information specifically stated in the first sentence of the passage. The author introduces Duverger's work by calling it the first study of *women's electoral participation ever to use election data and survey data together* (lines 3–5).

A   **Correct.** Duverger's work was unique because it used election data and survey data together.
B   The two data types had never before been used together in such a study; they may well have been used separately in many earlier political studies.
C   The second paragraph states that Duverger placed his findings in the context of historical processes, but not that he was unique in doing so (lines 15–17).
D   Duverger compared the frequency and direction of voting between men and women, not the effect that their relationships had on voting (line 27).
E   Duverger's work analyzed political activism, but the author does not claim that it was unique in doing so (lines 5–6).

The correct answer is A.

89.   Which of the following characteristics of a country is most clearly an example of a factor that Duverger, as described in the passage, failed to consider in his study?

(A)   A large population

(B)   A predominantly Protestant population

(C)   A predominantly urban population

(D)   A one-party government

(E)   Location in the heart of Europe

Inference

In the second paragraph, the author notes Duverger's *failure to consider … the influence of political regimes, the effects of economic factors, and the ramifications of political and social relations between women and men* (lines 22–27). This question requires checking this list from the passage against the possible answers; the only point of convergence is the system of government. A system of government in which there is only one political party is a type of political regime.

A   The author does not say that Duverger failed to consider the size of the population.
B   No evidence shows that Duverger failed to consider the predominance of a religion.
C   The author does not say that Duverger failed to consider the location of the population.
D   Correct. According to the author of the passage, Duverger failed to consider *the influence of political regimes.*
E   Duverger is not faulted for failing to consider the location of the countries that he studied.

The correct answer is D.

90.   The author implies that Duverger's actual findings are

(A)   limited because they focus on only four countries
(B)   inaccurate in their description of the four countries in the early 1950s
(C)   out-of-date in that they are inapplicable in the four countries today
(D)   flawed because they are based on unsound data
(E)   biased by Duverger's political beliefs

Inference

Since the question uses the word *implies*, the answer involves making an inference based on the information in the text. The second paragraph evaluates Duverger's work. The author notes that Duverger *placed his findings in the context of many of the historical processes.* Because these contexts have changed since 1955, the author holds that *Duverger's approach has proved more durable than his actual findings.* The actual findings, then, are out-of-date and irrelevant to the countries today.

A   The limitations the author brings up in the second paragraph have no connection to the number of countries studied.
B   The limitations the author brings up in the second paragraph do not suggest that the findings were inaccurate; rather, they were, in the author's view, significantly incomplete.

C   **Correct.** The actual findings, unlike the research method, are out-of-date and inapplicable today.
D   The limitations the author brings up in the second paragraph do not suggest that Duverger's data were unsound; rather, in the author's view, they were incomplete and have become dated.
E   The limitations the author brings up in the second paragraph do not suggest that Duverger's findings were politically biased; rather, in the author's view, they did not take full enough account of politics.

The correct answer is C.

91.   The passage implies that, in comparing four European countries, Duverger found that the voting rates of women and men were most different in the country in which women

(A)   were most politically active
(B)   ran for office most often
(C)   held the most conservative political views
(D)   had the most egalitarian relations with men
(E)   had possessed the right to vote for the shortest time

Inference

The comparison of voting rates is discussed at the end of the first paragraph and forms the basis for the required inference. Duverger found that *women voted somewhat less frequently than men* but that this difference narrowed *the longer the women had the vote* (lines 9–11). That is, there was an ongoing process of convergence in voting rates for women and men, as the time period for which women had the vote lengthened. This suggests that at one end, when women had been voting for the shortest time, voting rates were most dissimilar, and at the other end, when women had been voting for the longest time, the rates were most similar.

A   Women's political activism is not suggested as a reason for the difference.

B   Women's political candidacy is not suggested as a reason for the difference.

C   Women's political views are not suggested as a reason for the difference.

D   Women's egalitarian relations with men are not suggested as a reason for the difference.

E   **Correct.** Duverger's finding is of (apparently steady, ongoing) convergence in voting-frequency rates between women and men over time. This supports the inference that the shorter the time period, the less convergence—i.e., the more divergence—there is in voting-frequency rates.

The correct answer is E.

92.   The author implies that some behavioralist research involving the multinational study of women's political participation that followed Duverger's study did which of the following?

(A)   Ignored Duverger's approach

(B)   Suffered from faults similar to those in Duverger's study

(C)   Focused on political activism

(D)   Focused on the influences of political regimes

(E)   Focused on the political and social relations between women and men

Inference

The final sentence of the passage links Duverger's study to behavioralist work in general. After noting Duverger's failure to consider several important elements, the author observes, *Duverger's study foreshadowed the enduring limitations of the behavioralist approach to the multinational study of women's political participation* (lines 28–31). Thus, it is reasonable to infer that the author is of the opinion that the behavioralist research that followed Duverger's study suffered from the same limitations.

A   The author does not imply that other behavioralists ignored Duverger's approach.

B   **Correct.** The author says that Duverger's work revealed the *enduring limitations* also found in later behavioralist research.

C   This is not obviously a limitation at all, let alone one that Duverger's study suffered from.

D   This is not obviously a limitation at all, let alone one that Duverger's study suffered from.

E   This is not obviously a limitation at all, let alone one that Duverger's study suffered from.

The correct answer is B.

Questions 93–98 refer to the passage on page 402.

93.   According to the passage, senior managers use intuition in all of the following ways EXCEPT to

(A)   speed up the creation of a solution to a problem

(B)   identify a problem

(C)   bring together disparate facts

(D)   stipulate clear goals

(E)   evaluate possible solutions to a problem

Supporting ideas

To answer this question, look for information explicitly stated in the passage. The third paragraph of the passage describes the five ways that senior managers use intuition. To find the one way that is NOT described, go back to the paragraph and check the possible answers against the list of the ways provided in the paragraph. The list includes all the answer choices except stipulating clear goals.

A   Lines 39–40 state that intuition allows managers to *move rapidly to engender a plausible solution.*

B   Lines 22–23 explain that managers use intuition to *sense when a problem exists.*

C   Lines 28–29 say the third function of intuition is to *synthesize isolated bits of data and practice into an integrated picture.*

D   **Correct.** Stipulating clear goals is not linked with managers' use of intuition.

E   Lines 30–38 show that managers use intuition *as a check on the results of more rational analysis,* when they are *leery of solutions suggested by these methods.*

The correct answer is D.

94. The passage suggests which of the following about the "writers on management" mentioned in line 12?

   (A) They have criticized managers for not following the classical rational model of decision analysis.

   (B) They have not based their analyses on a sufficiently large sample of actual managers.

   (C) They have relied in drawing their conclusions on what managers say rather than on what managers do.

   (D) They have misunderstood how managers use intuition in making business decisions.

   (E) They have not acknowledged the role of intuition in managerial practice.

Inference

Answering this question depends on making an inference from the passage. The second paragraph dismisses most *writers on management* for displaying *a poor grasp of what intuition is* (line 15). The third paragraph, in contrast, describes Isenberg's research, which shows that *senior managers use intuition in at least five distinct ways* (lines 21–22), and those ways are then discussed in more detail. It can be inferred that Isenberg understands what most *writers on management* do not: how managers use intuition in making business decisions.

A The passage does not link these writers with such a critique of managers.

B No mention is made in the passage of the writers' methods.

C The passage does not indicate that the writers have examined words at the expense of actions.

D Correct. According to the passage, the writers do not understand what intuition is or how managers apply it.

E According to lines 12–15, the writers have acknowledged that *some practicing managers rely heavily on intuition*, but the writers fail to understand how or why.

The correct answer is D.

95. Which of the following best exemplifies "an 'Aha!' experience" (line 30) as it is presented in the passage?

   (A) A manager risks taking an action whose outcome is unpredictable to discover whether the action changes the problem at hand.

   (B) A manager performs well-learned and familiar behavior patterns in creative and uncharacteristic ways to solve a problem.

   (C) A manager suddenly connects seemingly unrelated facts and experiences to create a pattern relevant to the problem at hand.

   (D) A manager rapidly identifies the methodology used to compile data yielded by systematic analysis.

   (E) A manager swiftly decides which of several sets of tactics to implement in order to deal with the contingencies suggested by a problem.

Application

Finding an example involves applying the information in the passage to new situations. How do managers reach *an "Aha!" experience*? Lines 28–29 clearly explain that this experience is the result of the managers' ability *to synthesize isolated bits of data and practice into an integrated picture*. Managers connect apparently unrelated pieces of information and elements of their previous experience, and, through these unexpected connections, produce a unified picture or pattern.

A This managerial style is mentioned in the last paragraph, but not as defining the *"Aha!" experience*.

B Lines 23–27 indicate that managers use intuition *to perform well-learned behavior patterns rapidly*, but the result is not an *"Aha!" experience*.

C Correct. Through an intuitive appreciation of the subtle interrelationships of disparate facts and experiences, the manager all at once perceives the coherent overarching pattern or picture formed by the interconnections, which lines 28–29 define as an *"Aha!" experience*.

D Lines 34–38 show that managers do possess this ability, but it does not culminate in an *"Aha!" experience*.

E This managerial style is also related to the second function of intuition, *to perform well-learned behavior patterns rapidly* (lines 23–27), but does not define an *"Aha!" experience*.

The correct answer is C.

96. According to the passage, the classical model of decision analysis includes all of the following EXCEPT

   (A) evaluation of a problem
   (B) creation of possible solutions to a problem
   (C) establishment of clear goals to be reached by the decision
   (D) action undertaken in order to discover more information about a problem
   (E) comparison of the probable effects of different solutions to a problem

Supporting ideas

What does the passage say about the classical model of decision analysis? The first sentence defines the classical model as *clarifying goals, assessing the problem, formulating options, estimating likelihoods of success, making a decision, and only then taking action to implement the decision.* To solve this process-of-elimination question, check the given list against the possible answers in order to find the one that does not match. Note that the exact wording in the answers may differ from that in the passage; the match is based on underlying meaning.

A   Evaluating a problem is identified as *assessing the problem.*
B   Creating solutions is identified as *formulating options.*
C   Establishing goals is identified as *clarifying goals.*
D   **Correct.** Acting in order to learn more about the problem is not identified in the passage as part of the rational classical model. It does appear as part of the acting/thinking cycle in the last paragraph.
E   Comparing probable effects is identified as *estimating likelihoods of success.*

The correct answer is D.

97. It can be inferred from the passage that which of the following would most probably be one major difference in behavior between Manager X, who uses intuition to reach decisions, and Manager Y, who uses only formal decision analysis?

   (A) Manager X analyzes first and then acts; Manager Y does not.
   (B) Manager X checks possible solutions to a problem by systematic analysis; Manager Y does not.
   (C) Manager X takes action in order to arrive at the solution to a problem; Manager Y does not.
   (D) Manager Y draws on years of hands-on experience in creating a solution to a problem; Manager X does not.
   (E) Manager Y depends on day-to-day tactical maneuvering; Manager X does not.

Application

To answer this question, apply the information in the passage to the specific examples of Manager X, an intuitive decision maker, and Manager Y, who relies exclusively on formal decision analysis. The first paragraph distinguishes between the process of formal decision analysis, in which a decision is made and then action is taken (lines 4–5), and the process of intuition, in which action is integrated into the process of thinking (lines 10–11). The last paragraph reinforces the definition of the intuitive manager as one for whom *"thinking" is inseparable from acting* and *action is often part of defining the problem.* Manager X is likely to act as part of the process of solving a problem, but Manager Y is not.

A   Acting only after analysis characterizes the rational model, not intuition.
B   Systematic analysis is typical of the rational model, not intuition.
C   **Correct.** An intuitive manager acts as a step within the problem-solving process, but a manager who depends on formal decision analysis acts only after making a decision.
D   Drawing on experience is linked in the passage with intuition rather than with rational analysis; the passage does not suggest that managers who use formal decision analysis would ignore their experience in so doing.

E   Day-to-day tactical maneuvers are required of all managers.

The correct answer is C.

98.   The passage provides support for which of the following statements?

(A)   Managers who rely on intuition are more successful than those who rely on formal decision analysis.

(B)   Managers cannot justify their intuitive decisions.

(C)   Managers' intuition works contrary to their rational and analytical skills.

(D)   Logical analysis of a problem increases the number of possible solutions.

(E)   Intuition enables managers to employ their practical experience more efficiently.

Logical structure

This question asks the reader to select the statement for which there is the most justification in the passage. The entire passage places value on the use of intuition, so the answer to this question is bound to show a benefit of intuition. Lines 25–27 reveal that intuition is based on *years of painstaking practice and hands-on experience* and lines 38–40 explain that, in contrast to formal decision analysis, intuition allows managers to *move rapidly to engender a plausible solution*. Thus, intuition enables managers to apply their experience quickly and productively, that is, efficiently.

A   The first paragraph acknowledges that most successful managers are intuitive, but it does not go so far as to make this comparison.

B   There is no support for or against this statement in the passage; Isenberg's research shows why intuition is beneficial, but does not address how managers justify their decisions.

C   Intuition does not compete with rational analysis, but complements it; line 25 provides an assurance that intuition is *not arbitrary or irrational.*

D   The passage does not support this claim for logical analysis.

E   **Correct.** Managers can reach decisions more efficiently through an intuitive approach based on experience than through time-consuming formal analyses.

The correct answer is E.

Questions 99–103 refer to the passage on page 404.

99.   The passage is primarily concerned with

(A)   identifying two practices in medical research that may affect the accuracy of clinical trials

(B)   describing aspects of medical research that tend to drive up costs

(C)   evaluating an analysis of certain shortcomings of current medical research practices

(D)   describing proposed changes to the ways in which clinical trials are conducted

(E)   explaining how medical researchers have traditionally conducted clinical trials and how such trials are likely to change

Main idea

This question requires an understanding of what the passage as a whole is doing. The passage introduces Frazier and Mosteller as proposing changes to the ways clinical trials in medical research are currently conducted. The rest of the passage then describes these proposed changes together with the support Frazier and Mosteller provide for adopting these changes.

A   The passage identifies practices in medical research to help illustrate the basis for Frazier and Mosteller's proposed changes.

B   The passage mentions medical research costs as one example within the larger description of Frazier and Mosteller's proposed changes.

C   The passage is not concerned with evaluating Frazier and Mosteller's proposed changes.

D   **Correct.** The passage describes the changes proposed by Frazier and Mosteller to the way clinical trials are conducted.

E   The passage is not concerned with establishing the likelihood of any changes to the way medical research is conducted.

The correct answer is D.

100. Which of the following can be inferred from the passage about a study of the category of patients referred to in lines 21–23?

   (A) Its findings might have limited applicability.

   (B) It would be prohibitively expensive in its attempt to create ideal conditions.

   (C) It would be the best way to sample the total population of potential patients.

   (D) It would allow researchers to limit information collection without increasing the risk that important variables could be overlooked.

   (E) Its findings would be more accurate if it concerned treatments for a progressive disease than if it concerned treatments for a nonprogressive disease.

Inference

This question requires drawing an inference from information given in the passage. In describing the proposals put forth by Frazier and Mosteller, the passage states in lines 16–21 that they propose using more patients in clinical trials than are currently being used, and that the trials would thereby obtain *a more representative sample of the total population with the disease under study.* The passage then states that researchers often *restrict* (lines 21–23) their trials to certain types of patients, therefore limiting the applicability of their findings.

   A   Correct. The passage states that the researchers preferred to restrict the types of patients used in their studies, thereby using a less representative sample than if they used a more inclusive group of patients.

   B   The passage mentions the added expense of clinical trials only in relation to data storage, collection, and analysis.

   C   The passage describes the category of patients referred to as restricted and therefore unrepresentative of the total population.

   D   While the passage does mention the amount of data collected about an individual patient, that topic is not connected to the category of patients referred to in lines 21–23.

   E   The passage does not suggest that a study using the category of patients referred to would be more effective in investigating progressive diseases.

The correct answer is A.

101. It can be inferred from the passage that a study limited to patients like those mentioned in lines 21–23 would have which of the following advantages over the kind of study proposed by Frazier and Mosteller?

   (A) It would yield more data and its findings would be more accurate.

   (B) It would cost less in the long term, though it would be more expensive in its initial stages.

   (C) It would limit the number of variables researchers would need to consider when evaluating the treatment under study.

   (D) It would help researchers to identify subgroups of patients with secondary conditions that might also be treatable.

   (E) It would enable researchers to assess the value of an experimental treatment for the average patient.

Inference

This question requires understanding what the information in the passage implies. The passage explains that Frazier and Mosteller's proposal involves enrolling more patients in clinical trials (lines 18–19) than is the case with the category of patients referred to. The passage then explains that broadening the range of trial participants would allow an evaluation of particular treatments *under various conditions* and *for different patient subgroups* (lines 29–30). This strongly suggests that limiting the patients used to those described in the referred text would limit the number of variables researchers would need to consider.

   A   The passage suggests that not limiting the patients used in clinical trials will yield more data than restricting them will.

   B   The passage refers to the costs of clinical trials only as it concerns the collection, storage, and analysis of data collected from participants.

C   **Correct.** By limiting the patients used to those having the ailment under study, the passage suggests that researchers need to consider fewer variables in their assessment of a treatment.

D   The passage suggests that *not* limiting the types of patients used in clinical trials will better allow researchers to evaluate subgroups.

E   The passage suggests that limiting the types of patients available for clinical trials results in data for specific, rather than average, populations.

The correct answer is C.

102. The author mentions patients' ages (line 33) primarily in order to

(A)   identify the most critical variable differentiating subgroups of patients

(B)   cast doubt on the advisability of implementing Frazier and Mosteller's proposals about medical research

(C)   indicate why progressive diseases may require different treatments at different stages

(D)   illustrate a point about the value of enrolling a wide range of patients in clinical trials

(E)   substantiate an argument about the problems inherent in enrolling large numbers of patients in clinical trials

Evaluation

Answering this question requires understanding how a particular piece of information functions in the passage as a whole. The passage is concerned with describing the proposals of Frazier and Mosteller. One of these proposals, described in the second paragraph, involves broadening the range of participants used in clinical trials. The passage states that in following this proposal, Frazier and Mosteller suggest that the effectiveness of treatments can be assessed for different patient subgroups. To affirm the value of broadening the range of participants, the passage then cites two examples of criteria by which relevant subgroups might be identified: disease stages and patients' ages.

A   The passage makes no judgment as to the value of the subgroups it refers to in relation to broadened participation in clinical trials.

B   The passage does not call into question the potential effectiveness of Frazier and Mosteller's proposals.

C   The passage's example of patients' ages is not intended to be causally connected to its previous example regarding progressive diseases.

D   **Correct.** Patients' ages are referred to in the passage to identify subgroups that could be evaluated if the range of participants in clinical trials were broadened.

E   The passage refers to patients' ages in support of Frazier and Mosteller's proposal that more patients be used in clinical trials.

The correct answer is D.

103. According to the passage, which of the following describes a result of the way in which researchers generally conduct clinical trials?

(A)   They expend resources on the storage of information likely to be irrelevant to the study they are conducting.

(B)   They sometimes compromise the accuracy of their findings by collecting and analyzing more information than is strictly required for their trials.

(C)   They avoid the risk of overlooking variables that might affect their findings, even though doing so raises their research costs.

(D)   Because they attempt to analyze too much information, they overlook facts that could emerge as relevant to their studies.

(E)   In order to approximate the conditions typical of medical treatment, they base their methods of information collection on those used by hospitals.

Supporting ideas

This question asks for an identification of specific information given in the passage. The passage describes the proposals of Frazier and Mosteller as attempting to improve the way clinical trials have generally been conducted. In describing how current trials are generally conducted, the passage states that researchers collect *far more background information on patients than is strictly required for their trials* (lines 4–6) and that they therefore escalate the costs of the trials.

A   **Correct.** The passage states that researchers generally collect more information than they need to perform their clinical trials, which drives up the costs of the trials.
B   The passage makes no judgment about the accuracy of the information collected by researchers who currently hold clinical trials.
C   The passage states that the risk of overlooking relevant information in clinical trials is *never entirely eliminable* (lines 11–12).
D   The passage states that researchers generally collect more information than is relevant, not that they overlook relevant information.
E   The passage states that, in general, researchers currently collect more information than hospitals do (line 6).

The correct answer is A.

Questions 104–110 refer to the passage on page 406.

104. The author is primarily concerned with

   (A) advocating a return to an older methodology
   (B) explaining the importance of a recent theory
   (C) enumerating differences between two widely used methods
   (D) describing events leading to a discovery
   (E) challenging the assumptions on which a theory is based

Main idea

Examine the entire passage to find the author's primary concern. An analysis of this passage shows that the author introduces a recent theory in the first paragraph, explains the practical importance of the theory in the second, and discusses the methods of exploration the theory makes possible in the third and fourth paragraphs. The author is primarily concerned with presenting a new theory and showing why it is important.

A   The only older methodology cited in the passage, *simple prospecting methods*, leads to only an *occasional discovery* (lines 15–17); there is no indication that the author favors this.
B   **Correct.** The author describes a recent theory of ore formation and discusses its importance.
C   Three methods of exploration are described in the third paragraph, but differences among them are not discussed.
D   The passage describes a theory and the practice derived from it; it does not describe a series of events leading to a discovery.
E   The author describes two theories of ore formation in the first paragraph but does not challenge the assumptions on which either one is based.

The correct answer is B.

105. According to the passage, the widely held view of Archean-age gold-quartz vein systems is that such systems

   (A) were formed from metamorphic fluids
   (B) originated in molten granite-like bodies
   (C) were formed from alluvial deposits
   (D) generally have surface expression
   (E) are not discoverable through chemical tests

Supporting ideas

This question asks for information explicitly stated in the first paragraph where Archean-age gold-quartz vein systems are discussed. The recent theory is *contrary* to the *widely held* theory that Archean-age gold-quartz vein systems *were deposited from metamorphic fluids* (lines 6–7).

A   **Correct.** The widely held theory explains that the systems were *deposited from metamorphic fluids* (line 7).

B   It is the recent theory that holds that the systems were formed *from magmatic fluids that originated from molten granite–like bodies* (lines 3–4); the recent theory is not *the widely held view*.

C   Alluvial deposits are mentioned only in the context of *simple prospecting methods* (lines 14–16); there is nothing in the passage explicitly linking alluvial deposits to metamorphic fluids.

D   Lines 17–19 explain that most deposits *not yet discovered ... have no surface expression*, but there is no mention in the passage of widely held beliefs concerning surface expressions of the metamorphic fluids.

E   *Sensitive chemical tests* are able to detect deposits where mineralization has occurred (lines 27–29).

The correct answer is A.

106. The passage implies that which of the following steps would be the first performed by explorers who wish to maximize their chances of discovering gold?

   (A)   Surveying several sites known to have been formed more than two billion years ago

   (B)   Limiting exploration to sites known to have been formed from metamorphic fluid

   (C)   Using an appropriate conceptual model to select a site for further exploration

   (D)   Using geophysical methods to analyze rocks over a broad area

   (E)   Limiting exploration to sites where alluvial gold has previously been found

Inference

Since the question uses the word *implies*, the answer will be an inference based on what the passage says about exploration. The third and fourth paragraphs describe the process of exploration. The high-technology methods are of no use to the explorer if the sites have not mineralized, *and to maximize the chances of discovery the explorer must therefore pay particular attention to selecting the ground formations most likely to be mineralized* (lines 30–35). Conceptual models based on observation and ore-formation theories allow the explorer to identify the areas most likely to be mineralized (lines 39–46).

A   Nothing in the passage indicates that a large portion of two-billion-year-old sites will have gold in them; it only indicates that if they are gold-quartz vein systems, they will be over two billion years old.

B   The widely held view, rather than the recent theory that is the focus of the passage, argued that gold-quartz vein systems were formed from metamorphic fluids. The passage says the recent theory has *considerable practical importance*, suggesting the benefits of applying the recent theory rather than this widely held view.

C   **Correct.** Conceptual models lead the explorer to the sites most likely to have mineralized.

D   Geophysical techniques are of no use unless ground formations in an area have been mineralized (lines 24–32).

E   The *simple prospecting methods* that find alluvial gold lead to only an *occasional discovery*; *most deposits not yet discovered ... are buried* (lines 15–19).

The correct answer is C.

107. Which of the following statements about discoveries of gold deposits is supported by information in the passage?

(A) The number of gold discoveries made annually has increased between the time of the original gold rushes and the present.

(B) New discoveries of gold deposits are likely to be the result of exploration techniques designed to locate buried mineralization.

(C) It is unlikely that newly discovered gold deposits will ever yield as much as did those deposits discovered during the original gold rushes.

(D) Modern explorers are divided on the question of the utility of simple prospecting methods as a source of new discoveries of gold deposits.

(E) Models based on the theory that gold originated from magmatic fluids have already led to new discoveries of gold deposits.

Supporting ideas

This question requires consideration of explicit information throughout the passage. The second paragraph explains that *most deposits not yet discovered … are buried* (lines 17–19), so the explorer's best means of discovering them is the use of *conceptual models* to identify the sites most likely to have buried minerals (lines 35–38). At that point, the explorer may use the high-technology methods possible when buried mineralization is present (lines 22–29).

A   The passage does not discuss the number of gold discoveries.

B   **Correct.** Since most gold deposits are buried, explorers must find the sites most likely to contain buried minerals.

C   The passage does not discuss the yield of gold discoveries.

D   While *simple prospecting methods* lead only to an *occasional discovery*, modern explorers are not said to dispute their utility (lines 15–17).

E   The passage does not say that gold deposits have already been found by using the models based on this recent theory.

The correct answer is B.

108. It can be inferred from the passage that which of the following is easiest to detect?

(A) A gold-quartz vein system originating in magmatic fluids

(B) A gold-quartz vein system originating in metamorphic fluids

(C) A gold deposit that is mixed with granite

(D) A gold deposit that has shed alluvial gold

(E) A gold deposit that exhibits chemical halos

Application

To answer this question, apply what the passage says about gold deposits to the examples in the answer choices. The second paragraph states that the gold deposits discovered during the gold rushes were *exposed at the Earth's surface*; they were found because *they had shed trails of alluvial gold that were easily traced by simple prospecting methods* (lines 11–16). Most deposits have not been detected because they are buried and have *no surface expression*. Thus the simplest gold to find would be that in a deposit that had shed alluvial gold.

A   The recent theory holds that gold-quartz vein systems are formed from magmatic fluids, but does not say that these systems have easily detectable surface expressions; the passage states that they form deep beneath the surface of Earth, which makes it unlikely that they will be easy to find.

B   The widely held view contends that gold-quartz vein systems are formed from metamorphic fluids, but does not say if these have easily detectable surface expressions.

C   The passage does not comment on gold deposits mixed with granite, although the recent theory does mention *molten granite-like bodies deep beneath the surface of the Earth* (lines 4–5).

D   **Correct.** Finding gold deposits that have shed alluvial gold at the Earth's surface is far easier than finding buried gold deposits.

E   One complex, difficult subsurface exploration method involves chemical tests detecting the subtle chemical halos that surround mineralized areas; clearly this is not the *easiest* means of detecting gold deposits.

The correct answer is D.

109. The theory mentioned in lines 1–5 relates to the conceptual models discussed in the passage in which of the following ways?

    (A) It may furnish a valid account of ore-forming processes, and, hence, can support conceptual models that have great practical significance.

    (B) It suggests that certain geological formations, long believed to be mineralized, are in fact mineralized, thus confirming current conceptual models.

    (C) It suggests that there may not be enough similarity across Archean-age gold-quartz vein systems to warrant the formulation of conceptual models.

    (D) It corrects existing theories about the chemical halos of gold deposits, and thus provides a basis for correcting current conceptual models.

    (E) It suggests that simple prospecting methods still have a higher success rate in the discovery of gold deposits than do more modern methods.

Logical structure

This question requires considering the conceptual models described in lines 35–41 in light of the recent theory (lines 1–5), which the author assures the reader has *considerable practical importance* (lines 10–11). The conceptual models are derived from observation and from *theories of ore-forming processes*. Therefore, the recent theory may explain ore formation in a way that leads to the development of an updated model, and that model may then aid in the discovery of gold deposits.

A   **Correct.** The theory provides an explanation of ore formation, which aids in creating a conceptual model that may help explorers find gold deposits.

B   The theory does not confirm models, but contributes to forming them.

C   The practical value of the theory is that it can help to formulate models.

D   The theory does not challenge theories about chemical halos but rather contributes to the development of conceptual models that might allow for the broader application of chemical halos.

E   The theory does not compare methods of discovering gold deposits.

The correct answer is A.

110. According to the passage, methods of exploring for gold that are widely used today are based on which of the following facts?

    (A) Most of the Earth's remaining gold deposits are still molten.

    (B) Most of the Earth's remaining gold deposits are exposed at the surface.

    (C) Most of the Earth's remaining gold deposits are buried and have no surface expression.

    (D) Only one type of gold deposit warrants exploration, since the other types of gold deposits are found in regions difficult to reach.

    (E) Only one type of gold deposit warrants exploration, since the other types of gold deposits are unlikely to yield concentrated quantities of gold.

Supporting ideas

This question concerns factual information stated in the passage. In contrast to the gold deposits discovered at the Earth's surface, *most deposits not yet discovered have gone undetected because they are buried and have no surface expression* (lines 17–19). The *methods widely used today* must search for buried minerals rather than minerals on the surface (lines 22–29).

A   The passage mentions neither molten gold nor the method to detect it.

B   The passage explicitly says that most deposits are buried.

C   **Correct.** The passage explicitly states that most gold deposits are buried, leaving no traces at the Earth's surface.

D   The passage neither distinguishes between types of gold nor describes inaccessible regions.

E   The passage does not relate types of gold to yields of gold deposits.

The correct answer is C.

Questions 111–114 refer to the passage on page 408.

111. The passage mentions which of the following as a factor that affects the role of *P. ochraceus* as a keystone species within different habitats?

   (A) The degree to which the habitat is sheltered from waves

   (B) The degree to which other animals within a habitat prey on mussels

   (C) The fact that mussel populations are often not dominant within some habitats occupied by *P. ochraceus*

   (D) The size of the *P. ochraceus* population within the habitat

   (E) The fact that there is great species diversity within some habitats occupied by *P. ochraceus*

Supporting idea

This question depends on recognizing what the passage states about the factors affecting *P. ochraceus*'s role as a keystone species, which is different in different habitats. According to the passage, *P. ochraceus* consumes and suppresses mussel populations in some habitats—specifically, those that are wave-exposed—making it a keystone predator in those habitats. But in wave-sheltered habitats, *P. ochraceus* does not play the same role in suppressing mussel populations.

   A   Correct. The passage clearly states that *P. ochraceus*'s role in wave-exposed habitats differs from its role in wave-sheltered habitats.

   B   The passage says that the impact of *P. ochraceus* predation on mussels is not strong in wave-sheltered habitats, but this is not—at least not at all sites—because other animals are preying on the mussels; rather, at least at some sites, it is because mussels are controlled by sand burial.

   C   The passage does not suggest that mussel populations are dominant in any habitats occupied by *P. ochraceus*.

D   The size of the *P. ochraceus* population affects the size of the mussel population within wave-exposed habitats, but the passage does not suggest that *P. ochraceus*'s role as a keystone species depends on the size of its population within those habitats.

E   The only other species the passage mentions in conjunction with *P. ochraceus* habitats is the mussel; the passage does not address species diversity in these habitats.

The correct answer is A.

112. Which of the following hypothetical experiments most clearly exemplifies the method of identifying species' roles that the author considers problematic?

   (A) A population of seals in an Arctic habitat is counted in order to determine whether it is the dominant species in that ecosystem.

   (B) A species of fish that is a keystone species in one marine ecosystem is introduced into another marine ecosystem to see whether the species will come to occupy a keystone role.

   (C) In order to determine whether a species of monkey is a keystone species within a particular ecosystem, the monkeys are removed from that ecosystem and the ecosystem is then studied.

   (D) Different mountain ecosystems are compared to determine how geography affects a particular species' ability to dominate its ecosystem.

   (E) In a grassland experiencing a changing climate, patterns of species extinction are traced in order to evaluate the effect of climate changes on keystone species in that grassland.

Application

Answering this question depends on recognizing what the author says about identifying species' roles in habitats and then extending that to another situation. The author considers a particular method of studying keystone species problematic: removing a suspected keystone species from its habitat and observing what happens to the ecosystem. The author finds this problematic because interactions among species are complex.

A   The author does not discuss counting the members of a population as a problematic way of determining whether that population is a dominant species.

B   The method that the author finds problematic has to do with observing what happens to an ecosystem when a keystone species is removed from it, not with observing what happens to a different ecosystem when the species is introduced into it.

C   **Correct.** The author states explicitly that removing a species from a habitat in order to determine its keystone status is problematic. Removing the monkeys from their habitat is a clear example of this problematic practice.

D   Comparison of habitats in order to determine geography's effect on a particular species' dominance would most likely find favor with the author, for this is the approach the author seems to advocate in investigating *P. ochraceus*'s keystone status.

E   The author does not discuss tracing patterns of extinction or changing climates in the passage.

The correct answer is C.

113. Which of the following, if true, would most clearly support the argument about keystone status advanced in the last sentence of the passage (lines 24–31)?

(A)   A species of bat is primarily responsible for keeping insect populations within an ecosystem low, and the size of the insect population in turn affects bird species within that ecosystem.

(B)   A species of iguana occupies a keystone role on certain tropical islands, but does not play that role on adjacent tropical islands that are inhabited by a greater number of animal species.

(C)   Close observation of a savannah ecosystem reveals that more species occupy keystone roles within that ecosystem than biologists had previously believed.

(D)   As a keystone species of bee becomes more abundant, it has a larger effect on the ecosystem it inhabits.

(E)   A species of moth that occupies a keystone role in a prairie habitat develops coloration patterns that camouflage it from potential predators.

Evaluation

To answer this question, focus on the argument advanced in the last sentence of the passage and identify what information would support that argument. In the last sentence of the passage, the author claims that keystone status depends on context. The author then offers three contextual factors that may affect a species' keystone status: geography, community diversity (i.e., the number of species in a given habitat), and length of species interaction. Evidence supporting this argument would show that context is important to a species' keystone status.

A   This scenario does not indicate anything about keystone status; this is simply a description of how species populations in a single ecosystem affect one another.

B   **Correct.** That the iguana is a keystone species in a location that has limited species diversity but not a keystone species in a location that has greater species diversity suggests that keystone status does indeed depend on context. Thus, this example supports the author's argument in the last sentence of the passage.

C   That biologists were mistaken about keystone species in a particular ecosystem does not have a bearing on whether keystone status is context dependent.

D   It is not surprising that an increase in a species' population would lead to that species having a larger effect on its ecosystem—but this does not speak directly to the question of whether keystone status itself depends on context.

E   A keystone species enhancing its ability to survive in a single ecosystem does not lend any support to the idea that keystone status depends on context. The moth's keystone status would have to undergo some change for this to have a bearing on the question of context.

The correct answer is B.

114. The passage suggests which of the following about the identification of a species as a keystone species?

(A) Such an identification depends primarily on the species' relationship to the dominant species.

(B) Such an identification can best be made by removing the species from a particular ecosystem and observing changes that occur in the ecosystem.

(C) Such an identification is likely to be less reliable as an ecosystem becomes less diverse.

(D) Such an identification seems to depend on various factors within the ecosystem.

(E) Such an identification can best be made by observing predation behavior.

Inference

Answering this question requires identifying how the passage suggests that keystone species should be identified. The passage identifies a particular way in which keystone status should *not* be determined: removing a species and observing what happens to the ecosystem. The passage also argues that keystone status depends strongly on context: that is, an ecosystem's characteristics, including its geography and inhabitants, determine its keystone species.

A   While the passage uses an example of a keystone species, *P. ochraceus*, which preys on a species that would, in the keystone species' absence, be dominant, there is nothing to suggest that a keystone species *must* have a particular relationship with the dominant, or potentially dominant, species in an ecosystem.

B   The passage explicitly states that this method of identification would be problematic.

C   A reduction in an ecosystem's diversity might alter which species occupy keystone roles in that ecosystem, the passage suggests, but there is no indication that identifying such species would become more difficult.

D   **Correct.** If, as the passage suggests, keystone status for any given species depends on the context of the ecosystem in which it lives, then it is likely that identifying keystone species depends strongly on understanding what factors of the ecosystem contribute to creating keystone status. The passage lists such factors as geography, community diversity, and species interaction.

E   While the passage uses a predator, *P. ochraceus*, as its example of a keystone species, there is no indication that predation is an essential component of the actual definition of keystone species (*one whose effects are much larger than would be predicted from its abundance*).

The correct answer is D.

Questions 115–119 refer to the passage on page 410.

115. The passage is primarily concerned with

(A) defending a controversial approach

(B) criticizing an accepted view

(C) summarizing research findings

(D) contrasting competing theories

(E) describing an innovative technique

Main idea

Figuring out the authors' primary concern depends on a careful review of the passage as a whole. The first paragraph identifies the larger question that is the context for the authors' investigation. The second paragraph presents the part of the question the authors researched, concluding with their unexpected results. The third paragraph explains the importance of these findings in relation to the larger question of the universe's possible "*close.*" The authors' primary purpose in this passage is to summarize the findings of their research.

A   The authors do not discuss approaches to the question they research.

B   The authors mention that their findings do not conform to Kepler's law, but the passage's primary focus is on summarizing research findings and not on criticizing any particular view.

C   Correct. This passage presents a summation of the findings of the authors' research.

D   The authors do not contrast different theories in this passage.

E   The authors do not discuss new techniques in this passage.

The correct answer is C.

116. The authors' study indicates that, in comparison with the outermost regions of a typical spiral galaxy, the region just outside the nucleus can be characterized as having

(A)   higher rotational velocity and higher luminosity

(B)   lower rotational velocity and higher luminosity

(C)   lower rotational velocity and lower luminosity

(D)   similar rotational velocity and higher luminosity

(E)   similar rotational velocity and similar luminosity

Inference

In the second paragraph, the authors observe that *outside the bright nucleus of a typical spiral galaxy luminosity falls off rapidly* (lines 20–21); the region just outside the nucleus may thus be characterized as having higher luminosity than the outermost regions of a spiral galaxy. Their research finds that *the rotational velocity in spiral galaxies either remains constant with increasing distance from the center or increases slightly* (lines 27–30). The region just outside the nucleus may thus be characterized as sharing with the outermost regions of a spiral galaxy a similar rotational velocity.

A   This region was expected to have higher rotational velocity, but the research findings did not corroborate this hypothesis; it is correct that the region has higher luminosity.

B   The region does have higher luminosity, but not lower rotational velocity.

C   The region has neither lower luminosity nor lower rotational velocity.

D   Correct. The region has similar rotational velocity and higher luminosity.

E   The region has similar rotational velocity but higher luminosity.

The correct answer is D.

117. The authors' suggestion that "as much as 90 percent of the mass of the universe is not radiating at any wavelength with enough intensity to be detected on the Earth" (lines 34–37) would be most weakened if which of the following were discovered to be true?

(A)   Spiral galaxies are less common than types of galaxies that contain little nonluminous matter.

(B)   Luminous and nonluminous matter are composed of the same basic elements.

(C)   The bright nucleus of a typical spiral galaxy also contains some nonluminous matter.

(D)   The density of the observable universe is greater than most previous estimates have suggested.

(E)   Some galaxies do not rotate or rotate too slowly for their rotational velocity to be measured.

Application

The authors' conclusion about nonluminous matter is based on their study of the rotational velocity of spiral galaxies. If spiral galaxies were found to be atypical of galaxies, then it would be possible that, in those other galaxies, nonluminous matter does not increase as luminous matter decreases. If this were the case, the authors' conclusion would be based on a sample of galaxies not representative of the whole, and their argument would be seriously weakened.

A **Correct.** The authors' conclusion assumes that spiral galaxies are typical of all galaxies; information calling that assumption into question weakens the argument.

B The relation rather than the composition of luminous and nonluminous mass is relevant to the conclusion.

C Nonluminous mass increases as luminous mass decreases: This finding does not rule out that the nucleus contains some nonluminous mass; the argument is not affected.

D The density of the observable universe is only *a fraction* of the density needed to *"close"* the universe, so even if this density were greater, it is not likely to exceed the density of nonluminous matter.

E The authors are concerned only with measurable rotational velocity.

The correct answer is A.

118. It can be inferred from information presented in the passage that if the density of the universe were equivalent to significantly less than three hydrogen atoms per cubic meter, which of the following would be true as a consequence?

(A) Luminosity would be a true indicator of mass.

(B) Different regions in spiral galaxies would rotate at the same velocity.

(C) The universe would continue to expand indefinitely.

(D) The density of the invisible matter in the universe would have to be more than 70 times the density of the luminous matter.

(E) More of the invisible matter in spiral galaxies would have to be located in their nuclei than in their outer regions.

Inference

An inference is drawn from stated information. This question refers to the first paragraph, where the authors explain that *the critical density of matter needed to brake the expansion and "close" the universe is equivalent to three hydrogen atoms per cubic meter* (lines 7–9). If the density is significantly less, then the universe will not *"close"* but continue to expand indefinitely.

A The authors' finding that luminosity is not a true indicator of mass is not derived from the conclusion that the density is less than three hydrogen atoms per cubic meter.

B The authors' finding that different regions rotate at similar velocities does not come from the hypothesis about the density of the universe.

C **Correct.** If the critical density needed to *"close"* the universe is equivalent to three hydrogen atoms per cubic meter, then a density of significantly less than this amount means that the universe will continue its expansion.

D This statement would be true of the hypothetical *"close"* of the universe, but if the density is less than three hydrogen atoms per cubic meter, the universe will continue its expansion.

E This statement cannot be inferred from the hypothesis about the density of the universe.

The correct answer is C.

119. The authors propose all of the following as possibly contributing to the "missing matter" in spiral galaxies EXCEPT

(A) massive black holes

(B) small black holes

(C) small, dim stars

(D) massive stars

(E) large planets

Supporting ideas

This question asks the reader to find the list of possible explanations for the *"missing"* or *dark matter* that the authors give in the passage and to check that list against the possible answers. Using the process of elimination will show which answer is not included on the authors' list. In the final paragraph, the authors write, *Such dark matter could be in the form of extremely dim stars of low mass, of large planets like Jupiter, or of black holes, either small or massive* (lines 37–40).

A   The authors include massive black holes.
B   The authors include small black holes.
C   The authors include small, dim stars.
D   Correct. The authors do not include massive stars in their list of possible explanations for *"missing matter."*
E   The authors include large planets.

The correct answer is D.

Questions 120–127 refer to the passage on page 412.

120. The primary purpose of the passage is to

(A)   advocate a more positive attitude toward technological change

(B)   discuss the implications for employees of the modernization of a telephone exchange

(C)   consider a successful challenge to the constructivist view of technological change

(D)   challenge the position of advocates of technological determinism

(E)   suggest that the social causes of technological change should be studied in real situations

Main idea

This question asks for an assessment of what the passage as a whole is doing. The passage introduces Clark's study as a *solid contribution* (lines 3–4) to the debate between technological determinists and social constructivists. In the second paragraph, Braverman is introduced as holding a position of social constructivism, a position that Clark takes issue with. In the final paragraph, the passage holds that Clark *refutes the extremes of the constructivists* (line 33), and Clark's arguments challenging social constructivism are then described.

A   The passage takes no position on the merits of technological change but is concerned only with the role of such change in society.
B   The passage mentions telephone exchange workers as an example that helps illustrate the more central debate between determinists and constructivists.
C   Correct. The passage is mainly concerned with portraying Clark's view as a successful challenge to constructivism.
D   The passage describes Clark's view as a successful challenge to social constructivism, not technological determinism.
E   The passage is concerned with describing a challenge to social constructivism and not with suggesting the context in which technological change ought to be studied.

The correct answer is C.

121. Which of the following statements about the modernization of the telephone exchange is supported by information in the passage?

(A)   The new technology reduced the role of managers in labor negotiations.

(B)   The modernization was implemented without the consent of the employees directly affected by it.

(C)   The modernization had an impact that went significantly beyond maintenance routines.

(D)   Some of the maintenance workers felt victimized by the new technology.

(E)   The modernization gave credence to the view of advocates of social constructivism.

Supporting ideas

This question requires recognizing information contained in the passage. The passage states in the first paragraph that Clark's study focused on the modernization of a telephone exchange and the effect this had on maintenance work and workers. After describing Braverman's analysis in the second paragraph as being at odds with Clark's views, the passage discusses Clark's views in more detail in the final paragraph. As part of this discussion, the passage notes that Clark shows how a change from *maintenance-intensive electromechanical switches to semielectronic switching systems* at the telephone exchange *altered work tasks, skills, training opportunities, administration, and organization of workers* (lines 41–46). Thus, the passage shows that the modernization of the telephone exchange affected much more than maintenance routines.

A   The passage does not discuss whether new technology reduces the role of managers in labor negotiations.

B   The passage does not discuss the role of employee consent in the modernization of the telephone exchange.

C   Correct. The passage states that the modernization of the telephone exchange affected tasks, skills, training, administration, and the organization of workers.

D   The passage does not suggest that maintenance workers felt victimized by the modernization of the telephone exchange.

E   The passage describes modernization as a fact viewable from a perspective of social constructivism or technological determinism, but that does not in itself support either view.

The correct answer is C.

122. Which of the following most accurately describes Clark's opinion of Braverman's position?

(A)   He respects its wide-ranging popularity.

(B)   He disapproves of its misplaced emphasis on the influence of managers.

(C)   He admires the consideration it gives to the attitudes of the workers affected.

(D)   He is concerned about its potential to impede the implementation of new technologies.

(E)   He is sympathetic to its concern about the impact of modern technology on workers.

Inference

Answering this question requires inferring what the passage's author likely believes. The passage describes Braverman's position as one of mainstream social constructivism (lines 23–24), a position that Clark takes issue with. Although it describes Braverman's position, the rest of the passage is devoted to showing how Clark's position takes issue with Braverman's. In the second paragraph, the passage describes Clark as holding that *technology can be a primary determinant of social and managerial organization* (lines 11–12), which suggests that managers are sometimes subordinate to technological change. In lines 16–19, however, Braverman is described as holding that *the shape of a technological system is subordinate to the manager's desire to wrest control of the labor process from the workers*, which shows that Clark and Braverman are at odds on this point.

A   Since the passage says that Clark believes an important insight *has been obscured by the recent sociological fashion* that Braverman's views exemplify (lines 12–15), one cannot infer that Clark respects the popularity of Braverman's views.

B   Correct. The passage shows that Clark believes managers to have less influence over how technology affects an organization than Braverman claims that they have.

C   The passage does not indicate that Clark admires any aspect of Braverman's position.

D   The passage does not indicate that Clark considers impediments to modernization.

E   The passage does not indicate that Clark is sympathetic to any concerns attributed to Braverman.

The correct answer is B.

123. The information in the passage suggests that which of the following statements from hypothetical sociological studies of change in industry most clearly exemplifies the social constructivists' version of technological determinism?

    (A) It is the available technology that determines workers' skills, rather than workers' skills influencing the application of technology.

    (B) All progress in industrial technology grows out of a continuing negotiation between technological possibility and human need.

    (C) Some organizational change is caused by people; some is caused by computer chips.

    (D) Most major technological advances in industry have been generated through research and development.

    (E) Some industrial technology eliminates jobs, but educated workers can create whole new skills areas by the adaptation of the technology.

Application

This question requires understanding different points of view discussed in the passage. In the first paragraph, the passage mentions the debate involving technological determinism and social constructivism. In the second and third paragraphs, the passage uses Braverman's analysis to illustrate the social constructivists' position and in the third paragraph suggests that the constructivists are *misrepresenting technological determinism* (lines 25–26). In lines 31–32, the constructivists are reported to hold that technological determinism views technology as *existing outside society, capable of directly influencing skills and work organization.*

A **Correct.** This statement is consistent with the constructivists' view that technological determinism sees technology as outside of society, influencing workers' skills.

B The passage states that the constructivists hold that *technological determinists are supposed to believe … that machinery imposes appropriate forms of order on society* (lines 27–29), suggesting that no negotiation is present.

C According to the description of them in the passage, constructivists portray technological determinists as believing that technology, not people, drives organizational change.

D The passage does not portray either constructivists or determinists as being concerned with technological research and development.

E The passage does not portray either constructivists or determinists as being concerned with technology-driven job elimination or creation.

The correct answer is A.

124. The information in the passage suggests that Clark believes that which of the following would be true if social constructivism had not gained widespread acceptance?

    (A) Businesses would be more likely to modernize without considering the social consequences of their actions.

    (B) There would be greater understanding of the role played by technology in producing social change.

    (C) Businesses would be less likely to understand the attitudes of employees affected by modernization.

    (D) Modernization would have occurred at a slower rate.

    (E) Technology would have played a greater part in determining the role of business in society.

Inference

Answering this question involves understanding a point of view as it is described in the passage. The passage aligns Clark's study closely with the technological determinists, summarizing his view in lines 11–12: *technology can be a primary determinant of social and managerial organization.* In the following sentence, the passage states that Clark believes that *this possibility is obscured by the recent sociological fashion, exemplified by Braverman's analysis* (lines 12–15). After illustrating Braverman's analysis, the passage then states that it represents *social constructivism.*

A   According to the passage, Clark holds that constructivists obscure how modernization might have social consequences.

B   Correct. According to the passage, Clark sees constructivism as obscuring the possibility that technology plays a primary role in social change.

C   The passage does not discuss how the attitudes of employees are perceived by their employers.

D   The passage describes a debate about the history and sociology of technology; it does not suggest that sociological analyses affect the pace of modernization.

E   The passage describes a debate about the history and sociology of technology; it does not suggest that sociological analyses affect the role that technology plays in business.

The correct answer is B.

125. According to the passage, constructivists employed which of the following to promote their argument?

(A)   Empirical studies of business situations involving technological change

(B)   Citation of managers supportive of their position

(C)   Construction of hypothetical situations that support their view

(D)   Contrasts of their view with a misstatement of an opposing view

(E)   Descriptions of the breadth of impact of technological change

Supporting ideas

Answering this question involves recognizing information given in the passage. The passage indicates that a debate exists between technological determinists and social constructivists, suggesting that these views are in opposition. The passage goes on to state that *constructivists gain acceptance by misrepresenting technological determinism* (lines 25–26). This misrepresentation is presented as the *alternative to constructivism* (lines 29–30), suggesting that constructivists promoted their own view by contrasting it with a misrepresentation of determinists' views.

A   The passage mentions empirical studies in relation to Clark's study but not Braverman's analysis.

B   The passage does not mention that managers were supportive of any particular point of view within the sociology of technology.

C   The passage does not mention any hypothetical situations as being used by the constructivists in support of their view.

D   Correct. The passage indicates that the constructivists have come into fashion by contrasting their own views with a misrepresentation of the views of technological determinists.

E   The passage does not describe the constructivists as making determinations regarding the degree of impact that technological change has on social or managerial organization.

The correct answer is D.

126. The author of the passage uses the expression "are supposed to" in line 27 primarily in order to

(A)   suggest that a contention made by constructivists regarding determinists is inaccurate

(B)   define the generally accepted position of determinists regarding the implementation of technology

(C)   engage in speculation about the motivation of determinists

(D)   lend support to a comment critical of the position of determinists

(E)   contrast the historical position of determinists with their position regarding the exchange modernization

Evaluation

This question requires understanding how a particular phrase functions in the passage as a whole. In the third paragraph the passage states that *constructivists gain acceptance by misrepresenting technological determinism* (lines 25–26) and follows this claim with an example of this misrepresentation, stating that *technological determinists are supposed to believe, for example* (lines 27–28). This line implies that the constructivist view of the determinists is inaccurate.

A **Correct.** The passage uses the expression in part to provide an example of the constructivists' misrepresentation of the determinists.

B The passage indicates that the view attributed to the determinists is a misrepresentation, not one that is generally accepted by determinists.

C The expression in the passage is part of a discussion about the motivation of constructivists, not determinists.

D The expression in the passage is part of a discussion that is critical of the constructivists, not the determinists.

E The passage does not describe either the historical position of determinists or their position on the exchange modernization.

The correct answer is A.

127. Which of the following statements about Clark's study of the telephone exchange can be inferred from information in the passage?

(A) Clark's reason for undertaking the study was to undermine Braverman's analysis of the function of technology.

(B) Clark's study suggests that the implementation of technology should be discussed in the context of conflict between labor and management.

(C) Clark examined the impact of changes in the technology of switching at the exchange in terms of overall operations and organization.

(D) Clark concluded that the implementation of new switching technology was equally beneficial to management and labor.

(E) Clark's analysis of the change in switching systems applies only narrowly to the situation at the particular exchange that he studied.

Inference

This question requires understanding what the passage implies in its discussion of a point of view. The details of Clark's views are discussed primarily in the final paragraph. The passage states that on an empirical level, Clark demonstrates that technological change regarding switches at the telephone exchange *altered work tasks, skills, training opportunities, administration, and organization of workers* (lines 44–46). The passage goes on to state Clark's contention that these changes even influenced negotiations between management and labor unions.

A The passage indicates that Clark's study addressed the extremes of both technological determinism and social constructivism. It cites Braverman as a proponent of social constructivism but provides no evidence that Clark's motivation in beginning his study was specifically to target an analysis offered by Braverman.

B The passage indicates that Clark attributed some organizational change to the way labor and management negotiated the introduction of technology but does not mention conflict between them.

C **Correct.** According to the passage, Clark concludes that changes to the technology of switches had an influence on several aspects of the overall operations and organization of the telephone exchange.

D The passage does not indicate that Clark assesses the benefits of technological change to either labor or management.

E The passage indicates that Clark believes the change in switching technology influenced many aspects of the overall operations of the telephone exchange.

The correct answer is C.

Questions 128–133 refer to the passage on page 414.

128. According to the passage, the five well-known plant hormones are not useful in controlling the growth of crops because

(A) it is not known exactly what functions the hormones perform

(B) each hormone has various effects on plants

(C) none of the hormones can function without the others

(D) each hormone has different effects on different kinds of plants

(E) each hormone works on only a small subset of a cell's genes at any particular time

Supporting ideas

To answer this question, look for information that is provided in the passage. Lines 16–20 explain that each of the five plant hormones *has more than one effect on the growth and development of plants*; for this reason, they *are not very useful in artificially controlling the growth of crops.*

A   Lines 20–25 describe in detail the multiple functions of the hormone auxin.
B   **Correct.** The hormones *have so many simultaneous effects* on plants that they are not useful in controlling the growth of crops.
C   The passage provides no evidence to support this reason.
D   No information is given in the passage to support this reason.
E   The hormones' multiple effects on plant growth, not their specific effect at the cellular level, make them ineffective at artificially controlling crop growth.

The correct answer is B.

129. The passage suggests that the place of hypothalamic hormones in the hormonal hierarchies of animals is similar to the place of which of the following in plants?

(A) Plant cell walls

(B) The complement of genes in each plant cell

(C) A subset of a plant cell's gene complement

(D) The five major hormones

(E) The oligosaccharins

Inference

This question asks for information that is not directly stated in the passage. It requires examining the analogy between the action of hormones in animals and in plants, which is the subject of the third and fourth paragraphs. In animals, hypothalamic hormones stimulate the pituitary gland to synthesize and release many different hormones; this process causes hormones from the adrenal cortex to be released. A similar *hierarchy of hormones* may exist in plants. The pleiotropic plant hormones may activate the enzymes that, in turn, release oligosaccharins from the cell wall. It is reasonable to infer that, in triggering the action, the plant hormones may act in a way similar to the hypothalamic hormones in animals.

A   Plant cell walls do not activate enzymes as the hypothalamic hormones activate the pituitary gland.
B   The passage states that all cells of a plant start out with the same complement of genes (lines 1–2), but this statement is not part of the analogy.
C   Line 5 refers to the subset of genes, but it is not a part of the analogy.
D   **Correct.** Like hypothalamic hormones in animals, the five major plant hormones may be responsible for releasing the catalysts for growth.
E   The oligosaccharins are part of the hierarchy, but they are not equivalent to the hypothalamic hormones in releasing other hormones.

The correct answer is D.

130. The passage suggests that which of the following is a function likely to be performed by an oligosaccharin?

(A) To stimulate a particular plant cell to become part of a plant's root system

(B) To stimulate the walls of a particular cell to produce other oligosaccharins

(C) To activate enzymes that release specific chemical messengers from plant cell walls

(D) To duplicate the gene complement in a particular plant cell

(E) To produce multiple effects on a particular subsystem of plant cells

Inference

Answering this question requires making an inference based on the information in the passage. The analogy between animal and plant hormones describes a process that ends, in animals, with *specific effects on target organs all over the body* (lines 33–34). While the pleiotropic plant hormones have multiple effects, the oligosaccharins are described as *more specific chemical messengers* (lines 43–44). It is reasonable to infer that oligosaccharins affect a specific part of a plant's growth.

A **Correct.** This is the only response that gives an example of an effect on a specific aspect of plant growth and development.

B The last paragraph explains that enzymes release oligosaccharins. The passage provides no evidence that oligosaccharins stimulate the release of other oligosaccharins.

C The pleiotropic plant hormones, not the oligosaccharins, may activate the enzymes (lines 41–43).

D The passage does not discuss such duplication.

E The oligosaccharins, as *more specific chemical messengers*, have a specific effect, not multiple effects, on plant growth.

The correct answer is A.

131. The author mentions specific effects that auxin has on plant development in order to illustrate the

    (A) point that some of the effects of plant hormones can be harmful

    (B) way in which hormones are produced by plants

    (C) hierarchical nature of the functioning of plant hormones

    (D) differences among the best-known plant hormones

    (E) concept of pleiotropy as it is exhibited by plant hormones

Logical structure

To answer this question, reread the section where auxin is discussed. The second paragraph explains that each of the five major pleiotropic hormones, including auxin, *has more than one effect on the growth and development of plants*. The author then lists auxin's multiple effects as an example of the principle of pleiotropy in plants.

A The passage does not discuss harmful effects.

B The passage discusses the effects of hormones, not their production.

C Auxin is used to exemplify the many different effects of a pleiotropic hormone, not its role in a hierarchy of hormones.

D The differences among the five major hormones are not discussed.

E **Correct.** The author lists auxin's multiple effects to illustrate how pleiotropic hormones affect plant growth.

The correct answer is E.

132. According to the passage, which of the following best describes a function performed by oligosaccharins?

    (A) Regulating the daily functioning of a plant's cells

    (B) Interacting with one another to produce different chemicals

    (C) Releasing specific chemical messengers from a plant's cell walls

    (D) Producing the hormones that cause plant cells to differentiate to perform different functions

    (E) Influencing the development of a plant's cells by controlling the expression of the cells' genes

Supporting ideas

To answer this question, look for information that is provided in the passage. Oligosaccharins are *regulatory molecules* (line 13). They form part of the complex system that turns on, or expresses, a small subset of genes in a particular kind of cell. As explained in the first paragraph, this process allows plant cells to differentiate and form different plant structures. Unlike the five major plant hormones, the oligosaccharins affect a specific aspect of the plant's growth (lines 14–17).

A   The passage does not discuss the daily functioning of a plant's cells.

B   The passage provides no evidence of this interaction.

C   The oligosaccharins *are fragments of the cell wall* (line 39) and the *specific chemical messengers from the cell wall* (lines 43–44).

D   The oligosaccharins are not said to produce hormones.

E   Correct. Oligosaccharins are part of the system that turns on, or expresses, the subset of a cell's genes that allows cells to grow into different plant structures.

The correct answer is E.

133. The passage suggests that, unlike the pleiotropic hormones, oligosaccharins could be used effectively to

(A)   trace the passage of chemicals through the walls of cells

(B)   pinpoint functions of other plant hormones

(C)   artificially control specific aspects of the development of crops

(D)   alter the complement of genes in the cells of plants

(E)   alter the effects of the five major hormones on plant development

Inference

The passage does not explicitly state how oligosaccharins could be used, but a use can be inferred. The second paragraph establishes that the pleiotropic hormones are not useful in artificially controlling crop growth because of their multiple, diverse effects. Oligosaccharins are contrasted with the hormones because they have specific effects. Thus it is reasonable to infer that oligosaccharins might be used to control specific aspects of crop growth.

A   Passage of chemicals through cell walls is not discussed.

B   The passage does not indicate that oligosaccharins act in this way.

C   Correct. Because the oligosaccharins have specific rather than multiple effects, they might have the potential to be used to control specific aspects of a crop's growth.

D   The oligosaccharins are not said to alter the cells' complement of genes.

E   The passage does not show that oligosaccharins alter the hormones' effects.

The correct answer is C.

Questions 134–139 refer to the passage on page 416.

134. The author indicates explicitly that which of the following records has been a source of information in her investigation?

(A)   United States Immigration Service reports from 1914 to 1930

(B)   Payrolls of southern manufacturing firms between 1910 and 1930

(C)   The volume of cotton exports between 1898 and 1910

(D)   The federal census of 1910

(E)   Advertisements of labor recruiters appearing in southern newspapers after 1910

Supporting ideas

Since the question uses the word *explicitly*, it is clear that the answer can be found in the passage. In lines 27–30, the author refers to the number of African American workers in *manufacturing and mechanical pursuits*, a phrase cited as coming from the federal census and indicating that she was using census data. While she probably used other sources as well, no other source is explicitly mentioned.

A   Immigration Service reports are not mentioned in the passage.

B   Payroll records are not mentioned in the passage.

C   While the decline of the cotton industry is mentioned, records of exports are not.

D   Correct. The federal census is indicated as a source of information on the employment of African American workers.

E   Labor recruiters and the African American press are mentioned, but there is no mention of data being collected from labor recruiting ads.

The correct answer is D.

135. In the passage, the author anticipates which of the following as a possible objection to her argument?

    (A) It is uncertain how many people actually migrated during the Great Migration.

    (B) The eventual economic status of the Great Migration migrants has not been adequately traced.

    (C) It is not likely that people with steady jobs would have reason to move to another area of the country.

    (D) It is not true that the term "manufacturing and mechanical pursuits" actually encompasses the entire industrial sector.

    (E) Of the African American workers living in southern cities, only those in a small number of trades were threatened by obsolescence.

Logical structure

Answering questions about the author's line of argument requires following the steps in the logical structure of that argument. The author argues that many of the African American migrants to the North may have lived and worked in southern urban areas, not rural areas. In lines 33–36, she recognizes that some people may find it *surprising to argue* that African Americans with steady jobs would leave and proceeds to offer *an explanation* based on southern labor conditions. She thus anticipates the objection that workers would not leave steady jobs.

A   The actual number of people migrating is not part of the author's argument, which concerns whether the migrants came from urban or rural backgrounds.

B   The eventual economic status is outside the scope of the argument.

C   **Correct.** The author anticipates this objection and answers it by citing southern labor conditions.

D   The author claims that *"manufacturing and mechanical pursuits"* encompassed roughly *the entire industrial sector* (lines 29–31) but does not address—either explicitly or implicitly—any possible objections relating to this claim.

E   The number of industrial workers leaving southern cities specifically because of job obsolescence is not at issue and is thus not the basis for a potential objection. In the final paragraph, the author is simply presenting her case that wage pressures affected southern African American urban workers in general, in both artisan trades and newly developed industries.

The correct answer is C.

136. According to the passage, which of the following is true of wages in southern cities in 1910?

    (A) They were being pushed lower as a result of increased competition.

    (B) They had begun to rise so that southern industry could attract rural workers.

    (C) They had increased for skilled workers but decreased for unskilled workers.

    (D) They had increased in large southern cities but decreased in small southern cities.

    (E) They had increased in newly developed industries but decreased in the older trades.

Supporting ideas

The information that this question asks for is stated in the passage and can be found by careful rereading. The last paragraph is about working conditions in the South. Lines 52–55 show that an influx of rural workers had increased competition for the available industrial jobs and driven wages lower.

A   **Correct.** Lines 52–55 indicate that wages were going down as more workers arrived from rural areas and competed for jobs.

B   Rural workers arrived in the city because of the boll weevil infestation, not because of the promise of higher wages, and their arrival depressed wages.

C   The passage refers to wages for industrial jobs but does not distinguish between the wages of skilled workers and unskilled workers in this respect.

D   The passage does not discuss wage differences between large and small southern cities.

E   The passage provides no information on differences in wages between older trades and new industries.

The correct answer is A.

137. The author cites each of the following as possible influences in an African American worker's decision to migrate north in the Great Migration EXCEPT

(A) wage levels in northern cities

(B) labor recruiters

(C) competition from rural workers

(D) voting rights in northern states

(E) the African American press

Supporting ideas

Use the process of elimination to answer this question regarding what specifically does NOT appear in the passage. Four of the five answers are mentioned as influences on migration, and one is not. Match each answer with its mention in the passage; the choice that does not have a match is the correct answer. In this case, the only answer not mentioned is *voting rights*.

A   Northern wage levels are mentioned in lines 49–51.

B   Labor recruiters are mentioned in line 48.

C   Competition from rural workers is mentioned in lines 52–54.

D   **Correct.** Voting rights in northern states are not mentioned in the passage; the author has not cited them as a possible influence on a migrant's decision.

E   The African American press is mentioned in lines 48–49.

The correct answer is D.

138. It can be inferred from the passage that the "easy conclusion" mentioned in line 58 is based on which of the following assumptions?

(A) People who migrate from rural areas to large cities usually do so for economic reasons.

(B) Most people who leave rural areas to take jobs in cities return to rural areas as soon as it is financially possible for them to do so.

(C) People with rural backgrounds are less likely to succeed economically in cities than are those with urban backgrounds.

(D) Most people who were once skilled workers are not willing to work as unskilled workers.

(E) People who migrate from their birthplaces to other regions of a country seldom undertake a second migration.

Inference

The question directs one's attention to line 58 and the phrase *easy conclusion*. In this context, *easy* has the negative connotation of "facile" or "simplistic" and suggests the author's disagreement with the conclusion that the economic problems of the migrants to northern urban areas were linked to their rural backgrounds. The *conclusion* derived from this link is first discussed in lines 17–19, where lack of economic success in the North is tied to a rural background.

A   The author does assume economic motives for migration, but this assumption is not linked to the conclusion about difficulties arising from a rural background.

B   This point is not discussed in the passage and is not related to the conclusion that a rural background is linked to economic problems.

C   Correct. The conclusion referred to in line 58 is based on the assumption that rural background will hinder economic success in urban settings.

D   The conclusion refers to all people from rural backgrounds and does not distinguish between skilled and unskilled workers.

E   The conclusion about the economic difficulties of migrants from rural backgrounds makes no assumptions about whether people migrate more than once.

The correct answer is C.

139. The primary purpose of the passage is to

(A)   support an alternative to an accepted methodology

(B)   present evidence that resolves a contradiction

(C)   introduce a recently discovered source of information

(D)   challenge a widely accepted explanation

(E)   argue that a discarded theory deserves new attention

Main idea

Answering questions about primary purpose requires thinking about the underlying structure of the passage. In the first paragraph, the author describes the Great Migration and mentions the assumption that most migrants came from rural areas. Some people then concluded that the migrants' economic difficulties were due to their rural background. In the second paragraph, the author speculates that many migrants could have come from urban areas, and in the third paragraph, she offers information that supports her position. Essentially, if the migrants came from urban areas, their subsequent economic difficulties cannot be attributed to their nonexistent rural background. An analysis of the structure of the passage thus reveals that the author is presenting a generally accepted view and then challenging it.

A   The author is showing the weakness in an explanation; there is no discussion of a methodology or of an alternative methodology.

B   The reasoning presented in the passage contradicts what the author describes as prevailing ideas but does not resolve any previous contradiction.

C   The author does not mention any source of information that was previously unavailable. While census records are briefly mentioned, they are hardly a recently discovered source of information.

D   Correct. The author first discusses a widely accepted explanation of the economic difficulties of African American migrants and then challenges that explanation.

E   The author argues against an explanation she thinks should be discarded. She does not discuss any previously discarded theory.

The correct answer is D.

8.0 Critical Reasoning

8.0 Critical Reasoning

Critical reasoning questions appear in the Verbal section of the GMAT® exam. The Verbal section uses multiple-choice questions to measure your ability to read and comprehend written material, to reason and to evaluate arguments, and to correct written material to conform to standard written English. Because the Verbal section includes content from a variety of topics, you may be generally familiar with some of the material; however, neither the passages nor the questions assume knowledge of the topics discussed. Critical reasoning questions are intermingled with reading comprehension and sentence correction questions throughout the Verbal section of the test.

You will have 75 minutes to complete the Verbal section, or about 1¾ minutes to answer each question. Although critical reasoning questions are based on written passages, these passages are shorter than reading comprehension passages. They tend to be less than 100 words in length and generally are followed by one or two questions. For these questions, you will see a split computer screen. The written passage will remain visible as each question associated with that passage appears in turn on the screen. You will see only one question at a time.

Critical reasoning questions are designed to test the reasoning skills involved in (1) making arguments, (2) evaluating arguments, and (3) formulating or evaluating a plan of action. The materials on which questions are based are drawn from a variety of sources. The GMAT exam does not suppose any familiarity with the subject matter of those materials.

In these questions, you are to analyze the situation on which each question is based, and then select the answer choice that most appropriately answers the question. Begin by reading the passages carefully, then reading the five answer choices. If the correct answer is not immediately obvious to you, see whether you can eliminate some of the wrong answers. Reading the passage a second time may be helpful in illuminating subtleties that were not immediately evident.

Answering critical reasoning questions requires no specialized knowledge of any particular field; you don't have to have knowledge of the terminology and conventions of formal logic. The sample critical reasoning questions in this chapter illustrate the variety of topics the test may cover, the kinds of questions it may ask, and the level of analysis it requires.

The following pages describe what critical reasoning questions are designed to measure and present the directions that will precede questions of this type. Sample questions and explanations of the correct answers follow.

8.1 What Is Measured

Critical reasoning questions are designed to provide one measure of your ability to reason effectively in the following areas:

- **Argument construction**

  Questions in this category may ask you to recognize such things as the basic structure of an argument, properly drawn conclusions, underlying assumptions, well-supported explanatory hypotheses, and parallels between structurally similar arguments.

- **Argument evaluation**

  These questions may ask you to analyze a given argument and to recognize such things as factors that would strengthen or weaken the given argument; reasoning errors committed in making that argument; and aspects of the method by which the argument proceeds.

- **Formulating and evaluating a plan of action**

  This type of question may ask you to recognize such things as the relative appropriateness, effectiveness, or efficiency of different plans of action; factors that would strengthen or weaken the prospects of success of a proposed plan of action; and assumptions underlying a proposed plan of action.

8.2 Test-Taking Strategies

1. **Read very carefully the set of statements on which a question is based.**

   Pay close attention to

   - what is put forward as factual information

   - what is not said but necessarily follows from what is said

   - what is claimed to follow from facts that have been put forward

   - how well substantiated are any claims that a particular conclusion follows from the facts that have been put forward

   In reading the arguments, it is important to pay attention to the logical reasoning used; the actual truth of statements portrayed as fact is not important.

2. **Identify the conclusion.**

   The conclusion does not necessarily come at the end of the text; it may come somewhere in the middle or even at the beginning. Be alert to clues in the text that an argument follows logically from another statement or statements in the text.

3. **Determine exactly what each question asks.**

   You might find it helpful to read the question first, before reading the material on which it is based; don't assume that you know what you will be asked about an argument. An argument may have obvious flaws, and one question may ask you to detect them. But another question may direct you to select the one answer choice that does NOT describe a flaw in the argument.

4. **Read all the answer choices carefully.**

   Do not assume that a given answer is the best without first reading all the choices.

8.3 The Directions

These are the directions you will see for critical reasoning questions when you take the GMAT exam. If you read them carefully and understand them clearly before going to sit for the test, you will not need to spend too much time reviewing them when you are at the test center and the test is under way.

For these questions, select the best of the answer choices given.

8.4 Practice Questions

Each of the underlined critical reasoning questions is based on a short argument, a set of statements, or a plan of action. For each question, select the best answer of the choices given.

1. Snowmaking machines work by spraying a mist that freezes immediately on contact with cold air. Because the sudden freezing kills bacteria, QuickFreeze is planning to market a wastewater purification system that works on the same principle. The process works only when temperatures are cold, however, so municipalities using it will still need to maintain a conventional system.

   Which of the following, if true, provides the strongest grounds for a prediction that municipalities will buy QuickFreeze's purification system despite the need to maintain a conventional purification system as well?

   (A) Bacteria are not the only impurities that must be removed from wastewater.

   (B) Many municipalities have old wastewater purification systems that need to be replaced.

   (C) Conventional wastewater purification systems have not been fully successful in killing bacteria at cold temperatures.

   (D) During times of warm weather, when it is not in use, QuickFreeze's purification system requires relatively little maintenance.

   (E) Places where the winters are cold rarely have a problem of water shortage.

2. Homeowners aged 40 to 50 are more likely to purchase ice cream and are more likely to purchase it in larger amounts than are members of any other demographic group. The popular belief that teenagers eat more ice cream than adults must, therefore, be false.

   The argument is flawed primarily because the author

   (A) fails to distinguish between purchasing and consuming

   (B) does not supply information about homeowners in age groups other than 40 to 50

   (C) depends on popular belief rather than on documented research findings

   (D) does not specify the precise amount of ice cream purchased by any demographic group

   (E) discusses ice cream rather than more nutritious and healthful foods

3. Suncorp, a new corporation with limited funds, has been clearing large sections of the tropical Amazon forest for cattle ranching. This practice continues even though greater profits can be made from rubber tapping, which does not destroy the forest, than from cattle ranching, which does destroy the forest.

   Which of the following, if true, most helps to explain why Suncorp has been pursuing the less profitable of the two economic activities mentioned above?

   (A) The soil of the Amazon forest is very rich in nutrients that are important in the development of grazing lands.

   (B) Cattle-ranching operations that are located in tropical climates are more profitable than cattle-ranching operations that are located in cold-weather climates.

(C)   In certain districts, profits made from cattle ranching are more heavily taxed than profits made from any other industry.

(D)   Some of the cattle that are raised on land cleared in the Amazon are killed by wildcats.

(E)   The amount of money required to begin a rubber-tapping operation is twice as high as the amount needed to begin a cattle ranch.

4.   According to a prediction of the not-so-distant future published in 1940, electricity would revolutionize agriculture. Electrodes would be inserted into the soil, and the current between them would kill bugs and weeds and make crop plants stronger.

Which of the following, if true, most strongly indicates that the logic of the prediction above is flawed?

(A)   In order for farmers to avoid electric shock while working in the fields, the current could be turned off at such times without diminishing the intended effects.

(B)   If the proposed plan for using electricity were put into practice, farmers would save on chemicals now being added to the soil.

(C)   It cannot be taken for granted that the use of electricity is always beneficial.

(D)   Since weeds are plants, electricity would affect weeds in the same way as it would affect crop plants.

(E)   Because a planting machine would need to avoid coming into contact with the electrodes, new parts for planting machines would need to be designed.

5.   A company is considering changing its policy concerning daily working hours. Currently, this company requires all employees to arrive at work at 8 a.m. The proposed policy would permit each employee to decide when to arrive—from as early as 6 a.m. to as late as 11 a.m.

The adoption of this policy would be most likely to decrease employees' productivity if the employees' job functions required them to

(A)   work without interruption from other employees

(B)   consult at least once a day with employees from other companies

(C)   submit their work for a supervisor's eventual approval

(D)   interact frequently with each other throughout the entire workday

(E)   undertake projects that take several days to complete

6.   Parland's alligator population has been declining in recent years, primarily because of hunting. Alligators prey heavily on a species of freshwater fish that is highly valued as food by Parlanders, who had hoped that the decline in the alligator population would lead to an increase in the numbers of these fish available for human consumption. Yet the population of this fish species has also declined, even though the annual number caught for human consumption has not increased.

Which of the following, if true, most helps to explain the decline in the population of the fish species?

(A)   The decline in the alligator population has meant that fishers can work in some parts of lakes and rivers that were formerly too dangerous.

(B)   Over the last few years, Parland's commercial fishing enterprises have increased the number of fishing boats they use.

(C)   The main predator of these fish is another species of fish on which alligators also prey.

(D)   Many Parlanders who hunt alligators do so because of the high market price of alligator skins, not because of the threat alligators pose to the fish population.

(E)   In several neighboring countries through which Parland's rivers also flow, alligators are at risk of extinction as a result of extensive hunting.

7. The amount of time it takes for most of a worker's occupational knowledge and skills to become obsolete has been declining because of the introduction of advanced manufacturing technology (AMT). Given the rate at which AMT is currently being introduced in manufacturing, the average worker's old skills become obsolete and new skills are required within as little as five years.

Which of the following plans, if feasible, would allow a company to prepare most effectively for the rapid obsolescence of skills described above?

(A) The company will develop a program to offer selected employees the opportunity to receive training six years after they were originally hired.

(B) The company will increase its investment in AMT every year for a period of at least five years.

(C) The company will periodically survey its employees to determine how the introduction of AMT has affected them.

(D) Before the introduction of AMT, the company will institute an educational program to inform its employees of the probable consequences of the introduction of AMT.

(E) The company will ensure that it can offer its employees any training necessary for meeting their job requirements.

8. In virtually any industry, technological improvements increase labor productivity, which is the output of goods and services per person-hour worked. In Parland's industries, labor productivity is significantly higher than it is in Vergia's industries. Clearly, therefore, Parland's industries must, on the whole, be further advanced technologically than Vergia's are.

The argument is most vulnerable to which of the following criticisms?

(A) It offers a conclusion that is no more than a paraphrase of one of the pieces of information provided in its support.

(B) It presents as evidence in support of a claim information that is inconsistent with other evidence presented in support of the same claim.

(C) It takes one possible cause of a condition to be the actual cause of that condition without considering any other possible causes.

(D) It takes a condition to be the effect of something that happened only after the condition already existed.

(E) It makes a distinction that presupposes the truth of the conclusion that is to be established.

9. While many people think of genetic manipulation of food crops as being aimed at developing larger and larger plant varieties, some plant breeders have in fact concentrated on discovering or producing dwarf varieties, which are roughly half as tall as normal varieties.

Which of the following would, if true, most help to explain the strategy of the plant breeders referred to above?

(A) Plant varieties used as food by some are used as ornamentals by others.

(B) The wholesale prices of a given crop decrease as the supply of it increases.

(C) Crops once produced exclusively for human consumption are often now used for animal feed.

(D) Short plants are less vulnerable to strong wind and heavy rains.

(E) Nations with large industrial sectors tend to consume more processed grains.

10. Traverton's city council wants to minimize the city's average yearly expenditures on its traffic signal lights and so is considering replacing the incandescent bulbs currently in use with arrays of light-emitting diodes (LEDs) as the incandescent bulbs burn out. Compared to incandescent bulbs, LED arrays consume significantly less energy and cost no more to purchase. Moreover, the costs associated with the conversion of existing fixtures so as to accept LED arrays would be minimal.

Which of the following would it be most useful to know in determining whether switching to LED arrays would be likely to help minimize Traverton's yearly maintenance costs?

(A)   Whether the expected service life of LED arrays is at least as long as that of the currently used incandescent bulbs

(B)   Whether any cities have switched from incandescent lights in their traffic signals to lighting elements other than LED arrays

(C)   Whether the company from which Traverton currently buys incandescent bulbs for traffic signals also sells LED arrays

(D)   Whether Traverton's city council plans to increase the number of traffic signal lights in Traverton

(E)   Whether the crews that currently replace incandescent bulbs in Traverton's traffic signals know how to convert the existing fixtures so as to accept LED arrays

11. The Maxilux car company's design for its new luxury model, the Max 100, included a special design for the tires that was intended to complement the model's image. The winning bid for supplying these tires was submitted by Rubco. Analysts concluded that the bid would only just cover Rubco's costs on the tires, but Rubco executives claim that winning the bid will actually make a profit for the company.

Which of the following, if true, most strongly justifies the claim made by Rubco's executives?

(A)   In any Maxilux model, the spare tire is exactly the same make and model as the tires that are mounted on the wheels.

(B)   Rubco holds exclusive contracts to supply Maxilux with the tires for a number of other models made by Maxilux.

(C)   The production facilities for the Max 100 and those for the tires to be supplied by Rubco are located very near each other.

(D)   When people who have purchased a carefully designed luxury automobile need to replace a worn part of it, they almost invariably replace it with a part of exactly the same make and type.

(E)   When Maxilux awarded the tire contract to Rubco, the only criterion on which Rubco's bid was clearly ahead of its competitors' bids was price.

12. Which of the following most logically completes the passage?

Most bicycle helmets provide good protection for the top and back of the head, but little or no protection for the temple regions on the sides of the head. A study of head injuries resulting from bicycle accidents showed that a large proportion were caused by blows to the temple area. Therefore, if bicycle helmets protected this area, the risk of serious head injury in bicycle accidents would be greatly reduced, especially since _____.

(A)   among the bicyclists included in the study's sample of head injuries, only a very small proportion had been wearing a helmet at the time of their accident

(B)   even those bicyclists who regularly wear helmets have a poor understanding of the degree and kind of protection that helmets afford

(C)   a helmet that included protection for the temples would have to be somewhat larger and heavier than current helmets

(D)   the bone in the temple area is relatively thin and impacts in that area are thus very likely to cause brain injury

(E)   bicyclists generally land on their arm or shoulder when they fall to the side, which reduces the likelihood of severe impacts on the side of the head

13. In order to reduce the number of items damaged while in transit to customers, packaging consultants recommended that the TrueSave mail-order company increase the amount of packing material so as to fill any empty spaces in its cartons. Accordingly, TrueSave officials instructed the company's packers to use more packing material than before, and the packers zealously acted on these instructions and used as much as they could. Nevertheless, customer reports of damaged items rose somewhat.

Which of the following, if true, most helps to explain why acting on the consultants' recommendation failed to achieve its goal?

(A) The change in packing policy led to an increase in expenditure on packing material and labor.

(B) When packing material is compressed too densely, it loses some of its capacity to absorb shock.

(C) The amount of packing material used in a carton does not significantly influence the ease with which a customer can unpack the package.

(D) Most of the goods that TrueSave ships are electronic products that are highly vulnerable to being damaged in transit.

(E) TrueSave has lost some of its regular customers as a result of the high number of damaged items they received.

14. Wood smoke contains dangerous toxins that cause changes in human cells. Because wood smoke presents such a high health risk, legislation is needed to regulate the use of open-air fires and wood-burning stoves.

Which of the following, if true, provides the most support for the argument above?

(A) The amount of dangerous toxins contained in wood smoke is much less than the amount contained in an equal volume of automobile exhaust.

(B) Within the jurisdiction covered by the proposed legislation, most heating and cooking is done with oil or natural gas.

(C) Smoke produced by coal-burning stoves is significantly more toxic than smoke from wood-burning stoves.

(D) No significant beneficial effect on air quality would result if open-air fires were banned within the jurisdiction covered by the proposed legislation.

(E) In valleys where wood is used as the primary heating fuel, the concentration of smoke results in poor air quality.

15. A certain automaker aims to increase its market share by deeply discounting its vehicles' prices for the next several months. The discounts will cut into profits, but because they will be heavily advertised the manufacturer hopes that they will attract buyers away from rival manufacturers' cars. In the longer term, the automaker envisions that customers initially attracted by the discounts may become loyal customers.

In assessing the plan's chances of achieving its aim, it would be most useful to know which of the following?

(A) Whether the automaker's competitors are likely to respond by offering deep discounts on their own products

(B) Whether the advertisements will be created by the manufacturer's current advertising agency

(C) Whether some of the automaker's models will be more deeply discounted than others

(D) Whether the automaker will be able to cut costs sufficiently to maintain profit margins even when the discounts are in effect

(E) Whether an alternative strategy might enable the automaker to enhance its profitability while holding a constant or diminishing share of the market

16. In Washington County, attendance at the movies is just large enough for the cinema operators to make modest profits. The size of the county's population is stable and is not expected to increase much. Yet there are investors ready to double the number of movie screens in the county within five years, and they are predicting solid profits both for themselves and for the established cinema operators.

Which of the following, if true about Washington County, most helps to provide a justification for the investors' prediction?

(A) Over the next ten years, people in their teenage years, the prime moviegoing age, will be a rapidly growing proportion of the county's population.

(B) As distinct from the existing cinemas, most of the cinemas being planned would be located in downtown areas, in hopes of stimulating an economic revitalization of those areas.

(C) Spending on video purchases, as well as spending on video rentals, has been increasing modestly each year for the past ten years.

(D) The average number of screens per cinema is lower among existing cinemas than it is among cinemas still in the planning stages.

(E) The sale of snacks and drinks in cinemas accounts for a steadily growing share of most cinema operators' profits.

17. Hollywood restaurant is replacing some of its standard tables with tall tables and stools. The restaurant already fills every available seat during its operating hours, and the change in seating arrangements will not result in an increase in the restaurant's seating capacity. Nonetheless, the restaurant's management expects revenue to increase as a result of the seating change without any concurrent change in menu, prices, or operating hours.

Which of the following, if true, provides the best reason for the expectation?

(A) One of the taller tables takes up less floor space than one of the standard tables.

(B) Diners seated on stools typically do not linger over dinner as long as diners seated at standard tables.

(C) Since the restaurant will replace only some of its standard tables, it can continue to accommodate customers who do not care for the taller tables.

(D) Few diners are likely to avoid the restaurant because of the new seating arrangement.

(E) The standard tables being replaced by tall tables would otherwise have to be replaced with new standard tables at a greater expense.

18. Hunter: **Many people blame hunters alone for the decline in Greenrock National Forest's deer population over the past ten years.** Yet clearly, black bears have also played an important role in this decline. In the past ten years, the forest's protected black bear population has risen sharply, and examination of black bears found dead in the forest during the deer hunting season showed that a number of them had recently fed on deer.

In the hunter's argument, the portion in boldface plays which of the following roles?

(A) It is the main conclusion of the argument.

(B) It is a finding that the argument seeks to explain.

(C) It is an explanation that the argument concludes is correct.

(D) It provides evidence in support of the main conclusion of the argument.

(E) It introduces a judgment that the argument opposes.

19. A major network news organization experienced a drop in viewership in the week following the airing of a controversial report on the economy. The network also received a very large number of complaints regarding the report. The network, however, maintains that negative reactions to the report had nothing to do with its loss of viewers.

Which of the following, if true, most strongly supports the network's position?

(A) The other major network news organizations reported similar reductions in viewership during the same week.

(B) The viewers who registered complaints with the network were regular viewers of the news organization's programs.

(C) Major network news organizations publicly attribute drops in viewership to their own reports only when they receive complaints about those reports.

(D) This was not the first time that this network news organization has aired a controversial report on the economy that has inspired viewers to complain to the network.

(E) Most network news viewers rely on network news broadcasts as their primary source of information regarding the economy.

20. Physician: The hormone melatonin has shown promise as a medication for sleep disorders when taken in synthesized form. Because the long-term side effects of synthetic melatonin are unknown, however, I cannot recommend its use at this time.

    Patient: Your position is inconsistent with your usual practice. You prescribe many medications that you know have serious side effects, so concern about side effects cannot be the real reason you will not prescribe melatonin.

    The patient's argument is flawed because it fails to consider that

    (A) the side effects of synthetic melatonin might be different from those of naturally produced melatonin
    (B) it is possible that the physician does not believe that melatonin has been conclusively shown to be effective
    (C) sleep disorders, if left untreated, might lead to serious medical complications
    (D) the side effects of a medication can take some time to manifest themselves
    (E) known risks can be weighed against known benefits, but unknown risks cannot

21. In recent years, many cabinetmakers have been winning acclaim as artists. But since furniture must be useful, cabinetmakers must exercise their craft with an eye to the practical utility of their product. For this reason, cabinetmaking is not art.

    Which of the following is an assumption that supports drawing the conclusion above from the reason given for that conclusion?

    (A) Some furniture is made to be placed in museums, where it will not be used by anyone.
    (B) Some cabinetmakers are more concerned than others with the practical utility of the products they produce.
    (C) Cabinetmakers should be more concerned with the practical utility of their products than they currently are.
    (D) An object is not an art object if its maker pays attention to the object's practical utility.
    (E) Artists are not concerned with the monetary value of their products.

22. Only a reduction of 10 percent in the number of scheduled flights using Greentown's airport will allow the delays that are so common there to be avoided. Hevelia airstrip, 40 miles away, would, if upgraded and expanded, be an attractive alternative for fully 20 percent of the passengers using Greentown airport. Nevertheless, experts reject the claim that turning Hevelia into a full-service airport would end the chronic delays at Greentown.

    Which of the following, if true, most helps to justify the experts' position?

    (A) Turning Hevelia into a full-service airport would require not only substantial construction at the airport itself, but also the construction of new access highways.
    (B) A second largely undeveloped airstrip close to Greentown airport would be a more attractive alternative than Hevelia for many passengers who now use Greentown.
    (C) Hevelia airstrip lies in a relatively undeveloped area but would, if it became a full-service airport, be a magnet for commercial and residential development.
    (D) If an airplane has to wait to land, the extra jet fuel required adds significantly to the airline's costs.
    (E) Several airlines use Greentown as a regional hub, so that most flights landing at Greentown have many passengers who then take different flights to reach their final destinations.

23. Male bowerbirds construct elaborately decorated nests, or bowers. Basing their judgment on the fact that different local populations of bowerbirds of the same species build bowers that exhibit different building and decorative styles, researchers have concluded that the bowerbirds' building styles are a culturally acquired, rather than a genetically transmitted, trait.

    Which of the following, if true, would most strengthen the conclusion drawn by the researchers?

(A) There are more common characteristics than there are differences among the bower-building styles of the local bowerbird population that has been studied most extensively.

(B) Young male bowerbirds are inept at bower-building and apparently spend years watching their elders before becoming accomplished in the local bower style.

(C) The bowers of one species of bowerbird lack the towers and ornamentation characteristic of the bowers of most other species of bowerbird.

(D) Bowerbirds are found only in New Guinea and Australia, where local populations of the birds apparently seldom have contact with one another.

(E) It is well known that the song dialects of some songbirds are learned rather than transmitted genetically.

24. Plan: Concerned about the welfare of its senior citizens, the government of Runagia decided two years ago to increase by 20 percent the government-provided pension paid to all Runagians age sixty-five and older.

Result: Many Runagian senior citizens are no better off financially now than they were before the increase.

Further information: The annual rate of inflation since the pension increase has been below 5 percent, and the increased pension has been duly received by all eligible Runagians.

In light of the further information, which of the following, if true, does most to explain the result that followed implementation of the plan?

(A) The majority of senior citizens whose financial position has not improved rely entirely on the government pension for their income.

(B) The Runagian banking system is so inefficient that cashing a pension check can take as much as three weeks.

(C) The prices of goods and services that meet the special needs of many senior citizens have increased at a rate much higher than the rate of inflation.

(D) The pension increase occurred at a time when the number of Runagians age sixty-five and older who were living below the poverty level was at an all-time high.

(E) The most recent pension increase was only the second such increase in the last ten years.

25. A drug that is highly effective in treating many types of infection can, at present, be obtained only from the bark of the ibora, a tree that is quite rare in the wild. It takes the bark of 5,000 trees to make one kilogram of the drug. It follows, therefore, that continued production of the drug must inevitably lead to the ibora's extinction.

Which of the following, if true, most seriously weakens the argument above?

(A) The drug made from ibora bark is dispensed to doctors from a central authority.

(B) The drug made from ibora bark is expensive to produce.

(C) The leaves of the ibora are used in a number of medical products.

(D) The ibora can be propagated from cuttings and grown under cultivation.

(E) The ibora generally grows in largely inaccessible places.

26. When a polygraph test is judged inconclusive, this is no reflection on the examinee. Rather, such a judgment means that the test has failed to show whether the examinee was truthful or untruthful. Nevertheless, employers will sometimes refuse to hire a job applicant because of an inconclusive polygraph test result.

Which of the following conclusions can most properly be drawn from the information above?

(A) Most examinees with inconclusive polygraph test results are in fact untruthful.

(B) Polygraph tests should not be used by employers in the consideration of job applicants.

(C) An inconclusive polygraph test result is sometimes unfairly held against the examinee.

(D) A polygraph test indicating that an examinee is untruthful can sometimes be mistaken.

(E) Some employers have refused to consider the results of polygraph tests when evaluating job applicants.

27. For similar cars and comparable drivers, automobile insurance for collision damage has always cost more in Greatport than in Fairmont. Police studies, however, show that cars owned by Greatport residents are, on average, slightly less likely to be involved in a collision than cars in Fairmont. Clearly, therefore, insurance companies are making a greater profit on collision-damage insurance in Greatport than in Fairmont.

    In evaluating the argument, it would be most useful to compare

    (A) the level of traffic congestion in Greatport with the level of traffic congestion in Fairmont

    (B) the cost of repairing collision damage in Greatport with the cost of repairing collision damage in Fairmont

    (C) the rates Greatport residents pay for other forms of insurance with the rates paid for similar insurance by residents of Fairmont

    (D) the condition of Greatport's roads and streets with the condition of Fairmont's roads and streets

    (E) the cost of collision-damage insurance in Greatport and Fairmont with that in other cities

28. Last year a record number of new manufacturing jobs were created. Will this year bring another record? Well, a new manufacturing job is created either within an existing company or by the start-up of a new company. Within existing firms, new jobs have been created this year at well below last year's record pace. At the same time, there is considerable evidence that the number of new companies starting up will be no higher this year than it was last year, and surely **the new companies starting up this year will create no more jobs per company than did last year's start-ups**. Clearly, it can be concluded that **the number of new jobs created this year will fall short of last year's record**.

    In the argument given, the two portions in boldface play which of the following roles?

    (A) The first is a prediction that, if accurate, would provide support for the main conclusion of the argument; the second is that main conclusion.

    (B) The first is a prediction that, if accurate, would provide support for the main conclusion of the argument; the second is a conclusion drawn in order to support that main conclusion.

    (C) The first is an objection that the argument rejects; the second is the main conclusion of the argument.

    (D) The first is an objection that the argument rejects; the second presents a conclusion that could be drawn if that objection were allowed to stand.

    (E) The first is a claim that has been advanced in support of a position that the argument opposes; the second is a claim advanced in support of the main conclusion of the argument.

29. The tulu, a popular ornamental plant, does not reproduce naturally, and is only bred and sold by specialized horticultural companies. Unfortunately, the tulu is easily devastated by a contagious fungal rot. The government ministry plans to reassure worried gardeners by requiring all tulu plants to be tested for fungal rot before being sold. However, infected plants less than 30 weeks old have generally not built up enough fungal rot in their systems to be detected reliably. And many tulu plants are sold before they are 24 weeks old.

    Which of the following, if performed by the government ministry, could logically be expected to overcome the problem with their plan to test for the fungal rot?

    (A) Releasing a general announcement that tulu plants less than 30 weeks old cannot be effectively tested for fungal rot

    (B) Requiring all tulu plants less than 30 weeks old to be labeled as such

    (C) Researching possible ways to test tulu plants less than 24 weeks old for fungal rot

    (D) Ensuring that tulu plants not be sold before they are 30 weeks old

    (E) Quarantining all tulu plants from horticultural companies at which any case of fungal rot has been detected until those tulu plants can be tested for fungal rot

30. The Eurasian ruffe, a fish species inadvertently introduced into North America's Great Lakes in recent years, feeds on the eggs of lake whitefish, a native species, thus threatening the lakes' natural ecosystem. To help track the ruffe's spread, government agencies have produced wallet-sized cards about the ruffe. The cards contain pictures of the ruffe and explain the danger they pose; the cards also request anglers to report any ruffe they catch.

    Which of the following, if true, would provide most support for the prediction that the agencies' action will have its intended effect?

    (A) The ruffe has spiny fins that make it unattractive as prey.

    (B) Ruffe generally feed at night, but most recreational fishing on the Great Lakes is done during daytime hours.

    (C) Most people who fish recreationally on the Great Lakes are interested in the preservation of the lake whitefish because it is a highly prized game fish.

    (D) The ruffe is one of several nonnative species in the Great Lakes whose existence threatens the survival of lake whitefish populations there.

    (E) The bait that most people use when fishing for whitefish on the Great Lakes is not attractive to ruffe.

31. Which of the following most logically completes the argument?

    Ferber's syndrome, a viral disease that frequently affects cattle, is transmitted to these animals through infected feed. Even though chickens commercially raised for meat are often fed the type of feed identified as the source of infection in cattle, Ferber's syndrome is only rarely observed in chickens. This fact, however, does not indicate that most chickens are immune to the virus that causes Ferber's syndrome, since _____ .

(A) chickens and cattle are not the only kinds of farm animal that are typically fed the type of feed liable to be contaminated with the virus that causes Ferber's syndrome

(B) Ferber's syndrome has been found in animals that have not been fed the type of feed liable to be contaminated with the virus that can cause the disease

(C) resistance to some infectious organisms such as the virus that causes Ferber's syndrome can be acquired by exposure to a closely related infectious organism

(D) chickens and cattle take more than a year to show symptoms of Ferber's syndrome, and chickens commercially raised for meat, unlike cattle, are generally brought to market during the first year of life

(E) the type of feed liable to be infected with the virus that causes Ferber's syndrome generally constitutes a larger proportion of the diet of commercially raised chickens than of commercially raised cattle

32. Last year the rate of inflation was 1.2 percent, but for the current year it has been 4 percent. We can conclude that inflation is on an upward trend and the rate will be still higher next year.

    Which of the following, if true, most seriously weakens the conclusion above?

    (A) The inflation figures were computed on the basis of a representative sample of economic data rather than all of the available data.

    (B) Last year a dip in oil prices brought inflation temporarily below its recent stable annual level of 4 percent.

    (C) Increases in the pay of some workers are tied to the level of inflation, and at an inflation rate of 4 percent or above, these pay raises constitute a force causing further inflation.

    (D) The 1.2 percent rate of inflation last year represented a 10-year low.

    (E) Government intervention cannot affect the rate of inflation to any significant degree.

33. Which of the following most logically completes the argument below?

Although the number of large artificial satellites orbiting the Earth is small compared to the number of small pieces of debris in orbit, the large satellites interfere more seriously with telescope observations because of the strong reflections they produce. Because many of those large satellites have ceased to function, the proposal has recently been made to eliminate interference from nonfunctioning satellites by exploding them in space. This proposal, however, is ill conceived, since _____.

(A) many nonfunctioning satellites remain in orbit for years

(B) for satellites that have ceased to function, repairing them while they are in orbit would be prohibitively expensive

(C) there are no known previous instances of satellites' having been exploded on purpose

(D) the only way to make telescope observations without any interference from debris in orbit is to use telescopes launched into extremely high orbits around the Earth

(E) a greatly increased number of small particles in Earth's orbit would result in a blanket of reflections that would make certain valuable telescope observations impossible

34. Thyrian lawmaker: Thyria's Cheese Importation Board inspects all cheese shipments to Thyria and rejects shipments not meeting specified standards. Yet only 1 percent is ever rejected. Therefore, since the health consequences and associated economic costs of not rejecting that 1 percent are negligible, whereas the board's operating costs are considerable, for economic reasons alone the board should be disbanded.

Consultant: I disagree. The threat of having their shipments rejected deters many cheese exporters from shipping substandard product.

The consultant responds to the lawmaker's argument by

(A) rejecting the lawmaker's argument while proposing that the standards according to which the board inspects imported cheese should be raised

(B) providing evidence that the lawmaker's argument has significantly overestimated the cost of maintaining the board

(C) objecting to the lawmaker's introducing into the discussion factors that are not strictly economic

(D) pointing out a benefit of maintaining the board, which the lawmaker's argument has failed to consider

(E) shifting the discussion from the argument at hand to an attack on the integrity of the cheese inspectors

35. Which of the following best completes the passage below?

The computer industry's estimate that it loses millions of dollars when users illegally copy programs without paying for them is greatly exaggerated. Most of the illegal copying is done by people with no serious interest in the programs. Thus, the loss to the industry is quite small, because _____.

(A) many users who illegally copy programs never find any use for them

(B) most people who illegally copy programs would not purchase them even if purchasing them were the only way to obtain them

(C) even if the computer industry received all the revenue it claims to be losing, it would still be experiencing financial difficulties

(D) the total market value of all illegal copies is low in comparison to the total revenue of the computer industry

(E) the number of programs that are frequently copied illegally is low in comparison to the number of programs available for sale

36. The growing popularity of computer-based activities was widely expected to result in a decline in television viewing, since it had been assumed that people lack sufficient free time to maintain current television-viewing levels while spending increasing amounts of free time on the computer. That assumption, however, is evidently false: In a recent mail survey concerning media use, a very large majority of respondents who report increasing time spent per week using computers report no change in time spent watching television.

Which of the following would it be most useful to determine in order to evaluate the argument?

(A) Whether a large majority of the survey respondents reported watching television regularly

(B) Whether the amount of time spent watching television is declining among people who report that they rarely or never use computers

(C) Whether the type of television programs a person watches tends to change as the amount of time spent per week using computers increases

(D) Whether a large majority of the computer owners in the survey reported spending increasing amounts of time per week using computers

(E) Whether the survey respondents' reports of time spent using computers included time spent using computers at work

37. In the last decade there has been a significant decrease in coffee consumption. During this same time, there has been increasing publicity about the adverse long-term effects on health of the caffeine in coffee. Therefore, the decrease in coffee consumption must have been caused by consumers' awareness of the harmful effects of caffeine.

Which of the following, if true, most seriously calls into question the explanation above?

(A) On average, people consume 30 percent less coffee today than they did 10 years ago.

(B) Heavy coffee drinkers may have mild withdrawal symptoms, such as headaches, for a day or so after significantly decreasing their coffee consumption.

(C) Sales of specialty types of coffee have held steady as sales of regular brands have declined.

(D) The consumption of fruit juices and caffeine-free herbal teas has increased over the past decade.

(E) Coffee prices increased steadily in the past decade because of unusually severe frosts in coffee-growing nations.

38. Which of the following best completes the passage below?

When the products of several competing suppliers are perceived by consumers to be essentially the same, classical economics predicts that price competition will reduce prices to the same minimal levels and all suppliers' profits to the same minimal levels. Therefore, if classical economics is true, and given suppliers' desire to make as much profit as possible, it should be expected that _____.

(A) in a crowded market widely differing prices will be charged for products that are essentially the same as each other

(B) as a market becomes less crowded as suppliers leave, the profits of the remaining suppliers will tend to decrease

(C) each supplier in a crowded market will try to convince consumers that its product differs significantly from its competitors' products.

(D) when consumers are unable to distinguish the products in a crowded market, consumers will judge that the higher-priced products are of higher quality

(E) suppliers in crowded markets will have more incentive to reduce prices and thus increase sales than to introduce innovations that would distinguish their product from their competitors' products

39. Which of the following most logically completes the argument?

Sviatovin is a medieval Moringian text whose author and exact date of composition are unknown. However, the events in the life of Prince Sviatov that the text describes occurred in 1165, and in the diagram of Sviatov's family that accompanies the text his father, who died in 1167, is identified as still living. Thus *Sviatovin* must have been written between 1165 and 1167, assuming that _____.

(A) the life of Prince Sviatov is not the subject of any other medieval Moringian texts

(B) the author of *Sviatovin* intended it to provide as accurate a report about Prince Sviatov's exploits as possible

(C) the diagram accurately represents the composition of Sviatov's family at the time *Sviatovin* was written

(D) *Sviatovin* is the earliest Moringian text whose composition can be dated to within a few years

(E) *Sviatovin* was not written by Sviatov's father himself

40. Crowding on Mooreville's subway frequently leads to delays, because it is difficult for passengers to exit from the trains. Subway ridership is projected to increase by 20 percent over the next 10 years. The Mooreville Transit Authority plans to increase the number of daily train trips by only 5 percent over the same period. Officials predict that this increase is sufficient to ensure that the incidence of delays due to crowding does not increase.

Which of the following, if true, provides the strongest grounds for the officials' prediction?

(A) By changing maintenance schedules, the Transit Authority can achieve the 5 percent increase in train trips without purchasing any new subway cars.

(B) The Transit Authority also plans a 5 percent increase in the number of bus trips on routes that connect to subways.

(C) For most commuters who use the subway system, there is no practical alternative public transportation available.

(D) Most of the projected increase in ridership is expected to occur in off-peak hours when trains are now sparsely used.

(E) The 5 percent increase in the number of train trips can be achieved without an equal increase in Transit Authority operational costs.

41. Installing scrubbers in smokestacks and switching to cleaner-burning fuel are the two methods available to Northern Power for reducing harmful emissions from its plants. Scrubbers will reduce harmful emissions more than cleaner-burning fuels will. Therefore, by installing scrubbers, Northern Power will be doing the most that can be done to reduce harmful emissions from its plants.

Which of the following is an assumption on which the argument depends?

(A) Switching to cleaner-burning fuel will not be more expensive than installing scrubbers.

(B) Northern Power can choose from among various kinds of scrubbers, some of which are more effective than others.

(C) Northern Power is not necessarily committed to reducing harmful emissions from its plants.

(D) Harmful emissions from Northern Power's plants cannot be reduced more by using both methods together than by the installation of scrubbers alone.

(E) Aside from harmful emissions from the smokestacks of its plants, the activities of Northern Power do not cause significant air pollution.

42. Trancorp currently transports all its goods to Burland Island by truck. The only bridge over the channel separating Burland from the mainland is congested, and trucks typically spend hours in traffic. Trains can reach the channel more quickly than trucks, and freight cars can be transported to Burland by barges that typically cross the channel in an hour. Therefore, to reduce shipping time, Trancorp plans to switch to trains and barges to transport goods to Burland.

Which of the following would be most important to know in determining whether Trancorp's plan, if implemented, is likely to achieve its goal?

(A) Whether transportation by train and barge would be substantially less expensive than transportation by truck

(B) Whether there are boats that can make the trip between the mainland and Burland faster than barges can

(C) Whether loading the freight cars onto barges is very time consuming

(D) Whether the average number of vehicles traveling over the bridge into Burland has been relatively constant in recent years

(E) Whether most trucks transporting goods into Burland return to the mainland empty

43. Some anthropologists study modern-day societies of foragers in an effort to learn about our ancient ancestors who were also foragers. A flaw in this strategy is that forager societies are extremely varied. Indeed, any forager society with which anthropologists are familiar has had considerable contact with modern, non-forager societies.

Which of the following, if true, would most weaken the criticism made above of the anthropologists' strategy?

(A) All forager societies throughout history have had a number of important features in common that are absent from other types of societies.

(B) Most ancient forager societies either dissolved or made a transition to another way of life.

(C) All anthropologists study one kind or another of modern-day society.

(D) Many anthropologists who study modern-day forager societies do not draw inferences about ancient societies on the basis of their studies.

(E) Even those modern-day forager societies that have not had significant contact with modern societies are importantly different from ancient forager societies.

44. Contrary to earlier predictions, demand for sugarcane has not increased in recent years. Yet, even though prices and production amounts have also been stable during the last three years, sugarcane growers last year increased their profits by more than 10 percent over the previous year's level.

Any of the following statements, if true about last year, helps to explain the rise in profits EXCEPT:

(A) Many countries that are large consumers of sugarcane increased their production of sugarcane-based ethanol, yet their overall consumption of sugarcane decreased.

(B) Sugarcane growers have saved money on wages by switching from paying laborers an hourly wage to paying them by the amount harvested.

(C) The price of oil, the major energy source used by sugarcane growers in harvesting their crops, dropped by over 20 percent.

(D) Many small sugarcane growers joined together to form an association of sugarcane producers and began to buy supplies at low group rates.

(E) Rainfall in sugarcane-growing regions was higher than it had been during the previous year, allowing the growers to save money on expensive artificial irrigation.

45. Which of the following most logically completes the argument below?

Davison River farmers are currently deciding between planting winter wheat this fall or spring wheat next spring. Winter wheat and spring wheat are usually about equally profitable. Because of new government restrictions on the use of Davison River water for irrigation, per acre yields for winter wheat, though not for spring wheat, would be much lower than average. Therefore, planting spring wheat will be more profitable than planting winter wheat, since _____.

(A) the smaller-than-average size of a winter wheat harvest this year would not be compensated for by higher winter wheat prices

(B) new crops of spring wheat must be planted earlier than the time at which standing crops of winter wheat are ready to be harvested

(C) the spring wheat that farmers in the Davison River region plant is well adapted to the soil of the region

(D) spring wheat has uses that are different from those of winter wheat

(E) planting spring wheat is more profitable than planting certain other crops, such as rye

46. If the county continues to collect residential trash at current levels, landfills will soon be overflowing and parkland will need to be used in order to create more space. Charging each household a fee for each pound of trash it puts out for collection will induce residents to reduce the amount of trash they create; this charge will therefore protect the remaining county parkland.

Which of the following is an assumption made in drawing the conclusion above?

(A) Residents will reduce the amount of trash they put out for collection by reducing the number of products they buy.

(B) The collection fee will not significantly affect the purchasing power of most residents, even if their households do not reduce the amount of trash they put out.

(C) The collection fee will not induce residents to dump their trash in the parklands illegally.

(D) The beauty of county parkland is an important issue for most of the county's residents.

(E) Landfills outside the county's borders could be used as dumping sites for the county's trash.

47. Certain genetically modified strains of maize produce a powerful natural insecticide. The insecticide occurs throughout the plant, including its pollen. Maize pollen is dispersed by the wind and frequently blows onto milkweed plants that grow near maize fields. Caterpillars of monarch butterflies feed exclusively on milkweed leaves. When these caterpillars are fed milkweed leaves dusted with pollen from modified maize plants, they die. Therefore, by using genetically modified maize, farmers put monarch butterflies at risk.

Which of the following would it be most useful to determine in order to evaluate the argument?

(A) Whether the natural insecticide is as effective against maize-eating insects as commercial insecticides typically used on maize are

(B) Whether the pollen of genetically modified maize contains as much insecticide as other parts of these plants

(C) Whether monarch butterfly caterpillars are actively feeding during the part of the growing season when maize is releasing pollen

(D) Whether insects that feed on genetically modified maize plants are likely to be killed by insecticide from the plant's pollen

(E) Whether any maize-eating insects compete with monarch caterpillars for the leaves of milkweed plants growing near maize fields

48. Although computers can enhance people's ability to communicate, computer games are a cause of underdeveloped communication skills in children. After-school hours spent playing computer games are hours not spent talking with people. Therefore, children who spend all their spare time playing these games have less experience in interpersonal communication than other children have.

The argument depends on which of the following assumptions?

(A) Passive activities such as watching television and listening to music do not hinder the development of communication skills in children.

(B) Most children have other opportunities, in addition to after-school hours, in which they can choose whether to play computer games or to interact with other people.

(C) Children who do not spend all of their after-school hours playing computer games spend at least some of that time talking with other people.

(D) Formal instruction contributes little or nothing to children's acquisition of communication skills.

(E) The mental skills developed through playing computer games do not contribute significantly to children's intellectual development.

49. Maize contains the vitamin niacin, but not in a form the body can absorb. Pellagra is a disease that results from niacin deficiency. When maize was introduced into southern Europe from the Americas in the eighteenth century, it quickly became a dietary staple, and many Europeans who came to subsist primarily on maize developed pellagra. Pellagra was virtually unknown at that time in the Americas, however, even among people who subsisted primarily on maize.

    Which of the following, if true, most helps to explain the contrasting incidence of pellagra described above?

    (A) Once introduced into southern Europe, maize became popular with landowners because of its high yields relative to other cereal crops.

    (B) Maize grown in the Americas contained more niacin than maize grown in Europe did.

    (C) Traditional ways of preparing maize in the Americas convert maize's niacin into a nutritionally useful form.

    (D) In southern Europe many of the people who consumed maize also ate niacin-rich foods.

    (E) Before the discovery of pellagra's link with niacin, it was widely believed that the disease was an infection that could be transmitted from person to person.

50. One variety of partially biodegradable plastic beverage container is manufactured from small bits of plastic bound together by a degradable bonding agent such as cornstarch. Since only the bonding agent degrades, leaving the small bits of plastic, no less plastic refuse per container is produced when such containers are discarded than when comparable nonbiodegradable containers are discarded.

    Which of the following, if true, most strengthens the argument above?

    (A) Both partially biodegradable and non-biodegradable plastic beverage containers can be crushed completely flat by refuse compactors.

    (B) The partially biodegradable plastic beverage containers are made with more plastic than comparable nonbiodegradable ones in order to compensate for the weakening effect of the bonding agents.

    (C) Many consumers are ecology-minded and prefer to buy a product sold in the partially biodegradable plastic beverage containers rather than in nonbiodegradable containers, even if the price is higher.

    (D) The manufacturing process for the partially biodegradable plastic beverage containers results in less plastic waste than the manufacturing process for nonbiodegradable plastic beverage containers.

    (E) Technological problems with recycling currently prevent the reuse as food or beverage containers of the plastic from either type of plastic beverage container.

51. Rye sown in the fall and plowed into the soil in early spring leaves a residue that is highly effective at controlling broad-leaved weeds, but unfortunately for only about forty-five days. No major agricultural crop matures from seed in as little as forty-five days. Synthetic herbicides, on the other hand, although not any longer-lasting, can be reapplied as the crop grows. Clearly, therefore, for major agricultural crops, plowing rye into the soil can play no part in effective weed control.

    The argument is most vulnerable to the objection that it fails to

    (A) consider that there might be minor, quick-growing crops that do mature in forty-five days or less

    (B) identify any alternative method of weed control that could be used instead of the method it rejects

    (C) distinguish among the various kinds of synthetic herbicides

    (D) allow for the possibility of combining the two weed-control methods it mentions

    (E) allow for the possibility that plants other than rye, handled the same way, might have the same effect

52. Most employees in the computer industry move from company to company, changing jobs several times in their careers. However, Summit Computers is known throughout the industry for retaining its employees. Summit credits its success in retaining employees to its informal, nonhierarchical work environment.

    Which of the following, if true, most strongly supports Summit's explanation of its success in retaining employees?

    (A) Some people employed in the computer industry change jobs if they become bored with their current projects.

    (B) A hierarchical work environment hinders the cooperative exchange of ideas that computer industry employees consider necessary for their work.

    (C) Many of Summit's senior employees had previously worked at only one other computer company.

    (D) In a nonhierarchical work environment, people avoid behavior that might threaten group harmony and thus avoid discussing with their colleagues any dissatisfaction they might have with their jobs.

    (E) The cost of living near Summit is relatively low compared to areas in which some other computer companies are located.

53. Insurance Company X is considering issuing a new policy to cover services required by elderly people who suffer from diseases that afflict the elderly. Premiums for the policy must be low enough to attract customers. Therefore, Company X is concerned that the income from the policies would not be sufficient to pay for the claims that would be made.

    Which of the following strategies would be most likely to minimize Company X's losses on the policies?

    (A) Attracting middle-aged customers unlikely to submit claims for benefits for many years

    (B) Insuring only those individuals who did not suffer any serious diseases as children

    (C) Including a greater number of services in the policy than are included in other policies of lower cost

    (D) Insuring only those individuals who were rejected by other companies for similar policies

    (E) Insuring only those individuals who are wealthy enough to pay for the medical services

54. The fewer restrictions there are on the advertising of legal services, the more lawyers there are who advertise their services, and the lawyers who advertise a specific service usually charge less for that service than the lawyers who do not advertise. Therefore, if the state removes any of its current restrictions, such as the one against advertisements that do not specify fee arrangements, overall consumer legal costs will be lower than if the state retains its current restrictions.

    If the statements above are true, which of the following must be true?

    (A) Some lawyers who now advertise will charge more for specific services if they do not have to specify fee arrangements in the advertisements.

    (B) More consumers will use legal services if there are fewer restrictions on the advertising of legal services.

    (C) If the restriction against advertisements that do not specify fee arrangements is removed, more lawyers will advertise their services.

    (D) If more lawyers advertise lower prices for specific services, some lawyers who do not advertise will also charge less than they currently charge for those services.

    (E) If the only restrictions on the advertising of legal services were those that apply to every type of advertising, most lawyers would advertise their services.

55. Which of the following most logically completes the argument given below?

    People in isolated rain-forest communities tend to live on a largely vegetarian diet, and they eat little salt. Few of them suffer from high blood pressure, and their blood pressure does not tend to increase with age, as is common in industrialized countries. Such people often do develop high blood pressure when they move to cities and adopt high-salt diets. Though suggestive, these facts do not establish salt as the culprit in high blood pressure, however, because _____.

(A)   genetic factors could account for the lack of increase of blood pressure with age among such people

(B)   people eating high-salt diets and living from birth in cities in industrialized societies generally have a tendency to have high blood pressure

(C)   it is possible to have a low-salt diet while living in a city in an industrialized country

(D)   there are changes in other aspects of diet when such people move to the city

(E)   salt is a necessity for human life, and death can occur when the body loses too much salt

56.   Even though most universities retain the royalties from faculty members' inventions, the faculty members retain the royalties from books and articles they write. Therefore, faculty members should retain the royalties from the educational computer software they develop.

The conclusion above would be more reasonably drawn if which of the following were inserted into the argument as an additional premise?

(A)   Royalties from inventions are higher than royalties from educational software programs.

(B)   Faculty members are more likely to produce educational software programs than inventions.

(C)   Inventions bring more prestige to universities than do books and articles.

(D)   In the experience of most universities, educational software programs are more marketable than are books and articles.

(E)   In terms of the criteria used to award royalties, educational software programs are more nearly comparable to books and articles than to inventions.

57.   In order to withstand tidal currents, juvenile horseshoe crabs frequently burrow in the sand. Such burrowing discourages barnacles from clinging to their shells. When fully grown, however, the crabs can readily withstand tidal currents without burrowing, and thus they acquire substantial populations of barnacles. Surprisingly, in areas where tidal currents are very weak, juvenile horseshoe crabs are found not to have significant barnacle populations, even though they seldom burrow.

Which of the following, if true, most helps to explain the surprising finding?

(A)   Tidal currents do not themselves dislodge barnacles from the shells of horseshoe crabs.

(B)   Barnacles most readily attach themselves to horseshoe crabs in areas where tidal currents are weakest.

(C)   The strength of the tidal currents in a given location varies widely over the course of a day.

(D)   A very large barnacle population can significantly decrease the ability of a horseshoe crab to find food.

(E)   Until they are fully grown, horseshoe crabs shed their shells and grow new ones several times a year.

58.   Red blood cells in which the malarial-fever parasite resides are eliminated from a person's body after 120 days. Because the parasite cannot travel to a new generation of red blood cells, any fever that develops in a person more than 120 days after that person has moved to a malaria-free region is not due to the malarial parasite.

Which of the following, if true, most seriously weakens the conclusion above?

(A)   The fever caused by the malarial parasite may resemble the fever caused by flu viruses.

(B)   The anopheles mosquito, which is the principal insect carrier of the malarial parasite, has been eradicated in many parts of the world.

(C)   Many malarial symptoms other than the fever, which can be suppressed with antimalarial medication, can reappear within 120 days after the medication is discontinued.

(D)   In some cases, the parasite that causes malarial fever travels to cells of the spleen, which are less frequently eliminated from a person's body than are red blood cells.

(E)   In any region infested with malaria-carrying mosquitoes, there are individuals who appear to be immune to malaria.

59. Which of the following most logically completes the passage?

A recent government study links the high rates of respiratory ailments in Groverston to airborne pollutants released by the Woodco plywood manufacturing plant there. To address the problem, the government imposed strict regulations on emissions which will go into effect in four years. Although Woodco plans to cut its emissions in half two years ahead of schedule, it is unlikely that the rate of respiratory ailments will decline before the regulations go into effect, since _____.

(A) the number of facilities capable of treating respiratory ailments is not likely to increase

(B) reducing emissions even further than planned would necessitate decreasing production at Woodco

(C) it is difficult to make accurate, long-term predictions about emissions

(D) not all respiratory ailments are caused by airborne pollutants

(E) three new plywood manufacturing plants are about to go into production in Groverston

60. Neither a rising standard of living nor balanced trade, by itself, establishes a country's ability to compete in the international marketplace. Both are required simultaneously since standards of living can rise because of growing trade deficits and trade can be balanced by means of a decline in a country's standard of living.

If the facts stated in the passage above are true, a proper test of a country's ability to be competitive is its ability to

(A) balance its trade while its standard of living rises

(B) balance its trade while its standard of living falls

(C) increase trade deficits while its standard of living rises

(D) decrease trade deficits while its standard of living falls

(E) keep its standard of living constant while trade deficits rise

61. When there is less rainfall than normal, the water level of Australian rivers falls and the rivers flow more slowly. Because algae whose habitat is river water grow best in slow-moving water, the amount of algae per unit of water generally increases when there has been little rain. By contrast, however, following a period of extreme drought, algae levels are low even in very slow-moving river water.

Which of the following, if true, does most to explain the contrast described above?

(A) During periods of extreme drought, the populations of some of the species that feed on algae tend to fall.

(B) The more slowly water moves, the more conducive its temperature is to the growth of algae.

(C) When algae populations reach very high levels, conditions within the river can become toxic for some of the other species that normally live there.

(D) Australian rivers dry up completely for short intervals in periods of extreme drought.

(E) Except during periods of extreme drought, algae levels tend to be higher in rivers in which the flow has been controlled by damming than in rivers that flow freely.

62. When hypnotized subjects are told that they are deaf and are then asked whether they can hear the hypnotist, they reply, "No." Some theorists try to explain this result by arguing that the selves of hypnotized subjects are dissociated into separate parts, and that the part that is deaf is dissociated from the part that replies.

Which of the following challenges indicates the most serious weakness in the attempted explanation described above?

(A) Why does the part that replies not answer, "Yes"?

(B) Why are the observed facts in need of any special explanation?

(C) Why do the subjects appear to accept the hypnotist's suggestion that they are deaf?

(D) Why do hypnotized subjects all respond the same way in the situation described?

(E) Why are the separate parts of the self the same for all subjects?

63. A prominent investor who holds a large stake in the Burton Tool Company has recently claimed that **the company is mismanaged**, citing as evidence the company's failure to slow production in response to a recent rise in its inventory of finished products. It is doubtful whether an investor's sniping at management can ever be anything other than counterproductive, **but in this case it is clearly not justified**. It is true that an increased inventory of finished products often indicates that production is outstripping demand, but in Burton's case it indicates no such thing. Rather, the increase in inventory is entirely attributable to products that have already been assigned to orders received from customers.

In the argument given, the two boldfaced portions play which of the following roles?

(A) The first states the position that the argument as a whole opposes; the second provides evidence to undermine the support for the position being opposed.

(B) The first states the position that the argument as a whole opposes; the second is evidence that has been used to support the position being opposed.

(C) The first states the position that the argument as a whole opposes; the second states the conclusion of the argument as a whole.

(D) The first is evidence that has been used to support a position that the argument as a whole opposes; the second provides information to undermine the force of that evidence.

(E) The first is evidence that has been used to support a position that the argument as a whole opposes; the second states the conclusion of the argument as a whole.

64. Excavation of the ancient city of Kourion on the island of Cyprus revealed a pattern of debris and collapsed buildings typical of towns devastated by earthquakes. Archaeologists have hypothesized that the destruction was due to a major earthquake known to have occurred near the island in A.D. 365.

Which of the following, if true, most strongly supports the archaeologists' hypothesis?

(A) Bronze ceremonial drinking vessels that are often found in graves dating from years preceding and following A.D. 365 were also found in several graves near Kourion.

(B) No coins minted after A.D. 365 were found in Kourion, but coins minted before that year were found in abundance.

(C) Most modern histories of Cyprus mention that an earthquake occurred near the island in A.D. 365.

(D) Several small statues carved in styles current in Cyprus in the century between A.D. 300 and A.D. 400 were found in Kourion.

(E) Stone inscriptions in a form of the Greek alphabet that was definitely used in Cyprus after A.D. 365 were found in Kourion.

65. Which of the following most logically completes the passage?

Pecan growers get a high price for their crop when pecans are comparatively scarce, but the price drops sharply when pecans are abundant. Thus, in high-yield years, growers often hold back part of their crop in refrigerated warehouses for one or two years, hoping for higher prices in the future. This year's pecan crop was the smallest in five years. It is nonetheless quite possible that a portion of this year's crop will be held back, since _____.

(A) each of the last two years produced record-breaking pecan yields

(B) the quality of this year's pecan crop is no worse than the quality of the pecan crops of the previous five years

(C) pecan prices have not been subject to sharp fluctuations in recent years

(D) for some pecan growers, this year's crop was no smaller than last year's

(E) the practice of holding back part of one year's crop had not yet become widespread the last time the pecan crop was as small as it was this year

66. To protect certain fledgling industries, the government of Country Z banned imports of the types of products those industries were starting to make. As a direct result, the cost of those products to the buyers, several export-dependent industries in Z, went up, sharply limiting the ability of those industries to compete effectively in their export markets.

Which of the following conclusions about Country Z's adversely affected export-dependent industries is best supported by the passage?

(A) Profit margins in those industries were not high enough to absorb the rise in costs mentioned above.

(B) Those industries had to contend with the fact that other countries banned imports from Country Z.

(C) Those industries succeeded in expanding the domestic market for their products.

(D) Steps to offset rising materials costs by decreasing labor costs were taken in those industries.

(E) Those industries started to move into export markets that they had previously judged unprofitable.

67. Several industries have recently switched at least partly from older technologies powered by fossil fuels to new technologies powered by electricity. It is thus evident that less fossil fuel is being used as a result of the operations of these industries than would have been used if these industries had retained their older technologies.

Which of the following, if true, most strengthens the argument above?

(A) Many of the industries that have switched at least partly to the new technologies have increased their output.

(B) Less fossil fuel was used to manufacture the machinery employed in the new technologies than was originally used to manufacture the machinery employed in the older technologies.

(C) More electricity is used by those industries that have switched at least partly to the new technologies than by those industries that have not switched.

(D) Some of the industries that have switched at least partly to the new technologies still use primarily technologies that are powered by fossil fuels.

(E) The amount of fossil fuel used to generate the electricity needed to power the new technologies is less than the amount that would have been used to power the older technologies.

68. Scientists have modified feed corn genetically, increasing its resistance to insect pests. Farmers who tried out the genetically modified corn last season applied less insecticide to their corn fields and still got yields comparable to those they would have gotten with ordinary corn. Ordinary corn seed, however, costs less, and what these farmers saved on insecticide rarely exceeded their extra costs for seed. Therefore, for most feed-corn farmers, switching to genetically modified seed would be unlikely to increase profits.

Which of the following would it be most useful to know in order to evaluate the argument?

(A) Whether there are insect pests that sometimes reduce feed-corn yields, but against which commonly used insecticides and the genetic modification are equally ineffective

(B) Whether the price that farmers receive for feed corn has remained steady over the past few years

(C) Whether the insecticides typically used on feed corn tend to be more expensive than insecticides typically used on other crops

(D) Whether most of the farmers who tried the genetically modified corn last season applied more insecticide than was actually necessary

(E) Whether, for most farmers who plant feed corn, it is their most profitable crop

69. Which of the following most logically completes the argument?

    By competing with rodents for seeds, black ants help control rodent populations that pose a public health risk. However, a very aggressive species of black ant, the Loma ant, which has recently invaded a certain region, has a venomous sting that is often fatal to humans. Therefore, the planned introduction into that region of ant flies, which prey on Loma ants, would benefit public health, since _____.

    (A) ant flies do not attack black ants other than Loma ants

    (B) Loma ants are less effective than many bird species in competing with rodents for seeds

    (C) certain other species of black ants are more effective than Loma ants in competing with rodents for seeds

    (D) the sting of Loma ants can also be fatal to rodents

    (E) some pesticides that could be used to control Loma ants are harmful to the environment

70. Community activist: If Morganville wants to keep its central shopping district healthy, it should prevent the opening of a huge SaveAll discount department store on the outskirts of Morganville. Records from other small towns show that whenever SaveAll has opened a store outside the central shopping district of a small town, within five years the town has experienced the bankruptcies of more than a quarter of the stores in the shopping district.

    The answer to which of the following would be most useful for evaluating the community activist's reasoning?

    (A) Have community activists in other towns successfully campaigned against the opening of a SaveAll store on the outskirts of their towns?

    (B) Do a large percentage of the residents of Morganville currently do almost all of their shopping at stores in Morganville?

    (C) In towns with healthy central shopping districts, what proportion of the stores in those districts suffer bankruptcy during a typical five-year period?

    (D) What proportion of the employees at the SaveAll store on the outskirts of Morganville will be drawn from Morganville?

    (E) Do newly opened SaveAll stores ever lose money during their first five years of operation?

71. In comparison to the standard typewriter keyboard, the EFCO keyboard, which places the most-used keys nearest the typist's strongest fingers, allows faster typing and results in less fatigue. Therefore, replacement of standard keyboards with the EFCO keyboard will result in an immediate reduction of typing costs.

    Which of the following, if true, would most weaken the conclusion drawn above?

    (A) People who use both standard and EFCO keyboards report greater difficulty in the transition from the EFCO keyboard to the standard keyboard than in the transition from the standard keyboard to the EFCO keyboard.

    (B) EFCO keyboards are no more expensive to manufacture than are standard keyboards and require less frequent repair than do standard keyboards.

    (C) The number of businesses and government agencies that use EFCO keyboards is increasing each year.

    (D) The more training and experience an employee has had with the standard keyboard, the more costly it is to train that employee to use the EFCO keyboard.

    (E) Novice typists can learn to use the EFCO keyboard in about the same amount of time that it takes them to learn to use the standard keyboard.

72. In the past the country of Malvernia has relied heavily on imported oil. Malvernia recently implemented a program to convert heating systems from oil to natural gas. Malvernia currently produces more natural gas each year than it uses, and oil production in Malvernian oil fields is increasing at a steady pace. If these trends in fuel production and usage continue, therefore, Malvernian reliance on foreign sources for fuel is likely to decline soon.

Which of the following would it be most useful to establish in evaluating the argument?

(A) When, if ever, will production of oil in Malvernia outstrip production of natural gas?

(B) Is Malvernia among the countries that rely most on imported oil?

(C) What proportion of Malvernia's total energy needs is met by hydroelectric, solar, and nuclear power?

(D) Is the amount of oil used each year in Malvernia for generating electricity and fuel for transportation increasing?

(E) Have any existing oil-burning heating systems in Malvernia already been converted to natural-gas-burning heating systems?

73. An overly centralized economy, not the changes in the climate, is responsible for the poor agricultural production in Country X since its new government came to power. Neighboring Country Y has experienced the same climatic conditions, but while agricultural production has been falling in Country X, it has been rising in Country Y.

Which of the following, if true, would most weaken the argument above?

(A) Industrial production also is declining in Country X.

(B) Whereas Country Y is landlocked, Country X has a major seaport.

(C) Both Country X and Country Y have been experiencing drought conditions.

(D) The crops that have always been grown in Country X are different from those that have always been grown in Country Y.

(E) Country X's new government instituted a centralized economy with the intention of ensuring an equitable distribution of goods.

74. Which of the following most logically completes the argument below?

Using broad-spectrum weed killers on weeds that are competing with crops for sunlight, water, and nutrients presents a difficulty: how to keep the crop from being killed along with the weeds. For at least some food crops, specially treated seed that produces plants resistant to weed killers is under development. This resistance wears off as the plants mature. Therefore, the special seed treatment will be especially useful for plants that _____.

(A) produce their crop over an extended period of time, as summer squash does

(B) produce large seeds that are easy to treat individually, as corn and beans do

(C) provide, as they approach maturity, shade dense enough to keep weeds from growing

(D) are typically grown in large tracts devoted to a single crop

(E) are cultivated specifically for the seed they produce rather than for their leaves or roots

75. Because no employee wants to be associated with bad news in the eyes of a superior, information about serious problems at lower levels is progressively softened and distorted as it goes up each step in the management hierarchy. The chief executive is, therefore, less well informed about problems at lower levels than are his or her subordinates at those levels.

The conclusion drawn above is based on the assumption that

(A) problems should be solved at the level in the management hierarchy at which they occur

(B) employees should be rewarded for accurately reporting problems to their superiors

(C) problem-solving ability is more important at higher levels than it is at lower levels of the management hierarchy

(D) chief executives obtain information about problems at lower levels from no source other than their subordinates

(E) some employees are more concerned about truth than about the way they are perceived by their superiors

76. Although the earliest surviving Greek inscriptions written in an alphabet date from the eighth century B.C., **the fact that the text of these Greek inscriptions sometimes runs from right to left and sometimes from left to right** indicates that the Greeks adopted alphabetic writing at least two centuries before these inscriptions were produced. After all, the Greeks learned alphabetic writing from the Phoenicians, and presumably, along with the alphabet, they also adopted the then-current Phoenician practice with respect to the direction of text. **And although Phoenician writing was originally inconsistent in direction, by the eighth century B.C. Phoenician was consistently written from right to left and had been for about two centuries**.

In the argument given, the two portions in boldface play which of the following roles?

(A) The first and the second each describe evidence that has been used to challenge the position that the argument seeks to establish.

(B) The first is evidence that forms the basis for an objection to the position that the argument seeks to establish; the second is that position.

(C) The first is evidence that forms the basis for an objection to the position that the argument seeks to establish; the second is a consideration that is introduced to counter the force of that evidence.

(D) The first and the second each provide evidence in support of the position that the argument seeks to establish.

(E) The first provides evidence in support of the position that the argument seeks to establish; the second is that position.

77. A recent report determined that although only 3 percent of drivers on Maryland highways equipped their vehicles with radar detectors, 33 percent of all vehicles ticketed for exceeding the speed limit were equipped with them. Clearly, drivers who equip their vehicles with radar detectors are more likely to exceed the speed limit regularly than are drivers who do not.

The conclusion drawn above depends on which of the following assumptions?

(A) Drivers who equip their vehicles with radar detectors are less likely to be ticketed for exceeding the speed limit than are drivers who do not.

(B) Drivers who are ticketed for exceeding the speed limit are more likely to exceed the speed limit regularly than are drivers who are not ticketed.

(C) The number of vehicles that were ticketed for exceeding the speed limit was greater than the number of vehicles that were equipped with radar detectors.

(D) Many of the vehicles that were ticketed for exceeding the speed limit were ticketed more than once in the time period covered by the report.

(E) Drivers on Maryland highways exceeded the speed limit more often than did drivers on other state highways not covered in the report.

78. **In countries where automobile insurance includes compensation for whiplash injuries sustained in automobile accidents, reports of having suffered such injuries are twice as frequent as they are in countries where whiplash is not covered.** Presently, no objective test for whiplash exists, so it is true that spurious reports of whiplash injuries cannot be readily identified. Nevertheless, these facts do not warrant the conclusion drawn by some commentators that in the countries with the higher rates of reported whiplash injuries, half of the reported cases are spurious. Clearly, **in countries where automobile insurance does not include compensation for whiplash, people often have little incentive to report whiplash injuries that they actually have suffered.**

In the argument given, the two boldfaced portions play which of the following roles?

(A) The first is a claim that the argument disputes; the second is a conclusion that has been based on that claim.

(B) The first is a claim that has been used to support a conclusion that the argument accepts; the second is that conclusion.

(C) The first is evidence that has been used to support a conclusion for which the argument provides further evidence; the second is the main conclusion of the argument.

(D) The first is a finding whose implications are at issue in the argument; the second is a claim presented in order to argue against deriving certain implications from that finding.

(E) The first is a finding whose accuracy is evaluated in the argument; the second is evidence presented to establish that the finding is accurate.

79. When demand for a factory's products is high, more money is spent at the factory for safety precautions and machinery maintenance than when demand is low. Thus the average number of on-the-job accidents per employee each month should be lower during periods when demand is high than when demand is low and less money is available for safety precautions and machinery maintenance.

Which of the following, if true about a factory when demand for its products is high, casts the most serious doubt on the conclusion drawn above?

(A) Its employees ask for higher wages than they do at other times.

(B) Its management hires new workers but lacks the time to train them properly.

(C) Its employees are less likely to lose their jobs than they are at other times.

(D) Its management sponsors a monthly safety award for each division in the factory.

(E) Its old machinery is replaced with modern, automated models.

80. A sudden increase in the production of elephant ivory artifacts on the Mediterranean coast of North Africa occurred in the tenth century. Historians explain this increase as the result of an area opening up as a new source of ivory and argue on this basis that the important medieval trade between North Africa and East Africa began at this period.

Each of the following, if true, provides some support for the historians' account described above EXCEPT:

(A) In East Africa gold coins from Mediterranean North Africa have been found at a tenth-century site but at no earlier sites.

(B) The many surviving letters of pre-tenth-century North African merchants include no mention of business transactions involving East Africa.

(C) Excavations in East Africa reveal a tenth-century change in architectural style to reflect North African patterns.

(D) Documents from Mediterranean Europe and North Africa that date back earlier than the tenth century show knowledge of East African animals.

(E) East African carvings in a style characteristic of the tenth century depict seagoing vessels very different from those used by local sailors but of a type common in the Mediterranean.

81. Which of the following most logically completes the argument?

    The attribution of the choral work *Lacrimae* to the composer Pescard (1400–1474) has been regarded as tentative, since it was based on a single treatise from the early 1500s that named Pescard as the composer. Recently, several musical treatises from the late 1500s have come to light, all of which name Pescard as the composer of *Lacrimae*. Unfortunately, these newly discovered treatises lend no support to the attribution of *Lacrimae* to Pescard, since

    _____.

    (A) the treatise from the early 1500s misidentifies the composers of some of the musical works it considers

    (B) the author of the treatise from the early 1500s had no very strong evidence on which to base the identification of Pescard as the composer of *Lacrimae*

    (C) there are works that can conclusively be attributed to Pescard that are not even mentioned in the treatise from the early 1500s

    (D) the later treatises probably had no source for their attribution other than the earlier treatise

    (E) no known treatises from the 1600s identify Pescard as the composer of *Lacrimae*

82. Journalist: In physics journals, the number of articles reporting the results of experiments involving particle accelerators was lower last year than it had been in previous years. Several of the particle accelerators at major research institutions were out of service the year before last for repairs, so it is likely that the low number of articles was due to the decline in availability of particle accelerators.

    Which of the following, if true, most seriously undermines the journalist's argument?

    (A) Every article based on experiments with particle accelerators that was submitted for publication last year actually was published.

    (B) The average time scientists must wait for access to a particle accelerator has declined over the last several years.

    (C) The number of physics journals was the same last year as in previous years.

    (D) Particle accelerators can be used for more than one group of experiments in any given year.

    (E) Recent changes in the editorial policies of several physics journals have decreased the likelihood that articles concerning particle-accelerator research will be accepted for publication.

83. Many people suffer an allergic reaction to certain sulfites, including those that are commonly added to wine as preservatives. However, since there are several winemakers who add sulfites to none of the wines they produce, people who would like to drink wine but are allergic to sulfites can drink wines produced by these winemakers without risking an allergic reaction to sulfites.

    Which of the following is an assumption on which the argument depends?

    (A) These winemakers have been able to duplicate the preservative effect produced by adding sulfites by means that do not involve adding any potentially allergenic substances to their wine.

    (B) Not all forms of sulfite are equally likely to produce the allergic reaction.

    (C) Wine is the only beverage to which sulfites are commonly added.

    (D) Apart from sulfites, there are no substances commonly present in wine that give rise to an allergic reaction.

    (E) Sulfites are not naturally present in the wines produced by these winemakers in amounts large enough to produce an allergic reaction in someone who drinks these wines.

84. Networks of blood vessels in bats' wings serve only to disperse heat generated in flight. This heat is generated only because bats flap their wings. Thus paleontologists' recent discovery that the winged dinosaur Sandactylus had similar networks of blood vessels in the skin of its wings provides evidence for the hypothesis that Sandactylus flew by flapping its wings, not just by gliding.

In the passage, the author develops the argument by

(A) forming the hypothesis that best explains several apparently conflicting pieces of evidence

(B) reinterpreting evidence that had been used to support an earlier theory

(C) using an analogy with a known phenomenon to draw a conclusion about an unknown phenomenon

(D) speculating about how structures observed in present-day creatures might have developed from similar structures in creatures now extinct

(E) pointing out differences in the physiological demands that flight makes on large, as opposed to small, creatures

85. Keith: Compliance with new government regulations requiring the installation of smoke alarms and sprinkler systems in all theaters and arenas will cost the entertainment industry $25 billion annually. Consequently, jobs will be lost and profits diminished. Therefore, these regulations will harm the country's economy.

Laura: The $25 billion spent by some businesses will be revenue for others. Jobs and profits will be gained as well as lost.

Laura responds to Keith by

(A) demonstrating that Keith's conclusion is based on evidence that is not relevant to the issue at hand

(B) challenging the plausibility of the evidence that serves as the basis for Keith's argument

(C) suggesting that Keith's argument overlooks a mitigating consequence

(D) reinforcing Keith's conclusion by supplying a complementary interpretation of the evidence Keith cites

(E) agreeing with the main conclusion of Keith's argument but construing that conclusion as grounds for optimism rather than for pessimism

86. When trying to identify new technologies that promise to transform the marketplace, market researchers survey the managers of those companies that are developing new technologies. Such managers have an enormous stake in succeeding, so they invariably overstate the potential of their new technologies. Surprisingly, however, market researchers typically do not survey a new technology's potential buyers, even though it is the buyers—not the producers—who will ultimately determine a technology's commercial success.

Which of the following, if true, best accounts for the typical survey practices among market researchers?

(A) If a new technology succeeds, the commercial benefits accrue largely to the producers, not to the buyers, of that technology.

(B) People who promote the virtues of a new technology typically fail to consider that the old technology that is currently in use continues to be improved, often substantially.

(C) Investors are unlikely to invest substantial amounts of capital in a company whose own managers are skeptical about the commercial prospects of a new technology they are developing.

(D) The potential buyers for not-yet-available technologies can seldom be reliably identified.

(E) The developers of a new technology are generally no better positioned than its potential buyers to gauge how rapidly the new technology can be efficiently mass-produced.

87. In the United States, of the people who moved from one state to another when they retired, the percentage who retired to Florida has decreased by three percentage points over the past ten years. Since many local businesses in Florida cater to retirees, these declines are likely to have a noticeably negative economic effect on these businesses and therefore on the economy of Florida.

Which of the following, if true, most seriously weakens the argument given?

(A) People who moved from one state to another when they retired moved a greater distance, on average, last year than such people did ten years ago.

(B) People were more likely to retire to North Carolina from another state last year than people were ten years ago.

(C) The number of people who moved from one state to another when they retired has increased significantly over the past ten years.

(D) The number of people who left Florida when they retired to live in another state was greater last year than it was ten years ago.

(E) Florida attracts more people who move from one state to another when they retire than does any other state.

88. Businesses are suffering because of a lack of money available for development loans. To help businesses, the government plans to modify the income-tax structure in order to induce individual taxpayers to put a larger portion of their incomes into retirement savings accounts, because as more money is deposited in such accounts, more money becomes available to borrowers.

Which of the following, if true, raises the most serious doubt regarding the effectiveness of the government's plan to increase the amount of money available for development loans for businesses?

(A) When levels of personal retirement savings increase, consumer borrowing always increases correspondingly.

(B) The increased tax revenue the government would receive as a result of business expansion would not offset the loss in revenue from personal income taxes during the first year of the plan.

(C) Even with tax incentives, some people will choose not to increase their levels of retirement savings.

(D) Bankers generally will not continue to lend money to businesses whose prospective earnings are insufficient to meet their loan repayment schedules.

(E) The modified tax structure would give all taxpayers, regardless of their incomes, the same tax savings for a given increase in their retirement savings.

89. Since it has become known that **several of a bank's top executives have been buying shares in their own bank,** the bank's depositors, who had been worried by rumors that the bank faced impending financial collapse, have been greatly relieved. They reason that, since top executives evidently have faith in the bank's financial soundness, those worrisome rumors must be false. Such reasoning might well be overoptimistic, however, since **corporate executives have been known to buy shares in their own company in a calculated attempt to dispel negative rumors about the company's health.**

In the argument given, the two boldfaced portions play which of the following roles?

(A) The first describes evidence that has been taken as supporting a conclusion; the second gives a reason for questioning that support.

(B) The first describes evidence that has been taken as supporting a conclusion; the second states a contrary conclusion that is the main conclusion of the argument.

(C) The first provides evidence in support of the main conclusion of the argument; the second states that conclusion.

(D) The first describes the circumstance that the argument as a whole seeks to explain; the second gives the explanation that the argument seeks to establish.

(E) The first describes the circumstance that the argument as a whole seeks to explain; the second provides evidence in support of the explanation that the argument seeks to establish.

90. A new law gives ownership of patents—documents providing exclusive right to make and sell an invention—to universities, not the government, when those patents result from government-sponsored university research. Administrators at Logos University plan to sell any patents they acquire to corporations in order to fund programs to improve undergraduate teaching.

Which of the following, if true, would cast the most doubt on the viability of the college administrators' plan described above?

(A) Profit-making corporations interested in developing products based on patents held by universities are likely to try to serve as exclusive sponsors of ongoing university research projects.

(B) Corporate sponsors of research in university facilities are entitled to tax credits under new federal tax-code guidelines.

(C) Research scientists at Logos University have few or no teaching responsibilities and participate little if at all in the undergraduate programs in their field.

(D) Government-sponsored research conducted at Logos University for the most part duplicates research already completed by several profit-making corporations.

(E) Logos University is unlikely to attract corporate sponsorship of its scientific research.

91. Environmentalist: The commissioner of the Fish and Game Authority would have the public believe that increases in the number of marine fish caught demonstrate that this resource is no longer endangered. This is a specious argument, as unsound as it would be to assert that the ever-increasing rate at which rain forests are being cut down demonstrates a lack of danger to that resource. The real cause of the increased fish-catch is a greater efficiency in using technologies that deplete resources.

The environmentalist's statements, if true, best support which of the following as a conclusion?

(A) The use of technology is the reason for the increasing encroachment of people on nature.

(B) It is possible to determine how many fish are in the sea in some way other than by catching fish.

(C) The proportion of marine fish that are caught is as high as the proportion of rain forest trees that are cut down each year.

(D) Modern technologies waste resources by catching inedible fish.

(E) Marine fish continue to be an endangered resource.

92. In the country of Veltria, the past two years' broad economic recession has included a business downturn in the clothing trade, where sales are down by about 7 percent as compared to two years ago. Clothing wholesalers have found, however, that the proportion of credit extended to retailers that was paid off on time fell sharply in the first year of the recession but returned to its prerecession level in the second year.

Which of the following, if true, most helps to explain the change between the first and the second year of the recession in the proportion of credit not paid off on time?

(A) The total amount of credit extended to retailers by clothing wholesalers increased between the first year of the recession and the second year.

(B) Between the first and second years of the recession, clothing retailers in Veltria saw many of their costs, rent and utilities in particular, increase.

(C) Of the considerable number of clothing retailers in Veltria who were having financial difficulties before the start of the recession, virtually all were forced to go out of business during its first year.

(D) Clothing retailers in Veltria attempted to stimulate sales in the second year of the recession by discounting merchandise.

(E) Relatively recession-proof segments of the clothing trade, such as work clothes, did not suffer any decrease in sales during the first year of the recession.

93. Commentator: The theory of trade retaliation states that countries closed out of any of another country's markets should close some of their own markets to the other country in order to pressure the other country to reopen its markets. If every country acted according to this theory, no country would trade with any other.

The commentator's argument relies on which of the following assumptions?

(A) No country actually acts according to the theory of trade retaliation.

(B) No country should block any of its markets to foreign trade.

(C) Trade disputes should be settled by international tribunal.

(D) For any two countries, at least one has some market closed to the other.

(E) Countries close their markets to foreigners to protect domestic producers.

94. As a construction material, bamboo is as strong as steel and sturdier than concrete. Moreover, in tropical areas bamboo is a much less expensive construction material than either steel or concrete and is always readily available. In tropical areas, therefore, building with bamboo makes better economic sense than building with steel or concrete, except where land values are high.

Which of the following, if true, most helps to explain the exception noted above?

(A) Buildings constructed of bamboo are less likely to suffer earthquake damage than are steel and concrete buildings.

(B) Bamboo is unsuitable as a building material for multistory buildings.

(C) In order to protect it from being damaged by termites and beetles, bamboo must be soaked, at some expense, in a preservative.

(D) In some tropical areas, bamboo is used to make the scaffolding that is used during large construction projects.

(E) Bamboo growing in an area where land values are increasing is often cleared to make way for construction.

95. Studies in restaurants show that the tips left by customers who pay their bill in cash tend to be larger when the bill is presented on a tray that bears a credit-card logo. Consumer psychologists hypothesize that simply seeing a credit-card logo makes many credit-card holders willing to spend more because it reminds them that their spending power exceeds the cash they have immediately available.

Which of the following, if true, most strongly supports the psychologists' interpretation of the studies?

(A) The effect noted in the studies is not limited to patrons who have credit cards.

(B) Patrons who are under financial pressure from their credit-card obligations tend to tip less when presented with a restaurant bill on a tray with a credit-card logo than when the tray has no logo.

(C) In virtually all of the cases in the studies, the patrons who paid bills in cash did not possess credit cards.

(D) In general, restaurant patrons who pay their bills in cash leave larger tips than do those who pay by credit card.

(E) The percentage of restaurant bills paid with a given brand of credit card increases when that credit card's logo is displayed on the tray with which the bill is presented.

96. Although parapsychology is often considered a pseudoscience, it is in fact a genuine scientific enterprise, for it uses scientific methods such as controlled experiments and statistical tests of clearly stated hypotheses to examine the questions it raises.

The conclusion above is properly drawn if which of the following is assumed?

(A) If a field of study can conclusively answer the questions it raises, then it is a genuine science.

(B) Since parapsychology uses scientific methods, it will produce credible results.

(C) Any enterprise that does not use controlled experiments and statistical tests is not genuine science.

(D) Any field of study that employs scientific methods is a genuine scientific enterprise.

(E) Since parapsychology raises clearly statable questions, they can be tested in controlled experiments.

97. Hotco oil burners, designed to be used in asphalt plants, are so efficient that Hotco will sell one to the Clifton Asphalt plant for no payment other than the cost savings between the total amount the asphalt plant actually paid for oil using its former burner during the last two years and the total amount it will pay for oil using the Hotco burner during the next two years. On installation, the plant will make an estimated payment, which will be adjusted after two years to equal the actual cost savings.

Which of the following, if it occurred, would constitute a disadvantage for Hotco of the plan described above?

(A) Another manufacturer's introduction to the market of a similarly efficient burner

(B) The Clifton Asphalt plant's need for more than one new burner

(C) Very poor efficiency in the Clifton Asphalt plant's old burner

(D) A decrease in the demand for asphalt

(E) A steady increase in the price of oil beginning soon after the new burner is installed

98. **Delta Products Inc. has recently switched at least partly from older technologies using fossil fuels to new technologies powered by electricity.** The question has been raised whether it can be concluded that **for a given level of output Delta's operation now causes less fossil fuel to be consumed than it did formerly.** The answer, clearly, is yes, since the amount of fossil fuel used to generate the electricity needed to power the new technologies is less than the amount needed to power the older technologies, provided level of output is held constant.

In the argument given, the two boldfaced portions play which of the following roles?

(A) The first identifies the content of the conclusion of the argument; the second provides support for that conclusion.

(B) The first provides support for the conclusion of the argument; the second identifies the content of that conclusion.

(C) The first states the conclusion of the argument; the second calls that conclusion into question.

(D) The first provides support for the conclusion of the argument; the second calls that conclusion into question.

(E) Each provides support for the conclusion of the argument.

99. An experiment was done in which human subjects recognize a pattern within a matrix of abstract designs and then select another design that completes that pattern. The results of the experiment were surprising. The lowest expenditure of energy in neurons in the brain was found in those subjects who performed most successfully in the experiments.

Which of the following hypotheses best accounts for the findings of the experiment?

(A) The neurons of the brain react less when a subject is trying to recognize patterns than when the subject is doing other kinds of reasoning.

(B) Those who performed best in the experiment experienced more satisfaction when working with abstract patterns than did those who performed less well.

(C) People who are better at abstract pattern recognition have more energy-efficient neural connections.

(D) The energy expenditure of the subjects' brains increases when a design that completes the initially recognized pattern is determined.

(E) The task of completing a given design is more capably performed by athletes, whose energy expenditure is lower when they are at rest.

100. Debater: The average amount of overtime per month worked by an employee in the manufacturing division of the Haglut Corporation is 14 hours. Most employees of the Haglut Corporation work in the manufacturing division. Furthermore, the average amount of overtime per month worked by any employee in the company generally does not fluctuate much from month to month. Therefore, each month, most employees of the Haglut Corporation almost certainly work at least some overtime.

The debater's argument is most vulnerable to criticism on which of these grounds?

(A) It takes for granted that the manufacturing division is a typical division of the corporation with regard to the average amount of overtime its employees work each month.

(B) It takes for granted that if a certain average amount of overtime is worked each month by each employee of the Haglut Corporation, then approximately the same amount of overtime must be worked each month by each employee of the manufacturing division.

(C)   It confuses a claim from which the argument's conclusion about the Haglut Corporation would necessarily follow with a claim that would follow from the argument's conclusion only with a high degree of probability.

(D)   It overlooks the possibility that even if, on average, a certain amount of overtime is worked by the members of some group, many members of that group may work no overtime at all.

(E)   It overlooks the possibility that even if most employees of the corporation work some overtime each month, any one corporate employee may, in some months, work no overtime.

101.   Which of the following most logically completes the argument?

The irradiation of food kills bacteria and thus retards spoilage. However, it also lowers the nutritional value of many foods. For example, irradiation destroys a significant percentage of whatever vitamin B1 a food may contain. Proponents of irradiation point out that irradiation is no worse in this respect than cooking. However, this fact is either beside the point, since much irradiated food is eaten raw, or else misleading, since _____.

(A)   many of the proponents of irradiation are food distributors who gain from foods' having a longer shelf life

(B)   it is clear that killing bacteria that may be present on food is not the only effect that irradiation has

(C)   cooking is usually the final step in preparing food for consumption, whereas irradiation serves to ensure a longer shelf life for perishable foods

(D)   certain kinds of cooking are, in fact, even more destructive of vitamin B1 than carefully controlled irradiation is

(E)   for food that is both irradiated and cooked, the reduction of vitamin B1 associated with either process individually is compounded

102.   One way to judge the performance of a company is to compare it with other companies. This technique, commonly called "benchmarking," permits the manager of a company to discover better industrial practices and can provide a justification for the adoption of good practices.

Any of the following, if true, is a valid reason for benchmarking the performance of a company against companies with which it is not in competition rather than against competitors EXCEPT:

(A)   Comparisons with competitors are most likely to focus on practices that the manager making the comparisons already employs.

(B)   Getting "inside" information about the unique practices of competitors is particularly difficult.

(C)   Since companies that compete with each other are likely to have comparable levels of efficiency, only benchmarking against noncompetitors is likely to reveal practices that would aid in beating competitors.

(D)   Managers are generally more receptive to new ideas that they find outside their own industry.

(E)   Much of the success of good companies is due to their adoption of practices that take advantage of the special circumstances of their products or markets.

103.   For a trade embargo against a particular country to succeed, a high degree of both international accord and ability to prevent goods from entering or leaving that country must be sustained. A total blockade of Patria's ports is necessary to an embargo, but such an action would be likely to cause international discord over the embargo.

The claims above, if true, most strongly support which of the following conclusions?

(A)   The balance of opinion is likely to favor Patria in the event of a blockade.

(B)   As long as international opinion is unanimously against Patria, a trade embargo is likely to succeed.

(C)   A naval blockade of Patria's ports would ensure that no goods enter or leave Patria.

(D)   Any trade embargo against Patria would be likely to fail at some time.

(E)   For a blockade of Patria's ports to be successful, international opinion must be unanimous.

104. Theater Critic: The play *La Finestrina*, now at Central Theater, was written in Italy in the eighteenth century. The director claims that this production is as similar to the original production as is possible in a modern theater. Although the actor who plays Harlequin the clown gives a performance very reminiscent of the twentieth-century American comedian Groucho Marx, Marx's comic style was very much within the comic acting tradition that had begun in sixteenth-century Italy.

     The considerations given best serve as part of an argument that

     (A)   modern audiences would find it hard to tolerate certain characteristics of a historically accurate performance of an eighteenth-century play

     (B)   Groucho Marx once performed the part of the character Harlequin in *La Finestrina*

     (C)   in the United States the training of actors in the twentieth century is based on principles that do not differ radically from those that underlay the training of actors in eighteenth-century Italy

     (D)   the performance of the actor who plays Harlequin in *La Finestrina* does not serve as evidence against the director's claim

     (E)   the director of *La Finestrina* must have advised the actor who plays Harlequin to model his performance on comic performances of Groucho Marx

105. The cost of producing radios in Country Q is 10 percent less than the cost of producing radios in Country Y. Even after transportation fees and tariff charges are added, it is still cheaper for a company to import radios from Country Q to Country Y than to produce radios in Country Y.

     The statements above, if true, best support which of the following assertions?

     (A)   Labor costs in Country Q are 10 percent below those in Country Y.

     (B)   Importing radios from Country Q to Country Y will eliminate 10 percent of the manufacturing jobs in Country Y.

     (C)   The tariff on a radio imported from Country Q to Country Y is less than 10 percent of the cost of manufacturing the radio in Country Y.

     (D)   The fee for transporting a radio from Country Q to Country Y is more than 10 percent of the cost of manufacturing the radio in Country Q.

     (E)   It takes 10 percent less time to manufacture a radio in Country Q than it does in Country Y.

106. Exposure to certain chemicals commonly used in elementary schools as cleaners or pesticides causes allergic reactions in some children. Elementary school nurses in Renston report that the proportion of schoolchildren sent to them for treatment of allergic reactions to those chemicals has increased significantly over the past ten years. Therefore, either Renston's schoolchildren have been exposed to greater quantities of the chemicals, or they are more sensitive to them than schoolchildren were ten years ago.

     Which of the following is an assumption on which the argument depends?

     (A)   The number of school nurses employed by Renston's elementary schools has not decreased over the past ten years.

     (B)   Children who are allergic to the chemicals are no more likely than other children to have allergies to other substances.

     (C)   Children who have allergic reactions to the chemicals are not more likely to be sent to a school nurse now than they were ten years ago.

     (D)   The chemicals are not commonly used as cleaners or pesticides in houses and apartment buildings in Renston.

     (E)   Children attending elementary school do not make up a larger proportion of Renston's population now than they did ten years ago.

107. Although the discount stores in Goreville's central shopping district are expected to close within five years as a result of competition from a SpendLess discount department store that just opened, those locations will not stay vacant for long. In the five years since the opening of Colson's, a nondiscount department store, a new store has opened at the location of every store in the shopping district that closed because it could not compete with Colson's.

     Which of the following, if true, most seriously weakens the argument?

(A) Many customers of Colson's are expected to do less shopping there than they did before the SpendLess store opened.

(B) Increasingly, the stores that have opened in the central shopping district since Colson's opened have been discount stores.

(C) At present, the central shopping district has as many stores operating in it as it ever had.

(D) Over the course of the next five years, it is expected that Goreville's population will grow at a faster rate than it has for the past several decades.

(E) Many stores in the central shopping district sell types of merchandise that are not available at either SpendLess or Colson's.

108. Kale has more nutritional value than spinach. But since collard greens have more nutritional value than lettuce, it follows that kale has more nutritional value than lettuce.

Any of the following, if introduced into the argument as an additional premise, makes the argument above logically correct EXCEPT:

(A) Collard greens have more nutritional value than kale.

(B) Spinach has more nutritional value than lettuce.

(C) Spinach has more nutritional value than collard greens.

(D) Spinach and collard greens have the same nutritional value.

(E) Kale and collard greens have the same nutritional value.

109. Last year all refuse collected by Shelbyville city services was incinerated. This incineration generated a large quantity of residual ash. In order to reduce the amount of residual ash Shelbyville generates this year to half of last year's total, the city has revamped its collection program. This year city services will separate for recycling enough refuse to reduce the number of truckloads of refuse to be incinerated to half of last year's number.

Which of the following is required for the revamped collection program to achieve its aim?

(A) This year, no materials that city services could separate for recycling will be incinerated.

(B) Separating recyclable materials from materials to be incinerated will cost Shelbyville less than half what it cost last year to dispose of the residual ash.

(C) Refuse collected by city services will contain a larger proportion of recyclable materials this year than it did last year.

(D) The refuse incinerated this year will generate no more residual ash per truckload incinerated than did the refuse incinerated last year.

(E) The total quantity of refuse collected by Shelbyville city services this year will be no greater than that collected last year.

110. Although custom prosthetic bone replacements produced through a new computer-aided design process will cost more than twice as much as ordinary replacements, custom replacements should still be cost-effective. Not only will surgery and recovery time be reduced, but custom replacements should last longer, thereby reducing the need for further hospital stays.

Which of the following must be studied in order to evaluate the argument presented above?

(A) The amount of time a patient spends in surgery versus the amount of time spent recovering from surgery

(B) The amount by which the cost of producing custom replacements has declined with the introduction of the new technique for producing them

(C) The degree to which the use of custom replacements is likely to reduce the need for repeat surgery when compared with the use of ordinary replacements

(D) The degree to which custom replacements produced with the new technique are more carefully manufactured than are ordinary replacements

(E) The amount by which custom replacements produced with the new technique will drop in cost as the production procedures become standardized and applicable on a larger scale

111. Springfield Fire Commissioner: The vast majority of false fire alarms are prank calls made anonymously from fire alarm boxes on street corners. Since virtually everyone has access to a private telephone, these alarm boxes have outlived their usefulness. Therefore, we propose to remove the boxes. Removing the boxes will reduce the number of prank calls without hampering people's ability to report a fire.

Which of the following, if true, most strongly supports the claim that the proposal, if carried out, will have the announced effect?

(A) The fire department traces all alarm calls made from private telephones and records where they came from.

(B) Maintaining the fire alarm boxes costs Springfield approximately $5 million annually.

(C) A telephone call can provide the fire department with more information about the nature and size of a fire than can an alarm placed from an alarm box.

(D) Responding to false alarms significantly reduces the fire department's capacity for responding to fires.

(E) On any given day, a significant percentage of the public telephones in Springfield are out of service.

112. The difficulty with the proposed high-speed train line is that a used plane can be bought for one-third the price of the train line, and the plane, which is just as fast, can fly anywhere. The train would be a fixed linear system, and we live in a world that is spreading out in all directions and in which consumers choose the free-wheel systems (cars, buses, aircraft), which do not have fixed routes. Thus a sufficient market for the train will not exist.

Which of the following, if true, most severely weakens the argument presented above?

(A) Cars, buses, and planes require the efforts of drivers and pilots to guide them, whereas the train will be guided mechanically.

(B) Cars and buses are not nearly as fast as the high-speed train will be.

(C) Planes are not a free-wheel system because they can fly only between airports, which are less convenient for consumers than the high-speed train's stations would be.

(D) The high-speed train line cannot use currently underutilized train stations in large cities.

(E) For long trips, most people prefer to fly rather than to take ground-level transportation.

113. The average hourly wage of television assemblers in Vernland has long been significantly lower than that in neighboring Borodia. Since Borodia dropped all tariffs on Vernlandian televisions three years ago, the number of televisions sold annually in Borodia has not changed. However, recent statistics show a drop in the number of television assemblers in Borodia. Therefore, updated trade statistics will probably indicate that the number of televisions Borodia imports annually from Vernland has increased.

Which of the following is an assumption on which the argument depends?

(A) The number of television assemblers in Vernland has increased by at least as much as the number of television assemblers in Borodia has decreased.

(B) Televisions assembled in Vernland have features that televisions assembled in Borodia do not have.

(C) The average number of hours it takes a Borodian television assembler to assemble a television has not decreased significantly during the past three years.

(D) The number of televisions assembled annually in Vernland has increased significantly during the past three years.

(E) The difference between the hourly wage of television assemblers in Vernland and the hourly wage of television assemblers in Borodia is likely to decrease in the next few years.

114. Normally, the pineal gland governs a person's sleep-wake cycle by secreting melatonin in response to the daily cycle of light and darkness as detected by the eye. Nonetheless, many people who are totally blind due to lesions in the visual cortex of the brain easily maintain a 24-hour sleep-wake cycle. So the neural pathway by which the pineal gland receives information from the eye probably does not pass through the visual cortex.

For purposes of evaluating the argument it would be most useful to establish which of the following?

(A)   Whether melatonin supplements help people who have difficulty maintaining a 24-hour sleep cycle to establish such a pattern

(B)   Whether the melatonin levels of most totally blind people who successfully maintain a 24-hour sleep-wake cycle change in response to changes in exposure to light and darkness

(C)   Whether melatonin is the only substance secreted by the pineal gland

(D)   Whether most people who do not have a 24-hour sleep-wake cycle nevertheless have a cycle of consistent duration

(E)   Whether there are any people with normal vision whose melatonin levels respond abnormally to periods of light and darkness

115.   Guidebook writer: I have visited hotels throughout the country and have noticed that in those built before 1930 the quality of the original carpentry work is generally superior to that in hotels built afterward. Clearly carpenters working on hotels before 1930 typically worked with more skill, care, and effort than carpenters who have worked on hotels built subsequently.

Which of the following, if true, most seriously weakens the guidebook writer's argument?

(A)   The quality of original carpentry in hotels is generally far superior to the quality of original carpentry in other structures, such as houses and stores.

(B)   Hotels built since 1930 can generally accommodate more guests than those built before 1930.

(C)   The materials available to carpenters working before 1930 were not significantly different in quality from the materials available to carpenters working after 1930.

(D)   The better the quality of original carpentry in a building, the less likely that building is to fall into disuse and be demolished.

(E)   The average length of apprenticeship for carpenters has declined significantly since 1930.

116.   Scientists typically do their most creative work before the age of forty. It is commonly thought that this happens because aging by itself brings about a loss of creative capacity. However, studies show that **of scientists who produce highly creative work beyond the age of forty, a disproportionately large number entered their field at an older age than is usual**. Since by the age of forty the large majority of scientists have been working in their field for at least fifteen years, the studies' finding strongly suggests that the real reason why scientists over forty rarely produce highly creative work is not that they have aged but rather that **scientists over forty have generally spent too long in their field**.

In the argument given, the two portions in boldface play which of the following roles?

(A)   The first is a claim, the accuracy of which is at issue in the argument; the second is a conclusion drawn on the basis of that claim.

(B)   The first is an objection that has been raised against a position defended in the argument; the second is that position.

(C)   The first is evidence that has been used to support an explanation that the argument challenges; the second is that explanation.

(D)   The first is evidence that has been used to support an explanation that the argument challenges; the second is a competing explanation that the argument favors.

(E)   The first provides evidence to support an explanation that the argument favors; the second is that explanation.

117. Northern Air has dozens of flights daily into and out of Belleville Airport, which is highly congested. Northern Air depends for its success on economy and quick turnaround and consequently is planning to replace its large planes with Skybuses, whose novel aerodynamic design is extremely fuel efficient. The Skybus's fuel efficiency results in both lower fuel costs and reduced time spent refueling.

Which of the following, if true, could present the most serious disadvantage for Northern Air in replacing their large planes with Skybuses?

(A) The Skybus would enable Northern Air to schedule direct flights to destinations that currently require stops for refueling.

(B) Aviation fuel is projected to decline in price over the next several years.

(C) The fuel efficiency of the Skybus would enable Northern Air to eliminate refueling at some of its destinations, but several mechanics would lose their jobs.

(D) None of Northern Air's competitors that use Belleville Airport are considering buying Skybuses.

(E) The aerodynamic design of the Skybus causes turbulence behind it when taking off that forces other planes on the runway to delay their takeoffs.

118. It is true of both men and women that those who marry as young adults live longer than those who never marry. This does not show that marriage causes people to live longer, since, as compared with other people of the same age, young adults who are about to get married have fewer of the unhealthy habits that can cause a person to have a shorter life, most notably smoking and immoderate drinking of alcohol.

Which of the following, if true, most strengthens the argument above?

(A) Marriage tends to cause people to engage less regularly in sports that involve risk of bodily harm.

(B) A married person who has an unhealthy habit is more likely to give up that habit than a person with the same habit who is unmarried.

(C) A person who smokes is much more likely than a nonsmoker to marry a person who smokes at the time of marriage, and the same is true for people who drink alcohol immoderately.

(D) Among people who marry as young adults, most of those who give up an unhealthy habit after marriage do not resume the habit later in life.

(E) Among people who as young adults neither drink alcohol immoderately nor smoke, those who never marry live as long as those who marry.

119. The earliest Mayan pottery found at Colha, in Belize, is about 3,000 years old. Recently, however, 4,500-year-old stone agricultural implements were unearthed at Colha. These implements resemble Mayan stone implements of a much later period, also found at Colha. Moreover, the implements' designs are strikingly different from the designs of stone implements produced by other cultures known to have inhabited the area in prehistoric times. Therefore, there were surely Mayan settlements in Colha 4,500 years ago.

Which of the following, if true, most seriously weakens the argument?

(A) Ceramic ware is not known to have been used by the Mayan people to make agricultural implements.

(B) Carbon-dating of corn pollen in Colha indicates that agriculture began there around 4,500 years ago.

(C) Archaeological evidence indicates that some of the oldest stone implements found at Colha were used to cut away vegetation after controlled burning of trees to open areas of swampland for cultivation.

(D) Successor cultures at a given site often adopt the style of agricultural implements used by earlier inhabitants of the same site.

(E) Many religious and social institutions of the Mayan people who inhabited Colha 3,000 years ago relied on a highly developed system of agricultural symbols.

120. Codex Berinensis, a Florentine copy of an ancient Roman medical treatise, is undated but contains clues to when it was produced. Its first 80 pages are by a single copyist, but the remaining 20 pages are by three different copyists, which indicates some significant disruption. Since a letter in handwriting identified as that of the fourth copyist mentions a plague that killed many people in Florence in 1148, Codex Berinensis was probably produced in that year.

    Which of the following, if true, most strongly supports the hypothesis that Codex Berinensis was produced in 1148?

    (A) Other than Codex Berinensis, there are no known samples of the handwriting of the first three copyists.

    (B) According to the account by the fourth copyist, the plague went on for 10 months.

    (C) A scribe would be able to copy a page of text the size and style of Codex Berinensis in a day.

    (D) There was only one outbreak of plague in Florence in the 1100s.

    (E) The number of pages of Codex Berinensis produced by a single scribe becomes smaller with each successive change of copyist.

121. The spacing of the four holes on a fragment of a bone flute excavated at a Neanderthal campsite is just what is required to play the third through sixth notes of the diatonic scale—the seven-note musical scale used in much of Western music since the Renaissance. Musicologists therefore hypothesize that the diatonic musical scale was developed and used thousands of years before it was adopted by Western musicians.

    Which of the following, if true, most strongly supports the hypothesis?

    (A) Bone flutes were probably the only musical instrument made by Neanderthals.

    (B) No musical instrument that is known to have used a diatonic scale is of an earlier date than the flute found at the Neanderthal campsite.

    (C) The flute was made from a cave-bear bone and the campsite at which the flute fragment was excavated was in a cave that also contained skeletal remains of cave bears.

    (D) Flutes are the simplest wind instrument that can be constructed to allow playing a diatonic scale.

    (E) The cave-bear leg bone used to make the Neanderthal flute would have been long enough to make a flute capable of playing a complete diatonic scale.

122. Outsourcing is the practice of obtaining from an independent supplier a product or service that a company has previously provided for itself. Since a company's chief objective is to realize the highest possible year-end profits, any product or service that can be obtained from an independent supplier for less than it would cost the company to provide the product or service on its own should be outsourced.

    Which of the following, if true, most seriously weakens the argument?

    (A) If a company decides to use independent suppliers for a product, it can generally exploit the vigorous competition arising among several firms that are interested in supplying that product.

    (B) Successful outsourcing requires a company to provide its suppliers with information about its products and plans that can fall into the hands of its competitors and give them a business advantage.

    (C) Certain tasks, such as processing a company's payroll, are commonly outsourced, whereas others, such as handling the company's core business, are not.

    (D) For a company to provide a product or service for itself as efficiently as an independent supplier can provide it, the managers involved need to be as expert in the area of that product or service as the people in charge of that product or service at an independent supplier are.

    (E) When a company decides to use an independent supplier for a product or service, the independent supplier sometimes hires members of the company's staff who formerly made the product or provided the service that the independent supplier now supplies.

123. Museums that house Renaissance oil paintings typically store them in environments that are carefully kept within narrow margins of temperature and humidity to inhibit any deterioration. Laboratory tests have shown that the kind of oil paint used in these paintings actually adjusts to climatic changes quite well. If, as some museum directors believe, **paint is the most sensitive substance in these works**, then by relaxing the standards for temperature and humidity control, **museums can reduce energy costs without risking damage to these paintings**. Museums would be rash to relax those standards, however, since results of preliminary tests indicate that gesso, a compound routinely used by Renaissance artists to help paint adhere to the canvas, is unable to withstand significant variations in humidity.

    In the argument above, the two portions in boldface play which of the following roles?

    (A) The first is an objection that has been raised against the position taken by the argument; the second is the position taken by the argument.

    (B) The first is the position taken by the argument; the second is the position that the argument calls into question.

    (C) The first is a judgment that has been offered in support of the position that the argument calls into question; the second is a circumstance on which that judgment is, in part, based.

    (D) The first is a judgment that has been offered in support of the position that the argument calls into question; the second is that position.

    (E) The first is a claim that the argument calls into question; the second is the position taken by the argument.

124. Vargonia has just introduced a legal requirement that student-teacher ratios in government-funded schools not exceed a certain limit. All Vargonian children are entitled to education, free of charge, in these schools. When a recession occurs and average incomes fall, the number of children enrolled in government-funded schools tends to increase. Therefore, though most employment opportunities contract in economic recessions, getting a teaching job in Vargonia's government-funded schools will not be made more difficult by a recession.

    Which of the following would be most important to determine in order to evaluate the argument?

    (A) Whether in Vargonia there are any schools not funded by the government that offer children an education free of charge

    (B) Whether the number of qualified applicants for teaching positions in government-funded schools increases significantly during economic recessions

    (C) What the current student-teacher ratio in Vargonia's government-funded schools is

    (D) What proportion of Vargonia's workers currently hold jobs as teachers in government-funded schools

    (E) Whether in the past a number of government-funded schools in Vargonia have had student-teacher ratios well in excess of the new limit

8.5 Answer Key

1.	C	32.	B	63.	C	94.	B
2.	A	33.	E	64.	B	95.	B
3.	E	34.	D	65.	A	96.	D
4.	D	35.	B	66.	A	97.	E
5.	D	36.	E	67.	E	98.	B
6.	C	37.	E	68.	C	99.	C
7.	E	38.	C	69.	A	100.	D
8.	C	39.	C	70.	A	101.	A
9.	D	40.	D	71.	D	102.	E
10.	A	41.	A	72.	C	103.	D
11.	D	42.	C	73.	D	104.	D
12.	D	43.	A	74.	C	105.	C
13.	B	44.	A	75.	A	106.	C
14.	E	45.	A	76.	B	107.	B
15.	A	46.	C	77.	B	108.	A
16.	A	47.	C	78.	B	109.	D
17.	B	48.	C	79.	B	110.	C
18.	E	49.	C	80.	D	111.	A
19.	A	50.	B	81.	C	112.	C
20.	E	51.	D	82.	E	113.	C
21.	D	52.	B	83.	C	114.	B
22.	E	53.	A	84.	C	115.	D
23.	B	54.	C	85.	C	116.	E
24.	C	55.	D	86.	D	117.	E
25.	D	56.	E	87.	B	118.	E
26.	C	57.	E	88.	A	119.	D
27.	B	58.	D	89.	A	120.	D
28.	A	59.	E	90.	D	121.	E
29.	D	60.	E	91.	E	122.	B
30.	C	61.	D	92.	C	123.	D
31.	D	62.	A	93.	D	124.	B

8.6 Answer Explanations

The following discussion is intended to familiarize you with the most efficient and effective approaches to critical reasoning questions. The particular questions in this chapter are generally representative of the kinds of critical reasoning questions you will encounter on the GMAT exam. Remember that it is the problem solving strategy that is important, not the specific details of a particular question.

1. Snowmaking machines work by spraying a mist that freezes immediately on contact with cold air. Because the sudden freezing kills bacteria, QuickFreeze is planning to market a wastewater purification system that works on the same principle. The process works only when temperatures are cold, however, so municipalities using it will still need to maintain a conventional system.

    Which of the following, if true, provides the strongest grounds for a prediction that municipalities will buy QuickFreeze's purification system despite the need to maintain a conventional purification system as well?

    (A) Bacteria are not the only impurities that must be removed from wastewater.

    (B) Many municipalities have old wastewater purification systems that need to be replaced.

    (C) Conventional wastewater purification systems have not been fully successful in killing bacteria at cold temperatures.

    (D) During times of warm weather, when it is not in use, QuickFreeze's purification system requires relatively little maintenance.

    (E) Places where the winters are cold rarely have a problem of water shortage.

Evaluation of a Plan

Situation   QuickFreeze is planning to market wastewater purification systems that work by spraying a mist that freezes on contact with cold air. The sudden freezing kills bacteria. Because the system works only at cold temperatures, municipalities using it will still need to maintain a conventional system.

Reasoning   *Which statement provides the strongest grounds for thinking that at least some municipalities will buy the purification system despite the need to maintain a conventional purification system as well?* The passage tells us why a municipality using a QuickFreeze wastewater purification system would still need a conventional system. But why would a municipality want the QuickFreeze system *in addition to* a conventional system? If conventional systems are not fully effective at cold temperatures, the QuickFreeze system would allow municipalities that sometimes experience cold temperatures to purify their wastewater more effectively.

A   There is no basis in the passage for determining whether the QuickFreeze system will help remove impurities other than bacteria from wastewater. If it does not, this answer choice implies that the QuickFreeze system would not be sufficient for purifying wastewater. This would actually undermine the prediction.

B   The passage states that municipalities using the QuickFreeze system would still need a conventional system. Thus, the old conventional wastewater systems would still need to be replaced with new conventional systems. This answer choice provides no reason to think municipalities would buy the QuickFreeze system.

C **Correct.** This statement, if true, would strengthen the prediction, because it provides a valid reason why the QuickFreeze system could be needed alongside conventional ones: it is more effective in cold weather.

D Although this claim does undercut one reason for thinking municipalities might *not* be likely to purchase the QuickFreeze system, it provides little reason to think that they will purchase such a system. Perhaps in times of cold weather, the QuickFreeze system is very expensive to maintain.

E The issue of whether or not there are water shortages in places where winters are cold is not directly relevant. If conventional wastewater systems are sufficient to purify water in such places, municipalities would not need the QuickFreeze system (as they would still need to maintain a conventional purification system).

The correct answer is C.

2. Homeowners aged 40 to 50 are more likely to purchase ice cream and are more likely to purchase it in larger amounts than are members of any other demographic group. The popular belief that teenagers eat more ice cream than adults must, therefore, be false.

The argument is flawed primarily because the author

(A) fails to distinguish between purchasing and consuming

(B) does not supply information about homeowners in age groups other than 40 to 50

(C) depends on popular belief rather than on documented research findings

(D) does not specify the precise amount of ice cream purchased by any demographic group

(E) discusses ice cream rather than more nutritious and healthful foods

Argument Evaluation

Situation   Adults aged 40 to 50 buy more ice cream than does any other demographic group (for example, teenagers). Does this mean that adults consume more ice cream than teenagers do?

Reasoning   *A flawed assumption underlies the reasoning: the assumption that the buyers of the ice cream are also the eaters of the ice cream.* Although the demographic group homeowners aged 40 to 50 purchases more ice cream than does any other demographic group, it is quite likely that much of the ice cream purchased by those homeowners is for consumption by family members rather than for exclusive consumption by the purchaser. This leaves open the possibility that teenagers may indeed be the largest consumers of ice cream.

A **Correct.** The failure to make this distinction led to the making of the flawed assumption.

B This is false: The argument tells us (indirectly) that homeowners aged 40 to 50 buy more ice cream than does any other group—which allows us to infer that they buy more than do homeowners aged 30 to 40, for example. But even if the argument had stated such information explicitly, it would not have offered any better support for its conclusion.

C There is nothing in the argument to suggest that the information given is based on popular belief.

D Providing precise information about the quantity of ice cream purchased by homeowners aged 40 to 50 would not improve the argument at all.

E The subject is ice cream, not nutrition, so this point is irrelevant.

The correct answer is A.

3. Suncorp, a new corporation with limited funds, has been clearing large sections of the tropical Amazon forest for cattle ranching. This practice continues even though greater profits can be made from rubber tapping, which does not destroy the forest, than from cattle ranching, which does destroy the forest.

Which of the following, if true, most helps to explain why Suncorp has been pursuing the less profitable of the two economic activities mentioned above?

(A) The soil of the Amazon forest is very rich in nutrients that are important in the development of grazing lands.

(B) Cattle-ranching operations that are located in tropical climates are more profitable than cattle-ranching operations that are located in cold-weather climates.

(C) In certain districts, profits made from cattle ranching are more heavily taxed than profits made from any other industry.

(D) Some of the cattle that are raised on land cleared in the Amazon are killed by wildcats.

(E) The amount of money required to begin a rubber-tapping operation is twice as high as the amount needed to begin a cattle ranch.

Argument Construction

Situation   Suncorp is a new corporation with limited funds. It has been clearing large sections of the tropical Amazon forest for ranching, even though rubber-tapping would be more profitable.

Reasoning   *What would explain why Suncorp is clearing sections of the rain forest for ranching, even though rubber tapping would be more profitable?* Because Suncorp has limited funds, if rubber tapping has much higher start-up costs, Suncorp might not have enough money to start rubber-tapping operations. If cattle ranching has much lower start-up costs than rubber tapping, Suncorp might be able to afford such an operation.

A   This statement gives a reason why cattle ranching in the Amazon might be more profitable than one might otherwise think it would be. However, we already know from the passage that rubber tapping would be more profitable than cattle ranching. So, this answer choice does not help explain why cattle ranching might be preferable to rubber tapping.

B   The comparison between the profitableness of cattle ranching in tropical climates and in cold-weather climates is irrelevant. The passage only covers cattle ranching in the tropical Amazon forest. This answer choice would at most explain why Suncorp is undertaking cattle ranching in the Amazon rather than in some cold-weather location.

C   This statement makes what needs to be explained *harder* to understand, for it indicates that cattle ranching in the Amazon might be less profitable than one would otherwise think.

D   Like answer choice (C), this statement indicates a disadvantage of cattle ranching in the Amazon. So, it does not explain why cattle ranching would be preferred to some other economic activity.

E   **Correct.** Because it costs less to begin cattle ranching than it does to begin rubber tapping, Suncorp—which has limited funds—would have a reason to pursue cattle ranching over a potentially more profitable activity.

The correct answer is E.

4. According to a prediction of the not-so-distant future published in 1940, electricity would revolutionize agriculture. Electrodes would be inserted into the soil, and the current between them would kill bugs and weeds and make crop plants stronger.

   Which of the following, if true, most strongly indicates that the logic of the prediction above is flawed?

   (A) In order for farmers to avoid electric shock while working in the fields, the current could be turned off at such times without diminishing the intended effects.

   (B) If the proposed plan for using electricity were put into practice, farmers would save on chemicals now being added to the soil.

   (C) It cannot be taken for granted that the use of electricity is always beneficial.

   (D) Since weeds are plants, electricity would affect weeds in the same way as it would affect crop plants.

   (E) Because a planting machine would need to avoid coming into contact with the electrodes, new parts for planting machines would need to be designed.

Evaluation of a Plan

Situation   In 1940, electricity was predicted to revolutionize agriculture. This prediction suggested that electric current running between electrodes inserted into the soil would kill bugs and weeds while encouraging the growth of crop plants.

Reasoning   *Which point most suggests that the logic used in formulating the prediction is flawed?* Electricity will revolutionize agriculture, it is said, because current can be run through electrodes placed in the soil. This current will kill bugs and weeds while strengthening plants. But how will the current accomplish this feat? More specifically, how will it kill one kind of plant (weeds) while strengthening another (crop plants)?

A   The logic of the prediction has nothing to do with whether the current can be turned on and off; rather, it is concerned with the current itself and its effects.

B   Rather than suggesting that the logic of the prediction is flawed, this serves to support the prediction: Farmers' saving on chemicals would be part of the predicted agricultural revolution.

C   The argument does not take for granted that the use of electricity is always beneficial; it merely suggests that it would be of great benefit to agriculture.

D   Correct. This statement properly identifies a problem with the prediction: It provides no reason to believe that the electricity would affect crop plants and weeds differently.

E   Rather than suggesting that the logic of the prediction is flawed, this serves to support the prediction: Changes in planting machines would be part of the predicted agricultural revolution.

The correct answer is D.

5. A company is considering changing its policy concerning daily working hours. Currently, this company requires all employees to arrive at work at 8 a.m. The proposed policy would permit each employee to decide when to arrive—from as early as 6 a.m. to as late as 11 a.m.

The adoption of this policy would be most likely to decrease employees' productivity if the employees' job functions required them to

(A) work without interruption from other employees

(B) consult at least once a day with employees from other companies

(C) submit their work for a supervisor's eventual approval

(D) interact frequently with each other throughout the entire workday

(E) undertake projects that take several days to complete

Evaluation of a Plan

Situation   A company considers changing all employees' starting time from 8 a.m. to individually flexible arrival hours, anytime from 6 to 11 a.m.

Reasoning   *Under what conditions could this plan cause employees' productivity to decline?* Consider the job functions defined in the answer choices and determine which entails requirements that would most likely be in conflict with the proposed plan. A plan that allows a five-hour range of start times would make it far more difficult for employees to coordinate their schedules. This would make it difficult, if not impossible, for employees to collaborate with each other throughout the workday and could well decrease productivity.

A   Working without interruption would likely mean improved productivity.

B   Assuming that all employees are in the same time zone (we are not told otherwise), the flexible hours would still leave plenty of time for at least one daily consultation during the regular business hours of the workday.

C   *Eventual approval* indicates that the flexibility exists to permit employees' submissions at any time.

D   Correct. The wide range of flexibility in regards to working hours would make frequent interaction difficult, if not impossible, and would be likely to decrease employees' productivity.

E   We are not told that the projects involve significant interaction; so such projects would be accomplished just as easily on the proposed flexible schedule.

The correct answer is D.

6.   Parland's alligator population has been declining in recent years, primarily because of hunting. Alligators prey heavily on a species of freshwater fish that is highly valued as food by Parlanders, who had hoped that the decline in the alligator population would lead to an increase in the numbers of these fish available for human consumption. Yet the population of this fish species has also declined, even though the annual number caught for human consumption has not increased.

Which of the following, if true, most helps to explain the decline in the population of the fish species?

(A)   The decline in the alligator population has meant that fishers can work in some parts of lakes and rivers that were formerly too dangerous.

(B)   Over the last few years, Parland's commercial fishing enterprises have increased the number of fishing boats they use.

(C)   The main predator of these fish is another species of fish on which alligators also prey.

(D)   Many Parlanders who hunt alligators do so because of the high market price of alligator skins, not because of the threat alligators pose to the fish population.

(E)   In several neighboring countries through which Parland's rivers also flow, alligators are at risk of extinction as a result of extensive hunting.

Argument Construction

Situation   Due to hunting, Parland's alligator population has been declining. Parlanders had hoped that the population of a certain prized species of freshwater fish that alligators prey on would have increased as a result, but the population of this freshwater fish has actually declined.

Reasoning   *What would explain why the population of the freshwater species has declined?* Suppose alligators prey not only on the prized freshwater fish but also on another species of fish that is the main predator of those fish. If there are fewer alligators to prey on the predator fish, there may well be more of the predator fish. An increase in the population of the predator fish could help explain why the population of the prized freshwater fish has declined: there are now more of the predator fish around to prey on them.

A   Though this statement suggests that the population of the prized fish species may have declined due to their being caught in greater numbers by fishers, the passage tells us that the number of these fish caught for human consumption has not increased. Therefore this statement cannot explain the species' decline in population.

B   The passage tells us that the number of fish caught for human consumption has not increased. This answer choice does not provide any explanation for why the population of these fish has declined.

C   **Correct.** Since alligators prey on the predator fish, a decline in the alligator population could result in an increase in the population of the predator fish, which could lead to an increase in nonhuman consumption of the prized freshwater fish.

D   We already know from the passage that hunting has led to a decline in the population of alligators. It is irrelevant what motivated the hunting of alligators.

E   The fact that alligators are at risk of extinction due to hunting in neighboring countries does not help explain why the prized freshwater fish species is declining in population. If it is puzzling why the fish population is declining despite the reduction in Parland's alligator population, it would be just as puzzling if the alligator population elsewhere was declining.

The correct answer is C.

7. The amount of time it takes for most of a worker's occupational knowledge and skills to become obsolete has been declining because of the introduction of advanced manufacturing technology (AMT). Given the rate at which AMT is currently being introduced in manufacturing, the average worker's old skills become obsolete and new skills are required within as little as five years.

    Which of the following plans, if feasible, would allow a company to prepare most effectively for the rapid obsolescence of skills described above?

    (A) The company will develop a program to offer selected employees the opportunity to receive training six years after they were originally hired.

    (B) The company will increase its investment in AMT every year for a period of at least five years.

    (C) The company will periodically survey its employees to determine how the introduction of AMT has affected them.

    (D) Before the introduction of AMT, the company will institute an educational program to inform its employees of the probable consequences of the introduction of AMT.

    (E) The company will ensure that it can offer its employees any training necessary for meeting their job requirements.

Evaluation of a Plan

Situation   The introduction of AMT is making workers' occupational skills obsolete within as little as five years.

Reasoning   *Which plan will be most effective in helping the company prepare for the expected rapid obsolescence in occupational knowledge and skills?* It should be clear that some type of training or retraining will be involved, since (at least in certain types of industry) it is unlikely that any company in that industry can afford to avoid introducing AMT if its market competitors are doing so.

A   Providing training only to *selected* employees and only after their skills have already become obsolete is not likely to be an effective response.

B   This plan only accelerates the problem and does not address the employees' skills.

C   Periodic surveys may provide information to employers but will not be enough to prevent employees' skills from becoming obsolete.

D   Having knowledge of the consequences does not prevent those consequences; employees' skills will still become obsolete.

E   **Correct.** This would ensure that all employees have the most current occupational knowledge and skills needed for their jobs

The correct answer is E.

8. In virtually any industry, technological improvements increase labor productivity, which is the output of goods and services per person-hour worked. In Parland's industries, labor productivity is significantly higher than it is in Vergia's industries. Clearly, therefore, Parland's industries must, on the whole, be further advanced technologically than Vergia's are.

The argument is most vulnerable to which of the following criticisms?

(A) It offers a conclusion that is no more than a paraphrase of one of the pieces of information provided in its support.

(B) It presents as evidence in support of a claim information that is inconsistent with other evidence presented in support of the same claim.

(C) It takes one possible cause of a condition to be the actual cause of that condition without considering any other possible causes.

(D) It takes a condition to be the effect of something that happened only after the condition already existed.

(E) It makes a distinction that presupposes the truth of the conclusion that is to be established.

Argument Evaluation

Situation   Technological improvements in nearly every industry increase labor productivity, which is the output of goods and services per person-hour worked. Because labor productivity is significantly higher in Parland than Vergia, Parland's industries are, in general, more technologically advanced than Vergia's.

Reasoning   *To which criticism is the argument most vulnerable?* Though one factor, such as technological advancements, may lead to greater labor productivity, it may not be the only such factor, or even a necessary factor, leading to great labor productivity. Therefore, the mere fact that one region's labor is more productive than another's is not sufficient to establish that the former region is more technologically advanced than the latter region is.

A   The conclusion is not merely a paraphrase of the pieces of information provided in its support. Indeed, the problem with the argument is that the conclusion goes too far beyond what the premises merit.

B   The premises of the argument are not inconsistent with one another.

C   **Correct.** This accurately describes the flaw in the argument because the reasons given in the argument for its conclusion would be good reasons *only if* there were no other plausible explanations for Parland's greater labor productivity.

D   The argument does not mention how long Parland has had more productive labor, or when technological improvements would have occurred.

E   Neither of the premises contains anything that presupposes the conclusion to be true.

The correct answer is C.

9. While many people think of genetic manipulation of food crops as being aimed at developing larger and larger plant varieties, some plant breeders have in fact concentrated on discovering or producing dwarf varieties, which are roughly half as tall as normal varieties.

    Which of the following would, if true, most help to explain the strategy of the plant breeders referred to above?

    (A) Plant varieties used as food by some are used as ornamentals by others.
    (B) The wholesale prices of a given crop decrease as the supply of it increases.
    (C) Crops once produced exclusively for human consumption are often now used for animal feed.
    (D) Short plants are less vulnerable to strong wind and heavy rains.
    (E) Nations with large industrial sectors tend to consume more processed grains.

Evaluation of a Plan

Situation   Some plant breeders have concentrated on discovering or producing certain species of food crop plants to be roughly half as tall as normal varieties.

Reasoning   *Why would some plant breeders concentrate on discovering or producing smaller varieties of certain food crops?* Presumably these breeders would not seek smaller varieties of plant crops unless the smaller size conveyed some benefit. If short plants were less vulnerable to strong wind and heavy rains, they would be apt to be more productive, other things being equal. Plant breeders would have reason to try to discover or produce such hardier varieties.

A   This statement doesn't indicate whether those who use the plants as ornamentals desire shorter varieties.

B   At most this suggests that higher productivity is not as much of an advantage as it otherwise would be. But there is nothing in the passage that indicates that smaller varieties would be more productive than normal-sized plants.

C   No reason is given for thinking that smaller varieties of plants are more conducive to use for animal feed than are larger varieties.

D   Correct. This answer choice is correct because—unlike the other choices—it helps explain why smaller plant varieties could sometimes be preferable to larger varieties. A plant that is less vulnerable to wind and rain is apt to suffer less damage. This is a clear advantage that would motivate plant breeders to try to discover or produce smaller varieties.

E   This has no direct bearing on the question posed. Processed grains are not even mentioned in the passage, let alone linked to smaller plant varieties.

The correct answer is D.

10. Traverton's city council wants to minimize the city's average yearly expenditures on its traffic signal lights and so is considering replacing the incandescent bulbs currently in use with arrays of light-emitting diodes (LEDs) as the incandescent bulbs burn out. Compared to incandescent bulbs, LED arrays consume significantly less energy and cost no more to purchase. Moreover, the costs associated with the conversion of existing fixtures so as to accept LED arrays would be minimal.

Which of the following would it be most useful to know in determining whether switching to LED arrays would be likely to help minimize Traverton's yearly maintenance costs?

(A) Whether the expected service life of LED arrays is at least as long as that of the currently used incandescent bulbs

(B) Whether any cities have switched from incandescent lights in their traffic signals to lighting elements other than LED arrays

(C) Whether the company from which Traverton currently buys incandescent bulbs for traffic signals also sells LED arrays

(D) Whether Traverton's city council plans to increase the number of traffic signal lights in Traverton

(E) Whether the crews that currently replace incandescent bulbs in Traverton's traffic signals know how to convert the existing fixtures so as to accept LED arrays

Evaluation of a Plan

Situation   The city council of Traverton is considering replacing burned-out incandescent traffic signal lights with LED arrays. The LED arrays consume less energy than incandescent bulbs do while costing no more than those bulbs. Further, the cost of converting existing fixtures to accept LED arrays would be minimal.

Reasoning   *What would it be most important to know in determining whether the switch to LEDs would minimize the city's yearly maintenance costs?* LEDs cost no more than incandescent bulbs, and they consume less energy. This suggests that the overall cost of LEDs is lower than that of incandescent bulbs. Is there any circumstance under which the costs associated with LEDs might be higher? They might be higher if more LEDs than incandescent bulbs had to be purchased every year—and that would be necessary if LEDs burn out more quickly than incandescent bulbs do.

A   **Correct.** Unless the answer to this question were yes rather than no, the switch to LED arrays would not help minimize Traverton's yearly maintenance costs. So it is essential to know the answer to this question in order to determine whether switching to LEDs would help.

B   The existence of another possible alternative to incandescent lights does not have any bearing on the question of whether switching from incandescent lights to LEDs would help.

C   The source from which Traverton acquires its lights, be they incandescent or LEDs, is unimportant.

D   Increasing the number of traffic signal lights in Traverton would probably increase the city's yearly maintenance costs, but it would do so regardless of whether those lights use LEDs or incandescent bulbs.

E   Since the goal of switching to LED arrays is to help minimize yearly expenditures on maintenance, a potential one-time cost—that of training workers to convert the existing fixtures—is not relevant. Further, it is not necessarily the case that the crews that currently replace the incandescent bulbs would be the ones converting the existing fixtures—and even if they were, the account of the plan states that conversion costs would be minimal.

The correct answer is A.

11. The Maxilux car company's design for its new luxury model, the Max 100, included a special design for the tires that was intended to complement the model's image. The winning bid for supplying these tires was submitted by Rubco. Analysts concluded that the bid would only just cover Rubco's costs on the tires, but Rubco executives claim that winning the bid will actually make a profit for the company.

Which of the following, if true, most strongly justifies the claim made by Rubco's executives?

(A) In any Maxilux model, the spare tire is exactly the same make and model as the tires that are mounted on the wheels.

(B) Rubco holds exclusive contracts to supply Maxilux with the tires for a number of other models made by Maxilux.

(C) The production facilities for the Max 100 and those for the tires to be supplied by Rubco are located very near each other.

(D) When people who have purchased a carefully designed luxury automobile need to replace a worn part of it, they almost invariably replace it with a part of exactly the same make and type.

(E) When Maxilux awarded the tire contract to Rubco, the only criterion on which Rubco's bid was clearly ahead of its competitors' bids was price.

Argument Construction

Situation   Rubco won a bid for supplying tires for the Max 100, a new luxury model by Maxilux. The bid would barely cover the cost of the tires, but Rubco executives claim that winning the bid will be profitable.

Reasoning   *What would support the executives' claim?* Rubco is not expected to make a profit from supplying the tires for the new cars, so we must look for some other way that Rubco could derive a profit as a result of winning the bid. If by winning the bid Rubco created an inevitable market for itself in replacement tires—on which Rubco could earn a profit—then the executives' claim may be justified.

A   We have already been told that the bid is expected to barely cover the costs of supplying the tires on the new cars, so the analysts mentioned in the passage have presumably already taken into account that there is a spare tire supplied for the Max 100.

B   If winning the bid led Rubco to win more exclusive contracts with the Maxilux, that might help support the executives' claim. But this statement indicates only that Rubco *already* has several exclusive contracts to supply Maxilux with tires, not that winning the bid has led to, or will lead to, more such contracts, which is what would be needed.

C   As in answer choice (A), this is relevant to the costs of supplying the tires for the Max 100, but presumably this was taken into account by the analysts when they concluded that the bid would barely cover Rubco's costs on the tires.

D   Correct. This indicates that by winning the bid Rubco has created a way to profit from the contract with Maxilux, specifically, by creating a market for replacement tires.

E   This is likely one of the reasons that Rubco's bid only just covers the Rubco's costs on the tires; it does nothing to justify the executives' claims that the bid will lead to a profit for Rubco.

The correct answer is D.

12. Which of the following most logically completes the passage?

    Most bicycle helmets provide good protection for the top and back of the head, but little or no protection for the temple regions on the sides of the head. A study of head injuries resulting from bicycle accidents showed that a large proportion were caused by blows to the temple area. Therefore, if bicycle helmets protected this area, the risk of serious head injury in bicycle accidents would be greatly reduced, especially since _____.

    (A) among the bicyclists included in the study's sample of head injuries, only a very small proportion had been wearing a helmet at the time of their accident

    (B) even those bicyclists who regularly wear helmets have a poor understanding of the degree and kind of protection that helmets afford

    (C) a helmet that included protection for the temples would have to be somewhat larger and heavier than current helmets

    (D) the bone in the temple area is relatively thin and impacts in that area are thus very likely to cause brain injury

    (E) bicyclists generally land on their arm or shoulder when they fall to the side, which reduces the likelihood of severe impacts on the side of the head

Argument Construction

Situation   Bicycle helmets protect the top and back of the head, but not the sides or temples. A study found that a large proportion of head injuries caused by biking accidents were caused by blows to the temple area.

Reasoning   *Why would the risk of serious head injury in bicycle accidents be greatly reduced if bicycle helmets protected the temple regions?* If for some reason a serious head injury is particularly likely when there is impact to the temple area, then bicycle helmets that protect that area would be apt to reduce the number of serious head injuries from bicycle accidents. One such reason is that the bone in the temple area is relatively thin.

A   This point is irrelevant because it gives us no information about the seriousness or the likelihood of injuries due to impact to the temple area.

B   Whether bicyclists who regularly wear helmets have a good understanding of what protection their helmets afford is not relevant as to whether serious head injuries are particularly likely to occur from impact to the temple area.

C   This point is relevant only to what a helmet that protected the temple area would be like, not to the seriousness of injuries resulting from impact to that area. If anything, this point counts as a reason *against* the conclusion, not *for* it. If such helmets are heavier and larger, they may be used less than they otherwise would be. If fewer helmets are used, then improvements to helmet design will have less of an effect in reducing serious head injuries.

D   Correct. This statement provides a reason why the temple area of the rider's head needs protection: impacts to this area are very likely to cause brain injuries.

E   This is largely irrelevant. Even if it suggests that head injuries do not generally result from bicyclists falling to the side, it does not indicate that such injuries are rare or that there is not great risk of serious injury in those cases in which there is impact to the temple area.

The correct answer is D.

13. In order to reduce the number of items damaged while in transit to customers, packaging consultants recommended that the TrueSave mail-order company increase the amount of packing material so as to fill any empty spaces in its cartons. Accordingly, TrueSave officials instructed the company's packers to use more packing material than before, and the packers zealously acted on these instructions and used as much as they could. Nevertheless, customer reports of damaged items rose somewhat.

Which of the following, if true, most helps to explain why acting on the consultants' recommendation failed to achieve its goal?

(A)   The change in packing policy led to an increase in expenditure on packing material and labor.

(B)   When packing material is compressed too densely, it loses some of its capacity to absorb shock.

(C)   The amount of packing material used in a carton does not significantly influence the ease with which a customer can unpack the package.

(D)   Most of the goods that TrueSave ships are electronic products that are highly vulnerable to being damaged in transit.

(E)   TrueSave has lost some of its regular customers as a result of the high number of damaged items they received.

Evaluation of a Plan

Situation   Mail-order company TrueSave wants to reduce the number of items damaged while in transit to customers. Packaging consultants recommended that to achieve this goal, the company should use more packing material to fill empty spaces in its cartons. The company's packers began using as much packing material as they could, yet reports of damaged items rose rather than fell.

Reasoning   *What would help explain why the company's acting on the recommendation did not achieve its goal?* The recommendation involved increasing the amount of packing material, so there must have been something about that increase that led to more damage. More damage would be likely to result if stuffing more packing material into shipping boxes made the packaging less effective.

A   An increase in expenditure on packing material and labor might affect the company's profitability, but it would have no effect on whether items were damaged in transit.

B   **Correct.** This statement adequately explains why more items, rather than fewer, were damaged in transit.

C   If customers were able to remove their items just as easily from boxes filled with more packing material as from boxes using less packing material, the items would be unaffected by an increase in the amount of packing material used.

D   The kind of goods TrueSave ships most frequently is not relevant to the question of why increasing the amount of packing material failed to reduce the number of items damaged in transit, since they most likely shipped this same kind of goods both before and after making the recommended change.

E   The loss of regular customers helps explain why TrueSave turned to the packaging consultants for help, but it does not help explain why those consultants' recommendation failed to reduce the number of items damaged in transit.

The correct answer is B.

14. Wood smoke contains dangerous toxins that cause changes in human cells. Because wood smoke presents such a high health risk, legislation is needed to regulate the use of open-air fires and wood-burning stoves.

Which of the following, if true, provides the most support for the argument above?

(A) The amount of dangerous toxins contained in wood smoke is much less than the amount contained in an equal volume of automobile exhaust.

(B) Within the jurisdiction covered by the proposed legislation, most heating and cooking is done with oil or natural gas.

(C) Smoke produced by coal-burning stoves is significantly more toxic than smoke from wood-burning stoves.

(D) No significant beneficial effect on air quality would result if open-air fires were banned within the jurisdiction covered by the proposed legislation.

(E) In valleys where wood is used as the primary heating fuel, the concentration of smoke results in poor air quality.

Argument Construction

Situation   Wood smoke is hazardous, so restrictive legislation is needed.

Reasoning   *Which point supports the need for legislation?* The argument for legislation is based on the position that wood smoke is hazardous to people's health. Any evidence of physical harm resulting from wood smoke supports the argument that legislation is needed. Undoubtedly, poor air quality caused by a high concentration of wood smoke presents just such a health risk.

A   If wood smoke were as dangerous as car exhaust, this might support the idea of regulating it just as exhaust emissions are regulated; but this statement tells us it is less dangerous.

B   This point suggests less of a need for legislation.

C   This information provides no support for the idea that the use of wood-burning stoves should be regulated.

D   The lack of benefit from banning open-air fires is a point against the legislation.

E   **Correct.** This supports the argument in favor of legislation.

The correct answer is E.

15. A certain automaker aims to increase its market share by deeply discounting its vehicles' prices for the next several months. The discounts will cut into profits, but because they will be heavily advertised the manufacturer hopes that they will attract buyers away from rival manufacturers' cars. In the longer term, the automaker envisions that customers initially attracted by the discounts may become loyal customers.

In assessing the plan's chances of achieving its aim, it would be most useful to know which of the following?

(A) Whether the automaker's competitors are likely to respond by offering deep discounts on their own products

(B) Whether the advertisements will be created by the manufacturer's current advertising agency

(C) Whether some of the automaker's models will be more deeply discounted than others

(D) Whether the automaker will be able to cut costs sufficiently to maintain profit margins even when the discounts are in effect

(E) Whether an alternative strategy might enable the automaker to enhance its profitability while holding a constant or diminishing share of the market

Evaluation of a Plan

Situation   An automaker is planning to offer deep discounts on its vehicles' prices in order to increase its market share. The automaker's profit margins will be reduced by this action. By advertising the discounts, the automaker hopes to attract customers who might otherwise be inclined to buy rival manufacturers' cars. These customers would ideally then develop loyalty to the automaker's cars.

Reasoning   *What would it be most useful to know in assessing whether offering deep discounts will enable the automaker to increase its market share?* To achieve an increase in market share, the automaker would have to take customers away from other automakers. Under what circumstances would other automakers be able to retain their customers, if those customers are more likely to purchase cars from automakers that offer deep discounts (and then remain loyal to those automakers)? The other automakers might try to retain their customers by matching the discounts. Thus it would be useful to know whether the other automakers would indeed offer such discounts.

A   **Correct.** If the answer to this question were yes, the plan would probably not achieve its aim of increasing market share. If the answer were no, the plan would have a good chance of succeeding.

B   Since there is no information about the effectiveness of the automaker's current advertising, it would not be useful to know whether the same advertising agency will produce the ads publicizing the discount.

C   Knowing whether some models will be more deeply discounted than others might help in assessing which of the automaker's models will sell best, but it would not help in assessing the overall chance of the automaker increasing its market share.

D   The discounts the automaker plans to offer will cut into profits, according to the information given, so the question of whether the automaker can maintain profit margins while the discounts are in effect has already been answered.

E   While it might be useful to the automaker to know about alternative strategies, such knowledge does not help in assessing the likelihood that the plan under discussion will achieve its aim.

The correct answer is A.

16. In Washington County, attendance at the movies is just large enough for the cinema operators to make modest profits. The size of the county's population is stable and is not expected to increase much. Yet there are investors ready to double the number of movie screens in the county within five years, and they are predicting solid profits both for themselves and for the established cinema operators.

    Which of the following, if true about Washington County, most helps to provide a justification for the investors' prediction?

    (A) Over the next ten years, people in their teenage years, the prime moviegoing age, will be a rapidly growing proportion of the county's population.

    (B) As distinct from the existing cinemas, most of the cinemas being planned would be located in downtown areas, in hopes of stimulating an economic revitalization of those areas.

    (C) Spending on video purchases, as well as spending on video rentals, has been increasing modestly each year for the past ten years.

    (D) The average number of screens per cinema is lower among existing cinemas than it is among cinemas still in the planning stages.

    (E) The sale of snacks and drinks in cinemas accounts for a steadily growing share of most cinema operators' profits.

Evaluation of a Plan

Situation   Movie attendance in Washington County is large enough (though barely so) to allow the cinemas to make a modest profit. The county's population is expected to remain approximately the same. Despite this, investors wish to double the number of movie screens in the county. They expect both that the new screens will be profitable and that the established cinema operators will continue to maintain their profits.

Reasoning   *What piece of information would most help justify the investors' expectation?* To make twice the number of movie screens profitable, movie attendance in Washington County would have to increase. But how could this happen, given that the county's population is not expected to change? Clearly, some people in Washington County will need to go to the movies more often than they do now. This might happen if some of the population of Washington County were to age into a demographic that is likely to go to the movies more frequently.

A   **Correct.** This statement tells us that over the next ten years, a larger proportion of the population will probably be moviegoers and this could significantly increase movie attendance in Washington County.

B   While stimulating downtown revitalization is a worthy goal, this does not help explain why more people would be likely to go to the movies in Washington County. Further, it raises the question of whether theaters in a revitalized downtown would draw business away from theaters in other locations, thus reducing the established cinema operators' profits.

C   This provides a reason to doubt the investors' prediction, because if spending on videos is increasing, people are probably less likely to see movies in movie theaters.

D   Regardless of how many screens each new cinema has relative to the established cinemas, none of them will be profitable if they cannot attract sufficient numbers of cinemagoers.

E   Cinemas' profitability depending on their sales of snacks and drinks does not explain why more people would go to the cinema in the first place.

The correct answer is A.

17. Hollywood restaurant is replacing some of its standard tables with tall tables and stools. The restaurant already fills every available seat during its operating hours, and the change in seating arrangements will not result in an increase in the restaurant's seating capacity. Nonetheless, the restaurant's management expects revenue to increase as a result of the seating change without any concurrent change in menu, prices, or operating hours.

Which of the following, if true, provides the best reason for the expectation?

(A) One of the taller tables takes up less floor space than one of the standard tables.

(B) Diners seated on stools typically do not linger over dinner as long as diners seated at standard tables.

(C) Since the restaurant will replace only some of its standard tables, it can continue to accommodate customers who do not care for the taller tables.

(D) Few diners are likely to avoid the restaurant because of the new seating arrangement.

(E) The standard tables being replaced by tall tables would otherwise have to be replaced with new standard tables at a greater expense.

Argument Construction

Situation   Hollywood restaurant is replacing some of its tables with taller tables and stools, and the management expects this will increase revenue, despite the fact that the restaurant already fills all of its available seats and that this change will not increase seating capacity. Furthermore, there will not be any change in menu, prices, or operating hours.

Reasoning   *What would strongly support the management's expectation?* Since the new seating will not increase the restaurant's seating capacity, the management's expectations must be based on a belief that the change to taller tables and stools will somehow change diners' behavior, perhaps by leading them to order more food, or to stay at their tables for a shorter time, thereby allowing the restaurant to serve more diners during its operating hours without increasing seating capacity. If diners seated at tall tables and on tall stools spend less time lingering over their dinners, then they will leave sooner, opening up the tables for more diners. Because the restaurant, before the change, already fills every available seat during its operating hours, it is reasonable to think that it will be able to serve more diners than it currently does, thereby selling more food and thus increasing revenue.

A   This would be relevant if we could infer from it that seating capacity will increase. However, the passage indicates that the new seating arrangement will not result in greater capacity.

B   Correct. Because the restaurant will be able to serve more meals during its operating hours, the restaurant's revenue can be expected to increase.

C   This may indicate that the restaurant is less likely to alienate customers who do not care for tall tables and stools, but that only supports the claim that the restaurant will not lose customers and therefore lose revenue; it does not indicate that the restaurant will see revenue increase.

D   Again, this merely indicates that there will not be a loss—or much loss—of revenue, not that there will be an increase in revenue.

E   Less expensive tables will decrease the restaurant's costs, but it will not increase the restaurant's revenue.

The correct answer is B.

18. Hunter: **Many people blame hunters alone for the decline in Greenrock National Forest's deer population over the past ten years.** Yet clearly, black bears have also played an important role in this decline. In the past ten years, the forest's protected black bear population has risen sharply, and examination of black bears found dead in the forest during the deer hunting season showed that a number of them had recently fed on deer.

    In the hunter's argument, the portion in boldface plays which of the following roles?

    (A) It is the main conclusion of the argument.

    (B) It is a finding that the argument seeks to explain.

    (C) It is an explanation that the argument concludes is correct.

    (D) It provides evidence in support of the main conclusion of the argument.

    (E) It introduces a judgment that the argument opposes.

Argument Construction

Situation   The hunter claims that hunters have been identified by many people as the sole cause of the decline in Greenrock National Forest's deer population. But the hunter argues that black bears have also contributed to the deer population decline. Black bears are protected and have increased in number, and they have been found to have fed recently on deer.

Reasoning   *What role in the argument is played by the hunter's statement that many people blame hunters alone for the decline in the national forest's deer population?* In this statement, the hunter claims that many people have judged hunters responsible for the decline. The hunter then goes on to offer evidence supporting a different judgment: that hunters are *not* solely responsible, but that black bears are also to blame.

A   The hunter's main conclusion is that black bears have also contributed to the decline in the deer population.

B   The argument seeks to offer a reason for the finding that the deer population has declined, not the finding that people blame hunters for that decline.

C   The hunter does not conclude that blaming hunters for the decline in the deer population is correct; rather, the hunter suggests that black bears should also be blamed.

D   The hunter believes that hunters are *not* solely responsible for the decline in the deer population, so people's suggestion that they *are* responsible does not support the hunter's main conclusion.

E   **Correct.** The boldfaced statement cites a judgment that the hunter attributes to many people, and that the hunter argues is incorrect. The hunter opposes the judgment that hunters alone are responsible for the decline in the deer population.

The correct answer is E.

19. A major network news organization experienced a drop in viewership in the week following the airing of a controversial report on the economy. The network also received a very large number of complaints regarding the report. The network, however, maintains that negative reactions to the report had nothing to do with its loss of viewers.

Which of the following, if true, most strongly supports the network's position?

(A) The other major network news organizations reported similar reductions in viewership during the same week.

(B) The viewers who registered complaints with the network were regular viewers of the news organization's programs.

(C) Major network news organizations publicly attribute drops in viewership to their own reports only when they receive complaints about those reports.

(D) This was not the first time that this network news organization has aired a controversial report on the economy that has inspired viewers to complain to the network.

(E) Most network news viewers rely on network news broadcasts as their primary source of information regarding the economy.

Argument Construction

Situation   A major network news organization aired a controversial report on the economy, and the following week the network's viewership declined. The network claims that the loss of viewers was not connected with negative reactions to the report.

Reasoning   *Which statement most strongly supports the network's position?* If other major news network organizations had similar drops in viewership, it is implausible to think that the controversial report accounted for the other organizations' drops in viewership. On the other hand, it is not implausible to suppose that whatever did cause the drop in the viewership experienced by other network news organizations—e.g., holidays, weather, popular non-news programming—also had that effect on the organization that ran the controversial report. This would give some reason to believe that it was not the report that accounts for the organization's drop in viewership.

A   **Correct.** This statement indicates that something other than the airing of the report could account for the subsequent drop in the organization's viewership.

B   If anything, this statement tends to undermine the network's claim, because it suggests that the report offended people who otherwise might have continued to watch the organization's programming.

C   Since the network did in fact receive complaints about the report, this statement is irrelevant.

D   The fact that the network has received complaints before about controversial reports on the economy that the network's news organization has aired tells us nothing about whether this recent report caused a subsequent drop in viewership.

E   The fact that viewers turn to network news broadcasts as their primary source of information about the economy tells us nothing about whether viewers might stop watching a particular network news organization's programs as a result of its airing a controversial report on the economy.

The correct answer is A.

20. Physician: The hormone melatonin has shown promise as a medication for sleep disorders when taken in synthesized form. Because the long-term side effects of synthetic melatonin are unknown, however, I cannot recommend its use at this time.

    Patient: Your position is inconsistent with your usual practice. You prescribe many medications that you know have serious side effects, so concern about side effects cannot be the real reason you will not prescribe melatonin.

    The patient's argument is flawed because it fails to consider that

    (A)   the side effects of synthetic melatonin might be different from those of naturally produced melatonin
    (B)   it is possible that the physician does not believe that melatonin has been conclusively shown to be effective
    (C)   sleep disorders, if left untreated, might lead to serious medical complications
    (D)   the side effects of a medication can take some time to manifest themselves
    (E)   known risks can be weighed against known benefits, but unknown risks cannot

Argument Evaluation

Situation   The physician refuses to prescribe synthetic melatonin to treat sleep disorders despite this medication's promise. The reason the physician offers for this refusal is that the long-term side effects of synthetic melatonin are unknown. The patient responds that because the physician prescribes other medications that are known to have serious side effects, it cannot be a concern for synthetic melatonin's side effects that is prompting the physician's refusal to prescribe that medication.

Reasoning   *What does the patient's argument fail to consider?* The patient says that the inconsistency in the physician's position lies in the physician's unwillingness to prescribe synthetic melatonin coupled with a willingness to prescribe other medications that are known to have serious side effects. But notice that the physician does not say that synthetic melatonin has *serious* side effects; rather, the physician points out that the long-term side effects of synthetic melatonin are unknown. The physician most likely prescribes medications that have serious side effects because the medications' benefits outweigh the risks posed by their side effects. In the case of synthetic melatonin, however, this kind of decision cannot be made.

A   The patient's argument has to do with whether the physician's refusal to prescribe synthetic melatonin is consistent with the physician's usual prescription practices. The question of whether naturally produced melatonin has different side effects than synthetic melatonin has no bearing on that argument.

B   It is quite reasonable for the patient's argument not to mention this possibility, especially since the physician expresses a belief that synthetic melatonin may be effective—but expresses no belief about whether or not it has been conclusively shown to be effective.

C   Awareness that sleep disorders can lead to serious medical complications most likely prompts the patient's desire for treatment—but the patient's not mentioning this possible consequence of sleep disorders does not indicate a flaw in the argument.

D   The patient makes clear that the physician prescribes medications that have serious side effects; the time those side effects take to manifest themselves is not relevant to the argument.

E   **Correct.** The patient's argument is flawed in failing to consider this key difference between known risks and unknown risks. If the patient had considered this key difference, the patient would have realized that the physician's position is not at all inconsistent, and that the physician's refusal to prescribe is genuinely based on a concern about an unknown risk.

The correct answer is E.

21. In recent years, many cabinetmakers have been winning acclaim as artists. But since furniture must be useful, cabinetmakers must exercise their craft with an eye to the practical utility of their product. For this reason, cabinetmaking is not art.

    Which of the following is an assumption that supports drawing the conclusion above from the reason given for that conclusion?

    (A) Some furniture is made to be placed in museums, where it will not be used by anyone.

    (B) Some cabinetmakers are more concerned than others with the practical utility of the products they produce.

    (C) Cabinetmakers should be more concerned with the practical utility of their products than they currently are.

    (D) An object is not an art object if its maker pays attention to the object's practical utility.

    (E) Artists are not concerned with the monetary value of their products.

Argument Construction

Situation Cabinetmaking is not art because furniture must be made with an eye to its usefulness.

Reasoning *What assumption is made in the argument?* The argument claims that cabinetmakers, when making furniture, must take usefulness into account. It concludes that cabinetmaking is not art. However, the reasoning has a gap: Some information that is not explicitly stated is needed to make the argument succeed. This need for additional information can be met, at least in part, by adding an assumption such as this: Nothing created with a view to its usefulness is a work of art.

A The destination of the object after its creation is not the issue.

B The extent to which some cabinetmakers *actually consider* utility is irrelevant, since the reasoning claims that utility must be considered in the successful manufacture of furniture.

C The argument primarily concerns truly successful cabinetmaking, whether it is art or not, and the role utility plays in (successful) cabinetmaking. It does not address the issue of whether or not current cabinetmakers give adequate consideration to utility or whether or not today's cabinetmakers produce truly successful and useful furniture.

D Correct. This option, unlike the other four, provides information that helps fill the gap in the argument.

E The issue of monetary value is not raised at all in the argument.

The correct answer is D.

22. Only a reduction of 10 percent in the number of scheduled flights using Greentown's airport will allow the delays that are so common there to be avoided. Hevelia airstrip, 40 miles away, would, if upgraded and expanded, be an attractive alternative for fully 20 percent of the passengers using Greentown airport. Nevertheless, experts reject the claim that turning Hevelia into a full-service airport would end the chronic delays at Greentown.

Which of the following, if true, most helps to justify the experts' position?

(A) Turning Hevelia into a full-service airport would require not only substantial construction at the airport itself, but also the construction of new access highways.

(B) A second largely undeveloped airstrip close to Greentown airport would be a more attractive alternative than Hevelia for many passengers who now use Greentown.

(C) Hevelia airstrip lies in a relatively undeveloped area but would, if it became a full-service airport, be a magnet for commercial and residential development.

(D) If an airplane has to wait to land, the extra jet fuel required adds significantly to the airline's costs.

(E) Several airlines use Greentown as a regional hub, so that most flights landing at Greentown have many passengers who then take different flights to reach their final destinations.

Evaluation of a Plan

Situation   To avoid the delays now common at Greentown's airport, the number of scheduled flights there would need to be reduced by 10 percent. If the nearby Hevelia airstrip were expanded and upgraded, it would be an attractive alternative for 20 percent of Greentown airport's passengers. Still, experts do not believe that the delays at Greentown would end even if Hevelia were turned into a full-service airport.

Reasoning   *Which statement most supports the experts' position?* If the number of flights at Greentown's airport did not drop by at least 10 percent, despite the fact that 20 percent of the passengers who currently use Greentown's airport would find nearby Hevelia airstrip an attractive alternative, then the delays would not be avoided. Airlines generally use certain airports as regional hubs—an airport through which an airline routes most of its traffic— so, even if many passengers would be willing to use Hevelia airstrip, the number of flights at Greentown may not decline significantly, or at all.

A   The experts' position concerns what would happen to the flight delays at Greentown airport *if* the Hevelia airstrip were converted into a full-service airport. So the fact that there are great costs involved in making such a conversion—possibly making such a conversion unlikely—has no bearing on the effects such a conversion would have on flight delays at Greentown *if* the conversion were to be carried out.

B   This statement indicates that the undeveloped airstrip near Greentown might be a better way to alleviate flight delays at Greentown, but it tells us nothing about the effects that converting the Hevelia airstrip to a full-service airport would have were it to be carried out.

C   This in no way explains why converting the Hevelia airstrip into a full-service airport would not alleviate the problem with flight delays at Greentown.

D   This provides a reason to think that reducing the number of flights at Greentown might make the airport more efficient. But that has no bearing on the effect that converting the Hevelia airstrip to a full-service airport might have on flight delays at Greentown.

E   **Correct.** This statement provides support for the experts' position because it gives a reason for thinking that the number of scheduled flights at Greentown would not be reduced, even if Hevelia airstrip became an attractive alternative for some 20 percent of Greentown's passengers.

The correct answer is E.

23. Male bowerbirds construct elaborately decorated nests, or bowers. Basing their judgment on the fact that different local populations of bowerbirds of the same species build bowers that exhibit different building and decorative styles, researchers have concluded that the bowerbirds' building styles are a culturally acquired, rather than a genetically transmitted, trait.

Which of the following, if true, would most strengthen the conclusion drawn by the researchers?

(A) There are more common characteristics than there are differences among the bower-building styles of the local bowerbird population that has been studied most extensively.

(B) Young male bowerbirds are inept at bower-building and apparently spend years watching their elders before becoming accomplished in the local bower style.

(C) The bowers of one species of bowerbird lack the towers and ornamentation characteristic of the bowers of most other species of bowerbird.

(D) Bowerbirds are found only in New Guinea and Australia, where local populations of the birds apparently seldom have contact with one another.

(E) It is well known that the song dialects of some songbirds are learned rather than transmitted genetically.

Argument Evaluation

Situation   Male bowerbirds of the same species but living in different habitats build nests of widely varying styles. Researchers conclude that this nest-building behavior is culturally acquired rather than genetically transmitted.

Reasoning   *What evidence supports the researchers' conclusion?* The researchers base their conclusion upon the different styles of nests and probably the assumption that the nests would all be similar if the bower-building behavior was only transmitted through the genes of the species. What would lend support to this reasoning? If young male bowerbirds have no inherent aptitude for nest building and must learn it over a period of years by watching older male bowerbirds, then the argument that bowerbirds acquire their nest-building preferences culturally rather than genetically is strengthened.

A   The greater number of similarities than differences in style in one population could be attributed to either cultural acquisition or genetic transmission, so the conclusion is not strengthened.

B   **Correct.** Compared with the other options, this information provides the most additional support for the researchers' conclusion.

C   The cited differences are among populations of the same species; differences between species are outside the scope of the conclusion.

D   Since no information is given about the nest-building styles of these populations (whether or not they are of the same species), the fact that they have little contact neither strengthens nor weakens the conclusion.

E   This statement provides an example of learned bird behavior, and so provides a little additional support for the conclusion, but not as much additional support as does answer choice (B).

The correct answer is B.

24. Plan: Concerned about the welfare of its senior citizens, the government of Runagia decided two years ago to increase by 20 percent the government-provided pension paid to all Runagians age sixty-five and older.

    Result: Many Runagian senior citizens are no better off financially now than they were before the increase.

    Further information: The annual rate of inflation since the pension increase has been below 5 percent, and the increased pension has been duly received by all eligible Runagians.

    In light of the further information, which of the following, if true, does most to explain the result that followed implementation of the plan?

    (A) The majority of senior citizens whose financial position has not improved rely entirely on the government pension for their income.

    (B) The Runagian banking system is so inefficient that cashing a pension check can take as much as three weeks.

    (C) The prices of goods and services that meet the special needs of many senior citizens have increased at a rate much higher than the rate of inflation.

    (D) The pension increase occurred at a time when the number of Runagians age sixty-five and older who were living below the poverty level was at an all-time high.

    (E) The most recent pension increase was only the second such increase in the last ten years.

Evaluation of a Plan

Situation   Two years ago, Runagia's government attempted to improve senior citizens' welfare by increasing senior citizens' pensions by 20 percent. Unfortunately, many of those senior citizens' welfare did not improve. This result occurred despite inflation being relatively low—below 5 percent—and all appropriate people receiving their increased pensions.

Reasoning   *What would do most to explain why many of Runagia's senior citizens are no better off than they were before their pensions increased?* Many of Runagia's senior citizens were not helped by receiving more money. Clearly, these senior citizens used nearly 20 percent more money than they did before to maintain the same standard of living. Usually, this could be explained by high inflation—but the further information informs us that the annual rate of inflation was well below the percentage of the pension increase. The annual rate of inflation is, however, an average calculated over a large number of goods and services. The prices of some goods and services rise more than the prices of other goods and services. It could be the case that the goods and services senior citizens need are those that have risen most in price. If this were the case, their pension increase could have been insufficient to raise their standard of living.

A   Regardless of what someone relies on for their income, a 20 percent increase in that income would be expected to raise that person's standard of living.

B   The 20 percent increase in pensions occurred two years ago. Whatever problems a three-week delay in the cashing of pension checks caused would be unlikely to persist over two years.

C   **Correct.** This statement properly identifies a reason why the plan's result was that many Runagian senior citizens were no better off than they were before the increase.

D   Even if it were true that an all-time high number of Runagians over sixty-five were living below the poverty line at the time of the pension increase, it would still be expected that such an increase would leave them better off financially than they were before the increase.

E   Regardless of how many pension increases there were in the past, the current 20 percent increase could reasonably be expected to leave its recipients better off financially than they were before the increase.

The correct answer is C.

25. A drug that is highly effective in treating many types of infection can, at present, be obtained only from the bark of the ibora, a tree that is quite rare in the wild. It takes the bark of 5,000 trees to make one kilogram of the drug. It follows, therefore, that continued production of the drug must inevitably lead to the ibora's extinction.

Which of the following, if true, most seriously weakens the argument above?

(A) The drug made from ibora bark is dispensed to doctors from a central authority.

(B) The drug made from ibora bark is expensive to produce.

(C) The leaves of the ibora are used in a number of medical products.

(D) The ibora can be propagated from cuttings and grown under cultivation.

(E) The ibora generally grows in largely inaccessible places.

Argument Evaluation

Situation   The extinction of the rare ibora tree is inevitable if production of an effective infection-fighting drug continues.

Reasoning   *Which point most weakens the argument?* The production of the drug requires such an enormous amount of bark that, the argument concludes, the continuing existence of the rare tree is in jeopardy. But the argument assumes that killing the trees in the wild is the only way to obtain the needed bark. Can the tree be cultivated? If so, the majority of the trees in the wild could be left to flourish.

A   The method of the drug's distribution is irrelevant, unless the central authority can limit the drug's production from the bark of wild ibora trees. But this information is not provided.

B   The cost of producing the drug does not affect the outcome for the tree unless it deters production.

C   The existence of uses for other parts of the tree opens the possibility that the ibora-bark drug would cause no increase in destruction of trees other than what exists already. If this information were provided, it would weaken support for the conclusion. Since it is not provided, this option does not significantly weaken the argument.

D   **Correct.** This information most weakens the argument.

E   Difficulty of access to the trees could provide a disincentive to their harvesting—but we are not told that it would prevent their harvesting.

The correct answer is D.

26. When a polygraph test is judged inconclusive, this is no reflection on the examinee. Rather, such a judgment means that the test has failed to show whether the examinee was truthful or untruthful. Nevertheless, employers will sometimes refuse to hire a job applicant because of an inconclusive polygraph test result.

    Which of the following conclusions can most properly be drawn from the information above?

    (A) Most examinees with inconclusive polygraph test results are in fact untruthful.

    (B) Polygraph tests should not be used by employers in the consideration of job applicants.

    (C) An inconclusive polygraph test result is sometimes unfairly held against the examinee.

    (D) A polygraph test indicating that an examinee is untruthful can sometimes be mistaken.

    (E) Some employers have refused to consider the results of polygraph tests when evaluating job applicants.

Argument Construction

Situation   Employers sometimes refuse to hire job applicants because of inconclusive polygraph tests, even though inconclusive tests reveal only the failure of the test itself to determine the truthfulness or untruthfulness of the person tested.

Reasoning   *What conclusion can be drawn from this information?* Inconclusive polygraph results do not reveal anything about the person tested; they reveal only the failure of the polygraph test. Nevertheless, employers may choose not to hire an applicant whose polygraph test has had an inconclusive result. It is reasonable to conclude that these employers unfairly treat the lack of firm polygraph results as counting against the candidate—not against the polygraph test.

A   This statement makes a judgment that is explicitly contradicted in the passage, which states that an inconclusive polygraph result *is no reflection on the examinee.*

B   This sweeping conclusion is not as well supported by the passage as is answer choice (C). The passage discusses only inconclusive polygraph results.

C   **Correct.** Given the information in the passage, one can infer that inconclusive polygraph tests are sometimes used unfairly against job applicants—if one makes the reasonable assumption that judging a job applicant unsuitable is unfair if the judgment is based merely on the failure of a particular technique to provide reliable evidence.

D   The passage is concerned only with inconclusive tests, not cases when the polygraph test is mistaken.

E   Information about employers who do not consider polygraph tests is irrelevant to the discussion.

The correct answer is C.

27. For similar cars and comparable drivers, automobile insurance for collision damage has always cost more in Greatport than in Fairmont. Police studies, however, show that cars owned by Greatport residents are, on average, slightly less likely to be involved in a collision than cars in Fairmont. Clearly, therefore, insurance companies are making a greater profit on collision-damage insurance in Greatport than in Fairmont.

In evaluating the argument, it would be most useful to compare

(A) the level of traffic congestion in Greatport with the level of traffic congestion in Fairmont

(B) the cost of repairing collision damage in Greatport with the cost of repairing collision damage in Fairmont

(C) the rates Greatport residents pay for other forms of insurance with the rates paid for similar insurance by residents of Fairmont

(D) the condition of Greatport's roads and streets with the condition of Fairmont's roads and streets

(E) the cost of collision-damage insurance in Greatport and Fairmont with that in other cities

Argument Evaluation

Situation A particular kind of insurance, that for collision damage, costs more in Greatport than in Fairmont. The cars of Greatport residents are, however, less likely to be involved in collisions than are cars of Fairmont residents. So insurance companies must be making a greater profit on collision-damage insurance in Greatport than in Fairmont.

Reasoning *What would it help to consider in evaluating the argument?* Insurance companies would make greater profits on collision-damage insurance in Greatport than they make in Fairmont if they pay out less money in response to Greatport residents' claims than they do in response to Fairmont's residents' claims. That Greatport residents' cars are involved in fewer collisions than are Fairmont's residents' cars supports this—if there are fewer collisions overall, then the insurance companies might pay out less money overall. But the number of collisions is only one factor contributing to how much money an insurance company pays out in response to claims; another factor is the amount of damage inflicted on the cars involved in collisions and how much it costs to repair that damage. These costs would need to be considered before concluding that insurance companies' profits on collision-damage insurance are greater in Greatport than in Fairmont.

A The level of traffic congestion probably contributes to the frequency of collisions in each town. The information given, however, includes the statement that Greatport cars are less likely to be involved in collisions than are Fairmont cars. Why this occurs—whether, for example, traffic congestion is a contributory factor—is not relevant.

B Correct. This is clearly a factor that would affect the profitability of insurance in the two towns—and is therefore highly relevant to evaluating the argument, especially its conclusion.

C The argument's conclusion is about insurance companies' profits on collision-damage insurance alone, so other types of insurance, and the rates paid for them, are not relevant.

D The condition of the roads and streets in each town probably contributes to the frequency of collisions in each town. The information given, however, includes the statement that Greatport cars are less likely to be involved in collisions than are Fairmont cars. Why this is so—whether, for example, the condition of the roads is a contributory cause—is not relevant.

E Since the argument is concerned solely with collision-insurance costs and profits in Greatport and Fairmont, comparing the cost of insurance in those towns with the cost of insurance elsewhere would provide no useful insight.

The correct answer is B.

28. Last year a record number of new manufacturing jobs were created. Will this year bring another record? Well, a new manufacturing job is created either within an existing company or by the start-up of a new company. Within existing firms, new jobs have been created this year at well below last year's record pace. At the same time, there is considerable evidence that the number of new companies starting up will be no higher this year than it was last year, and surely **the new companies starting up this year will create no more jobs per company than did last year's start-ups**. Clearly, it can be concluded that **the number of new jobs created this year will fall short of last year's record**.

In the argument given, the two portions in boldface play which of the following roles?

(A)　The first is a prediction that, if accurate, would provide support for the main conclusion of the argument; the second is that main conclusion.

(B)　The first is a prediction that, if accurate, would provide support for the main conclusion of the argument; the second is a conclusion drawn in order to support that main conclusion.

(C)　The first is an objection that the argument rejects; the second is the main conclusion of the argument.

(D)　The first is an objection that the argument rejects; the second presents a conclusion that could be drawn if that objection were allowed to stand.

(E)　The first is a claim that has been advanced in support of a position that the argument opposes; the second is a claim advanced in support of the main conclusion of the argument.

Argument Construction

Situation　The question posed is whether this year will, like last year, see a record number of new manufacturing jobs. Among the evidence presented is the assertion that any new manufacturing job is created by an existing company or as part of the start-up of a new company. New jobs have been created by existing firms at a slower pace than last year. It is unlikely that more new companies will be started up this year than were started last year; further, the argument suggests that this year's new companies are unlikely to create more jobs per company than did last year's new companies. For all these reasons, the argument concludes, this year's job creation will not equal that of last year.

Reasoning　*What roles do the two portions in boldface play in the argument?* The first boldfaced portion states that this year's new companies will create no more jobs per company than did last year's new companies. The speaker does not know this for a fact, since it has not yet happened; it is thus a prediction. If it turns out to be the case, it would support the idea that job creation this year will fall short of last year's—which is, in turn, the conclusion that the argument reaches.

A　**Correct.** This statement properly identifies the roles played in the argument by the two portions in boldface.

B　This properly identifies the role played in the argument by the first portion in boldface. The second is, of course, a conclusion, but it is not drawn in order to support the main conclusion; rather, it is the main conclusion.

C　This properly identifies the role played by the second portion in boldface. The first portion in boldface, however, states that companies starting up this year will create no more jobs than last year's start-ups. The argument does not reject this idea; rather, it relies on it.

D　The first portion in boldface states that companies starting up this year will create no more jobs than last year's start-ups. The argument does not reject this idea; rather, it relies on it. The second portion in boldface does present a conclusion, but since the first portion is not an objection, any description that relies on that mischaracterization is in error.

E　The second portion in boldface is not merely a claim; it is, rather, the main conclusion of the argument. The first portion in boldface is a claim, but it is not advanced in support of a position that the argument opposes; rather, it supports the argument's main conclusion.

The correct answer is A.

29. The tulu, a popular ornamental plant, does not reproduce naturally, and is only bred and sold by specialized horticultural companies. Unfortunately, the tulu is easily devastated by a contagious fungal rot. The government ministry plans to reassure worried gardeners by requiring all tulu plants to be tested for fungal rot before being sold. However, infected plants less than 30 weeks old have generally not built up enough fungal rot in their systems to be detected reliably. And many tulu plants are sold before they are 24 weeks old.

Which of the following, if performed by the government ministry, could logically be expected to overcome the problem with their plan to test for the fungal rot?

(A) Releasing a general announcement that tulu plants less than 30 weeks old cannot be effectively tested for fungal rot

(B) Requiring all tulu plants less than 30 weeks old to be labeled as such

(C) Researching possible ways to test tulu plants less than 24 weeks old for fungal rot

(D) Ensuring that tulu plants not be sold before they are 30 weeks old

(E) Quarantining all tulu plants from horticultural companies at which any case of fungal rot has been detected until those tulu plants can be tested for fungal rot

Evaluation of a Plan

Situation   There is a contagious fungal rot that devastates the tulu, a popular ornamental plant. To reassure worried gardeners, the government ministry plans to require that tulu plants be tested for the rot before being sold. However, many tulu plants are sold before they are 24 weeks old, yet fungal rot in plants less than 30 weeks old generally cannot be detected reliably.

Reasoning   *What could the government ministry do to overcome the problem?* The problem arises from the fact that tulu plants are frequently sold before they are 24 weeks old, which is too soon for any fungal rot that is present to have built up enough in their root systems to be detected. Since the goal of the testing is to ensure that infected tulu plants not be sold, an obvious solution would be to make sure that no plants are sold before they are old enough for fungal rot to have built up to a detectable level. Thus, tulu plants should not be sold before they are 30 weeks old.

A   Releasing such an announcement would help overcome the problem if it guaranteed that no one would buy or sell tulu plants before the plants were 30 weeks old, but it is far from certain that such an announcement would guarantee this.

B   Since some people may not be aware of the significance of such labeling, such labeling might have very little effect.

C   There is no guarantee that such research will be successful at reducing the age at which tulu plants can be reliably tested.

D   **Correct.** If the government *ensures* that no tulu plants less than 30 weeks of age are sold, then the specific problem mentioned in the passage would be overcome.

E   This will not help overcome the problem. Such a quarantine program might lead horticultural companies to start selling tulu plants *only* if they are less than 24 weeks old, thereby minimizing the chance of quarantine by minimizing the chance of detection.

The correct answer is D.

30.   The Eurasian ruffe, a fish species inadvertently introduced into North America's Great Lakes in recent years, feeds on the eggs of lake whitefish, a native species, thus threatening the lakes' natural ecosystem. To help track the ruffe's spread, government agencies have produced wallet-sized cards about the ruffe. The cards contain pictures of the ruffe and explain the danger they pose; the cards also request anglers to report any ruffe they catch.

Which of the following, if true, would provide most support for the prediction that the agencies' action will have its intended effect?

(A)   The ruffe has spiny fins that make it unattractive as prey.

(B)   Ruffe generally feed at night, but most recreational fishing on the Great Lakes is done during daytime hours.

(C)   Most people who fish recreationally on the Great Lakes are interested in the preservation of the lake whitefish because it is a highly prized game fish.

(D)   The ruffe is one of several nonnative species in the Great Lakes whose existence threatens the survival of lake whitefish populations there.

(E)   The bait that most people use when fishing for whitefish on the Great Lakes is not attractive to ruffe.

Evaluation of a Plan

Situation   The Eurasian ruffe, a species not native to the Great Lakes, is threatening the native lake whitefish. Government agencies hope that wallet-sized cards identifying the ruffe, explaining the danger they pose, and asking anglers to report their ruffe catches will help them track the ruffe's spread.

Reasoning   *What point would support the idea that the agencies' action will have its intended effect?* The cards are intended to help government agencies track the ruffe's spread. They will be useful for this purpose only if anglers actually report the ruffe they catch. Thus anything that increases the odds of anglers' doing such reporting would make it more likely that the cards will have their intended effect.

A   If ruffe are unattractive as prey, they will probably spread more quickly in the Great Lakes. This will most likely have little effect on whether the wallet-sized cards will help government agencies track the ruffe.

B   If ruffe feed at night, while fishing is done in the daytime, it is unlikely that anglers would catch ruffe. Thus few catches would be reported to government agencies, making it more difficult for those agencies to track the spread of ruffe.

C   **Correct.** This statement properly identifies a point that supports the prediction that the agencies' action will have its intended effect—that is, those who are interested in preserving the lake whitefish will be likely to report catches of ruffe, which threaten whitefish, thus enabling the agencies' tracking of the spread of ruffe.

D   That the ruffe is one of several nonnative species threatening the Great Lakes lessens the odds that the whitefish will survive, but this has no effect on the question of whether the wallet-sized cards will help government agencies track the ruffe's spread.

E   This would make it likely that anglers would catch few ruffe. If anglers do not catch many ruffe, there will not be many to report to government agencies, which would in turn make it more difficult for those agencies to track the ruffe's spread.

The correct answer is C.

31. Which of the following most logically completes the argument?

    Ferber's syndrome, a viral disease that frequently affects cattle, is transmitted to these animals through infected feed. Even though chickens commercially raised for meat are often fed the type of feed identified as the source of infection in cattle, Ferber's syndrome is only rarely observed in chickens. This fact, however, does not indicate that most chickens are immune to the virus that causes Ferber's syndrome, since _____.

    (A) chickens and cattle are not the only kinds of farm animal that are typically fed the type of feed liable to be contaminated with the virus that causes Ferber's syndrome

    (B) Ferber's syndrome has been found in animals that have not been fed the type of feed liable to be contaminated with the virus that can cause the disease

    (C) resistance to some infectious organisms such as the virus that causes Ferber's syndrome can be acquired by exposure to a closely related infectious organism

    (D) chickens and cattle take more than a year to show symptoms of Ferber's syndrome, and chickens commercially raised for meat, unlike cattle, are generally brought to market during the first year of life

    (E) the type of feed liable to be infected with the virus that causes Ferber's syndrome generally constitutes a larger proportion of the diet of commercially raised chickens than of commercially raised cattle

Argument Construction

Situation   Certain feed given to cows and to chickens commercially raised for meat is infected with the virus that causes Ferber's syndrome. Cows are frequently affected by this disease, while it is rarely observed in chickens. But (for a reason the argument omits) this does not suggest that chickens are immune to the virus.

Reasoning   *What point would most logically complete the argument?* How could it be the case that chickens are infected, yet Ferber's syndrome is only rarely observed in them? The important point here is that Ferber's syndrome is not *observed* in chickens. A disease is usually observed to be present on the basis of its symptoms. Those symptoms might not be present, or might not *yet* be present, in chickens that are infected with the virus. If the chickens were used for meat before they began showing symptoms, then they would not be observed to have Ferber's syndrome, but this would not indicate that they were immune to the virus.

A   That other animals are fed the potentially contaminated feed is not relevant to the question of whether chickens are immune to the virus.

B   The idea that there could be a source of the virus other than contaminated feed does not have any bearing on whether chickens are immune to the virus.

C   The idea that there is a way for animals to acquire a resistance to the virus that causes Ferber's syndrome suggests that some animals, possibly chickens, might be immune to the virus. This is the opposite of what the argument is trying to establish.

D   Correct. This statement properly identifies a point that logically completes the argument: It provides a reason why infected chickens would fail to show symptoms of Ferber's syndrome.

E   If chickens' diets contain proportionally more of the potentially infected feed than cattle's diets do, it is even more surprising that Ferber's syndrome is not observed in chickens—far from providing a reason not to conclude that chickens are immune to the virus; this makes it seem even more likely that they are immune.

The correct answer is D.

32. Last year the rate of inflation was 1.2 percent, but for the current year it has been 4 percent. We can conclude that inflation is on an upward trend and the rate will be still higher next year.

    Which of the following, if true, most seriously weakens the conclusion above?

    (A)   The inflation figures were computed on the basis of a representative sample of economic data rather than all of the available data.

    (B)   Last year a dip in oil prices brought inflation temporarily below its recent stable annual level of 4 percent.

    (C)   Increases in the pay of some workers are tied to the level of inflation, and at an inflation rate of 4 percent or above, these pay raises constitute a force causing further inflation.

    (D)   The 1.2 percent rate of inflation last year represented a 10-year low.

    (E)   Government intervention cannot affect the rate of inflation to any significant degree.

Argument Evaluation

Situation   The rate of inflation was 1.2 percent last year but is 4 percent in the current year. It is therefore expected to rise above 4 percent next year.

Reasoning   *What point most weakens this conclusion?* The conclusion is based on an *upward trend* that is derived from data for two years. Data from only two years provide rather weak evidence of a *trend*. Additional evidence that provides a context for the annual inflation rates during the most recent two-year period will promote a more solid evaluation of this prediction of next year's inflation rate. If inflation has recently been *stable* at 4 percent, and the temporary drop the previous year is accounted for by lower oil prices, then the basis for the prediction seems quite weak.

A   As long as the sample was representative, the figures should be accurate. This point does not weaken the conclusion.

B   **Correct.** This statement suggests that the 1.2 percent inflation rate is an unusual occurrence in recent years. Especially because the dip below the stable 4 percent rate was *temporary*, this unusual occurrence cannot be used as the basis for predicting a trend.

C   This statement explains one process by which inflation increases and tends to support the conclusion that inflation will continue to rise.

D   This information implies, for example, that two years ago, the inflation rate was higher than 1.2 percent. This raises the possibility (without stating it) that last year and the year preceding mark a trend of declining inflation (and that the current year's 4 percent is an aberration). However, if the inflation rate two years ago was only slightly higher than 1.2 percent (for example, 1.25 percent), then it would be difficult to regard these two numbers as signaling a trend of declining inflation. We do not have enough information here to regard this as a significant weakener. The information is sufficient to justify a little doubt about the argument's conclusion—but not at all specific enough to undermine the argument's conclusion as much as does answer choice (B).

E   The failure of government intervention to affect the rate of inflation could be seen to support, not weaken, the conclusion.

The correct answer is B.

33. Which of the following most logically completes the argument below?

Although the number of large artificial satellites orbiting the Earth is small compared to the number of small pieces of debris in orbit, the large satellites interfere more seriously with telescope observations because of the strong reflections they produce. Because many of those large satellites have ceased to function, the proposal has recently been made to eliminate interference from nonfunctioning satellites by exploding them in space. This proposal, however, is ill conceived, since _____.

(A) many nonfunctioning satellites remain in orbit for years

(B) for satellites that have ceased to function, repairing them while they are in orbit would be prohibitively expensive

(C) there are no known previous instances of satellites' having been exploded on purpose

(D) the only way to make telescope observations without any interference from debris in orbit is to use telescopes launched into extremely high orbits around the Earth

(E) a greatly increased number of small particles in Earth's orbit would result in a blanket of reflections that would make certain valuable telescope observations impossible

Evaluation of a Plan

Situation   Many large artificial satellites orbiting earth no longer function. Reflections from these satellites interfere with telescope observations. A proposal has been made to eliminate this interference by exploding these satellites in space.

Reasoning   *Why is the proposal ill conceived?* If exploding the large artificial satellites—thereby creating a large amount of debris—would result in an increase in interference with telescope observation, the proposal would be self-defeating, and therefore would be ill conceived.

A   The fact that many nonfunctioning satellites remain in orbit for years would seem to make the proposal *more* attractive. If large nonfunctioning artificial satellites generally do not remain in orbit for years—e.g., if they fall out of orbit—then there might be no need to explode the satellites. Therefore this statement is not correct.

B   This statement, too, makes the proposal more attractive—the opposite of what is called for. If nonfunctioning satellites cannot be repaired, then that eliminates one possible reason for not blowing them up.

C   The fact that there are no known instances of intentional explosions of satellites does not show that the plan is ill conceived. At most this might suggest that the consequences of such an explosion are not well understood, but even that is not very strongly suggested. For instance, if large artificial satellites have accidentally blown up, scientists may have studied the results and have good reason to believe that no ill-effects will result from exploding the satellites.

D   This is not a cogent reason for thinking the proposal to be ill conceived. Even if the proposal would not eliminate *all interference* with ground based telescopes, it might still greatly reduce interference.

E   **Correct.** If exploding large nonfunctioning satellites would lead to more interference, then we have a reason to think that the proposal is ill conceived.

The correct answer is E.

34. Thyrian lawmaker: Thyria's Cheese Importation Board inspects all cheese shipments to Thyria and rejects shipments not meeting specified standards. Yet only 1 percent is ever rejected. Therefore, since the health consequences and associated economic costs of not rejecting that 1 percent are negligible, whereas the board's operating costs are considerable, for economic reasons alone the board should be disbanded.

    Consultant: I disagree. The threat of having their shipments rejected deters many cheese exporters from shipping substandard product.

    The consultant responds to the lawmaker's argument by

    (A) rejecting the lawmaker's argument while proposing that the standards according to which the board inspects imported cheese should be raised

    (B) providing evidence that the lawmaker's argument has significantly overestimated the cost of maintaining the board

    (C) objecting to the lawmaker's introducing into the discussion factors that are not strictly economic

    (D) pointing out a benefit of maintaining the board, which the lawmaker's argument has failed to consider

    (E) shifting the discussion from the argument at hand to an attack on the integrity of the cheese inspectors

Argument Construction

Situation   The Thyrian lawmaker argues that the Cheese Importation Board should be disbanded, because its operating costs are high and it rejects only a small percentage of the cheese it inspects. The consultant disagrees, pointing out that the board's inspections deter those who export cheese to Thyria from shipping substandard cheese.

Reasoning   *What strategy does the consultant use in the counterargument?* The consultant indicates to the lawmaker that there is a reason to retain the board that the lawmaker has not considered. The benefit the board provides is not that it identifies a great deal of substandard cheese and rejects it (thus keeping the public healthy), but that the possibility that their cheese could be found substandard is what keeps exporters from attempting to export low-quality cheese to Thyria.

A   The consultant does reject the lawmaker's argument, but the consultant does not propose higher standards. Indeed, in suggesting that the board should be retained, the consultant implies that the board's standards are appropriate.

B   The consultant does not provide any evidence related to the board's cost.

C   The only point the lawmaker raises that is not strictly economic is about the health consequences of disbanding the board, but the consultant does not address this point at all.

D   **Correct.** This statement properly identifies the strategy the consultant employs in his or her counterargument. The consultant points out that the board provides a significant benefit that the lawmaker did not consider.

E   The consultant does not attack the integrity of the cheese inspectors; to the contrary, the consultant says that their inspections deter the cheese exporters from shipping substandard cheese.

The correct answer is D.

35. Which of the following best completes the passage below?

The computer industry's estimate that it loses millions of dollars when users illegally copy programs without paying for them is greatly exaggerated. Most of the illegal copying is done by people with no serious interest in the programs. Thus, the loss to the industry is quite small, because _____.

(A) many users who illegally copy programs never find any use for them

(B) most people who illegally copy programs would not purchase them even if purchasing them were the only way to obtain them

(C) even if the computer industry received all the revenue it claims to be losing, it would still be experiencing financial difficulties

(D) the total market value of all illegal copies is low in comparison to the total revenue of the computer industry

(E) the number of programs that are frequently copied illegally is low in comparison to the number of programs available for sale

Argument Construction

Situation   The computer industry's estimate of its losses due to illegally copied programs is exaggerated—and actually quite small—because most of the illegal copying is done by people who are not greatly interested in the programs.

Reasoning   *Why would the loss to the industry be said to be small?* The industry's loss due to illegal copying of programs must be evaluated in terms of the sales lost; the actual loss to the industry is directly related to the legitimate sales opportunities that have been lost. Would the people illegally copying the programs buy them if they could not otherwise obtain them? If it were true that most of them have *no serious interest in the programs*, they would be unlikely to purchase them. In this case, few sales would be lost and the loss to the industry could be considered small.

A   What users do (or do not do) with programs once they have them does not help to show that the loss to the industry is small.

B   **Correct.** This information provides a reason supporting the claim that the industry has not lost potential sales.

C   The greater financial difficulties of the industry do not help to show that the loss incurred because of the illegally copied programs is small.

D   This comparison is faulty: The loss is not being considered in the context of total industry revenues but in the context of total sales of programs.

E   This information does not provide a good reason for the claim that the loss to the industry is small. Even if the number of programs frequently copied is low, the number of copies made from each program might be huge (for the most popular programs).

The correct answer is B.

36. The growing popularity of computer-based activities was widely expected to result in a decline in television viewing, since it had been assumed that people lack sufficient free time to maintain current television-viewing levels while spending increasing amounts of free time on the computer. That assumption, however, is evidently false: In a recent mail survey concerning media use, a very large majority of respondents who report increasing time spent per week using computers report no change in time spent watching television.

Which of the following would it be most useful to determine in order to evaluate the argument?

(A) Whether a large majority of the survey respondents reported watching television regularly

(B) Whether the amount of time spent watching television is declining among people who report that they rarely or never use computers

(C) Whether the type of television programs a person watches tends to change as the amount of time spent per week using computers increases

(D) Whether a large majority of the computer owners in the survey reported spending increasing amounts of time per week using computers

(E) Whether the survey respondents' reports of time spent using computers included time spent using computers at work

Argument Evaluation

Situation   The argument is intended to debunk the assumption that people lack sufficient free time to maintain television-viewing levels while spending increasing amounts of free time on the computer. To do so, it cites a survey of media use in which a large majority of respondents who spend increasing amounts of time using computers also claim to have not altered the amount of time they spend watching television.

Reasoning   *What would it be most useful to know in order to evaluate the argument?* The argument uses the survey results to claim that people have enough free time to both maintain their television viewing levels and spend increasing amounts of free time on the computer. But the survey, as reported here, did not address whether people are spending their *free time* on the computer; the respondents reported increasing *time* spent per week using computers. Since the argument is about free time, it is important to know whether this is actually what the respondents were reporting.

A   The argument is concerned with the *change* in the amount of television watched by those whose computer use increased, so whether the survey's respondents reported watching television regularly is irrelevant.

B   The argument is concerned with the change in the amount of television watched by those whose computer use has increased, so it does not matter whether the amount of time spent watching television among people who do not use computers is declining, remaining the same, or increasing.

C   The argument is concerned with the *amount* of television watched by those whose computer use has increased, not the type of television programs such a person does or does not watch.

D   The argument here is concerned with people who report spending increasing amounts of time on the computer; what computer owners do is a separate question.

E   **Correct.** This statement properly identifies something that would be useful to know in evaluating the argument: whether the survey data included time spent using computers at work—if it did, this would make the data misleading as evidence for the argument's conclusion.

The correct answer is E.

37. In the last decade there has been a significant decrease in coffee consumption. During this same time, there has been increasing publicity about the adverse long-term effects on health of the caffeine in coffee. Therefore, the decrease in coffee consumption must have been caused by consumers' awareness of the harmful effects of caffeine.

Which of the following, if true, most seriously calls into question the explanation above?

(A) On average, people consume 30 percent less coffee today than they did 10 years ago.

(B) Heavy coffee drinkers may have mild withdrawal symptoms, such as headaches, for a day or so after significantly decreasing their coffee consumption.

(C) Sales of specialty types of coffee have held steady as sales of regular brands have declined.

(D) The consumption of fruit juices and caffeine-free herbal teas has increased over the past decade.

(E) Coffee prices increased steadily in the past decade because of unusually severe frosts in coffee-growing nations.

Argument Evaluation

Situation   The decrease in coffee consumption in the last decade can be explained by consumers' increased awareness of the detrimental effects of the caffeine in coffee.

Reasoning   *What point weakens this explanation?* A conclusion offering an explanation for some occurrence may be weakened when another explanation at least as compelling as the original is offered. Coffee consumption may have decreased over the decade for some reason other than consumers' awareness of the adverse health effects of caffeine. If the price of coffee has increased in the same period that consumption has decreased, then the decrease may well be the result of consumers' attention to price rather than their attention to health. Higher prices would offer a good alternative explanation that would weaken the original explanation.

A   This point merely tells us how much coffee consumption has decreased; it does not make the explanation offered in the conclusion any less likely to be correct.

B   Withdrawal symptoms would occur only after decreased consumption has occurred and so cannot explain why the decrease occurred.

C   Suppose that the specialty coffees that had their sales hold steady were all caffeine-free coffees; note that nothing rules this out. If this were the case, the explanation would remain plausible.

D   An increase in the consumption of these drinks could plausibly be the result of some coffee drinkers switching to these drinks to avoid the negative effects of caffeine.

E   **Correct.** This statement properly identifies a plausible alternative explanation and therefore undermines the given explanation.

The correct answer is E.

38. Which of the following best completes the passage below?

    When the products of several competing suppliers are perceived by consumers to be essentially the same, classical economics predicts that price competition will reduce prices to the same minimal levels and all suppliers' profits to the same minimal levels. Therefore, if classical economics is true, and given suppliers' desire to make as much profit as possible, it should be expected that _____.

    (A) in a crowded market widely differing prices will be charged for products that are essentially the same as each other

    (B) as a market becomes less crowded as suppliers leave, the profits of the remaining suppliers will tend to decrease

    (C) each supplier in a crowded market will try to convince consumers that its product differs significantly from its competitors' products.

    (D) when consumers are unable to distinguish the products in a crowded market, consumers will judge that the higher-priced products are of higher quality

    (E) suppliers in crowded markets will have more incentive to reduce prices and thus increase sales than to introduce innovations that would distinguish their product from their competitors' products

Argument Construction

Situation   Classical economics holds that prices and profits are minimal when consumers perceive the products of competing suppliers to be the same.

Reasoning   *According to classical economics, what strategy are suppliers most likely to use to maximize profits in such a situation?* The given information states that the force driving prices and profits down in this case is the consumers' perception that the competing products are *essentially the same*. It is reasonable to assume that, with prices already at *minimal levels*, it is not possible to lower them any more. What can be done? The suppliers' most likely strategy would then be to change the consumers' perception of their products. It can be expected that an individual supplier would try to convince consumers that its product greatly differs from (and is certainly preferable to) the products of its competitors.

A   According to classical economics, *prices* will be reduced by competition *to the same minimal levels* as long as the products *are perceived by consumers to be essentially the same*, and nothing indicates that they will not be; therefore there is no reason to believe that prices will differ widely.

B   The passage discusses the conditions of a crowded market, not a market that is becoming less crowded.

C   **Correct.** This statement properly suggests that the most likely strategy for any one supplier in a crowded market is convincing consumers that its product is very different from those of its competitors.

D   According to classical economics, *prices* will be reduced *to the same minimal levels* when consumers are unable to distinguish among the products; therefore none of the products will be priced higher than any others.

E   The passage gives no indication of what classical economics says about the attractiveness to suppliers of reducing prices versus introducing innovations.

The correct answer is C.

39.   Which of the following most logically completes the argument?

Sviatovin is a medieval Moringian text whose author and exact date of composition are unknown. However, the events in the life of Prince Sviatov that the text describes occurred in 1165, and in the diagram of Sviatov's family that accompanies the text his father, who died in 1167, is identified as still living. Thus *Sviatovin* must have been written between 1165 and 1167, assuming that _____.

(A)   the life of Prince Sviatov is not the subject of any other medieval Moringian texts

(B)   the author of *Sviatovin* intended it to provide as accurate a report about Prince Sviatov's exploits as possible

(C)   the diagram accurately represents the composition of Sviatov's family at the time Sviatovin was written

(D)   *Sviatovin* is the earliest Moringian text whose composition can be dated to within a few years

(E)   *Sviatovin* was not written by Sviatov's father himself

Argument Construction

Situation   A medieval Moringian text was written about Prince Sviatov. It is not known exactly when the text was written, but the events described in it occurred in 1165 and a diagram in the text indicates that Sviatov's father—who died in 1167—was alive at the time it was composed.

Reasoning   *What completion of the blank would provide the best reason for believing the argument's conclusion?* The argument's conclusion is that the book *Sviatovin* was written between 1165 and 1167. The reasoning given is this: It could not have been written before 1165 because it includes events that took place in that year. It could not have been written after 1167 because Sviatov's father died in that year. A diagram in the book suggests he was alive when the book was written. Was the diagram correct in that suggestion? The argument depends on assuming that it was.

A   The argument focuses on one text and its date of composition. The argument does not need to make any assumptions about other texts.

B   The argument does not assume this. Issues about the accurate reporting of Sviatov's exploits (or about the author's intention to report them accurately) are irrelevant to the argument, which hinges on the accuracy of the diagram that accompanies the text. The diagram does not report Sviatov's exploits.

C   **Correct.** The reasoning in the argument assumes that the diagram was correct in representing the Prince's father as still living when the text was composed. If his father was not living when the text was written, then the information that his father actually died in 1167 is no guarantee that the text was composed by then.

D   See the explanation for answer choice (A) above. The degree of precision with which scholars have succeeded in dating other Moringian texts is entirely irrelevant.

E   The conclusion concerns when *Sviatovin* was written and not by whom it was written. If, contrary to answer choice (E), it were known that the author was Sviatov's father, this would actually provide strong support for the argument's conclusion. Thus answer choice (E) does not provide a good reason for the argument's conclusion.

The correct answer is C.

40. Crowding on Mooreville's subway frequently leads to delays, because it is difficult for passengers to exit from the trains. Subway ridership is projected to increase by 20 percent over the next 10 years. The Mooreville Transit Authority plans to increase the number of daily train trips by only 5 percent over the same period. Officials predict that this increase is sufficient to ensure that the incidence of delays due to crowding does not increase.

Which of the following, if true, provides the strongest grounds for the officials' prediction?

(A) By changing maintenance schedules, the Transit Authority can achieve the 5 percent increase in train trips without purchasing any new subway cars.

(B) The Transit Authority also plans a 5 percent increase in the number of bus trips on routes that connect to subways.

(C) For most commuters who use the subway system, there is no practical alternative public transportation available.

(D) Most of the projected increase in ridership is expected to occur in off-peak hours when trains are now sparsely used.

(E) The 5 percent increase in the number of train trips can be achieved without an equal increase in Transit Authority operational costs.

Argument Construction

Situation   Ridership on the Mooreville subway, which often experiences delays due to crowding, is expected to increase 20 percent over the next 10 years. Despite plans to increase the number of daily trains only 5 percent during those 10 years, officials predict that delays due to crowding will not increase.

Reasoning   *What would provide the strongest grounds for the officials' prediction that delays due to crowding will not increase?* Delays due to crowding probably would increase if the extra 20 percent total ridership occurred at typically busy times, even if the total 5 percent increase in the number of daily trains were to occur at those typically busy times. The increases in daily trains would clearly not be enough to absorb the extra ridership. If the increase in ridership were to occur at other times of day, however, perhaps when the subway trains were less crowded overall, the system would be able to absorb the extra passengers without an increase in delays due to crowding.

A   While this supports the idea that the Transit Authority can economically increase the number of train trips, it provides no information about whether the trains will be crowded.

B   Increasing the number of bus trips on routes that connect to subways would be likely to lead to more people to ride the subways. This makes it less likely that the officials' prediction—that delays due to overcrowding will not increase—will turn out to have been accurate.

C   This suggests that subway ridership will remain high, and thus that delays caused by overcrowding will continue.

D   Correct. This statement properly identifies a situation in which the officials' prediction is likely to turn out to have been accurate. The ridership will be increasing during times when more passengers will not create delays, since they will merely fill empty seats on existing trains.

E   While this supports the idea that the Transit Authority can economically increase the number of train trips, it provides no information about whether the trains will be crowded.

The correct answer is D.

41. Installing scrubbers in smokestacks and switching to cleaner-burning fuel are the two methods available to Northern Power for reducing harmful emissions from its plants. Scrubbers will reduce harmful emissions more than cleaner-burning fuels will. Therefore, by installing scrubbers, Northern Power will be doing the most that can be done to reduce harmful emissions from its plants.

Which of the following is an assumption on which the argument depends?

(A) Switching to cleaner-burning fuel will not be more expensive than installing scrubbers.

(B) Northern Power can choose from among various kinds of scrubbers, some of which are more effective than others.

(C) Northern Power is not necessarily committed to reducing harmful emissions from its plants.

(D) Harmful emissions from Northern Power's plants cannot be reduced more by using both methods together than by the installation of scrubbers alone.

(E) Aside from harmful emissions from the smokestacks of its plants, the activities of Northern Power do not cause significant air pollution.

Argument Construction

Situation   A power plant can reduce emissions by installing scrubbers and also by switching to cleaner-burning fuel; installing scrubbers reduces emissions more than switching fuels. By installing scrubbers, the company is doing the most that it can do.

Reasoning   *What assumption does the argument depend on?* The assumption will be a statement that has to be true in order for the argument's premises to provide a solid reason for believing its conclusion. Here, the conclusion that the company is doing the most that it can do is based on believing that choosing one or the other of the two options will be more effective than choosing both options together. This argument assumes, then, that installing the scrubbers alone is just as effective as both installing scrubbers *and* switching to cleaner-burning fuel.

A   The relative costs of the two options indicate nothing about whether by installing scrubbers the company will have done the most that it can to reduce harmful emissions.

B   Even if the company installs the most efficient scrubbers, it may be that there is more that Northern Power could do to reduce harmful emissions.

C   Even if the company is fully committed to reducing harmful emissions, it could be that installing scrubbers is the most it can do to reduce harmful emissions.

D   **Correct.** If harmful emissions could be reduced even more by using both methods, then installing scrubbers alone will not be the most that the company can do to reduce harmful emissions.

E   Even if this were not assumed and the company's other activities did cause significant air pollution, it could still be that installing scrubbers is the most that the company can do to reduce harmful emissions *from its plants*; perhaps any of its other activities that do cause significant air pollution have nothing to do with its plants—for example, pollution coming from trucks the company uses.

The correct answer is D.

42. Trancorp currently transports all its goods to Burland Island by truck. The only bridge over the channel separating Burland from the mainland is congested, and trucks typically spend hours in traffic. Trains can reach the channel more quickly than trucks, and freight cars can be transported to Burland by barges that typically cross the channel in an hour. Therefore, to reduce shipping time, Trancorp plans to switch to trains and barges to transport goods to Burland.

Which of the following would be most important to know in determining whether Trancorp's plan, if implemented, is likely to achieve its goal?

(A) Whether transportation by train and barge would be substantially less expensive than transportation by truck

(B) Whether there are boats that can make the trip between the mainland and Burland faster than barges can

(C) Whether loading the freight cars onto barges is very time consuming

(D) Whether the average number of vehicles traveling over the bridge into Burland has been relatively constant in recent years

(E) Whether most trucks transporting goods into Burland return to the mainland empty

Evaluation of a Plan

Situation   Transporting goods to Burland Island by truck takes many hours, because the trucks must take the congested single bridge that reaches the island. Trains can get goods to the channel separating Burland from the mainland more quickly than trucks can, and the freight cars can then be loaded onto barges that can cross the channel in an hour. Trancorp plans to reduce shipping time by switching from trucks to trains and barges.

Reasoning   *What would it be most important to know in determining whether Trancorp will achieve its goal of reducing shipping time?* Trancorp's plan could fail to reduce shipping time if there were some aspect of the new shipping process, involving the trains and the barges, that took more time than anticipated.

A   The goal of Trancorp's plan is to reduce shipping time. This might lower costs—but whether or not it does so is not directly relevant to whether or not the plan's goal is achieved.

B   Trancorp's plan involves the use of barges. If some boats can make the trip between the mainland and Burland faster than barges can, that might be something to consider for the future, but it has nothing to do with whether the current plan will reduce shipping time.

C   **Correct.** This statement properly identifies something that would be important in determining whether Trancorp's plan for reducing shipping time will achieve its goal—that is, whether loading the freight cars onto the barges will use up all the time saved by not using trucks.

D   Regardless of variation in traffic, the bridge, according to the information provided in the passage, is congested and typically causes trucking delays. Given this information, the degree of variation is not helpful in evaluating Transcorp's plan.

E   The state of the trucks returning to the mainland has nothing to do with whether Trancorp's plan for reducing shipping time will achieve its goal.

The correct answer is C.

43. Some anthropologists study modern-day societies of foragers in an effort to learn about our ancient ancestors who were also foragers. A flaw in this strategy is that forager societies are extremely varied. Indeed, any forager society with which anthropologists are familiar has had considerable contact with modern, non-forager societies.

Which of the following, if true, would most weaken the criticism made above of the anthropologists' strategy?

(A) All forager societies throughout history have had a number of important features in common that are absent from other types of societies.

(B) Most ancient forager societies either dissolved or made a transition to another way of life.

(C) All anthropologists study one kind or another of modern-day society.

(D) Many anthropologists who study modern-day forager societies do not draw inferences about ancient societies on the basis of their studies.

(E) Even those modern-day forager societies that have not had significant contact with modern societies are importantly different from ancient forager societies.

Argument Evaluation

Situation   Studying contemporary foraging societies in order to understand ancient foragers is flawed because forager societies are so widely varied and also because the contemporary foragers have had so much contact with modern societies.

Reasoning   *Which point weakens this argument?* The argument rejects the comparison of modern-day foraging societies to ancient ones because of the variety of existing forager societies and because the modern-day foragers have been in contact with other modern cultures. What situation would support making this comparison? What if modern-day foragers remain similar to ancient foragers because of nonchanging features of foraging societies throughout history? If these are features that are not shared with other cultures, then the argument that anthropologists cannot learn about ancient foragers by studying their modern counterparts is weakened.

A   **Correct.** This statement properly identifies the factor that weakens the argument: A comparison could well be a valuable source of understanding if all foraging societies are shown to share certain features not found in other societies.

B   This point slightly strengthens, rather than weakens, the argument.

C   This point does not address the issue of comparing a modern society to an ancient society.

D   The reason for this could be that these anthropologists know that such a comparison is not useful; thus this point does not weaken the argument.

E   This point strengthens, rather than weakens, the argument.

The correct answer is A.

44. Contrary to earlier predictions, demand for sugarcane has not increased in recent years. Yet, even though prices and production amounts have also been stable during the last three years, sugarcane growers last year increased their profits by more than 10 percent over the previous year's level.

    Any of the following statements, if true about last year, helps to explain the rise in profits EXCEPT:

    (A) Many countries that are large consumers of sugarcane increased their production of sugarcane-based ethanol, yet their overall consumption of sugarcane decreased.

    (B) Sugarcane growers have saved money on wages by switching from paying laborers an hourly wage to paying them by the amount harvested.

    (C) The price of oil, the major energy source used by sugarcane growers in harvesting their crops, dropped by over 20 percent.

    (D) Many small sugarcane growers joined together to form an association of sugarcane producers and began to buy supplies at low group rates.

    (E) Rainfall in sugarcane-growing regions was higher than it had been during the previous year, allowing the growers to save money on expensive artificial irrigation.

Argument Construction

Situation   Even though demand for sugar cane has not increased, and although prices and production amounts have been stable, sugarcane growers experienced a 10 percent rise in profits last year.

Reasoning   *Which piece of information does NOT help to explain the rise in profits?* All the answer choices will show a reason that profits rose except one. Consider each one to determine which situation would NOT be likely to contribute to increased profits. Any changes that lowered costs for the sugarcane growers WOULD be able to contribute to a rise in their profits. On the other hand, if it is true that many historically large consumers of sugarcane reduced their overall consumption last year, then the lower demand for sugarcane would be unlikely to drive increases in profits. Such a decrease in total consumption would be more likely to drive prices and profits down than up.

A   **Correct.** This statement properly identifies a factor that does not explain a rise in profits; it indicates a drop in consumption among certain countries without indicating a corresponding increase in consumption elsewhere or any decreases in costs for growers.

B   Saving money on wages would lower costs and thus contribute to a rise in profits.

C   Saving money on oil would lower costs and thus contribute to a rise in profits.

D   Saving money on supplies bought at a lower rate would lower costs and thus contribute to a rise in profits.

E   Saving money on irrigation would lower costs and thus contribute to a rise in profits.

The correct answer is A.

45. Which of the following most logically completes the argument below?

Davison River farmers are currently deciding between planting winter wheat this fall or spring wheat next spring. Winter wheat and spring wheat are usually about equally profitable. Because of new government restrictions on the use of Davison River water for irrigation, per acre yields for winter wheat, though not for spring wheat, would be much lower than average. Therefore, planting spring wheat will be more profitable than planting winter wheat, since _____.

(A) the smaller-than-average size of a winter wheat harvest this year would not be compensated for by higher winter wheat prices

(B) new crops of spring wheat must be planted earlier than the time at which standing crops of winter wheat are ready to be harvested

(C) the spring wheat that farmers in the Davison River region plant is well adapted to the soil of the region

(D) spring wheat has uses that are different from those of winter wheat

(E) planting spring wheat is more profitable than planting certain other crops, such as rye

Argument Construction

Situation   Farmers in the Davison River region must choose between planting winter wheat in the fall and planting spring wheat next spring. The crops tend to be equally profitable. This year's winter wheat crop yield is likely to be lower than average. The spring wheat yield should not be lower than average. Thus, for these reasons (plus one that the argument omits), spring wheat will be more profitable than winter wheat.

Reasoning   *Which point would logically complete the argument?* What would ensure spring wheat's profitability over winter wheat? Since the yield per acre of winter wheat is likely to be lower than usual, there will most likely be less winter wheat to sell. Winter wheat could match its usual profitability if the price farmers receive for it were to rise. If its price does not rise, however, it is unlikely to match its usual profitability. It would thus be unlikely to match spring wheat's profitability.

A   **Correct.** If this is true, it would mean that smaller-than-average winter wheat yields would translate into lower-than-usual profits on winter wheat (while spring wheat would be as profitable as winter wheat would normally be). This would justify the conclusion that spring wheat will be more profitable than winter wheat.

B   This provides support for the idea that farmers must choose between planting winter wheat and planting spring wheat, but it does not help determine which would be more profitable to plant.

C   This does not help explain why spring wheat is likely to be more profitable than winter wheat, because it gives no information about how well winter wheat is adapted to the soil of the region.

D   That spring wheat and winter wheat have different uses is not helpful in supporting a conclusion about which kind of wheat will be more profitable. It might help to know which of their uses are more profitable than others.

E   Since the question is whether it will be more profitable to plant winter wheat or to plant spring wheat, the fact that spring wheat is more profitable than nonwheat crops is not relevant.

The correct answer is A.

46. If the county continues to collect residential trash at current levels, landfills will soon be overflowing and parkland will need to be used in order to create more space. Charging each household a fee for each pound of trash it puts out for collection will induce residents to reduce the amount of trash they create; this charge will therefore protect the remaining county parkland.

    Which of the following is an assumption made in drawing the conclusion above?

    (A) Residents will reduce the amount of trash they put out for collection by reducing the number of products they buy.

    (B) The collection fee will not significantly affect the purchasing power of most residents, even if their households do not reduce the amount of trash they put out.

    (C) The collection fee will not induce residents to dump their trash in the parklands illegally.

    (D) The beauty of county parkland is an important issue for most of the county's residents.

    (E) Landfills outside the county's borders could be used as dumping sites for the county's trash.

Argument Construction

Situation   Landfills will overflow and parkland will have to be used instead if current trash collection levels continue. Charging fees per pound of trash collected will inhibit trash growth and protect parkland.

Reasoning   *What assumption underlies the conclusion?* The assumption will be a statement that has to be true in order for the argument's premises to provide a solid reason for believing its conclusion. To reach the conclusion that the plan will protect the parkland, the argument must assume that county residents will comply with the new fee, reducing both the trash they generate and the need to convert parkland to landfills. It is assumed that residents will not resort to some illegal means of avoiding the new fee, and it is certainly assumed that they will not contribute to the destruction of parklands by dumping trash in them illegally.

A   Even though the fee may indirectly have this effect, the argument need not assume that it will; perhaps residents will continue to buy as much, but will make longer use of the product, or recycle it.

B   The argument would be stronger if this were assumed NOT to be true.

C   **Correct.** This statement properly identifies the fact that the argument rests on the assumption that the fee will not create illegal dumping.

D   The argument need not assume this, and nothing in the argument indicates that it does. Financial incentives could be enough to make the desired outcome happen even if residents are indifferent to the parkland's beauty.

E   The argument assumes that residents will reduce the amount of trash that they create, not that they will find other places to dispose of it.

The correct answer is C.

47.   Certain genetically modified strains of maize produce a powerful natural insecticide. The insecticide occurs throughout the plant, including its pollen. Maize pollen is dispersed by the wind and frequently blows onto milkweed plants that grow near maize fields. Caterpillars of monarch butterflies feed exclusively on milkweed leaves. When these caterpillars are fed milkweed leaves dusted with pollen from modified maize plants, they die. Therefore, by using genetically modified maize, farmers put monarch butterflies at risk.

Which of the following would it be most useful to determine in order to evaluate the argument?

(A)   Whether the natural insecticide is as effective against maize-eating insects as commercial insecticides typically used on maize are

(B)   Whether the pollen of genetically modified maize contains as much insecticide as other parts of these plants

(C)   Whether monarch butterfly caterpillars are actively feeding during the part of the growing season when maize is releasing pollen

(D)   Whether insects that feed on genetically modified maize plants are likely to be killed by insecticide from the plant's pollen

(E)   Whether any maize-eating insects compete with monarch caterpillars for the leaves of milkweed plants growing near maize fields

Argument Evaluation

Situation   Monarch butterfly caterpillars die when fed milkweed leaves dusted with the pollen of certain genetically modified strains of maize. A natural insecticide occurs throughout the maize plant and in its pollen, which blows onto milkweed growing near maize fields. Caterpillars of monarch butterflies eat only milkweed leaves, so farmers who use this genetically modified maize are endangering monarch butterflies.

Reasoning   *What would it be most useful to know in evaluating the argument?* We know that the caterpillars eat only milkweed leaves, but we do not know when, in the course of their development, they do so. Monarch butterflies would be at risk only if the caterpillars were to eat the milkweed leaves when those leaves had maize pollen on them. So it would be useful to know if the caterpillars eat milkweed leaves when maize pollen is likely to be present.

A   The argument addresses whether farmers put monarch butterflies at risk by using genetically modified maize. The effectiveness of the natural insecticide that maize produces, relative to other insecticides, is not relevant to determining whether monarch butterflies are being endangered.

B   The amount of insecticide in the rest of the plant, as opposed to in its pollen, has nothing to do with whether the use of the maize puts monarch butterflies at risk. All that matters is the amount of insecticide in the pollen, and we know that this is sufficient to kill the caterpillars.

C   **Correct.** This question properly identifies something that it would be useful to know in evaluating whether monarch butterflies are actually at risk—that is, whether caterpillars will be eating milkweed leaves when those leaves are likely to have pollen on them.

D   Since the issue at hand is whether farmers are endangering monarch butterflies, the question of the maize pollen's impact on other insects—that is, those that feed on maize—is irrelevant.

E   Competition from maize-eating insects attracted to the area by the planting of maize might affect the monarch butterfly population, but simply knowing that such insects might compete with the caterpillars for milkweed leaves does not give any information on whether they would be able to compete *successfully* for those leaves.

The correct answer is C.

48. Although computers can enhance people's ability to communicate, computer games are a cause of underdeveloped communication skills in children. After-school hours spent playing computer games are hours not spent talking with people. Therefore, children who spend all their spare time playing these games have less experience in interpersonal communication than other children have.

    The argument depends on which of the following assumptions?

    (A) Passive activities such as watching television and listening to music do not hinder the development of communication skills in children.

    (B) Most children have other opportunities, in addition to after-school hours, in which they can choose whether to play computer games or to interact with other people.

    (C) Children who do not spend all of their after-school hours playing computer games spend at least some of that time talking with other people.

    (D) Formal instruction contributes little or nothing to children's acquisition of communication skills.

    (E) The mental skills developed through playing computer games do not contribute significantly to children's intellectual development.

Argument Construction

Situation   Spending after-school hours playing computer games does not enhance communication skills because children are not talking with other people during this time. Children who spend all their spare time playing computer games do not have as much interpersonal communication as other children do.

Reasoning   *What assumption does this argument depend on?* The unstated assumption in an argument will be a statement that has to be true in order for the argument's premises to provide a solid reason for believing its conclusion. Here, playing computer games is said to replace talking with people. Thus the argument assumes that children who do not spend all their spare time playing computer games instead spend at least some of that time talking with people.

A   This need not be assumed. The argument is not committed to any claim about the effects that watching television or listening to music may have on the development of communication skills in children.

B   The argument is limited to after-school hours or spare time.

C   **Correct.** This statement properly identifies the assumption on which the argument is based.

D   This could be false and the argument could still be sound; perhaps children who spend all their spare time playing computer games receive no formal instruction.

E   This could be false and the argument could still be sound as long as the intellectual development the games contribute to does not contribute to the development of communication skills.

The correct answer is C.

49. Maize contains the vitamin niacin, but not in a form the body can absorb. Pellagra is a disease that results from niacin deficiency. When maize was introduced into southern Europe from the Americas in the eighteenth century, it quickly became a dietary staple, and many Europeans who came to subsist primarily on maize developed pellagra. Pellagra was virtually unknown at that time in the Americas, however, even among people who subsisted primarily on maize.

Which of the following, if true, most helps to explain the contrasting incidence of pellagra described above?

(A) Once introduced into southern Europe, maize became popular with landowners because of its high yields relative to other cereal crops.

(B) Maize grown in the Americas contained more niacin than maize grown in Europe did.

(C) Traditional ways of preparing maize in the Americas convert maize's niacin into a nutritionally useful form.

(D) In southern Europe many of the people who consumed maize also ate niacin-rich foods.

(E) Before the discovery of pellagra's link with niacin, it was widely believed that the disease was an infection that could be transmitted from person to person.

Argument Construction

Situation Maize was introduced into southern Europe from the Americas in the eighteenth century and quickly became a dietary staple. Maize contains niacin but not in a form that the body can absorb. Many Europeans who came to subsist primarily on maize developed pellagra, a disease that results in niacin deficiency. However, the disease rarely occurred among people in the Americas who subsisted primarily on maize.

Reasoning *Which statement most helps to explain why Europeans who subsisted primarily on maize developed pellagra but people in the Americas who subsisted on maize did not?* The apparent cause of the disease in the Europeans who subsisted primarily on maize was that they did not get sufficient niacin in their diets. Maize contains niacin but not in a form that the human body can absorb without further processing. The way people in the Americas prepared maize converted the niacin into a "nutritionally useful form" and that explains why they were getting enough niacin to prevent pellagra. Although the passage does not say so, the information it gives somewhat suggests that the Europeans may have lacked the appropriate traditional preparation methods (e.g., the passage says that maize *quickly* became a dietary staple).

A The fact that maize became popular in Europe does not explain why Europeans subsisting on it developed pellagra and people in the Americas did not.

B If the niacin in maize cannot be readily absorbed by the body, then the fact that there was more niacin in the American-consumed maize does little to explain why people in the Americas did not get pellagra.

C **Correct.** This helps explain the contrast between maize consumers in the Americas and those in Europe. The people of the Americas who subsisted primarily on maize did not suffer from pellagra; because of the way they prepared maize, subsisting on it did not lead to a niacin deficiency. For a *complete* explanation, we would also need the information that the European maize consumers had no preparation methods that could make niacin in maize nutritionally available.

D This answer choice, far from explaining why southern maize-eating Europeans got pellagra, actually makes it even more puzzling why they got it, given that pellagra results from niacin deficiency.

E The question concerns what actually caused pellagra to occur in one population and not in another. Answer choice (E) concerns only the beliefs that people had at one time concerning the causes of pellagra. So it has no bearing on the explanation that is being sought.

The correct answer is C.

50. One variety of partially biodegradable plastic beverage container is manufactured from small bits of plastic bound together by a degradable bonding agent such as cornstarch. Since only the bonding agent degrades, leaving the small bits of plastic, no less plastic refuse per container is produced when such containers are discarded than when comparable nonbiodegradable containers are discarded.

Which of the following, if true, most strengthens the argument above?

(A) Both partially biodegradable and nonbiodegradable plastic beverage containers can be crushed completely flat by refuse compactors.

(B) The partially biodegradable plastic beverage containers are made with more plastic than comparable nonbiodegradable ones in order to compensate for the weakening effect of the bonding agents.

(C) Many consumers are ecology-minded and prefer to buy a product sold in the partially biodegradable plastic beverage containers rather than in nonbiodegradable containers, even if the price is higher.

(D) The manufacturing process for the partially biodegradable plastic beverage containers results in less plastic waste than the manufacturing process for nonbiodegradable plastic beverage containers.

(E) Technological problems with recycling currently prevent the reuse as food or beverage containers of the plastic from either type of plastic beverage container.

Argument Evaluation

Situation   One kind of partially biodegradable beverage container produces as much plastic refuse per container as a nonbiodegradable container does because only the bonding agent, not the plastic, degrades once the container is discarded.

Reasoning   *Which point strengthens the argument?* The information that strengthens the argument will help rule out a possible objection to the argument. In this case, one possible objection would be that the partially biodegradable containers might contain less plastic given that the container is made up in part of the degradable bonding agent. So, discovering that the partially biodegradable containers actually use more plastic than comparable nonbiodegradable ones in order to compensate for the weakness of the biodegradable bonding agent would strengthen the argument.

A   Nonbiodegradable plastic containers can be crushed completely flat. To say that biodegradable ones can be completely crushed also is perfectly compatible with saying that they contain less plastic.

B   **Correct.** This statement properly identifies a point that strengthens the argument by saying that the container actually produces more plastic refuse.

C   Consumers' preferences are not relevant to the argument about residual plastic.

D   The argument is not concerned with waste from manufacturing processes, but only with the product itself.

E   No reason is given to indicate that the inability to reuse the plastic from either type of container is related to the amount of plastic in either container.

The correct answer is B.

51. Rye sown in the fall and plowed into the soil in early spring leaves a residue that is highly effective at controlling broad-leaved weeds, but unfortunately for only about forty-five days. No major agricultural crop matures from seed in as little as forty-five days. Synthetic herbicides, on the other hand, although not any longer-lasting, can be reapplied as the crop grows. Clearly, therefore, for major agricultural crops, plowing rye into the soil can play no part in effective weed control.

The argument is most vulnerable to the objection that it fails to

(A) consider that there might be minor, quick-growing crops that do mature in forty-five days or less

(B) identify any alternative method of weed control that could be used instead of the method it rejects

(C) distinguish among the various kinds of synthetic herbicides

(D) allow for the possibility of combining the two weed-control methods it mentions

(E) allow for the possibility that plants other than rye, handled the same way, might have the same effect

Argument Evaluation

Situation   Broad-leaved weeds can be controlled in the spring for forty-five days by plowing fall-sown rye into the soil. But major agricultural crops take more than forty-five days to mature, and the rye-sowing process cannot be repeated. Synthetic herbicides last no longer than forty-five days, but they can be reapplied as necessary. Based on these facts, it is concluded that plowing rye into the soil cannot be part of effective weed control for major crops.

Reasoning   *To what objection is the argument vulnerable?* Note that the conclusion of the argument is emphatic: Plowing rye into the soil can play *no* part in effective weed control. Does the argument support this strong a conclusion? The argument fails to address whether it would be feasible to use plowed-in rye to control weeds for the first forty-five days of crop growth, and use applications of herbicide for the rest of the growing season. This might not be the case, but it should be addressed before it is concluded that plowing rye into the soil *cannot* be part of effective weed control.

A   The argument is concerned with whether plowing rye into the soil can be used in weed control for major crops, so the existence of minor crops for which rye could be used, because its weed-controlling qualities would last throughout their maturation, is irrelevant.

B   The argument *does* identify a method of weed control that can be used instead of rye: synthetic herbicides.

C   That there are many types of synthetic herbicides is not important to the argument; what is important is that at least some of them can be reapplied as crops grow.

D   **Correct.** This statement properly identifies a possibility that the argument fails to consider.

E   The argument is concerned with whether rye can be used to control weeds. That there might be other plants that could have the same effect is not relevant.

The correct answer is D.

52. Most employees in the computer industry move from company to company, changing jobs several times in their careers. However, Summit Computers is known throughout the industry for retaining its employees. Summit credits its success in retaining employees to its informal, nonhierarchical work environment.

Which of the following, if true, most strongly supports Summit's explanation of its success in retaining employees?

(A) Some people employed in the computer industry change jobs if they become bored with their current projects.

(B) A hierarchical work environment hinders the cooperative exchange of ideas that computer industry employees consider necessary for their work.

(C) Many of Summit's senior employees had previously worked at only one other computer company.

(D) In a nonhierarchical work environment, people avoid behavior that might threaten group harmony and thus avoid discussing with their colleagues any dissatisfaction they might have with their jobs.

(E) The cost of living near Summit is relatively low compared to areas in which some other computer companies are located.

Argument Evaluation

Situation   A computer company attributes its success in retaining employees to its informal, nonhierarchical work environment.

Reasoning   *Which point most supports the company's explanation?* The company says that employees stay at the company for one reason: its work environment. The explanation can therefore be supported only by a point that relates to the specific work environment. If employees feel that a more formal, hierarchical structure would interfere with their ability to do their jobs, the argument is strengthened.

A   Neither this point nor the passage indicates that an informal, nonhierarchical work environment would be less boring than others.

B   **Correct.** This statement properly identifies a point that strengthens the company's argument, relating the work environment to job satisfaction and therefore to employees' remaining at the company.

C   The previous work experience of senior employees is irrelevant.

D   While this point shows how the work environment might reduce discussion of job dissatisfaction, it does not indicate that there will be less dissatisfaction.

E   This point presents an alternate explanation—employees stay due to low cost of living—and so tends to weaken the company's argument.

The correct answer is B.

53. Insurance Company X is considering issuing a new policy to cover services required by elderly people who suffer from diseases that afflict the elderly. Premiums for the policy must be low enough to attract customers. Therefore, Company X is concerned that the income from the policies would not be sufficient to pay for the claims that would be made.

    Which of the following strategies would be most likely to minimize Company X's losses on the policies?

    (A) Attracting middle-aged customers unlikely to submit claims for benefits for many years
    (B) Insuring only those individuals who did not suffer any serious diseases as children
    (C) Including a greater number of services in the policy than are included in other policies of lower cost
    (D) Insuring only those individuals who were rejected by other companies for similar policies
    (E) Insuring only those individuals who are wealthy enough to pay for the medical services

Evaluation of a Plan

Situation   An insurance company considers an affordable policy for the elderly, but the company's income from the policies must exceed expenditures on claims.

Reasoning   *What strategy will minimize the company's losses?* The insurance company's proposed plan would include a high-risk group, the elderly, who are likely to submit claims immediately. By expanding the customer base to include those who are less likely to submit claims for many years, the company will increase its income and thus minimize its losses.

A   **Correct.** This statement properly identifies a strategy that minimizes policy losses.

B   No connection is made between childhood diseases and geriatric diseases, so this point is irrelevant.

C   Offering more services would tend to increase costs, and thus losses.

D   Individuals rejected by other companies are more likely to make claims that would increase losses.

E   People who are wealthy enough to pay for the services themselves would buy insurance only if the policies were reasonably priced and they planned to make claims on the policies; this point is irrelevant.

The correct answer is A.

54. The fewer restrictions there are on the advertising of legal services, the more lawyers there are who advertise their services, and the lawyers who advertise a specific service usually charge less for that service than the lawyers who do not advertise. Therefore, if the state removes any of its current restrictions, such as the one against advertisements that do not specify fee arrangements, overall consumer legal costs will be lower than if the state retains its current restrictions.

If the statements above are true, which of the following must be true?

(A) Some lawyers who now advertise will charge more for specific services if they do not have to specify fee arrangements in the advertisements.

(B) More consumers will use legal services if there are fewer restrictions on the advertising of legal services.

(C) If the restriction against advertisements that do not specify fee arrangements is removed, more lawyers will advertise their services.

(D) If more lawyers advertise lower prices for specific services, some lawyers who do not advertise will also charge less than they currently charge for those services.

(E) If the only restrictions on the advertising of legal services were those that apply to every type of advertising, most lawyers would advertise their services.

Argument Construction

Situation   Consumer legal costs will be reduced if the state removes even one restriction on lawyers' advertisements because the fewer the restrictions, the greater the number of lawyers who advertise, and lawyers who advertise charge less than lawyers who do not advertise.

Reasoning   *What conclusion can logically be drawn?* The argument sets up an inverse proportion: the fewer the number of restrictions on ads, the greater the number of lawyers who advertise. This is true of all restrictions and all lawyers. Therefore, removing any one restriction necessarily increases the number of lawyers who advertise.

A   The lawyers may charge more, but nothing in the passage rules out the possibility that no lawyer will charge more.

B   No evidence in the passage indicates that there will be an increased use of legal services.

C   **Correct.** This statement properly identifies a conclusion that logically follows, because reducing any restriction will increase the number of lawyers who advertise.

D   Nothing in the passage indicates that lawyers who continue not to advertise will be compelled to lower their fees.

E   The argument concerns numbers of advertisers rather than types; it remains possible that few lawyers would advertise.

The correct answer is C.

55. Which of the following most logically completes the argument given below?

People in isolated rain-forest communities tend to live on a largely vegetarian diet, and they eat little salt. Few of them suffer from high blood pressure, and their blood pressure does not tend to increase with age, as is common in industrialized countries. Such people often do develop high blood pressure when they move to cities and adopt high-salt diets. Though suggestive, these facts do not establish salt as the culprit in high blood pressure, however, because _____.

(A) genetic factors could account for the lack of increase of blood pressure with age among such people

(B) people eating high-salt diets and living from birth in cities in industrialized societies generally have a tendency to have high blood pressure

(C) it is possible to have a low-salt diet while living in a city in an industrialized country

(D) there are changes in other aspects of diet when such people move to the city

(E) salt is a necessity for human life, and death can occur when the body loses too much salt

Argument Construction

Situation   People in isolated communities who eat low-salt diets tend not to have high blood pressure or to experience age-related increases in blood pressure. When these people move to industrialized areas and adopt high-salt diets, many do develop high blood pressure. Nevertheless, (for a reason the argument omits) one cannot conclude that salt causes high blood pressure.

Reasoning   *What idea would logically complete the argument?* It may seem reasonable to say that salt causes high blood pressure when it is observed that when people who eat little salt begin eating salt, they develop high blood pressure. But look more closely at the circumstances under which these people began eating more salt: They moved from isolated rain-forest communities, where they ate vegetarian diets, to cities. It is most likely the case that such a move would entail dietary changes other than just an increase in salt consumption, and so it is possible that those changes contribute to their developing high blood pressure.

A   If genetic factors accounted for such people's lack of increase of blood pressure with age, then their blood pressure would not increase when they moved to cities and adopted high-salt diets.

B   If people who eat high-salt diets tend to have high blood pressure, it would support the idea that salt is indeed the culprit in high blood pressure.

C   The argument is concerned with what happens when people from rain-forest communities move to cities *and adopt high-salt diets*, so the fact that it is possible to have a low-salt diet in a city is not relevant.

D   Correct. This statement properly identifies a reason why salt might not be responsible for high blood pressure: There could be some other dietary factor that, when adopted, causes high blood pressure.

E   The argument is concerned with the effects of high-salt diets. The fact that consuming too little salt can cause death says nothing about whether consuming too much salt is harmful.

The correct answer is D.

56. Even though most universities retain the royalties from faculty members' inventions, the faculty members retain the royalties from books and articles they write. Therefore, faculty members should retain the royalties from the educational computer software they develop.

    The conclusion above would be more reasonably drawn if which of the following were inserted into the argument as an additional premise?

    (A) Royalties from inventions are higher than royalties from educational software programs.
    (B) Faculty members are more likely to produce educational software programs than inventions.
    (C) Inventions bring more prestige to universities than do books and articles.
    (D) In the experience of most universities, educational software programs are more marketable than are books and articles.
    (E) In terms of the criteria used to award royalties, educational software programs are more nearly comparable to books and articles than to inventions.

Argument Construction

Situation   Faculty members get the royalties from their books, but universities get the royalties from faculty inventions. Faculty members should get the royalties from their educational computer software.

Reasoning   *What premise should be added to the argument?* This argument does not support its conclusion very well without an underlying assumption regarding the nature of computer programs. If, in terms of the criteria used to award royalties, educational computer programs are more like books and articles than like inventions, faculty members should retain the royalties. On the other hand, if they are more like inventions, then universities should retain the royalties. The conclusion states that faculty members should receive royalties for educational software without stating that software is more comparable to books and articles than to inventions. The missing premise must show the relationship between educational software and either inventions or books and articles.

A   The same may be true of books and articles.

B   This point does not indicate whether educational software is more comparable to inventions or to books and articles.

C   This point could be true even if, with regard to the relevant criteria, educational software is more comparable to inventions than to books and articles.

D   This point does not indicate whether educational software is more comparable to inventions or to books and articles.

E   **Correct.** This statement properly identifies a premise that establishes the relationship required to complete the argument.

The correct answer is E.

57.   In order to withstand tidal currents, juvenile horseshoe crabs frequently burrow in the sand. Such burrowing discourages barnacles from clinging to their shells. When fully grown, however, the crabs can readily withstand tidal currents without burrowing, and thus they acquire substantial populations of barnacles. Surprisingly, in areas where tidal currents are very weak, juvenile horseshoe crabs are found not to have significant barnacle populations, even though they seldom burrow.

Which of the following, if true, most helps to explain the surprising finding?

(A)   Tidal currents do not themselves dislodge barnacles from the shells of horseshoe crabs.

(B)   Barnacles most readily attach themselves to horseshoe crabs in areas where tidal currents are weakest.

(C)   The strength of the tidal currents in a given location varies widely over the course of a day.

(D)   A very large barnacle population can significantly decrease the ability of a horseshoe crab to find food.

(E)   Until they are fully grown, horseshoe crabs shed their shells and grow new ones several times a year.

Argument Construction

Situation   Juvenile horseshoe crabs withstand tidal currents by burrowing in the sand. This action makes barnacles less likely to cling to their shells. Adult horseshoe crabs can withstand currents, so they do not burrow, and barnacles become more likely to cling to their shells. Surprisingly, however, juvenile horseshoe crabs that do not burrow, because tidal currents do not threaten them, do not have significant numbers of barnacles clinging to their shells.

Reasoning   *What would most help explain the finding that nonburrowing juvenile horseshoe crabs do not have significant barnacle populations?* The finding suggests that there is some way in which nonburrowing juvenile horseshoe crabs either discourage barnacles from clinging to their shells, or get rid of the barnacles that do cling to their shells. Identifying how this is accomplished will explain the finding.

A   This gives a reason why juvenile horseshoe crabs that do not burrow *would* have significant barnacle populations.

B   If barnacles in areas of weak tidal currents readily attach themselves to horseshoe crabs, then it would be more likely for juvenile horseshoe crabs in such areas to have significant barnacle populations.

C   The areas under discussion are those where tidal currents are very weak. The strength of currents may vary widely there, but presumably they are still weak compared to other areas.

D   The surprising finding under discussion is why certain juvenile horseshoe crabs do not have significant barnacle populations, despite failing to engage in behavior that dislodges barnacles. That a very large barnacle population can hurt a horseshoe crab does not help explain such a finding.

E   **Correct.** This statement properly identifies something that helps explain the surprising finding: If juvenile horseshoe crabs regularly shed their shells, they also regularly shed the barnacles that cling to those shells. Thus juvenile horseshoe crabs would most likely be found not to have significant barnacle populations.

The correct answer is E.

58. Red blood cells in which the malarial-fever parasite resides are eliminated from a person's body after 120 days. Because the parasite cannot travel to a new generation of red blood cells, any fever that develops in a person more than 120 days after that person has moved to a malaria-free region is not due to the malarial parasite.

    Which of the following, if true, most seriously weakens the conclusion above?

    (A) The fever caused by the malarial parasite may resemble the fever caused by flu viruses.

    (B) The anopheles mosquito, which is the principal insect carrier of the malarial parasite, has been eradicated in many parts of the world.

    (C) Many malarial symptoms other than the fever, which can be suppressed with antimalarial medication, can reappear within 120 days after the medication is discontinued.

    (D) In some cases, the parasite that causes malarial fever travels to cells of the spleen, which are less frequently eliminated from a person's body than are red blood cells.

    (E) In any region infested with malaria-carrying mosquitoes, there are individuals who appear to be immune to malaria.

Argument Evaluation

Situation The malarial-fever parasite lives in red blood cells, but these cells are eliminated after 120 days. If the infected person moves to a malaria-free region, any new fever that occurs after 120 days cannot be due to the malarial-fever parasite.

Reasoning *What weakens the conclusion?* The passage says that the malarial parasites that reside in red blood cells are eliminated after 120 days. What if malarial parasites can also reside in other places in a person's body? If for instance the parasites can reside in the spleen, from which they are not eliminated as frequently, as well as in red blood cells, they may not be eliminated within 120 days. Therefore, they could cause malarial fever after the 120-day period. In that case, the conclusion ruling out a new generation of malarial parasites as the cause of new fever is unfounded.

A   The issue is not about a similarity of symptoms but about where the parasites reside.

B   The existence of malaria-free regions is not in question.

C   The argument gives no reason to postulate any significant connection between the discontinuation of medication and the issue of whether symptoms can persist after a patient has been in a malaria-free region for 120 days.

D   Correct. This statement properly identifies a point that weakens the conclusion.

E   This tells us only that some individuals are immune; it does not help us determine whether those who are not can have symptoms occur more than 120 days after moving into a malaria-free area.

The correct answer is D.

59. Which of the following most logically completes the passage?

A recent government study links the high rates of respiratory ailments in Groverston to airborne pollutants released by the Woodco plywood manufacturing plant there. To address the problem, the government imposed strict regulations on emissions which will go into effect in four years. Although Woodco plans to cut its emissions in half two years ahead of schedule, it is unlikely that the rate of respiratory ailments will decline before the regulations go into effect, since _____.

(A) the number of facilities capable of treating respiratory ailments is not likely to increase

(B) reducing emissions even further than planned would necessitate decreasing production at Woodco

(C) it is difficult to make accurate, long-term predictions about emissions

(D) not all respiratory ailments are caused by airborne pollutants

(E) three new plywood manufacturing plants are about to go into production in Groverston

Argument Construction

Situation   A government study linked high rates of respiratory illness in Groverston to air pollutants released by a plywood manufacturing plant. A government-imposed restriction on emissions will go into effect in four years. But the Woodco manufacturing plant plans to cut its emissions in half two years ahead of schedule.

Reasoning   *Which of the possible completions of the passage will provide the most support for the argument's conclusion?* The argument's conclusion is that the rate of respiratory illness is unlikely to decline before the regulations go into effect four years from now. That is a surprising claim, given that the existing plywood factory is going to *halve* its emissions two years from now—so this claim requires additional support (to be provided by completing the blank). Such additional support is provided by the information that three new plywood manufacturing plants will soon be starting production in Groverston. This suggests that even if Groverston reduces its emissions by half over the next two years—and even if each of the three new plants have only, let's say, *one quarter* of the emissions of the existing plant as currently operated—the *total amount* of airborne pollutants from plywood manufacture in the Groverston area will not decline. Since the total airborne pollution from the plants will not decline, we should not expect that the rate of respiratory illnesses from such pollution would decline either.

A   The argument focuses on the incidence of respiratory ailments in Groverston, not on the availability of treatment facilities for such ailments once they occur. So this statement is largely irrelevant to the argument.

B   This information provides no support for the argument's conclusion. It merely indicates a practical difficulty Woodco would have in making more than a 50 percent reduction in its emissions. However, even with the 50 percent emissions reduction that Woodco plans to implement in two years, the rate of respiratory ailments should decline.

C   First, it is not clear that a prediction about levels of emissions in Groverston three or four years from now is a *long-term prediction*. More to the point, if it would be very difficult to predict the emissions even two years from now, that would not support a conclusion that rates of respiratory ailments are unlikely to decline. Rather, it would support the conclusion that we do not know whether rates will decline.

D   This information raises the possibility that within the next four years, an increase in the occurrence of factors *other than* airborne pollutants might make a decline in respiratory ailments unlikely. However, the passage provides no information whatsoever that implies an increase in the occurrence of such "other" factors.

E   **Correct.** This helps to support the conclusion that rates of respiratory ailments in Groverston are unlikely to decline before the new government regulations go into effect.

The correct answer is E.

60. Neither a rising standard of living nor balanced trade, by itself, establishes a country's ability to compete in the international marketplace. Both are required simultaneously since standards of living can rise because of growing trade deficits and trade can be balanced by means of a decline in a country's standard of living.

    If the facts stated in the passage above are true, a proper test of a country's ability to be competitive is its ability to

    (A) balance its trade while its standard of living rises
    (B) balance its trade while its standard of living falls
    (C) increase trade deficits while its standard of living rises
    (D) decrease trade deficits while its standard of living falls
    (E) keep its standard of living constant while trade deficits rise

Argument Evaluation

Situation   A country's ability to compete in the international marketplace depends on both a rising standard of living and balanced trade.

Reasoning   *What must a country do to be considered competitive?* The passage states that there are two conditions that must be met simultaneously: The standard of living must rise, and trade must be balanced. While it is possible for the standard of living to rise when trade is not balanced and for trade to be balanced while the standard of living is falling, neither of these situations allows the country to be considered competitive internationally. The country must both balance trade and have a rising standard of living.

A   **Correct.** This statement properly identifies the two requirements the country must meet at the same time.
B   One of the two conditions is not met; the standard of living must be rising, not falling.
C   One of the two conditions is not met; trade must be balanced.
D   Neither of the conditions is met; trade must be balanced, and the standard of living must be rising.
E   Neither of the conditions is met; the standard of living must be rising, not constant, and trade must be balanced.

The correct answer is A.

61. When there is less rainfall than normal, the water level of Australian rivers falls and the rivers flow more slowly. Because algae whose habitat is river water grow best in slow-moving water, the amount of algae per unit of water generally increases when there has been little rain. By contrast, however, following a period of extreme drought, algae levels are low even in very slow-moving river water.

   Which of the following, if true, does most to explain the contrast described above?

   (A) During periods of extreme drought, the populations of some of the species that feed on algae tend to fall.

   (B) The more slowly water moves, the more conducive its temperature is to the growth of algae.

   (C) When algae populations reach very high levels, conditions within the river can become toxic for some of the other species that normally live there.

   (D) Australian rivers dry up completely for short intervals in periods of extreme drought.

   (E) Except during periods of extreme drought, algae levels tend to be higher in rivers in which the flow has been controlled by damming than in rivers that flow freely.

Argument Construction

Situation   When Australian rivers flow slowly due to little rain, algae populations in those rivers increase. But after periods of extreme drought, algae levels are low even in water moving at speeds that would normally show population increases.

Reasoning   *What would explain the contrast between algae levels in slow-moving water resulting from little rain and slow-moving water after a drought?* There must be some difference between what happens during periods in which there is simply less rainfall than normal and periods in which there is extreme drought, a difference that affects the algae population.

A   This indicates one of the consequences of drought, and slightly suggests that this might be due to a lower algae level. But it does nothing to explain why algae levels might be lower after a drought.

B   This could explain why some rivers that are slow-moving and have little water might have a high algae level—but not why the algae level is low in such rivers after a period of drought.

C   This explains why levels of other species might be low when algae populations are high, not why algae populations are high when there is little rain, but low following a period of extreme drought.

D   Correct. This statement properly identifies something that helps explain the contrast. According to the information given, the habitat of the algae under discussion is river water. If the river dries up, the algae will probably not survive. Then after the drought, algae population levels would likely take a while to rise again.

E   This emphasizes that there is a contrast between what happens to algae during periods of extreme drought and what happens to them at other times, but it does not help explain that contrast.

The correct answer is D.

62. When hypnotized subjects are told that they are deaf and are then asked whether they can hear the hypnotist, they reply, "No." Some theorists try to explain this result by arguing that the selves of hypnotized subjects are dissociated into separate parts, and that the part that is deaf is dissociated from the part that replies.

Which of the following challenges indicates the most serious weakness in the attempted explanation described above?

(A) Why does the part that replies not answer, "Yes"?

(B) Why are the observed facts in need of any special explanation?

(C) Why do the subjects appear to accept the hypnotist's suggestion that they are deaf?

(D) Why do hypnotized subjects all respond the same way in the situation described?

(E) Why are the separate parts of the self the same for all subjects?

Argument Evaluation

Situation   People under hypnosis are told they are deaf. When asked by the hypnotist if they can hear, they hear the question and respond, "No." A theory explains this puzzling result by stating that the hypnotized subjects dissociate the part of themselves that is deaf from the part that replies to the question.

Reasoning   *Which question points to a weakness in the theory?* According to the theory, hypnotized people dissociate themselves into separate parts: the hearing part and the deaf part. Then, they must be using the hearing part of themselves when they respond to the hypnotist's question; obviously, if they were using the deaf part of themselves at that point, they would not hear or thus respond at all. So, if they are using the hearing part of themselves, as the theorists maintain, why would they respond "No" to the question, "Can you hear me?" The hearing part would more logically answer "Yes."

A   **Correct.** This statement properly identifies a challenge that demonstrates the weakness in the theory.

B   This question does not address a weakness in the explanation; instead it asks why there needs to be an explanation at all.

C   The theorists' explanation, if true, can help answer this question, so this challenge does not indicate a weakness.

D   The theorists' explanation, if true, can help answer this question, so this challenge does not indicate a weakness.

E   The theorists' explanation does not address why the parts of the self are the same for all subjects, so this question does not get to a weakness of their argument.

The correct answer is A.

63. A prominent investor who holds a large stake in the Burton Tool Company has recently claimed that **the company is mismanaged**, citing as evidence the company's failure to slow production in response to a recent rise in its inventory of finished products. It is doubtful whether an investor's sniping at management can ever be anything other than counterproductive, **but in this case it is clearly not justified**. It is true that an increased inventory of finished products often indicates that production is outstripping demand, but in Burton's case it indicates no such thing. Rather, the increase in inventory is entirely attributable to products that have already been assigned to orders received from customers.

In the argument given, the two boldfaced portions play which of the following roles?

(A) The first states the position that the argument as a whole opposes; the second provides evidence to undermine the support for the position being opposed.

(B) The first states the position that the argument as a whole opposes; the second is evidence that has been used to support the position being opposed.

(C) The first states the position that the argument as a whole opposes; the second states the conclusion of the argument as a whole.

(D) The first is evidence that has been used to support a position that the argument as a whole opposes; the second provides information to undermine the force of that evidence.

(E) The first is evidence that has been used to support a position that the argument as a whole opposes; the second states the conclusion of the argument as a whole.

Argument Evaluation

Situation   An investor states that Burton Tool must be mismanaged because it has failed to slow production in response to increasing inventory of finished products. This criticism is unjustified because the finished inventory has already been assigned to orders received.

Reasoning   *Which option identifies the roles played by the boldfaced portions?* The first boldfaced portion expresses the investor's claim that the company is mismanaged. The argument asserts, in the second boldfaced portion, that this claim by the investor is unjustified. The passage then goes on to support this assertion.

A   The second boldfaced portion does not provide evidence to undermine the support for the position being opposed; instead, it states that this position is unjustified.

B   The second boldfaced portion is not said to have been used as evidence for the position being opposed; instead, it states that this position is unjustified.

C   **Correct.** This option correctly identifies the roles played in the argument by the boldfaced portions.

D   The first boldfaced portion is not *evidence for* the position being opposed; it *is* that position.

E   Again, first is not *evidence for* the position being opposed; it *is* that position.

The correct answer is C.

64. Excavation of the ancient city of Kourion on the island of Cyprus revealed a pattern of debris and collapsed buildings typical of towns devastated by earthquakes. Archaeologists have hypothesized that the destruction was due to a major earthquake known to have occurred near the island in A.D. 365.

Which of the following, if true, most strongly supports the archaeologists' hypothesis?

(A) Bronze ceremonial drinking vessels that are often found in graves dating from years preceding and following A.D. 365 were also found in several graves near Kourion.

(B) No coins minted after A.D. 365 were found in Kourion, but coins minted before that year were found in abundance.

(C) Most modern histories of Cyprus mention that an earthquake occurred near the island in A.D. 365.

(D) Several small statues carved in styles current in Cyprus in the century between A.D. 300 and A.D. 400 were found in Kourion.

(E) Stone inscriptions in a form of the Greek alphabet that was definitely used in Cyprus after A.D. 365 were found in Kourion.

Argument Evaluation

Situation   The excavation of Kourion reveals a pattern of destruction typical in towns destroyed by earthquakes. Archaeologists suggest Kourion was destroyed when an earthquake hit nearby in A.D. 365.

Reasoning   *Which statement best supports the archaeologists' hypothesis?* An earthquake struck near Cyprus in A.D. 365; this fact is not disputed. If this earthquake is the one responsible for the devastation of Kourion, then there should be evidence of active occupation before A.D. 365, but no evidence of activity after that date. The dates on the coins found on the site suggest that life in Kourion was flourishing before A.D. 365; the total lack of coins after the year of the earthquake supports the idea that the city had been destroyed.

A   The existence of vessels made both before and after A.D. 365 suggests that Kourion was not destroyed by the earthquake.

B   **Correct.** This statement properly identifies evidence that supports the archaeologists' hypothesis.

C   The occurrence of the earthquake is not in question; this statement simply confirms a fact already assumed in the argument.

D   The existence of statues carved in styles current after the date of the earthquake (A.D. 365–A.D. 400) argues against the town's destruction in A.D. 365.

E   The existence of inscriptions using an alphabet common only after the earthquake argues against the theory that the earthquake destroyed Kourion.

The correct answer is B.

65. Which of the following most logically completes the passage?

Pecan growers get a high price for their crop when pecans are comparatively scarce, but the price drops sharply when pecans are abundant. Thus, in high-yield years, growers often hold back part of their crop in refrigerated warehouses for one or two years, hoping for higher prices in the future. This year's pecan crop was the smallest in five years. It is nonetheless quite possible that a portion of this year's crop will be held back, since _____.

(A) each of the last two years produced record-breaking pecan yields

(B) the quality of this year's pecan crop is no worse than the quality of the pecan crops of the previous five years

(C) pecan prices have not been subject to sharp fluctuations in recent years

(D) for some pecan growers, this year's crop was no smaller than last year's

(E) the practice of holding back part of one year's crop had not yet become widespread the last time the pecan crop was as small as it was this year

Argument Construction

Situation   The price of pecans tends to drop sharply in years when pecans are abundant. So in high-yield years, growers often hold back part of the harvest in refrigerated warehouses. This year's harvest was the smallest in five years.

Reasoning   *What would provide the best completion of the argument?* The argument's conclusion is that some of this year's crop might be held back. The blank to be completed should provide a reason in support of that conclusion. What would lead us to believe that some of this year's crop might go into cold storage even though the crop was unusually small? Only in high-yield years does this usually happen. But suppose there is *already* a large quantity of pecans in cold storage from previous harvests. Given this information, it would make perfect sense to expect that the pecans already in cold storage would be marketed first, while some of the latest crop would be stored. This would avoid the market oversupply and lower producer prices that might result if both all of this year's crop and all of the already stored pecans were marketed this year.

A   **Correct.** This answer choice provides information that makes it more probable that the conclusion is true.

B   The argument provides no information whatsoever that would suggest the decision to store or not to store pecans is based on evaluation of the crop's quality.

C   This information is of little or no relevance. It is reasonable to think that predictions about pecan prices this year would affect the decision to store or not to store. But the information in this answer choice sheds little or no light on what this year's pecan prices might be, given that, as the passage tells us, this year's crop is exceptionally small.

D   It is not surprising that some growers had crops this year that were as big as their crops the year before. But what matters, what affects the price of pecans, is the overall size of total pecan production and the abundance or scarcity of pecans at the time.

E   This piece of history about marketing and storage practices explains why pecans were not placed in storage in previous small-yield years, but it provides no reason to believe that some of the new pecan crop will be stored this year.

The correct answer is A.

66. To protect certain fledgling industries, the government of Country Z banned imports of the types of products those industries were starting to make. As a direct result, the cost of those products to the buyers, several export-dependent industries in Z, went up, sharply limiting the ability of those industries to compete effectively in their export markets.

Which of the following conclusions about Country Z's adversely affected export-dependent industries is best supported by the passage?

(A) Profit margins in those industries were not high enough to absorb the rise in costs mentioned above.

(B) Those industries had to contend with the fact that other countries banned imports from Country Z.

(C) Those industries succeeded in expanding the domestic market for their products.

(D) Steps to offset rising materials costs by decreasing labor costs were taken in those industries.

(E) Those industries started to move into export markets that they had previously judged unprofitable.

Argument Construction

Situation   Country Z bans the importation of products that would compete with those that some of its new industries are beginning to make. Consequently, the export-dependent local industries that buy these products must pay more for them, and these exporters are now less competitive in their markets.

Reasoning   *What conclusion can be drawn about the export–dependent industries?* Any conclusion must be supported by the facts in the passage. The export-dependent industries could no longer compete effectively when they had to purchase necessary products at greater expense from local industries. The export-dependent industries' inability to adjust successfully to the rise in costs suggests that staying competitive in their markets required tight cost control to maintain their profit margins. It is reasonable to conclude then that their profit margins were not high enough for them to be able to absorb the increased costs caused by their new need to purchase domestically made products.

A   **Correct.** This statement properly identifies the conclusion that the export-dependent industries were low-margin businesses that could not successfully accommodate the higher prices of the domestically made products.

B   No information about other countries' ban of imports from Country Z is given in the passage.

C   Not enough information is given in the passage to support this conclusion.

D   No information about cutting labor costs is given in the passage.

E   No information about the industries' moving into different markets is given in the passage.

The correct answer is A.

67. Several industries have recently switched at least partly from older technologies powered by fossil fuels to new technologies powered by electricity. It is thus evident that less fossil fuel is being used as a result of the operations of these industries than would have been used if these industries had retained their older technologies.

Which of the following, if true, most strengthens the argument above?

(A) Many of the industries that have switched at least partly to the new technologies have increased their output.

(B) Less fossil fuel was used to manufacture the machinery employed in the new technologies than was originally used to manufacture the machinery employed in the older technologies.

(C) More electricity is used by those industries that have switched at least partly to the new technologies than by those industries that have not switched.

(D) Some of the industries that have switched at least partly to the new technologies still use primarily technologies that are powered by fossil fuels.

(E) The amount of fossil fuel used to generate the electricity needed to power the new technologies is less than the amount that would have been used to power the older technologies.

Argument Evaluation

Situation Several industries have now switched, at least partly, to technologies using electricity rather than fossil fuels. Thus, less fossil fuel will be consumed as a result of the operation of these industries than otherwise would have been.

Reasoning *Which option most strengthens the argument?* One way to strengthen an argument is to eliminate or minimize one of its flaws or weaknesses. Because the conclusion is stated in terms of "fossil fuel consumed *as a result* of the operation of these industries," the claim would encompass even any fossil fuel that might be used to generate the electricity that the newer technologies use. Yet the premise of the argument does not address this issue. So the argument is strengthened if it turns out that less fossil fuel was used to produce the electricity than would have been used to power the older technologies.

A In an indirect way, this option slightly weakens rather than strengthens the argument. For *if* fossil fuels are used to produce the electricity now used by the industries and *if* it is because of these newer technologies that output has increased, the argument's conclusion is *less* likely.

B It does not matter how much fossil fuel was used to manufacture the older technologies *originally*. That has no bearing on whether more fossil fuel would have been expended as a result of the *continued operation* of the industries if the partial switch to newer technologies had not occurred.

C This is what we would expect, but it in no way strengthens the argument.

D This may seem to weaken the argument by indicating that the switch from older technologies will have less of an impact on fossil fuel consumption by these industries than we might have assumed. But since the conclusion makes no claim about how much consumption has been reduced, it is not clear that this option has any bearing on the strength of the argument one way or the other.

E **Correct.** This is the option that most strengthens the argument.

The correct answer is E.

68. Scientists have modified feed corn genetically, increasing its resistance to insect pests. Farmers who tried out the genetically modified corn last season applied less insecticide to their corn fields and still got yields comparable to those they would have gotten with ordinary corn. Ordinary corn seed, however, costs less, and what these farmers saved on insecticide rarely exceeded their extra costs for seed. Therefore, for most feed-corn farmers, switching to genetically modified seed would be unlikely to increase profits.

    Which of the following would it be most useful to know in order to evaluate the argument?

    (A) Whether there are insect pests that sometimes reduce feed-corn yields, but against which commonly used insecticides and the genetic modification are equally ineffective
    (B) Whether the price that farmers receive for feed corn has remained steady over the past few years
    (C) Whether the insecticides typically used on feed corn tend to be more expensive than insecticides typically used on other crops
    (D) Whether most of the farmers who tried the genetically modified corn last season applied more insecticide than was actually necessary
    (E) Whether, for most farmers who plant feed corn, it is their most profitable crop

Argument Evaluation

Situation   Farmers who grew feed corn genetically engineered to be pest resistant got yields comparable to those of farmers growing ordinary feed corn, but did so while using less pesticide. Since the amount saved on pesticide was rarely in excess of the extra costs for the genetically modified corn, most farmers will probably not increase profits by choosing the genetically engineered variety.

Reasoning   *Which would be most useful to know in evaluating the argument?* To answer a question such as this, one should look for information that would strengthen or weaken the argument. If one had information that the farmers growing the genetically modified corn could have increased their yields last year at lower cost, this would be helpful in evaluating the argument, because this would show that the argument is weak.

A   It does not matter to the argument whether there are pests against which pesticides and genetic resistance are equally ineffective, because that is compatible with there being pests against which they are not equally effective.

B   Whether prices of feed corn go up or down affects the comparison groups equally.

C   The relative cost of insecticides for other crops has no bearing on the argument because the argument is concerned with only feed corn.

D   Correct. This option provides the information that it would be most useful to know in evaluating the argument. It shows that farmers growing genetically modified corn last year could have attained higher profits than they in fact did.

E   The argument concerns only the relative profitability of growing one variety of feed corn versus another.

The correct answer is D.

69.   Which of the following most logically completes the argument?

By competing with rodents for seeds, black ants help control rodent populations that pose a public health risk. However, a very aggressive species of black ant, the Loma ant, which has recently invaded a certain region, has a venomous sting that is often fatal to humans. Therefore, the planned introduction into that region of ant flies, which prey on Loma ants, would benefit public health, since _____.

(A)   ant flies do not attack black ants other than Loma ants

(B)   Loma ants are less effective than many bird species in competing with rodents for seeds

(C)   certain other species of black ants are more effective than Loma ants in competing with rodents for seeds

(D)   the sting of Loma ants can also be fatal to rodents

(E)   some pesticides that could be used to control Loma ants are harmful to the environment

Argument Construction

Situation   Black ants help to control populations of rodents by competing with them for seeds. But a very aggressive species of black ant, the Loma ant, has a sting that can be fatal to humans. Ant flies prey on Loma ants and their presence can thereby benefit public health.

Reasoning   *Which of the possible completions of the passage provides the most support for the conclusion?* The argument's conclusion is that introducing ant flies into the region where Loma ants have recently invaded would benefit public health. We know from the passage that black ants, generally, benefit public health by keeping down rodent populations. However, the sting of Loma ants, a species of black ant, can be fatal to humans. Ant flies prey on Loma ants. To that extent their introduction in the region would tend to benefit public health by making fatal Loma stinging of humans less likely. But if these ant flies also prey on black ants other than the Loma ants, then to that extent they would undermine another public health benefit associated with controlling rodents. Thus, the information that ant flies do not prey on black ants other than Loma ants would provide strong logical support for the conclusion.

A   **Correct.** This most logically completes the argument because it addresses a potential downside of introducing the ant flies into the region. The potential downside is that it might reduce the desirable effect that other species of black ants have in keeping down the rodent populations.

B   We have no idea whether the bird species that are more effective than Loma ants at competing with rodents for seeds are even present in the region in question.

C   This does not help the conclusion very much because we do not know *from the passage* whether ant flies prey on other species of black ants besides Loma ants.

D   If anything, this is a reason *not to introduce ant flies* into the region. This answer choice at least suggests that Loma ants might have some positive effect on public health because they might keep down rodent populations by reducing their survival chances.

E   This provides very little support for the conclusion. It does not exclude the possibility that there are pesticides—perhaps several—that would control Loma ants effectively without harming the environment. So it is not a strong reason for introducing ant flies.

The correct answer is A.

70. Community activist: If Morganville wants to keep its central shopping district healthy, it should prevent the opening of a huge SaveAll discount department store on the outskirts of Morganville. Records from other small towns show that whenever SaveAll has opened a store outside the central shopping district of a small town, within five years the town has experienced the bankruptcies of more than a quarter of the stores in the shopping district.

    The answer to which of the following would be most useful for evaluating the community activist's reasoning?

    (A) Have community activists in other towns successfully campaigned against the opening of a SaveAll store on the outskirts of their towns?

    (B) Do a large percentage of the residents of Morganville currently do almost all of their shopping at stores in Morganville?

    (C) In towns with healthy central shopping districts, what proportion of the stores in those districts suffer bankruptcy during a typical five-year period?

    (D) What proportion of the employees at the SaveAll store on the outskirts of Morganville will be drawn from Morganville?

    (E) Do newly opened SaveAll stores ever lose money during their first five years of operation?

Argument Evaluation

Situation   Morganville should stop SaveAll from opening a store on its outskirts if it wants to keep its shopping district healthy. Other small towns have experienced bankruptcies in 25 percent of the stores in their central shopping district within five years after such openings.

Reasoning   *Which option provides the information that it would be most useful to know in evaluating the argument?* The argument contends that if SaveAll opens a store in Morganville, then that will somehow undermine the health of the shopping district. Two basic questions arise when evaluating the bankruptcy data from other small towns: (1) Did the opening of SaveAlls cause any of these bankruptcies? No information is given about bankruptcy rates in small towns without SaveAlls. (2) Is a 25 percent bankruptcy rate over five years *unhealthy*?

A   This has to do with the likelihood that the SaveAll will open; and not with what will happen if it does.

B   The conclusion would be supported just as well—or as poorly—if this question were answered with a yes as with a no.

C   **Correct.** This option provides the information that it would be most useful to know in evaluating the argument.

D   This may be important in determining the effect the SaveAll would have on Morganville residents, but the argument has only to do with SaveAll's effect on the economic health of the shopping district.

E   Whether SaveAlls tend to make or lose money in their first five years has no obvious bearing on whether they are apt to undermine the health of the town's shopping districts.

The correct answer is C.

71. In comparison to the standard typewriter keyboard, the EFCO keyboard, which places the most-used keys nearest the typist's strongest fingers, allows faster typing and results in less fatigue. Therefore, replacement of standard keyboards with the EFCO keyboard will result in an immediate reduction of typing costs.

Which of the following, if true, would most weaken the conclusion drawn above?

(A) People who use both standard and EFCO keyboards report greater difficulty in the transition from the EFCO keyboard to the standard keyboard than in the transition from the standard keyboard to the EFCO keyboard.

(B) EFCO keyboards are no more expensive to manufacture than are standard keyboards and require less frequent repair than do standard keyboards.

(C) The number of businesses and government agencies that use EFCO keyboards is increasing each year.

(D) The more training and experience an employee has had with the standard keyboard, the more costly it is to train that employee to use the EFCO keyboard.

(E) Novice typists can learn to use the EFCO keyboard in about the same amount of time that it takes them to learn to use the standard keyboard.

Argument Evaluation

Situation   Compared to the standard typewriter keyboard, the EFCO keyboard promotes faster typing while producing less fatigue. Replacing standard keyboards with EFCO keyboards promises immediate reduction of typing costs.

Reasoning   *What point would weaken the conclusion about reduced typing costs?* Whenever a word like *immediate* is part of an argument, it is wise to be alert. Given the comparison with the standard keyboard, it could well be that over the longer term the EFCO keyboard will save money. What problems might there be initially, however, that would counteract the possibility of *immediate* savings? Personnel must first be retrained on the new EFCO keyboard, and it is possible that the costs of the training could offset any short-term savings. If the more experience employees have had with the standard keyboard, the more costly the initial training, then adopting the new keyboard could have high short-term costs that preclude *immediate* savings.

A   The greater ease of changing from the standard keyboard to the EFCO keyboard for typists experienced in both would support, not weaken, the conclusion.

B   The fewer repairs required by EFCO keyboards should save money in the long run; immediate costs will not go up since the price of both keyboards is the same. The conclusion is not weakened.

C   The increasing use of EFCO keyboards supports the conclusion, because it suggests that other offices have found the switch advantageous.

D   Correct. This statement properly identifies information that weakens the conclusion that savings will be immediate.

E   For new typists, training time is the same for both keyboards; this statement does not weaken the conclusion.

The correct answer is D.

72. In the past the country of Malvernia has relied heavily on imported oil. Malvernia recently implemented a program to convert heating systems from oil to natural gas. Malvernia currently produces more natural gas each year than it uses, and oil production in Malvernian oil fields is increasing at a steady pace. If these trends in fuel production and usage continue, therefore, Malvernian reliance on foreign sources for fuel is likely to decline soon.

    Which of the following would it be most useful to establish in evaluating the argument?

    (A) When, if ever, will production of oil in Malvernia outstrip production of natural gas?
    (B) Is Malvernia among the countries that rely most on imported oil?
    (C) What proportion of Malvernia's total energy needs is met by hydroelectric, solar, and nuclear power?
    (D) Is the amount of oil used each year in Malvernia for generating electricity and fuel for transportation increasing?
    (E) Have any existing oil-burning heating systems in Malvernia already been converted to natural-gas-burning heating systems?

Argument Evaluation

Situation   Malvernia has relied heavily on imported oil, but recently began a program to convert heating systems from oil to natural gas. Malvernia produces more natural gas than it uses, so it will probably reduce its reliance on imported oils if these trends continue.

Reasoning   *Which option provides the information that it would be most useful to know in evaluating the argument?* In other words, we are looking for the option which—depending on whether it was answered yes or no—would either most weaken or most strengthen the argument. The argument indicates that Malvernia will be using less oil for heating and will be producing more oil domestically. But the conclusion that Malvernia's reliance on foreign oil will decline, assuming the current trends mentioned continue, would be seriously undermined if there was something in the works that was bound to offset these trends, for instance, if it turned out that the country's need for oil was going to rise drastically in the coming years.

A   Since both counteract the need for imported oil, it makes little difference to the argument whether domestic oil production exceeds domestic natural gas.

B   Whether there are many countries that rely more on foreign oil than Malvernia would have little impact on whether Malvernia's need for foreign oil can be expected to decline.

C   Since there is no information in the argument about whether Malvernia can expect an increase or decrease from these other energy sources, it does not matter how much they now provide.

D   Correct. This option provides the information that it would be most useful to know in evaluating the argument.

E   The argument tells us that a program has begun *recently* to convert heating systems from oil to gas. So, even if no such conversions have been completed, the argument still indicates that they can be expected to occur.

The correct answer is D.

73. An overly centralized economy, not the changes in the climate, is responsible for the poor agricultural production in Country X since its new government came to power. Neighboring Country Y has experienced the same climatic conditions, but while agricultural production has been falling in Country X, it has been rising in Country Y.

Which of the following, if true, would most weaken the argument above?

(A) Industrial production also is declining in Country X.

(B) Whereas Country Y is landlocked, Country X has a major seaport.

(C) Both Country X and Country Y have been experiencing drought conditions.

(D) The crops that have always been grown in Country X are different from those that have always been grown in Country Y.

(E) Country X's new government instituted a centralized economy with the intention of ensuring an equitable distribution of goods.

Argument Evaluation

Situation   Two countries sharing similar climate conditions differ widely in agricultural production, one experiencing a rise and the other a decline. The decline is blamed on an overly centralized economy.

Reasoning   *What point most weakens the argument that the economy is to blame?* If a factor other than the economy could account for the differences in agricultural production, then the argument is weakened. If the two countries grow different kinds of crops that may react differently to the same climate conditions, then the types of crops, rather than the economy could be responsible for the differences in production.

A   This weakly suggests that the overly centralized economy of Country X is to blame for its poor agricultural production; this strengthens the argument more than it weakens it.

B   The availability of a seaport does not explain the differences in agricultural production.

C   Similar climate conditions have already been established in the argument.

D   Correct. This statement properly identifies a factor that weakens the argument.

E   The government's intention when instituting the economy does not have any bearing on whether the economy is responsible for the decline or not.

The correct answer is D.

74. Which of the following most logically completes the argument below?

Using broad-spectrum weed killers on weeds that are competing with crops for sunlight, water, and nutrients presents a difficulty: how to keep the crop from being killed along with the weeds. For at least some food crops, specially treated seed that produces plants resistant to weed killers is under development. This resistance wears off as the plants mature. Therefore, the special seed treatment will be especially useful for plants that _____.

(A) produce their crop over an extended period of time, as summer squash does

(B) produce large seeds that are easy to treat individually, as corn and beans do

(C) provide, as they approach maturity, shade dense enough to keep weeds from growing

(D) are typically grown in large tracts devoted to a single crop

(E) are cultivated specifically for the seed they produce rather than for their leaves or roots

Argument Construction

Situation   A difficulty in using broad-spectrum weed killers is keeping them from killing the food crops along with the weeds. Specially treated seed is being developed that will protect certain food crop plants in their earlier stages of growth.

Reasoning   *Which is the best completion for the conclusion?* The conclusion is incompletely stated as "Therefore, the special seed treatment will be especially useful for plants that _____." The question is what sorts of plants does the passage suggest the seed treatment would be especially useful for. We have been told that this treatment makes the plants resistant to weed killer, but that this resistance wears off when the plant matures. So the treatment will be most useful with plants that are not harmed by weed killer and that suffer no significant disadvantage when the resistance wears off as the plant matures. Choice (C) is the correct answer choice because it describes a sort of plant that can combat weeds and requires no weed killer once the plant matures.

A   Given that the seed treatment wears off as the plant matures, it would not be especially useful for plants that produce their crops over an extended period.

B   We have not been told whether small seeds are more difficult to treat, and so we have no basis to conclude that the special seed treatment would be *especially useful* for plants that have large seeds that are easy to treat individually. We have also been given no reason to think that it is better to treat seeds individually.

C   Correct. Plants that, as they approach maturity, produce shade dense enough to keep weeds from growing, would benefit from resistance to weed killer when young and would not need weed killer when they have matured and lost their resistance.

D   We have been given no reason to think that the seed treatment would be especially useful for plants grown in a large tract devoted to a single crop. For example, why would it be less useful for small tracts with a variety of crops?

E   A plant harvested for its roots, fruits, or leaves, rather than for its seeds, would derive no less an advantage from resistance to weed killers in earlier stages of growth.

The correct answer is C.

75. Because no employee wants to be associated with bad news in the eyes of a superior, information about serious problems at lower levels is progressively softened and distorted as it goes up each step in the management hierarchy. The chief executive is, therefore, less well informed about problems at lower levels than are his or her subordinates at those levels.

The conclusion drawn above is based on the assumption that

(A) problems should be solved at the level in the management hierarchy at which they occur

(B) employees should be rewarded for accurately reporting problems to their superiors

(C) problem-solving ability is more important at higher levels than it is at lower levels of the management hierarchy

(D) chief executives obtain information about problems at lower levels from no source other than their subordinates

(E) some employees are more concerned about truth than about the way they are perceived by their superiors

Argument Construction

Situation   No employee wants to report bad news to a superior, so information about problems is softened and distorted as it goes up the ranks of management. As a result, chief executives know less about problems at lower levels than their subordinates do.

Reasoning   *What assumption is being made in this argument?* This passage contends that information travels step by step upward through an organization, and that information becomes increasingly distorted along the route with each additional individual's reluctance to be candid with a superior about problems. What must be true about this information flow to support the conclusion? In order to conclude that chief executives are *less well informed* about problems than their subordinates, the argument must logically assume that they have no source of information except their subordinates.

A   This argument is not about how problems should be solved, only about how chief executives learn of them.

B   No recommendation for solving the problem is assumed; only the method of discovering the problem is assumed.

C   Problem-solving ability plays no role in the argument.

D   Correct. This statement properly identifies an assumption that underlies the argument.

E   This statement undermines the assertion made in the first sentence of the passage and so cannot be assumed.

The correct answer is D.

76. Although the earliest surviving Greek inscriptions written in an alphabet date from the eighth century B.C., **the fact that the text of these Greek inscriptions sometimes runs from right to left and sometimes from left to right** indicates that the Greeks adopted alphabetic writing at least two centuries before these inscriptions were produced. After all, the Greeks learned alphabetic writing from the Phoenicians, and presumably, along with the alphabet, they also adopted the then-current Phoenician practice with respect to the direction of text. **And although Phoenician writing was originally inconsistent in direction, by the eighth century B.C. Phoenician was consistently written from right to left and had been for about two centuries**.

In the argument given, the two portions in boldface play which of the following roles?

(A) The first and the second each describe evidence that has been used to challenge the position that the argument seeks to establish.

(B) The first is evidence that forms the basis for an objection to the position that the argument seeks to establish; the second is that position.

(C) The first is evidence that forms the basis for an objection to the position that the argument seeks to establish; the second is a consideration that is introduced to counter the force of that evidence.

(D) The first and the second each provide evidence in support of the position that the argument seeks to establish.

(E) The first provides evidence in support of the position that the argument seeks to establish; the second is that position.

Argument Evaluation

Situation   The oldest surviving Greek inscriptions written in an alphabet are from the eighth century B.C. and run from both left to right and right to left. Therefore, it is likely that the Greeks adopted alphabetic writing at least two centuries before these inscriptions were made. The Greeks adopted their alphabet from the Phoenicians, who wrote in both directions up until two centuries prior to the eighth century.

Reasoning   *What roles do the two boldfaced portions play in the argument?* The conclusion of the argument is that the Greeks adopted alphabetic writing at least two centuries before the oldest surviving Greek inscriptions were written in the eighth century B.C. The first and second boldfaced portions work together to support this conclusion.

A   The first and second portions are not used to challenge the position the argument seeks to establish, but to support it.

B   The first is evidence for the conclusion, not for an objection to it; the second is as well.

C   The first is evidence for the conclusion, not for an objection to it; the second is as well.

D   **Correct.** This option correctly identifies the roles played by the boldfaced portions.

E   The second boldfaced portion is not the conclusion, but evidence for that conclusion.

The correct answer is D.

77. A recent report determined that although only 3 percent of drivers on Maryland highways equipped their vehicles with radar detectors, 33 percent of all vehicles ticketed for exceeding the speed limit were equipped with them. Clearly, drivers who equip their vehicles with radar detectors are more likely to exceed the speed limit regularly than are drivers who do not.

The conclusion drawn above depends on which of the following assumptions?

(A) Drivers who equip their vehicles with radar detectors are less likely to be ticketed for exceeding the speed limit than are drivers who do not.

(B) Drivers who are ticketed for exceeding the speed limit are more likely to exceed the speed limit regularly than are drivers who are not ticketed.

(C) The number of vehicles that were ticketed for exceeding the speed limit was greater than the number of vehicles that were equipped with radar detectors.

(D) Many of the vehicles that were ticketed for exceeding the speed limit were ticketed more than once in the time period covered by the report.

(E) Drivers on Maryland highways exceeded the speed limit more often than did drivers on other state highways not covered in the report.

Argument Construction

Situation   Although only 3 percent of drivers on Maryland's highways have radar detectors in their vehicles, 33 percent of vehicles recently ticketed for driving over the speed limit on Maryland highways have had radar detectors. Drivers who have radar detectors are thus more likely to exceed the speed limit regularly than drivers who do not.

Reasoning   *What assumption must be true for the conclusion to be drawn?* The argument moves from a particular example, that is, the percentage of vehicles ticketed for exceeding the speed limit that were equipped with radar detectors, to a generalization about the regular driving behaviors of all drivers who have radar detectors in their vehicles. The reasoning links the example to the generalization with an assumption. What can the assumption be? Only if the drivers ticketed in this instance are assumed to make a regular habit of exceeding the speed limit can the conclusion be drawn that drivers with radar detectors are more likely to do so *regularly* than drivers who are not ticketed.

A   While this statement about being ticketed may be true, the conclusion pertains to the recurrent exceeding of the speed limit, so this statement is not relevant.

B   Correct. This statement properly identifies the conclusion's necessary assumption about ticketed drivers' being more likely to drive in excess of the speed limit than nonticketed drivers.

C   This statement is about the number of vehicles ticketed, not about the regular habits of drivers, so it is not assumed for the conclusion.

D   While this additional information could help support the conclusion, it is not a necessary assumption in the conclusion because it is about the particular example of the drivers in Maryland, not about drivers' habits in general.

E   Learning that Maryland drivers are not representative of other drivers undermines the conclusion about all drivers, so it is clearly not assumed.

The correct answer is B.

78. **In countries where automobile insurance includes compensation for whiplash injuries sustained in automobile accidents, reports of having suffered such injuries are twice as frequent as they are in countries where whiplash is not covered.** Presently, no objective test for whiplash exists, so it is true that spurious reports of whiplash injuries cannot be readily identified. Nevertheless, these facts do not warrant the conclusion drawn by some commentators that in the countries with the higher rates of reported whiplash injuries, half of the reported cases are spurious. Clearly, **in countries where automobile insurance does not include compensation for whiplash, people often have little incentive to report whiplash injuries that they actually have suffered.**

In the argument given, the two boldfaced portions play which of the following roles?

(A) The first is a claim that the argument disputes; the second is a conclusion that has been based on that claim.

(B) The first is a claim that has been used to support a conclusion that the argument accepts; the second is that conclusion.

(C) The first is evidence that has been used to support a conclusion for which the argument provides further evidence; the second is the main conclusion of the argument.

(D) The first is a finding whose implications are at issue in the argument; the second is a claim presented in order to argue against deriving certain implications from that finding.

(E) The first is a finding whose accuracy is evaluated in the argument; the second is evidence presented to establish that the finding is accurate.

Argument Evaluation

Situation   Reported whiplash injuries are twice as common in countries where car insurance companies pay compensation for such injuries as they are in countries where insurance companies do not. Although there is no objective test for whiplash, this does not mean, as some suggest, that half of the reports of such injuries are fake. It could simply be that where insurance will not pay for such injuries, people are less inclined to report them.

Reasoning   *What roles do the two boldfaced portions play in the argument?* The first portion tells us about the correlation between reported cases of whiplash in countries and the willingness of insurance companies in those countries to compensate for whiplash injuries. The argument next states that whiplash is difficult to objectively verify. The argument then asserts that *although* this last fact, taken together with the first boldfaced portion, has led some to infer that over half of the reported cases in countries with the highest whiplash rates are spurious, such an inference is unwarranted. The second boldfaced portion then helps to explain why such an inference is not necessarily warranted by offering an alternative explanation.

A   The claim made in the first boldfaced portion is never disputed in the argument; at dispute is how to account for the fact that this claim is true. The second is not the argument's conclusion.

B   In a manner of speaking, perhaps, the argument uses the first portion to support its conclusion; but there is no indication that it has been used elsewhere to do so. In any case, the second boldfaced portion is not the argument's conclusion.

C   The first has been used to support a conclusion that the argument *rejects*; the second boldfaced portion is not the argument's conclusion.

D   **Correct.** This option correctly identifies the roles played in the argument by the boldfaced portions.

E   The accuracy of the first boldfaced portion is never questioned in the argument; nor is the second intended to somehow help show that the first is accurate. Rather, the argument assumes that the first portion is accurate.

The correct answer is D.

79. When demand for a factory's products is high, more money is spent at the factory for safety precautions and machinery maintenance than when demand is low. Thus the average number of on-the-job accidents per employee each month should be lower during periods when demand is high than when demand is low and less money is available for safety precautions and machinery maintenance.

Which of the following, if true about a factory when demand for its products is high, casts the most serious doubt on the conclusion drawn above?

(A) Its employees ask for higher wages than they do at other times.

(B) Its management hires new workers but lacks the time to train them properly.

(C) Its employees are less likely to lose their jobs than they are at other times.

(D) Its management sponsors a monthly safety award for each division in the factory.

(E) Its old machinery is replaced with modern, automated models.

Argument Evaluation

Situation   Because more money is spent on safety precautions and machinery maintenance at a factory when demand for its product is high, the average number of job-related accidents per employee at the factory should be lower when demand is high.

Reasoning   *What point casts doubt on the conclusion?* Consider what other conditions can result from high demand for a factory's products. What if, when demand is high, more employees are hired to meet the demand? If, in the effort to increase production, there is not enough time for proper training, then it is likely that the new, poorly trained employees will have more job-related accidents than experienced, well-trained workers.

A   If employers consented to employees' request and diverted money from safety to wages, this statement might cast doubt on the conclusion. However, no such reallocation of resources is implied, and the passage conclusively states that more money *is* spent on safety precautions and machinery maintenance when demand for the product is high. Therefore this statement is irrelevant.

B   Correct. This statement properly identifies a point that undermines the conclusion.

C   Increased job security could result in an increased number of workers, which might increase the total number of accidents. However, the conclusion is about the number of accidents *per employee*, so this point is irrelevant.

D   Actively promoting safety with an award would tend to support the argument, not weaken it.

E   Replacing outdated machinery with more modern machinery could result in a safer workplace; this point could strengthen the conclusion.

The correct answer is B.

80.   A sudden increase in the production of elephant ivory artifacts on the Mediterranean coast of North Africa occurred in the tenth century. Historians explain this increase as the result of an area opening up as a new source of ivory and argue on this basis that the important medieval trade between North Africa and East Africa began at this period.

Each of the following, if true, provides some support for the historians' account described above EXCEPT:

(A)   In East Africa gold coins from Mediterranean North Africa have been found at a tenth-century site but at no earlier sites.

(B)   The many surviving letters of pre-tenth-century North African merchants include no mention of business transactions involving East Africa.

(C)   Excavations in East Africa reveal a tenth-century change in architectural style to reflect North African patterns.

(D)   Documents from Mediterranean Europe and North Africa that date back earlier than the tenth century show knowledge of East African animals.

(E)   East African carvings in a style characteristic of the tenth century depict seagoing vessels very different from those used by local sailors but of a type common in the Mediterranean.

Argument Evaluation

Situation   There was a sudden increase in the production of ivory artifacts in an area of North Africa in the tenth century. Historians say this was brought about by a new source of ivory opening up, and argue from this that important trade between North Africa and East Africa began at this time.

Reasoning   *Which option does NOT provide support for the historians' account?* The historians' account posits new trade between North and East Africa opening in the tenth century and infers this from the increase in ivory production in North Africa that occurred at about this time. Thus, an option that identifies some connection between North and East Africa which predates the tenth century would not support but rather undermine the historians' account.

A   That gold coins may have first been traded between East Africa and North Africa supports the idea that important trade between these areas opened up at this time.

B   This is support for the historians' conclusion, because if there had been important trade between East Africa and North Africa prior to the tenth century, there likely would have been some mention of it in at least some of the letters that survive from that period.

C   This change in architectural design suggests that North Africa began to influence East Africa around this time. Opening up of new trade would explain the emergence of this new influence.

D   Correct. This is the one option that does not support the historians' account.

E   The fact that East African carvings that are possibly from tenth century depict ships not from East Africa but possibly from North Africa would support the idea that trade was occurring at this time.

The correct answer is D.

81. Which of the following most logically completes the argument?

    The attribution of the choral work *Lacrimae* to the composer Pescard (1400–1474) has been regarded as tentative, since it was based on a single treatise from the early 1500s that named Pescard as the composer. Recently, several musical treatises from the late 1500s have come to light, all of which name Pescard as the composer of *Lacrimae*. Unfortunately, these newly discovered treatises lend no support to the attribution of *Lacrimae* to Pescard, since _____.

    (A) the treatise from the early 1500s misidentifies the composers of some of the musical works it considers

    (B) the author of the treatise from the early 1500s had no very strong evidence on which to base the identification of Pescard as the composer of *Lacrimae*

    (C) there are works that can conclusively be attributed to Pescard that are not even mentioned in the treatise from the early 1500s

    (D) the later treatises probably had no source for their attribution other than the earlier treatise

    (E) no known treatises from the 1600s identify Pescard as the composer of *Lacrimae*

Argument Construction

Situation   A choral work has been tentatively attributed to Pescard based on a single treatise from the early 1500s. But several treatises from the late 1500s have recently been discovered, and all of them attribute the work to Pescard.

Reasoning   *Which of the answer choices provides the strongest reason for the conclusion?* The argument's conclusion is that the newly discovered late-1500 treatises lend no support to the attribution of *Lacrimae* to Pescard. It is worth noting that prior to the conclusion the passage provides information which suggests that these newly discovered treatises *do* lend support to the attribution. So the question is: Why don't they? A good reason for thinking they do not is that the newly discovered treatises probably derive solely from the attribution given in the earlier text. Thus the attributions in the later treatises are only as reliable as the attribution in the earlier treatise—and the argument suggests that that reliability has not been conclusively established.

A   This makes the treatise from the early 1500s less reliable, but it does not explain why the newly discovered treatises are unreliable.

B   Like answer choice (A), this is irrelevant. The question is not why the treatise from the early 1500s fails to lend support to the attribution but why the treatises from the late 1500s fail to do so.

C   This is irrelevant because it does not refer to the newly discovered treatises whose attribution of *Lacrimae* is at issue.

D   **Correct.** The question is whether these newly discovered treatises lend *additional* support. *Lacrimae* has already been tentatively attributed to Pescard based on the text from the early 1500s. So, if the later treatises base their attribution solely on the earlier treatise, then they provide no additional support beyond that already provided by the earlier treatise.

E   This leaves open the possibility that there was no treatise at all in the 1600s that discussed Pescard or *Lacrimae*. Also, it fails to provide significant evidence either for or against Pescard's having composed *Lacrimae*. But even if it did provide such evidence, it would be irrelevant because the issue is why the late-1500 treatises fail to provide significant support for the attribution of *Lacrimae* to Pescard, not whether Pescard composed the work.

The correct answer is D.

82. Journalist: In physics journals, the number of articles reporting the results of experiments involving particle accelerators was lower last year than it had been in previous years. Several of the particle accelerators at major research institutions were out of service the year before last for repairs, so it is likely that the low number of articles was due to the decline in availability of particle accelerators.

    Which of the following, if true, most seriously undermines the journalist's argument?

    (A) Every article based on experiments with particle accelerators that was submitted for publication last year actually was published.

    (B) The average time scientists must wait for access to a particle accelerator has declined over the last several years.

    (C) The number of physics journals was the same last year as in previous years.

    (D) Particle accelerators can be used for more than one group of experiments in any given year.

    (E) Recent changes in the editorial policies of several physics journals have decreased the likelihood that articles concerning particle-accelerator research will be accepted for publication.

Argument Evaluation

Situation   A journalist attributes the low number of articles about particle accelerators in physics journals to the fact that several accelerators at major research institutions had been out of service the previous year.

Reasoning   *What point undermines the journalist's argument?* The journalist assumes that the researchers' lack of access to the accelerators is responsible for the decline in the number of articles. What else could explain fewer articles? What if the decline is due, not to the availability of the accelerators for experiments, but to policies regarding publishing articles related to such experiments? An alternate explanation is that changes in the editorial policies of physics journals, rather than the effect of the out-of-service accelerators, could well be responsible for the lower number of published articles about particle-accelerator research.

A   This statement rules out the possibility that submitted articles were not published, and eliminating this alternate explanation tends to support the argument.

B   A decline in waiting time would seem to promote more articles about accelerator research being written and published, not fewer.

C   While the decline in articles could be explained by a decline in the number of journals, this statement eliminates that alternate explanation.

D   If the accelerators can be used for multiple experiments, then it is reasonable to expect more articles related to them, not fewer.

E   **Correct.** This statement properly identifies a point that undermines the journalist's reasoning.

The correct answer is E.

83. Many people suffer an allergic reaction to certain sulfites, including those that are commonly added to wine as preservatives. However, since there are several winemakers who add sulfites to none of the wines they produce, people who would like to drink wine but are allergic to sulfites can drink wines produced by these winemakers without risking an allergic reaction to sulfites.

Which of the following is an assumption on which the argument depends?

(A) These winemakers have been able to duplicate the preservative effect produced by adding sulfites by means that do not involve adding any potentially allergenic substances to their wine.

(B) Not all forms of sulfite are equally likely to produce the allergic reaction.

(C) Wine is the only beverage to which sulfites are commonly added.

(D) Apart from sulfites, there are no substances commonly present in wine that give rise to an allergic reaction.

(E) Sulfites are not naturally present in the wines produced by these winemakers in amounts large enough to produce an allergic reaction in someone who drinks these wines.

Argument Construction

Situation   People who are allergic to certain sulfites can avoid risking an allergic reaction by drinking wine from one of the several producers that does not add sulfites.

Reasoning   *On what assumption does the argument depend?* Drinking wine to which no sulfites have been *added* will not prevent exposure to sulfites if, for instance, sulfites occur naturally in wines. In particular, if the wines that do not have sulfites added have sulfites present naturally in quantities sufficient to produce an allergic reaction, drinking these wines will not prevent an allergic reaction. The argument therefore depends on assuming that this is not the case.

A   The argument does not require this because the conclusion does not address allergic reactions to substances other than sulfites.

B   The argument specifically refers to "certain sulfites" producing allergic reactions. It is entirely compatible with certain other forms of sulfites not producing allergic reactions in anyone.

C   This is irrelevant. The argument does not claim that one can avoid having an allergic reaction to sulfites *from any source* just by restricting one's wine consumption to those varieties to which no sulfites have been added.

D   Once again, the argument's conclusion does not address allergic reactions to substances other than sulfites in wine.

E   **Correct.** The argument relies on this assumption.

The correct answer is E.

84. Networks of blood vessels in bats' wings serve only to disperse heat generated in flight. This heat is generated only because bats flap their wings. Thus paleontologists' recent discovery that the winged dinosaur Sandactylus had similar networks of blood vessels in the skin of its wings provides evidence for the hypothesis that Sandactylus flew by flapping its wings, not just by gliding.

In the passage, the author develops the argument by

(A) forming the hypothesis that best explains several apparently conflicting pieces of evidence

(B) reinterpreting evidence that had been used to support an earlier theory

(C) using an analogy with a known phenomenon to draw a conclusion about an unknown phenomenon

(D) speculating about how structures observed in present-day creatures might have developed from similar structures in creatures now extinct

(E) pointing out differences in the physiological demands that flight makes on large, as opposed to small, creatures

Argument Evaluation

Situation   The network of blood vessels in bats' wings is compared with a similar structure in the wings of the dinosaur Sandactylus to explain how the dinosaur flew.

Reasoning   *How is this argument developed?* The author first shows that a physical characteristic of bats' wings is directly related to their style of flight. The author then argues that the similar structure found in the wings of Sandactylus is evidence that the dinosaur had a style of flight similar to that of bats. The structure of this argument is a comparison, or analogy, between a known phenomenon (bats) and an unknown one (Sandactylus).

A   The evidence of the blood vessels in the wings does not conflict with other evidence.

B   The evidence of the blood vessels in the wings is used to support only one theory—that Sandactylus flew by flapping its wings as well as by gliding; no evidence is discussed in relation to any earlier theory.

C   **Correct.** This statement properly identifies how the argument compares the wings of bats and of Sandactylus in order to draw a conclusion about how the dinosaur flew.

D   The argument is not about how the structures in the bats developed from the structures in the dinosaurs, but rather about how Sandactylus flew.

E   The comparison between bats and Sandactylus points out similarities, not differences.

The correct answer is C.

85. Keith: Compliance with new government regulations requiring the installation of smoke alarms and sprinkler systems in all theaters and arenas will cost the entertainment industry $25 billion annually. Consequently, jobs will be lost and profits diminished. Therefore, these regulations will harm the country's economy.

Laura: The $25 billion spent by some businesses will be revenue for others. Jobs and profits will be gained as well as lost.

Laura responds to Keith by

(A) demonstrating that Keith's conclusion is based on evidence that is not relevant to the issue at hand
(B) challenging the plausibility of the evidence that serves as the basis for Keith's argument
(C) suggesting that Keith's argument overlooks a mitigating consequence
(D) reinforcing Keith's conclusion by supplying a complementary interpretation of the evidence Keith cites
(E) agreeing with the main conclusion of Keith's argument but construing that conclusion as grounds for optimism rather than for pessimism

Argument Construction

Situation Keith argues that the cost of new regulations will result in a loss of jobs and profits, hurting the national economy. Laura points out that while one industry will suffer, others will gain by supplying the goods and services required by the regulations.

Reasoning *What is the strategy Laura uses in the counterargument?* Laura uses the same evidence, the $25 billion spent on meeting new regulations, but comes to a different conclusion. While Keith focuses on the losses to one industry, Laura looks at the gains to other industries. By suggesting a consequence that Keith did not mention, she places the outcome in a more positive light.

A Laura accepts the relevance of Keith's evidence and uses it herself when she replies that *the $25 billion spent by some businesses will be revenue for others*.

B Laura does not challenge Keith's evidence; she uses the same evidence as the basis of her own argument.

C Correct. This statement properly identifies the strategy Laura employs in her counterargument. Laura points out that Keith did not consider that, in this case, losses for one industry mean gains for others.

D Laura rejects rather than reinforces Keith's conclusion; while he notes the losses in jobs and profits that will harm the economy, she points out that *jobs and profits will be gained as well as lost*.

E Laura does not agree with Keith's main conclusion that the regulations will harm the national economy; she argues instead that gains in other industries will compensate for the losses in one industry.

The correct answer is C.

86. When trying to identify new technologies that promise to transform the marketplace, market researchers survey the managers of those companies that are developing new technologies. Such managers have an enormous stake in succeeding, so they invariably overstate the potential of their new technologies. Surprisingly, however, market researchers typically do not survey a new technology's potential buyers, even though it is the buyers—not the producers—who will ultimately determine a technology's commercial success.

Which of the following, if true, best accounts for the typical survey practices among market researchers?

(A) If a new technology succeeds, the commercial benefits accrue largely to the producers, not to the buyers, of that technology.

(B) People who promote the virtues of a new technology typically fail to consider that the old technology that is currently in use continues to be improved, often substantially.

(C) Investors are unlikely to invest substantial amounts of capital in a company whose own managers are skeptical about the commercial prospects of a new technology they are developing.

(D) The potential buyers for not-yet-available technologies can seldom be reliably identified.

(E) The developers of a new technology are generally no better positioned than its potential buyers to gauge how rapidly the new technology can be efficiently mass-produced.

Argument Construction

Situation   Market researchers seeking to identify new technologies that have the potential to transform the marketplace survey managers of companies developing new technologies, but typically not the potential buyers of new technologies, even though managers tend to overstate the potential of their new technologies and it is the buyers who determine the products' commercial success.

Reasoning   *What best explains why it is managers, not buyers, that the market researchers survey?* Why, despite the information in the passage, are managers of technology companies surveyed while potential buyers are typically not? A partial explanation would be that it is difficult to reliably determine who the potential buyers of new technologies will be. If market researchers cannot identify who the potential buyers of as-yet unavailable technologies will be, that explains why they are not typically surveyed—and why the next best alternative may be to survey managers.

A   This answer choice tells us who would benefit from commercial success of new technologies. But it says nothing about whose opinion would be most valuable in predicting the commercial success of new technologies.

B   At most, this could help explain why managers overstate the potential of their new technologies. But it does not explain the motives of market researchers in relying on the managers' rather than buyers' opinions about new technologies.

C   Given that managers of technology companies will want to attract investors, this helps to explain why the managers would tend to overstate the potential of their new technologies. But it does not help to explain the survey practices.

D   **Correct.** This accounts for why potential buyers of new technologies are not typically sought out in surveys by market researchers: It is difficult to determine in advance who they are.

E   This, like answer choice (C), tends to make the practices of market researchers more difficult rather than easier to understand. If developers of new technologies are no better at gauging how rapidly a new technology can be mass-produced (a factor affecting commercial success), then all the more reason to survey potential buyers rather than the managers.

The correct answer is D.

87. In the United States, of the people who moved from one state to another when they retired, the percentage who retired to Florida has decreased by three percentage points over the past ten years. Since many local businesses in Florida cater to retirees, these declines are likely to have a noticeably negative economic effect on these businesses and therefore on the economy of Florida.

Which of the following, if true, most seriously weakens the argument given?

(A) People who moved from one state to another when they retired moved a greater distance, on average, last year than such people did ten years ago.

(B) People were more likely to retire to North Carolina from another state last year than people were ten years ago.

(C) The number of people who moved from one state to another when they retired has increased significantly over the past ten years.

(D) The number of people who left Florida when they retired to live in another state was greater last year than it was ten years ago.

(E) Florida attracts more people who move from one state to another when they retire than does any other state.

Argument Evaluation

Situation   Of those people who move to another state when they retire, the percentage moving to Florida has declined. This trend is apt to harm Florida's economy because many businesses there cater to retirees.

Reasoning   *Which of the options most weakens the argument?* The argument draws its conclusion from data about the *proportion* of emigrating retirees moving to Florida. Yet what matters more directly to the conclusion (and to Florida's economy) is the *absolute number* of retirees immigrating to Florida. That number could have remained constant or even risen if the absolute number of emigrating retirees itself increased while the proportion going to Florida decreased.

A   This has no obvious bearing on the argument one way or another. It makes it more likely, perhaps, that a person in a distant state will retire to Florida, but less likely that one in a neighboring state will do so.

B   This has no bearing whether fewer people have been retiring to Florida over the last ten years.

C   **Correct.** This is the option that most seriously weakens the argument.

D   This makes it *more* likely that Florida's economy will be harmed because of decreasing numbers of retirees, but has no real bearing on the argument which concludes specifically that *declines in the proportion of emigrating retirees moving to Florida* will have a negative effect on the state's economy.

E   This is irrelevant. At issue is how the numbers of retirees in Florida from one year compare to the next, not how those numbers compare with numbers of retirees in other states.

The correct answer is C.

88. Businesses are suffering because of a lack of money available for development loans. To help businesses, the government plans to modify the income-tax structure in order to induce individual taxpayers to put a larger portion of their incomes into retirement savings accounts, because as more money is deposited in such accounts, more money becomes available to borrowers.

    Which of the following, if true, raises the most serious doubt regarding the effectiveness of the government's plan to increase the amount of money available for development loans for businesses?

    (A) When levels of personal retirement savings increase, consumer borrowing always increases correspondingly.

    (B) The increased tax revenue the government would receive as a result of business expansion would not offset the loss in revenue from personal income taxes during the first year of the plan.

    (C) Even with tax incentives, some people will choose not to increase their levels of retirement savings.

    (D) Bankers generally will not continue to lend money to businesses whose prospective earnings are insufficient to meet their loan repayment schedules.

    (E) The modified tax structure would give all taxpayers, regardless of their incomes, the same tax savings for a given increase in their retirement savings.

Evaluation of a Plan

Situation   Because the lack of available money for development loans is harming businesses, the government plans to modify the income-tax structure, encouraging taxpayers to put more money into retirement accounts. This plan is intended to ensure that with more money put into these accounts, more money will in turn be available to business borrowers.

Reasoning   *What potential flaw in this plan might prevent it from being effective?* What is the expectation behind the plan? The government's plan supposes that the money invested in retirement accounts will be available to business borrowers in the form of development loans. Consider what circumstances might hinder that availability. What if consumer borrowers compete with businesses? If it is known that, historically, increased savings in personal retirement accounts corresponds with increased consumer borrowing, then the government's effort to target businesses as the beneficiaries of this plan could well fail.

A   **Correct.** This statement properly identifies a reason that the government's plan could be less effective in meeting its goal.

B   A predicted revenue shortfall does not directly affect the plan's effectiveness in reaching its stated goal, and might be deemed an acceptable cost of achieving that goal.

C   As long as the total amount deposited in personal retirement accounts increases sufficiently, the decision of *some people* not to increase their contributions will not keep the plan from achieving its goal.

D   The plan would increase the money available specifically for development loans, not existing loans.

E   The universal tax savings does not affect the effectiveness of the plan.

The correct answer is A.

89. Since it has become known that **several of a bank's top executives have been buying shares in their own bank**, the bank's depositors, who had been worried by rumors that the bank faced impending financial collapse, have been greatly relieved. They reason that, since top executives evidently have faith in the bank's financial soundness, those worrisome rumors must be false. Such reasoning might well be overoptimistic, however, since **corporate executives have been known to buy shares in their own company in a calculated attempt to dispel negative rumors about the company's health**.

In the argument given, the two boldfaced portions play which of the following roles?

(A) The first describes evidence that has been taken as supporting a conclusion; the second gives a reason for questioning that support.

(B) The first describes evidence that has been taken as supporting a conclusion; the second states a contrary conclusion that is the main conclusion of the argument.

(C) The first provides evidence in support of the main conclusion of the argument; the second states that conclusion.

(D) The first describes the circumstance that the argument as a whole seeks to explain; the second gives the explanation that the argument seeks to establish.

(E) The first describes the circumstance that the argument as a whole seeks to explain; the second provides evidence in support of the explanation that the argument seeks to establish.

Argument Evaluation

Situation   Top executives at a bank that has been rumored to be in financial trouble have been buying shares in the bank. Bank depositors see this as a good sign, because they believe that it indicates that the executives have faith in the bank. However, corporate executives sometimes do this just to dispel rumors about a company's health.

Reasoning   *What is the role that the two boldfaced portions play in the argument?* The first boldfaced portion states that bank executives are buying bank shares, which the passage indicates is taken by bank depositors to be evidence of the executives' faith in the bank. The passage then tells us what some have inferred from this, and finally offers in the second boldfaced statement evidence that undermines this inference.

A   **Correct.** This option correctly identifies the roles played by the boldfaced portions.

B   This correctly describes the first statement's role, but the second statement is not offered as a conclusion—no evidence is given for it; rather it is evidence for something else.

C   Again, the second statement is not offered as a conclusion; no evidence is given for it.

D   The second statement is not itself offered as an explanation of why these bank executives are investing in the bank; if it were, that would mean that the bank executives are doing so *because* corporate executives are known to do such things in a calculated effort to dispel worries. Furthermore the argument does not conclude that this other explanation (which the boldfaced portion points to) is correct, only that the one inferred by depositors may not be.

E   Again, the argument is not so much seeking to establish an explanation of its own as it is trying to undermine that inferred by the depositors.

The correct answer is A.

90. A new law gives ownership of patents—documents providing exclusive right to make and sell an invention—to universities, not the government, when those patents result from government-sponsored university research. Administrators at Logos University plan to sell any patents they acquire to corporations in order to fund programs to improve undergraduate teaching.

    Which of the following, if true, would cast the most doubt on the viability of the college administrators' plan described above?

    (A) Profit-making corporations interested in developing products based on patents held by universities are likely to try to serve as exclusive sponsors of ongoing university research projects.

    (B) Corporate sponsors of research in university facilities are entitled to tax credits under new federal tax-code guidelines.

    (C) Research scientists at Logos University have few or no teaching responsibilities and participate little if at all in the undergraduate programs in their field.

    (D) Government-sponsored research conducted at Logos University for the most part duplicates research already completed by several profit-making corporations.

    (E) Logos University is unlikely to attract corporate sponsorship of its scientific research.

Evaluation of a Plan

Situation   Universities own the patents resulting from government-sponsored research at their institutions. One university plans to sell its patents to corporations to fund a program to improve teaching.

Reasoning   *Which point casts doubt on the university's plan?* The university's plan assumes there will be a market for its patents, and that the corporations will want to buy them. What might make this untrue? If some of the corporations have already done the same or similar research, they will not be prospective buyers of the university's patents.

A   This point is irrelevant to the plan to sell patents in order to fund a program.

B   The university plans to sell the patents to the corporations, not to invite the corporations to sponsor research.

C   This point is irrelevant to the university's plan to sell off patents since the plan does not specify that the research scientists will be involved in the programs to improve undergraduate teaching.

D   Correct. This statement properly identifies a factor that casts doubt on the university's plan to sell its patents to corporations.

E   The plan concerns selling patents resulting from government-sponsored research, not attracting corporate sponsorship for research.

The correct answer is D.

91. Environmentalist: The commissioner of the Fish and Game Authority would have the public believe that increases in the number of marine fish caught demonstrate that this resource is no longer endangered. This is a specious argument, as unsound as it would be to assert that the ever-increasing rate at which rain forests are being cut down demonstrates a lack of danger to that resource. The real cause of the increased fish-catch is a greater efficiency in using technologies that deplete resources.

The environmentalist's statements, if true, best support which of the following as a conclusion?

(A) The use of technology is the reason for the increasing encroachment of people on nature.

(B) It is possible to determine how many fish are in the sea in some way other than by catching fish.

(C) The proportion of marine fish that are caught is as high as the proportion of rain forest trees that are cut down each year.

(D) Modern technologies waste resources by catching inedible fish.

(E) Marine fish continue to be an endangered resource.

Argument Construction

Situation   A public official argues that increased catches show that marine fish are no longer endangered. An environmentalist attacks the position and cites technology as the cause of the increased catch.

Reasoning   *What conclusion do the environmentalist's statements support?* The environmentalist casts doubt by saying the commissioner *would have the public believe* that the increased catch shows that the fish are no longer endangered; the phrasing indicates that the environmentalist believes just the reverse. The environmentalist does believe the marine fish are endangered, and, after attacking the commissioner's argument as *specious*, or false, and offering an analogy to make that argument look ridiculous, the environmentalist gives an alternate explanation for the increased catch that is consistent with that belief.

A   Although the environmentalist claims that technology causes people's greater encroachment on nature in this single instance, there is nothing in the argument to suggest that such encroachment caused by technology is a general trend.

B   The environmentalist's claims imply that the number of fish caught is not a reliable indicator of how many are left in the ocean but do not give any indication that it is possible to find out by any other means, either.

C   The environmentalist creates an analogy between fish caught and rain forest trees cut down but does not compare their proportion.

D   Nothing about how the fish can be used, including whether they are edible or inedible, plays any role in the environmentalist's argument.

E   **Correct.** This statement properly identifies a conclusion supported by the environmentalist's statements: The marine fish are endangered.

The correct answer is E.

92. In the country of Veltria, the past two years' broad economic recession has included a business downturn in the clothing trade, where sales are down by about 7 percent as compared to two years ago. Clothing wholesalers have found, however, that the proportion of credit extended to retailers that was paid off on time fell sharply in the first year of the recession but returned to its prerecession level in the second year.

Which of the following, if true, most helps to explain the change between the first and the second year of the recession in the proportion of credit not paid off on time?

(A) The total amount of credit extended to retailers by clothing wholesalers increased between the first year of the recession and the second year.

(B) Between the first and second years of the recession, clothing retailers in Veltria saw many of their costs, rent and utilities in particular, increase.

(C) Of the considerable number of clothing retailers in Veltria who were having financial difficulties before the start of the recession, virtually all were forced to go out of business during its first year.

(D) Clothing retailers in Veltria attempted to stimulate sales in the second year of the recession by discounting merchandise.

(E) Relatively recession-proof segments of the clothing trade, such as work clothes, did not suffer any decrease in sales during the first year of the recession.

Argument Evaluation

Situation   Two years of recession in Veltria included a downturn in the clothing trade where sales are down 7 percent from two years ago. Yet, in the second year of the recession, the proportion of credit extended from clothing wholesalers to retailers that was paid off on time has returned to its prerecession level, after having fallen sharply during the first year.

Reasoning   *Which option would most help to explain the change between the first and second year in the proportion of credit paid off on time?* The apparent discrepancy in the passage that needs explaining is between the downturn in the clothing trade over the last two years and the return to prerecession rates in the proportion of credit extended to clothing retailers that was paid on time. How can the proportion this past year be similar to what it would be in a normal year? After all, one would expect retailers to have a harder time paying off credit in a recession. And what changed in the past year to bring this about? If the first year of the recession drove out of business many of the retailers who were most apt to get behind in their payments to wholesalers, then that would explain how the rate at which credit was being paid on time could be as high in the second year of the recession as it was before the recession.

A   The fact that the absolute amount of credit that was extended to retailers went up in the second year does not help to explain why the *proportion that was paid on time* also went up.

B   If anything, this would suggest that more retailers would have trouble paying their credit to wholesalers on time.

C   **Correct.** This is the option that most helps to explain the phenomenon.

D   Just because retailers *tried* to stimulate sales does not mean that they succeeded, and the passage tells us that the downturn in sales in the clothing trade continued into the second year.

E   This does not change the fact that there was a downturn in sales of clothing during the first year. Furthermore, the question is why the rate of unpaid credit dropped in the *second* year of the recession.

The correct answer is C.

93. Commentator: The theory of trade retaliation states that countries closed out of any of another country's markets should close some of their own markets to the other country in order to pressure the other country to reopen its markets. If every country acted according to this theory, no country would trade with any other.

    The commentator's argument relies on which of the following assumptions?

    (A) No country actually acts according to the theory of trade retaliation.

    (B) No country should block any of its markets to foreign trade.

    (C) Trade disputes should be settled by international tribunal.

    (D) For any two countries, at least one has some market closed to the other.

    (E) Countries close their markets to foreigners to protect domestic producers.

Argument Construction

Situation   The theory of trade retaliation is explained as the action and reaction of closing markets between trading nations; no country would ever trade with another, the observation is offered, if every country acted according to the theory.

Reasoning   *What assumption underlies this argument?* What makes the commentator conclude that no country would be trading if the theory were operative? The commentator must perceive of some condition as a given here. The argument assumes an initial action, a country's closing of a market to a trading partner, that is followed by a reaction, the retaliatory closing of a market by that partner. In this unending pattern of action-reaction, at least one of the two countries must have a market closed to the other.

A   The argument does not assume that no country acts according to the theory, just that not all countries do so.

B   The commentator's argument is about what the theory of trade retaliation predicts, not about what trade policies countries ought to follow, and a statement about the latter is not an assumption for the former.

C   This alternative scenario—trade disputes settled by international tribunal rather than by trade retaliation—plays no role in the argument.

D   Correct. This statement properly identifies the assumption required to create the never-ending action-reaction pattern.

E   The argument does not pertain to countries' initial reasons for closing their markets to foreign trade, only to the consequences of doing so.

The correct answer is D.

94. As a construction material, bamboo is as strong as steel and sturdier than concrete. Moreover, in tropical areas bamboo is a much less expensive construction material than either steel or concrete and is always readily available. In tropical areas, therefore, building with bamboo makes better economic sense than building with steel or concrete, except where land values are high.

Which of the following, if true, most helps to explain the exception noted above?

(A) Buildings constructed of bamboo are less likely to suffer earthquake damage than are steel and concrete buildings.

(B) Bamboo is unsuitable as a building material for multistory buildings.

(C) In order to protect it from being damaged by termites and beetles, bamboo must be soaked, at some expense, in a preservative.

(D) In some tropical areas, bamboo is used to make the scaffolding that is used during large construction projects.

(E) Bamboo growing in an area where land values are increasing is often cleared to make way for construction.

Argument Construction

Situation Bamboo is as strong as steel and sturdier than concrete when used as a construction material. In tropical areas, bamboo is much less expensive and is always readily available.

Reasoning *What explains the exception specified in the conclusion?* The argument's conclusion is that in tropical areas bamboo is a more economical building material than steel or concrete, *except where land values are high.* The information in the passage makes clear why bamboo is a more economical building material in tropical areas than are concrete or steel. So the question is: Why must an exception be made for areas where land values are high? Multistory buildings are particularly desirable in areas where land values are high, but bamboo may not be suitable for such buildings.

A This explains why bamboo would be preferable to steel or concrete in tropical areas especially prone to earthquakes. However, there is no clear connection to be made between areas where land values are high and areas especially prone to earthquakes.

B Correct. Multistory buildings provide a greater area of floor space for a given site area, and in that sense are more economical. A single-story building with the same floor space will occupy a much bigger site, so the higher the land values, the more likely it is that a multistory building will be built on that land. Thus, given this information, bamboo is less suitable for areas where land values are high.

C This undermines, to some extent, the claim that bamboo is an economical building material. But it does nothing to explain why it would be less economical specifically in areas where land values are high.

D This is irrelevant. Bamboo is used to build scaffolding for construction projects and as a building material for permanent structures. There is no way to infer from this that bamboo is less economical specifically in areas where land values are high.

E The fact that bamboo is cleared from an area to make room for construction in no way implies that bamboo would not be a suitable and economical building material for the area once it has been cleared.

The correct answer is B.

95. Studies in restaurants show that the tips left by customers who pay their bill in cash tend to be larger when the bill is presented on a tray that bears a credit-card logo. Consumer psychologists hypothesize that simply seeing a credit-card logo makes many credit-card holders willing to spend more because it reminds them that their spending power exceeds the cash they have immediately available.

Which of the following, if true, most strongly supports the psychologists' interpretation of the studies?

(A) The effect noted in the studies is not limited to patrons who have credit cards.

(B) Patrons who are under financial pressure from their credit-card obligations tend to tip less when presented with a restaurant bill on a tray with a credit-card logo than when the tray has no logo.

(C) In virtually all of the cases in the studies, the patrons who paid bills in cash did not possess credit cards.

(D) In general, restaurant patrons who pay their bills in cash leave larger tips than do those who pay by credit card.

(E) The percentage of restaurant bills paid with a given brand of credit card increases when that credit card's logo is displayed on the tray with which the bill is presented.

Argument Evaluation

Situation Studies have found that restaurant customers give more generous tips when their bills are brought on trays bearing a credit-card logo. Psychologists speculate that this is because the logo reminds customers of their ability to spend more money than they have.

Reasoning *Which of the options most helps to support the psychologists' explanation of the studies?* The psychologists' hypothesis is that the credit-card logos on the trays bring to the minds of those who tip more the fact that they have more purchasing power than merely the cash that they have at hand. This explanation would not be valid even if those people who are *not* reminded of their own excess purchasing power—if in fact they have any such power—when they see such a logo nonetheless tip more in such trays. Thus, if restaurant patrons who are under financial pressure from their credit-card obligations do not tip more when their bills are presented on trays bearing credit-card logos, then the psychologists' interpretation of the studies is supported.

A This undermines the psychologists' interpretation, for it shows that the same phenomenon occurs even when the alleged cause has been removed.

B **Correct.** This option identifies the result that would most strengthen the psychologists' interpretation.

C This undermines the psychologists' interpretation by showing that the same phenomenon occurs even when the alleged cause has been removed; patrons cannot be reminded of something that is not there.

D To the extent that this bears on the interpretation of the study, it weakens it. Patrons *using* credit cards are surely aware that they have credit, and yet they spend *less* generously.

E This does not support the idea that being reminded that one has a credit card induces one to be *more generous*, only that it induces one to *use* that credit card.

The correct answer is B.

96. Although parapsychology is often considered a pseudoscience, it is in fact a genuine scientific enterprise, for it uses scientific methods such as controlled experiments and statistical tests of clearly stated hypotheses to examine the questions it raises.

The conclusion above is properly drawn if which of the following is assumed?

(A) If a field of study can conclusively answer the questions it raises, then it is a genuine science.

(B) Since parapsychology uses scientific methods, it will produce credible results.

(C) Any enterprise that does not use controlled experiments and statistical tests is not genuine science.

(D) Any field of study that employs scientific methods is a genuine scientific enterprise.

(E) Since parapsychology raises clearly statable questions, they can be tested in controlled experiments.

Argument Construction

Situation   The argument states that parapsychology is a genuine science because it uses scientific methods.

Reasoning   *What assumption does the argument make?* The argument asserts that parapsychology is a science, *for it uses scientific methods*. The argument thus assumes that the use of scientific methods proves that a field of study is a genuine science.

A   The argument is based on an assumption about how the questions are investigated rather than on how well they are answered.

B   The argument is not about whether the results are credible, so this assumption is irrelevant.

C   The argument does not concern what is *not* genuine science, so there is no need for this assumption.

D   **Correct.** This statement properly identifies the argument's assumption that the use of scientific method is sufficient to make an enterprise genuine science.

E   This assumption does not make the connection required by the argument between the use of scientific methods and a field of study's status as genuine science.

The correct answer is D.

97. Hotco oil burners, designed to be used in asphalt plants, are so efficient that Hotco will sell one to the Clifton Asphalt plant for no payment other than the cost savings between the total amount the asphalt plant actually paid for oil using its former burner during the last two years and the total amount it will pay for oil using the Hotco burner during the next two years. On installation, the plant will make an estimated payment, which will be adjusted after two years to equal the actual cost savings.

    Which of the following, if it occurred, would constitute a disadvantage for Hotco of the plan described above?

    (A) Another manufacturer's introduction to the market of a similarly efficient burner

    (B) The Clifton Asphalt plant's need for more than one new burner

    (C) Very poor efficiency in the Clifton Asphalt plant's old burner

    (D) A decrease in the demand for asphalt

    (E) A steady increase in the price of oil beginning soon after the new burner is installed

Evaluation of a Plan

Situation Hotco produces a very efficient oil burner. It sells a burner to an asphalt plant, stating that the price of the burner is how much money the plant saves on oil using the new burner.

Reasoning *Hotco will be at a disadvantage if which of the following occurs?* Hotco is to be paid based on how much money the plant saves on oil over a two-year period. There is an assumption that a number of factors will remain relatively stable from the previous two years to the next two years. What is a factor that could cause a disadvantage for Hotco? If the price of oil goes up, then the plant will experience smaller savings than Hotco anticipated, despite the plant's using less oil than previously because of its new, more efficient burners. If the plant's savings go down, Hotco will not get the payment it is expecting.

A The burner is already installed, so a competitor is not a problem.

B The plant's need for multiple burners should be an opportunity for Hotco, not a disadvantage.

C If the old burner was very inefficient, the new burner should save a great deal of money that would ultimately go to Hotco.

D If demand decreases, less oil would need to be purchased, and Hotco would get more money.

E **Correct.** This statement properly identifies a factor that would constitute a disadvantage for the plan: since the payment for the burner is based on savings in oil purchases, any increases in the price of oil will decrease savings and thus decrease payments to Hotco.

The correct answer is E.

98. **Delta Products Inc. has recently switched at least partly from older technologies using fossil fuels to new technologies powered by electricity.** The question has been raised whether it can be concluded that **for a given level of output Delta's operation now causes less fossil fuel to be consumed than it did formerly.** The answer, clearly, is yes, since the amount of fossil fuel used to generate the electricity needed to power the new technologies is less than the amount needed to power the older technologies, provided level of output is held constant.

In the argument given, the two boldfaced portions play which of the following roles?

(A) The first identifies the content of the conclusion of the argument; the second provides support for that conclusion.

(B) The first provides support for the conclusion of the argument; the second identifies the content of that conclusion.

(C) The first states the conclusion of the argument; the second calls that conclusion into question.

(D) The first provides support for the conclusion of the argument; the second calls that conclusion into question.

(E) Each provides support for the conclusion of the argument.

Argument Evaluation

Situation   Delta switched from technologies using fossil fuels to ones using electricity. It has been asked whether this results in less fossil fuel used per level of output. The answer is that it does.

Reasoning   *What roles do the two boldfaced portions play in the argument?* The first boldfaced statement is simply asserted by the passage. But the second boldfaced statement, when it is first introduced, is not asserted to be true, but rather is identified as something that might be inferred from the first statement. By the end of the passage the argument concludes that the second statement is true.

A   This option simply reverses the roles that the statements play in the argument.

B   **Correct.** This option identifies the roles the boldfaced portions play.

C   Nothing in the passage is intended to support the first statement; and the second statement is not supposed to call the first into question.

D   This correctly identifies the role of the first statement, but the second boldfaced portion does not call the argument's conclusion into question—it is part of a sentence that refers to the question whether that conclusion can be drawn from the first statement.

E   Again, this is only half right. The second boldfaced portion is not offered as support for the conclusion; if it were offered as such support, the argument would be guilty of circular reasoning, since the second boldfaced portion states exactly what the argument concludes.

The correct answer is B.

99. An experiment was done in which human subjects recognize a pattern within a matrix of abstract designs and then select another design that completes that pattern. The results of the experiment were surprising. The lowest expenditure of energy in neurons in the brain was found in those subjects who performed most successfully in the experiments.

Which of the following hypotheses best accounts for the findings of the experiment?

(A) The neurons of the brain react less when a subject is trying to recognize patterns than when the subject is doing other kinds of reasoning.

(B) Those who performed best in the experiment experienced more satisfaction when working with abstract patterns than did those who performed less well.

(C) People who are better at abstract pattern recognition have more energy-efficient neural connections.

(D) The energy expenditure of the subjects' brains increases when a design that completes the initially recognized pattern is determined.

(E) The task of completing a given design is more capably performed by athletes, whose energy expenditure is lower when they are at rest.

Argument Construction

Situation   Experimental subjects worked with pattern recognition and completion. The subjects who performed best showed the lowest expenditure of energy in neurons in the brain.

Reasoning   *Which hypothesis best accounts for the findings?* In order to account for the findings, the hypothesis must suggest a plausible link between successful performance and the energy expenditure of neurons in the brain. Consider each answer choice, and evaluate its plausibility and logic. Where is there a reasonably direct relationship between the given factors and the conclusion that is drawn? Understand that hypotheses based on factors not included in the experiment cannot be used to account for the findings.

A   The experiment did not compare types of reasoning so this hypothesis does not account for the results.

B   No information is provided about subjects' satisfaction, so this hypothesis is not warranted.

C   **Correct.** This statement properly identifies a hypothesis that connects subjects' performance with their energy expenditure and so could account for the experiment's results.

D   The most successful subjects would presumably not have completed fewer patterns than average, so the posited increase in energy would likely lead to higher energy expenditures for them, not lower.

E   No information is offered on the subjects, so no hypothesis about athletes is warranted.

The correct answer is C.

100. Debater: The average amount of overtime per month worked by an employee in the manufacturing division of the Haglut Corporation is 14 hours. Most employees of the Haglut Corporation work in the manufacturing division. Furthermore, the average amount of overtime per month worked by any employee in the company generally does not fluctuate much from month to month. Therefore, each month, most employees of the Haglut Corporation almost certainly work at least some overtime.

The debater's argument is most vulnerable to criticism on which of these grounds?

(A) It takes for granted that the manufacturing division is a typical division of the corporation with regard to the average amount of overtime its employees work each month.

(B) It takes for granted that if a certain average amount of overtime is worked each month by each employee of the Haglut Corporation, then approximately the same amount of overtime must be worked each month by each employee of the manufacturing division.

(C) It confuses a claim from which the argument's conclusion about the Haglut Corporation would necessarily follow with a claim that would follow from the argument's conclusion only with a high degree of probability.

(D) It overlooks the possibility that even if, on average, a certain amount of overtime is worked by the members of some group, many members of that group may work no overtime at all.

(E) It overlooks the possibility that even if most employees of the corporation work some overtime each month, any one corporate employee may, in some months, work no overtime.

Argument Evaluation

Situation Most of the employees of the Haglut Corporation work in the manufacturing division, where employees average 14 hours per month in overtime. The average amount of overtime per month for employees at Haglut does not fluctuate much from month to month.

Reasoning *What is the argument's greatest weakness?* The argument's conclusion is that *almost certainly* each month most of the employees of Haglut work at least some overtime. Answer choice (D) identifies the argument's greatest weakness because it points out how the conclusion of the argument could be false even if all of the supporting information were true. For example, it could be that less than half of the employees work any overtime at all, but those that do work overtime work much more than 14 hours per month.

A The argument leaves open the possibility that in some divisions of the corporation, the average monthly overtime of its employees is quite different from 14 hours, even if (as the argument states) that average does not change much from month to month.

B The argument does not assume that there is a monthly amount of overtime worked by each employee of the manufacturing division equivalent to the company-wide average monthly overtime per employee.

C This does not identify a weakness that can be detected in the argument. Since the claims mentioned here are not specified, the passage provides no evidence that clearly indicates that this type of confusion is playing a role in the argument.

D Correct. The argument ignores the possibility that most of the employees of Haglut work no overtime at all in a particular month—which is quite consistent with the argument's assertion that the average number of monthly overtime hours per employee within the manufacturing division is 14.

E The possibility described by this is not overlooked by the argument, because this possibility is consistent with the conclusion. It could easily be that most employees of the corporation work some overtime each month—as the conclusion envisions—but that there are always some employees who do not work any overtime.

The correct answer is D.

101. Which of the following most logically completes the argument?

The irradiation of food kills bacteria and thus retards spoilage. However, it also lowers the nutritional value of many foods. For example, irradiation destroys a significant percentage of whatever vitamin B1 a food may contain. Proponents of irradiation point out that irradiation is no worse in this respect than cooking. However, this fact is either beside the point, since much irradiated food is eaten raw, or else misleading, since _____.

(A) many of the proponents of irradiation are food distributors who gain from foods' having a longer shelf life

(B) it is clear that killing bacteria that may be present on food is not the only effect that irradiation has

(C) cooking is usually the final step in preparing food for consumption, whereas irradiation serves to ensure a longer shelf life for perishable foods

(D) certain kinds of cooking are, in fact, even more destructive of vitamin B1 than carefully controlled irradiation is

(E) for food that is both irradiated and cooked, the reduction of vitamin B1 associated with either process individually is compounded

Argument Construction

Situation Irradiation kills bacteria but it also lowers the amount of nutrients—including vitamin B1—in foods. Proponents try to dismiss this concern by arguing that cooking destroys B1 as well. That point is said to be misleading.

Reasoning *Which option most logically completes the argument?* For the proponents' claim to be misleading it needs to be suggesting something about irradiation that is false. By stating that irradiation destroys no more B1 than cooking does, the proponent seems to be suggesting that any food that is going to be cooked might as well be irradiated because it will end up with the same amount of B1 either way. But if the effects of radiation and cooking combine to destroy more B1 than cooking or irradiation alone would, then the proponents' claim suggests something that is false.

A This might make the assurances of the proponents less credible but it does not make their claim misleading.

B Nothing about the proponents' claim suggests that the only effect irradiation has is to kill bacteria.

C The fact that cooking and irradiation have different purposes does not indicate that the proponents' claim suggests something that is false.

D If anything, this strengthens the proponents' point by minimizing the relative damage caused by irradiation.

E **Correct.** This option most logically completes the argument.

The correct answer is E.

102. One way to judge the performance of a company is to compare it with other companies. This technique, commonly called "benchmarking," permits the manager of a company to discover better industrial practices and can provide a justification for the adoption of good practices.

     Any of the following, if true, is a valid reason for benchmarking the performance of a company against companies with which it is not in competition rather than against competitors EXCEPT:

     (A) Comparisons with competitors are most likely to focus on practices that the manager making the comparisons already employs.

     (B) Getting "inside" information about the unique practices of competitors is particularly difficult.

     (C) Since companies that compete with each other are likely to have comparable levels of efficiency, only benchmarking against noncompetitors is likely to reveal practices that would aid in beating competitors.

     (D) Managers are generally more receptive to new ideas that they find outside their own industry.

     (E) Much of the success of good companies is due to their adoption of practices that take advantage of the special circumstances of their products or markets.

Argument Construction

Situation "Benchmarking" is a technique for judging the performance of a company by comparing it with other companies. The goal is to find and adopt better industrial practices.

Reasoning *Which one condition does NOT recommend benchmarking against noncompetitors? Which one condition IS a well-founded reason to benchmark against competitors?* First, sort through the given information and the answer choices for the question to gain an understanding of the potential advantages or disadvantages of comparing a company to its competitors or to noncompetitors. What are the reasons in favor of benchmarking against noncompetitors? Information about noncompeting companies is easier to obtain; it can offer new insights; and it may be easier to put into practice. Why then might a manager choose to benchmark against competitors? Competing companies do share special circumstances involving products and markets. If companies are often successful because of practices related to these special circumstances within their industry, then benchmarking against competitors will reveal these practices and so be more fruitful than benchmarking against noncompetitors.

A Since benchmarking against competitors would yield few new practices, it would be better to benchmark against noncompetitors.

B If information about competitors is hard to obtain, benchmarking against noncompetitors is preferable.

C Since benchmarking against noncompetitors would yield practices useful in beating competitors, benchmarking against noncompetitors is preferable.

D If managers are more likely to adopt new practices learned from benchmarking against noncompetitors, then this technique is preferable.

E **Correct.** This statement properly identifies the rationale that supports a company's benchmarking against its competitors.

The correct answer is E.

103. For a trade embargo against a particular country to succeed, a high degree of both international accord and ability to prevent goods from entering or leaving that country must be sustained. A total blockade of Patria's ports is necessary to an embargo, but such an action would be likely to cause international discord over the embargo.

The claims above, if true, most strongly support which of the following conclusions?

(A) The balance of opinion is likely to favor Patria in the event of a blockade.

(B) As long as international opinion is unanimously against Patria, a trade embargo is likely to succeed.

(C) A naval blockade of Patria's ports would ensure that no goods enter or leave Patria.

(D) Any trade embargo against Patria would be likely to fail at some time.

(E) For a blockade of Patria's ports to be successful, international opinion must be unanimous.

Argument Construction

Situation   The success of a trade embargo requires both international accord and the ability to enforce the embargo. In the case of Patria, an embargo would require a total blockade of the ports, but the blockade itself would likely lead to international discord.

Reasoning   *What conclusion can be drawn from this information?* A conclusion must be based only on the information provided. Since the given information discusses the general conditions for a successful trade embargo and the conditions specific to the possible embargo in Patria, the conclusion should be about the likelihood of success for a trade embargo against Patria. Since international accord is necessary for the success of an embargo but the blockade required in this case would create international discord, the contradictions of this paradoxical situation make any embargo unlikely to succeed.

A   Although international discord would likely result from a blockade, no information allows a conclusion to be drawn about the balance of opinion.

B   This conclusion is not justified because a successful embargo requires both international accord and the ability to enforce the embargo.

C   This statement simply defines the purpose of a blockade; it is not a conclusion from the information given.

D   **Correct.** This statement properly identifies a conclusion supported by the claims.

E   The necessary condition for success is *a high degree of international accord*, not unanimity, so this conclusion cannot be justified.

The correct answer is D.

104. Theater Critic: The play *La Finestrina*, now at Central Theater, was written in Italy in the eighteenth century. The director claims that this production is as similar to the original production as is possible in a modern theater. Although the actor who plays Harlequin the clown gives a performance very reminiscent of the twentieth-century American comedian Groucho Marx, Marx's comic style was very much within the comic acting tradition that had begun in sixteenth-century Italy.

The considerations given best serve as part of an argument that

(A) modern audiences would find it hard to tolerate certain characteristics of a historically accurate performance of an eighteenth-century play

(B) Groucho Marx once performed the part of the character Harlequin in *La Finestrina*

(C) in the United States the training of actors in the twentieth century is based on principles that do not differ radically from those that underlay the training of actors in eighteenth-century Italy

(D) the performance of the actor who plays Harlequin in *La Finestrina* does not serve as evidence against the director's claim

(E) the director of *La Finestrina* must have advised the actor who plays Harlequin to model his performance on comic performances of Groucho Marx

Argument Construction

Situation   The director of the local production of *La Finestrina* says it is as similar to the original production as is possible in a modern theater. The actor playing Harlequin gives a performance reminiscent of Groucho Marx, whose comic style falls within an acting tradition which began in sixteenth-century Italy.

Reasoning   *For which of the options would the consideration given best serve as an argument?* The actor's performance was reminiscent of someone who fell within a tradition going back to sixteenth-century Italy. The play was written, and therefore was likely first performed, in eighteenth-century Italy. All of this suggests that there could be a similarity between the performances of Harlequin in the local production and in the original production. While the two performances *might* have been quite dissimilar, there is nothing *here* that supports that.

A   Regardless of how plausible this option might be on its own merits, the passage provides no support for it because the passage provides no information about the characteristics of a historically accurate performance of an eighteenth-century play.

B   The passage neither says this nor implies it.

C   The passage says nothing about the training of actors, so this option would be supported by the passage only in a very roundabout, indirect way.

D   Correct. This is the option that the considerations most support.

E   That the performance reminded the theater critic of Groucho Marx hardly shows that the similarity was intentional, let alone that it was at the director's instruction.

The correct answer is D.

105. The cost of producing radios in Country Q is 10 percent less than the cost of producing radios in Country Y. Even after transportation fees and tariff charges are added, it is still cheaper for a company to import radios from Country Q to Country Y than to produce radios in Country Y.

The statements above, if true, best support which of the following assertions?

(A) Labor costs in Country Q are 10 percent below those in Country Y.

(B) Importing radios from Country Q to Country Y will eliminate 10 percent of the manufacturing jobs in Country Y.

(C) The tariff on a radio imported from Country Q to Country Y is less than 10 percent of the cost of manufacturing the radio in Country Y.

(D) The fee for transporting a radio from Country Q to Country Y is more than 10 percent of the cost of manufacturing the radio in Country Q.

(E) It takes 10 percent less time to manufacture a radio in Country Q than it does in Country Y.

Argument Construction

Situation   One country's manufacturing costs for a product are 10 percent higher than another country's. Even with tariffs and transportation costs, importing is a less expensive option than local production.

Reasoning   *What conclusion can be drawn from this information?* Because production costs are 10 percent higher in Country Y than in Country Q, importing radios is less expensive only if the combined costs of tariffs and transportation are less than 10 percent of the manufacturing costs.

A   Lower labor costs may explain the lower production costs in Country Q, but there may be a variety of other reasons as well.

B   It is possible that manufacturing jobs would be decreased, but no evidence in the passage leads to that conclusion.

C   **Correct.** This statement properly identifies the point that, for importing to be less expensive, tariffs and transportation costs together must be less than 10 percent of manufacturing costs. Therefore, tariffs alone must be less than 10 percent

D   If transportation costs were more than 10 percent, importing would be more expensive, not less.

E   Less production time may explain the lower costs in Country Q, but there may be a variety of other reasons as well.

The correct answer is C.

106. Exposure to certain chemicals commonly used in elementary schools as cleaners or pesticides causes allergic reactions in some children. Elementary school nurses in Renston report that the proportion of schoolchildren sent to them for treatment of allergic reactions to those chemicals has increased significantly over the past ten years. Therefore, either Renston's schoolchildren have been exposed to greater quantities of the chemicals, or they are more sensitive to them than schoolchildren were ten years ago.

Which of the following is an assumption on which the argument depends?

(A) The number of school nurses employed by Renston's elementary schools has not decreased over the past ten years.

(B) Children who are allergic to the chemicals are no more likely than other children to have allergies to other substances.

(C) Children who have allergic reactions to the chemicals are not more likely to be sent to a school nurse now than they were ten years ago.

(D) The chemicals are not commonly used as cleaners or pesticides in houses and apartment buildings in Renston.

(E) Children attending elementary school do not make up a larger proportion of Renston's population now than they did ten years ago.

Argument Construction

Situation   Some children have allergic reactions to some of the chemicals commonly used in elementary schools as cleaners and pesticides. The number of children sent to elementary school nurses in Renston for allergic reactions to such chemicals has risen significantly over the past ten years.

Reasoning   *What must the argument assume?* The argument's conclusion presents just two alternatives: either the children are exposed to more of the chemicals than children in earlier years, *or* they are more sensitive. But there is a third possible explanation for the significant increase in school-nurse visits that the school nurses have reported: that children are just more inclined to go to the school nurse when they experience an allergic reaction than were children several years ago. For the conclusion to follow from its premises, the argument must assume that this is not the correct explanation.

A   If the number of elementary school nurses in Renston elementary schools had decreased over the past ten years, that would in no way explain the rise in the proportion of children reporting to school nurses for allergic reactions.

B   Only school-nurse visits for allergic reactions to the cleaners and pesticides used in elementary schools are in question in the argument. Of course there could be school-nurse visits for allergic reactions to other things, but that issue does not arise in the argument.

C   **Correct.** This can be seen by considering whether the argument would work if we assume that this were false, i.e., that a school-nurse visit *is* more likely in such cases. As noted above, this provides an alternative to the two explanations that the conclusion claims are the sole possibilities.

D   This does not need to be assumed by the argument. The argument's conclusion suggests that children may in recent years have had greater exposure to the chemicals, not that this exposure has occurred exclusively in the schools. The argument does not rely on this latter assumption.

E   The argument does not need to make this assumption. The argument is framed in terms of proportions of children having school-nurse visits for certain allergic reactions. *How many* children there are or what proportion such children are of Renston's total population is not directly relevant to the argument.

The correct answer is C.

107. Although the discount stores in Goreville's central shopping district are expected to close within five years as a result of competition from a SpendLess discount department store that just opened, those locations will not stay vacant for long. In the five years since the opening of Colson's, a nondiscount department store, a new store has opened at the location of every store in the shopping district that closed because it could not compete with Colson's.

Which of the following, if true, most seriously weakens the argument?

(A) Many customers of Colson's are expected to do less shopping there than they did before the SpendLess store opened.

(B) Increasingly, the stores that have opened in the central shopping district since Colson's opened have been discount stores.

(C) At present, the central shopping district has as many stores operating in it as it ever had.

(D) Over the course of the next five years, it is expected that Goreville's population will grow at a faster rate than it has for the past several decades.

(E) Many stores in the central shopping district sell types of merchandise that are not available at either SpendLess or Colson's.

Argument Evaluation

Situation   Due to competition from a recently opened SpendLess discount department store, discount stores in Goreville's central shopping district are expected to close within five years. But those locations will not be vacant long, for new stores have replaced all those that closed because of the opening five years ago of a Colson's nondiscount department store.

Reasoning   *The question is which option would most weaken the argument?* The arguer infers that stores that leave because of the SpendLess will be replaced in their locations by other stores because that is what happened after the Colson's department came in. Since the reasoning relies on a presumed similarity between the two cases, any information that brings to light a relevant dissimilarity would weaken the argument. If the stores that were driven out by Colson's were replaced mostly by discount stores, that suggests that the stores were replaced because of a need that no longer exists after the opening of SpendLess.

A   The fact that Colson's may be seeing fewer customers does not mean that the discount stores that close will not be replaced; they might be replaced by stores that in no way compete with Colson's or SpendLess.

B   **Correct.** This option most seriously weakens the argument.

C   If anything, this strengthens the argument by indicating that Goreville's central shopping district is thriving.

D   This, too, strengthens the argument because one is more likely to open a new store in an area with a growing population.

E   Because this statement does not indicate whether any of these stores that offer goods not sold at SpendLess or Colson's will be among those that are closing, it is not possible to determine what effect it has on the strength of the argument.

The correct answer is B.

108. Kale has more nutritional value than spinach. But since collard greens have more nutritional value than lettuce, it follows that kale has more nutritional value than lettuce.

    Any of the following, if introduced into the argument as an additional premise, makes the argument above logically correct EXCEPT:

    (A) Collard greens have more nutritional value than kale.

    (B) Spinach has more nutritional value than lettuce.

    (C) Spinach has more nutritional value than collard greens.

    (D) Spinach and collard greens have the same nutritional value.

    (E) Kale and collard greens have the same nutritional value.

Argument Construction

Situation Using the symbol > to mean "has (or have) more nutritional value than," this statement can be expressed as kale > spinach, and collard greens > lettuce. The conclusion that kale > lettuce remains valid if all but one of the premises is added.

Reasoning *Which premise makes the conclusion incorrect?* The information given in the passage is that kale > spinach and that collard greens > lettuce. This is not enough to conclude that kale > lettuce; another premise is needed to establish the relative nutritional value of kale and lettuce. Look at each premise offered in the answers to see whether the conclusion kale > lettuce remains valid. The ranking of vegetables may change with the additional premises; the conclusion, kale > lettuce, must not change. Find the one answer that does NOT support the conclusion.

A **Correct.** This statement properly identifies an additional premise that would invalidate the argument. If collard greens > kale, then it is possible that lettuce > kale, because the ranking could be collard greens > lettuce > kale > spinach.

B If spinach > lettuce, then kale > lettuce because kale > spinach.

C If spinach > collard greens, then kale > lettuce because the ranking would then be kale > spinach > collard greens > lettuce.

D If spinach = collard greens, then kale > lettuce because the ranking would be kale > spinach = collard greens > lettuce.

E If kale = collard greens, then kale > lettuce because kale = collard greens > lettuce.

The correct answer is A.

109. Last year all refuse collected by Shelbyville city services was incinerated. This incineration generated a large quantity of residual ash. In order to reduce the amount of residual ash Shelbyville generates this year to half of last year's total, the city has revamped its collection program. This year city services will separate for recycling enough refuse to reduce the number of truckloads of refuse to be incinerated to half of last year's number.

Which of the following is required for the revamped collection program to achieve its aim?

(A) This year, no materials that city services could separate for recycling will be incinerated.

(B) Separating recyclable materials from materials to be incinerated will cost Shelbyville less than half what it cost last year to dispose of the residual ash.

(C) Refuse collected by city services will contain a larger proportion of recyclable materials this year than it did last year.

(D) The refuse incinerated this year will generate no more residual ash per truckload incinerated than did the refuse incinerated last year.

(E) The total quantity of refuse collected by Shelbyville city services this year will be no greater than that collected last year.

Argument Construction

Situation   To cut in half the residual ash produced at its incinerator, the city will separate for recycling enough refuse to cut in half the number of truckloads of refuse going to the incinerator.

Reasoning   *Which option is required if the city's revamped collection program is to achieve its aim?* Cutting the number of truckloads of refuse in half must reduce the amount of residual ash to half last year's level. But if removal of the recycled refuse does not proportionately reduce the amount of ash, this will not happen. So if the amount of residual ash produced per truckload increases after recycling, then the amount of ash produced will not be cut in half by cutting in half the number of truckloads.

A   This merely indicates that no further reduction of ash through recycling could be achieved this year; it indicates nothing about how much the ash will be reduced.

B   This suggests a further benefit from recycling, but does not bear on the amount of ash that will be produced.

C   Since no information is provided about how much, if any, recyclable materials were removed from the refuse last year, this does not affect the reasoning.

D   Correct. This states a requirement for the collection program to achieve its aim.

E   This is not a requirement because even if the city collects more refuse this year, it could still cut in half the amount of residual ash by cutting in half the number of truckloads going to the incinerator.

The correct answer is D.

110. Although custom prosthetic bone replacements produced through a new computer-aided design process will cost more than twice as much as ordinary replacements, custom replacements should still be cost-effective. Not only will surgery and recovery time be reduced, but custom replacements should last longer, thereby reducing the need for further hospital stays.

Which of the following must be studied in order to evaluate the argument presented above?

(A) The amount of time a patient spends in surgery versus the amount of time spent recovering from surgery

(B) The amount by which the cost of producing custom replacements has declined with the introduction of the new technique for producing them

(C) The degree to which the use of custom replacements is likely to reduce the need for repeat surgery when compared with the use of ordinary replacements

(D) The degree to which custom replacements produced with the new technique are more carefully manufactured than are ordinary replacements

(E) The amount by which custom replacements produced with the new technique will drop in cost as the production procedures become standardized and applicable on a larger scale

Argument Evaluation

Situation   Custom prosthetic bone replacements, although twice as expensive as ordinary replacements, should be cost-effective because they reduce the time of surgery, recovery, and potential future hospitalizations.

Reasoning   *What research study would help in evaluating this argument?* The custom replacements must be compared with the ordinary replacements on the basis of the costs of surgery, recovery, and potential repeat hospitalizations. Repeat surgery involves all three kinds of costs; the extent to which such repeat surgery can be avoided is a sound measure of the cost-effectiveness of the two types of replacements.

A   Comparing time in surgery with time in recovery does not lead to a conclusion about the two kinds of replacements and their cost-effectiveness.

B   The cost-effectiveness of the custom replacements is being projected in the current moment; a previous decline in production costs would already have been taken into account.

C   **Correct.** This statement properly identifies evidence of cost-effectiveness that would assist in evaluating the argument.

D   The analysis is about cost-effectiveness; it is not about the level of care taken in manufacture.

E   Anticipating a future drop in production costs is outside the scope of the analysis, which should be based on current conditions.

The correct answer is C.

111. Springfield Fire Commissioner: The vast majority of false fire alarms are prank calls made anonymously from fire alarm boxes on street corners. Since virtually everyone has access to a private telephone, these alarm boxes have outlived their usefulness. Therefore, we propose to remove the boxes. Removing the boxes will reduce the number of prank calls without hampering people's ability to report a fire.

Which of the following, if true, most strongly supports the claim that the proposal, if carried out, will have the announced effect?

(A) The fire department traces all alarm calls made from private telephones and records where they came from.

(B) Maintaining the fire alarm boxes costs Springfield approximately $5 million annually.

(C) A telephone call can provide the fire department with more information about the nature and size of a fire than can an alarm placed from an alarm box.

(D) Responding to false alarms significantly reduces the fire department's capacity for responding to fires.

(E) On any given day, a significant percentage of the public telephones in Springfield are out of service.

Argument Evaluation

Situation   It is proposed that fire alarm boxes on street corners be removed. Doing so will reduce the number of prank calls without hampering people's ability to report fires. Most false alarms are prank calls made from these boxes. They have outlived their usefulness, as most people now have private telephones.

Reasoning   *Which option most strongly supports the claim that removing the alarm boxes will reduce the number of prank calls without hampering people's ability to report a fire?* The argument already provides some evidence that (1) removing the boxes will reduce prank calls—because that is where most such call are now made from—and that (2) doing so will not hamper people's ability to report fires—virtually everyone already has a private telephone from which they could report a fire. So for an option to be correct it must support either (1) or (2) or both, and provide more such support than the other options. If prank calls from private telephones are traced back to their origin, that should deter people from making such calls.

A   **Correct.** This option provides the most support for the claim.

B   This may provide a reason for supporting the proposal, but it provides no support for either (1) or (2).

C   This indicates that it is better to receive fire calls from telephones than from alarm boxes—other things being equal—but that supports neither (1) nor (2). There is still the possibility that the only person aware that a fire has started is near an alarm box but lacks access to a telephone.

D   This merely indicates that it would be good if the proposal had the intended effects.

E   This actually *weakens* support for (2), by enhancing the possibility that the only person aware that a fire has started is near an alarm box but lacks access to a working telephone.

The correct answer is A.

112. The difficulty with the proposed high-speed train line is that a used plane can be bought for one-third the price of the train line, and the plane, which is just as fast, can fly anywhere. The train would be a fixed linear system, and we live in a world that is spreading out in all directions and in which consumers choose the free-wheel systems (cars, buses, aircraft), which do not have fixed routes. Thus a sufficient market for the train will not exist.

Which of the following, if true, most severely weakens the argument presented above?

(A)   Cars, buses, and planes require the efforts of drivers and pilots to guide them, whereas the train will be guided mechanically.

(B)   Cars and buses are not nearly as fast as the high-speed train will be.

(C)   Planes are not a free-wheel system because they can fly only between airports, which are less convenient for consumers than the high-speed train's stations would be.

(D)   The high-speed train line cannot use currently underutilized train stations in large cities.

(E)   For long trips, most people prefer to fly rather than to take ground-level transportation.

Argument Evaluation

Situation   A free-wheel system of transportation, the airplane, is as fast as a fixed linear system, the high-speed train. Because people prefer free-wheel systems that do not have fixed routes, the high-speed train will never find a sufficient market.

Reasoning   *What is the potential weakness in this argument?* The passage argues that consumers will choose to fly rather than use the high-speed train. The argument is based upon a consumer preference for free-wheel systems over fixed linear systems. The definition of a free-wheel system is one that does *not have fixed routes*. The argument is weakened by any challenge to the definition of flying as a free-wheel transportation system. It is true that airplanes may be able to go almost anywhere, but commercial airlines do establish fixed routes and necessarily must travel to and from airports. Furthermore, if airports are less conveniently located for consumers than are train terminals, consumers might well prefer the more convenient of the two fixed-route alternatives.

A   The method of guidance is irrelevant to the argument about free-wheel versus fixed linear systems.

B   The passage compares the speed and system models of airplanes and high-speed trains. The argument does not incorporate buses and cars, which are included only to give examples of free-wheel systems, and so this statement is irrelevant.

C   **Correct.** This statement properly identifies the weakness in the argument: Airplanes are not truly a free-wheel system because they are restricted to traveling between airports. Additionally, airports tend to be less conveniently located than train terminals, which has further potential to weaken the argument in favor of airplanes.

D   The inability of high-speed trains to use some convenient train stations strengthens, rather than weakens, the argument in favor of airplanes.

E   Consumer preference for air travel over ground travel on long trips strengthens, rather than weakens, the argument in favor of airplanes.

The correct answer is C.

113. The average hourly wage of television assemblers in Vernland has long been significantly lower than that in neighboring Borodia. Since Borodia dropped all tariffs on Vernlandian televisions three years ago, the number of televisions sold annually in Borodia has not changed. However, recent statistics show a drop in the number of television assemblers in Borodia. Therefore, updated trade statistics will probably indicate that the number of televisions Borodia imports annually from Vernland has increased.

Which of the following is an assumption on which the argument depends?

(A) The number of television assemblers in Vernland has increased by at least as much as the number of television assemblers in Borodia has decreased.

(B) Televisions assembled in Vernland have features that televisions assembled in Borodia do not have.

(C) The average number of hours it takes a Borodian television assembler to assemble a television has not decreased significantly during the past three years.

(D) The number of televisions assembled annually in Vernland has increased significantly during the past three years.

(E) The difference between the hourly wage of television assemblers in Vernland and the hourly wage of television assemblers in Borodia is likely to decrease in the next few years.

Argument Construction

Situation   Television assemblers in Vernland are paid less than those in neighboring Borodia. The number of televisions sold in Borodia has not dropped since its tariffs on Borodian TVs were lowered three years ago, but the number of TV assemblers in Borodia has. So TV imports from Vernland have likely increased.

Reasoning   *What assumption does the argument depend on?* The fact that fewer individuals in Borodia are working as TV assemblers is offered as evidence that TV imports from Vernland into Borodia have likely increased. That piece of evidence is relevant *only* as an indication that the number of TVs being produced within Borodia has decreased. But a drop in the number of TV assemblers does not indicate a drop in the number of TVs being assembled *if* the number of TVs an average assembler puts together has increased. Thus, the argument must be assuming that the average time it takes an assembler to put together a TV has not significantly decreased.

A   The argument does not rely on any information about the number of television assemblers in Vernland nor for that matter on the number of TVs assembled in Vernland.

B   The argument need not assume there is any difference in the features of the TVs produced in the two countries. Increased sales of Vernlandian TVs in Borodia could be due to any number of other reasons, such as price or quality.

C   Correct. This option states an assumption on which the argument depends.

D   The argument does not depend upon this being so: Vernland's domestic TV sales (or perhaps its exports to countries other than Borodia) may have decreased by more than its imports into Borodia have increased.

E   The argument's conclusion addresses what *has* happened; the argument in no way relies on any assumptions about what may or may not happen in the coming years.

The correct answer is C.

114. Normally, the pineal gland governs a person's sleep-wake cycle by secreting melatonin in response to the daily cycle of light and darkness as detected by the eye. Nonetheless, many people who are totally blind due to lesions in the visual cortex of the brain easily maintain a 24-hour sleep-wake cycle. So the neural pathway by which the pineal gland receives information from the eye probably does not pass through the visual cortex.

For purposes of evaluating the argument it would be most useful to establish which of the following?

(A)   Whether melatonin supplements help people who have difficulty maintaining a 24-hour sleep cycle to establish such a pattern

(B)   Whether the melatonin levels of most totally blind people who successfully maintain a 24-hour sleep-wake cycle change in response to changes in exposure to light and darkness

(C)   Whether melatonin is the only substance secreted by the pineal gland

(D)   Whether most people who do not have a 24-hour sleep-wake cycle nevertheless have a cycle of consistent duration

(E)   Whether there are any people with normal vision whose melatonin levels respond abnormally to periods of light and darkness

Argument Evaluation

Situation   Normally, a person's sleep-wake cycle is governed by the pineal gland secreting melatonin in response to the daily cycle of light and darkness as detected by the eye. Yet many people who are totally blind due to lesions of the visual cortex easily maintain a 24-hour sleep-wake cycle.

Reasoning   *What additional information would be most helpful in evaluating the argument?* The argument's conclusion is that the neural pathway by which the pineal gland receives information probably does not pass through the visual cortex. This is suggested by the fact that people without a well-functioning visual cortex (e.g., people with a certain type of blindness) can nonetheless maintain a 24-hour sleep-wake cycle. Is it by the pineal gland's secretion of melatonin that they do so? The argument tells us that *normally* (i.e., in sighted people), this is the mechanism for sleep regulation. But the argument depends on assuming that a similar mechanism is operating in people who are blind but have well-regulated sleep cycles. The best choice will be the one that helps us decide whether that assumption is correct.

A   This question would not give us an answer that would help in evaluating the argument. A "no" answer would not clarify whether the pineal gland-melatonin mechanism operates in people who are blind. A "yes" answer would do no better. The question refers only to people who have sleep dysfunctions (which the argument does not address).

B   **Correct.** Answering this question would provide the most useful information for evaluating the argument. A "yes" answer would help confirm a key assumption of the argument: that blind people rely on the pineal gland-melatonin mechanism for sleep regulation. A "no" answer would help disconfirm that assumption.

C   Whether or not there are other substances secreted by the pineal gland makes no difference to the reasoning. The argument relies on the premise that the pineal gland governs the sleep cycle *by secreting melatonin*. For example, if the pineal gland sometimes secreted adrenaline, that would still have no bearing on the argument.

D   The consistency or inconsistency of the duration of some people's sleep patterns has no relevance to the reasoning. Their sleep patterns could be due to any of a number of factors.

E   This does not help, for there could be sighted people whose melatonin levels respond abnormally simply because of a pineal-gland abnormality.

The correct answer is B.

115. Guidebook writer: I have visited hotels throughout the country and have noticed that in those built before 1930 the quality of the original carpentry work is generally superior to that in hotels built afterward. Clearly carpenters working on hotels before 1930 typically worked with more skill, care, and effort than carpenters who have worked on hotels built subsequently.

Which of the following, if true, most seriously weakens the guidebook writer's argument?

(A) The quality of original carpentry in hotels is generally far superior to the quality of original carpentry in other structures, such as houses and stores.

(B) Hotels built since 1930 can generally accommodate more guests than those built before 1930.

(C) The materials available to carpenters working before 1930 were not significantly different in quality from the materials available to carpenters working after 1930.

(D) The better the quality of original carpentry in a building, the less likely that building is to fall into disuse and be demolished.

(E) The average length of apprenticeship for carpenters has declined significantly since 1930.

Argument Evaluation

Situation   The original carpentry in hotels built before 1930 shows superior care, skill, and effort to that in hotels built after 1930. This leads to the conclusion that carpenters working on hotels before 1930 were superior in skill, care, and effort to those that came after.

Reasoning   *Which option most seriously weakens the argument?* The argument draws an inference from a comparison between carpentry in hotels of different eras to a judgment about the carpenters working on hotels in those eras. One way to weaken this inference is by finding some way in which the carpentry in the hotels may be unrepresentative of the skill, care, and effort of the carpenters working in the eras. The comparison is between the carpentry evident in hotels of the two eras *that still exist.* Thus, if there is some reason to think that hotels with good carpentry survive longer than those with bad carpentry, then still-existing hotels from the older era will have disproportionately more good carpentry, even assuming no difference between the skill, care, and effort of the carpenters from the two eras.

A   This option applies equally to both eras, so it has no bearing on the argument.

B   It is not clear whether carpenters working on larger hotels would exercise more, less, or the same skill and care as those working on smaller hotels; thus this option does not weaken the argument.

C   The argument does not rely, even implicitly, on there being any difference in the quality of materials used in the two eras, so it does not weaken the argument to point out that no such difference exists.

D   Correct. This weakens the reasoning in the argument by showing a respect in which the comparison between *existing* hotels is unrepresentative.

E   The longer a carpenter works as an apprentice, the more skill he or she is apt to have upon becoming a full-fledged carpenter. So this option would tend to slightly strengthen rather than weaken the argument.

The correct answer is D.

116. Scientists typically do their most creative work before the age of forty. It is commonly thought that this happens because aging by itself brings about a loss of creative capacity. However, studies show that **of scientists who produce highly creative work beyond the age of forty, a disproportionately large number entered their field at an older age than is usual**. Since by the age of forty the large majority of scientists have been working in their field for at least fifteen years, the studies' finding strongly suggests that the real reason why scientists over forty rarely produce highly creative work is not that they have aged but rather that **scientists over forty have generally spent too long in their field**.

In the argument given, the two portions in boldface play which of the following roles?

(A) The first is a claim, the accuracy of which is at issue in the argument; the second is a conclusion drawn on the basis of that claim.

(B) The first is an objection that has been raised against a position defended in the argument; the second is that position.

(C) The first is evidence that has been used to support an explanation that the argument challenges; the second is that explanation.

(D) The first is evidence that has been used to support an explanation that the argument challenges; the second is a competing explanation that the argument favors.

(E) The first provides evidence to support an explanation that the argument favors; the second is that explanation.

Argument Evaluation

Situation   It is generally thought that the reason scientists tend to do their most creative work before age forty is that creative capacity declines with age. Yet those scientists who do creative work after forty tend, disproportionately, to have started their careers in science later in life. So a better explanation is that many scientists over forty have just been at it too long.

Reasoning   *What roles do the two portions of the argument that are in boldface play?* The argument describes a phenomenon and what is commonly thought to explain it. Then, the first boldfaced statement introduces evidence that suggests that there may be another explanation. After this evidence is further developed, the argument then concludes that there is indeed a better explanation for the phenomenon; that explanation is stated in the second boldfaced portion.

A   The accuracy of the first statement is never called into question by the argument; rather, it is relied upon as the basis for the argument's conclusion.

B   The first statement is not an objection against the position the argument defends; instead, it is a basis for that position.

C   The first statement is not used to support a position the argument challenges, and the second statement is the explanation the argument supports, not the one it challenges.

D   The second statement is indeed an explanation that the argument favors; but the first statement is not used to support a competing explanation that the argument challenges.

E   **Correct.** This option correctly identifies the roles played by the boldfaced portions of the argument.

The correct answer is E.

117. Northern Air has dozens of flights daily into and out of Belleville Airport, which is highly congested. Northern Air depends for its success on economy and quick turnaround and consequently is planning to replace its large planes with Skybuses, whose novel aerodynamic design is extremely fuel efficient. The Skybus's fuel efficiency results in both lower fuel costs and reduced time spent refueling.

Which of the following, if true, could present the most serious disadvantage for Northern Air in replacing their large planes with Skybuses?

(A) The Skybus would enable Northern Air to schedule direct flights to destinations that currently require stops for refueling.

(B) Aviation fuel is projected to decline in price over the next several years.

(C) The fuel efficiency of the Skybus would enable Northern Air to eliminate refueling at some of its destinations, but several mechanics would lose their jobs.

(D) None of Northern Air's competitors that use Belleville Airport are considering buying Skybuses.

(E) The aerodynamic design of the Skybus causes turbulence behind it when taking off that forces other planes on the runway to delay their takeoffs.

Evaluation of a Plan

Situation   An airline flies in and out of a highly congested airport many times a day. Because the airline's success depends on low costs and quick turnaround, it plans to replace its current planes with Skybuses, whose more fuel-efficient design will reduce both fuel costs and the time spent refueling.

Reasoning   *What could be a serious disadvantage of the plan?* Since it is given that the Skybuses provide fuel economy and quicker refueling, what could be a disadvantage of the proposed plan? What if the use of the particular aircraft somehow contributed to the congestion at the busy airport or caused slower turnaround? While the Skybus's design promotes fuel economy, if it also creates turbulence on takeoff, the turbulence would then delay the takeoffs of any other planes. Since the airport is congested and the airline flies through it many times a day, such takeoff delays would ultimately impede Northern Air's turnaround time, as well as its success.

A   The ability to schedule direct flights would be an advantage, not a disadvantage.

B   The decline in the price of aviation fuel might make the plan seem less pressing, and it could conceivably complicate the issue of whether the expected savings would justify the investment in new planes. However, lower fuel costs would not diminish the crucial time-saving advantage of Skybuses, and any hypotheses about their relevance to the overall decision are purely speculative.

C   The ability to eliminate refueling is an advantage to the airline. The loss of jobs could, in theory, have some negative effect on the airline due to lowered morale among remaining employees. However, *several* does not support a hypothesis that the effect would be very significant, and any hypotheses about whether it might override the benefits are purely speculative.

D   The decisions made by other airlines are irrelevant to the plan.

E   **Correct.** This statement properly identifies a potentially serious disadvantage to the plan.

The correct answer is E.

118. It is true of both men and women that those who marry as young adults live longer than those who never marry. This does not show that marriage causes people to live longer, since, as compared with other people of the same age, young adults who are about to get married have fewer of the unhealthy habits that can cause a person to have a shorter life, most notably smoking and immoderate drinking of alcohol.

Which of the following, if true, most strengthens the argument above?

(A) Marriage tends to cause people to engage less regularly in sports that involve risk of bodily harm.

(B) A married person who has an unhealthy habit is more likely to give up that habit than a person with the same habit who is unmarried.

(C) A person who smokes is much more likely than a nonsmoker to marry a person who smokes at the time of marriage, and the same is true for people who drink alcohol immoderately.

(D) Among people who marry as young adults, most of those who give up an unhealthy habit after marriage do not resume the habit later in life.

(E) Among people who as young adults neither drink alcohol immoderately nor smoke, those who never marry live as long as those who marry.

Argument Evaluation

Situation   We should not conclude that getting married causes one to live longer based merely on the fact that those who marry young tend to live longer than those who never marry at all. Those who marry young tend to have fewer unhealthy habits to begin with, such as drinking and smoking, than do those who will never marry.

Reasoning   *Which of the options most strengthens the argument?* The argument is trying to show that the difference in longevity between the two groups need not be *caused by* marital status. The argument relies on the fact that even before marriage those who will be married tend to live healthier lifestyles than those who will never marry. Yet, even if those who are apt to live longer are more apt to marry young, it could still be that marriage *further enhances* one's longevity. So, by showing that a person who gets married young tends to live about as long as one who had been living an equally healthy lifestyle as a young adult but who never got married, the argument is greatly strengthened.

A   To the extent that risk of bodily harm decreases longevity, this weakens rather than strengthens the argument.

B   This option, too, weakens the argument rather than strengthens it, since it suggests that marriage does indeed enhance one's longevity.

C   Even if a person with unhealthy habits who marries is more likely to wind up with a spouse with unhealthy habits than is a person with healthy habits who marries, that tells us nothing about whether the average person who gets married gets a boost in longevity.

D   This option does not tell us whether it is also true of those who never marry that most of them who give up an unhealthy habit as a young adult ever resume that habit later in life. Thus, by itself, this option has no bearing on the strength of the argument.

E   **Correct.** This strengthens the argument against the causal connection between marriage and longevity by showing that the longevity difference disappears when the longevity of those who marry young is compared with young adults with similar health habits who will never marry.

The correct answer is E.

119. The earliest Mayan pottery found at Colha, in Belize, is about 3,000 years old. Recently, however, 4,500-year-old stone agricultural implements were unearthed at Colha. These implements resemble Mayan stone implements of a much later period, also found at Colha. Moreover, the implements' designs are strikingly different from the designs of stone implements produced by other cultures known to have inhabited the area in prehistoric times. Therefore, there were surely Mayan settlements in Colha 4,500 years ago.

Which of the following, if true, most seriously weakens the argument?

(A) Ceramic ware is not known to have been used by the Mayan people to make agricultural implements.

(B) Carbon-dating of corn pollen in Colha indicates that agriculture began there around 4,500 years ago.

(C) Archaeological evidence indicates that some of the oldest stone implements found at Colha were used to cut away vegetation after controlled burning of trees to open areas of swampland for cultivation.

(D) Successor cultures at a given site often adopt the style of agricultural implements used by earlier inhabitants of the same site.

(E) Many religious and social institutions of the Mayan people who inhabited Colha 3,000 years ago relied on a highly developed system of agricultural symbols.

Argument Evaluation

Situation   Recently, 4,500-year-old stone agricultural implements have been found in Colha, a location where 3,000-year-old Mayan pottery had previously been found. The implements resemble other Mayan implements of a much later time that were also found in Colha, and they are unlike the implements used by other local cultures in prehistoric times. These recently discovered implements thus prove that Mayan culture was established in Colha 4,500 years ago.

Reasoning   *Which point weakens the argument?* First, identify a crucial underlying assumption. The argument assumes the distinctive 4,500-year-old implements must be Mayan because they are similar to implements the Mayans are known to have used there much later. What if there is another reason for the similarity? What if a culture that comes to an already inhabited site tends to adapt its implements to the style of the resident culture's implements? In that case, the Mayans could have come to the already established community of Colha at some later point, and the later Mayan agricultural tools could be copies of the earlier culture's tools.

A   The argument does not suggest that the Mayans used ceramics for implements, so this point does not weaken the argument; it is irrelevant to it.

B   Since the point of the argument is who, specifically, established a settlement in Colha 4,500 years ago, the evidence that some unidentified people were practicing agriculture there at that time neither strengthens nor weakens the argument.

C   Discovering how the implements were used does not explain who was using them, so this information is not relevant to the conclusion.

D   **Correct.** This statement properly identifies the weakness in the argument that the similarity between the 4,500-year-old implements and the later Mayan implements may be attributed to the Mayans' adopting the style of implements used earlier by another culture.

E   That the Mayans relied on agricultural symbols at that time is nearly irrelevant to the issue of whether the earlier implements belonged to their culture. To the extent that this is relevant, it very slightly supports, rather than weakens, the argument; *highly developed* suggests that Mayans had been practicing agriculture for a long time.

The correct answer is D.

120. Codex Berinensis, a Florentine copy of an ancient Roman medical treatise, is undated but contains clues to when it was produced. Its first 80 pages are by a single copyist, but the remaining 20 pages are by three different copyists, which indicates some significant disruption. Since a letter in handwriting identified as that of the fourth copyist mentions a plague that killed many people in Florence in 1148, Codex Berinensis was probably produced in that year.

Which of the following, if true, most strongly supports the hypothesis that Codex Berinensis was produced in 1148?

(A) Other than Codex Berinensis, there are no known samples of the handwriting of the first three copyists.

(B) According to the account by the fourth copyist, the plague went on for 10 months.

(C) A scribe would be able to copy a page of text the size and style of Codex Berinensis in a day.

(D) There was only one outbreak of plague in Florence in the 1100s.

(E) The number of pages of Codex Berinensis produced by a single scribe becomes smaller with each successive change of copyist.

Argument Evaluation

Situation   The Florentine copy of an ancient Roman work is undated but provides clues as to the time it was produced. The first 80 pages of Codex Berinenis are the work of one copyist. The fact that the last 20 pages are the work of a succession of three different copyists is an indication of serious turmoil at the time the copying was done. Since a letter in the fourth copyist's handwriting reveals that a plague killed many people there in 1148, Codex Berinenis was probably produced in that year.

Reasoning   *Which information supports the hypothesis dating the Codex to 1148?* Consider the basis of the hypothesis: the succession of copyists indicating the work was significantly disrupted, and the fourth copyist's letter indicating the plague of 1148 caused serious loss of life. From this it is argued that the plague of 1148 was the reason for the multiple copyists and that the work can thus be dated to that year. What if there were multiple plagues? In that case, Codex Berinensis could have been produced at another time. If instead only one plague occurred in the 1100s, the elimination of that possibility supports the hypothesis that the work was done in 1148.

A   Examples of the copyists' handwriting might help date Codex Berinensis; the absence of handwriting samples does not help support 1148 as the date.

B   The length of the plague, while it may account for the succession of copyists, does not help support the particular year the work was done.

C   The amount of work a copyist could achieve each day does not provide any information about the year the work appeared.

D   Correct. This statement properly identifies a circumstance that supports the hypothesis.

E   The productivity or tenure of the various copyists is irrelevant to establishing the date.

The correct answer is D.

121. The spacing of the four holes on a fragment of a bone flute excavated at a Neanderthal campsite is just what is required to play the third through sixth notes of the diatonic scale—the seven-note musical scale used in much of Western music since the Renaissance. Musicologists therefore hypothesize that the diatonic musical scale was developed and used thousands of years before it was adopted by Western musicians.

Which of the following, if true, most strongly supports the hypothesis?

(A) Bone flutes were probably the only musical instrument made by Neanderthals.

(B) No musical instrument that is known to have used a diatonic scale is of an earlier date than the flute found at the Neanderthal campsite.

(C) The flute was made from a cave-bear bone and the campsite at which the flute fragment was excavated was in a cave that also contained skeletal remains of cave bears.

(D) Flutes are the simplest wind instrument that can be constructed to allow playing a diatonic scale.

(E) The cave-bear leg bone used to make the Neanderthal flute would have been long enough to make a flute capable of playing a complete diatonic scale.

Argument Evaluation

Situation   The arrangement of the holes in a bone fragment from a Neanderthal campsite match part of the scale used in Western music since the Renaissance. Musicologists hypothesize from this that the scale was developed thousands of years before Western musicians adopted it.

Reasoning   *Which of the options, if true, would provide the most support for the musicologists' hypothesis?* One way to approach this question is to ask yourself, "If this option were false, would the hypothesis be *less* likely to be true?" If the Neanderthal bone fragment could *not* have been part of a flute that encompassed *the entire* seven-note diatonic scale, then the bone fragment's existence would not provide strong support for the hypothesis.

A   To the extent that this is even relevant, it tends to weaken the hypothesis; it makes less likely the possibility that Neanderthals used other types of musical instruments employing the diatonic scale.

B   This also weakens the hypothesis, because it states that there is no known evidence of a certain type that would support the hypothesis.

C   The fact that the cave-bear bone fragment that was apparently a flute came from a site where many other cave-bear skeletal remains were found has little bearing on the hypothesis, and in no way supports it.

D   This does not strengthen the hypothesis, for even if the option were false—even if a simpler instrument could be constructed that employed the diatonic scale—the existence of a flute employing the diatonic scale would provide no less support for the hypothesis.

E   **Correct.** This option most strongly supports the hypothesis.

The correct answer is E.

122. Outsourcing is the practice of obtaining from an independent supplier a product or service that a company has previously provided for itself. Since a company's chief objective is to realize the highest possible year-end profits, any product or service that can be obtained from an independent supplier for less than it would cost the company to provide the product or service on its own should be outsourced.

Which of the following, if true, most seriously weakens the argument?

(A) If a company decides to use independent suppliers for a product, it can generally exploit the vigorous competition arising among several firms that are interested in supplying that product.

(B) Successful outsourcing requires a company to provide its suppliers with information about its products and plans that can fall into the hands of its competitors and give them a business advantage.

(C) Certain tasks, such as processing a company's payroll, are commonly outsourced, whereas others, such as handling the company's core business, are not.

(D) For a company to provide a product or service for itself as efficiently as an independent supplier can provide it, the managers involved need to be as expert in the area of that product or service as the people in charge of that product or service at an independent supplier are.

(E) When a company decides to use an independent supplier for a product or service, the independent supplier sometimes hires members of the company's staff who formerly made the product or provided the service that the independent supplier now supplies.

Argument Evaluation

Situation In order to realize the highest year-end profits, a company should outsource any service or product that can be obtained from an independent supplier for less than it would cost the company to provide that service or product itself.

Reasoning *What weakens this argument?* When could outsourcing a service or product result in a business disadvantage or lower profits? It is clear that the company must give independent suppliers enough information to enable them to provide the contracted products and services, but this means that the company can lose control over who has possession of such critical information. If the information becomes known to the company's competitors and gives them a business advantage, the company's profitability may be harmed rather than helped by outsourcing. This possibility weakens the argument.

A This would strengthen the argument since the pricing competition among independent suppliers is an advantage for the company.

B **Correct.** This statement properly identifies one disadvantage of outsourcing: the company no longer controls access to its information and plans. With the increased possibility of competitors' gaining access to its proprietary information, the company's business is put at risk.

C Providing examples of the tasks typically outsourced or handled internally does not affect the argument.

D Expertise in a particular area is an advantage of outsourcing and thus a strength of the argument.

E The supplier's hiring of members of the company's staff to handle work no longer performed within the company is not shown to be a disadvantage.

The correct answer is B.

123. Museums that house Renaissance oil paintings typically store them in environments that are carefully kept within narrow margins of temperature and humidity to inhibit any deterioration. Laboratory tests have shown that the kind of oil paint used in these paintings actually adjusts to climatic changes quite well. If, as some museum directors believe, **paint is the most sensitive substance in these works**, then by relaxing the standards for temperature and humidity control, **museums can reduce energy costs without risking damage to these paintings**. Museums would be rash to relax those standards, however, since results of preliminary tests indicate that gesso, a compound routinely used by Renaissance artists to help paint adhere to the canvas, is unable to withstand significant variations in humidity.

In the argument above, the two portions in boldface play which of the following roles?

(A) The first is an objection that has been raised against the position taken by the argument; the second is the position taken by the argument.

(B) The first is the position taken by the argument; the second is the position that the argument calls into question.

(C) The first is a judgment that has been offered in support of the position that the argument calls into question; the second is a circumstance on which that judgment is, in part, based.

(D) The first is a judgment that has been offered in support of the position that the argument calls into question; the second is that position.

(E) The first is a claim that the argument calls into question; the second is the position taken by the argument.

Argument Evaluation

Situation   Museums house Renaissance paintings under strictly controlled climatic conditions to prevent deterioration. This is costly. But the paint in these works actually adjusts well to climate changes. On the other hand, another compound routinely used in these paintings, gesso, does not react well to changes in humidity.

Reasoning   *What roles do the two boldfaced statements play in the argument?* The first statement is not asserted by the author of the argument, but rather attributed as a belief to some museum directors. What the argument itself asserts is that IF this belief is true THEN the second boldfaced statement is true. But the argument then goes on to offer evidence that the first statement is false and so concludes that museum directors would be ill-advised to assume that the second statement was true.

A   This option mistakenly claims that the argument adopts the second statement as its position, when in fact the argument calls this position into question.

B   Rather than adopting the first statement, the argument offers evidence that calls it into question.

C   This option contends that the first statement is a judgment that is based on the second; in fact the opposite is true.

D   Correct. This option properly identifies the roles the two portions in boldface play in the argument.

E   While the argument does call the first statement into question, it also calls the second statement into question.

The correct answer is D.

124. Vargonia has just introduced a legal requirement that student-teacher ratios in government-funded schools not exceed a certain limit. All Vargonian children are entitled to education, free of charge, in these schools. When a recession occurs and average incomes fall, the number of children enrolled in government-funded schools tends to increase. Therefore, though most employment opportunities contract in economic recessions, getting a teaching job in Vargonia's government-funded schools will not be made more difficult by a recession.

Which of the following would be most important to determine in order to evaluate the argument?

(A) Whether in Vargonia there are any schools not funded by the government that offer children an education free of charge

(B) Whether the number of qualified applicants for teaching positions in government-funded schools increases significantly during economic recessions

(C) What the current student-teacher ratio in Vargonia's government-funded schools is

(D) What proportion of Vargonia's workers currently hold jobs as teachers in government-funded schools

(E) Whether in the past a number of government-funded schools in Vargonia have had student-teacher ratios well in excess of the new limit

Argument Evaluation

Situation   During a recession, the number of children in government-funded schools in Vargonia tends to increase. Vargonian children are entitled to a free education in these schools. A new law requires student-teacher ratios in these schools to remain below a certain limit.

Reasoning   *Which of the five questions would provide us with the best information for evaluating the argument?* The argument's conclusion is that recessions do not make teaching jobs in Vargonia's government-funded schools harder to get. During recessions, the reasoning goes, more students will enroll in Vargonia's government-funded schools than in non-recession times. Implicit in the argument is the thought that, because the new law sets an upper limit on the average number of students per teacher, schools that get an influx of new students would have to hire more teachers. During a recession, however, there might be much more competition in the labor market for teachers because many more qualified people are applying for teaching jobs.

A   This information is not significant in the context of the argument, which does not need to assume that only government-funded schools provide free education.

B   **Correct.** Getting an answer to this question would provide us with specific information useful in evaluating the argument. A "yes" answer to this question would suggest that competition for teaching jobs in Vargonian government-funded schools would be keener during recessions. A "no" answer would suggest that the level of competition would decrease during recessions.

C   Discovering the current student-teacher ratio in Vargonia's schools would be of no value, by itself, in evaluating the argument. We do not know what the new upper limit on the student-teacher ratio is, and we do not know whether Vargonia is currently in a recession.

D   Finding out whether the proportion this refers to is 1 percent, for example, or 4 percent, would tell us nothing about whether getting teaching jobs at government-funded schools in Vargonia becomes more difficult during a recession. Among other things, we do not know whether Vargonia is currently in a recession, and we do not know what proportion of Vargonia's workers would be qualified candidates for teaching jobs.

E   This is of no relevance in evaluating the argument because, presumably, the new limit on student-teacher ratios will be complied with. Thus, even if student-teacher ratios in the past would have exceeded the new limit, the argument concerns whether, *in the future*, getting a teaching job in Vargonia's government-funded schools will be made more difficult by a recession.

The correct answer is B.

9.0 Sentence Correction

9.0 Sentence Correction

Sentence correction questions appear in the Verbal section of the GMAT® exam. The Verbal section uses multiple-choice questions to measure your ability to read and comprehend written material, to reason and evaluate arguments, and to correct written material to express ideas effectively in standard written English. Because the Verbal section includes passages from several different content areas, you may be generally familiar with some of the material; however, neither the passages nor the questions assume detailed knowledge of the topics discussed. Sentence correction questions are intermingled with critical reasoning and reading comprehension questions throughout the Verbal section of the test. You will have 75 minutes to complete the Verbal section, or about 1¾ minutes to answer each question.

Sentence correction questions present a statement in which words are underlined. The questions ask you to select from the answer options the best expression of the idea or relationship described in the underlined section. The first answer choice always repeats the original phrasing, whereas the other four provide alternatives. In some cases, the original phrasing is the best choice. In other cases, the underlined section has obvious or subtle errors that require correction. These questions require you to be familiar with the stylistic conventions and grammatical rules of standard written English and to demonstrate your ability to improve incorrect or ineffective expressions. Sentence correction questions may include English-language idioms, which are standard constructions not derived from the most basic rules of grammar and vocabulary, but idioms are not intended to measure any specialized knowledge of colloquilisms or regionalisms.

You should begin these questions by reading the sentence carefully. Note whether there are any obvious grammatical errors as you read the underlined section. Then read the five answer choices carefully. If there was a subtle error you did not recognize the first time you read the sentence, it may become apparent after you have read the answer choices. If the error is still unclear, see whether you can eliminate some of the answers as being incorrect. Remember that in some cases, the original selection may be the best answer.

9.1 Basic English Grammar Rules

Sentence correction questions ask you to recognize and potentially correct at least one of the following grammar rules. However, these rules are not exhaustive. If you are interested in learning more about English grammar as a way to prepare for the GMAT exam, there are several resources available on the Web.

Agreement

Standard English requires elements within a sentence to be consistent. There are two types of agreement: noun-verb and pronoun.

Noun-verb agreement: Singular subjects take singular verbs, whereas plural subjects take plural verbs.
Examples:
Correct: "I walk to the store." Incorrect: "I walks to the store."
Correct: "We go to school." Incorrect: "We goes to school."
Correct: "The number of residents has grown." Incorrect: "The number of residents have grown."
Correct: "The masses have spoken." Incorrect: "The masses has spoken."

Pronoun agreement: A pronoun must agree with the noun or pronoun it refers to in person, number, and gender.

Examples:

Correct: "When you dream, you are usually asleep." Incorrect: "When one dreams, you are usually asleep."

Correct: "When the kids went to sleep, they slept like logs." Incorrect: "When the kids went to sleep, he slept like a log."

Diction

Words should be chosen to reflect correctly and effectively the appropriate part of speech. There are several words that are commonly used incorrectly. When answering sentence correction questions, pay attention to the following conventions.

Among/between: Among is used to refer to relationships involving more than two objects. *Between* is used to refer to relationships involving only two objects.

Examples:

Correct: "We divided our winnings among the three of us." Incorrect: "We divided our winnings between the three of us."

Correct: "She and I divided the cake between us." Incorrect: "She and I divided the cake among us."

As/like: As can be a preposition meaning "in the capacity of," but more often is a conjunction of manner and is followed by a verb. *Like* is generally used as a preposition, and therefore is followed by a noun, an object pronoun, or a verb ending in *-ing*.

Examples:

Correct: "I work as a librarian." Incorrect: "I work like a librarian."

Correct: "Do as I say, not as I do." Incorrect: "Do like I say, not like I do."

Correct: "It felt like a dream." Incorrect: "It felt as a dream."

Correct: "People like you inspire me." Incorrect: "People as you inspire me."

Correct: "There's nothing like biking on a warm, autumn day." Incorrect: "There's nothing as biking on a warm autumn day."

Mass and count words: Mass words are nouns quantified by an amount rather than by a number. *Count* nouns can be quantified by a number.

Examples:

Correct: "We bought a loaf of bread." Incorrect: "We bought one bread."

Correct: "He wished me much happiness." Incorrect: "He wished me many happinesses."

Correct: "We passed many buildings." Incorrect: "We passed much buildings."

Pronouns: Myself should not be used as a substitute for *I* or *me*.

Examples:

Correct: "Mom and I had to go to the store." Incorrect: "Mom and myself had to go to the store."

Correct: "He gave the present to Dad and me." Incorrect: "He gave the present to Dad and myself."

Grammatical Construction

Good grammar requires complete sentences. Be on the lookout for improperly formed constructions.

Fragments: Parts of a sentence that are disconnected from the main clause are called fragments.
Example:
Correct: "We saw the doctor and his nurse at the party." Incorrect: "We saw the doctor at the party. And his nurse."

Run-on sentences: A run-on sentence is two independent clauses that run together without proper punctuation.
Examples:
Correct: "Jose Canseco is still a feared batter; most pitchers don't want to face him."
Incorrect: "Jose Canseco is still a feared batter most pitchers don't want to face him."

Constructions: Avoid wordy, redundant constructions.
Example:
Correct: "We could not come to the meeting because of a conflict." Incorrect: "The reason we could not come to the meeting is because of a conflict."

Idiom

It is important to avoid nonstandard expressions, although English idioms sometimes do not follow conventional grammatical rules. Be careful to use the correct idiom when using the constructions and parts of speech.

Prepositions: Specific prepositions have specific purposes.
Examples:
Correct: "She likes to jog in the morning." Incorrect: "She likes to jog on the morning."
Correct: "They ranged in age from 10 to 15." Incorrect: "They ranged in age from 10 up to 15."

Correlatives: Word combinations such as "not only … but also" should be followed by an element of the same grammatical type.
Examples:
Correct: "I have called not only to thank her but also to tell her about the next meeting."
Incorrect: "I have called not only to thank her but also I told her about the next meeting."

Forms of comparison: Many forms follow precise constructions. *Fewer* refers to a specific number, whereas *less than* refers to a continuous quantity. *Between … and* is the correct form to designate a choice. *Farther* refers to distance, whereas *further* refers to degree.
Examples:
Correct: "There were fewer children in my class this year." Incorrect: "There were less children in my class this year."
Correct: "There was less devastation than I was told." Incorrect: "There was fewer devastation than I was told."
Correct: "We had to choose between chocolate and vanilla." Incorrect: "We had to choose between chocolate or vanilla." (It is also correct to say, "We had to choose chocolate or vanilla.")
Correct: "I ran farther than John, but he took his weight training further than I did."
Incorrect: "I ran further than John, but he took his weight training farther than I did."

Logical Predication

Watch out for phrases that detract from the logical argument.

Modification problems: Modifiers should be positioned so it is clear what word or words they are meant to modify. If modifiers are not positioned clearly, they can cause illogical references or comparisons, or distort the meaning of the statement.
Examples:
Correct: "I put the cake that I baked by the door." Incorrect: "I put the cake by the door that I baked."
Correct: "Reading my mind, she gave me the delicious cookie." Incorrect: "Reading my mind, the cookie she gave me was delicious."
Correct: "In the Middle Ages, the world was believed to be flat." Incorrect: "In the Middle Ages, the world was flat."

Parallelism

Constructing a sentence that is parallel in structure depends on making sure that the different elements in the sentence balance each other; this is a little bit like making sure that the two sides of a mathematical equation are balanced. To make sure that a sentence is grammatically correct, check to see that phrases, clauses, verbs, and other sentence elements parallel each other.

Examples:
Correct: "I took a bath, went to sleep, and woke up refreshed." Incorrect: "I took a bath, sleeping, and waking up refreshed."
Correct: "The only way to know is to take the plunge." Incorrect: "The only way to know is taking the plunge."

Rhetorical Construction

Good sentence structure avoids constructions that are awkward, wordy, redundant, imprecise, or unclear, even when they are free of grammatical errors.
Example:
Correct: "Before we left on vacation, we watered the plants, checked to see that the stove was off, and set the burglar alarm." Incorrect: "Before we left to go on our vacation, we watered, checked to be sure that the stove had been turned off, and set it."

Verb Form

In addition to watching for problems of agreement or parallelism, make sure that verbs are used in the correct tense. Be alert to whether a verb should reflect past, present, or future tense.
Example:
Correct: "I went to school yesterday." "I go to school every weekday." "I will go to school tomorrow."

Each tense also has a perfect form (used with the past participle—e.g., walked, ran), a progressive form (used with the present participle—e.g., walking, running), and a perfect progressive form (also used with the present participle—e.g., walking, running).

Present perfect: Used with *has* or *have,* the present perfect tense describes an action that occurred at an indefinite time in the past or that began in the past and continues into the present.
Examples:
Correct: "I have traveled all over the world." (at an indefinite time)
Correct: "He has gone to school since he was five years old." (continues into the present)

Past perfect: This verb form is used with *had* to show the order of two events that took place in the past.
Example:
Correct: "By the time I left for school, the cake had been baked."

Future perfect: Used with *will have,* this verb form describes an event in the future that will precede another event.
Example:
Correct: "By the end of the day, I will have studied for all my tests."

Present progressive: Used with *am, is,* or *are,* this verb form describes an ongoing action that is happening now.
Example:
Correct: "I am studying for exams." "The student is studying for exams." "We are studying for exams."

Past progressive: Used with *was* or *were,* this verb form describes something that was happening when another action occurred.
Example:
Correct: "The student was studying when the fire alarm rang." "They were studying when the fire broke out."

Future progressive: Used with *will be* or *shall be,* this verb tense describes an ongoing action that will continue into the future.
Example:
Correct: "The students will be studying for exams throughout the month of December."

Present perfect progressive: Used with *have been* or *has been,* this verb tense describes something that began in the past, continues into the present, and may continue into the future.
Example:
Correct: "The student has been studying hard in the hope of acing the test."

Past perfect progressive: Used with *had been,* this verb form describes an action of some duration that was completed before another past action occurred.
Example:
Correct: "Before the fire alarm rang, the student had been studying."

Future perfect progressive: Used with *will have been,* this verb form describes a future, ongoing action that will occur before a specified time.
Example:
Correct: "By the end of next year, the students will have been studying math for five years."

9.2 Study Suggestions

There are two basic ways you can study for sentence correction questions:

- **Read material that reflects standard usage.**
  One way to gain familiarity with the basic conventions of standard written English is simply to read. Suitable material will usually be found in good magazines and nonfiction books, editorials in outstanding newspapers, and the collections of essays used by many college and university writing courses.

- **Review basic rules of grammar and practice with writing exercises.**
  Begin by reviewing the grammar rules laid out in this chapter. Then, if you have school assignments (such as essays and research papers) that have been carefully evaluated for grammatical errors, it may be helpful to review the comments and corrections.

9.3 What Is Measured

Sentence correction questions test three broad aspects of language proficiency:

- **Correct expression**
  A correct sentence is grammatically and structurally sound. It conforms to all the rules of standard written English, including noun-verb agreement, noun-pronoun agreement, pronoun consistency, pronoun case, and verb tense sequence. A correct sentence will not have dangling, misplaced, or improperly formed modifiers; unidiomatic or inconsistent expressions; or faults in parallel construction.

- **Effective expression**
  An effective sentence expresses an idea or relationship clearly and concisely as well as grammatically. This does not mean that the choice with the fewest and simplest words is necessarily the best answer. It means that there are no superfluous words or needlessly complicated expressions in the best choice.

- **Proper diction**
  An effective sentence also uses proper diction. (Diction refers to the standard dictionary meanings of words and the appropriateness of words in context.) In evaluating the diction of a sentence, you must be able to recognize whether the words are well chosen, accurate, and suitable for the context.

9.4 Test-Taking Strategies

1. **Read the entire sentence carefully.**
   Try to understand the specific idea or relationship that the sentence should express.

2. **Evaluate the underlined passage for errors and possible corrections before reading the answer choices.**
   This strategy will help you discriminate among the answer choices. Remember, in some cases the underlined passage is correct.

3. **Read each answer choice carefully.**

   The first answer choice always repeats the underlined portion of the original sentence. Choose this answer if you think that the sentence is best as originally written, but do so *only after* examining all the other choices.

4. **Try to determine how to correct what you consider to be wrong with the original sentence.**

   Some of the answer choices may change things that are not wrong, whereas others may not change everything that is wrong.

5. **Make sure that you evaluate the sentence and the choices thoroughly.**

   Pay attention to general clarity, grammatical and idiomatic usage, economy and precision of language, and appropriateness of diction.

6. **Read the whole sentence, substituting the choice that you prefer for the underlined passage.**

   A choice may be wrong because it does not fit grammatically or structurally with the rest of the sentence. Remember that some sentences will require no correction. When the given sentence requires no correction, choose the first answer.

9.5 The Directions

These are the directions that you will see for sentence correction questions when you take the GMAT exam. If you read them carefully and understand them clearly before going to sit for the test, you will not need to spend too much time reviewing them once you are at the test center and the test is under way.

Sentence correction questions present a sentence, part or all of which is underlined. Beneath the sentence, you will find five ways of phrasing the underlined passage. The first answer choice repeats the original underlined passage; the other four are different. If you think the original phrasing is best, choose the first answer; otherwise choose one of the others.

This type of question tests your ability to recognize the correctness and effectiveness of expression in standard written English. In choosing your answer, follow the requirements of standard written English; that is, pay attention to grammar, choice of words, and sentence construction. Choose the answer that produces the most effective sentence; this answer should be clear and exact, without awkwardness, ambiguity, redundancy, or grammatical error.

9.6 Practice Questions

Each of the <u>sentence correction</u> questions presents a sentence, part or all of which is underlined. Beneath the sentence you will find five ways of phrasing the underlined part. The first of these repeats the original; the other four are different. Follow the requirements of standard written English to choose your answer, paying attention to grammar, word choice, and sentence construction. Select the answer that produces the most effective sentence; your answer should make the sentence clear, exact, and free of grammatical error. It should also minimize awkwardness, ambiguity, and redundancy.

1. In a review of 2,000 studies of human behavior that date back to the 1940s, two Swiss <u>psychologists, declaring that since most of the studies had failed to control for such variables as social class and family size,</u> none could be taken seriously.

    (A) psychologists, declaring that since most of the studies had failed to control for such variables as social class and family size,

    (B) psychologists, declaring that most of the studies failed in not controlling for such variables like social class and family size, and

    (C) psychologists declared that since most of the studies, having failed to control for such variables as social class and family size,

    (D) psychologists declared that since most of the studies fail in controlling for such variables like social class and family size,

    (E) psychologists declared that since most of the studies had failed to control for variables such as social class and family size,

2. Manufacturers rate batteries in watt-hours; <u>if they rate the watt-hour higher, the longer</u> the battery can be expected to last.

    (A) if they rate the watt-hour higher, the longer

    (B) rating the watt-hour higher, it is that much longer

    (C) the higher the watt-hour rating, the longer

    (D) the higher the watt-hour rating, it is that much longer that

    (E) when the watt-hour rating is higher, the longer it is

3. Although a surge in retail sales <u>have raised hopes that there is a recovery finally</u> under way, many economists say that without a large amount of spending the recovery might not last.

    (A) have raised hopes that there is a recovery finally

    (B) raised hopes for there being a recovery finally

    (C) had raised hopes for a recovery finally being

    (D) has raised hopes that a recovery is finally

    (E) raised hopes for a recovery finally

4. At the end of the 1930s, Duke Ellington was looking for a composer to assist him—<u>someone not only who could arrange music for his successful big band, but mirroring his eccentric writing style as well in order to finish</u> the many pieces he had started but never completed.

    (A) someone not only who could arrange music for his successful big band, but mirroring his eccentric writing style as well in order to finish

    (B) someone who could not only arrange music for his successful big band, but also mirror his eccentric writing style in order to finish

    (C) someone who not only could arrange music for his successful big band, but also to mirror his eccentric writing style in finishing

    (D) that being someone who could not only arrange music for his successful big band, but mirroring his eccentric writing style for finishing

    (E) being someone not only who could arrange music for his successful big band, but mirror his eccentric writing style as well, finishing

5. Of all the vast tides of migration that have swept through history, <u>maybe none is more concentrated as</u> the wave that brought 12 million immigrants onto American shores in little more than three decades.

   (A) maybe none is more concentrated as

   (B) it may be that none is more concentrated as

   (C) perhaps it is none that is more concentrated than

   (D) maybe it is none that was more concentrated than

   (E) perhaps none was more concentrated than

6. Diabetes, together with its serious complications, <u>ranks as the nation's third leading cause of death, surpassed only</u> by heart disease and cancer.

   (A) ranks as the nation's third leading cause of death, surpassed only

   (B) rank as the nation's third leading cause of death, only surpassed

   (C) has the rank of the nation's third leading cause of death, only surpassed

   (D) are the nation's third leading causes of death, surpassed only

   (E) have been ranked as the nation's third leading causes of death, only surpassed

7. The intricate structure of the compound insect eye, <u>having hundreds of miniature eyes called ommatidia, help explain why scientists have assumed that it</u> evolved independently of the vertebrate eye.

   (A) having hundreds of miniature eyes called ommatidia, help explain why scientists have assumed that it

   (B) having hundreds of miniature eyes that are called ommatidia, helps explain why scientists have assumed that they

   (C) with its hundreds of miniature eyes that are called ommatidia, helps explain scientists' assuming that they

   (D) with its hundreds of miniature eyes called ommatidia, help explain scientists' assuming that it

   (E) with its hundreds of miniature eyes called ommatidia, helps explain why scientists have assumed that it

8. In late 1997, the chambers inside the pyramid of the Pharaoh Menkaure at Giza were closed to visitors for cleaning and repair <u>due to moisture exhaled by tourists, which raised its humidity to such levels so that salt from the stone was crystallizing</u> and fungus was growing on the walls.

   (A) due to moisture exhaled by tourists, which raised its humidity to such levels so that salt from the stone was crystallizing

   (B) due to moisture that tourists had exhaled, thereby raising its humidity to such levels that salt from the stone would crystallize

   (C) because tourists were exhaling moisture, which had raised the humidity within them to levels such that salt from the stone would crystallize

   (D) because of moisture that was exhaled by tourists raising the humidity within them to levels so high as to make the salt from the stone crystallize

   (E) because moisture exhaled by tourists had raised the humidity within them to such levels that salt from the stone was crystallizing

9. In 1979 lack of rain reduced India's rice production to about 41 million tons, nearly 25 percent <u>less than those of the 1978 harvest</u>.

   (A) less than those of the 1978 harvest

   (B) less than the 1978 harvest

   (C) less than 1978

   (D) fewer than 1978

   (E) fewer than that of India's 1978 harvest

10. The widely accepted big bang theory holds <u>that the universe began in an explosive instant ten to twenty billion years ago and has been expanding</u> ever since.

   (A) that the universe began in an explosive instant ten to twenty billion years ago and has been expanding

   (B) that the universe had begun in an explosive instant ten to twenty billion years ago and had been expanding

   (C) that the beginning of the universe was an explosive instant ten to twenty billion years ago that has expanded

   (D) the beginning of the universe to have been an explosive instant ten to twenty billion years ago that is expanding

   (E) the universe to have begun in an explosive instant ten to twenty billion years ago and has been expanding

11. <u>Like the idolization accorded the Brontës and Brownings,</u> James Joyce and Virginia Woolf are often subjected to the kind of veneration that blurs the distinction between the artist and the human being.

   (A) Like the idolization accorded the Brontës and Brownings,
   (B) As the Brontës' and Brownings' idolization,
   (C) Like that accorded to the Brontës and Brownings,
   (D) As it is of the Brontës and Brownings,
   (E) Like the Brontës and Brownings,

12. Carnivorous mammals can endure what would otherwise be lethal levels of body heat because they have a heat-exchange network <u>which kept</u> the brain from getting too hot.

   (A) which kept
   (B) that keeps
   (C) which has kept
   (D) that has been keeping
   (E) having kept

13. There are several ways to build solid walls using just mud or clay, but the most extensively used method has been <u>the forming of bricks out of mud or clay, and, after some preliminary air drying or sun drying, they are laid</u> in the wall in mud mortar.

   (A) the forming of bricks out of mud or clay, and, after some preliminary air drying or sun drying, they are laid
   (B) forming the mud or clay into bricks, and, after some preliminary air drying or sun drying, to lay them
   (C) having bricks formed from mud or clay, and, after some preliminary air drying or sun drying, they were laid
   (D) to form the mud or clay into bricks, and, after some preliminary air drying or sun drying, to lay them
   (E) that bricks were formed from mud or clay, which, after some preliminary air drying or sun drying, were laid

14. Rising inventories, <u>when unaccompanied correspondingly by increases in sales, can lead</u> to production cutbacks that would hamper economic growth.

   (A) when unaccompanied correspondingly by increases in sales, can lead
   (B) when not accompanied by corresponding increases in sales, possibly leads
   (C) when they were unaccompanied by corresponding sales increases, can lead
   (D) if not accompanied by correspondingly increased sales, possibly leads
   (E) if not accompanied by corresponding increases in sales, can lead

15. Many experts regarded the large increase in credit card borrowing in March not as a sign that households were pressed for cash and forced to borrow, <u>rather a sign of confidence by households that they could safely</u> handle new debt.

   (A) rather a sign of confidence by households that they could safely
   (B) yet as a sign of households' confidence that it was safe for them to
   (C) but a sign of confidence by households that they could safely
   (D) but as a sign that households were confident they could safely
   (E) but also as a sign that households were confident in their ability safely to

16. A surge in new home sales and a drop in weekly unemployment <u>claims suggest that the economy might not be as weak as some analysts previously thought</u>.

   (A) claims suggest that the economy might not be as weak as some analysts previously thought
   (B) claims suggests that the economy might not be so weak as some analysts have previously thought
   (C) claims suggest that the economy might not be as weak as have been previously thought by some analysts
   (D) claims, suggesting about the economy that it might not be so weak as previously thought by some analysts
   (E) claims, suggesting the economy might not be as weak as previously thought to be by some analysts

17. Sunspots, vortices of gas associated with strong electromagnetic activity, <u>are visible as dark spots on the surface of the Sun but have never been sighted on</u> the Sun's poles or equator.

    (A) are visible as dark spots on the surface of the Sun but have never been sighted on

    (B) are visible as dark spots that never have been sighted on the surface of the Sun

    (C) appear on the surface of the Sun as dark spots although never sighted at

    (D) appear as dark spots on the surface of the Sun, although never having been sighted at

    (E) appear as dark spots on the Sun's surface, which have never been sighted on

18. Warning that computers in the United States are not secure, the National Academy of Sciences has urged the nation to revamp computer security procedures, institute new emergency response teams, <u>creating a special nongovernment organization to take</u> charge of computer security planning.

    (A) creating a special nongovernment organization to take

    (B) creating a special nongovernment organization that takes

    (C) creating a special nongovernment organization for taking

    (D) and create a special nongovernment organization for taking

    (E) and create a special nongovernment organization to take

19. <u>A pioneer journalist, Nellie Bly's exploits included</u> circling the globe faster than Jules Verne's fictional Phileas Fogg.

    (A) A pioneer journalist, Nellie Bly's exploits included

    (B) The exploits of Nellie Bly, a pioneer journalist, included

    (C) Nellie Bly was a pioneer journalist including in her exploits the

    (D) Included in the pioneer journalist Nellie Bly's exploits are

    (E) The pioneer journalist's exploits of Nellie Bly included

20. Retail sales rose 0.8 of 1 percent in August, intensifying expectations <u>that personal spending in the July–September quarter more than doubled that of</u> the 1.4 percent growth rate in personal spending for the previous quarter.

    (A) that personal spending in the July–September quarter more than doubled that of

    (B) that personal spending in the July–September quarter would more than double

    (C) of personal spending in the July–September quarter, that it more than doubled

    (D) of personal spending in the July–September quarter more than doubling that of

    (E) of personal spending in the July–September quarter, that it would more than double that of

21. The commission has directed advertisers to restrict the use of the word "natural" to foods that do not contain color or flavor additives, chemical preservatives, <u>or nothing that has been</u> synthesized.

    (A) or nothing that has been

    (B) or that has been

    (C) and nothing that is

    (D) or anything that has been

    (E) and anything

22. <u>Plants are more efficient at acquiring carbon than are fungi,</u> in the form of carbon dioxide, and converting it to energy-rich sugars.

    (A) Plants are more efficient at acquiring carbon than are fungi,

    (B) Plants are more efficient at acquiring carbon than fungi,

    (C) Plants are more efficient than fungi at acquiring carbon,

    (D) Plants, more efficient than fungi at acquiring carbon,

    (E) Plants acquire carbon more efficiently than fungi,

23. The Iroquois were primarily planters, <u>but supplementing</u> their cultivation of maize, squash, and beans with fishing and hunting.

    (A) but supplementing

    (B) and had supplemented

    (C) and even though they supplemented

    (D) although they supplemented

    (E) but with supplementing

24. <u>As contrasted with the honeybee,</u> the yellow jacket can sting repeatedly without dying and carries a potent venom that can cause intense pain.

    (A) As contrasted with the honeybee,
    (B) In contrast to the honeybee's,
    (C) Unlike the sting of the honeybee,
    (D) Unlike that of the honeybee,
    (E) Unlike the honeybee,

25. <u>Neuroscientists, having amassed a wealth of knowledge over the past twenty years about the brain and its development from birth to adulthood, are</u> now drawing solid conclusions about how the human brain grows and how babies acquire language.

    (A) Neuroscientists, having amassed a wealth of knowledge over the past twenty years about the brain and its development from birth to adulthood, are
    (B) Neuroscientists, having amassed a wealth of knowledge about the brain and its development from birth to adulthood over the past twenty years, and are
    (C) Neuroscientists amassing a wealth of knowledge about the brain and its development from birth to adulthood over the past twenty years, and are
    (D) Neuroscientists have amassed a wealth of knowledge over the past twenty years about the brain and its development from birth to adulthood,
    (E) Neuroscientists have amassed, over the past twenty years, a wealth of knowledge about the brain and its development from birth to adulthood,

26. Tropical bats play important roles in the rain forest ecosystem, aiding in the dispersal of cashew, date, and fig seeds; <u>pollinating banana, breadfruit, and mango trees; and indirectly help produce</u> tequila by pollinating agave plants.

    (A) pollinating banana, breadfruit, and mango trees; and indirectly help produce
    (B) pollinating banana, breadfruit, and mango trees; and indirectly helping to produce
    (C) pollinating banana, breadfruit, and mango trees; and they indirectly help to produce
    (D) they pollinate banana, breadfruit, and mango trees; and indirectly help producing
    (E) they pollinate banana, breadfruit, and mango trees; indirectly helping the producing of

27. None of the attempts to specify the causes of crime explains why most of the people exposed to the alleged causes do not commit crimes and, conversely, why so many of those not so exposed <u>have</u>.

    (A) have
    (B) has
    (C) shall
    (D) do
    (E) could

28. In virtually all types of tissue in every animal species, dioxin induces the production of enzymes that are the organism's <u>trying to metabolize, or render harmless, the chemical that is irritating it</u>.

    (A) trying to metabolize, or render harmless, the chemical that is irritating it
    (B) trying that it metabolize, or render harmless, the chemical irritant
    (C) attempt to try to metabolize, or render harmless, such a chemical irritant
    (D) attempt to try and metabolize, or render harmless, the chemical irritating it
    (E) attempt to metabolize, or render harmless, the chemical irritant

29. Emily Dickinson's letters to Susan Huntington <u>Dickinson were written over a period beginning a few years before Susan's marriage to Emily's brother and ending shortly before Emily's death in 1886, outnumbering</u> her letters to anyone else.

    (A) Dickinson were written over a period beginning a few years before Susan's marriage to Emily's brother and ending shortly before Emily's death in 1886, outnumbering
    (B) Dickinson were written over a period that begins a few years before Susan's marriage to Emily's brother and ended shortly before Emily's death in 1886, outnumber
    (C) Dickinson, written over a period beginning a few years before Susan's marriage to Emily's brother and that ends shortly before Emily's death in 1886 and outnumbering
    (D) Dickinson, which were written over a period beginning a few years before Susan's marriage to Emily's brother, ending shortly before Emily's death in 1886, and outnumbering
    (E) Dickinson, which were written over a period beginning a few years before Susan's marriage to Emily's brother and ending shortly before Emily's death in 1886, outnumber

30. Paleontologists believe that fragments of a primate jawbone unearthed in Burma and estimated <u>at 40 to 44 million years old provide evidence of</u> a crucial step along the evolutionary path that led to human beings.

    (A) at 40 to 44 million years old provide evidence of
    (B) as being 40 to 44 million years old provides evidence of
    (C) that it is 40 to 44 million years old provides evidence of what was
    (D) to be 40 to 44 million years old provide evidence of
    (E) as 40 to 44 million years old provides evidence

31. <u>Unlike the conviction held by many of her colleagues that genes were</u> relatively simple and static, Barbara McClintock adhered to her own more complicated ideas about how genes might operate, and in 1983, at the age of 81, was awarded a Nobel Prize for her discovery that the genes in corn are capable of moving from one chromosomal site to another.

    (A) Unlike the conviction held by many of her colleagues that genes were
    (B) Although many of her colleagues were of the conviction of genes being
    (C) Contrary to many of her colleagues being convinced that genes were
    (D) Even though many of her colleagues were convinced that genes were
    (E) Even with many of her colleagues convinced of genes being

32. Galileo was convinced that natural phenomena, as manifestations of the laws of physics, would appear the same to someone on the deck of a ship moving smoothly and uniformly through the <u>water as a</u> person standing on land.

    (A) water as a
    (B) water as to a
    (C) water; just as it would to a
    (D) water, as it would to the
    (E) water; just as to the

33. <u>Because an oversupply of computer chips has sent prices plunging,</u> the manufacturer has announced that it will cut production by closing its factories for two days a month.

    (A) Because an oversupply of computer chips has sent prices plunging,
    (B) Because of plunging prices for computer chips, which is due to an oversupply,
    (C) Because computer chip prices have been sent plunging, which resulted from an oversupply,
    (D) Due to plunging computer chip prices from an oversupply,
    (E) Due to an oversupply, with the result that computer chip prices have been sent plunging,

34. Beyond the immediate cash flow crisis that the museum faces, its survival depends on <u>if it can broaden its membership and leave</u> its cramped quarters for a site where it can store and exhibit its more than 12,000 artifacts.

    (A) if it can broaden its membership and leave
    (B) whether it can broaden its membership and leave
    (C) whether or not it has the capability to broaden its membership and can leave
    (D) its ability for broadening its membership and leaving
    (E) the ability for it to broaden its membership and leave

35. By 1940, the pilot Jacqueline Cochran held seventeen official national and international speed records, <u>and she earned them at a time when aviation was still so new for many of the planes she flew to be</u> of dangerously experimental design.

    (A) and she earned them at a time when aviation was still so new for many of the planes she flew to be
    (B) earning them at a time that aviation was still so new for many of the planes she flew to be
    (C) earning these at a time where aviation was still so new that many of the planes she flew were
    (D) earned at a time in which aviation was still so new such that many of the planes she flew were
    (E) earned at a time when aviation was still so new that many of the planes she flew were

36. Along with the drop in producer prices announced yesterday, the strong retail sales figures released today seem <u>like it is indicative that</u> the economy, although growing slowly, is not nearing a recession.

    (A) like it is indicative that
    (B) as if to indicate
    (C) to indicate that
    (D) indicative of
    (E) like an indication of

37. Dressed as a man and using the name Robert Shurtleff, Deborah Sampson, the first woman to draw a soldier's pension, joined the Continental Army in 1782 at the age of <u>22, was injured three times, and was discharged in 1783 because she had become</u> too ill to serve.

    (A) 22, was injured three times, and was discharged in 1783 because she had become
    (B) 22, was injured three times, while being discharged in 1783 because she had become
    (C) 22 and was injured three times, and discharged in 1783, being
    (D) 22, injured three times, and was discharged in 1783 because she was
    (E) 22, having been injured three times and discharged in 1783, being

38. Bengal-born writer, philosopher, and educator Rabindranath Tagore had the greatest admiration <u>for Mohandas K. Gandhi the person and also as a politician, but Tagore had been</u> skeptical of Gandhi's form of nationalism and his conservative opinions about India's cultural traditions.

    (A) for Mohandas K. Gandhi the person and also as a politician, but Tagore had been
    (B) for Mohandas K. Gandhi as a person and as a politician, but Tagore was also
    (C) for Mohandas K. Gandhi not only as a person and as a politician, but Tagore was also
    (D) of Mohandas K. Gandhi as a person and as also a politician, but Tagore was
    (E) of Mohandas K. Gandhi not only as a person and as a politician, but Tagore had also been

39. Although schistosomiasis is not often fatal, <u>it is so debilitating that it has become an economic</u> drain on many developing countries.

    (A) it is so debilitating that it has become an economic
    (B) it is of such debilitation, it has become an economical
    (C) so debilitating is it as to become an economic
    (D) such is its debilitation, it becomes an economical
    (E) there is so much debilitation that it has become an economical

40. The Organization of Petroleum Exporting Countries (OPEC) had long been expected to announce a reduction in output to bolster sagging oil prices, but officials of the organization just recently announced that the group will pare daily production by 1.5 million barrels by the beginning of next <u>year, but only if non-OPEC nations, including Norway, Mexico, and Russia, were to trim output</u> by a total of 500,000 barrels a day.

    (A) year, but only if non-OPEC nations, including Norway, Mexico, and Russia, were to trim output
    (B) year, but only if the output of non-OPEC nations, which includes Norway, Mexico, and Russia, is trimmed
    (C) year only if the output of non-OPEC nations, including Norway, Mexico, and Russia, would be trimmed
    (D) year only if non-OPEC nations, which includes Norway, Mexico, and Russia, were trimming output
    (E) year only if non-OPEC nations, including Norway, Mexico, and Russia, trim output

41. In 1850, Lucretia Mott published her *Discourse on Women*, <u>arguing in a treatise for women to have equal political and legal rights</u> and for changes in the married women's property laws.

    (A) arguing in a treatise for women to have equal political and legal rights
    (B) arguing in a treatise for equal political and legal rights for women
    (C) a treatise that advocates women's equal political and legal rights
    (D) a treatise advocating women's equal political and legal rights
    (E) a treatise that argued for equal political and legal rights for women

42. To develop more accurate population forecasts, demographers <u>have to know a great deal more than now about the social and economic</u> determinants of fertility.

    (A) have to know a great deal more than now about the social and economic

    (B) have to know a great deal more than they do now about the social and economical

    (C) would have to know a great deal more than they do now about the social and economical

    (D) would have to know a great deal more than they do now about the social and economic

    (E) would have to know a great deal more than now about the social and economic

43. Laos has a land area <u>about the same as Great Britain but only four million in population, where many</u> are members of hill tribes ensconced in the virtually inaccessible mountain valleys of the north.

    (A) about the same as Great Britain but only four million in population, where many

    (B) of about the same size as Great Britain is, but in Laos there is a population of only four million, and many

    (C) that is about the same size as Great Britain's land area, but in Laos with a population of only four million people, many of them

    (D) comparable to the size of Great Britain, but only four million in population, and many

    (E) comparable to that of Great Britain but a population of only four million people, many of whom

44. The plot of *The Bostonians* centers on the <u>rivalry between Olive Chancellor, an active feminist, with her charming and cynical cousin, Basil Ransom,</u> when they find themselves drawn to the same radiant young woman whose talent for public speaking has won her an ardent following.

    (A) rivalry between Olive Chancellor, an active feminist, with her charming and cynical cousin, Basil Ransom,

    (B) rivals Olive Chancellor, an active feminist, against her charming and cynical cousin, Basil Ransom,

    (C) rivalry that develops between Olive Chancellor, an active feminist, and Basil Ransom, her charming and cynical cousin,

    (D) developing rivalry between Olive Chancellor, an active feminist, with Basil Ransom, her charming and cynical cousin,

    (E) active feminist, Olive Chancellor, and the rivalry with her charming and cynical cousin Basil Ransom,

45. Quasars, at billions of light-years from Earth the most distant observable objects in the universe, <u>believed to be</u> the cores of galaxies in an early stage of development.

    (A) believed to be

    (B) are believed to be

    (C) some believe them to be

    (D) some believe they are

    (E) it is believed that they are

46. In ancient Thailand, <u>much of the local artisans' creative energy was expended for the creation of Buddha images and when they constructed and decorated the temples that enshrined them</u>.

    (A) much of the local artisans' creative energy was expended for the creation of Buddha images and when they constructed and decorated the temples that enshrined them

    (B) much of the local artisans' creative energy was expended on the creation of Buddha images and on construction and decoration of the temples in which they were enshrined

    (C) much of the local artisans' creative energy was expended on the creation of Buddha images as well as constructing and decoration of the temples in which they were enshrined

    (D) creating images of Buddha accounted for much of the local artisans' creative energy, and also constructing and decorating the temples enshrining them

    (E) the creation of Buddha images accounted for much of the local artisans' creative energy as well as construction and decoration of the temples that enshrined them

47. In 1713, Alexander Pope began <u>his translation of the *Iliad*, a work that, taking him seven years until completion, and that literary critic Samuel Johnson, Pope's contemporary, pronounced</u> the greatest translation in any language.

    (A) his translation of the *Iliad*, a work that, taking him seven years until completion, and that literary critic Samuel Johnson, Pope's contemporary, pronounced

    (B) his translation of the *Iliad*, a work that took him seven years to complete and that literary critic Samuel Johnson, Pope's contemporary, pronounced

    (C) his translation of the *Iliad*, a work that had taken seven years to complete and that literary critic Samuel Johnson, Pope's contemporary, pronounced it as

    (D) translating the *Iliad*, a work that took seven years until completion and that literary critic Samuel Johnson, Pope's contemporary, pronounced it as

    (E) translating the *Iliad*, a work that had taken seven years to complete and literary critic Samuel Johnson, Pope's contemporary, pronounced it

48. <u>It is called a sea, but the landlocked Caspian is actually the largest lake on Earth, which covers</u> more than four times the surface area of its closest rival in size, North America's Lake Superior.

    (A) It is called a sea, but the landlocked Caspian is actually the largest lake on Earth, which covers

    (B) Although it is called a sea, actually the landlocked Caspian is the largest lake on Earth, which covers

    (C) Though called a sea, the landlocked Caspian is actually the largest lake on Earth, covering

    (D) Though called a sea but it actually is the largest lake on Earth, the landlocked Caspian covers

    (E) Despite being called a sea, the largest lake on Earth is actually the landlocked Caspian, covering

49. The automotive conveyor-belt system, which Henry Ford modeled after an assembly-line technique introduced by Ransom Olds, reduced <u>from a day and a half to 93 minutes the required time of assembling a Model T</u>.

    (A) from a day and a half to 93 minutes the required time of assembling a Model T

    (B) the time being required to assemble a Model T, from a day and a half down to 93 minutes

    (C) the time being required to assemble a Model T, a day and a half to 93 minutes

    (D) the time required to assemble a Model T from a day and a half to 93 minutes

    (E) from a day and a half to 93 minutes, the time required for the assembling of a Model T

50. According to some analysts, the gains in the stock market reflect growing confidence <u>that the economy will avoid the recession that many had feared earlier in the year and instead come</u> in for a "soft landing," followed by a gradual increase in business activity.

    (A) that the economy will avoid the recession that many had feared earlier in the year and instead come

    (B) in the economy to avoid the recession, what many feared earlier in the year, rather to come

    (C) in the economy's ability to avoid the recession, something earlier in the year many had feared, and instead to come

    (D) in the economy to avoid the recession many were fearing earlier in the year, and rather to come

    (E) that the economy will avoid the recession that was feared earlier this year by many, with it instead coming

51. A new study suggests that the conversational pace of everyday life may be so brisk <u>it hampers the ability of some children for distinguishing discrete sounds and words and, the result is, to make</u> sense of speech.

    (A) it hampers the ability of some children for distinguishing discrete sounds and words and, the result is, to make

    (B) that it hampers the ability of some children to distinguish discrete sounds and words and, as a result, to make

    (C) that it hampers the ability of some children to distinguish discrete sounds and words and, the result of this, they are unable to make

    (D) that it hampers the ability of some children to distinguish discrete sounds and words, and results in not making

    (E) as to hamper the ability of some children for distinguishing discrete sounds and words, resulting in being unable to make

52. To Josephine Baker, Paris was her home long before it was fashionable to be an expatriate, and she remained in France during the Second World War as a performer and an intelligence agent for the Resistance.

    (A) To Josephine Baker, Paris was her home long before it was fashionable to be an expatriate,

    (B) For Josephine Baker, long before it was fashionable to be an expatriate, Paris was her home,

    (C) Josephine Baker made Paris her home long before to be an expatriate was fashionable,

    (D) Long before it was fashionable to be an expatriate, Josephine Baker made Paris her home,

    (E) Long before it was fashionable being an expatriate, Paris was home to Josephine Baker,

53. The nineteenth-century chemist Humphry Davy presented the results of his early experiments in his "Essay on Heat and Light," a critique of all chemistry since Robert Boyle as well as a vision of a new chemistry that Davy hoped to found.

    (A) a critique of all chemistry since Robert Boyle as well as a vision of a

    (B) a critique of all chemistry following Robert Boyle and also his envisioning of a

    (C) a critique of all chemistry after Robert Boyle and envisioning as well

    (D) critiquing all chemistry from Robert Boyle forward and also a vision of

    (E) critiquing all the chemistry done since Robert Boyle as well as his own envisioning of

54. The report recommended that the hospital should eliminate unneeded beds, expensive services should be consolidated, and use space in other hospitals.

    (A) should eliminate unneeded beds, expensive services should be consolidated, and use space in other hospitals

    (B) should eliminate unneeded beds, expensive services should be consolidated, and other hospitals' space be used

    (C) should eliminate unneeded beds, expensive services should be consolidated, and to use space in other hospitals

    (D) eliminate unneeded beds, consolidate expensive services, and other hospitals' space used

    (E) eliminate unneeded beds, consolidate expensive services, and use space in other hospitals

55. Many house builders offer rent-to-buy programs that enable a family with insufficient savings for a conventional down payment to be able to move into new housing and to apply part of the rent to a purchase later.

    (A) programs that enable a family with insufficient savings for a conventional down payment to be able to move into new housing and to apply

    (B) programs that enable a family with insufficient savings for a conventional down payment to move into new housing and to apply

    (C) programs; that enables a family with insufficient savings for a conventional down payment to move into new housing, to apply

    (D) programs, which enables a family with insufficient savings for a conventional down payment to move into new housing, applying

    (E) programs, which enable a family with insufficient savings for a conventional down payment to be able to move into new housing, applying

56. Elizabeth Barber, the author of both *Prehistoric Textiles*, a comprehensive work on cloth in the early cultures of the Mediterranean, and also of *Women's Work*, a more general account of early cloth manufacture, is an expert authority on textiles in ancient societies.

    (A) also of *Women's Work*, a more general account of early cloth manufacture, is an expert authority on

    (B) also *Women's Work*, a more general account of cloth manufacture, is an expert authority about

    (C) of *Women's Work*, a more general account about early cloth manufacture, is an authority on

    (D) of *Women's Work*, a more general account about early cloth manufacture, is an expert authority about

    (E) *Women's Work*, a more general account of early cloth manufacture, is an authority on

57. Many of the earliest known images of Hindu deities in India date from the time of the Kushan <u>Empire, fashioned either from the spotted sandstone of Mathura or</u> Gandharan grey schist.

    (A) Empire, fashioned either from the spotted sandstone of Mathura or

    (B) Empire, fashioned from either the spotted sandstone of Mathura or from

    (C) Empire, either fashioned from the spotted sandstone of Mathura or

    (D) Empire and either fashioned from the spotted sandstone of Mathura or from

    (E) Empire and were fashioned either from the spotted sandstone of Mathura or from

58. <u>That educators have not anticipated the impact of microcomputer technology can hardly be said that it is their fault</u>: Alvin Toffler, one of the most prominent students of the future, did not even mention microcomputers in *Future Shock*, published in 1970.

    (A) That educators have not anticipated the impact of microcomputer technology can hardly be said that it is their fault

    (B) That educators have not anticipated the impact of microcomputer technology can hardly be said to be at fault

    (C) It can hardly be said that it is the fault of educators who have not anticipated the impact of microcomputer technology

    (D) It can hardly be said that educators are at fault for not anticipating the impact of microcomputer technology

    (E) The fact that educators are at fault for not anticipating the impact of microcomputer technology can hardly be said

59. A leading figure in the Scottish Enlightenment, <u>Adam Smith's two major books are to democratic capitalism what</u> Marx's *Das Kapital* is to socialism.

    (A) Adam Smith's two major books are to democratic capitalism what

    (B) Adam Smith's two major books are to democratic capitalism like

    (C) Adam Smith's two major books are to democratic capitalism just as

    (D) Adam Smith wrote two major books that are to democratic capitalism similar to

    (E) Adam Smith wrote two major books that are to democratic capitalism what

60. The Olympic Games helped to keep peace among the pugnacious states of the Greek <u>world in that a sacred truce was proclaimed during the festival's month</u>.

    (A) world in that a sacred truce was proclaimed during the festival's month

    (B) world, proclaiming a sacred truce during the festival's month

    (C) world when they proclaimed a sacred truce for the festival month

    (D) world, for a sacred truce was proclaimed during the month of the festival

    (E) world by proclamation of a sacred truce that was for the month of the festival

61. While <u>all states face similar industrial waste problems, the predominating industries and the regulatory environment of the states obviously determines</u> the types and amounts of waste produced, as well as the cost of disposal.

    (A) all states face similar industrial waste problems, the predominating industries and the regulatory environment of the states obviously determines

    (B) each state faces a similar industrial waste problem, their predominant industries and regulatory environment obviously determine

    (C) all states face a similar industrial waste problem; their predominating industries and regulatory environment obviously determines

    (D) each state faces similar industrial waste problems, the predominant industries and the regulatory environment of each state obviously determines

    (E) all states face similar industrial waste problems, the predominant industries and the regulatory environment of each state obviously determine

62. Rivaling the pyramids of Egypt or even the ancient cities of the Maya as an achievement, <u>the army of terra-cotta warriors created to protect Qin Shi Huang, China's first emperor, in his afterlife is more than 2,000 years old and took 700,000 artisans more than 36 years to complete</u>.

    (A) the army of terra-cotta warriors created to protect Qin Shi Huang, China's first emperor, in his afterlife is more than 2,000 years old and took 700,000 artisans more than 36 years to complete

(B)   Qin Shi Huang, China's first emperor, was protected in his afterlife by an army of terra-cotta warriors that was created more than 2,000 years ago by 700,000 artisans who took more than 36 years to complete it

(C)   it took 700,000 artisans more than 36 years to create an army of terra-cotta warriors more than 2,000 years ago that would protect Qin Shi Huang, China's first emperor, in his afterlife

(D)   more than 2,000 years ago, 700,000 artisans worked more than 36 years to create an army of terra-cotta warriors to protect Qin Shi Huang, China's first emperor, in his afterlife

(E)   more than 36 years were needed to complete the army of terra-cotta warriors that 700,000 artisans created 2,000 years ago to protect Qin Shi Huang, China's first emperor, in his afterlife

63.   When Congress reconvenes, some newly elected members from rural states will try <u>and establish tighter restrictions for the amount of grain farmers are to be allowed to grow and to encourage</u> more aggressive sales of United States farm products overseas.

(A)   and establish tighter restrictions for the amount of grain farmers are to be allowed to grow and to encourage

(B)   and establish tighter restrictions on the amount of grain able to be grown by farmers and encouraging

(C)   establishing tighter restrictions for the amount of grain farmers are allowed to grow and to encourage

(D)   to establish tighter restrictions on the amount of grain capable of being grown by farmers and encouraging

(E)   to establish tighter restrictions on the amount of grain farmers will be allowed to grow and to encourage

64.   Doctors generally agree that such factors as cigarette smoking, eating rich foods high in fats, and alcohol consumption <u>not only do damage by themselves but also aggravate</u> genetic predispositions toward certain diseases.

(A)   not only do damage by themselves but also aggravate

(B)   do damage by themselves but also are aggravating to

(C)   are damaging by themselves but also are aggravating

(D)   not only do damage by themselves, they are also aggravating to

(E)   are doing damage by themselves, and they are also aggravating

65.   Digging in sediments in northern China, <u>evidence has been gathered by scientists suggesting that complex life-forms emerged much earlier than they had</u> previously thought.

(A)   evidence has been gathered by scientists suggesting that complex life-forms emerged much earlier than they had

(B)   evidence gathered by scientists suggests a much earlier emergence of complex life-forms than had been

(C)   scientists have gathered evidence suggesting that complex life-forms emerged much earlier than

(D)   scientists have gathered evidence that suggests a much earlier emergence of complex life-forms than that which was

(E)   scientists have gathered evidence which suggests a much earlier emergence of complex life-forms than that

66.   In a plan to stop the erosion of East Coast beaches, the Army Corps of Engineers proposed building parallel to shore a breakwater of rocks that would rise six feet above the waterline and <u>act as a buffer, so that it absorbs</u> the energy of crashing waves and protecting the beaches.

(A)   act as a buffer, so that it absorbs

(B)   act like a buffer so as to absorb

(C)   act as a buffer, absorbing

(D)   acting as a buffer, absorbing

(E)   acting like a buffer, absorb

67. The 32 species that make up the dolphin family are closely related to whales and in fact <u>include the animal known as the killer whale, which can grow to be 30 feet long and is</u> famous for its aggressive hunting pods.

    (A) include the animal known as the killer whale, which can grow to be 30 feet long and is

    (B) include the animal known as the killer whale, growing as big as 30 feet long and

    (C) include the animal known as the killer whale, growing up to 30 feet long and being

    (D) includes the animal known as the killer whale, which can grow as big as 30 feet long and is

    (E) includes the animal known as the killer whale, which can grow to be 30 feet long and it is

68. Outlining his strategy for nursing the troubled conglomerate back to health, the chief <u>executive's plans were announced on Wednesday for cutting the company's huge debt by selling nearly $12 billion in assets over the next 18 months.</u>

    (A) executive's plans were announced on Wednesday for cutting the company's huge debt by selling nearly $12 billion in assets over the next 18 months

    (B) executive's plans, which are to cut the company's huge debt by selling nearly $12 billion in assets over the next 18 months, were announced on Wednesday

    (C) executive's plans for cutting the company's huge debt by selling nearly $12 billion in assets over the next 18 months were announced on Wednesday

    (D) executive announced plans Wednesday to cut the company's huge debt by selling nearly $12 billion in assets over the next 18 months

    (E) executive announced plans Wednesday that are to cut the company's huge debt by selling nearly $12 billion in assets over the next 18 months

69. Affording strategic proximity to the Strait of Gibraltar, Morocco was also of interest to the French throughout the first half of the twentieth century because they assumed that <u>if they did not hold it, their grip on Algeria was always insecure</u>.

    (A) if they did not hold it, their grip on Algeria was always insecure

    (B) without it their grip on Algeria would never be secure

    (C) their grip on Algeria was not ever secure if they did not hold it

    (D) without that, they could never be secure about their grip on Algeria

    (E) never would their grip on Algeria be secure if they did not hold it

70. The first trenches <u>that were cut into a 500-acre site at Tell Hamoukar, Syria, have yielded strong evidence for centrally administered complex societies in northern regions of the Middle East that were arising simultaneously with but</u> independently of the more celebrated city-states of southern Mesopotamia, in what is now southern Iraq.

    (A) that were cut into a 500-acre site at Tell Hamoukar, Syria, have yielded strong evidence for centrally administered complex societies in northern regions of the Middle East that were arising simultaneously with but

    (B) that were cut into a 500-acre site at Tell Hamoukar, Syria, yields strong evidence that centrally administered complex societies in northern regions of the Middle East were arising simultaneously with but also

    (C) having been cut into a 500-acre site at Tell Hamoukar, Syria, have yielded strong evidence that centrally administered complex societies in northern regions of the Middle East were arising simultaneously but

    (D) cut into a 500-acre site at Tell Hamoukar, Syria, yields strong evidence of centrally administered complex societies in northern regions of the Middle East arising simultaneously but also

    (E) cut into a 500-acre site at Tell Hamoukar, Syria, have yielded strong evidence that centrally administered complex societies in northern regions of the Middle East arose simultaneously with but

71. Along the major rivers that traverse the deserts of northeast Africa, the Middle East, and northwest India, the combination of a reliable supply of water and good growing conditions both encouraged farming traditions that, in places, endure in at least 6,000 years.

    (A) good growing conditions both encouraged farming traditions that, in places, endure in
    (B) good growing conditions encouraged farming traditions that have, in places, endured for
    (C) of good growing conditions have encouraged farming traditions that, in places, endured for
    (D) of good growing conditions both encouraged farming traditions that have, in places, endured
    (E) of good growing conditions encouraged farming traditions that have, in places, been enduring for

72. His studies of ice-polished rocks in his Alpine homeland, far outside the range of present-day glaciers, led Louis Agassiz in 1837 to propose the concept of an age in which great ice sheets had existed in now currently temperate areas.

    (A) in which great ice sheets had existed in now currently temperate areas
    (B) in which great ice sheets existed in what are now temperate areas
    (C) when great ice sheets existed where there were areas now temperate
    (D) when great ice sheets had existed in current temperate areas
    (E) when great ice sheets existed in areas now that are temperate

73. Unlike the original National Museum of Science and Technology in Italy, where the models are encased in glass or operated only by staff members, the Virtual Leonardo Project, an online version of the museum, encourages visitors to "touch" each exhibit, which thereby activates the animated functions of the piece.

    (A) exhibit, which thereby activates
    (B) exhibit, in turn an activation of
    (C) exhibit, and it will activate
    (D) exhibit and thereby activate
    (E) exhibit which, as a result, activates

74. Despite its covering the entire planet, Earth has a crust that is not seamless or stationary, rather it is fragmented into mobile semirigid plates.

    (A) Despite its covering the entire planet, Earth has a crust that is not seamless or stationary, rather it is
    (B) Despite the fact that it covers the entire planet, Earth's crust is neither seamless nor is it stationary, but is
    (C) Despite covering the entire planet, Earth's crust is neither seamless nor is it stationary, but rather
    (D) Although it covers the entire planet, Earth's crust is neither seamless nor stationary, but rather
    (E) Although covering the entire planet, Earth has a crust that is not seamless or stationary, but

75. More and more in recent years, cities are stressing the arts as a means to greater economic development and investing millions of dollars in cultural activities, despite strained municipal budgets and fading federal support.

    (A) to greater economic development and investing
    (B) to greater development economically and investing
    (C) of greater economic development and invest
    (D) of greater development economically and invest
    (E) for greater economic development and the investment of

76. Combining enormous physical strength with higher intelligence, the Neanderthals appear as equipped for facing any obstacle the environment could put in their path, but their relatively sudden disappearance during the Paleolithic era indicates that an inability to adapt to some environmental change led to their extinction.

    (A) appear as equipped for facing any obstacle the environment could put in their path,
    (B) appear to have been equipped to face any obstacle the environment could put in their path,
    (C) appear as equipped to face any obstacle the environment could put in their paths,
    (D) appeared as equipped to face any obstacle the environment could put in their paths,
    (E) appeared to have been equipped for facing any obstacle the environment could put in their path,

77. A 1972 agreement between Canada and the United States reduced the amount of phosphates that municipalities had been allowed to dump into the Great Lakes.

(A) reduced the amount of phosphates that municipalities had been allowed to dump

(B) reduced the phosphate amount that municipalities had been dumping

(C) reduces the phosphate amount municipalities have been allowed to dump

(D) reduced the amount of phosphates that municipalities are allowed to dump

(E) reduces the amount of phosphates allowed for dumping by municipalities

78. A proposal has been made to trim the horns from rhinoceroses to discourage poachers; the question is whether tourists will continue to visit game parks and see rhinoceroses after their horns are trimmed.

(A) whether tourists will continue to visit game parks and see rhinoceroses after their horns are

(B) whether tourists will continue to visit game parks to see one once their horns are

(C) whether tourists will continue to visit game parks to see rhinoceroses once the animals' horns have been

(D) if tourists will continue to visit game parks and see rhinoceroses once the animals' horns are

(E) if tourists will continue to visit game parks to see one after the animals' horns have been

79. Ryūnosuke Akutagawa's knowledge of the literatures of Europe, China, and that of Japan were instrumental in his development as a writer, informing his literary style as much as the content of his fiction.

(A) that of Japan were instrumental in his development as a writer, informing his literary style as much as

(B) that of Japan was instrumental in his development as a writer, and it informed both his literary style as well as

(C) Japan was instrumental in his development as a writer, informing both his literary style and

(D) Japan was instrumental in his development as a writer, as it informed his literary style as much as

(E) Japan were instrumental in his development as a writer, informing both his literary style in addition to

80. The only way for growers to salvage frozen citrus is to process them quickly into juice concentrate before they rot when warmer weather returns.

(A) to process them quickly into juice concentrate before they rot when warmer weather returns

(B) if they are quickly processed into juice concentrate before warmer weather returns to rot them

(C) for them to be processed quickly into juice concentrate before the fruit rots when warmer weather returns

(D) if the fruit is quickly processed into juice concentrate before they rot when warmer weather returns

(E) to have it quickly processed into juice concentrate before warmer weather returns and rots the fruit

81. Fossils of the arm of a sloth found in Puerto Rico in 1991, and dated at 34 million years old, made it the earliest known mammal of the Greater Antilles Islands.

(A) sloth found in Puerto Rico in 1991, and dated at 34 million years old, made it the earliest known mammal of

(B) sloth, that they found in Puerto Rico in 1991, has been dated at 34 million years old, thus making it the earliest mammal known on

(C) sloth that was found in Puerto Rico in 1991, was dated at 34 million years old, making this the earliest known mammal of

(D) sloth, found in Puerto Rico in 1991, have been dated at 34 million years old, making the sloth the earliest known mammal on

(E) sloth which, found in Puerto Rico in 1991, was dated at 34 million years old, made the sloth the earliest known mammal of

82. Defense attorneys have occasionally argued that their clients' misconduct stemmed from a reaction to something ingested, but in attributing criminal or delinquent behavior to some food allergy, the perpetrators are in effect told that they are not responsible for their actions.

(A) in attributing criminal or delinquent behavior to some food allergy,

(B) if criminal or delinquent behavior is attributed to an allergy to some food,

(C) in attributing behavior that is criminal or delinquent to an allergy to some food,

(D)   if some food allergy is attributed as the cause of criminal or delinquent behavior,

(E)   in attributing a food allergy as the cause of criminal or delinquent behavior,

83.   A report by the American Academy for the Advancement of Science has concluded that <u>much of the currently uncontrolled dioxins to which North Americans are exposed comes</u> from the incineration of wastes.

(A)   much of the currently uncontrolled dioxins to which North Americans are exposed comes

(B)   much of the currently uncontrolled dioxins that North Americans are exposed to come

(C)   much of the dioxins that are currently uncontrolled and that North Americans are exposed to comes

(D)   many of the dioxins that are currently uncontrolled and North Americans are exposed to come

(E)   many of the currently uncontrolled dioxins to which North Americans are exposed come

84.   Recently physicians have determined that stomach ulcers are <u>not caused by stress, alcohol, or rich foods, but</u> a bacterium that dwells in the mucous lining of the stomach.

(A)   not caused by stress, alcohol, or rich foods, but

(B)   not caused by stress, alcohol, or rich foods, but are by

(C)   caused not by stress, alcohol, or rich foods, but by

(D)   caused not by stress, alcohol, and rich foods, but

(E)   caused not by stress, alcohol, and rich foods, but are by

85.   According to a recent poll, owning and living in a freestanding house on its own land is still a goal of a majority of young adults, <u>like that of earlier generations</u>.

(A)   like that of earlier generations

(B)   as that for earlier generations

(C)   just as earlier generations did

(D)   as have earlier generations

(E)   as it was of earlier generations

86.   In 2000, a mere two dozen products accounted for half the increase in spending on prescription drugs, <u>a phenomenon that is explained not just because of more expensive drugs but by the fact that doctors are writing</u> many more prescriptions for higher-cost drugs.

(A)   a phenomenon that is explained not just because of more expensive drugs but by the fact that doctors are writing

(B)   a phenomenon that is explained not just by the fact that drugs are becoming more expensive but also by the fact that doctors are writing

(C)   a phenomenon occurring not just because of drugs that are becoming more expensive but because of doctors having also written

(D)   which occurred not just because drugs are becoming more expensive but doctors are also writing

(E)   which occurred not just because of more expensive drugs but because doctors have also written

87.   According to scientists who monitored its path, <u>an expanding cloud of energized particles ejected from the Sun recently triggered a large storm in the magnetic field that surrounds Earth, which brightened the Northern Lights and also possibly knocking</u> out a communications satellite.

(A)   an expanding cloud of energized particles ejected from the Sun recently triggered a large storm in the magnetic field that surrounds Earth, which brightened the Northern Lights and also possibly knocking

(B)   an expanding cloud of energized particles ejected from the Sun was what recently triggered a large storm in the magnetic field that surrounds Earth, and it brightened the Northern Lights and also possibly knocked

(C)   an expanding cloud of energized particles ejected from the Sun recently triggered a large storm in the magnetic field that surrounds Earth, brightening the Northern Lights and possibly knocking

(D)   a large storm in the magnetic field that surrounds Earth, recently triggered by an expanding cloud of energized particles, brightened the Northern Lights and it possibly knocked

(E)   a large storm in the magnetic field surrounding Earth was recently triggered by an expanding cloud of energized particles, brightening the Northern Lights and it possibly knocked

88. Often visible as smog, <u>ozone is formed in the atmosphere from</u> hydrocarbons and nitrogen oxides, two major pollutants emitted by automobiles, react with sunlight.

    (A) ozone is formed in the atmosphere from
    (B) ozone is formed in the atmosphere when
    (C) ozone is formed in the atmosphere, and when
    (D) ozone, formed in the atmosphere when
    (E) ozone, formed in the atmosphere from

89. Salt deposits and moisture threaten to destroy the Mohenjo-Daro excavation in Pakistan, the site of an ancient civilization <u>that flourished at the same time as the civilizations</u> in the Nile Delta and the river valleys of the Tigris and Euphrates.

    (A) that flourished at the same time as the civilizations
    (B) that had flourished at the same time as had the civilizations
    (C) that flourished at the same time those had
    (D) flourishing at the same time as those did
    (E) flourishing at the same time as those were

90. The results of the company's cost-cutting measures are evident in its profits, <u>which increased 5 percent during the first 3 months of this year after it fell</u> over the last two years.

    (A) which increased 5 percent during the first 3 months of this year after it fell
    (B) which had increased 5 percent during the first 3 months of this year after it had fallen
    (C) which have increased 5 percent during the first 3 months of this year after falling
    (D) with a 5 percent increase during the first 3 months of this year after falling
    (E) with a 5 percent increase during the first 3 months of this year after having fallen

91. In an effort to reduce their inventories, Italian vintners have cut prices; their wines <u>have been priced to sell, and they are</u>.

    (A) have been priced to sell, and they are
    (B) are priced to sell, and they have
    (C) are priced to sell, and they do
    (D) are being priced to sell, and have
    (E) had been priced to sell, and they have

92. <u>Thelonious Monk, who was a jazz pianist and composer, produced a body of work both rooted</u> in the stride-piano tradition of Willie (The Lion) Smith and Duke Ellington, yet in many ways he stood apart from the mainstream jazz repertory.

    (A) Thelonious Monk, who was a jazz pianist and composer, produced a body of work both rooted
    (B) Thelonious Monk, the jazz pianist and composer, produced a body of work that was rooted both
    (C) Jazz pianist and composer Thelonious Monk, who produced a body of work rooted
    (D) Jazz pianist and composer Thelonious Monk produced a body of work that was rooted
    (E) Jazz pianist and composer Thelonious Monk produced a body of work rooted both

93. Nobody knows exactly how many languages there are in the world, partly because of the difficulty of distinguishing between a language <u>and the sublanguages or dialects within it, but those who have tried to count typically have found</u> about five thousand.

    (A) and the sublanguages or dialects within it, but those who have tried to count typically have found
    (B) and the sublanguages or dialects within them, with those who have tried counting typically finding
    (C) and the sublanguages or dialects within it, but those who have tried counting it typically find
    (D) or the sublanguages or dialects within them, but those who tried to count them typically found
    (E) or the sublanguages or dialects within them, with those who have tried to count typically finding

94. <u>Heating-oil prices are expected to be higher this year than last because refiners are paying about $5 a barrel more for crude oil than they were</u> last year.

    (A) Heating-oil prices are expected to be higher this year than last because refiners are paying about $5 a barrel more for crude oil than they were
    (B) Heating-oil prices are expected to rise higher this year over last because refiners pay about $5 a barrel for crude oil more than they did
    (C) Expectations are for heating-oil prices to be higher this year than last year's because refiners are paying about $5 a barrel for crude oil more than they did

(D)   It is the expectation that heating-oil prices will be higher for this year over last because refiners are paying about $5 a barrel more for crude oil now than what they were

(E)   It is expected that heating-oil prices will rise higher this year than last year's because refiners pay about $5 a barrel for crude oil more than they did

95.   One of the primary distinctions <u>between our intelligence with that of other primates may lay not so much in any specific skill but</u> in our ability to extend knowledge gained in one context to new and different ones.

(A)   between our intelligence with that of other primates may lay not so much in any specific skill but

(B)   between our intelligence with that of other primates may lie not so much in any specific skill but instead

(C)   between our intelligence and that of other primates may lie not so much in any specific skill as

(D)   our intelligence has from that of other primates may lie not in any specific skill as

(E)   of our intelligence to that of other primates may lay not in any specific skill but

96.   <u>Even though Clovis points, spear points with longitudinal grooves chipped onto their faces, have been found all over North America, they are named for the New Mexico site where they were first discovered in 1932.</u>

(A)   Even though Clovis points, spear points with longitudinal grooves chipped onto their faces, have been found all over North America, they are named for the New Mexico site where they were first discovered in 1932.

(B)   Although named for the New Mexico site where first discovered in 1932, Clovis points are spear points of longitudinal grooves chipped onto their faces and have been found all over North America.

(C)   Named for the New Mexico site where they have been first discovered in 1932, Clovis points, spear points of longitudinal grooves chipped onto the faces, have been found all over North America.

(D)   Spear points with longitudinal grooves that are chipped onto the faces, Clovis points, even though named for the New Mexico site where first discovered in 1932, but were found all over North America.

(E)   While Clovis points are spear points whose faces have longitudinal grooves chipped into them, they have been found all over North America, and named for the New Mexico site where they have been first discovered in 1932.

97.   Some anthropologists believe that the genetic homogeneity evident in the world's people is the result of a "population bottleneck"—<u>at some time in the past our ancestors suffered an event, greatly reducing their numbers</u> and thus our genetic variation.

(A)   at some time in the past our ancestors suffered an event, greatly reducing their numbers

(B)   that at some time in the past our ancestors suffered an event that greatly reduced their numbers

(C)   that some time in the past our ancestors suffered an event so that their numbers were greatly reduced,

(D)   some time in the past our ancestors suffered an event from which their numbers were greatly reduced

(E)   some time in the past, that our ancestors suffered an event so as to reduce their numbers greatly,

98.   Ranked as one of the most important of Europe's young playwrights, Franz Xaver Kroetz has written 40 plays; his works—translated into more than 30 languages—are produced more often <u>than any</u> contemporary German dramatist.

(A)   than any

(B)   than any other

(C)   than are any

(D)   than those of any other

(E)   as are those of any

99. <u>The stars, some of them at tremendous speeds, are in motion just as the planets are, yet being</u> so far away from Earth that their apparent positions in the sky do not change enough for their movement to be observed during a single human lifetime.

(A) The stars, some of them at tremendous speeds, are in motion just as the planets are, yet being

(B) Like the planets, the stars are in motion, some of them at tremendous speeds, but they are

(C) Although like the planets the stars are in motion, some of them at tremendous speeds, yet

(D) As the planets, the stars are in motion, some of them at tremendous speeds, but they are

(E) The stars are in motion like the planets, some of which at tremendous speeds are in motion but

100. <u>Heavy commitment by an executive to a course of action, especially if it has worked well in the past, makes it likely to miss signs of incipient trouble or misinterpret them when they do appear.</u>

(A) Heavy commitment by an executive to a course of action, especially if it has worked well in the past, makes it likely to miss signs of incipient trouble or misinterpret them when they do appear.

(B) An executive who is heavily committed to a course of action, especially one that worked well in the past, makes missing signs of incipient trouble or misinterpreting ones likely when they do appear.

(C) An executive who is heavily committed to a course of action is likely to miss or misinterpret signs of incipient trouble when they do appear, especially if it has worked well in the past.

(D) Executives' being heavily committed to a course of action, especially if it has worked well in the past, makes them likely to miss signs of incipient trouble or misinterpreting them when they do appear.

(E) Being heavily committed to a course of action, especially one that has worked well in the past, is likely to make an executive miss signs of incipient trouble or misinterpret them when they do appear.

101. As rainfall began to decrease in the Southwest about the middle of the twelfth century, most of the Monument Valley Anasazi abandoned their homes to join other clans <u>whose access to water was less limited</u>.

(A) whose access to water was less limited

(B) where there was access to water that was less limited

(C) where they had less limited water access

(D) with less limitations on water access

(E) having less limitations to water access

102. Yellow jackets number among the 900 or so species of the world's social wasps, <u>wasps living in a highly cooperative and organized society where they consist almost entirely of</u> females—the queen and her sterile female workers.

(A) wasps living in a highly cooperative and organized society where they consist almost entirely of

(B) wasps that live in a highly cooperative and organized society consisting almost entirely of

(C) which means they live in a highly cooperative and organized society, almost all

(D) which means that their society is highly cooperative, organized, and it is almost entirely

(E) living in a society that is highly cooperative, organized, and it consists of almost all

103. El Niño, the periodic abnormal warming of the sea surface off Peru, <u>a phenomenon in which changes in the ocean and atmosphere combine allowing the warm water that has accumulated</u> in the western Pacific to flow back to the east.

(A) a phenomenon in which changes in the ocean and atmosphere combine allowing the warm water that has accumulated

(B) a phenomenon where changes in the ocean and atmosphere are combining to allow the warm water that is accumulating

(C) a phenomenon in which ocean and atmosphere changes combine and which allows the warm water that is accumulated

(D) is a phenomenon in which changes in the ocean and atmosphere combine to allow the warm water that has accumulated

(E) is a phenomenon where ocean and atmosphere changes are combining and allow the warm water accumulating

104. Beatrix Potter, in her book illustrations, carefully coordinating them with her narratives, capitalized on her keen observation and love of the natural world.

    (A) Beatrix Potter, in her book illustrations, carefully coordinating them with her narratives,

    (B) In her book illustrations, carefully coordinating them with her narratives, Beatrix Potter

    (C) In her book illustrations, which she carefully coordinated with her narratives, Beatrix Potter

    (D) Carefully coordinated with her narratives, Beatrix Potter, in her book illustrations

    (E) Beatrix Potter, in her book illustrations, carefully coordinated them with her narratives and

105. Marconi's conception of the radio was as a substitute for the telephone, a tool for private conversation; instead, it is precisely the opposite, a tool for communicating with a large, public audience.

    (A) Marconi's conception of the radio was as a substitute for the telephone, a tool for private conversation; instead, it is

    (B) Marconi conceived of the radio as a substitute for the telephone, a tool for private conversation, but which is

    (C) Marconi conceived of the radio as a tool for private conversation that could substitute for the telephone; instead, it has become

    (D) Marconi conceived of the radio to be a tool for private conversation, a substitute for the telephone, which has become

    (E) Marconi conceived of the radio to be a substitute for the telephone, a tool for private conversation, other than what it is,

106. Originally developed for detecting air pollutants, a technique called proton-induced X-ray emission, which can quickly analyze the chemical elements in almost any substance without destroying it, is finding uses in medicine, archaeology, and criminology.

    (A) Originally developed for detecting air pollutants, a technique called proton-induced X-ray emission, which can quickly analyze the chemical elements in almost any substance without destroying it,

    (B) Originally developed for detecting air pollutants, having the ability to analyze the chemical elements in almost any substance without destroying it, a technique called proton-induced X-ray emission

    (C) A technique originally developed for detecting air pollutants, called proton-induced X-ray emission, which can quickly analyze the chemical elements in almost any substance without destroying it,

    (D) A technique originally developed for detecting air pollutants, called proton-induced X-ray emission, which has the ability to analyze the chemical elements in almost any substance quickly and without destroying it,

    (E) A technique that was originally developed for detecting air pollutants and has the ability to analyze the chemical elements in almost any substance quickly and without destroying the substance, called proton-induced X-ray emission,

107. While it costs about the same to run nuclear plants as other types of power plants, it is the fixed costs that stem from building nuclear plants that makes it more expensive for them to generate electricity.

    (A) While it costs about the same to run nuclear plants as other types of power plants, it is the fixed costs that stem from building nuclear plants that makes it more expensive for them to generate electricity.

    (B) While the cost of running nuclear plants is about the same as for other types of power plants, the fixed costs that stem from building nuclear plants make the electricity they generate more expensive.

    (C) Even though it costs about the same to run nuclear plants as for other types of power plants, it is the fixed costs that stem from building nuclear plants that makes the electricity they generate more expensive.

    (D) It costs about the same to run nuclear plants as for other types of power plants, whereas the electricity they generate is more expensive, stemming from the fixed costs of building nuclear plants.

    (E) The cost of running nuclear plants is about the same as other types of power plants, but the electricity they generate is made more expensive because of the fixed costs stemming from building nuclear plants.

108. <u>Authoritative parents are more likely than permissive parents to have children who as adolescents are self-confident, high in self-esteem, and responsibly independent.</u>

   (A)   Authoritative parents are more likely than permissive parents to have children who as adolescents are self-confident, high in self-esteem, and responsibly independent.

   (B)   Authoritative parents who are more likely than permissive parents to have adolescent children that are self-confident, high in self-esteem, and responsibly independent.

   (C)   Children of authoritative parents, rather than permissive parents, are the more likely to be self-confident, have a high self-esteem, and to be responsibly independent as adolescents.

   (D)   Children whose parents are authoritative rather than being permissive, are more likely to have self-confidence, a high self-esteem, and be responsibly independent when they are an adolescent.

   (E)   Rather than permissive parents, the children of authoritative parents are the more likely to have self-confidence, a high self-esteem, and to be responsibly independent as an adolescent.

109. Among the objects found in the excavated temple were small terra-cotta effigies left by supplicants who were either asking the goddess Bona Dea's aid <u>in healing physical and mental ills or thanking her for such help</u>.

   (A)   in healing physical and mental ills or thanking her for such help

   (B)   in healing physical and mental ills and to thank her for helping

   (C)   in healing physical and mental ills, and thanking her for helping

   (D)   to heal physical and mental ills or to thank her for such help

   (E)   to heal physical and mental ills or thanking her for such help

110. <u>Published in Harlem, the owner and editor of The Messenger were two young journalists, Chandler Owen and A. Philip Randolph, who would later make his reputation as a labor leader.</u>

   (A)   Published in Harlem, the owner and editor of The Messenger were two young journalists, Chandler Owen and A. Philip Randolph, who would later make his reputation as a labor leader.

   (B)   Published in Harlem, two young journalists, Chandler Owen and A. Philip Randolph, who would later make his reputation as a labor leader, were the owner and editor of The Messenger.

   (C)   Published in Harlem, The Messenger was owned and edited by two young journalists, A. Philip Randolph, who would later make his reputation as a labor leader, and Chandler Owen.

   (D)   The Messenger was owned and edited by two young journalists, Chandler Owen and A. Philip Randolph, who would later make his reputation as a labor leader, and published in Harlem.

   (E)   The owner and editor being two young journalists, Chandler Owen and A. Philip Randolph, who would later make his reputation as a labor leader, The Messenger was published in Harlem.

111. A mutual fund having billions of dollars in assets will typically invest that money in hundreds of <u>companies, rarely holding more than one percent</u> of the shares of any particular corporation.

   (A)   companies, rarely holding more than one percent

   (B)   companies, and it is rare to hold at least one percent or more

   (C)   companies and rarely do they hold more than one percent

   (D)   companies, so that they rarely hold more than one percent

   (E)   companies; rarely do they hold one percent or more

112. Construction of the Roman Colosseum, <u>which was officially known as the Flavian Amphitheater, began in A.D. 69, during the reign of Vespasian,</u> was completed a decade later, during the reign of Titus, who opened the Colosseum with a one-hundred-day cycle of religious pageants, gladiatorial games, and spectacles.

   (A)   which was officially known as the Flavian Amphitheater, began in A.D. 69, during the reign of Vespasian,

   (B)   officially known as the Flavian Amphitheater, begun in A.D. 69, during the reign of Vespasian, and

   (C)   which was officially known as the Flavian Amphitheater, began in A.D. 69, during the reign of Vespasian, and

(D)   officially known as the Flavian Amphitheater and begun in A.D. 69, during the reign of Vespasian it

(E)   officially known as the Flavian Amphitheater, which was begun in A.D. 69, during the reign of Vespasian, and

113.   As a baby emerges from the darkness of the womb with a rudimentary sense of vision, it would be rated about 20/500, or legally blind if it were an adult with such vision.

(A)   As a baby emerges from the darkness of the womb with a rudimentary sense of vision, it would be rated about 20/500, or legally blind if it were an adult with such vision.

(B)   A baby emerges from the darkness of the womb with a rudimentary sense of vision that would be rated about 20/500, or legally blind as an adult.

(C)   As a baby emerges from the darkness of the womb, its rudimentary sense of vision would be rated about 20/500; qualifying it to be legally blind if an adult.

(D)   A baby emerges from the darkness of the womb with a rudimentary sense of vision that would be rated about 20/500; an adult with such vision would be deemed legally blind.

(E)   As a baby emerges from the darkness of the womb, its rudimentary sense of vision, which would deemed legally blind for an adult, would be rated about 20/500.

114.   Starfish, with anywhere from five to eight arms, have a strong regenerative ability, and if one arm is lost it quickly replaces it, sometimes by the animal overcompensating and growing an extra one or two.

(A)   one arm is lost it quickly replaces it, sometimes by the animal overcompensating and

(B)   one arm is lost it is quickly replaced, with the animal sometimes overcompensating and

(C)   they lose one arm they quickly replace it, sometimes by the animal overcompensating,

(D)   they lose one arm they are quickly replaced, with the animal sometimes overcompensating,

(E)   they lose one arm it is quickly replaced, sometimes with the animal overcompensating,

115.   Because there are provisions of the new maritime code that provide that even tiny islets can be the basis for claims to the fisheries and oil fields of large sea areas, they have already stimulated international disputes over uninhabited islands.

(A)   Because there are provisions of the new maritime code that provide that even tiny islets can be the basis for claims to the fisheries and oil fields of large sea areas, they have already stimulated

(B)   Because the new maritime code provides that even tiny islets can be the basis for claims to the fisheries and oil fields of large sea areas, it has already stimulated

(C)   Even tiny islets can be the basis for claims to the fisheries and oil fields of large sea areas under provisions of the new maritime code, already stimulating

(D)   Because even tiny islets can be the basis for claims to the fisheries and oil fields of large sea areas under provisions of the new maritime code, this has already stimulated

(E)   Because even tiny islets can be the basis for claims to the fisheries and oil fields of large sea areas under provisions of the new maritime code, which is already stimulating

116.   The original building and loan associations were organized as limited life funds, whose members made monthly payments on their share subscriptions, then taking turns drawing on the funds for home mortgages.

(A)   subscriptions, then taking turns drawing

(B)   subscriptions, and then taking turns drawing

(C)   subscriptions and then took turns drawing

(D)   subscriptions and then took turns, they drew

(E)   subscriptions and then drew, taking turns

117.   Gall's hypothesis of there being different mental functions localized in different parts of the brain is widely accepted today.

(A)   of there being different mental functions localized in different parts of the brain is widely accepted today

(B)   of different mental functions that are localized in different parts of the brain is widely accepted today

(C)   that different mental functions are localized in different parts of the brain is widely accepted today

(D)   which is that there are different mental functions localized in different parts of the brain is widely accepted today

(E)   which is widely accepted today is that there are different mental functions localized in different parts of the brain

118. Mauritius was a British colony for almost 200 years, <u>excepting for</u> the domains of administration and teaching, the English language was never really spoken on the island.

    (A) excepting for
    (B) except in
    (C) but except in
    (D) but excepting for
    (E) with the exception of

119. George Sand (Aurore Lucile Dupin) was one of the first European writers to consider the rural poor <u>to be legitimate subjects for literature and portray these</u> with sympathy and respect in her novels.

    (A) to be legitimate subjects for literature and portray these
    (B) should be legitimate subjects for literature and portray these
    (C) as being legitimate subjects for literature and portraying them
    (D) as if they were legitimate subjects for literature and portray them
    (E) legitimate subjects for literature and to portray them

120. The World Wildlife Fund has declared that global warming, <u>a phenomenon most scientists agree to be caused by human beings in burning fossil fuels,</u> will create havoc among migratory birds by altering the environment in ways harmful to their habitats.

    (A) a phenomenon most scientists agree to be caused by human beings in burning fossil fuels,
    (B) a phenomenon most scientists agree that is caused by fossil fuels burned by human beings,
    (C) a phenomenon that most scientists agree is caused by human beings' burning of fossil fuels,
    (D) which most scientists agree on as a phenomenon caused by human beings who burn fossil fuels,
    (E) which most scientists agree to be a phenomenon caused by fossil fuels burned by human beings,

121. New theories propose that catastrophic impacts of asteroids and comets may have caused reversals in the Earth's magnetic field, the onset of ice ages, <u>splitting apart continents</u> 80 million years ago, and great volcanic eruptions.

    (A) splitting apart continents
    (B) the splitting apart of continents
    (C) split apart continents
    (D) continents split apart
    (E) continents that were split apart

122. A firm that specializes in the analysis of handwriting claims <u>from a one-page writing sample that it can assess</u> more than 300 personality traits, including enthusiasm, imagination, and ambition.

    (A) from a one-page writing sample that it can assess
    (B) from a one-page writing sample it has the ability of assessing
    (C) the ability, from a one-page writing sample, of assessing
    (D) to be able, from a one-page writing sample, to assess
    (E) being able to assess, from a one-page writing sample

123. Sales of wines declined in the late 1980s, but <u>they began to grow again after the 1991 report that linked moderate consumption of alcohol, and particularly of red wine, with a reduced risk of heart disease</u>.

    (A) they began to grow again after the 1991 report that linked moderate consumption of alcohol, and particularly of red wine, with a reduced risk of heart disease
    (B) after the 1991 report that linked a reduced risk of heart disease with a moderate alcohol consumption, particularly red wine, they began growing again
    (C) in a 1991 report, moderate alcohol consumption, and particularly of red wine, which was linked with a reduced risk of heart disease, caused them to begin to grow again
    (D) with a reduced risk of heart disease linked in a 1991 report with moderate alcohol consumption, in particular red wine, they began growing again
    (E) a reduced risk of heart disease linked to moderate alcohol consumption in a 1991 report, and in particular red wine, started them growing again

124. <u>She was less successful after she had emigrated to New York compared to</u> her native Germany, photographer Lotte Jacobi nevertheless earned a small group of discerning admirers, and her photographs were eventually exhibited in prestigious galleries across the United States.

    (A) She was less successful after she had emigrated to New York compared to
    (B) Being less successful after she had emigrated to New York as compared to
    (C) Less successful after she emigrated to New York than she had been in
    (D) Although she was less successful after emigrating to New York when compared to
    (E) She had been less successful after emigrating to New York than in

125. Today, because of improvements in agricultural technology, the same amount of acreage produces <u>double the apples that it has</u> in 1910.

    (A) double the apples that it has
    (B) twice as many apples as it did
    (C) as much as twice the apples it has
    (D) two times as many apples as there were
    (E) a doubling of the apples that it did

126. The use of lie detectors is based on the assumption that lying produces emotional reactions in an individual <u>that, in turn, create unconscious physiological responses</u>.

    (A) that, in turn, create unconscious physiological responses
    (B) that creates unconscious physiological responses in turn
    (C) creating, in turn, unconscious physiological responses
    (D) to create, in turn, physiological responses that are unconscious
    (E) who creates unconscious physiological responses in turn

127. Joan of Arc, a young Frenchwoman who claimed to be divinely inspired, turned the tide of English victories in her country by liberating the city of Orléans and <u>she persuaded Charles VII of France to claim his throne</u>.

    (A) she persuaded Charles VII of France to claim his throne
    (B) persuaded Charles VII of France in claiming his throne
    (C) persuading that the throne be claimed by Charles VII of France
    (D) persuaded Charles VII of France to claim his throne
    (E) persuading that Charles VII of France should claim the throne

128. Australian embryologists have found evidence <u>that suggests that the elephant is descended from an aquatic animal, and its trunk originally evolving</u> as a kind of snorkel.

    (A) that suggests that the elephant is descended from an aquatic animal, and its trunk originally evolving
    (B) that has suggested the elephant descended from an aquatic animal, its trunk originally evolving
    (C) suggesting that the elephant had descended from an aquatic animal with its trunk originally evolved
    (D) to suggest that the elephant had descended from an aquatic animal and its trunk originally evolved
    (E) to suggest that the elephant is descended from an aquatic animal and that its trunk originally evolved

129. Cajuns speak a dialect brought to southern Louisiana by the 4,000 Acadians who migrated there in 1755; their language is basically seventeenth-century French <u>to which has been added English, Spanish, and Italian words</u>.

    (A) to which has been added English, Spanish, and Italian words
    (B) added to which is English, Spanish, and Italian words
    (C) to which English, Spanish, and Italian words have been added
    (D) with English, Spanish, and Italian words having been added to it
    (E) and, in addition, English, Spanish, and Italian words are added

130. Over 75 percent of the energy produced in France derives from nuclear power, while in Germany it is just over 33 percent.

    (A) while in Germany it is just over 33 percent
    (B) compared to Germany, which uses just over 33 percent
    (C) whereas nuclear power accounts for just over 33 percent of the energy produced in Germany
    (D) whereas just over 33 percent of the energy comes from nuclear power in Germany
    (E) compared with the energy from nuclear power in Germany, where it is just over 33 percent

131. Although the term "psychopath" is popularly applied to an especially brutal criminal, in psychology it is someone who is apparently incapable of feeling compassion or the pangs of conscience.

    (A) it is someone who is
    (B) it is a person
    (C) they are people who are
    (D) it refers to someone who is
    (E) it is in reference to people

132. Although appearing less appetizing than most of their round and red supermarket cousins, heirloom tomatoes, grown from seeds saved during the previous year—they are often green and striped, or have plenty of bumps and bruises—heirlooms are more flavorful and thus in increasing demand.

    (A) Although appearing less appetizing than most of their round and red supermarket cousins, heirloom tomatoes, grown from seeds saved during the previous year
    (B) Although heirloom tomatoes, grown from seeds saved during the previous year, appear less appetizing than most of their round and red supermarket cousins
    (C) Although they appear less appetizing than most of their round and red supermarket cousins, heirloom tomatoes, grown from seeds saved during the previous year
    (D) Grown from seeds saved during the previous year, heirloom tomatoes appear less appetizing than most of their round and red supermarket cousins
    (E) Heirloom tomatoes, grown from seeds saved during the previous year, although they appear less appetizing than most of their round and red supermarket cousins

133. Last week local shrimpers held a news conference to take some credit for the resurgence of the rare Kemp's ridley turtle, saying that their compliance with laws requiring that turtle-excluder devices be on shrimp nets protect adult sea turtles.

    (A) requiring that turtle-excluder devices be on shrimp nets protect
    (B) requiring turtle-excluder devices on shrimp nets is protecting
    (C) that require turtle-excluder devices on shrimp nets protect
    (D) to require turtle-excluder devices on shrimp nets are protecting
    (E) to require turtle-excluder devices on shrimp nets is protecting

134. Recently implemented "shift-work equations" based on studies of the human sleep cycle have reduced sickness, sleeping on the job, fatigue among shift workers, and have raised production efficiency in various industries.

    (A) fatigue among shift workers, and have raised
    (B) fatigue among shift workers, and raised
    (C) and fatigue among shift workers while raising
    (D) lowered fatigue among shift workers, and raised
    (E) and fatigue among shift workers was lowered while raising

135. Spanning more than 50 years, Friedrich Müller began his career in an unpromising apprenticeship as a Sanskrit scholar and culminated in virtually every honor that European governments and learned societies could bestow.

    (A) Müller began his career in an unpromising apprenticeship as
    (B) Müller's career began in an unpromising apprenticeship as
    (C) Müller's career began with the unpromising apprenticeship of being
    (D) Müller had begun his career with the unpromising apprenticeship of being
    (E) the career of Müller has begun with an unpromising apprenticeship of

136. <u>Whereas in mammals the tiny tubes that convey nutrients to bone cells are arrayed in parallel lines, in birds the tubes</u> form a random pattern.

    (A) Whereas in mammals the tiny tubes that convey nutrients to bone cells are arrayed in parallel lines, in birds the tubes
    (B) Whereas the tiny tubes for the conveying of nutrients to bone cells are arrayed in mammals in parallel lines, birds have tubes that
    (C) Unlike mammals, where the tiny tubes for conveying nutrients to bone cells are arrayed in parallel lines, birds' tubes
    (D) Unlike mammals, in whom the tiny tubes that convey nutrients to bone cells are arrayed in parallel lines, the tubes in birds
    (E) Unlike the tiny tubes that convey nutrients to bone cells, which in mammals are arrayed in parallel lines, in birds the tubes

137. Joachim Raff and Giacomo Meyerbeer are examples of the kind of composer who receives popular acclaim while living, <u>often goes into decline after death, and never regains popularity again</u>.

    (A) often goes into decline after death, and never regains popularity again
    (B) whose reputation declines after death and never regains its status again
    (C) but whose reputation declines after death and never regains its former status
    (D) who declines in reputation after death and who never regained popularity again
    (E) then has declined in reputation after death and never regained popularity

138. Most efforts to combat such mosquito-borne diseases <u>like malaria and dengue have focused either on the vaccination of humans or on exterminating</u> mosquitoes with pesticides.

    (A) like malaria and dengue have focused either on the vaccination of humans or on exterminating
    (B) like malaria and dengue have focused either on vaccinating of humans or on the extermination of
    (C) as malaria and dengue have focused on either vaccinating humans or on exterminating
    (D) as malaria and dengue have focused on either vaccinating of humans or on extermination of
    (E) as malaria and dengue have focused on either vaccinating humans or exterminating

139. In no other historical sighting did Halley's Comet cause such a worldwide sensation as <u>did its return in 1910–1911</u>.

    (A) did its return in 1910–1911
    (B) had its 1910–1911 return
    (C) in its return of 1910–1911
    (D) its return of 1910–1911 did
    (E) its return in 1910–1911

140. Rock samples taken from the remains of an asteroid about twice the size of the 6-mile-wide asteroid that eradicated the dinosaurs <u>has been dated to be 3.47 billion years old and thus is</u> evidence of the earliest known asteroid impact on Earth.

    (A) has been dated to be 3.47 billion years old and thus is
    (B) has been dated at 3.47 billion years old and thus
    (C) have been dated to be 3.47 billion years old and thus are
    (D) have been dated as being 3.47 billion years old and thus
    (E) have been dated at 3.47 billion years old and thus are

9.7 Answer Key

1.	E	36.	C	71.	B	106.	A
2.	C	37.	A	72.	B	107.	B
3.	D	38.	B	73.	D	108.	A
4.	B	39.	A	74.	D	109.	A
5.	E	40.	E	75.	A	110.	C
6.	A	41.	E	76.	B	111.	A
7.	E	42.	D	77.	D	112.	C
8.	E	43.	E	78.	C	113.	D
9.	B	44.	C	79.	C	114.	B
10.	A	45.	B	80.	E	115.	B
11.	B	46.	B	81.	D	116.	C
12.	B	47.	B	82.	B	117.	C
13.	D	48.	C	83.	E	118.	C
14.	E	49.	D	84.	C	119.	E
15.	D	50.	A	85.	E	120.	C
16.	A	51.	B	86.	B	121.	B
17.	A	52.	D	87.	C	122.	D
18.	E	53.	A	88.	B	123.	A
19.	B	54.	E	89.	A	124.	C
20.	B	55.	B	90.	C	125.	B
21.	D	56.	E	91.	C	126.	A
22.	C	57.	E	92.	D	127.	D
23.	D	58.	D	93.	A	128.	B
24.	E	59.	E	94.	A	129.	C
25.	A	60.	D	95.	C	130.	C
26.	B	61.	E	96.	A	131.	D
27.	D	62.	A	97.	B	132.	B
28.	E	63.	E	98.	D	133.	B
29.	E	64.	A	99.	B	134.	C
30.	D	65.	C	100.	E	135.	B
31.	D	66.	C	101.	A	136.	A
32.	B	67.	A	102.	B	137.	C
33.	A	68.	D	103.	D	138.	E
34.	B	69.	B	104.	C	139.	C
35.	E	70.	E	105.	C	140.	E

9.8 Answer Explanations

The following discussion of sentence correction is intended to familiarize you with the most efficient and effective approaches to these kinds of questions. The particular questions in this chapter are generally representative of the kinds of sentence correction questions you will encounter on the GMAT exam.

1. In a review of 2,000 studies of human behavior that date back to the 1940s, two Swiss psychologists, declaring that since most of the studies had failed to control for such variables as social class and family size, none could be taken seriously.

   (A) psychologists, declaring that since most of the studies had failed to control for such variables as social class and family size,

   (B) psychologists, declaring that most of the studies failed in not controlling for such variables like social class and family size, and

   (C) psychologists declared that since most of the studies, having failed to control for such variables as social class and family size,

   (D) psychologists declared that since most of the studies fail in controlling for such variables like social class and family size,

   (E) psychologists declared that since most of the studies had failed to control for variables such as social class and family size,

   Verb form; Diction

   The subject of the sentence, *two Swiss psychologists*, needs a main verb. The *-ing* verb form *declaring* cannot, on its own, be the main verb of a correct English sentence. Furthermore, the clause that addresses the reason for not taking the studies also seriously needs a subject (*most of the studies*) and a verb (*had failed*).

   A   The sentence needs a verb form that agrees in person and number with the subject *two Swiss psychologists* and that is in the appropriate tense.

   B   In addition to the problem with *declaring*, explained above, in this version of the sentence the phrase *failed in not controlling for* is awkward and does not mean the same thing as *failed to control for*. Also, the expression *such X like Y* is incorrect in English; the correct usage is *such X as Y*.

   C   The correct form for the sentence's main verb *declared* is used here, but *having failed* is a participial form and as such cannot be the main verb in the clause.

   D   English has a rule of sequence of tenses: once a verb form is marked for past tense, the following verb forms that describe the same object or event have to be in the past tense as well. Thus, *fail* is the wrong verb form. The expression *such X like Y* is incorrect in English; the correct usage is *such X as Y*.

   E   **Correct.** The subject *two Swiss psychologists* is followed by a verb in the past tense (*declared*); the dependent clause *since … family size* also has the correct verb form (*had failed*).

   The correct answer is E.

2. Manufacturers rate batteries in watt-hours; <u>if they rate the watt-hour higher, the longer</u> the battery can be expected to last.

   (A) if they rate the watt-hour higher, the longer
   (B) rating the watt-hour higher, it is that much longer
   (C) the higher the watt-hour rating, the longer
   (D) the higher the watt-hour rating, it is that much longer that
   (E) when the watt-hour rating is higher, the longer it is

Logical predication; Grammatical construction; Parallelism

There is a cause-and-effect connection between the watt-hour rating and the battery life; therefore, the phrases describing the cause and effect have to be expressed in two parallel grammatical constructions using the two comparative forms of the modifiers *higher* and *longer*.

A Because of the way this version is constructed, the pronoun *they*, referring to *manufacturers*, illogically suggests that the manufacturers can make the batteries last longer simply by rating them higher. The cause and effect is also unparallel.

B *Rating the watt-hour higher* needs a subject; this faulty construction is known as a dangling modifier. It is possible to construe it as referring to *manufacturers*, which would be confusing. See explanation of (A) above.

C **Correct.** This version uses the correct logical and grammatical structure *the higher X, ... the longer Y.*

D This version is unparallel and ungrammatical. The correct form is *the higher X, the longer Y.*

E This version is unparallel and ungrammatical. The correct form is *the higher X, the longer Y.*

The correct answer is C.

3. Although a surge in retail sales <u>have raised hopes that there is a recovery finally</u> under way, many economists say that without a large amount of spending the recovery might not last.

   (A) have raised hopes that there is a recovery finally
   (B) raised hopes for there being a recovery finally
   (C) had raised hopes for a recovery finally being
   (D) has raised hopes that a recovery is finally
   (E) raised hopes for a recovery finally

Agreement; Rhetorical construction

The subject of the first clause, the singular noun *surge*, must take the singular verb *has raised* rather than the plural *have raised*. It is superfluous and pointless to say that people hope both that *there is* a recovery and that such a recovery *is underway*. In this context, *there is* adds nothing and can be omitted to create a more concise sentence.

A Subject and verb do not agree; *there is ... finally underway* is awkward and wordy.

B *For there being* is awkward and wordy.

C *Had raised* is the wrong verb tense; *for ... being* is awkward and wordy.

D **Correct.** In this sentence, the subject and verb agree, and the verb is in the appropriate tense; *a recovery is finally* is clear and concise.

E *For a recovery finally* is awkward and—to the extent that it can be seen as grammatical—does not make sense.

The correct answer is D.

4. At the end of the 1930s, Duke Ellington was looking for a composer to assist him—<u>someone not only who could arrange music for his successful big band, but mirroring his eccentric writing style as well in order to finish</u> the many pieces he had started but never completed.

   (A) someone not only who could arrange music for his successful big band, but mirroring his eccentric writing style as well in order to finish
   (B) someone who could not only arrange music for his successful big band, but also mirror his eccentric writing style in order to finish
   (C) someone who not only could arrange music for his successful big band, but also to mirror his eccentric writing style in finishing

(D) that being someone who could not only arrange music for his successful big band, but mirroring his eccentric writing style for finishing

(E) being someone not only who could arrange music for his successful big band, but mirror his eccentric writing style as well, finishing

Rhetorical construction; Parallelism

In describing the qualities Duke Ellington sought in a composer, the sentence uses the construction *not only … but also….* In this construction the clauses need to be parallel—for example, *not only subject verb, but also subject verb.*

A   This version is wordy, awkward, and unparallel. Furthermore, the two verbs in the *not only … but also…* construction have to be in the same form, while here we have *arrange* and *mirroring.*

B   Correct. This version exemplifies a truly parallel construction. Here, *not only* and *but also* are directly in front of the verbs they introduce. The verbs denoting the two qualities in the sought-after composer are the same form: *arrange, mirror.*

C   This version is awkward and unparallel. The two verbs have to be in the same form, while here we have *arrange* and *to mirror.* Finally, the best way to express the causal relationship between the composer's qualities and finishing Ellington's pieces is to use the conjunction *in order to.*

D   Instead of the shorter and clearer *someone who,* this version uses the longer phrase *that being someone who,* which is overly wordy. Furthermore, the verbs are not in the same form and so the construction is unparallel. Finally, the best way to express the causal relationship between the composer's qualities and finishing Ellington's pieces is to use the conjunction *in order to.*

E   Placing *being* in front of *someone* is potentially misleading; it could illogically refer to Ellington himself. The *not only … but also …* construction is also unparallel. Finally, the best way to express the causal relationship between this composer's qualities and finishing Ellington's pieces is to use the conjunction *in order to.*

The correct answer is B.

5. Of all the vast tides of migration that have swept through history, <u>maybe none is more concentrated as</u> the wave that brought 12 million immigrants onto American shores in little more than three decades.

(A) maybe none is more concentrated as

(B) it may be that none is more concentrated as

(C) perhaps it is none that is more concentrated than

(D) maybe it is none that was more concentrated than

(E) perhaps none was more concentrated than

Idiom; Verb form

This sentence depends on the comparative structure *x is more than y.* Here, an idiomatically incorrect construction *x (none) is more as y (the wave)* is used. In addition, the second part of the sentence uses the past tense verb *brought,* indicating that the event is over. The verb used in the comparative construction must also be past tense, *x (none) was more concentrated than y (the wave). Maybe* and *perhaps* are interchangeable; *perhaps* is slightly more formal.

A   Incorrect idiom is used for comparison; *is concentrated* is the wrong tense.

B   Incorrect idiom is used for comparison; *it may be that* is wordy.

C   *It is none that is more …* is wordy; also, in this context, *it* must refer to something (unlike in phrases such as "it is clear that …"), yet it does not plausibly refer to anything.

D   As in (C), *it is none that was more …* is wordy; *it* must refer to something, yet it does not plausibly refer to anything.

E   Correct. The correct comparative construction is used in this sentence; the verb is past tense.

The correct answer is E.

6. Diabetes, together with its serious complications, <u>ranks as the nation's third leading cause of death, surpassed only</u> by heart disease and cancer.

   (A) ranks as the nation's third leading cause of death, surpassed only

   (B) rank as the nation's third leading cause of death, only surpassed

   (C) has the rank of the nation's third leading cause of death, only surpassed

   (D) are the nation's third leading causes of death, surpassed only

   (E) have been ranked as the nation's third leading causes of death, only surpassed

Agreement; Logical predication

This sentence correctly matches the singular verb, *ranks*, with the singular subject, *diabetes*, and uses the present tense to indicate a current situation. The phrase following *diabetes* is set off by a pair of commas, indicating that it is descriptive information that may be dropped from the sentence; it is not a part of the subject. *Only* is placed with precision next to the group of words it actually limits, *by heart disease and cancer*. Placed before *surpassed*, *only* would more ambiguously limit *surpassed*.

A **Correct.** In the original sentence, the subject and verb agree, and the proper tense is used; *only* is correctly placed next to the phrase it limits.

B *Rank* does not agree with *diabetes*; *only* limits *surpassed* rather than *by heart disease and cancer*.

C *Has the rank of* is wordy and unidiomatic; *only* limits *surpassed* rather than *by heart disease and cancer*.

D Construction *are … causes* does not agree with *diabetes*.

E Construction *have been ranked … causes* does not agree with *diabetes* and uses the wrong verb tense; *only* limits *surpassed* rather than *by heart disease and cancer*.

The correct answer is A.

7. The intricate structure of the compound insect eye, <u>having hundreds of miniature eyes called ommatidia, help explain why scientists have assumed that it</u> evolved independently of the vertebrate eye.

   (A) having hundreds of miniature eyes called ommatidia, help explain why scientists have assumed that it

   (B) having hundreds of miniature eyes that are called ommatidia, helps explain why scientists have assumed that they

   (C) with its hundreds of miniature eyes that are called ommatidia, helps explain scientists' assuming that they

   (D) with its hundreds of miniature eyes called ommatidia, help explain scientists' assuming that it

   (E) with its hundreds of miniature eyes called ommatidia, helps explain why scientists have assumed that it

Agreement; Logical predication

This sentence addresses why scientists have decided that the vertebrate eye and the insect eye evolved independently of each other. The insect eye is much more intricate, with hundreds of miniature eyes. The sentence needs to be clear as to what has *hundreds of miniature eyes*. The *structure* or the *insect eye*? Furthermore, the singular subject *intricate structure* requires the singular verb *helps*.

A This wording misleadingly suggests that *the intricate structure* has *miniature eyes*, while the correct subject of the predicate *having* is *the compound insect eye*. Subject-verb agreement is violated.

B This wording misleads as in (A). Furthermore, the pronoun at the end of the underlined part of the sentence should refer back to *the compound insect eye*, so it cannot be plural.

C The phrase *helps explain scientists' assuming* correctly agrees with the subject *structure*. However, it is nonstandard and awkward; the use of *assuming* with the possessive is unwarranted. Finally, the pronoun at the end of the underlined part of the sentence should refer back to *the compound insect eye*, so it cannot be plural.

D   The subject *structure* and the verb *help* do not agree in number. As in (C), *explain scientists' assuming* is verbose and awkward, and the use of the *assuming* with the possessive makes the construction unnecessarily complex.

E   **Correct.** The phrase *with its hundreds* correctly refers back to *the compound insect eye.* The verb *helps* correctly agrees with the subject *structure.* Finally, the pronoun *it* correctly refers to the singular noun *the compound insect eye.*

The correct answer is E.

8.   In late 1997, the chambers inside the pyramid of the Pharaoh Menkaure at Giza were closed to visitors for cleaning and repair <u>due to moisture exhaled by tourists, which raised its humidity to such levels so that salt from the stone was crystallizing</u> and fungus was growing on the walls.

(A)   due to moisture exhaled by tourists, which raised its humidity to such levels so that salt from the stone was crystallizing

(B)   due to moisture that tourists had exhaled, thereby raising its humidity to such levels that salt from the stone would crystallize

(C)   because tourists were exhaling moisture, which had raised the humidity within them to levels such that salt from the stone would crystallize

(D)   because of moisture that was exhaled by tourists raising the humidity within them to levels so high as to make the salt from the stone crystallize

(E)   because moisture exhaled by tourists had raised the humidity within them to such levels that salt from the stone was crystallizing

Agreement; Parallelism

The plural subject *chambers* requires plural pronouns. The sentence explains a causal sequence: visitors' breath introduced moisture that caused salt to crystallize, which caused the chambers to be closed for cleaning and repair. The phrase *due to* makes this causal sequence somewhat ambiguous, seeming to suggest that the repairs were due to humidity from visitors' breath.

A   *Due to* is an imprecise expression of the causal connection between the tourists' breath and the closing of the museum for cleaning; the singular pronoun *its* does not agree with the plural antecedent *chambers.*

B   It is not at all clear what the reference is for the pronoun *its; fungus was growing* should be parallel to *salt ... was crystallizing* (not *would crystallize*) because it is another effect of the humidity.

C   The pronoun *them* seems to refer to *tourists*, which is nonsensical; the entire construction is awkward and wordy; *would crystallize* is not parallel to *was growing.*

D   Once again, *them* seems to refer to tourists; the entire construction is awkward, wordy, and ambiguous; *crystallize* is not parallel to *was growing.*

E   **Correct.** The causal sequence is clear, and *them* clearly refers to *chambers.*

The correct answer is E.

9. In 1979 lack of rain reduced India's rice production to about 41 million tons, nearly 25 percent <u>less than those of the 1978 harvest</u>.

    (A)   less than those of the 1978 harvest
    (B)   less than the 1978 harvest
    (C)   less than 1978
    (D)   fewer than 1978
    (E)   fewer than that of India's 1978 harvest

Logical predication; Diction

The crucial part of this sentence is the latter part, where India's 1979 production of 41 million tons of rice is compared to the production of the previous year. What was produced in 1979 was 25 percent less than what was produced in 1978. The grammatical means of comparison have to express correctly this relationship between the two harvests. It helps if you think of 41 million tons of rice as the collective equivalent of the 1979 harvest.

A   This version exhibits redundant word choice. The pronoun *those* refers to the tons of the 1978 harvest. Both harvests are measured in tons, and it is clearer and simpler to compare with the harvest itself, not with the tons of the harvest.

B   Correct. This version correctly compares the 1978 harvest with the 1979 harvest.

C   This version is illogical. It compares rice production in tons with a year, 1978.

D   In addition to the problem described in (C) above, this version uses the wrong comparative adjective. *Fewer* refers to countable nouns, while *less* refers to quantities. Since the comparative adjective should refer to rice production, *fewer* is not appropriate.

E   Since the comparative adjective should refer to rice production, *fewer* is not appropriate. Furthermore, the pronoun *that* refers back to India's rice production [*fewer than **the rice production** of India's 1978 harvest*] and is redundant. The word *harvest* is sufficient here to express the comparison.

The correct answer is B.

10. The widely accepted big bang theory holds <u>that the universe began in an explosive instant ten to twenty billion years ago and has been expanding</u> ever since.

    (A)   that the universe began in an explosive instant ten to twenty billion years ago and has been expanding
    (B)   that the universe had begun in an explosive instant ten to twenty billion years ago and had been expanding
    (C)   that the beginning of the universe was an explosive instant ten to twenty billion years ago that has expanded
    (D)   the beginning of the universe to have been an explosive instant ten to twenty billion years ago that is expanding
    (E)   the universe to have begun in an explosive instant ten to twenty billion years ago and has been expanding

Logical predication; Verb form

The sentence describes the central tenet of a theory about how the universe began. The focus of the second clause should be consistently on the subject *the universe*, and all verbs in the clause beginning with *that* must describe what the universe did at the initial explosive moment.

A   Correct. Both verbs in the second clause correctly take *universe* as their subject.

B   *Had begun* is the wrong tense because it describes action that occurred farther in the past than some other, specified past action.

C   The relative clause *that has expanded* describes *instant*, which makes no sense.

D   *The beginning of the universe to have been ...* is unnecessarily indirect and wordy; illogically suggests that *beginning* is expanding, not the universe.

E   The verb phrases *to have begun* and *has been expanding* both reference the same subject of the clause, *universe*, and therefore need to be parallel.

The correct answer is A.

11. <u>Like the idolization accorded the Brontës and Brownings,</u> James Joyce and Virginia Woolf are often subjected to the kind of veneration that blurs the distinction between the artist and the human being.

(A) Like the idolization accorded the Brontës and Brownings,

(B) As the Brontës' and Brownings' idolization,

(C) Like that accorded to the Brontës and Brownings,

(D) As it is of the Brontës and Brownings,

(E) Like the Brontës and Brownings,

Logical predication

This sentence intends to compare nineteenth- and twentieth-century writers. Instead the comparison becomes ambiguous and illogical. *Like* must be used to compare similar elements: *Joyce* and *Woolf* are *like* the *Brontës* and the *Brownings*; they are not *like* the *idolization*.

A *The idolization accorded* is not comparable to Joyce and Woolf.

B The conjunction *as* may introduce a clause but not a phrase; Joyce and Woolf are compared to *idolization* rather than to the writers.

C *That* is ambiguous, and Joyce and Woolf are compared to *that* rather than to the writers.

D *It* is ambiguous; *as it is of* is awkward and wordy; the twentieth-century writers are compared to *it* rather than to the nineteenth-century writers.

E **Correct.** In this sentence, *like* introduces a clear and concise comparison that correctly links the nineteenth-and twentieth-century writers.

The correct answer is E.

12. Carnivorous mammals can endure what would otherwise be lethal levels of body heat because they have a heat-exchange network <u>which kept</u> the brain from getting too hot.

(A) which kept

(B) that keeps

(C) which has kept

(D) that has been keeping

(E) having kept

Verb form; Rhetorical construction

The use of the past tense (*kept*) is incorrect because a current situation is discussed; the present tense (*keeps*) is consistent with the other verbs in the sentence. In (A) and (C), *which* introduces a restrictive clause. Some writers follow the convention that *which* can only be used for nonrestrictive clauses, but insistence on this rule is controversial, and both (A) and (C) can be rejected on other grounds.

A *Kept* is the wrong tense.

B **Correct.** The verb *keeps* indicates a current situation and is consistent with the other verbs in the sentence. The sentence is clear and concise.

C Mistaken shift in tense: In this sentence the present tense expresses a timeless general principle; in contrast, *has kept* indicates a more definite context and time period and suggests that the heat-exchange network may no longer have this effect.

D *Has been keeping* is the wrong tense.

E *Having* is awkward and imprecise; *kept* is the wrong tense.

The correct answer is B.

13. There are several ways to build solid walls using just mud or clay, but the most extensively used method has been <u>the forming of bricks out of mud or clay, and, after some preliminary air drying or sun drying, they are laid</u> in the wall in mud mortar.

    (A) the forming of bricks out of mud or clay, and, after some preliminary air drying or sun drying, they are laid

    (B) forming the mud or clay into bricks, and, after some preliminary air drying or sun drying, to lay them

    (C) having bricks formed from mud or clay, and, after some preliminary air drying or sun drying, they were laid

    (D) to form the mud or clay into bricks, and, after some preliminary air drying or sun drying, to lay them

    (E) that bricks were formed from mud or clay, which, after some preliminary air drying or sun drying, were laid

Parallelism; Verb form

The purpose of the sentence is to describe the historically most popular method of building walls. The first clause announces this topic and the second clause describes the particular method. The clearest, most efficient way to accomplish these two pieces of business is to use a parallel structure. The *ways to build* in the first clause is narrowed to the single way *to form* and *to lay* in the second clause. There is no need to alternate the verb phrases between active and passive voice or to shift tenses.

A   The active gerund phrase *the forming of bricks* does not fit with the passive verb phrase that follows (*they are laid*).

B   The verb phrases *forming the mud …* and *to lay them* are not parallel.

C   In addition to faulty parallelism between *having bricks formed* and *they were laid*, the tense in the second half of the sentence unaccountably shifts from present to past.

D   Correct. The phrases *to form* and *to lay* in the second clause are parallel to *to build* in the first clause.

E   The relative clause beginning with *which* apparently (but nonsensically) describes the closest nouns, *mud or clay*, rather than *bricks*.

The correct answer is D.

14. Rising inventories, <u>when unaccompanied correspondingly by increases in sales, can lead</u> to production cutbacks that would hamper economic growth.

    (A) when unaccompanied correspondingly by increases in sales, can lead

    (B) when not accompanied by corresponding increases in sales, possibly leads

    (C) when they were unaccompanied by corresponding sales increases, can lead

    (D) if not accompanied by correspondingly increased sales, possibly leads

    (E) if not accompanied by corresponding increases in sales, can lead

Diction; Agreement

The modifying phrase *when … sales* is needlessly difficult to understand. The adverb *correspondingly* is incorrectly and ambiguously used; using the adjective *corresponding* to modify *increases in sales* makes the intended meaning clearer. *Unaccompanied* is not wrong but *not accompanied* more effectively expresses the intended negation.

A   *Unaccompanied correspondingly* is awkward and ambiguous.

B   Plural subject *inventories* does not agree with the singular verb *leads*.

C   Wrong tense: past tense *were* indicates a completed event, but *can lead* indicates a possibility that continues.

D   *Correspondingly increased sales* is awkward and unclear; verb (*leads*) does not agree with the subject (*inventories*).

E   Correct. *Not accompanied* emphasizes the negative and is preferable to *unaccompanied* in this usage; *corresponding* modifies *increases in sales*; the modifier is clear and comprehensible, and there is no subject-verb agreement problem.

The correct answer is E.

15. Many experts regarded the large increase in credit card borrowing in March not as a sign that households were pressed for cash and forced to borrow, <u>rather a sign of confidence by households that they could safely</u> handle new debt.

(A)   rather a sign of confidence by households that they could safely

(B)   yet as a sign of households' confidence that it was safe for them to

(C)   but a sign of confidence by households that they could safely

(D)   but as a sign that households were confident they could safely

(E)   but also as a sign that households were confident in their ability safely to

Idiom; Logical predication; Parallelism

The structure of this sentence expresses negation and affirmation: *Many experts regarded X not as a sign that Y, but as a sign of Z.* The idiomatic choice of words for this construction should involve two clauses introduced by *not as … but as….* It is also important to connect logically the adjective *confident* with the noun it describes, that is, *households.* If the adjective *confident* or its equivalent noun *confidence* is related to other words in the sentence, the message loses clarity and power.

A   The idiomatic choice of words to express the negation of one clause and the affirmation of another is *not as … but as….* The affirmed clause is incorrectly introduced by *rather.* Furthermore, the preposition *by* does not express the idea that households are confident. The placement of the restrictive clause *that they could safely handle new debt* after *households* could also cause confusion.

B   The idiomatic choice of words to express the negation of one clause and the affirmation of another is *not as … but as….* The affirmed clause is incorrectly introduced by *yet as.* The wording *it was safe for them [households] to handle new debt* changes the intended meaning, making the households less clearly an agent in the handling.

C   The idiomatic choice of words to express the negation of one clause and the affirmation of another is *not as … but as….* The affirmed clause is incorrectly introduced by *but* without the *as.* Furthermore, the preposition *by* does not express the idea that households are confident.

D   **Correct.** This version provides the correct logical structure. It also expresses the confidence of households using the most succinct and direct wording.

E   The use of the word *also* is misleading here. If the first embedded clause is negated, the affirmed second clause cannot also be true. In addition, *in their ability*, while expressing the same idea as *could*, is redundant and *safely to handle* is awkward; the wording in (D) is superior.

The correct answer is D.

16.   A surge in new home sales and a drop in weekly unemployment <u>claims suggest that the economy might not be as weak as some analysts previously thought</u>.

(A)   claims suggest that the economy might not be as weak as some analysts previously thought

(B)   claims suggests that the economy might not be so weak as some analysts have previously thought

(C)   claims suggest that the economy might not be as weak as have been previously thought by some analysts

(D)   claims, suggesting about the economy that it might not be so weak as previously thought by some analysts

(E)   claims, suggesting the economy might not be as weak as previously thought to be by some analysts

Agreement; Grammatical construction

The plural subject of this sentence (*surge* and *drop*) requires a plural verb, *suggest.* The object of this verb, the clause beginning with *that*, should be presented in as clear and direct a manner as possible.

A   **Correct.** The plural subject is matched with a plural verb.

B   The singular verb *suggests* does not match the plural subject of the sentence.

C   The sentence offers no plural subject to fit the passive verb *have been thought.*

D   This construction is awkward, wordy, and imprecise; it also lacks a main verb; there is no reason to use passive voice, and *suggesting about the economy that it might …* introduces extra words that contribute nothing to the meaning of this sentence fragment.

E   The passive construction makes this unnecessarily wordy; the lack of a main verb makes this a sentence fragment.

The correct answer is A.

17. Sunspots, vortices of gas associated with strong electromagnetic activity, <u>are visible as dark spots on the surface of the Sun but have never been sighted on</u> the Sun's poles or equator.

    (A) are visible as dark spots on the surface of the Sun but have never been sighted on

    (B) are visible as dark spots that never have been sighted on the surface of the Sun

    (C) appear on the surface of the Sun as dark spots although never sighted at

    (D) appear as dark spots on the surface of the Sun, although never having been sighted at

    (E) appear as dark spots on the Sun's surface, which have never been sighted on

Logical predication; Parallelism

The correct parallel structure in the original sentence emphasizes the contrast between where sunspots are found (*are visible … Sun*) and where they are not (*have never been sighted … equator*). *Sunspots* is the subject of the sentence; *are* is the verb of the first part of the contrast, and *have been sighted* is the verb of the second. (The adjective *visible* is a complement and is parallel to the past participle *sighted*.) Both parts of the sentence conclude with phrases indicating location. The contrast itself is indicated by the conjunction *but*.

A Correct. This sentence clearly and correctly draws a contrast between where sunspots are found and where they are not.

B The modifying clause *that never … Sun* distorts the meaning of the sentence; also, without punctuation, the phrase *on the surface of the Sun the Sun's poles or equator* is ungrammatical and makes no sense.

C *Although* typically introduces a subordinate clause, which has a subject and a verb, but here there is no subject and *sighted* is not a complete verb.

D *Although* usually introduces a subordinate clause, but there is no subject of the clause and *having been sighted* is not a complete verb phrase.

E This phrasing makes the sentence somewhat awkward and unclear.

The correct answer is A.

18. Warning that computers in the United States are not secure, the National Academy of Sciences has urged the nation to revamp computer security procedures, institute new emergency response teams, <u>creating a special nongovernment organization to take</u> charge of computer security planning.

    (A) creating a special nongovernment organization to take

    (B) creating a special nongovernment organization that takes

    (C) creating a special nongovernment organization for taking

    (D) and create a special nongovernment organization for taking

    (E) and create a special nongovernment organization to take

Parallelism; Grammatical construction

This sentence contains a list of three elements, all of which should be parallel. The last element should be preceded by the conjunction *and*. In this sentence, the last element must be made parallel to the previous two: to (1) *revamp computer security procedures*, (2) *institute new emergency response teams*, and (3) *create a special nongovernment organization to take charge of computer security planning*. Omitting *and* causes the reader to anticipate still another element in the series when there is none. Using the participle *creating* not only violates parallelism but also causes misreading since the participial phrase could modify the first part of the sentence. *To* does not need to be repeated with *institute* and *create* because it is understood.

A *Creating* is not parallel to *to revamp* and *institute*; *and* is needed in this series.

B *Creating* violates the parallelism of the previous two elements; *and* is needed in this series; since the organization does not yet exist, *that takes* is illogical.

C *Creating* is not parallel to *to revamp* and *institute*; *and* is needed in this series; *to* has the sense of *in order to*, but *for taking* is neither precise nor idiomatic.

D In the construction *create … to take*, the sense of *to* is *in order to*; *for taking* is not idiomatically correct.

E   **Correct.** The three elements in the series are parallel in this sentence, and the last is preceded by *and*.

The correct answer is E.

19. A pioneer journalist, Nellie Bly's exploits included circling the globe faster than Jules Verne's fictional Phileas Fogg.

   (A)   A pioneer journalist, Nellie Bly's exploits included
   (B)   The exploits of Nellie Bly, a pioneer journalist, included
   (C)   Nellie Bly was a pioneer journalist including in her exploits the
   (D)   Included in the pioneer journalist Nellie Bly's exploits are
   (E)   The pioneer journalist's exploits of Nellie Bly included

Logical predication; Modification

This sentence intends to discuss Nellie Bly, a pioneer journalist who counts among her exploits a very fast trip around the globe. The current construction is misleading because it suggests that Bly's exploits, not Bly herself, were a pioneer journalist.

A   In this answer choice, *a pioneer journalist* incorrectly modifies *exploits*, rather than *Nellie Bly*.
B   **Correct.** This version correctly attributes the modifier *a pioneer journalist* to *Nellie Bly*.
C   The wording of this version is illogical because it makes *Nellie Bly* the subject of the verb *including*.
D   Since this event clearly happened in the past, the tense of the verb *are* is wrong. Piling on too many descriptive words for the noun *exploits* [*the pioneer journalist Nellie Bly's exploits*] makes the phrase unwieldy and awkward.
E   This version can be construed as entailing that the pioneer journalist and Nellie Bly are two different people, one exploiting the other.

The correct answer is B.

20. Retail sales rose 0.8 of 1 percent in August, intensifying expectations that personal spending in the July–September quarter more than doubled that of the 1.4 percent growth rate in personal spending for the previous quarter.

   (A)   that personal spending in the July–September quarter more than doubled that of
   (B)   that personal spending in the July–September quarter would more than double
   (C)   of personal spending in the July–September quarter, that it more than doubled
   (D)   of personal spending in the July–September quarter more than doubling that of
   (E)   of personal spending in the July–September quarter, that it would more than double that of

Verb form; Logical predication

The sentence explains the expectations that resulted from a past retail sales trend. Since expectations look to the future but are not yet realized, the relative clause explaining these expectations should be conditional, employing the auxiliary verb *would*.

A   The simple past-tense verb form does not express the forward-looking sense of *expectations*.
B   **Correct.** By using the verb *would double*, this concise sentence indicates that the expectation has not yet been realized.
C   This construction is awkward, announcing the topic (*personal spending*) and then elaborating in a relative clause that restates this topic as *it*.
D   Although this option is not technically wrong, it is less clear and graceful than (B).
E   Like (C), this sentence is awkward and unnecessarily wordy, announcing the topic and then using an additional clause to elaborate on it.

The correct answer is B.

21. The commission has directed advertisers to restrict the use of the word "natural" to foods that do not contain color or flavor additives, chemical preservatives, <u>or nothing that has been</u> synthesized.

    (A) or nothing that has been
    (B) or that has been
    (C) and nothing that is
    (D) or anything that has been
    (E) and anything

Idiom; Logical predication

The use of *do not* and *nothing* in the same sentence creates a double negative and reverses the intended meaning. *Anything* should be used instead of *nothing*. Logically, a "natural" food cannot contain any prohibited ingredient, so the list of prohibited ingredients must be connected by *or*.

A   The use of *nothing* creates a double negative.

B   *That has been synthesized* distorts the meaning by referring to foods, rather than to something added to a food.

C   The use of *nothing* creates a double negative; *and* should be *or*.

D   **Correct.** This sentence correctly avoids a double negative and uses parallel elements.

E   *And* distorts the meaning of the sentence.

The correct answer is D.

22. <u>Plants are more efficient at acquiring carbon than are fungi,</u> in the form of carbon dioxide, and converting it to energy-rich sugars.

    (A) Plants are more efficient at acquiring carbon than are fungi,
    (B) Plants are more efficient at acquiring carbon than fungi,
    (C) Plants are more efficient than fungi at acquiring carbon,
    (D) Plants, more efficient than fungi at acquiring carbon,
    (E) Plants acquire carbon more efficiently than fungi,

Logical predication; Grammatical construction

This sentence compares how efficiently plants and fungi acquire carbon and convert it into sugars. The sentence construction needs to make clear that plants and fungi are the two topics being compared, and it must also clarify that *in the form of carbon dioxide* refers to *carbon* rather than to either *plants* or *fungi*.

A   According to the sentence grammar, *in the form of carbon dioxide* describes *fungi*, which is nonsensical.

B   This sentence claims that plants acquire carbon more efficiently than they acquire fungi, which is also nonsensical; *the form of carbon dioxide* still modifies *fungi*.

C   **Correct.** The sentence clearly compares plants to fungi, and *in the form of carbon dioxide* correctly modifies *carbon*.

D   This sentence is grammatically incomplete; there is no verb for the subject *plants*.

E   As in (B), this sentence claims that plants acquire carbon more efficiently than they acquire fungi; it is also grammatically incomplete because *and converting* does not clearly refer to anything.

The correct answer is C.

23. The Iroquois were primarily planters, <u>but supplementing</u> their cultivation of maize, squash, and beans with fishing and hunting.

    (A)   but supplementing
    (B)   and had supplemented
    (C)   and even though they supplemented
    (D)   although they supplemented
    (E)   but with supplementing

Grammatical construction; Verb form

The participle *supplementing* would normally be expected to modify the first clause, describing or extending its meaning, but the logic of this sentence demands a contrast, not an extension. Consequently, the second part of the sentence must be revised to emphasize the contrast properly. The logic of the sentence also argues against a construction that would set the two clauses and the importance of their content equal when they clearly should not be. The best solution is to have the main clause describe the primary activity, and a subordinate clause, *although they supplemented*, describe the supplementary activity.

A   The construction using *supplementing* fails to support the intended meaning of the sentence.

B   *And* does not convey contrast; *had supplemented* is the past perfect tense but the simple past is required to match *were*.

C   *And* does not convey contrast and should be omitted; *and even though* creates a sentence fragment.

D   Correct. Using *although* creates a subordinate clause in this sentence and logically links that clause with the main clause; the simple past *supplemented* parallels the simple past *were*.

E   *But with* is awkward and unclear; *supplementing* is a modifier when a contrasting clause is needed.

The correct answer is D.

24. <u>As contrasted with the honeybee,</u> the yellow jacket can sting repeatedly without dying and carries a potent venom that can cause intense pain.

    (A)   As contrasted with the honeybee,
    (B)   In contrast to the honeybee's,
    (C)   Unlike the sting of the honeybee,
    (D)   Unlike that of the honeybee,
    (E)   Unlike the honeybee,

Idiom; Logical predication

The intent of the sentence is to contrast the honeybee and the yellow jacket. Correct idioms for such a contrast include *in contrast with x, y; in contrast to x, y;* and *unlike x, y.* In all these idioms, *x* and *y* must be grammatically and logically parallel. *As contrasted with* is not a correct idiom.

A   *As contrasted with* is not a correct idiom.

B   Because of its apostrophe, *the honeybee's* is not parallel to *the yellow jacket.*

C   *The sting of the honeybee* is not parallel to *the yellow jacket.*

D   *That of the honeybee* is not parallel to *the yellow jacket.*

E   Correct. This sentence uses a correct idiom, and *the honeybee* is properly parallel to *the yellow jacket.*

The correct answer is E.

25. <u>Neuroscientists, having amassed a wealth of knowledge over the past twenty years about the brain and its development from birth to adulthood, are</u> now drawing solid conclusions about how the human brain grows and how babies acquire language.

    (A) Neuroscientists, having amassed a wealth of knowledge over the past twenty years about the brain and its development from birth to adulthood, are

    (B) Neuroscientists, having amassed a wealth of knowledge about the brain and its development from birth to adulthood over the past twenty years, and are

    (C) Neuroscientists amassing a wealth of knowledge about the brain and its development from birth to adulthood over the past twenty years, and are

    (D) Neuroscientists have amassed a wealth of knowledge over the past twenty years about the brain and its development from birth to adulthood,

    (E) Neuroscientists have amassed, over the past twenty years, a wealth of knowledge about the brain and its development from birth to adulthood,

Grammatical construction; Logical predication

This sentence introduces the subject (*Neuroscientists*), pauses to explain what neuroscientists have accomplished in the past twenty years, and then concludes by explaining what neuroscientists are presently doing as a result of their past accomplishments. The second part of the sentence—the explanation—interrupts the flow of the sentence from the subject (*Neuroscientists*) to the predicate (*are now drawing solid conclusions …*); it should therefore be bracketed by commas. The sentence construction should provide a main verb for the subject *neuroscientists*.

A **Correct.** The explanatory phrase between the subject and predicate is set off by commas, and the main clause contains both a subject (*Neuroscientists*) and a corresponding verb (*are now drawing*).

B *And are* indicates that *are* follows a previous verb, but in fact the sentence has not yet provided a first main verb for the subject *Neuroscientists*; the sentence is therefore incomplete; *over the … years* appears to be modifying *adulthood*.

C *Amassing*, like *having amassed*, functions as an adjective, not a verb; the sentence therefore lacks the first main verb implied by the compound verb construction *and are now drawing.…*

D The final descriptor in present tense, *now drawing conclusions* … does not fit the opening clause, which is in present-perfect tense (*have amassed a wealth …*) and seems to modify *adulthood*.

E Like (D), this sentence attempts to attach a present-tense descriptor to a present-perfect clause.

The correct answer is A.

26. Tropical bats play important roles in the rain forest ecosystem, aiding in the dispersal of cashew, date, and fig seeds; <u>pollinating banana, breadfruit, and mango trees; and indirectly help produce</u> tequila by pollinating agave plants.

    (A) pollinating banana, breadfruit, and mango trees; and indirectly help produce

    (B) pollinating banana, breadfruit, and mango trees; and indirectly helping to produce

    (C) pollinating banana, breadfruit, and mango trees; and they indirectly help to produce

    (D) they pollinate banana, breadfruit, and mango trees; and indirectly help producing

    (E) they pollinate banana, breadfruit, and mango trees; indirectly helping the producing of

Logical predication; Parallelism

This sentence expresses a list of the roles tropical bats play in the rain forest ecosystem. Since these roles are enumerated in a list, and since the first member of the list is already provided, it is necessary to maintain the same structure for the rest of the members of the list in order to maintain parallelism and clarity. Note that semicolons separate the members of the list, leaving the commas to mark series of items within each member of the list.

A   In this version, the third member of the list does not maintain the *-ing* verb form that the two previous members use.

B   Correct. This version correctly maintains the parallel structure (*aiding in … ; pollinating … ; and helping …*).

C   In this version, the third member of the list does not maintain the *-ing* verb form of the two previous members of the list. In addition, this member of the list includes a subject (*they*) while the other members do not, again violating parallelism.

D   In order to maintain parallelism the verb that is the member of the list has to be in the *-ing* form, not its complement. Thus, the *-ing* has to be on the verb *help*, not on *produce*.

E   Although this version maintains parallelism throughout, the phrase *helping the producing* is an incorrect construction in English.

The correct answer is B.

27.   None of the attempts to specify the causes of crime explains why most of the people exposed to the alleged causes do not commit crimes and, conversely, why so many of those not so exposed <u>have</u>.

   (A)   have
   (B)   has
   (C)   shall
   (D)   do
   (E)   could

Grammatical construction; Parallelism

The sentence compares one group of people, *most of the people exposed to the alleged causes*, with another group of people, *so many of those not so exposed*. To maintain the comparison, the verb in the second part should match the verb in the first part. Since the first verb is *do not commit*, the second verb should be the parallel *do*. There is no need to repeat *commit crimes* since it is understood in this construction.

A   Verb should be *do*, not *have*.

B   Verb should be *do*, not *has*.

C   Verb should be *do*, not *shall*.

D   **Correct.** This sentence correctly uses the verb *do* to complete the comparison and maintain the parallelism with *do not commit*.

E   Verb should be *do*, not *could*.

The correct answer is D.

28.   In virtually all types of tissue in every animal species, dioxin induces the production of enzymes that are the organism's <u>trying to metabolize, or render harmless, the chemical that is irritating it</u>.

   (A)   trying to metabolize, or render harmless, the chemical that is irritating it
   (B)   trying that it metabolize, or render harmless, the chemical irritant
   (C)   attempt to try to metabolize, or render harmless, such a chemical irritant
   (D)   attempt to try and metabolize, or render harmless, the chemical irritating it
   (E)   attempt to metabolize, or render harmless, the chemical irritant

Diction; Rhetorical construction

The *-ing* form of a verb can be used as a noun (e.g., *running* is her favorite sport), but it is often awkward, particularly when used with a possessive, as in this case. Substituting the noun *attempt* for the gerund *trying* eliminates the problem. While *chemical that is irritating it* and *chemical irritating it* are both grammatically correct and could be appropriate in some usages, they are excessively wordy for this context.

A   *Trying* is awkward, especially in this construction with *organism's*.

B   *Trying that it metabolize* is ungrammatical.

C   *Attempt to try* is redundant.

D   *Attempt to try and* is redundant.

E   **Correct.** In this sentence, the noun *attempt* replaces the gerund *trying* in this construction with *organism's*.

The correct answer is E.

29. Emily Dickinson's letters to Susan Huntington <u>Dickinson were written over a period beginning a few years before Susan's marriage to Emily's brother and ending shortly before Emily's death in 1886, outnumbering</u> her letters to anyone else.

(A) Dickinson were written over a period beginning a few years before Susan's marriage to Emily's brother and ending shortly before Emily's death in 1886, outnumbering

(B) Dickinson were written over a period that begins a few years before Susan's marriage to Emily's brother and ended shortly before Emily's death in 1886, outnumber

(C) Dickinson, written over a period beginning a few years before Susan's marriage to Emily's brother and that ends shortly before Emily's death in 1886 and outnumbering

(D) Dickinson, which were written over a period beginning a few years before Susan's marriage to Emily's brother, ending shortly before Emily's death in 1886, and outnumbering

(E) Dickinson, which were written over a period beginning a few years before Susan's marriage to Emily's brother and ending shortly before Emily's death in 1886, outnumber

Parallelism; Grammatical construction

The main point of the sentence is that Dickinson's letters to her sister-in-law outnumber her letters to anyone else. To emphasize this point, *outnumber* should be the main verb, and the description introduced by the passive verb *were written* needs to be changed from a main clause to an adjectival phrase.

A The long, wordy opening clause gives too much emphasis to the period when Dickinson's letters were written; it is unclear what *outnumbering* refers to.

B The verbs describing the letter-writing period (*begins* and *ended*) are not parallel.

C The verbs describing the letter-writing period need to be in parallel form and agree in tense—e.g., *beginning* and *ending* or *that began* and *that ended*; this is a fragment because it lacks a main verb for *letters*.

D The lack of a main verb for the subject of the sentence, *letters*, makes this a fragment.

E **Correct.** The information about the period when Dickinson's letters were written is contained in an adjectival phrase set off by commas, and the main verb *outnumber* refers clearly to *letters*.

The correct answer is E.

30. Paleontologists believe that fragments of a primate jawbone unearthed in Burma and estimated <u>at 40 to 44 million years old provide evidence of</u> a crucial step along the evolutionary path that led to human beings.

(A) at 40 to 44 million years old provide evidence of

(B) as being 40 to 44 million years old provides evidence of

(C) that it is 40 to 44 million years old provides evidence of what was

(D) to be 40 to 44 million years old provide evidence of

(E) as 40 to 44 million years old provides evidence of what was

Idiom; Agreement

The verb *estimated* should be followed by the infinitive *to be*, not the preposition *at*—unless the writer intends to indicate a location at which someone made the estimate. The jawbone fragments *were estimated to be* a certain age. The plural subject *fragments* requires the plural verb *provide*.

A *Estimated* is incorrectly followed by *at*.

B *Estimated* should be followed by *to be*, not *as being*; the singular verb *provides* incorrectly follows the plural subject *fragments*.

C Introducing a clause, *that it is …* , creates an ungrammatical sentence; the singular verb *provides* does not agree with the plural subject *fragments*.

D **Correct.** In this sentence, the verb *estimated* is correctly followed by the infinitive *to be*.

E The singular verb *provides* does not match the plural subject *fragments*.

The correct answer is D.

31. <u>Unlike the conviction held by many of her colleagues that genes were</u> relatively simple and static, Barbara McClintock adhered to her own more complicated ideas about how genes might operate, and in 1983, at the age of 81, was awarded a Nobel Prize for her discovery that the genes in corn are capable of moving from one chromosomal site to another.

    (A) Unlike the conviction held by many of her colleagues that genes were

    (B) Although many of her colleagues were of the conviction of genes being

    (C) Contrary to many of her colleagues being convinced that genes were

    (D) Even though many of her colleagues were convinced that genes were

    (E) Even with many of her colleagues convinced of genes being

Rhetorical construction; Idiom; Logical predication

The sentence compares a widely held conviction about genes with McClintock's adherence to her own ideas, then goes on to describe McClintock's accomplishments. The sentence must not compare widespread convictions with McClintock herself. The clearest and most efficient way to make the comparison is to introduce McClintock's colleagues' convictions in a dependent clause, followed by a main clause that introduces McClintock's different way of doing things and goes on to explain how successful she was.

A   Incorrect comparison between *conviction* and *Barbara McClintock*.

B   *Were of the conviction of genes being relatively simple* is wordy and awkward.

C   *Contrary to many of her colleagues being convinced* is wordy and awkward.

D   Correct. A dependent clause describing the beliefs of McClintock's colleagues is followed by the main clause presenting the contrasting beliefs of McClintock.

E   *Even with many of her colleagues … is wordy and indirect.*

The correct answer is D.

32. Galileo was convinced that natural phenomena, as manifestations of the laws of physics, would appear the same to someone on the deck of a ship moving smoothly and uniformly through the <u>water as a</u> person standing on land.

    (A) water as a

    (B) water as to a

    (C) water; just as it would to a

    (D) water, as it would to the

    (E) water; just as to the

Idiom; Parallelism

The second part of this sentence is a comparison. The correct, parallel, and idiomatic structure makes the comparison clear. In this case, a phenomenon appears *the same to x (someone) as to y (a person).* The two parts of the comparison must be parallel.

A   Without the preposition *to*, the sentence is neither idiomatic nor parallel.

B   Correct. The sentence uses the correct idiom, and the two parts of the comparison are parallel.

C   The use of a semicolon creates a sentence fragment.

D   The idiom is *the same to x as to y*, but this change would make it incorrect: *the same to x, as it would to y*, which also introduces a problem of agreement between the plural *phenomena* and the singular *it*.

E   The use of a semicolon introduces a sentence fragment.

The correct answer is B.

33. <u>Because an oversupply of computer chips has sent prices plunging,</u> the manufacturer has announced that it will cut production by closing its factories for two days a month.

   (A) Because an oversupply of computer chips has sent prices plunging,

   (B) Because of plunging prices for computer chips, which is due to an oversupply,

   (C) Because computer chip prices have been sent plunging, which resulted from an oversupply,

   (D) Due to plunging computer chip prices from an oversupply,

   (E) Due to an oversupply, with the result that computer chip prices have been sent plunging,

Agreement; Rhetorical construction

This sentence describes a causal sequence of events: The oversupply of chips caused prices to plunge, which in turn caused the manufacturer to announce factory closings to cut production. The clearest, most efficient way to express this sequence is to present the events in chronological order, as they occurred.

A **Correct.** Events are presented concisely, in chronological order.

B Because *which* refers to plural *prices*, it should be followed by *are*, not *is*.

C The violation of chronological order is confusing; reference of *which* is ambiguous.

D This backward description of the events behind the announcement of factory closings is confusing and awkward.

E *Due to* followed by *with the result* is redundant and unnecessarily wordy.

The correct answer is A.

34. Beyond the immediate cash flow crisis that the museum faces, its survival depends on <u>if it can broaden its membership and leave</u> its cramped quarters for a site where it can store and exhibit its more than 12,000 artifacts.

   (A) if it can broaden its membership and leave

   (B) whether it can broaden its membership and leave

   (C) whether or not it has the capability to broaden its membership and can leave

   (D) its ability for broadening its membership and leaving

   (E) the ability for it to broaden its membership and leave

Idiom; Verb form

This sentence requires the correct use of an idiom: *Depends on* should be followed by *whether*, not *if*, because this is an interrogative clause following a preposition.

A *Depends on if* is not a correct idiomatic expression.

B **Correct.** *Depends on whether* is the correct idiom to use in this sentence.

C Adding *it has the capability to* creates an unnecessarily wordy construction.

D *Its ability* should be followed by *to broaden*, not *for broadening*.

E *The ability for it to broaden* is wordy, awkward, and ungrammatical.

The correct answer is B.

35. By 1940, the pilot Jacqueline Cochran held seventeen official national and international speed records, <u>and she earned them at a time when aviation was still so new for many of the planes she flew to be</u> of dangerously experimental design.

   (A) and she earned them at a time when aviation was still so new for many of the planes she flew to be

   (B) earning them at a time that aviation was still so new for many of the planes she flew to be

   (C) earning these at a time where aviation was still so new that many of the planes she flew were

   (D) earned at a time in which aviation was still so new such that many of the planes she flew were

   (E) earned at a time when aviation was still so new that many of the planes she flew were

Rhetorical construction; Diction

Since this is a complex sentence with a lot of elements, its rhetorical construction is crucial in order to maintain effective communication. The underlined part emphasizes that on top of earning seventeen speed records, the pilot Jacqueline Cochran did so at a time when planes were of dangerous experimental design because aviation was still so new.

A   This version is too wordy and does not contribute to clarity. Economical, clear expression connects *earned* directly with the noun *speed records*, which it modifies.

B   Here, the word *earning* takes the pilot herself, not the *records*, as its subject. However, *earning* is close to *the records*, not to *Jacqueline Cochran*, making this sentence hard to process. In addition, the causal relationship between aviation being new and planes being of experimental design is more effectively communicated by the structure *so new that many X were Y*, not by the structure *so new for many X to be Y*.

C   The word *earning* takes the pilot herself, not the records, as its subject. However, *earning* is close to *the records*, not to *Jacqueline Cochran*, making this sentence hard to understand. Furthermore, the use of *where* to modify *time* is wrong; *where* refers to place.

D   The correct pronoun for *time* is *when*. The word *such* is redundant within *so new that many X were Y*.

E   **Correct.** The word *earned* is close to the noun it modifies, *speed records*. This version uses the clearest expression of causal relationship: *so new that many X were Y*.

The correct answer is E.

36.   Along with the drop in producer prices announced yesterday, the strong retail sales figures released today seem <u>like it is indicative that</u> the economy, although growing slowly, is not nearing a recession.

(A)   like it is indicative that
(B)   as if to indicate
(C)   to indicate that
(D)   indicative of
(E)   like an indication of

Grammatical construction; Agreement

In this sentence, the verb *seem* should be followed by an infinitive, *to indicate*; the relative pronoun *that* correctly introduces the clause, but *it* does not agree with *sales figures*.

A   Singular *it* does not agree with plural *sales figures*.

B   Verb *seem* may be followed by *as if* in some contexts, but here the result is an ungrammatical and illogical construction.

C   **Correct.** In this sentence, the verb *seem* is correctly followed by the infinitive *to indicate*, and the pronoun *that* correctly introduces a clause.

D   *Indicative of* cannot introduce a clause.

E   *An indication of* is wordy and cannot introduce a clause.

The correct answer is C.

37. Dressed as a man and using the name Robert Shurtleff, Deborah Sampson, the first woman to draw a soldier's pension, joined the Continental Army in 1782 at the age of <u>22, was injured three times, and was discharged in 1783 because she had become</u> too ill to serve.

    (A) 22, was injured three times, and was discharged in 1783 because she had become
    (B) 22, was injured three times, while being discharged in 1783 because she had become
    (C) 22 and was injured three times, and discharged in 1783, being
    (D) 22, injured three times, and was discharged in 1783 because she was
    (E) 22, having been injured three times and discharged in 1783, being

Parallelism; Logical predication

This sentence introduces Deborah Sampson with a description of Sampson when she first enlisted, and goes on to describe her career in the Continental Army. The information about her historical significance interrupts the chronological flow of the sentence and must therefore be set off with commas. The sequence of events that marks her career must be presented as a parallel series of items.

A **Correct.** The phrase that describes Deborah Sampson as *the first woman to draw a soldier's pension* intervenes between the subject and predicate of the main verb and thus is appropriately set off with commas; the three verbs in the main clause are in parallel form.

B *While being* … indicates that Sampson was injured at the same time she was discharged from the Army.

C *Discharged* should be in passive voice—*was discharged*—because Sampson did not do this herself.

D *Injured* needs to be in passive voice.

E *Having been injured* … indicates that all Sampson's injuries as well as her discharge occurred in 1783.

The correct answer is A.

38. Bengal-born writer, philosopher, and educator Rabindranath Tagore had the greatest admiration <u>for Mohandas K. Gandhi the person and also as a politician, but Tagore had been</u> skeptical of Gandhi's form of nationalism and his conservative opinions about India's cultural traditions.

    (A) for Mohandas K. Gandhi the person and also as a politician, but Tagore had been
    (B) for Mohandas K. Gandhi as a person and as a politician, but Tagore was also
    (C) for Mohandas K. Gandhi not only as a person and as a politician, but Tagore was also
    (D) of Mohandas K. Gandhi as a person and as also a politician, but Tagore was
    (E) of Mohandas K. Gandhi not only as a person and as a politician, but Tagore had also been

Rhetorical construction; Parallelism

This sentence describes the writer and philosopher Tagore's two types of feelings for Gandhi. The underlined part of the sentence has to express correctly the time line of these two feelings (they happened simultaneously). The underlined part also has to express the correct relationship between the complements of admiration and skepticism.

A To maintain parallelism, it is important for two conjoined phrases to be of the same grammatical type. Thus, it is appropriate to conjoin *Gandhi the person and the politician,* or *Gandhi as a person and as a politician,* but it is nonstandard in English to mix and match. In addition, the use of the past perfect tense *had been* places the skepticism earlier on the time line than the admiration, which is misleading.

B **Correct.** This version correctly conjoins two parallel phrases, *Gandhi as a person and as a politician,* and, in using two simple past tenses to introduce the two emotions, marks them as holding at the same time.

C   The phrase *not only X but also Y* matches the meaning of this sentence: Tagore had not only admiration but also skepticism. However *not only* has to precede *admiration* for this rhetorical construction to be parallel.

D   The noun *admiration* as it is positioned in this sentence should take the preposition *for*, not *of*, since it refers to a person. The adverb *also* is redundant because it expresses the same meaning as the conjunction *and*.

E   As in (D), the noun *admiration* should take the preposition *for*. As in (C), the rhetorical structure of *not only X but also Y* is violated. Finally, the use of the past perfect tense *had been* is misleading with respect to the time line.

The correct answer is B.

39.   Although schistosomiasis is not often fatal, it is so debilitating that it has become an economic drain on many developing countries.

(A)   it is so debilitating that it has become an economic

(B)   it is of such debilitation, it has become an economical

(C)   so debilitating is it as to become an economic

(D)   such is its debilitation, it becomes an economical

(E)   there is so much debilitation that it has become an economical

Idiom

This sentence correctly uses the idiomatic construction *so x that y* where *y* is a subordinate clause that explains or describes *x*: *So debilitating that it has become....* *It* clearly refers to *schistosomiasis*, which is correctly modified by the adjective *debilitating*.

A   **Correct.** In this sentence, the pronoun reference is clear, and the *so x that y* construction is concise.

B   The noun *debilitation* creates an awkward, wordy alternative and a slight change in meaning; the subordinate clause is not introduced by *that*; *economical* does not have the same meaning as *economic*.

C   The construction *so x as to y* is not a correct idiom.

D   The construction introduced by *such* is awkward and wordy; *debilitation* is also awkward and slightly different in meaning; *that* is omitted; *economical* does not have the same meaning as *economic*.

E   The noun *debilitation* creates an awkward, wordy alternative and a slight change in meaning; *economical* does not have the same meaning as *economic*.

The correct answer is A.

40. The Organization of Petroleum Exporting Countries (OPEC) had long been expected to announce a reduction in output to bolster sagging oil prices, but officials of the organization just recently announced that the group will pare daily production by 1.5 million barrels by the beginning of next <u>year, but only if non-OPEC nations, including Norway, Mexico, and Russia, were to trim output</u> by a total of 500,000 barrels a day.

(A) year, but only if non-OPEC nations, including Norway, Mexico, and Russia, were to trim output

(B) year, but only if the output of non-OPEC nations, which includes Norway, Mexico, and Russia, is trimmed

(C) year only if the output of non-OPEC nations, including Norway, Mexico, and Russia, would be trimmed

(D) year only if non-OPEC nations, which includes Norway, Mexico, and Russia, were trimming output

(E) year only if non-OPEC nations, including Norway, Mexico, and Russia, trim output

Rhetorical construction; Logical predication

The underlined part of this sentence deals with the conditions under which OPEC members will lower their own oil production by 1.5 million barrels by the beginning of next year. The important thing to notice here is the following logical relation: *X will do something only if Y does something else.*

A   This version has redundant words, *were to* in front of *trim* that do not add anything more in meaning. Furthermore, *were to trim* is not the proper verb form to accompany *will pare*. The addition of *but* before *only* is also redundant.

B   This version uses the passive construction in the conditional clause *only if the output … is trimmed.* This use of the passive voice makes this sentence vague; it is now unclear who needs to trim the output of non-OPEC nations. Finally, the addition of *but* before *only* is redundant.

C   As in (B), this version also introduces vagueness by using the passive construction. In addition, *would* in front of the passive verb *be trimmed* is redundant.

D   This version uses an active verb, but in the past progressive form, *were trimming.* The progressive tense denotes actions in progress, so its use is not normally warranted in conditional sentences such as this one.

E   **Correct.** This version uses the correct and most concise conditional structure, without redundancies.

The correct answer is E.

41. In 1850, Lucretia Mott published her *Discourse on Women,* <u>arguing in a treatise for women to have equal political and legal rights</u> and for changes in the married women's property laws.

(A) arguing in a treatise for women to have equal political and legal rights

(B) arguing in a treatise for equal political and legal rights for women

(C) a treatise that advocates women's equal political and legal rights

(D) a treatise advocating women's equal political and legal rights

(E) a treatise that argued for equal political and legal rights for women

Parallelism; Rhetorical construction

Mott's *Discourse* was a treatise, and it is redundant and confusing to present her as both publishing her *Discourse* and *arguing in a treatise,* as though they were two separate things. The verb *arguing* must be followed by a prepositional phrase beginning with *for,* but the verb *advocating* simply takes a direct object.

A   After *published her Discourse … arguing in a treatise* is wordy and imprecise.

B   *Arguing in a treatise* is redundant and awkward.

C   The verb *advocates* does not work idiomatically with the prepositional phrase *for changes.…*

D   The verbal *advocating* does not work idiomatically with the prepositional phrase *for changes.…*

E   **Correct.** The title of Mott's publication is followed by a phrase describing the treatise, and *argued* is followed by *for.*

The correct answer is E.

42. To develop more accurate population forecasts, demographers <u>have to know a great deal more than now about the social and economic</u> determinants of fertility.

   (A) have to know a great deal more than now about the social and economic

   (B) have to know a great deal more than they do now about the social and economical

   (C) would have to know a great deal more than they do now about the social and economical

   (D) would have to know a great deal more than they do now about the social and economic

   (E) would have to know a great deal more than now about the social and economic

Verb form; Logical predication

This sentence explains a hypothetical situation and therefore calls for a conditional—or contrary-to-fact—construction, because in order to more accurately predict population, demographers *would have to know* more than they presently know. A present-tense verb is required to describe the current state of demographers' knowledge, and the comparison made by the sentence must be between current and conditional knowledge, not between knowledge and time of knowing (*now*).

A   Wrong comparison—between knowledge and time (*now*); conditional verb is needed.

B   Conditional verb is needed; *economical* is the wrong adjective.

C   *Economical* is the wrong adjective.

D   Correct. Conditional knowledge, indicated by *would have to know*, is correctly compared to current knowledge.

E   Wrong comparison—between what demographers need to know and *now*.

The correct answer is D.

43. Laos has a land area <u>about the same as Great Britain but only four million in population, where many</u> are members of hill tribes ensconced in the virtually inaccessible mountain valleys of the north.

   (A) about the same as Great Britain but only four million in population, where many

   (B) of about the same size as Great Britain is, but in Laos there is a population of only four million, and many

   (C) that is about the same size as Great Britain's land area, but in Laos with a population of only four million people, many of them

   (D) comparable to the size of Great Britain, but only four million in population, and many

   (E) comparable to that of Great Britain but a population of only four million people, many of whom

Logical predication; Grammatical construction

The comparison in this sentence is between the land area of Laos and the land area of Great Britain, not between the land area of Laos and Great Britain. The phrase about the population of Laos is most clearly and efficiently expressed in an appositive using a relative pronoun to refer back to *people* rather than the more abstract *population*. Using this construction keeps the appropriate emphasis on the two main claims being made about Laos, one describing its land area and the other its sparse population.

A   The comparison between land area and Great Britain is incorrect; *where* is an inappropriate referent to *population*, which does not designate a place.

B   Inappropriate comparison between land area and Great Britain; the *there is …* construction is wordy and imprecise.

C   The reference of *them* is unclear and the expression is generally awkward.

D   The coordinating conjunction *and* gives undue emphasis to the claim that many of the people in Laos live in inaccessible places.

E   Correct. The land area of Laos is correctly compared to *that of* Great Britain; *whom* refers appropriately to *people*.

The correct answer is E.

44. The plot of *The Bostonians* centers on the <u>rivalry between Olive Chancellor, an active feminist, with her charming and cynical cousin, Basil Ransom,</u> when they find themselves drawn to the same radiant young woman whose talent for public speaking has won her an ardent following.

    (A) rivalry between Olive Chancellor, an active feminist, with her charming and cynical cousin, Basil Ransom,

    (B) rivals Olive Chancellor, an active feminist, against her charming and cynical cousin, Basil Ransom,

    (C) rivalry that develops between Olive Chancellor, an active feminist, and Basil Ransom, her charming and cynical cousin,

    (D) developing rivalry between Olive Chancellor, an active feminist, with Basil Ransom, her charming and cynical cousin,

    (E) active feminist, Olive Chancellor, and the rivalry with her charming and cynical cousin Basil Ransom,

    Idiom; Rhetorical construction

    Olive Chancellor and Basil Ransom are rivals. The situation can be expressed with the construction *the rivalry between x and y* or the construction *the rivals x and y*. The construction *rivalry between … with* is incorrect.

    A *With* is incorrect in the construction *the rivalry between x and y*.

    B *Against* is incorrect in the construction *the rivals x and y*.

    C **Correct.** This sentence uses the construction *the rivalry between x and y* correctly; it also clearly identifies both parties in the rivalry.

    D *With* is incorrect in the construction *the rivalry between x and y*.

    E This sentence does not make it clear that Olive is a party to the rivalry.

    The correct answer is C.

45. Quasars, at billions of light-years from Earth the most distant observable objects in the universe, <u>believed to be</u> the cores of galaxies in an early stage of development.

    (A) believed to be

    (B) are believed to be

    (C) some believe them to be

    (D) some believe they are

    (E) it is believed that they are

    Grammatical construction

    The original sentence is not actually a sentence; it is a sentence fragment since it lacks a verb: *believed to be* on its own is a participial phrase. The verb *are* must be placed before *believed to be* to create a complete sentence.

    A This sentence fragment lacks a verb.

    B **Correct.** The verb *are believed to be* grammatically completes the sentence and connects *quasars* to *cores*.

    C The clause *some believe them to be* does not supply a verb to accompany *quasars* as the subject of the sentence, and the clause supplies an object *them* so that *quasars* cannot be the object, making the sentence ungrammatical.

    D The clause *some believe they are* does not complete the clause begun by *quasars*, making the sentence ungrammatical.

    E The clause *it is believed that they are* does not complete the clause begun by *quasars*, making the sentence ungrammatical.

    The correct answer is B.

46. In ancient Thailand, <u>much of the local artisans' creative energy was expended for the creation of Buddha images and when they constructed and decorated the temples that enshrined them</u>.

    (A) much of the local artisans' creative energy was expended for the creation of Buddha images and when they constructed and decorated the temples that enshrined them

    (B) much of the local artisans' creative energy was expended on the creation of Buddha images and on construction and decoration of the temples in which they were enshrined

(C) much of the local artisans' creative energy was expended on the creation of Buddha images as well as constructing and decoration of the temples in which they were enshrined

(D) creating images of Buddha accounted for much of the local artisans' creative energy, and also constructing and decorating the temples enshrining them

(E) the creation of Buddha images accounted for much of the local artisans' creative energy as well as construction and decoration of the temples that enshrined them

Idiom; Parallelism; Rhetorical construction

The main point of the sentence is that artisans in ancient Thailand spent most of their creative energy on three tasks: creating Buddha images, and constructing and decorating temples to enshrine the Buddhas. These three tasks must be described in parallel forms. The verb *expended* should be followed by the preposition *on*, not *for*.

A *For* is the wrong preposition; the *and when …* clause introduces faulty parallelism; it is unclear what *they* refers to.

B **Correct.** The three activities are presented in parallel form: creation of Buddha images and construction and *decoration of the temples*.

C *Constructing* violates the parallelism otherwise maintained by *creation* and *decoration*.

D The *and also* phrase is awkwardly set apart from the main claim of the sentence—which is that all three tasks consumed much of the artisans' energy.

E This construction is awkward and unnecessarily wordy and says something different—that the images accounted for the construction and decoration of temples.

The correct answer is B.

47. In 1713, Alexander Pope began <u>his translation of the Iliad, a work that, taking him seven years until completion, and that literary critic Samuel Johnson, Pope's contemporary, pronounced</u> the greatest translation in any language.

(A) his translation of the *Iliad*, a work that, taking him seven years until completion, and that literary critic Samuel Johnson, Pope's contemporary, pronounced

(B) his translation of the *Iliad*, a work that took him seven years to complete and that literary critic Samuel Johnson, Pope's contemporary, pronounced

(C) his translation of the *Iliad*, a work that had taken seven years to complete and that literary critic Samuel Johnson, Pope's contemporary, pronounced it as

(D) translating the *Iliad*, a work that took seven years until completion and that literary critic Samuel Johnson, Pope's contemporary, pronounced it as

(E) translating the *Iliad*, a work that had taken seven years to complete and literary critic Samuel Johnson, Pope's contemporary, pronounced it

Logical predication; Grammatical construction

Pope's translation of the *Iliad*, not the *Iliad* itself, took seven years to complete. The main point of the sentence is that Pope began this translation in 1713, and every other comment about it must be subordinated to that opening claim, in parallel relative clauses.

A *A work that …* requires a verb; without it, the sentence is a fragment.

B **Correct.** Pope's *translation* is described as *a work*, which is then described concisely in two dependent clauses.

C The pronoun *it* after *pronounced* is redundant, an ungrammatical reference to *a work*, which has already been referenced by the relative pronoun *that*.

D The appositive phrase *a work …* incorrectly refers to the *Iliad*, not Pope's translation.

E The appositive phrase *a work …* incorrectly refers to the *Iliad*; the coordinating conjunction introduces inappropriate emphasis on Johnson's description, and the expression is awkward and unclear.

The correct answer is B.

48. <u>It is called a sea, but the landlocked Caspian is actually the largest lake on Earth, which covers</u> more than four times the surface area of its closest rival in size, North America's Lake Superior.

    (A) It is called a sea, but the landlocked Caspian is actually the largest lake on Earth, which covers

    (B) Although it is called a sea, actually the landlocked Caspian is the largest lake on Earth, which covers

    (C) Though called a sea, the landlocked Caspian is actually the largest lake on Earth, covering

    (D) Though called a sea but it actually is the largest lake on Earth, the landlocked Caspian covers

    (E) Despite being called a sea, the largest lake on Earth is actually the landlocked Caspian, covering

Logical predication; Grammatical construction

The topic of this sentence is a single large body of water, the Caspian Sea. The wording needs to make it clear that being *the largest lake on Earth* and *covering more than four times the surface area of ... Lake Superior* are both predicated of this one subject.

A   The referent of *which* is unclear. Grammatically, its antecedent cannot be *the landlocked Caspian*, so it must be either *Earth* or *the largest lake on Earth*. The latter is a little odd, because the sentence has already said that the lake in question is the Caspian, so one would expect *and* instead of *which*. For these reasons and because *Earth* immediately precedes *which*, the sentence appears to say, illogically, that Earth covers more than four times the surface area of Lake Superior.

B   As in (A), this appears to say, illogically, that Earth covers more than four times the surface area of Lake Superior.

C   **Correct.** The wording is direct, unambiguous, and grammatically correct.

D   The structure here is grammatically incoherent.

E   *Despite being called a sea* indicates, somewhat illogically, that the largest lake being called a sea would lead one to expect it not to be the Caspian. This makes little sense, especially to those who are familiar with the name *Caspian Sea*.

The correct answer is C.

49. The automotive conveyor-belt system, which Henry Ford modeled after an assembly-line technique introduced by Ransom Olds, reduced <u>from a day and a half to 93 minutes the required time of assembling a Model T</u>.

    (A) from a day and a half to 93 minutes the required time of assembling a Model T

    (B) the time being required to assemble a Model T, from a day and a half down to 93 minutes

    (C) the time being required to assemble a Model T, a day and a half to 93 minutes

    (D) the time required to assemble a Model T from a day and a half to 93 minutes

    (E) from a day and a half to 93 minutes, the time required for the assembling of a Model T

Rhetorical construction; Idiom

The underlined portion of the original sentence is awkward because the verb *reduced* is followed by a prepositional phrase rather than the direct object *time*. Changing this structure so that the object immediately follows the verb, *reduced the time*, also allows an idiomatic error to be corrected. *Required* should be followed by an infinitive, *to assemble*, rather than a prepositional phrase, *of assembling*. The phrase indicating time should be used to complete the sentence: *reduced the time required to assemble a Model T from a day and a half to 93 minutes*.

A   Placement of phrases creates an awkward construction; *required … of assembling* is not idiomatic.

B   *Being required* and *down to* are wordy constructions; the comma is unnecessary.

C   *Being required* is wordy; the construction *from … to* indicates time, not *to* alone.

D   Correct. This sentence has a clear, concise, and idiomatic construction.

E   Beginning with the prepositional phrase is awkward; the comma is unnecessary; *required for the assembling of* is wordy and awkward.

The correct answer is D.

50.   According to some analysts, the gains in the stock market reflect growing confidence <u>that the economy will avoid the recession that many had feared earlier in the year and instead come</u> in for a "soft landing," followed by a gradual increase in business activity.

(A)   that the economy will avoid the recession that many had feared earlier in the year and instead come

(B)   in the economy to avoid the recession, what many feared earlier in the year, rather to come

(C)   in the economy's ability to avoid the recession, something earlier in the year many had feared, and instead to come

(D)   in the economy to avoid the recession many were fearing earlier in the year, and rather to come

(E)   that the economy will avoid the recession that was feared earlier this year by many, with it instead coming

Grammatical construction; Rhetorical construction

The original sentence successfully avoids the problems that may occur in a long sentence with multiple modifiers. Two subordinate clauses begin with *that*, and one of them is contained within another. *That many had feared earlier in the year* clearly defines *the recession*. *That the economy will avoid … and instead* (*will* understood) *come…* is the subordinate clause that follows the main clause; its subject, *economy*, is followed by two parallel verbs, *will avoid* and (*will* understood) *come*. *Instead* before the second verb properly indicates contrast.

A   Correct. This sentence contains two correct subordinate clauses introduced by *that*.

B   *What* cannot replace *that*; *the economy to avoid the recession* is awkward and unclear; *rather to come* does not complete the second part of the sentence idiomatically.

C   *Earlier in the year* should follow *many had feared*, rather than preceding it; *instead to come* does not complete the second part of the sentence idiomatically.

D   *The recession* must be followed by *that*; *were fearing* is the wrong tense; *rather to come* does not complete the second part of the sentence idiomatically.

E   The passive voice construction *that was feared …* is weak and wordy; *with it instead coming* is awkward, wordy, and ungrammatical.

The correct answer is A.

51. A new study suggests that the conversational pace of everyday life may be so brisk <u>it hampers the ability of some children for distinguishing discrete sounds and words and, the result is, to make</u> sense of speech.

(A) it hampers the ability of some children for distinguishing discrete sounds and words and, the result is, to make

(B) that it hampers the ability of some children to distinguish discrete sounds and words and, as a result, to make

(C) that it hampers the ability of some children to distinguish discrete sounds and words and, the result of this, they are unable to make

(D) that it hampers the ability of some children to distinguish discrete sounds and words, and results in not making

(E) as to hamper the ability of some children for distinguishing discrete sounds and words, resulting in being unable to make

Rhetorical construction; Parallelism; Diction

The sentence describes a hypothesized causal series: The fast conversational pace impairs children's ability to distinguish individual sounds and words, and this, in turn, impairs their ability to make sense of speech. These two consequences, both impaired abilities, are most clearly and efficiently expressed in parallel infinitive phrases (*to distinguish* and *to make*). The explanatory phrase *as a result* before the second infinitive clarifies the sequence. The term *ability* should be followed by the preposition *to*, not *for*.

A *For* is the wrong preposition to follow *ability*; the phrase *and, the result, is* introduces a new clause which indicates that children's inability to distinguish sounds enables them to make sense of speech.

B **Correct.** The two abilities hampered by the fast pace of conversation are described with the parallel infinitive phrases *to distinguish* and *to make*.

C *The result of this* is a new subject that grammatically requires a new verb; the phrase is wordy and unclear.

D This version of the sentence nonsensically suggests that the pace of speech results in not making sense of speech, removing the children from the picture as the ones who are affected.

E The phrase is awkward, wordy, and unclear; *for* is the incorrect preposition to follow ability.

The correct answer is B.

52. <u>To Josephine Baker, Paris was her home long before it was fashionable to be an expatriate,</u> and she remained in France during the Second World War as a performer and an intelligence agent for the Resistance.

(A) To Josephine Baker, Paris was her home long before it was fashionable to be an expatriate,

(B) For Josephine Baker, long before it was fashionable to be an expatriate, Paris was her home,

(C) Josephine Baker made Paris her home long before to be an expatriate was fashionable,

(D) Long before it was fashionable to be an expatriate, Josephine Baker made Paris her home,

(E) Long before it was fashionable being an expatriate, Paris was home to Josephine Baker,

Rhetorical construction; Parallelism

This compound sentence (consisting of two independent clauses joined by the coordinating conjunction *and*) would be most clearly expressed if Josephine Baker were the subject of the first clause since *she* is the subject of the second clause: *Josephine Baker made Paris her home* would clearly parallel *she remained in France*. The adverb clause *long … expatriate* is best placed before the main clause.

A *To Josephine Baker … her* is redundant and awkward; the subject of the first main clause is *Paris* rather than *Baker*.

B *For Josephine Baker … her* is redundant and awkward; putting two introductory elements together before the main clause is awkward.

C Inversion of the expected word order in *to be an expatriate was unfashionable* is awkward.

D **Correct.** The clearest, most economical order for this sentence is to put the adverb clause first, and make *Baker* the subject of the first main clause, parallel to *she* in the second.

E *Being* is awkward; *Baker* should be the subject of the first main clause, parallel to *she* in the second main clause.

The correct answer is D.

53. The nineteenth-century chemist Humphry Davy presented the results of his early experiments in his "Essay on Heat and Light," <u>a critique of all chemistry since Robert Boyle as well as a vision of a</u> new chemistry that Davy hoped to found.

    (A) a critique of all chemistry since Robert Boyle as well as a vision of a
    (B) a critique of all chemistry following Robert Boyle and also his envisioning of a
    (C) a critique of all chemistry after Robert Boyle and envisioning as well
    (D) critiquing all chemistry from Robert Boyle forward and also a vision of
    (E) critiquing all the chemistry done since Robert Boyle as well as his own envisioning of

Parallelism; Rhetorical construction

The main objective of the sentence is to describe "Essay on Heat and Light" as Davy's presentation of his own experiments and to further explain that the essay served as both a critique of previous chemistry and a vision of a new kind of chemistry. The clearest, most effective form for providing this explanation of the essay's function is to make *critique* and *vision* both appositives of "Essay on Heat and Light," and to present them in a parallel structure.

A **Correct.** The phrases describing the essay's function are presented in parallel form.

B *Critique* and *his envisioning* are not parallel; the phrase *and also his envisioning* is unnecessarily wordy; it is also unclear to whom *his* refers.

C The two descriptors are not parallel.

D The two descriptors are not parallel.

E The meaning is confused in the assertion that Davy critiqued his own vision of chemistry.

The correct answer is A.

54. The report recommended that the hospital <u>should eliminate unneeded beds, expensive services should be consolidated, and use space in other hospitals</u>.

    (A) should eliminate unneeded beds, expensive services should be consolidated, and use space in other hospitals
    (B) should eliminate unneeded beds, expensive services should be consolidated, and other hospitals' space be used
    (C) should eliminate unneeded beds, expensive services should be consolidated, and to use space in other hospitals
    (D) eliminate unneeded beds, consolidate expensive services, and other hospitals' space used
    (E) eliminate unneeded beds, consolidate expensive services, and use space in other hospitals

Grammatical construction; Parallelism

The underlined portion of the sentence is incoherent and runs together two sentences (*the … beds*; *expensive … consolidated*). Making the report's three recommendations into a series of three grammatically parallel elements corrects this problem. Since the report *recommended*, it is redundant to use *should*. Each of the three parallel elements may consist of a verb and an object: 1) *eliminate unneeded beds*, 2) *consolidate expensive services*, and 3) *use space in other hospitals*.

A Incoherent construction includes a run-on sentence; following *recommended*, *should* is redundant.

B Following *recommended*, *should* is redundant; three elements in the series are not parallel.

C Following *recommended*, *should* is redundant; the second and third elements are not parallel to the first.

D *Other hospitals' space* used is awkward and not parallel to the other two elements.

E **Correct.** In this concise sentence, each of the three parallel elements in the series consists of a verb and an object.

The correct answer is E.

55. Many house builders offer rent-to-buy <u>programs that enable a family with insufficient savings for a conventional down payment to be able to move into new housing and to apply</u> part of the rent to a purchase later.

(A) programs that enable a family with insufficient savings for a conventional down payment to be able to move into new housing and to apply

(B) programs that enable a family with insufficient savings for a conventional down payment to move into new housing and to apply

(C) programs; that enables a family with insufficient savings for a conventional down payment to move into new housing, to apply

(D) programs, which enables a family with insufficient savings for a conventional down payment to move into new housing, applying

(E) programs, which enable a family with insufficient savings for a conventional down payment to be able to move into new housing, applying

Rhetorical construction; Logical predication

In a lengthy sentence consisting of many phrases, it is essential to determine which phrases and words are necessary to the sentence and which words may be eliminated because they are unnecessary. The relative pronoun *that* correctly refers to *programs* and introduces the subordinate clause; *family* is followed by two phrases that are clear and correct. *To be able to move*, however, is needlessly wordy, repeating the meaning of *enable*, and can be reduced to *to move*. This creates a parallel construction in which *programs … enable a family … to move … and to apply*.

A　*To be able to move* is wordy and *able* is redundant after *enable*; *to apply* is not logically parallel to the infinitive phrase *(able) to move*.

B　**Correct.** In this sentence, eliminating the wordy construction *to be able* allows *to move* to be parallel to *to apply*.

C　Insofar as this is grammatical, using a semicolon here causes *that* to refer too broadly to the entire previous clause rather than specifically to *programs*; the two infinitives should be joined by the conjunction *and*, not separated by a comma.

D　*Enables* does not agree with the plural subject; *applying* following a nonrestrictive clause suggests incorrectly that the builders, not the family, are applying the rent.

E　The comma after *programs* is incorrect because the clause is meant to be restrictive; as in (D), *applying* will alter the meaning of the sentence.

The correct answer is B.

56. Elizabeth Barber, the author of both *Prehistoric Textiles*, a comprehensive work on cloth in the early cultures of the Mediterranean, and <u>also of *Women's Work*, a more general account of early cloth manufacture, is an expert authority on</u> textiles in ancient societies.

(A) also of *Women's Work*, a more general account of early cloth manufacture, is an expert authority on

(B) also *Women's Work*, a more general account of cloth manufacture, is an expert authority about

(C) of *Women's Work*, a more general account about early cloth manufacture, is an authority on

(D) of *Women's Work*, a more general account about early cloth manufacture, is an expert authority about

(E) *Women's Work*, a more general account of early cloth manufacture, is an authority on

Rhetorical construction; Idiom; Parallelism

Using a lot of parenthetical elements, this sentence communicates the main idea that Elizabeth Barber is an authority on textiles in ancient societies. It is the main rhetorical goal of the sentence to position the parenthetical elements so that they do not obscure the main idea. The parenthetical descriptions need to be streamlined enough to be informative, but not too long. In addition, several versions repeat *of* before the title *Women's Work* and doing so makes the sentence unparallel; the first *of* comes before *both* and so should distribute over both clauses.

A   The use of *also of* before *Women's Work* is redundant and unparallel. It is sufficient to connect the two book titles like this: *both X and Y.* The meanings of the two nouns *expert* and *authority* largely overlap, so there is no need to modify one with the other.

B   The use of *also* before *Women's Work* is redundant. It is sufficient to connect the two book titles like this: *both X and Y.* The meanings of the two nouns *expert* and *authority* largely overlap, so there is no need to modify one with the other. Finally, the noun *authority* takes the preposition *on*, not *about.*

C   As in (A), repeating the preposition *of* before *Women's Work* makes the sentence unparallel. The noun *account* takes the preposition *of,* not *about.*

D   As in (A) and (C), repeating the preposition *of* before *Women's Work* makes the sentence unparallel. The noun *account* takes the preposition *of,* not *about.* It is redundant to modify *authority* with *expert* because they express the same idea. Finally, the noun *authority* takes the preposition *on*, not *about.*

E   **Correct.** This version is parallel, uses the most concise structure of the parenthetical descriptions, eschews the redundant modification of *authority,* and employs the correct prepositions.

The correct answer is E.

57. Many of the earliest known images of Hindu deities in India date from the time of the Kushan <u>Empire, fashioned either from the spotted sandstone of Mathura or</u> Gandharan grey schist.

(A) Empire, fashioned either from the spotted sandstone of Mathura or

(B) Empire, fashioned from either the spotted sandstone of Mathura or from

(C) Empire, either fashioned from the spotted sandstone of Mathura or

(D) Empire and either fashioned from the spotted sandstone of Mathura or from

(E) Empire and were fashioned either from the spotted sandstone of Mathura or from

Logical predication; Parallelism

The sentence makes two claims about the earliest known images of Hindu deities in India: They date from the Kushan Empire, and they are made from sandstone or schist. The clearest, most effective way to incorporate these two claims into a single sentence is to provide two parallel predicates for the single subject, *the earliest known images of Hindu deities in India.* The two options of media, presented as either/or choices, must also be given in parallel structure: *either from … or from … or from either … or. …*

A   Placement of the modifier *fashioned …* suggests that the *Empire* (the closest noun), not the images of the deities, was fashioned out of these materials; to parallel *either from,* the preposition *from* should also follow *or.*

B   Parallelism requires that *either* precede the first appearance of *from* or that the second appearance of *from* be eliminated.

C   As in (A) and (B), the placement of the modifier after *Empire* is misleading; parallelism requires that the phrase *fashioned from,* or another comparable verb and preposition, follow *or.*

D   Parallelism requires that a verb follow *or,* since a verb follows *either.*

E   **Correct.** Two verbs, *date* and *were fashioned,* introduce parallel predicates for the subject, *earliest known images;* the choices of media are correctly presented with the structure *either from … or from.*

The correct answer is E.

58. <u>That educators have not anticipated the impact of microcomputer technology can hardly be said that it is their fault</u>: Alvin Toffler, one of the most prominent students of the future, did not even mention microcomputers in *Future Shock*, published in 1970.

(A) That educators have not anticipated the impact of microcomputer technology can hardly be said that it is their fault

(B) That educators have not anticipated the impact of microcomputer technology can hardly be said to be at fault

(C) It can hardly be said that it is the fault of educators who have not anticipated the impact of microcomputer technology

(D) It can hardly be said that educators are at fault for not anticipating the impact of microcomputer technology

(E) The fact that educators are at fault for not anticipating the impact of microcomputer technology can hardly be said

Grammatical construction; Rhetorical construction

Although it is possible to begin a sentence with a subordinate clause beginning with *that*, this inverted construction often results in errors such as those found here. In the original sentence, the subordinate clause *that … technology* is followed by the main verb, *can … be said*, but then the verb is followed by yet another subordinate clause, *that it is their fault*. The best way to solve this problem is by putting the sentence in the expected order, with the main clause (*It can hardly be said*) preceding the subordinate clause (*that …*). For greater clarity and concision, the two subordinate clauses should be condensed into one: *educators are at fault for not anticipating the impact of microcomputer technology*.

A   Inverting the usual order results in an ungrammatical construction in which the main verb is both preceded and followed by a subordinate clause.

B   *Can hardly be said to be at fault* does not grammatically complete the subordinate clause.

C   Construction *that it is … who have not* is wordy and awkward; it also distorts meaning and lacks completion.

D   **Correct.** This sentence has the main clause followed by one subordinate clause correctly introduced by *that*.

E   *The fact* is wordy; the inverted construction does not successfully convey the meaning of the sentence.

The correct answer is D.

59. A leading figure in the Scottish Enlightenment, <u>Adam Smith's two major books are to democratic capitalism what</u> Marx's *Das Kapital* is to socialism.

(A) Adam Smith's two major books are to democratic capitalism what

(B) Adam Smith's two major books are to democratic capitalism like

(C) Adam Smith's two major books are to democratic capitalism just as

(D) Adam Smith wrote two major books that are to democratic capitalism similar to

(E) Adam Smith wrote two major books that are to democratic capitalism what

Idiom; Logical predication

A leading figure in the Scottish Enlightenment describes Adam Smith, not his two books, so the name of Adam Smith must immediately follow the opening phrase. The comparison between Smith's books and Marx's book is expressed as a ratio, so the correct idiomatic expression is *x is to y what a is to b*.

A   The opening phrase is a dangling modifier because it describes Smith, not his books.

B   The opening phrase is a dangling modifier; *like* is an incorrect word for making the comparison.

C   The opening phrase is a dangling modifier; *just as* is an incorrect term for the comparison.

D   *Similar to* is an incorrect conclusion to the comparison introduced by *are to*.

E   **Correct.** The opening phrase is followed by the subject that it modifies, Adam Smith, and the comparison of the two men's work is presented idiomatically.

The correct answer is E.

60. The Olympic Games helped to keep peace among the pugnacious states of the Greek <u>world in that a sacred truce was proclaimed during the festival's month</u>.

(A) world in that a sacred truce was proclaimed during the festival's month

(B) world, proclaiming a sacred truce during the festival's month

(C) world when they proclaimed a sacred truce for the festival month

(D) world, for a sacred truce was proclaimed during the month of the festival

(E) world by proclamation of a sacred truce that was for the month of the festival

Idiom; Rhetorical construction

This sentence depends on using the correct conjunction to join two independent clauses. *In that* is a conjunction that means *inasmuch as*; because *in that* has largely gone out of use, it is considered stilted and overly formal. It also uses two words when one would do. In this sentence, the second clause explains the first one, so the conjunction *for*, meaning *because*, is the most appropriate choice for joining the two independent clauses of the compound sentence. *Festival's month* is an awkward and imprecise use of the possessive; *during the month of the festival* is clearer.

A   *In that* is stilted and overly formal.

B   It is not clear who would be doing the *proclaiming*; a clause is preferable to a phrase here.

C   *They* is ambiguous, possibly referring to either the *states* or the *Games*. The phrase *truce for the festival month* loses the sense that it's to take place for the duration of the month.

D   **Correct.** In this sentence, the conjunction *for* joins the two clauses correctly and economically.

E   Wordy and awkward construction.

The correct answer is D.

61. While <u>all states face similar industrial waste problems, the predominating industries and the regulatory environment of the states obviously determines</u> the types and amounts of waste produced, as well as the cost of disposal.

(A) all states face similar industrial waste problems, the predominating industries and the regulatory environment of the states obviously determines

(B) each state faces a similar industrial waste problem, their predominant industries and regulatory environment obviously determine

(C) all states face a similar industrial waste problem; their predominating industries and regulatory environment obviously determines

(D) each state faces similar industrial waste problems, the predominant industries and the regulatory environment of each state obviously determines

(E) all states face similar industrial waste problems, the predominant industries and the regulatory environment of each state obviously determine

Agreement; Grammatical construction

This sentence requires careful attention to number and agreement. The main clause has a compound subject, *the predominating industries and the regulatory environment*, which must take a plural verb, *determine*, rather than the singular verb shown in the original sentence. The sentence begins with the conjunction *while*, here used to mean *although*, and contrasts the similar situation of *all states* with the varying conditions of *each state*. The point of the main clause is that all *states* do not share the same *predominating industries* and *regulatory environment*, so it is more logical and correct to have the *regulatory environment* of *each state*.

A   Compound subject does not agree with the singular verb *determines*; main clause should call attention to the conditions of *each state*, not *the states*.

B   *Each state* must be compared to all other states; *their* does not agree with *each*.

C   Using a semicolon results in a sentence fragment; subject and verb do not agree.

D   *Each state* must be compared to all other states; subject and verb do not agree.

E   **Correct.** This sentence makes the clear distinction between the problem *all states* share and the conditions *each state* faces; subject and verb agree.

The correct answer is E.

62. Rivaling the pyramids of Egypt or even the ancient cities of the Maya as an achievement, <u>the army of terra-cotta warriors created to protect Qin Shi Huang, China's first emperor, in his afterlife is more than 2,000 years old and took 700,000 artisans more than 36 years to complete</u>.

(A) the army of terra-cotta warriors created to protect Qin Shi Huang, China's first emperor, in his afterlife is more than 2,000 years old and took 700,000 artisans more than 36 years to complete

(B) Qin Shi Huang, China's first emperor, was protected in his afterlife by an army of terra-cotta warriors that was created more than 2,000 years ago by 700,000 artisans who took more than 36 years to complete it

(C) it took 700,000 artisans more than 36 years to create an army of terra-cotta warriors more than 2,000 years ago that would protect Qin Shi Huang, China's first emperor, in his afterlife

(D) more than 2,000 years ago, 700,000 artisans worked more than 36 years to create an army of terra-cotta warriors to protect Qin Shi Huang, China's first emperor, in his afterlife

(E) more than 36 years were needed to complete the army of terra-cotta warriors that 700,000 artisans created 2,000 years ago to protect Qin Shi Huang, China's first emperor, in his afterlife

Logical predication; Rhetorical construction

The opening modifier, *Rivaling the pyramids ...* describes *the army of terra-cotta warriors*, which must immediately follow the modifier. The placement of the predicates that follow is important; they must clarify two things about the army of terra-cotta warriors: how old it is and how long it took to complete. The clearest and most effective way to express these two assertions is as parallel verb phrases, *is more than 2,000 years old* and *took ... more than 36 years to complete*.

A **Correct.** The opening phrase correctly modifies the subject, *the army of terra-cotta warriors*; the placement of modifiers and predicates in the main clause makes the meaning of the sentence clear.

B Opening phrase is a dangling modifier because it does not describe the subject *Qin Shi Huang*; in addition, the sentence is awkward and unclear.

C Opening phrase is a dangling modifier because it does not describe the subject *it*; the sequence of information presented is confusing and unclear.

D Opening phrase is a dangling modifier because it does not describe the subject *700,000 artisans*.

E Opening phrase is a dangling modifier because it does not describe the subject *more than 36 years*.

The correct answer is A.

63. When Congress reconvenes, some newly elected members from rural states will try <u>and establish tighter restrictions for the amount of grain farmers are to be allowed to grow and to encourage</u> more aggressive sales of United States farm products overseas.

(A) and establish tighter restrictions for the amount of grain farmers are to be allowed to grow and to encourage

(B) and establish tighter restrictions on the amount of grain able to be grown by farmers and encouraging

(C) establishing tighter restrictions for the amount of grain farmers are allowed to grow and to encourage

(D) to establish tighter restrictions on the amount of grain capable of being grown by farmers and encouraging

(E) to establish tighter restrictions on the amount of grain farmers will be allowed to grow and to encourage

Idiom; Parallelism

Although *try and* is an idiom often used in colloquial language, in this sentence, *to* is needed after *will try* to maintain parallelism: *to establish* and *to encourage*. The correct preposition following *restrictions* is not *for* but *on*. *Are to be allowed to grow* is wordy; the infinitive *to be* should be omitted for a tighter and clearer expression.

A   *To* should replace *and* before *establish*; *restrictions* is incorrectly followed by *for* rather than *on*; *to be* is wordy and should be omitted.

B   Here, the passive-voice construction *able to be grown by* is weak and wordy; the constructions *and establish … and encouraging …* are not parallel.

C   *Will try establishing* does not show intent or purpose; *restrictions* must be followed by *on*, not *for*; parallelism is lost.

D   Passive-voice construction *capable of being grown by* is weak and wordy; *encouraging* and *to establish* are not parallel.

E   **Correct.** *To establish* indicates purpose and parallels *to encourage*; *restrictions* is correctly followed by *on*; the wordiness of the verb phrase has been eliminated.

The correct answer is E.

64.   Doctors generally agree that such factors as cigarette smoking, eating rich foods high in fats, and alcohol consumption <u>not only do damage by themselves but also aggravate</u> genetic predispositions toward certain diseases.

(A)   not only do damage by themselves but also aggravate

(B)   do damage by themselves but also are aggravating to

(C)   are damaging by themselves but also are aggravating

(D)   not only do damage by themselves, they are also aggravating to

(E)   are doing damage by themselves, and they are also aggravating

Verb form; Logical predication

This correctly written sentence uses the construction *not only x … but also y*; *x* is the simple present verb *do damage* and *y* is the parallel verb *aggravate*. The simple present tense should be used for a general statement such as this one. When used as a verb, *aggravate* clearly means to make worse; the adjective *aggravating* is instead widely interpreted to mean *annoying*.

A   **Correct.** This sentence correctly uses the *not only … but also* construction to explain the parallel effects of the factors.

B   *Are aggravating to* is not parallel to *do damage*; *aggravating* suggests a different meaning than does *aggravate*; using *but also* without using *not only* is incorrect.

C   The form *are aggravating* distorts the meaning of the sentence; using *but also* without using *not only* is incorrect.

D   Using *not only* without using *but also* is incorrect; *are aggravating to* is not parallel to *do damage*; *aggravating* suggests a different meaning.

E   Simple present tense, rather than the present progressive, should be used to present a general statement; *aggravating* distorts meaning.

The correct answer is A.

65. Digging in sediments in northern China, <u>evidence has been gathered by scientists suggesting that complex life-forms emerged much earlier than they had</u> previously thought.

    (A) evidence has been gathered by scientists suggesting that complex life-forms emerged much earlier than they had

    (B) evidence gathered by scientists suggests a much earlier emergence of complex life-forms than had been

    (C) scientists have gathered evidence suggesting that complex life-forms emerged much earlier than

    (D) scientists have gathered evidence that suggests a much earlier emergence of complex life-forms than that which was

    (E) scientists have gathered evidence which suggests a much earlier emergence of complex life-forms than that

Logical predication; Modification

In principle, the relationship described in the first part of the underlined portion could be expressed with *scientists* as the subject (*scientists gathered evidence*) or with *evidence* as the subject (*evidence was gathered by scientists*). The latter construction could be effective in some contexts, but here its relationship to the rest of the sentence appears to commit the writer to the claim that the evidence was digging in China.

A   This version has a dangling participle, *digging. … Digging in sediments in northern China* must modify *scientists*, not *evidence*. The passive structure of the main clause also creates an inadvisable distance between the words *evidence* and *suggesting*. Furthermore, the dependent clause starting with *suggesting* may be construed with either the evidence or the scientists, which makes this version unnecessarily ambiguous.

B   This version has a dangling participle, *digging. … Digging in sediments in northern China* must modify *scientists*, not *evidence*.

C   **Correct.** Choosing *scientists* as the subject of *gathered*, this version corrects the dangling participle. It also uses a parallel active form of the verb *emerge*, and does not use redundant material.

D   In this context it would be preferable to use a verb (*emerged*). The phrasing used here (*suggests a much earlier emergence of*) sounds more stilted and is less clear and direct. In addition, inserting *that which* before *previously thought* is not only redundant but incorrect English.

E   The problems described in (D) above are also in evidence here.

The correct answer is C.

66. In a plan to stop the erosion of East Coast beaches, the Army Corps of Engineers proposed building parallel to shore a breakwater of rocks that would rise six feet above the waterline and <u>act as a buffer, so that it absorbs</u> the energy of crashing waves and protecting the beaches.

    (A) act as a buffer, so that it absorbs

    (B) act like a buffer so as to absorb

    (C) act as a buffer, absorbing

    (D) acting as a buffer, absorbing

    (E) acting like a buffer, absorb

Parallelism; Idiom

The last part of the sentence describes the breakwater and should consist of two grammatically parallel phrases, *absorbing … and protecting*, in order to show two equal functions. *Act* followed by *like* means *to behave or comport oneself* and describes the action of a person: *He acted like a fool*. Here, *act as* describes the function of a thing; *the breakwater … acts as a buffer*. As an inanimate object, a breakwater cannot "behave" itself; it must be performing some function.

A   *So that it absorbs* should be *absorbing* to parallel *protecting*.

B   *Act as* is the proper idiom to describe things; *so as to absorb* is awkward and should be changed to *absorbing* to be parallel to *protecting*.

C   **Correct.** The idiom *act as* is used correctly in this sentence; *absorbing* is properly parallel to *protecting*.

D   Modifying clause is *that would rise … and* (*would* understood) *act*; *acting* cannot be used instead of *act*.

E   Modifying clause is *that would rise … and* (*would* understood) *act*; *acting* cannot be used instead of *act*; *absorb* is not parallel to *protecting*.

The correct answer is C.

67.   The 32 species that make up the dolphin family are closely related to whales and in fact <u>include the animal known as the killer whale, which can grow to be 30 feet long and is</u> famous for its aggressive hunting pods.

(A)   include the animal known as the killer whale, which can grow to be 30 feet long and is

(B)   include the animal known as the killer whale, growing as big as 30 feet long and

(C)   include the animal known as the killer whale, growing up to 30 feet long and being

(D)   includes the animal known as the killer whale, which can grow as big as 30 feet long and is

(E)   includes the animal known as the killer whale, which can grow to be 30 feet long and it is

Rhetorical construction; Agreement

The subject of the sentence is *the 32 species that make up the dolphin family*, and the sentence makes two claims about them: They are closely related, and they include the killer whale. The relative pronoun *which* restates the object of the second verb, reintroducing *the animal known as the killer whale* as the subject of a relative clause followed by two parallel verbs: *can grow* and *is famous*.

A   **Correct.** In this concise sentence, verbs agree in number with their subjects and the relative pronoun *which* indicates clearly that *the animal known as the killer whale* is the subject of the verbs in the dependent clause.

B   Changing the verb to the participial *growing* introduces ambiguity, because it could refer back to the subject of the sentence (*32 species*).

C   The participial *growing* might refer to *the 32 species*; the introduction of *being* is unnecessarily wordy and adds nothing in terms of meaning.

D   *as big as* is an idiomatically incorrect expression of the comparison; the plural verb form *include* is needed to match the plural subject *the 32 species*.

E   *It* simply restates the subject of the previous phrase, introducing more words but no additional meaning; the singular verb form *includes* should be the plural form *include*.

The correct answer is A.

68. Outlining his strategy for nursing the troubled conglomerate back to health, the chief <u>executive's plans were announced on Wednesday for cutting the company's huge debt by selling nearly $12 billion in assets over the next 18 months</u>.

    (A) executive's plans were announced on Wednesday for cutting the company's huge debt by selling nearly $12 billion in assets over the next 18 months

    (B) executive's plans, which are to cut the company's huge debt by selling nearly $12 billion in assets over the next 18 months, were announced on Wednesday

    (C) executive's plans for cutting the company's huge debt by selling nearly $12 billion in assets over the next 18 months were announced on Wednesday

    (D) executive announced plans Wednesday to cut the company's huge debt by selling nearly $12 billion in assets over the next 18 months

    (E) executive announced plans Wednesday that are to cut the company's huge debt by selling nearly $12 billion in assets over the next 18 months

Logical predication; Verb form

In this sentence, the opening dependent clause beginning *Outlining his strategy* is a dangling modifier. Furthermore, the verb form for *announce* should make it clear that the chief executive is doing the announcing. In addition, *to cut* is a clearer phrase than *for cutting* in this sentence.

A The subject of the opening clause should be *executive*, not *plans*. The passive verb form *were announced* suggests that someone other than the chief executive is outlining the strategy. Putting the phrase *were announced* between *plans* and *for cutting* makes it somewhat unclear whether *for cutting* ... is intended to modify *announced* or *plans*.

B In addition to having a dangling modifier and the wrong form of the verb *announce*, this sentence is made less clear by separating the subject and verb with the long clause beginning with *which are*.

C This version has the same issues as in (A) and (B) and is made less clear by separating the subject and verb with the long clause beginning with *for cutting*.

D Correct. The opening clause properly modifies *chief executive* and the verb form *announced* makes it clear that the chief executive is doing the announcing.

E Although the opening clause correctly modifies *chief executive* in this version, the words *that are* are extraneous and also suggest that the plans themselves are doing the cutting and selling.

The correct answer is D.

69. Affording strategic proximity to the Strait of Gibraltar, Morocco was also of interest to the French throughout the first half of the twentieth century because they assumed that <u>if they did not hold it, their grip on Algeria was always insecure</u>.

    (A) if they did not hold it, their grip on Algeria was always insecure

    (B) without it their grip on Algeria would never be secure

    (C) their grip on Algeria was not ever secure if they did not hold it

    (D) without that, they could never be secure about their grip on Algeria

    (E) never would their grip on Algeria be secure if they did not hold it

Rhetorical construction; Verb form

Conditional constructions require specific verb tenses. For a past condition, the subordinate clause introduced by *if* uses the past indicative, and the main clause uses the conditional *if x happened, then y would happen.*

A   Verb *was* should be the conditional *would be*; wordy and imprecise.

B   Correct. This clear, concise sentence correctly uses the conditional *would never be*.

C   Verb *was* should be the conditional *would be*; pronoun *it* is ambiguous and could refer to either *Morocco* or *Algeria*.

D   *It*, not *that*, should be used to refer back to *Morocco*; *could never be secure about their grip* is awkward.

E   Inverted word order is awkward and confusing; *it* could refer to either *Morocco* or *Algeria*.

The correct answer is B.

70. The first trenches <u>that were cut into a 500-acre site at Tell Hamoukar, Syria, have yielded strong evidence for centrally administered complex societies in northern regions of the Middle East that were arising simultaneously with but</u> independently of the more celebrated city-states of southern Mesopotamia, in what is now southern Iraq.

(A) that were cut into a 500-acre site at Tell Hamoukar, Syria, have yielded strong evidence for centrally administered complex societies in northern regions of the Middle East that were arising simultaneously with but

(B) that were cut into a 500-acre site at Tell Hamoukar, Syria, yields strong evidence that centrally administered complex societies in northern regions of the Middle East were arising simultaneously with but also

(C) having been cut into a 500-acre site at Tell Hamoukar, Syria, have yielded strong evidence that centrally administered complex societies in northern regions of the Middle East were arising simultaneously but

(D) cut into a 500-acre site at Tell Hamoukar, Syria, yields strong evidence of centrally administered complex societies in northern regions of the Middle East arising simultaneously but also

(E) cut into a 500-acre site at Tell Hamoukar, Syria, have yielded strong evidence that centrally administered complex societies in northern regions of the Middle East arose simultaneously with but

Rhetorical construction; Agreement; Grammatical construction

This sentence, explaining interconnections among a number of events, needs to be streamlined as much as possible in order to become understandable. To this end, unnecessary words and structures should be eliminated. Prominent among these are the relative clauses beginning with *that*. Additionally, the subject of this sentence is the plural *trenches*, which requires a plural verb.

A   *That were cut …* and *that were arising …* are unnecessarily wordy and create an unnecessarily complicated and confusing sentence structure.

B   In addition to the unnecessarily wordy relative clauses, the singular verb *yields* does not agree with the plural subject *trenches*.

C   *Having been cut …* is unnecessarily wordy; *arising simultaneously* must be followed by the preposition *with* in order to make sense.

D   The singular verb *yields* does not agree with the plural subject *trenches*; *also* adds no meaning to the sentence.

E   Correct. Unnecessary clauses and phrases are avoided, and the subject and verb of the main clause agree in number.

The correct answer is E.

71. Along the major rivers that traverse the deserts of northeast Africa, the Middle East, and northwest India, the combination of a reliable supply of water and <u>good growing conditions both encouraged farming traditions that, in places, endure in</u> at least 6,000 years.

(A) good growing conditions both encouraged farming traditions that, in places, endure in

(B) good growing conditions encouraged farming traditions that have, in places, endured for

(C) of good growing conditions have encouraged farming traditions that, in places, endured for

(D) of good growing conditions both encouraged farming traditions that have, in places, endured

(E) of good growing conditions encouraged farming traditions that have, in places, been enduring for

Logical predication; Rhetorical construction

The time line of this sentence, captured by the use of verb tenses, is of utmost importance. A combination of factors (in the past) encouraged farming traditions that are still with us today. The conditions for the use of the present perfect tense *have endured* are in place.

A   The word *both* repeats the meaning of *combination* and is thus redundant. The use of the present tense (*endure*) is not justified by the time line of the whole sentence. The correct preposition for this type of construction is *for* (an amount of time), not *in*.

B   Correct. This version correctly employs the present perfect tense with the appropriate adverbial *for at least 6,000 years*.

C   The repetition of the preposition *of* before *good growing conditions* makes no sense. It seems to indicate that there is both a combination of a reliable supply of water and a combination of good growing conditions.

D   The preposition *of* should not be repeated in front of *good growing conditions*. The word *both* repeats the meaning of *combination* and is thus redundant.

E   The preposition *of* should not be repeated in front of *good growing conditions*. The use of the present perfect progressive *have been*

enduring is not grammatically incorrect, but it is rhetorically inappropriate and sounds exaggerated.

The correct answer is B.

72. His studies of ice-polished rocks in his Alpine homeland, far outside the range of present-day glaciers, led Louis Agassiz in 1837 to propose the concept of an age <u>in which great ice sheets had existed in now currently temperate areas</u>.

(A) in which great ice sheets had existed in now currently temperate areas

(B) in which great ice sheets existed in what are now temperate areas

(C) when great ice sheets existed where there were areas now temperate

(D) when great ice sheets had existed in current temperate areas

(E) when great ice sheets existed in areas now that are temperate

Verb form; Rhetorical construction

In which or *when* can be used interchangeably in this sentence. The verb form here should be the simple past *existed* rather than the past perfect *had existed*. *Now currently* is redundant because both adverbs express the same idea.

A   *Had existed* should be *existed*; *now currently* is redundant.

B   Correct. The simple past verb tense is correctly used in this sentence; *now* is placed and used correctly.

C   *Where there were areas now temperate* is wordy and confusing.

D   *Had existed* should be *existed*; *current* should be *currently*; *in current temperate areas* is unclear.

E   *Now* is an adverb and should be placed just after the verb *are*.

The correct answer is B.

73.   Unlike the original National Museum of Science and Technology in Italy, where the models are encased in glass or operated only by staff members, the Virtual Leonardo Project, an online version of the museum, encourages visitors to "touch" each <u>exhibit, which thereby activates</u> the animated functions of the piece.

(A)   exhibit, which thereby activates

(B)   exhibit, in turn an activation of

(C)   exhibit, and it will activate

(D)   exhibit and thereby activate

(E)   exhibit which, as a result, activates

Grammatical construction; Logical predication

The relative pronoun *which* requires an antecedent, and there is none provided in this sentence. It makes more sense to make the visitors the agents responsible for the action of both the verbs—*touch* and *activate*. Because *to "touch"* is an infinitive, the second verb form must be, as well, though the *to* may be implied.

A   *Which* has no antecedent in the sentence, so it is unclear what activated the display.

B   *In turn an activation* ... seems to be the subject of a new clause, but it has no verb, so the sentence is incomplete.

C   There is no antecedent for *it* because *touch* is a verb.

D   **Correct.** The agent of the action is clearly indicated by the grammatical structure of the sentence; visitors are encouraged *to "touch"* ... *and thereby (to) activate.*

E   *Which* has no antecedent in this sentence.

The correct answer is D.

74.   <u>Despite its covering the entire planet, Earth has a crust that is not seamless or stationary, rather it is</u> fragmented into mobile semirigid plates.

(A)   Despite its covering the entire planet, Earth has a crust that is not seamless or stationary, rather it is

(B)   Despite the fact that it covers the entire planet, Earth's crust is neither seamless nor is it stationary, but is

(C)   Despite covering the entire planet, Earth's crust is neither seamless nor is it stationary, but rather

(D)   Although it covers the entire planet, Earth's crust is neither seamless nor stationary, but rather

(E)   Although covering the entire planet, Earth has a crust that is not seamless or stationary, but

Idiom; Parallelism; Logical predication

A dangling modifier is an error in sentence structure whereby a participle is associated with a word other than the one intended or with no particular word at all. In this sentence, *Earth* is the closest word to the participial clause, and so the latter means that Earth is covering the entire planet (itself), which is a contradiction.

A   This version has a dangling participle. The addition of *it is* before *fragmented* is unwarranted and makes the sentence ungrammatical. *Neither ... nor ... but rather* would make the intended relationship among *seamless, stationary,* and *fragmented* clearer and more precise than *not ... or ... rather.*

B   Parallel structure is disrupted by the addition of *is it* after *nor* and by the addition of *is* after *but.*

C   Parallel structure is disrupted by the addition of *is it* after *nor.*

D   **Correct.** *Despite* and *although* are very close in meaning. However, *despite* is a preposition and needs to be followed by a noun or noun phrase, while *although* is a conjunction and should be followed by a finite clause. This version uses *although* correctly. The parallel structure is also clear and correct.

E   *Although* is a conjunction and should be followed by a finite clause with a subject, not by a participle. In addition, the first clause represents a dangling modifier. Omitting *rather* from the parallel structure *neither X nor Y but rather Z* is possible, but not optimal.

The correct answer is D.

75. More and more in recent years, cities are stressing the arts as a means <u>to greater economic development and investing</u> millions of dollars in cultural activities, despite strained municipal budgets and fading federal support.

(A) to greater economic development and investing
(B) to greater development economically and investing
(C) of greater economic development and invest
(D) of greater development economically and invest
(E) for greater economic development and the investment of

Diction; Parallelism

The idiom *as a means to* correctly communicates that *stressing the arts* is a method for achieving *greater economic development*. The idiom *as a means of* would incorrectly suggest that *stressing the arts* is a kind of *greater economic development*. The adjective *economic* is needed to modify the noun *development*, and *investing* must be parallel to *stressing*.

A **Correct.** The idiom *as a means to* is correct in this sentence; *stressing* and *investing* are parallel.
B Adverb *economically* is the wrong part of speech and conveys the incorrect meaning.
C *Of* should be *to* to form the correct idiom; *invest* should be *investing* to parallel *stressing*.
D *Of* should be *to* to form the correct idiom; adverb *economically* is the wrong part of speech and conveys the incorrect meaning; *invest* should be *investing* to parallel *stressing*.
E *As a means for* is not idiomatic; *the investment of* is awkward and is not parallel to *stressing*.

The correct answer is A.

76. Combining enormous physical strength with higher intelligence, the Neanderthals <u>appear as equipped for facing any obstacle the environment could put in their path,</u> but their relatively sudden disappearance during the Paleolithic era indicates that an inability to adapt to some environmental change led to their extinction.

(A) appear as equipped for facing any obstacle the environment could put in their path,
(B) appear to have been equipped to face any obstacle the environment could put in their path,
(C) appear as equipped to face any obstacle the environment could put in their paths,
(D) appeared as equipped to face any obstacle the environment could put in their paths,
(E) appeared to have been equipped for facing any obstacle the environment could put in their path,

Verb form; Diction

Because Neanderthals "disappeared," the verb describing their apparent abilities cannot be present tense, so *as equipped* must be changed to *to have been equipped*. The expression *equipped to face* is clearer and more direct than *equipped for facing*.

A *As equipped* indicates that Neanderthals still appear this way; *equipped* should be followed by an infinitive form instead of a prepositional phrase.
B **Correct.** The verb tense clearly indicates that the current evidence is about Neanderthals in the past.
C *As equipped* does not indicate that Neanderthals appeared this way in the past; while individual Neanderthals may well have followed different paths, this sentence is about the single evolutionary path taken by Neanderthals as a species.
D Present-tense *appear* is needed to parallel present-tense *indicates* and to reinforce that this is current evidence about Neanderthals in the past; as in (C), *paths* should be singular.
E *For facing* is an incorrect substitution of a prepositional phrase for an infinitive.

The correct answer is B.

77. A 1972 agreement between Canada and the United States <u>reduced the amount of phosphates that municipalities had been allowed to dump</u> into the Great Lakes.

    (A) reduced the amount of phosphates that municipalities had been allowed to dump
    (B) reduced the phosphate amount that municipalities had been dumping
    (C) reduces the phosphate amount municipalities have been allowed to dump
    (D) reduced the amount of phosphates that municipalities are allowed to dump
    (E) reduces the amount of phosphates allowed for dumping by municipalities

    Verb form; Idiom

    An agreement that occurred in 1972 is correctly described with the past tense verb *reduced*. Since the dumping continued after the date of the agreement, the past perfect verb *had been allowed* should instead be the present *are allowed* (if the agreement remained in effect when the sentence was written) or the past *were allowed* (if the agreement was no longer in effect when the sentence was written). Since *were allowed* does not appear in any of the options, we can assume that the correct verb tense is *are allowed*. The phrase *amount of phosphates* is clear and idiomatically correct, whereas *phosphate amount* is not idiomatic.

    A *Had been allowed* should be *are allowed*.

    B *The phosphate amount* should be *the amount of phosphates*; the omission of some form of *allow* is incorrect since the agreement changed not the amount dumped, but the amount permitted to be dumped.

    C Present tense *reduces* should be the past tense *reduced*; *the phosphate amount* should be *the amount of phosphates*; *have been allowed* should be *are allowed*.

    D Correct. The past tense *reduced* is correctly used in this sentence to describe a past action, and the present tense *are allowed* is used to describe the present situation.

    E Present tense *reduces* should be the past tense *reduced*; *allowed for dumping* is an incorrect idiom; *allowed for dumping by municipalities* is awkward.

    The correct answer is D.

78. A proposal has been made to trim the horns from rhinoceroses to discourage poachers; the question is <u>whether tourists will continue to visit game parks and see rhinoceroses after their horns are</u> trimmed.

    (A) whether tourists will continue to visit game parks and see rhinoceroses after their horns are
    (B) whether tourists will continue to visit game parks to see one once their horns are
    (C) whether tourists will continue to visit game parks to see rhinoceroses once the animals' horns have been
    (D) if tourists will continue to visit game parks and see rhinoceroses once the animals' horns are
    (E) if tourists will continue to visit game parks to see one after the animals' horns have been

    Logical predication; Diction; Verb form

    The tourists are visiting for the purpose of seeing the rhinoceroses; purpose is expressed by using *to*, not *and*. Since *their* could refer to either *tourists* or *rhinoceroses*, *animals' horns* is needed to avoid the ludicrous suggestion that the visitors' horns are being trimmed. The verb following *after* should be the present-perfect *have been trimmed* to reflect that the trimming must occur before the tourists arrive.

    A *And see* should be *to see*; *their* is ambiguous; *are* should be *have been*.

    B *One* is ambiguous; *their* clearly and absurdly refers to *tourists*; *are* should be *have been*.

    C Correct. In this sentence, *to* correctly precedes *see*; it is clear that the horns belong to the animals; and *have been* is the correct tense following *once*.

    D *And see* should be *to see*; *are* should be *have been*.

    E *One* is ambiguous.

    The correct answer is C.

79. Ryūnosuke Akutagawa's knowledge of the literatures of Europe, China, and <u>that of Japan were instrumental in his development as a writer, informing his literary style as much as</u> the content of his fiction.

(A) that of Japan were instrumental in his development as a writer, informing his literary style as much as

(B) that of Japan was instrumental in his development as a writer, and it informed both his literary style as well as

(C) Japan was instrumental in his development as a writer, informing both his literary style and

(D) Japan was instrumental in his development as a writer, as it informed his literary style as much as

(E) Japan were instrumental in his development as a writer, informing both his literary style in addition to

Logical predication; Agreement

When a verb follows a complex noun phrase made up of several parts, it agrees with the first noun in the phrase. In this case, *knowledge of the literatures of Europe, China, and Japan* is a singular noun and the correct verb form is *was*, not *were*. The various parts of an enumeration have to be alike: *the literatures of Europe, China, and Japan*. The logical relationship between the predicates is important.

A This version of the sentence violates the correct subject-verb agreement, and the correct structure of enumeration is disrupted by the addition of *that of* in front of *Japan*.

B The correct structure of enumeration is disrupted by the addition of *that of* in front of *Japan*. *Both ... as well as ...* is incorrect usage.

C **Correct.** The structure of the enumeration (*Europe, China, and Japan*) as well as the conjunction structure (*both X and Y*) are correct. The logical relationships among the parts of the sentence are clearly expressed.

D This phrasing makes it unclear what the writer is claiming. It appears to indicate that the effect of Akutagawa's knowledge on his development as a writer was due to the fact that both of the aspects of his writing were influenced to the same extent. However, it is implausible to suppose that this is what the

writer intends. Furthermore, the comparison is ambiguous: did his knowledge inform his style as much as it informed the content, or did it inform his style as much as the content informed his style?

E The subject-verb agreement in this version is incorrect. *Both X in addition to Y* is incorrect usage.

The correct answer is C.

80. The only way for growers to salvage frozen citrus is <u>to process them quickly into juice concentrate before they rot when warmer weather returns</u>.

(A) to process them quickly into juice concentrate before they rot when warmer weather returns

(B) if they are quickly processed into juice concentrate before warmer weather returns to rot them

(C) for them to be processed quickly into juice concentrate before the fruit rots when warmer weather returns

(D) if the fruit is quickly processed into juice concentrate before they rot when warmer weather returns

(E) to have it quickly processed into juice concentrate before warmer weather returns and rots the fruit

Parallelism; Agreement

Parallelism requires that the same word forms perform the same functions in the sentence. Here, the linking verb *is* requires two infinitives: *to salvage ... to process* (or *to have ... processed*). A pronoun must match the noun it refers to. *Citrus* is singular and requires the singular pronoun *it*, not the plural pronouns *them* and *they*.

A *Citrus* does not agree with *them* and *they*.

B *If they are quickly processed* is not parallel to the infinitive *to salvage*; *they* does not agree with *citrus*.

C *For them to be processed quickly* is not parallel to the infinitive *to salvage*; *them* does not agree with *citrus*.

D *If the fruit is quickly processed* is not parallel to the infinitive *to salvage*; *they* does not agree with *fruit*.

E **Correct.** This sentence has correct parallel infinitives and uses the words *it* and *fruit* to refer unambiguously to *citrus*. The use of *before* rather than *when* also clearly establishes the cause-and-effect relationship between weather and rotting.

The correct answer is E.

81. Fossils of the arm of a <u>sloth found in Puerto Rico in 1991, and dated at 34 million years old, made it the earliest known mammal of</u> the Greater Antilles Islands.

(A) sloth found in Puerto Rico in 1991, and dated at 34 million years old, made it the earliest known mammal of

(B) sloth, that they found in Puerto Rico in 1991, has been dated at 34 million years old, thus making it the earliest mammal known on

(C) sloth that was found in Puerto Rico in 1991, was dated at 34 million years old, making this the earliest known mammal of

(D) sloth, found in Puerto Rico in 1991, have been dated at 34 million years old, making the sloth the earliest known mammal on

(E) sloth which, found in Puerto Rico in 1991, was dated at 34 million years old, made the sloth the earliest known mammal of

Agreement; Logical predication

The subject of the sentence is the plural *fossils*, not *sloth*, and therefore requires a plural verb. *It* therefore does not have a singular antecedent. To clarify the identification of the oldest known mammal, the noun *the sloth* must be explicitly identified.

A Because *sloth* is the object of a preposition and not the subject of the sentence, there is no reasonable antecedent for the pronoun *it*; in this construction, the subject of *made* is *fossils*, but it makes no sense to say that the *fossils* made it the earliest mammal.

B The introduction of the mysterious *they*, a pronoun without a reference, adds confusion to this sentence; the singular verb does not agree with the plural subject.

C The relative clause *that was* … is wordy and awkward; the singular verb does not agree with the plural subject.

D **Correct.** The plural verb agrees with its plural subject, and *the sloth* is explicitly identified as *the earliest known mammal*.

E The singular verb does not agree with the plural subject.

The correct answer is D.

82. Defense attorneys have occasionally argued that their clients' misconduct stemmed from a reaction to something ingested, but <u>in attributing criminal or delinquent behavior to some food allergy,</u> the perpetrators are in effect told that they are not responsible for their actions.

(A) in attributing criminal or delinquent behavior to some food allergy,

(B) if criminal or delinquent behavior is attributed to an allergy to some food,

(C) in attributing behavior that is criminal or delinquent to an allergy to some food,

(D) if some food allergy is attributed as the cause of criminal or delinquent behavior,

(E) in attributing a food allergy as the cause of criminal or delinquent behavior,

Logical predication; Idiom

The original sentence contains a misplaced modifier. The modifying phrase (*in attributing …*) incorrectly describes *perpetrators* when it should describe *defense attorneys*. The correct idiom in the active voice is one *attributes x* (an effect) *to y* (a cause). In the passive voice, *x* (the effect) *is attributed to y* (the cause). The best way to correct the sentence is to transform the modifying phrase into a subordinate clause that uses the idiom correctly: *criminal or delinquent behavior* (*x*) *is attributed to* (verb phrase) *an allergy to some food* (*y*).

A Misplaced modifier.

B **Correct.** In this sentence, the modification error has been eliminated with the use of the correct idiom, *is attributed to*.

C Modifier describes *perpetrators*, not *attorneys*; wordy and imprecise.

D *X is attributed as the cause of y* is not the correct idiom.

E Modifier incorrectly describes *perpetrators*; idiom is misused.

The correct answer is B.

83. A report by the American Academy for the Advancement of Science has concluded that <u>much of the currently uncontrolled dioxins to which North Americans are exposed comes</u> from the incineration of wastes.

    (A) much of the currently uncontrolled dioxins to which North Americans are exposed comes

    (B) much of the currently uncontrolled dioxins that North Americans are exposed to come

    (C) much of the dioxins that are currently uncontrolled and that North Americans are exposed to comes

    (D) many of the dioxins that are currently uncontrolled and North Americans are exposed to come

    (E) many of the currently uncontrolled dioxins to which North Americans are exposed come

Diction; Agreement

Much is used for an uncountable quantity such as effort or rain; *many* must be used for a countable quantity such as people or *dioxins*. As the subject of the subordinate clause, *many* must then be followed by the plural verb *come* rather than the singular *comes*.

A   *Much* is used instead of *many*.

B   *Much* is used instead of *many*.

C   *Much* is used instead of *many*; *that are* is wordy.

D   *That are* is wordy; to maintain the parallel in this construction, *that* would have to be repeated in the clause *that North Americans are exposed to*.

E   **Correct.** In this concise sentence, *many* is correctly used with *dioxins*, and the subject and verb agree.

The correct answer is E.

84. Recently physicians have determined that stomach ulcers are <u>not caused by stress, alcohol, or rich foods, but</u> a bacterium that dwells in the mucous lining of the stomach.

    (A) not caused by stress, alcohol, or rich foods, but

    (B) not caused by stress, alcohol, or rich foods, but are by

    (C) caused not by stress, alcohol, or rich foods, but by

    (D) caused not by stress, alcohol, and rich foods, but

    (E) caused not by stress, alcohol, and rich foods, but are by

Parallelism; Diction

The formula used in this sentence *not this but that* requires parallel elements following *not* and *but*. This means that *not by stress, alcohol, or rich foods* must be balanced by *but by a bacterium*. … There is no need to repeat the verb *are caused*, or even the auxiliary verb *are*, because the verb precedes the *not by … but by …* formula. The substitution of the conjunction *and* for the conjunction *or* changes the meaning of the sentence: *Stress, alcohol and rich foods* identifies the combination of these three factors as a suggested cause of stomach ulcers, whereas *stress, alcohol, or rich foods* offers three individual possibilities. There is no way to tell which one of these is the intended meaning of the sentence.

A   To preserve parallelism, *but* should be followed by *by*.

B   There is no reason to repeat the auxiliary verb *are*.

C   **Correct.** This sentence correctly uses the *not by … but by …* formula.

D   To preserve parallelism, *but* should be followed by *by*.

E   To preserve parallelism, *but* should be followed by *by*.

The correct answer is C.

85. According to a recent poll, owning and living in a freestanding house on its own land is still a goal of a majority of young adults, <u>like that of earlier generations</u>.

    (A) like that of earlier generations

    (B) as that for earlier generations

    (C) just as earlier generations did

    (D) as have earlier generations

    (E) as it was of earlier generations

Parallelism

This sentence compares a single goal shared by generations. The second part of the sentence must have the same structure as the first part: a clause with a subject and a verb. The phrase *owning ... land* is the subject of the first clause; in the correct sentence, the pronoun *it* refers back to this phrase and is the subject of the second clause. The first verb *is* also parallels the second verb *was*. The prepositional phrases *of a majority of young adults* and *of earlier generations* are parallel and correct.

A Phrase, without subject and verb, is not parallel to the main clause.

B Phrase, without subject and verb, is not parallel to the main clause.

C Subject and verb of the second clause—*earlier generations did*—are not parallel to those of the main clause.

D The verb *have* is not parallel to *is* in the main clause and also does not make sense without a past participle.

E **Correct.** In this sentence *as* shows comparison and introduces a subordinate clause in which all grammatical elements correspond to those in the main clause.

The correct answer is E.

86. In 2000, a mere two dozen products accounted for half the increase in spending on prescription drugs, <u>a phenomenon that is explained not just because of more expensive drugs but by the fact that doctors are writing</u> many more prescriptions for higher-cost drugs.

(A) a phenomenon that is explained not just because of more expensive drugs but by the fact that doctors are writing

(B) a phenomenon that is explained not just by the fact that drugs are becoming more expensive but also by the fact that doctors are writing

(C) a phenomenon occurring not just because of drugs that are becoming more expensive but because of doctors having also written

(D) which occurred not just because drugs are becoming more expensive but doctors are also writing

(E) which occurred not just because of more expensive drugs but because doctors have also written

Rhetorical construction; Idiom

This sentence explains that a few high-cost products account for increased spending for two reasons—rising drug prices and more prescriptions for high-priced drugs. To present these two causes, the sentence employs a formula that requires parallel elements: *not just because of x, but because of y*, with *x* and *y* assuming the same grammatical form. One way to create this parallelism is to phrase both contributing causes as noun clauses beginning with *the fact that*. To streamline the sentence, unnecessary words and redundancies should be eliminated. One such redundancy is the repetition of meaning in *explained* and *because of*.

A It is redundant and confusing to say that the phenomenon in question is *explained ... because of*; the sentence structure is not parallel.

B **Correct.** This sentence correctly uses parallel structure.

C The phrasing *drugs that are becoming* and *doctors having also written* are awkward and confusing; the placement of *also* is incorrect.

D The structure of this sentence is not parallel.

E The placement of *also* is incorrect; the structure of the sentence is not parallel.

The correct answer is B.

87. According to scientists who monitored its path, <u>an expanding cloud of energized particles ejected from the Sun recently triggered a large storm in the magnetic field that surrounds Earth, which brightened the Northern Lights and also possibly knocking</u> out a communications satellite.

(A) an expanding cloud of energized particles ejected from the Sun recently triggered a large storm in the magnetic field that surrounds Earth, which brightened the Northern Lights and also possibly knocking

(B) an expanding cloud of energized particles ejected from the Sun was what recently triggered a large storm in the magnetic field that surrounds Earth, and it brightened the Northern Lights and also possibly knocked

(C) an expanding cloud of energized particles ejected from the Sun recently triggered a large storm in the magnetic field that surrounds Earth, brightening the Northern Lights and possibly knocking

(D) a large storm in the magnetic field that surrounds Earth, recently triggered by an expanding cloud of energized particles, brightened the Northern Lights and it possibly knocked

(E) a large storm in the magnetic field surrounding Earth was recently triggered by an expanding cloud of energized particles, brightening the Northern Lights and it possibly knocked

Logical predication; Rhetorical construction; Verb form

The timing and logical relationships among the events described in this sentence are of utmost importance. The scientists monitored a cloud ejected from the Sun. The cloud triggered a large storm, whose consequences were the brightening of the Northern Lights and the possible knocking out of a satellite. The latter two events are in a conjunction, so they should be represented by similar verb forms.

A   In this context, the shift in verb form from *which brightened* to *and also possibly knocking* is ungrammatical. The two verbs should be in the same verb form for parallel construction.

B   *X was what triggered Y* is wordy and awkward, and its meaning is unclear in this

context. Given the most plausible intended meaning of the sentence, the two conjunctions *and … and …* in the last clause are redundant. The comma after *Earth* turns the final part of the sentence into an independent clause, and it is unclear whether this is part of what the scientists claimed or a separate claim made by the writer.

C   **Correct.** The conjoined elements are of parallel forms, and the logical relations between the events are clear and concisely communicated.

D   The wording in this answer choice makes the intended meaning unclear. The information that the cloud particles were ejected from the Sun is lost. The sentence is ungrammatical; the second conjoined main verb, *knocked*, needs no pronoun subject *it* because its subject is *a large storm*.

E   The wording in this answer choice makes the intended meaning unclear. The information that the cloud particles were ejected from the Sun is lost. The two conjoined verbs are of different form; the second conjoined verb includes an unnecessary pronoun subject.

The correct answer is C.

88. Often visible as smog, <u>ozone is formed in the atmosphere from</u> hydrocarbons and nitrogen oxides, two major pollutants emitted by automobiles, react with sunlight.

(A) ozone is formed in the atmosphere from

(B) ozone is formed in the atmosphere when

(C) ozone is formed in the atmosphere, and when

(D) ozone, formed in the atmosphere when

(E) ozone, formed in the atmosphere from

Grammatical construction; Idiom

The preposition *from* is incorrect because *ozone is formed from x and y react* is not a grammatical structure. Replacing *from* with the subordinating conjunction *when* makes the sentence complete: *Ozone is formed when x and y react*. A main clause is followed by a subordinate clause.

A   The preposition *from* introduces an incoherent and ungrammatical construction.

B **Correct.** The conjunction *when* introduces a subordinate clause, which completes the sentence correctly and coherently.

C *And when* distorts the meaning, suggesting that ozone is formed in two ways.

D Omitting the main verb, *is*, results in a sentence fragment.

E These changes result in a sentence fragment.

The correct answer is B.

89. Salt deposits and moisture threaten to destroy the Mohenjo-Daro excavation in Pakistan, the site of an ancient civilization <u>that flourished at the same time as the civilizations</u> in the Nile Delta and the river valleys of the Tigris and Euphrates.

(A) that flourished at the same time as the civilizations

(B) that had flourished at the same time as had the civilizations

(C) that flourished at the same time those had

(D) flourishing at the same time as those did

(E) flourishing at the same time as those were

Verb form; Agreement

The underlined portion of the sentence is a relative clause that describes *an ancient civilization*; the clause correctly uses the simple past tense, *flourished*, to describe civilizations that existed simultaneously.

A **Correct.** In this sentence, the relative clause correctly uses the simple past tense.

B Use of the past perfect, *had flourished*, is incorrect because it indicates a time prior to another action; the second *had* is redundant and unnecessary.

C Plural pronoun *those* cannot refer to the singular *civilization* and thus lacks a referent; *as* is missing but necessary; *had* is the wrong verb tense.

D Plural pronoun *those* cannot refer to the singular *civilization* and thus lacks a referent; *did* is awkward and unnecessary.

E Plural pronoun *those* cannot refer to the singular *civilization* and thus lacks a referent; *were* is awkward and unnecessary.

The correct answer is A.

90. The results of the company's cost-cutting measures are evident in its profits, <u>which increased 5 percent during the first 3 months of this year after it fell</u> over the last two years.

(A) which increased 5 percent during the first 3 months of this year after it fell

(B) which had increased 5 percent during the first 3 months of this year after it had fallen

(C) which have increased 5 percent during the first 3 months of this year after falling

(D) with a 5 percent increase during the first 3 months of this year after falling

(E) with a 5 percent increase during the first 3 months of this year after having fallen

Verb form; Agreement; Idiom

This sentence describes two sequentially ordered indicators by which the results of a company's cost-cutting measures can be seen. The first indicator to be identified, a 5 percent increase in profits, occurred <u>after</u> the indicator mentioned next. The sentence therefore needs to clarify the sequence by presenting the first-identified indicator in a clause with a verb tense that indicates a later time period than the verb tense in the clause presenting the second-identified indicator. The subject of the relative clause, *which*, refers to the plural noun *profits*, so subsequent pronouns referring to these profits must also be plural.

A The verb tenses do not distinguish between the times at which these indicators occurred; the singular *it* does not agree with the plural *profits*.

B The verb tenses do not distinguish between the times when the indicators occurred; the singular *it* does not agree with the plural *profits*.

C **Correct.** The verb tenses clearly indicate the sequence of events.

D It is not clear what connection is being described by *with*; the prepositional phrase makes the sentence wordy and unclear.

E It is not clear what connection is being described by *with*; the prepositional phrase makes the sentence wordy and unclear.

The correct answer is C.

91. In an effort to reduce their inventories, Italian vintners have cut prices; their wines <u>have been priced to sell, and they are</u>.

    (A) have been priced to sell, and they are
    (B) are priced to sell, and they have
    (C) are priced to sell, and they do
    (D) are being priced to sell, and have
    (E) had been priced to sell, and they have

Verb form

In the underlined segment, the second verb does not need to repeat the word *sell* because it is understood from the previous verb phrase *priced to sell*. However, the second verb must be correctly conjugated with the understood *sell*. *They are sell* is not a correct verb form; *they do sell* is correct.

A   *They are* would require *selling* to complete it, not *sell*.

B   *They have* would require *sold* to complete it, not *sell*.

C   **Correct.** This sentence properly uses *they do* in place of *they do sell*, a grammatically correct verb.

D   *Have* would require *sold* to complete it, not *sell*; omitting the subject *they* requires that the comma be omitted as well.

E   *They have* would require *sold* to complete it, not *sell*; the past-perfect *had been priced* suggests illogically that the wines were already *priced to sell* before the vintners cut prices; moreover, since the past-perfect tense indicates that one event in the past occurred prior to another event in the past, the past-tense *did* would be required rather than the present-tense *have*.

The correct answer is C.

92. <u>Thelonious Monk, who was a jazz pianist and composer, produced a body of work both rooted</u> in the stride-piano tradition of Willie (The Lion) Smith and Duke Ellington, yet in many ways he stood apart from the mainstream jazz repertory.

    (A) Thelonious Monk, who was a jazz pianist and composer, produced a body of work both rooted

(B) Thelonious Monk, the jazz pianist and composer, produced a body of work that was rooted both

(C) Jazz pianist and composer Thelonious Monk, who produced a body of work rooted

(D) Jazz pianist and composer Thelonious Monk produced a body of work that was rooted

(E) Jazz pianist and composer Thelonious Monk produced a body of work rooted both

Grammatical construction; Rhetorical construction

The subject of the sentence is *Thelonious Monk*, and the sentence tells about two things that he did: *produced* and *stood apart*. The work he produced was rooted in the mainstream (*stride piano*) jazz tradition, yet at the same time, he deviated from this tradition. The use of a relative clause (*who was a jazz pianist …*) or an appositive (*the jazz pianist …*) introduces unnecessary wordiness and grammatical complexity. Since only one point is being made about Monk's body of work, the appearance of the word *both* in the clause presenting the claim about Monk's work is deceptive as well as grammatically incorrect.

A   The relative clause introduces wordiness and confusion.

B   The appositive introduces wordiness and unnecessary grammatical complexity.

C   The sentence is a fragment because the main subject, *Thelonious Monk*, has no verb.

D   **Correct.** The sentence concisely identifies Thelonious Monk and expresses the single point about his work without unnecessary or misleading words.

E   The appearance of *both* is misleading, since only one point is being made about where Monk's musical roots are located.

The correct answer is D.

93. Nobody knows exactly how many languages there are in the world, partly because of the difficulty of distinguishing between a language <u>and the sublanguages or dialects within it, but those who have tried to count typically have found</u> about five thousand.

    (A) and the sublanguages or dialects within it, but those who have tried to count typically have found

(B) and the sublanguages or dialects within them, with those who have tried counting typically finding

(C) and the sublanguages or dialects within it, but those who have tried counting it typically find

(D) or the sublanguages or dialects within them, but those who tried to count them typically found

(E) or the sublanguages or dialects within them, with those who have tried to count typically finding

Agreement; Idiom

This sentence first introduces a condition that makes it difficult to count languages and then, with the conjunction *but*, introduces the topic of those who defy these difficulties and try to count the world's languages anyway. Connecting these two parts of the sentence with *but* indicates that the second clause of the sentence is counter to expectation. The challenges of the task are explained using the example of a single language and its many sublanguages or dialects. When this example is referred to with a pronoun, the pronoun should be singular; when the languages being counted are referred to with a pronoun, this pronoun must be plural.

A Correct. The pronoun *it* agrees in number to its singular antecedent, and *but* indicates that the idea expressed in the final clause defies expectations.

B The plural pronoun *them* incorrectly refers to the singular antecedent *language*; connecting the two clauses with the preposition *with* loses the sense that counting languages despite the difficulties defies expectations.

C The second appearance of *it*, referring to world languages, is incorrect because it does not agree in number with *languages*.

D The conjunction *or* is incorrect—the idiomatic expression is *distinguishing between x and y*; the plural pronoun *them* does not agree with the singular antecedent *language*.

E The plural pronoun *them* incorrectly refers to the singular antecedent, *language; with* is an imprecise connector for the two clauses, losing the *counter-to-expectation* relationship between them.

The correct answer is A.

94. <u>Heating-oil prices are expected to be higher this year than last because refiners are paying about $5 a barrel more for crude oil than they were</u> last year.

(A) Heating-oil prices are expected to be higher this year than last because refiners are paying about $5 a barrel more for crude oil than they were

(B) Heating-oil prices are expected to rise higher this year over last because refiners pay about $5 a barrel for crude oil more than they did

(C) Expectations are for heating-oil prices to be higher this year than last year's because refiners are paying about $5 a barrel for crude oil more than they did

(D) It is the expectation that heating-oil prices will be higher for this year over last because refiners are paying about $5 a barrel more for crude oil now than what they were

(E) It is expected that heating-oil prices will rise higher this year than last year's because refiners pay about $5 a barrel for crude oil more than they did

Rhetorical construction; Idiom

The sentence connects a comparison between this year's and last year's heating-oil prices with a comparison between this year's and last year's crude-oil prices. The most efficient, parallel expression of those comparisons is to use two comparative expressions, *higher than* and *more than*.

A Correct. This sentence expresses the comparison in succinct, parallel phrases.

B The comparative form, *higher*, anticipates the comparative term *than*, not *over*; in the second clause, the comparative terms *more than* should immediately follow *$5 a barrel*.

C *Expectations are for* … is an unnecessarily wordy and indirect expression; the possessive *year's* is not parallel with the adverbial phrase *this year*.

D *It is the expectation that* … is wordy and awkward; *for* and *what* are unnecessary.

E *It is expected that* … is wordy and awkward; the possessive *last year's* does not parallel the adverbial phrase *this year*.

The correct answer is A.

95. One of the primary distinctions <u>between our intelligence with that of other primates may lay not so much in any specific skill but</u> in our ability to extend knowledge gained in one context to new and different ones.

   (A) between our intelligence with that of other primates may lay not so much in any specific skill but

   (B) between our intelligence with that of other primates may lie not so much in any specific skill but instead

   (C) between our intelligence and that of other primates may lie not so much in any specific skill as

   (D) our intelligence has from that of other primates may lie not in any specific skill as

   (E) of our intelligence to that of other primates may lay not in any specific skill but

Diction; Idiom

When using the term *distinction* to indicate difference, the correct preposition to use is *between*. In this sentence, the distinction *may lie* in a certain ability that humans do not share with other primates. The verb *may lay* is transitive, requiring a direct object.

A   *With* is the incorrect comparative term to follow *distinctions between*; *lay* is the incorrect verb.

B   *With* is the incorrect comparative term to follow *distinctions between*.

C   Correct. The preposition *between* and the intransitive verb *may lie* are correct in this sentence.

D   *From* is the incorrect preposition to use with *distinction*; without *so much*, which is used in (C), *as* seems to introduce a comparison for *specific skill* rather than a distinction.

E   *Of* is the incorrect preposition to use with *distinction*, and *to* is an incorrect comparative term; *lay* is the incorrect verb.

The correct answer is C.

96. <u>Even though Clovis points, spear points with longitudinal grooves chipped onto their faces, have been found all over North America, they are named for the New Mexico site where they were first discovered in 1932.</u>

   (A) Even though Clovis points, spear points with longitudinal grooves chipped onto their faces, have been found all over North America, they are named for the New Mexico site where they were first discovered in 1932.

   (B) Although named for the New Mexico site where first discovered in 1932, Clovis points are spear points of longitudinal grooves chipped onto their faces and have been found all over North America.

   (C) Named for the New Mexico site where they have been first discovered in 1932, Clovis points, spear points of longitudinal grooves chipped onto the faces, have been found all over North America.

   (D) Spear points with longitudinal grooves that are chipped onto the faces, Clovis points, even though named for the New Mexico site where first discovered in 1932, but were found all over North America.

   (E) While Clovis points are spear points whose faces have longitudinal grooves chipped into them, they have been found all over North America, and named for the New Mexico site where they have been first discovered in 1932.

Verb form; Rhetorical construction; Logical predication

Even though, *although*, and *while* introduce clauses that <u>appear</u> to be logically incompatible but in fact are not. In this sentence, the apparent incompatibility that must be clearly expressed is that although the spear points are named for a particular place in New Mexico, they are in fact found throughout North America. Because their discovery took place in 1932 and is not ongoing, the correct verb tense is simple past, not present perfect.

A   **Correct.** The *even though* clause expresses clearly that the seeming incompatibility is between where the spear points have been found (*all over North America*) and the naming of the spear points for a single site in New Mexico.

B   The sentence structure indicates that the expected incompatibility is between the geographically based name of the points and their physical properties, which makes no sense; *where discovered* is missing a subject—the correct form is *where they were first discovered*.

C   *Have been first discovered* is the wrong tense, since the discovery is a discrete event completed in the past.

D   The sequence of information in this sentence is confusing; *even though* and *but* both introduce information that is contrary to expectation, so to use them both to describe a single apparent contradiction is redundant and nonsensical.

E   *While* introduces a description of Clovis points and suggests that this appears incompatible with their appearance all over North America, which makes no sense; *have been first discovered* is the wrong tense.

The correct answer is A.

97. Some anthropologists believe that the genetic homogeneity evident in the world's people is the result of a "population bottleneck"—<u>at some time in the past our ancestors suffered an event, greatly reducing their numbers</u> and thus our genetic variation.

(A)   at some time in the past our ancestors suffered an event, greatly reducing their numbers

(B)   that at some time in the past our ancestors suffered an event that greatly reduced their numbers

(C)   that some time in the past our ancestors suffered an event so that their numbers were greatly reduced,

(D)   some time in the past our ancestors suffered an event from which their numbers were greatly reduced

(E)   some time in the past, that our ancestors suffered an event so as to reduce their numbers greatly,

Grammatical construction; Parallelism

The underlined part of this sentence is an explanatory rewording of the clause that follows *believe. Scientists believe that X*—[in other words,] *that Y*. In this construction, X and Y are parallel clauses.

A   The omission of *that* after the dash makes the function of the final clause unclear. The structure makes that clause appear to be an awkward and rhetorically puzzling separate assertion that the writer has appended to the prior claim about what the anthropologists believe. The agent or cause of *reducing* is unclear.

B   **Correct.** Repetition of *that* effectively signals the paraphrasing of the belief.

C   The preposition *at* before *some time* is missing; without *at* the adverb *sometime* would be needed instead of this two-word noun phrase. The modifier of *event* is expressed with a wordy passive construction, which destroys the parallelism between it and what follows.

D   Repetition of *that* signals the paraphrasing of the belief and is therefore needed. The preposition *at* before *some time* is missing. The modifier of *event* is expressed with a wordy passive construction, which destroys the parallelism between it and what follows.

E   *That* is repeated in the paraphrase, but in the wrong place. A possible, and absurd, reading of this version is that our ancestors suffered an event in order to willfully reduce their own numbers and thus our genetic variation.

The correct answer is B.

98. Ranked as one of the most important of Europe's young playwrights, Franz Xaver Kroetz has written 40 plays; his works—translated into more than 30 languages—are produced more often <u>than any</u> contemporary German dramatist.

    (A) than any
    (B) than any other
    (C) than are any
    (D) than those of any other
    (E) as are those of any

Logical predication

The original sentence says Kroetz's *works ... are produced more often than any ... dramatist*. A *dramatist* cannot be *produced* and cannot be compared to *works*. Kroetz's *works* must be compared to *works* of other dramatists: *Kroetz's works ... are produced more often than those* (works) *of any other dramatist*.

A   Illogical comparison between *works* and *dramatist*.

B   Illogical comparison between *works* and *any other dramatist*.

C   Illogical comparison between *works* and *dramatist*.

D   Correct. In this sentence, Kroetz's *works* are compared to *those* (the pronoun referring to *works*) of other dramatists.

E   *More often* must be completed by *than*, not as; the phrase *those of any* illogically includes Kroetz's works.

The correct answer is D.

99. <u>The stars, some of them at tremendous speeds, are in motion just as the planets are, yet being</u> so far away from Earth that their apparent positions in the sky do not change enough for their movement to be observed during a single human lifetime.

    (A) The stars, some of them at tremendous speeds, are in motion just as the planets are, yet being
    (B) Like the planets, the stars are in motion, some of them at tremendous speeds, but they are

    (C) Although like the planets the stars are in motion, some of them at tremendous speeds, yet
    (D) As the planets, the stars are in motion, some of them at tremendous speeds, but they are
    (E) The stars are in motion like the planets, some of which at tremendous speeds are in motion but

Grammatical construction; Rhetorical construction

The first part of the original sentence intends to compare stars and planets; the comparison would be more effective at the beginning of the sentence: *Like the planets, the stars*. This alternative construction would lead the reader to expect the verb *are* immediately following the subject, and then the completion of the clause, *in motion*. The modifying phrase, *some of them at tremendous speeds*, is best placed after *motion*. This whole construction, *Like the planets, the stars are in motion, some of them at tremendous speeds*, is a main clause and must be followed by a comma before a coordinating conjunction (such as *yet* or *but*) introduces a second main clause. The second clause must have a subject and a verb; *being* is neither and must be replaced with *they are*.

A   Placements of the modifying phrase and the comparison are awkward and ineffective; *being* provides neither a subject nor a verb for the second main clause.

B   Correct. The comparison is clear and effective in this sentence; the second clause includes a subject and a verb.

C   Both *although* and *yet* indicate contrast, so only one of them may be used; wordy, awkward phrasing leads to an ungrammatical construction that lacks a subject and verb for the second clause.

D   The preposition *like* must be used for a comparison of two nouns; the subordinating conjunction *as* would need to introduce a subordinate clause.

E   Placement of *like the planets* is awkward; *some of which* is awkward and ambiguous; *are in motion* is said twice; subject and verb of the second clause are omitted.

The correct answer is B.

100. <u>Heavy commitment by an executive to a course of action, especially if it has worked well in the past, makes it likely to miss signs of incipient trouble or misinterpret them when they do appear.</u>

   (A) Heavy commitment by an executive to a course of action, especially if it has worked well in the past, makes it likely to miss signs of incipient trouble or misinterpret them when they do appear.
   (B) An executive who is heavily committed to a course of action, especially one that worked well in the past, makes missing signs of incipient trouble or misinterpreting ones likely when they do appear.
   (C) An executive who is heavily committed to a course of action is likely to miss or misinterpret signs of incipient trouble when they do appear, especially if it has worked well in the past.
   (D) Executives' being heavily committed to a course of action, especially if it has worked well in the past, makes them likely to miss signs of incipient trouble or misinterpreting them when they do appear.
   (E) Being heavily committed to a course of action, especially one that has worked well in the past, is likely to make an executive miss signs of incipient trouble or misinterpret them when they do appear.

Rhetorical construction; Logical predication

This sentence explains that an executive who is blindly committed to a proven course of action is likely to overlook or misinterpret indicators that the plan may no longer be working. The sentence needs to make clear *who* may misinterpret these indicators.

A The passive construction causes the sentence to be wordy and confusing; the reference for *it* is ambiguous, leaving the reader with questions about who or what is likely to miss these signs.

B The sentence structure indicates that the *executive*, not his or her strategy, causes signs to be overlooked; the modifier *when they do appear* is misplaced.

C The reference for the pronoun *it* is unclear because many nouns have intervened between the appearance of the logical referent (*course of action*) and *it*.

D *Misinterpreting* should be an infinitive verb form to parallel *miss*; the phrasing throughout the sentence is wordy and awkward.

E **Correct.** The grammatical structure of this sentence and the appropriate placement of modifiers expresses the meaning clearly and concisely.

The correct answer is E.

101. As rainfall began to decrease in the Southwest about the middle of the twelfth century, most of the Monument Valley Anasazi abandoned their homes to join other clans <u>whose access to water was less limited</u>.

   (A) whose access to water was less limited
   (B) where there was access to water that was less limited
   (C) where they had less limited water access
   (D) with less limitations on water access
   (E) having less limitations to water access

Diction; Logical predication

In the original sentence, the underlined clause provides a clear, correct, and succinct comparison, explaining the reason for the migration. The possessive pronoun *whose* correctly refers to its immediate antecedent, *clans*, and modifies *access*. For those other clans, access to water was *less limited* than it was for the Anasazi.

A **Correct.** This sentence uses a clear, concise clause that correctly connects *access to water* with *clans* by using the possessive pronoun *whose*.

B *Where there was … that was* is awkward, wordy, and redundant.

C *They* is ambiguous and might refer to either the *Anasazi* or *other clans*; *less limited water access* is awkward.

D *Limitations* is a countable quantity, so it must be modified by *fewer*, not *less*.

E *Limitations* is a countable quantity, so it must be modified by *fewer*, not *less*.

The correct answer is A.

102. Yellow jackets number among the 900 or so species of the world's social wasps, <u>wasps living in a highly cooperative and organized society where they consist almost entirely of</u> females—the queen and her sterile female workers.

    (A)   wasps living in a highly cooperative and organized society where they consist almost entirely of

    (B)   wasps that live in a highly cooperative and organized society consisting almost entirely of

    (C)   which means they live in a highly cooperative and organized society, almost all

    (D)   which means that their society is highly cooperative, organized, and it is almost entirely

    (E)   living in a society that is highly cooperative, organized, and it consists of almost all

Idiom; Logical predication; Rhetorical construction

This sentence identifies yellow jackets as one of 900 types of social wasps and provides an explanation of the term *social wasps*. In this explanation, the society or population—not the individual wasps themselves—consists almost entirely of females. The three descriptors of social wasps (*cooperative, organized*, and *consisting almost entirely of females*) are most effectively expressed in parallel structures.

A   *They*, referring to wasps, is an incorrect subject for *consist*.

B   **Correct.** The three descriptors of the wasp society are in parallel form, and *consisting* properly modifies *society*.

C   The sentence structure makes it unclear what *almost all females* describes.

D   *And it is …* violates the parallelism of the three descriptors of social wasps.

E   *And it consists …* violates the parallelism of the three descriptors.

The correct answer is B.

103. El Niño, the periodic abnormal warming of the sea surface off Peru, <u>a phenomenon in which changes in the ocean and atmosphere combine allowing the warm water that has accumulated</u> in the western Pacific to flow back to the east.

    (A)   a phenomenon in which changes in the ocean and atmosphere combine allowing the warm water that has accumulated

    (B)   a phenomenon where changes in the ocean and atmosphere are combining to allow the warm water that is accumulating

    (C)   a phenomenon in which ocean and atmosphere changes combine and which allows the warm water that is accumulated

    (D)   is a phenomenon in which changes in the ocean and atmosphere combine to allow the warm water that has accumulated

    (E)   is a phenomenon where ocean and atmosphere changes are combining and allow the warm water accumulating

Grammatical construction; Logical predication

This accumulation of phrases and clauses results in a sentence fragment; there is no main verb. This problem is easily solved by inserting the verb to be: *El Niño … is a phenomenon….* The clause defining *phenomenon* is clear (*in which changes in the ocean and atmosphere combine*), but the subsequent phrase, *allowing …* is not. If the participial phrase were to modify the previous clause, a comma would have to be inserted between *combine* and *allowing*. A better choice would be to follow *combine* with *to allow*, showing purpose. In this sense, the environmental changes *combine* (intransitive) in order to allow the water to flow back east.

A   Lacking a main verb, this construction is a sentence fragment; *allowing* should be replaced by *to allow*.

B   This construction is a sentence fragment; present progressive verb form (*are combining, is accumulating*) indicates action in progress, which does not accurately describe a periodically occurring phenomenon.

C   This construction is a sentence fragment; making a separate clause *and which allows …* prevents the relationships from being easily understood.

D   **Correct.** The addition of *is* completes the sentence; *combine to allow* shows the purpose of the changes.

E   *Where* cannot correctly refer to *phenomenon*; *are combining* is the wrong verb form; the relationships among the parts of the sentence are unclear.

The correct answer is D.

104. Beatrix Potter, in her book illustrations, carefully coordinating them with her narratives, capitalized on her keen observation and love of the natural world.

    (A) Beatrix Potter, in her book illustrations, carefully coordinating them with her narratives,

    (B) In her book illustrations, carefully coordinating them with her narratives, Beatrix Potter

    (C) In her book illustrations, which she carefully coordinated with her narratives, Beatrix Potter

    (D) Carefully coordinated with her narratives, Beatrix Potter, in her book illustrations

    (E) Beatrix Potter, in her book illustrations, carefully coordinated them with her narratives and

Logical predication; Rhetorical construction

This sentence awkwardly presents two phrases intended to modify *Beatrix Potter* and loses the clarity and logic of the meaning. In the original sentence, these modifiers sound choppy and create too much separation between the subject, *Beatrix Potter*, and the verb *capitalized*. Beginning the sentence with *In her book illustrations* and following that phrase with the relative clause *which she carefully coordinated with her narratives* allows the subject, *Beatrix Potter*, to be united with the verb, *capitalized*, for a stronger main clause.

A The participial phrase does not clearly modify the noun in the preceding phrase; use of the present progressive form of the verb confuses the sequence of time with respect to the past tense of the main verb *capitalized*.

B Phrase *carefully coordinating* ... illogically modifies the noun that immediately precedes it: *book illustrations*; Potter, not the illustrations, did the coordinating.

C **Correct.** The correct placement of the modifying elements makes this sentence easier to understand; the use of *which* clearly links the two elements.

D *Carefully coordinated* ... absurdly modifies *Beatrix Potter* rather than *her illustrations*.

E The participial phrase does not clearly modify *book illustrations*; the relationships among the parts of the sentence are unclear.

The correct answer is C.

105. Marconi's conception of the radio was as a substitute for the telephone, a tool for private conversation; instead, it is precisely the opposite, a tool for communicating with a large, public audience.

    (A) Marconi's conception of the radio was as a substitute for the telephone, a tool for private conversation; instead, it is

    (B) Marconi conceived of the radio as a substitute for the telephone, a tool for private conversation, but which is

    (C) Marconi conceived of the radio as a tool for private conversation that could substitute for the telephone; instead, it has become

    (D) Marconi conceived of the radio to be a tool for private conversation, a substitute for the telephone, which has become

    (E) Marconi conceived of the radio to be a substitute for the telephone, a tool for private conversation, other than what it is,

Rhetorical construction; Logical predication

The main point of this sentence is to explain that while Marconi felt the radio would substitute for the phone as an instrument of private communication, in fact it has become an instrument of mass communication. It is less wordy to use *Marconi* as the subject of the active verb *conceived* than to use the subject *conception* with the static verb *was*. The pronoun *it* positioned as the subject of the final verb *has become* refers back to *radio*. Versions of the sentence that use the relative pronoun *which* indicate that the telephone has become a mass medium.

A The nominalized subject, *conception*, leads to a wordy and awkward sentence.

B The reference for the relative pronoun *which* is ambiguous; the sentence as a whole is awkward.

C **Correct.** An active verb makes the first clause more concise; *it* in the second clause clearly refers to *the radio*.

D *Conceived of* ... should be followed by *as* rather than *to be*.

E *Conceived of* ... should be followed by *as* rather than *to be*; *other than what it is* is awkward, wordy, and redundant, overlapping the meaning of *precisely the opposite*. ...

The correct answer is C.

106. <u>Originally developed for detecting air pollutants, a technique called proton-induced X-ray emission, which can quickly analyze the chemical elements in almost any substance without destroying it,</u> is finding uses in medicine, archaeology, and criminology.

(A) Originally developed for detecting air pollutants, a technique called proton-induced X-ray emission, which can quickly analyze the chemical elements in almost any substance without destroying it,

(B) Originally developed for detecting air pollutants, having the ability to analyze the chemical elements in almost any substance without destroying it, a technique called proton-induced X-ray emission

(C) A technique originally developed for detecting air pollutants, called proton-induced X-ray emission, which can quickly analyze the chemical elements in almost any substance without destroying it,

(D) A technique originally developed for detecting air pollutants, called proton-induced X-ray emission, which has the ability to analyze the chemical elements in almost any substance quickly and without destroying it,

(E) A technique that was originally developed for detecting air pollutants and has the ability to analyze the chemical elements in almost any substance quickly and without destroying the substance, called proton-induced X-ray emission,

Rhetorical construction

The original sentence successfully avoids the problems that may occur in a long sentence with multiple modifiers. The sentence opens with the modifier *originally developed for detecting air pollutants*. This participial phrase is immediately followed by the word *technique* that it modifies; *technique* is in turn followed by the phrase *called proton-induced X-ray emission*. Finally, the nonrestrictive clause *which … destroying it* is correctly placed next to *emission* and set off from the rest of the sentence by a pair of commas.

A **Correct.** The modifiers are all correctly placed and punctuated; the meaning is clear.

B Placement of two long modifiers at the beginning of the sentence is awkward and makes it difficult to locate the subject; second modifier (*having…*) actually modifies the first modifier.

C *Called proton–induced X-ray emission* should be placed next to *a technique* and should not be set off by commas; relative clause introduced by *which* incorrectly and illogically modifies *emission*.

D *Called proton–induced X-ray emission* should be placed next to *a technique* and should not be set off by commas; relative clause introduced by *which* incorrectly and illogically modifies *emission*; *has the ability to* is wordy.

E *Called proton–induced X-ray emission* should be placed next to *a technique* and should not be set off by commas; *has the ability to* is wordy.

The correct answer is A.

107. <u>While it costs about the same to run nuclear plants as other types of power plants, it is the fixed costs that stem from building nuclear plants that makes it more expensive for them to generate electricity.</u>

(A) While it costs about the same to run nuclear plants as other types of power plants, it is the fixed costs that stem from building nuclear plants that makes it more expensive for them to generate electricity.

(B) While the cost of running nuclear plants is about the same as for other types of power plants, the fixed costs that stem from building nuclear plants make the electricity they generate more expensive.

(C) Even though it costs about the same to run nuclear plants as for other types of power plants, it is the fixed costs that stem from building nuclear plants that makes the electricity they generate more expensive.

(D) It costs about the same to run nuclear plants as for other types of power plants, whereas the electricity they generate is more expensive, stemming from the fixed costs of building nuclear plants.

(E) The cost of running nuclear plants is about the same as other types of power plants, but the electricity they generate is made more expensive because of the fixed costs stemming from building nuclear plants.

Agreement; Logical predication

The emphatic construction *it is X that does Y* (as in the phrase *it is Jane who knows the answer*) should be used only when there is a compelling reason to emphasize the doer of the action. In this sentence, the emphatic construction is used without good reason.

A   This sentence uses the emphatic structure *it is … that* without justification. The singular verb *makes* violates the agreement within the structure. The verb *makes* should agree with the notional subject (*the fixed costs*), not with the pronoun *it*.

B   **Correct.** This answer choice clearly and succinctly compares the two types of costs.

C   In addition to using the more cumbersome emphatic structure, this version violates the agreement within the structure. The verb should agree with the notional subject (*the fixed costs*), not with the pronoun *it*.

D   The preposition *for* is redundant in comparing the two objects of *run*. Since it is not clear what *stemming …* refers to, this is a dangling modifier.

E   The passive construction *electricity … is made more expensive because of …* is wordy and cumbersome. The preposition *for* is necessary in the comparison of the costs.

The correct answer is B.

108. <u>Authoritative parents are more likely than permissive parents to have children who as adolescents are self-confident, high in self-esteem, and responsibly independent.</u>

(A)   Authoritative parents are more likely than permissive parents to have children who as adolescents are self-confident, high in self-esteem, and responsibly independent.

(B)   Authoritative parents who are more likely than permissive parents to have adolescent children that are self-confident, high in self-esteem, and responsibly independent.

(C)   Children of authoritative parents, rather than permissive parents, are the more likely to be self-confident, have a high self-esteem, and to be responsibly independent as adolescents.

(D)   Children whose parents are authoritative rather than being permissive, are more likely to have self-confidence, a high self-esteem, and be responsibly independent when they are an adolescent.

(E)   Rather than permissive parents, the children of authoritative parents are the more likely to have self-confidence, a high self-esteem, and to be responsibly independent as an adolescent.

Grammatical construction; Logical predication

The sentence compares authoritative parents to permissive parents in terms of the kinds of adolescent children they are likely to have. Versions of the sentence that compare parents to children are nonsensical. The three characteristics most likely exemplified by children of authoritative parents should be presented in parallel structure.

A   **Correct.** The sentence effectively compares authoritative parents to permissive parents and expresses the characteristics of the children in parallel form.

B   The sentence is a fragment, since the main subject, *authoritative parents*, has no verb.

C   To preserve parallelism, the infinitive marker *to* should appear only before the first verb in the series OR it should appear before all three verbs; the sentence seems to be comparing children and parents.

D   The word *being* destroys the parallelism between *authoritative* and *permissive*; the single predicate noun *adolescent* does not agree with the plural subject *they*.

E   This sentence unintentionally compares children and parents.

The correct answer is A.

109. Among the objects found in the excavated temple were small terra-cotta effigies left by supplicants who were either asking the goddess Bona Dea's aid <u>in healing physical and mental ills or thanking her for such help</u>.

    (A) in healing physical and mental ills or thanking her for such help

    (B) in healing physical and mental ills and to thank her for helping

    (C) in healing physical and mental ills, and thanking her for helping

    (D) to heal physical and mental ills or to thank her for such help

    (E) to heal physical and mental ills or thanking her for such help

Parallelism; Idiom

This correct sentence uses parallel structure to explain that *supplicants were either asking … or thanking*. The correlative pair *either/or* is correctly used since each element is followed by the same part of speech: *either asking … or thanking*. The pair of correlative conjunctions *either … or* always work together; *either* may only be followed by *or*. The noun *aid* is correctly followed by *in healing* rather than by the infinitive *to heal*.

A **Correct.** The original sentence uses parallel structure to make its point; the idioms are correctly used.

B *And* is incorrect following *either*, and its use changes the meaning of the sentence; *to thank* is not parallel to *asking*; *for helping* is awkward.

C No comma should be used following *ills*; *and* is incorrect following *either*, and its use changes the meaning of the sentence; *for helping* is awkward.

D *To heal* is incorrect following *aid*; *to thank* is not parallel to *asking*.

E *To heal* is incorrect following *aid*.

The correct answer is A.

110. <u>Published in Harlem, the owner and editor of *The Messenger* were two young journalists, Chandler Owen and A. Philip Randolph, who would later make his reputation as a labor leader.</u>

    (A) Published in Harlem, the owner and editor of *The Messenger* were two young journalists, Chandler Owen and A. Philip Randolph, who would later make his reputation as a labor leader.

    (B) Published in Harlem, two young journalists, Chandler Owen and A. Philip Randolph, who would later make his reputation as a labor leader, were the owner and editor of *The Messenger*.

    (C) Published in Harlem, *The Messenger* was owned and edited by two young journalists, A. Philip Randolph, who would later make his reputation as a labor leader, and Chandler Owen.

    (D) *The Messenger* was owned and edited by two young journalists, Chandler Owen and A. Philip Randolph, who would later make his reputation as a labor leader, and published in Harlem.

    (E) The owner and editor being two young journalists, Chandler Owen and A. Philip Randolph, who would later make his reputation as a labor leader, *The Messenger* was published in Harlem.

Logical predication; agreement

A modifying phrase must be placed near the word it modifies. Here, the incorrect placement of the modifying phrase *published in Harlem* makes the phrase describe *the owner and editor* when it should describe *The Messenger*. The use of the singular *owner and editor* is puzzling: did one journalist own and the other edit? Or did they jointly own and edit? It is also unclear which of the two journalists is described in the clause beginning *who*.

A *Published in Harlem* incorrectly modifies *the owner and editor*; references are unclear.

B *Published in Harlem* incorrectly modifies *two young journalists*; references are unclear.

C **Correct.** In this sentence, the modifier correctly describes *The Messenger*; the verbs indicate that both journalists played both roles; and the relative clause clearly shows Randolph, not Owen, as the owner of the reputation.

D The relative clause (*who … leader*) lacks a clear antecedent; placement of *published in Harlem* is awkward and unclear.

E *Being* introduces an awkward construction; the relative clause (*who … leader*) does not have a clear antecedent.

The correct answer is C.

111. A mutual fund having billions of dollars in assets will typically invest that money in hundreds of <u>companies, rarely holding more than one percent</u> of the shares of any particular corporation.

    (A)   companies, rarely holding more than one percent

    (B)   companies, and it is rare to hold at least one percent or more

    (C)   companies and rarely do they hold more than one percent

    (D)   companies, so that they rarely hold more than one percent

    (E)   companies; rarely do they hold one percent or more

Agreement; Logical predication

The participial phrase starting with *rarely holding* is predicated of the main subject *a mutual fund*. It elaborates on the effect of the main clause verb: since a mutual fund invests in hundreds of companies, it rarely holds more than one percent in any particular corporation.

A   **Correct.** The participle *holding* in the embedded clause correctly refers to *a mutual fund*. It also correctly expresses the cause-and-effect relationship between investing in many companies and holding little in each company.

B   The antecedent of *it is rare to hold* is not clear. The use of *it is rare* instead of *rarely* could be misleading.

C   The use of *and* between the clauses makes them both main clauses. Thus, the cause-and-effect relationship between investing and holding is lost. The referent of *they* is unclear. It makes no sense to suppose that it refers to the hundreds of companies. Since it presumably refers to *a mutual fund*, it should be singular.

D   The pronoun *they* refers to *a mutual fund* and thus should be singular.

E   The pronoun *they* refers to *a mutual fund* and thus should be singular.

The correct answer is A.

112. Construction of the Roman Colosseum, <u>which was officially known as the Flavian Amphitheater, began in A.D. 69, during the reign of Vespasian,</u> was completed a decade later, during the reign of Titus, who opened the Colosseum with a one-hundred-day cycle of religious pageants, gladiatorial games, and spectacles.

    (A)   which was officially known as the Flavian Amphitheater, began in A.D. 69, during the reign of Vespasian,

    (B)   officially known as the Flavian Amphitheater, begun in A.D. 69, during the reign of Vespasian, and

    (C)   which was officially known as the Flavian Amphitheater, began in A.D. 69, during the reign of Vespasian, and

    (D)   officially known as the Flavian Amphitheater and begun in A.D. 69, during the reign of Vespasian it

    (E)   officially known as the Flavian Amphitheater, which was begun in A.D. 69, during the reign of Vespasian, and

Grammatical construction; Verb form

The main subject of the sentence is *Construction*, and it has two main verbs: *began* and *was completed*. These two verbs should be connected by the conjunction *and* to preserve their equal grammatical status. Both verbs should be in simple past tense.

A   The conjunction is missing before the second main verb, *was completed*.

B   *Begun* is the wrong verb form.

C   **Correct.** The two verbs of the main clause are in simple past tense and are joined with *and*.

D   There is no need to use the pronoun *it* as the subject of *was completed*, because *Roman Colosseum* (modified by phrases describing its name and the time it was begun) already serves as the subject of the final verb.

E   The appearance of the relative pronoun as the subject of the main verbs deprives the term *construction* of a verb and makes this sentence a fragment.

The correct answer is C.

113. As a baby emerges from the darkness of the womb with a rudimentary sense of vision, it would be rated about 20/500, or legally blind if it were an adult with such vision.

(A) As a baby emerges from the darkness of the womb with a rudimentary sense of vision, it would be rated about 20/500, or legally blind if it were an adult with such vision.

(B) A baby emerges from the darkness of the womb with a rudimentary sense of vision that would be rated about 20/500, or legally blind as an adult.

(C) As a baby emerges from the darkness of the womb, its rudimentary sense of vision would be rated about 20/500; qualifying it to be legally blind if an adult.

(D) A baby emerges from the darkness of the womb with a rudimentary sense of vision that would be rated about 20/500; an adult with such vision would be deemed legally blind.

(E) As a baby emerges from the darkness of the womb, its rudimentary sense of vision, which would deemed legally blind for an adult, would be rated about 20/500.

Grammatical construction

This sentence fails to convey its meaning because its construction is faulty. It begins with a subordinate clause, whose subject is *a baby*; the subject of the main clause, *it* appears to refer back to *baby*. However, reading the main clause reveals that *it* is intended to refer to the *sense of vision* the first time it is used and to the *baby* the second time. The whole sentence must be revised, and the relationships between the two parts of the sentence must be clarified.

A   Repeated use of *it* creates confusion because the referent is not clear.

B   The final phrase is awkwardly and ambiguously attached to the sentence.

C   The use of a semicolon instead of a comma creates a sentence fragment.

D   **Correct.** One independent clause describes a baby's vision, the other an adult's; the two independent but linked main clauses are correctly separated with a semicolon in this version of the sentence.

E   Subordinate clause beginning with *which* is awkward and ambiguous.

The correct answer is D.

114. Starfish, with anywhere from five to eight arms, have a strong regenerative ability, and if one arm is lost it quickly replaces it, sometimes by the animal overcompensating and growing an extra one or two.

(A) one arm is lost it quickly replaces it, sometimes by the animal overcompensating and

(B) one arm is lost it is quickly replaced, with the animal sometimes overcompensating and

(C) they lose one arm they quickly replace it, sometimes by the animal overcompensating,

(D) they lose one arm they are quickly replaced, with the animal sometimes overcompensating,

(E) they lose one arm it is quickly replaced, sometimes with the animal overcompensating,

Agreement; Idiom

In a conditional sentence *if X, (then) Y*, rhetorical flow is enhanced by the two clauses sharing the same structure. If one clause is passive, the other should be passive; if one clause is active, the other should be active, too.

A   The conditional clause has a passive verb, while the result clause has an active verb. The pronoun *it* should be plural since it refers to *starfish*. We know that *starfish* is plural in this sentence because it agrees with *have* in the main clause.

B   **Correct.** The conditional structure is clear and correct.

C   This answer choice allows the unintended reading that the animal replaces the missing arm by overcompensating. The logical connection between *overcompensating* and *growing* is unclear.

D   The conditional clause has an active verb, while the result clause has a passive verb. The second *they* should refer to *arm*, so the agreement is not correct. The logical connection between *overcompensating* and *growing* is unclear.

E   The conditional clause has an active verb, while the result clause has a passive verb. The logical connection between *overcompensating* and *growing* is unclear.

The correct answer is B.

115. <u>Because there are provisions of the new maritime code that provide that even tiny islets can be the basis for claims to the fisheries and oil fields of large sea areas, they have already stimulated</u> international disputes over uninhabited islands.

    (A) Because there are provisions of the new maritime code that provide that even tiny islets can be the basis for claims to the fisheries and oil fields of large sea areas, they have already stimulated

    (B) Because the new maritime code provides that even tiny islets can be the basis for claims to the fisheries and oil fields of large sea areas, it has already stimulated

    (C) Even tiny islets can be the basis for claims to the fisheries and oil fields of large sea areas under provisions of the new maritime code, already stimulating

    (D) Because even tiny islets can be the basis for claims to the fisheries and oil fields of large sea areas under provisions of the new maritime code, this has already stimulated

    (E) Because even tiny islets can be the basis for claims to the fisheries and oil fields of large sea areas under provisions of the new maritime code, which is already stimulating

    Logical predication; Grammatical construction

    In this sentence, the *there are … that …* construction contributes nothing more than unnecessary words. The sentence needs to make clear whether *provisions* or *code* is the subject of the main verb *stimulated*.

    A The *there are … that …* construction is unnecessarily wordy; in the predicate nominative instead of the subject position, *provisions* is not an obvious referent for the pronoun *they*.

    B **Correct.** In this sentence, *the new maritime code* is clearly the antecedent of *it* in the main clause and thus the subject of *has already stimulated*.

    C *Under provisions of the new maritime code* is a misplaced modifier, seeming to describe *sea areas*; the sentence does not make clear what is *stimulating … disputes*.

    D The referent of *this* is unclear.

    E The sentence is a fragment, opening with a dependent clause (*Because … code*) and concluding with a relative clause, but lacking a main, independent clause.

    The correct answer is B.

116. The original building and loan associations were organized as limited life funds, whose members made monthly payments on their share <u>subscriptions, then taking turns drawing</u> on the funds for home mortgages.

    (A) subscriptions, then taking turns drawing
    (B) subscriptions, and then taking turns drawing
    (C) subscriptions and then took turns drawing
    (D) subscriptions and then took turns, they drew
    (E) subscriptions and then drew, taking turns

    Verb form; Parallelism

    The *members* performed a sequence of two actions: first they *made monthly payments* … and then *took turns drawing*. The two actions must be expressed by the parallel past tense verbs *made* and *took*. The substitution of *taking* for *took* disrupts the parallelism and makes the sentence hard to understand.

    A The participle *taking* is not parallel to the verb *made*.

    B Adding *and* does not solve the lack of parallelism.

    C **Correct.** In this sentence, the second verb, *took*, is parallel to the first verb, *made*; the two verbs are correctly joined by *and* as compound verbs with the same subject, *members*.

    D Illogical construction creates a run-on sentence.

    E Construction is illogical, failing to show what the members *drew*; the final phrase makes no sense.

    The correct answer is C.

117. Gall's hypothesis <u>of there being different mental functions localized in different parts of the brain is widely accepted today</u>.

    (A) of there being different mental functions localized in different parts of the brain is widely accepted today

    (B) of different mental functions that are localized in different parts of the brain is widely accepted today

    (C) that different mental functions are localized in different parts of the brain is widely accepted today

    (D) which is that there are different mental functions localized in different parts of the brain is widely accepted today

    (E) which is widely accepted today is that there are different mental functions localized in different parts of the brain

Grammatical construction

Gall's hypothesis is contained in the clause *that different mental functions are localized in different parts of the brain* (noun + marker *that* + content clause). A series of phrases provides neither the same clarity nor grammatical correctness.

A   *Of there being* is not a precise expression; a clause identifying Gall's hypothesis is needed: *that* introduces a clause that complements the noun *hypothesis*.

B   This construction distorts meaning by separating parts of the description.

C   **Correct.** This sentence uses a clause that identifies Gall's hypothesis clearly and correctly.

D   *Which is* and *there are* introduce a wordy and awkward construction.

E   *Which is widely accepted today* implies that Gall's other theories are not accepted today, distorting the meaning of the sentence.

The correct answer is C.

118. Mauritius was a British colony for almost 200 years, <u>excepting for</u> the domains of administration and teaching, the English language was never really spoken on the island.

    (A) excepting for
    (B) except in
    (C) but except in
    (D) but excepting for
    (E) with the exception of

Idiom; Grammatical construction

This two-clause sentence describes an apparent incompatibility: as a British colony, Mauritius might be expected to be English-speaking, but in fact it was not. To describe this apparent contradiction and to avoid a comma splice, the clauses should be joined by the conjunction *but*. *Domains* describes places *in* which English is spoken; *for* is the incorrect preposition. *Excepting* is not idiomatic English in this case.

A   The lack of a conjunction causes a comma splice; *excepting for* is non-idiomatic.

B   The lack of a conjunction causes a comma splice.

C   **Correct.** The two independent clauses are separated by *but*, and *except in* is an appropriate idiom.

D   *Excepting for* is non-idiomatic.

E   The lack of a conjunction causes a comma splice.

The correct answer is C.

119. George Sand (Aurore Lucile Dupin) was one of the first European writers to consider the rural poor <u>to be legitimate subjects for literature and portray these</u> with sympathy and respect in her novels.

    (A) to be legitimate subjects for literature and portray these

    (B) should be legitimate subjects for literature and portray these

    (C) as being legitimate subjects for literature and portraying them

    (D) as if they were legitimate subjects for literature and portray them

    (E) legitimate subjects for literature and to portray them

Idiom; Diction; Parallelism

When *consider* means *think of* or *believe after careful deliberation*, it does not require *as* or any other expression before the object. The most concise phrase is *to consider the rural poor legitimate subjects for literature*. This phrase should have a parallel in *to portray them with sympathy and respect*. While it is not essential to repeat *to*, the repetition elegantly reinforces the parallelism. The correct pronoun must follow *portray*: Sand portrayed *them*. The pronoun *them* refers to the rural poor and is the direct object. *These* (pl. of *this*) is a demonstrative pronoun, and here it is unclear what it is pointing to as its antecedent: *Subjects* is the nearest plural noun antecedent, but *these* could also point to something not in the sentence, an unknown noun. Only the objective form of the pronoun (*them*) clearly points back to its antecedent *the rural poor*.

A   *To be* is unnecessary; *these* must be replaced by *them*.

B   *Should be* is wordy and requires *that* following *consider*; *these* should be *them*.

C   *As being* is awkward and unnecessary; *portraying* and *to consider* are not parallel.

D   *As if they were* distorts the meaning.

E   **Correct.** In this sentence, the correct idiom is used with the verb *consider*; the correct pronoun, *them*, replaces the incorrect *these*; *to consider* and *to portray* are parallel.

The correct answer is E.

120. The World Wildlife Fund has declared that global warming, <u>a phenomenon most scientists agree to be caused by human beings in burning fossil fuels,</u> will create havoc among migratory birds by altering the environment in ways harmful to their habitats.

    (A) a phenomenon most scientists agree to be caused by human beings in burning fossil fuels,

    (B) a phenomenon most scientists agree that is caused by fossil fuels burned by human beings,

    (C) a phenomenon that most scientists agree is caused by human beings' burning of fossil fuels,

    (D) which most scientists agree on as a phenomenon caused by human beings who burn fossil fuels,

    (E) which most scientists agree to be a phenomenon caused by fossil fuels burned by human beings,

Logical predication; Rhetorical construction

The underlined portion of the sentence is an appositive defining *global warming* as a phenomenon caused by the burning of fossil fuels by humans. Because this appositive intervenes between the subject (*global warming*) and verb (*will create*) of a clause, it should be expressed as clearly and economically as possible so as not to confuse the meaning of the sentence as a whole.

A   *To be caused* and *in burning* are wordy, awkward, and indirect.

B   *That is* should immediately follow *phenomenon*, not *agree*.

C   **Correct.** The phrase *human beings' burning* is more economical than constructions with prepositional phrases or relative clauses.

D   The phrasing is wordy and indirect.

E   The phrasing is wordy and the meaning is imprecise; it is not fossil fuels that cause global warming—it is the burning of fossil fuels by humans.

The correct answer is C.

121. New theories propose that catastrophic impacts of asteroids and comets may have caused reversals in the Earth's magnetic field, the onset of ice ages, <u>splitting apart continents</u> 80 million years ago, and great volcanic eruptions.

    (A) splitting apart continents
    (B) the splitting apart of continents
    (C) split apart continents
    (D) continents split apart
    (E) continents that were split apart

Parallelism

This sentence lists four effects of catastrophic impacts; each effect, except the one included in the underlined portion, is given in noun form: *reversals, the onset, eruptions*. *Splitting* is a verb and thus not parallel to the other nouns in the series; in the second option *splitting* is a noun. *Splitting* may be transformed into a noun by adding the article *the*.

A   *Splitting*, a verb, is not parallel to *reversals, the onset*, and *eruptions*, and its role as a member in the series is unclear.

B   **Correct.** *The splitting* is a gerund, or noun form, and is properly used in this sentence; it is parallel to the other nouns.

C   Verb *split* is not parallel to *reversals, the onset*, and *eruptions*.

D   If the impacts truly caused continents, the verb *created* would be used, but it makes no sense to say *impacts caused continents* and this phrase is not parallel to the other noun phrases.

E   This option is similar to the previous option: *continents* cannot be said to be *caused*.

The correct answer is B.

122. A firm that specializes in the analysis of handwriting claims <u>from a one-page writing sample that it can assess</u> more than 300 personality traits, including enthusiasm, imagination, and ambition.

    (A) from a one-page writing sample that it can assess
    (B) from a one-page writing sample it has the ability of assessing
    (C) the ability, from a one-page writing sample, of assessing
    (D) to be able, from a one-page writing sample, to assess
    (E) being able to assess, from a one-page writing sample

Idiom; Rhetorical construction

The meaning of this sentence becomes lost in an awkward and ungrammatical construction. The verb *claims* may be followed by one of two correct constructions: *claims that* + a subordinate clause, or *claims* + the infinitive. When the prepositional phrase *from a one-page writing sample* is placed between *claims* and *that*, the result confuses and distorts the meaning by suggesting that the claim is contained in the writing sample. Instead, the firm claims *to be able ... to assess*. The prepositional phrase should be placed between a pair of commas to show clearly that it is additional information not crucial to understanding the sentence.

A   Prepositional phrase following the verb distorts the meaning of the sentence.

B   Placing the prepositional phrase after *claims* distorts meaning; *that* is omitted; *the ability of assessing* is wordy and awkward.

C   *The ability ... of assessing* is wordy and awkward.

D   **Correct.** The correct idiomatic construction (*claims to be able to assess*) is used in this sentence, and the prepositional phrase is set off in a pair of commas to prevent misreading.

E   *Claims ... being able* is not a correct idiom.

The correct answer is D.

123. Sales of wines declined in the late 1980s, but <u>they began to grow again after the 1991 report that linked moderate consumption of alcohol, and particularly of red wine, with a reduced risk of heart disease</u>.

   (A) they began to grow again after the 1991 report that linked moderate consumption of alcohol, and particularly of red wine, with a reduced risk of heart disease

   (B) after the 1991 report that linked a reduced risk of heart disease with a moderate alcohol consumption, particularly red wine, they began growing again

   (C) in a 1991 report, moderate alcohol consumption, and particularly of red wine, which was linked with a reduced risk of heart disease, caused them to begin to grow again

   (D) with a reduced risk of heart disease linked in a 1991 report with moderate alcohol consumption, in particular red wine, they began growing again

   (E) a reduced risk of heart disease linked to moderate alcohol consumption in a 1991 report, and in particular red wine, started them growing again

Logical predication; Rhetorical construction

This sentence explains why a trend of declining wine sales reversed after the publication of a 1991 report suggesting that moderate consumption of red wine correlated with reduced risk of heart disease. The phrase *particularly of red wine* modifies *consumption of alcohol*, and the sentence must make clear that it is *moderate consumption*, not *red wine* that the report links to *reduced risk*.

A   **Correct.** In the second clause, *they* refers correctly to *sales of wines*; the relative clause beginning with *that* clearly indicates that the report *linked moderate consumption … with a reduced risk*.

B   *Particularly red wine* cannot describe consumption—the preposition *of* is needed; the placement of *they* so far from the position of the antecedent *Sales* makes the sentence awkward and difficult to decode.

C   The clause beginning with *which* refers to *red wine* in this construction, erroneously suggesting that wine rather than *moderate consumption* of alcohol correlates with reduced risk of heart disease; *particularly of red wine* is not parallel to *moderate alcohol consumption*; it needs to follow *moderate consumption of alcohol* to make sense.

D   Without the preposition *of*, the sentence indicates that red wine is a kind of consumption—which makes no sense.

E   The incorrect placement of the modifier *in a 1991 report* suggests that wine is being consumed (albeit in moderation) in the report itself.

The correct answer is A.

124. She was less successful after she had emigrated to New York compared to her native Germany, photographer Lotte Jacobi nevertheless earned a small group of discerning admirers, and her photographs were eventually exhibited in prestigious galleries across the United States.

    (A) She was less successful after she had emigrated to New York compared to

    (B) Being less successful after she had emigrated to New York as compared to

    (C) Less successful after she emigrated to New York than she had been in

    (D) Although she was less successful after emigrating to New York when compared to

    (E) She had been less successful after emigrating to New York than in

Idiom; Grammatical construction; Logical predication

This sentence compares the success Jacobi experienced after moving to New York to the success she had previously experienced in Germany. The phrase *less successful* anticipates the conclusion of the comparison with the phrase *than*.... The main subject of the sentence is *photographer Lotte Jacobi*, and the main verb is *earned*. The opening clause *She was less successful ...* therefore creates a comma splice if the comma is not followed by a conjunction. The most efficient way to incorporate the information about Jacobi's comparative successes in Germany and in New York is to turn this clause into an adjectival phrase describing Jacobi.

A   *Less successful ...* anticipates *than* rather than *compared to ...*; a comma is insufficient to join two independent clauses into a single sentence.

B   *As compared to* is an incorrect way to complete the comparison introduced by *less*; *Being ...* is unnecessarily wordy and awkward.

C   **Correct.** The idiomatic construction *less successful ... than* is incorporated into an introductory adjectival phrase modifying *Lotte Jacobi*.

D   *When compared to* is an incorrect phrase to complete the comparison introduced by *less*.

E   A comma is insufficient to join two independent clauses into a single sentence; past-perfect tense is misleading, since it refers to Jacobi's experience in New York, which in fact followed her experience in Germany.

The correct answer is C.

125. Today, because of improvements in agricultural technology, the same amount of acreage produces double the apples that it has in 1910.

    (A) double the apples that it has

    (B) twice as many apples as it did

    (C) as much as twice the apples it has

    (D) two times as many apples as there were

    (E) a doubling of the apples that it did

Logical predication; Diction; Verb form

The sentence compares the number of apples produced today with the number of apples produced in 1910. The phrase *double the apples* is not very exact but it could be understood to mean *twice as many* or *as many as*; the verb form *has* confounds the sequence of events and makes the comparison illogical. An action that occurred in 1910 requires a verb in the past tense. The two elements being compared must be grammatically parallel. *The same amount ... produces* is paralleled by *as it did* (*produce* understood). The subjects *amount* and *it* are parallel, as are the verbs *produces* and *did* (*produce*).

A   The comparative construction *as many as* is needed; the verb tense *has* is incorrect with *in 1910*.

B   **Correct.** *As many as* is used for a countable quantity; the two elements being compared are parallel; the verb is in the past tense.

C   *Much* is used where *many* is required; the verb tense *has* is incorrect with *in 1910*.

D   *Two times* is wordy; *there were* is vague because it does not refer to *amount of acreage*.

E   *A doubling of the apples* is awkward and, when joined with *that it did*, suggests doubling the apples themselves, not the amount of apples.

The correct answer is B.

126. The use of lie detectors is based on the assumption that lying produces emotional reactions in an individual that, in turn, create unconscious physiological responses.

(A) that, in turn, create unconscious physiological responses

(B) that creates unconscious physiological responses in turn

(C) creating, in turn, unconscious physiological responses

(D) to create, in turn, physiological responses that are unconscious

(E) who creates unconscious physiological responses in turn

Agreement; Rhetorical construction; Logical predication

This sentence describes a cause-and-effect sequence; in the underlined portion of the sentence, the relative pronoun *that* refers to the plural noun *reactions*. The verb in the relative clause must therefore be a plural verb. The causal sequence is most clearly expressed by a relative clause that turns the object *emotional reactions* (from the clause *lying causes emotional reactions in an individual*) into the subject (*that*) of a new clause (*that in turn create unconscious physiological responses*). *In turn* is best placed before the verb of the second relative clause, *create*, to clarify that a chain of events is being described.

A **Correct.** This construction clearly indicates the causal sequence.

B The singular verb *creates* does not agree with the subject referenced by the relative pronoun *that* (*reactions*).

C This construction is less successful at clarifying the chain of events because *creating* seems to refer back to *lying*; if used as a participial, *creating* would have to be preceded by a comma.

D This construction does not make clear the causal chain of events, because it is unclear which noun *to create* should attach to; the infinitive construction implies intent, which does not really make sense.

E Because *reactions* is not a person, *who* is the wrong relative pronoun to use.

The correct answer is A.

127. Joan of Arc, a young Frenchwoman who claimed to be divinely inspired, turned the tide of English victories in her country by liberating the city of Orléans and she persuaded Charles VII of France to claim his throne.

(A) she persuaded Charles VII of France to claim his throne

(B) persuaded Charles VII of France in claiming his throne

(C) persuading that the throne be claimed by Charles VII of France

(D) persuaded Charles VII of France to claim his throne

(E) persuading that Charles VII of France should claim the throne

Parallelism

Because this sentence consists of many parts, including lengthy modifiers (*a young Frenchwoman …* ; *by liberating …*), it is crucial to make the basic structure of it—the subject and verbs of the main clause—as clear and as concisely expressed as possible. *Joan of Arc* is the subject, *turned* is the first verb of the main clause, and *persuaded* is the second verb; so the sentence should be *Joan … turned … and persuaded*. Inserting *she* before the second verb both violates the parallelism and adds an unnecessary word.

A *Persuaded*, not *she persuaded*, is parallel to *turned*.

B The idiomatic construction is *persuade x to do y*, not *persuade x in doing y*.

C Here *persuading* is linked to *liberating*, but even if it were said that Joan did *turn the tide of English victories* by *persuading* Charles to claim the throne, a person cannot be said to *persuade* a clause (*that the thrown be claimed*), a person persuades another person or other entity; *be claimed by* is wordy.

D **Correct.** In this sentence, *persuaded* is parallel to *turned*, and the idiomatic construction *persuade x to do y* is used.

E Parallel form links *persuading* and *liberating* when *persuaded* should be parallel to *turned*; *persuading that x* is not a correct idiom: a person can only persuade another person or other entity.

The correct answer is D.

128. Australian embryologists have found evidence <u>that suggests that the elephant is descended from an aquatic animal, and its trunk originally evolving</u> as a kind of snorkel.

(A) that suggests that the elephant is descended from an aquatic animal, and its trunk originally evolving

(B) that has suggested the elephant descended from an aquatic animal, its trunk originally evolving

(C) suggesting that the elephant had descended from an aquatic animal with its trunk originally evolved

(D) to suggest that the elephant had descended from an aquatic animal and its trunk originally evolved

(E) to suggest that the elephant is descended from an aquatic animal and that its trunk originally evolved

Parallelism; Verb form

The clearest, most economical way of expressing the two things suggested by Australian embryologists' evidence is to format them as relative clauses serving as parallel direct objects of the verb *suggest*. It is awkward and confusing to string together relative clauses: *evidence that suggests that the elephant....* A clearer way of making this connection is to turn the verb *suggests* into a participle modifying *evidence*. The word *descended* is a predicate adjective following the present-tense verb *is* and describing the present-day elephant. The verb *evolved* should be past tense because it describes how the trunk of the elephant *originally* evolved, not how it is evolving today.

A The string of relative phrases is awkward and confusing; the phrase following the conjunction *and* is not parallel with the relative clause *that the elephant is descended....*

B The evidence *still* suggests these things about the evolution of the elephant and its trunk, so the present-perfect verb tense is inaccurate.

C *Had descended* is the wrong verb tense; *with* cannot be followed by an independent clause.

D *Had descended* is the wrong tense; the phrase following the conjunction *and* does not parallel the relative clause that precedes the conjunction.

E **Correct.** The two dependent clauses beginning with *that* are in parallel form and contain verbs in the correct tenses.

The correct answer is E.

129. Cajuns speak a dialect brought to southern Louisiana by the 4,000 Acadians who migrated there in 1755; their language is basically seventeenth-century French <u>to which has been added English, Spanish, and Italian words</u>.

(A) to which has been added English, Spanish, and Italian words

(B) added to which is English, Spanish, and Italian words

(C) to which English, Spanish, and Italian words have been added

(D) with English, Spanish, and Italian words having been added to it

(E) and, in addition, English, Spanish, and Italian words are added

Agreement; Logical predication

The sentence describes the Cajun language as *seventeenth-century French* and then modifies that description by noting the addition of words from other languages. Since *words* is a plural noun, a plural verb is required. The inverted word order in the original sentence is awkward.

A The singular *has* does not agree in number with *English, Spanish, and Italian words*; the verb should be the plural *have*; the inversion of the subject and the verb is awkward.

B Verb must be plural; since the action began in the past, the present perfect form *have been added* is required.

C **Correct.** The relative clause in this sentence has the correct verb form, and its placement makes it clear that it modifies the noun *French*. The clause also follows normal subject-verb word order.

D *With* does not concisely modify the noun *French*; *having been added to it* is a wordy expression.

E   Verb tense is incorrect; it is not clear that the construction modifies the noun *French*.

The correct answer is C.

130. Over 75 percent of the energy produced in France derives from nuclear power, <u>while in Germany it is just over 33 percent</u>.

    (A)   while in Germany it is just over 33 percent
    (B)   compared to Germany, which uses just over 33 percent
    (C)   whereas nuclear power accounts for just over 33 percent of the energy produced in Germany
    (D)   whereas just over 33 percent of the energy comes from nuclear power in Germany
    (E)   compared with the energy from nuclear power in Germany, where it is just over 33 percent

Rhetorical construction; Logical predication

This sentence compares percentages and uses the prepositional phrases *in France* and *in Germany* to distinguish the percentage of energy in each country coming from nuclear power. This information is most efficiently and clearly presented in two clauses joined by the conjunction *whereas*, which signifies a difference between the situations in the two countries. Each clause must identify what the percentage refers to—that is, the portion of the respective country's energy that comes from nuclear power.

A   *While* is somewhat ambiguous, since it might indicate simultaneity rather than contrast; the referent of *it* is ambiguous, raising questions about just what two things are being compared.

B   This sentence compares *75 percent* to *Germany;* it is not clear what *33 percent* refers to.

C   **Correct.** The two clauses joined by *whereas* indicate clearly that the comparison is between the different percentages of energy coming from nuclear power.

D   The use of the definite article *the* makes it seem as though the energy being referred to in this part of the sentence is that of France.

E   This construction is wordy and unclear; the referent of *it* is ambiguous.

The correct answer is C.

131. Although the term "psychopath" is popularly applied to an especially brutal criminal, in psychology <u>it is someone who is</u> apparently incapable of feeling compassion or the pangs of conscience.

    (A)   it is someone who is
    (B)   it is a person
    (C)   they are people who are
    (D)   it refers to someone who is
    (E)   it is in reference to people

Logical predication; Grammatical construction; Agreement

The intent of the sentence is to define the term "psychopath." In this sentence, the pronoun *it* refers back to *the term* and seems illogically to refer forward to *someone*. Logically, an inanimate *term* cannot be *a person* or *someone*. The sentence needs to be reworded so that it is clear that "psychopath" is a term used to define a specific kind of person.

A   This construction illogically asserts that *the term* is a person.

B   This construction illogically asserts that *the term* is a person.

C   Plural pronoun *they* does not agree with the singular noun *the term* and cannot refer to *psychopath*; this construction also asserts that *the term* is a person.

D   **Correct.** In this sentence, the verb *refers* clearly links the term to a particular kind of person; the alignment of pronouns and antecedents is both logical and grammatical.

E   To be correct, this construction needs a main verb such as *used*; the construction *is used in reference to* is awkward and much wordier than the single word *refers*; the plural *people* should be singular.

The correct answer is D.

132. <u>Although appearing less appetizing than most of their round and red supermarket cousins, heirloom tomatoes, grown from seeds saved during the previous year</u>—they are often green and striped, or have plenty of bumps and bruises—heirlooms are more flavorful and thus in increasing demand.

(A) Although appearing less appetizing than most of their round and red supermarket cousins, heirloom tomatoes, grown from seeds saved during the previous year

(B) Although heirloom tomatoes, grown from seeds saved during the previous year, appear less appetizing than most of their round and red supermarket cousins

(C) Although they appear less appetizing than most of their round and red supermarket cousins, heirloom tomatoes, grown from seeds saved during the previous year

(D) Grown from seeds saved during the previous year, heirloom tomatoes appear less appetizing than most of their round and red supermarket cousins

(E) Heirloom tomatoes, grown from seeds saved during the previous year, although they appear less appetizing than most of their round and red supermarket cousins

Rhetorical construction; Grammatical construction

The intended meaning could be communicated more effectively by mentioning heirloom tomatoes as early as possible in the sentence, so that we know that the writer is comparing heirloom tomatoes with supermarket tomatoes. The placement of *heirloom tomatoes* and *heirlooms* makes the sentence ungrammatical.

A   This is ungrammatical. If *heirloom tomatoes* is the subject of *are more flavorful* ... then *heirlooms* has no predicate and is nonsensically superfluous. If *heirlooms* is the subject, *heirloom tomatoes* has no predicate.

B   **Correct.** The noun *heirloom tomatoes* is mentioned early in the sentence, followed by a parenthetical definition, and is the subject of the verb *appear*, and *heirlooms* is the subject of *are*.

C   The noun *heirloom tomatoes* appears too late in the sentence. Parsing is made harder by introducing the pronoun *they* and revealing

its antecedent later in the sentence. The sentence is also ungrammatical. If *heirloom tomatoes* is the subject of *are more flavorful* ... then *heirlooms* has no predicate and is nonsensically superfluous. If *heirlooms* is the subject, *heirloom tomatoes* has no predicate.

D   Beginning the sentence with the explanatory clause *grown from seeds* ... gives it too much importance. It could be construed as the reason why heirloom tomatoes appear less appetizing, which is contrary to the truth. The sentence is also ungrammatical.

E   Rhetorical structure requires that *although* appear in the beginning of the clause to which it pertains. Placing it later necessitates the pronoun *they* with antecedent *heirloom tomatoes*, which is redundant. The sentence is also ungrammatical.

The correct answer is B.

133. Last week local shrimpers held a news conference to take some credit for the resurgence of the rare Kemp's ridley turtle, saying that their compliance with laws <u>requiring that turtle-excluder devices be on shrimp nets protect</u> adult sea turtles.

(A) requiring that turtle-excluder devices be on shrimp nets protect

(B) requiring turtle-excluder devices on shrimp nets is protecting

(C) that require turtle-excluder devices on shrimp nets protect

(D) to require turtle-excluder devices on shrimp nets are protecting

(E) to require turtle-excluder devices on shrimp nets is protecting

Rhetorical construction; Agreement

The subject of the clause introduced by *saying that* is the singular noun *compliance*. This subject requires the singular form of the verb *protect*. The clearest, most economical way to describe the laws in question is to follow the word *laws* with a present participle *requiring*. To use an infinitive, *to require*, seems to indicate that requiring these devices is the objective of the laws, when in fact the objective is to protect the sea turtles.

A   The plural verb *protect* does not agree with the singular subject *compliance*.

B   **Correct.** The singular verb *is protecting* agrees with the singular subject *compliance*, and the participial phrase beginning with *requiring* concisely and accurately describes the laws.

C   The relative clause *that require* introduces unnecessary wordiness; the plural verb *protect* does not agree with the singular subject *compliance*.

D   *To require* obscures the purpose of the laws; the plural verb phrase *are protecting* does not agree with the singular subject *compliance*.

E   *To require* obscures the purpose of the laws.

The correct answer is B.

134. Recently implemented "shift-work equations" based on studies of the human sleep cycle have reduced sickness, sleeping on the job, <u>fatigue among shift workers, and have raised</u> production efficiency in various industries.

(A) fatigue among shift workers, and have raised

(B) fatigue among shift workers, and raised

(C) and fatigue among shift workers while raising

(D) lowered fatigue among shift workers, and raised

(E) and fatigue among shift workers was lowered while raising

Grammatical construction

Implementing the equations has reduced *sickness, sleeping on the job,* and *fatigue*; at the same time, it has increased *efficiency*. The three parallel elements (*have reduced x, y, and z*) require *and* before the final element.

A   The omission of *and* before *fatigue* creates an unclear sentence.

B   The omission of *and* before *fatigue* creates an unclear sentence.

C   **Correct.** The use of *and* in this sentence unites the three parallel elements; the phrase *while raising* provides a clear contrast with *have reduced*.

D   *And* is required to link the parallel elements; the verb *reduced* applies to all three parallel elements, so inserting *lowered* before *fatigue* illogically suggests that fatigue actually increased.

E   The insertion of *was lowered* destroys the parallel structure, and thus *while raising* has no logical referent here.

The correct answer is C.

135. Spanning more than 50 years, Friedrich <u>Müller began his career in an unpromising apprenticeship as</u> a Sanskrit scholar and culminated in virtually every honor that European governments and learned societies could bestow.

(A) Müller began his career in an unpromising apprenticeship as

(B) Müller's career began in an unpromising apprenticeship as

(C) Müller's career began with the unpromising apprenticeship of being

(D) Müller had begun his career with the unpromising apprenticeship of being

(E) the career of Müller has begun with an unpromising apprenticeship of

Logical predication; Idiom

What spanned more than 50 years? It was Müller's career that spanned 50 years and *culminated in virtually every honor*. The correct subject of the sentence must be *Müller's career*.

A   *Müller's career*, not *Müller*, should be the subject of the sentence.

B   **Correct.** Using *Müller's career* as the subject of the sentence solves the modification problem with *spanning* … and provides a logical subject for *culminated*.

C   *Apprenticeship of being* is an incorrect idiom; *apprenticeship as* is correct.

D   *Müller's career*, not *Müller*, should be the subject of the sentence; past perfect tense is inappropriate; *apprenticeship of being* is an incorrect idiom.

E   *Müller's career* is preferable to *the career of Müller*; present perfect tense is incorrect; *apprenticeship of* should be *apprenticeship as*.

The correct answer is B.

136. <u>Whereas in mammals the tiny tubes that convey nutrients to bone cells are arrayed in parallel lines, in birds the tubes</u> form a random pattern.

    (A) Whereas in mammals the tiny tubes that convey nutrients to bone cells are arrayed in parallel lines, in birds the tubes

    (B) Whereas the tiny tubes for the conveying of nutrients to bone cells are arrayed in mammals in parallel lines, birds have tubes that

    (C) Unlike mammals, where the tiny tubes for conveying nutrients to bone cells are arrayed in parallel lines, birds' tubes

    (D) Unlike mammals, in whom the tiny tubes that convey nutrients to bone cells are arrayed in parallel lines, the tubes in birds

    (E) Unlike the tiny tubes that convey nutrients to bone cells, which in mammals are arrayed in parallel lines, in birds the tubes

Idiom; Rhetorical construction; Parallelism

Whereas introduces two contrasting situations or events and should be followed by parallel structures. In this sentence, *whereas* is immediately followed by a clause beginning with the prepositional phrase *in mammals*; this means that the second part of the sentence must also be a clause that opens with a preposition that functions in the same way—in this case, *in birds*. This structure clarifies that the things being contrasted are the *tubes* in mammals and the *tubes* in birds. Incorrect versions of the sentence grammatically contrast *tubes* and *birds*, *mammals* and *tubes*, or *birds* and *mammals*.

A **Correct.** Parallel structures make clear that the tubes in mammals are being contrasted with the tubes in birds.

B The faulty parallelism results in a sentence that is confusing and unnecessarily wordy.

C The sentence compares *mammals* and *birds' tubes*.

D Because of faulty parallelism, this sentence also compares *mammals* and *tubes in birds*.

E This structure is wordy and confusing because of faulty parallelism.

The correct answer is A.

137. Joachim Raff and Giacomo Meyerbeer are examples of the kind of composer who receives popular acclaim while living, <u>often goes into decline after death, and never regains popularity again</u>.

    (A) often goes into decline after death, and never regains popularity again

    (B) whose reputation declines after death and never regains its status again

    (C) but whose reputation declines after death and never regains its former status

    (D) who declines in reputation after death and who never regained popularity again

    (E) then has declined in reputation after death and never regained popularity

Verb tense; Parallelism

Faulty parallelism in the relative clause *who receives … goes … regains …* makes it unclear who or what is being described. The original clause begins by describing a certain kind of composer. As written, with *who* as the subject of *goes* and *regains*, the last two descriptions illogically continue to refer to the kind of composer. Logically it must be the reputation that declines after the composer's death.

A Illogically suggests the composer goes into decline after death; redundant *again*.

B The two clauses are not parallel, lack a coordinating conjunction, and do not describe the same thing; redundant *again*.

C **Correct.** This sentence presents the proper logic while maintaining parallel structure and consistent verb tense.

D The verb tenses are inconsistent with present tense used in the first phrase; redundant *again*.

E The verb tenses are inconsistent with present tense used in the first phrase; to maintain parallelism, the verbs must be *receives … declines … regains*.

The correct answer is C.

138. Most efforts to combat such mosquito-borne diseases <u>like malaria and dengue have focused either on the vaccination of humans or on exterminating</u> mosquitoes with pesticides.

    (A) like malaria and dengue have focused either on the vaccination of humans or on exterminating
    (B) like malaria and dengue have focused either on vaccinating of humans or on the extermination of
    (C) as malaria and dengue have focused on either vaccinating humans or on exterminating
    (D) as malaria and dengue have focused on either vaccinating of humans or on extermination of
    (E) as malaria and dengue have focused on either vaccinating humans or exterminating

Diction; Parallelism

The phrase *such ... diseases like malaria and dengue* is not a correct way in English to indicate that the two diseases mentioned are examples of a larger category; the correct expression is *such ... as....*

A This use of *such ... like ...* is incorrect English; the correct expression is *such ... as....* It is better to keep the preposition *on* close to the verb it goes with, *focus*, so as not to repeat it.

B The correct expression is *such ... as....* It is better to keep the preposition *on* close to the verb it goes with, *focus*, so as not to repeat it. This use of the gerund *vaccinating* (followed by *of*) would normally be preceded by *the*, but this would make the phrase awkward. It would be preferable to use *vaccination*, which is parallel to *extermination*.

C This answer choice incorrectly repeats the preposition *on* before *exterminating*.

D This answer choice incorrectly repeats the preposition *on* before *extermination*. This use of the gerund *vaccinating* (followed by *of*) would normally be preceded by *the*, but this would make the phrase awkward. It would be preferable to use *vaccination*, which is parallel to *extermination*.

E **Correct.** This version uses *either ... or ...* correctly and appropriately uses the parallel forms *vaccinating* and *exterminating*.

The correct answer is E.

139. In no other historical sighting did Halley's Comet cause such a worldwide sensation as <u>did its return in 1910–1911</u>.

    (A) did its return in 1910–1911
    (B) had its 1910–1911 return
    (C) in its return of 1910–1911
    (D) its return of 1910–1911 did
    (E) its return in 1910–1911

Parallelism; Verb form; Logical predication

The single subject of this sentence is *Halley's Comet*, and its single verb phrase is *did cause*. The comparison presented by the sentence is between adverbial phrases describing times when the comet was seen. Grammatically, the items being compared are parallel prepositional phrases beginning with the preposition *in: in no other sighting* and *in its return in 1910–1911*. This is the clearest, most economical way of presenting the information. The options that introduce a second verb (*did* or *had*) violate the parallelism and introduce a comparison between the comet itself (subject of the verb *did cause*) and the comet's return (subject of the verb *did* or *had*).

A This sentence implies a comparison between the comet and its return.

B This sentence implies a comparison between the comet and its return; *had* is the wrong auxiliary verb form because it must be followed by *caused* instead of *cause*.

C **Correct.** The parallel prepositional phrases in this sentence correctly compare times when the comet was sighted.

D This sentence implies a comparison between the comet and its return.

E This sentence violates parallelism, implying a comparison between a prepositional phrase and a noun phrase.

The correct answer is C.

140. Rock samples taken from the remains of an asteroid about twice the size of the 6-mile-wide asteroid that eradicated the dinosaurs <u>has been dated to be 3.47 billion years old and thus is</u> evidence of the earliest known asteroid impact on Earth.

    (A) has been dated to be 3.47 billion years old and thus is

    (B) has been dated at 3.47 billion years old and thus

    (C) have been dated to be 3.47 billion years old and thus are

    (D) have been dated as being 3.47 billion years old and thus

    (E) have been dated at 3.47 billion years old and thus are

Agreement; Idiom

The plural subject of this sentence, *Rock samples*, requires plural verb phrases—*have been dated* and *are* rather than *has been dated* and *is*. The idiomatic way of expressing estimation of age is with the phrase *dated at*.

A   The subject and verbs do not agree; *dated to be … is* not idiomatic.

B   The subject and verb do not agree; the conjunction *and thus* should be followed by a verb.

C   *Dated to be* is not idiomatic.

D   *As being* is not idiomatic; the conjunction *and thus* should be followed by a verb.

E   **Correct.** The plural verbs match the plural subject, and the wording of the sentence is idiomatic.

The correct answer is E.

10.0 Integrated Reasoning

10.0 Integrated Reasoning

The Integrated Reasoning section measures your ability to understand and evaluate multiple sources and types of information—graphic, numeric, and verbal—as they relate to one another; use quantitative and verbal reasoning to solve complex problems; and solve multiple problems in relation to one another. This section includes text passages, tables, graphs, and other visual information from a variety of content areas; however, the materials and questions do not assume detailed knowledge of the topics discussed. The Integrated Reasoning section differs from the Quantitative and Verbal sections in two important ways: 1) It involves both mathematical and verbal reasoning, either separately or in combination, and 2) questions are answered using four different response formats rather than only traditional multiple-choice.

Four types of questions are used in the Integrated Reasoning section:

- Multi-Source Reasoning
- Table Analysis
- Graphics Interpretation
- Two-Part Analysis

Use your unique access code found in the back of this book to access 50 Integrated Reasoning practice questions with full answer explanations.

10.1 What Is Measured

Integrated Reasoning questions assess your ability to apply, evaluate, infer, recognize, and strategize.

Apply concepts presented in the information

Apply questions measure your ability to understand principles, rules, or other concepts in the information provided and apply them to a new context or predict consequences that would follow if new information were incorporated into the context provided. You may be asked to

- decide whether new examples would comply with or violate rules established in the information provided
- determine how a trend present in the information provided would be affected by new scenarios
- use principles established in the information provided to draw conclusions about new data

Evaluate information qualitatively

Evaluate questions measure your ability to make judgments about the quality of information. For example, you may be asked to

- decide whether a claim made in one source is supported or undermined by information provided in another source
- determine whether the information provided is sufficient to justify a course of action

- judge the strength of evidence offered in support of an argument or plan
- identify errors or gaps in the information provided

Draw inferences from the information

Infer questions ask about information or ideas that are not explicitly stated in the materials provided but can be derived from them. For example, you may be asked to

- calculate the probability of an outcome on the basis of given data
- indicate whether statements follow logically from the information provided
- determine the meaning of a term within the context in which it is used
- identify the rate of change in data gathered over time

Recognize parts or relationships in the information

Recognize questions measure your ability to identify information that is directly presented in the materials provided, including specific facts or details and relationships between pieces of information. For example, you may be asked to

- identify areas of agreement and disagreement between sources of information
- determine the strength of correlation between two variables
- indicate which element in a table has a given rank in a combination of categories
- identify facts provided as evidence in an argument

Make strategic decisions or judgments based on the information

Strategize questions ask about the means of achieving a goal within the context of particular needs or constraints. For example, you may be asked to

- choose a plan of action that minimizes risks and maximizes value
- identify tradeoffs required to reach a goal
- specify the mathematical formula that will yield a desired result
- determine which means of completing a task are consistent within given constraints

10.2 The Question Types

The four Integrated Reasoning question types are described in detail below.

Multi-Source Reasoning

Multi-Source Reasoning questions begin with two or three sources of information, each labeled with a tab, which appear on the left side of a split computer screen. One or more of the sources will contain a written passage. The other sources may be tables, graphs, diagrams, or other types of visual information. Only one source of information will be displayed at a time. To view a different source, select its tab from those that appear above the source currently displayed.

The sources of information are accompanied by questions that will ask you to synthesize, compare, interpret, or apply the information presented. As each question associated with the sources appears in turn on the right side of the screen, the initial source will appear again on the left side. You can click on the tabs to view any of the sources as many times as needed. However, you will see only one question at a time and cannot go back to earlier questions.

There are two question formats for Multi-Source Reasoning:

- Multiple-choice questions
- Multiple–dichotomous choice questions

For multiple-choice questions, select the best of the five answer choices given. Read each question and series of answer choices carefully. Make sure you understand exactly what the question is asking and what the answer choices are.

Multiple–dichotomous choice questions provide three phrases, statements, numerical values, or algebraic expressions that require an indication as to whether each meets a certain condition. For example, you may be asked whether

- each statement is true, according to the sources
- each statement or numerical value is consistent with the sources
- each statement or algebraic expression would solve a problem described in the sources
- the value of each algebraic expression can be determined on the basis of the sources

In answering both kinds of Multi-Source Reasoning questions, be aware of the information from each source provided and try to determine the process that works best for you. One strategy is to examine the sources carefully and thoroughly, another is to skim the sources the first time through, or to read the first question before examining the sources. Read each question carefully and make sure you understand *exactly* what the question is asking. If necessary, go back to the sources to review relevant information.

You will have 30 minutes to complete the Integrated Reasoning section, or an average of 2 minutes and 30 seconds to answer each multiple-choice or multiple–dichotomous choice question. Keep in mind, however, that you will need time to examine the source materials that accompany the questions—and that time must be factored into the per-question average.

Table Analysis

Table Analysis questions present a table similar to a spreadsheet. It can be sorted on any of its columns by selecting the column's title from a drop-down menu. There may be a brief text explaining the table or providing additional information. The question then presents three phrases, statements, numerical values, or algebraic expressions, and you must indicate for each one whether or not it meets a certain condition. For example, you may be asked whether

- each statement is true (yes or no), according to the information in the table
- each statement or numerical value is consistent or inconsistent with the information in the table
- each statement or numerical value can or cannot be determined on the basis of the information in the table

Read the question thoroughly to make sure you understand what is being asked. Then consider each phrase, statement, numerical value, or algebraic expression to learn what information in the table you need to make your decision. In analyzing the table, you may need to, for example,

- determine statistics such as mean, median, mode, or range

- determine ratios, proportions, or probabilities

- identify correlations between two sets of data

- compare an entry's rank in two or more of the table's categories

You will have 30 minutes to complete the Integrated Reasoning section, or an average of 2 minutes and 30 seconds to answer each question. Keep in mind, however, that each Table Analysis question has three parts that all need to be answered in the time allowed.

Graphics Interpretation

Graphics Interpretation questions present a graph, diagram, or other visual representation of information, followed by one or more statements containing a total of two blanks. The blanks should be filled in with the option from each drop-down menu in order to create the most accurate statement or statements on the basis of the information provided.

Many of the graphs included in Graphics Interpretation questions involve two variables plotted on vertical and horizontal axes. Graphs of this type include *bar graphs*, *line graphs*, *scatterplots*, and *bubble graphs*. To read these graphs, determine what information is represented on each axis. Do this by carefully examining any information that may be provided, including labels on the axes, scales on the axes, the title of the graph, and accompanying text. To find the value of a data point on the graph, determine the corresponding values on the horizontal and vertical axes.

In the simple *bar graph* below, the first bar indicates that 7 units were sold on Monday of Week 1.

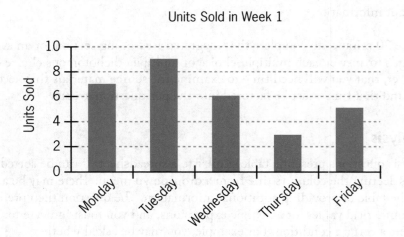

The same information is presented below as a *line graph*. Each point indicates the total number of units sold on a given day. The slope of the line connecting the points shows how the sales changed over time; a positive slope indicates that sales increased from the previous day, and a negative slope indicates that sales decreased.

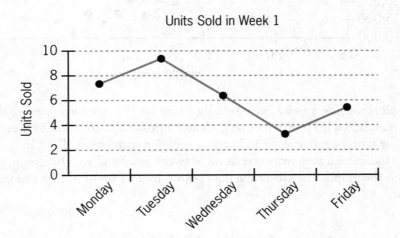

A third variable can be indicated with an additional vertical axis. In the following graph, the bars indicate the number of units sold on each day, which corresponds to the scale on the left axis. The line graph shows what percent of the total units were sold on each day. The scale for the percentages is shown on the right axis.

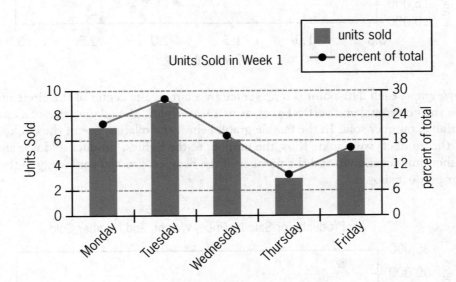

In a *scatterplot*, each dot is a single data point. In the scatterplot at the top of the next page, each dot represents a type of computer product offered for sale. A dot's position relative to the vertical axis indicates the product's price, and its position relative to the horizontal axis indicates its weight. Thus, the product that weighs 1.0 kg costs approximately 32,000 rupees.

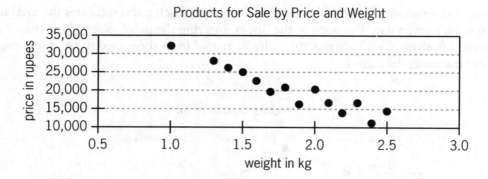

Some scatterplots include a *trend line*—usually a *least squares regression line*—that shows the trend of the data. A trend line with positive slope indicates a positive correlation between the two variables, and a trend line with negative slope indicates a negative correlation. Thus, in the scatterplot below, the trend line indicates a negative correlation between price and weight among the products represented on the graph. The closer the data points are to a trend line, the more strongly the data are correlated.

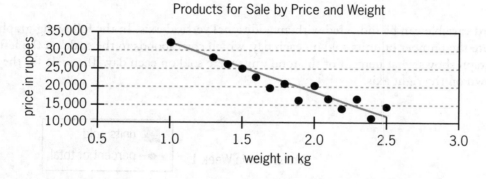

In a *bubble graph*, each data point is represented by a circle. The center of the circle indicates the values on the horizontal and vertical axes, as in a scatterplot. The relative size of a circle introduces a third variable, number sold. In the bubble graph below, the relative size of the circles indicates how many of the products were sold. Thus, the number of the lightest product sold was smaller than that of any other product shown, and the number of the heaviest product sold was greater than that of any other product shown.

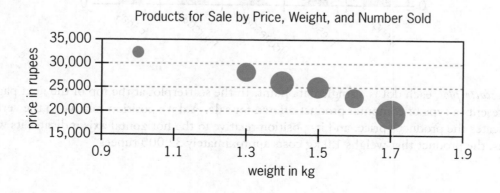

Other common kinds of graphics do not use vertical and horizontal axes. These include *pie charts*, *flow charts*, and *organization charts*.

A *pie chart* uses a circle divided into sectors to show what percent of the whole is represented by each component part. The circle represents the whole, and the relative size of each sector indicates its percent of the whole. Since the whole is 100%, the sum of the percentages of all the sectors is 100 (plus or minus a bit to account for rounding). Below is a pie chart created from the data used in the bar graph and line graph shown earlier. In this example, labels indicating the exact percents are not supplied, but it is still possible to gauge the size of the sectors relative to one another: the smallest percent of sales was on Thursday, and the largest was on Tuesday. In addition, the two radii that mark the boundaries of the Tuesday sector form an obtuse angle, which indicates that the sector is greater than one-fourth of the circle. Thus, Tuesday's sales comprised more than 25% of total sales.

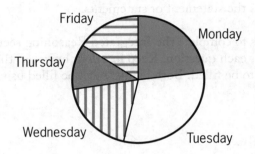

A *flow chart* is a diagram that shows the steps in a process. Often, the steps are represented by symbols, which are connected by arrows showing the flow of the process. Flow charts generally progress from top to bottom or from left to right. In the simple flow chart below, rectangles indicate steps to be completed. The diamond shape indicates a decision point: if the consultant is new, the process continues to the next step, *Append tax forms*. If the consultant is not new, that step is bypassed and the contract is mailed.

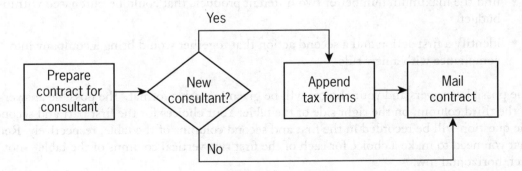

An *organization chart* represents the structure of an organization. Often, hierarchical relationships are shown with vertical lines and lateral relationships are shown with horizontal lines. In the organization chart at the top of the next page, each rectangle represents an employee or group of employees at a small restaurant. All the employees in the second row of rectangles report to the restaurant manager. In the third row, the food preparation staff and cleaning staff both report to the kitchen manager, and the serving staff report to the serving staff manager.

For all kinds of Graphics Interpretation questions, be sure to read the question carefully to be sure you understand what is being asked. Then read the statement or statements to determine what information you need to learn from the graphic. Finally, choose the answer from each drop-down menu that best completes the statement or statements.

You will have 30 minutes to complete the Integrated Reasoning section, or an average of 2 minutes and 30 seconds to answer each question. Keep in mind, however, that each Graphics Interpretation question has two blanks to be filled. Both blanks must be filled using the drop-down menus in the time allowed.

Two-Part Analysis

Two-Part Analysis questions present a brief written scenario or problem and ask you to make two choices related to that information. These choices are connected to each other in some way; for example, they might be two steps involved in solving a problem or two components required to successfully complete a task. In Two-Part Analysis questions you may be asked to, for example,

- calculate the proportions of two different components in a mixture
- determine something that would be lost and something that would be gained in a trade-off
- find the maximum number of two different products that could be purchased within a certain budget
- identify a first action and a second action that together would bring a company into compliance with a new rule

The possible answers and your choices will be given in a table format. The possible answers are listed in the third column, on the right side of the table. Your choices for the first part and second part of the question will be recorded in the first and second columns of the table, respectively. Remember that you need to make a choice for each of the first two vertical columns of the table—not one for each horizontal row.

In answering Two-Part Analysis questions, read the scenario or problem carefully. Be sure you understand what the question is asking. Read all the answer options to be sure that your choices are the best of all those available, and be careful to mark your choices in the proper columns.

You will have 30 minutes to complete the Integrated Reasoning section, or an average of 2 minutes and 30 seconds to answer each question. Keep in mind, however, that you must make the two choices for each Two-Part Analysis question within that average amount of time.

10.3 Test-Taking Strategies

Multi-Source Reasoning Questions

1. **Do not expect to be completely familiar with the material presented in Multi-Source Reasoning sets.**

   You may find some graphs, charts, tables, or verbal passages easier to understand than others. All of the material is designed to be challenging, but if you have familiarity with the subject matter, do not let this knowledge influence your answer choices. Answer all questions on the basis of what is given by the various sources of information.

2. **Analyze each source of information carefully, because the questions require a detailed understanding of the information presented.**

   Text passages often build ideas sequentially, so note as you read how each statement adds to the main idea of the passage as a whole. Some of the passages used with Multi-Source Reasoning items will be purely descriptive while others may contain strong opinions.

   Given that the graphic elements of Multi-Source Reasoning items come in various forms—such as tables, graphs, diagrams, or charts—briefly familiarize yourself with the information presented. If scales are provided, note the marked values and labels. Also note the major graphical elements of the information presented.

3. **Read the questions carefully, making sure you understand what is being asked.**

   Some of the questions will require you to recognize discrepancies among different sources of information, others will ask you to draw inferences using information from different sources, while others may require you to determine which one of the information sources is relevant. You can refer back to any of the sources at any time while you are answering the Multi-Source Reasoning questions.

4. **Select the answer choices that have the most support based on the information provided.**

   You may find it helpful to briefly familiarize yourself with the overall information given in the sources and then to focus more closely on the specific information needed to answer the question.

Table Analysis Questions

1. **Examine the table and accompanying text to determine the type of information provided.**

   Orienting yourself to the data at the outset will make it easier to locate the information necessary for completing the question.

2. **Read the question carefully.**

   The question will contain the condition that each phrase, statement, numerical value, or algebraic expression does or does not meet (for example, *is or is not consistent with the information provided*, or *can or cannot be inferred from the information provided*). Clearly understanding the condition will help you to clarify the choice to be made in each case.

3. **Read each phrase, statement, numerical value, or algebraic expression carefully to determine the data analysis required.**

Often, the phrase, statement, numerical value, or algebraic expression indicates a relationship that can be clarified by sorting the table on one or more of its columns. Careful reading can help you work more efficiently by using table sorts strategically to identify data of interest.

4. **Judge each phrase, statement, numerical value, or algebraic expression carefully on the basis of the condition specified.**

For each phrase, statement, numerical value, or algebraic expression, the two answer choices (such as *yes* or *no*, *true* or *false*, *consistent* or *inconsistent*) are mutually exclusive. Thus, you can focus your attention on whether or not the given condition has been met.

Graphics Interpretation Questions

1. **Read the graphic carefully.**

Quickly familiarize yourself with the information presented in the graphic. If scales are provided (on the axes, for example), make note of the marked values. If there are labels, be sure to note any discrepancy between the units in the graph and the units discussed in the text.

2. **Read any accompanying text carefully.**

If there is accompanying text, it may clarify the meaning of the graphic. Text might also present information that is not contained in the graphic but that is needed for answering the question.

3. **Scan the choices in the drop-down menu before you do any work.**

Some statements could be completed equally well with very general responses as with very specific responses. Checking the menu options gives you additional information about the task involved.

4. **Choose the option that best completes the statement.**

More than one option in a drop-down menu may seem plausible to you; in each menu choose the one that makes the statement most accurate or logical. If the drop-down menu is preceded by a phrase such as "nearest to" or "closest to," choose the option that is closest to the exact answer you compute. You may find that reading the entire statement again with your answer choice in place is a helpful way to check your work.

Two-Part Analysis Questions

1. **Read the information given carefully.**

All of the material presented is designed to be challenging, but if you have familiarity with the subject matter, do not let this knowledge influence your answer choices. Answer the question only on the basis of what is given.

2. **Determine exactly what the question is asking.**

Do not assume that the headings in the two response columns are complete descriptions of the tasks to be performed. Pay close attention to how the question describes the tasks. Often the headings in the two response columns are shorthand references to the tasks and may lack some details that could help you to better understand what you are supposed to do.

3. **Remember that only two choices are to be made.**

Select one answer in each of the first two columns of the response table. You do not need to make a choice for each *row* of the table. The third column contains possible answers for the two choices to be made.

4. **Do not choose an answer before reviewing all of the available answer choices.**
    Do not assume that you have chosen the best answers in the two columns without reading all of the available options.

5. **Determine whether tasks are dependent or independent.**
    Some Two-Part Analysis questions pose two independent tasks that can be carried out individually, and others pose one task with two dependent parts, each of which must be carried out correctly to create a single correct response. With questions of the dependent type, the question asked cannot be answered coherently without making both choices, so be sure to examine your answers in relation to one another.

6. **Keep in mind that one answer choice can be the correct response for both columns.**
    If the tasks associated with the two response columns are *not* mutually exclusive, it is possible that one answer choice satisfies the conditions associated with both response columns.

10.4 The Directions

These directions are similar to the directions given for the four question types in the Integrated Reasoning section of the GMAT® exam. Understanding them clearly before taking the test will save you time during the test.

- **Multi-Source Reasoning.** Click on the tabs and examine all the relevant information from text, charts, and tables to answer the questions.

- **Table Analysis.** Analyze the table, sorting on columns as needed, to determine whether each of the options presented meets the given criterion or not.

- **Graphics Interpretation.** Interpret the graph or graphical image and select from each drop-down menu the option that creates the most accurate statement based on the information provided.

- **Two-Part Analysis.** Read the information provided, review the options presented in the table, and indicate which option meets the criterion presented in the first column and which option meets the criterion presented in the second column. Make only two selections, one in each column.

For the Integrated Reasoning section, an onscreen calculator is available. To access the calculator, click "Calculator" on the blue bar at the upper left of the screen. Note that the calculator can be dragged to any part of the screen.

You can view explanations of the format of the specific Integrated Reasoning questions anytime while working through this section by clicking on HELP.

11.0   Analytical Writing Assessment

11.0 Analytical Writing Assessment

The Analytical Writing Assessment (AWA) consists of one 30-minute writing task called the Analysis of an Argument. In this section, you must read a brief argument, analyze the reasoning behind it, and then write a critique of the argument. You are not asked to state your opinion but rather to analyze the one given. You may, for example, consider what questionable assumptions underlie the author's thinking, what alternative explanations or counterexamples might weaken the conclusion, or what sort of evidence could help strengthen or refute the argument.

For this task, you will use the computer keyboard to type your response. You will be able to use typical word-processing functions—that is, you can cut, copy, paste, undo, and redo. These functions can be accessed either by using the keyboard or by using the mouse to click on icons on the screen. You will be able to take notes when planning your response.

It is important that you plan carefully before you begin writing. Read the specific analytical writing task several times to make sure you understand exactly what is expected. Think about how you might present your analysis. You may want to sketch an outline to help you plan and organize. Keep in mind the 30-minute time limit as you plan your response—keep your analysis brief enough to give you plenty of time to write a first draft, read it over carefully, and make any necessary corrections or revisions before you run out of time. As you write, try to keep your language clear, your sentences concise, and the flow of your ideas logical. State your premise clearly at the beginning, and make sure you present a strong conclusion at the end.

11.1 What Is Measured

The Analytical Writing Assessment is designed as a direct measure of your ability to think critically and communicate your ideas. More specifically, the Analysis of an Argument task tests your ability to formulate an appropriate and constructive critique of a prescribed conclusion based upon a specific line of thinking.

The argument that you will analyze may concern a topic of general interest, possibly related to business or to a variety of other subjects. It is important to note, however, that no Analysis of an Argument question presupposes any specific knowledge of business or other specific content areas. Only your capacity to write analytically is assessed.

Professional essay raters, including college and university faculty members from various subject-matter areas, including but not limited to management education, will evaluate your essay. For information on how readers are qualified, visit mba.com. Readers are trained to be sensitive and fair in evaluating the responses of nonnative speakers of English. A computer scoring program will also evaluate your essays. Your responses will be scored on the basis of:

- the overall quality of your ideas
- your ability to organize, develop, and express those ideas
- how well you provide relevant supporting reasons and examples
- your ability to control the elements of standard written English

11.2 Test-Taking Strategies

1. **Read the question carefully.**
   Make sure you have taken all parts of a question into account before you begin to respond to it.

2. **Do not start to write immediately.**
   Take a few minutes to think about the question and plan a response before you begin writing. You may find it helpful to write a brief outline or jot down some ideas on the erasable notepad provided. Take care to organize your ideas and develop them fully, but leave time to reread your response and make any revisions that you think would improve it.

3. **Focus on the task of analyzing and critiquing a line of thinking or reasoning.**
   Get used to asking yourself questions such as the following: *What questionable assumptions might underlie the thinking? What alternative explanations might be given? What counterexamples might be raised? What additional evidence might prove useful in fully and fairly evaluating the reasoning?*

4. **Develop fully any examples you use.**
   Do not simply list your examples—explain how they illustrate your point.

5. **Discuss alternative explanations or counterexamples.**
   These techniques allow you to introduce illustrations and examples drawn from your observations, experiences, and reading.

6. **Make sure your response reads like a narrative.**
   Your response should not read like an outline. It should use full sentences, a coherent organizational scheme, logical transitions between points, and appropriately introduced and developed examples.

11.3 The Directions

These are the directions that you will see for the Analysis of an Argument essay. If you read them carefully and understand them clearly before going to sit for the test, you will not need to spend too much time reviewing them when you take the GMAT® exam. They read as follows:

ANALYSIS OF AN ARGUMENT

In this section, you will be asked to write a critique of the argument presented. *You are* not *asked to present your own views on the subject*.

Writing Your Response: Take a few minutes to evaluate the argument and plan a response before you begin writing. Be sure to leave enough time to reread your response and make any revisions that you think are necessary.

Evaluation of Your Response: Scores will reflect how well you:

- organize, develop, and express your ideas about the argument presented

- provide relevant supporting reasons and examples

- control the elements of standard written English

11.4 GMAT® Scoring Guide: Analysis of an Argument

6 Outstanding

A 6 paper presents a cogent, well-articulated critique of the argument and demonstrates mastery of the elements of effective writing.

A typical paper in this category exhibits the following characteristics:

- clearly identifies important features of the argument and analyzes them insightfully

- develops ideas cogently, organizes them logically, and connects them with clear transitions

- effectively supports the main points of the critique

- demonstrates control of language, including diction and syntactic variety

- demonstrates facility with the conventions of standard written English but may have minor flaws

5 Strong

A 5 paper presents a well-developed critique of the argument and demonstrates good control of the elements of effective writing.

A typical paper in this category exhibits the following characteristics:

- clearly identifies important features of the argument and analyzes them in a generally thoughtful way

- develops ideas clearly, organizes them logically, and connects them with appropriate transitions

- sensibly supports the main points of the critique

- demonstrates control of language, including diction and syntactic variety

- demonstrates facility with the conventions of standard written English but may have occasional flaws

4 Adequate

A 4 paper presents a competent critique of the argument and demonstrates adequate control of the elements of writing.

A typical paper in this category exhibits the following characteristics:

- identifies and analyzes important features of the argument

- develops and organizes ideas satisfactorily but may not connect them with transitions

- supports the main points of the critique

- demonstrates sufficient control of language to convey ideas with reasonable clarity

- generally follows the conventions of standard written English but may have some flaws

3 Limited

A 3 paper demonstrates some competence in analytical writing skills and in its control of the elements of writing but is plainly flawed.

A typical paper in this category exhibits one or more of the following characteristics:

- does not identify or analyze most of the important features of the argument, although some analysis of the argument is present
- mainly analyzes tangential or irrelevant matters, or reasons poorly
- is limited in the logical development and organization of ideas
- offers support of little relevance and value for points of the critique
- does not convey meaning clearly
- contains occasional major errors or frequent minor errors in grammar, usage, and mechanics

2 Seriously Flawed

A 2 paper demonstrates serious weaknesses in analytical writing skills.

A typical paper in this category exhibits one or more of the following characteristics:

- does not present a critique based on logical analysis, but may instead present the writer's own views on the subject
- does not develop ideas, or is disorganized and illogical
- provides little, if any, relevant or reasonable support
- has serious and frequent problems in the use of language and in sentence structure
- contains numerous errors in grammar, usage, and mechanics that interfere with meaning

1 Fundamentally Deficient

A 1 paper demonstrates fundamental deficiencies in analytical writing skills.

A typical paper in this category exhibits more than one of the following characteristics:

- provides little evidence of the ability to understand and analyze the argument
- provides little evidence of the ability to develop an organized response
- has severe and persistent errors in language and sentence structure
- contains a pervasive pattern of errors in grammar, usage, and mechanics that results in incoherence

0 No Score

A paper in this category is off topic, not written in English, is merely attempting to copy the topic, or consists only of keystroke characters.

NR Blank

11.5 Sample: Analysis of an Argument

Read the statement and the instructions that follow it, and then make any notes that will help you plan your response.

The following appeared as part of an article in a daily newspaper:

"The computerized on-board warning system that will be installed in commercial airliners will virtually solve the problem of midair plane collisions. One plane's warning system can receive signals from another's transponder—a radio set that signals a plane's course—in order to determine the likelihood of a collision and recommend evasive action."

Discuss how well reasoned you find this argument. In your discussion, be sure to analyze the line of reasoning and the use of evidence in the argument. For example, you may need to consider what questionable assumptions underlie the thinking and what alternative explanations or counterexamples might weaken the conclusion. You can also discuss what sort of evidence would strengthen or refute the argument, what changes in the argument would make it more logically sound, and what, if anything, would help you better evaluate its conclusion.

Sample Paper 6

The argument that this warning system will virtually solve the problem of midair plane collisions omits some important concerns that must be addressed to substantiate the argument. The statement that follows the description of what this warning system will do simply describes the system and how it operates. This alone does not constitute a logical argument in favor of the warning system, and it certainly does not provide support or proof of the main argument.

Most conspicuously, the argument does not address the cause of the problem of midair plane collisions, the use of the system by pilots and flight specialists, or who is involved in the midair plane collisions. First, the argument assumes that the cause of the problem is that the planes' courses, the likelihood of collisions, and actions to avoid collisions are unknown or inaccurate. In a weak attempt to support its claim, the argument describes a system that makes all of these things accurately known. But if the cause of the problem of midair plane collisions is that pilots are not paying attention to their computer systems or flight operations, the warning system will not solve the collision problem. Second, the argument never addresses the interface between individuals and the system and how this will affect the warning system's objective of obliterating the problem of collisions. If the pilot or flight specialist does not conform to what the warning system suggests, midair collisions will not be avoided. Finally, if planes other than commercial airliners are involved in the collisions, the problem of these collisions cannot be solved by a warning system that will not be installed on non-commercial airliners. The argument also does not address what would happen in the event that the warning system collapses, fails, or does not work properly.

Because the argument leaves out several key issues, it is not sound or persuasive. If it included the items discussed above instead of solely explaining what the system supposedly does, the argument would have been more thorough and convincing.

Explanation of Score 6

This response is, as the scoring guide requires of a 6, "cogent" and "well articulated": all the points made not only bear directly on the argument to be analyzed, but also contribute to a single, integrated development of the writer's critique. The writer begins by making the controlling point that a mere description of the warning system's mode of operation cannot serve as a true argument proving the system's effectiveness, since the description overlooks several major considerations. The writer then identifies these considerations—what causes midair collisions, how pilots will actually use the commercial airline warning system, what kinds of airplanes are typically involved in midair collisions—and, citing appropriate counterexamples (e.g., what if pilots do not pay attention to their instruments?), explains fully how each oversight undermines the conclusion that the warning system will virtually eliminate midair plane collisions.

Throughout, the writer complements the logically organized development of this critique with good, clear prose that demonstrates the ability not only to control language and vary sentence structure but also to express ideas forcibly (e.g., "the argument never addresses the interface between individuals and the system"). Of course, as in any response written under time constraints, occasional minor flaws can be found. For example, "the argument assumes that the cause of the problem is that the planes' courses, the likelihood of collisions, and actions to avoid collisions are unknown or inaccurate" is wordy and imprecise: how can a course, a likelihood, or actions be inaccurate? But flaws such as these, minor and infrequent, do not interfere with the overall clarity and forcefulness of this outstanding response.

Sample Paper 4

The argument is not logically convincing. It does not state whether all planes can receive signals from each other. It does not state whether planes constantly receive signals. If they only receive signals once every certain time interval, collisions will not definitely be prevented. Further if they receive a signal right before they are about to crash, they cannot avoid each other.

The main flaw in the argument is that it assumes that the two planes, upon receiving each other's signals, will know which evasive action to take. For example, the two planes could be going towards each other and then receive the signals. If one turns at an angle to the left and the other turns at an angle to the right, the two planes will still crash. Even if they receive an updated signal, they will not have time to avoid each other.

The following argument would be more sound and persuasive. The new warning system will solve the problem of midair plane collisions. Each plane will receive constant, continual signals from each other. If the two planes are headed in a direction where they will crash, the system will coordinate the signals, and tell one plane to go one way, and the other plane to go another way. The new system will ensure that the two planes will turn in different directions so they don't crash by trying to prevent the original crash. In addition, the two planes will be able to see themselves and the other on a computer screen, to aid in the evasive action.

Explanation of Score 4

This response competently cites a number of deficiencies in the argument presented: the information given about the nature of the signals sent and received and the evasive action recommended does not warrant the conclusion that the onboard warning system "will virtually solve the problem of midair plane collisions." However, in discussing these insufficiencies in the argument, the response reveals an unevenness in the quality of its reasoning. For example, while it is perfectly legitimate to point out that the argument assumes too much and says too little about the evasive action that will be recommended by the warning system, it is farfetched to suggest that the system might be so poorly designed as to route two approaching airplanes to the same spot. Likewise, while it is fair to question the effectiveness of a warning signal about which the argument says so little, it is not reasonable to assume that the system would be designed to space signals so far apart that they would prove useless. Rather than invent implausibly bad versions of the warning system to prove that it might be ineffective, a stronger response would analyze unexplored possibilities inherent in the information that is given—for example, the possibility that pilots might not be able to respond quickly and effectively to the radio signals the argument says they will receive when the new system is installed. The "more sound and persuasive argument" in the last paragraph, while an improvement on the original, continues to overlook this possibility and also assumes that other types of aircraft without transponders will pose no problems.

The organization of ideas, while generally sound, is sometimes weakened by needless repetition of the same points, as in sentences 4 and 5 of the last paragraph. The writing contains minor instances of awkwardness (e.g., "Each plane will receive constant, continual signals from each other" in paragraph 3), but is free of flaws that make understanding difficult. However, though the writing is generally clean and clear, the syntax does not show much variety. A few sentences begin with "if" clauses, but almost all the rest, even those that begin with a transitional phrase such as "for example" or "in addition," conform to a "subject, verb, complement" pattern. The first paragraph, in which the second and third sentences begin the same way ("It does not state"), is particularly repetitious.

Sample Paper 2

This argument has no information about air collisions. I think most cases happen in new airports because the air traffic I heavy. In this case sound airport control could solve the problem.

I think this argument is logically reasonable. Its assumption is that plane collisions are caused by planes that don't know each others positions. So pilots can do nothing, if they know each others position through the system it will solve the problem.

If it can provide evidence the problem is lack of knowledge of each others positions, it will be more sound and persuasive.

More information about air collisions is helpful, (the reason for air collisions).

Explanation of Score 2

This response is seriously flawed in several ways. First of all, it has very little substance. The writer appears to make only one point—that while it seems reasonable to assume that midair collisions would be less likely if pilots were sure of each other's positions, readers cannot adequately judge this assumption without more information about where, why, and how such collisions occur. This point, furthermore, is neither explained by a single reason beyond what is given in the topic nor supported by a single example. Legitimate though it is, it cannot, alone and undeveloped, serve as an adequate response to the argument.

Aside from being undeveloped, the response is confusing. At the outset, it seems to be critical of the argument. The writer begins by pointing to the inadequacy of the information given; then speculates, without evidence, that "most cases happen in new airports"; and then suggests that the problem should be addressed by improving "airport control," not (it is implied) by installing onboard warning systems. After criticizing the argument in the first paragraph, the writer confusingly seems to endorse it in the second. Then, in the remainder of the response, the writer returns to a critical stance.

The general lack of coherence is reflected in the serious and frequent writing problems that make meaning hard to determine—for example, the elliptical and ungrammatical "So pilots can do nothing, if they know each others position through the system it will solve the problem" (paragraph 2) or "If it can provide evidence the problem is lack of knowledge of each others positions, it will be more sound and persuasive" (paragraph 3). The prose suffers from a variety of basic errors in grammar, usage, and mechanics.

11.6 Analysis of an Argument Sample Topics

The following appeared as part of an annual report sent to stockholders by Olympic Foods, a processor of frozen foods:

"Over time, the costs of processing go down because as organizations learn how to do things better, they become more efficient. In color film processing, for example, the cost of a 3-by-5-inch print fell from 50 cents for five-day service in 1970 to 20 cents for one-day service in 1984. The same principle applies to the processing of food. And since Olympic Foods will soon celebrate its 25th birthday, we can expect that our long experience will enable us to minimize costs and thus maximize profits."

Discuss how well reasoned you find this argument. In your discussion be sure to analyze the line of reasoning and the use of evidence in the argument. For example, you may need to consider what questionable assumptions underlie the thinking and what alternative explanations or counterexamples might weaken the conclusion. You can also discuss what sort of evidence would strengthen or refute the argument, what changes in the argument would make it more logically sound, and what, if anything, would help you better evaluate its conclusion.

The following appeared in a memorandum from the business department of the Apogee Company:

"When the Apogee Company had all its operations in one location, it was more profitable than it is today. Therefore, the Apogee Company should close down its field offices and conduct all its operations from a single location. Such centralization would improve profitability by cutting costs and helping the company maintain better supervision of all employees."

Discuss how well reasoned … etc.

The following appeared in a memorandum issued by a large city's council on the arts:

"In a recent citywide poll, 15 percent more residents said that they watch television programs about the visual arts than was the case in a poll conducted five years ago. During these past five years, the number of people visiting our city's art museums has increased by a similar percentage. Since the corporate funding that supports public television, where most of the visual arts programs appear, is now being threatened with severe cuts, we can expect that attendance at our city's art museums will also start to decrease. Thus some of the city's funds for supporting the arts should be reallocated to public television."

Discuss how well reasoned … etc.

The following appeared in a report presented for discussion at a meeting of the directors of a company that manufactures parts for heavy machinery:

"The falling revenues that the company is experiencing coincide with delays in manufacturing. These delays, in turn, are due in large part to poor planning in purchasing metals. Consider further that the manager of the department that handles purchasing of raw materials has an excellent background in general business, psychology, and sociology, but knows little about the properties of metals. The company should, therefore, move the purchasing manager to the sales department and bring in a scientist from the research division to be manager of the purchasing department."

Discuss how well reasoned … etc.

The following appeared in an announcement issued by the publisher of *The Mercury*, a weekly newspaper:

"Since a competing lower-priced newspaper, *The Bugle*, was started five years ago, *The Mercury*'s circulation has declined by 10,000 readers. The best way to get more people to read *The Mercury* is to reduce its price below that of *The Bugle*, at least until circulation increases to former levels. The increased circulation of *The Mercury* will attract more businesses to buy advertising space in the paper."

Discuss how well reasoned ... etc.

The following appeared as part of an article in a magazine devoted to regional life:

"Corporations should look to the city of Helios when seeking new business opportunities or a new location. Even in the recent recession, Helios's unemployment rate was lower than the regional average. It is the industrial center of the region, and historically it has provided more than its share of the region's manufacturing jobs. In addition, Helios is attempting to expand its economic base by attracting companies that focus on research and development of innovative technologies."

Discuss how well reasoned ... etc.

The following appeared in the health section of a magazine on trends and lifestyles:

"People who use the artificial sweetener aspartame are better off consuming sugar, since aspartame can actually contribute to weight gain rather than weight loss. For example, high levels of aspartame have been shown to trigger a craving for food by depleting the brain of a chemical that registers satiety, or the sense of being full. Furthermore, studies suggest that sugars, if consumed after at least 45 minutes of continuous exercise, actually enhance the body's ability to burn fat. Consequently, those who drink aspartame-sweetened juices after exercise will also lose this calorie-burning benefit. Thus it appears that people consuming aspartame rather than sugar are unlikely to achieve their dietary goals."

Discuss how well reasoned ... etc.

The following appeared in the editorial section of a corporate newsletter:

"The common notion that workers are generally apathetic about management issues is false, or at least outdated: a recently published survey indicates that 79 percent of the nearly 1,200 workers who responded to survey questionnaires expressed a high level of interest in the topics of corporate restructuring and redesign of benefits programs."

Discuss how well reasoned ... etc.

The following appeared in the opinion column of a financial magazine:

"On average, middle-aged consumers devote 39 percent of their retail expenditure to department store products and services, while for younger consumers the average is only 25 percent. Since the number of middle-aged people will increase dramatically within the next decade, department stores can expect retail sales to increase significantly during that period. Furthermore, to take advantage of the trend, these stores should begin to replace some of those products intended to attract the younger consumer with products intended to attract the middle-aged consumer."

Discuss how well reasoned ... etc.

The following appeared in the editorial section of a local newspaper:

"This past winter, 200 students from Waymarsh State College traveled to the state capitol building to protest against proposed cuts in funding for various state college programs. The other 12,000 Waymarsh students evidently weren't so concerned about their education: they either stayed on campus or left for winter break. Since the group who did not protest is far more numerous, it is more representative of the state's college students than are the protesters. Therefore the state legislature need not heed the appeals of the protesting students."

Discuss how well reasoned ... etc.

The following appeared in the editorial section of a local newspaper:

"In the first four years that Montoya has served as mayor of the city of San Perdito, the population has decreased and the unemployment rate has increased. Two businesses have closed for each new business that has opened. Under Varro, who served as mayor for four years before Montoya, the unemployment rate decreased and the population increased. Clearly, the residents of San Perdito would be best served if they voted Montoya out of office and reelected Varro."

Discuss how well reasoned ... etc.

The following appeared as part of a promotional campaign to sell advertising space in the *Daily Gazette* to grocery stores in the Marston area:

"Advertising the reduced price of selected grocery items in the *Daily Gazette* will help you increase your sales. Consider the results of a study conducted last month. Thirty sale items from a store in downtown Marston were advertised in *The Gazette* for four days. Each time one or more of the 30 items was purchased, clerks asked whether the shopper had read the ad. Two-thirds of the 200 shoppers asked answered in the affirmative. Furthermore, more than half the customers who answered in the affirmative spent over $100 at the store."

Discuss how well reasoned ... etc.

The following appeared as part of a campaign to sell advertising time on a local radio station to local businesses:

"The Cumquat Café began advertising on our local radio station this year and was delighted to see its business increase by 10 percent over last year's totals. Their success shows you how you can use radio advertising to make your business more profitable."

Discuss how well reasoned ... etc.

The following appeared as part of a newspaper editorial:

"Two years ago Nova High School began to use interactive computer instruction in three academic subjects. The school dropout rate declined immediately, and last year's graduates have reported some impressive achievements in college. In future budgets the school board should use a greater portion of the available funds to buy more computers, and all schools in the district should adopt interactive computer instruction throughout the curriculum."

Discuss how well reasoned ... etc.

The following appeared as a part of an advertisement for Adams, who is seeking re-election as governor:

"Re-elect Adams, and you will be voting for proven leadership in improving the state's economy. Over the past year alone, 70 percent of the state's workers have had increases in their wages, 5,000 new jobs have been created, and six corporations have located their headquarters here. Most of the respondents in a recent poll said they believed that the economy is likely to continue to improve if Adams is re-elected. Adams's opponent, Zebulon, would lead our state in the wrong direction, because Zebulon disagrees with many of Adams's economic policies."

Discuss how well reasoned ... etc.

The following appeared as part of an article in the education section of a Waymarsh city newspaper:

"Throughout the last two decades, those who earned graduate degrees found it very difficult to get jobs teaching their academic specialties at the college level. Those with graduate degrees from Waymarsh University had an especially hard time finding such jobs. But better times are coming in the next decade for all academic job seekers, including those from Waymarsh. Demographic trends indicate that an increasing number of people will be reaching college age over the next 10 years; consequently, we can expect that the job market will improve dramatically for people seeking college-level teaching positions in their fields."

Discuss how well reasoned ... etc.

The following appeared in an article in a consumer-products magazine:

"Two of today's best-selling brands of full-strength prescription medication for the relief of excess stomach acid, Acid-Ease and Pepticaid, are now available in milder nonprescription forms. Doctors have written 76 million more prescriptions for full-strength Acid-Ease than for full-strength Pepticaid. So people who need an effective but milder nonprescription medication for the relief of excess stomach acid should choose Acid-Ease."

Discuss how well reasoned ... etc.

The following is an excerpt from a memo written by the head of a governmental department:

"Neither stronger ethics regulations nor stronger enforcement mechanisms are necessary to ensure ethical behavior by companies doing business with this department. We already have a code of ethics that companies doing business with this department are urged to abide by, and virtually all of these companies have agreed to follow it. We also know that the code is relevant to the current business environment because it was approved within the last year, and in direct response to specific violations committed by companies with which we were then working—not in abstract anticipation of potential violations, as so many such codes are."

Discuss how well reasoned ... etc.

The following appeared as part of an article in the travel section of a newspaper:

"Over the past decade, the restaurant industry in the country of Spiessa has experienced unprecedented growth. This surge can be expected to continue in the coming years, fueled by recent social changes: personal incomes are rising, more leisure time is available, single-person households are more common, and people have a greater interest in gourmet food, as evidenced by a proliferation of publications on the subject."

Discuss how well reasoned ... etc.

The following appeared in an article in a health and fitness magazine:

"Laboratory studies show that Saluda Natural Spring Water contains several of the minerals necessary for good health and that it is completely free of bacteria. Residents of Saluda, the small town where the water is bottled, are hospitalized less frequently than the national average. Even though Saluda Natural Spring Water may seem expensive, drinking it instead of tap water is a wise investment in good health."

Discuss how well reasoned ... etc.

The following appeared as part of an editorial in an industry newsletter:

"While trucking companies that deliver goods pay only a portion of highway maintenance costs and no property tax on the highways they use, railways spend billions per year maintaining and upgrading their facilities. The government should lower the railroad companies' property taxes, since sending goods by rail is clearly a more appropriate mode of ground transportation than highway shipping. For one thing, trains consume only a third of the fuel a truck would use to carry the same load, making them a more cost-effective and environmentally sound mode of transport. Furthermore, since rail lines already exist, increases in rail traffic would not require building new lines at the expense of taxpaying citizens."

Discuss how well reasoned ... etc.

The following appeared in the editorial section of a newspaper:

"As public concern over drug abuse has increased, authorities have become more vigilant in their efforts to prevent illegal drugs from entering the country. Many drug traffickers have consequently switched from marijuana, which is bulky, or heroin, which has a market too small to justify the risk of severe punishment, to cocaine. Thus enforcement efforts have ironically resulted in an observed increase in the illegal use of cocaine."

Discuss how well reasoned ... etc.

The following appeared in a speech delivered by a member of the city council:

"Twenty years ago, only half of the students who graduated from Einstein High School went on to attend a college or university. Today, two-thirds of the students who graduate from Einstein do so. Clearly, Einstein has improved its educational effectiveness over the past two decades. This improvement has occurred despite the fact that the school's funding, when adjusted for inflation, is about the same as it was 20 years ago. Therefore, we do not need to make any substantial increase in the school's funding at this time."

Discuss how well reasoned ... etc.

The following appeared in a memo from the customer service division to the manager of Mammon Savings and Loan:

"We believe that improved customer service is the best way for us to differentiate ourselves from competitors and attract new customers. We can offer our customers better service by reducing waiting time in teller lines from an average of six minutes to an average of three. By opening for business at 8:30 instead of 9:00, and by remaining open for an additional hour beyond our current closing time, we will be better able to accommodate the busy schedules of our customers. These changes will enhance our bank's image as the most customer-friendly bank in town and give us the edge over our competition."

Discuss how well reasoned ... etc.

The following appeared as part of an article in a magazine on lifestyles:

"Two years ago, City L was listed fourteenth in an annual survey that ranks cities according to the quality of life that can be enjoyed by those living in them. This information will enable people who are moving to the state in which City L is located to confidently identify one place, at least, where schools are good, housing is affordable, people are friendly, the environment is safe, and the arts flourish."

Discuss how well reasoned … etc.

The following appeared in a memorandum from a member of a financial management and consulting firm:

"We have learned from an employee of Windfall, Ltd., that its accounting department, by checking about 10 percent of the last month's purchasing invoices for errors and inconsistencies, saved the company some $10,000 in overpayments. In order to help our clients increase their net gains, we should advise each of them to institute a policy of checking all purchasing invoices for errors. Such a recommendation could also help us get the Windfall account by demonstrating to Windfall the rigorousness of our methods."

Discuss how well reasoned … etc.

The following appeared in a newspaper editorial:

"As violence in movies increases, so do crime rates in our cities. To combat this problem we must establish a board to censor certain movies, or we must limit admission to persons over 21 years of age. Apparently our legislators are not concerned about this issue since a bill calling for such actions recently failed to receive a majority vote."

Discuss how well reasoned … etc.

The following appeared in the editorial section of a local newspaper:

"Commuter use of the new subway train is exceeding the transit company's projections. However, commuter use of the shuttle buses that transport people to the subway stations is below the projected volume. If the transit company expects commuters to ride the shuttle buses to the subway rather than drive there, it must either reduce the shuttle bus fares or increase the price of parking at the subway stations."

Discuss how well reasoned … etc.

The following was excerpted from the speech of a spokesperson for Synthetic Farm Products, Inc.:

"Many farmers who invested in the equipment needed to make the switch from synthetic to organic fertilizers and pesticides feel that it would be too expensive to resume synthetic farming at this point. But studies of farmers who switched to organic farming last year indicate that their current crop yields are lower. Hence their purchase of organic farming equipment, a relatively minor investment compared to the losses that would result from continued lower crop yields, cannot justify persisting on an unwise course. And the choice to farm organically is financially unwise, given that it was motivated by environmental rather than economic concerns."

Discuss how well reasoned … etc.

The following appeared in a newspaper story giving advice about investments:

"As overall life expectancy continues to rise, the population of our country is growing increasingly older. For example, more than 20 percent of the residents of one of our more populated regions are now at least 65 years old, and occupancy rates at resort hotels in that region declined significantly during the past six months. Because of these two related trends, a prudent investor would be well advised to sell interest in hotels and invest in hospitals and nursing homes instead."

Discuss how well reasoned … etc.

The following appeared as part of the business plan of an investment and financial consulting firm:

"Studies suggest that an average coffee drinker's consumption of coffee increases with age, from age 10 through age 60. Even after age 60, coffee consumption remains high. The average cola drinker's consumption of cola, however, declines with increasing age. Both of these trends have remained stable for the past 40 years. Given that the number of older adults will significantly increase as the population ages over the next 20 years, it follows that the demand for coffee will increase and the demand for cola will decrease during this period. We should, therefore, consider transferring our investments from Cola Loca to Early Bird Coffee."

Discuss how well reasoned … etc.

The following appeared in the editorial section of a West Cambria newspaper:

"A recent review of the West Cambria volunteer ambulance service revealed a longer average response time to accidents than was reported by a commercial ambulance squad located in East Cambria. In order to provide better patient care for accident victims and to raise revenue for our town by collecting service fees for ambulance use, we should disband our volunteer service and hire a commercial ambulance service."

Discuss how well reasoned … etc.

The following is part of a business plan being discussed at a board meeting of the Perks Company:

"It is no longer cost-effective for the Perks Company to continue offering its employees a generous package of benefits and incentives year after year. In periods when national unemployment rates are low, Perks may need to offer such a package in order to attract and keep good employees, but since national unemployment rates are now high, Perks does not need to offer the same benefits and incentives. The money thus saved could be better used to replace the existing plant machinery with more technologically sophisticated equipment, or even to build an additional plant."

Discuss how well reasoned … etc.

The following appeared as part of a plan proposed by an executive of the Easy Credit Company to the president:

"The Easy Credit Company would gain an advantage over competing credit card services if we were to donate a portion of the proceeds from the use of our cards to a well-known environmental organization in exchange for the use of its symbol or logo on our card. Since a recent poll shows that a large percentage of the public is concerned about environmental issues, this policy would attract new customers, increase use among existing customers, and enable us to charge interest rates that are higher than the lowest ones available."

Discuss how well reasoned … etc.

The following appeared as part of a recommendation from the financial planning office to the administration of Fern Valley University:

"In the past few years, Fern Valley University has suffered from a decline in both enrollments and admissions applications. The reason can be discovered from our students, who most often cite poor teaching and inadequate library resources as their chief sources of dissatisfaction with Fern Valley. Therefore, in order to increase the number of students attending our university, and hence to regain our position as the most prestigious university in the greater Fern Valley metropolitan area, it is necessary to initiate a fund-raising campaign among the alumni that will enable us to expand the range of subjects we teach and to increase the size of our library facilities."

Discuss how well reasoned … etc.

The following appeared in an article in a college departmental newsletter:

"Professor Taylor of Jones University is promoting a model of foreign language instruction in which students receive 10 weeks of intensive training, then go abroad to live with families for 10 weeks. The superiority of the model, Professor Taylor contends, is proved by the results of a study in which foreign language tests given to students at 25 other colleges show that first-year foreign language students at Jones speak more fluently after only 10 to 20 weeks in the program than do 9 out of 10 foreign language majors elsewhere at the time of their graduation."

Discuss how well reasoned … etc.

The following appeared as part of an article in the business section of a local newspaper:

"Motorcycle X has been manufactured in the United States for more than 70 years. Although one foreign company has copied the motorcycle and is selling it for less, the company has failed to attract motorcycle X customers—some say because its product lacks the exceptionally loud noise made by motorcycle X. But there must be some other explanation. After all, foreign cars tend to be quieter than similar American-made cars, but they sell at least as well. Also, television advertisements for motorcycle X highlight its durability and sleek lines, not its noisiness, and the ads typically have voice-overs or rock music rather than engine-roar on the sound track."

Discuss how well reasoned … etc.

The following appeared in the editorial section of a campus newspaper:

"Because occupancy rates for campus housing fell during the last academic year, so did housing revenues. To solve the problem, campus housing officials should reduce the number of available housing units, thereby increasing the occupancy rates. Also, to keep students from choosing to live off-campus, housing officials should lower the rents, thereby increasing demand."

Discuss how well reasoned ... etc.

The following appeared in an Avia Airlines departmental memorandum:

"On average, 9 out of every 1,000 passengers who traveled on Avia Airlines last year filed a complaint about our baggage-handling procedures. This means that although some 1 percent of our passengers were unhappy with those procedures, the overwhelming majority were quite satisfied with them; thus it would appear that a review of the procedures is not important to our goal of maintaining or increasing the number of Avia's passengers."

Discuss how well reasoned ... etc.

The following appeared as part of an article in a weekly newsmagazine:

"The country of Sacchar can best solve its current trade deficit problem by lowering the price of sugar, its primary export. Such an action would make Sacchar better able to compete for markets with other sugar-exporting countries. The sale of Sacchar's sugar abroad would increase, and this increase would substantially reduce Sacchar's trade deficit."

Discuss how well reasoned ... etc.

The following appeared as part of an article in a trade publication:

"Stronger laws are needed to protect new kinds of home-security systems from being copied and sold by imitators. With such protection, manufacturers will naturally invest in the development of new home-security products and production technologies. Without stronger laws, therefore, manufacturers will cut back on investment. From this will follow a corresponding decline not only in product quality and marketability, but also in production efficiency, and thus ultimately a loss of manufacturing jobs in the industry."

Discuss how well reasoned ... etc.

The following appeared in the opinion section of a national newsmagazine:

"To reverse the deterioration of the postal service, the government should raise the price of postage stamps. This solution will no doubt prove effective, since the price increase will generate larger revenues and will also reduce the volume of mail, thereby eliminating the strain on the existing system and contributing to improved morale."

Discuss how well reasoned ... etc.

The following appeared in an article in the health section of a newspaper:

"There is a common misconception that university hospitals are better than community or private hospitals. This notion is unfounded, however: the university hospitals in our region employ 15 percent fewer doctors, have a 20 percent lower success rate in treating patients, make far less overall profit, and pay their medical staff considerably less than do private hospitals. Furthermore, many doctors at university hospitals typically divide their time among teaching, conducting research, and treating patients. From this it seems clear that the quality of care at university hospitals is lower than that at other kinds of hospitals."

Discuss how well reasoned … etc.

The following is part of a business plan created by the management of the Megamart grocery store:

"Our total sales have increased this year by 20 percent since we added a pharmacy section to our grocery store. Clearly, the customer's main concern is the convenience afforded by one-stop shopping. The surest way to increase our profits over the next couple of years, therefore, is to add a clothing department along with an automotive supplies and repair shop. We should also plan to continue adding new departments and services, such as a restaurant and a garden shop, in subsequent years. Being the only store in the area that offers such a range of services will give us a competitive advantage over other local stores."

Discuss how well reasoned … etc.

The following appeared as part of a column in a popular entertainment magazine:

"The producers of the forthcoming movie *3003* will be most likely to maximize their profits if they are willing to pay Robin Good several million dollars to star in it—even though that amount is far more than any other person involved with the movie will make. After all, Robin has in the past been paid a similar amount to work in several films that were very financially successful."

Discuss how well reasoned … etc.

The following appeared in a memorandum from the directors of a security and safety consulting service:

"Our research indicates that over the past six years no incidents of employee theft have been reported within ten of the companies that have been our clients. In analyzing the security practices of these ten companies, we have further learned that each of them requires its employees to wear photo identification badges while at work. In the future, therefore, we should recommend the use of such identification badges to all of our clients."

Discuss how well reasoned … etc.

The following appeared as part of an article in the business section of a local newspaper:

"The owners of the Cumquat Café evidently made a good business decision in moving to a new location, as can be seen from the fact that the Café will soon celebrate its second anniversary there. Moreover, it appears that businesses are not likely to succeed at the old location: since the Café's move, three different businesses—a tanning salon, an antique emporium, and a pet-grooming shop—have occupied its former spot."

Discuss how well reasoned … etc.

The following appeared in the editorial section of a local newspaper:

"The profitability of Croesus Company, recently restored to private ownership, is a clear indication that businesses fare better under private ownership than under public ownership."

Discuss how well reasoned ... etc.

The following appeared in the editorial section of a local newspaper:

"If the paper from every morning edition of the nation's largest newspaper were collected and rendered into paper pulp that the newspaper could reuse, about 5 million trees would be saved each year. This kind of recycling is unnecessary, however, since the newspaper maintains its own forests to ensure an uninterrupted supply of paper."

Discuss how well reasoned ... etc.

The following appeared as part of a business plan recommended by the new manager of a musical rock group called Zapped:

"To succeed financially, Zapped needs greater name recognition. It should therefore diversify its commercial enterprises. The rock group Zonked plays the same type of music that Zapped plays, but it is much better known than Zapped because, in addition to its concert tours and four albums, Zonked has a series of posters, a line of clothing and accessories, and a contract with a major advertising agency to endorse a number of different products."

Discuss how well reasoned ... etc.

The following appeared in a magazine article on trends and lifestyles:

"In general, people are not as concerned as they were a decade ago about regulating their intake of red meat and fatty cheeses. Walk into the Heart's Delight, a store that started selling organic fruits and vegetables and whole-grain flours in the 1960s, and you will also find a wide selection of cheeses made with high butterfat content. Next door, the owners of the Good Earth Café, an old vegetarian restaurant, are still making a modest living, but the owners of the new House of Beef across the street are millionaires."

Discuss how well reasoned ... etc.

The following editorial appeared in the Elm City paper:

"The construction last year of a shopping mall in downtown Oak City was a mistake. Since the mall has opened, a number of local businesses have closed, and the downtown area suffers from an acute parking shortage, and arrests for crime and vagrancy have increased in the nearby Oak City Park. Elm City should pay attention to the example of the Oak City mall and deny the application to build a shopping mall in Elm City."

Discuss how well reasoned ... etc.

The following appeared as part of an editorial in a weekly newsmagazine:

"Historically, most of this country's engineers have come from our universities; recently, however, our university-age population has begun to shrink, and decreasing enrollments in our high schools clearly show that this drop in numbers will continue throughout the remainder of the decade. Consequently, our nation will soon be facing a shortage of trained engineers. If we are to remain economically competitive in the world marketplace, then we must increase funding for education—and quickly."

Discuss how well reasoned ... etc.

The following appeared in an Excelsior Company memorandum:

"The Excelsior Company plans to introduce its own brand of coffee. Since coffee is an expensive food item, and since there are already many established brands of coffee, the best way to gain customers for the Excelsior brand is to do what Superior, the leading coffee company, did when it introduced the newest brand in its line of coffees: conduct a temporary sales promotion that offers free samples, price reductions, and discount coupons for the new brand."

Discuss how well reasoned ... etc.

The following appeared as part of an article in a health club trade publication:

"After experiencing a decline in usage by its members, Healthy Heart fitness center built an indoor pool. Since usage did not increase significantly, it appears that health club managers should adopt another approach—lowering membership fees rather than installing expensive new features."

Discuss how well reasoned ... etc.

The following appeared as part of an article in a popular arts-and-leisure magazine:

"The safety codes governing the construction of public buildings are becoming far too strict. The surest way for architects and builders to prove that they have met the minimum requirements established by these codes is to construct buildings by using the same materials and methods that are currently allowed. But doing so means that there will be very little significant technological innovation within the industry, and hence little evolution of architectural styles and design—merely because of the strictness of these safety codes."

Discuss how well reasoned ... etc.

The following is from a campaign by Big Boards Inc. to convince companies in River City that their sales will increase if they use Big Boards billboards for advertising their locally manufactured products:

"The potential of Big Boards to increase sales of your products can be seen from an experiment we conducted last year. We increased public awareness of the name of the current national women's marathon champion by publishing her picture and her name on billboards in River City for a period of three months. Before this time, although the champion had just won her title and was receiving extensive national publicity, only five percent of 15,000 randomly surveyed residents of River City could correctly name the champion when shown her picture; after the three-month advertising experiment, 35 percent of respondents from a second survey could supply her name."

Discuss how well reasoned … etc.

The following appeared as part of an article on government funding of environmental regulatory agencies:

"When scientists finally learn how to create large amounts of copper from other chemical elements, the regulation of copper mining will become unnecessary. For one thing, since the amount of potentially available copper will no longer be limited by the quantity of actual copper deposits, the problem of over-mining will quickly be eliminated altogether. For another, manufacturers will not need to use synthetic copper substitutes, the production of which creates pollutants. Thus, since two problems will be settled—over-mining and pollution—it makes good sense to reduce funding for mining regulation and either save the money or reallocate it where it is needed more."

Discuss how well reasoned … etc.

The following appeared as part of an article in a popular science magazine:

"Scientists must typically work 60 to 80 hours a week if they hope to further their careers; consequently, good and affordable all-day child care must be made available to both male and female scientists if they are to advance in their fields. Moreover, requirements for career advancement must be made more flexible so that preschool-age children can spend a significant portion of each day with a parent."

Discuss how well reasoned … etc.

The following appeared as part of a recommendation by one of the directors of the Beta Company:

"The Alpha Company has just reduced its workforce by laying off 15 percent of its employees in all divisions and at all levels, and it is encouraging early retirement for other employees. As you know, the Beta Company manufactures some products similar to Alpha's, but our profits have fallen over the last few years. To improve Beta's competitive position, we should try to hire a significant number of Alpha's former workers, since these experienced workers can provide valuable information about Alpha's successful methods, will require little training, and will be particularly motivated to compete against Alpha."

Discuss how well reasoned … etc.

The following appeared in the letters-to-the-editor section of a local newspaper:

"*Muscle Monthly*, a fitness magazine that regularly features pictures of bodybuilders using state-of-the-art exercise machines, frequently sells out, according to the owner of Skyview Newsstand. To help maximize fitness levels in our town's residents, we should, therefore, equip our new community fitness center with such machines."

Discuss how well reasoned ... etc.

The following appeared as part of an article in the business section of a local newspaper:

"The Cumquat Café made a mistake in moving to a new location. After one year at the new spot, it is doing about the same volume of business as before, but the owners of the RoboWrench plumbing supply wholesale outlet that took over its old location are apparently doing better: RoboWrench is planning to open a store in a neighboring city."

Discuss how well reasoned ... etc.

The following appeared in a memorandum from the director of human resources to the executive officers of Company X:

"Last year, we surveyed our employees on improvements needed at Company X by having them rank, in order of importance, the issues presented in a list of possible improvements. Improved communications between employees and management was consistently ranked as the issue of highest importance by the employees who responded to the survey. As you know, we have since instituted regular communications sessions conducted by high-level management, which the employees can attend on a voluntary basis. Therefore, it is likely that most employees at Company X now feel that the improvement most needed at the company has been made."

Discuss how well reasoned ... etc.

The following appeared in a memorandum from the vice president of Road Food, an international chain of fast-food restaurants:

"This past year, we spent almost as much on advertising as did our main competitor, Street Eats, which has fewer restaurants than we do. Although it appeared at first that our advertising agency had created a campaign along the lines we suggested, in fact our total profits were lower than those of Street Eats. In order to motivate our advertising agency to perform better, we should start basing the amount that we pay it on how much total profit we make each year."

Discuss how well reasoned ... etc.

The following appeared in the promotional literature for Cerberus dog food:

"Obesity is a great problem among pet dogs, just as it is among their human owners. Obesity in humans is typically caused by consuming more calories than the body needs. For humans, a proper diet for losing weight is a reduced-calorie diet that is high in fiber and carbohydrates but low in fat. Therefore, the best way for dog owners to help their dogs lose weight in a healthy way is to restrict the dog's diet to Cerberus reduced-calorie dog food, which is high in fiber and carbohydrates but low in fat."

Discuss how well reasoned ... etc.

The following appeared in an article in a travel magazine:

"After the airline industry began requiring airlines to report their on-time rates, Speedee Airlines achieved the number one on-time rate, with more than 89 percent of its flights arriving on time each month. And now Speedee is offering more flights to more destinations than ever before. Clearly, Speedee is the best choice for today's business traveler."

Discuss how well reasoned … etc.

───────────────────────

The following appeared in a memorandum to the planning department of an investment firm:

"Costs have begun dropping for several types of equipment currently used to convert solar energy into electricity. Moreover, some exciting new technologies for converting solar energy are now being researched and developed. Hence we can expect that solar energy will soon become more cost efficient and attractive than coal or oil as a source of electrical power. We should, therefore, encourage investment in Solario, a new manufacturer of solar-powered products. After all, Solario's chief executive was once on the financial planning team for Ready-to-Ware, a software engineering firm that has shown remarkable growth since its recent incorporation."

Discuss how well reasoned … etc.

───────────────────────

The following appeared in a memorandum from a company's marketing department:

"Since our company started manufacturing and marketing a deluxe air filter six months ago, sales of our economy filter—and company profits—have decreased significantly. The deluxe air filter sells for 50 percent more than the economy filter, but the economy filter lasts for only one month while the deluxe filter can be used for two months before it must be replaced. To increase repeat sales of our economy filter and maximize profits, we should discontinue the deluxe air filter and concentrate all our advertising efforts on the economy filter."

Discuss how well reasoned … etc.

───────────────────────

The following appeared in a memorandum from the president of a company that makes shampoo:

"A widely publicized study claims that HR2, a chemical compound in our shampoo, can contribute to hair loss after prolonged use. This study, however, involved only 500 subjects. Furthermore, we have received no complaints from our customers during the past year, and some of our competitors actually use more HR2 per bottle of shampoo than we do. Therefore, we do not need to consider replacing the HR2 in our shampoo with a more expensive alternative."

Discuss how well reasoned … etc.

The following appeared in the editorial section of a local newspaper:

"The tragic crash of a medical helicopter last week points out a situation that needs to be addressed. The medical-helicopter industry supposedly has more stringent guidelines for training pilots and maintaining equipment than do most other airline industries, but these guidelines do not appear to be working: statistics reveal that the rate of medical-helicopter accidents is much higher than the rate of accidents for nonmedical helicopters or commercial airliners."

Discuss how well reasoned ... etc.

The following appeared as part of a recommendation from the business manager of a department store:

"Local clothing stores reported that their profits decreased, on average, for the three-month period between August 1 and October 31. Stores that sell products for the home reported that, on average, their profits increased during this same period. Clearly, consumers are choosing to buy products for their homes instead of clothing. To take advantage of this trend, we should reduce the size of our clothing departments and enlarge our home furnishings and household products departments."

Discuss how well reasoned ... etc.

The following appeared in a letter to the editor of a regional newspaper:

"In response to petitions from the many farmers and rural landowners throughout our region, the legislature has spent valuable time and effort enacting severe laws to deter motorists from picking fruit off the trees, trampling through the fields, and stealing samples of foliage. But how can our local lawmakers occupy themselves with such petty vandalism when crime and violence plague the nation's cities? The fate of apples and leaves is simply too trivial to merit their attention."

Discuss how well reasoned ... etc.

The following appeared as part of an editorial in a campus newspaper:

"With an increasing demand for highly skilled workers, this nation will soon face a serious labor shortage. New positions in technical and professional occupations are increasing rapidly, while at the same time the total labor force is growing slowly. Moreover, the government is proposing to cut funds for aid to education in the near future."

Discuss how well reasoned ... etc.

The following appeared as part of a memorandum from a government agency:

"Given the limited funding available for the building and repair of roads and bridges, the government should not spend any money this year on fixing the bridge that crosses the Styx River. This bridge is located near a city with a weakening economy, so it is not as important as other bridges; moreover, the city population is small and thus unlikely to contribute a significant enough tax revenue to justify the effort of fixing the bridge."

Discuss how well reasoned ... etc.

The following appeared as part of an article in an entertainment magazine:

"A series of books based on the characters from a popular movie are consistently best sellers in local bookstores. Seeking to capitalize on the books' success, Vista Studios is planning to produce a movie sequel based on the books. Due to the success of the books and the original movie, the sequel will undoubtedly be profitable."

Discuss how well reasoned ... etc.

The following appeared in a letter to the editor of a popular science and technology magazine:

"It is a popular myth that consumers are really benefiting from advances in agricultural technology. Granted, consumers are, on the average, spending a decreasing proportion of their income on food. But consider that the demand for food does not rise in proportion with real income. As real income rises, therefore, consumers can be expected to spend a decreasing proportion of their income on food. Yet agricultural technology is credited with having made our lives better."

Discuss how well reasoned ... etc.

The following appeared in the editorial section of a local newspaper:

"This city should be able to improve existing services and provide new ones without periodically raising the taxes of the residents. Instead, the city should require that the costs of services be paid for by developers who seek approval for their large new building projects. After all, these projects can be highly profitable to the developers, but they can also raise a city's expenses and increase the demand for its services."

Discuss how well reasoned ... etc.

The following appeared in the editorial section of a local newspaper:

"In order to avoid the serious health threats associated with many landfills, our municipality should build a plant for burning trash. An incinerator could offer economic as well as ecological advantages over the typical old-fashioned type of landfill: incinerators can be adapted to generate moderate amounts of electricity, and ash residue from some types of trash can be used to condition garden soil."

Discuss how well reasoned ... etc.

The following appeared in the editorial section of a monthly business newsmagazine:

"Most companies would agree that as the risk of physical injury occurring on the job increases, the wages paid to employees should also increase. Hence it makes financial sense for employers to make the workplace safer: they could thus reduce their payroll expenses and save money."

Discuss how well reasoned ... etc.

The following appeared as part of a company memorandum:

"Adopting an official code of ethics regarding business practices may in the long run do our company more harm than good in the public eye. When one of our competitors received unfavorable publicity for violating its own code of ethics, it got more attention from the media than it would have if it had had no such code. Rather than adopt an official code of ethics, therefore, we should instead conduct a publicity campaign that stresses the importance of protecting the environment and assisting charitable organizations."

Discuss how well reasoned ... etc.

The following appeared in the editorial section of a daily newspaper:

"Although forecasts of presidential elections based on opinion polls measure current voter preference, many voters keep changing their minds about whom they prefer until the last few days before the balloting. Some do not even make a final decision until they enter the voting booth. Forecasts based on opinion polls are therefore little better at predicting election outcomes than a random guess would be."

Discuss how well reasoned ... etc.

The following appeared in the editorial section of a newspaper in the country of West Cambria:

"The practice of officially changing speed limits on the highways—whether by increasing or decreasing them—is a dangerous one. Consider what happened over the past decade whenever neighboring East Cambria changed its speed limits: an average of 3 percent more automobile accidents occurred during the week following the change than had occurred during the week preceding it—even when the speed limit was lowered. This statistic shows that the change in speed limit adversely affected the alertness of drivers."

Discuss how well reasoned ... etc.

The following appeared as part of a memorandum from the vice president of Nostrum, a large pharmaceutical corporation:

"The proposal to increase the health and retirement benefits that our employees receive should not be implemented at this time. An increase in these benefits is not only financially unjustified, since our last year's profits were lower than those of the preceding year, but also unnecessary, since our chief competitor, Panacea, offers its employees lower health and retirement benefits than we currently offer. We can assume that our employees are reasonably satisfied with the health and retirement benefits that they now have since a recent survey indicated that two-thirds of the respondents viewed them favorably."

Discuss how well reasoned ... etc.

The following appeared as part of an article on trends in television:

"A recent study of viewers' attitudes toward prime-time television programs shows that many of the programs that were judged by their viewers to be of high quality appeared on (noncommercial) television networks, and that, on commercial television, the most popular shows are typically sponsored by the bestselling products. Thus, it follows that businesses who use commercial television to promote their products will achieve the greatest advertising success by sponsoring only highly rated programs—and, ideally, programs resembling the highly rated noncommercial programs on public channels as much as possible."

Discuss how well reasoned ... etc.

The following appeared as part of an article in the business section of a daily newspaper:

"Company A has a large share of the international market in video-game hardware and software. Company B, the pioneer in these products, was once a $12 billion-a-year giant but collapsed when children became bored with its line of products. Thus Company A can also be expected to fail, especially given the fact that its games are now in so many American homes that the demand for them is nearly exhausted."

Discuss how well reasoned ... etc.

The following appeared as part of an article in a photography magazine:

"When choosing whether to work in color or in black-and-white, the photographer who wishes to be successful should keep in mind that because color photographs are more true to life, magazines use more color photographs than black-and-white ones, and many newspapers are also starting to use color photographs. The realism of color also accounts for the fact that most portrait studios use more color film than black-and-white film. Furthermore, there are more types of color film than black-and-white film available today. Clearly, photographers who work in color have an advantage over those who work in black-and-white."

Discuss how well reasoned ... etc.

The following appeared as part of a letter to the editor of a local newspaper:

"It makes no sense that in most places 15-year-olds are not eligible for their driver's license while people who are far older can retain all of their driving privileges by simply renewing their license. If older drivers can get these renewals, often without having to pass another driving test, then 15-year-olds should be eligible to get a license. Fifteen-year-olds typically have much better eyesight, especially at night; much better hand-eye coordination; and much quicker reflexes. They are also less likely to feel confused by unexpected developments or disoriented in unfamiliar surroundings, and they recover from injuries more quickly."

Discuss how well reasoned ... etc.

The following appeared in an ad for a book titled *How to Write a Screenplay for a Movie*:

"Writers who want to succeed should try to write film screenplays rather than books, since the average film tends to make greater profits than does even a best-selling book. It is true that some books are also made into films. However, our nation's film producers are more likely to produce movies based on original screenplays than to produce films based on books, because in recent years the films that have sold the most tickets have usually been based on original screenplays."

Discuss how well reasoned ... etc.

The following appeared as part of an article in a daily newspaper:

"The computerized onboard warning system that will be installed in commercial airliners will virtually solve the problem of midair plane collisions. One plane's warning system can receive signals from another's transponder—a radio set that signals a plane's course—in order to determine the likelihood of a collision and recommend evasive action."

Discuss how well reasoned ... etc.

The following appeared in a memorandum from the ElectroWares company's marketing department:

"Since our company started manufacturing and marketing a deluxe light bulb six months ago, sales of our economy light bulb—and company profits—have decreased significantly. Although the deluxe light bulb sells for 50 percent more than the economy bulb, it lasts twice as long. Therefore, to increase repeat sales and maximize profits, we should discontinue the deluxe light bulb."

Discuss how well reasoned ... etc.

The following is taken from an editorial in a local newspaper:

"Over the past decade, the price per pound of citrus fruit has increased substantially. Eleven years ago, Megamart charged 15 cents a pound for lemons, but today it commonly charges over a dollar a pound. In only one of these last 11 years was the weather unfavorable for growing citrus crops. Evidently, then, citrus growers have been responsible for the excessive increase in the price of citrus fruit, and strict pricing regulations are needed to prevent them from continuing to inflate prices."

Discuss how well reasoned ... etc.

The following appeared as part of an article in a local newspaper:

"Over the past three years the tartfish industry has changed markedly: fishing technology has improved significantly, and the demand for tartfish has grown in both domestic and foreign markets. As this trend continues, the tartfish industry on Shrimp Island can expect to experience the same overfishing problems that are already occurring with mainland fishing industries: without restrictions on fishing, fishers see no reason to limit their individual catches. As the catches get bigger, the tartfish population will be dangerously depleted while the surplus of tartfish will devalue the catch for fishers. Government regulation is the only answer: tartfish-fishing should be allowed only during the three-month summer season, when tartfish reproduce and thus are most numerous, rather than throughout the year."

Discuss how well reasoned ... etc.

The following appeared in a proposal from the development office at Platonic University:

"Because Platonic University has had difficulty in meeting its expenses over the past three years, we need to find new ways to increase revenues. We should consider following the example of Greene University, which recently renamed itself after a donor who gave it $100 million. If Platonic University were to advertise to its alumni and other wealthy people that it will rename either individual buildings or the entire university itself after the donors who give the most money, the amount of donations would undoubtedly increase."

Discuss how well reasoned … etc.

The following appeared as part of an article in the business section of a local newspaper:

"Hippocrene Plumbing Supply recently opened a wholesale outlet in the location once occupied by the Cumquat Café. Hippocrene has apparently been quite successful there because it is planning to open a large outlet in a nearby city. But the Cumquat Café, one year after moving to its new location, has seen its volume of business drop somewhat from the previous year's. Clearly, the former site was the better business location, and the Cumquat Café has made a mistake in moving to its new address."

Discuss how well reasoned … etc.

The following appeared in the editorial section of a local paper:

"Applications for advertising spots on KMTV, our local cable television channel, decreased last year. Meanwhile a neighboring town's local channel, KOOP, changed its focus to farming issues and reported an increase in advertising applications for the year. To increase applications for its advertisement spots, KMTV should focus its programming on farming issues as well."

Discuss how well reasoned … etc.

The following appeared as part of an article in a computer magazine:

"A year ago Apex Manufacturing bought its managers computers for their homes and paid for telephone connections so that they could access Apex computers and data files from home after normal business hours. Since last year, productivity at Apex has increased by 15 percent. Other companies can learn from the success at Apex: given home computers and access to company resources, employees will work additional hours at home and thereby increase company profits."

Discuss how well reasoned … etc.

The following was excerpted from an article in a farming trade publication:

"Farmers who switched from synthetic to organic farming last year have seen their crop yields decline. Many of these farmers feel that it would be too expensive to resume synthetic farming at this point, given the money that they invested in organic farming supplies and equipment. But their investments will be relatively minor compared to the losses from continued lower crop yields. Organic farmers should switch to synthetic farming rather than persist in an unwise course. And the choice to farm organically is financially unwise, given that it was motivated by environmental rather than economic concerns."

Discuss how well reasoned … etc.

The following appeared in a letter to prospective students from the admissions office at Plateau College:

"Every person who earned an advanced degree in science or engineering from Olympus University last year received numerous offers of excellent jobs. Typically, many graduates of Plateau College have gone on to pursue advanced degrees at Olympus. Therefore, enrolling as an undergraduate at Plateau College is a wise choice for students who wish to ensure success in their careers."

Discuss how well reasoned ... etc.

The following appeared in a memorandum sent by a vice-president of the Nadir Company to the company's human resources department:

"Nadir does not need to adopt the costly 'family-friendly' programs that have been proposed, such as part-time work, work at home, and jobsharing. When these programs were made available at the Summit Company, the leader in its industry, only a small percentage of employees participated in them. Rather than adversely affecting our profitability by offering these programs, we should concentrate on offering extensive training that will enable employees to increase their productivity."

Discuss how well reasoned ... etc.

The following appeared as part of an article in a trade magazine for breweries:

"Magic Hat Brewery recently released the results of a survey of visitors to its tasting room last year. Magic Hat reports that the majority of visitors asked to taste its low-calorie beers. To boost sales, other small breweries should brew low-calorie beers as well."

Discuss how well reasoned ... etc.

The following appeared in an editorial from a newspaper serving the town of Saluda:

"The Saluda Consolidated High School offers more than 200 different courses from which its students can choose. A much smaller private school down the street offers a basic curriculum of only 80 different courses, but it consistently sends a higher proportion of its graduating seniors on to college than Consolidated does. By eliminating at least half of the courses offered there and focusing on a basic curriculum, we could improve student performance at Consolidated and also save many tax dollars."

Discuss how well reasoned ... etc.

The following appeared as part of an article in the book section of a newspaper:

"Currently more and more books are becoming available in electronic form—either free-of-charge on the Internet or for a very low price-per-book on compact disc. Thus literary classics are likely to be read more widely than ever before. People who couldn't have purchased these works at bookstore prices will now be able to read them for little or no money; similarly, people who find it inconvenient to visit libraries and wait for books to be returned by other patrons will now have access to whatever classic they choose from their home or work computers. This increase in access to literary classics will radically affect the public taste in reading, creating a far more sophisticated and learned reading audience than has ever existed before."

Discuss how well reasoned ... etc.

The following appeared as an editorial in a magazine concerned with educational issues:

"In our country, the real earnings of men who have only a high-school degree have decreased significantly over the past 15 years, but those of male college graduates have remained about the same. Therefore, the key to improving the earnings of the next generation of workers is to send all students to college. Our country's most important educational goal, then, should be to establish enough colleges and universities to accommodate all high school graduates."

Discuss how well reasoned ... etc.

The following appeared as part of a business plan created by the management of the Take Heart Fitness Center:

"After opening the new swimming pool early last summer, Take Heart saw a 12 percent increase in the use of the center by its members. Therefore, in order to increase membership in Take Heart, we should continue to add new recreational facilities in subsequent years: for example, a multipurpose game room, a tennis court, and a miniature golf course. Being the only center in the area offering this range of activities would give us a competitive advantage in the health and recreation market."

Discuss how well reasoned ... etc.

The following appeared in a letter from a staff member in the office of admissions at Argent University:

"The most recent nationwide surveys show that undergraduates choose their major field primarily based on their perception of job prospects in that field. At our university, economics is now the most popular major, so students must perceive this field as having the best job prospects. Therefore, we can increase our enrollment if we focus our advertising and recruiting on publicizing the accomplishments of our best-known economics professors and the success of our economics graduates in finding employment."

Discuss how well reasoned ... etc.

The following appeared as part of a memorandum from the loan department of the Frostbite National Bank:

"We should not approve the business loan application of the local group that wants to open a franchise outlet for the Kool Kone chain of ice cream parlors. Frostbite is known for its cold winters, and cold weather can mean slow ice cream sales. For example, even though Frostbite is a town of 10,000 people, it has only one ice cream spot—the Frigid Cow. Despite the lack of competition, the Frigid Cow's net revenues fell by 10 percent last winter."

Discuss how well reasoned ... etc.

The following appeared as part of a letter to the editor of a local newspaper:

"Bayview High School is considering whether to require all of its students to wear uniforms while at school. Students attending Acorn Valley Academy, a private school in town, earn higher grades on average and are more likely to go on to college. Moreover, Acorn Valley reports few instances of tardiness, absenteeism, or discipline problems. Since Acorn Valley requires its students to wear uniforms, Bayview High School would do well to follow suit and require its students to wear uniforms as well."

Discuss how well reasoned ... etc.

The following appeared in a memo to the Saluda town council from the town's business manager:

"Research indicates that those who exercise regularly are hospitalized less than half as often as those who don't exercise. By providing a well-equipped gym for Saluda's municipal employees, we should be able to reduce the cost of our group health insurance coverage by approximately 50 percent and thereby achieve a balanced town budget."

Discuss how well reasoned ... etc.

The following appeared in a memorandum written by the assistant manager of a store that sells gourmet food items from various countries:

"A local wine store made an interesting discovery last month: it sold more French than Italian wine on days when it played recordings of French accordion music, but it sold more Italian than French wine on days when Italian songs were played. Therefore, I recommend that we put food specialties from one particular country on sale for a week at a time and play only music from that country while the sale is going on. By this means we will increase our profits in the same way that the wine store did, and we will be able to predict more precisely what items we should stock at any given time."

Discuss how well reasoned ... etc.

The following appeared in a memorandum from the director of research and development at Ready-to-Ware, a software engineering firm:

"The package of benefits and incentives that Ready-to-Ware offers to professional staff is too costly. Our quarterly profits have declined since the package was introduced two years ago, at the time of our incorporation. Moreover, the package had little positive effect, as we have had only marginal success in recruiting and training high-quality professional staff. To become more profitable again, Ready-to-Ware should, therefore, offer the reduced benefits package that was in place two years ago and use the savings to fund our current research and development initiatives."

Discuss how well reasoned ... etc.

The following appeared as a memorandum from the vice-president of the Dolci candy company:

"Given the success of our premium and most expensive line of chocolate candies in a recent taste test and the consequent increase in sales, we should shift our business focus to producing additional lines of premium candy rather than our lower-priced, ordinary candies. When the current economic boom ends and consumers can no longer buy major luxury items, such as cars, they will still want to indulge in small luxuries, such as expensive candies."

Discuss how well reasoned ... etc.

The following appeared in a memorandum from the business office of the Lovin' Cupful, a national restaurant chain:

"The Lovin' Cupful franchises in our northeast region have begun serving customers Almost, a brand new powdered instant tea, in place of brewed tea. Waiters report that only about 2 percent of the customers have complained, and that customers who want refills typically ask for 'more tea.' It appears, then, that 98 percent of the customers are perfectly happy with the switch, or else they cannot tell powdered instant from brewed tea. Therefore, in order to take advantage of the lower price per pound of Almost, all of our restaurants should begin substituting it for brewed tea."

Discuss how well reasoned ... etc.

The following appeared in a memorandum from the director of marketing for a pharmaceutical company:

"According to a survey of 5,000 urban residents, the prevalence of stress headaches increases with educational level, so that stress headaches occur most often among people with graduate-school degrees. It is well established that, nationally, higher educational levels usually correspond with higher levels of income. Therefore, in marketing our new pain remedy, Omnilixir, we should send free samples primarily to graduate students and to people with graduate degrees, and we should concentrate on advertising in professional journals rather than in general interest magazines."

Discuss how well reasoned ... etc.

The following appeared as part of an editorial in the Waymarsh city newspaper:

"Last year the parents of first graders in our school district expressed satisfaction with the reading skills their children developed but complained strongly about their children's math skills. To remedy this serious problem and improve our district's elementary education, everyone in the teacher-training program at Waymarsh University should be required to take more courses in mathematics."

Discuss how well reasoned ... etc.

The following appeared in a letter to the editor of a River City newspaper:

"The Clio Development Group should not be permitted to build a multilevel parking garage on Dock Street since most of the buildings on the block would have to be demolished. Because these buildings were erected decades ago, they have historic significance and must therefore be preserved as economic assets in the effort to revitalize a restored riverfront area. Recall how Lakesburg has benefited from business increases in its historic downtown center. Moreover, there is plenty of vacant land for a parking lot elsewhere in River City."

Discuss how well reasoned ... etc.

The following appeared in a corporate planning memorandum for a company that develops amusement parks:

"Because travel from our country to foreign countries has increased dramatically in recent years, our next project should be a 'World Tour' theme park with replicas of famous foreign buildings, rides that have international themes, and refreshment stands serving only foods from the country represented by the nearest ride. The best location would be near our capital city, which has large percentages of international residents and of children under the age of 16. Given the advantages of this site and the growing interest in foreign countries, the 'World Tour' theme park should be as successful as our space-travel theme park, where attendance has increased tenfold over the past decade."

Discuss how well reasoned ... etc.

The following appeared in a memorandum from the publisher to the staff of *The Clarion*, a large metropolitan newspaper:

"During the recent campaign for mayor, a clear majority of city readers who responded to our survey indicated a desire for more news about city government. To increase circulation, and thus our profits, we should therefore consistently devote a greater proportion of space in all editions of *The Clarion* to coverage of local news."

Discuss how well reasoned ... etc.

The following appeared in a memorandum from the assistant manager of Pageturner Books:

"Over the past two years, Pageturner's profits have decreased by 5 percent, even though we have added a popular café as well as a music section selling CDs and tapes. At the same time, we have experienced an increase in the theft of merchandise. We should therefore follow the example of Thoreau Books, which increased its profits after putting copies of its most frequently stolen books on a high shelf behind the payment counter. By doing likewise with copies of the titles that our staff reported stolen last year, we too can increase profitability."

Discuss how well reasoned ... etc.

The following appeared in a letter to the editor of a River City newspaper:

"The Clio Development Group's plan for a multilevel parking garage on Dock Street should be approved in order to strengthen the economy of the surrounding area. Although most of the buildings on the block would have to be demolished, they are among the oldest in the city and thus of little current economic value. Those who oppose the project should realize that historic preservation cannot be the only consideration: even Athens or Jerusalem will knock down old buildings to put up new ones that improve the local economy."

Discuss how well reasoned ... etc.

The following appeared in a memorandum from the owner of Carlo's Clothing to the staff:

"Since Disc Depot, the music store on the next block, began a new radio advertising campaign last year, its business has grown dramatically, as evidenced by the large increase in foot traffic into the store. While the Disc Depot's owners have apparently become wealthy enough to retire, profits at Carlo's Clothing have remained stagnant for the past three years. In order to boost our sales and profits, we should therefore switch from newspaper advertising to frequent radio advertisements like those for Disc Depot."

Discuss how well reasoned ... etc.

The following appeared as part of the business plan of the Capital Idea investment firm:

"Across town in the Park Hill district, the Thespian Theater, Pizzazz Pizza, and the Niblick Golf Club have all had business increases over the past two years. Capital Idea should therefore invest in the Roxy Playhouse, the Slice-o'-Pizza, and the Divot Golf Club, three new businesses in the Irongate district. As a condition, we should require them to participate in a special program: Any customer who patronizes two of the businesses will receive a substantial discount at the third. By motivating customers to patronize all three, we will thus contribute to the profitability of each and maximize our return."

Discuss how well reasoned ... etc.

The following appeared as part of an article in a newsletter for farmers:

"Users of Solacium, a medicinal herb now grown mainly in Asia, report that it relieves tension and promotes deep sleep. A recent study indicates that a large number of college students who took pills containing one of the ingredients in Solacium suffered less anxiety. To satisfy the anticipated demands for this very promising therapeutic herb and to reap the financial benefits, farmers in this country should begin growing it."

Discuss how well reasoned ... etc.

The following appeared in a memorandum from the president of Aurora, a company that sells organic milk (milk produced without the use of chemical additives):

"Sales of organic food products in this country have tripled over the past five years. If Aurora is to profit from this continuing trend, we must diversify and start selling products such as organic orange juice and organic eggs in addition to our regular product line. With the recent increase of articles in health magazines questioning the safety of milk and other food products, customers are even more likely to buy our line of organic products. And to help ensure our successful expansion, we should hire the founder of a chain of health-food stores to serve as our vice president of marketing."

Discuss how well reasoned ... etc.

The following appeared in a memorandum from the human resources department of Diversified Manufacturing:

"Managers at our central office report that their employees tend to be most productive in the days immediately preceding a vacation. To help counteract our declining market share, we could increase the productivity of our professional staff members, who currently receive four weeks paid vacation a year, by limiting them to a maximum of one week's continuous vacation time. They will thus take more vacation breaks during a year and give us more days of maximum productivity."

Discuss how well reasoned ... etc.

The following appeared in a memorandum from a regional supervisor of post office operations:

"During a two-week study of postal operations, the Presto City post office handled about twice as many items as the Lento City post office, even though the cities are about the same size. Moreover, customer satisfaction appears to be higher in Presto City, since the study found fewer complaints regarding the Presto City post office. Therefore, the postmasters at these two offices should exchange assignments: the Presto City postmaster will solve the problems of inefficiency and customer dissatisfaction at the Lento City office while the Lento City postmaster learns firsthand the superior methods of Presto City."

Discuss how well reasoned ... etc.

The following appeared in a memorandum written by the managing director of the Exeunt Theater Company:

"Now that we have moved to a larger theater, we can expect to increase our revenues from ticket sales. To further increase profits, we should start producing the plays that have been most successful when they were performed in our nation's largest cities. In addition, we should hire the Adlib Theater Company's director of fund-raising, since corporate contributions to Adlib have increased significantly over the three years that she has worked for Adlib."

Discuss how well reasoned … etc.

The following appeared in a memorandum from the human resources department of HomeStyle, a house remodeling business:

"This year, despite HomeStyle's move to new office space, we have seen a decline in both company morale and productivity, and a corresponding increase in administrative costs. To rectify these problems, we should begin using a newly developed software package for performance appraisal and feedback. Managers will save time by simply choosing comments from a preexisting list; then the software will automatically generate feedback for the employee. The human resources department at CounterBalance, the manufacturer of the countertops we install, reports satisfaction with the package."

Discuss how well reasoned … etc.

The following appeared as part of an article in a weekly newsmagazine:

"The country of Oleum can best solve the problem of its balance-of-trade deficit by further increasing the tax on its major import, crude oil. After Oleum increased the tax on imported crude oil four months ago, consumption of gasoline declined by 20 percent. Therefore, by imposing a second and significantly higher tax increase next year, Oleum will dramatically decrease its balance of trade deficit."

Discuss how well reasoned … etc.

The following appeared as part of a business plan by the Capital Idea investment firm:

"In recent years the worldwide demand for fish has grown, and improvements in fishing technology have made larger catches, and thus increased supply, possible: for example, last year's tuna catch was 9 percent greater than the previous year's. To capitalize on these trends, we should therefore invest in the new tartfish processing plant on Tartfish Island, where increasing revenues from tourism indicate a strong local economy."

Discuss how well reasoned … etc.

The following appeared in a speech by a stockholder of Consolidated Industries at the company's annual stockholders' meeting:

"In the computer hardware division last year, profits fell significantly below projections, the product line decreased from 20 to only 5 items, and expenditures for employee benefits increased by 15 percent. Nevertheless, Consolidated's board of directors has approved an annual salary of more than $1 million for our company's chief executive officer. The present board members should be replaced because they are unconcerned about the increasing costs of employee benefits and salaries, in spite of the company's problems generating income."

Discuss how well reasoned ... etc.

The following appeared in a memorandum from the business planning department of Avia Airlines:

"Of all the cities in their region, Beaumont and Fletcher are showing the fastest growth in the number of new businesses. Therefore, Avia should establish a commuter route between them as a means of countering recent losses on its main passenger routes. And to make the commuter route more profitable from the outset, Avia should offer a 1/3 discount on tickets purchased within two days of the flight. Unlike tickets bought earlier, discount tickets will be nonrefundable, and so gain from their sale will be greater."

Discuss how well reasoned ... etc.

The following appeared in a memorandum from the vice president of Gigantis, a development company that builds and leases retail store facilities:

"Nationwide over the past five years, sales have increased significantly at outlet stores that deal exclusively in reduced-price merchandise. Therefore, we should publicize the new mall that we are building at Pleasantville as a central location for outlet shopping and rent store space only to outlet companies. By taking advantage of the success of outlet stores, this plan should help ensure full occupancy of the mall and enable us to recover quickly the costs of building the mall."

Discuss how well reasoned ... etc.

The following appeared in a memorandum written by the chair of the music department to the president of Omega University:

"Mental health experts have observed that symptoms of mental illness are less pronounced in many patients after group music-therapy sessions, and job openings in the music-therapy field have increased during the past year. Consequently, graduates from our degree program for music therapists should have no trouble finding good positions. To help improve the financial status of Omega University, we should therefore expand our music-therapy degree program by increasing its enrollment targets."

Discuss how well reasoned ... etc.

The following appeared in a memorandum to the work-group supervisors of the GBS Company:

"The CoffeeCart beverage and food service located in the lobby of our main office building is not earning enough in sales to cover its costs, and so the cart may discontinue operating at GBS. Given the low staff morale, as evidenced by the increase in the number of employees leaving the company, the loss of this service could present a problem, especially since the staff morale questionnaire showed widespread dissatisfaction with the snack machines. Therefore, supervisors should remind the employees in their group to patronize the cart—after all, it was leased for their convenience so that they would not have to walk over to the cafeteria on breaks."

Discuss how well reasoned ... etc.

The following appeared as part of an article in a trade magazine:

"During a recent trial period in which government inspections at selected meat-processing plants were more frequent, the amount of bacteria in samples of processed chicken decreased by 50 percent on average from the previous year's level. If the government were to institute more frequent inspections, the incidence of stomach and intestinal infections throughout the country could thus be cut in half. In the meantime, consumers of Excel Meats should be safe from infection because Excel's main processing plant has shown more improvement in eliminating bacterial contamination than any other plant cited in the government report."

Discuss how well reasoned ... etc.

Appendix A   Percentile Ranking Tables

Verbal and Quantitative scores range from 0 to 60. Verbal scores below 9 and above 44 and Quantitative scores below 7 and above 50 are rare. Verbal and Quantitative scores measure different skills and cannot be compared with one another.

Verbal Score

Percentage Ranking*	Score
99%	45-51
97%	44
95%	42-43
92%	41
89%	40
87%	39
83%	38
81%	37
79%	36
74%	35
69%	34
66%	33
64%	32
58%	31
56%	30
53%	29
48%	28
43%	27.8—Mean Score
40%	26
35%	25
33%	24
29%	23
27%	22
23%	21
20%	20
16%	19
15%	18
12%	17
10%	16
8%	15
7%	14
6%	13
4%	12
3%	11
2%	9-10
1%	7-8
0%	6

Sample Size: 787,205
Standard Deviation: 9.07

Quantitative Score

Percentage Ranking*	Score
98%	51
92%	50
85%	49
80%	48
76%	47
73%	46
71%	45
66%	44
64%	43
59%	42
57%	41
55%	40
50%	39
48%	38
46%	37
43%	36.6—Mean Score
42%	36
38%	35
36%	34
34%	33
31%	32
27%	31
26%	30
23%	29
21%	28
18%	27
17%	26
14%	25
13%	24
12%	23
10%	22
9%	21
8%	20
7%	19
6%	18
5%	17
4%	14-16
3%	13
2%	10-12
1%	7-9
0%	6

Sample Size: 787,205
Standard Deviation: 10.83

* **Percentage Ranking** indicates the percentage of the test-taking population that scored below a given numerical score.

Your Total score is based on your performance in the Verbal and Quantitative sections and ranges from 200 to 800. About two-thirds of test-takers score between 400 and 600.

Analytical Writing Assessment scores range from 0 to 6 and represent the average of two independent ratings. If the independent scores vary by more than a point, a third reader adjudicates, but because of ongoing training and monitoring, discrepancies are rare.

Your Analytical Writing Assessment score is computed and reported separately from the other sections of the test and has no effect on your Verbal, Quantitative, or Total scores.

Total Score

Percentage Ranking*	Score
99%	760-800
98%	750
97%	740
96%	730
94%	720
92%	710
90%	700
88%	690
85%	680
84%	670
81%	660
79%	650
74%	640
73%	630
70%	620
67%	610
63%	600
60%	590
57%	580
54%	570
51%	560
48%	550
45%	542.0 —Mean Score
40%	530
39%	520
36%	510
34%	500
31%	490
29%	480
26%	470
23%	460
21%	450
19%	440
17%	430
16%	420
14%	410
13%	400
11%	390
10%	380
9%	370
8%	360
6%	340-350
5%	330
4%	320
3%	290-310
2%	260-280
1%	220-250
0%	200-210

Sample Size: 787,205
Standard Deviation: 120.54

Analytical Writing Assessment Score

Percentage Ranking*	Score
91%	6
77%	5.5
57%	5
38%	4.5
36%	4.4 —Mean Score
20%	4
10%	3.5
6%	3
4%	2.5
3%	0.5-2
0%	0

Sample Size: 787,205
Standard Deviation: 1.17

* **Percentage Ranking** indicates the percentage of the test-taking population that scored below a given numerical score.

Appendix B   Answer Sheets

Diagnostic Answer Sheet - Quantitative

1.   27.
2.   28.
3.   29.
4.   30.
5.   31.
6.   32.
7.   33.
8.   34.
9.   35.
10.   36.
11.   37.
12.   38.
13.   39.
14.   40.
15.   41.
16.   42.
17.   43.
18.   44.
19.   45.
20.   46.
21.   47.
22.   48.
23.
24.
25.
26.

Diagnostic Answer Sheet - Verbal

1.   27.
2.   28.
3.   29.
4.   30.
5.   31.
6.   32.
7.   33.
8.   34.
9.   35.
10.   36.
11.   37.
12.   38.
13.   39.
14.   40.
15.   41.
16.   42.
17.   43.
18.   44.
19.   45.
20.   46.
21.   47.
22.   48.
23.   49.
24.   50.
25.   51.
26.   52.

Problem Solving Answer Sheet

1.	32.	63.	94.	125.	156.	187.	218.
2.	33.	64.	95.	126.	157.	188.	219.
3.	34.	65.	96.	127.	158.	189.	220.
4.	35.	66.	97.	128.	159.	190.	221.
5.	36.	67.	98.	129.	160.	191.	222.
6.	37.	68.	99.	130.	161.	192.	223.
7.	38.	69.	100.	131.	162.	193.	224.
8.	39.	70.	101.	132.	163.	194.	225.
9.	40.	71.	102.	133.	164.	195.	226.
10.	41.	72.	103.	134.	165.	196.	227.
11.	42.	73.	104.	135.	166.	197.	228.
12.	43.	74.	105.	136.	167.	198.	229.
13.	44.	75.	106.	137.	168.	199.	230.
14.	45.	76.	107.	138.	169.	200.	
15.	46.	77.	108.	139.	170.	201.	
16.	47.	78.	109.	140.	171.	202.	
17.	48.	79.	110.	141.	172.	203.	
18.	49.	80.	111.	142.	173.	204.	
19.	50.	81.	112.	143.	174.	205.	
20.	51.	82.	113.	144.	175.	206.	
21.	52.	83.	114.	145.	176.	207.	
22.	53.	84.	115.	146.	177.	208.	
23.	54.	85.	116.	147.	178.	209.	
24.	55.	86.	117.	148.	179.	210.	
25.	56.	87.	118.	149.	180.	211.	
26.	57.	88.	119.	150.	181.	212.	
27.	58.	89.	120.	151.	182.	213.	
28.	59.	90.	121.	152.	183.	214.	
29.	60.	91.	122.	153.	184.	215.	
30.	61.	92.	123.	154.	185.	216.	
31.	62.	93.	124.	155.	186.	217.	

Data Sufficiency Answer Sheet

1.	36.	71.	106.	141.
2.	37.	72.	107.	142.
3.	38.	73.	108.	143.
4.	39.	74.	109.	144.
5.	40.	75.	110.	145.
6.	41.	76.	111.	146.
7.	42.	77.	112.	147.
8.	43.	78.	113.	148.
9.	44.	79.	114.	149.
10.	45.	80.	115.	150.
11.	46.	81.	116.	151.
12.	47.	82.	117.	152.
13.	48.	83.	118.	153.
14.	49.	84.	119.	154.
15.	50.	85.	120.	155.
16.	51.	86.	121.	156.
17.	52.	87.	122.	157.
18.	53.	88.	123.	158.
19.	54.	89.	124.	159.
20.	55.	90.	125.	160.
21.	56.	91.	126.	161.
22.	57.	92.	127.	162.
23.	58.	93.	128.	163.
24.	59.	94.	129.	164.
25.	60.	95.	130.	165.
26.	61.	96.	131.	166.
27.	62.	97.	132.	167.
28.	63.	98.	133.	168.
29.	64.	99.	134.	169.
30.	65.	100.	135.	170.
31.	66.	101.	136.	171.
32.	67.	102.	137.	172.
33.	68.	103.	138.	173.
34.	69.	104.	139.	174.
35.	70.	105.	140.	

Reading Comprehension Answer Sheet

1.	32.	63.	94.	125.
2.	33.	64.	95.	126.
3.	34.	65.	96.	127.
4.	35.	66.	97.	128.
5.	36.	67.	98.	129.
6.	37.	68.	99.	130.
7.	38.	69.	100.	131.
8.	39.	70.	101.	132.
9.	40.	71.	102.	133.
10.	41.	72.	103.	134.
11.	42.	73.	104.	135.
12.	43.	74.	105.	136.
13.	44.	75.	106.	137.
14.	45.	76.	107.	138.
15.	46.	77.	108.	139.
16.	47.	78.	109.	
17.	48.	79.	110.	
18.	49.	80.	111.	
19.	50.	81.	112.	
20.	51.	82.	113.	
21.	52.	83.	114.	
22.	53.	84.	115.	
23.	54.	85.	116.	
24.	55.	86.	117.	
25.	56.	87.	118.	
26.	57.	88.	119.	
27.	58.	89.	120.	
28.	59.	90.	121.	
29.	60.	91.	122.	
30.	61.	92.	123.	
31.	62.	93.	124.	

Critical Reasoning Answer Sheet

1.	32.	63.	94.
2.	33.	64.	95.
3.	34.	65.	96.
4.	35.	66.	97.
5.	36.	67.	98.
6.	37.	68.	99.
7.	38.	69.	100.
8.	39.	70.	101.
9.	40.	71.	102.
10.	41.	72.	103.
11.	42.	73.	104.
12.	43.	74.	105.
13.	44.	75.	106.
14.	45.	76.	107.
15.	46.	77.	108.
16.	47.	78.	109.
17.	48.	79.	110.
18.	49.	80.	111.
19.	50.	81.	112.
20.	51.	82.	113.
21.	52.	83.	114.
22.	53.	84.	115.
23.	54.	85.	116.
24.	55.	86.	117.
25.	56.	87.	118.
26.	57.	88.	119.
27.	58.	89.	120.
28.	59.	90.	121.
29.	60.	91.	122.
30.	61.	92.	123.
31.	62.	93.	124.

Sentence Correction Answer Sheet

1.	32.	63.	94.	125.
2.	33.	64.	95.	126.
3.	34.	65.	96.	127.
4.	35.	66.	97.	128.
5.	36.	67.	98.	129.
6.	37.	68.	99.	130.
7.	38.	69.	100.	131.
8.	39.	70.	101.	132.
9.	40.	71.	102.	133.
10.	41.	72.	103.	134.
11.	42.	73.	104.	135.
12.	43.	74.	105.	136.
13.	44.	75.	106.	137.
14.	45.	76.	107.	138.
15.	46.	77.	108.	139.
16.	47.	78.	109.	140.
17.	48.	79.	110.	
18.	49.	80.	111.	
19.	50.	81.	112.	
20.	51.	82.	113.	
21.	52.	83.	114.	
22.	53.	84.	115.	
23.	54.	85.	116.	
24.	55.	86.	117.	
25.	56.	87.	118.	
26.	57.	88.	119.	
27.	58.	89.	120.	
28.	59.	90.	121.	
29.	60.	91.	122.	
30.	61.	92.	123.	
31.	62.	93.	124.	

Integrated Reasoning Answer Sheet

1A.	11A.	21A.	31A.	42A.
1B.	11B.	21B.	31B.	42B.
1C.	11C.	21C.		
			32A.	43A.
2A.	12.	22A.	32B.	43B.
2B.		22B.		
2C.	13A.	22C.	33A.	44A.
	13B.		33B.	44B.
3.	13C.	23A.		
		23B.	34A.	45A.
4A.	14A.	23C.	34B.	45B.
4B.	14B.			
4C.	14C.	24A.	35A.	46A.
		24B.	35B.	46B.
5A.	15.	24C.		
5B.			36A.	47A.
5C.	16A.	25A.	36B.	47B.
	16B.	25B.		
6.	16C.		37A.	48A.
		26A.	37B.	48B.
7A.	17A.	26B.		
7B.	17B.		38A.	49A.
7C.	17C.	27A.	38B.	49B.
		27B.		
8A.	18.		39A.	50A.
8B.		28A.	39B.	50B.
8C.	19A.	28B.		
	19B.		40A.	
9.	19C.	29A.	40B.	
		29B.		
10A.	20A.		41A.	
10B.	20B.	30A.	41B.	
10C.	20C.	30B.		

CAUTION!

THE PENALTIES FOR CHEATING ON THE GMAT® EXAM ARE SEVERE.

THE FOLLOWING IS CONSIDERED CHEATING:

- Hiring someone to take the test.
- Taking the test for someone else.
- Memorizing test questions.
- Sharing answers with others.

THE PENALTIES FOR CHEATING ARE:

- Cancellation of your scores.
- Ban on future testing.
- School notification.
- Possible legal prosecution.

HAS SOMEONE BEEN TRYING TO GET YOU TO ACT ILLEGALLY?

FILE A REPORT VIA EMAIL: PVTESTSECURITY@PEARSON.COM